Peru

THIS EDITION WRITTEN AND RESEARCHED BY

Carolyn McCarthy,

Greg Benchwick, Alex Egerton, Phillip Tang, Luke Waterson

PLAN YOUR TRIP

ON THE ROAD

RICHARD MASCHMEYER/GETTY IMAGES ©

REED BOAT, LAKE TITICACA P171

BONCHAN/SHUTTERSTOCK ©

ANTICUCHOS P509

JOHN COLETTI/GETTY IMAGES ©

Contents

PARAGLIDER, PLAYA COSTA VERDE P77

ON THE ROAD

MATT MUNRO/GETTY IMAGES ©

TRADITIONAL PERUVIAN MARINERA DANCE P319

DANITA DELIMONT/GETTY IMAGES ©

WALL DECORATION, CHAN CHAN P325

Contents

WOOLLY MONKEYS, PARQUE NACIONAL MANU P461

UNDERSTAND

SURVIVAL GUIDE

SPECIAL FEATURES

Welcome to Peru

Peru is as complex as its most intricate and exquisite weavings. Festivals mark ancient rites, the urban vanguard beams innovation and nature brims with splendid diversity.

All Things Ancient

Visitors pilgrimage to the glorious Inca citadel of Machu Picchu, yet this feted site is just a flash in a 5000-year history of peoples. Explore the dusted remnants of Chan Chan, the largest pre-Columbian ruins in all the Americas. Fly over the puzzling geoglyphs etched into the arid earth at Nazca. Or venture into the wilds that hem the fortress of Kuélap. Lima's great museums reveal the sophistication, skill and passion of these lost civilizations. Visit remote communities and see how old ways live on. Immerse yourself, and you will leave Peru having gotten a little closer to the past.

Pleasure & the Palate

One existential question haunts all Peruvians: what to eat? Ceviche with slivers of fiery chili and corn, slow-simmered stews, velvety Amazonian chocolate – in the capital of Latin cooking, the choices dazzle. Geographic and cultural diversity has brought ingredients ranging from highland tubers to tropical jungle fruits to a complex cuisine of Spanish, indigenous, African and Asian influence. Fusion existed here long before it came with airs. Explore the bounty of food markets. Sample grilled *anticuchos* (beef skewers) on the street corners and splurge on exquisite *novoandina* (nouvelle cuisine).

Life is a Carnival

Welcome to a place of mythical beliefs where ancient pageants unwind to the tune of booming brass bands. Peru's rich cultural heritage is never more real and visceral than when you are immersed streetside in the swirling madness of a festival. Deities of old are reincarnated as Christian saints, pilgrims climb mountains in the dead of night and icons are paraded through crowded plazas as once were the mummies of Inca rulers. History is potent here and still pulsing, and there is no better way to experience it.

Oh, Adventure

Giant sand dunes, chiseled peaks and Pacific breaks a few heartbeats away from the capital's rush-hour traffic: from downtown Lima to smack-dab nowhere, this vast country translates to paradise for the active traveler. All the usual suspects – rafting, paragliding, ziplines and bike trails – are present. Spot scarlet macaws in the Amazon or catch the sunset over the dusty remnants of an ancient civilization. Take this big place in small bites and don't rush. Delays happen. Festivals can swallow you whole for days. And that's when you realize: in Peru the adventure usually lies in getting there.

Why I Love Peru

By Carolyn McCarthy, Writer

For me, Peru is the molten core of South America, a distillation of the oldest traditions and the finest building, weaving and art made by the most sophisticated cultures on the continent. In Peru the wildest landcapes – from frozen Andean peaks to the deep Amazon – help us reforge our connection to the natural world. It is also a cultural stew, where diverse peoples live side by side, negotiating modern life with humor and aplomb. Beyond that, the cuisine alone makes it worth the trip. Every return is rich and surprising.

For more about our writers, see page 576.

Above: Women working on embroidery beside a reed hut, Lake Titicaca (p184)

Peru

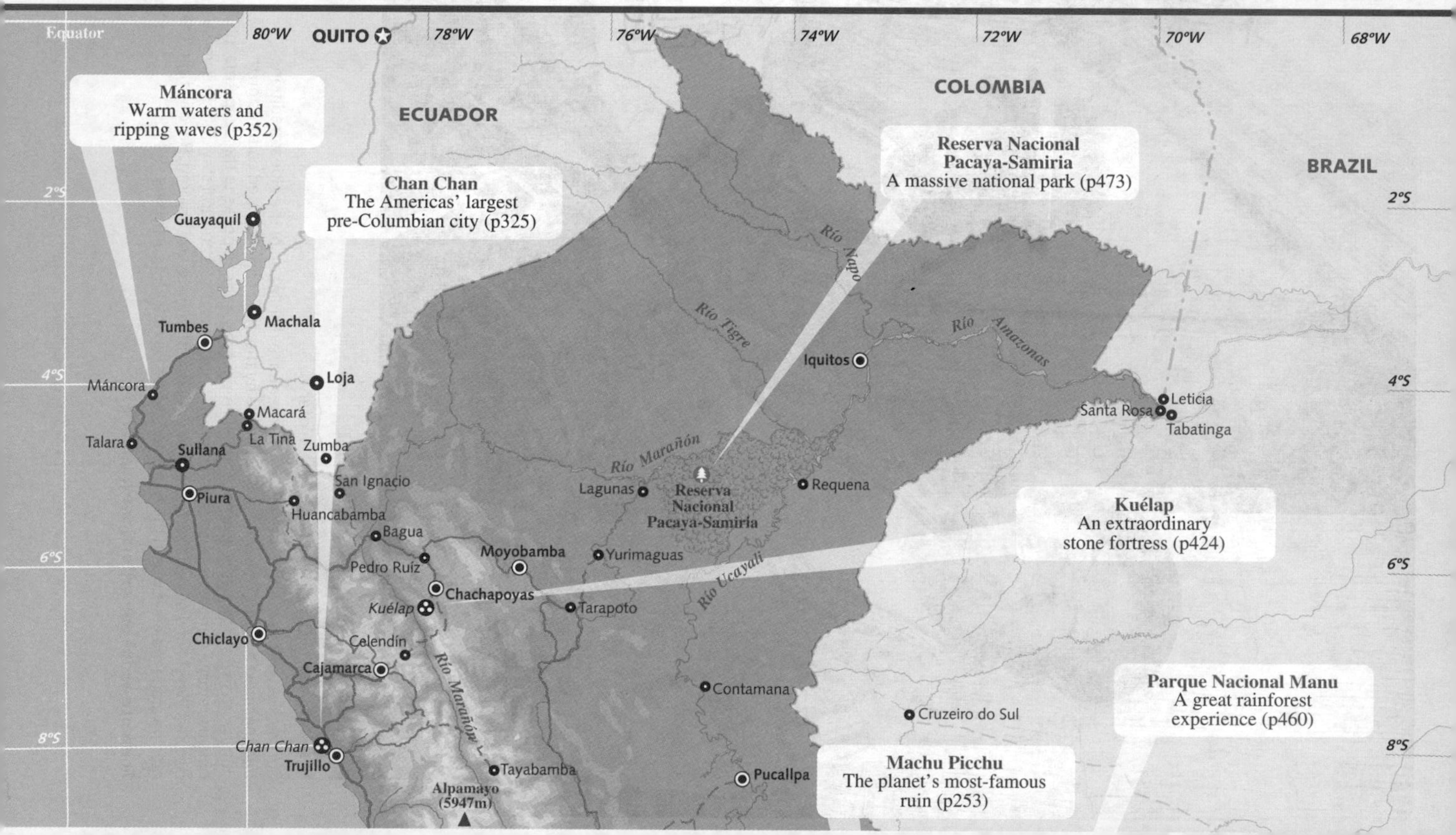

0 — 200 km
0 — 100 miles

Máncora
Warm waters and ripping waves (p352)

Chan Chan
The Americas' largest pre-Columbian city (p325)

Reserva Nacional Pacaya-Samiria
A massive national park (p473)

Kuélap
An extraordinary stone fortress (p424)

Parque Nacional Manu
A great rainforest experience (p460)

Machu Picchu
The planet's most-famous ruin (p253)

Equator
80°W
QUITO
78°W
76°W
74°W
72°W
70°W
68°W
2°S
4°S
6°S
8°S
ECUADOR
COLOMBIA
BRAZIL
Guayaquil
Machala
Tumbes
Loja
Máncora
Macará
La Tina
Talara
Sullana
Zumba
Piura
San Ignacio
Huancabamba
Bagua
Pedro Ruíz
Moyobamba
Chachapoyas
Kuélap
Chiclayo
Celendín
Cajamarca
Chan Chan
Trujillo
Tayabamba
Alpamayo (5947m)
Río Marañón
Río Napo
Río Tigre
Río Amazonas
Iquitos
Lagunas
Reserva Nacional Pacaya-Samiria
Requena
Yurimaguas
Tarapoto
Río Ucayali
Contamana
Pucallpa
Cruzeiro do Sul
Leticia
Santa Rosa
Tabatinga

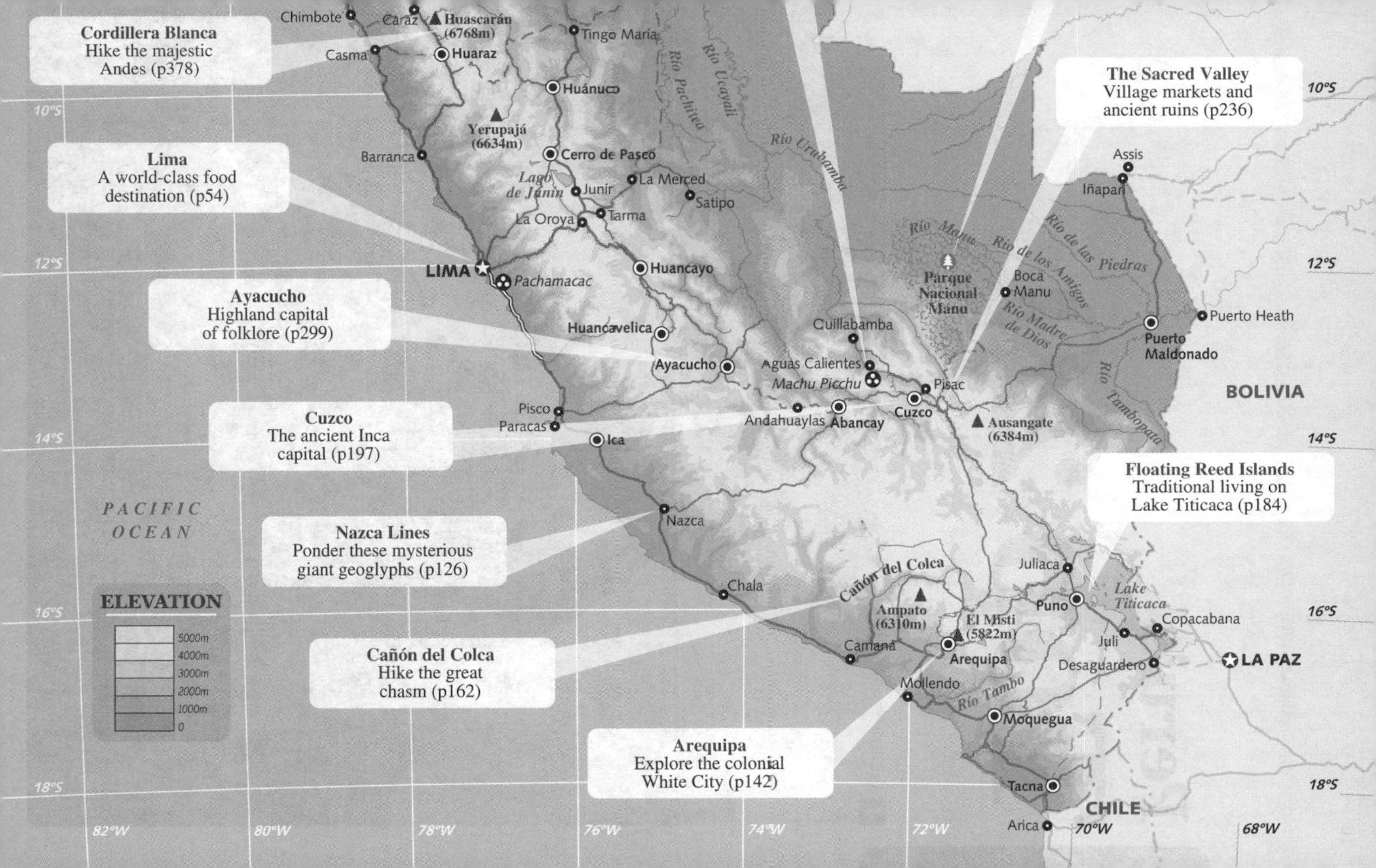

Cordillera Blanca
Hike the majestic Andes (p378)
Lima
A world-class food destination (p54)
Ayacucho
Highland capital of folklore (p299)
Cuzco
The ancient Inca capital (p197)
Nazca Lines
Ponder these mysterious giant geoglyphs (p126)
Cañón del Colca
Hike the great chasm (p162)
Arequipa
Explore the colonial White City (p142)
The Sacred Valley
Village markets and ancient ruins (p236)
Floating Reed Islands
Traditional living on Lake Titicaca (p184)
PACIFIC OCEAN
ELEVATION
5000m
4000m
3000m
2000m
1000m
0
BOLIVIA
CHILE
LA PAZ
LIMA
Chimbote
Caraz
Huascarán (6768m)
Casma
Huaraz
Tingo María
Huánuco
Yerupajá (6634m)
Barranca
Cerro de Pasco
Lago de Junín
Junín
La Merced
Satipo
La Oroya
Tarma
Pachamacac
Huancayo
Huancavelica
Ayacucho
Pisco
Paracas
Ica
Nazca
Chala
Camaná
Mollendo
Arequipa
El Misti (5822m)
Ampato (6310m)
Cañón del Colca
Moquegua
Tacna
Arica
Juliaca
Puno
Lake Titicaca
Juli
Copacabana
Desaguardero
Río Tambo
Río Pachitea
Río Ucayali
Río Urubamba
Río Manu
Parque Nacional Manu
Río de los Amigos
Río de las Piedras
Río Madre de Dios
Río Tambopata
Boca Manu
Assis
Iñapari
Puerto Heath
Puerto Maldonado
Cuillabamba
Aguas Calientes
Machu Picchu
Pisac
Cuzco
Andahuaylas
Abancay
Ausangate (6384m)
10°S
12°S
14°S
16°S
18°S
82°W
80°W
78°W
76°W
74°W
72°W
70°W
68°W

Peru's Top 20

1

Machu Picchu

1 A fantastic Inca citadel lost to the world until its rediscovery in the early 20th century, Machu Picchu (p253) stands as a ruin among ruins. With its emerald terraces, backed by steep peaks and Andean ridges that echo on the horizon, the sight simply surpasses the imagination. Beautiful it is. This marvel of engineering has withstood six centuries of earthquakes, foreign invasion and howling weather. Discover it for yourself, wander through its stone temples, and scale the dizzying heights of Wayna Picchu.

Floating Reed Islands, Lake Titicaca

2 Less a lake than a highland ocean, the Titicaca area is home to fantastical sights, but none more so than the surreal floating islands crafted entirely of tightly woven *totora* reeds. Centuries ago, the Uros people constructed the Islas Uros (p184; pictured below) in order to escape more aggressive mainland ethnic groups, such as the Incas. The reeds require near-constant renovation and are also used to build thatched homes, elegant boats and even archways and children's swing sets. See this wonder for yourself with a homestay visit that includes fishing and learning traditional customs.

PHILIP LEE HARVEY / LONELY PLANET ©

2

CHRIS CHEADLE / GETTY IMAGES ©

DAMIAN TURSKI / GETTY IMAGES ©

JEREMY RICHARDS / SHUTTERSTOCK ©

Hiking in the Cordillera Blanca

3 The dramatic peaks of the Cordillera Blanca (p378) stand sentinel over Huaraz and the surrounding region like an outrageously imposing granite Republican Guard. The range is the highest outside of the Himalayas, and 16 of its ostentatious summits breech 6000m, making it the continent's most challenging collection of summits-in-waiting. Glacial lakes, massive *Puya raimondii* plants and shards of sky-pointed rock all culminate in Parque Nacional Huascarán, where the Santa Cruz trek rewards the ambitious with a living museum of razor-sharp peaks.

Colonial Arequipa

4 Peru's second-largest metropolis bridges the gap between the Inca glories of Cuzco and the clamorous modernity of Lima. Crowned by some dazzling baroque-*mestizo* architecture hewn out of the local *sillar* (white volcanic rock), Arequipa (p142) is a Spanish colonial city that hasn't strayed far from its conception. Its ethereal natural setting, amid snoozing volcanoes and the high *pampa* is complemented by a 400-year-old monastery, a huge cathedral and some interesting Peruvian fusion cuisine showcased in traditional *picanterías* (spicy restaurants). Above: Iglesia de La Compañía (p146)

Parque Nacional Manu

5 Traverse three climatic zones from rearing Andean mountains to mist-swathed cloud forest on the lower slopes en route to the bowels of the jungle in Parque Nacional Manu (p460), the Amazon's best adventure. Manu has long been Peru's best-protected wilderness, brimming with opportunities to see fabled jungle creatures such as the anaconda, tapir, thousands of feasting macaws festooning clay licks, and jaguar. In this deep forest, tribespeople live as they have for centuries, with barely any contact with the outside world.

5

FRANS LEMMENS / GETTY IMAGES ©

Inca Trail

6 The continent's most famous pedestrian roadway, the Inca Trail (p41) snakes 43km, up stone steps and through thick cloud forest mists. A true pilgrimage, the four- to five-day trek ends at the famous Intipunku – or Sun Gate – where trekkers get their first glimpse of the extravagant ruins at Machu Picchu. While there are countless ancient roads all over Peru, the Inca Trail, with its mix of majestic views, staggering mountain passes and clusters of ruins, remains the favorite of travelers.

6

SHARPTOYOU / SHUTTERSTOCK ©

DANITA DELIMONT / GETTY IMAGES ©

CARLA NICHIATA / GETTY IMAGES ©

RALPH LEE HOPKINS / GETTY IMAGES ©

Cuzco

7 With ancient cobblestone streets, grandiose baroque churches and the remnants of Inca temples with centuries-old carvings, no city looms larger in Andean history than Cuzco (p197), a city that has been inhabited continuously since pre-Hispanic times. Once the capital of the Inca empire, tourist-thronged Cuzco also serves as the gateway to Machu Picchu. Mystic, commercial and chaotic, this unique city is still a stunner. Where else would you find ornately dressed women walking their llamas on leashes, a museum for magical plants, and the wildest nightlife in the high Andes?

Lima Cuisine

8 Some cities are known for their parks, or even their politics, but Lima (p54) is a city where life is often planned around the next meal. Consider it an experience worth savoring. The coastal capital is replete with options ranging from street carts to haute cuisine restaurants offering exquisite interpretations of Peru's unique fusion cuisine. Dishes are a complex blend of Spanish, indigenous, African and Asian influences (both Chinese and Japanese). There's a reason that its chefs and restaurants are feted in gourmet magazines, in world restaurant rankings and with international awards. Top: Ceviche

The Sacred Valley

9 Ragtag Andean villages, crumbling Inca military outposts and agricultural terraces used since time immemorial are linked by the Río Urubamba as it curves and widens, coursing through the Sacred Valley (p196). A strategic location between Cuzco and Machu Picchu makes this picturesque destination an ideal base to explore the area's famed markets and ruins. Accommodations range from inviting inns to top resorts, and adventure options include horseback riding, rafting and treks that take you through remote weaving and agricultural villages. Above: Mercado de Chinchero (p244)

Nazca Lines

10 Made by aliens? Laid out by prehistoric balloonists? Conceived as a giant astronomical chart? No two evaluations of Southern Peru's giant geoglyphs, communally known as the Nazca Lines (p130), are ever the same. The mysteries have been drawing in outsiders since the 1940s when German archaeologist Maria Reiche devoted half her life to studying them. But neither Reiche nor subsequent archaeologists have been able to fully crack the code. The lines remain unfathomed, enigmatic and loaded with historic intrigue, inspiring awe in all who pass.

Chavín de Huántar

11 The Unesco-recognized ruins of Chavín de Huántar (p397) were once a righteous ceremonial center. Today, the exceptional feat of engineering, dating between 1200 BC and 800 BC, features striking temple-like structures above ground and a labyrinthine complex of underground corridors, ducts and chambers that invite clambering through. Nearby, the outstanding Museo Nacional de Chavín, home to the lion's share of the intricate and horrifyingly carved tenon heads that once embellished Chavín's walls, helps piece together the enigma.

10

DANITA DELIMONT / GETTY IMAGES ©

11

DC_COLOMBIA / GETTY IMAGES ©

12

AURORA PHOTOS / ALAMY STOCK PHOTO ©

13

MATYAS REHAK / SHUTTERSTOCK ©

Semana Santa in Ayacucho

12 As if a week wasn't enough for a party, Ayacucho's Semana Santa (p302) lasts 10 days in the lead-up to Easter Sunday. The religious spectacle is moving, with vivid re-enactments of scenes, including the procession of Christ on a donkey through streets of flowers and palm fronds. But the after-show parties are the highlight. Fairs, feasts and pre-dawn fireworks take place on Easter Sunday after a Saturday during which it is believed that, since Christ died on Friday and rose on Sunday, no sin can be committed.

Kuélap

13 Lacking the budget, Unesco branding and – drum roll, please – the crowds of Machu Picchu, the stone fortress at Kuélap (p424) is second to Peru's most famous ruins in little else. Tucked away deep in cloud-forest territory at 3100m above the Río Urubamba near Chachapoyas, this remarkably preserved citadel is a testament to the enigmatic and strong-willed 'People of the Clouds.' Some 400 circular dwellings, some ornately adorned and surrounded by a towering rock wall, highlight this beautiful and mysterious stone beast in the clouds.

14

FRANCESCO DE MARCO / SHUTTERSTOCK ©

15

DC_COLOMBIA / GETTY IMAGES ©

Islas Ballestas

14 A collection of barren, guano-covered rocks protruding out of the Pacific Ocean, the Islas Ballestas (p115) support an extraordinary ecosystem of birds, sea mammals and fish (notably anchovies). They also represent one of Peru's most successful conservation projects; guano is managed by the Ministry of Agriculture while the archipelago is protected in a national reserve. Boat trips around the island's cliffs allow close encounters with barking sea lions, huddled Humboldt penguins and tens of thousands of birds.

Trujillo

15 Rising from the sand-strewn desert like a mirage of colonial color, old Trujillo (p324) boasts a dazzling display of preserved splendor. The city's historical center is full of elegant churches, mansions and otherwise unspoiled colonial constructions, which are steeped today in a modern motif that lends the city a lovely, livable feel. Tack on the vicinity of impressive Chimú ruins such as Chan Chan and Moche Huacas del Sol y de la Luna, and Trujillo easily trumps its northern rivals in style and grace.

Above: Basilica Menor Catedral (p315)

Cañón del Colca

16 It's deep, very deep, but the Colca Canyon (p162) is about more than statistics. In an area colonized by pre-Inca, Inca and Spanish civilizations, the culture here is as alluring as the endless trekking possibilities. Stretching 100km from end to end and plunging more than 3400m at its deepest part, the canyon has been embellished with terraced agricultural fields, pastoral villages, Spanish colonial churches and ruins that date back to pre-Inca times. Hike it, bike it, raft it or zipline it – just keep your eyes peeled for the emblematic condors.

Chan Chan

17 The extraordinary Chimú capital of Chan Chan (p325) is the largest pre-Columbian city in the Americas and the largest adobe city in the world. Once home to 60,000 inhabitants and a trove of treasures, Chan Chan today is a work in progress. Tour the Tschudi complex, the only one of the 10 walled citadels here nearly restored to its former glory. Despite numerous weather-batterings over the years, courtesy of El Niño, Chan Chan's ceremonial courtyards, decorative walls and labyrinthine audience rooms are remarkably resilient.

16

17

STEPHEN COLLECTOR / GETTY IMAGES ©

HUGHES HERVE / HEMIS.FR / GETTY IMAGES ©

EMIL VON MALTITZ / AGE FOTOSTOCK ©

Lima Museums

18 Want to understand what Peru's ancient civilizations were all about? Begin your trip here. Lima's museums (p54) hold millennia worth of treasures, from sublime ceramics and carved rock stelae to breathtaking textiles made centuries ago. Some of the best collections are at Museo Larco, Museo Andrés del Castillo and the Museo Nacional de Antropología, Arqueología e Historía del Perú. Extended evening hours at Museo Larco offer an alternative to conventional nightlife. Above: Chimú idol, Museo Larco

Surfing on the North Coast

19 Surfers hellbent on an endless summer flock to Peru's north coast for the chance to catch some of the world's longest and most consistent breaks. The coast's surf scene culminates in rowdy Máncora (p352), Peru's only tried and true beach resort. Not to be confused with the world's other famous North Shore, Máncora holds its own as far as South America is concerned, drawing surfers and sand worshippers alike to its crescent-shaped coast for year-round fun in the sun.

Reserva Nacional Pacaya-Samiria

20 Peru's biggest national park (p473) is home to weird and wonderful creatures rarely glimpsed elsewhere: Amazon manatees, pink river dolphins, 6m caimans and giant river turtles. Just getting here is challenge enough – guests can arrive via an exciting boat trip from Yurimaguas to Iquitos. But unlike other Peruvian reserves, this is a walk on the *really* wild side. Transport is by dug-out canoe, there are no fancy lodges and you'll need to spend several days roughing it to see the best stuff: welcome to pure, unadulterated nature.

Need to Know

For more information, see Survival Guide (p531)

Currency
Nuevo sol (S)

Language
Spanish, Aymara and Quechua

Visas
Generally not required for stays of up to 183 days.

Money
ATMs widely available in larger cities and towns. Credit cards accepted widely. Traveler's checks not widely accepted.

Cell Phones
Local SIM cards (and top-up credits) are cheap and widely available, and can be used on unlocked triband GSM 1900 world phones.

Time
Eastern Standard Time (EST), five hours behind Greenwich Mean Time (GMT); same as New York City, without Daylight Savings Time.

When to Go

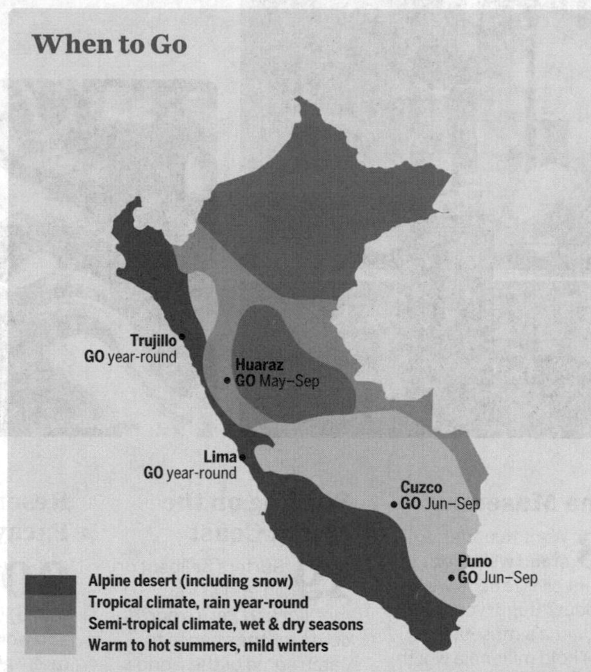

High Season
(Jun–Aug)

- Dry season in Andean highlands and eastern rainforest
- Best time for festivals and highland sports, including treks
- Busiest time due to North American and European holidays

Shoulder
(Sep–Nov & Mar–May)

- Spring and fall weather in the highlands
- Ideal for less-crowded visits
- September to November for good rainforest trekking

Low Season
(Dec–Feb)

- Rainy season in the highlands
- The Inca Trail closes during February for clean up
- High season for the coast and beach activities
- Very rainy in the Amazon, lasting through May

Useful Websites

Lonely Planet (www.lonelyplanet.com/peru) Destination information, hotel bookings, traveler forum and more.

Expat Peru (www.expatperu.com) Useful for government offices and customs regulations.

Latin America Network Information Center (www.lanic.utexas.edu) Informative links including academic research.

Living in Peru (www.livinginperu.com) An English-language guide with articles and reviews.

Peru Reports (http://perureports.com) Alternative English-language news.

Peruvian Times (www.peruviantimes.com) The latest news, in English.

Bus Portal Peru (https://busportal.pe) Tickets for buses throughout the country.

Important Numbers

Country code	☎51
International access code	4-digit carrier ☎00 + country code
Directory assistance	☎103
Tourist information (24hr)	☎511-574-800
Police	☎105

Exchange Rates

Australia	A$1	S2.72
Canada	C$1	S2.67
Europe	€1	S3.40
Japan	¥100	S3.28
New Zealand	NZ$1	S2.15
UK	UK£1	S4.22
USA	US$1	S2.60

For current exchange rates, see www.xe.com.

Daily Costs

Budget: Less than S300

- Inexpensive hotel room or dorm bed: S25-85
- Set lunches: less than S15; supermarkets have takeout
- Entry fee to historic sights: average S10

Midrange: S300–550

- Double room in midrange hotel: S140
- Multi-course lunch at midrange restaurant: S40
- Group tours from: S120

Top end: More than S550

- Double room in top-end hotel: S300
- Private city tour: from S180 per person
- Fine restaurant dinner: from S70

Opening Hours

Opening hours vary throughout the year. We've provided high-season opening hours; hours will generally decrease in the shoulder and low seasons.

Banks 9am–6pm Mon–Fri, some 9am–6pm Sat

Restaurants 10am–10pm, many close 3–6pm

Museums Often close on Monday

Government offices and businesses 9am–5pm Mon–Fri

Shops 9am–6pm, some open Saturday

Arriving in Peru

Aeropuerto Internacional Jorge Chávez (p543) Many flights arrive in the wee hours, so be sure to have a hotel booked ahead.

Bus The *combi* company La S (per person S2 to S3) runs various routes to Miraflores and beyond. It's south along Av Elmer Faucett.

Taxi S45, 30 minutes to one hour (rush hour) to Miraflores, Barranco or San Isidro, faster for downtown Lima.

Getting Around

Public transportation in Peru is cheap, with options plentiful and frequent.

Light Rail Lima's Metropolitano offers efficient, fast service to downtown.

Train Expensive and geared towards tourists.

Car Useful for traveling at your own pace, though cities can be difficult to navigate and secure parking is a must.

Bus Cheapest option with reclining seats on better long-distance buses.

Taxi A good option for sightseeing, shared taxis are common in the provinces.

For much more on **getting around**, see p546

What's New

Qhapaq Ñan

In 2014, the UN World Heritage Committee designated this Inca road system a World Heritage Site. Including Peru, it runs 14,000 miles from Colombia to Chile.

Lima Museums

From the upgraded MAC (Museo de Arte Contemporaneo) to the Lugar de Memoria, fashion's Museo Mario Testino and the new Casa de la Gastronomia Peruana, new attractions abound.

Museo Machu Picchu, Cuzco

A century after Hiram Bingham whisked the treasures of Machu Picchu to Yale, 500 of these Inca artifacts have returned to Peru and are displayed here at the Casa Concha.

Peruvian Craft Beer

Lima held 2014's inaugural Festival de Cerveza Artisanal to show off Peru's growing artisan beer movement. Look for new breweries in Lima, the Sacred Valley and even in hostels.

Coastal Adventures

Was bronzing really once the main sport of beachgoers to Peru? Now offerings include kite surfing near Paracas and paddleboarding outside Máncora, where you can also dive with sea turtles off a petrol platform.

Reserva Tingana, Moyobamba

Tours are now up and running to this accessible slice of jungle paradise run by the local community as part of a pioneering environmental protection program.

Mountain Bike Cañón del Pato

Freshly paved and still as spectacular, pedal along sheer cliffs and through dozens of tunnels in this gorge where the Cordilleras Negra and Blanca come together.

The Paved Road to Marcahuamachuco

Once a nightmare bone-rattling journey to these massive and seldom-visited ruins is now an easy cruise from either Trujillo or Cajamarca via this freshly minted road.

Jungle Lodges

Luxury has arrived to the Peruvian Amazon in the form of jungle lodges, such as the inimitable Treehouse, located at the confluence of the Parapa and Cumaceba rivers near Iquitos.

Nauta, Amazonian travel hub

The village of Nauta has become the starting point for many Iquitos jungle tours.

Amazon Adventure

New adventure parks at Monte Amazonico Lodge near Puerto Maldonado and Isla las Turunas in San Ramón ensure a lung-busting adrenalin rush.

Highland travel routes

The improved Lima–Cerro de Pasco route now offers a great backdoor option into the Central Highlands.

For more recommendations and reviews, see lonelyplanet.com/peru

If You Like...

Ancient Ruins

Kuélap Perched atop a limestone mountain, this monumental stone-fortified city is the best-preserved site of Chachapoyas. (p424)

Tambo Colorado An understated gem on the south coast, it's worth going with a guide for a fuller appreciation. (p118)

Cahuachi When in Nazca, it's worth checking out these expansive 2000-year-old pyramids and other ruins. (p129)

Wari The capital of the empire that ruled the roost in the highlands before the Inca invaded. (p307)

Huanuco Viejo Ascend to the high plains above La Unión for an exploration of this extensive Inca settlement. (p279)

Hiking

El Clásico The best trek in the Colca Canyon for seeing a bit of everything except for a paved road. (p167)

Ausangate In a stunning arena of tumbling glaciers, turquoise lakes and rural hamlets awaits the most challenging trek in the Cuzco region. (p268)

Santa Cruz trek This five-day favorite journeys through Andean hamlets and valleys, with excellent views of Huascarán, Peru's highest peak. (p379)

Lares Beautiful Andean landscapes are just a by-product, since the main draw here is remote village life in the Sacred Valley. (p45)

Quilcayhuanca–Cojup trek No crowds, no pack animals – just you and the spectacular peaks of the Cordillera Blanca in this very challenging trek. (p378)

Peruvian Delicacies

Cooking courses Learn from the masters in Arequipa. (p155)

Patarashca A seafood jungle dish cooked with tomatoes, sweet peppers, onions, garlic and *sascha culantro*, wrapped in a bijao leaf. (p436)

Chocolate Luxuriant Andean-style hot cocoa is spiked with chilis and honey at Choco Museo. (p205)

Picanterias The best of Arequipa's ultimate salt-of-the-earth eateries emphasize authenticity and spices. (p94)

Belén mercado Grab a crash course in real Amazonian grub with a trip to this manic floating market – yes, 'grub' as in the insect larvae... (p480)

Into the Wild

Potent scenery is not hard to find in Peru, where ecosystems range from parched desert to lush Amazonian rainforest and glaciated Andean peaks.

Cordillera Huayhuash Circuit A 10-day odyssey among alpine lakes with condors circling the 6000m peaks. (p385)

The source of the Amazon A three-day hike from the Colca Canyon to the genesis of the world's longest river. (p164)

Cotahuasi A 12-hour road journey from Arequipa lies the world's deepest canyon. (p169)

Choquequirao A remote sister site to Machu Picchu that requires four days of hard trekking. (p269)

Río Heath Parque Nacional Bahuaja-Sonene is one of Peru's largest, wildest, most biodiverse regions. (p455)

Pisco

Emblematic of Peru, this potent grape brandy is best known in sours but new fusions with jungle fruit and herbs make it even more quaffable. Follow its journey from producer to bartop.

Tacama Lays on free tours and tastings at its lovely colonial hacienda. (p121)

Museo del Pisco A chic Cuzco bar with an encyclopedic list of piscos and original cocktails that wow. (p228)

Lima bars Taste pisco sours at its source, El Bolivarcito (p95), and exotic remixes at bar-mansion Ayahuasca (p95).

Luanahuná Sip industrial-strength pisco at the Bodega Santa Maria – a day trip from Lima. (p109)

Time Traveling Cultures

In Peru, the traditions of indigenous cultures are easily witnessed in many religious or seasonal festivals. To get a more in-depth experience, check out the following.

Colca homestays Rustic homestays in the villages of Sibayo and Yanque offer a taste of rural canyon life. (p163)

Weaving villages Cuzco-based tour operators visit the more remote traditional villages around the Sacred Valley. (p238)

Nazca Beyond sighting the famous 'Lines,' the highly distinctive and colorful pottery amazes too. (p126)

Community tourism Stay with locals in the area of Huaraz. (p369)

Top: Trekking in the Cordillera Huayhuash (p384)

Bottom: Terra-cotta vessel in the distinctive Nazca style

Month by Month

TOP EVENTS

Q'oyoriti, May/June

Semana Santa, March/April

Carnaval, February/March

Verano Negro, February/March

Fiesta de la Vendimia, March

January

January through March is the busiest (and most expensive) season on the coast, also the best time to find beach facilities open and festivals rocking. In the mountains and canyons, it's rainy season and best avoided by trekkers and mountaineers.

Año Nuevo

New Year's Day, January 1, is particularly big in Huancayo, where the fiesta continues until Epiphany (January 6).

Dance of the Blacks

In the central highlands town of Huánuco, revelers wear costumes with black masks to commemorate slave forefathers who worked the area mines.

Fiesta de la Marinera

Trujillo's national dance festival is held the last week in January.

February

The Inca Trail is closed all month. Many Peruvian festivals echo the Roman Catholic calendar and are celebrated with great pageantry, especially in indigenous highland villages, where Catholic feast days are often linked with traditional agricultural festivals.

La Virgen de la Candelaria

Held on February 2, this highland fiesta, also known as Candlemas, is particularly colorful around Puno, where folkloric music and dance celebrations last for two weeks.

Carnaval

Held on the last few days before Lent (in February or March), this holiday is often 'celebrated' with weeks of water fights, so be warned. It's popular in the highlands, with the fiesta in Cajamarca being one of the biggest. It's also busy in the beach towns.

Lunahuaná Adventure Sports Festival

Lunahuaná has an active and growing adventure sports scene, especially river running. Check out this festival in late February/early March.

March

Beach resort prices go down and crowds disperse, though the coast remains sunny. Orchids bloom post–rainy season on the Inca Trail and Amazonian birds enact their mating rituals.

Verano Negro

A must for anyone with an interest in Afro-Peruvian culture, this festival in Chincha features plenty of music and dancing. It takes place in late February or early March.

Fiesta de la Vendimia

Celebrated big on the south coast's two main wine regions, Ica and

Lunahuaná. These harvest festivals involve some grape stomping.

April

Crowds and high season prices mark Holy Week, a boon of national tourism in March or April. Hotel prices spike to their highest and availability is low. Reserve way ahead.

Semana Santa

The week before Easter Sunday, Holy Week is celebrated with spectacular religious processions almost daily, with Ayacucho recognized as the biggest celebration in Peru, lasting a full 10 days. Arequipa and Huancayo also have Easter processions.

May

The heaviest rains have passed, leaving the highlands lush and green. With the return of drier weather, trekking season starts to take off in Huaraz and around Cuzco.

El Señor de Muruhuay

This big annual pilgrimage happens in late May – with processions and fireworks to accompany the religious fervour.

Noche en Blanco

Inspired by Europe's White Nights, the streets of Miraflores in Lima are closed to cars while arts, music and dance take over. Held in early May.

Festival of the Crosses

This fascinating religious festival is held on May 3 in Lima, Apurímac, Ayacucho, Junín, Ica and Cuzco.

Festival del Mar

The first week in May commemorates the arrival of Takaynamo, the man history tells us founded Chan Chan. They celebrate every other year in Huanchaco with surf contests, dancing and revelry.

Q'oyoriti

A fascinating indigenous pilgrimage to the holy mountain of Ausangate, outside Cuzco, in May or June. Though known by few outsiders, it's well worth checking out.

June

High season for international tourism runs June through August, with Machu Picchu requiring advance reservations for train tickets and entry. It's also the busiest time for festivals in and around Cuzco.

Spot the Marvelous Spatuletail

June is your best opportunity to spot this unique and endangered hummingbird in tracts of forest around the Rio Utcubamba valley near Chachapoyas.

Semana de Andinismo

Mountaineering aficionados descend on Huaraz to celebrate the Andes with hikes, rock climbing, paragliding, skiing and concerts.

Corpus Christi

Processions of this Catholic celebration in Cuzco are especially dramatic. Held on the ninth Thursday after Easter.

Inti Raymi

The Festival of the Sun; also the Feast of St John the Baptist and Peasant's Day, it's the greatest of Inca festivals, celebrating the winter solstice on June 24. It's certainly the spectacle of the year in Cuzco, attracting thousands of Peruvian and foreign visitors. It's also a big holiday in many jungle towns.

Selvámanos

Reggae, *cumbia* (Colombian salsa-like dance and musical style) and electronica rock the jungle at this new music festival held near Oxapampa, in a spectacular national park setting.

San Juan

The feast of San Juan is all debauchery in Iquitos, where dancing, feasting and cockfights go until the wee hours on the eve of the actual holiday of June 24.

San Pedro y San Pablo

The feasts of saints Peter and Paul provide more fiestas on June 29, especially around Lima and in the highlands.

Top: La Virgen del Carmen parade, in July

Bottom: Dancers perform for Inti Raymi, the Festival of the Sun, in June

July

The continuation of high-season tourism. In Lima the weather is marked by *garúa*, a thick, grey sea mist that lingers over the city for the next few months and brings a chill.

Fiesta del Santiago

Rio Mantaro Valley towns, especially Huancayo, dress up cattle and parade them through the streets. There's also singing and dancing, in what many believe is an ancient fertility right.

La Virgen del Carmen

Held on July 16, this holiday is mainly celebrated in the southern sierra – with Paucartambo and Pisac near Cuzco, and Pucará near Lake Titicaca being especially important centers.

Fiestas Patrias

The National Independence Days are celebrated nationwide on July 28 and 29; festivities in the southern sierra begin with the Feast of St James on July 25.

August

The last month of high tourist visitation throughout Peru is also the most crowded at Machu Picchu. Book reservations well ahead.

Feast of Santa Rosa de Lima

Commemorating the country's first saint, major processions are held on August 30 in Lima, Arequipa and

Junín to honor the patron saint of Lima and of the Americas.

September

Low season everywhere, September and October can still offer good weather to highland trekkers without the crowds, while migrating birds become another attraction for birders.

Mistura

For one week in September, this massive, internationally acclaimed food festival is held in Lima, drawing up to half a million visitors to sample the country's best restaurants and street food.

El Festival Internacional de la Primavera

A don't miss, the International Spring Festival in Trujillo features supreme displays of horsemanship, as well as dancing and cultural celebrations during the last week of September.

October

The best time to hit the Amazon runs from September to November when drier weather results in better wildlife-watching.

El Señor de Luren

Travel down to Ica in late October for this religious festival, marked by fireworks, processions and plenty of merriment.

Great Amazon River Raft Race

The longest raft race in the world flows between Nauta and Iquitos in September or early October.

La Virgen del Rosario

On October 4, this saint's celebration comes to Lima, Apurímac, Arequipa and Cuzco. Its biggest event is held in Ancash, with a symbolic confrontation between Moors and Christians.

El Señor de los Milagros

A major religious festival, the Lord of the Miracles celebration is held in Lima on October 18, around which time the bullfighting season starts.

November

A good month for festivals, with plenty of events to choose from. It's worth checking out the wild celebrations held in Puno. Waves return, calling all surfers to the coast.

Todos Santos

All Saints' Day is November 1, a religious precursor to the following day celebrated with Catholic masses.

Día de los Muertos

All Souls' Day is celebrated on November 2 with gifts of food, drink and flowers taken to family graves. It's especially colorful in the Andes where some of the 'gift' food and drink is consumed, and the atmosphere is festive rather than somber.

Puno Week

Starting November 5, this week-long festival involves several days of spectacular costumes and street dancing to celebrate the legendary emergence of the first Inca, Manco Cápac.

December

Beach season returns with warmer Pacific temperatures. Skip the Amazon, where heavy rains start falling from the end of the month through early April.

Fiesta de la Purísima Concepción

The Feast of the Immaculate Conception is a national holiday celebrated with religious processions in honor of the Virgin Mary. It's held on December 8.

Christmas Day

Held on December 25, Christmas is less secular and more religious, particularly as celebrated in the Andean highlands.

La Virgen del Carmen de Chincha

Frenzied dancing and all-night music in the *peñas* (bars or clubs featuring live folkloric music) of El Carmen on December 27.

Itineraries

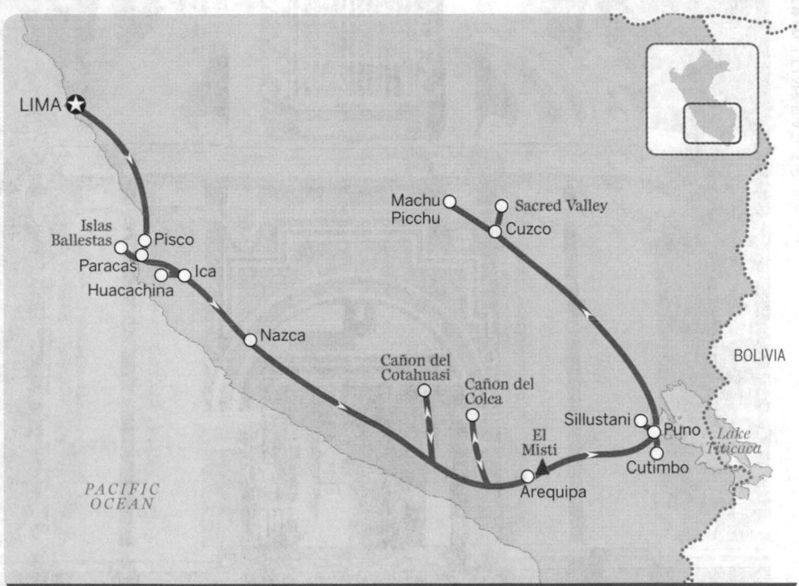

The Gringo Trail

This trip hits some of the pre-eminent highlights of the continent. Leaving **Lima**, journey south to **Pisco** and **Paracas**, where you can boat to the wildlife-rich **Islas Ballestas**, lodging in Paracas. Then it's on to **Ica**, Peru's wine and pisco capital, and the palm-fringed, dune-lined oasis of **Huacachina**, famous for sandboarding and a good place to overnight. Next is **Nazca** for a flight over the mysterious Nazca Lines.

Turn inland for the 'White City' of **Arequipa**, with its colonial architecture and stylish nightlife. Lace up your boots to trek the incredible **Cañón del Colca** or **Cañón del Cotahuasi** – perhaps the world's deepest – or climb **El Misti**, a postcard-perfect 5822m volcano. Continue upwards to **Puno**, Peru's port on **Lake Titicaca**, one of the world's highest navigable lakes. From here you can boat to traditional islands and explore the strange *chullpas* (ancient funerary towers) at **Sillustani** and **Cutimbo**.

Wind through the Andes to **Cuzco**, South America's oldest continuously inhabited city. Browse colorful markets and explore archaeological sites in the **Sacred Valley**, then trek to **Machu Picchu** via an adventurous alternative route.

Top: Colorful facade on Plaza de Armas (p315), Trujillo

Bottom: Rafting expedition on the Río Alto Madre de Dio (p456), Manu area

The Best of Peru

If you're set on getting a taste of everything, this whirlwind tour hits Peru's top must-see attractions. Give yourself a full month to fully take it all in.

Conquer your jet lag with the exquisite tastes of Peru in the restaurants of **Lima**, strolling through parks and museums between meals. Head south through the coastal desert to **Nazca**, for a flyover of the Nazca Lines before arriving in stylish, cosmopolitan **Arequipa**, with its mysterious monasteries, deep canyons and smoking volcanoes.

Fly high into the Andes to reach the ancient Inca capital of **Cuzco** for a few days of acclimatization, exploring the cobblestone city and visiting **Sacred Valley** villages to check out colorful markets selling textiles, talismans and dozens of types of tubers. Then board the train to **Machu Picchu**, the most visited archaeological site in South America.

From Cuzco, fly to **Puerto Maldonado** (or brave the 10-hour bus ride) where you can kick back at a wildlife lodge along one of the mighty rivers of the Amazon Basin. Alternatively, you can take an overland tour from Cuzco to the **Manu area**, with remote tracts of virgin forest holding diverse animals from kinkajous to caimans. It's one of the most biodiverse areas of the planet. Another option for exploring the Amazonian *selva* (jungle) is to first fly back to Lima, then onward to **Iquitos**, a bustling port that will launch you deeper into the jungle.

Back in Lima, take a bus or fly north to the adventurers' base camp of **Huaraz**, where a short trek will take you to the precipitous peaks of the **Cordillera Blanca**. A day trip to Chavín de Huántar will lead you to one of Peru's oldest ancient sites. Rumble back down to the coast at **Chimbote**, then dash north to historic **Trujillo**, which offers spicy northern dishes, surrounded by a cornucopia of archaeological sites. These include the ruins of the largest pre-Columbian city in the Americas, Chan Chan, and the fascinating Huacas del Sol y de la Luna. Finish up the journey by taking a seaside break at the bustling surf town of **Máncora**.

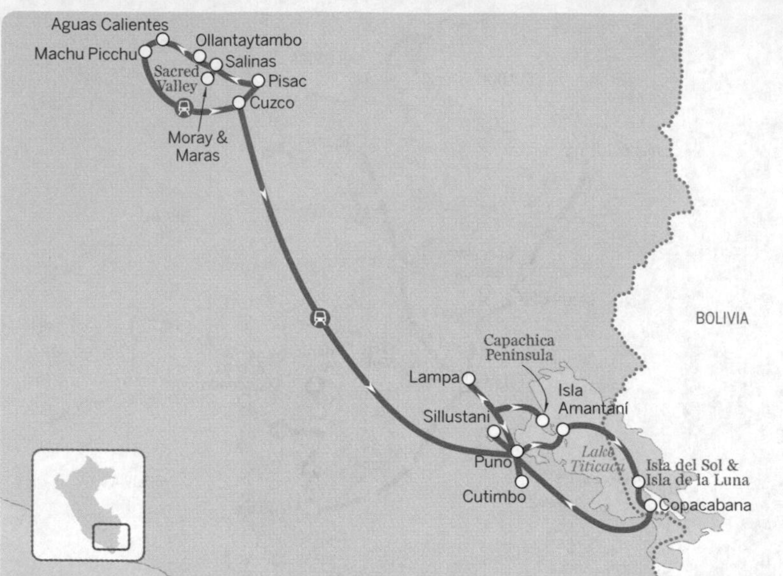

2 WEEKS The Inca Heartland

From Lima, fly to Cuzco but move on to the lower **Sacred Valley** to spend your first three to four days acclimating to the altitude. Visit the bustling market of **Pisac**, and see the ruins and ride horses at **Moray and Maras**. The best accommodations are in the quaint Inca village of **Ollantaytambo**, at a swank valley resort or area B&B.

From Ollantaytambo, hike the town ruins in the morning or visit the cool salt pans of **Salinas** and take an afternoon train to **Aguas Calientes**. Enjoy a leisurely dinner and tuck in early so you can take the first bus to the great Inca citadel of **Machu Picchu**. Spend the day browsing the ruins.

The following morning, hop on the train to **Cuzco**. Now that you're acclimated, spend a few days enjoying the colonial charms of this former Inca capital, taking a walking tour, visiting a few museums, admiring the splendors of **Qorikancha**, the Inca's most spectacular temple, and enjoying the city's outstanding cuisine.

Grab a comfortable tourist bus (or take the historic train) to the altiplano (Andean plateau) city of **Puno**. If you can coincide with a festival, this is the place to do it, with wild costumes, brass bands and fervent merriment. Otherwise, take in folkloric music at a dinner show or adventure to aquatic accommodations on the retired steamship *Yavari*.

From your base in Puno, the funerary towers of the Colla, Lupaca and Inca cultures can be found at **Sillustani** and **Cutimbo**, an easy day trip, and worth combining with lovely **Lampa** and its historic church. Take a boat tour of **Lake Titicaca**, visiting the famous reed islands and staying overnight in traditional family lodgings on **Isla Amantaní**. If you have a few extra days, take a catamaran tour, which also visits the Bolivian islands of **Isla del Sol** and **Isla de la Luna**, landing you in **Copacabana**, from where you can take a tourist bus back to Puno.

Returning to Puno, explore the coast of the **Capachica Peninsula**, home to places still steeped in the ancient traditions of the altiplano with nary another traveler in sight.

Get ready for the culture shock of big city living, and fly back to Lima.

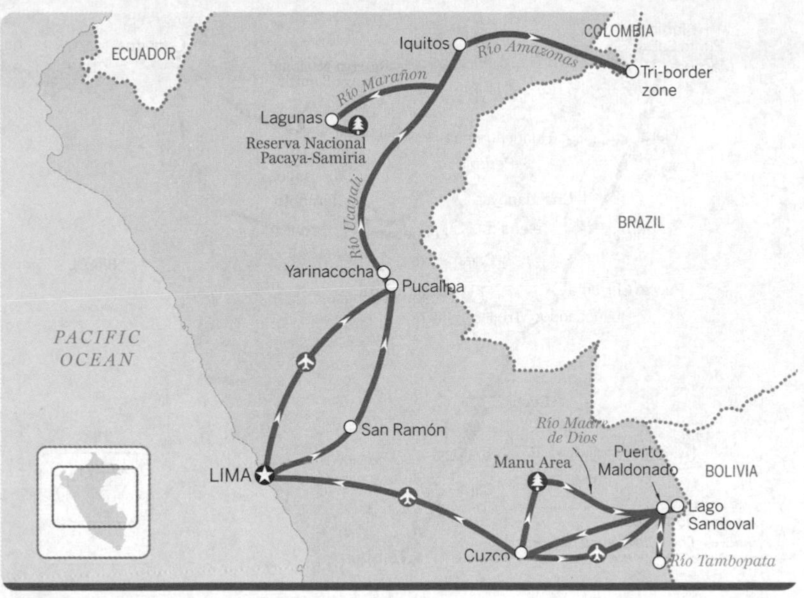

2–4 WEEKS Exploring Amazonia

More than half of Peru is jungle, populated by spectacular wildlife and tribal peoples. Go overland and drop dramatically away from the eastern slopes of the Andes to slip deep into the Amazon Basin, which stretches all the way to the Atlantic. This entire itinerary takes a month, or it can be divided by region into one- or two-week segments.

The most popular excursion starts from **Cuzco** and heads to the **Manu area**, itself the size of a small country, albeit one with kingdoms of jungle lodges. Another option is to fly from Cuzco to **Puerto Maldonado** and kick back in a thatch-roofed bungalow with a view, either along the **Río Madre de Dios**, the gateway to lovely **Lago Sandoval**, or along the **Río Tambopata**, where a national reserve protects one of the country's largest clay licks. The dry season (July and August) is traditionally the best time to return overland back to Cuzco, although the recent paving of this route means it's now possible outside these months.

Alternatively, return to Lima and turn your focus to the north. The easiest way to get there is to fly from Lima to **Pucallpa**, staying in a lodge or bungalow in nearby **Yarinacocha**. The lovely oxbow lake is ringed by tribal villages. You can visit some of these, including those of the matriarchal Shipibo people, renowned for their pottery. Hardcore overland travelers can opt to reach Pucallpa from Lima via the coffee-growing settlement of **San Ramón**.

From Pucallpa, begin the classic slow riverboat journey north along the **Río Ucayali** to **Iquitos**, the world's largest city with no road access! This northern jungle capital has a floating market and a bustling port, where you can catch a more comfortable cruise into Peru's largest national park, **Reserva Nacional Pacaya-Samiria**, via **Lagunas**. It's also tempting to float over into Brazil via the unique **tri-border zone**.

It's best to fly if your time is limited; if not, lose yourself for weeks on epic river and road journeys through jungle terrain. Bring bucket loads of patience and self-reliance – and a lot of luck never hurts.

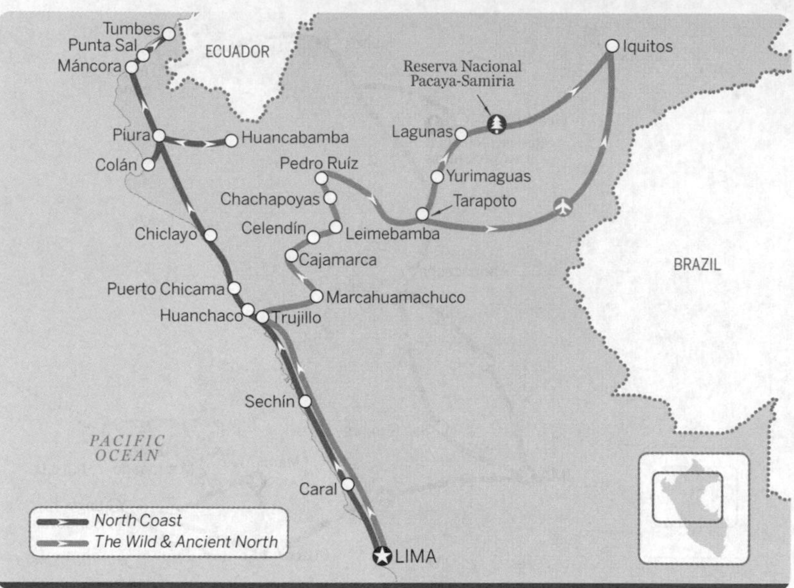

North Coast

The first stop north of **Lima** could be **Caral**, where the oldest known civilization in South America arose about 5000 years ago. Further north, spy ancient engravings of human sacrifice at **Sechín** and continue to **Trujillo**. Nearby attractions include the Moche pyramids of Huacas del Sol y de la Luna and ruins of the Chan Chan.

Off the sleepy beaches at **Huanchaco**, surfers paddle out to the breakers while local fishers trawl the coast. To the north, the surf spot of **Puerto Chicama** boasts one of the world's longest left-hand breaks. Then it's **Chiclayo**, with world-class museums nearby showcasing riches from the archaeological site of Sipán.

Craft-market hub **Piura** has great dining, while the witch doctors of **Huancabamba** are hidden away in the Andes. Peru's best beaches lie along the Pacific shoreline. Feast on fresh seafood and dance the balmy nights away at resorts such as **Colán**, **Máncora**, and **Punta Sal**.

The journey ends at **Tumbes**, a gateway to Ecuador and jumping-off point to endangered mangrove swamps, which teem with wildlife (mind the crocs!).

The Wild & Ancient North

From **Lima**, head to **Trujillo**, sampling the fiery coastal cuisine and exploring nearby ruins at Chan Chan and Huacas del Sol y de la Luna. From Trujillo, take the freshly paved scenic old highway to Cajamarca via the magnificent mountaintop ruins of **Marcahuamachuco**.

The lovely highland town of **Cajamarca** is where the conquistadors captured Inca Atahualpa. In the dry season, adventure on the slow, spectacular route to friendly **Celendín** and on to **Leimebamba** to see the Marvelous Spatuletail Hummingbird. Continue on to **Chachapoyas** where the cloud forest obscures the fantastic monolithic fortress of Kuélap.

From Chachapoyas, journey via **Pedro Ruíz** to **Tarapoto**, where you can hike in lush forest to waterfalls. Next, fly to the jungle city of **Iquitos** or continue via **Yurimaguas**, where cargo boats make the rugged two-day trip to Iquitos via the village of **Lagunas**, the entry point to the **Reserva Nacional Pacaya-Samiria**, for an unforgettable glimpse of the world's greatest river basin. At Iquitos, you can arrange boat trips that go deeper into the rainforest and on to Brazil or Colombia.

Plan Your Trip

Peru Outdoors

Scale icy Andean peaks. Raft one of the world's deepest canyons. Surf the heavenly Pacific curlers. Walk the flanks of a smoldering volcano known locally as a living deity. With its breathtaking, diverse landscapes, Peru is a natural adventure hub. So gear up and take the Band-Aids. You're in for one wild ride.

Hiking & Trekking

Pack the hiking boots because the variety of trails in Peru is downright staggering. The main trekking centers are Cuzco and Arequipa in the southern Andes, and Huaraz in the north. Hikers will find many easily accessible trails around Peru's archaeological ruins, which are also the final destinations for more challenging trekking routes.

History goes deep here – you may be hiking through terraced fields along ancient trade routes or trails used by Inca messengers. Yet even then, the fledgling status of some outdoor activities here means that, in certain times and places, you can get a whole mountain, sandy shore or complex of ruins to yourself.

Big plans are in the works for Qhapaq Ñan, the Inca road system that became a World Heritage Site in 2014. It spans a whopping 22,530km from Colombia to Chile and follows one of the most scenic routes possible, proving definitively that the Incas were master road builders. Tourism outfitters hope that the designation will spur investment into these often neglected trails. Look out for new trekking opportunities on this route.

Peru's most famous trek is the Inca Trail to Machu Picchu. Limited permits mean this guided-only trek sells out months in advance. For those who haven't planned so far in advance, there are worthwhile alternative routes. Other possibilities

Top 5 Wildlife-Watching Spots

Parque Nacional Manu

Jaguars, tapirs and monkeys inhabit this expansive rainforest park, among the continent's wildest, deep in the Amazon

Cañón del Colca

Andean condors glide over this rugged canyon, the second deepest in the world

Islas Ballestas

Colonies of honking sea lions and penguins claim these rocky Pacific outcrops off Peru's south coast

Parque Nacional Huascarán

Giant Puya raimondii plants burst with flowers while vicuñas and viscachas bustle around the high alpine landscape of the Cordillera Blanca

Tumbes

A rare mangrove forest on the northernmost coast, home to crocodiles, seabirds, flamingos and crabs around Cuzco include the spectacular six-day trek around the venerated Ausangate (6372m), which will take you over 5000m passes, through huge herds of alpacas and past tiny hamlets unchanged in centuries. Likewise, the isolated Inca site of Choquequirao is another intriguing destination for a trek.

In nearby Arequipa, you can head down some of the world's deepest canyons – the world-famous Cañón del Colca and the Cañón del Cotahuasi. The scenery is guaranteed to knock you off your feet, and it's easier going than some higher-altitude destinations. During the wet season, when some Andean trekking routes are impassable, Colca is invitingly lush and green. It's also the best place in Peru for DIY trekking between rural villages. The more remote and rugged Cañón del Cotahuasi is best visited with an experienced local guide and only during the dry season.

Outside Huaraz, the Cordillera Blanca can't be beat for vistas of rocky, snow-capped mountaintops, while the remote and rugged Cordillera Huayhuash is similarly stunning. The classic and favorite trekking route is the four-day journey from Llanganuco to Santa Cruz, where hardy mountaineers climb the 4760m Punta Union pass, surrounded by ice-clad peaks. Longer treks include the northern route around the dazzling Alpamayo, which requires at least a week. Shorter overnight trips in the area go to mountain base camps, alpine lakes and even along an old Inca road.

Cuzco and Huaraz (and, to a lesser degree, Arequipa) have outfitters that can provide equipment, guides and even *arrieros* (mule drivers). If you prefer to trek ultralight, you might want to purchase your own gear, especially a sleeping bag, as old-generation rental items tend to be heavy.

Whether you'll need a guide depends on where you trek. Certain areas of Peru, such as along the Inca Trail, require guides; in other places, such as in the Cordillera Huayhuash, there have been muggings, so it's best to be with a local. Thankfully, scores of other trekking routes are wonderfully DIY. Equip yourself with topographic maps for major routes in the nearest major gateway towns or, better yet, at the Instituto Geográfico Nacional (IGN) or at the South American Explorers Club in Lima.

Whatever adventure you choose, be prepared to spend a few days acclimating to the dizzying altitudes – or face a heavy-duty bout of altitude sickness.

Trekking is most rewarding during the dry season (May to September) in the Andes. Avoid the wet season (December to March), when rain makes some areas impassable.

RESPONSIBLE TREKKING

- Don't depend on open fires. Cook on a lightweight camp stove and dispose of butane cartridges responsibly.
- Carry out all rubbish.
- Contamination of water sources by human waste can lead to the transmission of all sorts of nasties. Where there is a toilet, use it. Where there is none, bury your waste. Dig a small hole 15cm deep and at least 100m from any watercourse. Cover the waste with soil and a rock. Pack out toilet paper.
- For washing, use biodegradable soap and a water container at least 50m away from any watercourses. Disperse the waste water widely to allow the soil to filter it fully.
- Do not feed the wildlife.
- Some trails pass through private property. It's polite to ask residents before crossing their property and to leave all livestock gates as you found them.
- Don't give children money, sweets or gifts. This encourages persistent begging, which has become a major problem on some busy routes. If you wish to help, consider donating directly to local schools, NGOs and other volunteer organizations.
- Keep a low profile: the gear you are carrying costs more than many locals earn in a month (or a year). Stow everything inside your tent at night.

Mountain, Rock & Ice Climbing

Peru has the highest tropical mountains in the world, offering some absolutely inspired climbs, though acclimatization to altitude is essential. The Cordillera Blanca, with its dozens of snowy peaks exceeding 5000m, is one of South America's top destinations.

The Andean town of Huaraz has tour agencies, outfitters, guides, information and climbing equipment for hire. Still, it's best to bring your own gear for serious ascents. Near Huaraz, Ishinca (5530m) and Pisco (5752m) provide two ascents easy enough for relatively inexperienced climbers.

For experts, these mountains are also good warm-up climbs for bigger adventures such as Huascarán (6768m), Peru's highest peak. Other challenging peaks include the stunning, knife-edged Alpamayo (5947m) and Yerupajá (6634m), Peru's second-highest mountain, located in the Cordillera Huayhuash.

Rock and ice climbing are also taking off around Huaraz, where a few outfitters have indoor climbing walls, rent out technical equipment and organize group trips.

In southern Peru, the snowy volcanic peaks around Arequipa can be scaled by determined novice mountaineers. The most popular climb is El Misti (5822m), a site of Inca human sacrifice. Despite its serious altitude, it is basically a very long, tough walk. Chachani (6075m) is one of the easier 6000m peaks in the world – though it still requires crampons, an ice ax and a good guide. Other tempting peaks tower above the Cañón del Colca.

For beginners looking to bag their first serious mountains, Peru may not be the best place to start. Not all guides know the basics of first aid or wilderness search and rescue. Check out a prospective guide's credentials carefully and seek out those who are personally recommended. Carefully check any rental equipment before setting out.

As with trekking, high-elevation climbing is best done during the dry season (mid-June to mid-July).

TOUCHING THE VOID

What inspires a person to endure inhospitable climes, hunger, exhaustion and a lack of oxygen in order to conquer forbidding mountain peaks? It's a question explored at length by Joe Simpson in his celebrated book, *Touching the Void: The True Story of One Man's Miraculous Survival*. This gripping narrative tells the story of a climb that Simpson undertook with his climbing partner, Simon Yates. The climb began well enough – with an extremely challenging and, ultimately, successful ascent on the jagged and steep Siula Grande in the Cordillera Huayhuash. But it ended in an accident that almost claimed one man's life. The book examines the thrills, rewards and agony of mountaineering. *Touching the Void* became an award-winning British documentary in 2003.

Rafting & Kayaking

River running is growing in popularity around Peru, with trips that range from a few hours to more than two weeks.

Cuzco is the launch point for the greatest variety of river-running options. Choices range from a few hours of mild rafting on the Urubamba to adrenaline-pumping rides on the Santa Teresa to several days on the Apurímac, technically the source of the Amazon (with world-class rafting between May and November). A river-running trip on the Tambopata, available from June through October, tumbles down the eastern slopes of the Andes, culminating in a couple of days of floating in unspoiled rainforest.

Arequipa is another rafting center. Here, the Río Chili is the most frequently run, with a half-day novice trip leaving daily between March and November. Further afield, the more challenging Río Majes features class II and III rapids. On the south coast, Lunahuaná, not far from Lima, is a prime spot for beginners and experts alike. Between December and April, rapids here can reach class IV.

JAN-NIKLAS KELTSCH / SHUTTERSTOCK ©

TODD LAWSON / GETTY IMAGES ©

Top: Sandboarding, Huacachina (p124)

Bottom: Rafting, Caraz (p391)

Note that rafting is not regulated in Peru. There are deaths every year and some rivers are so remote that rescues can take days. In addition, some companies are not environmentally responsible and leave camping beaches dirty. Book excursions only with reputable, well-recommended agencies and avoid cut-rate trips. A good operator will have insurance, provide you with a document indicating that they are registered, and have highly experienced guides with certified first-aid training who carry a properly stocked medical kit. Choose one that provides top-notch equipment, including self-bailing rafts, US Coast Guard–approved life jackets, first-class helmets and spare paddles. Many good companies raft rivers accompanied by a kayaker experienced in river rescue.

For more on river running in Peru, visit www.peruwhitewater.com.

Surfing, Kitesurfing & Paddleboarding

With consistent, uncrowded waves and plenty of remote breaks to explore, Peru has a mixed surfing scene that attracts dedicated locals and international die-hards alike. Kitesurfing and paddle-boarding are also emerging as popular sports.

Waves can be found from the moment you land. All along the southern part of Lima, surfers ride out popular point and beach breaks at Miraflores (known as Waikiki), Barranquito and La Herradura. Herradura's outstanding left-hand point break gets crowded when there is a strong swell. In-the-know surfers prefer the smaller crowds further south at Punta Hermosa. International and national championships are held at nearby Punta Rocas as well as Pico Alto, an experts-only 'kamikaze' reef break with some of the largest waves in Peru. Isla San Gallán, off the Península de Paracas, also provides experts with a world-class right-hand point break only accessible by boat; ask local fishermen or at hotels.

Peru's north coast has a string of excellent breaks. The most famous is Puerto Chicama, where rides of more than 2km are possible on what's considered the longest left-hand break in the world. Also, very consistent waves can be found at Pacasmayo, and outside Chiclayo at Pimentel and Santa Rosa. It's also worth checking out Lobitos and Máncora.

Máncora is a hub for paddleboarding and kitesurfing, which has also caught on in Paracas.

The water is cold from April to mid-December (as low as 15°C/60°F), when wet suits are generally needed. Indeed, many surfers wear wet suits year-round (2/3mm will suffice), even though the water is a little warmer (around 20°C, or 68°F, in the Lima area) from January to March. The far north coast (north of Talara) stays above 21°C (70°F) most of the year.

Though waves are generally not crowded, surfing can be a challenge – facilities are limited and equipment rental is expensive. The scene on the north coast is the most organized, with surf shops and hostels that offer advice, rent out boards and arrange surfing day trips. Huanchaco is a great base for these services. Serious surfers should bring their own board.

The best surfing websites include www.peruazul.com, www.vivamancora.com and www.wannasurf.com, with a comprehensive, highly detailed list of just about every break in Peru.

Good wave and weather forecasts can be found at www.magicseaweed.com and www.windguru.com.

Sandboarding

Sandboarding down the giant desert dunes is growing in popularity at Huacachina and around Nazca, on Peru's south coast. Nazca's Cerro Blanco (2078m) is the highest known sand dune in the world.

Some hotels and travel agencies offer tours in *areneros* (dune buggies), where you are hauled to the top of the dunes, then get picked up at the bottom. (Choose your driver carefully; some are notoriously reckless.)

For more information on sandboarding worldwide, check out *Sandboard Magazine* at www.sandboard.com.

Mountain Biking & Cycling

In recent years mountain biking has exploded in popularity. It is still a fledgling sport in Peru, but there is no shortage of incredible terrain. Single-track trails ranging from easy to expert await mountain bikers outside Huaraz, Arequipa and even Lima. If you're experienced, there are incredible mountain-biking possibilities around the Sacred Valley and downhill trips to the Amazon jungle, all accessible from Cuzco. Easier cycling routes include the wine country around Lunahuaná and in the Cañón del Colca, starting from Chivay.

Mountain-bike rental in Peru tends to be basic; if you are planning on serious biking it's best to bring your own. (Airline bicycle-carrying policies vary, so shop around.) You'll also need a repair kit and extra parts.

Swimming

Swimming is popular along Peru's desert coast from January to March, when the Pacific Ocean waters are warmest and skies are blue. Some of the best spots are just south of Lima. Far more attractive is the stretch of shore on the north coast, especially at laid-back Huanchaco, around Chiclayo and the perennially busy jet-set resorts of Máncora.

Only north of Talara does the water stay warm year-round. Watch for dangerous currents and note that beaches near major coastal cities are often polluted.

Scuba Diving

Scuba diving in Peru is limited. The water is cold except from mid-December to March. During these months the water is at its cloudiest, due to runoff from mountain rivers. Dive shops in Lima offer PADI certification classes, rent out scuba equipment and run trips to sea-lion colonies along the coast. Máncora is also a hub for scuba diving.

Horseback Riding

Horse rentals can be arranged in many tourist destinations, but the rental stock is not always treated well, so check your horse carefully before you saddle up. For a real splurge, take a ride on a graceful Peruvian *paso* horse. Descendants of horses with royal Spanish and Moorish lineage, such as those ridden by the conquistadors, are reputed to have the world's smoothest gait. Stables around Peru advertise rides for half a day or longer, especially in the Sacred Valley at Urubamba.

Paragliding

Popular paragliding sites include the coastal clifftops of suburban Miraflores in Lima and various points along the south coast, including Pisco and Paracas (even, possibly, over the Nazca Lines). There are few paragliding operators in Peru. Book ahead through the agencies in Lima.

Plan Your Trip

Trekking the Inca Trail

You have pictured its deep green gorges, the lost citadels and misty peaks that ebb in and out of view. It is nothing less than mind-bending to climb these stone stairways laid millennia ago, following the Andean route that evaded the Spanish for centuries. There is no doubt: trekking the Inca Trail is a traveler's rite of passage and the adventure of a lifetime. Logistics can be confusing, so preplanning is essential before you get your boots on the trail.

Planning Your Trek

When to Go

Organized groups leave year-round except in February, when the Inca trail is closed for maintenance and it rains so much that nobody in their right mind goes trekking. The coldest, driest and most popular months are June to August. But those who are well prepared with proper gear can enjoy the trail during any month it's open.

To skip the crowds, consider going before and after the rainy season: from March to May (best vegetation, orchids and birdlife) or September to November.

What to Expect

Even if you are not carrying a full backpack, this trek requires a good level of fitness. In addition to regularly exercising, you can get ready with hikes and long walks in the weeks before your trip (also a good time to test out your gear). Boots should be already worn in by the time you go. On the trail, you may have to deal with issues such as heat and altitude. Just don't rush it; keep a reasonable pace and you should do fine.

Alternative Routes to Machu Picchu

Two-day Inca Trail

A guided overnight route with the top highlights of the trail. Permits are limited, so book far in advance.

Lares

Best done with a guide, this culturally oriented option is a flexible multiday trek through quaint Andean villages, combined with train travel from Ollantaytambo to Aguas Calientes.

Salcantay Trek

A scenic, but demanding, five-day hike that ranges from jungle to alpine terrain, peaking at 4700m. It's possible to do independently or with a guide.

The Inca Jungle Trail

With hiking, biking and rafting options, this guided multisport route offers stages to Machu Picchu via Santa Teresa.

Booking Your Trip

It is important to book your trip at least six months in advance for dates between May and August. Outside these months, you may get a permit with a few weeks' notice, but it's very hard to predict. Only licensed operators can get permits, but you can check general availability at www.camino-inca.com.

Consider booking a five-day trip to lessen the pace and enjoy more wildlife and ruins. Other positives include less-crowded campsites and being able to stay at the most scenic one – Phuyupatamarka (3600m) – on the third evening.

Take some time to research your options – you won't regret it. It's best to screen agencies for a good fit before committing. Also make sure you have international travel insurance that covers adventure activities.

Regulations & Fees

The Inca Trail is the only trek in the Cuzco area that cannot be walked independently – you must go with a licensed operator. Prices range from US$550 to US$1465 and above.

Only 500 people each day (including guides and porters) are allowed to start the trail. You must go through an approved Inca Trail operator. Permits are issued to them on a first-come, first-served basis. You will need to provide your passport number to get a permit, and carry the passport with you to show at checkpoints along the trail. Be aware that if you get a new passport but had applied with your old, it may present a problem.

Permits are nontransferrable: name changes are not allowed.

BOOK AHEAD

Due to the Inca Trail's overwhelming popularity, you must book at least six weeks in advance for trips outside high season and six months to a full year beforehand for departures between late May and early September. The same goes for the abbreviated two-day route.

And if it's already booked for your dates? Check out the alternative routes (p45).

Choosing an Inca Trail Operator

While it may be tempting to quickly book your trek and move onto the next item on your To Do list, it's a good idea to examine the options carefully before sending that deposit. If price is your bottom line, keep in mind that the cheapest agencies may cut corners by paying their guides and porters lower wages. Other issues are substandard gear (ie leaky tents) and dull or lackadaisical guiding.

Yet paying more may not mean getting more, especially since international operators take their cut and hire local Peruvian agencies. Talk with a few agencies to get a sense of their quality of service. You might ask if the guide speaks English (fluently or just a little), request a list of what is included and inquire about group size and the kind of transportation used. Ensure that your tour includes a tent, food, a cook, one-day admission to the ruins and the return train fare.

If you have special dietary requirements, state them clearly before the trip, being clear about allergies (versus preference issues). Vegans will meet with a lot of quinoa and lentils. If possible, get confirmation in writing that your specific requirements will be met.

Porters who carry group gear – tents, food etc – are also included. You'll be expected to carry your own personal gear, including sleeping bag. If you are not an experienced backpacker, it may be a good idea to hire a porter to carry your personal gear; this usually costs around US$50 per day for about 10kg.

Part of the fun is meeting travelers from other parts of the world in your trekking group. Keep in mind that individual paces vary and the group dynamic requires some compromise.

For those who prefer more exclusive services, it's possible to organize private trips with an independent licensed guide (US$1250 to US$2000 per person). This can be expensive but for groups of six or more it may in fact be cheaper than the standard group treks. Prices vary considerably, so shop around.

Porter welfare is a major issue in the Cuzco region. Porter laws are enforced through fines and license suspensions by

PORTER WELFARE

In the past, Inca trail porters have faced excessively low pay, enormous carrying loads and poor working conditions. Relatively recent laws now stipulate a minimum payment of S170 to porters, adequate sleeping gear and food, and treatment for on-the-job injuries. At checkpoints on the trail, porter loads are weighed (each is allowed 20kg of group gear and 5kg of their own gear).

Yet there is still room for improvement and the best way to help is to choose your outfitter wisely. Conscientious operators do exist, but only a few are confident enough to charge the price that a well-equipped, well-organized, well-guided trip requires. A quality trip will set you back at least US$500. The cheaper trips cut costs and often affect porter welfare – on the Inca Trail and other trekking routes. Go with a well-recommended company.

There's more you can do on the trail:

- Don't overpack. Someone will have to carry the extra weight and porters may have to leave their own essential gear behind.
- Don't occupy the dining tent until late if it's where the porters sleep.
- Tip the cooks if you liked the food, and always tip your porters.
- Tip individuals directly and in soles. Don't leave it to the company or a guide to distribute.
- If you don't plan to use your gear again, items such as good sleeping bags are like gold to porters. Warm jackets, pocket tools and headlamps also make thoughtful end-of-trip tips.
- If you don't like what you see, complain to your guide and to the agency, and register an official complaint with iPerú (www.peru.info), either at a branch or online.

Though guides and outfitters are subject to annual review, it can take time to deactivate a company that has acted irresponsibly. It is important for trekkers to give feedback. To learn more about the life of porters, look for the documentary *Mi Chacra*, winner of the 2011 Banff Film Festival Grand Prize.

Peru's Ministerio de Trabajo (Ministry of Work).

Lonely Planet only lists operators who haven't been sanctioned at the time of research. Of course, there are other conscientious operators out there, and some offer treks as well as other tours around Peru.

Amazonas Explorer (☎84-25-2846; www.amazonas-explorer.com) Cuzco's longest-standing outfitter, with socially and environmentally responsible practices. Offers the five-day classic and alternative treks.

Aracari (☎in Lima 01-651-2424; www.aracari.com) A reputable Lima-based agency with high-end tours.

Aventours (☎84-22-4050; www.aventours.com; Saphi 456, Cuzco) A responsible outfitter with a long-tenured team.

Culturas Peru (☎84-24-3629; www.culturasperu.com; Tandapata 354-A, Cuzco) A highly knowledgeable and reputable, locally owned and run outfitter with sustainable practices.

Explorandes (☎in Lima 01-715-2323; www.explorandes.com) Offers five-day itineraries and a luxury version; ISO certified.

Intrepid Adventures (☎in Australia 61-3-9473-2626; www.intrepidtravel.com) A reputable Australian outfitter with sustainable practices.

Peruvian Odyssey (☎84-22-2105; www.peruvianodyssey.com; Pasaje Pumaqchupan 204, Cuzco) Operator with 20 years' experience; also offers alternative route via Santa Teresa.

Tambo Trek (☎84-23-7718; www.tambotreks.net) A pioneer outfitter, does classic and alternative routes, supports clean-up initiatives.

MICHAEL DEFREITAS / GETTY IMAGES ©

ED NORTON / GETTY IMAGES ©

Top: Machu Picchu (p253)

Bottom: The Salkantay trail to Machu Picchu

What to Bring

Trekking poles are highly recommended, as the Inca Trail features a cartilage-crunching number of downhill stone steps. Other items that will come in handy: first-aid kit, sunscreen, sandals for camp, a down jacket for cold nights, a waterproof jacket, a warm hat and gloves, sun hat, travel towel, broken-in hiking boots, warm trekking socks, thermal underwear top and bottom, a fleece, water bottle or hydration pack, insect repellent, long pants and sunglasses. Make sure that your pack is comfortable with weight and that you have enough camera batteries – there are no electrical outlets on the way.

Take cash (in Peruvian soles) for tipping; an adequate amount is S100 for a porter and S200 for a cook.

WATER TIP

When hiking the Inca trail, get your next day's water hot in a well-sealed bottle; you can use it as a sleeping bag warmer and it will be cool to drink by the time you're hiking.

Alternative Routes to Machu Picchu

For more information on alternative routes to Machu Picchu, the *Alternative Inca Trails Information Packet* from the South American Explorers Club is a great resource.

Two-Day Inca Trail

This 10km version of the Inca Trail gives a fairly good indication of what the longer trail is like. It's a real workout, and passes through some of the best scenery and most impressive ruins and terracing of the longer trail.

It's a steep three- or four-hour climb from Km 104 to Wiñay Wayna, then another two hours or so on fairly flat terrain to Machu Picchu. You may be on the trail a couple of hours longer, just to enjoy the views and explore. We advise taking the earliest train possible from Cuzco or Ollantaytambo.

The two-day trail means overnighting in Aguas Calientes and visiting Machu Picchu the next day, so it's really only one day of walking. The average price is US$400 to US$535.

Lares Valley Trek

This is not a specific track as such, but a walk along any of a number of different routes to Ollantaytambo through the dramatic Lares Valley. Starting at natural hot springs, the route wanders through rural Andean farming villages, lesser-known Inca archaeological sites, lush lagoons and river gorges. You'll finish by taking the train from Ollantaytambo to Aguas Calientes. Although this is more of a cultural trek than a technical trip, the mountain scenery is breathtaking, and the highest mountain pass (4450m) is certainly nothing to sneeze at. The average price is US$460.

Salkantay Trek

Salkantayis a longer, more spectacular trek, with a slightly more difficult approach to Machu Picchu than the Inca Trail. Its highest point is a high pass of over 4700m near the magnificent glacier-clad peak of Salkantay (6271m; 'Savage Mountain' in Quechua). From here you descend in spectacular fashion to the vertiginous valleys of the subtropics. It takes five to seven days to get to Machu Picchu, and the average price is US$400.

For a luxury approach, **Mountain Lodges of Peru** (☎84-26-2640; www.mountainlodgesofperu.com; per person US$2390-2990) offers high-quality guiding with accommodations in comfortable lodges with outdoor hot tubs. Prices vary according to high and low seasons.

Inca Jungle Trail: Back Door to Machu Picchu

Dreamed up by outfitters and guides, this multisport route between Cuzco and Machu Picchu travels via Santa Teresa with options to bike, hike and raft your way in two to five days. Some call it 'Machu Picchu via the back door.' The number of days and activities vary, but the backbone of tours on offer is the same.

The trip starts with a long, four- to five-hour drive from Cuzco to Abra

Málaga, with the high (4350m) pass between Ollantaytambo and the Amazon Basin. Somewhere on the Amazon side you'll board mountain bikes for the long ride down to Santa María. Starting on a paved road that turns to dirt after about 20km, it's an incredibly scenic descent from the glacial to the tropical, up to 71km total.

Some operators walk the 23km from Santa María to Santa Teresa; others send you by vehicle (one hour), arguing that it's not a particularly interesting hike, though there is a short section of preconquest *camino de hierro* (iron road) – the Inca version of a superhighway.

Either way you'll arrive in Santa Teresa to the welcome spectacle of the Cocalmayo hot springs. Some companies include rafting near Santa Teresa or the ziplines at Cola de Mono.

From Santa Teresa, you can walk the 20km to Machu Picchu, 12km of it along train tracks. There's nice river scenery but no particular attraction and it's usually dusty and hot. Alternatively, you can catch a bus and a train. You may reverse this route to get back to Cuzco, but it's much quicker to catch the train via the Sacred Valley.

Many varieties of this trip exist, and bare-bones versions may not include hotels or entry fees, so read the fine print. Whether you stay in a tent or a hostel, key factors in the trip price are bike quality, professional English-speaking guides and whether you walk or catch the train to Aguas Calientes. Three-day/two-night trips start from US$465, and usually include a guided tour of Machu Picchu and return train ticket to Ollantaytambo.

Gravity Peru (p214) offers the best-quality bikes. Other respected operators include **Reserv Cusco** (☎84-26-1548; www.reserv-cusco-peru.com; Plateros 326, Cuzco) and X-Treme Tourbulencia (p212).

Plan Your Trip

Travel with Children

Traveling with children to Peru can bring some distinct advantages. It is a family-oriented society and little ones are treasured. For parents, it makes an easy conversation starter with locals and ultimately aids in breaking down cultural barriers. In turn, Peru can be a great place for kids, with plenty of opportunities to explore and interact.

Peru for Kids

Peru is welcoming to kids, though it's best to take all the usual travel precautions – and be sure they have the appropriate vaccinations. Children will often get free or reduced admission rates at events and performances.

Practicalities

➡ **Public Transportation** In Peru, kids are welcome on public transportation. Often someone will give up a seat for a parent and child or offer to put your child on their lap. On buses, children aren't normally charged if they sit on their parent's lap.

➡ **Driving** Child seats are not widely available with rental cars so it is best if you bring one with you.

➡ **Expecting & New Mothers** Expecting mothers enjoy a boon of special parking spaces and grocery store lines. Breastfeeding in public is not uncommon, but most women discreetly cover themselves.

➡ **Babysitting** Babysitting services or children's activity clubs tend to be limited to upmarket hotels and resorts.

➡ **Public Toilets** In general, public toilets are poorly maintained. Always carry toilet paper. While a woman may take a young boy into the ladies' room, it would be socially unacceptable for a man to take a girl into the men's room.

Best Regions for Kids

Lima

Kids dig the Parque del Amor, Circuito Mágico del Agua, visiting markets and joining outdoor family events.

Cuzco & the Sacred Valley

Whether exploring the narrow passageways of the ancient city of Cuzco, visiting a traditional market or climbing high on the Via Ferrata, there's something here for all ages.

The Coast

Seaside resorts such as Paracas and Huanchaco provide beach fun and some surf. A gentle, sunny climate here helps keep your plans on target.

Machu Picchu

What could be more intriguing for teens than the mysteries of the Incas? Nearby, smaller sites such as Ollantaytambo, Pisac and Maras also make for exciting explorations.

➡ **Flights** Children under the age of 12 may receive discounts on airline travel, while infants under two pay only 10% of the fare, provided they sit on their parent's lap.

Health & Safety

The main issue in Peru is diet. Drink only filtered/bottled water for starters. It's also best to avoid raw vegetables unless you are assured they have been properly prepared. When traveling with young children, be particularly careful about their diet, as diarrhea can be especially dangerous to them. Children under two are particularly vulnerable to Hep A and typhoid fever, which can be contracted via contaminated food or water, as they are too young to be vaccinated against them.

Sun exposure can be dangerous, particularly at high altitudes, so make sure kids are adequately covered up and using sunscreen. Altitude sickness can also be an issue, so it's important that the family acclimates slowly. Taking children under three to high altitudes is not recommended. Consult your doctor on how to help kids cope with altitude sickness.

Children under nine months should not be taken to lower-altitude jungle areas because the yellow-fever vaccine is not safe for this age group.

All travelers to malaria-endemic countries such as Peru should visit their physician to obtain appropriate chemoprophylaxis based on their travel risk factors and age. Current guidelines suggest mefloquine, doxycycline and atovaquone-proguanil for travel to Peru, and all these can be used in children, with some limitations based on age and drug formulations. Some of these drugs need to be started two weeks before arrival in the country, so plan accordingly.

DEET-containing insect repellents can be used safely, but in concentrations of no higher than 30% for children according to the American Academy of Pediatrics (adults can safely use DEET concentrations of 50%). Insect repellents are not recommended for infants younger than two months of age (they should use an

ROCK PERU KID-STYLE

Peru has many ways to please young adventurers. Here are a few highlights.

Adventure

- ➡ Rafting near Cuzco
- ➡ Horseback riding in the Andean foothills
- ➡ Splashing about in the hot pools in Cañón del Colca's La Calera
- ➡ Canopy ziplining in the Sacred Valley
- ➡ Cycling the coastal paths of Lima
- ➡ Exploring ruins in Chachapoyas, Sacred Valley and Machu Picchu
- ➡ Spying wildlife in the Amazon

Entertainment

- ➡ Fiestas with traditional dances
- ➡ Bungee tramps and climbing walls in summer
- ➡ Llamas and alpacas at farms and petting zoos

Dining

- ➡ *Quintas* (places serving Andean food) with oversized grills and backyard ambience
- ➡ Picnics on rocky outcrops with a view to the world

Rainy Day Refuges

- ➡ Chiquity Club in Cuzco and *ludotecas* (educational centers) in Lima
- ➡ Making chocolates at the Choco Museos in Lima and Cuzco

infant carrier drape with mosquito netting instead).

Since street dogs are common, it's best to be up to date with rabies vaccinations. Most dogs are mild-mannered, but avoid those that seem aggressive.

Dining

While restaurants don't offer special kids' meals, most offer a variety of dishes suitable for children or may accommodate a special request. You can always order it *sin picante* (without spice). It is perfectly acceptable to split a dish between two children or an adult and a child. Don't wait to eat until everyone is too hungry – service can be quite slow. High chairs are available in some larger restaurants.

Adventure

Routine travel, such as train rides or jungle canoe trips, can amount to adventure for kids. In rural areas, community tourism is a great option. Many of the activities aimed at adults can be scaled down for children. Activities such as guided horseback rides and canyoning often have age limits (usually eight and up), but are invariably OK for teenagers. Some rivers may be suitable for children to float or raft; make sure outfitters have life vests and wet suits in appropriate sizes.

Planning

When to Go

Summer (between December and February) offers the most opportunities for good weather and beach fun, though the coast is enjoyed year-round. Avoid the highlands during the rainiest months (December to March). The highland dry season, between June and August, is ideal for exploring Cuzco and Machu Picchu, though these are also the busiest times.

Accommodations

Most midrange and top-end hotels will have reduced rates for children under 12 years of age, provided the child shares a room with parents. Cots are not normally available, except at the most exclusive hotels. Cabins or apartments, more common in beach destinations, usually make a good choice with options for self-catering.

What to Pack or Not to Pack

➡ If you're traveling with an infant, stock up on diapers (nappies) in Lima or other major cities before heading to rural areas. Also pack infant medicines, a thermometer and, of course, a favorite toy. Formula and baby food are easily found.

➡ It's handy to have hand sanitizer, as bathrooms may lack soap.

➡ Bring your favorite insect repellent. It's available here but nontoxic items are harder to find.

➡ It's a good idea to have diarrhea medication just in case.

➡ Kids should have comfortable outdoor clothing, a bathing suit, hats for the sun, a shell jacket and warm clothing for chilly days and nights. Before your trip, make sure everyone has adequate, broken-in shoes. Sandals can also be useful for the coast.

➡ A cheap digital camera or pair of binoculars can provide lots of entertainment.

➡ It's possible to rent children's bikes with helmets, as well as surf gear.

➡ Strollers are unlikely to be convenient in most places beyond cities.

➡ Baby backpacks are handy for market visits or getting onto the trails with tots or babies over six months old.

➡ Consider carefully the need to bring electronic games and tablet computers – they're bound to attract a lot of attention if used in public and it's probably best to limit their use to the hotel.

Before You Go

Keep the kids in mind as you plan your itinerary or include them in the trip planning from the get-go. If renting a car, ask ahead if you can book a child's seat, as they are not always available. Lonely Planet's *Travel with Children* provides good information, advice and anecdotes.

It's not necessary to be tied down to a schedule while traveling in Peru, as plenty of activities can be booked just a few days in advance.

Regions at a Glance

With parched coastal desert, jagged Andean peaks and the lush expanse of the Amazon rainforest, the regions of Peru feature cultures and landscapes brimming with diversity. In Lima, urban life is among the most sophisticated on the continent. In the provinces and remote areas, communities still follow age-old traditions. Within this dazzling cultural mosaic, solemn pilgrimages honor gods both Christian and indigenous, neon clubs pulse with reveling youth, and ancient ruins bring us back to prehistory. And then, there is Peruvian cuisine – sublime creations that alter with the landscape, made from ingredients both native and contemporary. Welcome to Peru – a blast to the senses.

Lima

Food
Culture
Nightlife

Novoandina & Beyond

Setting the foodie world on fire, Lima's signature pan-cultural cuisine introduces fresh, indigenous ingredients to sophisticated dishes. Join the half-million attending prestigious food festival Mistura.

From Clubs to Catacombs

Founded in the 15th century, Lima boasts culture in spades, from colonial catacombs and museums to clubs and galleries in funky Barranco.

La Noche

When the sun sets behind the Pacific and a million lights pop on, it's time to enjoy some Latin nightlife. Start with a pisco sour or *chilcano* in a weathered bar or velvet lounge. Later shake it 'til the wee hours to *cumbia,* house, techno, Latin rock or *reggaeton.*

p54

South Coast

History
Adventure
Wine

History Between the Lines

Two pre-Inca civilizations stamped their presence here. Nazca etched famous geoglyphs into the desert south of Ica while Paracas buried intricate textiles in necropolises near Pisco.

Adrenaline Fixes

There's excellent river running in Lunahuaná and sandboarding in desert oasis Huacachina and Cerro Blanco, the world's tallest sand dune. Surfers can rent a 4WD to discover unchartered breaks.

Desert Vineyards

Peru's best grapes grow in its well-irrigated southern desert. Beyond the wine and pisco capital of Ica there are decent wineries in Lunahuaná and Moquegua.

p106

Arequipa & Canyon Country

Trekking
Architecture
Food

Cañón del Colca

For many, trekking in Peru begins and ends on the Inca Trail. But if the crowds make you claustrophobic, come to the spectacular, isolated trails of Colca and Cotahuasi Canyons.

The White City

Arequipa is touted as one of the best-preserved Spanish colonial cities in the Americas, crafted uniquely out of white volcanic *sillar* rock. Less heralded are the exquisitely preserved baroque churches in Colca Canyon villages.

La Picantería

Long before Gastón Acurio, Arequipa was fusing Quechua, Spanish and Chinese influences to concoct a unique hybrid cuisine best showcased in the city's traditional restaurants.

p141

Lake Titicaca

Festivals
Culture
Detouring

Like a Virgin

With wild costumes and more than 300 traditional dances, Puno knows festivals. La Virgen de la Candelaria (celebrated February 2) celebrates the city's patron virgin with a thunderous street party that's the event of the year.

Reed Islands

Community tourism is the best way to understand life on this great blue expanse almost 4000m high. Islanders live in another dimension – from the surreal reed-made Uros to the rural rhythms of Isla Amantani.

Remote Wonders

Splurge on a visit to the nature preserve of Isla Suasi or spend a few days in rural homestays on the lakeshore to experience timeless Titicaca.

p171

Cuzco & the Sacred Valley

Ruins
Adventure
Culture

Sacred Valley Ruins

Overnight in Pisac or Ollantaytambo for full immersion in the Andean culture and landscape before the grand finale of Machu Picchu.

The Wilderness Plunge

Whiz from the high Andes to the jungle on a mountain bike, ascend sheer rock on the *via ferrata* (iron way) or trek the wild wilderness around Ausangate. Cuzco rivals Huaraz as Peru's adventure center.

The Quechua World

Inca culture permeates the relics, but living indigenous cultures have just as much to offer. Engage in community tourism, join the fervor of a festival or do the culturally fascinating Lares trek through remote Andean villages.

p196

Central Highlands

Architecture
Detouring
Festivals

Colonial Backroads

Forgotten cities such as Ayacucho and Huancavelica offer insight into Peru's colonial heyday. While they lack preservation funds, they haven't been spoiled by Western chain stores either: wander ancient streets and be transported in time.

Classic Andean Road Trips

Discover the Andes of the good old days: adventures through spectacular gorges on wheezing buses along abysmal roads to places seldom seen by tourists.

Holy Week Revelry

Here they take revelry seriously – one valley has a festival every day. Don't miss South America's best Semana Santa celebrations and the party towns of Río Mantaro.

p271

North Coast

Ruins
Food
Beaches

Tracing History

It's not hard to channel your inner Indiana Jones along Peru's north coast, where under nearly every grain of sand this sweeping dune desertscape reveals yet another largely intact antediluvian ruin.

Ceviche

There's no better stretch of sand for a seafood crusade. Don't miss Peru's iconic dish, ceviche (raw fish marinated in citrus and chili, served with onions, corn and sweet potato), a major player in the country's gastronomic renaissance.

Golden Sands

Go all the way to Peru for a beach vacation? Dip your toes into the ample sands of Huanchaco, Colán, Máncora or Punta Sal and you won't want to go back.

p309

Huaraz & the Cordilleras

Trekking
Outdoors
Ruins

Peru's Trekking Capital

The majestic peaks of the Blanca, Negra and Huayhuash cordilleras host the most iconic trails in South America. A nearly endless array of treks through diverse terrain with postcard-perfect scenery.

Aire Libre

Beyond trekking, these stately mountains offer a bounty of open-air adventures, from casual mountain biking, horseback riding and rock climbing to ice climbing and mountaineering endeavors.

Chavín de Huántar

The Unesco ruins at Chavín de Huántar are among Peru's most important and fascinating primordial sites, so break up your outdoor lovefest with a little ancient culture.

p364

Northern Highlands

Nature
Ruins
Food

Back to Nature

From the impressive 771m Gocta waterfall to birding opportunities galore and numerous new nature lodges, the Northern Highlands has some of Peru's most impressive landscapes.

Kuélap

Second only to Machu Picchu in awe, the excellently preserved ruins of Kuélap, tucked away in misty-eyed cloud forest near Chachapoyas, is reason alone to venture into this neck of the woods.

Lowland Flavors

Jungle-influenced recipes of Tarapoto and Chachapoyas offer original flavors, only just finding their way to renowned Lima restaurants. Wash it down with regional elixirs soaked in wild roots and vines.

p404

Amazon Basin

Adventure
Wildlife
Festivals

Old-Fashioned Exploration

Trekking amid foliage so thick you have to slice through it; navigating rivers in dug-out canoes like 17th-century explorers; soaring through the canopy on ziplines. It's tailor-made for adventures.

Elusive Animals

It's not just anacondas or giant creepy-crawlies, nor is it rose-colored river dolphins, the scarlet flash of cock-of-the-rocks found only in Manu's cloud forests, or jaguars – the search for these creatures makes for one wild adventure.

Hot Celebrations

The Amazon's two premier parties are among Peru's best – conveniently occurring within a week of each other in June: San Juan (Iquitos) and Selvámanos (Oxapampa).

p438

On the Road

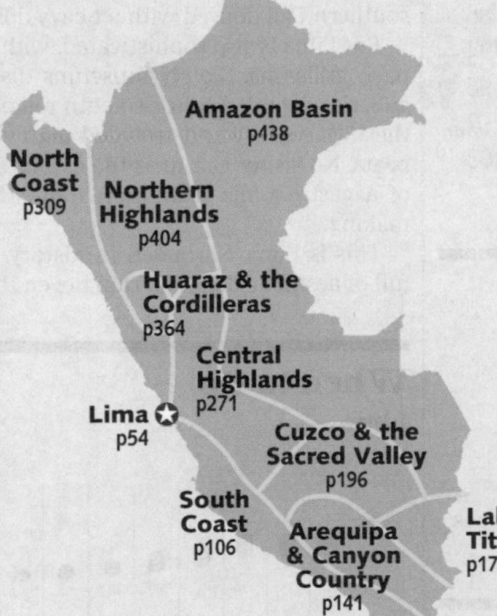
Amazon Basin
p438
North Coast
p309
Northern Highlands
p404
Huaraz & the Cordilleras
p364
Central Highlands
p271
Lima
p54
Cuzco & the Sacred Valley
p196
South Coast
p106
Arequipa & Canyon Country
p141
Lake Titicaca
p171

Lima

☎01 / POP 9.8 MILLION

Includes ➡

Best Places to Eat

- ➡ Central (p91)
- ➡ Astrid y Gastón Casa Moreyra (p88)
- ➡ ámaZ (p90)
- ➡ El Rincón que no Conoces (p93)

Best Places to Stay

- ➡ Hotel de Autor (p83)
- ➡ Casa Cielo (p82)
- ➡ Second Home Perú (p85)
- ➡ 3B Barranco B&B (p85)
- ➡ Casa Nuestra (p85)

Why Go?

When fog bundles its colonial facades and high rises, Lima's enchantments come across as all too subtle. After Cairo, this sprawling metropolis is the second-driest world capital, rising above a long coastline of crumbling cliffs. To enjoy it, climb on the wave of chaos that spans from high-rise condos built alongside pre-Columbian temples, and fast Pacific breakers rolling toward noisy traffic snarls. Think one part southern Cali doused with a heavy dose of *America Latina*.

But Lima is also sophisticated, with civilization that dates back millennia. Stately museums display sublime pottery; galleries debut edgy art; solemn religious processions recall the 18th century and crowded nightclubs dispense tropical beats. No visitor can miss the capital's culinary genius, part of a gastronomic revolution more than 400 years in the making.

This is Lima. Shrouded in history, gloriously messy and full of aesthetic delights. Don't even think of missing it.

When to Go

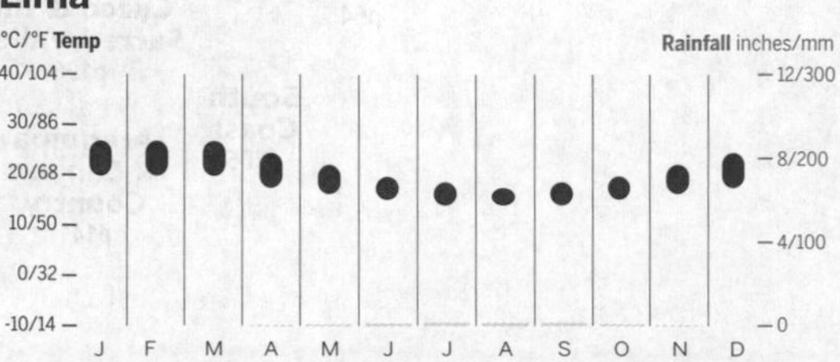

Year-round A mild and dry climate means comfortable capital visits year-round.

Dec–Mar The hottest, blue-sky months ideal for surf and sun on the coast.

Late Aug Colorful processions mark the festival of Santa Rosa de Lima, the country's first saint.

History

As ancient as it is new, Lima has survived regular apocalyptic earthquakes, warfare and the rise and fall of civilizations. This resilient city has welcomed a rebirth after each destruction. In pre-Hispanic times, the area served as an urban center for the Lima, Wari, Ichsma and even the Inca cultures in different periods.

When Francisco Pizarro sketched out the boundaries of his 'City of Kings' in January of 1535, there were roughly 200,000 indigenous people living in the area. By the 18th century, the Spaniards' tumbledown village of adobe and wood had given way to a viceregal capital, where fleets of ships arrived to transport the golden spoils of conquest back to Europe. After a disastrous earthquake wiped out much of the city in 1746, it was rebuilt with splendorous baroque churches and ample *casonas* (mansions). The city's prominence began to fade after independence in 1821, when other urban centers were crowned capitals of newly independent states.

In 1880, Lima was ransacked and occupied by the Chilean military during the War of the Pacific (1879–83). As part of the pillage, the Chileans made off with thousands of tomes from the National Library (they were returned in 2007). Postwar expansion meant that by the 1920s Lima was crisscrossed by a network of broad boulevards inspired by Parisian urban design. When another devastating earthquake struck in 1940, the city again had to rebuild.

By the mid-1900s the population was growing exponentially. An influx of rural poor took the metro area from 661,000 inhabitants in 1940 to 8.5 million by 2007. The migration was particularly intense during the 1980s, when armed conflicts in the Andes displaced many people. Shantytowns mushroomed, crime soared and the city fell into a period of steep decay. In 1992, the terrorist group Sendero Luminoso (Shining Path) detonated deadly truck bombs in middle-class Miraflores, marking one of Lima's darkest hours.

Today's Lima has been rebuilt to an astonishing degree. A robust economy and a vast array of municipal improvement efforts have repaved the streets, refurbished parks and created safer public areas to bring back a thriving cultural and culinary life.

Sights

The city's historic heart, Lima Centro (Central Lima) is a grid of crowded streets laid out in the 16th-century days of Francisco Pizarro, and home to most of the city's surviving colonial architecture. Well-to-do San Isidro is Lima's banking center and one of its most affluent settlements. It borders the contiguous, seaside neighborhood of Miraflores, which serves as Lima's contemporary core, bustling with commerce,

LIMA IN...

Two Days

Start with a **walking tour** (p67) of the city's colonial heart. For lunch, try the historic **El Cordano** (p86) or the lovely **Domus** (p86). Afterwards, view the Chancay pottery inside a pristine historic mansion at the **Museo Andrés del Castillo** (p64) and end the day with a most important pilgrimage: a pisco sour, either at **El Bolivarcito** (p95), the renowned bar inside the Gran Hotel Bolivar, or **Museo del Pisco** (p94).

On the second day, you can go pre-Columbian or contemporary: view breathtaking Moche pottery at the **Museo Larco** (p76) or see a gripping exhibit on the Internal Conflict at the **Museo de la Nación** (p66). In the afternoon, grab an espresso from **Cafe Bisetti** (p93) and stroll through the cliff-top gardens of **Barranco** (p73); you could also visit **Huaca Pucllana** (p73), the centuries-old adobe temple in the middle of Miraflores. Spend the evening sampling *novoandina* (nouvelle cuisine) at one of the city's many fine restaurants.

Three Days

Seeking something colonial? In the morning, visit the exquisite **Museo Pedro de Osma** (p75) in Barranco to view some of the most intriguing Cuzco School canvases and an abundance of relics from the days of the viceroyalty, followed by a visit next door to **MATE** (p75) to see photographer Mario Testino's exciting legacy. Otherwise, make the day trip to **Pachacamac** (p103) to stand amid arid ruins dating back almost two millennia. Spend the afternoon haggling for crafts at the **Mercado Indio** (p97) in Miraflores.

Lima Highlights

1. Biting into Peruvian delicacies at the innovative restaurants of **Miraflores** (p88).
2. Sipping potent pisco cocktails at the vintage bars and chic lounges of **Barranco** (p95).
3. Admiring pre-Columbian masterpieces, from sublime tapestries to intricate goldwork at **Museo Larco** (p76).
4. Exploring sandy ruins with several civilizations' worth of temples at **Pachacamac** (p103).
5. Leaping off the Miraflores cliff tops and **paragliding** (p77) among the high-rises with the Pacific Ocean filling the horizon.
6. Gazing upon the skulls of some of Latin America's most celebrated saints at the **Iglesia de Santo Domingo** (p63) in Lima Centro.
7. Strolling or cycling the lush **coastal parks** (p76).

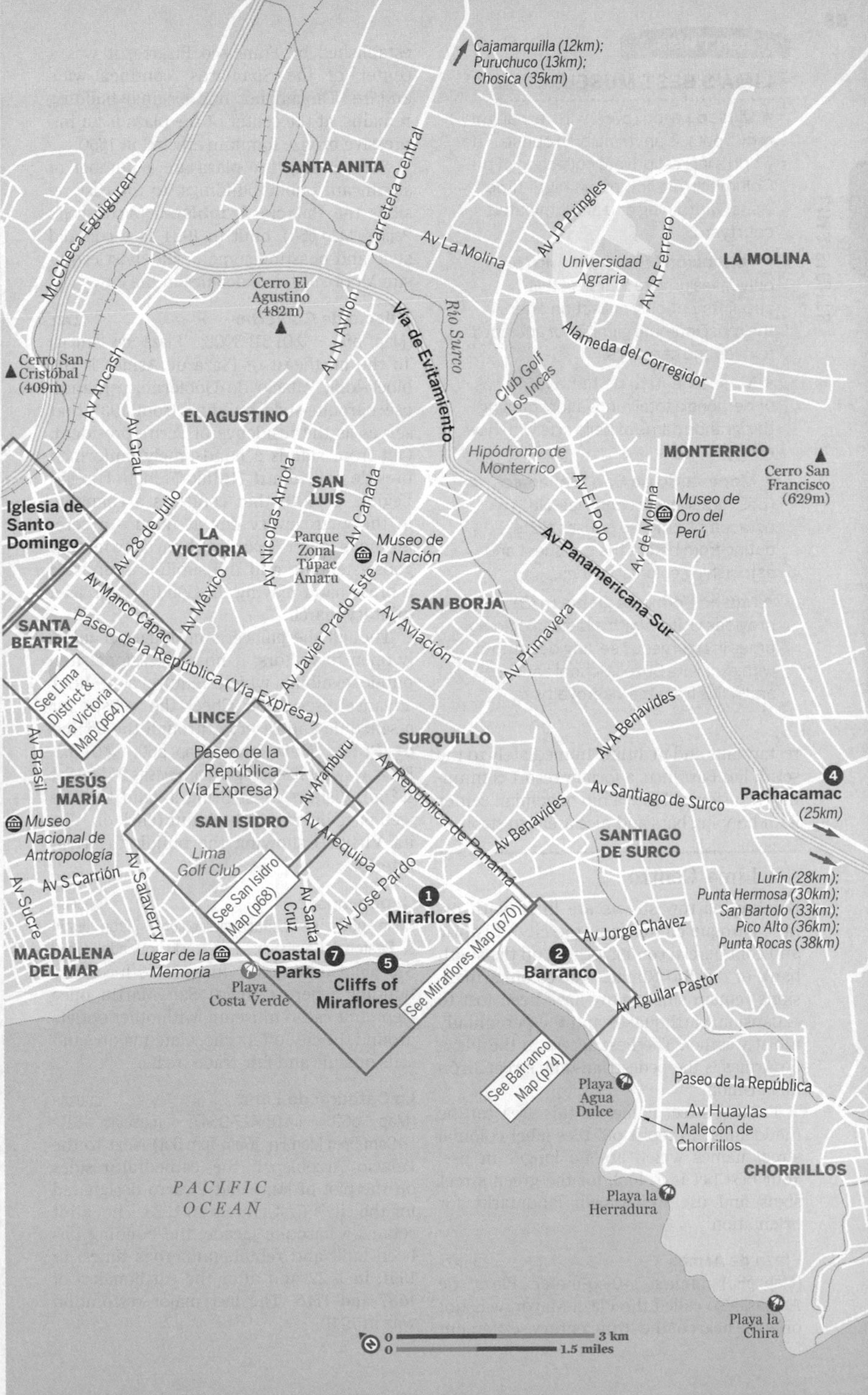
Cajamarquilla (12km); Puruchuco (13km); Chosica (35km)
SANTA ANITA
Carretera Central
McCheca Eguiguren
Av La Molina
Av J P Pringles
Av R Ferrero
Universidad Agraria
LA MOLINA
Cerro El Agustino (482m)
Av N Ayllon
Vía de Evitamiento
Río Surco
Alameda del Corregidor
Club Golf Los Incas
Cerro San Cristóbal (409m)
Av Ancash
EL AGUSTINO
Av Grau
Hipódromo de Monterrico
MONTERRICO
Cerro San Francisco (629m)
Av Nicolas Arriola
SAN LUIS
Av Canada
Av El Polo
Av de Molina
Museo de Oro del Perú
Iglesia de Santo Domingo
Av 28 de Julio
LA VICTORIA
Parque Zonal Túpac Amaru
Museo de la Nación
Av Panamericana Sur
Av Manco Cápac
Av México
Av Javier Prado Este
SAN BORJA
SANTA BEATRIZ
Paseo de la República (Vía Expresa)
Av Aviación
Av Primavera
See Lima District & La Victoria Map (p64)
LINCE
Av A Benavides
Av Brasil
Paseo de la República (Vía Expresa)
SURQUILLO
JESÚS MARÍA
Av Aramburu
Av República de Panamá
Av Santiago de Surco
4
Pachacamac (25km)
Museo Nacional de Antropología
SAN ISIDRO
Av Arequipa
Av Benavides
SANTIAGO DE SURCO
Lima Golf Club
Av S Carrión
Av Salaverry
See San Isidro Map (p68)
Av Santa Cruz
Av Jose Pardo
1
Miraflores
Lurín (28km); Punta Hermosa (30km); San Bartolo (33km); Pico Alto (36km); Punta Rocas (38km)
Av Sucre
See Miraflores Map (p70)
Av Jorge Chávez
MAGDALENA DEL MAR
Lugar de la Memoria
Coastal Parks
7
5
Cliffs of Miraflores
2
Barranco
Playa Costa Verde
Av Aguilar Pastor
See Barranco Map (p74)
Playa Agua Dulce
Paseo de la República
Av Huaylas
Malecón de Chorrillos
CHORRILLOS
PACIFIC OCEAN
Playa la Herradura
Playa la Chira
0 3 km
0 1.5 miles

DON'T MISS

LIMA'S BEST MUSEUMS

➡ **Museo Larco** (p76), with its naughty erotic pots, is anything but routine. The world's largest private collection of pre-Columbian art now offers night-time visits, with dining and an illuminated courtyard.

➡ **Fundación Museo Amano** (p72) only takes private tours, so this appointment-only collection offers the most intimate glimpse of ancient textiles and ceramics.

➡ **Museo de Arte de Lima** (p65) has undergone a total renovation infusing this grande dame of belle arts with new energy.

➡ **Monasterio de San Francisco** (p59) is a trove of centuries-old catacombs but also houses texts dating from before the conquest and astonishing colonial fittings.

➡ **Museo Pedro de Osma** (p75) provides visitors with a taste of colonial times in a gorgeous setting decorated with exquisite Cuzco School canvases and relics from the viceroyalty.

restaurants and nightlife. Immediately to the south lies Barranco, a former resort community transformed into a hip bohemian center with hopping bars and nice areas to stroll.

Lima Centro

Bustling narrow streets are lined with ornate baroque churches in the city's historic and commercial center, located on the south bank of the Río Rímac. Few colonial mansions remain since many have been lost to expansion, earthquakes and the perennially moist weather. The best access to the Plaza de Armas is the pedestrian-only street Jirón de la Unión.

Finding street names in this area can be maddening; to top it off, tiles label colonial street names which are no longer in use. Your best bet is to look for the green street signs and use well-known landmarks for orientation.

Plaza de Armas PLAZA

(Map p60) Lima's 140-sq-meter Plaza de Armas, also called the Plaza Mayor, was not only the heart of the 16th-century settlement established by Francisco Pizarro, it was a center of the Spaniards' continent-wide empire. Though not one original building remains, at the center of the plaza is an impressive bronze fountain erected in 1650.

Surrounding the plaza are a number of significant public buildings: to the east resides the **Palacio Arzobispal** (Archbishop's Palace; Map p60), built in 1924 in a colonial style and boasting some of the most exquisite Moorish-style balconies in the city.

Palacio de Gobierno PALACE

(Map p60; ☎01-311-3908; Plaza de Armas) To the northeast of Plaza de Armas is the block-long Palacio de Gobierno, a grandiose baroque-style building from 1937 that serves as the residence of Peru's president. Out front stands a handsomely uniformed presidential guard (think French Foreign Legion, c 1900) that conducts a changing of the guard every day at noon – a ceremonious affair that involves slow-motion goose-stepping and the sublime sounds of a brass band playing 'El Cóndor Pasa' as a military march.

Though the palace is no longer regularly open to visitors, it hosts occasional free public exhibits, which require a 48-hour advance reservation. Check the website for a schedule and reserve through the **Office of Public Relations** (Map p60; ☎01-311-3908; www.presidencia.gob.pe; ⌚visits 9-11am Sat & Sun). Visitors must bring a valid ID. The web page offers a virtual tour (click on 'Visita Virtual') showing the building's lavish interiors.

Choco Museo MUSEUM

(Map p60; www.chocomuseo.com; Jirón Junin & Peatonal Carabaya; 2hr workshop adult/child S75/55) Housed in a historic 16th-century building where General San Martin once slept, this cacao museum, with other outlets around the city, offers chocolate-making and sells organic and fair-trade treats.

La Catedral de Lima CHURCH

(Map p60; ☎01-427-9647; museum S10; ⌚9am-5pm Mon-Fri, 10am-1pm Sat) Next to the Palacio Arzobispal, the cathedral resides on the plot of land that Pizarro designated for the city's first church in 1535. Though it retains a baroque facade, the building has been built and rebuilt numerous times: in 1551, in 1622 and after the earthquakes of 1687 and 1746. The last major restoration was in 1940.

A craze for all things neoclassical in the late 18th century left much of the interior (and the interiors of many Lima churches) stripped of its elaborate baroque decor. Even so, there is plenty to see. The various chapels along the nave display more than a dozen altars carved in every imaginable style, and the ornate wood choir, produced by Pedro de Noguera in the early 17th century, is a masterpiece of rococo sculpture. A **museum**, in the rear, features paintings, vestments and an intricate sacristy.

By the cathedral's main door is the mosaic-covered chapel with the remains of Pizarro. Their authenticity came into question in 1977, after workers cleaning out a crypt discovered several bodies and a sealed lead box containing a skull that bore the inscription, 'Here is the head of the gentleman Marquis Don Francisco Pizarro, who found and conquered the kingdom of Peru...' After a battery of tests in the 1980s, a US forensic scientist concluded that the body previously on display was of an unknown official and that the brutally stabbed and headless body from the crypt was Pizarro's. Head and body were reunited and transferred to the chapel, where you can also view the inscribed lead box.

Guide services in Spanish, English, French, Italian and Portuguese are available for an additional fee.

Parque de la Muralla PARK

(Map p60; ☎01-427-4125; Amazonas, btwn Lampa & Av Abancay; ⏰9am-9pm) FREE During the 17th century, the heart of Lima was ringed by a *muralla* (city wall), much of which was torn down in the 1870s as the city expanded. However, you can view a set of excavated remains at the Parque de la Muralla, where, in addition to the wall, a small on-site **museum** (with erratic hours) details the development of the city and holds a few objects.

The park features a bronze statue of Francisco Pizarro created by American sculptor Ramsey MacDonald in the early 20th century. The figure once commanded center stage at the Plaza de Armas, but over the years has been displaced as attitudes toward Pizarro have grown critical. The best part: the figure isn't even Pizarro – it's an anonymous conquistador of the sculptor's invention. MacDonald made three copies of the statue. One was erected in the US; the other, Spain. The third was donated to the city of Lima after the artist's death in 1934 (and after Mexico rejected it). So now, Pizarro – or, more accurately, his proxy – sits at the edge of this park, a silent witness to a daily parade of amorous Peruvian teens.

Monasterio de San Francisco MONASTERY

(Map p60; ☎01-426-7377; www.museocatacumbas.com; cnr Lampa & Ancash; adult/child under 15 S7/1; ⏰9:30am-5:30pm) This bright-yellow Franciscan monastery and church is most famous for its bone-lined catacombs (containing an estimated 70,000 remains) and its remarkable library housing 25,000 antique texts, some of which predate the conquest. Admission includes a 30-minute guided tour in English or in Spanish. Tours leave as groups gather.

This baroque structure has many other treasures: the most spectacular is a geometric Moorish-style cupola over the main staircase, which was carved in 1625 (restored 1969) out of Nicaraguan cedar. In addition, the refectory contains 13 paintings of the biblical patriarch Jacob and his 12 sons, attributed to the studio of Spanish master Francisco de Zurbarán.

Casa de Pilatos HISTORIC BUILDING

(Map p60; ☎01-427-5814; Ancash 390; ⏰8am-1pm & 2-5pm Mon-Fri) FREE East of the plaza, the lovely red Casa de Pilatos is home to offices for the Tribunal Constitucional (Supreme Court). Access is a challenge: visitors are only allowed into the courtyard provided there aren't official meetings going on. Enter through the side door on Azángaro.

Museo de la Inquisición MUSEUM

(Map p60; ☎01-311-7777, ext 5160; www.congreso.gob.pe/museo.htm; Jirón Junín 548; ⏰9am-5pm) FREE A graceful neoclassical structure facing the Plaza Bolívar houses this diminutive museum where the Spanish Inquisition once plied its trade. In the 1800s, the building was expanded and rebuilt into the Peruvian senate. Today, guests can tour the basement, where morbidly hilarious wax figures are stretched on racks and flogged – to the delight of visiting

CALLE CONFUSION

The same street can have several names as it traverses Lima, such as Av Arequipa (aka Garcilaso de la Vega or Wilson). Some names reappear in different districts, so indicate the right neighborhood to taxi drivers. Streets also may change names – for practicality we have used the most common names.

Centro Histórico

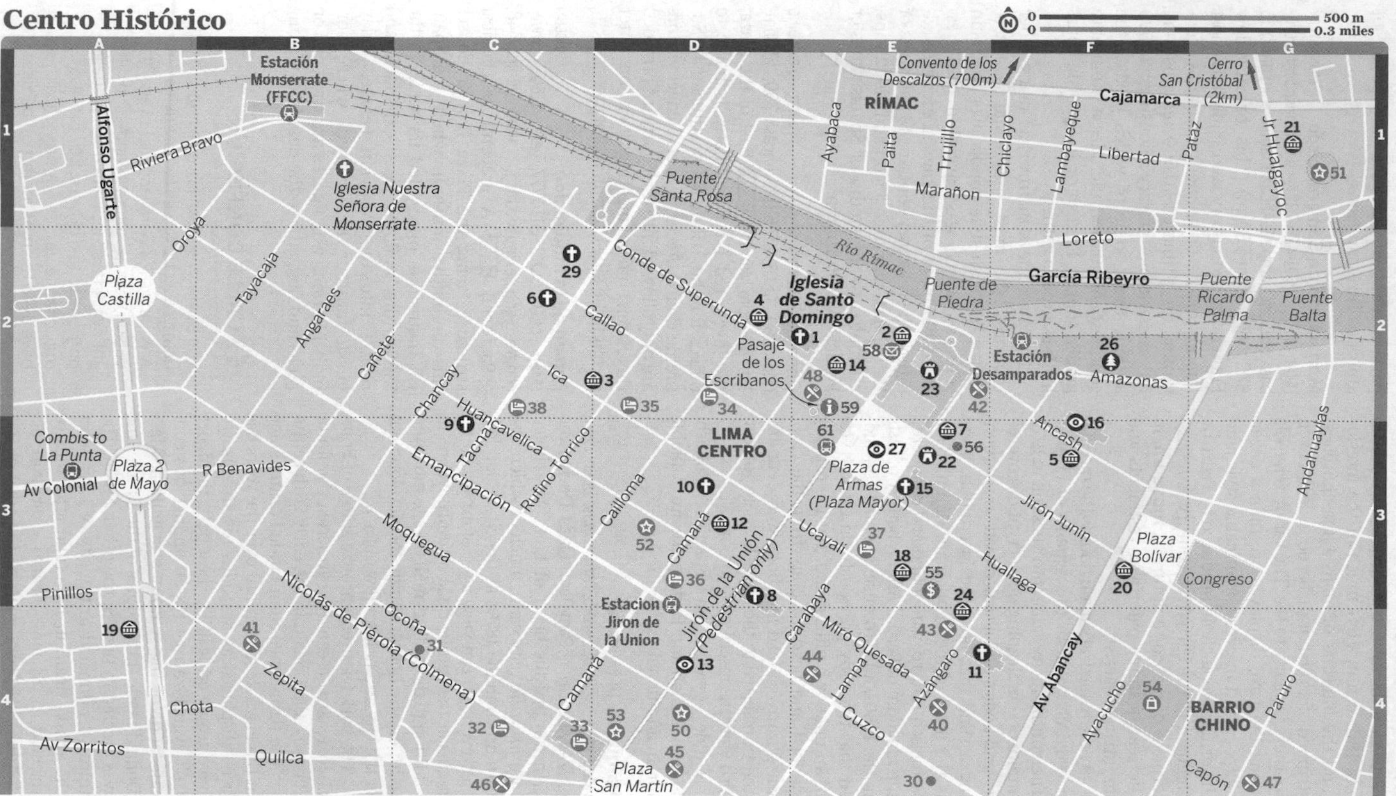

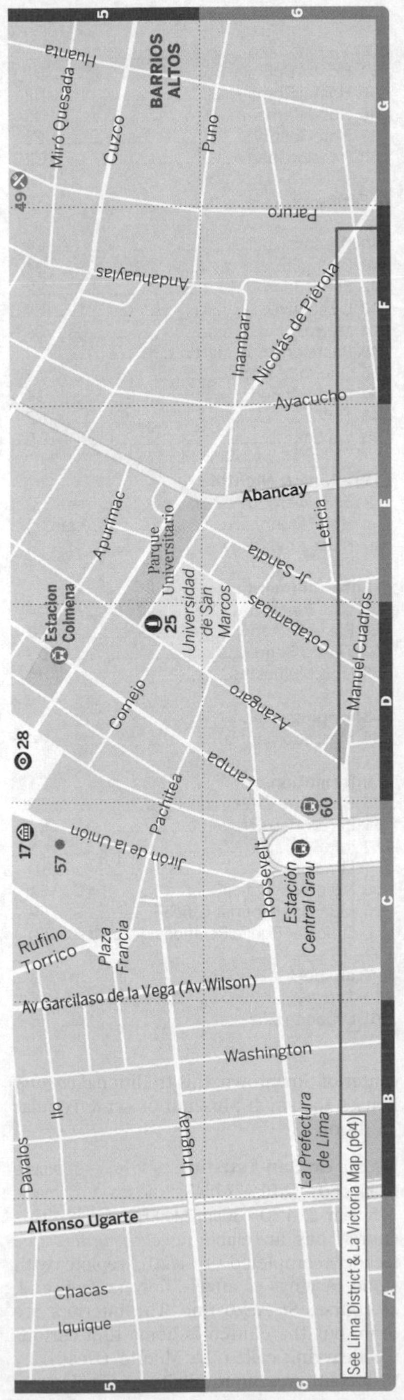

eight-year-olds. The old 1st-floor library retains a remarkable baroque wooden ceiling. After an obilgatory half-hour tour (in Spanish or English) guests can wander.

Iglesia de San Pedro CHURCH
(Map p60; ☎01-428-3010; www.sanpedrodelima.org; cnr Azángaro & Ucayali; ⏰8:30am-1pm & 2-4pm Mon-Fri) FREE This small 17th-century church is considered to be one of the finest examples of baroque colonial-era architecture in Lima. Consecrated by the Jesuits in 1638, it has changed little since. The interior is sumptuously decorated with gilded altars, Moorish-style carvings and glazed tiles.

Palacio Torre Tagle HISTORIC BUILDING
(Map p60; ☎01-427-3860; Ucayali 363; ⏰Mon-Fri) The most immaculate of Lima's historic *casonas* was completed in 1735, with its ornate baroque portico (the best one in Lima) and striking Moorish-style balconies. Unfortunately, it is now home to Peru's Foreign Ministry, so entry is restricted. Groups and educational organizations, however, can request a tour in advance via the **oficina cultural** (☎01-311-2400).

Museo Banco Central de Reserva del Perú MUSEUM
(Map p60; ☎01-613-2000, ext 2655; www.bcrp.gob.pe/proyeccion-institucional/museo.html; cnr Lampa & Ucayali; ⏰10am-4:30pm Tue-Fri, to 1pm Sat & Sun) FREE Housed in a graceful bank building, the Museo Banco Central de Reserva del Perú is a well-presented overview of several millennia of Peruvian art, from pre-Columbian gold and pottery to a selection of 19th- and 20th-century Peruvian canvases. Don't miss the watercolors by Pancho Fierro on the top floor, which provide an unparalleled view of dress and class in 19th-century Lima. Identification is required for admittance.

Iglesia de la Merced CHURCH
(Map p60; ☎01-427-8199; cnr Jirón de la Unión & Miró Quesada; ⏰10am-noon & 5-7pm) FREE The first Latin Mass in Lima was held in 1534 on a small patch of land now marked by the Iglesia de la Merced. Originally built in 1541, it was rebuilt several times over the course of the next two centuries. Most of today's structure dates to the 18th century. The most striking feature is the imposing granite facade, carved in the *churrigueresque* manner (a highly ornate style popular during the late Spanish baroque period).

Centro Histórico

Top Sights
1 Iglesia de Santo Domingo ... E2

Sights
2 Casa Aliaga ... E2
3 Casa de la Riva ... D2
4 Casa de Oquendo ... D2
5 Casa de Pilatos ... F3
6 Casa-Capilla de San Martín de Porres ... C2
7 Choco Museo ... E3
8 Iglesia de la Merced ... D3
9 Iglesia de las Nazarenas ... C3
10 Iglesia de San Agustín ... D3
11 Iglesia de San Pedro ... E4
12 Instituto Riva-Aguero ... D3
13 Jirón de la Unión ... D4
14 La Casa de La Gastronomia Peruana ... E2
15 La Catedral de Lima ... E3
16 Monasterio de San Francisco ... F3
17 Museo Andrés del Castillo ... C5
18 Museo Banco Central de Reserva del Perú ... E3
19 Museo de la Cultura Peruana ... A4
20 Museo de la Inquisición ... F3
21 Museo Taurino ... G1
22 Palacio Arzobispal ... E3
23 Palacio de Gobierno ... E2
24 Palacio Torre Tagle ... E4
25 Panteón de los Próceres ... D5
26 Parque de la Muralla ... F2
27 Plaza de Armas ... E3
28 Plaza San Martín ... D5
29 Santuario de Santa Rosa de Lima ... C2

Activities, Courses & Tours
30 Instituto Cultural Peruano-Norteamericano ... E4
31 Lima Tours ... C4

Sleeping
32 Familia Rodríguez ... C4
33 Gran Hotel Bolívar ... C4
34 Hostal Bonbini ... D2
35 Hostal Roma ... D2
36 Hotel Kamana ... D3
37 Hotel Maury ... E3
38 Pensión Ibarra ... C2

Eating
40 Domus ... E4
41 El Chinito ... B4
42 El Cordano ... E2
43 L'Eau Vive ... E4
44 Metro ... E4
45 Pastelería San Martín ... D4
46 Queirolo ... C4
47 Salon Capon ... G4
48 Tanta ... E2
49 Wa Lok ... G5

Drinking & Nightlife
El Bolivarcito ... (see 33)
Hotel Maury ... (see 37)
Museo del Pisco ... (see 7)

Entertainment
50 Cine Planet ... D4
51 Plaza de Acho ... G1
52 Teatro Segura ... D3
53 UVK Multicines ... D4

Shopping
54 Mercado Central ... F4

Information
55 Banco de Crédito del Perú ... E3
56 Fertur Peru Travel ... E3
57 InfoPerú ... C5
Lima Tours ... (see 31)
58 Main Post Office ... E2
59 Municipal Tourist Office ... E2
Office of Public Relations ... (see 23)

Transport
60 Tepsa ... C6
61 Urbanito Bus ... E3

Inside, the nave is lined with more than two-dozen magnificent baroque and Renaissance-style altars, some carved entirely out of mahogany. To the right as you enter is a large silver cross that once belonged to Father Pedro Urraca (1583–1657), renowned for having had a vision of the Virgin. This is a place of pilgrimage for Peruvian worshippers, who come to place a hand on the cross and pray for miracles.

Instituto Riva-Aguero HISTORIC BUILDING
(Map p60; ☎01-626-6600; Camaná 459; admission S2; ⏰10am-1pm, 2-7pm Mon-Fri) Toward the center of downtown, this traditional *casona* houses the small Museum of Art & Popular Tradition.

Iglesia de San Agustín CHURCH
(Map p60; ☎01-427-7548; cnr Ica & Camaná; ⏰8-9am & 4:30-7:30pm Mon-Fri) FREE This church has an elaborate *churrigueresque* facade (completed in 1720), replete with stone carvings of angels, flowers, fruit and, of course, St Augustine. The interiors are drab, but the church is home to a curious woodcarving called 'La Muerte' (Death) by 18th-century sculptor Baltazar Gavilán. As

one (probably fictional) story goes, Gavilán died in a state of madness after viewing his own chilling sculpture in the middle of the night. The piece sometimes travels, so call ahead.

Limited operating hours can make the church a challenge to visit.

Iglesia de las Nazarenas CHURCH

(Map p60; ☎01-423-5718; cnr Tacna & Huancavelica; ⏰7am-1pm & 5-9pm) FREE One of Lima's most storied churches was part of a 17th-century shantytown inhabited by former slaves. One of them painted an image of the Crucifixion on a wall here. It survived the devastating earthquake of 1655 and a church was built around it (the painting serves as the centerpiece of the main altar) in the 1700s. The church has been rebuilt many times since but the wall endures.

On October 18 each year a representation of the mural, known as 'El Señor de los Milagros' (Lord of Miracles), is carried around in a tens-of-thousands-strong procession that lasts for days.

Casa de la Riva HISTORIC BUILDING

(Map p60; Ica 426; admission S5; ⏰10am-1pm & 2-4pm Mon-Fri) This handsome, 18th-century mansion features beautiful wooden balconies, an elegant patio and period furnishings.

Casa-Capilla de San Martín de Porres CHURCH

(Map p60; ☎01-423-0707; Callao 535; ⏰9am-1pm & 3-6pm Mon-Fri, 9am-1pm Sat) FREE Right across the street from the Santuario de Santa Rosa de Lima, this building (now a center of religious study) commemorates the birthplace of San Martín. Visitors are welcome to view the bright interior patios and diminutive chapel.

Santuario de Santa Rosa de Lima CHURCH

(Map p60; ☎01-425-1279; cnr Tacna & Callao; ⏰7:30am-noon & 5-8pm) FREE Honoring the first saint of the Americas, this plain, terra-cotta-hued church on a congested avenue is located roughly at the site of her birth. The modest adobe sanctuary in the gardens was built in the 17th century for Santa Rosa's prayers and meditation.

Casa de Oquendo HISTORIC BUILDING

(Map p60; ☎01-427-7987; Conde de Superunda 298; ⏰9am-5pm Mon-Fri, to noon Sat) Two blocks to the north of the Casa de la Riva, the cornflower-blue Casa de Oquendo is a ramshackle turn-of-the-19th-century house (in its time, the tallest in Lima) with a creaky lookout tower that, on a clear day, has views of Callao. Arrange tours for small groups ahead of time with a suggested donation.

★Iglesia de Santo Domingo CHURCH

(Map p60; ☎01-427-6793; cnr Camaná & Conde de Superunda; ⏰9am-1pm & 5-7:30pm Mon-Sat) FREE One of Lima's most storied religious sites, the Iglesia de Santo Domingo and its expansive **convent** (admission S7) are built on land granted to the Dominican Friar Vicente de Valverde, who accompanied Pizarro throughout the conquest and was instrumental in persuading him to execute the captured Inca Atahualpa. Originally completed in the 16th century, this impressive pink church has been rebuilt and remodeled at various points since.

It is most renowned as the final resting place for three important Peruvian saints: San Juan Macías, Santa Rosa de Lima and San Martín de Porres (the continent's first black saint). The convent – a sprawling courtyard-studded complex lined with baroque paintings and clad in vintage Spanish tiles – contains the saints' tombs. The church, however, has the most interesting relics: the skulls of San Martín and Santa Rosa, encased in glass, in a shrine to the right of the main altar.

La Casa de La Gastronomia Peruana MUSEUM

(Map p60; ☎01-321-5627; Conde de Superunda 170; admission S3; ⏰9am-5pm Tue-Sun) This new museum provides a brief but helpful introduction to the world-famous Peruvian cuisine, with three rooms that present the Inca diet, regional cuisine, and the influence of immigration. Across the courtyard there's a room dedicated solely to quinoa.

Casa Aliaga HISTORIC BUILDING

(Map p60; ☎01-619-6900; www.casadealiaga.com; Jirón de la Unión 224; admission S30; ⏰9:30am-5pm, by reservation only) Innocuously tucked on a side street by the post office is Casa Aliaga, which stands on land given in 1535 to Jerónimo de Aliaga, one of Pizarro's followers, and which has been occupied by 16 generations of his descendants. It may not look like much from the outside, but the interiors are lovely, with vintage furnishings and tile work. It can also be visited via organized excursions with Lima Tours (p101).

Lima District & La Victoria

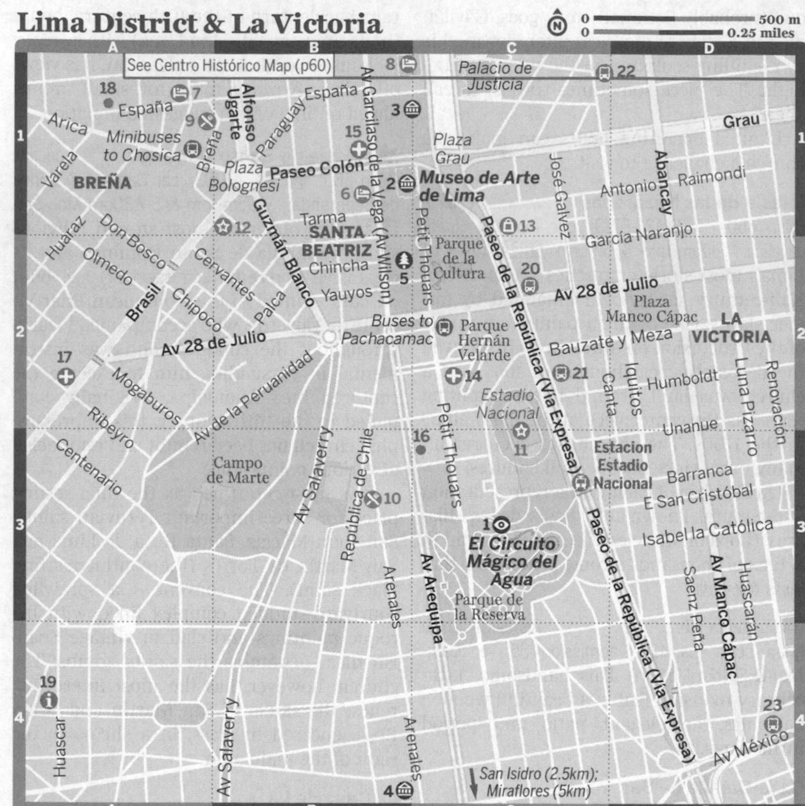

Jirón de la Unión
HISTORIC SITE

(Map p60) In the late 19th and early 20th centuries, the five pedestrian blocks on Jirón de la Unión, from the Plaza de Armas to Plaza San Martín, were *the* place to see and be seen. The street has long since lost its aristocratic luster, but the shells of neocolonial and art-deco buildings survive. Watch out for pickpockets who work the crowds during street performances.

Plaza San Martín
PLAZA

(Map p60) Built in the early 20th century, Plaza San Martín has come to life in recent years as the city has set about restoring its park and giving the surrounding beaux-arts architecture a much-needed scrubbing. It is especially lovely in the evenings, when illuminated. The plaza is named for the liberator of Peru, **José de San Martín**, who sits astride a horse at the center of the plaza.

At the base of the statue, don't miss the bronze rendering of **Madre Patria**, the symbolic mother of Peru. Commissioned in Spain under instruction to give the good lady a crown of flames, nobody thought to iron out the double meaning of the word flame in Spanish (llama), so the hapless craftsmen duly placed a delightful little llama on her head.

The once-stately Gran Hotel Bolívar (p80), built in the 1920s, presides over the square from the northwest.

Museo Andrés del Castillo
MUSEUM

(Map p60; ☎01-433-2831; www.madc.com.pe; Jirón de la Unión 1030; admission S10; ⏲9am-6pm, closed Tue) Housed in a pristine 19th-century mansion with Spanish-tile floors, this worthwhile new private museum showcases a vast collection of minerals, as well as breathtakingly displayed Nazca textiles and Chancay pottery, including some remarkable representations of Peruvian hairless dogs.

Lima District & La Victoria

Top Sights
1 El Circuito Mágico del Agua.................C3
2 Museo de Arte de Lima.........................B1

Sights
3 Museo de Arte Italiano..........................B1
4 Museo de Historia Natural...................B4
5 Parque de la Cultura............................B2

Sleeping
6 1900 Backpackers...............................B1
7 Hostal Iquique.....................................A1
8 Lima Sheraton.....................................B1

Eating
9 Cevichería la Choza Nautica................A1
10 Rovegno...B3

Entertainment
11 Estadio Nacional................................C3

12 Las Brisas del Titicaca........................B1

Shopping
13 Polvos Azules......................................C1

Information
14 Centro de La Mujer Peruana Flora Tristán..........................C2
15 Clínica Internacional...........................B1
16 Conadis...C3
17 Instituto Nacional de Salud del Niño...A2
18 Oficina de Migraciónes........................A1
19 Trekking & Backpacking Club..............A4

Transport
20 Civa..C2
21 Móvil Tours..C2
22 Ormeño...C1
23 Soyuz..D4

Panteón de los Próceres MONUMENT
(Map p60; ☎01-427-8157; Parque Universitario; ⊙10am-5pm) Located inside a little-visited 18th-century Jesuit church, this monument pays tribute to Peruvian battle heroes, from Túpac Amaru II, the 18th-century Quechua leader who led an indigenous uprising, to José de San Martín, who led the country to independence in the 1820s. The mosaic-lined crypt holds the remains of Ramón Castilla, the four-time Peruvian president who saw the country through a good piece of the 19th century. The impressive baroque altar, carved out of Ecuadorean mahogany, dates to the 1500s.

Museo de la Cultura Peruana MUSEUM
(Museum of Peruvian Culture; Map p60; ☎01-423-5892; www.limacultura.pe/directorio-cultural/museo-nacional-de-la-cultura-peruana; Alfonso Ugarte 650; admission S5; ⊙10am-5pm Tue-Sat) About half-a-dozen blocks west of the Plaza San Martín, on a traffic-choked thoroughfare, resides the Museo de la Cultura Peruana, a repository of Peruvian folk art. The collection, consisting of elaborate *retablos* (religious dioramas) from Ayacucho, historic pottery from Puno and works in feathers from the Amazon, is displayed in a building whose exterior facade is inspired by pre-Columbian architecture.

Parque de la Cultura PARK
(Map p64) Originally known as Parque de la Exposición, this newly revamped park has gardens and a small amphitheater for outdoor performances. Two of Lima's major art museums reside here.

★**Museo de Arte de Lima** MUSEUM
(Map p64; ☎01-204-0000; www.mali.pe; Paseo Colón 125; adult/child S12/4; ⊙10am-8pm Tue, Thu & Fri, to 5pm Sat & Sun) Known locally as MALI, Lima's principal fine-art museum is housed in a striking beaux-arts building that was recently renovated. Subjects span from pre-Columbian to contemporary art, and there are also guided visits to special exhibits. On Sunday, entry is just S1. A satellite museum is under construction in Barranco.

Museo de Arte Italiano MUSEUM
(Italian Art Museum; Map p64; ☎01-321-5622; Paseo de la República 250; adult/child S6/1; ⊙10am-5pm Mon-Fri) Just north of MALI, the Museo de Arte Italiano exhibits a tepid collection of 19th- and 20th-century Italian academic art. Its best attribute is the glittering Venetian mosaics on the exterior walls.

★**El Circuito Mágico del Agua** FOUNTAIN
(Map p64; Parque de la Reserva, Av Petit Thouars, cuadra 5; admission S4; ⊙3:30-10:30pm) This indulgent series of illuminated fountains is so over the top it can't help but induce stupefaction among even the most hardened traveling cynic. A dozen different fountains – all splendiferously illuminated – are capped, at the end, by a laser light show at the 120m-long Fuente de la Fantasía (Fantasy Fountain). The whole display is set to a medley of tunes comprised of everything

from Peruvian waltzes to ABBA. Has to be seen to be believed.

Access to the area is free by day when fountains are off.

Museo de Historia Natural MUSEUM

(Natural History Museum; Map p64; ☎01-471-0117; museohn.unmsm.edu.pe; Arenales 1256, Jesús María; adult/child S7/5; ⏰9am-5pm Mon-Sat, 10am-1:30pm Sun) One block west of *cuadra* 12 off Av Arequipa, south of the Parque de la Reserva, the Museo de Historia Natural run by the Universidád de San Marcos has a modest taxidermy collection that provides a useful overview of Peruvian fauna, with guided tours (S25) available.

Rímac

Rímac can be a rough neighborhood. Taxis or organized tours are the best options for most sights.

Museo Taurino MUSEUM

(Bullfight Museum; Map p60; ☎01-481-1467; Hualgayoc 332; admission S5; ⏰9am-4:30pm Mon-Fri) Plaza de Acho, Lima's bullring, was built on this site north of the Río Rímac in 1766. Some of the world's most famous toreadors passed through here, among them the renowned Manolete from Spain. A visit includes a free guided tour inspecting cluttered displays of weapons, paintings, photographs and the gilded outfits worn by a succession of bullfighters – gore holes, blood stains and all.

Cerro San Cristóbal LOOKOUT

This 409m-high hill to the northeast of Lima Centro has a **mirador** (lookout) at its crown, with views of Lima stretching off to the Pacific (in winter expect to see nothing but fog). From the Plaza de Armas, taxis can take you to the summit (from S16) or you can wait for the **Urbanito bus** (Map p60; ☎01-428-5841; www.urbanito.com.pe; Jirón Manoa 391, Breña; per person S5; ⏰10am-7pm), on the southwest corner of the plaza, which does one-hour tours to the summit from 2pm on. Buses run every 30 minutes.

A huge **cross**, built in 1928 and illuminated at night, is a Lima landmark and the object of pilgrimages during Semana Santa (Holy Week) and the first Sunday in May. There is a small **museum** (admission S1).

Convento de los Descalzos MUSEUM

(☎01-481-0441; Manco Cápac 202A, Alameda de los Descalzos; adult/student S5/3; ⏰9:30am-1pm & 2:30-5:30pm) At the end of the attractive Alameda de los Descalzos, all but forgotten, is this 16th-century convent and museum, run by the Descalzos ('the Barefooted,' a reference to Franciscan friars). Visitors can see old winemaking equipment in the kitchen, a refectory, an infirmary and the monastic cells. There are also some 300 colonial paintings, including noteworthy canvases by renowned Cuzco School artist Diego Quispe Tito. Spanish-speaking guides give 45-minute tours. Taxis from the Plaza de Armas start at about S12.

East Lima

The city begins to rise into the foothills of the Andes as you turn east, an area carpeted with government buildings and teeming residential districts.

Museo de la Nación MUSEUM

(Museum of the Nation; ☎01-476-9878; Av Javier Prado Este 2466, San Borja) At the time of research, this museum was closed but may reopen soon; check iPerú (p100) for updates. In a brutalist concrete tower, it provides a cursory overview of Peru's civilizations, from Chavín stone carvings and the knotted-rope *quipus* (used for record-keeping) of the Incas to colonial artifacts. One must-see is the permanent exhibit **Yuyanapaq**. Quechua for 'to remember,' it's a moving photographic tribute to the Internal Conflict (1980–2000) created by Peru's Truth & Reconciliation Commission in 2003.

From San Isidro, you can catch one of the many buses or *combis* (minivans) heading east along Av Javier Prado Este toward La Molina.

Museo de Oro del Perú MUSEUM

(Gold Museum of Peru; ☎01-345-1292; www.museoroperu.com.pe; Alonso de Molina 1100, Monterrico; adult/child under 11 S33/16; ⏰10:30am-6pm) The now notorious Museo de Oro del Perú, a private museum, was a Lima must-see until 2001, when a study revealed that 85% of the museum's metallurgical pieces were fakes. It reopened with an assurance that works on display are bona fide, though descriptions classify certain pieces as 'reproductions.' The cluttered, poorly signed exhibits still leave something to be desired.

Of greater interest (and, in all likelihood, of greater authenticity) are the thousands of weapons presented in the **Arms Museum**, on the museum's ground floor.

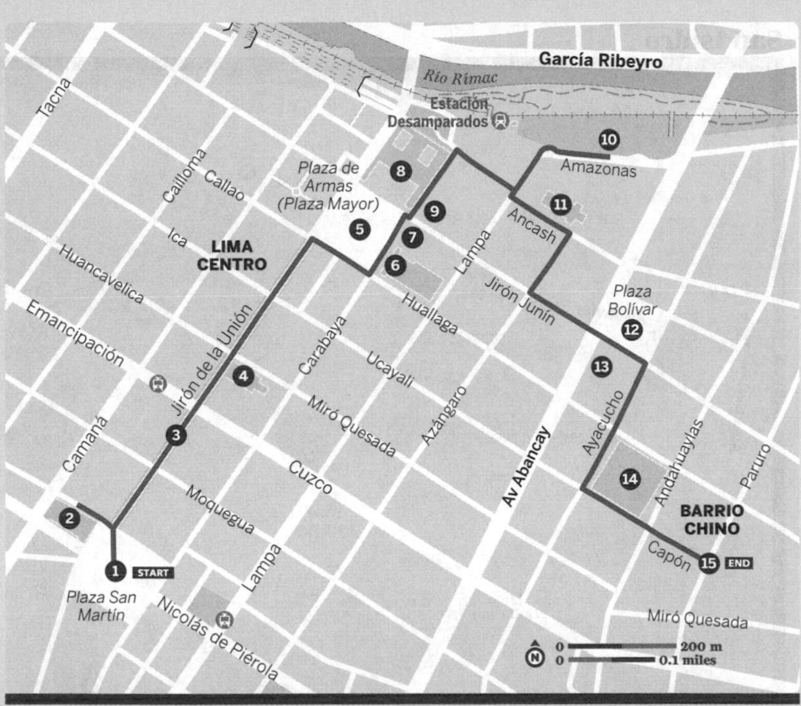

City Walk
Downtown Lima

START PLAZA SAN MARTÍN
FINISH BARRIO CHINO
LENGTH 3KM, TWO HOURS

Begin in ❶ **Plaza San Martín** (p64) to imbibe the faded grandeur of ❷ **Gran Hotel Bolívar** (p80), the city's first fine hotel. Walk the pedestrian street of ❸ **Jirón de la Unión** (p64); once the heart of aristocratic city life, it's now lined with cinemas and bargain shoe stores. To the right is ❹ **Iglesia de la Merced** (p61), originally built in 1541. It held the first Mass in Lima. Peek inside at the impressive mahogany altars.

The boulevard ends at the ❺ **Plaza de Armas** (p58), surrounded by palms and ornate canary-yellow buildings. In the era of the viceroys it served as market, bullpen and even execution site for the condemned. The restored ❻ **Catedral de Lima** (p58) houses the once-misplaced remains of conquistador Francisco Pizarro in an inscribed lead box. The adjacent ❼ **Palacio Arzobispal** (p58) has some of the city's best-preserved ornate Moorish balconies, perfectly designed for absconding people-watchers. To the northeast, the grandiose baroque ❽ **Palacio de Gobierno** (p58) serves as Peru's presidential palace – pass at noon for the ceremonious changing of the guard with a brass band tapping out 'El Condor Pasa.' Across the street, the ❾ **Museo del Pisco** (p94) merits a stop, though you might want to save it to cap your walk with a drink here instead.

The palace backs up against the Río Rimac. Follow behind it to ❿ **Parque de la Muralla** (p59), a spacious park alongside remains of the original city wall. Return via Amazonas to Lampa and ⓫ **Monasterio de San Francisco** (p59) to check out the monastery's compelling catacombs that hold skulls and bones laid out in geometric designs. Cross the avenida to ⓬ **Plaza Bolívar** and Congress, passing the ghoulish ⓭ **Museo de la Inquisición** (p59), where wax figures are tortured in the basement. Follow Ayacucho two blocks to the ⓮ **Mercado Central** (p98), with stalls of goods from soccer jerseys to tropical fruit. Take the pedestrian street Capón to **El Barrio Chino** (Chinatown) for a Cantonese lunch.

San Isidro

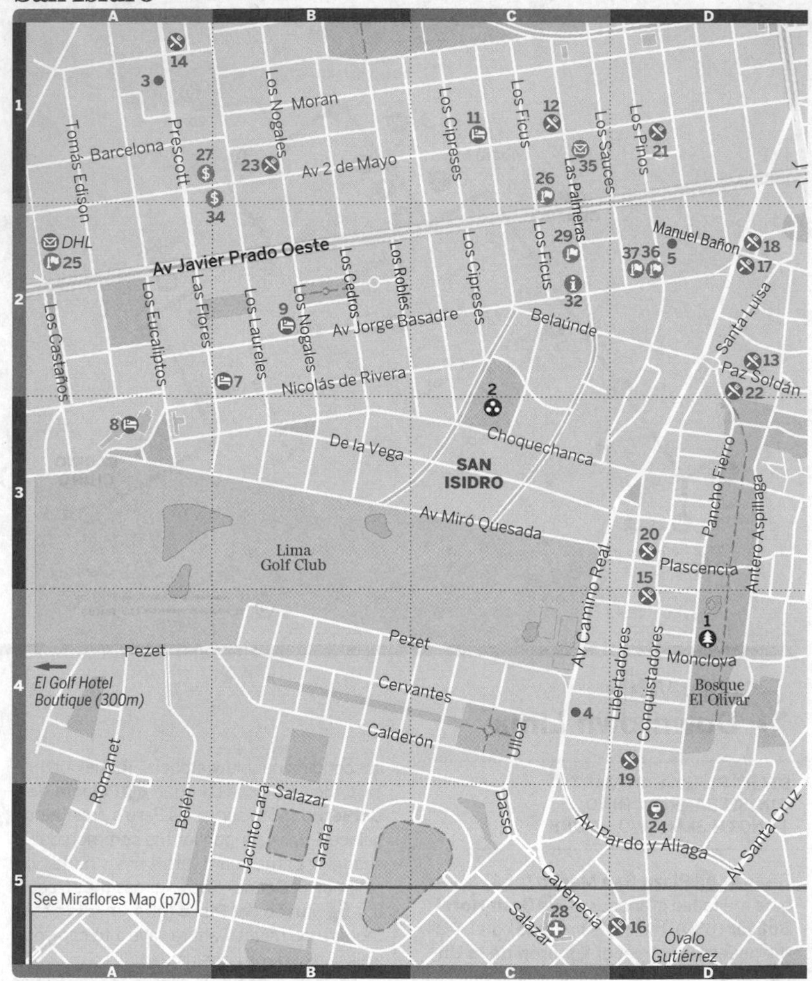

Here, in various jumbled rooms, you'll find rifles, swords and guns from every century imaginable, including a firearm that once belonged to Fidel Castro.

Go via taxi or *combi* from Museo de la Nación heading northeast on Angamos toward Monterrico and get off at the Puente Primavera. From there, it's a 15-minute stroll north to the museum.

Asociación Museo del Automóvil MUSEUM
(Automobile Museum; ☎01-368-0373; Av La Molina, cuadra 37, cnr Totoritas, La Molina; adult S20; ⌚9:30am-7pm) The Asociación Museo del Automóvil has an impressive array of classic cars dating back to 1901, from a Ford Model T to a Cadillac Fleetwood used by four Peruvian presidents.

San Isidro

A combination of middle- and upper-class residential neighborhoods offer some important sights of note.

Huaca Huallamarca RUINS
(Map p68; ☎01-222-4124; Nicolás de Rivera 201; adult/child S10/5; ⌚9am-5pm Tue-Sun) Nestled among condominium towers and sprawling

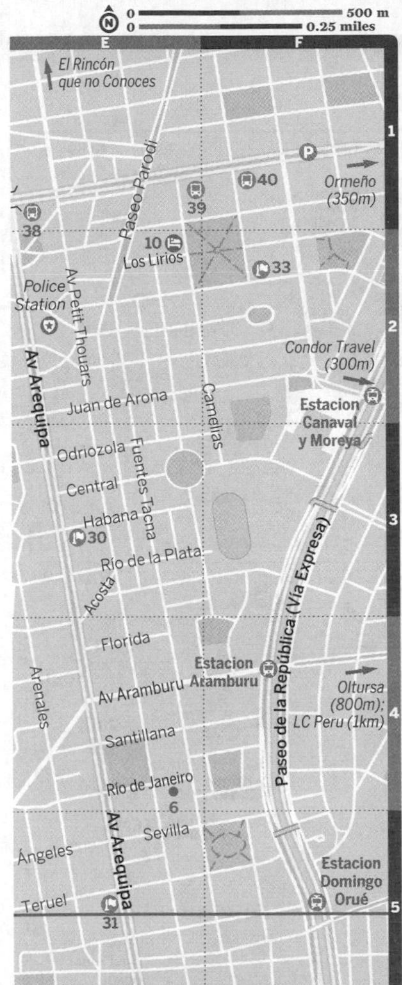

high-end homes, the simple Huaca Huallamarca is a highly restored adobe pyramid, produced by the Lima culture, that dates to somewhere between AD 200 and 500. A small on-site **museum**, complete with mummy, details its excavation.

Bosque El Olivar PARK

(Map p68) This tranquil park, a veritable oasis in the middle of San Isidro, consists of the remnants of an old **olive grove**, part of which was planted by the venerated San Martín de Porres in the 17th century.

San Isidro

Sights
- 1 Bosque El Olivar D4
- 2 Huaca Huallamarca C3

Activities, Courses & Tours
- 3 Centro de Idiomas A1
- 4 Idiomas Católica C4
- 5 InkaNatura D2
- 6 Rainbow Peruvian Tours E4

Sleeping
- 7 Casa Bella Perú B2
- 8 Country Club Lima Hotel A3
- 9 Hotel Basadre Suites B2
- 10 Malka Youth Hostel E2
- 11 Suites Antique C1

Eating
- 12 Antica C1
- 13 Astrid y Gastón Casa Moreyra D2
- 14 Coffee Road A1
- 15 Hanzo D4
- 16 La Balanza D5
- 17 Malabar D2
- 18 Matsuei D2
- 19 Punta Sal D4
- 20 Segundo Muelle D3
- 21 Spizza D1
- 22 Tanta D2
- 23 Vivanda B1

Drinking & Nightlife
- 24 Bravo Restobar D5

Information
- 25 Bolivian Embassy A2
- 26 Chilean Embassy C1
- 27 Citibank A1
- 28 Clínica Anglo-Americana C5
- 29 Ecuadorian Embassy C2
- 30 French Embassy E3
- 31 German Embassy E5
- 32 iPerú C2
- 33 Israeli Embassy F2
- 34 Scotiabank B1
- 35 Serpost C1
- 36 Spanish Consulate D2
- 37 Spanish Embassy D2

Transport
- 38 Colectivos to Chosica E1
- 39 Cruz del Sur E1
- 40 Tepsa F1

Miraflores

The city's bustling, modern hub – full of restaurants, shops and nightspots – overlooks the Pacific from a set of ragged cliffs.

Miraflores

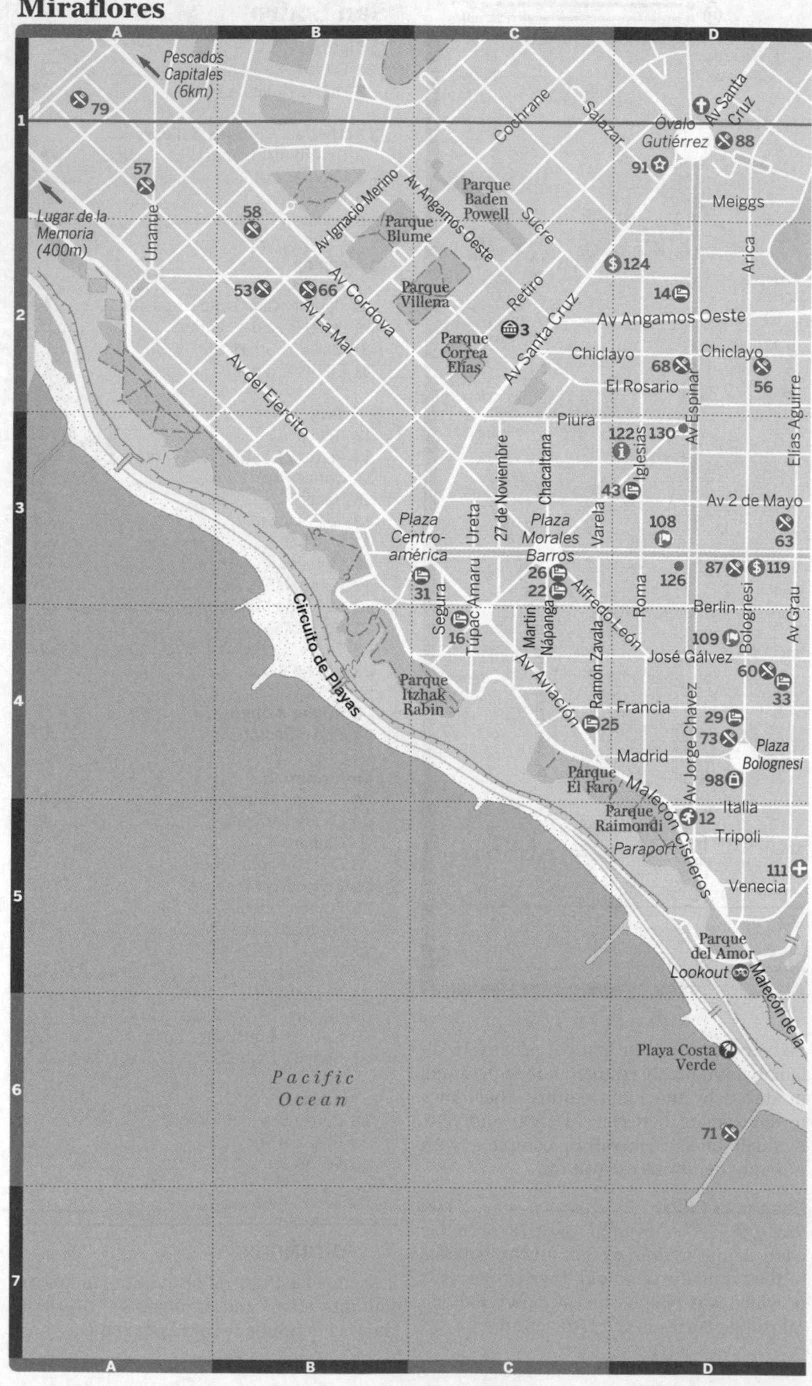

Pescados Capitales (6km)
Lugar de la Memoria (400m)
Unanue
Cochrane
Salazar
Óvalo Gutiérrez
Av Santa Cruz
Parque Baden Powell
Meiggs
Av Ignacio Merino
Av Angamos Oeste
Parque Blume
Sucre
Parque Villena
Retiro
Av Cordova
Av La Mar
Parque Correa Elías
Av Santa Cruz
Av Angamos Oeste
Arica
Chiclayo
El Rosario
Av Espinar
Av del Ejercito
Piura
Iglesias
Elías Aguirre
27 de Noviembre
Chacaltana
Av 2 de Mayo
Plaza Centro-américa
Ureta
Plaza Morales Barros
Varela
Segura
Tupac Amaru
Martin Nápanga
Alfredo León
Roma
Berlin
Bolognesi
Av Grau
Circuito de Playas
Ramón Zavala
José Gálvez
Av Aviación
Parque Itzhak Rabin
Francia
Av Jorge Chavez
Madrid
Plaza Bolognesi
Parque El Faro
Malecón Cisneros
Parque Raimondi
Italia
Tripoli
Paraport
Venecia
Parque del Amor
Lookout
Malecón de la
Playa Costa Verde
Pacific Ocean

0 500 m
0 0.25 miles
See San Isidro Map (p68)
See Barranco Map (p74)
Huaca Pucllana
Garcia Calderon
Ayacucho
Tarapacá
Montero
Domingo Elías
Av Arequipa
Paseo de la República (Vía Expresa)
Estacion Angamos
Av Angamos Este
Inca
Av República de Panamá
Santa Rosa
Carmen
Gonzales Prada
Plaza Manuel Solan
Independencia
Inclán
Piura
Av Petit Thouars
Gral Suárez
Parque Miranda
Enrique Palacios
Gonzales
Pershing
Colina
General Borgoño
Atahualpa
Av José Pardo
Óvalo
Av Ricardo Palma
Estacion Ricardo Palma
Cáceres
Libertad
Bellavista
Manuel Bonilla
Esperanza
Vargas Machuca
Pasaje Juan Figari
Benavides (Diagonal)
Parque Central
Cantuarias
Parque Las Tradiciones
Mariano Odicio
Diez Canseco
Parque Kennedy
Federico Recavarren
Av La Paz
Schell
Pedro Silva
Olcay
Trujillo
Av Casimiro Juan Ulloa
Psje Tarata
Malecón Balta
Alfredo Benavides
Estacion Benavides
Ramón Ribeyro
Parque L Prado
Bajada de Balta
Malecón 28 de Julio
Bolívar
Parque Reducto
Arias Araguez
Porta
Ocharán
Colón
Av José Larco
Av 28 de Julio
San Martín
Av Reducto
Jr Manco Cápac
Grimaldo del Solar
Juan Fanning
Diego Ferre
José Gonzáles
Las Dalias
Alcanfores
Santa Isabel
Estacion 28 de Julio
Reserva
Av Vasco Núñez de Balboa
Circuito de Playas
Parque Salazar
Arístides Aljovín
Av Armendariz
Parque Melitón Porras
Lookout
Carolinos
Parque Domodossola
San Ignacio de Loyola
Las Acacias

Miraflores

Sights

1 Casa de Ricardo Palma F3
2 Choco Museo E4
3 Fundación Museo Amano C2
4 Huaca Pucllana E1

Activities, Courses & Tours

5 Bike Tours of Lima F5
6 El Sol G5
7 Explorandes F6
8 Instituto Cultural Peruano-Norteamericano E2
9 Lima Vision E2
10 Mirabici E6
11 Peru Expeditions G4
12 Peru Fly D5
13 Peru Hands On F5

Sleeping

14 Albergue Miraflores House D2
15 Albergue Turístico Juvenil Internacional G4
16 Backpacker's Family House C4
17 Casa Andina F4
18 Casa Andina G6
19 Casa Andina F3
20 Casa Cielo E4
21 Casa San Martín E5
22 Condor's House C3
23 Dragonfly Hostel E5
24 Ekeko Hostel E1
25 El Faro Inn C4
26 Explorer's House C3
27 Flying Dog F4
28 Friend's House E5
29 Hitchhikers D4
30 Hostal El Patio F4
31 Hostal Torreblanca C3
32 Hotel Alemán E2
33 Hotel Antigua Miraflores D4
34 Hotel Ariosto F5
35 Hotel Bayview F6
36 Hotel de Autor F5
37 Hotel El Doral E3
38 Hotel Esperanza F4
39 Hotel Ibis F6
40 Hotel San Antonio Abad G5
41 Hotel Señorial F6
42 IFE Boutique Hotel G7
43 Inka Frog D3
44 JW Marriott Hotel Lima F6
45 La Casa Nostra G5
46 La Castellana F4
47 La Paz Apart Hotel F4
48 Miraflores Park Hotel F7
49 Terra Viva F5

Eating

50 Al Toke Pez G2
51 AlmaZen E4
52 ámaZ F6
53 Anticuchos de la Tía Grimanesa B2
54 Central F6
55 Dédalo Arte y Cafe E4
56 El Enano D2
57 El Mercado A1
58 El Pan de la Chola B2
59 El Punto Azul F5
60 El Rincón del Bigote D4
61 Fiesta G6
62 Haiti E4
63 IK D3
64 Kulcafé E4
65 La Lucha Sanguachería E4
66 La Mar B2
67 La Matilda E3
68 La Pascana de Madre Natura D2
69 La Picantería G3
70 La Preferida H6
71 La Rosa Nautica D6

Fundación Museo Amano MUSEUM

(Map p70; ☎01-441-2909; www.museoamano.org; Retiro 160; ⏲3-5pm Mon-Fri, by appointment only) FREE The well-designed Fundación Museo Amano features a fine private collection of ceramics, with a strong representation of wares from the Chimú and Nazca cultures. It also has a remarkable assortment of lace and other textiles produced by the coastal Chancay culture. Museum visits are allowed by a one-hour guided tour only, in Spanish or Japanese.

Lugar de la Memoria MUSEUM

(LUM; ☎01-261-8136; lugardelamemoria.org; Bajada San Martin 151) An ambitious state project to preserve the memory of victims of violence during Peru's tumultuous period from 1980 to 2000. This new postmodernist museum is still in the process of implementation, but has traveling open-air exhibits in the meanwhile (check the website for details). Exhibits reflect on events and commemorate victims to help Peruvians heal and embrace a strong stance on human rights. It's directed especially at younger generations who didn't experience the period, but proves fascinating to non-nationals as well.

Choco Museo MUSEUM

(Map p70; ☎01-445-9708; www.chocomuseo.com; Berlin 375; 2hr workshop adult/child S75/55; ⏲11am-8:30pm Sun-Thu, to 9:30pm Fri & Sat) FREE On-site chocolate production is the seducing factor of this 'museum' selling fondue and fair-trade hot cocoa. French-owned, it is

72 La Tiendecita Blanca ... F3
73 Las Brujas de Cachiche ... D4
74 Maido ... E5
75 Manolo ... F4
76 Panchita ... E3
77 Pardo's Chicken ... G5
78 Pastelería San Antonio ... G6
79 Pescados Capitales ... A1
80 Plaza Vea ... F2
81 Quattro D ... E2
82 Rafael ... E5
83 Raw Cafe ... E2
84 Restaurant Huaca Pucllana ... E1
85 Tanta ... G6
86 Vivanda ... F5
87 Vivanda ... D3
88 Wong ... D1

Drinking & Nightlife
89 Bodega Miraflores ... F4
90 Café Bar Habana ... F3
Huaringas ... (see 73)

Entertainment
91 Cine Planet ... D1
92 Cinerama ... F3
93 Cocodrilo Verde ... E4
Jazz Zone ... (see 96)
94 Teatro Británico ... E4
UVK Multicines ... (see 99)

Shopping
95 Alpamayo ... F4
96 Centro Comercial el Suche ... F5
97 CompuPalace ... F3
98 El Virrey ... D4
99 LarcoMar ... E6
100 Mercado Indio ... F2
Tatoo Adventure Gear ... (see 99)
101 Todo Camping ... E2

Information
102 Australian Embassy ... F5
103 Banco de Crédito del Perú ... E3
104 Banco de Crédito del Perú ... F6
105 Banco de Crédito del Perú ... F4
106 BBVA Continental ... F4
107 Belgian Embassy ... E2
Botica Fasa ... (see 72)
108 Brazilian Embassy ... D3
109 Canadian Embassy ... D4
110 Citibank ... F3
111 Clínica Good Hope ... D5
112 Federal Express ... E3
113 Fertur Peru Travel ... F4
114 InkaFarma ... F5
iPerú ... (see 99)
115 Irish Consulate ... G4
116 LAC Dólar ... F3
Netherlands Embassy ... (see 125)
117 Policía de Turismo ... E5
118 Scotiabank ... F6
119 Scotiabank ... D3
120 Serpost ... F2
121 Serpost ... F5
122 South American Explorers Club ... D3
Teleticket ... (see 88)
123 Tika Tours ... E3
124 Travex ... D2
125 UK Embassy ... F6

Transport
126 Avianca ... D3
Easy Taxi ... (see 99)
127 La S Combis to the Airport ... F3
128 LAN ... E3
129 Peruvian Airlines ... E3
130 Star Perú ... D3

well known for organic chocolate-making workshops, offered at least twice daily. Truffle workshops must be reserved in advance, but otherwise walk-ins are welcome.

Casa de Ricardo Palma HISTORIC BUILDING
(Map p70; ☎01-617-7115; Gral Suárez 189; adult/student S6/3; ⏲10am-1pm & 3-5pm Mon-Fri) This house was the home of the Peruvian author Ricardo Palma from 1913 until his death in 1919. A listless tour is included in the price.

Huaca Pucllana RUINS
(Map p70; ☎01-617-7138; cnr Borgoño & Tarapacá; adult/student S12/5; ⏲9am-4:30pm) Located near the Óvalo Gutiérrez, this *huaca* is a restored adobe ceremonial center from the Lima culture that dates back to AD 400. In 2010, an important discovery of four Wari mummies was made, untouched by looting. Though vigorous excavations continue, the site is accessible by regular guided tours in Spanish (for a tip). In addition to a tiny on-site **museum**, there's a celebrated **restaurant** that offers incredible views of the illuminated ruins at night.

Barranco

A tiny resort back at the turn of the 20th century, Barranco is lined with grand old *casonas,* many of which have been turned into eateries and hotels.

Museo de Arte Contemporaneo MUSEUM
(MAC; Map p74; ☎01-514-6800; www.maclima.pe; Av Grau 1511; adult/child S10/6; ⏲10am-6pm

Barranco

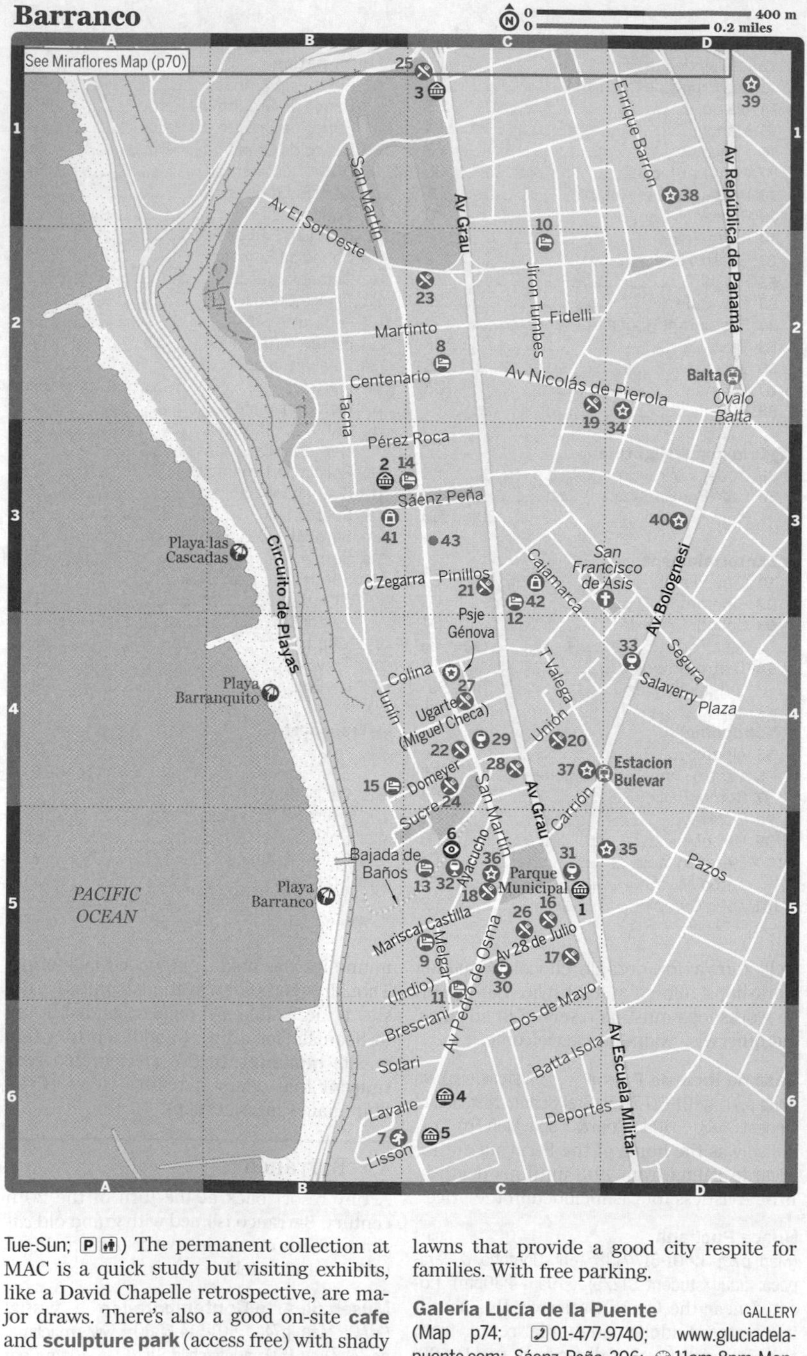

See Miraflores Map (p70)

Tue-Sun; P 🚻) The permanent collection at MAC is a quick study but visiting exhibits, like a David Chapelle retrospective, are major draws. There's also a good on-site **cafe** and **sculpture park** (access free) with shady lawns that provide a good city respite for families. With free parking.

Galería Lucía de la Puente GALLERY
(Map p74; ☎01-477-9740; www.gluciadelapuente.com; Sáenz Peña 206; ⏲11am-8pm Mon-

Barranco

Sights

1 Choco Museo C5
2 Galería Lucía de la Puente B3
3 Museo de Arte Contemporaneo C1
4 Museo Mario Testino C6
5 Museo Pedro de Osma C6
6 Puente de los Suspiros C5

Activities, Courses & Tours

7 Perú Bike B6

Sleeping

8 3B Barranco B&B C2
9 Backpackers Inn C5
10 Casa Nuestra C2
11 D'Osma B&B C5
12 Hostal Gémina C3
13 Hostal Kaminu C5
14 Hotel B C3
15 Second Home Perú B4

Eating

16 Blu C5
17 Burrito Bar C5
18 Cafe Bisetti C5
19 Café Tostado C2
20 Chifa Chung Yion C4
21 Delifrance C3
22 Isolina C4
23 La 73 .... C2
24 La Bodega Verde C4
25 La Bodega Verde C1
26 La Calandria C5
27 La Canta Rana C4
28 Las Mesitas C4

Drinking & Nightlife

29 Ayahuasca C4
30 Bar Piselli C5
31 Juanito's C5
32 Santos C5
33 Wahio's D4

Entertainment

34 El Dragón D2
35 La Candelaria D5
36 La Estación de Barranco C5
37 La Noche C4
38 La Oficina D1
39 La Peña del Carajo D1
40 Sargento Pimienta D3

Shopping

41 Dédalo B3
42 Las Pallas C3

Information

43 InteJ C3

Fri, from 3pm Sat) A magnificent two-story *casona* is home to Lima's most prestigious contemporary art gallery. Look for works by cutting-edge painters such as Fernando Gutiérrez, whose canvases often skewer Peruvian culture.

Puente de los Suspiros BRIDGE

(Bridge of Sighs; Map p74) A block west of the main plaza, look for this recently renovated, narrow wooden bridge over an old stone stairway that leads to the beach. Especially popular with couples on first dates, the bridge has inspired many a Peruvian folk song.

Choco Museo MUSEUM

(Map p74; ☎01-477-3584; www.chocomuseo.com; Av Grau 264; 2hr workshop adult/child S75/55; ⏰11am-10pm) A quickie cacao 101 museum better known for its daily chocolate-making workshops, with a few locations in the city. The specialty of this outlet is the bean-to-bar chocolate factory housed on-site. Fair-trade chocolate is also sold here.

Museo Mario Testino MUSEUM

(MATE; Map p74; ☎01-251-7755; www.mate.pe; Av Pedro de Osma 409; adult/student S15/5; ⏰11am-8pm Tue-Sun) A wonderful small museum dedicated to the work of the world-renowned photographer Mario Testino, a native of Peru and local *barranquino*. The permanent exhibition includes iconic portraits of Princess Diana, Kate Moss and notable actors. There's also beautiful portraits of Andean highlanders in traditional garb.

Museo Pedro de Osma MUSEUM

(Map p74; ☎01-467-0141; www.museopedrodeosma.org; Av Pedro de Osma 423; admission S20; ⏰10am-6pm Tue-Sun) Housed in a lovely beaux-arts mansion surrounded by gardens, this undervisited museum has an exquisite collection of colonial furniture, silverwork and art, some of which date back to the 1500s. Among the many fine pieces, standouts include a 2m-wide canvas that depicts a Corpus Christi procession in turn-of-the-17th-century Cuzco.

West Lima & Callao

To the west of downtown, cluttered lower-middle-class and poor neighborhoods eventually give way to the port city of Callao, where the Spanish once shipped their gold.

Travelers should approach Callao with caution, since some areas are dangerous, even during the day.

★Museo Larco MUSEUM
(☎01-461-1312; www.museolarco.org; Bolívar 1515, Pueblo Libre; adult/child under 15 S30/15; ⊙9am-10pm) In an 18th-century viceroy's mansion, this museum offers one of the largest, best-presented displays of ceramics in Lima. Founded by pre-Columbian collector Rafael Larco Hoyle in 1926, the collection includes over 50,000 pots, with ceramic works from the Cupisnique, Chimú, Chancay, Nazca and Inca cultures. Highlights include the sublime Moche portrait vessels, presented in simple, dramatically lit cases, and a Wari weaving in one of the rear galleries that contains 398 threads to the linear inch – a record.

There's also gold and jewels. Many visitors are lured here by a separately housed collection of pre-Columbian erotica illustrating all manner of sexual activity with comical explicitness. Don't miss the vitrine that depicts sexually transmitted diseases.

The highly recommended on-site **Café del Museo** faces a private garden draped in bougainvillea and is a perfect spot for ceviche.

Catch a bus from Av Arequipa in Miraflores marked 'Todo Bolívar' to Bolívar's 15th block. A painted blue line on the sidewalk links this building to the Museo Nacional de Antropología, Arqueología e Historía del Perú, about a 15-minute walk away.

Museo Nacional de Antropología, Arqueología e Historía del Perú MUSEUM
(National Anthropology, Archaeology & History Museum; ☎01-463-5070; http://mnaahp.cultura.pe; Plaza Bolívar, cnr San Martín & Vivanco, Pueblo Libre; adult/child S10/1; ⊙9am-5pm Tue-Sat, to 4pm Sun) Trace the history of Peru from the pre-ceramic period to the early republic. Displays include the famous Raimondi Stela, a 2.1m Chavín rock carving from one of the first Andean cultures to have a widespread, recognizable artistic style. Late-colonial and early republic paintings include an 18th-century *Last Supper* in which Christ and his disciples feast on *cuy* (guinea pig). The building was home to revolutionary heroes San Martín (from 1821 to 1822) and Bolívar (from 1823 to 1826).

From Miraflores, take a 'Todo Brasil' *combi* from Av Arequipa (just north from Óvalo) to *cuadra* 22 on the corner of Vivanco, then walk seven blocks up that street. A blue line connects this museum with Museo Larco.

Parque de Las Leyendas ZOO
(☎01-717-9878; www.leyendas.gob.pe; Av Las Leyendas 580-86, San Miguel; adult/child S10/5; ⊙9am-6pm) Located between Lima Centro and Callao, the zoo covers Peru's major geographical divisions: coast, mountains and jungle. There are 210 native animals, with a few imports (such as hippos). The conditions are OK, and the zoo is well maintained.

In Lima Centro, catch buses and *colectivos* (shared taxis) that travel past the park at Av Abancay and Garcilaso de la Vega every 30 minutes.

La Punta

A narrow peninsula that extends west into the Pacific Ocean, La Punta was once a fishing hamlet, and later, in the 19th century, an upscale summer beach resort. Today this pleasant upper-middle-class neighborhood, graced with neocolonial and art-deco homes, is a great spot to stroll by the ocean and enjoy a seafood lunch.

You can take a taxi from Miraflores (about S30). In Lima Centro, *combis* traveling to Callao run west along Av Colonial from the Plaza 2 de Mayo. Take the ones labeled 'La Punta.' A good spot to get out is Plaza Gálvez; from here, you can head west all along the waterside Malecón Figueredo, which offers magnificent views of craggy Isla San Lorenzo, just off the coast.

Fortaleza del Real Felipe FORT
(☎01-429-0532; Plaza Independencia, Callao; adult/child S12/3; ⊙9am-2pm) In the 1820s, the Spanish royalists made their last stand during the battle for independence at this historic fort, which was built in 1747 to guard against pirates. It still houses a small military contingent. Visits are by guided tours in Spanish only.

On the western flank of the fort, don't miss an opportunity to stroll through the truly bizarre **Parque Tématico de la Policía** (Police Park), a nicely landscaped garden that is dotted with police tanks and life-size statues of policemen in riot gear – a perfect place for those surreal family vacation photos.

Note that the nearby dock area is quite a rough neighborhood; travel by taxi.

Activities

Cycling

Popular excursions from Lima include the 31km ride to Pachacamac, where there are good local trails open between April and

December. Expert riders can inquire about the stellar downhill circuit from Olleros to San Bartolo south of Lima. For general information (in Spanish) on cycling, try **Federación Deportiva Peruana de Ciclismo** (☎01-346-3493; www.fedepeci.org; Av San Luis 1308, San Luis) or the Facebook page of **Ciclismo Sin Fronteras Miraflores**.

Dozens of bike shops are listed in Lima's Yellow Pages under 'Bicicletas.'

Bike Tours of Lima BICYCLE TOUR
(Map p70; ☎01-445-3172; www.biketoursoflima.com; Bolívar 150, Miraflores; 3hr tour S105; ⏰9am-7pm Mon-Sat) Highly recommended for organized day tours around Barranco, Miraflores and San Isidro, as well as Sunday excursions into downtown. Rentals available.

Perú Bike BICYCLE TOUR
(Map p74; ☎01-260-8225; www.perubike.com; Punta Sal D7, Surco; ⏰9am-1pm & 4-8pm Mon-Sat) A recommended shop that offers repairs. The mountain-biking tours run from conventional to more demanding routes, with downhill options and multiday trips to the Andes and jungle areas.

Mirabici BICYCLE RENTAL
(Map p70; ☎01-673-3908; www.mirabiciperu.pe; Costanera s/n; per hr S20; ⏰9:30am-6:30pm) On the coastal paths, a convenient stop for bicycle rentals also offering tours.

Paragliding

From the Miraflores cliff tops, tandem flights (S240 for 10 minutes) take off from the cliff-top 'paraport' at the Parque Raimondi to soar over coastal skyscrapers and gaze down at the surfers.

Peru Fly PARAGLIDING
(Map p70; ☎01-959-524-940; www.perufly.com) A paragliding school that also offers tandem flights in Miraflores.

Andean Trail Peru PARAGLIDING
(andeantrailperu.com) Offers tandem flights over Miraflores and Pachacamac, along with basic paragliding courses.

Swimming & Water Sports

Despite the newspaper warnings about pollution, *limeños* hit the beaches in droves in summer (January through March). **Playa Costa Verde** in Miraflores (nicknamed Waikiki) is a favorite of local surfers and has good breaks year-round. Barranco's beaches have waves that are better for long boards. There are seven other beaches in Miraflores and four more in Barranco. Serious surfers can also try **Playa La Herradura** in Chorrillos, which has waves up to 5m high during good swells. Do not leave your belongings unattended as theft is a problem.

Focus SURFING
(☎01-430-0444; www.focussurf.com; Leonardo da Vinci 208, Surquillo; ⏰8am-8pm Mon-Fri, 9am-1pm Sat) An established board fabrication outlet, they also offer lessons and run a surf camp south of Lima in Lurín.

Wayo Whilar SURFING
(☎01-254-1344; www.wayowhilar.com.pe; Alameda Garzas Reales Mz-FA 7, Chorillos; ⏰9am-7pm Mon-Thu, to 4pm Fri & Sat) The shop of a longtime Peruvian surfer who sells his own line of hand-shaped surfboards.

Perú Divers DIVING
(☎01-251-6231; www.perudivers.com; Av Defensores del Morro 175, Chorrillos) Deep-sea diving off Peru's southern coast is reasonably priced. Luis Rodríguez, a PADI-certified instructor, owns this excellent dive shop with equipment for sale, and offers certification and diving trips. Regular excursions visit a year-round sea-lion colony at Islas Palomino, off the coast of Callao.

Courses

Peru's clear, well-spoken Spanish makes it a hub for language schools. You will find plenty in Lima.

Centro de Idiomas LANGUAGE COURSE
(Map p68; ☎01-219-0151; www.up.edu.pe/idiomas; Prescott 333, San Isidro) Overseen by the Universidad del Pacífico, it offers a 40-hour semester-long course, available in five levels.

El Sol LANGUAGE COURSE
(Map p70; ☎01-242-7763; elsol.idiomasperu.com; Grimaldo del Solar 469, Miraflores) Private classes are S75 per hour; one-week courses start at S805.

Idiomas Católica LANGUAGE COURSE
(Map p68; ☎01-626-6500; www.idiomas.pucp.edu.pe; Av Camino Real 1037, San Isidro) Managed by the prestigious Catholic University, this program offers five two-hour group classes per week.

Instituto Cultural Peruano-Norteamericano LANGUAGE COURSE
(ICPNA; ☎01-706-7000; www.icpna.edu.pe) The institute's various branches, including one

in **Central Lima** (Map p60; Cuzco 446) and one in **Miraflores** (Map p70; Av Arequipa 4798), offer Spanish courses from qualified instructors.

 Tours

For guided tours of Lima and nearby archaeological sites such as Pachacamac, as well as trips around Peru, try these companies. In addition, travel agencies organize local, regional and national tours. It may be helpful to look for guides registered with **Agotur** (Asociación de Guías Oficiales de Turismo; www.agotur.com), the Peruvian guide organization. Another resource is www.leaplocal.com. Telephone numbers are for Peruvian daytime use only. Full-day tours in Lima usually start at around US$70.

Respons TOUR
(01-995-057-612; www.responsibletravelperu.com; Canarias, Chorrillos) High-end tours all over Peru, specializing in sustainable tourism.

Lima Tasty Tours FOOD TOUR
(01-958-313-939; www.limatastytours.com) Excellent gastronomic tours, with tailored options and insider access to lesser-known culinary treasures, available in English.

Jorge Riveros Cayo GUIDED TOUR
(01-944-324-637; jorge.riveros.cayo@gmail.com) A fluent English speaker and journalist offering recommended gastronomic tours, city excursions and longer custom trips with a cultural bent.

Explorandes ADVENTURE TOUR
(Map p70; 01-8423-8380; www.explorandes.com; Aristides Aljovín 484, Miraflores) The winner of various green travel awards. Outdoor travel is their focus, with a specialty in trekking, biking and adventure sports.

Ecoaventura Vida CULTURAL TOUR
(01-461-2555; www.ecoaventuravida.com; city walking tour US$70 or S231) In addition to city tours and adventure tourism throughout the country, Ecoaventura offers sustainable travel and homestays with Peruvian families.

InkaNatura ADVENTURE TOUR
(Map p68; 01-203-5000, in US 1-888-870-7378; www.inkanatura.com; Manuel Bañón 461, San Isidro) Quality tours throughout Peru, including Chachapoyas and the jungle.

Lima Vision TOUR
(Map p70; 01-447-7710; www.limavision.com; Chiclayo 444, Miraflores) Lima Vision has various four-hour city tours (S70), as well as day trips to the ruins at Pachacamac.

Peru Expeditions ADVENTURE TOUR
(Map p70; 01-447-2057; www.peru-expeditions.com; Paseo de la Republica 5662, office 1201, Miraflores) Books trips and organized tours around the region and beyond, and also specializes in 4WD excursions.

Peru Hands On TOUR
(Map p70; 999-542-728; www.peruhandson.com; apt 401, Av La Paz 887, Miraflores) A locally run agency specializing in standard and custom itineraries around Peru.

Mónica Tours GUIDED TOUR
(99-943-0796; www.monicatoursperu.com) Reader-recommended tours, in English.

Condor Travel TOUR
(01-615-3000; www.condortravel.com; Blondet 249, San Isidro) Recommended for top-end touring and custom itineraries throughout the Andes.

Festivals & Events

For local events, see local newspapers or visit *The Peru Guide* (www.theperuguide.com). Holidays specific to Lima include the Festival of Lima, Feast of Santa Rosa de Lima and El Señor de los Milagros.

Festival of Lima CULTURAL
Celebrates the anniversary of Lima's founding on January 18.

Feria de Santa Rosa de Lima RELIGIOUS
Held on August 30, this feast honors Santa Rosa, the venerated patron saint of Lima and the Americas. Believers visit the Santuario de Santa Rosa de Lima in the Centro Historico. From here a procession goes to the saint's hometown Santa Rosa de Quives near Lima.

El Señor de los Milagros RELIGIOUS
(Lord of Miracles) The city drapes itself in purple during this massive religious procession through Centro Histórico on October 18 in honor of the Christ from the Nazarenas church; smaller processions occur other Sundays in October.

Sleeping

From diminutive family *pensións* to glassy hotel towers armed with spas, Lima has every type of accommodations imaginable. It is also one of the most expensive destinations in the country (other than the tourist mecca of Cuzco).

The favored traveler neighborhood is Miraflores, offering a bounty of hostels, inns and upscale hotel chains and vigilant neighborhood security. The former seaside resort of Barranco nearby has become a hot neighborhood and is certainly one of the most walkable areas, with lots of gardens and colonial architecture. More upscale – and generally more tranquil – is the financial hub of San Isidro. Cheaper lodging can be found in Lima Centro, though it is rather removed from the city's hopping restaurants and nightclubs.

If arriving at night, it's worth contacting hotels in advance to arrange for airport pickup; even budget hostels can arrange this – sometimes for a few dollars less than the official airport service.

LAY OF THE LAND

With over 30 municipalities, Lima's historic heart is Lima Centro (Central Lima). Av Arequipa, one of the city's principal thoroughfares, plunges southeast toward well-to-do San Isidro, the contemporary seaside neighborhood of Miraflores, and Barranco to the south.

The principal bus routes connecting Central Lima with San Isidro and Miraflores run along broad avenues such as Tacna, Garcilaso de la Vega and Av Arequipa. These neighborhoods are also connected by the short highway Paseo de la República or Vía Expresa, known informally as *el zanjón* (the ditch).

Lima Centro

Offerings in the congested city center lag behind other neighborhoods. Central Lima has seen its high-end business slip away as upscale establishments have shifted to San Isidro and Miraflores. There is some good-value lodging with proximity to some of the most storied attractions. But keep in mind that it's mainly alive during the day and can feel abandoned at night. Although security has improved greatly, it is advisable to take taxis at night and to never display expensive camera gear or jewelry.

★1900 Backpackers HOSTEL $
(Map p64; ☎01-424-3358; www.1900hostel.com; Av Garcilaso de la Vega 1588; dm S25-37, s/d/tr incl breakfast 62/87/130; @📶) A downtown hot spot, this old mansion designed by Gustavo Eiffel is revamped with modern design touches, though it maintains the marble floors and other turn-of-the-century flourishes. For a hostel it's downright gorgeous. Rooms are smart and simple, with bunks shoulder-to-shoulder. There's a tiny kitchen and cool common spaces, like a pool room with bar and red chandelier.

Though the location is riddled with traffic exhaust during the day, there's the plus of having a premier museum right across the street.

Familia Rodríguez HOMESTAY $
(Map p60; ☎01-423-6465; jotajot@terra.com.pe; Nicolás de Piérola 730, No 201, apt 201; d incl breakfast S70; @📶) An early-20th-century building west of the Plaza San Martín houses a sprawling old apartment with parquet floors and spotless bathrooms in this tranquil, well-recommended family homestay. All bathrooms are shared.

Hostal Iquique HOTEL $
(Map p64; ☎01-433-4724; www.hostaliquique.com; Iquique 758; s/d without bathroom S54/90, s/d/tr incl breakfast S75/96/132; @) Recommended Iquique is basic but clean and safe, with small, dark, concrete rooms sporting remodeled bathrooms with hot showers. The rooftop terrace features a pool table, and guests get to use shared kitchen facilities. Credit cards are accepted.

Pensión Ibarra GUESTHOUSE $
(Map p60; ☎01-427-8603; pensionibarra@gmail.com; Tacna 359, No 152, 14th fl; s/d without bathroom from S25/35; 📶) Inside a scruffy concrete apartment block, the helpful Ibarra sisters keep seven basic guest rooms that are clean and stocked with firm beds. There is a shared kitchen and laundry service. A small balcony has views of the noisy city.

Hostal Roma HOTEL $
(Map p60; ☎01-427-7576; www.hostalroma.8m.com; Ica 326; s/d/tr S50/80/105; @📶) A relic from another era, Roma's 22 tidy rooms are dull (some are windowless) and quiet and set around a sunny interior courtyard. Beds sag – it's hard to expect more from a bargain –

but some units feature cable TV. An on-site cafe serves breakfast.

Hotel Kamana HOTEL $$
(Map p60; ☎427-7106, 01-426-7204; www.hotelkamana.com; Camaná 547; s/d/tr incl breakfast S152/193/234; ❄@📶) Popular with tour groups and business travelers, this staid and secure hotel has 46 tidy, carpeted rooms enlivened by colorful bedspreads. English and French are spoken. Credit cards accepted. An on-site restaurant-cafe is open 24 hours.

Hostal Bonbini HOTEL $$
(Map p60; ☎01-427-6477; www.hostalbonbini.com; Cailloma 209; s/d/tr incl breakfast S110/140/170; @📶) On a street cluttered with print shops, this comfy, 15-room hotel features simple, carpeted rooms, spick-and-span bathrooms and cable TV. Service could be more attentive, but credit cards are accepted.

Hotel Maury HOTEL $$
(Map p60; ☎01-428-8188; hotmaury@rcp.net.pe; Ucayali 201; s/d incl breakfast S135/165; ❄@📶) A longtime Lima outpost renowned for cultivating a new-fangled cocktail known as the pisco sour (grape brandy cocktail) back in the 1930s. While public areas retain old-world flourishes such as gilded mirrors and Victorian-style furniture, the 76 simple rooms are more modern, some feature Jacuzzi tubs and lockboxes. Credit cards accepted.

Gran Hotel Bolívar HISTORIC HOTEL $$$
(Map p60; ☎01-619-7171; www.granhotelbolivar.com.pe; Jirón de la Unión 958; s/d/tr S247/278/309; @) For aficionados of the gilded age, this venerable 1924 hotel was where Clark Gable, Mick Jagger and Robert Kennedy all tucked in. Though now frayed, there's a certain grand-dame finesse, and it's on Plaza San Martín. It's also employee-owned, a rarity in the hotel world, which translates to impeccable and entertaining service even from the bellhop.

Lima Sheraton HOTEL $$$
(Map p64; ☎01-619-3300; www.sheraton.com.pe; Paseo de la República 170; d S584; ❄@📶🏊) Housed in a brutalist high-rise that overlooks the equally dour Palacio de Justicia (Supreme Court), downtown's top hotel has more than 400 rooms and suites decorated in an array of desert tones. In addition to 24-hour room service, there are concierge services, two on-site restaurants, a bar, a gym, a swimming pool and a beauty salon.

San Isidro

Want to fit into San Isidro? Carry a tennis racket. With a hyper-exclusive golf course at its heart, this is the tree-lined cradle of Lima's elite who inhabit expansive modernist homes and sip cocktails at members-only social clubs. Accommodations are unapologetically upscale.

Malka Youth Hostel HOSTEL $
(Map p68; ☎01-222-5589; www.youthhostelperu.com; Los Lirios 165; dm S35, d incl breakfast with/without bathroom S128/112; @📶) A quiet hostel in a nice neighborhood just a block from a park, Malka is run by an amiable mother–daughter team. The house features 10 clean rooms, a nice garden space and a rock-climbing wall. There is a large shared kitchen and laundry facilities, a TV room with DVD player, luggage storage and a small on-site cafe serving light meals.

It's near the transit hub of Av Arequipa and Av Javier Prado.

Casa Bella Perú GUESTHOUSE $$
(Map p68; ☎01-421-7354; www.casabellaperu.net; Las Flores 459; d incl breakfast S232; @📶) A great midrange option in a relentlessly expensive area, this expansive former 1950s home has contemporary rooms accented by indigenous textiles. Fourteen varied units have comfy beds, firm pillows, oversized plasma TVs and remodeled bathrooms. There is a kitchen, an ample garden and a lounge. Credit cards accepted.

Hotel Basadre Suites HOTEL $$
(Map p68; ☎01-442-2423; www.hotelbasadre.com; Jorge Basadre 1310; s/d incl breakfast S217/248; ❄@🏊) A good option, this attentive inn has 20 attractive, contemporary rooms, some quite spacious. Built around a former private home, each room has a minibar, hairdryer, cable TV and lockbox. Breakfast, served in a small room by the garden, is abundant. Credit cards accepted; check the website for excellent special offers.

El Golf Hotel Boutique BOUTIQUE HOTEL $$$
(☎01-677-8888; www.elgolfhb.com; Valle Riesta 576; s/d/ste incl breakfast S340/433/494; ❄@📶🏊) This intimate hotel features 20 monochromatic rooms outfitted with soft sheets, slippers and marble baths. Service is proper and the on-site restaurant offers the

option of lunch or evening meals. It's on a serene residential street, two blocks west of the Lima Golf Club. Credit cards accepted.

Country Club Lima Hotel LUXURY HOTEL $$$

(Map p68; 01-611-9000; www.hotelcountry.com; Los Eucaliptos 590; d from S802;) Set on a sprawling lawn dotted with palms, this regal hotel occupies one of Lima's finest buildings, a sprawling 1927 structure built in the Spanish tradition. Clad in colorful tiles, wood-beam ceilings and replica Cuzco School paintings, its signature feature is a round stained-glass atrium where breakfast is served. The 83 rooms replete with amenities range from the luxurious Master Room to the opulent Presidential Suite. Credit cards accepted.

Suites Antique APARTMENT $$$

(Map p68; 01-222-1094; www.suites-antique.com; Av 2 de Mayo 954; s/d/ste incl breakfast S423/485/562;) Central and low-key, this small hotel features smart and bright decor, though prices are dear. The 23 spotless suites are spacious, with small kitchenettes equipped with microwaves and a minifridge. Breakfast is served at the cozy in-house cafe.

Miraflores

Overlooking the ocean, this neighborhood's pedestrian-friendly streets teem with cafes, restaurants, hotels, high-rises, banks, shops and nightclubs that pump everything from disco to *cumbia*. There are many quiet blocks, too.

Ekeko Hostel HOSTEL $

(Map p70; 01-635-5031; Garcia Calderon 274; dm/s/d without bathroom S31/50/93, d incl breakfast S99;) Tucked into a comfortable middle-class neighborhood, this spacious home features a huge kitchen and oversized breakfast table, plus nonstandard amenities, like hairdryers. Guests will enjoy the nice backyard and good service.

Dragonfly Hostel HOSTEL $

(Map p70; 01-654-3226; www.dragonflyhostels.com; Av 28 de Julio 190; dm S31-35, s without bathroom incl breakfast S70, d S78-99;) In a central location, this tiny 2nd-floor hostel proves a popular choice. Expect all the usual amenities: lockers, guest kitchen, bar and options for airport transfer. Rooms are brightly appointed and tidy. Guests can also chill on the rooftop and enjoy the hostel's very own (and good) artisan beer.

Hitchhikers HOSTEL $

(Map p70; 01-242-3008; www.hhikersperu.com; Bolognesi 400; dm/s/d without bathroom S28/65/70, s/d incl breakfast S70/84;) Occupying an enormous century-old *casona,* this longtime hostel has a wide array of rooms. Secure and sleeper-friendly, it includes a lounge with cable TV and a DVD library, while a bare outdoor patio has barbecue facilities and ping-pong. Also parks campers (S18). Overall, a good choice.

Condor's House HOSTEL $

(Map p70; 01-446-7267; www.condorshouse.com; Napanga 137; dm S25-30, d/tr S50/75;) In a good location, this hostel fosters mild chaos, with weekend barbecues and live music, ping-pong and a bar. Be warned: private doubles feature bunks, and baths have electric showers. There's a nice back patio for lounging, but not much locked storage space.

Backpacker's Family House HOSTEL $

(Map p70; 01-447-4572; www.backpackers-familyhouse.com; Juan Moore 304; dm/d incl breakfast S47/126;) A small brick home with parquet floors, graffiti murals and games like foosball and ping-pong. It's uncluttered but a little rundown, and we wish the beds had some backbone. Be warned, the top floor rooms have bathrooms one flight down.

Flying Dog HOSTEL $

(Map p70; 01-444-5753; www.flyingdogperu.com; Lima 457; dm S35, d with/without bathroom S115/135;) Of Flying Dog's four Lima hostels, this is the best, featuring a lovely outdoor garden bar and 3rd-floor lounge area with expansive views over Parque Kennedy. Two kitchens make for a shorter cooking queue, and the included breakfast is taken at the terrace restaurant across the park. The biggest outlet, across the park, is rather dusty and rundown.

Albergue Turístico Juvenil Internacional HOSTEL $

(Map p70; 01-446-5488; www.limahostell.com.pe; Av Casimiro Juan Ulloa 328; dm S52, s/d S157/185;) This first-generation youth hostel caters mostly to groups. Dorms are spotless, and spacious private rooms feature homey decorations, but the vibe is a little dull and the location isolated from main attractions. Infrastructure is a strength, with ample kitchen facilities and a spacious backyard with a pool.

Friend's House HOSTEL $
(Map p70; ☎01-446-6248; friendshouseperu@yahoo.com.mx; Jirón Manco Cápac 368; dm/s/d S27/35/60, s/d incl breakfast S40/70; 📶) Overtaken by young dudes, this backpacker haunt is unpretentious and sociable, though dorms are cramped and a little worn. There's kitchen privileges and a small lounge with cable TV.

Explorer's House HOSTEL $
(Map p70; ☎01-241-5002; www.explorershouse-lima.com; Alfredo León 158; dm/s/d without bathroom S25/60/70, d incl breakfast S80; @📶) Bare bones, this hostel is somewhat frayed with sofas on their last gasp, but shared bathrooms are clean. The management is very sweet and there's a shared kitchen, wi-fi and a rooftop terrace with views. It is popular with Spanish-speaking guests.

★**Casa Cielo** BOUTIQUE HOTEL $$
(Map p70; ☎01-242-1127; www.hotelcasacielo.com; Berlin 370; s/d S164/275; P📶) A beautiful option that's centrally located, offering top-notch service and great value. The look is modern Andino, with ceramic bulls and Mario Testino photographs set against a neutral palette. Rooms feature hypoallergenic pillows, double-pane windows and safe boxes, king beds go for US$10 extra. Buffet breakfasts are served at a top-floor cafe.

Hotel Antigua Miraflores INN $$
(Map p70; ☎01-241-6116; www.peru-hotels-inns.com; Av Grau 350; s/d/tr incl breakfast S284/328/439; ❄@📶) In a converted early-20th-century mansion, this quiet, atmospheric hotel with a lovely courtyard channels colonial charm. Rooms are equipped with the expected modern amenities, but the furnishings display baroque touches. Units vary in size and style; the more expensive ones have Jacuzzi tubs and kitchenettes.

Inka Frog HOTEL $$
(Map p70; ☎01-445-8979; www.inkafrog.com; Iglesias 271; s/d/tr incl breakfast S170/201/263; @📶) As lodgings go, this is among Lima's best values, targeted at mature hostel-goers wanting private rooms. Subdued and friendly, it features ample and spotless modern rooms with fans and flat-screen TVs; those on a cute roof patio feature air-conditioning at no extra cost. Enjoy the complimentary coffee hour on plush sofas. Staff is helpful and the street is refreshingly quiet.

Hostal El Patio GUESTHOUSE $$
(Map p70; ☎01-444-2107; www.hostalelpatio.net; Ernesto Diez Canseco 341A; s/d incl breakfast S126/156, s/d superior S156/186; @📶) On a quiet side street just steps from the Parque Kennedy, this gem of a guesthouse is named for its plant-filled courtyard with a trickling fountain. With a cheery English- and French-speaking owner, it features small, spotless rooms with cast-iron beds and colonial-style art. A few are equipped with small kitchenettes and minifridges. Check the website for special offers.

Casa San Martín INN $$
(Map p70; ☎243-3900, 01-241-4434; www.casasanmartinperu.com; San Martín 339; s/d/tr incl breakfast S185/260/325; @📶) Among the more atmospheric options, this Spanish Revival building is modern and uncluttered, with 20 pleasant, high-ceiling rooms with terra-cotta tiles and Andean textiles. Breakfast is served in a bright cafe that faces the terrace. Credit cards accepted.

Hotel Ibis HOTEL $$
(Map p70; ☎01-634-8888; www.ibishotel.com; Av José Larco 1140; d incl breakfast S241; @📶) This French hotel chain is a good option with a great location. There's a chic Ikea look, blackout curtains and soundproof windows. The hotel is cleverly divided into smoking and nonsmoking floors, though all rooms are on the small side. Biodegradable toiletries and water-saving policies are a plus. Breakfast is extra.

Albergue Miraflores House HOSTEL $$
(Map p70; ☎01-447-7748; www.alberguemirafloreshouse.com; Av Espinar 611; s/d/tr incl breakfast S180/225/300, d without bathroom S150; @📶) The owner's wanderlust sets the tone for this welcoming hostel tucked into a busy street. It's very dated but spotless, with the extra value of drums and guitars for impromtu jam sessions. Guests can make free international calls, there's plenty of on-site games and the location is central.

El Faro Inn HOTEL $$
(Map p70; ☎01-242-0339; www.elfaroinn.com; Francia 857; s/d incl breakfast S185/232; @📶) You'll find this quiet option behind a row of international flags (there is no sign) close to the relaxing cliff-top park on the north side

of Miraflores. Rooms are small but well appointed; some readers say the service lags.

Hotel San Antonio Abad HOTEL $$

(Map p70; ☎01-447-6766; www.hotelsanantonioabad.com; Ramón Ribeyro 301; s/d incl breakfast S210/280; ❄@📶) A bright-yellow mansion from the 1940s houses this pleasant, reader-recommended hotel. There are 24 ample dark-paneled rooms (some with air-con) with cable TV and soundproofed windows. Breakfast is served on a terrace facing the garden. Free airport pickup can be arranged with advance reservation. Credit cards are accepted.

Hotel Alemán HOTEL $$

(Map p70; ☎01-445-6999; www.hotelaleman.com.pe; Av Arequipa 4704; s/d/tr incl breakfast S216/247/278; @📶) A rowdy boulevard gives way to this surprisingly charming 23-room hotel built around a Spanish *casona*. Simple, stuccoed rooms are decorated with Peruvian textiles and colonial-style furnishings and cable TV, telephones, desks and minifridges. Credit cards accepted.

La Casa Nostra INN $$

(Map p70; ☎01-241-1718; www.lacasanostraperu.com; Grimaldo del Solar 265; s/d/tr incl breakfast S120/152/196; @📶) All the charm of this Spanish-style *casona* goes into the shared spaces, including a vintage wood-beamed ceiling in the lobby. By contrast, the seven rooms are clean but not very interesting, with mattresses that are a bit flat and narrow single beds.

Hotel Esperanza HOTEL $$

(Map p70; ☎01-444-2411; www.hotelesperanza.com.pe; Esperanza 350; s/d incl breakfast S139/186; 📶) A friendly spot. Baroque-style furniture and satin bedspreads provide an unusual juxtaposition to the somewhat monastic 39 brick rooms. Advantages: it is clean, functional and has a central location.

Hostal Torreblanca HOTEL $$

(Map p70; ☎01-447-3363; www.torreblancaperu.com; Av José Pardo 1453; d/tr incl breakfast S223/272) The lobby may be cramped and the hallways narrow, but the clean, modern rooms in this Spanish-style building are comfortable. A few on the top floor have wood-beamed ceilings, red tilework and fireplaces. Rooms have down duvets and feature cable TV, minibars and telephones. Credit cards are accepted.

Hotel Bayview HOTEL $$

(Map p70; ☎01-445-7321; www.bayviewhotel.com.pe; Las Dalias 276; s/d/tr incl breakfast S201/232/297; @📶) A simple, pleasant hotel with restaurant, painted salmon pink. It has carpeted rooms adorned with folksy Peruvian paintings and amenities like minibars and cable TV. A good value, it tends to fill up.

La Castellana INN $$

(Map p70; ☎01-444-4662; www.castellanahotel.com; Grimaldo del Solar 222; s/d/tr incl breakfast S180/212/252; 📶) In a stucco mansion, this 42-room inn has pleasant but dark rooms, many around a lovely garden courtyard where breakfast is served. Rooms sport '80s decor, some without wi-fi signals, so check ahead when booking.

Hotel Señorial HOTEL $$

(Map p70; ☎01-445-1870, 01-445-7306; www.senorial.com; José González 567; s/d/tr incl breakfast S250/355/433; @📶) This longtime hotel features over 100 rooms and a pleasant grassy courtyard. Think standard, with cable TV and perfunctory stabs at decoration. Credit cards accepted.

★ **Hotel de Autor** B&B $$$

(Map p70; ☎01-681-8074; www.hoteldeautor.com; Av 28 de Julio 562B, Quinta Bustos; d incl breakfast S541; P❄📶) Why can't every hotel be like this? Service is personal, breakfasts satisfying, and the style is classical and modern, with authentic travel memorabilia to help guide and inspire your journey throughout Peru. Rooms are spacious, all with king-size beds, luxuriant linens and writing desks. Balconies and claw-foot tubs add a dose of romance on this quiet, centrally located cul-de-sac.

Offers cruiser bikes on loan.

Miraflores Park Hotel LUXURY HOTEL $$$

(Map p70; ☎01-242-3000; www.mirafloresspark.com; Malecón de la Reserva 1035; d from S1236; ❄@📶🏊) The best of Lima's small luxury hotels, this Belmond property enjoys a glorious oceanside setting and every frill. The spiral grand staircase, gorgeous library, spa services and and infinity pool help foster the fairy-tale atmosphere.

Tragaluz, the on-site restaurant, is a hot spot for local 30- to 40-year-olds, with arthouse decor, international cuisine and a champion barman.

IFE Boutique Hotel BOUTIQUE HOTEL $$$
(Map p70; ☎01-677-2229; www.ifeboutique.com; San Ignacio de Loyola 646; d incl breakfast S380-618; ❄📶) A little, service-oriented boutique hotel in a convenient neighborhood. It's stylish and elegant, with eight rooms, their styles ranging from classical to pop art. King- and queen-size beds have luxuriant linens. Staff are helpful and amenities include LCD televisions, minibars, iPod docks and safe boxes.

JW Marriott Hotel Lima HOTEL $$$
(Map p70; ☎01-217-7000; www.marriotthotels.com/limdt; Malecón de la Reserva 615; d incl breakfast from S643; ❄@📶🏊) The lively five-star Marriott has a superb seafront location by the LarcoMar shopping mall, ideal for watching paragliders float outside the glass walls. The rooms sparkle and sport every amenity (though wi-fi costs extra): think minibar, plasma TV and whirlpool bath. There is also an executive lounge, restaurants, a bar, a casino and an open-air tennis court, sauna and pool.

Those nervous about their next flight can check the departure and arrival board in the lobby.

Casa Andina HOTEL $$$
(Map p70; ☎01-241-4050; www.casa-andina.com; Av 28 de Julio 1088; d incl breakfast S294; ❄@📶) This upmarket Peruvian chain has three hotels at various price points scattered around Miraflores. The San Antonio and Miraflores Centro (Map p70; ☎01-447-0263; Av Petit Thouars 5444; d incl breakfast S294; ❄@📶) branches are more affordable, with 50-plus rooms decorated in contemporary Andean color schemes.

Colección Privada (Map p70; ☎01-213-4300; Av La Paz 463, Colección Privada; d/ste incl breakfast from S470/578; ❄@📶🏊) is the luxury outpost, with 148 chic, earth-palette rooms that are spacious, sporting pre-Columbian flourishes and organic bath products.

Terra Viva HOTEL $$$
(Map p70; ☎01-637-1003; tierravivahoteles.com/tierra-viva-miraflores-larco; Bolívar 176-180; s/d incl breakfast S457/488) A cheerful addition to Lima, this immaculate Peruvian chain offers good service and modern rooms with lockboxes, berber carpets, king-size beds and woven Andean blankets that add a splash of color. Breakfast is served on the 8th-floor terrace.

La Paz Apart Hotel APARTMENT $$$
(Map p70; ☎01-242-9350; www.lapazaparthotel.com; Av La Paz 679; s/d ste incl breakfast S371/464, 2-bedroom ste S773; ❄@📶) This modern high-rise may have a businesslike demeanor, but the service is attentive and the rooms comfortable. Twenty-five super-clean suites, all equipped with kitchenettes, minifridges and separate sitting areas, are tastefully decorated. The most spacious sleeps up to five. The hotel also has a mini-gym and a small conference room.

Hotel El Doral HOTEL $$$
(Map p70; ☎01-242-7799; www.eldoral.com.pe; Av José Pardo 486; s/d incl breakfast S328/359; ❄@📶🏊) All business on the outside, these 39 shiny suites (think 1980s) face a pleasant, plant-filled interior. All units have cable TV, minibars and sitting areas – plus double-glazed windows to block out the noise. Breakfast is served on a rooftop terrace that faces the pool.

Hotel Ariosto HOTEL $$$
(Map p70; ☎01-444-1414; www.hotelariosto.com.pe; Av La Paz 769; s/d incl breakfast S340/371; ❄@📶) This seven-story hotel has colonial-meets-the-1960s Peruvian formality. A sprawling modernist lobby sports oversized leather couches and baroque art flourishes, while the 96 spacious, carpeted rooms are equipped with king-size beds. There is a small business center and a lounge area, and the buffet breakfast is immense. Rates include free airport pickup.

Barranco

At the turn of the 20th century, this was a summer resort for the upper-crust. In the 1960s, it was a center of bohemian life. Today, it is cluttered with restaurants and bustling bars, its graceful mansions converted into hotels of every price range.

Backpackers Inn HOSTEL $
(Map p74; ☎01-247-1326; www.barrancobackpackersperu.com; Mariscal Castilla 260; dm/tw incl breakfast S37/109) A British-run backpacker hangout housed in a weathered but essentially clean mansion on a quiet street with 24-hour security. Dorms are ample, some with ocean views.

There's a kitchen, eight rooms, help with trips and tours, a TV lounge and convenient access to Bajada de Baños, leading to the beach.

Hostal Kaminu B&B $

(Map p74; ☎01-252-8680; www.kaminu.com; Bajada de Baños 342; dm S30-35, d incl breakfast with/without bathroom S100/68; @) Tiny and rambling, this sardine-can hostel sits in the thick of Barranco nightlife – for better or worse. Highlights include an ambient rooftop deck.

★**3B Barranco B&B** B&B $$

(Map p74; ☎01-247-6915, 01-719-3868; www.3bhostal.com; Centenario 130; s/d incl breakfast S230/250; @ 📶) Cool, clean and modern, this service-oriented lodging is poised to be a traveler favorite. A common area charged with Warholesque pastiche art leads to 16 minimalist rooms with plush burlap-colored bed covers, granite vanities and windows opening on lightboxes of tended greenery. Good value.

★**Casa Nuestra** B&B $$

(Map p74; ☎01-248-8091; casanuestraperu.com; Jirón Tumbes 270; s/d S120/180, d without bathroom incl breakfast S155; @ 📶) With cool decor, murals and retro poster art, this sweet home sits on a quiet, shady side street. Run by an Italian-Peruvian couple, it provides a great base for exploring Barranco, with discounts for long stays. The 2nd-floor rooms are best – 1st floor digs remain a step behind in renovation. There's kitchen access and a lovely roof deck. By reservation only.

D'Osma B&B B&B $$

(Map p74; ☎01-251-4178; www.deosma.com; Av San Pedro de Osma 240; s/d incl breakfast from S115/180, d without bathroom S130; @ 📶) 🌿 A personable, family vibe brightens this unassuming little B&B, a cheap midrange option, with small carpeted rooms featuring skylights and fans. There's some English and German spoken, recycling and satisfying breakfasts with eggs and fruit. The only drawback is the noisy street outside – try for a back room.

Hostal Gémina HOTEL $$

(Map p74; ☎01-477-0712; hostalgemina.com; Av Grau 620; s/d/tr incl breakfast S105/150/195; @ 📶) Tucked into a small shopping gallery, this welcoming surprise offers 31 spacious units with 1970s style. Think ship-shape, accidental-retro. There's an ample living room, and clean rooms feature TVs and folksy textiles. Credit cards accepted.

★**Second Home Perú** B&B $$$

(Map p74; ☎01-247-5522; www.secondhome-peru.com; Domeyer 366; d/ste incl breakfast S386/556; @ 📶 🏊) With a fairy-tale feel, this lovely five-room Bavarian-style *casona* has claw-foot tubs, sculpted ironworks, a swimming pool and breathtaking views of the ocean. Run by the children of artist Victor Delfín, it features private gardens with his taurine sculptures, works of other artists and a sculpting studio available for rent. Credit cards accepted.

Hotel B BOUTIQUE HOTEL $$$

(Map p74; ☎01-206-0800; hotelb.pe; Sáenz Peña 204; d S1112; @ 📶) A notable newcomer, this refurbished mansion mixes modern with classical to dramatic effect. There are 17 eclectic rooms, though some can feel a bit overstuffed, surrounding a courtyard planted with a living wall of figs. Popular with nonguests, the lovely bar specializes in G&Ts and Gatsby moments. You can also visit the adjacent gallery or the rooftop with ocean views.

West Lima

Mami Panchita INN $$

(☎01-263-7203; www.mamipanchita.com; Av Federico Gallesi 198, San Miguel; s/d/tr incl breakfast S124/155/185; @ 📶) In a pleasant neighborhood near Miraflores, this Dutch-Peruvian guesthouse occupies a comfortable and sprawling Spanish-style house. The owners run an on-site travel agency. It's a great option for families, with rooms that are large and homey, a crib option and a flower-bedecked patio ideal for relaxing.

Eating

The gastronomic capital of the continent, Lima is where you will find some of the country's most sublime culinary creations: from simple *cevicherías* (ceviche counters) and corner *anticucho* (beef-heart skewer) stands to outstanding molecular cuisine. Lima's prime position on the coast gives it access to a wide variety of staggeringly fresh seafood, while its status as a centralized capital assures the presence of all manner of regional specialties.

You'll find cocktails infused with Amazon berries, nutty chicken stews from Arequipa *(ají de gallina)* and one of the country's most exquisite renderings (outside of Chiclayo) of Chiclayo-style *arroz con pato* (rice and duck), slowly simmered in cilantro, garlic and beer. The city has such a vast assortment of cuisine, in fact, that it's possible to spend weeks here without tasting it all. Pack your appetite; you'll need it.

Lima Centro

Miraflores and San Isidro may have the city's trendiest restaurants, but Lima's downtown spots offer cheap deals and history, from functional *comedores* (simple dining rooms) packed with office workers to atmospheric eateries that count Peruvian presidents among the clientele. *Menús* (set meals) in the vicinity of S10 can be found at many of the cheaper restaurants.

Domus PERUVIAN **$**

(Map p60; ☎01-427-0525; Miró Quesada 410; 3-course menús S20; ⏲7am-5pm Mon-Fri) A restored 19th-century mansion houses this modern-yet-intimate two-room restaurant that caters to journalists from the nearby offices of *El Comercio.* There is no à la carte dining, just a rotating daily list of well-executed Peruvian-Italian specialties that always includes a vegetarian option in the mix. Freshly squeezed juices accompany this well-tended feast.

El Chinito SANDWICHES **$**

(Map p60; ☎01-423-2197; Chancay 894; sandwiches S12; ⏲8am-10pm Mon-Sat, to 1pm Sun) Nearly half a century old, this venerable downtown outpost, clad in Spanish tile, is *the* spot for heaping sandwiches stuffed with a bevy of fresh-roasted meats: turkey, pork, beef, ham – and the most popular, *chicharrón* (fried pork) – all served with a traditional marinade of red onions, hot peppers and cilantro.

BEST CHEAP EATS

- Heaping sandwiches at **El Enano** (p88)
- Open-air ceviche at **Al Toke Pez** (p94)
- Hearty breads paired with olives and cheese at **El Pan de la Chola** (p88)
- Exotic herb and juice blends from **Kulcafé** (p89)
- Fish tacos from **Burrito Bar** (p93)
- DIY picnics from **Delifrance** (p93)

El Cordano CAFETERIA **$**

(Map p60; ☎01-427-0181; Ancash 202; mains S10-32; ⏲8am-9pm) A Lima institution since 1905, this old-world dining hall has served practically every Peruvian president for the last 100 years (the presidential palace is right across the street). Don't expect innovation here. It is known for its skillfully rendered *tacu tacu* (pan-fried rice and beans) and *butifarra* (French bread stuffed with country ham).

Pastelería San Martín BAKERY **$**

(Map p60; ☎01-428-9091; Nicolás de Piérola 987; snacks S6; ⏲9am-9pm Mon-Sat) Founded in 1930, this bare-bones bakery serves what is considered Lima's finest *turrón de Doña Pepa,* a dessert associated with the religious feast of El Señor de Los Milagros: flaky, sticky and achingly sweet, pair it with a stiff espresso.

Queirolo PERUVIAN **$**

(Map p60; ☎01-425-0421; Camaná 900; mains S12-38; ⏲9:30am-1am Mon-Sat) Lined with wine bottles, Queirolo is popular with office workers for cheap *menús* featuring staples such as *papa rellena* (stuffed potatoes). It is also popular for evening gatherings, when locals pop in for *chilcano de pisco* (pisco with ginger ale and lime juice) and chit-chat. Dinner offerings are sparse.

Rovegno DELI **$**

(Map p64; ☎01-424-8465; Arenales 456; mains S13-25, buffet S28; ⏲7am-10pm Mon-Sat) This cluttered bakery-deli-restaurant sells an assortment of decent wine, breads, cheeses, ham and olives, plus plenty of pastries in a rainbow of colors. Restaurant dishes are typical Peruvian specialties such as *lomo saltado* (beef stir-fried with onions and peppers).

Wa Lok CHINESE **$$**

(Map p60; ☎01-427-2750, 01-447-1329; Paruro 878; mains S15-80; ⏲9am-11pm Mon-Sat, to 10pm Sun) Serving seafood, fried rice as light and fresh as it gets, and sizzling meats that come on steaming platters, Wa Lok is among the best *chifas* (Chinese restaurants) in Chinatown. The 16-page Cantonese menu includes dumplings, noodles, stir-fries and a good selection of vegetarian options (try the braised tofu casserole). Portions are enormous; don't over-order.

Cevichería la Choza Nautica CEVICHE $$
(Map p64; ☎01-423-8087; www.chozanautica.com; Breña 204; ceviches S20-42, mains S19-45; ⏰8am-11pm Mon-Sat, to 9pm Sun) A surprisingly bright spot in a slightly dingy area, this popular *cevichería*, tended to by bow-tied waiters, offers more than a dozen types of ceviches and *tiraditos* (Japanese-style ceviche, without onions). There is also a long list of soups, seafood and rice dishes. Live music plays on busy nights.

L'Eau Vive FRENCH $$
(Map p60; ☎01-427-5612; Ucayali 370; mains S25-35, 3-course menús S30-50; ⏰12:30-3pm & 7:30-9:30pm Mon-Sat; ❄) In an 18th-century building, this very simple and unusual eatery is run by French Carmelite nuns. Expect French and other continental specialties (think *coquilles St Jacques*) with Peruvian influences. The food isn't jaw-dropping, but the real reason to come is to enjoy the strange serenade. Every night, after dinner (at around 9pm), the nuns gather to sing 'Ave Maria.'

Tanta CAFE $$
(Map p60; ☎01-428-3115; Pasaje de los Escribanos 142, Lima Centro; mains S21-46; ⏰9am-10pm Mon-Sat, to 6pm Sun) One of several informal bistros in the Gastón Acurio brand, Tanta serves Peruvian dishes, fusion pastas, heaping salads and sandwiches. It's a good bet in the city center where pickings are slim. The food is generally good but desserts shine: try the heavenly passionfruit cheesecake mousse. There are other branches in **Miraflores** (Map p70; ☎01-447-8377; Av 28 de Julio 888) and **San Isidro** (Map p68; ☎01-421-9708; Pancho Fierro 115).

Salon Capon CHINESE $$
(Map p60; ☎01-426-9286; Paruro 819; mains S12-48; ⏰9am-10pm Mon-Sat, to 7pm Sun) Across the street from Wa Lok, the smaller Salon Capon has a lengthy Cantonese menu, good dim sum and a traditional bakery that makes scrumptious, flaky egg tarts.

Self-Catering

Metro SUPERMARKET $
(Map p60; Cuzco 255; ⏰9am-10pm) In Lima Centro, the best supermarket is the block-long Metro in downtown, which also stocks prepared foods.

San Isidro

Chic dining rooms, frothy cocktails and fusion haute cuisine: San Isidro is a bastion of fine dining – and not much else. Those on a budget may prefer to prepare their own meals, or head to nearby Miraflores, which is generally cheaper.

> **A LA LIMEÑA**
>
> Many restaurants in Lima tone down the spices on some traditional dishes for foreign travelers. If you like your cooking spicy *(picante)*, tell them to turn up the heat by asking for your food *a la limeña* – Lima-style.

Coffee Road CAFE $
(Map p68; ☎01-637-2028; Av Prescott 380; mains S6-12; ⏰7:30am-10pm Mon-Sat, 1-9pm Sun) Calling all coffee snobs: this diminutive cafe of long bars and leather stools will brew you delicious espresso, Chemex, French press, Aeropress and more, using quality Peruvian beans. Some claim it's the best in town. Also serves quiches and desserts.

La Balanza BISTRO $$
(Map p68; ☎01-222-2659; Cavenecia 162; mains S32-60; ⏰1-4pm & 7pm-midnight Mon-Sat; ✎) A farm-to-table bistro serving satisfying meals, there's little wonder it's a hit with both families and couples on date night. Free-range chicken, organic salads and wonders like beet gnocchi with blue cheese burst with flavor. Enjoy it with a glass of *chicha morada* tinged with star anise. Green also permeates the ambience, with shelves of microgreens and cool recycled place mats.

Matsuei JAPANESE $$
(Map p68; ☎01-422-4323; Manuel Bañon 260; maki S30-55; ⏰12:30-3:30pm & 7:30-11pm Mon-Sat) Venerated Japanese super-chef Nobu Matsuhisa once co-owned this diminutive sushi bar. Don't let the modest appearance fool you: it serves some of the most spectacular sashimi and *maki* (sushi rolls) in Lima. A must-have: the *acevichado*, a roll stuffed with shrimp and avocado, then doused in a house-made mayo infused with ceviche broth. It makes your brain tingle.

Spizza PIZZERIA $$
(Map p68; ☎01-222-2228; Av 2 de Mayo 455; pizza S29-50; ⏰12:30-3:30pm & 7-11pm Mon-Sat, 12:30-10pm Sun) Never underestimate the value of a thin-crust margherita pizza blistered by a searing wood oven. Upholding Neapolitan tradition, this tiny brick

restaurant delivers the goods alongside artisan beer and sangria made with fresh hierba luisa mint.

Segundo Muelle CEVICHE $$
(Map p68; ☎01-421-1206; www.segundomuelle.com; Conquistadores 490; mains S32-40; ⏰noon-5pm) A mainstay of impeccable service and renowned ceviches with innovative twists. Try the *ceviche de mariscos a los tres ajíes,* a stack of mixed fish and shellfish bathed in three types of hot pepper sauce. The menu also features heaping rice and other seafood dishes, including a recommended *parrilla marina* (seafood grill).

Punta Sal CEVICHE $$
(Map p68; ☎01-441-7431; www.puntasal.com; Conquistadores 958; mains S24-40; ⏰11am-5pm) Another great seafood restaurant that has been around for decades, Punta Sal serves at least nine different kinds of ceviche. Try the assassin ceviche – a paradisaical mix of octopus, squid, crawfish, crab, flounder and mangrove cockles.

Hanzo JAPANESE $$
(Map p68; ☎01-422-6367; www.hanzo.com.pe; Conquistadores 598; mains S23-50; ⏰12:30-4pm & 7:30-11:30pm Mon-Sat, 12:30-4pm Sun) With a full bar, this atmospheric fusion house is a lively place for sushi but it's not for purists. *Maki acevichado* and butter rolls made with fried rice are playful nods to Peruvian influence.

Antica PIZZA $$
(Map p68; ☎01-222-9488; Av 2 de Mayo 732; mains S29-42; ⏰noon-midnight) On a street littered with European restaurants, this is one of the most reasonable: a woody, candle-bedecked spot serving house-made pasta, gnocchi and pizza from a wood-fired oven. It's popular with local families. There is antipasto, as well as a decent wine list strong on South American brands (from S40).

★Astrid y Gastón Casa Moreyra NOVOANDINA $$$
(Map p68; ☎01-442-2775; www.astridygaston.com; Av Paz Soldan 290; mains S53-89; ⏰12:30-3:30pm & 6:30pm-midnight Mon-Sat) The standard-bearer of *novoandina* cooking in Lima, Gastón Acurio's flagship French-influenced restaurant as run by Lima native Diego Muñoz remains a culinary tour de force. The seasonal menu features traditional Peruvian fare, but it's the exquisite fusion specialties that make this such a sublime fine-dining experience. The 28-course tasting menu showcases the depth and breadth of possibility here – just do it.

Guests may be treated to a kitchen visit to watch white-coated armies assembling plates with tweezer-precision. The setting is a gorgeous mansion with multiple dining rooms and sterling service, including a helpful sommelier.

Malabar FUSION $$$
(Map p68; ☎01-440-5200; www.malabar.com.pe; Av Camino Real 101; mains S52-68; ⏰12:30-4pm & 7:30-11pm Mon-Sat) With an Amazonian bent, chef Pedro Miguel Schiaffino's seasonal menu features deftly prepared delicacies such as crisp, seared *cuy* and Amazonian river snails bathed in spicy chorizo sauce. Don't forego the cocktails (the chef's father, a noted pisco expert, consulted on the menu) or desserts – perhaps the lightest and most refreshing in Lima.

Miraflores

By far the most varied neighborhood for eating, Miraflores carries the breadth and depth of Peruvian cooking at every price range imaginable, from tiny *comedores* with cheap lunchtime *menús* to some of the city's most revered gastronomic outposts. Pavement cafes are ideal for sipping pisco sours and people-watching.

Casual places with cheap *menús* abound on the tiny streets east of Av José Larco just off the Parque Kennedy.

El Enano SANDWICHES $
(Map p70; Chiclayo 699; sandwiches S8-12; ⏰6am-1am Sun-Thu, to 3am Fri & Sat) Grab a stool at the open-air counter and watch the masters at work. Fresh-roasted chicken, ham, turkey and *chicharrón* sandwiches on French bread are dressed with marinated onions and chilies. After one too many piscos, this is the cure. Exotic fresh juices are served in glass jars.

El Pan de la Chola CAFE $
(Map p70; Av La Mar 918; mains S8-18; ⏰8am-10pm Mon-Sat) In South America, finding real, crusty whole-grain bread is rarer than striking gold. Enter this small brick cafe baking four scrumptious varieties, with organic coffee from the Peruvian Amazon, greek yogurt and sweets. There's European-style seating at big wooden tables; grab a sandwich or share the tasting plate with bread, olives, hummus and fresh cheese.

CITY CUISINE

In Lima, food inspires as much reverence as religion. So, the agonizing question is, what to eat? Start by sampling these local staples.

➡ Lima's most tender beef-heart skewers, *anticuchos*, can be found at street carts and a posh Miraflores eatery, **Panchita** (p90).

➡ Sublime renditions of the country's most seductive dish, ceviche, can be found in places both economical, such as **El Rincón del Bigote** (p91), and upscale, such as **Pescados Capitales** (p92); for something truly different, try it seared at **Fiesta** (p92).

➡ The country's fusion cuisine, *criollo* cooking – a singular blend of Spanish, Andean, Chinese and African influences – is without parallel at neighborhood eateries **Isolina** (p93) and **El Rincón que No Conoces** (p93), in addition to the super-chic **Restaurant Huaca Pucllana** (p90).

➡ First-rate service, encyclopedic wine lists, and sculptural dishes that blend the traditional and the nouveau find their apex at **Astrid y Gastón Casa Moreyra** and **Central** (p91).

➡ Celebrating the humble potato, *causas* are cold potato dishes that are as beautiful as they are delectable, and are found in any traditional restaurant.

Anticuchos de la Tía Grimanesa BARBECUE $

(Map p70; Av Ignacio Merino 465; anticucho S12; ⏲5-11pm Mon-Sat) The legendary Doña Grimanesa presided over a humble *anticucho* (beef-heart skewers) cart for over 30 years and earned a flock of fans before getting her own place. With tender meat and homemade hot sauces, it's a simple pleasure.

Raw Cafe VEGAN $

(Map p70; ☎01-446-9456; Independencia 587; mains S10-18; ⏲9am-9pm Mon-Fri, to 6pm Sat; 🖉) The raw-food movement has arrived in Lima and this popular cafe is proof. Think beet burgers, pizzas with cashew cheese, salads with toasted coconut 'bacon', green juices and kombucha. Also serves organic coffee.

La Matilda CAFE $

(Map p70; ☎01-444-3187; Av 2 de Mayo 535; mains S8-25; ⏲9am-8pm Mon-Sat; 🖉) This Argentine teahouse and home store teems with vintage girly charm. Scrumptious homemade desserts are served on fine china with a selection of loose-leaf teas and coffee. There's also sandwiches and vegan options.

La Lucha Sanguachería SANDWICHES $

(Map p70; ☎01-241-5953; Benavides 308; sandwiches S13-16; ⏲8am-1am Sun-Thu, to 3am Fri & Sat) This all-hours corner sandwich shop is the perfect fix for the midnight munchies. *Lechon a la leña* (roasted pork) is their specialty, but there's also roast chicken or ham served in fluffy rolls with juice blended on the spot.

Kulcafé CAFE $

(Map p70; ☎993-325-5445; Bellavista 370; mains S8-12; ⏲8:30am-11pm Mon-Sat, 10am-10pm Sun; 📶) For German sweets, coffee drinks and smoothies, this is the spot. Don't go conventional – the 'sweet green' smoothie makes spinach, watermelon and mango delectable together. There are also organic foods and beautiful whole-grain bagels served in a cozy living-room atmosphere.

Pardo's Chicken PERUVIAN $

(Map p70; ☎01-446-4790; www.pardoschicken.pe; Alfredo Benavides 730; mains S17-25) Lima is littered with rotisserie chicken chains; this one is, hands down, the best. Go early for lunch as it fills up.

Dédalo Arte y Cafe CAFE $

(Map p70; Benavides 378; snacks S3-10; ⏲8am-9:30pm Mon-Sat; 📶) Caffeine fiends find their way to this discreet cafe on Parque Kennedy where coffee is as serious as a sacrament. You'll find the usual suspects plus rarer *ristretto* and Australian takes like a flat white. It's owned by the same family as the tasteful Barranco home-decor and accessories shop.

Pastelería San Antonio CAFE $

(Map p70; ☎01-241-3001; Av Vasco Núñez de Balboa 770; sandwiches S12-25; ⏲7am-9pm Mon-Thu, to 8pm Fri, 9am-6pm Sat) A cross-section of Miraflores society jams into this 50-year-old

SEAFOOD AT LA PUNTA

A quiet residential neighborhood with great views of the water, La Punta is perfect for a leisurely lunch. At the humble fish house **Manolo** (☎01-429-8453; Malecón Pardo s/n, cuadra 1; mains S15-38; ⏱11:30am-3:30pm) seafood die-hards line up for fresh ceviche, grilled fish and hearty soups. Or dine in style at the waterfront **La Rana Verde** (☎01-429-5279; Parque Gálvez s/n; mains S25-53; ⏱11:30am-6pm), ideal for Sunday dinner within view of the Isla San Lorenzo. Dishes are all deftly prepared and the *pulpo al olivo* is one of the best in Lima. It's located on the pier inside the Club Universitario de Regatas. A taxi ride from Miraflores runs at around S30.

institution for an infinite variety of sandwiches, as well as a wide selection of baked goods, including a dreamy chocolate croissant (ask for it warm).

Manolo CAFE $
(Map p70; ☎01-444-2244; www.manolochurros.com; Av José Larco 608; churros S4; ⏱7am-1am Sun-Thu, to 2am Fri & Sat) This thriving all-hours sidewalk cafe is best known for its piping-hot churros, which go smashingly well with a *chocolate caliente espeso* (thick hot chocolate) – perfect for dipping.

Haiti CAFE $
(Map p70; ☎01-445-0539; Diagonal 160; snacks S12) This nearly half-century-old cafe is like stepping into 1960s Lima: waiters in green jackets tend to coiffed ladies and chattering businessmen. It's good for dessert or a pressed-pork sandwich while you watch the world go by.

Quattro D ICE CREAM $
(Map p70; ☎01-445-4228; Av Angamos Oeste 408; mains S18-32, ice cream from S10; ⏱6:30am-11:45pm Mon-Thu, to 12:30am Fri & Sat, 7-11am Sun) A bustling cafe that serves hot pressed sandwiches, pasta and other dishes, in addition to a diabetes-inducing assortment of sweets and gelato (including a few sugar-free flavors).

Bodega Miraflores CAFE
(Map p70; Diez Canseco 109; coffee S3; ⏱9:30am-1pm & 3:30-7:30pm Mon-Sat) A frumpy spot with a grumpy counterman that serves strong, inky *cortados* (espresso with a dollop of steamed milk) made with coffee grown in Chanchamayo. Bagged, whole-bean coffee is available to take home.

★ámaZ AMAZONIAN $$
(Map p70; ☎01-221-9393; www.amaz.com.pe; Av La Paz 1079; mains S12-44; ⏱12:30-11:30pm Mon-Sat, 12:30-4:30pm Sun; 🖉) Chef Pedro Miguel's latest wonder is wholly dedicated to the abundance of the Amazon. Start with tart jungle-fruit cocktails and oversized *tostones* (plantain chips). Banana-leaf wraps, aka *juanes,* hold treasures like fragrant Peking duck with rice. There's excellent *encurtido* (pickled vegetables) and the generous vegetarian set menu for two (S270) is a delicious way to sample the diversity.

With a circular bar and coveted thatched-roof tables.

El Mercado SEAFOOD $$
(Map p70; ☎01-221-1322; Unanue 203; mains S15-58; ⏱12:30-5pm Tue-Sun) This hip, bare-bones ceviche joint just so happens to be spearheaded by culinary star Rafael Osterling. Diners pack in for fresh, fusion-style shellfish and eight distinct ceviches, but the seared-fish sandwiches (S15) prove great value. For dessert: cinnamon ice cream perfumed with anise.

Restaurant Huaca Pucllana PERUVIAN $$
(Map p70; ☎01-445-4042; www.resthuacapucllana.com; Gral Borgoño cuadra 8; mains S24-60; ⏱12:30pm-midnight Mon-Sat, to 4pm Sun) Overlooking the illuminated ruins at Huaca Pucllana, this sophisticated establishment serves a skillfully rendered array of contemporary Peruvian dishes (from grilled *cuy* to seafood chowders), along with a smattering of Italian-fusion specialties. Portions are large. Save room for the pisco and lemon parfait come dessert.

Panchita PERUVIAN $$
(Map p70; ☎01-242-5957; Av 2 de Mayo 298; mains S33-60; ⏱12:30-9pm Mon-Sat, to 5pm Sun) A Gastón Acurio homage to Peruvian street food in a contemporary setting ringed by folk art. *Anticuchos* are grilled over an open flame to melt-in-your-mouth perfection, particularly the charred octopus. Another winner is the crisp suckling pig with *tacu tacu*. There's also a great salad bar. Portions are big and filling so don't come alone. With outstanding service.

El Rincón del Bigote CEVICHE $$
(Map p70; José Galvez 529; mains S32-36; noon-4pm Tue-Sun) Go early. On weekends, locals and tourists line up for seating in this bare-bones ceviche house. The specialty is *almejas in su concha:* pair these marinated clams with a side of crisp yucca fries and a bottle of cold pilsner and you're in heaven.

El Punto Azul CEVICHE $$
(Map p70; 01-445-8078; San Martín 595; mains S22-40; noon-5pm) Awash in Caribbean blues, this pleasant family eatery dishes up fresh ceviches, *tiraditos* and family-sized rice dishes. Try their risotto with parmesan, shrimp and *ají amarillo* (yellow chili) – and don't miss the line-up of beautiful desserts. It gets packed, so show up before 1pm if you want a table. Excellent value.

AlmaZen VEGETARIAN $$
(Map p70; 01-243-0474; Federico Recavarren 298; mains S30-40; 9am-10pm Mon-Fri;) With soothing ambience, this vegetarian restaurant and teahouse offers a rotating daily selection of artfully prepared organic, vegan and gluten-free dishes. Their mango ceviche is second to none and juices, like *lulo,* are delicious. Come only if you're not in a rush – the service is dead slow. Between lunch and dinner, meal service stops but the cafe stays open.

★**Central** PERUVIAN $$$
(Map p70; 01-242-8515; centralrestaurante.com.pe; Santa Isabel 376; mains S52-88; 12:45-3:15pm & 7:45-11:15pm Mon-Fri) Part restaurant, part laboratory, Central reinvents Andean cuisine and rescues age-old Peruvian edibles you'd find nowhere else. Dining here is an experience, evidenced by the tender native potatoes served in edible clay. Chef Virgilio Martinez wants you to taste the Andes. He paid his dues in Europe and Asia's top kitchens, but it's his work here that dazzles.

Seafood – like the charred octopus starter – is a star, but classics like suckling pig deliver, served with pickled vegetables and spiced squash. A menu supplied by sustainable fish and a rooftop herb garden enhance the ultra-fresh appeal.

La Mar SEAFOOD $$$
(Map p70; 01-421-3365; www.lamarcebicheria.com; Av La Mar 770; mains S29-69; noon-5pm Mon-Fri, 11:45am-5:30pm Sat & Sun) A good-time *cevichería* with outstanding service and wonderful, mouthwatering ceviche and *tiraditos,* alongside *chifon chaufa* (fried rice) done light and fresh. This Gastón Acurio outpost is not much more than a polished cement patio bursting with VIPs. Try their delicious riff on a bloody Mary – the sublime bloody *locho,* seafood shells and all. Desserts deliver too. Does not take reservations.

DON'T MISS

MISTURA

One serious eating event, **Mistura** (www.mistura.pe; Parque de la Exposicion, Lima Centro) is Lima's prestigious week-long international food fair held every September. Get a ticket and sample an astonishing diversity of delicacies, from the finest restaurants to the best street food.

Maido JAPANESE $$$
(Map p70; 01-446-2512; www.maido.pe; San Martín 399; mains S35-78; 12:30-4pm & 7:30-11pm Mon-Sat, 12:30-4pm Sun) True artistry and exquisite flavors make Maido an excellent stop for top-notch Nikkei fare. The menu ranges from sushi to *okonomiyaki* and ramen, albeit with a Peruvian accent. Desserts – like the yucca *mochi* or a white chocolate egg with sorbet yolk – delight. Supports sustainable fishing.

Rafael NOVOANDINA $$$
(Map p70; 01-242-4149; www.rafaelosterling.com; San Martín 300; mains S39-78; 1-3pm & 8-11pm Mon-Wed, to midnight Thu-Sat) A consistent favorite of discerning palates, here Chef Rafael Osterling produces a panoply of fusion dishes, such as *tiradito* bathed in Japanese citrus or suckling goat stewed in Madeira wine. For slimmer budgets the crisp pizzas are divine. Make it past the generously poured cocktails and there's a decent and lengthy international wine list.

IK NOVOANDINA $$$
(Map p70; 01-652-1692; Elías Aguirre 179; mains S45-75; 12:30-3pm & 7:30-11pm Tue-Sat, 7:30-11pm Mon) Combining ancestral traditions with the Peruvian vanguard of molecular gastronomy is a tall order, but most feel that IK pulls it off with style. The restaurant is a tribute to a well-known local chef and its restorative atmosphere of living plants, natural sounds and light projections bring something new to the dining experience. Dishes are well balanced and meticulously presented.

With award-winning bartenders and a master sommelier to assist with the impressive wine selection.

Pescados Capitales SEAFOOD $$$
(Map p70; ☎01-421-8808; www.pescadoscapitales.com; Av La Mar 1337; mains S35-65; ⏰12:30-5pm) On a street once lined by clattering auto shops, this industrial-contemporary destination serves some of the finest ceviche around. Try the 'Ceviche Capital,' a mix of flounder, salmon and tuna marinated with red, white and green onions, bathed in a three-chili crème. A nine-page wine list offers a strong selection of Chilean and Argentinean vintages.

Fiesta PERUVIAN $$$
(Map p70; ☎01-242-9009; www.restaurantfiestagourmet.com; Av Reducto 1278; mains S40-65; ⏰noon-midnight Mon-Sat) The finest northern Peruvian cuisine in Lima is served at this busy establishment on Miraflores' eastern edge. The *arroz con pato a la chiclayana* (duck and rice Chiclayo-style) is achingly tender and *ceviche a la brasa* gets a quick sear so it's lightly smoky, yet tender. It has to be eaten to be believed.

Las Brujas de Cachiche PERUVIAN $$$
(Map p70; ☎01-444-5310; www.brujasdecachiche.com.pe; Bolognesi 460; mains S35-80; ⏰noon-midnight Mon-Sat, to 4pm Sun) A staple of quality Peruvian cooking with the live ambience of a tinkling piano, Brujas' menu has wonderfully prepared classics such as *ají de gallina,* as well as lesser-known specialties such as *carapulcra,* a dried potato stew. To try a bit of everything, hit the lunch buffet (S89).

La Tiendecita Blanca EUROPEAN $$$
(Map p70; ☎01-445-9797; Av José Larco 111; mains S38-72; ⏰7am-midnight) A Miraflores landmark for more than half a century, fans of Swiss cuisine will find potato *röstis,* fondues and a terrific selection of apple tarts, Napoleons and quiches at this graceful beaux-arts bistro on the square.

MORE, PLEASE

Want to eat like a local? When eating in homes, local *fondas* or *quintas* (informal family restaurants) you can ask for a generous portion by ordering it '*bien taipa*.' If you want seconds, say '*yapa!*' – it roughly translates as 'more, please.'

La Rosa Nautica SEAFOOD $$$
(Map p70; ☎01-445-0149; Circuito de Playas; mains S34-72; ⏰1-9pm) Location, location, location. Though you can get better seafood deals elsewhere, the views from this eatery on the historic pier are unparalleled. Go during happy hour (5pm to 7pm), when you can watch the last of the day's surfers skim along the crests of the waves. Take a taxi to the pier and walk the last 100m.

Self-Catering

On Saturdays, a small green market sets up at Parque Reducto, off Alfredo Benavides and Ribeyro. Likewise, try the neighborhood's excellent supermarkets.

La Preferida DELI $
(Map p70; ☎01-445-5180; Arias Araguez 698; mains S18-26, tapas S6; ⏰8am-5pm Mon-Sat) Located a couple of blocks north of Av 28 de Julio, just east of the Vía Expresa, this charming take-out place has gorgeous *causas* and fresh seafood specialties such as *pulpo al olivo* (octopus in olive sauce) and *choros a la chalaca* (mussels with a corn and tomato salsa) served in tapas-sized portions. A few stools accommodate diners.

There's a second location in LarcoMar.

La Pascana de Madre Natura CAFE $
(Map p70; Chiclayo 815; 🌿) A natural-food store and bakery.

Plaza Vea SUPERMARKET $
(Map p70; ☎01-625-8000; www.plazavea.com.pe; Av Arequipa 4651; ⏰8am-10pm) Big supermarket.

Vivanda SUPERMARKET $
(Map p70; www.vivanda.com.pe; Benavides 487; ⏰24hr) There are many supermarkets loaded with both local and imported food, drink, toiletries and medicines. One of the best is Vivanda, which rivals any North American mall hangout. There are also branches on José Pardo (Map p70; Av José Pardo) and in San Isidro (Map p68; Av 2 de Mayo 1420; ⏰8am-10pm).

Wong SUPERMARKET $
(Map p70; ☎01-625-0000, ext 1130; www.ewong.com; Óvalo Gutiérrez, Av Santa Cruz 771) A massive supermarket built around the courtyard of a vintage home; look out for the baroque-style staircase.

Barranco

Even as Barranco has gone upscale in recent years, with trendy restaurants serving everything fusion, the neighborhood still holds on to atmospheric, local spots where life is no more complicated than ceviche and beer. A number of informal restaurants serving *anticuchos* and cheap *menús* line Av Grau around the intersection with Unión.

★Blu ICE CREAM $
(Map p74; ☎01-247-3791; Av 28 de Julio 202; cones S9; ⏲noon-10pm Wed-Sat, to 8pm Sun) Creamy, dense chocolate, bright herbs, Madagascar vanilla or tart jungle fruit: this is Lima's best gelato, made fresh daily.

Burrito Bar MEXICAN $
(Map p74; ☎987-352-120; Av Grau 113; mains S12-18; ⏲1-11pm Tue-Sat, noon-5pm Sun) Londoner Stew created this Mexican fast, fresh food sensation after studying tortilla making on YouTube. The experiment was a smash hit, from Baja-style fish tacos to fresh salsas and thirst-quenching mint limeade. Also serves Sierra Andina microbrews. For dessert, the chocolate tamal is a no-brainer.

Delifrance BAKERY $
(Map p74; Av Grau 695; snacks S4-7; ⏲9am-8pm Tue-Sat, to 2pm Sun) Stock your picnic basket with authentic, fresh-baked *pain au chocolat,* baguettes, brioche, top-quality deli meats and cheeses or the lovely French desserts sold at this takeout center.

Cafe Bisetti CAFE $
(Map p74; ☎01-713-9565; Av Pedro de Osma 116; coffee S8-16; ⏲8am-9pm Mon-Fri, 10am-11pm Sat, 3-9pm Sun) Locals park their designer dogs out front of this roasting house with some of the finest lattes in town, well matched with fresh pastries or bitter chocolate pie. Check out the courses on roasting and tasting.

La Bodega Verde CAFE $
(Map p74; ☎01-247-8804; Sucre 335A; mains S18-23; ⏲9am-10pm Mon-Sat, to 8pm Sun; 📶👪) Set in a walled garden, this cafe and gallery is a pleasant spot to linger. Grab the Scrabble (or toys set out for kids) and order up a salad, *lúcuma* milkshake with fruit from the garden tree, tea served in a ceramic pot or organic coffee. Breakfast includes whole-grain breads. Sweets, like carrot cake, are especially good.

The **Museum of Contemporary Art location** (☎248-8559; Av Grau 1511, MAC; ⏲8am-8pm; 👪) has an enclosed park setting that's ideal for families.

DON'T MISS

EL RINCÓN QUE NO CONOCES

El Rincón que no Conoces (☎01-471-2171; Av Bernardo Alcedo 363, Lince; mains S21-55; ⏲12:30-5pm Tue-Sun) Worth the taxi trek to Lince, this mecca of *comida criolla* was founded by the late Teresa Izquierdo Gonzales, a home-trained cook who grew into a beloved national icon. It's *all* good. Try the creamy *ahí de gallina, causas* and heaping plates of *cordero al seco,* a tender lamb dish. Accompany it with *chicha morada,* a sweet corn drink served by the jar.

Just save room for the *pícarones,* airy pumpkin pastries dipped in sweet molasses. Go early and be prepared to wait, it's wildly popular.

La Calandria VEGETARIAN $
(Map p74; ☎01-248-7951; Av 28 de Julio 202; menu S14; ⏲8am-6pm; 🌿) A no-nonsense vegetarian dining room within a small organic dry-goods store, La Calandria delivers on healthy meals in ample portions. Consider it a quick fix.

Las Mesitas PERUVIAN $
(Map p74; ☎01-477-4199; Av Grau 341; mains S8-30; ⏲noon-2am) A vintage spot with little ambience beyond the terra-cotta-tile floors. Diners come for the cheap Peruvian classics, their *ahi de gallina* (chicken stew) is renowned. Or just stop in for a traditional dessert, like their wonderful *suspiro limeño* (a caramel-meringue sweet).

★Isolina PERUVIAN $$
(Map p74; ☎01-247-5075; Av San Martín 101; mains S22-48; ⏲10am-midnight) Go old school. This is home-style *criollo* food at its best. Isolina doesn't shy away from tripe and kidneys, but also offers loving preparations of succulent ribs, *causa escabechada* (with marinated onions) and vibrant green salads on the handwritten menu. Family-sized portions come in old-fashioned tins, but you could also make a lighter meal of starters like marinated clams or ceviche.

There may not be room for dessert, but it sure looks good. Pisco sours recommended.

La Canta Rana CEVICHE $$
(Map p74; ☎01-247-7274; Génova 101; mains S28-45; ⏲8am-11pm Tue-Sat) Around for decades, this unpretentious spot draped in flags and plastered in photos packs in the locals

with its offering of more than 17 different types of ceviche.

Café Tostado PERUVIAN **$$**
(Map p74; ☎01-247-7133; Av Nicolás de Pierola 222; mains S10-32, menú S20; ⏰12:30-9pm Mon-Sat, 7:30am-6pm Sun) Call it a cultural experience. This barely converted auto-repair shop long ago transformed into a bastion of traditional cooking, with long wooden tables and an open kitchen surrounded by scarred iron pots and drying noodles. Daily specials rotate but the sought-after signature dish is rabbit – which feeds up to three people for S45.

Award-winning Tunki coffee is served with *chicharrónes* (fried pork belly) on Sunday for a typical Peruvian breakfast.

Chifa Chung Yion CHINESE **$$**
(Map p74; ☎01-477-0550; Unión 126; mains S18-37; ⏰noon-5:30pm & 7pm-midnight) Known locally as the 'Chifa Unión,' this bustling restaurant is known for its heaping bowls of wonton soup and well-rendered fried rice with prawns. Servings are generous and the owner is always circulating among the old-timey curtained booths. Ample veggie options as well.

La 73 BISTRO **$$**
(Map p74; ☎01-247-0780; Av El Sol Oeste 175; mains S29-45; ⏰noon-midnight) Named for an iconic local bus, this contemporary bistro serves Peruvian–Mediterranean fare, with sustainable fish. Some dishes seem rushed, but standouts include homemade artichoke ravioli stuffed with goat cheese and duck risotto. The bar serves wine and pisco concoctions, or try the amazing herba luisa lemonade. To end on a sweet note, split the crisp, warm churros for dessert.

Surquillo

Al Toke Pez SEAFOOD **$**
(Map p70; Av Angamos Este 886; mains S10-20; ⏰11:30am-3:30pm Tue-Sun) Before sunrise, chef Tomas Matsufuji hits the fish market for today's catch and filets it to serve as super-fresh ceviche in his modest shop with a half-dozen stools lined at the counter on a busy avenue. His daily menu (S15) is a heaping plate of *chicharron de marisco* (fried seafood), ceviche and seafood rice done to perfection.

★**La Picantería** PERUVIAN **$$**
(Map p70; ☎01-241-6676; www.picanteriasdelperu.com; Santa Rosa 388, Surquillo; mains S20-52; ⏰noon-5:30pm Tue-Sat) Just blocks from the famous Surquillo market, diners share two long tables to feast on sea-urchin omelette, stuffed rocoto peppers and stewed osso buco. These traditional plates, hailing from both northern and southern Peru, come with an edge. Chef Héctor Solís knows chiles and doles out just enough heat to leave you at the edge of wanting more.

Drinking & Nightlife

Lima is overflowing with establishments of every description, from rowdy beer halls to high-end lounges to atmospheric old bars. Downtown has the cheapest prices while San Isidro, Miraflores and Barranco feature trendier lounges serving premium cocktails.

The club scene gets started well after midnight and keeps going until the break of dawn. Barranco and Miraflores are the best neighborhoods to go clubbing, but spots come and go, so ask around before heading out. Music styles and cover charges vary depending on the night of the week. For other options, hit 'Pizza Street' (Pasaje Juan Figari) in Miraflores, where a row of raucous clubs regularly spin their wares.

Cinemas, theaters, traveling art exhibits and concerts are covered in the daily *El Comercio,* with the most detailed listings found in Monday's 'Luces' section. Likewise, the information portal **Living in Peru** (www.livinginperu.com) maintains an up-to-date calendar of events. More youth oriented is **Oveja Negra** (ovejanegra.peru.com), a pocket-sized directory distributed free at restaurants and bars, which provides monthly listings of cultural and nightlife happenings.

Lima Centro

Nightlife downtown is for the nostalgic, composed largely of vintage hotel bars and period halls.

★**Museo del Pisco** BAR
(Map p60; ☎99-350-0013; museodelpisco.org; Jirón Junin 201; ⏰10am-midnight) The 'educational' aspect of this wonderful bar might get you in the door, but it's the congenial atmosphere and outstanding original cocktails that will keep you here. We loved the *asu mare* – a pisco martini with ginger, cucumber, melon and basil. A sister bar to the popular original in Cuzco, this one occupies the Casa del Oidor, a 16th-century *casona*.

At lunchtime there's a set menu. Watch the Facebook page for live-music news.

El Bolivarcito BAR

(Map p60; ☎01-427-2114; Jirón de la Unión 958) Facing the Plaza San Martín from the Gran Hotel Bolívar, this frayed yet bustling spot is known as 'La Catedral del Pisco' for purveying some of the first pisco sours in Peru. Order the double-sized *pisco catedral* if your liver can take it.

Hotel Maury BAR

(Map p60; ☎01-428-8188; Ucayali 201) Another vintage bar renowned for popularizing pisco sours. Intimate and old-world, it's lined with stained-glass windows and tended by a battalion of bow-tie-clad waiters.

San Isidro

Bravo Restobar COCKTAIL BAR

(Map p68; ☎01-221-5700; www.bravorestobar.com; Conquistadores 1005; ⏲12:30pm-midnight Sun-Fri, 7pm-3am Sat) With a backlit bar and stone-and-wood interiors, Bravo's able bartenders stir up an encyclopedic cocktail menu (try the *aguaymanto* sour, made with pisco and Amazonian berries). An excellent selection of small-batch piscos make this mellow San Isidro lounge a good spot to sip and be seen. Also serves lauded Italian-Peruvian fusion fare.

Miraflores

Old-world cafes with suited waiters serving frothy pisco sours, or raucous watering holes blaring techno and salsa – Miraflores has a little bit of everything. The area around the Parque Kennedy is particularly suited for sipping and people-watching. *Discotecas* have been getting a comeuppance recently, with various outlets closing due to discrimination.

Huaringas LOUNGE

(Map p70; ☎01-447-1883; Bolognesi 460; ⏲9pm-late Tue-Sat) A popular Miraflores bar and lounge located inside the Las Brujas de Cachiche restaurant, Huaringas serves a vast array of cocktails, including a well-recommended passionfruit sour. On busy weekends, there are DJs.

Café Bar Habana CAFE

(Map p70; ☎01-446-3511; www.cafebarhabana.com; Manuel Bonilla 107; ⏲6pm-late Mon-Sat) Boisterous Cuban proprietor Alexi García and his Peruvian wife, Patsy Higuchi, operate this homey establishment with delicious *mojitos*. The couple, both of whom are artists, sometimes display their works in the adjacent gallery.

Barranco

Barranco's bars and clubs are concentrated around the Parque Municipal, which is thronging with revelers on Friday and Saturday nights.

★Ayahuasca COCKTAIL BAR

(Map p74; ☎01-247-6751; ayahuascarestobar.com; San Martín 130; ⏲8pm-close Mon-Sat) Lounge in a stunning restored *casona* full of Moorish architectural flourishes. Few actually admire the architecture, most guests are busy checking out everyone else. The hyper-real decor includes a dangling mobile made with costumes used in Ayacucho folk dances. There's a long list of contemporary pisco cocktails, like the tasty Ayahuasca sour made with jungle fruit *tambo* and coca leaves.

Bar Piselli BAR

(Map p74; ☎01-252-6750; Av 28 de Julio 297; ⏲10am-11pm Mon-Thu, to 3am Fri & Sat) This neighborhood bar reminiscent of old Buenos Aires beats all for ambience. There's live music on Thursdays provoking boisterous sing-alongs of Peruvian classics.

Juanito's BAR

(Map p74; Av Grau 274; ⏲11:30am-2am Mon-Sat, noon-midnight Sun) This worn-in woody bar – it was a leftist hangout in the 1960s – is one of the mellowest haunts in Barranco. Decorated with a lifetime's worth of theater posters, this is where the writerly set arrives to swig *chilcano de pisco* and deconstruct the state of humanity. There's no sign; look for the crowded room lined with wine bottles.

Santos LOUNGE

(Map p74; ☎01-247-4609; Jirón Zapita 203; ⏲5pm-1am Mon-Thu, to 3am Fri & Sat; 📶) In a creaky old mansion, this funky and congenial bar has multiple rooms and a balcony with sea views (also perfect for people-watching). Local 20- and 30-somethings start their night out here with tapas and the daily two-for-one that goes until 9pm.

Wahio's BAR

(Map p74; ☎01-477-4110; Plaza Espinosa; ⏲Thu-Sat) A large and lively bar with a fair share of dreadlocks and a classic soundtrack of reggae, ska and dub attracting a young crowd.

☆ Entertainment

Some of the best events in the city – film screenings, art exhibits, theater and dance – are put on by the various cultural institutes, some of which have several branches. Check individual websites, newspapers or the web portal *The Peru Guide* (www.theperuguide.com) for listings.

Live Music

Many restaurants and bars feature small local acts, while bigger bands tend to play at the casinos or sporting arenas. Most of the following places take table reservations

El Dragón LIVE MUSIC
(Map p74; ☎01-715-5043; www.eldragon.com.pe; Av Nicolas de Pierola 168, Barranco; cover up to S20; ⏰Thu-Sat) With live music or DJs, this popular venue draws a diverse crowd for Latin rock, *tropicalismo,* soul and funk.

Cocodrilo Verde LIVE MUSIC
(Map p70; ☎01-242-7583; www.cocodriloverde.com; Francisco de Paola 226; minimum tab S25; ⏰6:30pm-close Mon-Sat) With great bands that range from popular music to jazz and bossa nova, this hip lounge is good for a night out.

La Noche LIVE MUSIC
(Map p74; ☎01-247-1012; www.lanoche.com.pe; Av Bolognesi 307, Barranco) This well-known tri-level bar is *the* spot to see rock, punk and Latin music acts in Lima, though drinks could be better.

La Estación de Barranco CLUB
(Map p74; ☎01-247-0344; www.laestaciondebarranco.com; Av Pedro de Osma 112, Barranco) A middling space that hosts a variety of jazz, cabaret, musical and comedy performances.

TELETICKET

Teleticket (Map p70; ☎01-613-8888; www.teleticket.com.pe) A handy place to buy tickets is Teleticket, a one-stop shopping broker that sells tickets to sporting events, concerts, theatre and some *peñas* (bars or clubs featuring live folkloric music), as well as the tourist train to Huancayo. The most convenient Teleticket offices can be found on the 2nd floor of the Wong supermarket at Óvalo Gutiérrez and inside the Metro supermarket in Lima Centro. The website has a full listing of locations all over Lima.

Jazz Zone CLUB
(Map p70; ☎01-241-8139; www.jazzzoneperu.com; Centro Comercial El Suche, Av La Paz 656, Miraflores; cover from S5) A variety of jazz, folk, *cumbia,* flamenco and other acts at this intimate, well-recommended club on the eastern side of Miraflores.

Sargento Pimienta CLUB
(Map p74; ☎01-247-3265; www.sargentopimienta.com.pe; Av Bolognesi 755, Barranco; admission from S15) A reliable spot in Barranco whose name means 'Sergeant Pepper.' The barnlike club hosts various theme nights and occasional live bands.

Peñas

Peruvian folk music and dance is performed on weekends at *peñas*. There are two main types of Peruvian music performed at these venues: *folklórica* and *criollo*. The first is more typical of the Andean highlands; the other, a coastal music driven by African-influenced beats. Admission varies; dinner is sometimes included in the price.

La Peña del Carajo LIVE PERFORMANCE
(☎01-247-7023; www.delcarajo.com.pe; Miranda 158) Locals recommend this high-energy *peña* that brings guests to their feet. Offering a variety of shows.

Las Brisas del Titicaca TRADITIONAL MUSIC
(Map p64; ☎01-715-6960; www.brisasdeltiticaca.com; Wakuski 168, Lima Centro; admission from S30) A lauded *folklórica* show near Plaza Bolognesi downtown, in an enormous venue.

La Candelaria TRADITIONAL MUSIC
(Map p74; ☎01-247-1314; www.lacandelariaperu.com; Av Bolognesi 292, Barranco; admission from S35) In Barranco, a show that incorporates both *folklórica* and *criollo* music and dancing.

La Oficina TRADITIONAL MUSIC
(Map p74; ☎01-247-6544; Enrique Barron 441, Barranco) A locally recommended traditional *criollo* performance space located near the intersection of Avs Grau and El Sol; see the Facebook page for details.

Cinemas

The latest international films (S16) are usually screened with Spanish subtitles, except children's movies, which are always dubbed. Some cinemas offer reduced admission midweek. Listings can be found online or in the cultural pages of the local newspapers.

Cine Planet CINEMA
(Map p60; ☎01-624-9500; www.cineplanet.com.pe; Jirón de la Unión 819) Large cinema with outlets throughout the city, including in **Miraflores** (Map p70; Av Santa Cruz 814).

Cinerama CINEMA
(Map p70; ☎01-243-0541; www.cinerama.com.pe; Av José Pardo 121, Miraflores) A cramped movie theater.

UVK Multicines CINEMA
(Map p70; ☎01-446-7336; www.uvkmulticines.com; LarcoMar, Malecón de la Reserva 610; admission S9-17) Has a 'CineBar,' where, for S23, you can sit in a theater with bar tables and have cocktails delivered to your seat. There's another branch on Plaza San Martín (Map p60; ☎01-428-6042; Ocoña 110; admission S6.50-8.50).

Theater

Teatro Británico THEATRE
(Map p70; ☎01-615-3434; www.britanico.edu.pe; Bellavista 527, Miraflores) Hosts a variety of worthwhile productions, including plays in English.

Teatro Segura THEATRE
(Map p60; ☎01-426-7189; Huancavelica 265, Lima Centro) Built in 1909, the gorgeous Teatro Segura puts on opera, plays and ballet.

Sports

Estadio Nacional STADIUM
(Map p64; Lima Centro) *Fútbol* is the national obsession, and Peru's Estadio Nacional, off *cuadras* 7 to 9 of Paseo de la República, is the venue for the most important matches and other events. Teleticket has listings and sales.

Plaza de Acho SPECTATOR SPORT
(Map p60; ☎481-1467; www.plazaacho.com; Jirón Hualgayoc 332, Rímac) Bullfighting remains popular in Lima, though it's controversial in some circles. The height of the season is in October, during the religious feast of El Señor de los Milagros, when Peru's best toreadors compete. Teleticket has listings.

Jockey Club of Peru HORSE RACING
(☎01-610-3000; www.hipodromodemonterrico.com.pe; Hipódromo de Monterrico) Located at the junction of the Panamericana Sur and Av Javier Prado, the horse track has races three to four days a week.

Shopping

Clothing, jewelry and handicrafts from all over Peru can generally be found in Lima. Shop prices tend to be high, but those with less capital can haggle their hearts out at the craft markets. Shopping hours are generally 10am to 8pm Monday to Saturday, with variable lunchtime hours. Credit cards and traveler's checks can be used at some spots, but you'll need photo identification.

Quality pisco can be bought duty-free at the airport just prior to departure.

Handicrafts

Small shops selling crafts dot the major tourist areas around Pasaje de los Escribanos in Lima Centro, and near the intersection of Diez Canseco and La Paz in Miraflores. To buy crafts directly from artisans, visit the Ichimay Wari collective (p106) in Lurín.

A number of Miraflores boutiques sell high-quality, contemporary alpaca knits.

Mercado Indio MARKET
(Map p70; Av Petit Thouars 5245, Miraflores) The best place to find everything from pre-Columbian-style clay pottery to alpaca rugs to knock-offs of Cuzco School canvases. Prices vary; shop around.

Feria Artesanal MARKET
(Av de la Marina, Pueblo Libre) Slightly cheaper than Mercado Indio is this crafts market in Pueblo Libre.

Centro Comercial el Suche MARKET
(Map p70; Av La Paz, Miraflores) A shady passageway with a jumble of handicrafts, antiques and jewelry stores.

Dédalo HANDICRAFTS
(Map p74; ☎01-652-5400; dedaloarte.blogspot.com; Sáenz Peña 295, Barranco; ⏰10am-8pm Mon-Sat 11am-7pm Sun) A vintage *casona* houses this contemporary crafts store with a lovely courtyard cafe.

Las Pallas HANDICRAFTS
(Map p74; ☎01-477-4629; www.laspallasperu.com; Cajamarca 212, Barranco; ⏰10am-7pm Mon-Sat) For special gifts, check out this handicrafts shop featuring a selection of the highest-quality products from all over Peru; it's even on the radar of Sotheby's. Ring the bell if the gate is closed during opening hours.

La Casa de la Mujer Artesana Manuela Ramos HANDICRAFTS
(☎01-423-8840; www.casadelamujerartesana.com; Av Juan Pablo Fernandini 1550, Pueblo Libre;

11am-1pm & 2-6pm Mon-Fri) Crafts cooperative whose proceeds support women's economic development programs, at *cuadra* 15 of Av Brasil.

Local Markets

Markets get crowded; watch your wallet.

Mercado Central MARKET
(Map p60; cnr Ayacucho & Ucayali, Lima Centro) From fresh fish to blue jeans, you can buy almost anything at this crowded market close to the Barrio Chino.

Polvos Azules MARKET
(Map p64; www.polvosazules.pe) Need a socket wrench, a suitcase and a T-shirt of Jesus Christ wearing an Alianza Lima soccer jersey? Then Polvos Azules is the place for you. This multilevel, popular market attracts people of all social strata for a mind-boggling assortment of cheap goods.

Shopping Malls

In San Isidro, Conquistadores street is cluttered with high-end boutiques, or you can experience the full-blown Peruvian mall-rat experience.

Jockey Plaza MALL
(Av Javier Prado Este 4200, Monterrico) A huge, upscale mall bursting with department stores, boutiques, movie theaters and a food court.

LarcoMar MALL
(Map p70; Malecón de la Reserva 610) A well-to-do outdoor mall wedged into the cliff top beneath the Parque Salazar, full of high-end clothing shops, trendy discotheques and a wide range of eateries. There's also a bowling alley.

Camping Equipment

A number of shops sell specialized clothing, backpacks and a variety of other gear.

Alpamayo OUTDOOR EQUIPMENT
(Map p70; 01-445-1671; 2nd fl, Av José Larco 345, Miraflores) Outdoor supplies.

Tatoo Adventure Gear OUTDOOR EQUIPMENT
(Map p70; 01-242-1938; www.tatoo.ws; LarcoMar, Malecón de la Reserva 610, Miraflores) Tatoo-brand outdoor clothes, some accessories.

Todo Camping OUTDOOR EQUIPMENT
(Map p70; 01-242-1318; Av Angamos Oeste 350, Miraflores) Sells fuel stoves and also climbing equipment.

Books & Electronics

El Virrey BOOKS
(Map p70; 01-444-4141; www.elvirrey.com; Bolognesi 510, Miraflores; 10am-7pm) Includes a room stocked with thousands of rare vintage editions.

CompuPalace ELECTRONICS
(Map p70; Av Petit Thouars 5358, Miraflores) You'll find rechargeable and lithium batteries, as well as computer parts, supplies and replacements at CompuPalace, a block-long electronics arcade.

Information

DANGERS & ANNOYANCES

Like any large Latin American city, Lima is a land of haves and have-nots, which has made stories about crime here the stuff of legend. Yet the city has greatly improved since the lawless 1980s and most visitors have a safe visit. Nonetheless, stay aware.

Airport The airport attracts crime – do not leave your belongings loosely attended and beware anyone who approaches you outside gates claiming your flight is delayed, offering transport to the airline office for assistance – this is an express kidnapping tactic used to drain credit cards at various city ATMs. Once you are at the airport, stay inside and don't linger outside the passenger-only area.

Neighborhoods Increased police and private security in Miraflores and in the cliff-top parks make them some of the city's safest areas. Barranco is mostly safe and pedestrian-friendly but has seen a few evening robberies at a few restaurants and bars. Security may increase by the time you read this, but it doesn't hurt to go out with the minimum and leave the rest in a hotel safe. The most dangerous neighborhoods are San Juan de Lurigancho, Los Olivos, Comas, Vitarte and El Agustino.

Precautions Do not wear flashy jewelry, and keep your camera in your bag when you are not using it. It is best to be discreet with cash and take only as much as you'll need for the day. Unless you need your passport for official purposes, leave it in a hotel safe box; a photocopy will do. Blending in helps, too: *limeños* save their shorts for the beach.

Theft The most common offense is theft, such as muggings. Do not resist robbery. You are unlikely to be physically hurt, but it is nonetheless best to keep a streetwise attitude.

Transportation Be wary at crowded events and the areas around bus stops and terminals. These bring out pickpockets – even in upscale districts. Late at night, it's preferable to take official taxis. The areas of Rímac, Callao,

Surquillo and La Victoria can get quite rough so approach with caution (taxis are best).

Touts Be skeptical of unaffiliated touts and taxi drivers who try to sell you tours or tell you that the hotel you've booked is closed or dodgy. Many of these are scam artists trying to steer you to places that pay them a commission.

EMERGENCY

Policía de Turismo (Tourist Police, Poltur; ☎01-225-8698; Av Javier Prado Este 2465, 5th fl, San Borja; ⏲24hr) Main division of the Policía Nacional (National Police) at Museo de la Nación. English-speaking officers who can provide theft reports for insurance claims or traveler's-check refunds. In heavily touristed areas, it is easy to identify members of Poltur by their white shirts.

Policía Nacional Head Office (☎01-460-0921; Moore 268, Magdalena del Mar; ⏲24hr)

IMMIGRATION

Oficina de Migraciónes (Immigration Office; Map p64; ☎01-200-1000; www.migraciones.gob.pe; Prolongación España 734, Breña; ⏲8am-1pm Mon-Fri) Contact the Oficina de Migraciónes for visa issues or to apply for residency. Tourists can stay in Peru for 183 days. If you plan to stay the full period, speak up when you get your entry stamp to get the maximum allotted time, otherwise you might be granted 30 or 90 days.

Keep the tourist card you receive upon entry into Peru in your passport for your entire stay; you will need it upon exiting the country. Peru no longer allows extensions to tourist cards. Readers have remarked that travelers have been able to make on-site payments for varied fees with certain flexible officials; this risky behavior is not condoned by Lonely Planet.

MEDICAL SERVICES

There are a number of clinics with emergency services and some English-speaking staff. Consultations start in the vicinity of S80 and climb from there, depending on the clinic and the doctor. Treatments and medications are an additional fee, as are appointments with specialists.

Pharmacies abound in Lima. **Botica Fasa** (Map p70; ☎01-619-0000; www.boticafasa.com.pe; cnr Av José Larco 129-35, Miraflores; ⏲24hr) and **InkaFarma** (Map p70; ☎01-315-9000, deliveries 01-314-2020; www.inkafarma.com.pe; Alfredo Benavides 425, Miraflores; ⏲24hr) are well-stocked chains and open 24 hours. They often deliver free of charge.

You can have eyeglasses made cheaply by one of the opticians along Miró Quesada in the vicinity of Camaná in Central Lima or around Schell and Av José Larco in Miraflores.

Clínica Anglo-Americana (☎01-436-9933; www.clinangloamericana.com.pe; Av La Fontana 362) A renowned (but expensive) hospital. There's a walk-in center in La Molina, near the US embassy and a branch in San Isidro (Map p68; ☎616-8900; Salazar 350).

Clínica Good Hope (Map p70; ☎01-610-7300; www.goodhope.org.pe; Malecón Balta 956) Quality care at good prices; there is also a dental unit.

Clínica Internacional (Map p64; ☎01-619-6161; www.clinicainternacional.com.pe; Garcilaso de la Vega 1420, Lima Centro) A well-equipped clinic with specialities in gastroenterology, neurology and cardiology.

Clínica Montesur (☎01-317-4000; www.clinicamontesur.com.pe; Av El Polo 505, Monterrico) Devoted exclusively to women's health.

Clínica San Borja (☎01-475-4000; www.clinicasanborja.com.pe; Av Guardia Civil 337, San Borja) Another reputable clinic, with cardiology services.

Instituto de Medicina Tropical (Hospital Nacional Cayetano Heredia; ☎01-482-3910, 01-482-3903; www.upch.edu.pe/tropicales; Av Honorio Delgado 430, San Martín de Porras) Good for treating tropical diseases; located within Hospital Nacional Cayetano Heredia. The immediate area around the hospital is safe, but the surrounding neighborhood can be rough.

Instituto Nacional de Salud del Niño (Map p64; ☎01-330-0066; www.isn.gob.pe; Brasil 600, Breña) A pediatric hospital; gives tetanus and yellow-fever jabs.

MONEY

Banks are plentiful and most have 24-hour ATMs, which tend to offer the best exchange rates. For extra security, use ATMs inside banks (as opposed to ones on the street or in supermarkets), cover the key pad as you enter passwords and graze the whole keypad to prevent infrared tracing of passwords. Avoid making withdrawals late at night.

Lima's *casas de cambio* (foreign-exchange bureaus) give similar or slightly better rates than banks for cash, although not traveler's checks. They're found downtown on Ocoña and Camaná, as well as along Av José Larco in Miraflores. Consider using street moneychangers carefully as counterfeit is a problem.

Banco de Crédito del Perú (BCP; Map p70; www.viabcp.com; cnr Av José Larco & José Gonzales; ⏲9am-6:30pm Mon-Fri, 9:30am-1pm Sat) Has 24-hour Visa and Plus ATMs; also gives cash advances on Visa, and changes Amex, Citicorp and Visa traveler's checks. The Central Lima (Map p60; ☎427-5600; cnr Lampa & Ucayali) branch has incredible stained-glass ceilings. There's another branch at José Pardo (Map p70; ☎445-1259; Av José Pardo 491).

BBVA Continental (Map p70; ☎01-595-0000; www.bbvacontinental.pe; Av José Larco 631; ⊙9am-6pm Mon-Fri, 9:30am-12:30pm Sat) A representative of Visa; its ATMs also take Cirrus, Plus and MasterCard.

Citibank (Map p68; ☎01-221-7000; www.citibank.com.pe; Av 2 de Mayo 1547; ⊙9am-6pm Mon-Fri, 9:30am-1pm Sat) This location and the one in Miraflores (Map p70; Av José Pardo 127) have 24-hour ATMs operating on the Cirrus, Maestro, MasterCard and Visa systems; they cash Citicorp traveler's checks.

LAC Dólar (Map p70; ☎01-242-4085; Av La Paz 211; ⊙9:30am-6pm Mon-Fri, 9am-2pm Sat) A reliable exchange house; can deliver cash to your hotel in exchange for traveler's checks.

Scotiabank (Map p68; ☎01-311-6000; www.scotiabank.com.pe; Av 2 de Mayo 1510-1550; ⊙9:15am-6pm Mon-Fri, to 12:30pm Sat) ATMs (24-hour) operate on the MasterCard, Maestro, Cirrus, Visa and Plus networks and dispense soles and US dollars. There are also branches at Miraflores Larco (Map p70; Av José Larco 1119) and Miraflores Pardo (Map p70; cnr Av José Pardo & Bolognesi).

Travex (Map p70; ☎01-630-9800; www.travex.com.pe; Av Santa Cruz 873, Miraflores; ⊙8am-5pm Mon-Fri) Buy traveler's checks or replace lost ones.

POST

Serpost, the national postal service, has outlets throughout Lima. Mail sent to you at Lista de Correos (Poste Restante), Correo Central, Lima, can be collected at the main post office in Central Lima. Take identification.

DHL (Map p68; ☎01-221-0816; www.dhl.com.pe; Av Dos de Mayo 635, San Isidro; ⊙9am-8pm Mon-Fri, to 1pm Sat)

Federal Express (FedEx; Map p70; ☎01-242-2280; www.fedex.com.pe; Pasaje Olaya 260, BSC Miraflores, Miraflores; ⊙9am-7pm Mon-Fri, 10am-3pm Sat)

Main Post Office (Map p60; ☎01-511-5000; www.serpost.com.pe; Pasaje Piura, Central Lima; ⊙8am-9pm Mon-Sat) Poste restante mail can be collected here, though it's not 100% reliable. Bring ID.

TOURIST INFORMATION

iPerú (☎01-574-8000; Aeropuerto Internacional Jorge Chávez) The government's reputable tourist bureau dispenses maps, offers good advice and can help handle complaints. The Miraflores office (Map p70; ☎01-445-9400; LarcoMar; ⊙11am-2pm & 3-8pm) is tiny but is highly useful on weekends. There's another branch in San Isidro (Map p68; ☎01-421-1627; Jorge Basadre 610; ⊙9am-6pm Mon-Fri).

Municipal Tourist Office (Map p60; ☎01-632-1300; www.munlima.gob.pe; Pasaje de los Escribanos 145, Lima Centro; ⊙9am-5pm Mon-Fri, 11am-3pm Sat & Sun) Of limited use; check the website for a small number of listings of local events and info on free downtown tours.

Trekking & Backpacking Club (Map p64; ☎01-423-2515; www.angelfire.com/mi2/tebac; Huascar 1152, Jesús María) Provides information, maps, brochures, equipment rental and guide information for independent trekkers.

SOUTH AMERICAN EXPLORERS

Now more than three decades old, the venerable **South American Explorers Club** (SAE; Map p70; ☎447-7731; www.saexplorers.org; Enrique Palacios 956, Miraflores; ⊙9:30am-4:30pm Mon-Fri, to 1pm Sat) is an indispensable resource for long-term travelers, journalists and scientists spending long periods in Peru, Ecuador, Bolivia and Argentina. It has an extensive library as well as a vast array of guides and maps for sale, including trail maps for the Inca Trail, Colca Canyon, Mt Ausangate, the Cordillera Blanca and Cordillera Huayhuash. You can also attend talks, get useful information on travel conditions in remote areas and research volunteer opportunities.

This member-supported, nonprofit organization helped launch the first clean-up of the Inca Trail and has supported local medicine drives. Annual dues are US$60 per person (US$90 per couple) or a US$30 membership is good for three months. There are additional clubhouses in Cuzco, Quito and Buenos Aires (find contact information online). You can sign up in person at one of the offices or via the website.

Members receive full use of the clubhouse and its facilities, including luggage storage, poste restante, a book exchange and discounts on items sold on-site. Members can also take advantage of the club's rooms for rent and get discounts at businesses throughout Peru. Members can look at their Lima Survival Kit, a helpful guide for new long-term residents.

Nonmembers are welcome to browse some of the information and purchase guides or maps.

TRAVEL AGENCIES

Travel agencies can organize airline bookings and other arrangements.

Fertur Peru Travel (Map p60; ☎01-427-1958, 01-427-2626; www.fertur-travel; Jirón Junín 211; ⊙9am-7pm Mon-Fri, to noon Sat) A highly recommended agency that can book local, regional and international travel, as well as create custom group itineraries. Discounts available for students and SAE members. There's another branch in Miraflores (Map p70; ☎01-242-1900; Schell 485).

InfoPerú (Map p60; ☎01-425-0414; infoperu.com.pe; Jirón de la Unión 1066, Lima Centro; ⊙9:30am-6pm Mon-Fri, 10am-2pm Sat) Books bus and plane tickets and dispenses reliable information on hotels and sightseeing.

InteJ (Map p74; ☎01-247-3230; www.intej.org; San Martín 240, Barranco; ⊙9:30am-12:45pm & 2-5:45pm Mon-Fri, 9:30am-12:45pm Sat) The official International Student Identity Card (ISIC) office, InteJ can arrange discounted air, train and bus fares, among other services.

Lima Tours (Map p60; ☎01-619-6900; www.limatours.com.pe; Nicolás de Piérola 589, 18th fl, Lima Centro; ⊙9:30am-6pm Mon-Fri, to 1pm Sat) A well-known, high-end agency that handles all manner of travel arrangements. Also organizes gay-friendly trips and basic gastronomic tours of Lima.

Tika Tours (Map p70; ☎01-719-9990; www.tikagroup.com.pe; José Pardo 332-350, Miraflores) Tour operator and travel agent, helpful for local information, as well as travel all over Peru.

USEFUL WEBSITES

- www.lonelyplanet.com/peru/lima
- www.livinginperu.com
- www.peru.travel
- www.saexplorers.org
- www.lima.dailysecret.com

ℹ Getting There & Away

AIR

Lima's Aeropuerto Internacional Jorge Chávez (p543) is stocked with the usual facilities plus a pisco boutique, a post office and luggage storage. Internet access is available on the 2nd floor.

All departure taxes are included in ticket prices. You can get flight information, buy tickets and reconfirm flights online or via telephone, but for ticket changes or problems, it's best to go to the airline office in person.

Avianca (Map p70; ☎01-511-8222; www.avianca.com; Av Jose Pardo 811; ⊙8:30am-7pm Mon-Fri, 9am-2pm Sat) Flies to Cuzco.

LAN (Map p70; ☎01-213-8200; www.lan.com; Av José Pardo 513, Miraflores) LAN goes to Arequipa, Chiclayo, Cuzco, Iquitos, Juliaca, Piura, Puerto Maldonado, Tacna, Tarapoto and Trujillo. Additionally it offers link services between Arequipa and Cuzco, Arequipa and Juliaca, Arequipa and Tacna, Cuzco and Juliaca, and Cuzco and Puerto Maldonado.

LC Peru (☎01-204-1313; www.lcperu.pe; Av Pablo Carriquirry 857, San Isidro) Flies from Lima to Andahuaylas, Ayacucho, Cajamarca, Huánuco, Huaraz, Iquitos and Huancayo (Jauja) on smaller turbo-prop aircraft.

Peruvian Airlines (Map p70; ☎01-716-6000; www.peruvianairlines.pe; Av José Pardo 495, Miraflores; ⊙9am-7pm Mon-Fri, to 5pm Sat) Flies to Arequipa, Cuzco, Piura, Iquitos, Pucallpa, Tarapoto and Tacna.

Star Perú (Map p70; ☎01-705-9000; www.starperu.com; Av Espinar 331, Miraflores) Flies to Ayacucho, Cuzco, Huanuco, Iquitos, Pucallpa, Puerto Maldonado and Tarapoto.

BUS

There is no central bus terminal; each company operates its ticketing and departure points independently. Some companies have several terminals, so always clarify from which point a bus leaves when buying tickets. The busiest times of year are Semana Santa (the week before Easter Sunday) and the weeks surrounding Fiestas Patrias (July 28–29), when thousands of *limeños* make a dash out of the city and fares double. At these times, book well ahead.

Some stations are in rough neighborhoods. If possible, buy your tickets in advance and take a taxi when carrying luggage.

Civa (Map p64; ☎01-418-1111; www.civa.com.pe; cnr Av 28 de Julio & Paso de la Republica 569) For Arequipa, Cajamarca, Chachapoyas, Chiclayo, Cuzco, Ilo, Máncora, Nazca, Piura, Puno, Tacna, Tarapoto, Trujillo and Tumbes. The company also runs a more luxurious sleeper line called **Excluciva** (www.excluciva.com) to various coastal destinations.

Cruz del Sur (Map p68; www.cruzdelsur.com.pe; Av Javier Prado Este 1109) One of the biggest companies, serving the coast – as well as inland cities such as Arequipa, Cuzco, Huancayo and Huaraz – with three different classes of service: the cheaper Ideal, and the more luxurious Imperial and Cruzero.

Móvil Tours (Map p64; ☎01-716-8000; www.moviltours.com.pe; Paseo de la República 749) For Chachapoyas, Chiclayo, Huancayo, Huaraz and Tarapoto.

Oltursa (☎01-708-5000; www.oltursa.pe; Av Aramburu 1160, San Isidro) A short distance from San Isidro lies the main terminal for this very reputable company, which travels to Arequipa, Chiclayo, Ica, Máncora, Nazca, Paracas, Piura, Trujillo and Tumbes.

Ormeño (☎01-472-1710; www.grupo-ormeno.com.pe; Av Javier Prado Este 1059) A huge Lima bus company offering daily service to Arequipa,

Ayacucho, Cajamarca, Cañete, Chiclayo, Chincha, Cuzco, Huaraz, Ica, Ilo, Nazca, Paracas, Piura, Puno, Tacna, Trujillo and Tumbes, all of which leave from the terminal in La Victoria.

The Central Lima terminal (Map p64; ☎472-5000; www.grupo-ormeno.com.pe; Carlos Zavala Loayza 177) is for buying tickets or arranging transport on one of the smaller subsidiaries: Expreso Continental (northern Peru), Expreso Chinchano (south coast and Arequipa) and San Cristóbal (Puno and Cuzco).

It has three classes of service: Econo, Business and Royal.

Soyuz (Map p64; ☎01-205-2370; www.soyuz.com.pe; Av México 333, La Victoria) Frequent buses to Cañete, Chincha, Ica and Nazca.

Tepsa (Map p60; ☎01-428-4635, 01-427-5642; www.tepsa.com.pe; Paseo de la República 151A) Comfortable buses that travel to Arequipa, Cajamarca, Chiclayo, Cuzco, Ica, Lambayeque, Máncora, Nazca, Piura, Tacna, Trujillo and Tumbes. There's another station at Javier Prado (Map p68; ☎01-470-6666; www.tepsa.com.pe; Av Javier Prado Este 1091).

CAR

Lima has major intersections without stoplights, kamikaze bus drivers, spectacular traffic jams and little to no parking. If you are still game, a number of companies have 24-hour desks at the airport. Prices range from about S85 to S190 per day, not including surcharges, insurance and taxes (of about 19%). Delivery is possible.

Budget (☎01-204-4400; www.budgetperu.com)

Dollar (☎01-444-3050; www.dollar.com)

Hertz (☎01-445-5716; www.hertz.com.pe)

National (☎01-578-7878; www.nationalcar.com.pe)

TRAIN

Ferrocarril Central Andino (☎01-226-6363; www.ferrocarrilcentral.com.pe; adult/child one-way S120/85, return $195/130) A 12-hour odyssey along Andean mountainscapes and vertigo-inducing bridges, this tourist train climbs from sea level to 4829m – the second-highest point for passenger trains in the world – before descending to Huancayo at 3260m. The journey runs fortnightly from mid-April to mid-October. Confirm schedules in advance since the rail lines aren't always operational.

ℹ Getting Around

TO & FROM THE AIRPORT

The airport resides in the port city of Callao, about 12km west of downtown or 20km northwest of Miraflores. In a private taxi, allow at least an hour to the airport from San Isidro, Miraflores or Barranco; by *combi*, expect the journey to take at least two hours – with plenty of stops in between. Traffic is lightest before 6:30am.

As you come out of customs, inside the airport to the right is the official taxi service: **Taxi Green** (☎01-484-4001; www.taxigreen.com.pe).

Outside the airport perimeter itself, you will find 'local' taxis. Taking these does not always save you money, and safety is an issue – local hustlers use this as an opportunity to pick up foreign travelers and rob them. It is best to use the official airport taxis, or arrange pickup with your hotel.

BUSES FROM LIMA

DESTINATION	COST* (S)	DURATION (HR)
Arequipa	80/170	16-18
Ayacucho	70/160	9-11
Cajamarca	90/150	16
Chiclayo	60/125	12-14
Cuzco	110/210	22-23
Huancayo	35/80	7-8
Huaraz	60/160	8
Ica	30/80	4½-5½
Nazca	80/160	6-8
Piura	80/184	16
Puno	140/170	22
Tacna	115/190	18-22
Trujillo	40/125	9-10
Tumbes	80/200	20

*Prices are general estimates for normal/luxury buses.

The cheapest way to get to and from the airport is via the *combi* company known as **La S** (Map p70; per person from S2.50) – a giant letter 'S' is pasted to the front windshields – which runs various routes from the port of Callao to Miraflores and beyond. From the airport, these can be found heading south along Av Elmer Faucett. For the return trip to the airport, La S *combis* can be found traveling north along Av Petit Thouars and east along Av Angamos in Miraflores. The most central spot to find them is at the *paradero* (bus stop) on Av Petit Thouars, just north of Av Ricardo Palma. Expect to be charged additional fares for any seats that your bags may occupy. *Combi* companies change their routes regularly, so ask around before heading out.

BUS

The new trans-Lima electric express bus system, **El Metropolitano** (www.metropolitano.com.pe), is the fastest and most efficient way to get into the city center. Routes are few, though coverage is expanding to the northern part of the city. Ruta Troncal (S2.50) goes through Barranco, Miraflores and San Isidro to Plaza Grau in the center of Lima. Users must purchase a *tarjeta intelligente* (cards S4.50) that can be credited for use.

Otherwise, traffic-clogging caravans of **minivans** hurtle down the avenues with a *cobrador* (ticket taker) hanging out the door and shouting out the stops. Go by the destination placards taped to the windshield. Your best bet is to know the nearest major intersection or landmark close to your stop (eg Parque Kennedy) and tell that to the *cobrador* – he'll let you know whether you've got the right bus. *Combis* are generally slow and crowded, but startlingly cheap: fares run from S1 to S3, depending on the length of your journey.

The most useful **bus routes** link Central Lima with Miraflores along Av Arequipa or Paseo de la República. Minibuses along Garcilaso de la Vega (also called Av Wilson) and Av Arequipa are labeled 'Todo Arequipa' or 'Larco/Schell/Miraflores' when heading to Miraflores and, likewise, 'Todo Arequipa' and 'Wilson/Tacna' when leaving Miraflores for Central Lima. Catch these buses along Av José Larco or Av Arequipa in Miraflores. To get to Barranco, look for buses along Av Arequipa labeled 'Chorrillos/Huaylas/Metro' (some will also have signs that say 'Barranco'). You can also find these on the Diagonal, just west of the Parque Kennedy, in Miraflores.

TAXI

Lima's taxis lack meters, so negotiate fares before getting in. Fares vary depending on the length of the journey, traffic conditions, time of day (evening is more expensive) and your Spanish skills. Registered taxis or taxis hailed outside a tourist attraction charge higher rates. As a (very) rough guide, a trip within Miraflores costs around S5 to S10. From Miraflores to Central Lima is S10 to S15, to Barranco from S8 to S12, and San Isidro from S6 to S12. You can haggle fares – though it's harder during rush hour. If there are two or more passengers be clear on whether the fare is per person or for the car.

The majority of taxis in Lima are unregistered (unofficial); indeed, surveys have indicated that no less than one vehicle in seven here is a taxi. During the day, it's usually not a problem to use either. At night it is important to use registered taxis for your safety, which are traceable by the license number painted on the side. They should also have checkers, a rectangular authorization sticker with the word SETAME on the upper left corner of the windshield and may have yellow paint.

Registered taxis can be called by phone or found at taxi stands, such as the one outside the Sheraton in Central Lima or outside the LarcoMar shopping mall in Miraflores. Registered taxis cost about 30% more than regular street taxis but the security is worth it.

Easy Taxi (Map p70; LarcoMar) Download the app on your smartphone for fast service or cost estimates. Recommended.

Taxi Lima (☎ 01-271-1763)

Taxi Móvil (☎ 01-422-6890)

Taxi Real (☎ 01-215 1414; www.taxireal.com) Recommended.

Taxi Seguro (☎ 01-241-9292)

AROUND LIMA

On weekends and holidays, *limeños* head for the beach or the hills. From exploring ancient ruins to beach bumming, there is much to do outside of the city that is worthy of exploration if you have a few extra days.

Pachacamac

☎ 01

Situated about 31km southeast of the city center, the archaeological complex of **Pachacamac** (☎ 01-430-0168; pachacamac.perucultural.org.pe; admission S10; ⏰ 9am-4pm Tue-Sat, to 3pm Sun) is a pre-Columbian citadel made up of adobe and stone palaces and temple pyramids. If you've been to Machu Picchu, it may not look like much, but this was an important Inca site and a major city when the Spanish arrived. It began as a ceremonial center for the Lima culture beginning at about AD 100, and was later expanded by the Waris before being taken over by the Ichsma. The Incas added numerous other structures to the area upon their arrival in 1450. The name Pachacamac, which can be variously translated as 'He who Animated the World' or 'He who Created Land and Time,' comes from the Wari god, whose wooden, two-faced image can be seen in the on-site **museum**.

Most of the buildings are now little more than piles of rubble that dot the desert landscape, but some of the main temples have been excavated and their ramps and stepped sides revealed. You can climb the switchback trail to the top of the **Templo del Sol** (Temple of the Sun), which on clear days offers excellent views of the coast. The most remarkable structure on-site, however, is the Palacio de las Mamacuna (House of the Chosen Women), commonly referred to as the **Acllahuasi**, which boasts a series of Inca-style trapezoidal doorways. Unfortunately, a major earthquake in 2007 has left the structure highly unstable. As a result, visitors can only admire it from a distance. Without funding to repair the extensive damage, it has been listed as one of the planet's most endangered sites.

There is a **visitors center and cafe** at the site entrance, which is on the road to Lurín. A simple map can be obtained from the ticket office, and a track leads from here into the complex. Those on foot should allow at least two hours to explore. (In summer, take water and a hat – there is no shade to speak of once you hit the trail.) Those with a vehicle can drive from site to site.

Various agencies in Lima offer guided tours (half-day around S115 per person) that include transport and a guide. Mountain-bike tours can be an excellent option.

Alternatively, catch a minibus signed 'Pachacamac' from Av 28 de Julio or the sunken roadway at the corner of Andahuaylas and Grau in Central Lima (S3, 45 minutes); minibuses leave every 15 minutes during daylight hours. From Miraflores, take a bus on Av Benavides headed east to the Panamericana and Puente Primavera and change here for the bus signed 'Pachacamac/Lurín' (S3, 30 minutes). For both services, tell the driver to let you off near the *ruinas* (ruins) or you'll end up at Pachacamac village, about 1km beyond the entrance. To get back to Lima, flag down any bus outside the gate, but expect to stand. You can also hire a taxi (from S40 per hour) from Lima.

Southern Beaches

☎01

Every summer, *limeños* make a beeline for the beaches clustered along the Panamericana to the south. The exodus peaks on weekends, when, occasionally, the road is so congested that it becomes temporarily one-way. The principal beach towns include El Silencio, Señoritas, Caballeros, Punta Hermosa, Punta Negra, San Bartolo, Santa María, Naplo and Pucusana. Don't expect tropical resorts; this stretch of barren, coastal desert is lapped by cold water and strong currents. Inquire locally before swimming, as drownings occur annually. Surfboard rental is almost nonexistent; best to bring your own.

Popular with families is **San Bartolo**, which is cluttered with hostels at budget to midrange rates during the busy summer. Sitting above the bay, **Hostal 110** (☎01-430-7559; www.hostal110.com; Malecón San Martín Nte 110; d S150-170, extra person S30; 🅿) has 14 spacious and neat tiled rooms and apartments – some of which sleep up to six – staggered over a swimming pool on the cliffside. Guests pay the higher rate on Saturdays. On

ARTISAN STUDIOS OF LURÍN

Lurín is a working-class enclave 50km south of Central Lima on the Panamericana. At its southern edge, crafts collective **Ichimay Wari** (☎01-430-3674; www.ichimaywari.org; Jirón Jorge Chávez, Manzana 22, Lote A; ⏰8am-1pm & 2-5pm Mon-Fri) has its studios. Here, talented artisans from Ayacucho produce traditional *retablos* (religious dioramas), pottery, Andean-style Christmas decorations and the colorful clay trees known as *arbolitos de la vida* (trees of life). Your best bet is to make an appointment 24 hours in advance to tour individual studios and meet the artisans.

A taxi from Lima costs around S100 round-trip. By bus from the Puente Benavides or Puente Primavera, take one headed to Lurín, San Bartolo or San Miguel. Get off at the main stoplight in Lurín. From there, hail a *mototaxi* (motorcycle taxi) and ask them to take you south to the Barrio Artesano. Parts of Lurín can get rough; take taxis and keep your camera stowed.

the far southern edge of town (take a *mototaxi*), facing the soccer field, the recommended **Restaurant Rocío** (01-430-8184; www.restaurant-rocio.com; Urb Villa Mercedes, Mz A, Lte 5-6; mains S20-50; 11am-11pm) serves *leche de tigre* (seafood broth) and fresh fish grilled, fried and bathed in garlic.

Further south, **Punta Hermosa**, with its relentless waves, is *the* surfer spot. The town has plenty of accommodations. A good choice is the compact **Punta Hermosa Surf Inn** (01-230-7732, 505-8810-4144; www.puntahermosasurfinn.com; Bolognesi 407, cnr Pacasmayo; dm/s/d incl breakfast S55/70/150; @), which has six rooms, a cozy hangout area with hammocks and cable TV. Note: weekend rates are S30 higher for private rooms and S10 higher for shared rooms. The largest waves in Peru, which can reach a height of 10m, are found nearby at **Pico Alto** (at Panamericana Km 43).

Punta Rocas, a little further south, is also popular with experienced surfers (annual competitions are held here), who generally crash at the basic **Hostal Hamacas** (505-8810-4144; www.hostalhamacas.com; Panamericana Km 47; s/d with air-con S124/139, with fan S77/93), right on the beach. There are 15 rooms and five bungalows (which sleep six), all with private bathrooms, hot water and ocean views. There is an on-site **restaurant** during the high season (October to April). It also rents boards.

To get to these beaches, take a bus signed 'San Bartolo' from the Panamericana Sur at the Puente Primavera in Lima. You can get off at any of the beach towns along the route, but in many cases it will be a 1km to 2km hike down to the beach. (Local taxis are usually waiting by the road.) A one-way taxi from Lima runs between S70 and S110.

There are also beaches to the south, such as Pucusana.

Carretera Central

The Carretera Central (Central Hwy) heads directly east from Lima, following the Rímac valley into the foothills of the Andes and on to La Oroya in Peru's central highlands.

Minibuses to Chosica leave frequently from Arica at the Plaza Bolognesi. These can be used to travel to Puruchuco (S3, 50 minutes) and Chosica (S4, two hours). Recognizing sites from the road can be difficult, so let the driver know where you want to get off.

Puruchuco

01

The site of **Puruchuco** (01-321-5623; museopuruchuco.perucultural.org.pe; admission S5; guided groups S20; 8:30am-4pm Tue-Sun) hit the news in 2002 when about 2000 well-preserved mummy bundles were unearthed from the enormous Inca cemetery. It's one of the biggest finds of its kind, and the multitude of grave goods included a number of well-preserved *quipu*. The site has a highly reconstructed chief's house, with one room identified as a guinea-pig ranch. Situated amid the shantytown of Túpac Amaru, Puruchuco is 13km from Central Lima. (It is best to take a taxi, S30 one-way from Lima.) A signpost on the highway marks the turnoff, and from here it is several hundred meters along a road to the right.

Cajamarquilla

01

Another pre-Columbian site, **Cajamarquilla** (01-321-5623; 9am-4pm) is a crumbling adobe city that was built up by the Wari culture (AD 700–1100) on the site of a settlement originally developed by people of the Lima culture. A road to the left from Lima at about Km 10 (18km from Central Lima) goes to the Cajamarquilla zinc refinery, almost 5km from the highway. The ruins are located about halfway along the refinery road; take a turn to the right along a short road. There are signs, but ask the locals for the *zona arqueológica* if you have trouble finding them.

During research, this site was closed for restoration. Check with Puruchuco or iPerú (p100) for updates.

Chosica

01

About 40km from Lima lies the rustic mountain town of Chosica, which sits at 860m above sea level, above the fog line. In the early half of the 20th century, it was a popular weekend getaway spot for *limeños* intent on soaking up sun in winter. Today its popularity has declined, though some visitors still arrive for day trips. The plaza is lined with restaurants, and in the evenings *anticucho* vendors gather along some of the fountain-lined promenades. From Chosica, a minor road leads to the ruins of **Marcahuasi**.

South Coast

Includes ➡

Best Places to Eat

- ➡ Café Da Vinci (p138)
- ➡ As de Oro's (p114)
- ➡ Mamashana (p131)
- ➡ El Chorito (p120)

Best Places to Stay

- ➡ Casa-Hacienda San José (p111)
- ➡ Banana's Adventure (p125)
- ➡ Hotel El Molino (p110)
- ➡ Hotel Oro Viejo (p131)

Why Go?

This wild and lonely coast entrances visitors with teetering sand dunes, verdant desert oases, forgotten fishing villages, ancient earth drawings, and plenty of wild open space for the imagination to run wild.

It's a stark, dry corner of earth – caught between the Andes and the sea – that only comes to life in the fertile river valleys that produce wine and fruit, providing visitors with a fleeting relief from the relentless beat of the brown desolate desert.

Most adventures take you on a tried-and-true trail that begins with rafting in Lunahuaná, wildlife watching in the Islas Ballestas, sandboarding out of Huacachina and a requisite stop to the mysterious lines and odd geoglyphs that decorate the blank desert canvas outside Nazca. Step beyond the outlines of this Gringo Trail to discover virgin surf spots, vibrant agricultural villages and spirited and unassuming cultural beats.

When to Go

Nazca

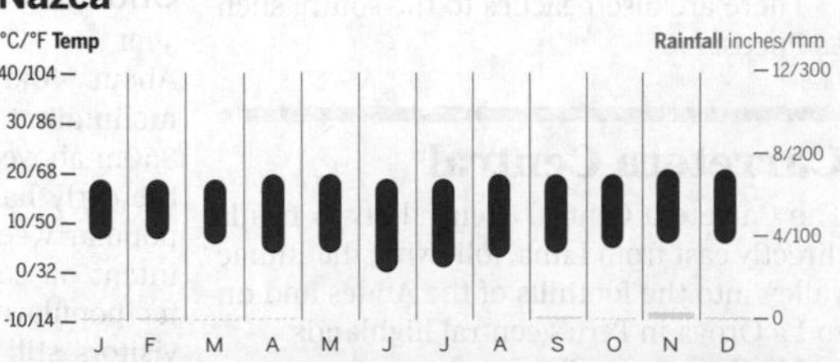

Jan–Mar High summer means the main coastal beach resorts are open and pulsating with energy.

Mar There are grape harvests and accompanying wine festivals in Lunahuaná and Ica.

Jun & Jul Cooler temperatures, fewer tourists and esoteric festivals are enjoyed in Chincha and Ica.

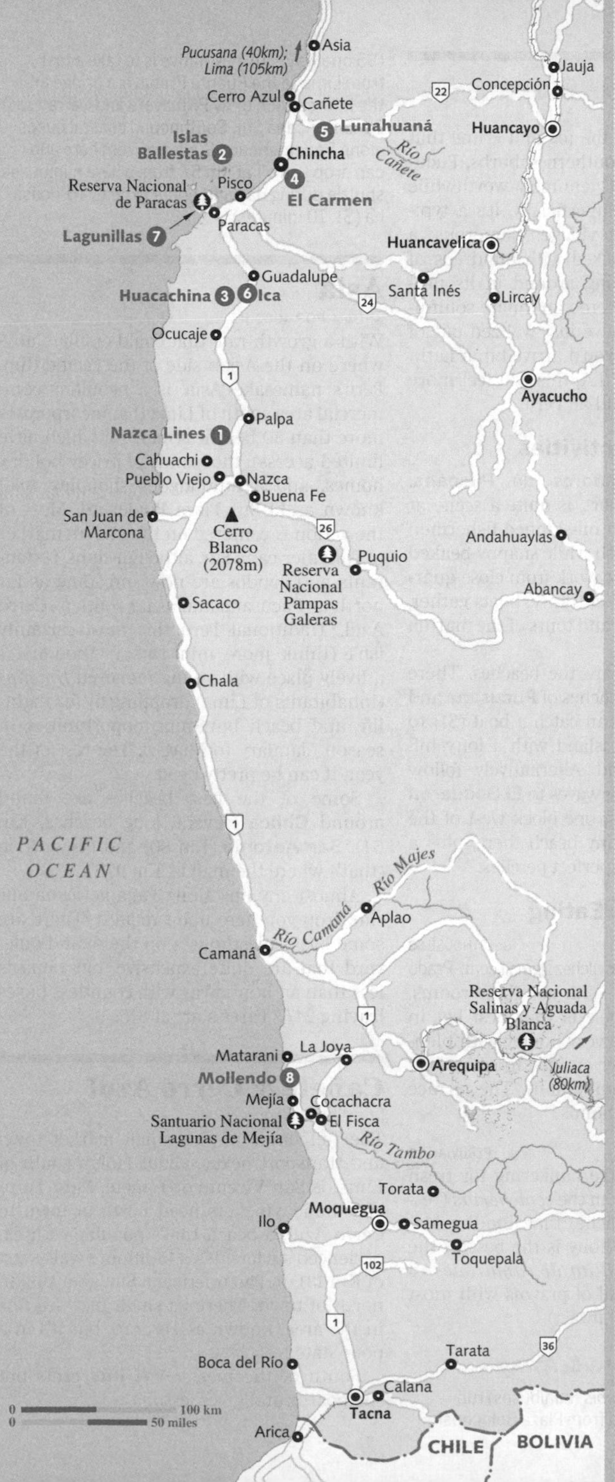

South Coast Highlights

1. Deciphering the mysteries of the **Nazca Lines** (p130) with a once-in-a-lifetime flight-seeing tour.
2. Capturing the wild and dodging guano bombs as you visit sea lion and bird colonies on a boat tour to **Islas Ballestas** (p115).
3. Watching the sun set atop a giant sand dune overlooking the desert oasis of **Huacachina** (p124).
4. Finding your rhythm with live Afro-Peruvian music and dance at **Casa-Hacienda San José** (p111) in El Carmen.
5. Rafting the rip-roarious rapids of Río Cañete in the adventure nexus of **Lunahuaná** (p109).
6. Tasting some of Peru's best wines and piscos at the **Bodega Tacama** (p121) near Ica.
7. Hiking across the deserted Paracas peninsula for a seafood lunch in **Lagunillas** (p118).
8. Extending your journey beyond the Gringo Trail with a surf safari to offbeat **Mollendo** (p134).

Pucusana

☎01 / POP 10,000

Materializing out of the fog and grime that hangs over Lima's southern suburbs, Pucusana marks the first genuinely worthwhile stop on the coast. Superficially, it's a typical Peruvian fishing village: clamorous, a little grubby and packed with hundreds of wooden boats bobbing around in its protected harbor. But there's an innate soulfulness here too. If you've just waltzed out of Miraflores thinking you'd arrived in a Latin American version of LA, this will feel more like the real warts-and-all Peru.

Sights & Activities

Gremio de Pescadores de Puscana, Pucusana's fishing port, is quite a scene at any time of day with oil-skinned fishermen battling with huge fish while snappy-beaked pelicans inspect their work from close quarters. Just outside the entrance, boats gather, offering fishing trips and tours of the marina (from S40).

Other drawcards are the beaches. There are the small town beaches of **Pucusana** and **Las Ninfas**, or you can catch a boat (S1) to **La Isla**, an offshore island with a lofty hill and a strand of sand. Alternatively, follow the sound of crashing waves to **El Boquerón** blowhole, located just one block west of the Malecón. There's a tiny beach there, plus a few restaurants with perfect perches.

Sleeping & Eating

Hospedaje 717 GUESTHOUSE **$$**
(☎01-430-9248; jramosvilchez@gmail.com; Prado 717; s/d S100/150; wi-fi) With just three rooms, this affable guesthouse is your best bet in town. The rooms are very homey with plenty of doilies and other antique touches. Just like staying with your granny. The terrace restaurant is a huge bonus.

Restaurante Jhony PERUVIAN **$$**
(mains S20-30) If you're hankering for fresh seafood, you'll find it in the *cevicherías* (restaurants serving ceviche) that line the Malecón. Restaurante Jhony is the best of the cluster; try the *tortillita de camarones* (a thick tasty omelet full of prawns with most of their anatomy still intact).

Getting There & Away

From central Lima, *combis* (minibuses) run frequently to Pucusana from Plaza Bolognesi (S5 one way). An alternative is to take a taxi from Lima to the Puente Primavera bridge at the intersection of Av Primavera and Carretera Panamericana Sur. Southbound coastal buses along Panamericana Sur leave from here and can drop you off at Km 57, from where minibuses shuttle during daylight hours to central Pucusana (S1, 10 minutes).

Asia

☎01 / POP 4000

With a growth rate that could emulate anywhere on the Asian side of the Pacific Rim, Peru's namesake 'Asia' is a nebulous commercial area south of Lima that incorporates more than 30 beaches (many of which have limited access), thousands of pricey holiday homes, and a humongous shopping mall known as El Sur Plaza Boulevard. Most of the action is centered on the 97.5km marker of Panamericana Sur, although clubs, restaurants and condos are now spreading as far north as Pucusana and as far south as Cerro Azul. Traditional Peru this most certainly isn't (think more mini-Dubai), though it's a lively place with young moneyed *limeños* (inhabitants of Lima) dropping by for nightlife and beach bumming opportunities in season (January to March). The rest of the year, it can be pretty dead.

Some of the best beaches are found around **Chilca** (several long beaches, Km 64), **San Antonio** (Km 80) and **Playa Asia** (that's where the mall is, Km 97.5).

Almost any bus along Panamericana Sur can drop you here upon request. There are some basic guesthouses on the main boulevard that are quite expensive, but Lima is less than an hour away with countless buses leaving 24/7. Fares start at S16.

Cañete & Cerro Azul

☎01 / POP 37,000

The full name of this small market town and transport nexus, about 145km south of Lima, is San Vicente de Cañete. Most Peruvian holidaymakers head north of town to Cerro Azul, a beach that's popular with experienced surfers. It's a 15-minute walk west of Km 131 on Panamericana Sur, about 15km north of town. There's a small Inca sea fort in the area, known as **Huarco**, but it's in a poor state.

South of the pier, a **VW Bus** rents out surfboards and gives lessons.

Sleeping & Eating

Cerro Azul Hostal HOTEL $$
(☎01-284-6052; www.cerroazulhostal.com; Puerto Viejo 106, Cerro Azul; r S180;) This surfer-friendly hostal with chamber-like rooms and rock-hard beds is less than 100m from the shoreline, just south of the pier.

Restaurant Juanito PERUVIAN $$
(Rivera del Mar; mains S20-25; ⌚8am-9pm) Restaurant Juanito is a popular local pick of the beachfront restaurants, all of which serve fresh seafood.

Getting There & Away

From Lima, buses for Pisco or Ica can drop you at Cañete and sometimes Cerro Azul (S15 to S21, 2½ hours). Buses back to Lima are invariably crowded, especially on Sunday from January to April. There are also *combis* between Cañete and Cerro Azul (S2.50, 30 minutes) or south to Chincha (S2, one hour).

Lunahuaná

☎01 / POP 3600 / ELEV 1700M

The small town of Lunahuaná rises like a slice of desert romance above the foggy and grubby coastal strip south of Lima. Reached via a winding 38km road that tracks east from the noisy settlement of Cañete, it appears almost magically, a thin strip of broccoli green amid the dusty desert that gleams with a touch of Middle Eastern promise. But, there are no Bedouin tents or wailing minarets here. Instead, Lunahuaná's life and times are split between wine-production and river running. Both owe their existence to the seasonably turbulent Rio Cañete, whose class IV rapids provide cheap thrills for brave rafters and a vital form of irrigation for the local vineyards.

Some people incorporate Luanahuaná into an overnighter from Lima, and it's certainly worth the effort. The best time to show up is during the second week of March for the grape harvest, **Fiesta de la Vendimia**. An **adventure-sports festival** is usually held in late February or early March.

Sights

Lunahuaná is small with little of architectural significance outside its main square, which is crowned by the **Iglesia Santiago Apostal** dating from 1690. The square's arched *portales* (walkways) hide bars and shops that specialize in wine and pisco.

SOUTH COAST SURF SPOTS

The South Coast is relatively virgin surf territory. Grab a four-by-four, boards and a case of *cerveza* (beer) to pioneer a huge swath of unexplored Pacific. Unfortunately, up north near Asia, many sections of coastline have been artificially 'privatized' by condo complexes, but there are still plenty of backwoods breaks to discover, with consistent winter swells. Here are some hints from www.magicseaweed.com.

➡ **Mollendo** (p134) has 1m to 2m waves on a 'mushy' beach break right in town, and there are a half-dozen named breaks south of here on the coastal road and around **Ilo** (p136).

➡ **Cerro Azul** (p108) is a top spot, with a long left point break.

➡ From **Tacna** (p137) head to the coast for top breaks, including **Boca del Río**, known for short fun rides; **Punta Colorado**, a bodyboarder fave; and a powerful left point break at **Caleta Sama**.

From the square, it's a five-minute walk up to a scenic **mirador** with great views of the town and its surrounding greenery.

Bodega Santa Maria WINERY
(www.bodegasantamaria.com; Km 39 Carr Cañete-Lunahuaná) A very civilized semi-industrial winery 1km north of town with flowery grounds and large wooden casks that retain the air of an Andalucian sherry bodega. Free samples of the sweet-ish wine (red, white and rosé) and powerful pisco varietals are laid on in an aromatic tasting room. It also sells locally made honey.

Catapalla VILLAGE
A tiny settlement 6km further up the valley from Lunahuaná, Catapalla is notable for one of the valley's oldest artisanal wineries, the venerable **La Reyna de Lunahuaná** (☎99-477-7117; ⌚7am-1pm & 2-5pm) FREE, which presides over the main plaza. The owners here can teach you the ABCs of pisco (Peruvian grape brandy) and wine production.

The village's other main feature is its **Puente Colgante** (suspension bridge) that hangs precariously over the Río Cañete's angry rapids. A one-way taxi ride to Catapalla from Lunahuaná should cost from S6, but you may have to wait until a car shows up for the return.

Incahuasi RUINS
(Km 39 Carr Cañete-Lunahuaná; admission S5; 9am-5pm) The most notable archaeological site in the Cañete Valley is Incahuasi, the rough-walled ruins of the military headquarters of the 10th Inca king Túpac Yupanqui, located on the western outskirts of Lunahuaná. It is thought that the original buildings date from 1438-ish, soon after the ascension of Emperor Pachacuti. You won't find a lot of signage or fellow travelers here, but therein lies the attraction. The ruins are on the main road 10km west of Lunahuaná.

A taxi should cost S10 to S12 round-trip.

Activities

River running

River running (rafting) can be done year-round, but the best time is between December and April, the rainy months in the Andes when the Río Cañete runs high. For rafting purposes, the river is split into three sections. The hardest (Ruta Alta) is the section east of Lunahuaná up to the village of Catapalla, which is graded III–IV in summer. The easier sections to the west between Lunahuaná and Paullo, and Paullo and Socsi are graded I–III and are only doable in the summer.

Reputable rafting companies include **Río Cañete Expediciones** (01-284-1271; www.riocanete.com), based at Camping San Jerónimo, and **Laberinto Explorer** (01-284-1057; laberinto_explorer@hotmail.com; Jiron Bolognesi 476), a couple of blocks from Lunahuaná's main plaza. Most trips require a minimum of four people (you'll be paired up onsite), and last between one and three hours. Costs range from S60 and S330.

Ziplining

Satisfying a growing international craze for ziplining (canopy tours), Luanahuaná has come up with a real corker fitted out with five cables that shoot vertigo-shunners over the Río Cañete for a total 'zip' distance of 2500m – one of Latin America's longest. The price for the full five lines is S100. Zippers launch into thin air from Camping San Jerónimo.

Abseiling

For a more vertical drop, you can abseil (rappel) down a cliff face overlooking the Cañete river approximately 7km north of town. Most agencies in Av Grau organize excursions.

Cycling

Located high above the car-crazed coast, Lunahuaná is easily cycled; indeed, bikes are a handy way of visiting some of the outlying sites and wine bodegas. Decent machines with gears generally cost S40 for two hours and can be procured from most of the travel companies on Av Grau.

Sleeping

Hostal Los Andes HOTEL $
(01-284-1041; Los Andes; s/d/tr S40/50/70;) A basic but dependable three-storied yellow block with some 2nd-floor rooms offering peek-a-boo river views. There's hot water and cable TV.

Camping San Jerónimo CAMPGROUND $
(01-284-1271; Carretera Cañete–Lunahuaná, Km 33; sites per person S15) This campground borders the river at the far west of town. Base camp for Río Cañete Expediciones, it has good facilities and a free artificial rock-climbing wall for guests.

Hostal Río Alto HOTEL $$
(01-284-1125; www.rioaltohotel.com; Km 39 Carr Cañete-Lunahuaná; s/d S156/177;) About 1km along the highway east of Lunahuaná, this friendly guesthouse looks down to the river from a shady terrace overrun with plants. Rooms, though plain, are modern and have hot showers.

★**Hotel El Molino** HOTEL $$$
(01-378-6061; www.hotelelmolino.com.pe; Malecon Araoz Km 39 Carretera Cañete-Lunahuana; s/d S350/550;) Not far from the 'beast' of Lima's southern suburbs lies the 'beauty' of El Molino, a lovingly tended hotel complex set on the banks of the Cañete river on the cusp of Luanahuná. The hotel opened in 2011 with boutique-style rooms encased in glassy river-facing units.

There are two pools, table football, and a fine restaurant in the beautifully landscaped grounds where tranquility reigns bar the odd triumphant whoop of a passing rafter.

Refugio de Santiago HOTEL $$$
(99-199-1259; www.refugiodesantiago.com; Km 31 Carr Cañete-Lunahuaná; r per person incl breakfast/full-board S240/450) This renovated colonial home a few kilometers west of Lunahuaná is the ultimate relaxing getaway. Rooms are rustic but elegant and the grounds feature a fragrant botanical garden and a restaurant that serves textbook local specialties (mains S32 to S48). The rates

also include guided walks through the local orchards.

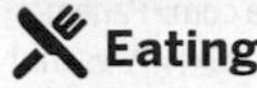

Eating

Sabores de mi Tierra PERUVIAN $
(Bolognesi 199; meals from S6) Cheap, earthy flavors served up for as little as S6 for a main plus starter. Try the chicken stew and prawn chowder.

Don Ignacio La Casa del Pisco PERUVIAN $
(Plaza de Armas; mains from S10) One of the best pisco-biased restaurants on the main square, where you can dilute the local 'rocket fuel' with typical food from the area, including memorable crawfish.

Getting There & Away

From Cañete, catch a *combi* to Imperial (S1, 10 minutes), from where *combis* also run to Lunahuaná (S3.50, 45 minutes). Faster *colectivos* (shared taxis) wait for passengers on the main road, just downhill from the plaza in Lunahuaná, and then race back to Imperial (S4, 25 minutes).

Chincha

☎056 / POP 194,000

Gloriously chaotic or frustratingly anarchic (depending on your tolerance for dust and noise), Chincha is Peru uncut and unpackaged, an unregulated mess of buses, taxis and jay-walking humanity. On the surface it could be any Peruvian town in any south coast province, but closer scrutiny unearths some engrossing details: sugar cane juice sellers, black African figurines offered as souvenirs, and menus advertising *criolla* (coastal) specialties. Chincha is a stronghold of Afro-Peruvian culture, a small and little-known component of the national whole that testifies to a brutal slave past.

Sights

There's not much to see in the city center, although the main square with its terracotta **church** and tall, sinuous palm trees is surprisingly pleasant.

★Casa-Hacienda San José MUSEUM
(☎056-31-3332; www.casahaciendasanjose.com; El Carmen; admission S20; ⏲9am-noon, 3-5pm Mon-Fri & 9am-noon Sat & Sun) Providing reason alone to make the trip down from Lima, this former slave plantation with its stately hacienda offers a rare opportunity for Afro-Peruvian historical immersion – some of it gilded, some of it gruesome.

One-hour tours of the hacienda and its famous catacombs include strolls through the original building, with its fine baroque chapel that dates from 1688.

Surviving artifacts include frescoes, agricultural equipment, and brutal remnants of a system once used to subjugate the slaves including an extensive web of catacombs and underground tunnels (which you explore with a candle). Should you arrive on a Sunday be sure to stay for the dinner buffet show (S70), which is accompanied by athletic Afro-Peruvian dancing in the shaded courtyard. A spectacularly ruined cotton factory, dating from 1913, sits next door.

El Carmen District VILLAGE
Veterans of Cuba have been known to double take in El Carmen, a place where African and Latin American cultures collide with hip-gyrating results. The small rustic 'village' is famous for its rhythm-heavy Afro-Peruvian music, heard in the *peñas* (bars and clubs featuring live folkloric music). The best lie about 15km outside town and there are two simple affairs on the town square.

The best times to visit are during the cultural festivals.

Ballumbrosio Estate HISTORIC BUILDING
(San José 325) The home of El Carmen's most famous dancing family is a museum to Afro-Peruvian culture and music breaks out here spontaneously most weekends. Pop in if you're in the village to view the photos and paintings and see what's up.

La Plazuela WINERY
(Av Benavides 501) The local wine industry is evident in the shops that line Av Benavides between the square and the bus station. La Plazuela will pour a few gratis mini-glasses of the eye-wateringly sweet local wine and the mega-strong pisco. The owners run a restaurant next door, should you fancy further top-ups.

Archaeological Sites

In ancient times, the small Chincha empire flourished in this region until it was clobbered by the Incas in the late 15th century. The best surviving archaeological sites in the area are **Tambo de Mora**, on the coast about 10km from Chincha, and the temple of **La Centinela** northwest of the city, about 8km off Panamericana Sur. Both can be visited by taxi (about S15 one way).

Festivals & Events

The abundance of local festivals includes the **Verano Negro** (late Feb–early Mar), **Fiestas Patrias** (July 28 & 29) and **La Virgen del Carmen de Chincha** (Dec 27). During these times, minibuses run from Chincha to El Carmen all night long, and the *peñas* are full of frenzied *limeños* (inhabitants of Lima) and locals dancing. One traditional dance not to try at home: 'El Alcatraz,' when a gyrating male dancer with a candle attempts to set fire to a handkerchief attached to the back of his partner's skirt.

Sleeping & Eating

Bare-bones cheap hotels and *chifas* (Chinese restaurants) surround Chincha's main plaza. Most fill up and double or triple their prices during festivals, though you can always avoid this problem by dancing all night and taking an early morning bus back to Lima or further south along the coast.

In El Carmen, a few local families will take in overnight guests and cook meals for between S10 and S20 per person per night – ask around.

Casa-Hacienda San José Hotel HISTORIC HOTEL $$
(056-31-3332; www.casahaciendasanjose.com; El Carmen; r from S200;) Extend your stay in El Carmen at this former slave plantation. It's the best-preserved historic hotel on the Peruvian Coast. The grounds are off-the-chart, with small gardens, antiques and a luscious pool. While the backside bungalows offer all the modern conveniences, a stay in the historic wing is where it's at.

If service improves, we'll definitely make this a top choice in future editions.

Casa Andina – Chincha Sausal BOUTIQUE HOTEL $$
(056-26-2451; www.casa-andina.com; Panamericana Sur Km 197.5; d S204;) A rather odd outpost of Peru's plushest hotel chain, glued to the frankly horrible Panamericana Sur 1km north of Chincha's bus station, the Sausal is aimed at the corporate business market and is thus a bit stuffy and officious. As to be expected, facilities are upper-crust with flowered grounds, luxury bed-linens and a decent restaurant.

Hostal El Condado HOTEL $$
(056-26-1424; Panamericana Sur Km195; r from S100;) An air freshener on the congested Panamericana Sur, El Condado rarely disappoints with super clean rooms, welcoming service and a rather nice restaurant where the portions aren't small.

Restaurant Doña Jita PERUVIAN $
(Av Benavides 293; mains from S6) Set menus are the order of the day here in a communal atmosphere. Choose from the two-course *ejecutivo* (executive; S10) or *económico* (economic; S6) *menú* (set meal). The garbanzo soup and *lomo saltado* (strips of beef stir-fried with onions, tomatoes, potatoes and chili) are among the best (and cheapest) you'll taste this side of Lima.

Getting There & Around

There are many companies based on the Panamericana Sur with buses running through Chincha en route between Lima (S20 to S23, 2½ hours) and Ica (S7 to S10, two hours). If you're headed to Pisco, most southbound buses can drop you off at the San Clemente turnoff on Panamericana Sur (S4), from where you can catch frequent *colectivos* and *combis* for the 6km trip into Pisco (S3). From Chincha, *combis* headed north to Cañete (S2, one hour) and south to

AFRO-PERUVIAN MUSIC & DANCE

The mesmerizing beats and lightning-speed movements of this traditional art form are guaranteed to make you want to get up and dance. During the colonial period, when Spanish colonizers banned the use of drums, African slaves working on Peruvian plantations began using hollow wooden crates (now called a *cajón*) and donkey jawbones to create percussion that now forms the base of this distinct musical style. Often music is accompanied by an impressive flamenco-style dance called *zapateo* and impassioned singing.

Over the past few decades, groups such as Perú Negro and the Ballumbrosio family have garnered quite a following both nationally and internationally, making it their mission to preserve Peru's African heritage through the performance of its music and dance. If you're in the right place at the right time, you can catch one of these shows in the community that is famous for it, El Carmen.

Paracas (S3, one hour) leave from near Plazuela Bolognesi.

Combis to El Carmen (S2-2.50, 30 minutes) leave from Chincha's central market area, a few blocks from the main plaza.

The plaza is 500m from Panamericana Sur where the coastal buses stop.

Pisco

056 / POP 58,200

Crushed by a 2007 earthquake that destroyed its infrastructure but not its spirit, Pisco is a town on the rebound, reinventing itself almost daily with the resilience of an immortal phoenix. Irrespective of the substantial damage, the town remains open for business, promoting itself, along with the nearby beach resort of El Chaco (Paracas), as a base for forays to the Paracas Reserve and Islas Ballestas, although El Chaco trumps it in terms of location and choice of facilities.

Pisco shares its name with the national beverage, a brandy that is made throughout the region. The area is of historical and archaeological interest, having hosted one of the most highly developed pre-Inca civilizations – the Paracas culture from 700 BC until AD 400. Later it acted as a base for Peru's revolutionary fever in the early 19th century.

Although the Pisco-Paracas area is spread out, it's easy to get around. Public transportation between Pisco and the harbor at Paracas, 15km further south along the coast, leaves from Pisco's market area or the main plaza in the El Chaco beach area of Paracas.

Sights & Activities

It is still perfectly viable to use Pisco as a base for tours of the Paracas Peninsula and the Islas Ballestas. Various agencies dot the central area.

Plaza de Armas PLAZA

Post-earthquake, Pisco's main Plaza de Armas is a mishmash of the vanquished and the saved. The equestrian **statue of José de San Martín**, sword bravely raised in defiance, falls into the latter category. Another survivor is the **Moorish Municipalidad** building (town hall), dating from 1929, whose wrecked shell awaits a major refurb. Pisco's biggest earthquake casualty was the colonial **San Clemente Cathedral**. A new modern red-bricked church has gone up in its place, financed with Spanish money – not so pretty, but an achievement all the same.

Commerce has returned to pedestrianized San Martin, which runs west from the plaza and is beautified with benches, flower-covered trellises and a refreshing fountain.

Aproturpisco TOURS

(056-50-7156; aproturpisco@hotmail.com; San Francisco 112) This laid-back but business-like travel company organizes trips to all the local sights, including Islas Ballestras (S70) and even the Nazca Lines (US$140). Guides speak six languages, including Hebrew.

Sleeping

Many hotels will pick you up from the San Clemente turnoff on the Panamericana Sur.

Posada Hispana Hotel HOTEL $

(056-53-6363; www.posadahispana.com; Bolognesi 236; s/d S50/70; P) This is as good as it gets. Rooms feature local textiles and hardwood accents. There's a rooftop terrace for kicking back. The restaurant is one of the best in town, with a S10 lunchtime *menú* (set meal) served in a two-level bamboo dining room.

Hostal La Casona HOTEL $

(056-53-2703; www.hostallacasona.com; San Juan de Dios 252; s S60-70, d S70-90; P) A massive wooden door serves as a slightly deceiving portal to this hotel half a block from the main square, which, though clean, isn't anywhere near as grand as its entryway suggests. The rooms can be a bit stale, but air out quickly.

Hostal Villa Manuelita HOTEL $$

(056-53-5218; www.villamanuelitahotel.com; San Francisco 227; s/d/tr incl breakfast S110/150/190; P) While it had to be heavily renovated post-earthquake, this hotel still retains the grandeur of its colonial foundations. Plus, it's very conveniently located only half a block from the plaza.

Eating & Drinking

Only a few cafes in Pisco open early enough for breakfast before an Islas Ballestas tour, so many hotels include breakfast in their rates.

La Concha de Tus Mares PERUVIAN $$

(Calle Muelle 992; mains S15-25) Old pictures of what Pisco used to look like pre-2007 adorn the walls of this nostalgic place next to the Colegio Alexander Von Humboldt about 1km south of the center. The fish comes in big portions and is lauded by the locals.

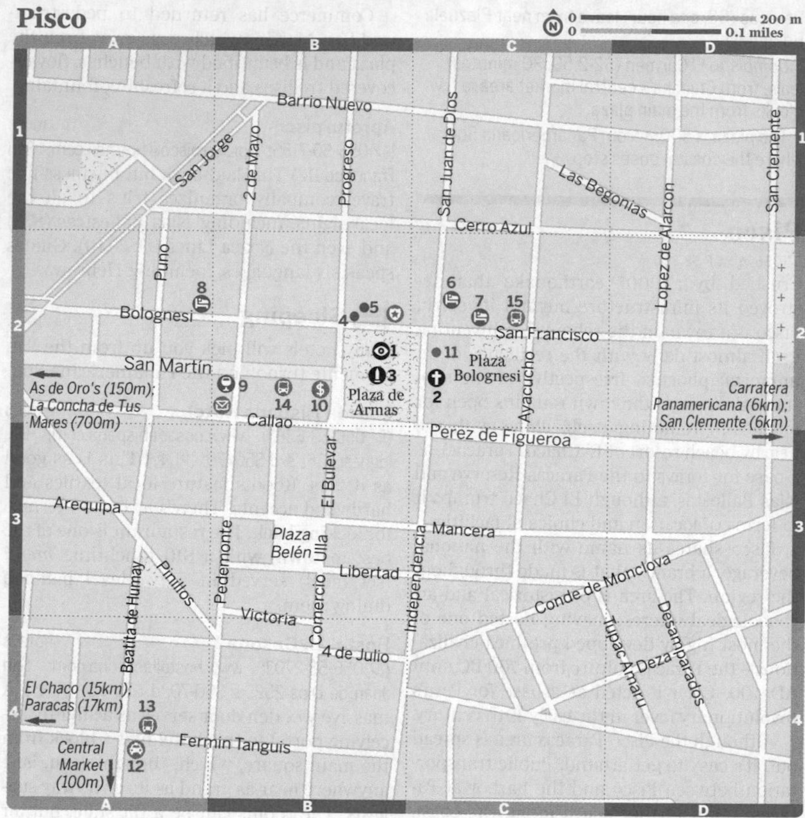

Pisco

Sights
1 Plaza de Armas ... B2
2 San Clemente Cathedral ... C2
3 Statue of José de San Martín ... B2

Activities, Courses & Tours
4 Aproturpisco ... B2
5 Paracas Overland ... B2

Sleeping
6 Hostal La Casona ... C2
7 Hostal Villa Manuelita ... C2
8 Posada Hispana Hotel ... A2

Drinking & Nightlife
9 Taberna de Don Jaime ... B2

Information
10 Interbank ... B2
11 Muncipalidad ... C2

Transport
12 Colectivos to Paracas and the San Clemente turnoff on the Panamerica ... A4
13 Combis to Paracas ... A4
14 Flores ... B2
15 Ormeño ... C2

★ **As de Oro's** PERUVIAN $$$
(www.asdeoros.com.pe; San Martín 472; mains S30-50; ⊙noon-midnight Tue-Sun) Talk about phoenix from the flames; the plush As de Oro serves up spicy mashed potato with octopus, plaice with butter and capers, and grilled prawns with fried yucca and tartare sauce at tables overlooking a small swimming pool, as the rest of the town struggles back to its feet.

Taberna de Don Jaime BAR
(☎056-53-5023; San Martín 203; ⊙4pm-2am) This clamorous tavern is a favorite with

locals and tourists alike. It is also a showcase for artisanal wines and piscos. On weekends, the crowds show up to dance to live Latin and rock tunes into the small hours.

Information

There's no tourist office in Pisco, but travel agencies on the main plaza and **police** (☎056-53-2884; San Francisco 132; ⊙24hr) help when they can. Everything else you'll need is found around the Plaza de Armas, including internet cafes.

DANGERS & ANNOYANCES

On its knees after the earthquake, Pisco acquired a reputation for crime, but the curtain is lifting. The commerce-packed streets should be fine during the daytime (there's a notable police presence in the city center). Nonetheless, it is best to utilize taxis after dark, particularly around the bus station and market areas. If you arrive late, get the ticket agent at your bus company office to hail you a reputable cab (*taxi de confianza*).

MONEY

Interbank (San Martín 101) Has a 24-hour global ATM.

Getting There & Around

Pisco is 6km west of Panamericana Sur, and only buses with Pisco as the final destination actually go there. **Ormeño** (☎056-53-2764; San Francisco), **Flores** (☎056-79-6643; San Martín) and **Soyuz** (www.soyuz.com.pe; Av Ernesto R Diez Canseco 4) offer multiple daily departures north to Lima and south to Ica and Arequipa. There's no direct service from Pisco to Nazca; you'll need to leave from Paracas or change buses in Ica. Indicative costs and durations are as follows:

DESTINATION	COST (S)	DURATION (HR)
Arequipa	60–144	12–15
Ica	5–15	1½–2
Lima	25–70	4½
Nazca	17–35	4

If you're not on a direct bus to either Pisco or Paracas, ask to be left at the San Clemente turnoff on Panamericana Sur, where fast and frequent *colectivos* wait to shuttle passengers to central Pisco's Plaza de Armas (S1.50, 10 minutes) or Paracas (S10, 20 minutes). In the reverse direction, *colectivos* for the San Clemente turnoff leave frequently from near Pisco's central market. After dark, avoid the dangerous market area and take a taxi instead (S5). From the San Clemente turnoff, you can flag down buses, which pass frequently heading either north or south.

Transportation from Pisco to Paracas is possible via *combi* (S1.50, 30 minutes) or *colectivo* (20 minutes), which leave frequently from near Pisco's central market (S3) or the center (S4-5).

Paracas (El Chaco)

The Paracas peninsula's main village, El Chaco – often referred to erroneously as 'Paracas' – is the primary embarkation point for trips to Islas Ballestas and the Reserva Nacional de Paracas. New condos and luxury hotels are found north and south of the village proper. It's a fun place with a lively traveler scene. Most of the action centers on the Malecón, where you'll find a pretty wide selection of restaurants and bars. Its natural attractions and long beaches stand out from many South Coast destinations, and many travelers end up spending at least two or even three nights here, allowing for a day tour to the islands, beachtime and an extended foray across the peninsula. The 2007 earthquake did a lot of damage to the town, but all systems are now go, with a new *malecón*, tourist dock and international airport.

Sights & Activities

The region's essential business is the boat tour of the Islas Ballestas and the one-day sojourn around the bald deserted Paracas peninsula. Birds and sea mammals are the lures here, but, lest we forget, this is also one of Peru's most important archaeological sites thanks primarily to the pre-Inca treasures unearthed by one of the country's most important archaeologists, Julio Tello in the 1920s.

El Chaco

Paracas History Museum MUSEUM
(Av Los Libertadores; admission S10; ⊙9am-5:30pm) Since most of the archaeological booty dug up nearby has been carted off to Lima, Paracas' tiny museum is left with only a few scraps, the most striking of which are the elongated human skulls.

Islas Ballestas

Grandiosely nicknamed the 'poor man's Galapagos,' the **Islas Ballestas** (tours S35, park entrance island only S10, island and peninsula S15) make for a memorable excursion. The only way to get there is on a boat tour, offered by many tour agencies, touts and hotels. Tours leave at 8am, 10am and noon from the Marina Turística de Paracas. The 8am tour usually has the calmest seas and best

BIRD-POO WAR

In the history of pointless wars, the 1864–66 skirmish between Spain and its former colonies of Peru and Chile might seem like the most pointless of them all. Ostensibly, its primary motivation was not self-preservation or saving the world from aliens, but guano, or, to put it less politely, bird-poo. But, although a thoroughly unpleasant substance when dropped from a great height onto your head, guano has long been a vital contributor to the Peruvian economy, and a resource worth protecting from prying outsiders. In the early 19th century, German botanist Alexander von Humboldt sent samples of it to Europe where innovative British farmers found it to be 30 times more efficient than cow dung when used as a fertilizer. By the 1850s a rapidly industrializing Britain was importing 200,000 tons of the crap annually to bolster its agriculture. Suddenly the white droppings that covered Peru's bird-filled Pacific Islands were worth the lion's share of the GDP. Spain understood as much in 1864 when, in an act of post-colonial petulance, it occupied the guano-rich Chincha Islands in an attempt to extract reparations from Peru over a small domestic incident in Lambayeque. Peru didn't hesitate to retaliate. A protracted naval war ensued that dragged in Chile, before the islands and their precious bird-poo were wrenched back from Spain in 1866.

In the conflict-free present, the industry remains lucrative. Layers of sun-baked, nitrogen-rich guano still cover the Chincha Islands, as well as the nearby Islas Ballestas, although the over-fishing of anchovies (the bird's main food source) in the 1960s and 1970s led to a worrying decline in supplies. Today guano production is closely (and peacefully) regulated by Peru's Ministry of Agriculture.

wildlife viewing. While the two-hour tours do not disembark onto the islands, they do get you startlingly close to an impressive variety of wildlife.

None of the small boats have a cabin, so dress to protect against the wind, spray and sun. The sea can get rough, so sufferers of motion sickness should take medication before boarding. Wear a hat (cheap ones are sold at the harbor), as it's not unusual to receive a direct hit of guano (droppings) from the seabirds.

On the outward boat journey, which takes about 30 minutes, you will stop just offshore to admire the famous **Candelabra Geoglyph**, a giant three-pronged figure etched into the sandy hills, which is more than 150m high and 50m wide. No one knows exactly who made the glyph, or when, or what it signifies, but theories abound. Some connect it to the Nazca Lines, while others propound that it served as a navigational guide for sailors and was based on the constellation of the Southern Cross (or even a masonic symbol). Some even believe it to have been inspired by a local cactus species with hallucinogenic properties.

A further hour is spent cruising around the islands' arches and caves and watching large herds of noisy sea lions sprawl on the rocks. The most common guano-producing birds in this area are the guanay cormorant, the Peruvian booby and the Peruvian pelican, seen in colonies several thousand strong. You'll see some extraction facilities on a couple of islands. The Peruvian government still extracts guano (it's a great natural fertilizer) from the islands, but only do so every eight years.

You'll also see cormorants, Humboldt penguins and, if you're lucky, dolphins. Although you can get close enough to the wildlife for a good look, some species, especially the penguins, are more visible with binoculars.

Back on shore, you can grab a bite to eat at one of the many waterfront restaurants near the dock in El Chaco, or you can continue on a tour of the Reserva Nacional de Paracas.

Reserva Nacional de Paracas

This vast desert **reserve** (park entrance Islas Ballestas only S10, island and peninsula S15) occupies most of the Península de Paracas. An alternative to tour operators, taxi drivers who function as guides often wait beyond the dock where passengers disembark in Paracas' beach village of El Chaco, and can take groups into the reserve for around S50 for a three-hour tour. You can also walk or rent a bike from El Chaco – just make sure to allow lots of time, and bring food and plenty of water. To get there, start at the

Reserva Nacional de Paracas

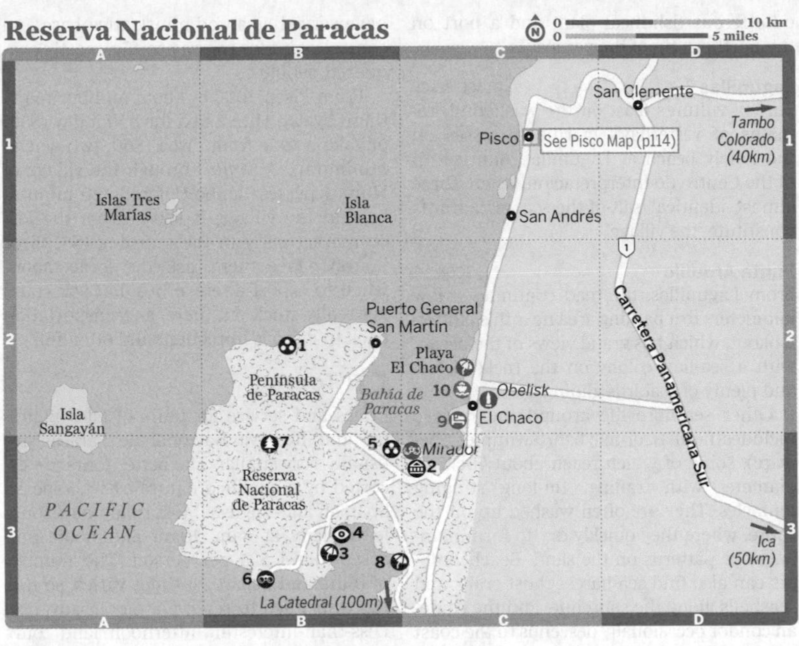

Reserva Nacional de Paracas

obelisk commemorating the landing of the liberator General José de San Martín that lies near the entrance to El Chaco village, and continue on foot along the tarmac road that heads to the south.

Centro de Interpretación MUSEUM
(7am-6pm) FREE Located 1.5km south of the entry point to Reserva Nacional de Paracas, this modest center's displays kick off with a 12-minute rather twee video aimed, it would seem, at wide-eyed teenagers.

The subsequent exhibits on fauna, archaeology and geology are weightier and more inspiring. The bay in front of the complex is the best spot to view Chilean flamingos, and there's a walkway down to a mirador (lookout), from where these birds can best be spotted from June through August.

Paracas Necropolis ARCHAEOLOGICAL SITE
A few hundred meters behind the visitor complex on Cerro Colorado are the 5000-year-old remains of a necropolis related to the Paracas culture, which predated the Incas by more than a thousand years. A stash of more than 400 funerary bundles was found here, each wrapped in many layers of colorful woven shrouds for which the Paracas culture is famous.

There's little to see now; indeed, signs warn you off the site. Lima's Museo Larco and Ica's Museo Regional de Ica exhibit some of the exquisite textiles and other finds from the site.

Beyond the visitor complex, the tarmac road continues around the peninsula to Puerto General San Martín, which has an odoriferous fish-meal plant and a port on the northern tip of the peninsula.

Lagunillas VILLAGE, BEACH
Turkey vultures feast on the washed-up remains of yesterday's marine carcasses on the lonely beach at Lagunillas, 5km south of the Centro de Interpretación, where three almost identical salt-of-the-sea restaurants constitute 'the village'

Punta Arquillo LOOKOUT
From Lagunillas, the road continues a few kilometers to a parking area near this clifftop lookout, which has grand views of the ocean, with a sea-lion colony on the rocks below and plenty of seabirds gliding by.

Other seashore life around the reserve includes flotillas of jellyfish (swimmers beware), some of which reach about 70cm in diameter with trailing, 1m-long stinging tentacles. They are often washed up on the shore, where they quickly dry to form mandala-like patterns on the sand. Beachcombers can also find sea hares, ghost crabs and seashells along the shoreline, and the Andean condor occasionally descends to the coast in search of rich pickings.

La Mina Beach BEACH
This beach is a short drive or walk south of Lagunillas on a dirt road. Sunbathers come here in summer (January to March) when you may find the odd mobile drinks concession set up. Camping is also allowed. Plan to bring all the water you will need, and never camp alone as robberies have been reported. Adjacent is the rockier **El Raspón beach**.

Yumaque Beach & La Catedral BEACH, LANDMARK
The reserve protrudes south a fair few kilometers below the Paracas Peninsula. Dirt roads branch off just east of Lagunillas to Yumaque beach and La Catedral. The latter – a majestic natural arch that jutted out into the sea – was destroyed by the 2007 earthquake. Formed over hundreds of thousands of years of wind and wave erosion, it got toppled in less than a minute. Today it is little more than a sea stack.

Tambo Colorado

An early Inca lowland outpost about 45km northeast of Pisco, **Tambo Colorado** (admission S10; dawn-dusk) was named for the red paint that once completely covered its adobe walls. It's one of the best-preserved sites on the south coast and is thought to have served as an administrative base and control point for passing traffic, mostly conquered peoples.

From Pisco, it takes about an hour to get there by car. Hire a taxi for half a day (S50) or take a tour from Pisco (S60, two-person minimum). A *combi* through the village of Humay passes Tambo Colorado 20 minutes beyond the village; it leaves from the Pisco market early in the morning (S8, three hours). Once there, ask the locals about when to expect a return bus, but you could get really stuck out there, as transportation back to Pisco is infrequent and often full.

Tours

Prices and service for tours of Islas Ballestas and Reserva Nacional de Paracas are usually very similar. The better tours are escorted by a qualified naturalist who speaks Spanish and English. Most island boat tours leave daily at 8am, 10am and noon, and cost around S35 per person. The number of tours and departure times varies, so it is recommended to reserve a day in advance. Less-than-interesting afternoon land tours of the Península de Paracas (S25) briefly stop at the national reserve's visitor center, breeze by coastal geological formations and spend a long time having lunch in a remote fishing village. Tours of the reserve can be combined with an Islas Ballestas tour to make a full-day excursion (S60). Paracas Backpackers House (p119) rents out bikes for S30 (full-day).

PeruKite KITESURFING
(99-456-7802; www.perukite.com; Paracas s/n, Paracas Restaurant) Paracas offers pretty great kitesurfing with limited chop, easy shallow access and good winds. This operation does courses running one hour (US$60), three hours (US$175) and six hours (two days, US$320).

Paracas Explorer GUIDED TOURS
(056-53-1487; www.paracasexplorer.com; Paracas 9) In the El Chaco village of Paracas, this backpacker travel agency offers the usual island and reserve tours, as well as multiday trips that take you to Ica and Nazca (US$80 to US$90 per person).

Paracas Overland GUIDED TOURS
(056-53-3855; www.paracasoverland.com.pe; San Francisco 111) Popular with backpackers, this agency offers tours of the Islas Ballestas with its own fleet of boats, as well as to

the Reserva Nacional de Paracas and Tambo Colorado. It can also arrange sandboarding trips to nearby dunes.

Sleeping

If arriving directly in Paracas, most hotels and hostels will pick you up from the bus terminal upon request.

Paracas Backpackers House HOSTEL $
(056-63-5623; www.paracasbackpackershouse.com.pe; Av Los Libertadores; dm S17.50, s without bathroom S40, d with/without bathroom S80/45;) Of the several 'backpackers hostels' on this strip, this is the original and still the most popular. Most rooms have private baths and look onto the terrace, with hammock and chill area. In front, two-bed 'bungalows' with shared baths offer good value, but don't catch breezes like the upper-storied rooms.

Dorms sleep eight to 10 people with the big-boy on top catching the best breezes.

Willy's House HOSTEL $
(95-688-0822; willyshouse@outlook.es; Calle San Martín; dm/r S20/60;) This upstart backpackers hostel has four-bed dorms, a back chillaxing area with billiards tables and solid clean private rooms. While the rooms could be a bit bigger, this is a strong budget buy. Self-caterers will appreciate the shared kitchen.

Bamboo Lodge HOTEL $$
(99-904-5654; bamboolodgeparacas@hotmail.com; Malecón s/n; r incl breakfast S160-180) If you can score one of the waterfront rooms with their own balconies, this is a top buy. If you only get a room in back, it still ain't half bad. With bamboo everywhere (go figure), simple, light, airy appointments and fab-tiled bathrooms throughout, this is a strong middleweight contender.

Hostal Santa Maria HOTEL $$
(056-77-5799; www.hostalsantamariaparacas.com; Av Paracas s/n, Plaza de Paracas; s/d/tr incl breakfast S80/100/120;) The rooms here are functional and admirably clean, all with cable TV, clean lines and fans to cool off from the considerable heat. There's a rooftop terrace and an annex just down the street. Staff members are knowledgeable and can help arrange tours, though they are sometimes preoccupied with looking after the restaurant next door.

Hospedaje del Pirata HOTEL $$
(056-54-5054; www.refugiodelpirata.com; Av Paracas 6; s S80-100, d S140-180, all incl breakfast;) Rooms are cramped and have poor light, but they get the job done, and some have ocean views. The upstairs terrace provides a pleasant setting to sip a pisco sour while watching the sunset. A fancier new-build across the street has a pool.

Ask nicely if you are staying in the old hotel, and they might just let you use the pool.

Hotel Gran Palma HOTEL $$$
(056-65-5932; www.hotelgranpalma.com; Calle 1 lot 3; s/d incl breakfast S170/260;) This newish hotel offers brain-surgery-clean rooms and breakfast on a pleasant rooftop terrace. The functional minimalist rooms sparkle, but leave little space for embellishment or storage. It's overpriced for what you get, and the service can be a bit abrupt.

Hotel Paracas RESORT $$$
(056-58-1333; www.luxurycollection.com/hotelparacas; Av Paracas 178; r S2048-2170, ste S2294-3155;) A dreamscape plucked from a tourist brochure with puffed cushions, permanently smiling staff, excellent kid's facilities and a luxuriously raked beach, this Starwood resort offers the best high-end rooms in town. The cabaña-style rooms have private balconies and monstrous master baths. Unfortunately, ocean views are limited from many rooms. There are three hotels, two pools and a private dock onsite.

Kayaks, paddle boards and catamarans are included.

Double-Tree Hilton RESORT $$$
(01-617-1000; www.doubletree.com; 2km south of El Chaco; r from US$229;) A top pick for resort styling, this all-suite hotel gives you private patios, a turquoise pool and killer ocean views. The large living areas in the rooms make this a great option for families.

Eating & Drinking

On the waterfront there are loads of lookalike beachfront restaurants serving fresh seafood throughout the day.

Punta Paracas CAFE, INTERNATIONAL $
(Blvd Turístico; mains S15-35; 7am-10pm) Coffee and chocolate brownies hit the spot at this open-all-day cafe that remains lively after most other places have closed.

★**El Chorito** PERUVIAN $$
(Paracas; mains S20-30; ⏲noon-9pm) The Italians come to the rescue in the clean, polished Chorito – part of the Hostal Santa Maria – where a welcome supply of Illy coffee saves you from the otherwise ubiquitous powdered Nescafé. The cooked-to-order fish dishes aren't bad either – all locally caught, of course.

Pisco and Olé PERUVIAN $$
(Malecón s/n; mains S25-35; 📶) Tonier than the other spots on the Malecón, this friendly eatery offers a standard array of Peruvian seafood mashups. The only difference is the affable service and the slightly European styling. It's also a great sunset cocktail spot.

Misk'i BAR
(Calle 1 ; ⏲6pm-close) Strong drinks and well-chilled vibes star at this root-down tourist resto-bar that serves up plenty of international dishes and has a perpetual reggae soundtrack that will keep you skankin' it easy.

Getting There & Around

A new international airport should be servicable by the time this book hits the press. Check to see if any of the Peruvian airlines are servicing the route.

A few buses run daily between Lima and the El Chaco beach district of Paracas (S40 to S55, 3½ hours) before continuing to other destinations south. These include **Cruz del Sur** (www.cruzdelsur.com.pe) and **Oltursa** (www.oltursa.com.pe); the latter also runs direct buses to Nazca, Ica, Arequipa and Lima from Paracas. Prices are the same as from Pisco. Most agencies in El Chaco sell bus tickets including Paracas Explorer (p118).

Transportation from Paracas to Pisco is possible via *combi* (S1.50, 30 minutes), or *colectivo* (S3-5, 20 minutes).

Most trips to Islas Ballestas depart from the new tourist port of **Marina Turística de Paracas** (Malecón s/n, El Chaco).

Ica

☎056 / POP 125,000 / ELEV 420M

Just when you thought the landscape was dry enough for Martians, out jumps Ica, Peru's agricultural 'miracle in the desert' that churns out bumper-crop after bumper-crop of asparagus, cotton and fruits, as well as laying claim to being the nation's leading (and best) wine producer. Ica, like Pisco, sustained significant earthquake damage in 2007 – the graceful cathedral and two other churches suffered serious damage and are undergoing lengthy repairs. Most people who make it this far bed down in infinitely more attractive Huacachina 4km to the west, but Ica has reasons to be cheerful too: the south coast's best museum (outside Arequipa) resides here, plus – arguably – the finest winery in Peru. If Nazca seems too much of a circus, it's also possible to organize Nazca Line excursions from Ica – the desert etchings lie 1½ hours to the south.

Sights & Activities

Ica's main square has been repainted post-Earthquake in generic mustard-yellow to reflect its 'city of eternal sun' moniker. The two sinuous obelisks in its center are supposed to signify the Nazca and Paracas cultures. Elsewhere, bustling commerce has returned.

Museo Regional de Ica MUSEUM
(Ayabaca cuadra 8; admission S10; ⏲8am-7pm Mon-Fri, 9am-6pm Sat & Sun) In the suburban neighborhood of San Isidro, Ica pulls out its trump card: a museum befitting a city three times the size. While it might not be the Smithsonian in terms of layout and design, this understated gem catalogs the two key pre-Inca civilizations on Peru's southern coast, namely the Paracas and Nazca cultures, the former famed for its intricate textiles and the latter for its instantly recognizable ceramics.

Any attempt to understand the region's ancient history should begin here where a whole gamut of locally excavated artifacts is on display.

Unfortunately, the museum's famous riches have attracted malign as well as benign interest. In 2004, the building was robbed, with thieves making off with three priceless textiles.

The museum is 2.5km southwest of the city center. Take a taxi from the Plaza de Armas (S3). You could walk, but it's usually not safe to do so alone, and even larger groups may get hassled.

Iglesia de La Merced CHURCH
(cnr Bolívar & Libertad) Ica's cathedral was the last church the Jesuits built in Peru before their expulsion. It was rebuilt in the late 19th century and contains a finely carved wooden altar. The effects of the 2007 earthquake caused a steeple and part of the roof to collapse. At the time of writing the church was closed for restorations.

Santuario de El Señor de Luren CHURCH
(Cutervo) This fine church has an image of the patron saint that is venerated by pilgrims during Semana Santa and again in October. The streets surrounding the Plaza de Armas display a few impressive Spanish colonial mansions, including along the first block of Libertad. The church tower fell in the 2007 earthquake, but the dome survived. Years later, it is still undergoing extensive renovations.

Iglesia de San Francisco CHURCH
(cnr Municipalidad & San Martín) This hulking church withstood the 2007 earthquake and continues to show off its fine stained-glass windows.

Centro Cultural de la Unica GALLERY
(Calle Bolívar 232; ⏲9am-5pm) FREE This art gallery sits in a restored courtyard next to the cathedral; expositions inside are small but packed with local talent.

Wineries

Ica is Peru's largest and most revered wine producer, though it's desert-defying vineyards are unlikely to get any Euro wine-snobs jumping on a plane anytime soon. The main drawback is 'sweetness'. Even Peru's *semi-seco* (medium-dry) wines are sweet by most yardsticks. Nonetheless, tours around the vineyards can be novel and worthwhile diversions. Most offer free sampling. Bodegas can be visited year-round, but the best time is during the grape harvest from late February until early April.

The countryside around Ica is also scattered with family-owned artisanal bodegas, including **San Juan de Bautista** about a 7km taxi (S7 one way) or *colectivo* (S1.50) ride from Ica's center. *Colectivos* leave from the corner of Municipalidad and Loreto.

Bodega Tacama WINE TASTING
(☎056-58-1030; www.tacama.com; Camino Real s/n, Tinguiña; ⏲9:30am-4:30pm Tue-Sun) FREE Possibly the most professional and lauded of Ica's wineries, Tacama is run out of a sprawling pink hacienda backed by striped fields lined by vines. Eschewing Peru's penchant for sickly sweet wines, Tacama produces some rather good chardonnays and malbecs that might one day give the Chileans a run for their money.

The half-hour free tour and sampling includes a *mirador* (lookout), a guide through the aging process (in French oak barrels, no less) and a glimpse of an old chapel damaged in the 2007 earthquake. Situated 11km northwest of town, you'll have to hire a taxi to get here (S15 each way).

Bodega Ocucaje WINE TASTING
(☎056-40-8011; www.ocucaje.com; Av Principal s/n; ⏲tastings 9am-noon & 2-5pm Mon-Fri, 9am-noon Sat, tours 11am-3pm Mon-Fri) FREE Some of Peru's finest wine is said to come from this bodega, but, unfortunately, it's fairly isolated, more than 30km south of Ica off the Panamericana Sur. Hiring a taxi to reach the winery costs around S30 each way, or you can join a local tour leaving from Ica.

Bodega Vista Alegre WINE TASTING
(www.vistaalegre.com.pe; Camino a La Tinguina, Km 2.5; admission S5; ⏲8am-noon & 1:45-4:45pm Mon-Fri, 7am-1pm Sat) About 3km northeast of Ica in the La Tinguiña district, this is the easiest of the large commercial wineries to visit (taxi one way S5). It's best to go in the morning, as the winery occasionally closes in the afternoon.

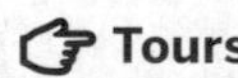

Tours

Desert Travel TOUR
(☎056-22-7215; desert_travel@hotmail.com; Calle Lima 171) Desert Travel offers city tours (S25, four hours), dune-buggy trips in Huacachina (S45) and even boat tours to Islas Ballestas (S50 to S60).

Festivals & Events

Ica Carnaval RELIGIOUS
(⏲Feb) Carnaval inspires the water-throwing antics typical of any Latin American carnaval, plus dancers in beautiful costumes.

Fiesta de la Vendimia HARVEST
(⏲early-mid-Mar) This famous grape-harvest festival includes all manner of processions, beauty contests, cockfights and horse shows, music and dancing and, of course, free-flowing pisco and wine.

Ica Week CULTURAL
(⏲mid-Jun) Celebration of the founding of the city by the Spanish conquistadors on June 17, 1563.

Tourist Week MUSIC, FOOD
(⏲mid-Sep) Tourist Week brings festivals, food, dancing and more.

El Señor de Luren RELIGIOUS
(⏲late Oct) This religious pilgrimage culminates in fireworks and a traditional procession of the faithful that keeps going all night.

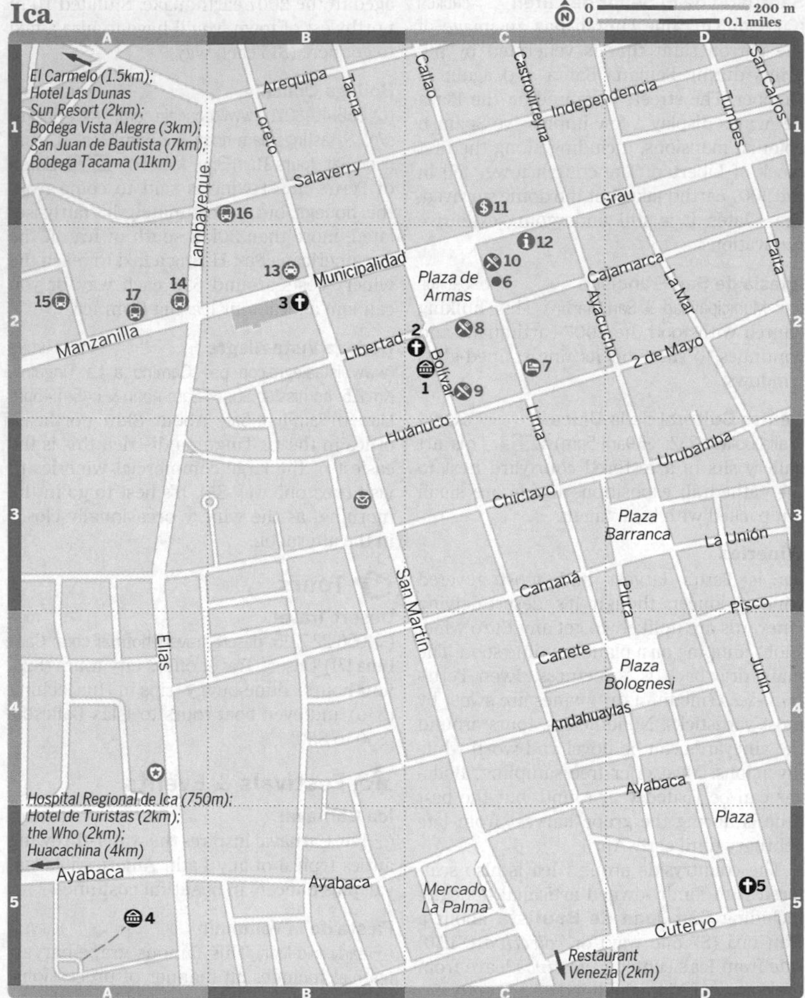

Sleeping

Beware that hotels fill up and double or triple their prices during the many festivals. Most budget travelers head for Huacachina, 4km west of the city, but Ica has several options.

Hostal Soyuz HOTEL $

(056-22-4138; Manzanilla 130; s/d/tr S40/50/70;) Sitting directly over the Soyuz bus terminal, this handy option for late arrivals or early departures has carpeted rooms with air-con and cable TV, but is only for heavy sleepers on account of the rumpus below. Check in is at the bus ticket desk.

El Carmelo HISTORIC HOTEL $$

(056-23-2191; www.elcarmelohotelhacienda.com; Carr Panamericana Sur Km 301; s/d/tr/q from S100/150/200/250;) This romantic roadside hotel on the outskirts of town inhabits a delightful 200-year-old hacienda that has undeniable rustic charm. There's a good restaurant plus a winery onsite. Take a taxi from the city center (S3).

Hotel Sol de Ica HOTEL $$

(056-23-6168; www.hotelsoldeica.com; Lima 265; s/d/tr incl buffet breakfast S145/180/230;) This three-story central hotel is hidden down a long dark passage behind

Ica

Sights

Activities, Courses & Tours

Sleeping

Eating

Information

Transport

reception that delivers more than it initially promises. Remarkably small rooms have natural wood touches, but don't sparkle (perhaps because of the mustard yellow sheets). The hotel has a large garden and swimming pool.

Hotel Las Dunas Sun Resort RESORT $$$
(☎056-25-6224; www.lasdunashotel.com; Av La Angostura 400, Panamericana Sur Km 300; s/d/tr from S400/600/800; P❄@📶≈) By far the most luxurious hotel in town, the sprawling Las Dunas resort is equipped with a swimming pool, sauna, tennis courts, mini-golf course, business center, restaurants and bars. Various excursions are offered (for an additional fee), including cycling, horseback riding, sandboarding and winery tours. Service can be haphazard, however. The resort is located off Panamericana Sur Km 300.

Eating

Several shops in the streets east of the plaza sell *tejas* (caramel-wrapped sweets flavored with fruits, nuts etc).

El Otro Peñoncito PERUVIAN, INTERNATIONAL $
(Bolívar 225; mains S9-26; ⏲8am-midnight Mon-Fri; 🖉) Ica's most historic and characterful restaurant serves a varied menu of Peruvian and international fare that includes plenty of options for vegetarians. The formal bartenders here shake a mean pisco sour.

Plaza 125 PERUVIAN $
(Lima 125; mains S10-16, menú S14) Your quick stop on the main square backs up homespun *lomo saltado* (strips of beef stir-fried with onions, tomatoes, potatoes and chili) with more internationally flavored chicken fillets. It's riotously popular with locals in a hurry, and the set lunch is a good deal.

Anita BAKERY $$
(Libertad 135; mains S15-36, menús from S12; ⏲8am-midnight) True, the bow-tied waiters are a bit over the top (this ain't the Ritz), but Anita does a mean stuffed avocado and the bakery counter knocks out some hard-to-resist cakes. Best restaurant in the main square by far.

Restaurant Venezia ITALIAN $$
(San Martín 1229; mains S12-29; ⏲lunch & dinner Tue-Sun) In a suburban location about 2.5km south of the town center, Venezia is a popular family-run Italian restaurant. Allow plenty of time as all plates are made fresh upon ordering.

Drinking

There's not much happening in Ica outside fiesta times, though if its gringo-dominated nightlife you're after, Huacachina calls like a desert siren. On Ica's Plaza de Armas, you'll find several wine and pisco tasting rooms to pop into for a quick tipple. South of the plaza along Lima, local bars and clubs advertise live music, DJs and dancing, but they're pretty rough. The craziest late-night disco, called **The Who** (www.discotecathewho.com; Av de Los Maestros 500; admission S10), is situated on the north side of the Hotel de Turistas, 3km southwest of the plaza; it's a S3 taxi ride.

Information

Tour agencies and internet cafes abound in the area around the Plaza de Armas.

BCP (Plaza de Armas) Has a Visa/MasterCard ATM and changes US dollars.

Dircetur (☎056-21-0332; www.dirceturica.gob.pe; Grau 148) Government-sponsored office of tourism.

Hospital Regional de Ica (☎056-23-4798; www.hrica.gob.pe; Prolongación Ayabaca s/n; ⌚24hr) For emergency services.

Police (☎056-23-5421; JJ Elias, 5th block; ⌚24hr) At the city center's edge.

Serpost (San Martín 521) Southwest of the Plaza de Armas.

DANGERS & ANNOYANCES

Ica experiences some petty theft. Take the normal precautions, particularly around the bus terminals and market areas.

Getting There & Away

Ica is a main destination for buses along the Panamericana Sur, so it's easy to get to/from Lima or Nazca. Most of the bus companies are clustered in a high-crime area at the west end of Salaverry, and also Manzanilla west of Lambayeque.

Soyuz (☎056-22-4138; www.soyuzonline.com.pe; Manzanilla 130) run the 'Perubus' to Lima via Chincha and Cañete with services leaving every 15 minutes. Watch your belongings on Soyuz, especially when people get on and off the bus, as petty theft is common. **Cruz del Sur** (☎0-801-11111; www.cruzdelsur.com.pe; Lambayeque 140) and **Ormeño** (☎056-21-5600; www.grupo-ormeno.com.pe; Lambayeque s/n) offer more luxurious services going north and south.

Buses from Ica:

DESTINATION	COST (S)	DURATION (HR)
Arequipa	50–144	12
Cañete	8	3
Chincha	6	2
Cuzco	140-165	14
Lima	25–41	4½
Nazca	12	2½
Pisco	4–15	1½–2

Some faster, but slightly more expensive *colectivos* and *combis* heading for Pisco and Nazca leave when full from near the intersection of Lambayeque and Municipalidad in Ica.

Ormeño as well as some small companies may serve destinations around Peru's central highlands, such as Ayacucho and Huancavelica.

Colectivos to Huacachina cost S6.50.

Huacachina

☎056 / POP 200

Imagine... It's 6pm and you're sitting atop a giant wind-sculpted sand dune watching the sun set psychedelically over a landscape of golden yellows and rusty reds. Two hundred meters below you lies a dreamy desert lagoon ringed by exotic palm trees, and furnished with a clutch of rustic yet suitably elegant hotels. It took you an exhausting 20 minutes to climb up to this lofty vantage point, but with a well-waxed sandboard wedged beneath your belly you'll be down in less than one.

While not as famous as Nazca to the south, Huacachina, an aesthetically perfect desert oasis 4km west of Ica, is a firmly established stopover on Southern Peru's well-trampled Gringo Trail, and with good reason. Sandboarding, dune-buggie rides and good-old romantic idling are the orders of the day here. This is backpacker central, so expect plenty of late-night disco parties and international flavors. Many people just make it here for a quick overnight and dune trip the next day, but a few days of relaxed strolls and dune climbs may just channel your inner chi.

Activities

Sand is an essential ingredient in most Huacachina activities.

Sandboarding

You can rent sandboards for S5 an hour to slide, surf or ski your way down the dunes, getting sand lodged into every bodily orifice. Snowboarding this isn't. There are no tow ropes or chair-lifts here. Instead you must stagger up the sugary dunes for your 45-second adrenaline rush. Make sure you are given wax (usually in the form of an old candle) when you rent your board as they are pretty useless without regular rub-downs. Start on the smaller slopes and don't be lulled into a false sense of security – several people have seriously injured themselves losing control of their sandboards. Most riders end up boarding belly down with their legs splayed out behind as emergency brakes. Don't forget to keep your mouth shut.

Dune Buggies

Many hotels offer thrill-rides in **areneros** (dune buggies) which head out early morning (8am-ish) and late afternoon (4pm-ish) to avoid the intense sun. They then stop at the top of the soft slopes, from where you can sandboard down and be picked up at the bottom. Word on the street is that some drivers take unnecessary risks, so ask around before choosing an operator. Make sure cameras are well protected, as sand can be damaging. The going rate for tours is S45 but ask first if sandboard rental is included and how long the tour lasts. Tours do not include a fee of S4, which must be paid upon entering the dunes (this doesn't apply to those entering on foot).

Litter is an issue on Huacachina's dunes, as it is in much of Peru. It ought to go without saying, but pack out all your rubbish when you visit these beautiful sandy behemoths.

Swimming & Boating

The lagoon's murky waters supposedly have curative properties, though you may find swimming in the hotel pools (of which there are half a dozen) more inviting. You can also hire boats – both rowing and pedal-powered – at a couple of points on the lagoon for S12 an hour.

Tours

Pretty much all the hotels can organize dune-buggy rides.

Pelican Travel ADVENTURE TOUR
(056-25-6567; www.pelicanperu.com; Perotti s/n) Pelican Travel runs two-hour dune-buggy tours (S45), trips to Paracas and the Islas Ballestas (S70), an overnight all-you-can-drink camping trip (S300), wine tours (S50), and their signature 'shitface-drinking-dancing' pub crawl (S80).

Sleeping

Hospedaje Mayo HOSTEL $
(056-22-9005; hospedajemayo@gmail.com; dm/s/d/tr S20/40/60/90;) Facing the southern dunes, this guesthouse turned hostel has clean, well-maintained rooms with cheery blue and tangerine bed covers. The dorm sleeps ten, and while it sports roof fans, it can get hot as an armadillo's bottom. There's a little pool out back, along with a Foosball table. Gol!!!

Casa de Arena HOSTEL $
(056-21-5274; www.casadearena.net; Balneario de Huacachina; dm S25, s/d S40/120, s/d without bathroom S35/100;) Cast with a rowdy reputation, the Arena knows how to party. The rooms come with or without bathrooms, allowing scrimpers to... well... scrimp. The boisterous Friday night disco can get wild. If you want peace, go elsewhere. If you want to party, this is the place.

★ **Banana's Adventure** HOSTEL $$
(056-23-7129; bananasadventure@hotmail.com; Perotti s/n; r per person incl breakfast and excursion S75-110;) This peaced-out crash pad on the north side of the lagoon only offers packaged stays. They include a room for the night – choose between four-bed dorms with super firm mattresses or elegant deluxe rooms with glass on all sides and modern fixings – plus a dune-buggy and sandboarding excursion the next day.

We don't love that you are roped into the package tour, but with huge windows, a fun bar and little dip pool, this is the best budget spot in town.

El Huacachinero Hotel HOTEL $$
(056-21-7435; www.elhuacachinero.com; Perotti; s/d/tr incl breakfast S176/202/265;) Recently upgraded, the Huacachinero has the finest restaurant in the oasis (by a stretch), a relaxing pool area (no blaring music), and immediate dune access via the back gate if you're up for a 45° one-step-forward-two-steps-back climb to the sunset of your dreams. Agreeably rustic rooms have super-comfortable beds and cane accents.

Hostería Suiza HOTEL $$
(056-23-8762; www.hosteriasuiza.com.pe; Balneario de Huacachina; s/d/tr/q incl breakfast S125/205/255/375;) This formal hotel on the northwest end of the Laguna has high-ceiling rooms and Moorish-meets-hacienda architectural features. The rooms looking onto the backyard garden and pool area are the best, with textured green bedspreads and newly remodeled modern bathrooms.

Hostal Curasi HOTEL $$
(056-21-6989; www.huacachinacurasi.com; Balneario de Huacachina; s/d incl breakfast S105/150;) This quiet oasis has a garden and pool in the middle to cool off on those hot south-coast days. The rooms have ocean-evoking bedspreads and a few über-kitsch oil paintings.

Hotel Mossone HISTORIC HOTEL $$$
(01-614-3900; www.dematourshoteles.com; Balneario de Huacachina; d/tr/ste S355/449/464;) At Huacachina's first hotel, the atmospheric central courtyard, with its chipped paving stones and wire-mesh aviary, looks like something out of Fidel Castro's time-warped Cuba. Rooms are huge. In fact you get two of them: a *sala* (sitting room) and a high-ceilinged bedroom. Unfortunately, the rooms are poorly prepared and dimly lit, losing the hotel points in the top-tier race.

Eating

Desert Nights INTERNATIONAL $

(Blvd de Huacachina; mains S15-25;) The menu might have been ripped off from anywhere else on the banana-pancake trail, but this international hostel with a decent and very popular cafe out front is somewhere you're guaranteed to meet other travelers. The excellent shade-grown Peruvian coffee is backed up by peanut butter and jam sandwiches, burgers, pizza and brownies.

House of Avinoam PIZZA $$

(Perotti; pizzas S15-25) The House of Avinoam in the Carola del Sur Lodge has a decent pizza restaurant and one of the oasis' larger and more atmospheric bars.

Drinking & Nightlife

Bars and discos in Huacachina are generally attached to the various hotels and clientele is mostly foreign. Fame and infamy belong to the boisterous Casa de Arena hostel (p125) and its weekend discos. Next door, the **Pub** (Balneario de Huacachina) is a cool bar/restaurant owned by the same people as Desert Nights.

Information

DANGERS & ANNOYANCES

Though safer than Ica, Huacachina is not a place to be lax about your personal safety or to forget to look after your property. Some guesthouses have reputations for ripping off travelers and also harassing young women with sexual advances. Check out all of your options carefully before accepting a room. Also, the few small stores around the lake offer plenty of souvenirs but are often out of the basics; come prepared!

Getting There & Away

The only way to get to Huacachina from Ica is by taxi (S5 to S7 one way).

Palpa

056 / POP 7200 / ELEV 300M

From Ica, the Panamericana Sur heads southeast through the small oasis of Palpa, famous for its orange groves.

Palpa Lines ARCHAEOLOGICAL SITE

Like Nazca, Palpa is surrounded by perplexing geoglyphs, the so-called Palpa Lines, which are serially overshadowed by the more famous, but less abundant, Nazca Lines to the south. The Palpa Lines display a greater profusion of human forms including the Familia Real de Paracas, a group of eight figures on a hillside.

Due to their elevated position, the figures are easier to view from terra firma at a *mirador* (lookout) 8km south of town. A small museum hut onsite offers further explanations in English and Spanish. The best way to see more of these lines is on a combined overflight from Nazca.

Nazca & Around

056 / ELEV 590M

It's hard to say the word 'Nazca' without following it immediately with the word 'Lines,' a reference not just to the ancient geometric lines that crisscross the Nazca desert, but to the enigmatic animal geoglyphs that accompany them. Like all great unexplained mysteries, these dramatic etchings on the pampa, thought to have been made by a pre-Inca civilization between AD 450 and 600, attract a variable fan base of archaeologists, scientists, history buffs, New Age mystics, curious tourists, and pilgrims on their way to (or back from) Machu Picchu.

Question marks still hang over how they were made and by whom, and the answers are often as much wild speculation as pure science (aliens? prehistoric balloonists?). Documented for the first time by North American scientist Paul Kosok in 1939 and declared a Unesco World Heritage Site in 1994, the lines today are the south coast's biggest tourist attraction, which means the small otherwise insignificant desert town of Nazca can be a bit of a circus.

Sights & Activities

Nazca Lines

The best-known lines are found in the desert 20km north of Nazca, and by far the best way to appreciate them is to get a bird's-eye view from a *sobrevuelo* (overflight).

Mirador LOOKOUT

(admission S2) You'll get only a sketchy idea of the Lines at this lookout on the Panamericana Sur 20km north of Nazca, which has an oblique view of three figures: the lizard, tree and hands (or frog, depending on your point of view). It's also a lesson in the damage to which the Lines are vulnerable. The Panamericana Sur runs smack through the tail of the lizard, which from nearby seems all but obliterated.

GREENPEACE DID WHAT TO THE NAZCA LINES?

The earth does deserve a voice, but for many Peruvians and world citizens, the Greenpeace action on December 8, 2014 that placed a message – 'Time For Change! The Future is Renewable. Greenpeace' – in large yellow letters next to the iconic hummingbird biomorphic geoglyph in the Nazca Lines was an act of vandalism, causing irreparable damage to a World Heritage Site.

Since the action – which was designed to attract the attention of world leaders attending a UN Climate Summit in Lima – Greenpeace has issued apologies, and three of the 20 people taking part have been publicly accused (with Greenpeace releasing the names of four more participants in hopes of having charges dropped for journalists that covered the brash environmental action).

Because of the delicate nature of these mysterious formations that date back 1500 years, nobody is permitted to walk on the Nazca Lines complex (these rules apply equally to backpackers and presidents). Only when using special weight-dispersing padded shoes do archaeologists enter the site.

And while Greenpeace points out that activists did not walk on the geoglyph itself, they did overturn rocks. Recent drone flights reveal disrupted areas where the protestors (or vandals depending on how you look at it) entered the site, and you can see remnants of the letter C. International outrage swirled around the incident. The Peruvian government is now looking at ways to restore the site and criminal proceedings are ongoing. It certainly leaves a lasting imprint on the global debate surrounding environmental protection, but how that legacy will be viewed is certainly up for interpretation.

Signs warning of landmines are a reminder that walking on the Lines is strictly forbidden. It irreparably damages them and, besides, you can't see anything at ground level. To get to the observation tower from Nazca, catch any bus or *colectivo* northbound along Panamericana Sur (S1.50, 30 minutes). Some tours (from S50 per person) also combine a trip to the *mirador* with visits to another natural viewpoint and the Maria Reiche Museum. About 1km south of the man-made *mirador* there is a **Mirador Natural** (free) on a small knoll-like hill with a close-up view of one of the geometric lines made by removing reddish pebbles from the grey earth.

Museo Maria Reiche MUSEUM

(admission S25; ⏲9am-6pm) When Maria Reiche, the German mathematician and long-term researcher of the Nazca Lines, died in 1998, her house, which stands 5km north of the *mirador* (lookout) along Panamericana Sur, was made into a small museum. Though the museum is disappointingly scant on information, you can see where she lived, amid the clutter of her tools and obsessive sketches.

The sun can be punishing, but it's possible to walk here from the *mirador* in a sweaty hour or so, or passing *colectivos* can sometimes take you (S1). To return to Nazca, just ask the guard to help you flag down any southbound bus or *colectivo*. A visit to the museum can also be arranged as part of a tour to the nearby *mirador*.

Museo Didáctico Antonini MUSEUM

(☎056-52-3444; Av de la Cultura 600; admission S20, plus camera S5; ⏲9am-7pm) On the east side of town, this excellent archaeological museum has an aqueduct running through the back garden, as well as interesting reproductions of burial tombs, a valuable collection of ceramic pan flutes and a scale model of the Lines.

You can get an overview of both the Nazca culture and a glimpse of most of Nazca's outlying sites here. Though the exhibit labels are in Spanish, the front desk lends foreign-language translation booklets for you to carry around. To get to the museum follow Bolognesi to the east out of town for 1km, or take a taxi (S2).

Nazca Planetarium PLANETARIUM

(☎056-52-2293; Nazca Lines Hotel, Bolognesi 147; admission S20; ⏲in English 7pm, in Spanish 8:15pm) This small planetarium is in the Nazca Lines Hotel and offers scripted evening lectures on the Lines with graphical displays on a domed projection screen that last approximately 45 minutes. Call ahead or check the posted schedules for show times.

Nazca

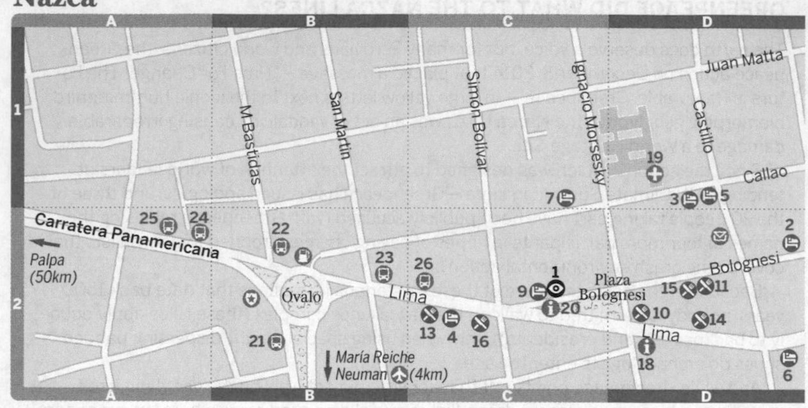

Nazca

Sights
- 1 Nazca Planetarium C2

Activities, Courses & Tours
- Alas Peruanas .... (see 4)
- Alegría Tours .... (see 4)
- Kunan Tours .... (see 8)

Sleeping
- 2 Casa Andina D2
- 3 Hospedaje Yemayá D1
- 4 Hotel Alegría C2
- 5 Hotel La Encantada D1
- 6 Hotel Nasca D2
- 7 Hotel Oro Viejo C1
- 8 Kunan Wasi Hotel E1
- 9 Nazca Lines Hotel C2

Eating
- 10 El Portón D2
- 11 La Encantada Cafe D2
- 12 La Estación Plaza Mayor E2
- 13 La Kañada C2
- 14 La Taberna D2
- 15 Mamashana D2
- 16 Rico Pollo C2

Information
- 17 BCP E2
- 18 DIRCETUR D2
- 19 Hospital de Apoyo Nazca D1
- 20 Information Booth C2

Transport
- 21 Colectivos and Minibuses to Chala B2
- 22 Colectivos and Minibuses to Ica B2
- 23 Cruz del Sur B2
- 24 Flores A2
- 25 Ormeño A2
- 26 Soyuz C2

Outlying Sights

Most outlying sights can be visited on tours from Nazca, although individual travelers or pairs may have to wait a day or two before the agency finds enough people who are also interested in going.

Chauchilla Cemetery ARCHAEOLOGICAL SITE

(admission S7.50; ⏲8am-2pm) The most popular excursion from Nazca, this cemetery, 30km south of Nazca, will satisfy any urges you have to see ancient bones, skulls and mummies. Dating back to the Ica-Chincha culture around AD 1000, the mummies were, until recently, scattered haphazardly across the desert, left by ransacking tomb-robbers.

Now they are seen carefully rearranged inside a dozen or so tombs, though cloth fragments and pottery and bone shards still litter the ground outside the demarcated trail. Organized tours last three hours and cost US$10 to US$35 per person.

Pardeones Ruins RUINS

(admission S10, incl entry to Cantallo Aqueducts) The Pardeones ruins, 2km southeast of town via Arica over the river, are not very well preserved, primarily because they were constructed from adobe rather than stone. Their position on a slope above the town is commanding, which is probably why the Incas used it as an administrative

control center between the mountains and the coast.

Cantallo Aqueducts ARCHAEOLOGICAL SITE

(admission S10, incl entry to Pardeones Ruins) About 4km southeast of town are the 30-plus underground Cantallo Aqueducts, which are still in working order and essential in irrigating the surrounding fields. Though it was once possible to enter the aqueducts through the spiraling *ventanas* (windows), which local people use to clean the aqueducts each year, entry is now prohibited; instead, you can take note of the Nazca's exceptional stonework from outside.

It's possible, but not necessarily safe, to walk to the aqueducts; at least, don't carry any valuables. Alternatively you can hire a taxi to take you there. This should cost around S40 to S50 round-trip. There are also tours from Nazca that take 2½ hours, cost from S15 per person and may be combined with a visit to see El Telar, a geoglyph found in the town of Buena Fe, and visits to touristy gold and ceramics workshops.

Cahuachi RUINS

(⏲9am-4pm) FREE A dirt road travels 25km west from Nazca to Cahuachi, the most important known Nazca center, which is still undergoing excavation. It consists of several pyramids, a graveyard and an enigmatic site called Estaquería, which may have been used as a place of mummification. Tours from Nazca take three hours, cost US$15 to US$50 per person, and may include a side trip to Pueblo Viejo, a nearby pre-Nazca residential settlement.

Going here with advanced reservations from a tour agency is recommended.

Reserva Nacional Pampas Galeras WILDLIFE RESERVE

This national reserve is a *vicuña* (threatened wild camelid) sanctuary, high in the mountains 90km east of Nazca on the road to Cuzco. It is the best place to see these shy animals in Peru, though tourist services are virtually nonexistent.

Every year in late May or early June is the *chaccu* (round-up), when hundreds of villagers round up the *vicuñas* for shearing and three festive days of traditional ceremonies, with music and dancing and, of course, drinking. Full-day or overnight tours from Nazca cost US$30 to US$90 per person.

Cerro Blanco ADVENTURE TOUR

Stand down all other pretenders. Cerro Blanco, 14km east of Nazca, is the highest sand dune in the world: 2078m above sea level and – more importantly – 1176m from base to summit. That's higher than the tallest mountain in England and numerous other countries. If Huacachina's sand didn't irrevocably ruin your underwear, this could be your bag.

Due to the dune's height and steepness it's best to organize an excursion from Nazca. Trips leave at about 4am to avoid the intense heat. The arduous climb to the top of the dune (buggies can't climb this behemoth) takes approximately three hours. Going down is counted more in minutes with some clear runs of up to 800m. Many agencies in Nazca offer this trip, including Kunan Tours.

☞ Tours

Most people fly over the Lines (US$80) then leave, but there's more to see around Nazca. If you take one of the many local tours, they typically include a torturously long stop at a potter's and/or gold-miner's workshop for a demonstration of their techniques (tips for those who show you their trade are expected, too).

Hotels tirelessly promote their own tours. Nazca Lines Hotel and Casa Andina are good options.

Alegría Tours ADVENTURE TOUR

(☎056-52-3775; www.alegriatoursperu.com; Hotel Alegría, Lima 168) Behemoth agency offers all the usual local tours, plus off-the-beaten-track and sandboarding

THE NAZCA LINES: ANCIENT MYSTERIES IN THE SAND

Spread over 500 sq km (310 sq mi) of arid, rock-strewn plain in the Pampa Colorada (Red Plain), the **Nazca Lines** are one of the world's great archaeological mysteries. Comprising more than 800 straight lines, 300 geometric figures (geoglyphs) and 70 animal and plant drawings (biomorphs), the lines are almost imperceptible on the ground. From above, they form a striking network of stylized figures and channels, many of which radiate from a central axis.

The figures are mostly etched out in single continuous lines, while the encompassing geoglyphs form perfect triangles, rectangles or straight lines running for several kilometers across the desert.

The lines were made by the simple process of removing the dark sun-baked stones from the surface of the desert and piling them up on either side of the lines, thus exposing the lighter, powdery gypsum-laden soil below. The most elaborate designs represent animals, including a 180m-long (590ft) lizard, a monkey with an extravagantly curled tail, and a condor with a 130m (426ft) wingspan. There's also a hummingbird, spider and an intriguing owl-headed person on a hillside, popularly referred to as an astronaut because of its goldfish-bowl shaped head, though some believe it's a priest with a mystical owl's head.

Endless questions remain. Who constructed the lines and why? And how did they know what they were doing when the lines can only be properly appreciated from the air? Maria Reiche (1903–98), a German mathematician and long-time researcher of the lines, theorized that they were made by the Paracas and Nazca cultures between 900 BC and AD 600, with some additions by the Wari settlers from the highlands in the 7th century. She also claimed that the lines were an astronomical calendar developed for agricultural purposes, and that they were mapped out through the use of sophisticated mathematics (and a long rope). However, the handful of alignments Reiche discovered between the sun, stars and lines were not enough to convince scholars.

Later, English documentary maker Tony Morrison hypothesized that the lines were walkways linking *huacas* (sites of ceremonial significance). A slightly more surreal suggestion from explorer Jim Woodman was that the Nazca people knew how to construct hot-air balloons and that they did, in fact, observe the lines from the air. Or, if you believe author George Von Breunig, the lines formed a giant running track.

A more down-to-earth theory, given the value of water in the sun-baked desert, was suggested by anthropologist Johann Reinhard, who believed that the lines were involved in mountain worship and a fertility/water cult. Recent work by the **Swiss-Liechtenstein Foundation** (SLSA; www.slsa.ch) agrees that they were dedicated to the worship of water, and it is thus ironic that their theory about the demise of the Nazca culture suggests that it was due not to drought but to destructive rainfall caused by a phenomenon such as El Niño!

About the only thing that is certain is that when the Nazca set about turning their sprawling desert homeland into an elaborate art canvas, they also began a debate that will keep archaeologists busy for many decades, if not centuries to come.

options. The tours are expensive for one person, so ask to join up with other travelers to receive a group discount. Alegría can arrange guides in Spanish, English, French and German in some cases.

Kunan Tours GUIDED TOUR
(☎056-52-4069; www.kunantours.com; Arica 419) Based out of the Kunan Wasi Hotel, this comprehensive travel company offers all the Nazca tours, plus excursions to Islas Ballestas, Huacachina and Chincha.

Sleeping

Prices drop by up to 50% outside of peak season, which runs from May until August.

Kunan Wasi Hotel HOTEL $
(☎056-52-4069; www.kunanwasihotel.com; Arica 419; s/d/tr S70/90/120; @ 📶) Very clean and very bright with each room conforming to a different color scheme, Kunan Wasi is run by English-speaking Yesenia. It's super friendly, immaculately clean, and travelers will love the top-floor terrace. Welcome to a perfectly packaged Nazca bargain.

Hospedaje Yemayá HOTEL $
(056-52-3146; www.hospedajeyemaya.com; Callao 578; s/d S45/60, s/d without bathroom S30/45;) An indefatigably hospitable family deftly deals with all of the backpackers that stream through their doorway. They offer a few floors of small but well cared for rooms with hot showers and cable TV. There's a sociable terrace with a handy washing machine and dryer.

Hotel Nasca HOTEL $
(056-52-2085; marionasca13@hotmail.com; Lima 438; s/d/tr S35/45/65) A rock-bottom, bargain-basement place with friendly, elderly owners. Army barracks–style rooms offer bare bones facilities; some have private baths.

★**Hotel Oro Viejo** HOTEL $$
(056-52-2284; www.hoteloroviejo.net; Callao 483; s/d/tr/ste incl buffet breakfast S150/200/240/450;) There's a decidedly oriental feel to this excellent midrange hotel with it's open gardens and glistening swimming pool. Occasional farming artifacts grace the common areas and lounge, while the well-fragranced rooms deliver comfort, quiet and relaxation. Ask for a new room out back.

Hotel La Encantada HOTEL $$
(056-52-2930; www.hotellaencantada.com.pe; Callao 592; s/d/tr S105/140/160;) While the rooms lack some tidiness (just below cleanliness and godliness in our books), this modernish hotel offers bright, freshly painted rooms and a pleasant terrace out front.

Hotel Alegría HOTEL $$
(056-52-2702; www.hotelalegria.net; Lima 168; s/d incl breakfast S210/240;) This is a classic travelers' haunt with a restaurant, manicured grounds and pool. It has narrow, carpeted business-standard rooms. All in all, it's an OK bet, but falls a bit short for the price.

Nazca Lines Hotel HOTEL $$$
(056-52-2293; www.peru-hotels.com/nazlines.htm; Bolognesi s/n; d/tr/ste incl breakfast S445/529/573;) Exceedingly tranquil considering its city center location, this lauded hotel is arranged around a large courtyard complete with lovely swimming pool and fountain. Classy touches include tilework and arches reminiscent of southern Spain, an onsite planetarium (with daily shows), a shop, a comfy lounge, and efficient but not officious service.

Choose between romantic garden-level rooms or more modern affairs on the second floor.

Casa Andina BOUTIQUE HOTEL $$$
(01-213-9718; www.casa-andina.com; Bolognesi 367; r incl breakfast buffet S433-484;) This Peruvian chain hotel, poised midway between the bus stations and the Plaza de Armas, offers contemporary Andean touches like leather lampshades and textile bed runners, creating a solid value proposition in the upmarket hotel category. The palm-filled courtyard and adjacent pool area are small but tasteful.

Eating & Drinking

West of the Plaza de Armas, Bolognesi is stuffed full of foreigner-friendly pizzerias, restaurants and bars.

Rico Pollo PERUVIAN $
(Lima 190; mains from S12) A local lunchtime phenomenon, this very cheap, very crowded chicken joint offers some of the best barbecued meat cuts on the south coast. For S12 you get a filling meal of chicken breast with fries and vegetables. Cakes and salads provide an excellent supporting act.

La Taberna PERUVIAN $
(Lima 321; mains from S15, menú S6; lunch & dinner;) It's a hole-in-the-wall place, and the scribbles covering every inch of wall are a testament to its popularity. Try the spicy fish topped with sauce and mixed shellfish challengingly named *Pescado a lo Macho* (no that doesn't mean Macho-man fish), or choose from a list of vegetarian options.

La Kañada PERUVIAN $
(Lima 160; mains S12-16, menú S10; 8am-11pm) Handy to the bus stations, this old standby serves up all the Peruvian standards. A decent list of cocktails includes *algarrobina* – a cocktail of pisco, milk and syrup from the *huarango* (carob) tree.

★**Mamashana** INTERNATIONAL $$
(056-21-1286; www.mamashana.com; Bolognesi 270; mains S20-35; 10am-11pm;) Head upstairs to take advantage of bird's-eye views of the street below at this international-traveler-set favorite. The food is quite good, and prepared with a worldwide audience in mind. Choose from steaks and seafood, and lasagna and hamburgers. The cane-thatched

OVERFLIGHTS OVERVIEW

Bad publicity wracked the Nazca Lines in 2010 when two small aircraft carrying tourists on *sobrevuelos* (overflights) crashed within eight months of each other causing a total of 13 fatalities. The crashes followed an equally catastrophic 2008 accident that killed five French tourists, along with another incident when a plane was forced to make an emergency landing on the Panamericana Sur in 2009.

In response to the incidents, some changes have been made. Fifteen plane companies have been streamlined into half a dozen, all planes now fly with two pilots, and prices have gone up to ensure that companies don't cut corners with poorly maintained aircraft or over-filled flights.

Nonetheless, it still pays to put safety before price when choosing your overflight company. Question anyone who offers less than US$80 for the standard 30-minute excursion and don't be afraid to probe companies on their safety records and flight policies. **Aeroparacas** (☎01-641-7000; www.aeroparacas.com) is one of the better airline companies. Other longstanding operators include **Aerodiana** (☎01-447-6824; www.aerodiana.com.pe) and **Alas Peruanas** (☎056-52-2444; www.alasperuanas.com). Some countries, including the UK and USA, still place warnings about overflights on their foreign office websites.

If you do opt for a flight, bear in mind that, because the small aircraft bank left and right, it can be a stomach-churning experience, so motion-sickness sufferers should consider taking medication. Looking at the horizon may help mild nausea.

Most airline companies use **Maria Reiche Neuman Airport**, 4km southwest of Nazca, although you can also depart from Pisco and Lima. On top of the tour fee the airport normally charges a departure tax of S20.

room and exposed wood lend a South American air.

La Encantada Cafe INTERNATIONAL **$$**
(www.hotellaencantada.com.pe; Bolognesi 282; mains S20-40) A top spot on the 'Boulevard' (Bolognesi), La Encantada sparkles in Nazca's dusty center with well-placed wine displays, great coffee and courteous and friendly wait staff. The extensive menu mixes Europhile flavors (pasta etc) with Peruvian favorites.

El Portón PERUVIAN **$$**
(www.elportonrestaurante.com; Ignacio Moreseky 120; mains S20-35) Fed with a regular diet of Nazca Lines tour groups, single diners could get lonely in this rambling place. The menu is anchored by above-average potatoes in a Huancayo sauce, stuffed avocados and some fancier mains. Musical trios drop by with *El Condor Pasa* on default setting.

La Estación Plaza Mayor STEAK **$$**
(cnr Calle Bolognesi & Arica; meals S15-25) This longstanding spot has a coal grill with a rustic wood-and-bamboo mezzanine seating area overlooking Plaza de Armas – barbecued meats dominate.

ℹ Information

BCP (Lima 495) Has a Visa/MasterCard ATM and changes US dollars.

Dircetur (Parque Bolognesi, 3rd fl) This government-sponsored tourist information office; can recommend local tour operators. There's an information booth in the park itself.

Hospital de Apoyo Nazca (☎056-52-2586; www.hospitalnasca.gob.pe; Callao s/n; ⏲24hr) For emergency services.

Information Booth Regularly staffed tourist information booth.

Police Station

Serpost (Castillo 379) Two blocks west of the Plaza de Armas.

DANGERS & ANNOYANCES

The town of Nazca is generally safe for travelers, though be wary when walking at night near either bridge to the south of town. Travelers arriving by bus will be met by persistent *jaladores* (agents) trying to sell tours or take arriving passengers to hotels. These touts may use the names of recommended places but are never to be trusted. Never hand over any money until you can personally talk to the hotel or tour-company owner and get a confirmed itinerary in writing. It's best to go with a reliable agency for land tours of the surrounding area, as a few violent assaults and robberies of foreign tourists have been reported.

Getting There & Around

Nazca is a major destination for buses on the Panamericana Sur and is easy to get to from Lima, Ica or Arequipa. Bus companies cluster at the west end of Calle Lima, near the *óvalo* (main roundabout) and about a block towards town on the same street. Buses to Arequipa generally originate in Lima, and to get a seat you have to pay the Lima fare.

Most long-distance services leave in the late afternoon or evening. **Cruz del Sur** (☎0801-11111; www.cruzdelsur.com.pe; Av Los Incas) and **Ormeño** (☎056-52-2058; www.grupo-ormeno.com.pe; Av Los Incas) have a few luxury buses daily to Lima. Intermediate points such as Ica and Pisco are more speedily served by smaller, *económico* (cheap) bus companies, such as **Flores** and **Soyuz** (☎056-52-1464), which run buses to Ica every half-hour from Av Los Incas. These buses will also drop you at Palpa (S3, one hour).

To go direct to Cuzco, several companies, including Cruz del Sur, take the paved road east via Abancay. This route climbs over 4000m and gets very cold, so wear your warmest clothes and bring your sleeping bag on board if you have one. Alternatively, some companies also offer direct buses to Cuzco via Arequipa.

Nazca Buses:

DESTINATION	COST (S)	DURATION (HR)
Arequipa	59–140	10–12
Camaná	60–120	7
Chala	15	3½
Cuzco	80–140	14
Lima	55–145	8
Ica	30–65	2½
Pisco	30–65	1½–2
Tacna	70–165	15

For Ica, fast *colectivos* (S15, two hours) and slower minibuses leave when full from near the **gas station** on the *óvalo*. On the south side of the main roundabout, antiquated *colectivos* wait for enough passengers to make the run down to Chala (S15, 2½ hours).

A taxi from central Nazca to the airport, 4km away, costs about S4.

Chala

☎054 / POP 2500

The tiny, ramshackle fishing village of Chala, about 170km from Nazca, presents intrepid travelers with an opportunity to break the journey to Arequipa and visit the archaeological site of **Puerto Inca** (⌚24hr) FREE. Fresh fish was once sent all the way to Cuzco by runners from here – no mean effort for some Omega 3! The well-marked turnoff is 10km north of town, at Km 603 along Panamericana Sur, from where a dirt road leads 3km west to the coastal ruins.

Near the ruins, **Hotel Puerto Inka** (☎054-69-2608; www.puertoinka.com.pe; Panamericana Sur Km 603; camping per person S15, s/d/tr/q incl breakfast S119/189/249/299; P≋♿) is a large resort set on a pretty private bay. It has a campground that costs S13 per person, with a shower complex by the sea. It also offers horseback riding and rents out bodyboards, kayaks and jet skis. The showers are brackish, but the bungalow rooms are pleasant enough. The restaurant is open for non-guests for lunch. Credit cards not accepted – bring cash.

Colectivos to Chala (S15, 2½ hours) leave when full from the *óvalo* (main roundabout) in Nazca from the early morning until mid-afternoon. Onward buses to Arequipa (S35, eight hours) stop in Chala at small ticket offices along the Panamericana Sur, with most buses departing in the evening.

Camaná

☎054 / POP 14,600

After leaving Chala in the dust, the Panamericana Sur heads south for 220km, clinging tortuously to sand dunes dropping down to the sea, until it reaches positively urban Camaná. This coastal city has long been a summer resort popular with *arequipeños* (inhabitants of Arequipa) who flock to its beaches, about 5km from the center. Unless you are starved for beachtime, there's not much reason to stay here.

At the beach there are a few sparse restaurants and hotels, some bearing scars from a 2001 tsunami, but most people end up staying in the city proper, with the beach turning to a ghost town at night outside of high season. Hotels get busy on summer weekends from January to April.

Housed in a large elegant building set in spacious gardens, **Hotel de Turistas** (☎054-57-1113; Lima 138; s/d incl breakfast S140/200; P@≋) is a cut above the competition. It has a restaurant and sweet water slide, and is just a short walk or taxi ride from the bus stations.

The main plaza is about a 15-minute walk toward the coast along the road where all the buses stop. To get to the coast, *colectivos*

OFF THE BEATEN TRACK

SANTUARIO NACIONAL LAGUNAS DE MEJÍA

About 6km southeast of Mejía along an unbroken line of beaches is this 690-hectare **sanctuary** (Carretera Mollendo, Km 32; admission S5; ⌚dawn-dusk) protects coastal lagoons that are the largest permanent lakes in 1500km of desert coastline. They attract more than 200 species of coastal and migratory birds, best seen in the very early morning.

The visitor center has maps of hiking trails leading through the dunes to *miradors* (lookouts). From Mollendo, *colectivos* pass by the visitor center (S3, 30 minutes) frequently during the daytime. Ask the staff to help you flag down onward transportation, which peters out by the late afternoon.

to La Punta beach (S1, 10 minutes) leave from the intersection where Av Lima turns into a pedestrian walkway.

Frequent bus services to Arequipa (S12 to S45, 3½ hours) are provided by several companies, all of which are found along Lima, including luxurious **Cruz del Sur** (☎0801-11111; www.cruzdelsur.com.pe; Lima 474), and the always economical **Flores** (☎054-57-1013; www.floreshnos.net; Lima 200). Cruz del Sur and other smaller bus companies also have daily services to Lima (S35 to S135, 12 hours) that stop at most intermediate coastal points, such as Chala (S15, 4½ hours) and Nazca (S45, seven hours).

Mollendo

☎054 / POP 22,800

The gringo trail takes a sharp left turn south of Camaná as it heads inland toward Arequipa, leaving the next stop on the coast, Mollendo, to diehard locals, a few intrepid surfers, plus a seasonal influx of beach-starved *arequipeños*. This is by far the prettiest beach town of the southern south coast, with a bunch of cool two-story wood buildings dating back 100 years. The village itself slopes down to an arching beach.

The town can be a little lacking in atmosphere (and people for that matter) outside of the summer season (January to April). Mollendo's history testifies to occupations by the Incas and the Chileans. More notoriously, it was the birthplace of Abimael Guzmán, aka Presidente Gonzalo, the philosophy professor turned political agitator who became leader of the Sendero Luminoso (Shining Path) in 1980. Among nonsunbathers, Mollendo is revered for its bird reserve at the nearby Lagunas de Mejía.

Sights & Activities

There are several named surf breaks (mostly lefts) on the coastal road south of the aquatic park. They tend to be good in winter, but close out when it gets too big.

Aquatic Park AMUSEMENT PARK
(adult/child S4/2) When temperatures are searing from January through to at least March, the beachside aquatic park opens alongside the sea, and beachfront discos stay thumping until the small hours of the morning.

El Castillo de Forga HISTORIC BUILDING
El Castillo de Forga was built in 1908 on a crag between two of the beaches just south of the city center by a rich *arequipeño* in love with European architecture. Once an eye-catching stately home, it is currently unoccupied. There have been proposals to turn it into a casino.

Sleeping & Eating

Reservations are a must during the high season (January to April).

Hostal La Casona HOTEL $
(☎054-53-3160; henrymagrove@hotmail.com; Arequipa 188-192; s/d S50/60; wifi) The cheapest town center option, La Casona has bright rooms with high-ceilings, cable TV and hot water. The staff can be stiff necked, but the atmosphere is casual.

Hotel Bahia del Puerto HOTEL $$
(☎054-53-2990; hotelbahiadelpuerto@hotmail.com; Ugarte 301; s/d incl breakfast S60/110; air-con, internet, wifi, pool) Mollendo's best hotel is a bargain. Some rooms have quick ocean views, big flat-screen TVs and handmade quilts.

El Hostalito HOTEL $$
(☎054-53-4365; el_hostalito_mollendo@yahoo.com; Blondell 169; s/d/tr incl breakfast S70/120/160; wifi) A good budget bet on the top of the hill two blocks south of the main plaza, this hotel offers small peeks at the ocean from its top-floor rooms. The rooms are small but cozy, with flower prints and fans. There's a small terrace out back.

★Marco Antonio PERUVIAN $$
(Comercio 258; mains S20-30; ⏲8am-8pm Mon-Sat, 8am-7pm Sun; 📶) This little cafe and eatery scores big on ambience, with classic old-time styling and a few modern touches. The seafood dishes are direct, unpretentious and delicious.

ℹ Getting There & Around

The *terminal terrestre* (bus station) is about 2km northwest of the center; there's a S1 departure tax. **Santa Ursula** (☎054-53-2586) have frequent bus departures throughout the day for Arequipa (S8, two hours). *Colectivos* wait outside the terminal to whisk arriving passengers down to the town's plazas and the beach (S1, 10 minutes) or you can walk.

Combis (S1.20, 20 minutes) and *colectivos* (S2, 15 minutes) to the beach resort of Mejía leave from the corner of Valdivia and Arequipa. Unfortunately, there are no direct buses onward to Moquegua or Tacna. *Colectivos* and minivans marked 'El Valle' leave Mollendo from the top end of Mariscal Castilla, by a gas station, and pass through Mejía and the Río Tambo Valley to reach Cocachacra (S4, 1½ hours). There you can immediately jump into a *colectivo* heading for El Fiscal (S3, 15 minutes), a flyblown gas station where crowded buses heading to Moquegua, Tacna, Arequipa and Lima regularly stop.

Moquegua

☎053 / POP 56,000 / ELEV 1420M

Clinging to the northern limits of the world's driest desert, Moquegua defies near zero annual rainfall by supporting a thriving wine industry and a valley full of green fields replete with grazing cows that look like they might have been peeled off the surface of northern France (it's the rivers, you know). The town itself has a picturesque main square, but there is little else to detain you from a fleeting, but by no means unpleasant, overnight stop.

Sights & Activities

The town's small and shady **Plaza de Armas** boasts a 19th-century wrought-iron fountain, thought by some to have been designed in a workshop run by Gustave Eiffel (of eponymous tower fame), and flower gardens that make it a welcome oasis away from the encroaching desert.

The foreign-funded **Museo Contisuyo** (☎053-46-1844; www.museocontisuyo.com; Tacna 294; admission S3; ⏲8am-1pm & 2:30-5:30pm Wed-Mon, 8am-noon & 4-8pm Tue) is an excellent little repository of local archaeological artifacts, including photographs of recent excavations, along with exhibitions of new works by local artists. The labels are in Spanish and English.

The town's oldest church, **Iglesia Matriz** (Plaza de Armas), mostly collapsed during a massive earthquake in 1868. You can still see the ruins today. Opposite you'll find an 18th-century Spanish **colonial jail**, with intimidating iron-grilled windows. At one corner of the Plaza de Armas, visitors can enter the **Casa Posada de Teresa Podesta** (cnr Ancash & Ayacucho; admission S2; ⏲10am-3pm Mon-Fri), a stately colonial mansion with its innards still intact.

Walk around the town center to see some of the typical sugarcane thatching, especially along Calle Moquegua, and have a peek inside **Catedral Santa Catalina** (Ayacucho), which houses the body of 18th-century St Fortunata, whose hair and nails are said to be still growing.

A **park** on a cliff high above the town is dominated by the **Cristo Blanco**, a white statue of Christ raised in 2002. There are swinging seats, a small suspension bridge, and expansive views over the Moquegua oasis and the surrounding desert.

Cerro Baúl

A worthwhile excursion outside the city is to the flat-topped and steep-sided hill of **Cerro Baúl**, 18km northeast of Moquegua, once a royal brewery built by the Wari people. As was the case with succeeding Inca traditions, it was upper-class Wari women who were the skilled brewers here. Archaeologists who are still at work excavating the site believe that it was ceremonially destroyed by fire after one last, drunken *chicha* (fermented corn beer) bash, though why it was abandoned in such a rush remains a mystery so far. The rugged walk to the top of the site, which boasts panoramic views, takes about an hour.

From Moquegua, a round-trip taxi costs about S30, or simply catch a *combi* (S1.50) or *colectivo* (S3) headed for Torata from central Moquegua and ask to be let off at Cerro Baúl.

Sleeping & Eating

It's best to pass up the cheap hostels near the bus stations in lieu of a safer option closer to the center of town.

Hostal Plaza HOTEL $
(☎053-46-1612; Ayacucho 675; s/d/tr S55/60/75; 📶) This is a neat spot by the plaza where some of the upstairs rooms have pretty views of the cathedral. The good-value digs are airy and sport large-screen cable TVs.

Hostal Arequipa HOTEL $
(☎053-46-1338; Arequipa 360; s/d/tr S50/60/70; 📶) Located on a busy main street not far from the plaza, the Arequipa has clean and inviting rooms with hot showers and cable TV. Service here is reasonably friendly and helpful.

Vissios Pizzeria PIZZA $
(Plaza de Armas 343; mains S13-23) A little more chic than your average pizza joint, Vissios has bright red walls, waiter service and modish photo prints on the wall. The roaring eat-in, take-out trade is spearheaded by pizzas, pastas and super-sweet Moquegua wine. Naples it isn't. Nonetheless, it's a welcome sight in the middle of the Peruvian desert.

Roda Fruta BREAKFAST $
(Moquegua 439; breakfast S8-12) Grab your eggs, granola, yogurt and fruit salad in this salubrious breakfast place with casual seating. There's another branch in Calle Arequipa.

Information

BCP (Moquegua 861) Has a 24-hour Visa/MasterCard ATM.

Municipal Tourist Office (Casa de la Cultura, Calle Moquegua; ⏲7am-4pm) Local government-run tourist office.

Getting There & Away

Buses leave from several small terminals downhill southwest of the Plaza de Armas. There you'll also find faster, though less safe and more expensive *colectivos* that leave when full for Ilo (S12, 1½ hours) and Arequipa (S30, 3½ hours).

Quality **Ormeño** (☎053-76-1149; www.grupo-ormeno.com.pe; Av La Paz 524) buses and cheaper **Flores** (☎053-46-2647; www.floreshnos.net; Av Ejercito s/n) options run north serving Lima via Nazca and Ica, and south to Tacna. Flores and a couple of other companies also head west to Ilo. Numerous companies serve Arequipa.

Several smaller companies, including **San Martín** (☎95-352-1550; Av La Paz 175), take a mostly paved route to Puno (S25, nine hours) via Desaguadero on the Bolivian border (S18, six hours), usually departing in the evening.

Moquegua Buses:

DESTINATION	COST (S)	DURATION (HR)
Arequipa	30	3½–4
Ilo	20–30	1½
Lima	50–144	16–20
Puno	25	9
Tacna	10	3

Ilo

☎053 / POP 58,700

Ilo is the ugly departmental port, about 95km southwest of Moquegua, used mainly to ship copper from the mine at Toquepala further south, and wine and avocados from Moquegua. Ilo does offer a pleasant boardwalk and a few beachside luxury hotels that fill with Peruvian vacationers in the summertime, but though the beach is long and curving, the waters are murky and unappealing for swimming.

Sights

Museo Municipal de Sitio MUSEUM
(☎053-83-5000; Centro Mallqui; admission S5; ⏲10am-3pm Mon-Sat, 10am-2pm Sun) About 15km inland at El Algarrobal is the Museo Municipal de Sitio, which hosts a surprisingly noteworthy collection of exhibits on the area's archaeology and agriculture, including ceramics, textiles, a collection of feather-topped hats and a mummified llama. A round-trip by taxi costs around S30.

Sleeping & Eating

There's no need to stay overnight, but if you get stuck there are plenty of options.

Hotel Kristal Azul HOTEL $$
(☎053-48-4050; Av 28 de Julio 664; s/d S60/90; 📶) Above a pizza restaurant two blocks from the bus station, this place is clean, if unremarkable, with breakfast included.

Los Corales SEAFOOD $$
(Malecón Miramar 504; mains S14-30; ⏲lunch & dinner; 📶) The prime shore-front position pretty much guarantees fresh seafood including local favorite, *pulpo al olvia* (octopus in olive oil), a cold appetizer.

Getting There & Away

Most buses leave from a terminal in the town center, a couple of blocks from the plaza and the beach.

Flores (☎053-48-2512; www.floreshnos.net; cnr Ilo & Matará) covers Tacna (S10, 3½ hours), Moquegua (S8, 1½ hours) and Arequipa (S18, 5½ hours) where you can connect for onward journeys.

Faster, slightly pricier *colectivos* to Tacna and sometimes Moquegua leave when full from the side streets near the smaller bus stations.

Tacna

☎052 / POP 262,700 / ELEV 460M

Patriotism puts up a steely rearguard action in Tacna, Peru's most southerly settlement, a city that belonged to Chile as recently as 1929 (a young Salvador Allende lived here for eight of his childhood years), but is now proudly and unequivocally part of Peru. Just in case you forget, there's an earnest flag-raising ceremony every Sunday morning in the main plaza, plus a raft of heroic statues, leafy avenues and hyperbolic museum exhibits all dedicated to Peru's glorious past.

For outsiders, Tacna's primary role is as a staging post on the way to its former nemesis, Chile. Cordial modern relations between the two countries make the border crossing a comparative breeze. If you're delayed in town, a trio of small museums and some Europhile bars and restaurants will smooth the wait.

Sights

Plaza de Armas SQUARE

Tacna's main plaza is studded with palm trees and large pergolas topped by bizarre mushroom-like features. The plaza, famously pictured on the front of Peru's S100 note, features a huge arch – a monument to the heroes of the War of the Pacific.

It is flanked by larger-than-life bronze statues of Admiral Grau and Colonel Bolognesi. Nearby, the 6m-high bronze **fountain** was created by the French engineer Gustave Eiffel, who also designed the **cathedral**, noted for its small but fine stained-glass windows and onyx high altar.

Museo Ferroviario MUSEUM

(☎052-24-5572; admission S5; ⌚8am-6pm) This museum located inside the train station – just ring the bell at the southern gates – gives the impression of stepping back in time. You can wander amid beautiful though poorly maintained 20th-century steam engines and rolling stock.

About a 15-minute walk south of the train station, a British locomotive built in 1859 and used as a troop train in the War of the Pacific is the centerpiece of **El Parque de la Locomotora**, an otherwise empty roadside park.

Casa Museo Basadre MUSEUM

(Plaza de Armas 212; admission by donation; ⌚9am-5pm) Named for a local historian born in 1903, this place is more convincing as a cultural center than a museum (though there's a handful of old photos and exhibits). Check out the posters inside for upcoming music and art shows.

Museo de Zela MUSEUM

(Zela 542; ⌚8am-noon & 3-5pm Mon-Sat) FREE The small, musty Museo de Zela provides a look at the interior of one of Tacna's oldest colonial buildings, the Casa de Zela.

Museo Histórico Regional MUSEUM

(Casa de la Cultura, Apurímac 202; admission S5; ⌚8am-noon & 1:30-5pm Mon-Fri) Patriotic like everything in Tacna, this museum above the town library broadcasts a grand somewhat triumphant air. Five huge canvases adorn the walls, and busts of erstwhile heroes such as Zela, Bolognesi and Ugarte sit among old swords, yellowed letters and details about the War of the Pacific against former foe Chile.

Sleeping

There's no shortage of hotels catering to Tacna's cross-border traffic. That said, almost all are overpriced and fill up very fast, especially with Chileans who cross the border for weekend shopping and dentistry trips.

Hostal Le Prince HOTEL $

(☎052-42-1252; Zela 728; s/d S70/80; P 📶) This is an economical and modern spot that's hard to resist if you aren't willing enough to cough up the extra cash to stay in one of the fancier digs in town.

Dorado Hotel HOTEL $$

(☎052-41-5741; www.doradohoteltacna.com; Av Arias Aragüez 145; s/d/tr incl breakfast S129/179/209; @ 📶) Posing as Tacna's grandest hotel, the Dorado is the sort of place where the curtains are heavy, the lobby sports shiny balustrades, and a bellboy will carry your bags to your room. While it can't emulate the exclusivity of a European city hotel, it makes a good job of trying.

Tacna

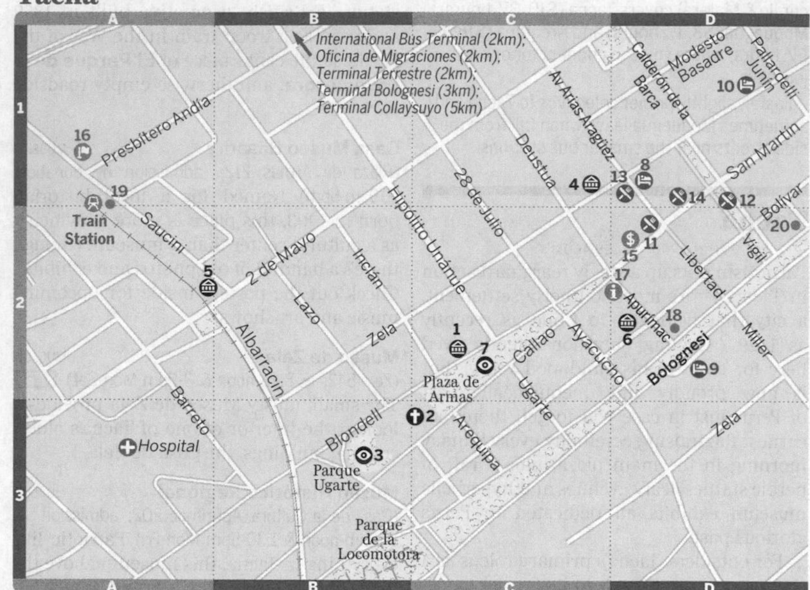

Gran Hotel Tacna HOTEL $$
(052-42-4193; www.granhoteltacna.com; Bolognesi 300; s/d incl breakfast S214/244;) Bringing the feeling of a 'resort' to the city center, the architecturally uninteresting Gran Hotel Tacna is certainly large, with numerous bars and restaurants, a shop, a pool and waistcoated waiters running around looking busy. It's not the classiest joint in town but it's certainly the most comprehensive (and expensive).

Eating

Popular local dishes include *patasca a la tacneña* (a thick, spicy vegetable-and-meat soup) and *picante a la tacneña* (hot peppered tripe – better than it sounds).

Café Verdi CAFE $
(Vigil 57; snacks S3-8, menú S7.50; 8:30am-9pm Mon-Sat) Verdi's an old-school cafe with baked goods and desserts, as well as affordable fixed lunches served at perennially busy tables. Half the clientele looks as if they've been coming here for 50 years. They probably have.

★ **Café Da Vinci** EUROPEAN $$
(Calle Arias Aragüez 122; mains S23-40; 11am-11pm) There's a Euro-feel to the food and decor in this wood-paneled domain where well-dressed wait staff give out Mona Lisa smiles along with menus that highlight fabulous baguettes, pizzas, generous glasses of dry red wine, and decent Peruvian staples. Pride of place goes to the real Italian espresso machine.

Uros Restaurante FUSION $$
(www.restauranteuros.com; Av San Martín 608; mains S22-35) Tacna's stab at *novoandina* (Peruvian nouvelle cuisine) avoids too many pretensions, if you can get past the (admittedly photogenic) photos of the food on the menu.

Mushna INTERNATIONAL $$
(Av Arias Aragüez 204; mains S25-35) A post-modern resto-bar that looks like it has drifted across from Arica, Chile. Food is presented with artistic panache in an interior that is more nightclub than restaurant. Cocktails abound.

Drinking

The small pedestrian streets of Libertad and Vigil are ground zero for Tacna's limited nightlife.

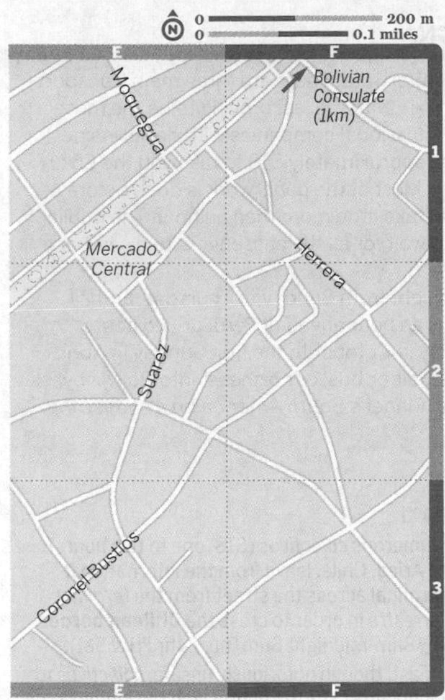

Tacna

Sights

1 Casa Museo Basadre ... C2
2 Cathedral ... C3
3 Fountain ... B3
4 Museo de Zela ... C1
5 Museo Ferroviario ... A2
6 Museo Histórico Regional ... D2
7 Plaza de Armas ... C2

Sleeping

8 Dorado Hotel ... D1
9 Gran Hotel Tacna ... D2
10 Hostal Le Prince ... D1

Eating

11 Café Da Vinci ... D2
12 Café Verdi ... D1
13 Mushna ... D1
14 Uros Restaurante ... D1

Information

15 BCP ... D2
16 Chilean Consulate ... A1
17 iPerú ... D2

Transport

18 LAN ... D2
19 PeruRail Ticket Office ... A1
20 Peruvian Airlines ... D2

Information

Internet cafes are everywhere, and most offer inexpensive local, long-distance and international phone calls. Chilean pesos, Peruvian nuevos soles and US dollars can all be easily exchanged in Tacna. There's a global ATM at the *terminal terrestre* (bus station).

BCP (San Martín 574) Has a Visa/MasterCard ATM and gives cash advances on Visa cards.

Bolivian Consulate (052-25-5121; Bolognesi 1751) Some nationalities (American included) may need to solicit a visa one month in advance and pay a US$135 entry fee. Some Bolivian borders will issue on-the-spot visas payable in US dollars. Check ahead.

Chilean Consulate (052-42-3063; Presbitero Andía s/n) Most travelers don't need a Chilean visa and head straight for the border instead.

Hospital (052-42-2121, 052-42-3361; Blondell s/n; 24hr) For emergency services.

iPerú (052-42-5514; San Martín 491; 8:30am-7:30pm Mon-Fri, to 2:30pm Sat) National tourist office, provides free information and brochures.

Oficina de Migraciones (Immigration Office; 052-24-3231; Circunvalación s/n, Urb Él Triángulo; 8am-4pm Mon-Fri) Immigration office.

Police (052-41-4141; Calderón de la Barca 353; 24hr) Police.

Getting There & Away

AIR

Tacna's **airport** (TCQ) is 5km west of town. **LAN** (052-42-8346; www.lan.com; Apurímac 101; 8:30am-7pm Mon-Fri, 9am-2pm Sat) and **Peruvian Airlines** (www.peruvian.pe; Av Bolognesi 670) both offer daily passenger services to Lima, and some seasonal services to Arequipa and Cuzco.

BUS

Most long-distance departures leave from the **terminal terrestre** (Hipólito Unánue), at the northeast edge of town, with the exception of some buses to Juliaca, Desaguadero and Puno, which leave from **Terminal Collaysuyo**, located in the district of Alta Alianza to the north of town.

Frequent buses (S10) to Arica, Chile, leave between 6am and 10pm from the international terminal across the street from the *terminal terrestre*.

San Martín (952-524-252; Terminal Collaysuyo s/n) runs overnight *económico* and luxury bus services to Puno via Desaguadero on

BORDER CROSSING: CHILE VIA TACNA

Border-crossing formalities are relatively straightforward. There are three main transport options: train, public bus or *colectivo* (shared taxi), with the last proving to be the most efficient. The five-passenger taxis are run by professional companies with desks inside Tacna's international bus terminal. They charge approximately S18 to take you the 65km to Arica in Chile with stops at both border posts. Most of the paperwork is done before you get in the car. On a good day the trip should take little more than an hour. The public bus is cheaper (S10), but slower, as you have to wait for all the passengers to disembark and clear customs.

The Chilean border post is open 8am to midnight from Sunday to Thursday, and 24 hours on Friday and Saturday. Note that Chile is an hour ahead of Peru, or two hours during daylight-saving time from the last Sunday in October to the first Sunday in April. From Arica, you can continue south into Chile by air or bus, or northeast into Bolivia by air or bus. For more information, consult Lonely Planet's *South America on a shoestring, Chile & Easter Island* and/or *Bolivia*.

the Bolivian border, finally ending up in Cuzco. These mostly leave in the evening from Terminal Collaysuyo. When choosing this route, opt for the nicest bus, or you could be in for a cold, bumpy ride with few bathroom breaks – trust us! Alternatively, you can also return to Arequipa and transfer there.

Long-distance buses are frequently stopped and searched by immigration and/or customs officials not far north of Tacna. Have your passport handy.

A S1 terminal-use tax is levied at the *terminal terrestre*. The usual suspects head to all destinations north including **Ormeño** (☎052-42-3292; www.grupo-ormeno.com.pe; Terminal Terrestre s/n) and more economical **Flores** (☎052-74-1150; www.floreshnos.net; Terminal Terrestre s/n).

Tacna Buses:

DESTINATION	COST (S)	DURATION (HR)
Arequipa	15–35	7
Cuzco	60–125	17
Ilo	10	3½
Lima	50–144	18–22
Moquegua	10	3
Puno	25–45	10

TAXI

Numerous *colectivos* (S18, one to two hours) to Arica, Chile, leave from the international terminal across the street from the *terminal terrestre* in order to cross the **Chilean border** (⏲8am-midnight Sun-Thu, 24hr Fri & Sat).

Fast, though notoriously unsafe, *colectivos* to Moquegua (S15, 2½ hours), and sometimes Ilo, leave when full from Mercado Grau, a short walk uphill from the *terminal terrestre*. Be sure to keep your wits about you in the dangerous market area.

TRAIN

Trains between Tacna's **train station** (Av 2 de Mayo) and Arica, Chile (S10/C$2000, 1½ hours) are the cheapest and most charming but also the slowest way to cross the border. Your passport is stamped at the station before boarding the train in Tacna. There is no stop at the actual border and you receive your entry stamp when you arrive in Chile near Arica's Plaza de Armas. Though this historic railway is a must for train buffs, service can be erratic and inconveniently timed. At the time of writing two trains a day were departing from Tacna at 4am and 6am. Return trains leave Arica at 4pm and 6pm. Always double check at the station for the latest schedules.

ℹ Getting Around

A taxi between the airport and the city center costs about S5. A taxi from the center to the bus terminals costs about S3.

Arequipa & Canyon Country

Includes ➡

Best Places to Eat

- ➡ Zingaro (p155)
- ➡ Tradición Arequipeña (p154)
- ➡ Zig Zag (p155)
- ➡ Chicha (p156)

Best Places to Stay

- ➡ Hotel Casona Solar (p152)
- ➡ Los Tambos Hostal (p153)
- ➡ Colca Lodge (p166)
- ➡ Casa Andina Classic (p153)

Why Go?

Arequipa province is Peru's big combo ticket. Authentic historical immersion and white-knuckle Andean adventure inhabit the same breathing space here. Imagine the cultural riches of one of South America's finest colonial cities just a few hours' drive from the world's two deepest canyons and you'll get a hint of the dramatic contrasts. Ample urban distractions can be found in Arequipa, the arty, audacious, unflappably resilient metropolis that lies in the shadow of El Misti volcano. Beckoning to the northwest lie the Colca and Cotahuasi canyons whose depth, while impressive, is a mere statistic compared to the Andean condors, epic treks, and long-standing Spanish, Inca and pre-Inca traditions that lurk in their midst. Other unusual apparitions include the lava-encrusted Valle de los Volcanes, the haunting Toro Muerto petroglyphs and the barren Paso de Patopampa where a main road ascends to 4910m, higher than any point in Western Europe or North America.

When to Go

Arequipa

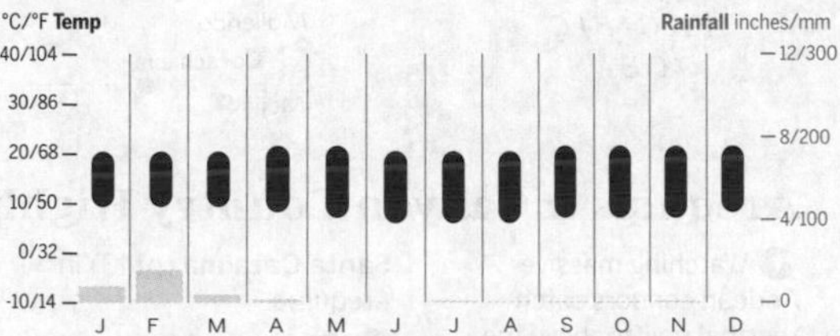

Mar–Apr Arequipa puts on a Semana Santa parade to rival the cities of former colonial power, Spain

Apr–Dec Outside rainy season, hiking in the Colca and Cotahuasi canyons is a sublime experience

Jun–Sep Your best chance of seeing Andean condors gliding above the Cañón del Colca

AREQUIPA

☎054 / POP 969,300 / ELEV 2350M

It's hard playing second fiddle to Cuzco and Machu Picchu on Peru's international tourist circuit, not that this little detail makes the average *arequipeño* jealous. Other Peruvians joke that you need a different passport to enter Peru's second-largest city, a metropolis one-tenth of the size of the capital Lima but pugnaciously equal to it in terms of cuisine, historical significance and confident self-awareness.

Guarded by not one but *three* dramatic volcanoes, the city enjoys a resplendent, if seismically precarious setting – earthquakes regularly wrack this region, the last big one causing significant damage in 2001. Fortunately, the city's architecture, a formidable ensemble of baroque buildings grafted out of the local white volcanic *sillar* rock, has

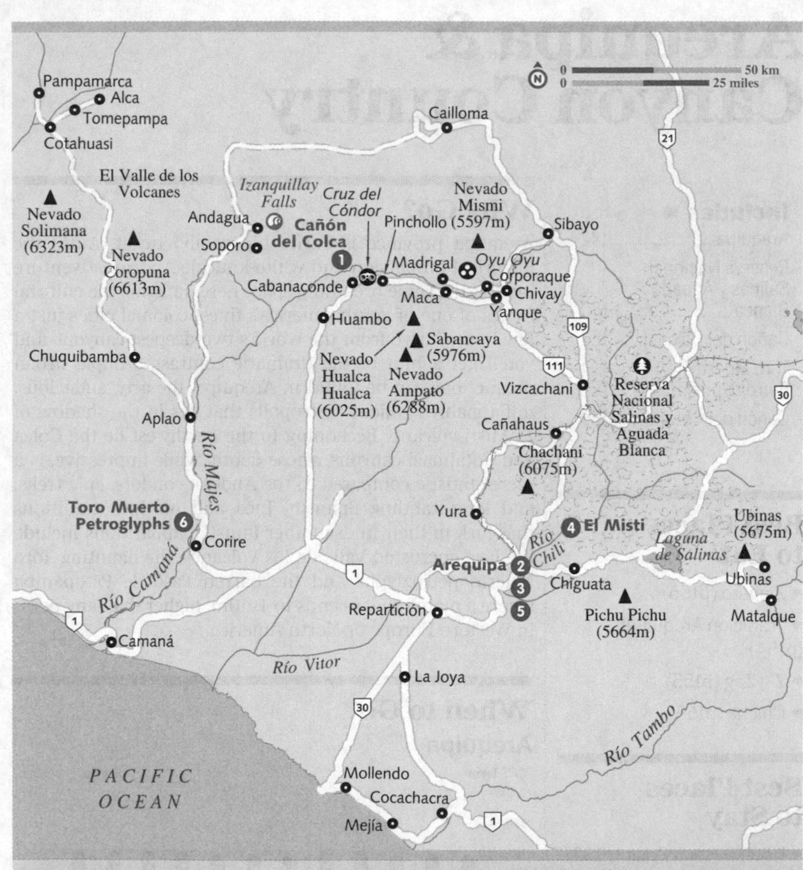

Arequipa & Canyon Country Highlights

1. Watching massive Andean condors catch thermal uplifts above the almost sheer walls of the **Cañón del Colca** (p162).
2. Getting a glimpse of austere, monastic life behind the high stone walls of the **Monasterio de Santa Catalina** (p143) in Arequipa.
3. Dining the traditional way in one of Arequipa's **picanterías** (p155).
4. Making a summit attempt on the almost perfectly symmetrical cone of **El Misti** (p161) volcano.
5. Studying the frozen remains of Juanita in the **Museo Santuarios Andinos** (p146).
6. Pondering the meaning of the mysterious **Toro Muerto petroglyphs** (p168).

so far withstood most of what mother earth has thrown at it. In 2000 the city's central core earned a well-deserved Unesco World Heritage listing – the sight of the gigantic cathedral, with the ethereal image of 5825m El Misti rising behind it, is worth a visit alone.

Pretty cityscapes aside, Arequipa has played a fundamental role in Peru's gastronomic renaissance; classic spicy dishes such as *rocoto relleno* (stuffed spicy red peppers), *chupe de camarones* (prawn chowder) and *ocopa* (boiled potato in a creamy, spicy sauce), best enjoyed in the city's communal *picantería* restaurants, all hail from here.

Arequipeños are a proud people fond of intellectual debate, especially about their fervent political beliefs, which historically found voice through regular demonstrations in the Plaza de Armas. Not surprisingly, the city has produced one of Latin America's most influential novelists, Mario Vargas Llosa, the literary genius who ran unsuccessfully for the Peruvian presidency in 1990.

History

Evidence of pre-Inca settlement by indigenous peoples from the Lake Titicaca area lead some scholars to think the Aymara people first named the city (*ari* means 'peak' and *quipa* means 'lying behind' in Aymara; hence, Arequipa is 'the place lying behind the peak' of El Misti). However, another oft-heard legend says that the fourth *inca* (king), Mayta Cápac, was traveling through the valley and became enchanted by it. He ordered his retinue to stop, saying, '*Ari, quipay*,' which translates as 'Yes, stay.' The city was refounded by the Spaniards on August 15, 1540, a date that is remembered with a week-long fair.

Arequipa is built in an area highly prone to natural disasters; the city was totally destroyed by earthquakes and volcanic eruptions in 1600 and has since been rocked by major earthquakes in 1687, 1868, 1958, 1960 and, most recently, in 2001. For this reason, many of the city's buildings are built low for stability. Despite the disasters, many fetching historic structures survive.

Sights

Monasterio de Santa Catalina MONASTERY

(☎054-22-1213; www.santacatalina.org.pe; Santa Catalina 301; admission S40; ⌚8am-5pm, to 8pm Tue & Thu, last entry 1hr before closing) Even if you have overdosed on colonial edifices, this convent shouldn't be missed. Occupying a whole block and guarded by imposing high walls, it is one of the most fascinating religious buildings in Peru. Nor is it just a religious building – the 20,000-sq-meter complex is almost a citadel within the city. It was founded in 1580 by a rich widow, doña María de Guzmán. Enter from the southeast corner.

The best way to visit Santa Catalina is to hire one of the informative guides, available for S20 from inside the entrance. Guides speak Spanish, English, French, German, Italian, Portuguese or Japanese. The tours last about an hour, after which you're welcome to keep exploring by yourself, until the gates close. The monastery is also open two evenings a week so that visitors can traipse through the shadowy grounds by candlelight as nuns would have done centuries ago.

Alternatively, you can wander around on your own without a guide, soaking up the meditative atmosphere and getting slightly lost (there's a finely printed miniature map on the back of your ticket if you're up for an orienteering challenge). A helpful way to begin is to focus a visit on the three main **cloisters**. After passing under the *silencio* (silence) arch you will enter the **Novice Cloister**, marked by a courtyard with a rubber tree at its center. After passing under this arch, novice nuns were required to zip their lips in a vow of solemn silence and resolve to a life of work and prayer. Nuns lived as novices for four years, during which time their wealthy families were expected to pay a dowry of 100 gold coins per year. At the end of the four years they could choose between taking their vows and entering into religious service, or leaving the convent – the latter would most likely have brought shame upon their family.

Graduated novices passed onto the **Orange Cloister**, named for the orange trees clustered at its center that represent renewal and eternal life. This cloister allows a peek into the **Profundis Room**, a mortuary where dead nuns were mourned. Paintings of the deceased line the walls. Artists were allotted 24 hours to complete these posthumous paintings, since painting the nuns while alive was out of the question.

Leading away from the Orange Cloister, **Córdova Street** is flanked by cells that served as living quarters for the nuns. These dwellings would house one or more nuns, along with a handful of servants, and ranged from austere to lavish depending on the wealth of the inhabitants. Ambling down

Arequipa

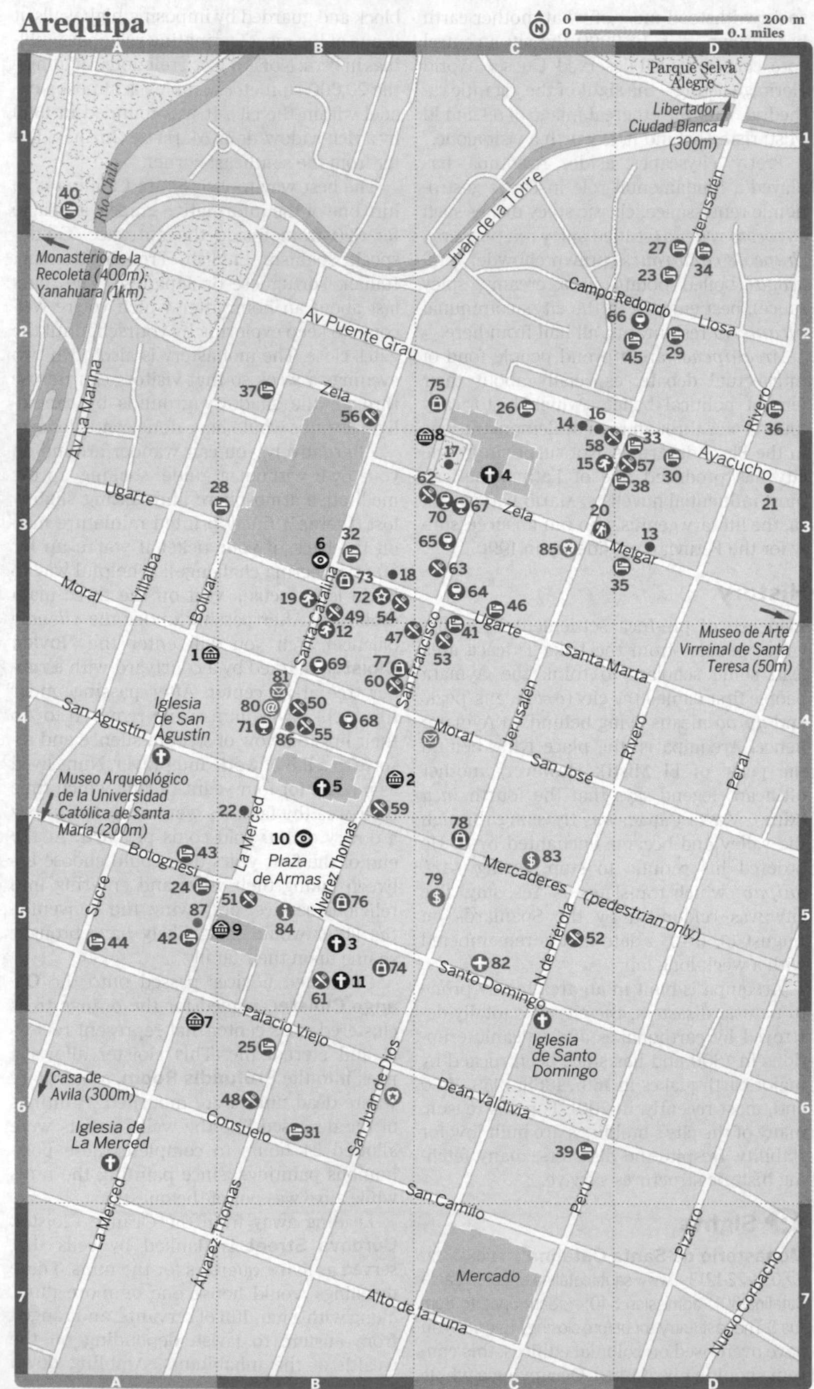
0 200 m
0 0.1 miles
A
B
C
D
1
2
3
4
5
6
7
Parque Selva Alegre
Libertador Ciudad Blanca (300m)
Río Chili
Monasterio de la Recoleta (400m); Yanahuara (1km)
Juan de la Torre
Jerusalén
Campo Redondo
Llosa
Av Puente Grau
Av La Marina
Zela
Rivero
Ayacucho
Ugarte
Melgar
Moral
Villalba
Bolívar
Santa Catalina
San Francisco
Santa Marta
Museo de Arte Virreinal de Santa Teresa (50m)
San Agustín
Iglesia de San Agustín
Museo Arqueológico de la Universidad Católica de Santa María (200m)
La Merced
Álvarez Thomas
Plaza de Armas
San José
Peral
Bolognesi
Mercaderes (pedestrian only)
Sucre
N de Piérola
Santo Domingo
Iglesia de Santo Domingo
Palacio Viejo
Casa de Avila (300m)
San Juan de Dios
Deán Valdivia
Consuelo
Iglesia de La Merced
Perú
San Camilo
Pizarro
Mercado
Nuevo Corbacho
Alto de la Luna

Arequipa

Sights

1 Casa de Moral ... A4
2 Casa Ricketts ... B4
3 Iglesia de La Compañía ... B5
4 Iglesia de San Francisco ... C3
5 La Catedral ... B4
6 Monasterio de Santa Catalina ... B3
Museo Arqueológico Chiribaya ... (see 8)
7 Museo de la Universidad Nacional de San Agustín ... A6
8 Museo Histórico Municipal ... C3
9 Museo Santuarios Andinos ... B5
10 Plaza de Armas ... B5
11 San Ignacio Chapel ... B5

Activities, Courses & Tours

12 Carlos Zárate Adventures ... B4
13 Centro Cultural Peruano Norteamericano ... D3
14 CEPESMA ... C2
15 Colca Trek ... C3
16 Ecotours ... C2
17 Free Walking Tour Peru ... C3
18 Instituto Cultural Peruano Alemán ... B3
19 Naturaleza Activa ... B3
20 Pablo Tour ... C3
Peru Camping Shop ... (see 33)
21 ROCIO ... D3
22 Tours Class Arequipa ... B4

Sleeping

23 Casa Andina Classic ... D2
24 Casablanca Hostal ... A5
25 Casona Terrace Hotel ... B6
26 Colonial House Inn ... C2
27 Hostal El Descanso del Fundador ... D2
28 Hostal las Torres de Ugarte ... B3
29 Hostal Núñez ... D2
30 Hostal Solar ... D3
31 Hotel Casona Solar ... B6
32 Hotel La Posada del Monasterio ... B3
33 Hotel Real Arequipa ... D3
34 La Casa de Mamayacchi (Arequipa Office) ... D2
35 La Casa de Melgar ... D3
36 La Casa de Sillar ... D2
37 La Hostería ... B2
38 La Posada del Cacique ... D3
39 La Posada del Parque ... C6
40 La Posada del Puente ... A1
41 Le Foyer ... C4
42 Los Andes Bed & Breakfast ... A5
43 Los Tambos Hostal ... A5
44 Point Hostel ... A5
45 Terruño de Yarabaya ... D2
46 Wild Rover Hostel ... C3

Eating

47 Café Fez-Istanbul ... B4
48 Cevichería Fory Fay ... B6
Chicha ... (see 73)
49 Crepisimo ... B3
50 El Carpriccio ... B4
51 El Super ... B5
52 El Super ... C5
53 El Turko ... C4
54 Hatunpa ... B3
55 Inkari Pub Pizzeria ... B4
56 La Trattoria del Monasterio ... B2
57 Lakshmivan ... D3
58 Los Leños ... C3
59 Manolo's ... B4
60 Nina-Yaku ... B4
61 Ribs Café ... B5
62 Zig Zag ... C3
63 Zingaro ... C3

Drinking & Nightlife

64 Brujas Bar ... C3
65 Casona Forum ... C3
66 Chelawasi Public House ... D2
67 Déjà Vu ... C3
68 Farren's Irish Pub ... B4
69 Museo del Pisco ... B4
70 Split ... C3
71 Zoom ... B4

Entertainment

72 Café Art Montréal ... B3

Shopping

73 Casona Santa Catalina ... B3
74 Claustros de la Campañía ... B5
75 Fundo El Fierro ... C2
76 Galería de Artesanías 'El Tumi de Oro' ... B5
77 Librería el Lector ... B4
78 Patio del Ekeko ... C5

Information

79 BCP ... C5
80 Ciber Market ... B4
81 DHL ... B4
82 InkaFarma ... C5
83 Interbank ... C5
84 iPerú ... B5
85 Policía de Turismo ... C3

Transport

86 LAN ... B4
87 Sky Airline ... A5

Toledo Street leads you to the cafe, which serves fresh-baked pastries and espressos, and finally to the communal washing area where servants washed in mountain runoff channeled into huge earthenware jars.

Heading down **Burgos Street** toward the cathedral's sparkling *sillar* tower, visitors may enter the musty darkness of the communal kitchen that was originally used as the church until the reformation of 1871. Just beyond, **Zocodober Square** (the name comes from the Arabic word for 'barter') was where nuns gathered on Sundays to exchange their handicrafts, such as soaps and baked goods. Continuing on, to the left you can enter the **cell** of the legendary Sor Ana, a nun renowned for her eerily accurate predictions about the future and the miracles she is said to have performed until her death in 1686.

Finally, the **Great Cloister** is bordered by the **chapel** on one side and the **art gallery**, which used to serve as a communal dormitory, on the other. This building takes on the shape of a cross. Murals along the walls depict scenes from the lives of Jesus and the Virgin Mary.

Museo Santuarios Andinos MUSEUM

(054-20-0345; La Merced 110; admission S20; 9am-6pm Mon-Sat, to 3pm Sun) There's an escalating drama to this theatrically presented museum, dedicated to the preserved body of a frozen 'mummy,' and its compulsory guided tour (free, but a tip is expected at the end). Spoiler: the climax is the vaguely macabre sight of poor Juanita, the 12-year-old Inca girl sacrificed to the gods in the 1450s and now eerily preserved in a glass refrigerator. Tours take about an hour and are conducted in Spanish, English and French.

Before presenting Juanita herself, well-versed student guides from the university lead you through a series of atmospheric, dimly lit rooms filled with artifacts from the expedition that found the 'mummy.' There is a beautifully shot 20-minute film about how Juanita, the so-called 'Ice Maiden,' was unearthed atop Nevado Ampato in 1995. From January to April, Juanita is switched for a different 'mummy.'

Plaza de Armas SQUARE

Arequipa's main plaza, unblemished by modern interference, is a museum of the city's *sillar* architecture – white, muscular and aesthetically unique. Impressive colonnaded balconies line three sides. The fourth is given over to Peru's widest cathedral, a humongous edifice with two soaring towers. Even this is dwarfed by the duel snowcapped sentinels of El Misti and Chanchani, both visible from various points in the central park.

Once the noisy stage for political protests and honking taxis, in mid-2015 protests and traffic were (controversially) banned in and around the plaza to make it more tourist friendly.

La Catedral CATHEDRAL

(054-23-2635; 7-11:30am & 5-7:30pm Mon-Sat, 7am-1pm & 5-7pm Sun) FREE On the Plaza de Armas, this building stands out for its stark white *sillar* and massive size – it is the only cathedral in Peru that stretches the length of a plaza. It also has a history of rising up from the ashes. The original structure, dating from 1656, was gutted by fire in 1844. Consequently rebuilt, it was then flattened by the 1868 earthquake. Most of what you see now has been rebuilt since then.

An earthquake in 2001 toppled one enormous tower, and made the other slump precariously, yet by the end of the next year the cathedral looked as good as new.

The interior is simple and airy, with a luminous quality, and the high vaults are uncluttered. It also has a distinctly international flair; it is one of fewer than 100 basilicas in the world entitled to display the Vatican flag, which is to the right of the altar. Both the altar and the 12 columns (symbolizing the 12 Apostles) are made of Italian marble. The huge Byzantine-style brass lamp hanging in front of the altar is from Spain and the pulpit was carved in France. In 1870, Belgium provided the impressive organ, said to be the largest in South America, though damage during shipping condemned the devout to wince at its distorted notes for more than a century.

Iglesia de La Compañía CHURCH

(9am-12:30pm & 3-6pm Sun-Fri, 11:30am-12:30pm & 3-6pm Sat) FREE If Arequipa's cathedral seems *too* big, an interesting antidote (proving that small can be beautiful) is this diminutive Jesuit church on the southeast corner of the Plaza de Armas. The facade is an intricately carved masterpiece of the *churrigueresque* style (think baroque and then some – a style hatched in Spain in the 1660s). The equally detailed altar, completely covered in gold leaf, takes the style further and will be eerily familiar to anyone who has visited Seville cathedral in Spain.

To the left of the altar is the **San Ignacio Chapel** (admission S4; ⌚9am-12:30pm & 3-6pm Sun-Fri, 11:30am-12:30pm & 3-6pm Sat), with a polychrome cupola smothered in unusual jungle-like murals of tropical flowers, fruit and birds, among which mingle warriors and angels.

Next door, and accessed via Calle Santo Domingo, the beautiful, semi-outdoor shopping center Claustros de la Campañía (p158) continues the ornate theme.

Monasterio de la Recoleta MONASTERY

(La Recoleta 117; admission S10; ⌚9am-noon & 3-5pm daily, to 8pm Wed & Fri) Bibliophiles will delight in this musty monastery's huge library, which contains more than 20,000 dusty books and maps; the oldest volume dates to 1494. Scholarship was an integral part of the Franciscans' order. The library is open for supervised visits; just ask at the entrance.

There is also a well-known museum of Amazonian artifacts (including preserved jungle animals) collected by the missionaries, and an extensive collection of pre-Conquest artifacts and religious art of the *escuela cuzqueña* (Cuzco School).

The monastery was constructed on the west side of the Río Chili in 1648 by Franciscan friars, though now it has been completely rebuilt. Guides speaking Spanish, English, French and Italian are available; a tip is expected.

It's located in a dicey neighborhood a short cab ride from the city center.

Museo de Arte Virreinal de Santa Teresa MUSEUM

(☎054-28-1188; Melgar 303; admission S20; ⌚9am-5pm Mon-Thu & Sat, to 8pm Fri) This gorgeous 17th-century Carmelite convent is open to the public as a living museum. The colonial-era buildings are justifiably famed for their decorative painted walls and restored rooms filled with priceless votive *objets d'art,* murals, precious metalwork, colonial-era paintings and other historical artifacts. It is all explained by student tour guides who speak Spanish, English, French, German and Portuguese; tips appreciated. A charming shop at the front of the complex sells baked goods and rose-scented soap made by the nuns.

Casa de Moral HISTORIC BUILDING

(☎054-21-4907; Moral 318; admission S5; ⌚9am-5pm Mon-Sat) Built in 1730, this stylized baroque house is named after the 200-year-old mulberry tree in its central courtyard. Owned by BCP (a bank) since 2003, it is now a museum notable for its antique maps, heavy furniture, religious art, and extensive Peruvian coin and banknote collection (courtesy of BCP). Explanations are in Spanish and English.

Casa Ricketts HISTORIC BUILDING

(Casa Tristán del Pozo; ☎054-21-5060; San Francisco 108; ⌚9am-6pm Mon-Fri, to 1pm Sat) FREE Built in 1738, the ornate Casa Ricketts has served as a seminary, archbishop's palace, school and home to well-to-do families. Today it is the most splendiferous working bank in the city – possibly even Peru. Even if you're not here for a transaction, it's worth nosing around its small gallery of Arequipan art, and dual interior courtyards with their puma-headed fountains.

La Mansión del Fundador HISTORIC BUILDING

(☎054-44-2460; www.lamansiondelfundador.com; admission S15; ⌚9am-5pm) This 17th-century mansion was once owned by Arequipa's founder Garcí Manuel de Carbajal, has been restored with original furnishings and paintings, and even has its own chapel. The mansion is in the village of Huasacache, 9km from Arequipa's city center, most easily reached by taxi (round-trip S20). Local city tours often stop here.

Iglesia de San Francisco CHURCH

(☎054-22-3048; Zela cuadra 1; admission S5; ⌚9am-12:30pm & 3-6:30pm Mon-Fri) Originally built in the 16th century, this church has been badly damaged by several earthquakes. It still stands, however, and visitors can see a large crack in the cupola – testimony to the power of quakes. Other colonial churches around the city center include **San Agustín**, **La Merced** and **Santo Domingo**.

Museo Arqueológico de la Universidad Católica de Santa María MUSEUM

(☎054-22-1083; Cruz Verde 303; by donation; ⌚8:30am-4pm Mon-Fri) This university-run museum has interesting little displays on local excavation sites, as well as some artifacts, including surprisingly well-preserved ancient ceramics. Guided tours are available in Spanish and English; tips are expected.

Museo Histórico Municipal MUSEUM

(Plazuela San Francisco 407; admission S10; ⌚9am-5pm Mon-Sat, to 1pm Sun) Arequipa's and Peru's historical trajectory is showcased in this educational, if unexciting museum, split into different rooms dedicated to different epochs.

There's pre-Hispanic, the independence era, the republic era and the War of the Pacific. Once you're done counting the many dead heroes, pop into the adjacent **Museo Arqueológico Chiribaya** (☎054-28-6528; La Merced 117; admission S15; ⏲8:30am-7pm Mon-Fri, 9am-3pm Sun), which houses an impressive collection of artifacts from the pre-Incan Chiribaya civilization, including well-preserved textiles and the only pre-Inca gold collection in southern Peru.

Museo de la Universidad Nacional de San Agustín MUSEUM
(UNAS; Álvarez Thomas 200; admission S2; ⏲9am-4pm Mon-Fri) One of many small university-run museums in Arequipa, this one's a little more esoteric than most with themes jumping between archaeological remains, baroque furniture and colonial art from the Peruvian Cuzco School.

Activities

Arequipa is the center for a raft of nebulous sights and activities dotted around the high country to the north and east of the city. Trekking, mountaineering and river running are the big three activities, but there are plenty more.

Trekking & Mountaineering

The spectacular canyons around Arequipa offer many excellent hiking options. Trekking agencies can arrange off-the-beaten-track routes to suit your timeline and fitness level.

Trekking solo in the well-traveled Cañón del Colca area is popular and easy, but, if you're nervous about hiking without guides or want to tackle more untrammeled routes, there are dozens of tour companies based in Arequipa that can arrange guided treks.

Superb mountains for climbing surround Arequipa. Adequate acclimatization for this area is essential and it's best to have spent some time in Cuzco or Puno immediately before a high-altitude expedition. Cold temperatures, which sometimes drop to -29°C at the highest camps, necessitate very warm clothing.

The Association of Mountain Guides of Peru warns that many guides are uncertified and untrained, so climbers are advised to go well informed about medical and wilderness-survival issues. Most agencies sell climbs as packages that include transport, so prices vary widely depending on the size of the group and the mountain, but the cost for a guide alone is around US$80 per day. Although you can trek year-round, the best (ie driest) time is from April to December.

Maps of the area can be obtained from Colca Trek in Arequipa or the Instituto Geográfico Nacional and South American Explorers Club in Lima. Carlos Zárate Adventures and Peru Camping Shop (p150) rent out tents, ice axes, crampons, stoves and boots.

Carlos Zárate Adventures ADVENTURE SPORTS
(☎054-20-2461; www.zarateadventures.com; Santa Catalina 204, Oficina 3) This highly professional company was founded in 1954 by Carlos Zárate, the great-grandfather of climbing in Arequipa. One of Zárate's sons, Miguel, was responsible, along with archaeologists, for unearthing Juanita 'the Ice Maiden' atop Mt Ampato in 1995. Now run by another son, experienced guide Carlos Zárate Flores, it offers various treks, and climbs all the local peaks.

Prices depend on group size and transportation method. It charges from US$250 per person for a group of four to climb El Misti, and US$220 for a three-day trek in the Cañón del Colca, both with private transport, guide, meals and all equipment.

Zárate's guides generally speak Spanish or English, but are also available in French when prearranged. It also rents out all kinds of gear to independent climbers and hikers including ice axes, crampons and hiking boots.

Colca Trek ADVENTURE SPORTS
(☎054-20-6217; www.colcatrek.com.pe; Jerusalén 401B) Colca Trek is an ecoconscious adventure-tour agency and shop run by the knowledgeable, English-speaking Vlado Soto. In addition to trekking tours, it organizes mountaineering, mountain-biking and river-running trips; and is one of the few shops selling decent topographical maps of the area. It is a venerable source of information for those hoping to explore the area on their own.

Be careful of copycat travel agencies that use the Colca Trek name and/or web addresses that are similar to the agency's official site.

Naturaleza Activa ADVENTURE SPORTS
(☎96-896-9544; naturactiva@yahoo.com; Santa Catalina 211) A favorite of those seeking adventure tours, and offering a full range of trekking, climbing and mountain-biking

options. A major advantage over going to an agency is that the people you speak to at Naturaleza Activa are actually the qualified guides, not salespeople, so can answer your questions with genuine knowledge. Guides speak English, French and German.

Pablo Tour TREKKING, ADVENTURE SPORTS
(☎054-20-3737; www.pablotour.com; Jerusalén 400 AB-1) Consistently recommended by readers, Pablo Tour's guides are experts in trekking and cultural tours in the region, and can furnish trekkers with all the necessary equipment and topographical maps.

River Running

Arequipa is one of Peru's premier bases for river running and kayaking. Many trips are unavailable during the rainy season (between December and March), when water levels can be dangerously high. For more information and advice, surf www.peruwhitewater.com.

The **Río Chili**, about 7km from Arequipa, is the most frequently run local river, with a half-day trip suitable for beginners leaving almost daily from April to November (from US$40). Further afield, you can also do relatively easy trips on the **Río Majes**, into which the Río Colca flows. The most commonly run stretches pass class II and III rapids.

A more off-the-beaten-track possibility is the remote **Río Cotahuasi**, a white-water adventure – not for the fainthearted – that reaches into the deepest sections of what is perhaps the world's deepest known canyon. Expeditions here are infrequent and only for the experienced, usually taking nine days and passing through class IV and V rapids. The **Río Colca** was first run back in 1981, but this is a dangerous, difficult trip, not to be undertaken lightly. A few outfitters will do infrequent and expensive rafting trips, and easier sections can be found upriver from the canyon.

Casa de Mauro RAFTING
(☎98-383-9729; lacasademauromajes@hotmail.com; Ongoro, Km 5; sites per person S15, dm S30) This convenient base camp for rafting the Río Majes is in the village of Ongoro, 190km by road west of Arequipa. The lodge offers 1½-hour trips for beginner to experienced rafters (per person S70). The lodge offers camping (per person S20) or triple rooms with private bathrooms (per room S130).

It is cheapest to take a Transportes del Carpio bus from Arequipa's *terminal terrestre* to Aplao (S12, three hours, hourly) and then a *combi* (minibus; S2) or a taxi (S15) to Ongoro.

JUANITA – THE 'ICE MAIDEN'

In 1992 local climber Miguel Zárate was guiding an expedition on Nevado Ampato (6288m) when he found curious wooden remnants, suggestive of a burial site, exposed near the icy summit. In September 1995 he convinced American mountaineer and archaeologist Johan Reinhard to climb the peak, which, following recent eruptions of nearby volcano Sabancaya, had been coated by ash, melting the snow below and exposing the site more fully. Upon arrival, they immediately found a statue and other offerings, but the burial site had collapsed and there was no sign of a body. Ingeniously, the team rolled rocks down the mountainside and, by following them, Zárate was able to spot the bundled mummy of an Inca girl, which had tumbled down the same path when the icy tomb had crumbled.

The girl had been wrapped and almost perfectly preserved by the icy temperatures for about 500 years. It was immediately apparent from the remote location of her tomb and from the care and ceremony surrounding her death (as well as the crushing blow to her right eyebrow) that this 12- to 14-year-old girl had been sacrificed to the gods at the summit. For the Incas, mountains were gods who could kill by volcanic eruption, avalanche or climatic catastrophes. These violent deities could only be appeased by sacrifices from their subjects, and the ultimate sacrifice was that of a child.

It took the men days to carry the frozen bundle down to the village of Cabanaconde. From here she was transported on a regal bed of frozen foodstuffs in Zárate's own domestic freezer to the Universidad Católica (Catholic University) in Arequipa to undergo a battery of scientific examinations. Quickly dubbed 'Juanita, the ice maiden,' the mummy was given her own museum in 1998 (Museo Santuarios Andinos). In total, almost two dozen similar Inca sacrifices have been discovered atop various Andean mountains since the 1950s.

Majes River Lodge RAFTING
(☎054-66-0219, 95-979-7731; www.majesriver.com) Offers easy one-hour rafting trips (S70) or more challenging three-hour trips that pass through class IV rapids (S120) on the Río Majes. Also available are single/double bungalows with solar hot-water showers (S100), camping, meals of fresh river shrimp and tours to the nearby Toro Muerto petroglyphs. Take a taxi (S12) or a *combi* (S2) from Aplao to the Majes River Lodge.

Ecotours ADVENTURE TOURS
(☎054-20-2562; Jerusalén 409) With 20 years in the business, Arequipa-based Ecotours organizes three-hour rafting (S85) trips on the Río Chili's class II to class IV rapids, or three-day excursions to the Cañón de Colca (S150) with meals and accommodations.

Mountain Biking

The Arequipa area has many mountain-biking possibilities. Many of the same companies that offer trekking or mountain-climbing trips also organize downhill volcano mountain-biking trips at Chachani and El Misti or can arrange tailor-made tours. If you have the experience and wherewithal, these agencies can rent you high-end bikes and offer expert trip-planning advice to help get you started on your own. For more basic machines, try **Peru Camping Shop** (☎054-22-1658; www.perucampingshop.com; Jerusalén 410), which rents out bikes by the half-day for S35 including helmet, gloves and a map of the area. It also organizes downhill cycling blasts in the vicinity of El Misti for S68 (one day) with transport.

Courses

Want to learn to speak Spanish? Immersion is the best way, and Arequipa provides plenty of opportunities to hook up on a course while practicing with the locals in the evenings. Book in with a recommended agency and you'll be reading Mario Vargas Llosa in the original before you know it.

Cepesma LANGUAGE
(☎054-95-996-1638; www.cepesmaidiomasceci.com; Av Puente Grau 108) You can take Spanish language courses of between two (US$16) to eight hours (US$64) per day. Cooking, dancing and volunteer opportunities are also available.

Juanjo LANGUAGE
(www.spanishlanguageperu.com; Los Arces 257A, Distrito Cayma) Recommended by travelers, Juanjo provides one-on-one Spanish classes from S350 per week, which include one free salsa lesson or cooking class. Homestays and volunteer work can also be arranged.

Rocio LANGUAGE
(☎054-22-4568; www.spanish-peru.com; Ayacucho 208) Charges S18 per hour for an individual Spanish class, while small group lessons cost S290 per 20-hour week. Ring bell number 21 at the communal entrance.

Centro Cultural Peruano Norteamericano LANGUAGE
(ICPNA; ☎054-39-1020; www.cultural.edu.pe; Melgar 109) Aside from offering a raft of cultural activities (theater, music and the like), the well-established Peru–North American cultural center bivouacked in a pleasant *casona* (large house) in the city center can organize Spanish lessons for foreigners from S35 for a 90-minute session.

Instituto Cultural Peruano Alemán LANGUAGE
(ICPA; ☎054-22-8130; www.icpa.org.pe; Ugarte 207) The Peruvian-German cultural center offers Spanish lessons in the city center for roughly S25 per hour.

Tours

The streets of Santa Catalina and Jerusalén harbor dozens of travel agencies offering ho-hum city tours and excursions to the canyon country, most with daily departures. While some agencies are professional, there are also plenty of carpetbaggers muscling in on the action, so shop carefully. Never accept tours from street touts and, where possible, pay for the tours in cash, as occasional credit-card fraud is reported.

The standard two-day tour of the Cañón del Colca (p162) costs S65 to S225 per person, depending on the season, group size and the comfort level of the hotel you choose in Chivay. Different agencies may sell you tickets for the same tours, so shop around. All tours leave Arequipa between 7am and 9am. Stops include the Reserva Nacional Salinas y Aguada Blanca (p160), Chivay, Calera hot springs (p163), an evening *peña* (bar or club featuring live folkloric music; at an additional fee) plus a visit to the Cruz del Cóndor (p167).

Al Travel Tours CULTURAL
(☎95-939-1436; www.aitraveltours.com; Av Lima 610, Vallecito) Owner Miguel Fernández offers some unique tours including a popular 'Re-

ality Tour' (from S60 per person, minimum two people), which visits a poor Arequipan neighborhood of stone-makers. A large part of your fee goes to the local workers' coops. Miguel is happy to visit you in your accommodations to explain the tours he offers.

Free Walking Tour Peru WALKING TOUR
(99-895-9567; http://fwtperu.com/fwt-arequipa.html; Plaza San Francisco; by donation; 12.15pm) FREE The quirky, passionate and knowledgeable guide (in a green vest) takes anybody who shows up on a 2½-hour English/Spanish/French walking tour of Arequipa's landmarks, such as San Lázaro church, while also visiting commercial places (with very little hard-sell) for taste-testing craft beer, chocolate tea and pisco. It's free but most participants are happy to tip the guide at the end.

Tours Class Arequipa BUS TOUR
(www.toursclassarequipa.com.pe; Portal de San Agustín 103, Plaza de Armas; 2.5/4.5 hours S35/45) This open-top bus tour is actually a handy way of seeing some of Arequipa's outer sights. Stops include Cayma and Yanahuara while the longer *campiña* (countryside) tour continues on to the Mansión del Fundador.

Festivals & Events

Semana Santa RELIGIOUS
(Holy Week) *Arequipeños* claim that their Semana Santa celebrations leading up to Easter are similar to the very solemn and traditional Spanish observances from Seville. Maundy Thursday, Good Friday and Holy Saturday processions are particularly colorful and sometimes end with the burning of an effigy of Judas.

Fiesta de la Virgen de Chapi RELIGIOUS
(May 1) Arequipa fills up for this festival, celebrated in the Yanahuara district.

August 15 CULTURAL
The founding day of the city is celebrated with parades, dancing, beauty pageants, climbing competitions on El Misti and other energetic events peppered through the fortnight leading up to August 14. The fireworks show in the Plaza de Armas on the evening of August 14 is definitely worth catching.

Sleeping

Central Arequipa is peppered with hotels of all shapes, sizes and prices. Due to the nature of the architecture in this Unesco World Heritage zone, many of them inhabit attractive, thick-walled *sillar* buildings. Cable TV and free wi-fi are pretty much a given in all but the bottom-rung places. Breakfast is also usually included though it is little more than bread, jam and coffee in the cheaper joints. Prices can fluctuate greatly even during high season (June to August).

La Casa de Sillar HOTEL $
(054-28-4249; www.lacasadesillar.com; Rivero 504; s with/without bathroom S45/35, d S70/60; @ wi-fi) Another of those thick-walled colonial mansions made – as the name implies – out of *sillar* rock hewn from El Misti, this one doesn't pretend to be boutique, but it does offer a fine bargain, especially if you're prepared to share a bathroom. Huge maps and an equally huge TV adorn a communal lounge.

Le Foyer HOSTEL $
(054-28-6473; www.hlefoyer.com; Ugarte 114; s/d/tr with bathroom 75/95/115, dm/d/tr without bathroom 25/60/85, all incl breakfast; @ wi-fi) There's a distinct New Orleans look to this cheap hostel-like hotel with its wraparound upstairs verandah where you can enjoy a standard bread and jam breakfast overlooking busy Calle Jerusalén. Rooms are nothing to brag about but the proximity to plenty of restaurants and nightlife (there's an alluring Mexican place downstairs) means you don't need GPS to find the action.

Wild Rover Hostel HOSTEL $
(054-21-2830; www.wildroverhostels.com; Calle Ugarte 111; dm/d S21/70; @ wi-fi pool) If halfway through your Peruvian sojourn you get a sudden compulsion to consume bangers and mash with Swedish backpackers in the familiar confines of an Irish pub, then the Wild Rover awaits you with open arms.

Los Andes Bed & Breakfast HOTEL, B&B $
(054-33-0015; www.losandesarequipa.com; La Merced 123; s/d without bathroom S31/50, with bathroom S48/72; @ wi-fi) There's a bit of a hospital feel to this hotel's giant rooms and ample communal kitchen, popular with climbing groups and long-term stays. But the pricing is good and it's a font of information for the surrounding area.

La Posada del Parque B&B $
(054-21-2275; www.parkhostel.net; Deán Valdivia 238A; dm/s/d incl breakfast S25/60/80; @ wi-fi) This B&B bargain near the market has high-ceilinged rooms that sit beneath

a wonderfully weathered terrace where El Misti appears so close you could almost hug it. There's a kitchen available and the owners can organize on-site Spanish lessons for S6 per hour.

Hotel Real Arequipa HOTEL $
(☎ 054-79-9248; hotelrealarequipa@hotmail.com; Jerusalén 412; r with/without bathroom S70/40; 📶) The rooms are basic and dark but there is a tidy kitchen and it is perfectly fine if you are counting your soles but don't want to stray far from the plaza.

Point Hostel HOSTEL $
(☎ 054-28-6920; www.thepointhostels.com; Palacio Viejo 325; dm/d incl breakfast S21/70; @📶) One of five Point backpackers hostels in Peru, this one is two blocks from the main square. It has a popular billiards table and bar, but beware – this is a place for people who like to socialize and don't necessarily need to be tucked up in bed quietly by 10pm.

Hostal Núñez HOSTEL $
(☎ 054-21-8648; www.hotel-nunez.de; Jerusalén 528; s/d with bathroom S100/120, without bathroom S50/80, all incl breakfast; 📶) On a street full of not-so-great guesthouses, this secure, friendly hostel is always stuffed with gringos. The colorful rooms sport frilly decor and cable TV, though the singles are a bit of a squeeze.

La Posada del Cacique HOTEL $
(☎ 054-20-2170; Jerusalén 404; s/d/tr S30/50/60; @📶) This 2nd-floor hostel has spacious, sunny rooms, a well-equipped shared kitchen, reliable hot water, and a tranquil rooftop sitting area. The father-son owners are great resources for local info and make guests feel right at home.

Hostal El Descanso del Fundador HOTEL $
(☎ 054-20-2341; Jerusalén 605; s/d S75/85; 📶) In a charming, pale-blue house on the cusp of the colonial core, this old mansion has a more classical feel than the heavier baroque abodes further south. Rooms are a little past their refurb date, but service is cute and helpful.

★ **Hotel Casona Solar** HOTEL $$
(☎ 054-22-8991; www.casonasolar.com; Consuelo 116; s/d/ste S158/240/354; 📶) Live like a colonial *caballero* (gentleman) in this gorgeous 'secret garden' situated – incredibly given its tranquility – only three blocks from the main square. Grand 18th-century rooms are crafted from huge *sillar* stones, some with mezzanine bedrooms. The service (same-day laundry, bus reservations, free airline check-in) is equally dazzling. Best value in the city – maybe even Peru.

Casablanca Hostal HOTEL $$
(☎ 054-22-1327; www.casablancahostal.com; Puente Bolognesi 104; s/d/tr incl breakfast S95/145/200; @) The *New York Times'* 'Frugal Traveler' wasn't the only budget-seeker to marvel at what he was getting for his money in this place. It has a prime corner location on the main plaza, beautiful exposed *sillar* brickwork and rooms large enough to keep a horse (or two) in. Service is discreet and breakfast is taken in a lovely sun-filled cafe.

Casona Terrace Hotel HOTEL $$
(☎ 054-21-2318; www.hotelcasonaterrace.com; Álvarez Thomas 211; s/d incl buffet breakfast S120/170; ❄@📶) A lovely old colonial home with rooms that have opted for modern simplicity over old-world splendor. The hotel is just one block from the main square but has secure entry and a roof terrace.

La Casa de Melgar HOTEL $$
(☎ 054-22-2459; www.lacasademelgar.com; Melgar 108; s/d incl buffet breakfast US$55/75; 📶) Housed in an 18th-century building, this hotel is nonetheless fitted with all the expected modern comforts. High-domed ceilings and unique decor lend the entire place an old-world feel. Comfy beds and tucked-away inner patios help make this a romantic hideaway within the city limits.

Terruño de Yarabaya HOTEL $$
(☎ 95-061-0077; www.terrunodeyarabaya.weebly.com; cnr Desaguadero 104-106 & Campo Redondo; s/d/ste incl breakfast S85/110/195; 📶) What a difference a garden makes. All the large rooms look onto the calming green space. Rooms and bathrooms are clean and modern with cable, microwave and fridge, while features such as reclaimed doors give an artistic touch. The attached cafe serves unexpected treats such as Japanese curries and tropical fruits, including the maple-flavoured *lúcuma,* which you can enjoy from your lawn chair.

Casa de Avila HOTEL $$
(☎ 054-21-3177; www.casadeavila.com; San Martín 116, Vallecito; s/d/tr incl breakfast S105/165/210; @📶) If the spacious courtyard garden doesn't swing it for you, the congenial personalized service ought to – this is not some 'yes sir, no sir' chain hotel. The place

also hosts Spanish-language courses and a unique cooking course in the sunny garden three times a week.

Hostal las Torres de Ugarte HOTEL $$
(054-28-3532; www.hotelista.com; Ugarte 401A; s/d/tr incl breakfast S144/176/211;) This is a friendly hostel in a quiet location behind the Monasterio de Santa Catalina. It has immaculate rooms with TVs and colorful woolly bedspreads. You'll just have to ignore the cacophonous echoing hallways. Rates drop considerably in low season.

Colonial House Inn GUESTHOUSE $$
(054-22-3533; colonialhouseinn@hotmail.com; Av Puente Grau 114; s/d S35/50;) Peaceful, if slightly run-down, colonial house with a rooftop terrace and garden with striking views of El Misti on clear days. Breakfast isn't included but the friendly staff can sometimes provide something basic, if you ask nicely.

Hostal Solar HOTEL $$
(054-24-1793; www.hostalsolar.com; Ayacucho 108; s/d incl breakfast S100/130;) This snazzy pick is clean and airy, with contemporary decor. Prices include airport pickup and a buffet breakfast served on the rooftop terrace.

Posada Nueva España HOTEL $$
(054-25-2941; Antiquilla 106, Yanahuara; s/d/tr incl breakfast S75/100/125;) This distinguished 19th-century colonial house has just more than a dozen rooms with solar hot showers. It's in the quaint suburb of Yanahuara; call for free pickups from central Arequipa. Spanish, French, German and English are spoken.

Los Tambos Hostal BOUTIQUE HOTEL $$$
(054-60-0900; www.lostambos.com.pe; Puente Bolognesi 129; d S219-289;) Breaking the mold in historic Arequipa is this modern boutique hotel, a marble roll from the main square, where small but significant extras and above-and-beyond service justify every sol of the asking price. Luring you in are chocolates on your pillow, aromatic soap selections, huge gourmet breakfasts (included), and free transportation to and from the airport or bus terminal.

Libertador Ciudad Blanca LUXURY HOTEL $$$
(054-21-5110; www.libertador.com.pe; Plaza Bolívar s/n, Selva Alegre; r S470, ste S600-725;) The grand dame of Arequipa's hotels, 1km north of the center. The stylish building is set in gardens with a pool and playground. It has spacious rooms and opulent public areas, plus its spa boasts a sauna, Jacuzzi and fitness room. The sedate restaurant serves fine Sunday brunch. Neighboring Selva Alegre park is beautiful, just don't wander far from the crowds.

La Hostería HOTEL $$$
(054-28-9269; www.lahosteriaqp.com.pe; Bolívar 405; s/d/ste incl breakfast S220/255/300;) Worth every sol is this picturesque colonial hotel with a flower-bedecked courtyard, light and quiet rooms (with minibar), carefully chosen antiques, a sunny terrace and a lounge. Some rooms suffer from street noise, so request one in the back. Apartment-style suites on the upper floors have stellar city views.

Casa Arequipa BOUTIQUE HOTEL $$$
(054-28-4219; www.arequipacasa.com; Av Lima 409, Vallecito; s/d S220/315;) Inside a cotton-candy pink colonial mansion in the gardens of suburban Vallecito, this gay-friendly B&B offers more than half a dozen guest rooms with fine design touches such as richly painted walls, pedestal sinks, antique handmade furnishings and alpaca-wool blankets. A sociable cocktail bar is in the lobby.

La Posada del Puente HOTEL $$$
(054-25-3132; www.posadadelpuente.com; Bolognesi 101; s/d S359/403;) Dipping down to the river, the extensive gardens of this high-end hotel make for a tranquil setting that's surprisingly removed from the bustling traffic above. Staying here gives you free access to the sports facilities and swimming pool at the nearby **Club Internacional** sports complex.

Casa Andina Classic BOUTIQUE HOTEL $$$
(054-213-9739; www.casa-andina.com; Jerusalén 603; r/ste incl breakfast S283/446;) Like most of the Casa Andina chain, this place flirts with boutique decor, but feels a tad overpriced when you factor in the rather dark restaurant, officious service and rooms that are basically just motel rooms with some deft color accents. The on-site spa claws back a little credibility with massages offered for S110 (one hour).

Hotel La Posada del Monasterio HOTEL $$$
(054-40-5728; www.hotelessanagustin.com.pe; Santa Catalina 300; s/d/tr incl buffet breakfast from US$70/80/100;) On a prime pedestrian corner, this hotel gracefully

inhabits an architectural mix-and-match building combining the best of the Old and New Worlds, especially popular with European tour groups. The comfortable modern rooms have all the expected facilities. From the rooftop terrace you can peer into the Santa Catalina convent across the street.

Eating

Hunker down. If you want to truly 'get' Arequipa, you have some serious food sampling to enjoy. Start with the basics: *rocoto relleno* and *chupe de camarones* and work up to the stuff you'll never find east of the Amazon (at least on a dinner plate) – guinea pig, anyone? Trendy upscale restaurants line Calle San Francisco north of the Plaza de Armas, while touristy outdoor cafes huddle together on Pasaje Catedral, behind the cathedral and away from the plaza.

Tradición Arequipeña PERUVIAN $
(☎054-42-6467; www.tradicionarequipena.com; Av Dolores 111; meals S18-40; ⌚11:30am-6pm Mon-Fri, 11:30am-1am Sat, 8:30am-6pm Sun) This locally famous restaurant has maze-like gardens, live *folklórica* and *criollo* music (upbeat coastal music), and offers a Sunday morning breakfast of *adobo de cerdo*, a traditional slow-cooked pork dish. It's 2km southeast of the center; a taxi ride here costs about S5.

Crepisimo CAFE, CREPERIE $
(www.crepisimo.com; Alianza Francesa, Santa Catalina 208; mains S7-16; ⌚8am-11pm Mon-Sat, noon-11pm Sun; 📶) All the essential components of a great cafe – food, setting, service, ambience – come together at Crepisimo in the French cultural center. In this chic colonial setting, the simple crepe is offered with 100 different types of filling, from Chilean smoked trout to exotic South American fruits, while casual wait staff serve you Parisian-quality coffee.

Café Fez-Istanbul MIDDLE EASTERN $
(San Francisco 229; mains S9-14; ⌚9am-midnight) The name suggests two cities, but the food is distinctly Middle Eastern rather than Moroccan. Falafels are the main draw – in a crepe or in a sandwich – served in a rather trendy resto-bar with a people-watching mezzanine floor. Other favorites include hummus, fresh cut fries and various sandwiches. Portions are snack fodder mainly, but in a cool environment.

Hatunpa PERUVIAN $
(Ugarte 208; dishes S11-15; ⌚12:30-9:30pm Mon-Sat) With just four tables and the common garden spud as its star ingredient, Hatunpa probably doesn't sound promising, but it has a fervent and fast-growing following. The trick? Potatoes originate in Peru and the *arequipeños* know how to embellish them with imaginative sauces and toppings such as alpaca, chorizo or veg. Even better, they're cheap (and filling) too.

El Turko TURKISH $
(www.elturko.com.pe; San Francisco 225; mains S7-16; ⌚8am-midnight Sun-Wed, 24hr Fri & Sat; 🖉) Part of an Ottoman empire of restaurants, this relaxed little joint serves a hungry crowd late-night kebabs, Middle Eastern salads and moist vegetarian falafel, with excellent coffee and sweet pastries during the day.

Ribs Café BARBECUE $
(☎054-28-8188; Álvarez Thomas 107; ribs from S26, empanadas S5-9; ⌚9am-9pm Mon-Sat) This surprising storefront cooks up barbecue ribs in a rainbow variety of sauces, ranging from chocolate to honey-mustard to red wine, as well as empanadas (meat or cheese turnovers) and solid American breakfasts.

Inkari Pub Pizzeria PIZZA $
(Pasaje Catedral; pizzas from S14; ⌚9am-11pm) You're pretty much guaranteed to meet a gringo at this predictably popular place behind the cathedral, which pampers to Western palates with a happy-hour special of personal pizza and *copa de vino* (glass of wine) for S18.

Manolo's PERUVIAN $
(☎054-21-9009; Mercaderes 107 & 113; mains S10-30; ⌚7:30am-midnight) Seeing double? Well, yes, actually. There are two Manolo's 20m apart in Arequipa's pedestrianized shopping thoroughfare, Calle Mercaderes. Shagged-out shoppers find it hard to resist the hiss of the coffee machine and the glint of the glass display case stuffed with thickly sliced cakes.

El Carpriccio CAFE $
(Santa Catalina 120; snacks from S10; ⌚12:30-10:30pm, to 11pm Fri & Sat; 📶) Coffee, carrot cake, quiche and wi-fi; the mezzanine of this refined cafe is where you come to write up your holiday blog.

El Super SUPERMARKET $
(⌚9am-2pm & 4-9pm Mon-Fri, 9am-9pm Sat, 9:30am-1:30pm Sun) There are El Super

YOU'VE TASTED IT, NOW COOK IT

If you recognize the name Gastón Acurio and concur that Peru is the gastronomical capital of Latin America, you may be inspired to enroll in an Arequipa **cooking course**. Local guide and qualified chef Miguel Fernández, who runs AI Travel, organizes **Peru Flavors**, a four-hour cooking course (S100, minimum two people) where you will learn to prepare a trio of appetizers and mains from the three different geographical regions of Peru: Amazonia, the Andes and the Coast. Dishes include *rocoto relleno* (stuffed spicy red peppers), *lomo saltado* (strips of beef stir-fried with onions, tomatoes, potatoes and chili) and *chupe de camerones* (prawn chowder).

Another popular option is the **Peruvian Cooking Experience** (054-213-177; www.peruviancookingexperience.com; San Martín 116, Vallecito), based at the Casa de Avila hotel, four blocks southwest of Plaza de Armas. Three-hour courses (11am to 2pm; S65) run Monday to Saturday. You can study the art of ceviche preparation or even opt for vegetarian recipes. Courses are available in Spanish and English. Maximum group size is six.

branches at Plaza de Armas (Plaza de Armas, Portal de la Municipalidad 130) and Piérola (N de Piérola, Cuadra 1, Piérola). You can pick up groceries at these supermarkets.

★ Zingaro PERUVIAN $$
(www.zingaro-restaurante.com; San Francisco 309; mains S30-49; noon-11pm Mon-Sat) In an old *sillar* building with wooden balconies, stained glass and a resident pianist, culinary legends are made. Zingaro is a leading font of gastronomic innovation, meaning it's an ideal place to try out *nouveau* renditions of Peruvian standards including alpaca ribs, ceviche, or perhaps your first *cuy* (guinea pig).

Two doors down (San Francisco 315), sister restaurant **Parrilla de Zingaro** specializes in Argentinian-style meats with equally splendid results.

Zig Zag PERUVIAN $$
(054-20-6020; www.zigzagrestaurant.com; Zela 210; mains S33-45; noon-midnight) Upscale but not ridiculously pricey, Zig Zag is a Peruvian restaurant with European inflections. It inhabits a two-story colonial house with an iron stairway designed by Gustave Eiffel (blimey, that bloke must have been busy). The menu classic is a meat selection served on a unique volcano-stone grill with various sauces. The fondues are also good.

Some heretics claim it's even better than famous Peruvian chef Gastón Acurio's Chicha (p156). The various set lunch *menús* (from S45) are an accessible way to taste test.

Nina-Yaku PERUVIAN, FUSION $$
(054-28-1432; San Francisco 211; menús S28, mains S28-38; 11am-11pm) Escaping the tumult of 'happening' Calle San Francisco, Nina-Yaku offers an atmosphere of whispered refinement along with affordable Arequipan specialties such as broccoli soufflé, potatoes in Huatacay sauce, and fettuccine pesto with alpaca.

Lakshmivan VEGETARIAN $$
(Jerusalén 400; mains S12-21, menús lunch S4-6, dinner S18-20; 9am-9pm;) Set in a colorful old building with a tiny outdoor courtyard, this place has various lunch and dinner *menús* (set meals) and an extensive à la carte selection, all with a South Asian flair.

La Trattoria del Monasterio ITALIAN $$
(054-20-4062; www.latrattoriadelmonasterio.com; Santa Catalina 309; mains S21-46; lunch from noon daily, dinner from 7pm Mon-Sat) A helping of epicurean delight is just next door to the austere Monasterio de Santa Catalina. The menu of Italian specialties was created with the help of superstar Peruvian chef Gastón Acurio, and is infused with the flavors of Arequipa. Reservations are essential.

La Nueva Palomino PERUVIAN $$
(Leoncio Prado 122; mains S14-29; noon-6pm) Definitely the local favorite, the atmosphere at this *picantería* is informal and can turn boisterous even during the week when groups of families and friends file in to eat local specialties and drink copious amounts of *chicha de jora* (fermented corn beer). The restaurant is in the Yanahuara district (2km northwest of the city center), east of the *mirador* (lookout).

El Charrua ARGENTINE $$
(054-34-6688; www.elcharrua.com; Cuesta del Olivo 318, Yanahuara; mains S28-55; 12:30-11pm Mon-Sat, noon-7pm Sun) This Argentine-Uruguayan

WORTH A TRIP

YANAHUARA

The peaceful neighborhood of Yanahuara makes a diverting excursion from the Arequipa city center, and it's within walking distance. Go west on Av Puente Grau over the Puente Grau (Grau Bridge) and continue on Av Ejército for half a dozen blocks. Turn right on Av Lima and walk five blocks to a small plaza, where you'll find the **Iglesia San Juan Bautista** (Plaza de Yanhuara) FREE, which dates from 1750. It has housed the highly venerated Virgen de Chapi since 2001, when the earthquake brought her original church tumbling down about her ears. The popular Fiesta de la Virgen de Chapi is held on May 1. At the side of the plaza there's a *mirador* (lookout) with stone archways inscribed with poetry and excellent views of Arequipa and El Misti.

Head back along Av Jerusalén, parallel to Av Lima, and just before reaching Av Ejército you'll see the well-known restaurant Sol de Mayo, where you can stop for a tasty lunch of typical *arequipeño* food. The round-trip walk should take around two hours. There are also *combis* (minibuses) to Yanahuara from along Av Puente Grau (and returning to the city from Yanahuara's plaza) every few minutes (S1, 10 minutes).

grill, with its dark-wood, gentlemen's club-style cocktail bar, is in the Yanahuara district adjacent to the *mirador*. Its terrace enjoys one of the best views in the city with the symmetrical hump of El Misti seemingly close enough to touch. The heavily meat-biased menu is well complemented by some robust malbec reds.

Not surprisingly, it isn't cheap. Its lunchtime *menús* (S35 to S65) offer better value.

El Tío Dario SEAFOOD **$$**
(☎054-27-0473; Callejon de Cabildo 100, Yanahuara; mains S27-45) Like fish? Like intimate secret-garden settings? Then, grab a taxi (or walk) out to the pleasant Yanahuara district for the ultimate in ceviche or grilled-fish dishes served in a flower-rich garden that frames superb volcano views. Tío Dario is through the charming archway to the left of Yanahuara *mirador*.

Los Leños PIZZA **$$**
(☎054-28-1818; Jerusalén 407; pizzas S12-46; ⌚5-11pm Tue-Sun) The indoor smoke from the wood-fire oven and smoking diners and staff can be a sight for sore eyes, but it's worth it for arguably the best pizza in Arequipa. Thin, crispy squares come soaked with flavour. Besides, the high-domed ceiling keeps the place airy.

Sol de Mayo PERUVIAN **$$**
(☎054-25-4148; Jerusalén 207, Yanahuara; mains S28-50) Serving good Peruvian food in the Yanahuara district, this *picantería* has live *música folklórica* every afternoon from 1pm to 4pm. Book a table in advance. You can combine a visit here with a stop at the *mirador* in Yanahuara.

Cevichería Fory Fay CEVICHE **$$**
(☎054-24-5454; Álvarez Thomas 221; mains S20-25; ⌚lunch) Small and to-the-point, it serves only the best ceviche (raw seafood marinated in lime juice) and nothing else. Pull up a chair at a rickety table and crack open a beer – limit one per person, though. By the way, the name is a phonetic spelling of how Peruvians say '45' in English.

Chicha PERUVIAN, FUSION **$$$**
(☎054-28-7360; www.chicha.com.pe; Santa Catalina 210; mains S28-49; ⌚noon-midnight Mon-Sat, to 9pm Sun) Peru's most famous chef, Gastón Acurio owns this wildly experimental place where the menu never veers far from Peru's Inca-Spanish roots. River prawns are a highlight in season (April to December), but Acurio prepares Peruvian staples with equal panache, along with tender alpaca burgers and earthy pastas.

Try the *tacu-tacu* (a Peruvian fusion dish of rice, beans and a protein), *lomo saltado* (strips of beef stir-fried with onions, tomatoes, potatoes and chili), or ceviche. Like many 'celeb' places, Chicha divides opinion between food snobs and purists. Step inside its fine colonial interior and join the debate.

Drinking & Nightlife

The nocturnal scene in Arequipa is pretty slow midweek but takes off on weekends. Arequipa's nightlife is as vital as Lima's, but confined to a smaller downtown area. Anyone who's anyone can be seen strolling Calle San Francisco sometime after 9pm on a Friday or Saturday, and many of the bars there offer happy-hour specials worth enjoying. The 300 block (between Ugarte and Zela) has the highest concentration of places to compare fashion notes.

Split PUB
(Zela 207; ⊙5pm-1am Mon-Wed, 6pm-2am Thu-Sat) Two bars split into upstairs and downstairs (with no ground level). Both are dark, narrow and popular with locals who like to kick-start the night with a strong drink such as Misti Colodo, a pisco piña colada; or drinks labelled 'Tóxicos' for a pot-luck concoction of alcohol. There are pizzas, crepes and pasta to tempt you to stay.

Déjà Vu COCKTAIL BAR
(San Francisco 319B; ⊙9am-late) With a rooftop terrace overlooking the church of San Francisco, this eternally popular haunt has a long list of crazy cocktails and a lethal happy hour every evening. After dark, decent DJs keep the scene alive on weekdays and weekends alike.

Chelawasi Public House MICROBREWERY
(Campo Redondo 102; beer S12; ⊙4pm-midnight Thu-Sat, to 10pm Sun) New to craft beer? The friendly Canadian-Peruvian owners will step you through the best beers from Peru's microbreweries, with bonus local travel advice. Arequipa's first craft-beer bar is a modern but unpretentious pub in the village-like San Lázaro area. You can even order pizza from nearby to eat at the handmade tables.

Museo del Pisco COCKTAIL BAR
(http://museodelpisco.org; cnr Santa Catalina & Moral; degustation for 1/2 people S45/60, drinks S16-32; ⊙noon-midnight) The name says museum, but the designer slabs of stone and glass, plus the menu of more than 100 piscos, says cocktail bar. Pick a favorite with a pisco degustation, which includes three mini craft piscos with an explanation in English by knowledgeable bar staff. Then mix your own (S30). Pace yourself with gourmet burgers and hummus.

Farren's Irish Pub PUB
(Pasaje Catedral; ⊙noon-11pm) Where would any city be without its themed Irish pub? Tucked behind the cathedral, this gringo haven has – guess what? – Guinness, pub grub and soccer on satellite TV.

Brujas Bar BAR
(San Francisco 300; ⊙5pm-late) Nordic-style pub with Union Jack flags, happy-hour cocktails and plenty of locals and expats having a chin-wag.

Casona Forum CLUB
(www.casonaforum.com; San Francisco 317) A five-in-one excuse for a good night out in a *sillar* building incorporating a pub (Retro), pool club (Zero), sofa bar (Chill Out), nightclub (Forum) and restaurant (Terrasse).

Zoom CLUB
(Santa Catalina 111) They're dancing by 8pm on a Saturday night in this youthful upstairs pub/club a block from the main square, with enough sectioned-off parts to find your own favorite nook. Beware of the tuneless karaoke.

☆ Entertainment

Avenida Dolores, 2km southeast of the center (a taxi costs around S5 one way), is where salsa and *cumbia* (Colombian salsa-like dance and musical style) music and dancing predominate.

Café Art Montréal LIVE MUSIC
(Ugarte 210; ⊙5pm-1am) This smoky, intimate little bar with live bands playing on a stage at the back would be equally at home as a bohemian student hangout on Paris' Left Bank.

Sports

Conducted *arequipeño* style, *peleas de toros* (bullfights) here are less bloodthirsty than most. They involve pitting two bulls against each other for the favors of a fertile female until one realizes he's beaten. The fights take place on Sundays between April and December. Ask at your hostel for the location of fights – they usually take place at stadiums on the outskirts of town. The three most important fights are in April, mid-August and early December (admission S18).

Shopping

Arequipa overflows with antique and artisan shops, especially on the streets around Monasterio de Santa Catalina. The most commonly bought items for sale are high-quality leather, alpaca and *vicuña* (threatened wild relative of alpacas) goods, and other handmade items.

Casona Santa Catalina CLOTHING, SOUVENIRS
(☎054-28-1334; www.santacatalina-sa.com.pe; Santa Catalina 210; ⊙most shops 10am-6pm) Inside this polished tourist complex, you'll find a few shops of major export brands, such as Sol Alpaca and Biondi Piscos.

Patio del Ekeko CLOTHING, SOUVENIRS
(☎054-21-5861; www.elekeko.pe; Mercaderes 141; ⌚10am-9pm Mon-Sat, 11am-8pm Sun) This high-end tourist mall has plenty of expensive but good alpaca- and vicuña-wool items, jewelry, ceramics and other arty souvenirs.

Galería de Artesanías 'El Tumi de Oro' CRAFT MARKET
(Portal de Flores 126; ⌚10am-6pm) A small artisan market under the *portales* (stone archways) on Plaza de Armas.

Claustros de la Campañía SHOPPING CENTER
(Santo Domingo) This is one of South America's most elegant shopping centers. Its ornate double courtyard is ringed by cloisters held up by *sillar* columns, etched with skillful carvings. You'll find a wine bodega, an ice-cream outlet, numerous alpaca-wool shops and a couple of elegant cafes on the courtyard. Young couples dot the upper levels enjoying the romantic setting and southerly views.

Fundo El Fierro CRAFT MARKET
(San Francisco 200; ⌚9am-8pm Mon-Sat, to 2pm Sun) The city's primary craft market occupies a beautiful colonial *sillar* courtyard next to the San Francisco church. Garments, paintings, handmade crafts and jewelry predominate, but you can also procure rare alpaca carpets from Cotahuasi. There's an artisanal fair with special stalls held here in August.

Librería el Lector BOOKS
(☎054-28-8677; San Francisco 213; ⌚9am-noon Mon-Sat) A two-for-one English book exchange and an excellent selection of new local-interest titles and guidebooks in a sharp, modern space.

Information

DANGERS & ANNOYANCES

Petty theft is often reported in Arequipa, so travelers are urged to hide their valuables. Most crime is opportunistic, so keep your stuff in sight while in restaurants and internet cafes. While the area south of the Plaza de Armas is reportedly safe after dark, be wary of wandering outside tourist zones at night. Take great care in Parque Selva Alegre, north of the city center, as muggings have been reported there. Instead of hailing a cab on the street, ask your hostel or tour operator to call you an official one; the extra time and money are worth the added safety. Only pay for tours in a recognized agency and never trust touts in the street – they bamboozle cash out of a surprisingly high number of travelers.

EMERGENCY

Policía de Turismo (Tourist Police; ☎054-20-1258; Jerusalén 315-317; ⌚24hr) May be helpful if you need an official theft report for insurance claims.

IMMIGRATION

Oficina de Migraciónes (Immigration Office; ☎054-42-1759; Urb Quinta Tristán, Parque 2, Distrito José Bustamante y Rivero; ⌚8am-3:30pm Mon-Fri) Come here for a visa extension.

INTERNET ACCESS

Most internet cafes charge about S1.50 per hour. Many also offer cheap local and international phone calls. All but the cheapest hotels offer free wi-fi as do many cafes.

MEDICAL SERVICES

Clínica Arequipa (☎054-25-3424, 054-25-3416; Bolognesi, near Puente Grau; ⌚8am-8pm Mon-Fri, to 12:30pm Sat) Arequipa's best and most expensive medical clinic.

Hospital Regional Honorio Delgado Espinoza (☎054-21-9702, 054-23-3812; Av Carrión s/n; ⌚24hr) Emergency 24-hour medical services.

InkaFarma (☎054-20-1565; Santo Domingo 113; ⌚24hr) One of Peru's biggest pharmacy chains; it's well stocked.

Paz Holandesa Policlinic (☎054-43-2281; www.pazholandesa.com; Av Chávez 527; ⌚8am-8pm Mon-Sat) This appointment-only travel clinic provides vaccinations. Doctors here speak English and Dutch. Profits go toward providing free medical services for underprivileged Peruvian children.

MONEY

There are money changers and ATMs on streets east of the Plaza de Armas. Global ATMs are easy to find in most areas frequented by travelers, including inside the Casona Santa Catalina complex, the bus terminal and the airport.

Both BCP and Interbank exchange US traveler's checks.

BCP (San Juan de Dios 125) Has a Visa ATM and changes US dollars.

Interbank (Mercaderes 217) Has a global ATM.

POST

DHL (☎054-22-5332; Santa Catalina 115; ⌚8:30am-7pm Mon-Fri, 9am-1pm Sat)

Serpost (Moral 118; ⌚8am-8pm Mon-Sat, 9am-1pm Sun)

TOURIST INFORMATION

Indecopi (☎054-21-2054; Hipólito Unanue 100A, Urb Victoria; ⌚8:30am-4pm Mon-Fri) This is the national tourist-protection agency that deals with complaints against local firms, including tour operators and travel agencies.

iPerú (☎054-22-3265; iperuarequipa@promperu.gob.pe; Portal de la Municipalidad 110, Plaza de Armas; ⏲9am-6pm Mon-Sat, to 1pm Sun) Government-supported source for objective information on local and regional attractions. There is also an office at the airport (☎054-44-4564; 1st fl, Main Hall, Aeropuerto Rodríguez Ballón; ⏲10am-7:30pm).

Getting There & Away

AIR

Arequipa's **Rodríguez Ballón International Airport** (AQP; ☎054-44-3458) is about 8km northwest of the city center.

LAN (☎054-20-1100; Santa Catalina 118C) has daily flights to Lima and Cuzco. **LCPeru** (☎01-204-1313; www.lcperu.pe) also offers daily flights to Lima. **Sky Airline** (☎054-28-2899; www.skyairline.cl; La Merced 121) flies to Santiago in Chile.

BUS

Night buses provide a convenient means to reach many far-off destinations in a city where options for air travel are limited, although some routes do have histories of accidents, hijackings and robberies. Paying a bit extra for a luxury bus service is often worth the added comfort and security. Exercise extreme care with your belongings on cheaper buses and refrain from keeping baggage in overhead luggage racks. It is also recommended that you carry extra food with you on long bus rides in case of a breakdown or road strike.

Arequipa Buses:

DESTINATION	COST (S)	DURATION (HR)
Cabanaconde	20	6
Camaná	50	7
Chivay	15	3½
Cotahuasi	40-45	10
Cuzco	70-135	6-11
Ica	45-120	11-15
Juliaca	20-80	6
Lima	80-160	14-17
Mollendo	10-15	2-2½
Moquegua	18	4
Nazca	59-154	10-12
Pisco	40-144	15
Puno	20-90	6
Tacna	20-57	6

International

From the Terrapuerto bus terminal, **Ormeño** (☎054-42-7788) has two buses a week to Santiago, Chile (US$140, 2½ days), and three a week to Buenos Aires, Argentina (US$200, three days).

Long-Distance

Most bus companies have departures from the *terminal terrestre* or the smaller Terrapuerto bus terminal; both are together on Av Andrés Avelino Cáceres, less than 3km south of the city center (take a taxi for S5). Check in advance which terminal your bus leaves from and keep a close watch on your belongings while you're waiting there. There's an S2 departure tax from either terminal. Both terminals have shops, restaurants and left-luggage facilities. The more chaotic *terminal terrestre* also has a global ATM and a tourist information office.

Dozens of bus companies have desks at the *terminal terrestre* so shop around. Prices range between superluxury **Cruz del Sur** (☎054-42-7375; www.cruzdelsur.com.pe) and **Ormeño** (☎054-42-3855) with 180-degree reclining 'bed' seats, and no-thrills **Flores** (☎054-42-9905, 054-43-2228; http://floresbuses.tripod.com), which travels to a greater variety of destinations including Mollendo, Moquegua and Ilo. Many buses useful for sightseeing in the canyon country leave from the *terminal terrestre* and Terrapuerto. Travel times and costs vary depending on road conditions. During the wet season (between December and April), expect significant delays.

The best companies serving the Cañón del Colca (Cabanaconde and Chivay) are **Andalucía** (☎054-44-5089) and **Reyna** (☎054-43-0612). Try to catch the earliest daylight departure, usually around 5am, and reserve tickets in advance if possible.

For buses to Corire (S12, three hours) to visit the Toro Muerto petroglyphs, both **Transportes del Carpio** and **Eros Tour** run hourly daytime services, from where you can continue on to Aplao in the Valle de Majes (S12, three hours) for river running. **Transportes Trebol** (☎054-42-5936) usually has a service departing around 4pm that continues to Andagua (S25, 10 to 12 hours) to visit El Valle de los Volcanes. The bus leaves Andagua for the return trip to Arequipa at around 5:30pm.

For the Cañón del Cotahuasi (S30, 12 hours), Reyna has a 4pm departure and **Transportes Alex** (☎054-42-4605) has a 4:30pm departure.

Getting Around

TO/FROM THE AIRPORT

There are no airport buses or shared taxis. An official taxi from downtown Arequipa to the airport costs around S25. It is possible to take a *combi* marked 'Río Seco' or 'Zamacola' from Av Puente Grau and Ejército that will let you off in a sketchy neighborhood about 700m from the airport entrance.

BUS

Combis go south along Bolívar to the *terminal terrestre* (S0.80, 25 minutes), next door to the Terrapuerto bus terminal, but it's a slow trip via the market area. A taxi costs about S8.

TAXI

You can often hire a taxi with a driver for less than renting a car from a travel agency. Local taxi companies include **Tourismo Arequipa** (☎054-45-8888) and **Taxitel** (☎054-45-2020). A short ride around town costs about S4, while a trip from the Plaza de Armas out to the bus terminals costs about S8. Whenever possible, try to call a recommended company to ask for a pickup as there have been numerous reports of travelers being scammed or assaulted by taxi drivers. If you must hail a taxi off the street, pick a regular size saloon (sedan) or estate (station wagon) over a compact yellow cab.

CANYON COUNTRY

Going to Arequipa and missing out on the Colca Canyon is like going to Cuzco and neglecting to visit Machu Picchu. For those with more time there's a whole load of other excursions that merit attention, including climbing the city's guardian volcano El Misti, rafting in the Majes canyon, visiting the petroglyphs at Toro Muerto, exploring El Valle de los Volcanes and trekking down into the world's deepest canyon at Cotahuasi. Most of these places can be visited by a combination of public bus and hiking. Alternatively, friends can split the cost of hiring a taxi or 4WD vehicle and driver; a two-day trip will set you back more than US$150.

Reserva Nacional Salinas y Aguada Blanca

The trouble with all those organized Colca Canyon tours is that they rush through one of southern Peru's finest protected reserves, **Reserva Nacional Salinas y Aguada Blanca** (☎054-25-7461; ⌚24hr) FREE, a vast Andean expanse of dozing volcanoes and brawny wildlife forging out an existence against the odds several kilometers above sea level. Drives take you up to an oxygen-deprived 4910m where, in between light-headed gasps for air, you can ponder weird wind-eroded rock formations, trek on old Inca trails and watch fleet-footed vicuñas run across the desolate pampa at speeds of up to 85km/h.

As a national reserve, Salinas y Aguada Blanca enjoys better protection than the Colca Canyon, primarily because no one lives here bar the odd isolated llama-herder. Its job is to protect a rich raft of high-altitude species such as the vicuñas, tarucas envinados (Andean deer), guanacos and various birds, most notably flamingos. Both El Misti and Chachani volcanoes are part of the reserve.

Arequipa to Chivay

Sights

Patahuasi LANDMARK

The only civilization between Arequipa and Chivay, save for a few scattered farmsteads, is this fork in the road that acts as a kind of truck/bus stop and fill-up point (buses head southeast for Puno every hour). A few snack shacks pepper the scruffy byway while a kilometer or so beyond the Puno turning you'll run into **El Chinito** (Hwy 34A s/n, San Antonio de Chucha; snacks from S5), the favored breakfast stop for early-morning tour buses. Next door to the restaurant sit various handicraft stores.

Close by and accessible via a short off-piste drive is the **Bosque de Piedras**, a surreal collection of mushroom-like stones eroded by the wind that stand sentinel over the Río Sumbay.

Pampa de Toccra WILDLIFE RESERVE

Pampa de Toccra, a high plain (pampa) that lies between El Misti/Chachani and the Colca Canyon, has an average height of around 4300m and supports plentiful bird and animal life. You're almost certain to see vicuñas roadside in the Zona de Vicuñas on the approach to Patahuasi. At a boggy and sometimes icy lake, waterfowl and flamingos reside in season. Nearby is a birdwatching *mirador*.

The **Centro de Interpretación de la Reserva Nacional Salinas** (⌚9am-5pm) FREE has detailed notes in English and Spanish about the area's geology and fauna. All four members of the South American camelid family thrive at the pampas in this region: the domesticated llama and alpaca, and the wild vicuña and (timid and rare) guanaco.

OFF THE BEATEN TRACK

LAGUNA DE SALINAS

This lake (4300m above sea level), east of Arequipa below Pichu Pichu and El Misti, is a salt lake that becomes a white salt flat during the dry months of May to December. Its size and the amount of water in it vary each year depending on the weather. During the rainy season (January to May) it is a good place to see all three flamingo species, as well as myriad other Andean water birds.

Buses to Ubinas (S13, 3½ hours) pass by the lake and can be caught on Av Sepulveda in Arequipa. A small ticket booth on Sepulveda sells tickets, and schedules vary so it is a good idea to inquire a day before you wish to go. You can hike around the lake, which can take about two days, then return on the packed daily afternoon bus at around 3pm (expect to stand).

One-day minibus tours from Arequipa cost about S150 per person; mountain-biking tours are also available.

Paso de Patopampa VIEWPOINT

The highest point on the road between Arequipa and Chivay is this almost lifeless pass which, at 4910m, is significantly higher than Europe's Mt Blanc and anywhere in North America's Rocky Mountains. If your red blood cells are up to it, disembark into the rarefied air at the **Mirador de los Volcanes** to view a muscular consortium of eight snowcapped volcanoes: Ubinas (5675m), El Misti (5822m), Chachani (6075m), Ampato (6310m), Sabancaya (5976m), Huaka Hualca (6025m), Mismi (5597m) and Chucura (5360m).

Less spectacular but no less amazing is the scrubby yareta, one of the few plants that can survive in this harsh landscape. Yaretas can live for several millennia and their annual growth rate is measured in millimeters rather than centimeters. Hardy ladies in traditional dress discreetly ply their wares at the *mirador* during the day – this must be the world's highest shopping center.

El Misti

Looming 5822m above Arequipa, the city's guardian volcano El Misti is the most popular climb in the area. It is technically one of the easiest ascents of any mountain of this size in the world, but it's hard work nonetheless and you normally need an ice axe and, sometimes, crampons. Hiring a guide is highly recommended. A two-day trip will usually cost between US$50 and US$70 per person. The mountain is best climbed from July to November, with the later months being the least cold. Below the summit is a sulfurous yellow crater with volcanic fumaroles hissing gas, and there are spectacular views down to the Laguna de Salinas and back to the city.

The ascent can be approached by many routes, some more worn-in than others, most of which can be done in two days. The Apurímac route is notorious for robberies. One popular route starts from Chiguata, and begins with a hard eight-hour slog uphill to reach base camp (4500m); from there to the summit and back takes eight hours, while the sliding return from base camp to Chiguata takes three hours or less. The Aguada Blanca route is restricted to a handful of official tour operators and allows climbers to arrive at 4100m before beginning to climb.

Determined climbers can reach the Chiguata route via public transportation. Buses going to Chiguata leave from Av Sepulveda in Arequipa (S8 one way, one hour) hourly beginning at 5:30am and will drop you off at an unmarked trailhead, from where you can begin the long trek to base camp. On the return trip, you should be able to flag down the same bus heading the opposite way. The more common method to reach the mountain is hiring a driver in a 4WD for around S250, who will take you up to 3300m and pick you up on the return.

Chachani

One of the easiest 6000m peaks in the world is Chachani (6075m), which is as close to Arequipa as El Misti. You will need crampons, an ice axe and good equipment. There are various routes up the mountain, one of which involves going by 4WD to Campamento de Azufrera at 4950m. From there you can reach the summit in about nine hours and return in under four hours.

Alternatively, for a two-day trip, there is a good spot to camp at 5200m. Other routes take three days but are easier to get to by 4WD (US$125 to US$180).

Other Mountains

Nevado Sabancaya (5976m) is part of a massif on the south rim of the Cañón del Colca that also includes extinct **Nevado Hualca Hualca** (6025m) and **Nevado Ampato** (6310m). Sabancaya erupted in 2014 after 15 dormant years, and should only be approached with a guide who understands the geologic activity of the area; neighboring Ampato is a fairly straightforward, if strenuous, three-day ascent, and you get safer views of the active Sabancaya from here.

Other mountains of interest near Arequipa include **Ubinas** (5675m), which used to be the easiest mountain to summit but from 2013 to 2015 it was spewing enough toxic ash that it is not recommended for climbing. **Nevado Mismi** (5597m) is a fairly easy three- or four-day climb on the north side of the Cañón del Colca. You can approach it on public transportation and, with a guide, find the lake that is reputedly the source of the Amazon. The highest mountain in southern Peru is the difficult **Nevado Coropuna** (6613m).

Cañón del Colca

It's not just the vastness and depth of the Colca that make it so fantastical, it's the shifts in its mood. There are more scenery changes along its 100km passage than there are in most European countries; from the barren steppe of Sibayo, through the ancient terraced farmland of Yanque and Chivay, into the steep-sided canyon proper beyond Cabanaconde that wasn't thoroughly explored until the 1980s. Of course one shouldn't turn a blind eye to the vital statistics. The Colca is the world's second-deepest canyon, a smidgen shallower than near neighbor, the Cotahausi, and twice as deep as the more famous Grand Canyon in the US. But, more than that, it is replete with history, culture, ruins, tradition and – rather like Machu Picchu – intangible Peruvian magic.

Despite its depth, the Cañón del Colca is geologically young. The Río Colca has cut into beds of mainly volcanic rocks, which were deposited less than 100 million years ago along the line of a major fault in the earth's crust. Though cool and dry in the hills above, the deep valley and generally sunny weather produce frequent updrafts on which soaring condors often float by at close range. Viscachas (burrowing rodents closely related to chinchillas) are also common around the canyon rim, darting furtively among the rocks. Cacti dot many slopes and, if they're in flower, you may be lucky enough to see tiny nectar-eating birds braving the spines to feed. In the depths of the canyon it can be almost tropical, with palm trees, ferns and even orchids in some isolated areas.

The local people are descendants of two conflicting groups that originally occupied the area, the Cabanas and the Collagua. These two groups used to distinguish themselves by performing cranial deformations, but nowadays use distinctively shaped hats and intricately embroidered traditional clothing to denote their ancestry. In the Chivay area at the east end of the canyon, the white hats worn by women are usually woven from straw and are embellished with lace, sequins and medallions. At the west end of the canyon, the hats have rounded tops and are made of painstakingly embroidered cotton.

Upper Canyon

The Upper Canyon (really still a valley at this stage) has a colder and harsher landscape than the terraced fields around Chivay and Yanque, and is only lightly visited. Pierced by a single road that plies northeast through the village of Tuti to Sibayo, the grassy terrain is inhabited by livestock while the still young river is ideal for rafting and trout-fishing.

SIBAYO

Sitting at an altitude of 3900m at the head of the canyon, Sibayo is a traditional rural village little touched by tourism. Many of the adobe houses still have old-fashioned straw roofs while the diminutive main plaza is framed by the recently restored **Iglesia San Juan Bautista**. Northeast of the town, a quiet spot by the river has been embellished by a small suspension bridge crossing the Colca called the **Puente Colgante Portillo**, plus a lookout, the **Mirador de Largarta**, named for a lizard-shaped mountain up the valley. It is possible to hike southwest down the canyon to Tuti and, ultimately, Chivay from here.

Sibayo has a handful of very basic homestays available in traditional houses. One such place is **Samana Wasi** (☎990-049-5793; Av Mariscal Castilla; r S25) where the eager-to-please owners can rustle up dinner (S15) and take you trout-fishing.

Combis (S10, 1 hour, hourly) for Sibayo leave from the market area in Chivay.

TUTI

Tuti is a tourist-lite village situated only 19km northeast of Colca-hub Chivay. With an economy centered on broad-bean cultivation and clothes-making, it is surrounded by some interesting sights all connected by hiking trails. The easiest excursion is to a couple of caves in the hills to the north clearly visible from the main road and accessible via a 3.5km grunt uphill from the village. From the same starting point, you can also hike 8km to an old abandoned village dating from the 1600s known colloquially as **Ran Ran** or 'Espinar de Tuti.' Continue beyond Ran Ran and you'll join the trail to the source of the Amazon on the north side of Nevado Mismi. Down in the valley you can catch a taxi or *colectivo* (shared transportation) from Chivay to Tuti and hike back to Chivay on a well-marked trail alongside the Río Colca. This stretch of the river is popular with rafters.

Middle Canyon

Behold the most accessible and popular segment of the canyon, a landscape dominated by agriculture and characterized by some of the most intensely terraced hillsides on earth. The greenery and accessibility has led to this becoming the canyon's busiest region with the bulk of the business centered in the small town of Chivay.

CHIVAY

☎054 / POP 7700 / ELEV 3630M

Chivay is the Colca Canyon's unashamedly disheveled nexus, a traditional town that has embraced tourism without (so far) losing its unkempt high-country identity. Long may it continue!

Around the market area and in the main square are good places to catch a glimpse of the decorative clothing worn by local Colca women. The town itself affords enchanting views of snowcapped peaks and terraced hillsides, and serves as a logical base from which to explore smaller towns further up the valley.

> **BOLETO TURÍSTICO**
>
> To access sites in the Cañón del Colca you need to purchase a *boleto turístico* (tourist ticket; S70) from a booth on the Arequipa road just outside Chivay. If you are taking an organized tour, the cost of the tour usually does not include this additional fee, and you will be asked for this in cash by your guide at the booth. If you are traveling alone, tickets can be purchased on most public buses entering or leaving Chivay, or in the town of Cabanaconde. Half of the proceeds from this ticket go to Arequipa for general maintenance and conservation of local tourist attractions, while the other half goes to the national agency of tourism.

Sights & Activities

Astronomical Observatory OBSERVATORY
(Planetario; ☎054-53-1020; Huayna Cápac; admission S25; ⊗Apr-Dec) No light pollution equals excellent Milky Way vistas. The Casa Andina hotel has a tiny observatory which holds nightly sky shows in Spanish and English. The price includes a 30-minute explanation and chance to peer into the telescope. It is closed between January and March as it is hard to catch a night with clear skies.

La Calera Hot Springs THERMAL BATHS
(admission S15; ⊗4:30am-7pm) If you've just bussed or driven in from Arequipa, a good way to acclimatize is to stroll 3km to La Calera Hot Springs and examine the canyon's (surprisingly shallow) slopes alfresco while lying in the naturally heated pools. The setting is idyllic and you'll be entertained by the whooping zipliners as they sail overhead. *Colectivos* from Chivay cost S1 to S2.

Hiking

Chivay is a good starting point for canyon hikes, both short and long. The view-embellished 7km path to Corporaque on the north side of the canyon starts on the north edge of town. Fork left on La Calera Hot Springs road, cross the Puente Inca, and follow the fertile fields to the village. Rather than retracing your steps, you can head downhill out of Corporaque past some small ruins and descend to the orange bridge across the Río Colca. From Yanque, on the southern bank, you can catch a passing bus

OFF THE BEATEN TRACK

SOURCE OF THE AMAZON TREK

For centuries it remained one of the world's greatest mysteries. Humans had landed probes on Mars and split the atom before they got around to finding and – more importantly – agreeing upon the source of the world's most voluminous and (debatably) longest river, the mighty Amazon. Everyone from Alexander von Humboldt to Jean-Michel Cousteau pitched in with their theories (often backed up with expensive expeditions) before the headwaters were finally pinpointed unequivocally in 2007: a fissure in a steep cliff situated at 5170m on the northern slopes of Nevado Mismi, 6992km from the Amazon's river mouth on Brazil's Atlantic coast. Here glacial melt-waters collect in Laguna McIntyre before flowing into the Apacheta, Apurímac, Ucayali and Marañón rivers whereupon they form the Amazon proper.

It is surprisingly easy to hike to the Amazon's source (marked inauspiciously by a wooden cross) from the Cañón del Colca. Paths ply north from the villages of Lari or Tuti. It's a two-day out-and-back hike from the latter village though some people prefer to undertake a three-day circuitous route starting in Lari and ending in Tuti, thus making a complete circle of Nevado Mismi. Alternatively, in the dry season, it is possible to get a 4WD to within 30 minutes hike of the Apacheta cliff. Carlos Zárate Adventures (p148) in Arequipa organizes memorable guided hikes. Soloists should come equipped with maps, food, tents and cold-weather clothing.

or *colectivo* for the 7km return to Chivay (or you can walk along the road). For a quicker trip, rent a mountain bike in Chivay.

To penetrate further west it's possible to continue on up the northern side of the canyon from Corporaque to the villages **Ichupampa**, **Lari** and, ultimately, **Madrigal**. Occasional *combis* run to these villages from the streets around the main market area in Chivay. Another option is to pitch northeast from near the Puente Inca and follow a path along the river to the villages of Tuti and Sibayo.

Ziplining

You can dangle terrifyingly over the Río Colca while entertaining bathers in La Calera Hot Springs (who relax below) doing the canyon's most modern sport – ziplining. The start point is just past La Calera Hot Springs, 3.5km from Chivay, but you can organize rides with one of the agencies in town or directly with **Colca Zip-lining** (☎95-898-9931; www.colcaziplining.com; 2/4 rides S50/100; ⊙from 9am Mon-Sat, from 10:30am Sun).

Sleeping

Though it's a tiny town, Chivay has plenty of budget guesthouses to choose from. The most convenient are on Siglo XX, off the plaza, for about S40 for a basic double.

Hostal La Pascana HOTEL $
(☎054-53-1001; Siglo XX 106; s/d/tr incl breakfast S50/70/100; wi-fi) La Pascana is a good old-fashioned crash pad that will probably seem like luxury after a few days hiking in the canyon. Simple rooms have blankets (thank heavens!), the staff is gracious and there's a small but decent restaurant. It's several notches above the other more modest guesthouses and lies adjacent to the plaza.

Hostal Estrella de David PENSION $
(☎054-53-1233; Siglo XX 209; s/d/tr S30/40/60) A simple, clean *hospedaje* (small, family-owned inn) with bathrooms and some rooms with cable TV. It's a couple of blocks from the plaza in the direction of the bus terminal. For budgeters, single rooms with shabby shared bathrooms are S20.

Inkari Lodge Colca LODGE $$
(☎95-900-350, 054-531-019; inkaricolca@hotmail.com; Espinar s/n; s/d incl breakfast S95/121/143) A seven-minute taxi ride above Chivay, the ragged cliffs huddle around the sprawling gardens here, while the sun sets over the mountains. The wooden rooms extend the chalet vibe, as does the cold, so keep that heater on. The hot showers are nearly as huge as the on-site restaurant, and nights are immaculately quiet, especially without wi-fi.

★**Hotel Pozo del Cielo** HOTEL $$$
(☎054-34-6547; www.pozodelcielo.com.pe; Calle Huascar s/n; d/ste S310/637; wi-fi) Looking a bit like something Gaudí might have crafted, 'Heaven's Well,' as the name translates, is all

low doorways, weirdly shaped rooms and winding paths. It's easy to imagine the seven dwarfs marching out. But, surrealism aside, this place works – a functional yet comfortable abode with an almost boutique-like feel to its individually crafted rooms and fine *mirador* restaurant.

Casa Andina BOUTIQUE HOTEL **$$$**
(☎054-53-1020, 054-53-1022; www.casa-andina.com; Huayna Cápac; s/d incl breakfast from S250;) The purposefully rustic rooms here inhabit thatched-roof stone cottages in neatly sculpted grounds. The best features are the unusual extras such as an observatory, oxygen (should you be feeling lightheaded for a lack of it) and nightly culture shows where local musicians and artisans mingle, and a shaman tells fortunes with coca leaves.

Eating

Innkas Café PERUVIAN **$**
(Plaza de Armas 705; mains S12-20; 7am-10pm) An old building with cozy window nooks warmed by modern gas heaters (and boy, do you need 'em). Maybe it's the altitude, but the *lomo saltado* tastes Gastón Acurio–good here. The sweet service is backed up by even sweeter cakes and coffee.

Aromas Caffee CAFE **$**
(www.aromascaffeecolca.com; cnr Plaza de Armas & Av Salaverry) The tiny cappuccino machine in this diminutive 'three's-a-crowd' cafe takes the conscientious barista about 10 minutes to manipulate, but your Peruvian coffee, when it emerges, is worth the wait.

Cusi Alina PERUVIAN **$$**
(Plaza de Armas 201; buffet S27;) One of a couple of restaurants in Chivay that offers an all-you-can-eat lunchtime buffet. The food represents a good Peruvian smorgasbord with plenty of vegetarian options. It's popular with tour buses, so get in before 1pm to enjoy more elbow room.

Information

There's a helpful **information office** (☎054-53-1143; Plaza de Armas 119; 8am-1pm & 3-7pm) right on the main plaza. The police station is next to the *municipalidad* (town hall) on the plaza. There is one ATM in town located on Calle Salaverry one block west of the main plaza. Some of the higher-end hotels and a few shops around town exchange US dollars, euros and traveler's checks at unfavorable rates. Internet access is available from a few internet cafes near the plaza.

Getting There & Around

The bus terminal is a 15-minute walk from the plaza. There are nine daily departures to Arequipa (S15, three hours), and four daily to Cabanaconde (S5, 2½ hours), stopping at towns along the southern side of the canyon and at Cruz del Cóndor.

Combis (S2 to S5) and *colectivo* taxis run to the surrounding villages from street corners in the market area, just north of the main plaza, or you can arrange a private taxi. Mountain bikes in varying condition can be readily hired from travel agencies on the plaza or at **BiciSport** (☎95-880-7652; Zaramilla 112; 9am-6pm) behind the market for about S5 per day.

Traveling onward to Cuzco from Chivay may be possible, but it's overly complicated and not recommended. Although some travelers have managed to catch *combis* to Puente Callalli and flag down a bus there, it's much safer and probably just as fast to return to Arequipa instead.

To get to Puno, it's cheaper to return to Arequipa but you'll save a few hours by taking a daily direct tourist bus from Chivay (stopping for food and photo ops) with **4M Express** (☎95-974-6330; www.4m-express.com; Chivay to Puno US$45) or **Rutas del Sur** (☎95-102-4754; chivay@rutasurperu.com; Av 22 de Agosto s/n; Chivay to Puno US$35), both leaving near Chivay's plaza at 1:30pm and arriving at Puno's plaza at 7:30pm. If you have taken a tour from Arequipa, let your guide know you don't plan on returning.

YANQUE

☎054 / POP 2100

Of the canyon's dozen or so villages, Yanque, 7km west of Chivay, has the prettiest and liveliest main square. It also sports the canyon's finest church (from the exterior, at least), the **Iglesia de la Inmaculada Concepción**, whose ornate doorway has an almost *churrigueresque* (a style from the late Spanish baroque period) look. Local children in traditional costume dance to music in the main square most mornings at around 7am, catching tourists on their way to the Cruz del Cóndor.

Sights

Museo Yanque MUSEUM
(http://yanqueperu.com; admission S5; 9am-6:30pm) Opposite the church on the plaza sits this university-run museum, unexpectedly comprehensive for a small village, which explains the culture of the Cañón del Colca in conscientious detail. Exhibits include information on Inca fabrics, cranial deformation, local agriculture, ecclesial

architecture and a mini-exposé on Juanita, the 'Ice Maiden.'

Baños Chacapi THERMAL BATHS
(admission S10; ⏲4am-7pm) From the plaza, a 30-minute walk down to the river brings you to these hot springs, a kind of poor-man's La Calera. The early-bird opening time is mainly for locals, many of whom don't have hot water in their houses.

Sleeping

Sumaq Huayta Wasi GUESTHOUSE $
(Casa Bella Flor; ☎92-929-2315; www.casabellaflor.com; Cusco 303) In Yanque, a number of simple, family-run guesthouses were started as part of a local development project; they are scattered around town, and offer lodging for S15 per room per night. Travelers have recommended Sumaq Huayta Wasi, just two blocks from the main plaza. It provides an excellent balance between tradition and comfort.

Hotel Collahua HOTEL $$
(☎054-22-6098; www.hotelcollahua.com; Av Collahua Cuadro 7; s/d/tr S75/95/105; 📶) A fairly upscale option, Hotel Collahua has bright rooms in independent bungalows over largish grounds where alpacas roam. There's a comprehensive restaurant on-site.

CORPORAQUE

Noncommercialized Corporaque has the valley's oldest church and not a lot else, unless you count the splendiferous views of canyon slopes covered in terraced fields.

Sights

Nonguests can use the thermal baths at the Colca Lodge for S35 (price includes one meal in the lodge restaurant).

Oyu Oyu RUIN
Though not visible from the road, the remnants of this pre-Incan settlement are reachable by a half-hour uphill hike, after which you can continue on to a waterfall whose source is the runoff from Nevado Mismi. Guides can be procured at the Colca Lodge.

Sleeping

La Casa de Mamayacchi INN $$
(www.lacasademamayacchi.com; d/tr incl breakfast from S223/293) Hidden away four blocks downhill from the main plaza, this inn is built with traditional materials and resides over terraced valley views. The cozy rooms have no TV, but there's a games library, fireplace and bar that make it sociable. Make advance reservations through the **Arequipa office** (☎054-24-1206; Jerusalén 606).

★Colca Lodge LUXURY HOTEL $$$
(☎054-28-2177; www.colca-lodge.com; d/ste incl breakfast S554/904; ❄📶🏊) Expensive but utterly romantic, this is the Colca Canyon packaged for the decadent, with artistically manicured grounds spreading majestically beside the rippling Río Colca. Lavish rooms come loaded with dapper dressing gowns, woodburning stoves, candles, coffee machines and king beds, but the real carrot is the alfresco thermal baths (37°C to 39°C) sculpted into whimsical pools beside the river.

For advance reservations, visit the **Arequipa office** (☎054-20-2587, 054-20-3604; Benavides 201).

LARI

Sleepy Lari, 16km west of Corporaque on the north side of the river, has the canyon's largest church. It is also a potential start point for the Source of the Amazon trek (p164), which can be looped back round to Tuti in the northeast. There's a rock-bottom hotel in the main square and a couple of bare-bones restaurants, but you're better off forging on to Chivay or Cabanaconde for an overnighter.

MADRIGAL

Madrigal is the last village on the canyon's north side reachable by road (unpaved by this point). Aside from its oversized church and scruffy digs at the **Hostal Municipalidad** (Plaza de Armas; r S12), Madrigal is a bucolic backwater perfect for a slow unflustered digestion of traditional Colca life. You can forge west on foot from here to two nearby archaeological sites: the **Fortaleza de Chimpa**, a walled Collagua citadel atop a hill, and the **Pueblo Perdido Matata**, some long-abandoned ruins.

PINCHOLLO

Pinchollo, about 30km from Chivay, is one of the valley's poorer villages. From here, a trail climbs toward **Hualca Hualca** (a snow-capped volcano of 6025m) to an active geothermal area set amid wild and interesting scenery. Though it's not very clearly marked, there's a rough four-hour trail up to a bubbling geyser that used to erupt dramatical-

'EL CLÁSICO' TREK

Short on time? Confused by the complicated web of Colca paths? Couldn't stand the crowds on the Inca Trail? What you need is 'El Clásico,' the unofficial name for a circular two- to three-day hike that incorporates the best parts of the mid-lower Colca Canyon below the Cruz del Cóndor and Cabanaconde.

Start by walking out of Cabanaconde on the Chivay road. At the San Miguel viewpoint, start a long 1200m descent into the canyon on a zigzagging path. Cross the Río Colca via a bridge and enter the village of **San Juan de Chuccho**. Accommodations are available here at the **Casa de Rivelino** (r without bathroom S15), with bungalows with warm water and a simple restaurant. Alternatively, you can ascend to the charming village of **Tapay**. Camping or overnight accommodations are available at **Hostal Isidro** – its owner is a guide and it has a shop, satellite phone and rental mules. On day two descend to the **Cinkumayu Bridge** before ascending to the villages of **Coshñirwa** and **Malata**. The latter has a tiny **Museo Familiar**, basically a typical local home where the owner will explain about the Colca culture. From Malata, descend to the beautiful **Sangalle** oasis (crossing the river again), with more overnight options, before ascending the lung-stretching 4km trail back to Cabanaconde (1200m of ascent).

Though it's easy to do solo, this classic trek can be easily organized with any reputable Arequipa travel agency.

ly before an earthquake contained it. Ask around for directions, or just head left uphill in the direction of the mountain, then follow the water channel to its end.

CRUZ DEL CÓNDOR

Some much hyped travel sights are anti-climactic in the raw light of day, but this is *not* one of them. No advance press can truly sell the **Cruz del Cóndor** (Chaq'lla; admission with boleto turístico), a famed viewpoint, also known locally as Chaq'lla, about 50km west of Chivay. A large family of Andean condors nests by the rocky outcrop and, weather and season permitting, they can be seen between approximately 8am and 10am gliding effortlessly on thermal air currents rising from the canyon, swooping low over onlookers' heads (condors rarely flap their wings). It's a mesmerizing scene, heightened by the spectacular 1200m drop to the river below and the sight of **Nevado Mismi** reaching more than 3000m above the canyon floor on the other side of the ravine.

Recently it has become more difficult to see the condors, mostly due to air pollution, including from travelers' campfires and tour buses. The condors are also less likely to appear on rainy days so it's best to visit during the dry season; they are unlikely to emerge at all in January and February. You won't be alone at the lookout. Expect a couple of hundred people for the 8am 'show' in season. Afterwards, it is possible to walk 12.5km from the viewpoint to Cabanaconde.

Lower Canyon

The narrow lower canyon is the Colca at its deepest. It runs roughly from Cabanaconde down to Huambo. Fruit trees can be found around Tapay and Sangalle, but otherwise the canyon supports no real economic activity.

CABANACONDE

☎054 / POP 2400 / ELEV 3290M

Only approximately 20% of Cañón del Colca visitors get as far as ramshackle Cabanaconde (most organized itineraries turn around at the Cruz del Cóndor). For those who make it, the attractions are obvious – less people, more authenticity and greater tranquility. Welcome to the *true* canyon experience. The Colca is significantly deeper here with steep, zigzagging paths tempting the fit and the brave to descend 1200m to the eponymous river. There are no ATMs in Cabanaconde. Stash some cash.

Activities

You've only half-experienced Colca if you haven't descended into the canyon by foot (the only method anywhere west of Madrigal). The shortest way in is via the spectacular two-hour hike from Cabanaconde down to the flower-filled greenery of **Sangalle** (also popularly known as 'the oasis') at the bottom of the canyon. The mountain walls create a tranquil oasis indeed, topped with a blanket of stars at night.

Here four sets of basic bungalows and camping grounds have sprung up, all costing from about S15 to S20 per person. There are two natural pools for swimming, the larger of which is claimed by Oasis Bungalows, which charges S5 to swim (free if you are staying in its bungalows). Paraíso Bungalows doesn't charge for the smaller swimming pool, and there is a local dispute over whether travelers should be charged to use the pools at all. Do not light campfires as almost half of the trees in the area have been destroyed in this manner, and cart all trash out with you. The return trek to Cabanaconde is a stiff climb and thirsty work; allow 1½ hours (superfit), two to 2½ hours (fit), three hours plus (average fitness). There's drink and food available in Sangalle.

Tours

Local guides can be hired by consulting with your hostel or the *municipalidad* in Cabanaconde. The going rate for guides is S30 to S60 per day, depending on the type of trek, season and size of the group. Renting a horse or mule, which is an excellent way to carry water into the canyon and waste out, can be arranged easily for about S60 per day.

Sleeping & Eating

Accommodation options are limited in Cabanaconde. Most people eat where they're sleeping, although there are a couple of cheap local restaurants near or on the main plaza.

★Pachamama HOSTEL $
(☎95-931-6322, 054-25-3879; www.pachamama-home.com; San Pedro 209; incl breakfast dm S25, d without/with bathroom S50/70; @) Run by the ultrafriendly and helpful Ludwig (who's fluent in English), Pachamama has plenty of room options (doubles, triples and other combos), a pizza oven, a fantastic crepe breakfast and an unexpectedly warm-hearted bar. One-way downhill bike excursions from the Cruz del Cóndor can be organized for S95, including transport there with the bikes to see the condors before the ride.

★Hotel Kuntur Wassi HOTEL $$
(☎054-81-2166; www.arequipacolca.com; Cruz Blanca s/n; s/d/ste incl breakfast S175/207/287; @) As upmarket as Cabanaconde gets, Kuntur Wassi is actually rather charming. It's built into the hillside above town, with stone bathrooms, trapezoidal windows overlooking the gardens and a nouveau-rustic feel. Suites have enormous bathtubs. There's also a bar, restaurant, library, laundry and foreign-currency exchange. It serves top-notch city-standard food.

La Posada del Conde HOTEL $$
(☎054-40-0408, 054-83-0033; www.posadadelconde.com; San Pedro s/n; s/d incl breakfast S95/128;) This small hotel mostly has double rooms, but they are well-cared-for with clean bathrooms. The rates often include a welcome *mate* (herbal tea) or pisco sour in the downstairs restaurant. The same people run a smaller, slightly plusher and pricier lodge up the road.

Restaurante Las Terrazas INTERNATIONAL $
(☎95-810-3553; www.villapastorcolca.com; Plaza de Armas s/n; snacks S10-15) Pizza, pasta, sandwiches and cheap Cuba Libres are offered at this restaurant overlooking the main square and its bucolic donkey traffic. There's also a computer terminal charitably offering free internet. Rooms are available.

Getting There & Away

Buses for Chivay (S5, 2½ hours) and Arequipa (S17, six hours) via Cruz del Cóndor leave Cabanaconde from the main plaza seven times per day with four companies, including **Andalucía** (☎054-44-5089) and **Reyna** (☎054-43-0612). Departure times change frequently though, so check with the bus company office on the main plaza. All buses will stop upon request at towns along the main road on the southern side of the canyon. Morning departures can get full with local farmers toward Chivay, so arrive a little earlier.

Toro Muerto Petroglyphs

A fascinating, mystical site in the high desert, Toro Muerto (meaning 'Dead Bull') is named for the herds of livestock that commonly died here from dehydration as they were escorted from the mountains to the coast. A barren hillside is scattered with white volcanic boulders carved with stylized people, animals and birds. Archaeologists have documented more than 5000 such petroglyphs spread over several square kilometers of desert. Though the cultural origins of this site remain unknown, most archaeologists date the mysterious drawings to the period of Wari domination, about 1200 years ago. Interpretations of the drawings vary widely; a guide can fill you in on some of the most common themes, or you can wander among the boulders yourself and formulate your own elaborate interpretation of the message these ancient images aim to tell.

To reach the site by public transportation, take a bus to Corire from Arequipa (S12, three hours). If you don't want to sleep in Corire, take an early bus (they start as early as 4am) and get off at a gas station just past the sign that denotes the beginning of the town of Corire. From there, you can walk the hot, dusty road about 2km uphill to a checkpoint where visitors must sign in. Otherwise, continue to Corire; from here you can catch a taxi to take you to where the petroglyphs start (from S45 round-trip if the taxi waits). In Corire, **Hostal Willy** (☎054-47-2046; Av Progreso; s/d/tr S40/45/60) has basic accommodations and can provide information on reaching the site. Bring plenty of water, sunblock and insect repellent (as there are plenty of mosquitoes en route).

Buses return from Corire to Arequipa once an hour, usually leaving at 30 minutes past the hour. The Toro Muerto petroglyphs can also be visited more conveniently on expensive full-day 4WD tours from Arequipa.

El Valle de los Volcanes

El Valle de los Volcanes is a broad valley, west of the Cañón del Colca and at the foot of Nevado Coropuna (6613m), famed for its unusual geological features. The valley floor is carpeted with lava flows from which rise many small (up to 200m high) cinder cones, some 80 in total, aligned along a major fissure, with each cone formed from a single eruption. Given the lack of erosion of some cones and minimal vegetation on the associated lava flows, the volcanic activity occurred no more than a few thousand years ago, and some was likely very recent – historical accounts suggest as recently as the 17th century.

The 65km-long valley surrounds the village of **Andagua**, near the snowy summit of Coropuna. Visitors seeking a destination full of natural wonders and virtually untouched by travelers will rejoice in this remote setting. From Andagua, a number of sites can be visited by foot or car. It is possible to hike to the top of the perfectly conical twin volcanoes which lie about 10km from town, though don't expect a clear-cut trail. Other popular hikes are to a nearby *mirador* at 3800m and to the 40m-high **Izanquillay** falls which are formed where the Río Andahua runs through a narrow lava canyon to the northeast of town. There are some *chullpas* (funerary towers) at **Soporo**, a two-hour hike or half-hour drive to the south of Andagua. En route to Soporo are the ruins of a pre-Columbian city named **Antaymarca**. An alternative way to enter the valley is by starting from Cabanaconde, crossing the Cañón del Colca, then hiking over a 5500m pass before descending into El Valle de los Volcanes. This trek requires at least five days (plus time for proper acclimatization beforehand), and is best to attempt with an experienced guide and pack mules.

There are several cheap and basic hostels and restaurants in Andagua, including the recommended **Hostal Volcanes** (☎054-83-4065; Calle 15 de Agosto; r S20). Camping is also possible, though you will need plenty of water and sun protection. To get to the valley from Arequipa, take a Reyna bus to Andagua (S45, 10 to 12 hours) which departs from Arequipa around 4pm. Return buses leave Andagua around 2pm. Some tour companies also visit El Valle de los Volcanes as part of expensive tours in 4WDs that may also include visits to the Cañón del Cotahuasi and Chivay.

Cañón del Cotahuasi

While the Cañón del Colca has stolen the limelight for many years, it is actually this remote canyon, 200km northwest of Arequipa as the condor flies, that is the deepest known canyon in the world. It is around twice the depth of the Grand Canyon, with stretches dropping down below 3500m. While the depths of the ravine are only accessible to experienced river runners, the rest of the fertile valley is rich in striking scenery and trekking opportunities. The canyon also shelters several traditional rural settlements that currently see only a handful of adventurous travelers.

Sights & Activities

The main access town is appropriately named **Cotahuasi** (population 3800) and is at 2620m above sea level on the southeast side of the canyon. Northeast of Cotahuasi and further up the canyon are the villages of **Tomepampa** (10km away; elevation 2500m) and **Alca** (20km away; 2660m), which also have basic accommodations. En route you'll pass a couple of **thermal baths** (admission S2).

Buses to the Sipia bridge (S3, one hour) leave the main plaza of Cotahuasi daily at 6:30am, from where you can begin a number of interesting hikes into the deepest parts of the canyon. Forty-five minutes up the trail, the **Sipia waterfall** is formed where the Río Cotahuasi takes an impressive 100m tumble; the viewpoint is from above. Another 1½ hours on a well-trodden track brings you to **Chaupo**, an oasis of towering cacti and remnants of pre-Incan dwellings. Camping is possible. From here a dusty path leads either up to **Velinga** and other remote communities where sleeping accommodations are available, or down to **Mallu**, a patch of verdant farmland at the river's edge where the owner, Ignacio, will allow you to pitch tents and borrow his stove for S12 per night. To get back to Cotahuasi, a return bus leaves the Sipia bridge around 11:30am daily.

Another possible day trip from Cotahuasi is to the hillside community of **Pampamarca**. From here, a two-hour hike up a steep switchbacking trail will bring you to an interesting group of rock formations, where locals have likened shapes in the rocks to mystical figures. A short walk from town brings you to a lookout with a view of the rushing 80m-high **Uscune falls**. To get to Pampamarca (S5, two hours), *combis* leave the main square in Cotahuasi twice daily around 7am and 2pm, and return shortly after arriving.

Trekking trips of several days' duration can be arranged in Arequipa; some can be combined with the Toro Muerto petroglyphs and, if you ask, they may return via a collection of dinosaur footprints on the west edge of the canyon.

Sleeping & Eating

In Pampamarca, ask around for basic **family guesthouses** (per person S10) that provide travelers with beds and meals.

Hostal Hatunhuasi GUESTHOUSE $

(☎054-58-1054, in Lima 01-531-0803; www.hatunhuasi.com; Centanario 309, Cotahuasi; s/d S30/60) A notch above the other options in town, this friendly guesthouse has plenty of rooms situated around a sunny inner courtyard and has hot water most of the time. Food can be prepared upon request, and the owners are good sources of hard-to-get information for travelers.

Hospedaje Casa Primavera INN $

(☎054-28-5089; primaverahostal@hotmail.com; Calle Union 112, Tomepampa; s/d incl breakfast S25/64) A good find in the tiny village of Tomepampa, this oldish hacienda-style building has a balcony, some floral embellishments and views. There is a variety of simple but clean rooms of different sizes.

Hotel Vallehermoso HOTEL $$

(☎054-58-1057; www.hotelvallehermoso.com; Calle Tacna 106-108, Cotahuasi; s/d/tr incl breakfast S75/140/195) Just what you probably wanted after a dusty 12-hour bus ride, Cotahuasi's poshest joint offers divine comfort in the middle of nowhere while never straying too far from rustic tradition. An on-site restaurant even tries its spin on *novoandina* (Peruvian nouvelle cuisine).

Hostal Alcalá GUESTHOUSE $

(☎054-83-0011; Plaza de Armas, Alca; s/d S25/40, dm/s/d without bathroom S10/15/25) In Alca, this guesthouse has a good mix of clean rooms and prices, including some of the most comfortable digs in the whole valley. There is 24-hour hot water here.

Getting There & Away

The 420km bus journey from Arequipa, half of which is on unpaved roads, takes 12 hours if the going is good. Over three-quarters of the way there, the road summits a 4500m pass between the huge glacier-capped mountains of Coropuna (6613m) and Solimana (6323m) before dropping down to Cotahuasi. Wild vicuña can also be spotted here running on the high altiplano. **Reyna** (☎054-43-0612) and **Transportes Alex** (☎054-42-4605) both run buses (S25) that leave Arequipa around 4pm. Buses return to Arequipa from Cotahuasi at around 5pm.

There are hourly *combis* from the Cotahuasi plaza up to Alca (S4, one hour) via Tomepampa (S2, 30 minutes). For Pampamarca, there are two daily buses (S5, two hours) departing in the early morning and again mid-afternoon.

Lake Titicaca

Includes ➡

Why Go?

In Andean belief, Titicaca is the birthplace of the sun. In addition, it's the largest lake in South America and the highest navigable body of water in the world. Banner blue skies contrast with bitterly cold nights. Enthralling and in many ways singular, the shimmering deep blue Lake Titicaca is the longtime home of highland cultures steeped in the old ways.

Pre-Inca Pukara, Tiwanaku and Collas all left a mark on the landscape. Today the region is a mix of crumbling cathedrals, desolate altiplano and checkerboard fields backed by rolling hills and high Andean peaks. In this world, crops are still planted and harvested by hand. *Campesinos* (peasants) wear sandals recycled from truck tires, women work in petticoats and bowler hats, and llamas are tame as pets.

It might at first appear austere, but ancient holidays are marked with riotous celebrations where elaborately costumed processions and brass bands start a frenzy that lasts for days.

Best Places to Stay & Eat

- ➡ Titilaka (p186)
- ➡ Casa Andina Isla Suasi (p186)
- ➡ Casa Panq'arani (p179)
- ➡ Capachica Community Homestays (p187)
- ➡ Mojsa (p181)

Best Festivals

- ➡ La Virgen de la Candelaria (p177)
- ➡ Puno Week (p178)
- ➡ Fiesta de San Juan (p178)
- ➡ Alacitas (p178)
- ➡ Feast of St James (p178)

When to Go

Puno

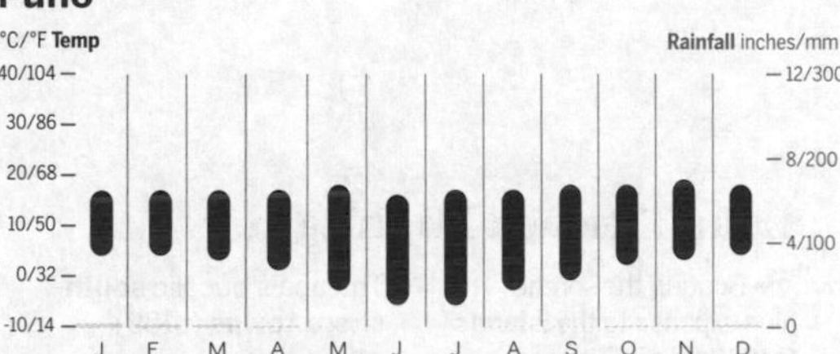

Early Feb For the marvelous spectacle of the festival of La Virgen de la Candelaria.

Jun–Aug Winter's dry season heralds cold, clear nights and bright sunny days.

Early Nov Puno Week celebrates the birth of Manco Cápac, the first Inca, in wild style.

Getting There & Around

There are daily flights to Juliaca (one hour from Puno) from Lima and Cuzco. Regular buses travel from Arequipa, Cuzco and Lima to Juliaca and Puno. There's also an iconic train route from Cuzco to Puno. If arriving from sea level, it's best to travel overland to better acclimate to the altitude.

It's also possible to arrive from Bolivia by bus or a packaged island tour of Lake Titicaca.

Juliaca

051 / ELEV 3826M

The region's only commercial airport makes Juliaca, the largest city on the altiplano, an unavoidable transit hub. The city bustles with commerce (and contraband) due to its handy location near the border. Daytime muggings and drunks on the street are not uncommon. Since Juliaca has little to offer

Lake Titicaca Highlights

1. Boating the serene blue expanse to the **islands** (p184) of Lake Titicaca.
2. Celebrating festivals with blaring bands and crazy costumes in **Puno** (p177), Peru's *capital folklórico*.
3. Admiring the elaborate temples that dwarf Lake Titicaca's bucolic **south-shore towns** (p189).
4. Hiking across farmland and climbing hills to ruins in **Ichu** (p189).
5. Visiting awe-inspiring funerary towers at **Sillustani** (p183) and **Cutimbo** (p183).
6. Recharging your batteries on sunny **Capachica Peninsula** (p187).
7. Stargazing and sleeping onboard the historic steamship **Yavari** (p174).
8. Crossing into Bolivia to explore the legendary **Isla del Sol**.

LAKE TITICACA JULIACA

travelers, it is advisable to stay in nearby Lampa or move on to Puno.

Hotels, restaurants, *casas de cambio* (foreign-exchange) and internet cafes abound along San Román, near Plaza Bolognesi. ATMs and banks are nearby on Nuñez.

If you are in a pinch, **Royal Inn Hotel** (051-32-1561; www.royalinnhoteles.com; San Román 158; s/d/tr incl breakfast S315/330/420) is an excellent upmarket choice. This towering hotel boasts recently revamped modern rooms with hot showers, heating and cable TV, plus one of Juliaca's best restaurants (mains from S20).

Getting There & Away

AIR

The **airport** (JUL; 051-32-4248) is 2km west of town. **LAN** (051-32-2228; San Román 125) has daily flights to/from Lima, Arequipa and Cuzco. **Avianca** (051-827-4951; www.avianca.com; Centro Comercial Real Plaza, Jirón Tumbes 391, Local LC-105; 11am-8pm Mon-Fri, to 6pm Sat & Sun) also flies to Lima.

Official airport taxis go to Puno (S80) and Juliaca (S10). A cheaper option is a *colectivo* (shared transportation, S15), a shuttle bus that goes directly to Puno and drops passengers at their hotels. For the return trip, most hotels in Puno can arrange trips in these minivans.

BUS & TAXI

The **terminal terrestre** (cnr Jirón San Martín & Av Miraflores) houses long-distance bus companies. Buses leave for Cuzco every hour from 5am to 11pm, and for Arequipa every hour from 2:30am to 11:30pm.

Buses to the coast leave from within walking distance of Plaza Bolognesi, on and around San Martín over the railway tracks; *combis* (minibuses) to Puno leave from Plaza Bolognesi.

Julsa (051-32-6602, 051-33-1952) has the most frequent departures to Arequipa; **Power** (051-32-1952) has the most frequent to Cuzco. **Civa**, **Ormeño** and **San Cristobal** run to Lima.

Sur Oriente has a daily bus to Tacna at 7pm. More centrally located, **San Martín** (051-32-7501) and other companies along Tumbes between Moquegua and Piérola go to Tacna (S30, 10 hours) via Moquegua.

Combis to Puno (S3.50, 50 minutes) leave from Plaza Bolognesi when full. *Combis* for Lampa (S2.50, 30 minutes) leave from Jirón Huáscar when full. *Combis* to Huancané (S3.50, one hour) leave every 15 minutes from Ballón and Sucre, about four blocks east of Apurímac and 1½ blocks north of Lambayeque. *Combis* to Capachica (S4, 1½ hours) leave from the **Terminal Zonal** (Av Tacna, cuadra 11). *Combis* to Escallani (S3.50, 1½ hours), via an incredibly scenic, unpaved back road, leave from the corner of Cahuide and Gonzáles Prada. All of these terminals are a S3 *mototaxi* (three-wheeled motorcycle-rickshaw taxi) ride from the center of town.

Juliaca Buses:

DESTINATION	COST* (S)	DURATION (HR)
Arequipa	15/50	6
Cuzco	20/40	5-6
Lima	80/170	20
Puno	3.50 (normal only)	1
Tacna	30/60	10-11

* Prices are estimates for normal/luxury buses.

Getting Around

Mototaxi is the best option for getting around. A ride to local destinations, including bus terminals, will cost about S3. Bus line 1B cruises around town and down Calle 2 de Mayo before heading to the airport (S0.60).

Lampa

051 / POP 2500 / ELEV 3860

This charming little town, 36km northwest of Juliaca, is known as La Ciudad Rosada (the Pink City) for its dusty, pink-colored buildings. A significant commercial center in colonial days, it still shows a strong Spanish influence. It's an excellent place to kill a few hours before flying out of Juliaca, or to spend a quiet night.

Sights

Just out of town is a pretty colonial **bridge**, and about 4km west is **Cueva de los Toros**, a bull-shaped cave with prehistoric carvings of llamas and other animals. The cave is on the right-hand side of the road heading west. Its entrance is part of a large, distinctive rock formation. En route you'll see several *chullpas* (funerary towers), not unlike the ones at Sillustani and Cutimbo.

Iglesia de Santiago Apostol CHURCH
(Plaza de Armas; tour S10; 9am-12:30pm & 2-4pm) Worth seeing and the pride of locals, this lime-mortar church includes fascinating features such as a life-sized sculpture of the *Last Supper;* Santiago (St James) atop a real stuffed horse, returning from the dead to trample the Moors; creepy catacombs; secret tunnels; a domed tomb topped by a wonderful copy of Michelangelo's *Pietà*; and

SWEET STEAMSHIP DREAMS

The oldest steamship on Lake Titicaca, the famed **Yavari** (051-36-9329; www.yavari.org; admission by donation; 8am-1pm & 3-5:30pm) has turned from British gunship to a museum and recommended bed and breakfast, with bunk-bed lodging and attentive service under the stewardship of its captain. And no, you don't have to be a navy buff reflecting on Titicaca. It's probably the most tranquil spot in Puno.

Its passage here was not easy. In 1862 the *Yavari* and its sister ship, the *Yapura*, were built in Birmingham and shipped as parts around Cape Horn to Arica (now northern Chile), moved by train to Tacna, and finally hauled by mule over the Andes to Puno. The incredible undertaking took six years.

After its assembly, the *Yavari* was launched on Christmas Day 1870. The *Yapura* was later renamed the *BAP Puno* and became a Peruvian Navy medical ship; it can still be seen in Puno. Both had coal-powered steam engines, but due to a shortage of coal, they were fuelled with dried llama dung.

After long years of service, the ship was decommissioned by the Peruvian Navy and the hull was left to rust on the lakeshore. In 1982, Englishwoman Meriel Larken visited the forgotten boat and decided to attempt to save this piece of Peruvian history. The Yavari Project was formed to buy and restore the vessel.

The *Yavari* is moored behind the Sonesta Posada Hotel del Inca, about 5km from the center of Puno. Its devoted crew happily gives guided tours. With prior notice, enthusiasts may even be able to see the engine fired up. Now with a restored engine, the *Yavari* motors across the lake seven times a year – though you will have to find out for yourself if it's still powered on llama dung.

hundreds of skeletons arranged in a ghoulishly decorative, skull-and-crossbones pattern. It truly has to be seen to be believed. Excellent Spanish-speaking guides are on hand daily.

Museo Kampac MUSEUM
(95-182-0085; cnr Ugarte & Ayacucho; suggested donation S5; 8am-6pm Mon-Fri) Staff at the shop opposite this museum, two blocks west of the Plaza de Armas, will give you a Spanish-language tour of this small but significant collection. It includes pre-Inca ceramics and monoliths, plus one mummy. They may also show you a unique vase inscribed with the sacred cosmology of the Incas.

Lampa Municipalidad TOWN HALL
(8am-6pm Mon-Fri) FREE In the small square beside the church, the town hall is recognizable by its murals depicting Lampa's history – past, present and future. Inside there's a gorgeous courtyard, a replica of the *Pietà* and a museum honoring noted Lampa-born painter Víctor Humareda (1920–86).

Sleeping & Eating

Lampa isn't all that geared up for overnight stays, but there are a few basic accommodations available. There are a couple of restaurants around the Plaza de Armas.

Casa Romero GUESTHOUSE
(952-71-9073; Aguirre 327; s/d/tr incl breakfast S55/80/120) Recommended, with friendly service, warm down duvets and well-appointed rooms. Full board is available with advance booking.

Getting There & Away

Combis for Lampa (S2.50, 30 minutes) leave when full from Jirón Huáscar in Juliaca. If you have time to kill after checking in at Juliaca airport, get a taxi to drop you off in Lampa (S5).

Pucará

051 / POP 675 / ELEV 3860M

More than 60km northwest of Juliaca, the sleepy village of Pucará is famous for its celebrations of **La Virgen del Carmen** on July 16 and its earth-colored pottery – including the ceramic *toritos* (bulls) often seen perched on the roofs of Andean houses for good luck. Several local workshops are open to the public and offer classes where you can make your own ceramics. Try the reader-recommended **Maki Pucará** (951-79-0618), on the highway near the bus stop.

The **Museo Lítico Pucará** (Jirón Lima; admission S10; 8:30am-5pm Tue-Sun), by the church, displays a surprisingly good selection of anthropomorphic monoliths from the town's pre-Inca site, **Kalasaya**. The ruins themselves sit above the town, a short walk up Jirón Lima away from the main plaza. One ticket gets you into both sites, though there's nobody to check your ticket at the ruin.

If you get stuck, there are some simple accommodations near the bus stop. Buses to Juliaca (S3.50, one hour) run from 6am to 8pm from Jirón 2 de Mayo.

Abra la Raya

From Ayaviri, the route climbs for almost another 100km to this Andean **mountain pass** (4470m), the highest point on the trip to Cuzco. Buses often stop here to allow passengers to take advantage of the photogenic view of snowcapped mountains and the cluster of handicrafts sellers. The pass also marks the departmental line between Puno and Cuzco.

Puno

051 / POP 141,100 / ELEV 3830M

With a regal plaza, concrete block buildings and crumbling bricks that blend into the hills, Puno has its share of both grit and cheer. It serves as the jumping-off point for Lake Titicaca and is a convenient stop for those traveling between Cuzco and La Paz. But it may just capture your heart with its own rackety charm.

Smoke from unvented fires wafts through Puno's streets, along with jangling waves of traffic, including *mototaxis* and *triciclos* (three-wheeled cycles) that edge pedestrians to the narrow slivers of sidewalks. Its urban center can feel contaminated and cold. But Puno's people are upbeat and ready to drop everything if there's a good time to be had.

As a trade (and contraband) hub between Peru, Bolivia and both coasts of South America, Puno is overwhelmingly commercial and forward-looking. For a glimpse of its colonial and naval identity, you only have to peruse the spots of old architecture, the colorful traditional dress worn by many inhabitants and scores of young cadets in the streets.

Puno is known as Peru's *capital folklórica* (folkloric capital) – its Virgen de la Candelaria parades are televised across the nation – and the associated drinking is the stuff of legend. Good times aren't restricted to religious festivals, though: some of Peru's most convivial bars are found in Puno.

STAYING HEALTHY AT ALTITUDE

Ascend to nearly 4000 meters direct from the coast and you run a real risk of getting *soroche* (altitude sickness). Plan on spending some time in elevation stops such as Arequipa (2350m) or Cuzco (3326m) first to acclimatize, or take it very easy after arriving in Puno. Higher-end hotels (and even some buses) offer oxygen, but this is a temporary fix; your body still needs to acclimatize at its own pace.

High altitude makes for extreme weather conditions. Nights get especially cold, so check if your hotel provides heating. During the winter months of June to August (the tourist high season), temperatures can drop well below freezing. Meanwhile, days are very hot and sunburn is a common problem.

Sights

Puno is handily compact. If you have energy to spare, you can walk into the center from the port or the bus terminals; otherwise, hop into a *mototaxi*. Everything in the town center is within easy walking distance. Jirón Lima, the main pedestrian street, fills in the early evening as *puneños* (inhabitants of Puno) come out to promenade.

Catedral de Puno CHURCH
(8am-noon & 3-6pm) FREE Puno's baroque cathedral, on the western flank of the Plaza de Armas, was completed in 1757. The interior is more spartan than you'd expect from the well-sculpted facade, except for the silver-plated altar, which, following a 1964 visit by Pope Paul VI, has a Vatican flag to its right.

Casa del Corregidor HISTORIC BUILDING
(051-35-1921; www.casadelcorregidor.pe; Deustua 576; 9am-8pm Mon-Sat, 10am-7pm Sun) FREE An attraction in its own right, this 17th-century house is one of Puno's oldest residences. A former community center, it now houses a small fair-trade arts-and-crafts store and a cafe.

Museo Carlos Dreyer MUSEUM
(Conde de Lemos 289; admission with English-speaking guide S15; 9am-7pm Mon-Fri, to 1pm Sat) This museum houses a fascinating collection of Puno-related archaeological artifacts and art. Upstairs there are three

Puno

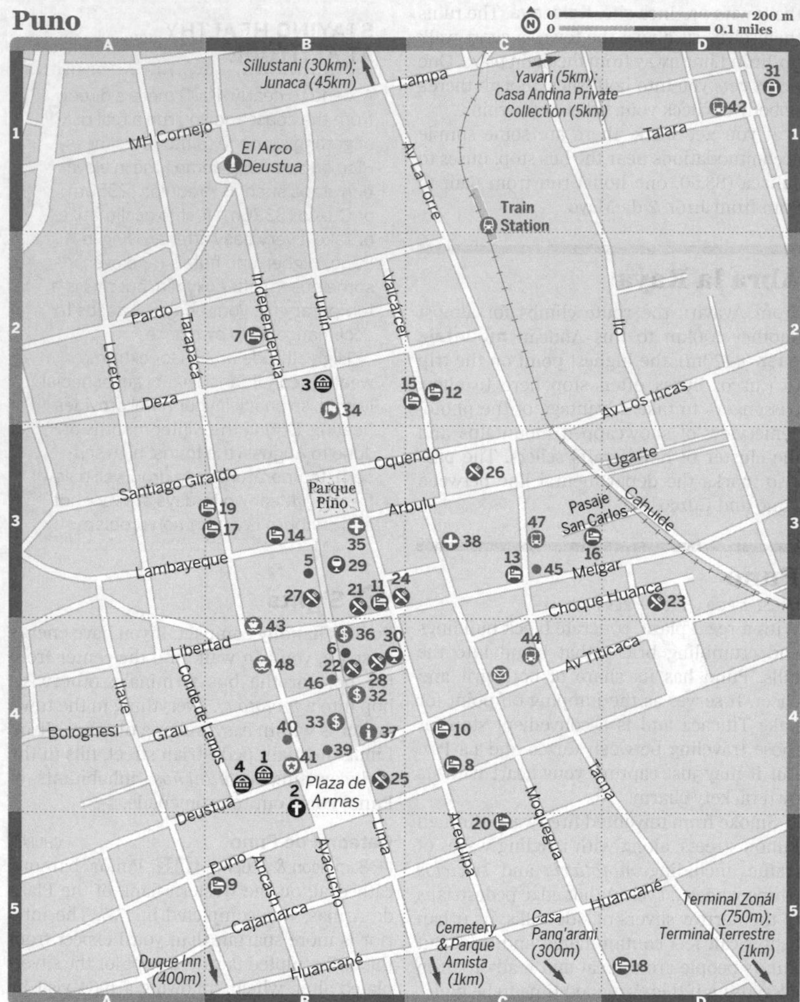

mummies and a full-scale fiberglass *chullpa* (funerary tower). It's around the corner from Casa del Corregidor (p175).

Coca Museum MUSEUM

(☎051-36-5087; Deza 301; admission S5; ⏰9am-1pm & 3-8pm) Tiny and quirky, this museum offers lots of interesting information – historical, medicinal, cultural – about the coca plant and its many uses. Presentation isn't that interesting, though: reams of text (in English only) are stuck to the wall and interspersed with photographs and old Coca-Cola ads. The display of traditional costumes is what makes a visit here worthwhile.

Though the relation between traditional dress and coca is unfathomable, it's a boon for making sense of the costumes worn in street parades.

The museum was closed for renovations at the time of research but should be open again by the time you read this.

Tours

It pays to shop around for a tour operator. Agencies abound and competition is fierce, leading to touting in streets and bus terminals, undeliverable promises, and prices so low as to undercut fair wages. Several of the

Puno

Sights

1 Casa del Corregidor B4
2 Catedral de Puno B4
3 Coca Museum B2
4 Museo Carlos Dreyer B4

Activities, Courses & Tours

All Ways Travel .... (see 1)
5 Edgar Adventures B3
Las Balsas Tours .... (see 6)
6 Nayra Travel B4

Sleeping

7 Casa Andina Classic B2
8 Casona Plaza Hotel C4
9 Conde de Lemos Inn B5
10 Hostal La Hacienda C4
11 Hostal Pukara B3
12 Hostal Uros C2
13 Hotel Casona Colón Inn C3
14 Hotel El Buho B3
15 Hotel Italia C2
16 Inka's Rest C3
17 Intiqa Hotel B3
18 Mosoq Inn D5
19 Posada Don Giorgio B3
20 Posada Luna Azul C5

Eating

21 Balcones de Puno B3
La Casa del Corregidor .... (see 1)
22 La Casona B4
23 Loving Hut D3
24 Machu Pizza B3
25 Mojsa B4
26 Supermercado Central C3
27 Tulipans B3
28 Ukuku's B4

Drinking & Nightlife

29 Ekeko's B3
30 Kamizaraky Rock Pub B4

Shopping

31 Mercado Bellavista D1

Information

32 Banco Continental B4
33 BCP B4
34 Bolivian Consulate B2
35 Botica Fasa B3
36 Interbank B4
37 iPerú B4
38 Medicentro Tourist's Health Clinic C3
39 Municipalidad B4
40 Oficina de Migraciónes B4
41 Policía de Turismo B4
Scotiabank .... (see 33)

Transport

42 Capachica Bus Stop D1
43 Crillon Tours B4
44 Inka Express C4
45 LAN C3
46 Star Perú B4
47 Tour Perú C3
48 Transturin B4

cheaper tour agencies have reputations for ripping off the islanders of Amantaní and Taquile, with whom travelers stay overnight, and whose living culture is one of the main selling points of these tours.

Island-hopping tours, even with the better agencies, are often disappointing: formulaic, lifeless and inflexible, the inevitable result of sheer numbers and repetition. If you only have a day or two though, a reputable tour can give a good taster and insight you might not otherwise get. If you have time, seeing the islands independently is recommended – you can wander around freely and spend longer in the places you like.

All Ways Travel CULTURAL TOUR
(☎051-35-3979; www.titicacaperu.com; 2nd fl, Deustua 576) Offers classic and 'nontourist' tours.

Edgar Adventures CULTURAL TOUR
(☎051-35-3444; www.edgaradventures.com; Lima 328) Longtime agency with positive community involvement.

Las Balsas Tours BOAT TOUR
(☎051-36-4362; www.balsastours.com; Lima 419 No 213, 2nd fl) Offers classic tours on a daily basis.

Nayra Travel BOAT TOUR
(☎051-36-4774; www.nayratravel.com; Lima 419 No 105) Local package-tour operator.

Festivals & Events

Many regional holidays and fiestas are celebrated for several days before and after the actual day. Most festivals also feature traditional music and dancing, as well as merry mayhem of all sorts.

La Virgen de la Candelaria RELIGION
(Candlemas; ⏲Feb 2-18) The region's most spectacular festival spreads out for several days around the actual date (Candlemas), depending upon which day of the week Candlemas falls. If it falls between Sunday and Tuesday, things get under way the previous Saturday; if Candlemas occurs between

Wednesday and Friday, celebrations will get going the following Saturday.

Puno Week CULTURAL

(⏲Nov) A huge celebration marking the legendary birth of Manco Cápac, the first Inca. Events are held the first week of November, centered on Puno Day (November 5).

Epiphany RELIGION

(⏲Jan 6) Also known as El Día de Los Reyes, this celebrates the day that the three wise men visited baby Jesus. Outside of every church, and in the Plaza de Armas, you will find women in traditional dress selling dolls for children to lay on church altars at Mass.

Fiesta de San Juan FESTIVAL

(Feast of St John the Baptist; ⏲Mar 8) St John is the patron saint of the ill and of hospitals and his image is carried around the main streets of Puno accompanied by prayers and songs for good health. There is food, fireworks and music.

Alasitas FESTIVAL

(⏲May 2-8) With the blessing of miniature objects, such as cars or houses, supplicants pray that the real thing will be obtained in the coming year. Features a miniature handicrafts fair in Puno on May 2.

Las Cruces FESTIVAL

(⏲May 3-4) Celebrations take place on Isla Taquile and in Huancané. Crosses (think of the + symbol, not crucifixes) are set up on the highest hills and people dance, eat and drink in honor of this Christian-Andean fusion green (representing life) cross.

Feast of St James FESTIVAL

(⏲Jul 25) Locals in their distinctive colorful dress and knitwear dance and play music to Taquile's patron saint. There are also fireworks. It's celebrated mostly on Isla Taquile.

Our Lady of Mercy FESTIVAL

(⏲Sep 24) The Lady being celebrated is the patroness of Peru. This festival is celebrated mainly in Juliaca with a 'Nuestra Señora de las Mercedes' feast, religious ceremonies and dancing. Images show the Lady of Mercy dressed in white praying for captive prisoners and people of every social class.

Sleeping

Inka's Rest HOSTEL $

(☎051-36-8720; www.inkasresthostel.com; Pasaje San Carlos 158; dm/d incl breakfast S23/70; @📶) Tucked into a small alley, this hostel earns high marks for service. Very clean, it features bunks with down duvets, and attractive old tile and parquet floors. There's a cute breakfast area as well as a guest kitchen and room with a huge flat-screen TV. Private rooms are less attractive. There is intercom entry but take a taxi if arriving at night.

FIESTAS & FOLKLORE AROUND LAKE TITICACA

The folkloric capital of Peru, Puno boasts as many as 300 traditional dances and celebrates numerous fiestas throughout the year. Although dances often occur during celebrations of Catholic feast days, many have their roots in precolonial celebrations usually tied in with the agricultural calendar. The dazzlingly ornate and imaginative costumes worn on these occasions are often worth more than an entire household's everyday clothes. Styles range from strikingly grotesque masks and animal costumes to glittering sequined uniforms.

Accompanying music uses a host of instruments, from Spanish-influenced brass and string instruments to percussion and wind instruments that have changed little since Inca times. These traditional instruments include *tinyas* (wooden hand drums) and *wankaras* (larger drums formerly used in battle), plus a chorus of *zampoñas* (panpipes), which range from tiny, high-pitched instruments to huge bass panpipes almost as tall as the musician. Keep an eye out for *flautas* (flutes): from simple bamboo pennywhistles called *quenas* to large blocks of hollowed-out wood. The most esoteric is the *piruru*, which is traditionally carved from the wing bone of an Andean condor.

Seeing street fiestas can be planned, but it's often simply a matter of luck. Some celebrations are localized to one town, but with others the whole region lets loose. Ask at the tourist office in Puno about any fiestas in the surrounding area while you're in town. The festivals we list are particularly important in the Lake Titicaca region, but many country-wide fiestas are celebrated here, too.

If you plan to visit during a festival, either make reservations in advance or show up a few days early, and expect to pay premium rates for lodgings.

Duque Inn HOTEL $
(☎051-20-5014; www.duqueinn.com; Ayaviri 152; s/d with bathroom S25/45, without bathroom S20/35) Cordial but kooky, this budget lodging is spruced up with satin bedspreads and chandeliers. Archaeologist owner Ricardo Conde is eccentric gold, offering free tours. It's a steal for budget travelers and serious trekkers. To find it, take Ilave for three blocks beyond Huancané, then turn right into Ayaviri. When you see the endless hill, you may want to splurge on taxis.

Hostal Uros HOTEL $
(☎051-35-2141; Valcárcel 135; s/d/tr S30/50/75; @📶) Serene but close to the action, this friendly, good-value hostel has its best rooms on the upper floors. The roomy light-filled patio can store bicycles or motorbikes. Ask for a room with a window. Heaters are S10 extra. If you're counting pennies, those with grubby shared bathroom are S5 cheaper per person.

★**Casa Panq'arani** B&B $$
(☎951-677-005, 051-36-4892; www.casapanqarani.com; Arequipa 1086; s/tw/d incl breakfast S80/135/145; 📶) This delightful traditional Puno home has a flower-filled courtyard and inviting rooms lining a 2nd-floor balcony. But the real draw is the sincere hospitality of owners Edgar and Consuelo. Rooms are ample, with comfortable beds with crocheted bedspreads and fresh flowers. There are ample sunny spots for lounging. Don't miss Consuelo's gourmet altiplano cooking (meals S35 with advance request).

Hotel Casona Colón Inn HOTEL $$
(☎051-35-1432; www.coloninn.com; Tacna 290 at Libertad; s/d/tr incl breakfast S150/180/225; @📶) An elegant European-owned *casona* with helpful staff, part of its charm is the Republican-era building, decorated with Cuzco-school paintings, frescos and a covered courtyard. The on-site restaurant specializes in Belgian and French cuisine; reservations are recommended. Rooms are smallish but with all amenities including portable heaters, while shared spaces are sumptuously colonial.

Mosoq Inn HOTEL $$
(☎051-36-7518; www.mosoqinnperu.com; Moquegua 673; s/d/tr incl breakfast S143/175/223; @📶) This modern hotel features 15 rooms distributed across three stories. High-quality mattresses ensure sound sleeping in ample, tangerine-hued rooms. There are also big closets, cable TV and space heaters, plus it has a business center.

Posada Luna Azul HOTEL $$
(☎95-159-0835; www.posadalunaazul.com; Cajamarca 242; s/d incl breakfast S60/90; 📶) The 'blue moon' name might conjure images of a cozy, tranquil night's rest. And this small hotel is tucked far enough away from the noise that it's true. The petite, clean, carpeted rooms have flat-screen TVs and good heaters, making them impressively warm all night, and the showers are strong and hot. Warmth at last in Puno.

Hotel Italia HOTEL $$
(☎051-36-7706; www.hotelitaliaperu.com; Valcárcel 122; s/d/tr S110/150/190; @📶) Snug rooms have parquet floors, cable TV, hot showers and heating, but vary in quality at this large, well-established spot. There are old-world touches with antique telephones and long-serving staff who are cordial and well groomed. The delicious buffet breakfast includes salty black olives and Puno's own triangular anise bread. Credit cards accepted.

Intiqa Hotel HOTEL $$
(☎051-36-6900; www.intiqahotel.com; Tarapacá 272; s/d incl breakfast S176/203; 📶) Yes, a mid-range Puno hotel with a sense of style. The 33 large, heated rooms feature snug duvets and earth tones, extra pillows, desks, flat-screen TVs and a safe box. The elevator is somewhat of a rarity in Puno. It offers free pickups from the *terminal terrestre*. Credit cards are accepted.

Hostal Pukara HOTEL $$
(☎051-368-448; www.pukaradeltitikaka.com; Libertad 328; s/d incl breakfast S70/120; @📶) Bright and cheery, Pukara leaves no corner undecorated, with an eye-catching four-story relief, murals and other touches. Rooms all have cable TV, phones and heating. Street-side rooms can be noisy all night. The buffet breakfast is served in a glass-covered rooftop cafe with a great view.

Hostal La Hacienda HOTEL $$
(☎051-35-6109; www.hhp.com.pe; Deustua 297; d/tr S178/223; @📶) This colonial-style hotel has lovely, airy common spaces, a mind-bending *Vertigo*-style spiral staircase and a 6th-floor dining room with panoramic views. After all that, rooms are a bit generic, but they're warm and comfortable with cable TV and phones. Some have bathtubs.

Hotel El Buho HOTEL **$$**
(051-36-6122; www.hotelbuho.com; Lambayeque 142; s/d/tw incl breakfast S120/180/220;) This quiet hotel features nice (but somewhat dull) rooms with paneled walls and carpets. The staff is helpful and there's a tour agency on-site. Booking on their website can be 25% cheaper.

Posada Don Giorgio HOTEL **$$**
(051-36-3648; www.posadadongiorgio.com; Tarapacá 238; s/d/tr S90/155/180;) A mellow spot with a barrage of cultures and exceptionally comfy rooms, Don Giorgio offers super-clean standard rooms. It's small enough to provide personal service, and rooms have phones, cable TV and deep armchairs.

Conde de Lemos Inn HOTEL **$$**
(051-36-9898; www.condelemosinn.com; Puno 675-681; s/d incl breakfast S130/165;) Housed in a startlingly jagged, glass-fronted ziggurat on the Plaza de Armas, this small hotel has been recommended by many travelers for its personable staff and high standards. Ask for a corner room with balcony.

Casa Andina Private Collection LUXURY HOTEL **$$$**
(051-213-9739; www.casa-andina.com; Av Sesqui Centenario 1970; d incl breakfast from S506;) On the outskirts of Puno, with lovely lakeside ambience, the exclusive version of this upscale chain features 46 rooms, gardens and a gourmet restaurant. It even has its own train stop for those coming from Cuzco. The look is rustic chic. Rooms feature impeccable white linens and subtle decor, some with chimneys and all with oxygen to help acclimatize. Credit cards are accepted.

Casa Andina Classic HOTEL **$$$**
(051-213-9739; www.casa-andina.com; Independencia 143; d incl breakfast S284;) The classic version of this fashionable Peruvian chain features snappy service and 50 tasteful rooms with muted colors, decorated with Andean folk motifs. Rooms feature heat, safes, blackout curtains and flat-screen TVs. Guests also get free oxygen and *mate* (a herbal tea) to help acclimate. A cozy dining space serves pizzas and soups postexcursion. Credit cards are accepted.

Casona Plaza Hotel HOTEL **$$$**
(051-36-5614; www.casonaplazahotel.com; Arequipa 655; r incl breakfast S318;) This well-run, central hotel with 64 rooms is one of the largest in Puno, but is often full. All rooms are good and bathrooms are great. They offer *matrimoniales* (matrimonial suites) especially for lovers – most are big enough to dance the *marinera* (Peru's national dance) between the bed and the lounge suite.

Eating

Most restaurants geared toward travelers are on Jirón Lima. To save a few soles, head a couple of blocks away. Many restaurants don't advertise their *menús* (set meals), which are cheaper than ordering à la carte. Locals eat *pollo a la brasa* (roast chicken) and economical *menús* on Jirón Tacna between Calles Puno and Libertad.

For a cheap snack, try *api* (hot, sweet corn juice) – a serious comfort food found in several places on Calle Oquendo between Parque Pino and the supermarket. Order it with a paper-thin, wickedly delicious envelope of deep-fried dough.

If you're feeling MSG-deprived, head to Calle Arbulú to fill up at a cheap (meals S9 to S11) and cheerful *chifa* (Chinese restaurant). For self-catering, head to **Supermercado Central** (Oquendo s/n; 8am-10pm), but be wary of pickpockets.

Loving Hut VEGETARIAN **$**
(www.lovinghut.com; Choque Huanca 188; mains S15-18, menú S12; 9am-6pm Mon-Sat;) Filling vegetarian lunches with salad, gluten, soy-meat and brown-rice options in Asian and Peruvian styles. Try the quinoa burger or *anticuchos veganos* (vegan beef skewers). The warm unsweetened soy milk or *mate* (tea) on tap makes the *menú* worth it alone.

Machu Pizza PIZZA **$**
(95-139-0652; Arequipa 409; mains S8-18; 5:30-11pm Mon-Sat, to 10pm Sun;) It might not be Colosseum authentic, but the *ají* (chili) aioli that you are given to spread over the thin-crust pizzas is a delicious Peruvian twist. The dim lighting, cozy mezzanine and back room, plus personal-sized pizzas make it a good place to dine alone or with your favorite person.

La Casa del Corregidor CAFE **$**
(drinks S4-9, snacks S8-21;) It's just off the plaza but feels like a world and era away. Vinyl records of Peru's yesteryear decorate the walls, while board games and clay teapots are ready to adorn the table. Try the good fresh infusions or alpaca barbecue sticks.

★ **Mojsa** PERUVIAN $$

(☎051-36-3182; Lima 394; mains S22-30; ⏰8am-10pm) The go-to place for locals and travelers alike, Mojsa lives up to its name, Aymara for 'delicious.' It has a thoughtful range of Peruvian and international food, including innovative trout dishes and a design-your-own salad option. All meals start with fresh bread and a bowl of local olives. In the evening, crisp brick-oven pizzas are on offer.

La Casona PERUVIAN $$

(☎051-35-1108; http://lacasona-restaurant.com; Lima 423, 2nd fl; mains S22-42) A solid choice for upscale *criollo* (spicy Peruvian fare with Spanish and African influences) and international food, even if portions are on the small side. Trout comes bathed in garlic or chili sauce. There's also pasta, salad and soup.

Tulipans PIZZA $$

(☎051-35-1796; Lima 394; mains S15-30; ⏰11am-10pm) Highly recommended for its yummy sandwiches, big plates of meat and piled-high vegetables, this cozy spot is warmed by the pizza oven in the corner. It also has a selection of South American wines. The courtyard patio is attractive for warm days – whenever those happen! Pizzas are only available at night. Tulipans is inside La Casona Parodi.

Balcones de Puno PERUVIAN $$

(☎051-36-5300; Libertad 354; mains S15-35) Dinner-show venue with traditional local food. The nightly show (7:30pm to 9pm) stands out for its quality and sincerity – no panpipe butchering of *El Cóndor Pasa* here. Save room for dessert, a major focus of dining here. Reserve ahead.

Ukuku's PERUVIAN $$

(Grau 172, 2nd fl; mains S20-27, dinner menú S25; ⏰noon-10pm; 📶🌿) Crowds of travelers and locals thaw out in this toasty restaurant, which dishes up good local and Andean food (try alpaca steak with baked apples, or the quinoa omelet), as well as pizza, pasta, Asian-style vegetarian fare and espresso drinks. The good-value dinner set menu includes a pisco.

Drinking & Nightlife

Central Puno's nightlife is geared toward tourists, with lively bars scattered around the bright lights on Jirón Lima (where touts hand out free-drink coupons) and next to the plaza on Jirón Puno.

Kamizaraky Rock Pub PUB

(Grau 158) With a classic-rock soundtrack, grungy cool bartenders and liquor-infused coffee drinks essential for staying warm during Puno's bone-chilling nights, it may be a hard place to leave.

Ekeko's CLUB

(Lima 355, 2nd fl; ⏰9pm-late) FREE Travelers and locals alike gravitate to this tiny, ultraviolet dance floor above a restaurant, splashed with psychedelic murals. It moves to a thumping mixture of modern beats and old favorites, from salsa to techno trance, which can be heard several blocks away.

Shopping

Artesanías (handicrafts, from musical instruments and jewelry to scale models of reed islands), wool and alpaca sweaters, and other typical tourist goods are sold in every second shop in the town center.

Feria HANDICRAFTS

(Av Costanera, Puno port; ⏰7am-5pm) This craft market sells the llama toys, rugs, alpaca sweaters, masks from Puno's 'La Virgen de Candelaria' festival and other handicrafts you'll see elsewhere in town and on the islands, but at prices more open to haggling. The dozens of nearly identical stalls are at the port entrance.

Mercado Bellavista MARKET

(Av El Sol) A market selling household goods and clothes. Watch out for pickpockets.

Information

DANGERS & ANNOYANCES

There are scenic lookouts on the hills above town, but as assaults and robberies have been reported (even by groups), it's not recommended to visit them unless there is a drastic improvement in security.

EMERGENCY

Policía de Turismo (Tourist Police; ☎051-35-3988; Deustua 558; ⏰24hr) There is a police officer on duty in the *terminal terrestre* (24 hours) – ask around if you need assistance.

IMMIGRATION

Bolivian Consulate (☎051-35-1251; fax 051-35-1251; Arequipa 136, 3rd fl; ⏰8am-4pm Mon-Fri)

Oficina de Migraciónes (Immigration Office; ☎051-35-7103; Ayacucho 270-280; ⏰8am-1pm & 2-4:15pm Mon-Fri) May help with student and business visas; doesn't give tourist-card extensions.

MEDICAL SERVICES

Botica Fasa (051-36-6862; Arequipa 314; 24hr) A well-stocked pharmacy that's attended 24 hours, though you may have to pound on the door late at night.

Medicentro Tourist's Health Clinic (051-36-5909, 951-62-0937; Moquegua 191; 24hr) English and French spoken; they will also come to your hotel.

MONEY

Bolivianos can be exchanged in Puno or at the border. You'll find an ATM inside the *terminal terrestre* that accepts most bank cards and dispenses US dollars and soles. **Scotiabank** (Jirón Lima 458), **Interbank** (Lima 444), **BCP** (Jirón Lima 444) and **Banco Continental** (Lima at Grau) all have branches and ATMs on Jirón Lima; there's another Banco Continental at Libertad.

POST

Serpost (Moquegua 267; 8am-8pm Mon-Sat)

TOURIST INFORMATION

iPerú (051-36-5088; Plaza de Armas, cnr Lima & Deustua; 9am-6pm Mon-Sat, to 1pm Sun) Puno's helpful and well-informed multilingual tourist office; also runs Indecopi, the tourist-protection agency, which registers complaints about travel agencies and hotels.

Getting There & Away

AIR

The nearest airport is in Juliaca, about an hour away. Hotels can book you a shuttle bus for around S15. Airlines with offices in Puno include **LAN** (051-36-7227; Tacna 299) and **Star Perú** (Jirón Lima 154).

BOAT

There are no passenger ferries across the lake from Puno to Bolivia, but you can get to La Paz via the lake in one or two days on high-class tours that visit Isla del Sol and other sites along the way. **Transturin** (051-35-2771; www.transturin.com; Ayacucho 148; 2-day tour US$255) has a bus/catamaran/bus combination, departing at 6:30am from Puno and arriving in La Paz at 7:30pm, or the following day at noon, with a night onboard. From Puno, **Crillon Tours** (051-35-2771; www.titicaca.com; Ayacucho 148) also visits Isla del Sol on the way to La Paz using hydrofoil boats. In total it's a 13-hour trip. Leon Tours is their Puno operator.

BUS

The **terminal terrestre** (051-36-4737; Primero de Mayo 703), three blocks down Ricardo Palma from Av El Sol, houses Puno's long-distance bus companies. The terminal has an ATM and charges a departure tax of S1.50, which you must pay in a separate booth before departure.

Buses leave for Cuzco every hour from 4am to 10pm, and for Arequipa every hour from 2am to 10pm. **Ormeño** (051-36-8176; www.grupo-ormeno.com.pe; Terminal Terrestre) is the safest, with the newest, fastest buses. **Cruz del Sur** (in Lima 01-311-5050; www.cruzdelsur.com.pe) has service to Arequipa. **Civa** (051-365-882; www.civa.com.pe) goes to Lima. **Tour Perú** (051-20-6088; www.tourperu.com.pe; Tacna 285) goes to Cuzco and also crosses to La Paz, Bolivia, via Copacabana, daily at 7:30am.

The most enjoyable way to get to Cuzco is via **Inka Express** (051-36-5654; www.inkaexpress.com; Tacna 346), whose luxury buses with panoramic windows depart every morning at 8am. Buffet lunch is included, along with an English-speaking tour guide and oxygen. The sites briefly visited en route include Andahuaylillas, Raqchi, Abra la Raya and Pucará. The trip takes about eight hours and costs S159 from Inka Express.

Puno Buses:

DESTINATION	COST* (S)	DURATION (HR)
Arequipa	25/75	5
Cuzco	30/80	6-7
Juliaca	3.50	1
Lima	140/170	18-21
Copacabana, Bolivia	20	3-4
La Paz, Bolivia	50	6

* Prices are estimates for normal/luxury buses.

Local *combis* to Chuquito, Juli, Pomata and the Bolivian border leave from **terminal zonál** (Simón Bolívar s/n), a few blocks northwest of *terminal terrestre*. Head out along Av El Sol until you see the hospital on your right, then turn left and you'll hit the *terminal zonál* (regional terminal) after two long blocks.

To get to Capachica (1¼ hours, S4), catch a *combi* from Jirón Talara, just off Av El Sol opposite the Mercado Bellavista. They leave once an hour from about 6am to 2pm. *Combis* to Luquina leave from opposite the Brahma Beer distributor on Manchero Rossi, about 1.5km south of town, every hour or so in the morning.

TRAIN

The train ride from Puno to Cuzco retains a certain renown from the days – now long gone – when the road wasn't paved and the bus journey was a nightmare. Train fares have skyrocketed in recent years and most travelers now take the bus. The fancy Andean Explorer train, which includes a glass-walled observation car and complimentary lunch, costs US$289; there's no cheaper option. This one's for train buffs, since it's only marginally more comfortable than the better buses, and the tracks run next to the road for much of the way, so the scenery, while wonderful, is comparable to a much cheaper bus ride.

Trains depart from Puno's **train station** (☎ 051-36-9179; www.perurail.com; Av La Torre 224; ⏰7am-noon & 3-6pm Mon-Fri, 7am-3pm Sat) at 8am, arriving at Cuzco around 6pm. Services run on Monday, Wednesday and Saturday from November to March, with an extra departure on Friday from April to October. Tickets can be purchased online.

ℹ Getting Around

A short taxi ride anywhere in town (and as far as the transport terminals) costs S4.50. *Mototaxis* are a bit cheaper at S2.50, and *triciclos* cheapest of all at S2 – but it's an uphill ride, so you may find yourself wanting to tip the driver more than the cost of the fare!

Around Puno

Sillustani

Sitting on rolling hills on the Lake Umayo peninsula, the funerary towers of **Sillustani** (admission S10) stand out for miles against the desolate altiplano landscape.

The ancient Colla people who once dominated the Lake Titicaca area were a warlike, Aymara-speaking tribe, who later became the southeastern group of the Incas. They buried their nobility in *chullpas* (funerary towers), which can be seen scattered widely around the hilltops of the region.

The most impressive of these towers are at Sillustani, where the tallest reaches a height of 12m. The cylindrical structures housed the remains of complete family groups, along with plenty of food and belongings for their journey into the next world. Their only opening was a small hole facing east, just large enough for a person to crawl through, which would be sealed immediately after a burial. Nowadays, nothing remains of the burials, but the *chullpas* are well preserved. The afternoon light is the best for photography, though the site can get busy at this time.

The walls of the towers are made from massive coursed blocks reminiscent of Inca stonework, but are considered to be even more complicated. Carved but unplaced blocks and a ramp used to raise them are among the site's points of interest, and you can also see the makeshift quarry. A few of the blocks are decorated, including a well-known carving of a lizard on one of the *chullpas* closest to the parking lot.

Sillustani is partially encircled by the sparkling Lago Umayo (3890m), which is home to a wide variety of plants and Andean water birds, plus a small island with vicuñas (threatened, wild relatives of llamas). Birdwatchers take note: this is one of the best sites in the area.

Tours to Sillustani leave Puno at around 2:30pm daily and cost from S30. The round-trip takes about 3½ hours and allows you about 1½ hours at the ruins. If you'd prefer more time at the site, hire a private taxi for S80 with one-hour waiting time. To save money, catch any bus to Juliaca and ask to be let off where the road splits (S3.50, 25 minutes). From there, occasional *combis* (S3, 20 minutes) go to the ruins.

For longer stays, **Atun Colla** (☎ 951-50-2390; Centro Artsenal, Atun Colla; r S20) offers *turismo vivencia* (homestays) from S20 per person per night. You can help your host family with farming, hike to lookouts and lesser-known archaeological sites, visit the tiny museum and eat dirt – this area is known for its edible *arcilla* (clay). Served up as a sauce on boiled potato, it goes down surprisingly well.

Cutimbo

Just over 20km from Puno, dramatic **Cutimbo** (admission S8) has an extraordinary position atop a table-topped volcanic hill surrounded by a fertile plain. Its modest number of well-preserved *chullpas*, built by the Colla, Lupaca and Inca cultures, come in both square and cylindrical shapes. You can still see the ramps used to build them. Look closely to find several monkeys, pumas and snakes carved into the structures.

This remote place receives few visitors, which makes it both enticing and potentially dangerous for independent travelers, especially women. Go in a group and keep an eye out for muggers. People are known to hide behind rocks at the top of the 2km trail that leads steeply uphill from the road.

Combis en route to Laraqueri leave the cemetery by Parque Amista, 1km from the center of Puno (S3, one hour). You can't miss the signposted site, which is on the left-hand side of the road – just ask the driver where to get off. Otherwise, the pricier options from Puno are taking a taxi (about S30 return with a 30-minute wait) or a package tour (US$59).

STRANGEST SIGHTS

Even if you don't believe in tales of alien colonies and strange sightings, Lake Titicaca has no shortage of the surreal.

➡ Islands made of **reeds** (p184)

➡ Michelangelo's **Pietà faked** (p173)

➡ An age-old tradition of **edible clay** (p183)

➡ Enormous **stone phalluses** (p189)

Lake Titicaca Islands

Lake Titicaca's islands are world famous for their peaceful beauty and the living tradition of their agrarian cultures, which date to pre-Columbian times. A homestay here offers a privileged glimpse of another way of life.

Be aware that not all islanders welcome tourism, which only stands to reason since not all benefit from tourism and may see the frequent intrusions into their daily life as disruptive. It's important to respect the privacy of islanders and show courtesy.

All travel agencies in Puno offer one- and two-day tours to Uros, Taquile and Amantaní. Travelers often complain that the guided island-hopping tours offer only a superficial view of the islands and their cultures. For more insight into the culture, it's recommended to travel independently if you have the time. All ferry tickets are valid for 15 days, so you can island-hop at will.

Islas Uros

Just 7km east of Puno, these unique **floating islands** (admission S8) are Lake Titicaca's top attraction. Their uniqueness is due to their construction. They have been created entirely with the buoyant *totora* reeds that grow abundantly in the shallows of the lake. The lives of the Uros people are interwoven with these reeds. Partially edible (tasting like nonsweet sugarcane), the reeds are also used to build homes, boats and crafts. The islands are constructed from many layers of the *totora*, which are constantly replenished from the top as they rot from the bottom, so the ground is always soft and springy.

Some islands also have elaborately designed versions of traditional tightly bundled reed boats on hand and other whimsical reed creations, such as archways and even swing sets. Be prepared to pay for a boat ride (S10) or to take photographs.

Intermarriage with the Aymara-speaking indigenous people has seen the demise of the pure-blooded Uros, who nowadays all speak Aymara. Always a small tribe, the Uros began their unusual floating existence centuries ago in an effort to isolate themselves from the aggressive Collas and Incas.

The popularity of the islands has led to aggressive commercialization in some cases. The most traditional reed islands are located further from Puno through a maze of small channels, only visited by private boat. Islanders there continue to live in a relatively traditional fashion and prefer not to be photographed.

Getting to the Uros is easy – there's no need to go with an organized tour, though you will miss out on the history lesson given by the guides. Ferries leave from the port for Uros (return trip S10) at least once an hour from 6am to 4pm. The community-owned ferry service visits two islands, on a rotation basis. Ferries to Taquile and Amantaní can also drop you off in the Uros.

An outstanding option is staying in the reed huts of Isla Khantati with boundless personality **Cristina Suaña** (☎951-69-5121, 951-47-2355; uroskhantati@hotmail.com; per person incl full board S180), an Uros native whose entrepreneurship earned her international accolades. Over a number of years, her family has built a number of impeccable semitraditional huts (with solar power and outhouses) that occupy half the tiny island, along with shady decks, cats and the occasional flamingo. The rates include transfers from Puno, fresh and varied meals, fishing, some cultural explanations, and the pleasure of the company of the effervescent Cristina. The hyper-relaxed pace means a visit here is not ideal for those with little time on their hands.

Isla Taquile

Inhabited for thousands of years, **Isla Taquile** (admission S8), 35km east of Puno, is a tiny 7-sq-km island with a population of about 2200 people. Taquile's lovely scenery is reminiscent of the Mediterranean. In the strong island sunlight, the deep, red-colored soil contrasts with the intense blue of the lake and the glistening backdrop of Bolivia's snowy Cordillera Real on the far side of the lake. Several hills boast Inca terracing on their sides and small ruins on top.

The natural beauty of the island makes it stand out. Quechua-speaking islanders are distinct from most of the surrounding Aymara-speaking island communities and maintain a strong sense of group identity. They rarely marry non-Taquile people.

Taquile has a fascinating tradition of handicrafts, and the islanders' creations are made according to a system of deeply ingrained social customs. Men wear tightly woven woolen hats that resemble floppy nightcaps, which they knit themselves – only men knit, learning from the age of eight. These hats are closely bound up with social symbolism: men wear red hats if they are married and red and white hats if they are single, and different colors can denote a man's current or past social position.

Taquile women weave thick, colorful waistbands for their husbands, which are worn with roughly spun white shirts and thick, calf-length black pants. Women wear eye-catching outfits comprising multilayered skirts and delicately embroidered blouses. These fine garments are considered some of the most well-made traditional clothes in Peru, and can be bought in the cooperative store on the island's main plaza.

Make sure you already have lots of small bills in local currency, because change is limited and there's nowhere to exchange dollars. You may want to bring extra money to buy some of the exquisite crafts sold in the cooperative store. A limited electricity supply was introduced to the island in the 1990s but it is not always available, so remember to bring a flashlight for an overnight stay.

Sights & Activities

Visitors are free to wander around, explore the ruins and enjoy the tranquility. The island is a wonderful place to catch a sunset and gaze at the moon, which looks twice as bright in the crystalline air, rising over the breathtaking peaks of the Cordillera Real. Take in the lay of the land while it's still light – with no roads, streetlights or big buildings to use as landmarks, travelers have been known to get so lost in the dark that they end up roughing it for the night.

A stairway of more than 500 steps leads from the dock to the center of the island. The climb takes a breathless 20 minutes if you're acclimatized – more if you're not.

BOAT TRAVEL ON LAKE TITICACA

Water-transport experiences on Titicaca are sometimes endurance events, so ask ahead about the boat you will be taking, and bring warm layers to stay out on deck. Three types of boats ply these waters. High-speed boats (*veloz*) take large groups of 30 to 40 people. *Lancha rápida*, the most common option, is slightly slower. The slowest form of travel are *embarcaciones artesenales*, which take twice as long as the speedboats. Ferries sometimes have truck motors and carry a lot of cargo – guaranteeing a slow ride. It's common to get woozy or seasick on boats that have in-cabin motors, which produce odor, particularly if you're confined in-cabin because of the cold or high seas.

Festivals & Events

Easter and **New Year's Day** are festive and rowdy. Many islanders go to Puno for La Virgen de Candelaria and Puno Week, when the island becomes somewhat deserted.

Fiesta de San Diego RELIGIOUS
(Feast of St James; Jul 25) The Fiesta de San Diego is a big feast day on Taquile. Dancing, music and general carousing go on for several days until the start of August, when islanders make traditional offerings to Pachamama (Mother Earth).

Sleeping & Eating

The *hospedajes* (small, family-owned inns) on Taquile offer basic accommodation for around S20 a night. Meals are additional (S10 to S15 for breakfast, S20 for lunch). Options range from a room in a family house to small guesthouses. Most offer indoor toilets and showers. Lodgings can either be booked with a tour operator or on your own once you arrive. As the community rotates visitors to lodgings, there is little room for choosing.

Restaurants all offer the same fare of *sopa de quinua* (quinoa soup – absolutely delicious everywhere on Lake Titicaca) and lake trout; dishes start at S20. Consider eating in the **Restaurante Comunál**, Taquile's only community-run food outlet.

TITILAKA

Secluded on the rugged shoreline of Lake Titicaca, luxury hotel **Titilaka** (in Lima 1-700-5105; www.titilaka.com; Lake Titicaca; s/d incl full board from US$648/1002; @) is a destination in itself. Huge picture windows drink in the serene landscapes in every direction. Rooms sport king-sized beds warmed by hot-water bottles, deep tubs, iPod docks and window ledge seating. There are games for kids, a spa and a gourmet restaurant.

The look is whimsical Euro-Andino, with a palette that ranges from neutral to flirty (think blushing rose and purple). Touches of exquisite folk art combine with the sculptures and black and white photography of well-known Peruvian artists. The staff is groomed to please.

Private guided tours give guests an intimate view of the islands. While most guests go for the three-day packages, the nightly rate includes full board and local excursions such as walks and kayaking. It's one hour south of Puno.

Getting There & Away

Ferries (round-trip S30; admission to island S8) leave from the Puno port for Taquile from 6:45am. If the ferry stops in Islas Uros, you will also have to pay the admission there. A ferry from Taquile to Puno leaves at 12:30pm. There's a ferry from Amantaní to Taquile every morning; it's also possible to get here by ferry from Llachón.

Isla Amantaní

Remote **Isla Amantaní** (admission S8), population 4000, is a few kilometers north of the smaller Taquile. Almost all trips to Amantaní involve an overnight stay with islanders. Guests help cook on open fires in dirt-floored kitchens. Witnessing the different aspects of rural life can create engaging and memorable experiences.

The villagers sometimes organize rousing traditional dances, letting travelers dress in their traditional party gear to dance the night away. Of course, your hiking boots might give you away. Don't forget to look up at the incredibly starry night sky as you stagger home.

The island is very quiet (no dogs allowed!), boasts great views and has no roads or vehicles. Several hills are topped by ruins, among the highest and best-known of which are **Pachamama** (Mother Earth) and **Pachatata** (Father Earth). These date to the Tiwanaku culture, a largely Bolivian culture that appeared around Lake Titicaca and expanded rapidly between 200 BC and AD 1000.

As with Taquile, the islanders speak Quechua, but their culture is more heavily influenced by the Aymara.

Sleeping & Eating

Amantaní Community Lodging HOMESTAY
(051-36-9714; r from S30) When you arrive, Amantaní Community Lodging, basically the island families, will allocate you to your accommodation according to a rotating system. Please respect this process, even if you are with a guided group. There's no problem with asking for families or friends to be together. A bed and full board starts at S30 per person per night.

Getting There & Away

Ferries (round-trip S30; admission to island S8) leave from the Puno port for Amantaní at 8am every day. There are departures from Amantaní to Taquile and Puno around 4pm every day – check, though, as times vary – and sometimes from Amantaní to Puno at around 8am, depending on demand.

Isla Suasi

On the northeastern part of the lake, this beautiful solar-powered island offers a total retreat into nature. The only privately owned island on Titicaca, it has been leased long term by a luxury hotel. Remote ecolodge **Casa Andina Isla Suasi** (1-213-9739; www.casa-andina.com; per person all-inclusive 2 days/1 night S1090) is as exclusive as resorts get. Terraced rooms are well appointed, with down duvets, fireplaces, peaked ceilings and lake views. With lush flower gardens, trails, wild vicuña (relatives of llamas) and spots for swimming (yes, people do swim here!), it's unique in the region for presenting more of a nature experience than a cultural one. Spa treatments and steam saunas with eucalyptus leaves provide a little pampering, and with games, canoes and guide-led activities, it's also a great destination for families. The island is a five-hour boat trip from Puno or a more than three-hour drive on dirt roads, with a short boat transfer from Cambria. A US$12 entry fee (included in lodging fees) helps local conservation projects.

The hotel provides daily transfers at 7:30am for guests from the pier in Puno, with stops to visit the Uros Islands and Isla Taquile.

Capachica Peninsula & Around

Poking far out into the northwestern part of the lake, midway between Juliaca and Puno, the Capachica Peninsula has the same beauty as the lake islands but without the crowds and commercial bent. Each *pueblito* (tiny town) boasts its own glorious scenery, ranging from pastoral and pretty to coweringly majestic. A few days here among the local people – handsome, dignified men in vests and black hats, and shy, smiling women in intricate headgear – with nothing to do but eat well, climb hills and trees, and stare at the lake, can provide a real retreat. Homestay is the only accommodation on offer and a major element of the fun.

Strung along the peninsula between the towns of Capachica and Llachón, the villages of Ccotos and Chifrón are linked by deserted, eminently walkable dirt roads and lackadaisical bus services (it's generally quicker to walk over the hill than drive around by the road). Escallani is further north, slightly off the peninsula proper, not far from Juliaca. Locals get to the mainland by *lancha* (small motorboat), which they are happy to hire out.

There is no internet reception on the peninsula, but cell phones work. There are no banks or ATMs and, as elsewhere in Peru, breaking big notes can be very difficult. Bring all the money you need, in bills of S20 or smaller if possible.

Travel agencies in Puno can get you to any of the peninsula's communities. **Cedesos** (☎051-36-7915; www.cedesos.org; Moquegua 348, 3rd fl) offers fully guided, standard and tailored trips to these communities and others in the area. This NGO works to improve local income and standards of living through tourism. It offers villagers training and cheap credit to ready themselves to receive tourists. Tours are not cheap, but they're well organized and come highly recommended by readers.

Most of the communities here offer the same deal on food and accommodations, similar to that encountered on Isla Amantaní. Families have constructed or adapted basic rooms for tourists in their homes, and charge around S25 per person per night for a bed, or about S65 for full board. Full board is recommended – each town has at least one shop, but supplies are limited and the meals provided by the families are healthy and tasty. Apart from trout, the diet is vegetarian, with emphasis on quinoa, potatoes and locally grown *habas* (broad beans).

Llachón and, to a lesser extent, Escallani are set up for travelers just turning up. For other communities, it's very important to arrange accommodations in advance, as hosts need to buy supplies and prepare. It's preferable to call rather than email. Generally, only Spanish is spoken.

Capachica

The peninsula's blisteringly forgettable commercial center has a couple of very basic restaurants and *hospedajes,* as well as a pretty church and an astonishingly oversized sports coliseum, all of which you can see from the bus. There's no reason to stop here unless you need to switch buses, or use the internet or a public telephone (there are a couple around the plaza); these services are unavailable elsewhere on the peninsula.

Llachón

Almost 75km northeast of Puno, this pretty little village community near the peninsula's southern tip offers fantastic views and short hikes to surrounding pre-Inca sites. The most developed of the peninsula's communities, thanks to locally managed tourism, it nevertheless feels far from the bright lights of modern Peru. With few cars and no dogs, it's an incredibly peaceful place to sit and enjoy stunning views of Lake Titicaca, while sheep, cows, pigs, llamas and kids wander by. From January to March, native birds are also a feature.

It's possible to simply turn up in town and ask around for accommodations.

Sleeping & Eating

Félix Turpo HOMESTAY $

(☎951-66-4828; hospedajesamary@hotmail.com; per person S25, full board S65) Community leader Félix Turpo has a gorgeous garden and the Capachica Peninsula's most spectacular view, overlooking Isla Taquile. It's also the spot to enjoy a rare hot shower, consisting of a black rubber pipe on a warm rock (it's recommended to shower during daylight hours).

Magno Cahui HOMESTAY $
(951-82-5316; hospedajetikawasi@yahoo.es; per person S25, full board S65) Magno Cahui, his wife and their very cute children have six cozy cabins built around his grandfather's stone altar. There is an incredible view of Lake Titicaca from here.

Valentín Quispe HOMESTAY $
(951-82-1392; llachon@yahoo.com; per person S25, full board S65) Local legend Valentín Quispe and his wife Lucila have a charming guesthouse hidden down a stone path, by an enchanting overgrown cemetery. They also rent out kayaks.

Richard Cahui Flores HOMESTAY $
(951-63-7382; hospedajesamary@hotmail.com; S25 per person, full board S65) Richard Cahui Flores works with lots of families and is the best point of contact for advance bookings. He will set you up with somebody else if he doesn't have space in his tranquil farmhouse.

Chifrón

If you found Llachón a bit too built-up, tiny somnolent Chifrón (population 24), off the main road in the northeast corner of the peninsula, is for you. Drowsing in rustling eucalypts above a deserted beach, three families offer very basic accommodations for a maximum of 15 people. This is truly a chance to experience another world. Contact **Emiliano** (951-91-9252, 951-91-9652; playachifron_01@hotmail.com) to arrange a stay.

Ccotos & Isla Ticonata

You can't get much further off the beaten track than Ccotos, two-thirds of the way down the peninsula's east coast. Nothing ever happens here except the annual Miss Playa (Miss Beach) competition, in which the donning of bathing suits stirs much controversy. Stay with the engaging **Alfonso Quispe** (951-85-6462; incasamanatours@yahoo.es) and his family, right on the edge of the lake. Catch your own fish for breakfast, bird-watch, hike to the lookout and some overgrown ruins, and relax on the beach,

ETHICAL COMMUNITY TOURISM

Since *turismo vivencial* (homestay tourism) took off around Puno, it has become the basis of the local tourism industry. There are dozens of tour agencies, in many cases offering the same thing at wildly different prices. The main difference for this discrepancy is the amount of money the agency pays to the host families. Nearly all the cheaper agencies (and some of the more expensive ones) pay little more than the cost of the visitors' meals. While it's difficult to find out which agencies fairly compensate the host families, the following tips can help you contribute to a better experience.

- Use one of our recommended agencies or one recommended by fellow travelers.
- Check that your guide rotates both homestays and floating-island visits.
- Insist on handing payment for your lodging to the family yourself.
- Expect to pay well for your homestay. Visitors must pay at least US$50 for a typical two-day island excursion for the host family to make a profit from your stay.
- Travel to the islands independently.
- Carry out your trash – islanders have no way of disposing of it.
- Bring gifts of things the islanders can't grow, such as fresh fruit or school supplies.
- Don't give candy or money to kids, so they don't learn to beg.
- Support communal enterprises, which benefit all. On Taquile, families take turns to run the Restaurante Comunál, which gives many people their only opportunity to benefit from the tidal wave of tourism that hits their island daily. Luquina Chico and Isla Ticonata run their tourism communally, through rotation of accommodations, profit-sharing, and shared work providing food, transport, guiding and activities.
- Consider visiting one of the communities around the lake. They're harder to get to than the islands but are less touristed – you'll see a living, agrarian community.

which is arguably Capachica's most beautiful (but it's a tough call).

A couple of hundred meters off Ccotos, Isla Ticonata is home to a fiercely united community and some significant mummies, fossils and archaeological sites. Isla Ticonata is only accessible by organized tour, and is a rare example of Lake Titicaca's local communities calling the shots over tour agencies, to the benefit of all. Tours can be booked in Puno at short notice through Cedesos (p187) or the travel agencies. Activities include fishing, dancing, cooking and helping till the family *chakras* (fields).

Escallani

You could spend days ogling the majestic views of reed beds, patchwork fields, craggy rocks and the perennially snowcapped Illimani (Bolivia's highest mountain, 6438m). The lake takes on a completely different aspect from the settlement of Escallani, located off the peninsula and on the way to Juliaca. **Rufino Paucar** (☎Spanish only 97-319-0552) and his large family have built a rambling complex of more than a dozen rustic, straw-thatched cabins high above the town. This area is a little more ready than other communities to receive guests unannounced – ask around at the plaza to find his place. There are also rumors of rock-climbing areas.

The trip from Juliaca to Escallani via Pusi by *micro* (small bus) is highly recommended for hardy travelers. The scenery on this unpaved road is unparalleled – sit on the left side of the bus if you're heading from Juliaca to Escallani so you can see the lake.

Getting There & Around

From Puno, catch a *combi* advertising either Capachica or Llachón from outside the Mercado Bellavista. All will stop in Capachica (S4, 80 minutes). From the plaza here continue to Llachón (S2.50, 45 minutes) or other destinations.

For Ccotos (S2, 35 minutes) or Escallani (S2.50, 45 minutes), *combis* leave the plaza of Capachica only on Sundays from 8am to 2pm. You could also take a taxi (S20) or *mototaxi* (S10) to Ccotos; it's a bit steeper for Escallani (S70).

For Chifrón from Capachica, take a *colectivo* (S1), taxi (S10) or *mototaxi* (S7). Alternately, you can hike over the hill from Llachón, or walk the 3km from Capachica.

Llachón is also accessible via the Taquile ferry. The easiest way to combine the two is to arrive by road, then have your host family in Llachón show you where to catch the ferry to Taquile.

South-Shore Towns

The road to Bolivia via Lake Titicaca's southern shore passes through bucolic villages noted for their colonial churches and beautiful views. Traveling this route is an easy way to get a relatively untouristed peek at the region's traditional culture. If you can coordinate the transportation connections, you can visit a few of the south-shore towns in a day trip from Puno or continue on to Bolivia.

For public transport to any south-shore town, go to Puno's *terminal zonál. Combis* leave when full. The route includes Ichu (S1, 15 minutes), Chucuito (S2, 30 minutes), Juli (S4, one hour), Pomata (S6, 1½ hours) and the Bolivian border at Yunguyo (S7, 2¼ hours) or Desaguadero (S7.50, 2½ hours). Direct transport to the towns closer to Puno is more frequent, but *combis* to most towns leave at least hourly – more often for closer destinations.

Ichu

Ten kilometers out of Puno, this rural community, spread across a gorgeous green valley, is home to a little-known ruin with superb views. It's a great place for a hike.

Leave the Panamericana at Ichu's second exit (after the service station) and head inland past the house marked 'Villa Lago 1960.' Walk 2km, bearing left at the junction, aiming for the two small, terraced hills you can see in the left of the valley. After bearing left at a second junction (you'll pass the school if you miss it), the road takes you between the two hills. Turn left again and head straight up the first one. Fifteen minutes of stiff climbing brings you to the top, where you'll be rewarded with the remains of a multilayered temple complex, and breathtaking 360-degree views.

This can be done as an easy half-day trip from Puno. Take plenty of water and food as there's no store.

Chucuito

☎051 / POP 1100

Sights

Templo de la Fertilidad TEMPLE
(Inca Uyu; admission S5; ⏲8am-5pm) Quiet Chucuito's principal attraction is the outlandish **Templo de la Fertilidad**. Its dusty grounds are scattered with large stone phalluses, some up to 1.2m in length. Local

guides tell various entertaining stories about the carvings, including tales of maidens sitting atop the stony joysticks to increase their fertility. Further uphill from the main road is the main plaza, which has two attractive colonial churches, **Santo Domingo** and **Nuestra Señora de la Asunción**.

You'll have to track down the elusive caretakers to get a glimpse inside.

Sleeping & Eating

There are a couple of very basic places to eat near the plaza. Both lodgings have upscale restaurants with touristy menus.

Albergue Las Cabañas CABINS **$$**
(051-36-8494; www.chucuito.com; Tarapacá 153; s/d/tr incl breakfast S64/96/126) This lodging near the main plaza has a charming, overgrown garden, rustic stone cabins and family bungalows complete with wood-burning fires.

Taypikala Lago HOTEL **$$$**
(051-79-2266; www.taypikala.com; Calle Sandia s/n; s/d/tr S$194/245/309) Across the highway, the swanky younger sister hotel of the original Taypikala offers even better views, with understated luxury and subtle architecture.

Luquina Chico

This tiny community, 53km east of Puno on the Chucuito Peninsula, is stunning. If you want to relax in a rural community, Luquina Chico also boasts the best standard of homestay accommodations of any community around the lake. The community is making economic strides thanks to tourism.

Sweeping views of Puno, Juliaca and all the islands of the lake can be taken in from both the headland's heights or the fertile flats by the lake. In the wet season, a lagoon forms, which attracts migrating wetland birds.

Chullpitas (miniature burial towers) are scattered all around this part of the peninsula. They are said to house the bodies of *gentiles,* little people who lived here in ancient times, before the sun was born and sent them underground.

Homestays (from S20) offer full board (S70). To get here, catch a *combi* labeled 'Luquina Chico' (S4.50, 1½ hours) from Puno, or take the ferry to or from Taquile and ask the driver to drop you off. Ask around about renting kayaks. **Edgar Adventures** can also get you here on a mountain bike, a somewhat grueling but extremely scenic three-hour ride along the peninsula.

Juli

051 / POP 8000

Past Chucuito, the road curves southeast away from the lake and through the commercial center of **Ilave**, best known for its livestock market and a lively sense of community justice, manifested most famously with the lynching of the town mayor in 2004. Ilave is best avoided in times of civil strife. Sleepy, friendly Juli is a more tourist-friendly stop. It's called Peru's *pequeña Roma* (little Rome) on account of its four colonial churches from the 16th and 17th centuries, which are slowly being restored. Churches are most likely to be open on Sundays, though opening hours here should not be taken as gospel. It's worth hammering on the door if one seems closed.

Dating from 1570, the adobe baroque church of **San Juan de Letrán** (admission S8; 8:30am-5pm Tue-Sun) contains richly framed *escuela cuzqueña* (Cuzco School) paintings that depict the lives of saints. The imposing 1557 church of **Nuestra Señora de la Asunción** (admission S8; 8:30am-5pm Tue-Sun) has an expansive courtyard approach that may awaken urges to oratory. Its interior is airy, and the pulpit is covered in gold leaf. The church of **Santa Cruz** has lost half its roof and remains closed for the foreseeable future. The 1560 stone church of **San Pedro**, on the main plaza, is in the best condition, with carved ceilings and a marble baptismal font. Mass is celebrated here every Sunday at 8am.

Sunday is also the day of Juli's market, the region's largest. Wednesday is a secondary market day.

Micros (S4.50, one hour) from the *terminal zonál* in Puno drop you off near the market, a 10-minute walk downhill from the center, but leave from Jirón Lima, two blocks up from the plaza. Internet cafes and basic guesthouses can be found around here.

Pomata

051 / POP 1800

Beyond Juli, the road continues southeast to Pomata, 105km from Puno. As you arrive, you'll see the Dominican church **Templo de Pomata Santiago Apóstolo** (admission S2) – totally out of proportion with the town it dominates, in terms of both size and splendor – dramatically located on top of a small hill. Founded in 1700, it is known for its windows made of translucent alabaster and its intricately carved baroque sandstone facade. Look for the puma carvings – the town's name means 'place of the puma' in Aymara.

Just out of Pomata, the road forks. The main road continues southeast through Zepita to the unsavory border town of Desaguadero. The left fork hugs the shore of Lake Titicaca and leads to another, more pleasant border crossing at Yunguyo. If you're going this way, consider stopping off at the **Mirador Natural de Asiru Patjata** lookout, a few kilometers from Yunguyo. Here, a 5000m-long rock formation resembles a *culebra* (snake), whose head is a viewpoint looking over to Isla del Sol. The area around here is known for its isolated villages and shamans.

Colectivos from the *terminal zonál* in Puno stop here (S8, 1½ hours); they are marked with signs for Yunguyo or Desaguadero.

Bolivian Shore

If you are drawn to the idea of staying longer in Bolivia, Lonely Planet's *Bolivia* guidebook has comprehensive information.

Copacabana

591-02 / POP 54,300 / ELEV 3808M

Just across the border from Yunguyo, Copacabana is a restful Bolivian town on Lake Titicaca's south shore. For centuries it has been the site of religious pilgrimages, and today local and international pilgrims flock to its fiestas. Small and bright, it makes a handy base for visiting famous Isla del Sol and Isla de la Luna. On the weekend it's full of visitors from La Paz; during the week, it snoozes.

In the 16th century the town was presented with an image of the Virgen de la Candelaria (now Bolivia's patron saint), sparking a slew of miracles. Copacabana's Moorish cathedral, where the Virgen is housed in a mystifyingly insalubrious chapel, is still a pilgrimage site.

Be prepared for heavy rains, especially during December and January, and chilly nights year-round.

Sights & Activities

Much of the action in Copacabana revolves around Plaza 2 de Febrero and 6 de Agosto, the main commercial drag, which runs east to west. The transportation hub is Av 16 de Julio at Plaza Sucre, where buses terminate. At the western end of 6 de Agosto is the lake and a walkway (Costañera), which traces the lakeshore.

Cathedral CHURCH

(6 de Agosto) FREE The sparkling white *mudéjar* cathedral, with its domes and colorful *azulejos* (blue Portuguese-style ceramic tiles), dominates the town.

The cathedral's black **Camarínde la Virgen de Candelaria statue**, carved by Inca Tupac Yupanqui's grandson, Francisco Yupanqui, is encased above the altar upstairs in the niche *(camarín)*; note, visiting hours can be unreliable. The statue is never moved from the cathedral, as superstition suggests that its disturbance would precipitate a devastating flood of Lake Titicaca.

The cathedral is a repository for both European and local religious art and the **Museo de la Catedral** (per person B$10, minimum 4) contains some interesting articles – offerings from hopeful individuals. Unfortunately, the museum is open only to groups of four or more (unless you're happy to pay) and you'll most probably need to chase down a sister to arrange your visit.

Cerro Calvario LOOKOUT

The summit of Cerro Calvario can be reached in half an hour and is well worth the climb, especially in the late afternoon to watch the sunset over the lake. The trail to the summit begins near the **church** at the end of Calle Destacamento, northwest of Plaza Sucre, and climbs past the 14 stations of the cross.

Museo Taypi MUSEUM

(Hotel Rosario del Lago, Paredes near Costañera) FREE Museo Taypi is a small, private cultural museum within the grounds of Hotel Rosario. It features a small, lovely collection of antiquities and cultural displays on the region. Here, too, is Jalsuri, a fair-trade craft shop selling quality *artesanía* (handicrafts).

Festivals & Events

Alasitas Festival SPIRITUAL

(Jan 24) People buy miniature objects (such as diplomas, passports, home appliances) in the hope that they will be converted into reality. Traditional music and dance fills the main plazas and an effigy of an Ekeko (a person representing abundance) is paraded around.

BORDER CROSSING: BOLIVIA

There are two viable routes from Puno to Bolivia. The north-shore route is very much off the beaten track and rarely used. There are two ways to go via the south shore: through either Yunguyo or Desaguadero. The only reason to go via Desaguadero is if you're pressed for time. The Yunguyo route is safer, prettier and far more popular; it passes through the chilled-out Bolivian lakeshore town of Copacabana, from where Isla del Sol – arguably the most significant site in Andean mythology – can be visited.

US citizens have to pay US$135 cash in US dollars for a tourist visa to enter Bolivia. This can be done at the border; and shops there can help with the two necessary photos and photocopies. Also, there's a Bolivian consulate in Puno. Citizens of the European Union and Australia don't need to pay a fee or provide photos.

Bolivian border agents often try to charge an unofficial B$30 (collaboration fee) to use the border. Politely refuse. Always keep your backpack with you when crossing the border.

Note that Peruvian time is one hour behind Bolivian time.

Via Yunguyo Toward Copacabana

There are two ways to do this. The quickest and easiest way is with a cross-border bus company such as **Tour Perú** (95-167-6600; Tacna 285 No 103) or **Ormeño** (p182). Purchase tickets at the terminal (or the more convenient Tour Perú ticket office in central Puno) at least one day in advance. The services stop at a *casa de cambio* (exchange bureau) at the border and waits for passengers to check through before continuing to Copacabana (S20 to S25, three to four hours). Here, another bus that's waiting can take you straight to La Paz (B$30, 3½ hours), with a changeover of 1½ hours.

The alternative is catching local transport – *micros* – from the *terminal zonál*. This much slower method of transport is only recommended if you want to stop at some or all of the south-shore towns. Leave as early as 8am to allow enough time. Between towns, *micros* (small buses) are regular, especially on Sunday, which is the market day in both Juli and Yunguyo. It's a great way to get off the beaten track and rub shoulders with locals.

Fiesta de la Virgen de Candelaria RELIGIOUS
(Feb 2-5) A bash honoring the patron saint of Copacabana and all Bolivia, with music, traditional Aymara dancing, drinking and feasting. Celebrations culminate with the corralling of 100 bulls.

Semana Santa RELIGIOUS
As part of the Holy Week celebrations, the town fills with pilgrims on Good Friday, with processions.

Bolivian Independence Day NATIONAL HOLIDAY
(Aug) Copacabana stages its biggest event during the first week in August. It's characterized by round-the-clock music, parades, brass bands, fireworks and amazing alcohol consumption. This coincides with a traditional pilgrimage that brings thousands of Peruvians into the town to visit the Virgin.

Tours

To visit Isla del Sol and Isla de la Luna, you can either take a ferry, or go the luxury route with a La Paz–based tour operator for a guided excursion (definitely adding a night or two in their hotels on Isla del Sol).

Sleeping

Hotels (many shoddy) keep springing up like reeds in Copacabana. Budget options abound, charging around B$30 per person (significantly more in high season and during festivals), especially along Calle Jáuregui.

Hostal Flores del Lago HOTEL $
(591-02-862-2117; www.hostalfloresdellago.com; Jáuregui; s/d/tr B$100/140/210;) A top-tier budget buy is this large four-story option on the north side of the harbor. The clean rooms are slightly damp, but you'll love the lake views and the friendly lobby area.

Hostal Sonia HOTEL $
(591-02-862-2019; hostalsoniacopacabana@gmail.com; Murillo 256; per person B$50; @) This lively spot has bright and cheery rooms, great views from the upstairs rooms and a top-floor terrace, making it one of the top budget bets in town. It's on the street on the east side of the cathedral.

★**Las Olas** BOUTIQUE HOTEL $$
(28622112, 7250-8668; www.hostallasolas.com; Michel Pérez 1-3; s/d/tr US$39/49/64, ste US$74;

Yunguyo is the end of the line. Catch a *triciclo* to Kasani or cross on foot – it's a pleasant 2km along Av Ejército. The *casas de cambio* here offer a better exchange rate than their Bolivian counterparts.

First visit the Peruvian police, followed by Control Migratorio (Immigration Office) on the left. Walk to the arch and the 'Welcome to Bolivia' sign for Bolivian immigration services.

A *combi* to Copacabana is B$3. *Combis* leave more frequently on Sunday; on weekdays you may have to wait up to an hour. If you are inclined to walk the 8km, it's a straightforward stroll around the lake.

The border is open from 7:30am until 6pm, Peruvian time.

Via Desaguadero Toward La Paz

If you're going straight from Puno to La Paz, unsavory Desaguadero is faster, slightly cheaper and more direct than Yunguyo. It's also less scenic and less safe, though perfectly fine if you are traveling by a tourist bus, which is only there briefly. Avoid spending the night in Desaguadero.

Combis leave Puno's *terminal zonál* for Desaguadero (S8, 2½ hours) throughout the day.

In Desaguadero, visit the Peruvian Dirección General de Migraciones y Naturalización to get stamped out of Peru. Then head to the building that says 'Migraciones Desaguadero,' to the left of the bridge, to complete Bolivian formalities.

Catch a *triciclo* to the Bolivian-side transport terminal, from where you can get to La Paz in 3½ hours either by *combi* or *colectivo* (shared transportation; B$30).

The border is open from 8:30am to 8:30pm, Bolivian time.

Note: the Peruvian police have a bad reputation here, sometimes demanding a nonexistent 'exit tax.' You are not required to visit the Peruvian police station before leaving the country, so if anyone asks you to accompany them there, politely but firmly refuse. There are no ATMs in Desaguadero, so bring cash from Puno if your nationality requires a tourist visa.

@) Creative and stylish with million-dollar vistas, this is a once-in-a-lifetime experience and well worth the splurge. There are kitchens, private terraces with hammocks, and a solar-powered Jacuzzi. Reserve ahead.

Hotel La Cúpula HOTEL $$
(591-02-862-2029; www.hotelcupula.com; Michel Pérez 1-3; rooms s/d/tr US$19/39/52, suites s/d/tr US$30/55/66;) An inviting oasis on the slopes of Cerro Calvario. Rooms are pretty basic (and beds will be too soft for some), but it's easy to love the gardens, hammocks, shared kitchen and friendly atmosphere. The helpful staff speak several languages. Best to reserve ahead.

Ecolodge Copacabana LODGE $$
(862-2500; www.ecocopacabana.com; Av Costañera s/n; per person incl breakfast B$180) Situated 20 minutes on foot along the Costañera (or a quick taxi ride), this eco-friendly place is right on the lake in a wonderful natural paradise. Quirky adobe rooms and self-equipped apartments are self-heated thanks to the mud bricks, and have solar-powered water. A garden of dahlias and gladioli affords great views of the lake.

Hotel Mirador HOTEL $$
(cnr Av Busch & Costañera; s/d B80/200) Stunning value (and popular with groups) for the impressive view of the lake that shines like a beacon from the end of the long rooms. The wooden floors, bathroom and TV are dated, but the sprawling size of the hotel gives it an LA motel charm.

Eating & Drinking

Tourist-focused restaurants line the bottom block of Calle 6 de Agosto, but varied and exciting food is not a feature of Copacabana. The local specialty is *trucha* (trout) farmed on Lake Titicaca. Competitive stalls along the beachfront serve it in every style. You'll find it in most set lunch and dinner *menús* (B$15 to B$30) all along 6 de Agosto. On a cold morning, head to the market for a cup of *api* – a hot, sweet, purple-corn drink.

Pit Stop BAKERY $
(Av 16 de Julio; snacks B$7-15; 10am-2pm & 4:30-7:30pm) Trust the Italians to bring proper

short espressos, rich brownies and dense cakes to Copacabana. You can find empanadas and pizza elsewhere in town, but Luciano and co. do it better at this hole in the wall where buses stop.

Restaurant Aransaya BOLIVIAN $

(Av 6 de Agosto 121; lunch menú B$15, mains B$30-45; ⏲lunch) Friendly local favorite for a cold beer and trout with all the trimmings. It's very traditional and popular with the locals. You'll find it just east of Plaza Sucre.

La Orilla INTERNATIONAL $$

(☎591-02-862-2267; Av 6 de Agosto s/n; mains B$45-52; ⏲4-9:30pm Mon-Sat; ✎) A cozy maritime-themed restaurant with fresh, crunchy, from-the-vine vegetables, crispy and supersavory pizzas, and interesting trout creations that incorporate spinach and bacon (mmm, bacon). It's near the lake end of the street.

La Cúpula Restaurant INTERNATIONAL $$

(www.hotelcupula.com; Michel Pérez 1-3; mains B$24-59; ⏲7:30am-3pm & 6-9pm daily, closed lunch Tue; ✎) The inventive use of local ingredients includes tasty vegetarian lasagna, and there's plenty for carnivores, too. Cheese fondue with authentic Gruyère cheese is to die for. The glassy surroundings maximize the fabulous view of the lake.

Kota Kahuaña INTERNATIONAL $$

(☎591-02-862-2141; Rigoberto Paredes near Costañera, inside Hotel Rosario; mains B$25-55) This hotel restaurant has excellent views, great service and well-prepared international dishes. Stuffed trout, an excellent salad bar, satisfying main courses and Bolivian wines ensure a fine-dining experience.

Flor de Mi Tierra BEER GARDEN

(cnr Av Costañera & 6 de Agosto; mains B$28-55, menús B$40-65) The top spot, literally, for a sunset drink is this resto-bar's roof terrace, while watching the lake smoulder bright orange. The burgers, pizza and trout are fine, though you're paying for the view.

ℹ Information

DANGERS & ANNOYANCES

Beware illegal minibuses and taxis offering service between Copacabana and La Paz: express kidnappings have been reported. Travelers are encouraged to take the formal tourist buses (or the larger buses) and travel by day.

During festivals stand far back from fireworks displays and be wary of light-fingered revelers. There are quite a few homeless dogs wandering the streets that are mostly harmless, if you keep your distance.

MEDICAL SERVICES

There is a basic hospital on the southern outskirts of town. For serious situations head straight to La Paz.

MONEY

Shops on Calle 6 de Agosto exchange foreign currency (dollars preferred). **Banco Fie ATM** (6 de Agosto at Plaza Sucre; ⏲24hr) is reliable, while **Banco Bisa ATM** (6 de Agosto & Pando) works only sometimes.

POST

Post Office (⏲8:30am-noon & 2:30-4pm Tue-Sun) On the north side of Plaza 2 de Febrero, but often closed or unattended.

TELEPHONE

Offices are dotted along 6 de Agosto and around town.

TOURIST INFORMATION

Centro de Información Turística

(☎72516220, 67179612; www.visitacopacabana.com; cnr Av 16 de Julio & 6 de Agosto; ⏲9am-1pm & 2-6pm Wed-Sun) There is a helpful English-speaking attendant, although only rudimentary information is available.

ℹ Getting There & Away

BUS

Most buses leave from near Plazas 2 de Febrero or Sucre. The more comfortable nonstop tour buses from Copacabana to La Paz (3½ hours) – mainly **Titicaca** (cnr Av 16 de Julio & 6 de Agosto) and **Vicuña Travel** (☎591-02-236-9052; cnr Av 16 de Julio & Max Paredes) – cost around B$30 and leave Copacabana at 1:30pm and 6:30pm. Tickets can be purchased from tour agencies or directly from the ticket offices. An hour outside of Copacabana, you will need to exit your bus at the Estrecho de Tiquina to cross via **ferry** (per person B$2, per car B$35-$40; ⏲5am-9pm) between the towns of San Pedro de Tiquina (tourist-info office is on the main plaza) and San Pablo de Tiquina. This is because people can't travel on the vehicle while it crosses the water.

Buses to Peru, including from Arequipa, Cuzco and Puno, depart and arrive in Copacabana from Av 6 de Agosto. You can also get to Puno by catching a public minibus from Plaza Sucre to the border at Kasani (B$5, 15 minutes).

BOAT

Buy your tickets for boat tours (though these 'tours' are really just shared boats with a silent driver) to Isla de la Luna and Isla del Sol from agencies on 6 de Agosto or from beach-front kiosks. A separate return service is available from both islands.

Asociación Unión Marines (Costañera; one-way B$30, round-trip B$50; departs Copacabana 8:30am & 1:30pm) Ferry service to the north and south of Isla del Sol, with a stop on the return at a floating island.

Titicaca Tours (Costañera; round-trip B$40; departs Copacabana 8:30am) Offers a round-trip boat tour that stops in Isla de la Luna for an hour, continuing to the southern end of Isla del Sol for a two-hour stop before heading back to Copacabana.

Isla del Sol & Isla de la Luna

The most famous island on Lake Titicaca is Isla del Sol (Island of the Sun), the legendary birthplace of Manco Cápac and his sister-wife Mama Ocllo, and indeed the sun itself. Both Isla del Sol and Isla de la Luna (Island of the Moon) have Inca ruins, reached by delightful walking trails through spectacular scenery dotted with traditional villages – there are no cars on the islands. Sunshine and altitude can take their toll, so bring extra water, food and sun block. You can visit the main sights in a day, but staying overnight is far more rejuvenating.

Water is a precious commodity. The island does not yet have access to water mains and supplies are carried by person or donkey. Please bear this in mind; think twice before taking showers.

Note: in high season (June to August and also during festivals) prices may double.

Sights & Activities

Isla del Sol's **Inca remains** include the **Chincana** labyrinth complex in the north, and fortress-like **Pilkokayna** and the verdant, gorgeous **Inca Stairway** in the south. The Chincana is the site of the sacred Titi Khar'ka (Rock of the Puma), which features in the Inca creation legend and gave the lake its name. The largest villages are Yumani to the south and Ch'allapampa in the north.

Far less touristed, quiet Isla de la Luna boasts the partially rebuilt ruins of the convent that housed virgins of the sun – women chosen at a young age to serve as nuns to the sun god Inti.

Sleeping & Eating

On Isla del Sol, basic hostels in restful beachside Cha'llapampa charge B$30 to B$40 per person for accommodations. There are a handful of basic restaurants and shops.

However, the most scenic spot to stay is Yumani, at the other end of the island. Far more developed, dozens of accommodations range from B$30 to B$100 per person, and there are relatively sophisticated dining options (pizza and vegetarian fare) on offer.

On Isla de la Luna, there are three hostels in the main settlement on the east side of the island, with ultrabasic rooms going for about B$20 to B$25 per person. Food in town will cost about B$25 to B$30 a meal. Ask around. The hotel on the east-side tourist dock costs B$20 per person, but you miss out on being in the main community.

If camping, it's best to ask permission from the local authority and then set up away from villages, avoiding cultivated land (a nominal payment of B$10 should be offered).

Getting There & Around

BOAT

To Isla de la Luna, travel by ferry from either Copacabana or Yampupata, or with a guided tour.

Tickets may be purchased at the ticket kiosks on the beach or from Copacabana agencies. Boats to the northern end of the island land at Cha'llapampa, while those going to the southern end land at either Pilko Kaina or the Escalera del Inca (Yumani).

Launches embark from Copacabana beach around 8:30am and 1:30pm daily. Depending on the season and the company, they may drop you off at a choice of the island's north or south (check with the agency). Return trips leave Yampupata at 10:30am and 3:30pm (B$20 one way), and Cha'llapampa at 1:30pm (B$20).

Most full-day trips go directly north to Cha'llapampa (two to 2½ hours). Boats anchor for 1½ hours only – you'll have just enough time to hike up to the Chincana ruins, and return again to catch the boat at 1pm to the Escalera del Inca and Pilko Kaina in the island's south. Here, you'll spend around two hours before departing for Copa.

Half-day trips generally go to the south of Isla del Sol only and give you just one hour to explore before the return boat departs from the same spot. Just enough time to climb the beautiful Escalera del Inca (Yumani) and back.

Those who wish to hike the length of the island can get off at Cha'llapampa in the morning and walk south to the Escalera del Inca for the return boat in the afternoon.

Alternatively, you can opt to stay overnight or longer on the island (highly recommended), then buy a one-way ticket to Copacabana with any of the boat companies.

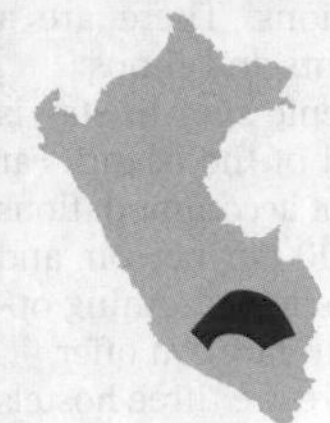

Cuzco & the Sacred Valley

Includes ➡

Best Places to Eat

- ➡ Cicciolina (p225)
- ➡ La Bodega 138 (p225)
- ➡ Huacatay (p243)
- ➡ Indio Feliz (p252)
- ➡ Marcelo Batata (p225)

Best Places to Stay

- ➡ Machu Picchu Pueblo Hotel (p251)
- ➡ Apu Lodge (p247)
- ➡ Ecopackers (p217)
- ➡ Niños Hotel (p218)
- ➡ Inkaterra La Casona (p220)

Why Go?

Incas deemed this spot the belly button of the world. A visit to Cuzco tumbles you back into the cosmic realm of ancient Andean culture – knocked down and fused with the colonial splendors of Spanish conquest, only to be repackaged as a thriving tourist mecca. Yet Cuzco is only the gateway. Beyond lies the Sacred Valley, Andean countryside dotted with villages, high altitude hamlets and ruins linked by trail and railway tracks to the continent's biggest draw – Machu Picchu.

Old ways are not forgotten here. Colorful textiles keep vivid the past, as do the wild fiestas and carnivals where pagan tradition meets solemn Catholic ritual. A stunning landscape careens from Andean peaks to orchid-rich cloud forests and Amazon lowlands. Explore it on foot or by fat tire, rafting wild rivers or simply braving the local buses to the remote and dust-worn corners of this far-reaching, culturally rich department.

When to Go

Cuzco

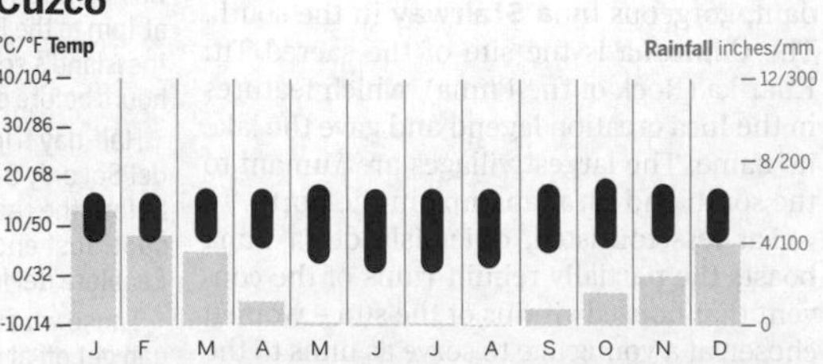

Jun–Aug High season for tourism, events and festivals; days are sunny and nights cold.

Late Jun Celebrate the solstice at Inti Raymi, the largest festival of the year.

Sep & Oct Shoulder season for tourism, with fewer crowds in Machu Picchu.

CUZCO

084 / POP 427,000 / ELEV 3326M

Cosmopolitan Inca capital, Cuzco (also Cusco, or Qosq'o in Quechua) today thrives with a measure of contradiction. Ornate cathedrals squat over Inca temples, massage hawkers ply the narrow cobblestone streets, a woman in traditional skirt and bowler offers bottled water to a pet llama while the finest boutiques sell alpaca knits for small fortunes. The foremost city of the Inca empire is now the undisputed archaeological capital of the Americas, as well as the continent's oldest continuously inhabited city. Few travelers to Peru will skip visiting this premier South American destination, also the gateway to Machu Picchu.

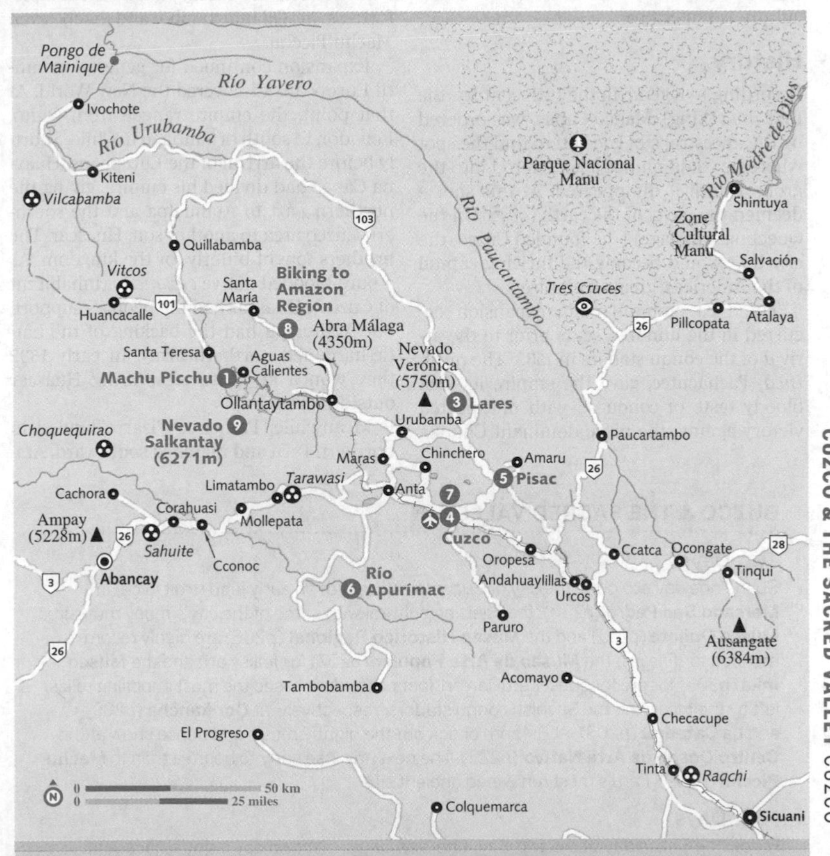

Cuzco & The Sacred Valley Highlights

1. Drinking in the sublime grandeur of **Machu Picchu** (p253).
2. Getting swept into the colorful frenzy of a traditional **festival** (p216).
3. Hiking through traditional villages and terraced agriculture on the spectacular **Lares trek** (p45).
4. Exploring the narrow streets and shops of bohemian **San Blas** (p207).
5. Wandering ancient ruins in the stunning settings of the **Sacred Valley** (p236).
6. Taking on the wild Apurímac or Tampobata Rivers on a **river-running trip** (p212).
7. Dining on haute cuisine or *cuy* (guinea pig): **Cuzco restaurants** (p224) can cater to any whim.
8. Barreling from the Andes down into the Amazon on a **mountain bike** (p213).
9. Trekking up from the tropics on the **Salkantay route** (p45) to Machu Picchu.

Visitors to Cuzco get a glimpse of the richest heritage of any South American city. Married to 21st-century hustle, at times it's a bit disconcerting (note the KFC and McDonald's behind the Inca stones). As rent soars on the Plaza de Armas and in trendy San Blas, locals are increasingly pushed to the margins. Foreign guests undoubtedly have the run of the roost, so showing respect toward today's incarnation of this powerhouse culture is imperative.

History

According to legend, in the 12th century, the first *inca* (king), Manco Capac, was ordered by the ancestral sun god Inti to find the spot where he could plunge a golden rod into the ground until it disappeared. At this spot – deemed the navel of the earth (*qosq'o* in the Quechua language) – he founded Cuzco, the city that would become the thriving capital of the Americas' greatest empire.

The Inca empire's main expansion occurred in the hundred years prior to the arrival of the conquistadors in 1532. The ninth *inca,* Pachacutec, gave the empire its first bloody taste of conquest, with unexpected victory against the more dominant Chanka tribe in 1438. His was the first wave of expansion that would create the Inca empire.

Pachacutec also proved himself a sophisticated urban developer, devising Cuzco's famous puma shape and diverting rivers to cross the city. He built fine buildings, including the famous Qorikancha temple and a palace on the present Plaza de Armas. Among the monuments he built in honor of Inca victories are Sacsaywamán, the temple-fortress at Ollantaytambo and likely even Machu Picchu.

Expansion continued for generations until Europeans discovered the New World. At that point, the empire ranged from Quito, Ecuador, to south of Santiago in Chile. Shortly before the arrival of the Europeans, Huayna Cápac had divided his empire, giving the northern part to Atahualpa and the southern Cuzco area to another son, Huascar. The brothers fought bitterly for the kingdom. As a pure-blooded native *cuzqueño* (inhabitant of Cuzco), Huascar had the people's support, but Atahualpa had the backing of the battle-hardened northern army. In early 1532 they won a key battle, capturing Huascar outside Cuzco.

Meanwhile, Francisco Pizarro landed in northern Peru and marched southward. Ata-

CUZCO & THE SACRED VALLEY IN...

Two Days

Spend one day exploring the city of Cuzco, starting with an early *jugo* (fruit juice) in **Mercado San Pedro** (p230), then getting cultural with some of the city's many museums. **Museo Quijote** (p210) and the **Museo Histórico Regional** (p206) are highly recommended for fine art; the **Museo de Arte Popular** (p207) for folksy art; and the **Museo Inka** (p205) for preconquest Peruvian artifacts. After lunch, see the most imposing relics left by the Incas and the Spanish conquistadors, respectively, at **Qorikancha** (p209) and **La Catedral** (p203). At 6:45pm check out the nightly music and dance show at the **Centro Qosqo de Arte Nativo** (p229). The next day, rise early to board a train to **Machu Picchu** (p249), Peru's most renowned ancient site.

Four Days

Follow the Cuzco day of the two-day itinerary. On the second day enjoy a decadent breakfast and explore **Sacsaywamán** (p235) in the morning. Then bus to ancient, cobbled **Ollantaytambo** (p245) and use the afternoon to hike through the ruins above town. Take an early morning train to **Aguas Calientes** (p249) and hop on a bus to **Machu Picchu** (p249). Wander through the marvels of the sprawling Inca citadel all day; get a guide for the inside story. Return to Ollantaytambo. There's still time to take local buses to the spectacular salt pans of **Salinas** (p243) on the way back to Cuzco.

One Week

Follow the Cuzco day of the two-day itinerary. On the second day, follow the **walking tour** (p211) up through arty San Blas to the impressive fortress of **Sacsaywamán**. Flag down local buses to the nearby ruins of **Q'enqo, Pukapukara** and **Tambomachay**. On the third day, start trekking the spectacular, rugged **Salkantay trail** to **Machu Picchu**.

hualpa himself had been too busy fighting the civil war to worry about a small band of foreigners, but by 1532 a fateful meeting had been arranged with the Spaniard in Cajamarca. It would radically change the course of South American history: Atahualpa was ambushed by a few dozen armed conquistadors, who succeeded in capturing him, killing thousands of indigenous tribes people and routing tens of thousands more.

In an attempt to regain his freedom, the *inca* offered a ransom of a roomful of gold and two rooms of silver, including gold stripped from the temple walls of Qorikancha. But after holding Atahualpa prisoner for a number of months, Pizarro murdered him anyway, and soon marched on to Cuzco. Mounted on horseback, protected by armor and swinging steel swords, thc Spanish cavalry was virtually unstoppable.

Pizarro entered Cuzco on November 8, 1533, by which time he had appointed Manco, a half-brother of Huascar and Atahualpa, as the new puppet leader. After a few years of toeing the line, however, the docile puppet rebelled. In 1536, Manco Inca set out to drive the Spaniards from his empire, laying siege to Cuzco with an army estimated at well over a hundred thousand people. A desperate last-ditch breakout and violent battle at Sacsaywamán saved the Spanish from complete annihilation.

Manco Inca was forced to retreat to Ollantaytambo and then into the jungle at Vilcabamba. After Cuzco was safely recaptured, looted and settled, the seafaring Spaniards turned their attentions to the newly founded colonial capital, Lima. Cuzco's importance quickly waned to that of another colonial backwater. All the gold and silver was gone, and many Inca buildings were pulled down to accommodate churches and colonial houses.

The Spanish kept chronicles in Cuzco, including Inca history as related by the Incas themselves. The most famous of these accounts is *The Royal Commentaries of the Incas,* written by Garcilaso de la Vega, the son of an Inca princess and a Spanish military captain.

Sights

While the city is sprawling, areas of interest to visitors are generally within walking distance, with some steep hills in between. The center of the city is the Plaza de Armas, while traffic-choked Av El Sol nearby is the main business thoroughfare. Walking just a few blocks north or east of the plaza will lead you onto steep, twisting cobblestone streets, little changed for centuries. The flatter areas to the south and west are the commercial center.

> **ACCLIMATIZATION**
>
> Those arriving from lower altitudes may experience altitude sickness. Take it easy the first few days of your visit or start in the slightly lower Sacred Valley.

The alley heading away from the northwest side of Plaza de Armas is Procuradores (Tax Collectors), nicknamed 'Gringo Alley' for its tourist restaurants, tour agents and other services. Watch out for predatory touts. Beside the hulking cathedral on the Plaza de Armas, narrow Calle Triunfo leads steeply uphill toward Plaza San Blas, the heart of Cuzco's eclectic, artistic *barrio* (neighborhood).

A resurgence of indigenous pride means many streets have been signposted with new Quechua names, although they are still commonly referred to by their Spanish names. The most prominent example is Calle Triunfo, which is signposted as Sunturwasi.

At tourist sites, freelance guides speak some English or other foreign languages. For more extensive tours at major sites, such as Qorikancha or the cathedral, always agree to a fair price in advance. Otherwise, a respectable minimum tip for a short tour is S5 per person in a small group, and a little more for individuals.

Opening hours are erratic and can change for any reason – from Catholic feast days to the caretaker slipping off for a beer with his mates. A good time to visit Cuzco's well-preserved colonial churches is in the early morning (from 6am to 8am), when they are open for Mass. Officially, they are closed to tourists at these times, but if you go in quietly and respectfully as a member of the congregation, you can see the church as it should be seen. Flash photography is not allowed inside churches or museums.

Central Cuzco

Plaza de Armas PLAZA

(Map p200) In Inca times, the plaza, called Huacaypata or Aucaypata, was the heart of the capital. Today it's the nerve center of the modern city. Two flags usually fly here – the red-and-white Peruvian flag and the rainbow-colored flag of Tahuantinsuyo.

Central Cuzco

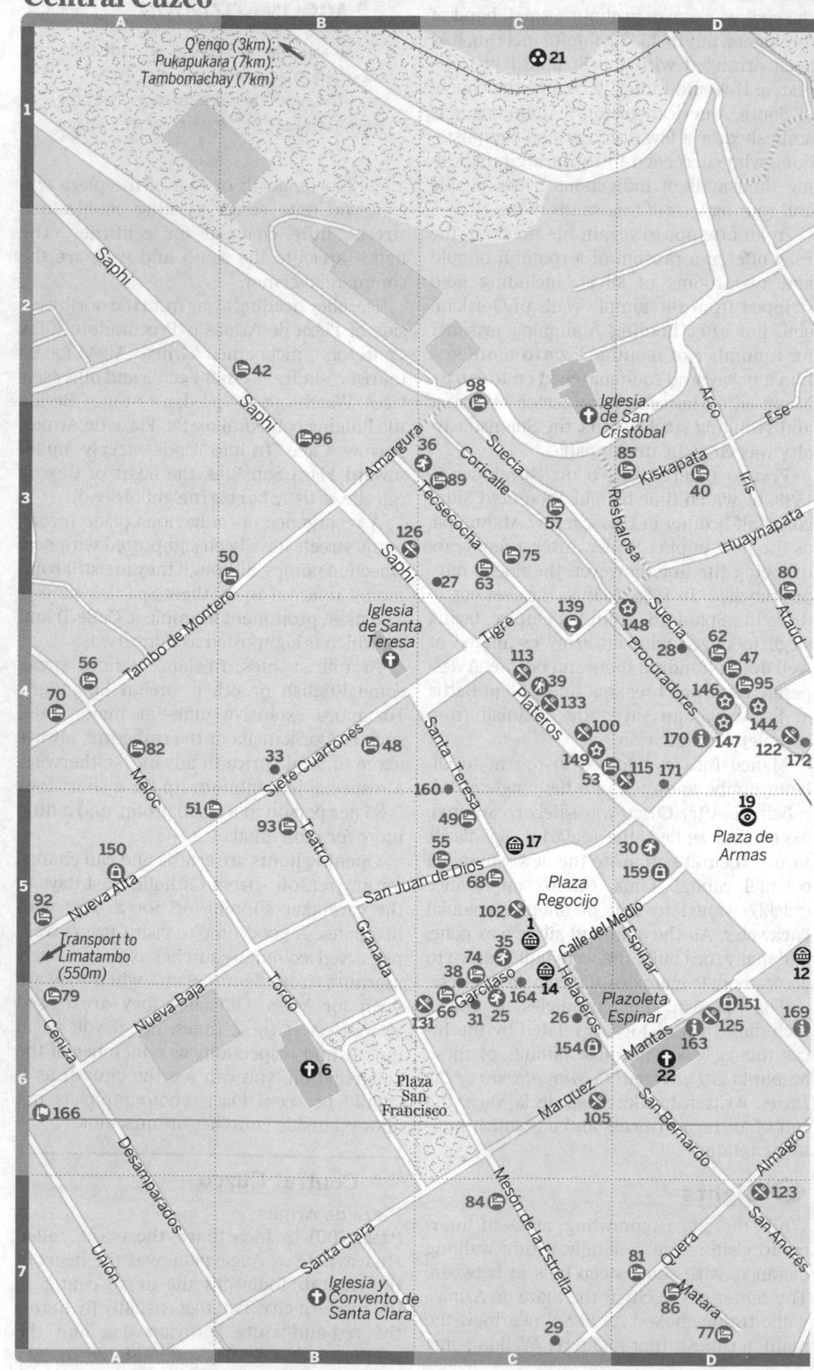

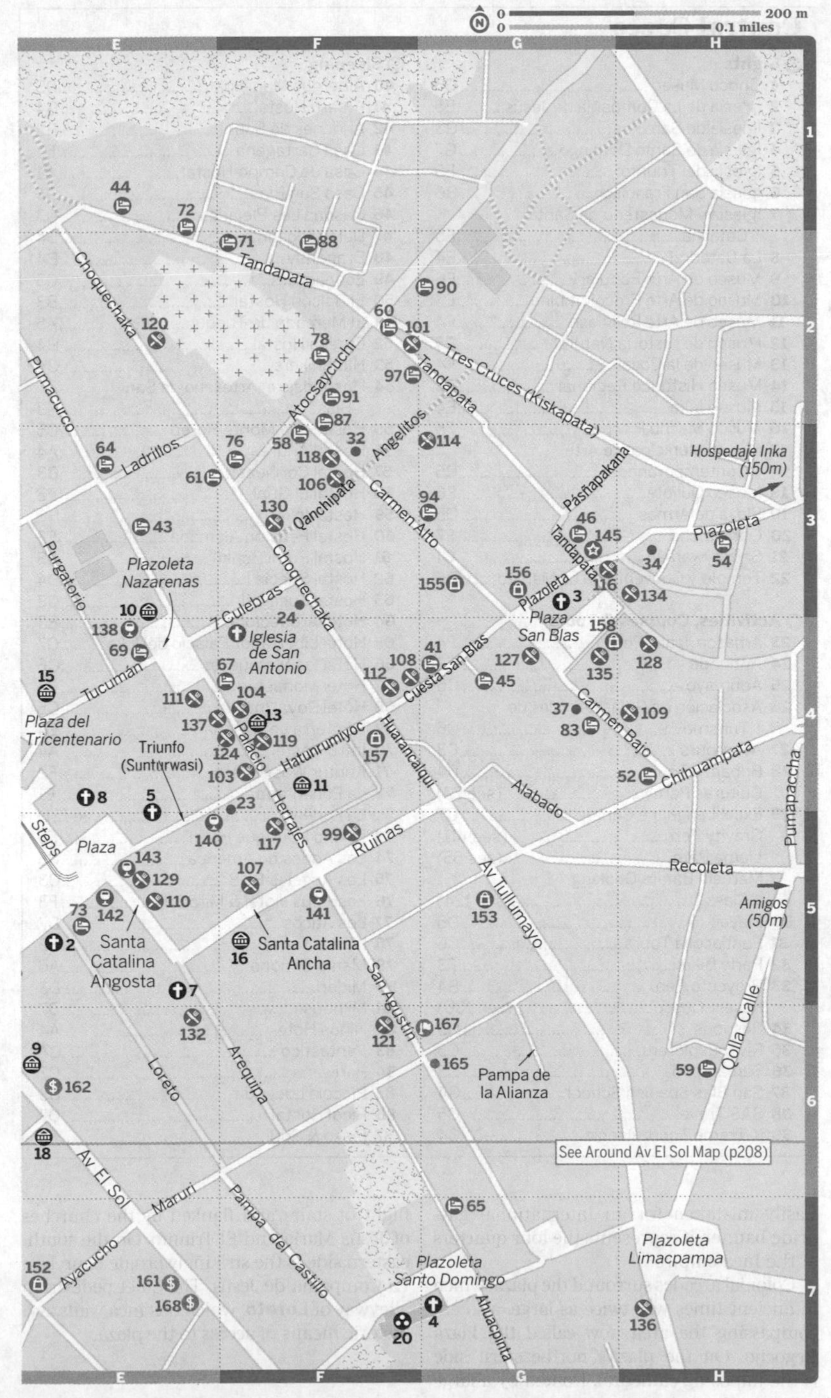
0 200 m
0 0.1 miles
E
F
G
H
1
2
3
4
5
6
7
Tandapata
Choquechaka
Atocsaycuchi
Tres Cruces (Kiskapata)
Pumacurco
Angelitos
Ladrillos
Qanchipata
Carmen Alto
Pasñapakana
Hospedaje Inka (150m)
Plazoleta
Purgatorio
Plazoleta Nazarenas
7 Culebras
Iglesia de San Antonio
Plazoleta
Plaza San Blas
Cuesta San Blas
Tucumán
Plaza del Tricentenario
Triunfo (Sunturwasi)
Palacio
Hatunrumiyoc
Huarancalqui
Carmen Bajo
Chihuampata
Alabado
Steps
Plaza
Herrajes
Ruinas
Av Tullumayo
Recoleta
Pumapaccha
Amigos (50m)
Santa Catalina Angosta
Santa Catalina Ancha
San Agustín
Loreto
Arequipa
Pampa de la Alianza
Qolla Calle
See Around Av El Sol Map (p208)
Av El Sol
Maruri
Pampa del Castillo
Ayacucho
Plazoleta Santo Domingo
Plazoleta Limacpampa
Ahuacpinta

Central Cuzco

Sights

1 Choco Museo ... C5
2 Iglesia de La Compañía de Jesús ... E5
3 Iglesia de San Blas ... G3
4 Iglesia de Santo Domingo ... G7
5 Iglesia del Triunfo ... E5
6 Iglesia San Francisco ... B6
7 Iglesia y Monasterio de Santa Catalina ... E5
8 La Catedral ... E4
9 Museo de Arte Popular ... E6
10 Museo de Arte Precolombino ... E3
11 Museo de Arte Religioso ... F4
12 Museo de Historia Natural ... D5
13 Museo de la Coca ... F4
14 Museo Histórico Regional ... C5
15 Museo Inka ... E4
16 Museo Machu Picchu ... F5
17 Museo Municipal de Arte Contemporáneo ... C5
18 Museo Quijote ... E6
19 Plaza de Armas ... D5
20 Qorikancha ... F7
21 Sacsaywamán ... C1
22 Templo y Convento de La Merced ... D6

Activities, Courses & Tours

23 Amazon Trails Peru ... F4
24 Antipode ... F3
25 Apumayo ... C6
26 Asociación de Guías Oficiales de Turismo ... C6
27 Aventours ... C3
28 Bonanza Tours ... D4
Culturas Peru ... (see 72)
29 Excel Language Center ... C7
Gravity Peru ... (see 141)
Llama Path ... (see 55)
Marcelo Batata Cooking Class ... (see 124)
30 Mayuc ... D5
31 Pantiacolla Tours ... C6
32 Party Bike ... F3
33 Proyecto Peru ... B4
Reserv Cusco ... (see 100)
34 Respons ... H3
35 River Explorers ... C5
36 Samana Spa ... C3
37 San Blas Spanish School ... G4
38 SAS Travel ... C5
39 X-Treme Tourbulencia ... C4

Sleeping

40 Albergue Municipal ... D3
41 Amaru Hostal ... G4
42 Andenes de Saphi ... B2
43 Casa Cartagena ... E3
44 Casa de Campo Hostal ... E1
45 Casa San Blas ... G4
46 Casona Les Pleiades ... G3
47 Del Prado Inn ... D4
48 Dragonfly ... B4
49 Ecopackers ... C5
50 El Balcón Hostal ... B3
51 El Mercado de Tunqui ... A5
52 Eureka Hostal ... H4
53 Hitchhikers ... C4
54 Hospedaje el Artesano de San Blas ... H3
55 Hospedaje Monte Horeb ... C5
56 Hostal Andrea ... A4
57 Hostal Corihuasi ... C3
58 Hostal El Grial ... F3
59 Hostal Inkarri ... H6
60 Hostal Pensión Alemana ... F2
61 Hostal Rumi Punku ... E3
62 Hostal Suecia I ... D4
63 Hostal Suecia II ... C3
64 Hotel Arqueólogo ... E3
65 Hotel Libertador Palacio del Inka ... G7
66 Hotel los Marqueses ... C6
67 Hotel Monasterio ... F4
68 Hotel Royal Inca I ... C5
69 Inkaterra La Casona ... E4
70 Intro Hostel ... A4
71 Kuntur Wasi Cusco ... F2
72 La Encantada ... E1
La Lune ... (see 121)
73 Loreto Boutique Hotel ... E5
74 Los Andes de America ... C5
75 Los Angeles B&B ... C3
76 Los Apus Hotel & Mirador ... F3
77 Los Aticos ... D7
78 Madre Tierra ... F2
79 Mama Simona ... A6
80 Midori ... D3
81 Milhouse ... D7
82 Niños Hotel ... A4
83 Pantastico ... G4
84 Pariwana ... C7
85 Piccola Locanda ... D3
86 Picol Hostal ... D7
87 Pisko & Soul ... F2

Easily mistaken for an international gay-pride banner, it represents the four quarters of the Inca empire.

Colonial arcades surround the plaza, which in ancient times was twice as large, also encompassing the area now called the Plaza Regocijo. On the plaza's northeastern side is the imposing cathedral, fronted by a large flight of stairs and flanked by the churches of Jesús María and El Triunfo. On the south-eastern side is the strikingly ornate church of La Compañía de Jesús. The quiet pedestrian alleyway of **Loreto**, which has Inca walls, is a historic means of access to the plaza.

88 Quinua Villa Boutique F2
89 Samana Spa B&B C3
90 Samay Wasi G2
91 Second Home Cusco F2
92 Tambo del Arriero A5
93 Teatro Inka B&B B5
94 Tierra Viva G3
95 Tierra Viva D4
96 Tierra Viva B3
97 Tika Wasi F2
98 WalkOn Inn C2

Eating
A Mi Manera .... (see 103)
99 Aldea Yanapay F5
100 Cafe Morena C4
101 Cafeteria 7&7 .... F2
102 Chicha C5
103 Cicciolina F4
104 Deli Monasterio F4
Divina Comedia .... (see 64)
105 El Ayllu C6
106 El Hada F3
107 Gato's Market F5
108 Granja Heidi F4
109 Greenpoint H4
110 Green's Organic E5
111 Inkazuela E4
112 Jack's Café F4
113 Jardín Secreto C4
114 Juanito's G3
115 Kintaro D4
116 Korma Sutra G3
117 La Bodega 138 .... F5
118 La Bohème F3
119 La Justina F4
120 La Quinta Eulalia E2
121 Le Soleil F6
122 Limo D4
123 Los Toldos D7
124 Marcelo Batata F4
125 Market D6
126 Mr. Soup B3
127 Pacha Papa G4
128 Pantastico H4
129 Papachos E5
130 Prasada F3
131 Q'ori Sara C6
132 Restaurante Egos E6
133 Restaurante Oblitas C4
134 Tacomania H3
135 The Meeting Place G4
136 Trujillo Restaurant H7
137 Uchu Peruvian Steakhouse E4

Drinking & Nightlife
138 Fallen Angel E4
139 La Chupiteria C4
Memoria .... (see 133)
140 Muse E5
141 Museo del Pisco F5
142 Norton Rats E5
143 Paddy Flaherty's E5

Entertainment
144 Inka Team D4
145 Km 0 .... G3
146 Mama Africa D4
147 Mythology D4
148 Roots D4
149 Ukuku's C4

Shopping
150 Aymi Wasi A5
151 Bookstore Kiosk D6
152 Centro Comercial de Cuzco E7
153 Inkakunaq Ruwaynin G5
154 Jerusalén C6
155 Taller and Museo Mérida G3
156 Taller Mendivil G3
157 Taller Mendivil F4
158 Taller Olave G4
159 Tatoo D5

Information
160 Action Valley C4
161 BBVA Continental E7
162 BCP E6
163 DIRCETUR D6
164 Eco Amazonia Lodge C5
165 Fertur Peru Travel G6
166 French Honorary Consulate A6
167 German Honorary Consulate G6
168 Interbank E7
169 iPerú D6
170 iPerú D4

Transport
171 Inca Rail D4
172 Peru Rail D4
Peru Rail .... (see 122)

It's worth visiting the plaza at least twice – by day and by night – as it takes on a strikingly different look after dark, all lit up.

La Catedral CHURCH

(Map p200; Plaza de Armas; admission S25; ⏲10am-5:45pm) A squatter on the site of Viracocha Inca's palace, the cathedral was built using blocks pilfered from the nearby Inca site of Sacsaywamán. Its construction started in 1559 and took almost a century. It is joined by **Iglesia del Triunfo** (1536) to its right and **Iglesia de Jesús María** (1733) to the left.

El Triunfo, Cuzco's oldest church, houses a vault containing the remains of the famous

STARGAZING WITH THE ANCIENTS

The Incas were the only culture in the world to define constellations of darkness as well as light. Astronomy wasn't taken lightly: some of Cuzco's main streets are designed to align with the stars at certain times of the year. Understanding their interest is a cool way to learn more about the Inca worldview. We recommend a visit to the **Cuzco Planetarium** (974-782-692; www.planetariumcusco.com; Carretera Sacsayhuamán, Km 2; per person S50) before you head out trekking and watching the night sky on your own. Think of how clever you'll feel pointing out the Black Llama to your fellow hikers. Reservations are essential. Price includes transfer from Plaza Regocijo.

Inca chronicler Garcilaso de la Vega, who was born in Cuzco in 1539 and died in Córdoba, Spain, in 1616. His remains were returned in 1978 by King Juan Carlos of Spain.

The cathedral is one of the city's greatest repositories of colonial art, especially for works from the *escuela cuzqueña* (Cuzco school), noted for its decorative combination of 17th-century European devotional painting styles with the color palette and iconography of indigenous Andean artists. A classic example is the frequent portrayal of the Virgin Mary wearing a mountain-shaped skirt with a river running around its hem, identifying her with Pachamama (Mother Earth).

One of the most famous paintings of the *escuela cuzqueña* is *The Last Supper* by Quechua artist Marcos Zapata. Found in the northeast corner of the cathedral, it depicts one of the most solemn occasions in the Christian faith, but graces it with a small feast of Andean ceremonial food; look for the plump and juicy-looking roast *cuy* (guinea pig) stealing the show with its feet held plaintively in the air.

Also look for the oldest surviving painting in Cuzco, showing the entire city during the great earthquake of 1650. The inhabitants can be seen parading around the plaza with a crucifix, praying for the earthquake to stop, which it miraculously did. This precious crucifix, called **El Señor de los Temblores** (Lord of the Earthquakes), can still be seen in the alcove to the right of the door leading into El Triunfo. Every year on Holy Monday, the señor is taken out on parade and devotees throw ñucchu flowers at him – these resemble droplets of blood and represent the wounds of crucifixion. The flowers leave a sticky residue that collects smoke from votive candles lit beneath the statue: this is why he's now black. Legend has it that under his skirt, he's lily white.

The sacristy of the cathedral is covered with paintings of Cuzco's bishops, starting with Vicente de Valverde, the friar who accompanied Pizarro during the conquest. The crucifixion at the back of the sacristy is attributed to the Flemish painter Anthony van Dyck, though some guides claim it to be the work of the 17th-century Spaniard Alonso Cano. The original wooden altar is at the very back of the cathedral, behind the present silver altar, and opposite both is the magnificently carved choir, dating from the 17th century. There are also many glitzy silver and gold side chapels with elaborate platforms and altars that contrast with the austerity of the cathedral's stonework.

The huge main doors of the cathedral are open to genuine worshippers between 6am and 10am. Religious festivals are a superb time to see the cathedral. During the feast of Corpus Christi, for example, it is filled with pedestals supporting larger-than-life statues of saints, surrounded by thousands of candles and bands of musicians honoring them with mournful Andean tunes.

Iglesia de La Compañía de Jesús CHURCH
(Map p200; Plaza de Armas; admission S15; 9-11:30am & 1-5:30pm) Built upon the palace of Huayna Cápac, the last Inca to rule an undivided, unconquered empire, the church was built by the Jesuits in 1571 and reconstructed after the 1650 earthquake. Two large canvases near the main door show early marriages in Cuzco in wonderful period detail. Local student guides are available to show you around the church, as well as the grand view from the choir on the 2nd floor, reached via rickety steps. Tips are gratefully accepted.

The Jesuits planned to make it the most magnificent of Cuzco's churches. The archbishop of Cuzco, however, complained that its splendor should not rival that of the cathedral, and the squabble grew to a point where Pope Paul III was called upon to arbitrate. His decision was in favor of the cathedral, but by the time word had reached Cuzco, La Compañía de Jesús was just about finished, complete with an incredible baroque facade and Peru's biggest altar, all crowned by a soaring dome.

Choco Museo MUSEUM
(Map p200; 084-24-4765; www.chocomuseo.com; Garcilaso 210; 10:30am-6:30pm;) FREE The wafting aromas of bubbling chocolate will mesmerize you from the start. While the museum is frankly lite, the best part of this French-owned enterprise is the organic chocolate-making workshops (S70 per person). You can also come for fondue or a fresh cup of fair-trade hot cocoa. It organizes chocolate farm tours close to Santa María. It's multilingual and kid-friendly.

Museo de Arte Precolombino MUSEUM
(Map p200; 084-23-3210; www.map.museolarco.org; Plazoleta Nazarenas 231; admission S20; 9am-10pm) Inside a Spanish colonial mansion with an Inca ceremonial courtyard, this dramatically curated pre-Columbian art museum showcases a stunningly varied, if selectively small, collection of archaeological artifacts previously buried in the vast storerooms of Lima's Museo Larco. Dating from between 1250 BC and AD 1532, the artifacts show off the artistic and cultural achievements of many of Peru's ancient cultures, with exhibits labeled in Spanish, English and French.

Highlights include the Nazca and Moche galleries of multicolored ceramics, *queros* (ceremonial Inca wooden drinking vessels) and dazzling displays of jewelry made with intricate gold- and silver-work.

Museo Inka MUSEUM
(Map p200; 084-23-7380; Tucumán near Ataúd; admission S10; 8am-6pm Mon-Fri, 9am-4pm Sat) The charmingly modest Museo Inka, a steep block northeast of the Plaza de Armas, is the best museum in town for those interested in the Incas. The restored interior is jam packed with a fine collection of metal- and gold-work, jewelry, pottery, textiles, mummies, models and the world's largest collection of *queros* (ceremonial Inca wooden drinking vessels). There's excellent interpretive information in Spanish, and English-speaking guides are usually available for a small fee.

The museum building, which rests on Inca foundations, is also known as the Admiral's House, after the first owner, Admiral Francisco Aldrete Maldonado. It was badly damaged in the 1650 earthquake and rebuilt by Pedro Peralta de los Ríos, the count of Laguna, whose crest is above the porch. Further damage from the 1950 earthquake has now been fully repaired, restoring the building to its position among Cuzco's finest colonial houses. Look for the massive stairway guarded by sculptures of mythical creatures, and the corner window column that from the inside looks like a statue of a bearded man but from the outside appears to be a naked woman. The ceilings are ornate, and the windows give good views straight out across the Plaza de Armas.

Downstairs in the sunny courtyard, highland Andean weavers demonstrate their craft and sell traditional textiles directly to the public.

Museo de Historia Natural MUSEUM
(Map p200; Plaza de Armas; admission S3; 9am-5pm Mon-Fri) The university-run natural history museum houses a somewhat motley

BOLETO TURÍSTICO & BOLETO RELIGIOSO

To visit most sites in the region, you will need Cuzco's official **boleto turístico** (adult/student under 26 with ISIC card S130/70), valid for 10 days. Among the 17 sites included are: Sacsaywamán, Q'enqo, Pukapukara, Tambomachay, Pisac, Ollantaytambo, Chinchero and Moray, as well as an evening performance of Andean dances and live music at the Centro Qosqo de Arte Nativo. While some inclusions are admitted duds, you can't visit any of them without it.

Three **partial boletos** (adult/student S70/35) cover the ruins immediately outside Cuzco, the museums in Cuzco, and the Sacred Valley ruins. They are valid for one day, except for the Sacred Valley option, which is valid for two.

Purchase *boletos turísticos* from **Dircetur/Cosituc** (%084-261-465; www.boletoturisticocusco.com; La Municipalidad, office 102, Av El Sol 103; h8am-6pm Mon-Fri) or at the sites themselves, except for the Centro Qosqo de Arte Nativo. Students must show valid ID.

The **boleto religioso** (adult/student S50/25), also valid for 10 days, secures entry to Cuzco's churches, the Museo de Arte Religioso and Cuzco's most significant display of contemporary art at Museo Quijote. It's available at any of the sites.

MACHU PICCHU TICKETS

Entrance tickets for Machu Picchu (p258) often sell out: buy them in advance in Cuzco. Travelers have reported problems purchasing tickets online. Authorized ticket agents (such as Peru Rail) are listed on the Machu Picchu website or visit Dircetur (p232) in Cuzco.

collection of stuffed local animals and birds and over 150 snakes from the Amazon. The entrance is hidden off the Plaza de Armas, to the right of Iglesia de La Compañía de Jesús.

Iglesia y Monasterio de Santa Catalina CHURCH

(Map p200; Arequipa s/n; admission S8; 8:30am-5:30pm Mon-Sat) This convent houses many colonial paintings of the *escuela cuzqueña* (Cuzco school), as well as an impressive collection of vestments and other intricate embroidery. The baroque side chapel features dramatic friezes, and many life-sized (and sometimes startling) models of nuns praying, sewing and going about their lives. The convent also houses 13 real, live contemplative nuns.

Templo y Convento de La Merced CHURCH

(Map p200; 084-23-1821; Mantas 121; admission S10; 8am-noon & 2-5pm Mon-Sat, cloister 8-11am) Cuzco's third most important colonial church, La Merced was destroyed in the 1650 earthquake, but was quickly rebuilt. To the left of the church, at the back of a small courtyard, is the entrance to the monastery and museum. Paintings based on the life of San Pedro Nolasco, who founded the order of La Merced in Barcelona in 1218, hang on the walls of the beautiful colonial cloister.

The church on the far side of the **cloister** contains the tombs of two of the most famous conquistadors: Diego de Almagro and Gonzalo Pizarro (brother of Francisco). Also on the far side of the cloister is a small religious museum that houses vestments rumored to have belonged to conquistador and friar Vicente de Valverde. The museum's most famous possession is a priceless solid-gold monstrance, 1.2m high and covered with rubies, emeralds and no fewer than 1500 diamonds and 600 pearls. Ask to see it if the display room is locked.

Museo de la Coca MUSEUM

(Map p200; 084-50-1020; museodelacoca@hotmail.com; Palacios 122; admission S10; 9am-6pm) A wonderful little museum that traces the uses of the coca leaf, from sacred ritual to its more insidious incarnations. Exhibits are labeled in both English and Spanish. Tips are suggested for guided visits. A good primer on Andean culture.

Museo Machu Picchu MUSEUM

(Casa Concha; Map p200; 084-25-5535; Santa Catalina Ancha 320; adult/child S20/10; 8am-5pm Mon-Fri, 9am-5pm Sat) This new museum exhibits 360 pieces from Machu Picchu returned by Yale University, including lithic and metals, ceramics and bones. Signs are in English and Spanish. Casa Concha is a beautiful restored colonial home which belonged to an aristocrat at the time of the conquest.

Museo Histórico Regional MUSEUM

(Map p200; Calle Garcilaso at Heladeros; adult/student under 26 with ISIC card S130/70; 8am-5pm Tue-Sun) This eclectic museum is housed in the colonial Casa Garcilaso de la Vega, the house of the Inca-Spanish chronicler who now lies buried in the cathedral. The chronologically arranged collection begins with arrowheads from the Preceramic Period and continues with ceramics and jewelry of the Wari, Pukara and Inca cultures. Admission is with the *boleto turístico* tourist card only, which is valid for 10 days and covers 16 other sites.

There is also a Nazca mummy, a few Inca weavings, some small gold ornaments and a strangely sinister scale model of the Plaza de Armas. A big, helpful chart in the courtyard outlines the timeline and characters of the *escuela cuzqueña*.

Museo Municipal de Arte Contemporáneo MUSEUM

(Map p200; Plaza Regocijo; adult/student under 26 with ISIC card S130/70; 9am-6pm Mon-Sat) The small collection of contemporary Andean art on display at this museum in the municipality building is really one for the fans. Museo Quijote has a much better collection, putting a representative range of Peru's contemporary artists on show, with interpretive information that puts art in context with history. Admission is with the *boleto turístico* tourist card only, which is valid for 10 days and covers 16 other sites.

Iglesia San Francisco CHURCH

(Map p200; Plaza San Francisco; museum admission S5; 6:30-8am & 5:30-8pm Mon-Sat, 6:30am-noon & 6:30-8pm Sun, museum 9am-noon & 3-5pm Mon-Fri, 9am-noon Sat) More austere than many of Cuzco's other churches, Iglesia

San Francisco dates from the 16th and 17th centuries and is one of the few that didn't need to be completely reconstructed after the 1650 earthquake. It has a large collection of colonial religious paintings and a beautifully carved cedar choir.

The attached **museum** houses supposedly the largest painting in South America, which measures 9m by 12m and shows the family tree of St Francis of Assisi, the founder of the order. Also of macabre interest are the two crypts, which are not totally underground. Inside are human bones, some of which have been carefully arranged in designs meant to remind visitors of the transitory nature of life.

Museo de Arte Religioso MUSEUM

(Map p200; cnr Hatunrumiyoc & Herrajes; admission S10; ⏲8-11am & 3-6pm Mon-Sat) Originally the palace of Inca Roca, the foundations of this museum were converted into a grand colonial residence and later became the archbishop's palace. The beautiful mansion is now home to a religious-art collection notable for the accuracy of its period detail, and especially its insight into the interaction of indigenous peoples with the Spanish conquistadors.

There are also some impressive ceilings and colonial-style tile work that's not original, having been replaced during the 1940s.

San Blas

Known as the artists' neighborhood, San Blas is nestled on a steep hillside next to the center. With classic architecture, its signature blue doors and narrow passageways without cars, it has become a hip attraction full of restaurants, watering holes and shops.

Iglesia de San Blas CHURCH

(Map p200; Plaza San Blas; admission S10; ⏲10am-6pm Mon-Sat, 2-6pm Sun) This simple adobe church is comparatively small, but you can't help but be awed by the baroque, gold-leaf principal altar. The exquisitely carved pulpit, made from a single tree trunk, has been called the finest example of colonial wood carving in the Americas.

Legend claims that its creator was an indigenous man who miraculously recovered from a deadly disease and subsequently dedicated his life to carving the pulpit for this church. Supposedly, his skull is nestled in the topmost part of the carving. In reality, no one is certain of the identity of either the skull or the woodcarver.

Avenida El Sol & Downhill

Museo de Arte Popular MUSEUM

(Map p200; Basement, Av El Sol 103; adult/student under 26 with ISIC card S130/70; ⏲9am-6pm Mon-Sat, 8am-1pm Sun) Winning entries in Cuzco's annual Popular Art Competition are displayed in this engaging museum. This is where the artisans and artists of San Blas showcase their talents in styles ranging from high art to cheeky, offering a fascinating, humorous take on ordinary life amid the pomp and circumstance of a once grandiose

WARNING: YOUR SACRED VISION FOR SALE

Shamanic ceremonies may be native to the Amazon, but they have become a hot commodity in Cuzco and the Sacred Valley. The psychedelic properties of the San Pedro and *ayahuasca* plants have earned them fame and piqued public curiosity and the interest of psychonauts who travel in search of these experiences. Extremely powerful drugs, they can be highly toxic and we don't recommend them.

Yet they are ubiquitous. In Cuzco, San Pedro is offered alongside massages by street hawkers; *ayahuasca* ceremonies are advertised in hostels. Of course, travelers will decide what is right and wrong for them. It's important to note that these are not recreational drugs. A real shaman knows the long list of dos and don'ts for practitioners, and may screen participants. Ceremonies can require multiple days for preparation, fasting and extended rituals.

It is hard not to be skeptical about a store-bought spiritual experience. Many *cuzqueños* (inhabitants of Cuzco) believe that it's a mockery to make these sacred ceremonies into moneymakers. Still, participating in a 'guided ceremony' can be safer than scarfing down a powerful narcotic by yourself, as long as you trust the practitioners (in some cases, female guests have been attacked while under the influence). Avoid casual opportunities. Serious operations often use a medical questionnaire. It's also advisable to look into ceremonies and ask previous participants about their experiences before signing up.

Around Av El Sol

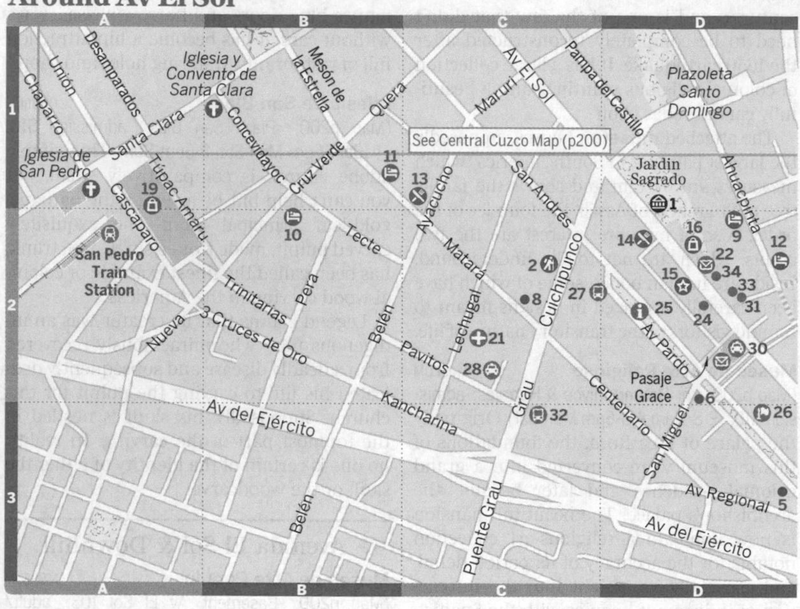

Around Av El Sol

Sights
1 Museo del Sitio de Qorikancha D1

Activities, Courses & Tours
2 Apu's Peru C2
3 Chaski Ventura F2
4 Fairplay F3
5 Manu Nature Tours D3
6 Milla Turismo D2
Peru Treks .... (see 27)
7 Peruvian Odyssey E2
8 SATO C2

Sleeping
9 Hostal San Juan Masías D2
10 Tierra Viva B2
11 Wild Rover B1
12 Yanantin Guest House D2

Eating
13 Mega C1
14 Valeriana D2

Entertainment
15 Centro Qosqo de Arte Nativo D2

Shopping
16 Center for Traditional Textiles of Cuzco D2
17 Centro Artesenal Cuzco E3
18 Mercado Modelo de Huanchac E2
19 Mercado San Pedro A1

Information
20 Clinica Pardo F1
21 Clínica Paredes C2
22 DHL D2
23 Dirección Regional de Cultura Cusco F1
24 Oficina de Migraciónes D2
25 South American Explorers D2
26 US Honorary Consulate D3

Transport
Avianca .... (see 15)
27 Bus to Estación Poroy C2
28 Colectivos to Chinchero, Ollantaytambo & Urubamba C2
29 Colectivos to Lucre E2
30 Combis to Airport D2
31 LAN D2
32 Minibuses to Chinchero, Ollantaytambo & Urubamba C3
33 Peruvian Airlines D2
34 Star Perú D2
35 Transport to Andahuaylillas, Piquillacta, Pisac, Tipón & Urcos E2

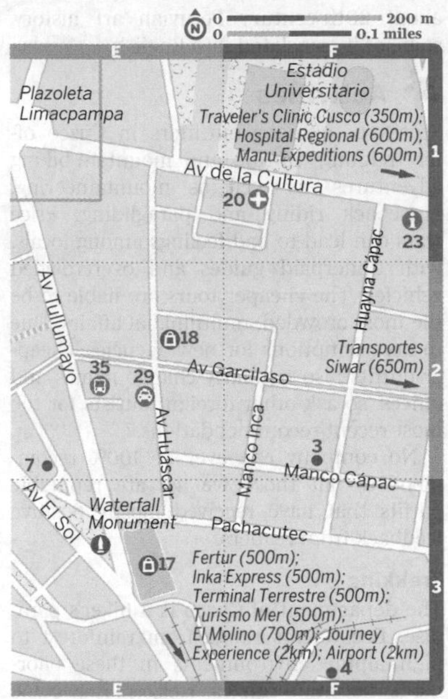

culture. Admission is with the *boleto turístico* tourist card only, which is valid for 10 days and covers 16 other sites.

Small-scale ceramic models depict drunken debauchery in the *picantería* (local restaurant), torture in the dentist's chair, carnage in the butcher shop, and even a caesarean section. There's also a display of photographs, many by renowned local photographer Martín Chambi, of Cuzco from the 1900s to the 1950s, including striking images of the aftermath of the 1950 earthquake in familiar streets.

Qorikancha RUIN

(Map p200; Plazoleta Santo Domingo; admission S10; ⏲8:30am-5:30pm Mon-Sat, 2-5pm Sun)

If you visit only one site in Cuzco, make it these Inca ruins, which form the base of the colonial church and convent of Santo Domingo. Qorikancha was once the richest temple in the Inca empire; all that remains today is the masterful stonework.

In Inca times, Qorikancha (Quechua for 'Golden Courtyard') was literally covered with gold. The temple walls were lined with some 700 solid-gold sheets, each weighing about 2kg. There were life-sized gold and silver replicas of corn, which were ceremonially 'planted' in agricultural rituals. Also reported were solid-gold treasures such as altars, llamas and babies, as well as a replica of the sun, which was lost. But within months of the arrival of the first conquistadors, this incredible wealth had all been looted and melted down.

Various other religious rites took place in the temple. It is said that the mummified bodies of several previous *incas* (kings) were kept here, brought out into the sunlight each day and offered food and drink, which was then ritually burnt. Qorikancha was also an observatory where high priests monitored celestial activities. Most of this is left to the imagination of the modern visitor, but the remaining stonework ranks with the finest Inca architecture in Peru. A curved, perfectly fitted 6m-high wall can be seen from both inside and outside the site. This wall has withstood all of the violent earthquakes that leveled most of Cuzco's colonial buildings.

Once inside the site, the visitor enters a courtyard. The octagonal font in the middle was originally covered with 55kg of solid gold. Inca chambers lie to either side of the courtyard. The largest, to the right, were said to be temples to the moon and the stars, and were covered with sheets of solid silver. The walls are perfectly tapered upward and, with their niches and doorways, are excellent examples of Inca trapezoidal architecture. The fitting of the individual blocks is so precise that in some places you can't tell where one block ends and the next begins.

Opposite these chambers, on the other side of the courtyard, are smaller temples dedicated to thunder and the rainbow. Three holes have been carved through the walls of this section to the street outside, which scholars think were drains, either for sacrificial *chicha* (fermented corn beer), blood or, more mundanely, rainwater. Alternatively, they may have been speaking tubes connecting the inner temple with the outside. Another feature of this side of the complex is the floor in front of the chambers: it dates from Inca times and is carefully cobbled with pebbles.

The temple was built in the mid-15th century during the reign of the 10th *inca*, Túpac Yupanqui. After the conquest, Francisco Pizarro gave it to his brother Juan, but he was not able to enjoy it for long – Juan died in the battle at Sacsaywamán in 1536. In his will, he bequeathed Qorikancha to the Dominicans, in whose possession it has remained ever since. Today's site is a bizarre combination of Inca and colonial architecture, topped with a roof of glass and metal.

COOL FOR KIDS: THE CHIQUITY CLUB

The excellent **Chiquity Club Activity Center** (084-23-3344; www.chiquityclubcusco.com; Marquez 259; child with parents S20; 9am-1pm & 3-7pm Mon-Fri, until 8pm Sat) offers a great way for young families to decompress. The brainchild of a bilingual Waldorf-trained teacher, this multifaceted space includes covered play areas, a climbing wall and a sandbox of 'fossils.' There's also a library with English-language books, an art room, a dress-up theater and a rockin' dark mini-disco, pulsing strobes and fun tunes. The ideal age for visitors is one to nine years old. It also offers babysitting services and activity kits to go.

Around the outside of the courtyard are colonial paintings depicting the life of St Dominic, which contain several representations of dogs holding torches in their jaws. These are God's guard dogs (*dominicanus* in Latin), hence the name of this religious order.

Iglesia de Santo Domingo CHURCH
(Map p200) FREE The church of Santo Domingo is next door to Qorikancha. Less baroque and ornate than many of Cuzco's churches, it is notable for its charming paintings of archangels depicted as Andean children in jeans and T-shirts. Opening hours are erratic.

Museo del Sitio de Qorikancha MUSEUM
(Map p208; Av El Son s/n; adult/student under 26 with ISIC card S130/70; 9am-6pm Mon-Sat, 8am-1pm Sun) There are sundry moth-bitten archaeological displays interpreting Inca and pre-Inca cultures at this small, mangy, underground archaeological museum, which is accessed off Av El Sol.

Admission is with the *boleto turistico* tourist card only, which is valid for 10 days and covers 16 other sites.

Museo Quijote MUSEUM
(Map p200; www.museoelquijote.com; Galería Banco la Nacion, Calle Almagro s/n; 9am-6pm Mom-Fri, 9am-1pm Sun) FREE In a new location housed inside a bank, this privately owned museum of contemporary art houses a diverse, thoughtful collection of painting and sculpture ranging from the folksy to the macabre. There's good interpretive information about 20th-century Peruvian art history, some of it translated into English.

Activities

Scores of outdoor outfitters in Cuzco offer trekking, rafting and mountain-biking adventures, as well as mountaineering, horseback riding and paragliding. Price wars can lead to bad feelings among locals, with underpaid guides and overcrowded vehicles. The cheaper tours are liable to be the most crowded, multilingual affairs. Due to tax exemptions for new agencies, cheaper outfits also regularly change names and offices, so ask other foreign tourists for the most recent recommendations.

No company can ever be 100% recommended, but those we list are reputable outfits that have received mostly positive feedback from readers.

Trekking

The department of Cuzco is a hiker's paradise. Ecosystems range from rainforest to high alpine environments in these enormous mountain ranges. Trekkers may come upon isolated villages and ruins lost in the undergrowth. Since altitudes vary widely, it is essential to properly acclimatize before undertaking any trek.

Of course, most come to hike the famed Inca Trail to Machu Picchu. Be aware that it's not the only 'Inca trail.' What savvy tourism officials and tour operators have christened the Inca Trail is just one of dozens of footpaths that the Incas built to reach Machu Picchu, out of thousands that crisscrossed the Inca empire. Some of these overland routes are still being dug out of the jungle by archaeologists. Many more have been developed for tourism, and an ever-increasing number of trekkers are choosing them.

For more detailed hiking information, purchase an *Alternative Inca Trails Information Packet* from South American Explorers (p232). Closer to Cuzco, imaginative operators have developed multiday Sacred Valley trekking itineraries that go well off the beaten track to little-visited villages and ruins.

Other recommended treks include Lares and Ausangate and, for archaeological sites, Choquequiraou and Vilcabamba.

The best time to go trekking in the Andes or the Amazon is during the colder dry season between May and September. Make reservations for treks during high seasons several months in advance, and up to a year

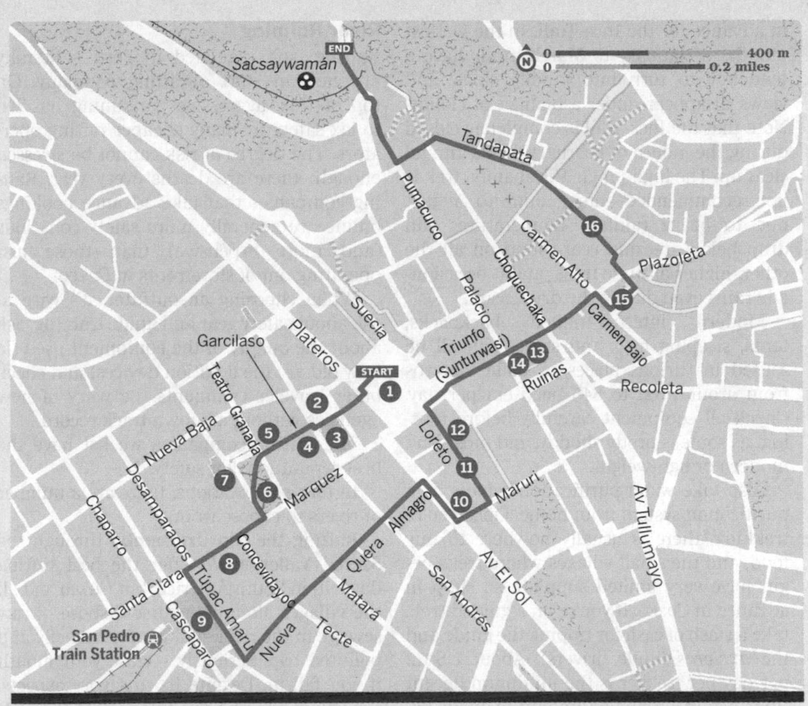

City Walk Cuzco

START PLAZA DE ARMAS
END SACSAYWAMÁN
DISTANCE 4KM
DURATION THREE HOURS, WITH STOPS

Start from the stunning **1 Plaza de Armas** (p199), stroll up Calle del Medio and head across **2 Plaza Regocijo**. On your left, a beautiful **3 building** houses restaurants and boutiques. Head up Calle Garcilaso, named for the Inca chronicler Garcilaso de la Vega, whose childhood home now houses the **4 Museo Histórico Regional** (p206). It sits amid colonial mansions; **5 Hotel los Marqueses** (p220) is particularly stunning.

On Sundays, Quechua-speaking country folk meet in **6 Plaza San Francisco**. Drop into the **7 church and museum of San Francisco** if you're so inclined. Past the colonial archway is the **8 church and convent of Santa Clara**. If it's open, peek inside at the mirrors, used in colonial times to entice curious indigenous people into the church for worship.

Just beyond is bustling **9 Mercado San Pedro** (p230). Order a juice, then step out onto Calle Nueva and follow to Av El Sol opposite the **10 Palacio de Justicia**. Head up Maruri and take a left into **11 Loreto**, which has Inca walls on both sides. The west wall belongs to Amaruqancha (Courtyard of the Serpents). The east wall is one of the oldest in Cuzco, belonging to the Aclla-huasi (House of the Chosen Women). Post conquest, it became part of the **12 closed convent of Santa Catalina**.

Return to the Plaza de Armas and turn right up Triunfo (Sunturwasi) and into Hatun-rumiyoc, another alley, named after the **13 12-sided stone**. This belongs to a wall of the palace of the sixth *inca*, Roca, which now houses the **14 Museo de Arte Religioso** (p207).

Hatunrumiyoc ends at Choquechaca. From here it's a short puff up to **15 Plaza San Blas**, Cuzco's bohemian HQ. Head left on **16 Tandapata** for classic cobblestones. Inca irrigation channels run down ancient stairways, and rock carvings adorn walls and stones in the path. Last, forge uphill to Sacsaywamán.

in advance for the Inca Trail. In the wettest months of January to March, trails have a tendency to turn into muddy slogs, and views disappear under a blanket of clouds. Note that the Inca Trail is completely closed during the month of February for its annual cleanup. The high jungle Vilcabamba trek is not recommended outside June to August due to heavy rainfall. Temperatures can drop below freezing year-round on all the other, higher-altitude treks, and it occasionally rains even during the dry season.

Modern internal-framed backpacks, tents, sleeping bags and stoves can all be rented in various places in Calle Plateros from around S21 to S45 per item per day. Check all equipment carefully before renting, as some is pretty shoddy, and most isn't modern or lightweight.

Also take water-purification tablets or a purification system from home. Once you're trekking, there is usually nowhere to buy food, and the small villages where treks begin have very limited supplies, so shop in advance in Cuzco. If you're on a guided trek, take a stash of cash for tipping the guide and the *arrieros* (mule drivers). About US$12 per day per trekker is the minimum decent tip to a guide; a similar amount to divide between *arrieros* is appropriate.

★ Apu's Peru HIKING
(Map p208; ☎084-23-3691; www.apus-peru.com; Cuichipunco 366) A recommended outfitter for the Inca Trail also offering conventional tours. Responsible and popular with travelers.

Eco Trek Peru HIKING
(☎084-24-7286; www.ecotrekperu.com) A trekking specialist.

X-Treme Tourbulencia HIKING
(Map p200; ☎084-22-4362; www.x-tremetourbulencia.com; Plateros 364) A recommended Cuzco-based tour operator offering multisport access to Machu Picchu via Santa Teresa and the Inca Jungle Trail. With multilingual guides.

Llama Path HIKING
(Map p200; ☎084-24-0822; www.llamapath.com; San Juan de Dios 250) Friendly, small trekking company that has received good reports from some travelers.

Peru Treks HIKING
(Map p208; ☎084-22-2722; www.perutreks.com; Av Pardo 540) Offers hiking tours to Machu Picchu.

River Running

Rafting isn't regulated in Peru – literally anyone can start a rafting company. On top of this, aggressive bargaining has led to lax safety by many cheaper rafting operators. The degree of risk cannot be stressed enough: there are deaths every year. Rafting companies that take advance bookings online are generally more safety conscious (and more expensive) than those just operating out of storefronts in Cuzco.

When choosing an outfitter, it's wise to ask about safety gear and guide training, ask about the quality of the equipment used (ie how old are the flotation devices) and check other traveler comments. Be wary of new agencies without a known track record.

The rafting companies we list have the best reputations for safety.

In terms of locations, there are a number of rivers to choose from.

Rafting the **Río Urubamba** through the Sacred Valley *could* offer the best rafting day trip in South America, but Cuzco and all the villages along its course dispose of raw sewage in the river, making for a smelly and polluted trip. Seriously – close your mouth if you fall in. Despite its unsavory aspects, the Ollantaytambo to Chilca (class II to III) section is surprisingly popular, offering 1½ hours of gentle rafting with only two rapids of note. Huarán and Huambutio to Pisac are other pollution-affected sections.

There are a variety of cleaner sections south of Cuzco on the upper Urubamba (also known as the Vilcanota), including the popular Chuquicahuana run (class III to IV+; class V+ in the rainy season). Another less-frenetic section is the fun and scenic Cusipata to Quiquihana (mainly class II to III). In the rainy season, these two sections are often combined. Closer to Cuzco, Pampa to Huambutio (class I to II) is a beautiful section, ideal for small children (three years and over) as an introduction to rafting.

Río Santa Teresa offers spectacular rafting in the gorge between the towns of Santa Teresa and Santa María, and downstream as far as Quillabamba. One word of warning: the section from Cocalmayo Hot Springs to Santa María consists of almost nonstop class IV to V rapids in a deep, inaccessible canyon. It should only be run with highly reputable operators, such as local experts Cola de Mono (p264). Be very aware, if considering a trip here, that guiding this section safely is beyond the powers of inexperienced (cheaper) rafting guides. This is not the place to economize. It's not a bad idea to raft another section in the area with your chosen operator before even considering it.

Run from May to November, the **Río Apurímac** offers three- to 10-day trips through deep gorges and protected rainforest. Apurímac features exhilarating rapids (classes IV and V) and wild, remote scenery with deep gorges. Sightings of condors and even pumas have been recorded. Four-day trips are the most relaxed and avoid the busier campsites, although three-day trips are more commonly offered. Camping is on sandy beaches, which have become increasingly overused. Sand flies can be a nuisance. Make sure your outfitter cleans up the campsite and practices a leave-no-trace ethic.

An even wilder expedition, the 10- to 12-day trip along the demanding **Río Tambopata** can only be run from May to October. The trip starts in the Andes, north of Lake Titicaca, and descends through the heart of the Parque Nacional Bahuaje-Sonene deep in the Amazon jungle. Just getting to the put-in from Cuzco is a two-day drive. The first days on the river are full of technically demanding rapids (classes III and IV) in wild Andean scenery, and the trip finishes with a couple of gentle floating days in the rainforest. Tapirs, capybara, caiman, giant otters and jaguars have all been seen by keen-eyed boaters.

Rivers further from Cuzco are days away from help in the event of illness or accident. It's essential to book a top-notch outfitter employing highly experienced rafting guides with first-aid certification and knowledge of swift-water rescue techniques.

Amazonas Explorer RAFTING
(☎084-25-2846; www.amazonas-explorer.com; Av Collasuyu 910 Miravalle) A professional international operator with top-quality equipment and guides, offering rafting trips on the Ríos Apurímac and Tambopata.

Apumayo RAFTING
(Map p200; ☎084-24-6018; www.apumayo.com; Jirón Ricardo Palma Ñ-11, Urb Santa Monica) A professional outfitter that takes advance international bookings for Río Tambopata trips. Also equipped to take travelers with disabilities.

River Explorers RAFTING
(Map p200; ☎084-26-0926; www.riverexplorers.com; Urb Kennedy A, B-15) This popular outfitter runs all sorts of sections, including trips of up to six days on the Río Apurímac.

Mayuc RAFTING
(Map p200; ☎084-24-2824; www.mayuc.com; Portal Confiturías 211) This monster operator, very popular with bargain hunters, dwarfs the competition.

Mountain Biking

Mountain-biking tours are a growing industry in Cuzco, and the local terrain is superb. Rental bikes are poor quality and it is most common to find *rígida* (single suspension) models, which can make for bone-chattering downhills. Good new or secondhand bikes are not easy to buy in Cuzco either. If you're a serious mountain biker, consider bringing your own bike from home. Selling it in Cuzco is eminently viable.

If you're an experienced rider, some awesome rides are quickly and easily accessible by public transportation. Take the Pisac bus (stash your bike on top) and ask to be let off at **Abra de Ccorao**. From here, you can turn right and make your way back to Cuzco via a series of cart tracks and single track; halfway down is a jump park constructed by local aficionados. This section has many variations and is known as **Yuncaypata**. Eventually, whichever way you go, you'll end up in Cuzco's southern suburbs, from where you can easily flag down a taxi to get you home.

If you head off the other side of the pass, to the left of the road, you'll find fast-flowing single track through a narrow valley, which makes it difficult to get lost. It brings you out on the highway in Ccorao. From here, follow the road through a flat section then a series of bends. Just as the valley widens out, turn left past a farmhouse steeply downhill to your left and into challenging single track through a narrow valley, including a hairy river crossing and some tricky, steep, rocky, loose descents at the end, reaching the village of Taray. From here it's a 10-minute ride along the river to Pisac, where you can catch a bus back to Cuzco.

Many longer trips are possible, but a professionally qualified guide and a support vehicle are necessary. The partly paved road down from **Abra Málaga to Santa María**, though not at all technical, is a must for any cyclist. It is part of the Inca Jungle Trail, offered by many Cuzco operators. **Maras to Salinas** is a great little mission. The **Lares Valley** offers challenging single track, which can be accessed from Cuzco in a long day. If heading to Manu in the Amazon Basin, you can break up the long bus journey by biking from **Tres Cruces to La Unión** – a beautiful, breathtaking downhill ride – or you could go all the way down by bike. The outfitters of Manu trips can arrange bicycle rental and guides. The descent to the **Río Apurímac** makes a great burn, as does the journey to the **Río Tambopata**, which boasts a descent of 3500m in five hours. A few bikers attempt the 500km-plus trip all the way to Puerto Maldonado, a great hot and sweaty challenge.

Gravity Peru ADVENTURE TOUR
(Map p200; ☎084-22-8032; www.gravityperu.com; Santa Catalina Ancha 398) Allied with well-known Gravity Bolivia, this professionally run operator is the only one offering double-suspension bikes for day trips. Its 'Back Door Machu Picchu' tour (via adventure options and biking) has become a hugely popular alternative to accessing the ruins. Highly recommended.

Amazonas Explorer ADVENTURE TOUR
(☎084-25-2846; www.amazonas-explorer.com; Av Collasuyu 910, Miravalle) Offers excellent two- to 10-day mountain-biking adventures; great for families, with kids' bikes available.

Party Bike ADVENTURE TOUR
(Map p200; ☎084-24-0399; www.partybiketravel.com; Carmen Alto 246) Traveler recommended, with downhills, tours to the valley and through Cuzco.

Horseback Riding

Most agencies can arrange a morning or afternoon's riding. Alternatively, you can walk to Sacsaywamán, where many ranches are located, and negotiate your own terms. Choose carefully, however, as horses may be in a sorry state. Select agencies will offer multiday trips to the area around Limatambo, and there are some first-rate ranches with highly trained, high-stepping thoroughbred Peruvian *paso* horses in Urubamba.

Bird-Watching

Serious birders should definitely get a hold of *Birds of the High Andes,* by Jon Fjeldså and Niels Krabbe. One of the best birding trips is from Ollantaytambo to Santa Teresa or Quillabamba, over Abra Málaga. This provides a fine cross section of habitats from 4600m to below 1000m. A good local field guide is *The Birds of Machu Picchu,* by Barry Walker.

Other Activities

For a post-trek splurge, a number of spas offer massage services, including **Samana Spa** (Map p200; ☎084-23-3721; www.samana-spa.com; Tecsecocha 536; ⊙10am-7pm Mon-Sat). Cheap massages touted in the street might get much more *intimate* than expected.

Sacred Valley Via Ferrata & Zipline ADVENTURE SPORTS
(☎974-360-269; www.naturavive.com; via ferrata or zipline per person S165, both S255) 'Iron Way' in Italian, this climb features a series of ladders, holds and bridges built into a sheer rock face in a stunning Sacred Valley setting. There's a 300m vertical ascent, a heart-hammering hanging bridge and a 100m rappel. A zipline is accessed by a 40-minute hike. Activities run three to four hours. Includes transfers to Cuzco or Urubamba, climbing and lunch.

First developed in the Italian Alps in WWII, it's a way for reasonably fit non-rock climbers to have some adrenaline-pumping fun. It was constructed and is operated by rock-climbing and high-mountain professionals. Its newest addition are clear 'skylodge suites' which are essentially capsules bolted to sheer rock that you can sleep (or stay awake) in.

Action Valley ADVENTURE SPORTS
(☎084-24-0835; www.actionvalley.com; ⊙9am-5pm Sun-Fri, closed mid-Jan–mid-Feb) A terror for acrophobes and a blast for kids and juvenile adults. Offerings include paintball (S77), a 10m climbing wall (S34), a 122m bungee jump (S253) and a bungee slingshot (S219). It's also possible to go paragliding (S216) from the *mirador* (lookout) of Racchi. The park is 11km outside Cuzco on Poroy road. Its **booking office** (Map p200; Santa Teresa 325) is in Cuzco.

Courses

Cuzco is one of the best places in South America to study Spanish. Shop around – competition is fierce and students benefit with free cultural and social activities. Salsa lessons and cooking nights are more or less ubiquitous.

The standard deal is 20 hours of classes per week, either individual or in groups of up to four people. Most schools will also let you pay by the hour or study more or less intensively. Rates average S15 per hour for group lessons and S29 per hour for private lessons.

Visit your school on a Friday to get tested and assigned to a group for a Monday start, or show up any time to start individual lessons. All schools can arrange family homestays and volunteer opportunities.

★Marcelo Batata Cooking Class COOKING COURSE
(Map p200; www.cuzcodining.com; Calle Palacio 135; courses S240; ⊙2pm) If you've fallen for Peruvian cooking, this four-hour course is a worthwhile foray. A fully stocked market pantry demystifies some of the exotic flavors of the region and the kitchen setup is comfortable. Includes appetizers, a pisco (Peruvian grape brandy) tasting and a main course. In English, Spanish or Portuguese. Accommodates vegetarians.

Amigos LANGUAGE COURSE
(☎084-24-2292; www.spanishcusco.com; Zaguan del Cielo B-23) A long-established nonprofit school with an admirable public-service record.

Excel Language Center LANGUAGE COURSE
(Map p200; ☎084-23-5298; www.excel-spanishlanguageprograms-peru.org; Cruz Verde 336) Spanish-language course, highly recommended for its professionalism.

Fairplay LANGUAGE COURSE
(Map p208; ☎984-78-9252; www.fairplay-peru.org; Pasaje Zavaleta C-5) A unique nonprofit NGO, Fairplay trains Peruvian single mothers to provide Spanish lessons and homestays. Students pay two-thirds of their class fees directly to their teachers. Individual classes only, priced according to the teacher's level of experience.

Proyecto Peru LANGUAGE COURSE
(Map p200; ☎084-24-0278; www.proyectoperucentre.org; Calle Seite Cuartones 290) Offers Quechua and business or medical Spanish. In a new downtown location.

San Blas Spanish School LANGUAGE COURSE
(Map p200; ☎084-24-7898; www.spanishschoolperu.com; Carmen Bajo 224) Students enjoy the informal teaching here, in tune with the school's location in the heart of bohemian San Blas.

Tours

Cuzco has hundreds of registered travel agencies, so ask other travelers for recommendations. Many of the small agencies clustered around Procuradores and Plateros earn commissions selling trips run by other outfitters, which can lead to organizational mix-ups. If the travel agency also sells ponchos, changes money and has an internet cabin in the corner, chances are it's not operating your tour.

Standard tours often travel in large groups and can be rushed. Classic options include a half-day tour of the city and/or nearby ruins, a half-day trip to the Sunday markets at Pisac or Chinchero and a full-day tour of the Sacred Valley (eg Pisac, Ollantaytambo and Chinchero). It's perfectly feasible to do these at your own pace with a licensed taxi driver or public transportation.

Agents also offer expensive Machu Picchu tours that include transportation, admission tickets to the archaeological site, an English-speaking guide and lunch. Since you only get to spend a few hours at the ruins, it's more enjoyable (not to mention much cheaper) to DIY and hire a guide at Machu Picchu.

Manu Expeditions (p216) and Manu Nature Tours (p458) also go into the jungle.

★Journey Experience ADVENTURE TOUR
(JOEX; ☎084-24-5642; www.joextravel.com; Av Tupac Amaru V-2-A, Progreso) A recommended outfitter for hiking and cultural activities.

Antipode ADVENTURE TOUR
(Map p200; ☎970-440-448; www.antipode-travel.com; Choquechaca 229) An attentive, French-run outfit offering classic tours, treks and shorter local adventure outings.

Chaski Ventura CULTURAL TOUR
(Map p208; ☎084-23-3952; www.chaskiventura.com; Manco Cápac 517) Pioneer of alternative and community tourism, with quality

TAXI TOURS

If you are short on time to see the sights outside Cuzco, consider taking a taxi tour. If you have two or more people, they can be a particularly good deal, and also allow you to take your time (or not) visiting various ruins and markets. From Cuzco, a tour of the Sacred Valley (possibly including Pisac, Ollantaytambo, Chinchero, Maras and Moray) runs around S180 (for the whole car); to the Southern Valley (with options to Tipón, Piquillacta and Raqchi) costs around S270.

One reliable option is **Virgin Estrella Taxi Tours** (☎974-955-374, 973-195-551) in Cuzco.

itineraries and guides, also involved in community development. Offers package trips to the jungle, overnights in Sacred Valley communities and Machu Picchu. French, English and Spanish spoken.

Fertur TOUR
(☎084-22-1304; www.fertur-travel.com; Calle Simon Bolivar F23) Local office of long-established, very reliable agency for flights and all conventional tours. Highly recommended by readers. The office is located near the bus terminal.

Milla Turismo TOUR
(Map p208; ☎084-23-1710; www.millaturismo.com; Av Pardo 800) Reputable conventional tour operator with travel agency services and recommended private tours with knowledgeable drivers.

Respons CULTURAL TOUR
(Responsible Travel Peru; Map p200; ☎084-23-3903; www.responsibletravelperu.com; Suyt'u Qhatu 777-B) High-end sustainable tour operator working with community development in the Sacred Valley. Offers a tour of a weaving community near Pisac and chocolate and coffee tours on the Inca Jungle Trail. Available in English, Spanish and French.

SAS Travel TOUR
(Map p200; ☎084-24-9194; www.sastravelperu.com; Calle Garcilaso 270) A direct operator with local owners. Offers high-end package tours to Machu Picchu, Inca Trail treks, jungle travel and Cuzco tours. While there's complaints that this outfitter charges more than the competition, traveler satisfaction is generally high.

SATO TOUR
(Map p208; ☎084-26-1505; www.southamericatravelsonline.com; Matara 437, interior-G) A reputable European agency working with local operators for trekking, hiking and rafting, also a last-minute specialist.

Turismo Caith CULTURAL TOUR
(☎084-23-3595; www.caith.org; Centro Yanapanakusun, Urb Ucchullo Alto, N4, Pasaje Santo Toribio) Leader in community tourism as well as standard single and multiday trips. Participants can help with educational projects.

Manu Expeditions ADVENTURE TOUR
(☎084-22-5990; www.manuexpeditions.com; Jr Los Geranios 2-G , Urb Mariscal Gamarra) Destinations include Manu Biosphere Reserve and horseback riding around the Sacred Valley.

Guides

Asociación de Guías Oficiales de Turismo GUIDED TOUR
(Agotur; Map p200; ☎084-24-9758; www.agoturcusco.com; Heladeros 157, 34-F) The official tourism guide association is a good way for travelers to contact guides.

Adam Weintraub GUIDED TOUR
(www.photoexperience.net) A native of Seattle, Adam has many years' experience in Peru and guides custom high-end photography tours and workshops over all of Peru, as well as shorter trips out of Cuzco.

Alain Machaca Cruz GUIDED TOUR
(☎984-056-635; www.alternativeincatrails.com) Recommended visits to the village of Paruro where you can make *chicha* (fermented corn beer) or see *cuy* (guinea pig) farms, multiday hikes to Choquequirao and other regional hikes. Quechua and English spoken.

Leo Garcia GUIDED TOUR
(☎984-70-2933, 984-75-4022; leogacia@hotmail.com) Personable, passionate and supremely knowledgeable about all things Inca, specializing in archaeology, history and anthropology.

Raul Castelo GUIDED TOUR
(☎084-24-3234, 984-692-270; www.topturperu.com) A recommended guide with his own transportation. Specializes in customized tours to the Sacred Valley, Machu Picchu, Cuzco, Cuzco–Puno and Lares.

Festivals & Events

Cuzco and the surrounding highlands celebrate many lively fiestas and holidays. In addition to national holidays, the most crowded times are around local festivals, when you should book all accommodations well in advance.

El Señor de los Temblores CULTURAL
(Lord of the Earthquakes) This procession on the Monday before Easter dates to the earthquake of 1650.

Crucifix Vigil FESTIVAL
(May 2 or 3) At this time, a Crucifix Vigil is held on all hillsides with crosses atop them.

Q'oyoriti CULTURAL
Less well-known than June's spectacular Inti Raymi are the more traditional Andean rites of this festival, which is held at the foot of Ausangate the Tuesday before Corpus Christi, in late May or early June.

Corpus Christi RELIGION

Held on the ninth Thursday after Easter, Corpus Christi usually occurs in early June and features fantastic religious processions and celebrations in the cathedral.

Inti Raymi CULTURAL

(Festival of the Sun) Cuzco's most important festival is held on June 24. It attracts tourists from all over Peru and the world, and the whole city celebrates in the streets. The festival culminates in a re-enactment of the Inca winter-solstice festival at Sacsaywamán. Despite its commercialization, it's still worth seeing the street dances and parades, as well as the pageantry at Sacsaywamán.

Santuranticuy Artisan Crafts Fair FESTIVAL

A crafts fair is held in the Plaza de Armas on December 24 (Christmas Eve).

Sleeping

Cuzco has hundreds of hotels of all types, and some of the highest room rates in Peru. Peak season is between June and August, especially during the 10 days before Inti Raymi on June 24 and during Fiestas Patrias (Independence Days) on July 28 and 29. Book in advance for these dates.

Prices are market-driven and vary dramatically according to the season and demand. Rates quoted are for high season.

Though the Plaza de Armas is the most central area, there are few bargains there. Accommodations along Av El Sol tend to be bland, expensive and set up for tour groups. Hilly San Blas has the best views and is deservedly popular. There are also many options west of the Plaza de Armas around Plaza Regocijo, in the commercial area towards the Mercado Central, and downhill from the center in the streets northeast of Av El Sol.

Many of Cuzco's guesthouses and hotels are located in charming colonial buildings with interior courtyards, which can echo resoundingly with noise from other guests or the street outside. Old stone buildings are notorious for having poor wi-fi connections – often it can only be accessed in a lobby. Many places that offer breakfast start serving as early as 5am to accommodate those heading out on tour. For this reason, early check-ins and check-outs are the rule.

With advance notice, most midrange and top-end places will pick you up for free at the airport, the train station or the bus terminal.

Inquire about hot water for showers, which may be sporadic. It helps to avoid showering at peak times, and it's always worth telling reception if you're having trouble – they may simply need to flick a switch or hook up a new gas canister.

Hotels claim to offer 24-hour hot-water showers, and midrange and above places generally include satellite TV. The top hotels all feature rooms with heating and telephone; exceptions are noted in the review. All top-end and some midrange hotels have oxygen tanks available, at a price, for altitude sufferers.

Cuzco's luxury hotels are usually booked solid during high season. Reserving through a travel agency or via the hotel's website may result in better rates.

Central Cuzco

Many of the side streets that climb northwest away from the plaza toward Sacsaywamán (especially Tigre, Tecsecocha, Suecia, Kiskapata, Resbalosa and 7 Culebras) are bursting with cheap crash pads. High-end hotels on the plaza offer premium rates for location.

★Ecopackers HOSTEL $

(Map p200; ☎084-23-1800; www.ecopackersperu.com; Santa Teresa 375; dm S35-52, d/ste S120/165; @📶) Thought has been put into this big backpacker haven that's a stone's throw from Plaza Regocijo. One of the all-inclusives (with bar, pool room and sunbathing), it ups the ante by being clean, friendly and service-minded. There's lovely wicker lounges in the courtyard and the sturdy beds are extra-long. There's also 24-hour security.

Pariwana HOSTEL $

(Map p200; ☎084-23-3751; www.pariwana-hostel.com; Av Mesón de la Estrella 136; dm S22-42, d/tr S150/195; @📶) Resembling spring break, this notably clean, newer hostel is among the better ones, filled with uni-types lounging on poufs and playing ping-pong in the courtyard of a huge colonial. Wi-fi connection comes in the common areas. Beds in newish dorms are well-spaced and the penthouse suite is well worth the splurge. The chic bar is invite-only. With an on-site travel agency.

Intro Hostel HOSTEL $

(Map p200; ☎084-223-869; www.introhosteles.com; Cuesta Santa Ana 515; dm S25-40, d S99, all incl breakfast; 📶) From the owners of 1900 Backpackers in Lima, this old colonial offers good service, an ample courtyard and nice, clean rooms. There's a covered outdoor cooking area, billiards and travel agency services. The reception operates 24 hours, take a taxi if it's late, since it's not in the most secure neighborhood.

Dragonfly HOSTEL $

(Map p200; www.dragonflyhostels.com; Seite Cuartones 245; dm S30-35, d/tr S95/120, s/d/tr without bathroom S48/90/99;) One of several 16th-century colonial buildings redone in candy colors, this hostel is French-run. Craft beer is made on-site, making it popular for an after-hours rendezvous at the bar. Guests have kitchen use and there's weekly barbecues. With friendly staff.

Wild Rover HOSTEL $

(Map p208; 084-22-1515; www.wildroverhostels.com; Matara 261; dm S21-38, d S90, all incl breakfast;) A clean and organized hostel attracting both Peruvian and internationals. There's a guarded entrance, women's dorm option and even a room with hairdryers and mirrors for party prep (sorry, women only). There's also a spacious cafe-bar and a smart locked cabinet with plugs for phones. Avoid rooms near the bar if you're turning in early.

Hostal Suecia I HOTEL $

(Map p200; 084-23-3282; www.hostalsuecia1.com; Suecia 332; s/d/tr incl breakfast S90/120/150;) Most rooms in this pint-sized guesthouse are very basic, but location and staff are fabulous and there's a sociable, stony, indoor courtyard. The two newer doubles on the top floor (311 and 312) are good value.

Milhouse HOSTEL $

(Map p200; 084-23-2151; www.milhousehostel.com; Quera 270; dm S29-38, d/tr S135/155;) Booming with backpackers, this busy colonial has all the standard features of a Cuzco hostel: beanbag chairs, ping-pong, travel agent service and happy hours. Rooms can seem a bit airless, but sports fans will appreciate the coordinated trips to local football matches. On a noisy street.

Mama Simona HOSTEL $

(Map p200; 084-26-0408; www.mamasimona.com; Calle Ceniza 364; dm S30-36, d with/without bathroom S90/72;) Styled for hipsters, with a crushed velvet sofa and oddball decor. Beds have nice down covers and the shared kitchen with picnic tables is undoubtedly cute. Stylish, comfortable and clean, it's two blocks northeast of Plaza San Francisco.

Albergue Municipal HOSTEL $

(Map p200; 084-25-2506; alberguegobierno-cusco@hotmail.com; Kiskapata 240; dm/d S15/40;) The Cuzco answer to the YMCA, it's a good, friendly choice for the tight of budget. Immaculate installations offer plenty of space, great views, kitchen access (breakfast only) and laundry facilities. All rooms have shared bathrooms. Look for its Facebook page.

Hospedaje Monte Horeb GUESTHOUSE $

(Map p200; 084-23-6775; montehorebcusco@yahoo.com; San Juan de Dios 260, 2nd fl; s/d/tr incl breakfast S84/120/165;) With an inner-courtyard entry and an inviting balcony, this serene and well-cared-for option has big, old-fashioned rooms, a curious mix of furnishings and beds as firm as an *intihuatana* stone. Thick blankets mean to make up for the lack of heat.

WalkOn Inn HOSTEL $

(Map p200; 084-23-5065; www.walkoninn.com.pe; Suecia 504; dm S25, s/d S100/110, s/d without bathroom S90/100;) A five-minute puff up from the Plaza de Armas, this quietish hostel has views but rather indifferent service. Breakfast is not included.

Hostal Suecia II HOTEL $

(Map p200; 084-23-9757; www.hostalsuecia2cusco.com; Tecsecocha 465; s/d/tr S60/80/100, s/d/tr without bathroom S50/60/80;) This long-standing backpacker favorite continues to offer excellent value with central location, friendly owners, a light, bright, flowery patio, decent rooms and a book-lending library. Its hostess, Señora Yolanda, has been here 20 years.

Hitchhikers HOSTEL $

(Map p200; 084-26-0079; www.hhikersperu.com; Saphi 440; dm/d S28/70;) In a very central location, this hostel is a bit rundown with sloping floors but it's ship-shape and clean. Rooms are on the cold side. With helpful staff.

Hostal Andrea GUESTHOUSE $

(Map p200; 084-23-6713; salemrey@hotmail.com; Cuesta Santa Ana 514; s/d S35/45, s/d without bathroom S13/30;) Cuzco's cheapest, this place is basic, but the kind, unassuming staff make it a reader favorite. Wi-fi is available only in the living room.

★ Niños Hotel HOTEL $$

(Map p200; 084-23-1424; www.ninoshotel.com; Meloc 442; s without bathroom S77, d with/without bathroom S170/155, tr S244;) Long beloved and highly recommended, this hotel is run by a Dutch-founded nonprofit foundation that serves underprivileged children in Cuzco. It is a rambling colonial with sunny courtyard. Refurbished rooms are bordered with bright trim and feature plaid throws and portable heaters. In the coldest months there's hot-water bottles to tuck in bed. A second branch is located at Fierro 476.

The public cafeteria features homemade cakes and breads as well as box lunches. Breakfast is not included.

Tierra Viva HOTEL **$$**
(Map p200; ☎084-60-1317; www.tierravivahoteles.com; Saphi 766; s/d incl breakfast S281/312; @📶) With modern stylings and notable service, this Peruvian hotel chain offers four comfortable options in downtown Cuzco. Doubles sport hardwood floors or Berber carpets, white linens and colorful throws. Buffet breakfast is available from 5am on. The location of this branch, back from the action, makes it a good compromise between central and peaceful.

Other branches are located at Centro (Map p208; ☎084-26-3300; Cruz Verde 390; d incl breakfast S255; @📶), San Blas (Map p200; ☎084-23-070; Carmen Alto 194; d incl breakfast S255; @📶) and Plaza de Armas (Map p200; ☎084-24-5858; Calle Suecia 345; d incl breakfast S320; 📶).

Hotel Arqueólogo BOUTIQUE HOTEL **$$**
(Map p200; ☎084-23-2569; www.hotelarqueologo.com; Pumacurco 408; d incl breakfast S337; @📶) Feeling luxurious but also lived-in, this antique French-owned guesthouse gives a real feel for Cuzco, down to the Inca stonework. Tasteful rooms with original murals and tapestries overlook a vast courtyard paved in river stones. Relax on the back lawn or sip a complimentary pisco sour in the fireplace lounge. The sale of local weavings helps fund public libraries. French, English and German are spoken. Superior rooms (S507) are a significant upgrade.

Andenes de Saphi HOTEL **$$**
(Map p200; ☎084-22-7561; www.andenesdesaphi.com; Saphi 848; s/d/tr S170/192/223; 📶) At the far end of Saphi, where the city starts to become more rural, this dependable, modern hotel has a rustic wooden construction with skylights and murals in every room.

Hostal Corihuasi GUESTHOUSE **$$**
(Map p200; ☎084-23-2233; www.corihuasi.com; Suecia 561; s/d/tr incl breakfast S151/183/216) A brisk walk uphill from the main plaza, this family-feel guesthouse inhabits a maze-like colonial building with postcard views. Amply sized rooms are outfitted in a warm, rustic style with alpaca-wool blankets, hand-woven rugs and solid wooden furnishings. Room 1 is the most in demand for its wraparound windows, ideal for soaking up panoramic sunsets. Airport transfer included.

El Balcón Hostal HOTEL **$$**
(Map p200; ☎084-23-6738; www.balconcusco.com; Tambo de Montero 222; s/d/tr incl breakfast S185/232/448; @📶) A reader favorite, this renovated 17th-century building features regional antiquities and 16 plain yet pleasant rooms, all with balconies, phone and TV. The garden blooms with fuchsias and offers great views over Cuzco.

Piccola Locanda GUESTHOUSE **$$**
(Map p200; ☎084-23-6775; www.piccolalocanda.com; Kiskapata 215; d with/without bathroom S170/140; @📶) A colorful Italian-owned lodging that's snug, with quixotic, bright rooms, plaza views and a cave-like cushioned lounge. Has an in-house responsible-travel operator, and sponsors community projects. Entrance is on Resbalosa.

Tambo del Arriero HOTEL **$$**
(Map p200; ☎084-26-0709; www.tambodelarriero.com; Nueva Alta 484; s/d/ste incl breakfast S278/371/464; 📶) A spacious and quiet courtyard hotel. Rooms are bordered with floral accents, with heated towel racks and down duvets. Some feature bathtubs. Breakfast comes buffet-style and it also offers free walking tours. If you like your space it's good value, though the neighborhood remains up-and-coming.

Midori HOTEL **$$**
(Map p200; ☎084-24-8144; www.midori-cusco.com; Ataúd 204; s/d/tr incl breakfast S240/310/390; @📶) Popular with small tour groups, this little hotel is classic and comfortable. Enormous rooms feature a living area, brocade fabrics and firm beds. Locally recommended, with some Japanese spoken.

Teatro Inka B&B GUESTHOUSE **$$**
(Map p200; ☎084-24-7372, in Lima 01-976-0523; www.teatroinka.com; Teatro 391; s/d/tr incl breakfast S145/190/225; @📶) An array of dark but decent doubles sit around an interior courtyard. While it isn't outstanding, it's inexpensive for a midrange option. The penthouse suite is well worth splashing out on.

Hotel los Marqueses HOTEL $$
(Map p200; ☎084-26-4249; www.hotel-marqueses.com; Calle Garcilaso 256; s/d/tr incl breakfast from S216/278/340; 📶) Romance pervades this colonial villa, built in the 16th century by Spanish conquistadors. Classic features include *escuela cuzqueña* (Cuzco school) paintings, courtyard fountains and balconies looking out on the cathedral on the Plaza de Armas. Rooms are large and airy, with some brass beds and carved wooden doors. Some have split-level sleeping areas and skylights. Most guests come on package tours. Wi-fi is available only on the patio.

Loreto Boutique Hotel HOTEL $$
(Map p200; ☎084-22-6352; www.loretoboutiquehotel.com; Loreto 115; s/d/tr incl breakfast S263/324/386) Maybe you're paying for the plaza location, since 'boutique' is an overstatement here. Dimly lit in daytime, Loreto has well-heeled, snug rooms bathed in neutrals. The best features are the four rooms with surviving Inca walls.

Samana Spa B&B B&B $$
(Map p200; ☎084-23-3721; www.samana-spa.com; Calle Teqsecocha 536; s/d S250/300; 📶) This spa and small hotel occupies a colonial building with stone walls and open beam ceilings. Ample rooms feature flat-screen TVs and electric heaters, but their best features are the big windows and private terraces to take in sweeping views over the tiled rooftops. Service could be smoother.

Los Angeles B&B HOTEL $$
(Map p200; ☎084-26-1101; www.losangelescusco.com; Tecsecocha 474; s/d/tr incl breakfast S110/140/150; @📶) Ambient and cheap, this old colonial features worn rooms with gold bedspreads, gelatinous mattresses and dark, carved furniture around a pleasant central courtyard with geraniums.

★ **Inkaterra La Casona** BOUTIQUE HOTEL $$$
(Map p200; ☎in Lima 01-610-0400; www.lacasona.info; Atocsaycuchi 616; stes incl breakfast from S1292; @📶) Hitting the perfect balance of cozy and high style, this renovated grand colonial in tiny Plazoleta Nazarenas is simply debonair. Rustic meets majestic with original features like oversized carved doors, rough-hewn beams and stone fireplaces, enhanced with radiant floors, glittering candelabras, plush divans and gorgeous Andean textiles.

Even though the TV is tucked away, tech isn't far with laptop loans and iPod docks. Service is impeccable and highly personal.

★ **Casa Cartagena** BOUTIQUE HOTEL $$$
(Map p200; ☎in Lima 01-242-3147; www.casacartagena.com; Pumacurco 336; stes from S927; @📶🏊) Fusing modern with colonial, this Italian-owned boutique hotel is dripping in style. Its 16 suites feature walls with oversized stripes, king-sized beds, iPod docks, bouquets of long-stemmed roses and enormous bathtubs lit by candles. There's a lovely on-site spa and room service is free.

Management boasts that both Neruda and Che Guevara bedded down in this historic mansion, actually a modest pension half a century ago: no word on how their politics fit in now.

La Lune BOUTIQUE HOTEL $$$
(Map p200; ☎984-347-070; www.onesuitehotelcusco.com; San Agustín 275; d incl breakfast S1081-1670; @📶) Christened the anti-hotel, it's hard to get more exclusive than this: a two-suite hotel with 24-hour concierge service from its French owner, Artur. He wants you to relax. So stays also include drinks from a full bar and a professional massage under a stained-glass window. So far, it has been a hit with visiting celebrities and diplomats.

Suites are luxuriant, with tasteful modern decor, organic bedding and an optional bed for Fido. Each suite takes a maximum of two guests; the pricier option comes with Jacuzzi (filled with rose petals at your bidding).

El Mercado de Tunqui DESIGN HOTEL $$$
(Map p200; ☎084-58-2640; www.elmercadohotel.com; Seite Cuartones 306; d/ste incl breakfast S918/1109; @📶) Modern and fresh meets colonial in this playful design hotel adorned with painted rocking horses and market carts. Activity centers on an open stone courtyard with loungers and evening bonfires. Large 2nd-floor rooms feature radiant heat – a luxury in these parts – as well as fireplaces. Breakfasts are varied, with made-to-order juices from an old-fashioned cart. With elevator access.

It's part of the Mountain Lodges of Peru, so most clients come here on package tours covering an active Sacred Valley circuit.

Hotel Monasterio LUXURY HOTEL $$$
(Map p200; ☎084-60-4000; www.belmond.com/hotel-monasterio-cusco; Calle Palacio 136; d from S1190; @📶) Arranged around graceful

16th-century cloisters, the five-star Monasterio has long been Cuzco's jewel, with majestic public areas and over 100 rooms surrounding genteel courtyards. Jesuit roots show in the irregular floor plans, though some of the renovations (eg a plasma TV that emerges from the foot of the bed) seem a little gauche.

In addition to two high-end restaurants, don't miss the chapel with its original gold-leaf paintings.

Los Andes de America HOTEL **$$$**
(Map p200; ☎084-60-6060; www.cuscoandes.com; Calle Garcilaso 150; s/d incl breakfast S278/340) A Best Western hotel noted for its buffet breakfast, which includes regional specialties such as *mote con queso* (cheese and corn) and *papa helada* (frozen potato). Rooms are warm and comfortable, bathrooms are big and relatively luxurious, and the atrium features a scale model of Machu Picchu.

Del Prado Inn HOTEL **$$$**
(Map p200; ☎084-224-442; www.delpradoinn.com; Suecia 310; s/d/tr incl buffet breakfast S226/402/448; @ 🛜) Del Prado is a solid option, with efficient staff and just over a dozen snug rooms reached by elevator. Some have tiny balconies with corner views of the plaza. Check out the original Inca walls in the dining room.

Hotel Royal Inca I HOTEL **$$$**
(Map p200; ☎084-23-1067; www.royalinkahotel.com; Plaza Regocijo 299; s/d incl breakfast S306/380; @ 🛜) Quiet as a mausoleum, this central hotel features good-quality rooms. Those in the colonial building are a bit dated but comfortable and luxurious, while the modern ones are big, bright and cheery. The oddest feature might be the mix of kitsch in the public areas, including gold masks and an oversized wall mural with an indigenous nature scene bordering on soft porn.

San Blas

Kuntur Wasi Cusco GUESTHOUSE **$**
(Map p200; ☎084-22-7570; www.hospedajekunturwasi.com; Tandapata 352; r per person incl breakfast S50) Quiet and economical, this simple hotel features ship-shape rooms, attentive service and free buffet breakfast. Interior rooms lack natural light, but feature pleasant decor and cozy down duvets. It's a hard bargain to beat.

Pantastico GUESTHOUSE **$**
(Map p200; ☎084-954-387; www.pan-tastico.com; Carmen Bajo 226; dm S35, s/d S75/105, s/d/tr without bathroom S50/90/120, all incl breakfast; @ 🛜) French-run with a friendly, bohemian air, this bed-and-bakery has good water pressure but beds that are a little bit saggy. Highlights include piping-hot bread at 5am and the residual warmth coming from the big oven. Offers cooking classes and travel-agency services. The one double with a view fetches S20 extra.

Pisko & Soul HOSTEL **$**
(Map p200; ☎084-22-1998; info@piskoandsoul.com; Carmen Alto 294; dm/s incl breakfast S47/72; @ 🛜) This Peruvian hostel goes for the Spanish language school formula, with free lessons, evening events and barbecues. Small dorms have snug down covers but the bathrooms could use some bleach.

Samay Wasi HOSTEL **$**
(Map p200; ☎084-25-3108; www.samaywasiperu.com; Atocsaycuchi 416; dm/d incl breakfast S34/85; @ 🛜) A friendly, rambling hostel clinging precariously to the hillside, hidden up a flight of stairs teetering way above town. There's a proper kitchen and ship-shape rooms. Some are a bit musty so ask to see a few. With major city views. Accepts credit cards.

Hospedaje el Artesano de San Blas GUESTHOUSE **$**
(Map p200; ☎084-26-3968; hospedajeartesano790@hotmail.com; Suytuccato 790; d/tr/q S56/83/108; 🛜) If you're wondering why it's such a deal, just try walking here with a full pack. Still, this peaceful and falling-down-charming colonial house has large rooms and a sunny patio with wi-fi reception. Kitchen available.

Hospedaje Inka GUESTHOUSE **$**
(☎084-23-1995; www.hospedajeinka.weebly.com; Suytuccato 848; dm/s/d incl breakfast S20/40/50; 🛜) This scruffy but charming converted hillside farmhouse high above Plaza San Blas affords some great views. There's erratic hot water, private bathrooms and a large farm kitchen available for cooking your own meals. Taxis can't climb the final uphill stretch, so be prepared for a stiff walk.

★**Quinua Villa Boutique** APARTMENT **$$**
(Map p200; ☎084-24-2646; www.quinua.com.pe; Pasaje Santa Rosa A-8; 2 or 3 person apt S294-464; 🛜) A clutch of cozy apartments high up on

the hill (staircase-only access), this charmer features suites themed according to historical periods in Peru, with playful touches like a bedspread completely made of used jeans. Thoughtful touches include fireplaces and kitchens stocked with a basket of cooking supplies. Also has safe boxes, LCD TVs and heaters; one suite features a sauna.

Second Home Cusco BOUTIQUE HOTEL **$$**
(Map p200; ☎084-23-5873; www.secondhomecusco.com; Atocsaycuchi 616; s/d incl breakfast S340/380; @ 📶) A cozy boutique lodging with three chic suites, featuring original artwork, adobe walls and skylights. Carlos Delfin, the affable and cosmopolitan English-speaking owner, orchestrates free airport pickups and private tours; he has even hunted down the best baguettes in town to serve at breakfast. Longer stays are discounted.

Hostal Pensión Alemana HOTEL **$$**
(Map p200; ☎084-22-6861; www.cuzco-stay.de; Tandapata 260; s/d/tr incl breakfast S183/219/276; @ 📶) Attentive and lovely, this polished Swiss-German lodge wouldn't look out of place in the Alps. Nice touches include air purifiers and complimentary tea and fruit. Couples should note there are very few matrimonial beds. Enjoy the tiled garden – rare in Cuzco – and the terraces with sweeping views.

Tika Wasi BOUTIQUE HOTEL **$$**
(Map p200; ☎084-23-1609; www.tikawasi.com; Tandapata 491; s/d/tr incl breakfast from S163/195/226; 📶) Behind a tall wall, this modern inn offers a personable option with bright, imaginatively themed rooms, with family photos and colonial accents. Rooms overlook small, sunny decks to hang out on. Breakfast is buffet. Non-nationals should be sure to get the tax subtracted from the room price.

La Encantada BOUTIQUE HOTEL **$$**
(Map p200; ☎084-24-2206; www.encantadaperu.com; Tandapata 354; s/d incl breakfast S278/340; @ 📶) Bright and cheerful, this modern boutique hotel features terraced gardens and immense views from iron-rail balconies. A circular staircase leads to small, tasteful rooms with soft linens and king-sized beds. The on-site spa helps hikers work out the aches and kinks. Be aware that checkout is at 9am.

Madre Tierra B&B **$$**
(Map p200; ☎084-24-8452; www.hostalmadretierra.com; Atocsaycuchi 647; s/d/tr S138/168/226; @ 📶) Warm and super cozy, with plenty of B&B-style luxury comfort touches, Madre Tierra is a vine-entwined, slightly claustrophobic little jewel box. Rooms have skylights and funky dimensions. Good value for money.

Amaru Hostal HOTEL **$$**
(Map p200; ☎084-22-5933; www.amaruhostal.com; Cuesta San Blas 541; s/d/tr incl breakfast S150/180/240; @ 📶) In a characterful old building in a prime location, Amaru is deservedly popular. Flowerpots sit outside well-kept rooms with styles that are a little dated. Some feature rocking chairs from which to admire the rooftop view. Rooms in the outer courtyard are noisy, and those at the back are newest.

Hostal Rumi Punku HOTEL **$$**
(Map p200; ☎084-22-1102; www.rumipunku.com; Choquechaca 339; s/d incl breakfast S294/340; @ 📶) Recognizable by the monumental Inca stonework around the entrance, Rumi Punku (Stone Door) is a stylish complex of old colonial houses, gardens and terraces. The rooftop terraces and other outdoor areas are utterly charming. Rooms ooze comfort and class, with central heating, wooden floors and European bedding.

It's probably not worth the upgrade to a superior room unless you want a bigger bed. Sauna and Jacuzzi are available for a minimal charge.

Casona Les Pleiades B&B **$$**
(Map p200; ☎084-50-6430; www.casona-pleiades.com; Tandapata 116; d/tr incl breakfast S205/260; @ 📶) A pleasant French-run B&B with a sunny courtyard featuring fresh flowers and balcony seating. The buffet breakfast is served in cozy booths. Heaters and lock-boxes are supplied in rooms.

Casa de Campo Hostal HOTEL **$$**
(Map p200; ☎084-24-4404; www.hotelcasadecampo.com; Tandapata 298; s/d/tr incl breakfast S155/170/247; @ 📶) The steep climb here might leave you on your knees, but the views astound. With a warm, friendly vibe, this hillside inn is almost perfect but installations are aging. Some rooms don't even have working electrical outlets (most have just one), so check before settling in. Breakfast includes a sprawling buffet that includes fresh fruit and cereal. Heaters cost extra.

Los Apus Hotel & Mirador HOTEL **$$**
(Map p200; ☎084-26-4243; www.losapushotel.com; Atocsaycuchi 515; s/d incl breakfast

S240/295; ❄@📶) With understated class, this longtime Swiss-run hotel features central heating, large bedrooms with down duvets and colonial-style art. It may seem overpriced, but you are also paying for the high-tech alarm system and an emergency water supply. A wheelchair-accessible room for travelers with disabilities is available.

Eureka Hostal HOTEL **$$**
(Map p200; ☎084-23-3505; www.peru-eureka.com; Chihuampata 591; s/d/tr S229/269/346; @📶) A funky blend of old and new, Eureka's stylish lobby and sun-soaked cafeteria invite further acquaintance. Rooms are comfortable but a little odd, with a child-like take on traditional motifs. Orthopedic mattresses and down quilts make them as comfortable as they are cool. Flexible tariffs can make it an even better deal.

Hostal El Grial HOTEL **$$**
(Map p200; ☎084-22-3012; www.hotelelgrial.com; Carmen Alto 112; s/d/tr S108/161/223) A good value in a rickety old wood-floored building; all rooms have orthopedic mattresses and some have views.

Casa San Blas BOUTIQUE HOTEL **$$$**
(Map p200; ☎084-23-7900; www.casasanblas.com; Tocuyeros 566; d/ste incl breakfast S420/510; @📶) Down a short passageway, this revamped colonial features smart, spare rooms with nice bedding, hardwood floors and Andean textiles. It has a cozy feel, though service is somewhat impersonal.

Avenida El Sol & Downhill

Hostal San Juan Masías GUESTHOUSE **$**
(Map p208; ☎084-43-1563; hostalsanjuanmasias.com; Ahuacpinta 600; s/d/tw S70/100/140, s/d/tw without bathroom S50/80/110, all incl breakfast; @) An excellent alternative guesthouse run by Dominican nuns on the grounds of the busy Colegio Martín de Porres, this place is clean, safe and friendly, and overlooks frequent volleyball matches on the courtyard. Simple, spotless rooms with heating are arranged off a long, sunny hallway. Two people will pay more for twin beds than one bed. Continental breakfast is included.

Yanantin Guest House GUESTHOUSE **$$**
(Map p208; ☎084-25-4205; www.yanantin.com; Ahuacpinta 775; d incl breakfast S148; 📶) This small guesthouse has an assortment of well-heeled, spotless rooms large enough for desks and coffee tables. Organic toiletries are offered and the comfy beds feature cotton sheets and down bedding. Good value.

Los Aticos HOTEL **$$**
(Map p200; ☎084-23-1710; www.losaticos.com; Quera 253, Pasaje Hurtado Álvarez; d/apt incl breakfast S155/201; @📶) Hidden in a small passageway, this sleepy spot is off the radar but well worth snagging. Rooms have comfy beds with down duvets and parquet floors. There's also self-service laundry and a full guest kitchen. The three mini-apartments sleep up to four and are good value for self-catering groups or families.

Hostal Inkarri HOTEL **$$**
(Map p200; ☎084-24-2692; www.inkarrihostal.com; Qolla Calle 204; s/d/tr incl breakfast S155/185/263; @📶) A roomy place with a pleasant stone courtyard, well-kept colonial terraces and whimsical collections of old sewing machines, phones and typewriters. Good value, but watch for rooms on the musty side.

Picol Hostal HOTEL **$$**
(Map p200; ☎084-24-9191; www.picolhostal.com; Quera 253, Pasaje Hurtado Álvarez; s/d/tr incl breakfast S90/130/150; 📶) In a bustling commercial district, this small hotel has agreeable staff and tiny, well-kept and airy doubles. The triples are a little too tight.

Hotel Libertador Palacio del Inka LUXURY HOTEL **$$$**
(Map p200; ☎084-23-1961; www.libertador.com.pe; Plazoleta Santo Domingo 259; d/ste US$803/2178; ❄@📶🏊) Opulence bedecks this colonial mansion built over Inca foundations. Parts of the building dating back to the 16th century, when Francisco Pizarro was an occupant. It's as luxurious and beautiful as you'd expect, with a fine interior courtyard, and ample renovated rooms. Just beware the 9am checkout.

Also features a Peruvian restaurant, bar, spa and business center.

Greater Cuzco

Hospedaje Turismo Caith GUESTHOUSE **$**
(☎084-23-3595; www.caith.org; Pasaje Sto Toribio N4, Urb Ucchullo Alto; s/d/tr incl breakfast S80/150/190; 📶) This rambling farmhouse-style hostel also runs an on-site girls foundation. Huge picture windows and various balconies and patios look toward the Plaza de Armas, a 20-minute walk or a five-minute taxi ride away. It's great for families – big rooms and cots are available,

and the rambling, grassy garden is a perfect place for kids to run around.

Torre Dorada Residencial GUESTHOUSE **$$**
(☎084-24-1698; www.torredorada.com; Los Cipreses N-5, Residencial Huancaro; s/d incl breakfast S325/402; @) With lovely and original decor in bright colors, Torre Dorada is a modern, family-run hotel in a quiet residential district close to the bus terminal. Though it isn't close to the action, guests rave about the high quality of service. It offers free shuttles to the airport, train stations and town center. Fluent English is spoken.

Hostal San Juan de Dios GUESTHOUSE **$$**
(☎084-24-0135; www.hostalsanjuandedios.com; Manzanares 264, Urb Manuel Prado; s/d incl breakfast S150/180; @ 📶) With a wonderful staff, this spotless guesthouse is part of a nonprofit enterprise that supports a hospital clinic and also provides job opportunities for young people with disabilities. The quiet, carpeted rooms have large windows; most have twin beds, though there's one matrimonial double. Staff help with everything from laundry services to making international phone calls.

It's a 30-minute walk from the city center, near shops and amenities.

Eating

Cuzco's location, nearly dropping off the eastern edge of the Andes, gives it access to an unbelievable range of crops from highland potatoes and quinoa to avocados, jungle fruit and *ají picante* (hot chili).

Most popular local restaurants are outside the historic center and focus on lunch; few open for dinner. Don't expect to encounter any language other than Spanish in these places, but the food is worth the effort! Pampa de Castillo is the street near Qorikancha where local workers lunch on Cuzco classics. Expect lots of *caldo de gallina* (chicken soup) and *chicharrón* (deep-fried pork) with corn, mint and, of course, potato, in a range of restaurants.

For self-caterers, small, overpriced grocery shops are located near the Plaza de Armas, including **Gato's Market** (Map p200; Santa Catalina Ancha 377; ⏲9am-11pm) and **Market** (Map p200; Mantas 119; ⏲8am-11pm). For a more serious stock-up head to supermarket **Mega** (Map p208; cnr Matará & Ayacucho; ⏲10am-8pm Mon-Sat, to 6pm Sun).

Central Cuzco

La Justina PIZZA **$**
(Map p200; ☎084-25-5474; Calle Palacio 110; pizzas S19-35; ⏲6-11pm Mon-Sat) Traipse through an uneven stone courtyard to this little gem, a pizza joint with wooden tables and gorgeous wood-fired pies. Original toppings include tomato, bacon and basil or spinach and garlic.

Mr. Soup INTERNATIONAL **$**
(Map p200; ☎084-25-3806; Saphi 448; mains S18-22; ⏲noon-10pm Tue-Sun) Sometimes you just want a huge bowl of soup. Serving fairly authentic udon curry, Thai tom kha, Andean quinoa soup and others, this tiny shop does the trick. Recipes were sourced from families, which helps gives them a homespun taste.

Pantastico BAKERY **$**
(Map p200; ☎084-25-4387; Tandapata 1024; mains S4-13; ⏲8:30am-8pm) For a little something sweet, this tiny bakery hits the spot, selling breads, empanadas and fat slabs of tart passion-fruit or coconut bread with fresh juice.

Deli Monasterio BAKERY **$**
(Map p200; Calle Palacio 136; mains S6-18; ⏲8am-9pm Mon-Sat, 10am-4pm Sun) Crusty, authentic baguettes are the highlight here (come early) but you can also get nice lunchboxes (perfect for day excursions) with gourmet and veggie options. The mini *pain au chocolat* and passion-fruit cookies aren't bad either.

Jardín Secreto PERUVIAN **$**
(Map p200; ☎084-26-2972; Plateros 380; mains S15-25; ⏲8am-2am) Run by the Pantastico people, this is a typical courtyard *picantería* (local restaurant) offering trout, *lomo saltado* (strips of beef stir-fried with onions, tomatoes, potatoes and chili) and fried rice. Attracts a mix of locals and visitors for its *menú* (S8), cheap 1L beers and live music (9:30pm). Bands range from rock and reggae to salsa, with *huayno* (Andean folk) on Sundays. Also offers cooking classes using a traditional clay oven.

Aldea Yanapay CAFE **$**
(Map p200; ☎084-25-5134; Ruinas 415, 2nd fl; lunch buffet S10, mains from S22; ⏲9am-11:30pm; 🌿) The stuffed animals, board games and decor perfectly evoke the circus you dreamed of running away with as a child. Aldea Yanapay is pitched at families but will appeal to anyone with a taste for the

ANDEAN CUISINE

Sunday lunch with a country stroll is a Cuzco ritual. Locals head to the villages south of town: Tipón is *the* place to eat *cuy* (guinea pig), Saylla is the home of *chicharrón* (deep-fried pork) and Lucre is renowned for duck. Look for the following foods in local restaurants, on the street and at festivals:

Anticucho Beef heart on a stick, punctuated by a potato, is the perfect street snack.

Caldo de gallina Healthy, hearty chicken soup is the local favorite to kick a hangover.

Chicharrones Definitely more than the sum of its parts: deep-fried pork served with corn, mint leaves, fried potato and onion.

Choclo con queso Huge, pale cobs of corn are served with a teeth-squeaking chunk of cheese in the Sacred Valley.

Cuy Guinea pig, raised on grains at home – what could be more organic? The faint of heart can ask for it served as a fillet (without the head and paws).

Lechón Suckling pig with plenty of crackling, served with tamales (corn cakes).

quixotic. Food includes burritos, falafel and tasty little fried things to pick at, and a great-value vegetarian lunch buffet.

Profits go to projects helping abandoned children. Highly recommended.

Los Toldos PERUVIAN **$**
(Map p200; cnr Almagro & San Andrés; mains S12-28; ⏲noon-11pm Mon-Sat) A local favorite for abundant cheap eats, this rotisserie restaurant features a worthwhile salad bar (try the black olive sauce). Most people can't go past the Peruvian classic *cuarto de pollo* (quarter of a chicken), done here to perfection.

El Ayllu CAFE **$**
(Map p200; Marquez 263; mains S7-16; ⏲6:30am-10pm Mon-Sat, to 1pm Sun) Longtime staff chat up clients and serve traditional pastries like *lengua de suegra* (mother-in-law's tongue; a sweet pastry confection) and pork sandwiches. Traditional breakfasts are worth trying and coffee is roasted the traditional local way – with orange, sugar and onion peels.

★La Bodega 138 PIZZA **$$**
(Map p200; ☎084-26-0272; Herrajes 138; mains S23-35; ⏲6:30-11pm Mon-Sat) Sometimes you are homesick for good atmosphere, uncomplicated menus and craft beer. In comes La Bodega, a fantastic laid-back enterprise run by a family in what used to be their home. Thin-crust pizzas are fired in the adobe oven, organic salads are fresh and the prices are reasonable. A true find. Cash only.

★Marcelo Batata PERUVIAN **$$**
(Map p200; Calle Palacio 121; mains S23-43; ⏲2-11pm) A sure bet for delectable Andean cuisine with a twist. Marcelo Batata innovates with traditional foods to show them at their best – like the humble tarwi pea, which makes a mean hummus. The chicken soup with *hierba Luisa* (a local herb), is exquisite, alongside satisfying beet *quinotto* (like risotto), tender *anticuchos* (beef skewers) and twice-baked Andean potatoes that offer crispy-creamy goodness.

A daring array of cocktails is best savored on the rooftop deck – the city views make it the best outdoor venue in Cuzco.

★Cicciolina INTERNATIONAL **$$**
(Map p200; ☎084-23-9510; Triunfo 393, 2nd fl; mains S35-55; ⏲8am-late) On the 2nd floor of a lofty colonial courtyard mansion, Cicciolina has long been among Cuzco's best restaurants. The eclectic, sophisticated food is divine, starting with house-marinated olives, continuing with crisp polenta squares with cured rabbit, huge green salads, charred octopus and satisfying mains like squid-ink pasta, beet ravioli and tender lamb. With impeccable service and warmly lit seating.

Uchu Peruvian Steakhouse PERUVIAN **$$**
(Map p200; ☎084-24-6598; Calle Palacio 135; mains S28-59; ⏲12:30-11pm) With a cozy, cavernous ambience of low-lit adobe, dark tables and bright turquoise walls, this chic eatery has a simple menu of meat (steak, alpaca or chicken) and fish cooked on hot volcanic stones at your table, served with delicious sauces. Starters are great – like the gingery ceviche with fish shipped fresh daily. Staff is knowledgeable and quick, a real treat.

Limo PERUVIAN $$
(Map p200; ☎084-24-068; Portal de Carnes 236, 2nd fl; mains S20-60; ⏰11am-11pm Mon-Sat) Tart pisco sours perfectly compliment Limo's Peruvian-Asian seafood creations. For starters, native potatoes and sauces are a fun change from the traditional bread basket. *Tiraditos* (raw fish in a fragrant sauce) simply melt on the tongue. Other hits are the creamy *causas* (potato dish) and *sudadito* (a mix of greens, corn and seared scallops). With elegant ambience and attentive service.

Cafe Morena PERUVIAN $$
(Map p200; Plateros 348B; mains S25-30; ⏰11am-10pm Mon-Sat) Popular and stylish, this chic cafe bridges the gap between gourmet Peruvian and kinder prices. Serves quinoa, burgers and Peruvian classics like *anticuchos* (beef skewers) in sumptuous sauces and hearty soups.

Green's Organic CAFE $$
(Map p200; ☎084-24-3399; Santa Catalina Angosta 235, 2nd fl; mains S28-46; ⏰11am-10pm; 📶✍) 🍃 With all-organic food and a bright farmhouse feel, Green's Organic oozes health. Inventive salads with options like roasted fennel, goat cheese, beets and spring greens are a welcome change of pace and the heartier fare includes pastas and alpaca dishes. Come early (or late) as it fills up fast and service is notably slow.

Trujillo Restaurant PERUVIAN $$
(Map p200; ☎084-233-465; Av Tullumayo 542, near Plaza Limacpampa; mains S17-37; ⏰9am-8pm Mon-Sat, to 5pm Sun) Run by a northern Peruvian family, this simple, spotless dining hall by Qorikancha nails northern classics such as *seco de cabrito* (goat stewed in beer and cilantro) and a variety of ceviches served with jars of *chicha morada* (a nonalcoholic purple maize drink). The *ají de gallina* (a creamy chicken stew served with rice and potatoes) is the best in all of Cuzco.

Kintaro JAPANESE $$
(Map p200; ☎084-22-6181; Plateros 326, 2nd fl; rolls S10-38; ⏰12-3:30pm & 6:30-10pm Mon-Sat) Local expats rave about the noodle bowls while the set lunch (S15) proves a good deal and provides a welcome change from familiar flavors. Also serves worthwhile sushi and sake. The alley entrance is a little hard to find.

Papachos BURGERS $$
(Map p200; www.papachos.com; Portal de Belen 115; mains S29-39; ⏰noon-midnight) You could do worse than satisfying your fast-food craving at a Gastón Acurio outlet. Papachos does big, beautiful burgers topped with goodies both exotic and comforting. There's veggie options, wings doused in Amazonian pepper sauce, and fish and chips.

Inkazuela INTERNATIONAL $$
(Map p200; ☎084-23-4924; Plazoleta Nazarenas 167, 2nd fl; mains S16-34; ⏰1pm-9:30pm Mon-Sat) Huge bowls of steaming Cuban-style meat stew, Caribbean coconut soup and Andean quinoa combinations are a warming godsend at this 2nd-floor cafe with low-lit ambience. Service is friendly and attentive.

A Mi Manera PERUVIAN $$
(Map p200; ☎084-22-2219; www.amimaneraperu.com; Triunfo 392, 2nd fl; mains S26-40; ⏰10am-10pm) For a reasonably priced night out, this romantic restaurant serves up traditional Peruvian cuisine and pasta. Offerings like steak in port sauce, spicy yucca or mashed muña potatoes comfort and satisfy.

Divina Comedia INTERNATIONAL $$
(Map p200; ☎084-23-2522; www.hotelarqueologo.com; Pumacurco 408; mains S25-45; ⏰noon-3pm & 6-11pm Mon-Sat) With sopranos singing live arias, this unusual upscale eatery fills a small niche of romantic dining with entertainment. The food combines Peruvian ingredients with Mediterranean influences; start with tapas. A notable specialty is duck, slow-cooked to utter tenderness.

Le Soleil FRENCH $$$
(Map p200; ☎084-24-0543; San Agustín 275; mains S41-72; ⏰12:30-3pm & 7-11:30pm Thu-Tue) Cuzco's go-to spot for traditional French cooking, this romantic white-linen restaurant does not disappoint. The menu features staples like brandied trout, baked ratatouille with goat cheese and herbs, and duck à l'orange. You can also go for a tasting menu (from S145). Ingredients like fish stock may be in non-meat dishes, so vegetarians should order carefully.

Chicha NOVOANDINA $$$
(Map p200; ☎084-24-0520; Regocijo 261, 2nd fl; mains S34-65) A Gastón Acurio venture serving up haute versions of Cuzco classics in an open kitchen. Their riff on *anticuchos* (beef skewers) is a delectable barbecued octopus with crisp herbed potato wedges. Other contenders include *rocoto relleno* (stuffed peppers), the wonton-style *sopa de galli-*

na (chicken soup) and *chairo* (beef soup) served in a clay pot.

The *chicha morada* (a nonalcoholic purple maize drink) is beyond fresh.

San Blas

Jack's Café CAFE $

(Map p200; ☎084-25-4606; Choquechaca 509; mains S12-26; ⏰7:30am-11:30pm) A line often snakes out the door at this consistently good Western-style eatery with Aussie roots. With fresh juices blended with mint or ginger, strong coffee and eggs heaped with smoked salmon or roasted tomatoes, it's easy to get out of bed. Also has nice cafe food, soups and good service.

La Bohème CREPERIE $

(Map p200; ☎084-23-5694; Carmen Alto 283; mains S6-18, menú S15; ⏰noon-10pm Tue-Sun) Diners rave about the crepes in this Marseillaise-owned cafe, crafted with fusion ingredients like caramelized onions, Andean cheese, mushrooms and béchamel. The set menu is a great deal. For dessert, try the signature crepe with salted butter and caramel.

Greenpoint VEGETARIAN $

(Map p200; ☎084-43-1146; Carmen Bajo 235; mains S8-22; ⏰8am-10pm; 🥬) Even non-vegetarians are repeat customers at this restaurant and bakery offering abundant set menu lunches. Highlights include the veggie sushi and mushroom ceviche. Enter through an interior patio. The best seating is on the 2nd-floor terrace. Also serves beer and wine.

El Hada ICE CREAM $

(Map p200; Qanchipata 596; ice cream from S10; ⏰8am-7pm) Served in fresh-made cones with a hint of vanilla or lemon peel, these exotic ice creams are ecstasy. Flavors like Indonesian cinnamon, bitter chocolate or roasted apples do not disappoint. Cap it off with an *espress* – Café Bisetti, Peru's best roaster, is offered.

The Meeting Place CAFE $

(Map p200; ☎084-24-0465; Plazoleta San Blas; mains S15-21; ⏰8:30am-4pm Mon-Sat; 📶) This British-Peruvian-owned cafe nails gringo breakfast. Start with organic coffee or nice loose-leaf teas, oversized waffles and egg combinations. The thick milkshakes have their devotees. With swift, friendly service and a good book exchange.

Juanito's SANDWICHES $

(Map p200; Angelitos 638; sandwiches S12-24; ⏰11am-10pm Mon-Sat) With the griddle hopping, this sandwich shop churns out satisfying made-to-order numbers with a variety of sauces. Vegetarians get big fried-egg sandwiches, and combos like chicken and walnuts prove tasty.

Prasada VEGETARIAN $

(Map p200; ☎084-25-3644; Qanchipata 269; mains S9-12; ⏰10am-9pm Mon-Fri, 10am-4pm Sat-Sun; 🥬) The best bang for your pesos, serving tacos, tortilla soup and lentil burgers with fresh toppings and generous servings. Pair with a jar of fresh-squeezed juice or kombucha and you're ready for the hike up to Sacsaywamán.

Cafeteria 7&7 CAFE $

(Map p200; Tandapata s/n; mains S7-9; ⏰10am-2pm & 4-10pm Mon-Sat, to 2pm Sun; 📶) A wonderful addition to the neighborhood, this sleek 3rd-story cafe bursts with city views. Yet the off-street location means it's quiet and conducive to chilling out. With white leather booths and a nice selection of homemade German cakes, light food like quinoa salads and espresso drinks. Also serves ice-cream sundaes.

Tacomania MEXICAN $

(Map p200; ☎984-132-032; Tandapata 917; mains S22; ⏰6-10pm) Serving nachos, burritos and tacos to just five tables, this simple Mexican restaurant is popular with expats. The tortilla chips are fragile, but chunky guacamole with red onion is a home run. If you ask for spicy, they'll deliver. With vegetarian options.

Granja Heidi CAFE $$

(Map p200; ☎084-23-8383; Cuesta San Blas 525, 2nd fl; mains S10-46; ⏰11:30am-9:30pm Mon-Sat) A cozy alpine cafe serving healthy fare that's consistently good, some of it provided from the small farm of the German owner. In addition to wonderful Peruvian fare (*rocoto relleno* is served vegetarian, with stuffed chili and peanuts), there are crepes and huge bowls of soups and salads. Save room for dessert.

La Quinta Eulalia PERUVIAN $$

(Map p200; ☎084-22-4951; Choquechaca 384; mains S25-54; ⏰9am-7pm Tue-Sun) This Cuzco classic has been in business for over half a century and its courtyard patio is a score on a sunny day. The chalkboard menu features the

THE LUCKY TOAD

Ever wondered what the locals do to relax instead of whiling away the hours over a game of darts or pool in the local bar? Well, next time you're in a *picantería* (local restaurant) or *quinta* (house serving typical Andean food), look out for a strange metal *sapo* (frog or toad) mounted on a large box and surrounded by various holes and slots. Men will often spend the whole afternoon drinking *chicha* (fermented corn beer) and beer while competing at this old test of skill in which players toss metal disks as close to the toad as possible. Top points are scored for landing one smack in the mouth. Legend has it that the game originated with Inca royals, who used to toss gold coins into Lake Titicaca in the hopes of attracting a *sapo*, believed to possess magical healing powers and to have the ability to grant wishes.

tenderest roast lamb, alpaca and traditional sides like the phenomenal *rocoto relleno* (spicy peppers stuffed with beef, peas and carrots topped with dribbling cheese). It is one of the best places to order *cuy* (guinea pig).

Pacha Papa PERUVIAN **$$**
(Map p200; ☎084-24-1318; Plazoleta Plaza San Blas 120; mains S23-45; ⊙11:30am-4pm & 7-11pm) Invoking a rustic highland ambience, this open courtyard with wooden tables serves up well-prepared Peruvian classics, cooked over a wood fire or in clay pots. It's also livened by a harpist on weekends. It's a good spot to try buttered corn in herbs, *ají de gallina* (creamy chicken stew) or oven-fired trout. *Cuy* (guinea pig) should be ordered in advance.

Korma Sutra INDIAN **$$**
(Map p200; ☎084-23-3023; Tandapata 909; mains S12-32; ⊙6-10pm Mon-Sat;) If you are craving spice, this London-style curry house will do the trick, with its garlicky naan, lassies and a variety of creamy kormas and curries. It's relaxing in the evening, with low-lit violet walls and cushioned booths.

Avenida El Sol & Downhill

Valeriana BAKERY **$**
(Map p208; ☎084-50-6941; Av del Sol 576; mains S2-14; ⊙7am-10pm Mon-Sat, 8am-9pm Sun;) Facing the sacred garden, this ambient bakery sells truffled cupcakes, whole wheat sandwiches and good veggie empanadas served on patterned china. There's also coffee drinks and refreshing juices blended with medicinal herbs. A fine stop to charge your batteries.

Greater Cuzco

Olas Bravas CEVICHE **$**
(☎084-43-9328; Mariscal Gamarra 11A; ceviche S25; ⊙9am-5pm) Most *cuzqueños* (Cuzco locals) think Olas Bravas offers the best ceviche in town, so it's often packed. Even if ceviche isn't your thing, this is a great place to try other *criollo* (coastal) dishes, such as *seco a la norteña* (goat stew). Check out the hammocks and the mural of the surfer.

Drinking & Nightlife

The European pubs are good places to track down those all-important soccer matches, with satellite TVs more or less permanently tuned into sports.

★ **Museo del Pisco** BAR
(Map p200; ☎084-26-2709; www.museodelpisco.org; Santa Catalina Ancha 398; ⊙11am-1am) When you've had your fill of colonial religious art, investigate this pisco museum, where the wonders of the national drink are extolled, exalted and – of course – sampled. Opened by an enthusiastic expat, this museum-bar is Pisco 101, combined with a tapas lounge. Grab a spot early for show-stopping live music (9pm to 11pm nightly).

Ambitions go far beyond the standard pisco sour to original cocktails like *valicha* (pisco with jungle fruit kion, spearmint and sour apple). Tapas, such as alpaca mini-burgers on sesame buns and *tiradito* (a Japanese-influenced version of ceviche) marinated in cumin-chili, sate your hunger. Look for special tastings and master distiller classes announced on the Facebook page.

Memoria BAR
(Map p200; ☎084-24-4111; Plateros 354; ⊙8pm-late) A wonderful, elegant bar with attentive bartenders and drinks that merit seconds. Check its Facebook page for events like live jazz, acoustic and techno music.

Fallen Angel COCKTAIL BAR
(Map p200; ☎084-25-8184; Plazoleta Nazarenas 221; ⊙6pm-late) This ultra-funky lounge redefines kitsch with glitter balls, fake fur and even bathtub-cum-aquarium tables complete with live goldfish. It isn't cheap, but

the decor really is worth seeing and the occasional theme parties held here are legendary.

Norton Rats PUB
(Map p200; cnr Santa Catalina Angosta & Plaza de Armas, 2nd fl; ⏲7am-late) Run by a motorcycle enthusiast, this unassuming expat-style bar overlooks the Plaza de Armas. It's a boon for people-watching, if you can get a balcony seat. Though known for delicious 200g burgers, it's also got TVs, darts and billiards to help you work up a thirst. Avoid the burritos. Happy hour is 7pm to 9pm.

La Chupiteria BAR
(Map p200; ☎984-725-241; Tecsecocha 400; ⏲8pm-4am) This popular, funky shot bar walks the wild side. Order from a huge drink list; the cocktail-filled teapots are served with shot glasses.

Paddy Flaherty's PUB
(Map p200; ☎084-24-7719; Triunfo 124; ⏲11am-late) This cramped little Irish pub is packed with random memorabilia, TVs, a working train set and homesick European travelers eating excellent-value hot sandwiches. Happy hours are from 7pm to 8pm and 10pm to 10:30pm.

☆ Entertainment

Clubs open early, but crank up a few notches after about 11pm. Happy hour is ubiquitous and generally entails two-for-one on beer or certain mixed drinks.

In popular *discotecas* (beware the word 'nightclub' – it is often used in Peru to indicate a brothel), especially right on the Plaza de Armas, both sexes should beware of drinks being spiked. The tried-and-true stops on the big night out in Cuzco are *discotecas* Inka Team, Roots and Ukuku's.

★Ukuku's LIVE MUSIC
(Map p200; ☎084-24-2951; Plateros 316; ⏲8pm-late) The most consistently popular nightspot in town, Ukuku's plays a winning combination of crowd pleasers – Latin and Western rock, reggae and *reggaetón* (a blend of Puerto Rican *bomba,* dancehall and hip-hop), salsa, hip-hop etc – and often hosts live bands. Usually full to bursting after midnight with as many Peruvians as foreign tourists, it's good, sweaty, dance-a-thon fun. Happy hour is 8pm to 10:30pm.

Roots CLUB
(Map p200; Tecsecocha s/n; ⏲8pm-late) This organic-feel club with an underground dance floor is ever-popular with locals and laid-back travelers alike.

Centro Qosqo de Arte Nativo PERFORMING ARTS
(Map p208; ☎084-22-7901; www.boletoturistico-cusco.net/arte-nativo.html; Av El Sol 604; adult/student under 26 with ISIC card S130/70) Has live nightly performances of Andean music and dance at 6:45pm. Admission is with the *boleto turístico* tourist card only, which is valid for 10 days and covers 16 other sights and venues.

Km 0 LIVE MUSIC
(Map p200; ☎084-23-6009; Tandapata 100; ⏲11am-late Tue-Sat, 5pm-late Sun & Mon) This convivial bar just off Plaza San Blas has a bit of everything. It serves good Thai food in the evening, and there's live music late every night – local musicians come here to jam after their regular gigs. Happy hour is 9pm to midnight.

Muse LIVE MUSIC
(Map p200; ☎084-25-3631, 984-23-1717; Triunfo 338, 2nd fl; 📶) Known as a good place to start your night out, this restaurant-lounge, a longtime Cuzco hangout, has very cool staff and live music in the evenings. Food includes good vegetarian options.

Inka Team CLUB
(Map p200; Portal de Carnes 298; ⏲8pm-late) Though it may change names, this place usually has the most up-to-the-minute electronic music collection, with trance, house and hip-hop mixed in with mainstream. There are chill-out sofas upstairs but this isn't the place for chat. A good mix of locals and tourists hang out here. Happy hour is 9pm to midnight.

Mythology CLUB
(Map p200; ☎084-25-5770; Portal de Carnes 298, 2nd fl; ⏲8pm-late) The party is always on at this crowded nightclub with a bouncy dance floor and tunes ranging from salsa to mainstream pop. Women be warned: the guys are not shy.

Mama Africa CLUB
(Map p200; Portal Harinas 191, 2nd fl; ⏲7pm-late) A favorite with Israelis, Mama Africa is the classic backpackers' hangout, usually packed with people sprawled across cushions or swaying to rock and reggae rhythms. Happy hour is 8:30pm to 11pm.

Shopping

San Blas – the plaza itself, Cuesta San Blas, Carmen Alto, and Tandapata east of the plaza – offers Cuzco's best shopping. It's the artisan quarter, packed with the workshops and showrooms of local craftspeople. Some offer the chance to watch artisans at work and see the interiors of colonial buildings while hunting down that perfect souvenir. Prices and quality vary greatly, so shop around and expect to bargain, except in the most expensive stores, where prices are often fixed. Some of the best-known include **Taller Olave** (Map p200; ☎084-23-1835; laza San Blas 651), which sells reproductions of colonial sculptures and pre-colonial ceramics. **Taller Mendivil** is nationally famous for its giraffe-necked religious figures and sun-shaped mirrors; it has outlets in **San Blas** (Map p200; ☎084-23-3247; Cuesta de San Blas, Plaza San Blas) and the **city center** (Map p200; ☎084-23-3247; cnr Hatunrumiyoc & Choquechaca). **Taller and Museo Mérida** (Map p200; ☎084-22-1714; Carmen Alto 133) offers striking earthenware statues that straddle the border between craft and art.

The same area is also home to an ever-evolving sprinkling of jewelry stores and quirky, one-off designer-clothes stores – a refreshing reminder that the local aesthetic is not confined to stridently colored ponchos and sheepskin-rug depictions of Machu Picchu. These and other mass-produced tourist tat, from textiles to teapots, are sold from pretty much every hole-in-the-wall in the historic center, and at the vast **Centro Artesenal Cuzco** (Map p208; cnr Avs El Sol & Tullumayo; ⌚9am-10pm).

If you're the type who likes to get your souvenir shopping done fast, **Aymi Wasi** (Map p200; Nueva Alta s/n) is for you. It's got *everything* – clothes, ornaments, toys, candles, jewelry, art, ceramics, handbags... Your friends and family will never suspect you bought all their gifts in one place! And it's all handmade and fair trade.

Cuzco is not known for its clothes-shopping, though there are a few cool stores hidden away in the **Centro Comercial de Cuzco** (Map p200; cnr Ayacucho & San Andrés; ⌚11am-10pm).

Tatoo (Map p200; ☎084-25-4211; Calle del Medio 130; ⌚9am-9:30pm) has brand-name outdoor clothing and technical gear at high prices. Many shops in Calle Plateros and Mercado El Molino have a good range of lower-quality, much cheaper gear.

Textiles

Center for Traditional Textiles of Cuzco HANDICRAFTS
(Map p208; Av El Sol 603A; ⌚7:30am-8:30pm) This nonprofit organization, founded in 1996, promotes the survival of traditional weaving. You may be able to catch a shop-floor demonstration illustrating different weaving techniques in all their finger-twisting complexity. Products for sale are high end.

For those who love textiles, there's a wonderful on-site museum (free).

Inkakunaq Ruwaynin HANDICRAFTS
(Map p200; ☎084-26-0942; www.tejidosandinos.com; inside CBC, Tullumayo 274; ⌚9am-7pm) This weaving cooperative with quality goods is run by 12 mountain communities from Cuzco and Apurimac; it's at the far end of the inner courtyard. There's also an online catalog.

Markets

Mercado San Pedro MARKET
(Map p208; Plazoleta San Pedro) Cuzco's central market is a must-see. Pig heads for *caldo* (soup), frogs (to enhance sexual performance), vats of fruit juice, roast *lechón* (suckling pig) and tamales (corn cakes) are just a few of the foods on offer. Around the edges are typical clothes, spells, incense and other random products to keep you entertained for hours.

Mercado Modelo de Huanchac MARKET
(Map p208; cnr Avs Garcilaso & Huascar) Huanchac is the local destination of choice for breakfast the morning after, specializing in the two hangover staples – jolting acid ceviche and greasy *chicharrón* (deep-fried pork).

El Molino MARKET
(Urbanizacion Ttio) Just beyond the *terminal terrestre* (bus station), this market is Cuzco's answer to the department store. It's a bargain hunter's paradise for clothes, housewares, bulk food and alcohol, *electrodomésticos* (electronic goods), camping gear, and pirated CDs and DVDs.

Bookstores

Many guesthouses, cafes and pubs have book exchanges. The best source of historical and archaeological information about the city and the surrounding area is the pocket-sized *Exploring Cuzco* by Peter Frost.

Bookstore Kiosk BOOKS
(Map p200; Mantas 113; ⌚9am-2pm & 4-9pm Mon-Sat) Novels and magazines in English

and German. Located just inside the door of the Centro Comercial de Cuzco.

Jerusalén BOOKS
(Map p200; ☎084-23-5428; Heladeros 143; ⏲10am-2pm & 4-8pm Mon-Sat) Cuzco's most extensive public book exchange (two used books, or one plus S8, will get you one book) plus used guidebooks, new titles and music CDs for sale.

Information

DANGERS & ANNOYANCES

Bags may be stolen from the backs of chairs in public places, or from overhead shelves in overnight buses. Walk around with a minimum of cash and belongings. If you keep your bag in your lap and watch out for pickpockets in crowded streets, transport terminals and markets, you are highly unlikely to be a victim of crime in Cuzco.

Robberies and even attacks in cabs have been reported. Use only official taxis, especially at night. (Look for the company's lit telephone number on top of the car.) Lock your doors from the inside, and never allow the driver to admit a second passenger. Readers have reported overcharging with *ticos* (taxi rickshaws).

Avoid walking by yourself late at night or very early in the morning. Revelers returning late from bars or setting off for the Inca Trail before sunrise are particularly vulnerable to 'choke and grab' attacks.

Don't buy drugs. Dealers and police often work together and Procuradores is one of several areas in which you can make a drug deal and get busted all within a couple of minutes. Drink spiking has been reported. Women especially should keep an eye on their glass and not accept drinks from strangers.

Take care not to overexert yourself during your first few days if you've flown in from lower elevations. You may find yourself quickly becoming winded while traipsing up and down Cuzco's narrow streets.

EMBASSIES & CONSULATES

Most foreign embassies and consulates are located in Lima, though Cuzco does have several honorary consul representatives.

Belgian Honorary Consulate (☎084-26-1517; Calle José Gabriel Cosio 307, Urb Magisterial)

French Honorary Consulate (Map p200; ☎084-24-9737; Nueva Baja 560)

German Honorary Consulate (Map p200; ☎084-24-2970; Calle San Agustin 307)

Italian Honorary Consulate (☎084-22-4398; Avenida Garcilaso, 700 Wanchaq)

UK Honorary Consulate (☎084-22-4135; Jiron Los Geranios 2-G, Mariscal Gamarra)

US Honorary Consulate (Map p208; ☎984-621-369, 084-23-1474; Av Pardo 845)

EMERGENCY

Policía de Turismo (PolTur, Tourist Police; ☎084-23-5123; Plaza Túpac Amaru s/n; ⏲24hr) If you have something stolen, you'll need to get an official police report for insurance claims.

IMMIGRATION

Oficina de Migraciónes (Immigration Office; Map p208; ☎084-22-2741; www.migraciones.gob.pe; Av El Sol 612; ⏲8am-4:15pm Mon-Fri, 9am-noon Sat) Can replace a lost Tarjeta Andina (tourist card) – be prepared for a lot of red tape.

INTERNET ACCESS

Internet cafes are found on almost every street corner. Many hotels and cafes offer free wireless.

LAUNDRY

Lavanderías (laundries) will wash, dry and fold your clothes from around S4 per kg. They're everywhere, but cluster just off the Plaza de Armas on Suecia, Procuradores and Plateros, and on Carmen Bajo in San Blas. The further you get from the Plaza de Armas, the cheaper they get.

LEFT LUGGAGE

If you're going trekking or on an overnight excursion, any hostel will store your bags for free. Always get a receipt and lock the bags. The bags should have identifying tags showing your name and the drop-off and expected pickup dates.

For soft-sided bags, we recommend placing them inside a larger plastic bag and sealing them shut with tape. Then sign your name across the seal, so that you can tell if your bag has been opened while you were away.

Keep all valuables (eg passport, credit cards, money) on your person. Trekkers are required to carry their passport with them on the Inca Trail.

MEDICAL SERVICES

Pharmacies abound along Av El Sol. Cuzco's medical facilities are limited; head to Lima for serious procedures.

Clinica Pardo (Map p208; ☎084-24-0997; Av de la Cultura 710; ⏲24hr) Well equipped and expensive – perfect if you're covered by travel insurance.

Clínica Paredes (Map p208; ☎084-22-5265; Lechugal 405; ⏲24hr) Consultations.

Hospital Regional (☎084-23-9792, emergencies 084-22-3691; Av de la Cultura s/n; ⏲24hr) Public and free, but wait times can be long and good care is not guaranteed.

Traveler's Clinic Cusco (084-22-1213; Puputi 148; 24hr) A private clinic with swift bilingual service and on-call doctor, deals mostly with altitude-sickness patients and travelers' illnesses. It's a 10-minute walk from San Blas.

MONEY

ATMs abound in and around the Plaza de Armas, and are also available at the airport, Huanchaq train station and the bus terminal. All accept Visa, most accept MasterCard. There are several big bank branches on Av El Sol; go inside for cash advances above daily ATM limits. *Casas de cambio* (foreign-exchange bureaus) give better exchange rates than banks, and are scattered around the main plazas and especially along Av El Sol. Moneychangers can be found outside banks, but rip-offs are common.

BBVA Continental (Map p200; Av El Sol 368; 9:15am-6:30pm Mon-Fri, 9:30am-12:30pm Sat)

BCP (Map p200; Av El Sol 189; 9am-6:30pm Mon-Thu, to 7:30pm Fri, to 1pm Sat)

Interbank (Map p200; Av El Sol 380; 9am-6:30pm Mon-Fri, 9:15am-12:30pm Sat)

POST

DHL (Map p208; 084-24-4167; Av El Sol 608; 8:30am-7pm Mon-Fri, 9am-1pm Sat) International express mail and package courier services.

Serpost (Map p208; Av El Sol 800; 8am-8pm Mon-Sat) General delivery (poste restante) mail is held here at the main post office; bring proof of identity.

TOURIST INFORMATION

Currently, Machu Picchu tickets can be purchased through DIRCETUR, IncaRail, Peru Rail and the bookstore of the Museo Histórico Regional (p206). Travel agencies are all too willing to help out with travel arrangements – for a hefty commission, of course.

DIRCETUR (Map p200; 084-58-2361, 084-58-2360; www.dirceturcusco.gob.pe; Mantas 117; 9am-8pm Mon-Fri, 9am-1pm Sat) The main place in Cuzco to purchase Machu Picchu entry tickets; closed on holidays.

Dirección Regional de Cultura Cusco (Map p208; 084-58-2030; www.drc-cusco.gob.pe; Av de La Cultura 238; 7:15am-6:30pm Mon-Sat) The organizing body for tourism in Cuzco.

Fertur Peru Travel (Map p200; 084-22-1304; www.fertur-travel.com; Calle San Agustín 317) Local office of long-established, very reliable agency for flights and all conventional tours.

iPerú (Map p200; 084-25-2974; www.peru.travel; Portal de Harinas 177, Plaza de Armas; 9am-7pm Mon-Fri, to 1pm Sat-Sun) Efficient and helpful. Excellent source for tourist information for both the region and entire country. There's an adjoining section of guarded ATMs. Also has a branch at the airport (Map p200; 084-23-7364; 6am-5pm).

South American Explorers (SAE; Map p208; 084-24-5484; www.saexplorers.org; Av Pardo 847; 9:30am-5pm Mon-Fri, to 1pm Sat;) SAE's Cuzco clubhouse has good-quality maps, books and brochures for sale, a huge stock of travel information and recommendations, wi-fi access, a book exchange and rooms for rent. Weekly events and limited volunteer information are available to nonmembers.

USEFUL WEBSITES

Andean Travel Web (www.andeantravelweb.com) More than 1000 pages of information.

Diario del Cusco (www.diariodelcusco.com) Online edition of the local newspaper (Spanish).

Municipalidad del Cusco (www.cusco.gob.pe) The city's official website.

Getting There & Away

AIR

Cuzco's **Aeropuerto Internacional Alejandro Velasco Astete** (CUZ; 084-22-2611) receives national and international flights. Most arrivals come in the morning since afternoon conditions make landings and takeoffs more difficult. If you have a tight connection, it's best to reserve the earliest flight available, as later ones are more likely to be delayed or canceled.

There are daily flights to Lima, Juliaca, Puerto Maldonado and Arequipa. Check in at least two hours ahead as overbooking errors are commonplace. During rainy season, flights to Puerto Maldonado are often seriously delayed. Departure taxes are included in ticket prices.

Official taxis from the airport to addresses near the city center cost S20 to S25.

Avianca (Map p208; 0800-18-2222; www.avianca.com; Av El Sol 602; 8:30am-7pm Mon-Fri, 9am-2pm Sat) Service to/from Lima Monday to Saturday.

LAN (Map p208; 084-25-5555; www.lan.com; Av El Sol 627B; 8:30am-7pm Mon-Sat, to 1pm Sun) Direct flights to Lima, Arequipa, Juliaca and Puerto Maldonado.

Peruvian Airlines (Map p208; 084-25-4890; www.peruvian.pe; Av El Sol 627-A; 9am-7:30pm Mon-Sat, to noon Sun)

Star Perú (Map p208; 01-705-9000; www.starperu.com; Av El Sol 679; 9am-1pm & 3-6:30pm Mon-Sat, 9am-12:30pm Sun)

BUS & TAXI

Travel times are approximate and apply when road conditions are good. Delays are likely during the rainy season, particularly to Puerto Maldonado or Lima via Abancay. This road is paved, but landslides can block the way in the rainy season.

International

All international services depart from the **terminal terrestre** (☎084-22-4471; Vía de Evitamiento 429), about 2km out of town towards the airport. Take a taxi (S14) or walk via Av El Sol. After it turns into Alameda Pachacutec, pedestrians can walk on the median. Straight after the tower and statue of Pachacutec, turn right, following the railway lines into a side street, which reaches the terminal in five minutes.

To Bolivia, **Transportes Internacional Litoral** (☎084-23-1155; www.litoral-miramar.com), **Tour Peru** (☎084-23-6463; www.tourperu.com.pe), **Transzela** (☎084-23-8223; www.transzela.com.pe) offer daily services to Copacabana (10 hours, S60 to S80) and, along with **Transporte Salvador** (☎084-23-3680), La Paz via Desaguadero (12 hours, S80 to S120). This is the quickest way to get to La Paz.

Ormeño (☎084-24-1426) travels to most South American capitals.

Long Distance

Buses to major cities leave from the *terminal terrestre*. Buses for more unusual destinations leave from elsewhere, so check carefully in advance. **Ormeño** (☎084-24-1426) and **Cruz del Sur** (☎084-74-0444; www.cruzdelsur.com.pe) have the safest, most comfortable buses. Of the cheaper options, **Tour Peru** (☎084-23-6463; www.tourperu.com.pe) and **Wari Palomino** (☎084-22-2694) have the best buses.

There are departures to Juliaca and Puno every hour from 4am to 11pm, and at random hours through the day. Cheap, slow options like **Libertad** (☎084-22-4571) stop to let passengers on and off along the way, so you can use them to access towns along the route. Mid-priced **Transportes Internacional Litoral** (☎084-23-1155; www.litoral-miramar.com) and **CIAL** (☎965-401-414) are faster and more comfortable.

The most enjoyable way to get to Puno is via **Inka Express** (☎084-24-7887; www.inka-express.com; Av 28 de Julio 211) or **Turismo Mer** (☎084-24-5171; www.turismomer.com; El Óvalo, Av La Paz A3), which run luxury buses every morning. The service includes lunch and an English-speaking tour guide, who talks about the four sites that are briefly visited along the way: Andahuaylillas, Raqchi, Abra la Raya and Pucará. The trip takes about eight hours and costs around S150.

Departures to Arequipa cluster around 6am to 7am and 7pm to 9:30pm. Ormeño offers a deluxe service at 9am.

Cruz del Sur and **CIVA** (☎084-24-9961; www.civa.com.pe) offer relatively painless services to Lima. Wari is the best of the cheaper options. Most buses to Lima stop in Nazca (13 hours) and Ica (16 hours). These buses go via Abancay and can suffer holdups in rainy season. Between January and April, it may be worth going via Arequipa (25 to 27 hours) instead.

Wari Palomino and **Expreso Los Chankas** (☎084-26-2909) depart every couple of hours through the day for Abancay and Andahuaylas (S45, nine hours). Change at Andahuaylas to get to Ayacucho via rough roads that get very cold at night. If you're going to Ayacucho by bus, wear all of your warm clothes and if you have a sleeping bag, bring it on board the bus.

San Martín (☎984-61-2520) and **Julsa** (☎084-24-4308, 951-298-798) offer direct buses to Tacna.

Various companies depart for Puerto Maldonado between 3pm and 4:30pm; CIVA is probably the best option.

Buses to Quillabamba via Santa María (4½ hrs) leave from the Santiago terminal, a brisk 20-minute walk from the center. Around the corner in Calle Antonio Lorena, many more companies offer air-conditioned, speedy comfort in the form of modern minivans that cost twice as much and cut a couple of hours off the trip. There are departures of both types of service at 8am, 10am, 1pm and 8pm. Change at Santa María to get to Santa Teresa. From Cuzco, only **Turismo Cusco Imperial** (☎940-223-356; Terminal Santiago) goes to Santa Teresa (S25, six hours), three times daily.

Transportes Siwar (☎993-407-105; Av Tito Condemayta 1613) and other companies have buses to Ocongate and Tinqui (S10, three hours), the start of the Ausangante trek, leaving from behind the Coliseo Cerrado every half hour.

Several buses and minivans depart daily to Paucartambo (S9 to S12, three hours) from Paradero Control in distrito de San Jerónimo – a taxi will know where to drop you off.

Cuzco Buses:

DESTINATION	COST* (S)	DURATION (HR)
Abancay	20/30	5
Arequipa	40/100	10
Ayacucho	65/95	16
Copacabana (Bolivia)	60/80	10
Ica	100/190	16
Juliaca	30/40	5
La Paz (Bolivia)	80/120	12
Lima	100/190	21
Nazca	100/140	13
Puerto Maldonado	50/70	10
Puno	20/70	6
Quillabamba	25/35	6½
Tacna	70/100	15

*Prices are estimates for normal/luxury buses

Regional Services

The government may soon restrict the use of old *colectivos;* note that some of these services may be cut or reduced in the future. Most services run from at least 5am until 7pm. Early and late services may charge more.

➡ Minibuses to Calca (S6, 1½ hours) via Pisac (S4, one hour) leave frequently from the terminal at Tullumayo 207.

➡ Minibuses to Urubamba (S8, 1½ hours) via Pisac leave frequently from the terminal in Puputi 208, just north of Av de la Cultura.

➡ Minibuses to Urubamba (S6, 1½ hours) and Ollantaytambo (S12, two hours) via Chinchero (S4, one hour) leave from near the Puente Grau. Just around the corner on Pavitos, faster *colectivos* leave when full for Urubamba (S7, one hour) and Ollantaytambo (S10 to S15, 1½ hours) via Chinchero.

➡ *Colectivos* to Urcos (S5, one hour) via Tipón (S1, 40 minutes), Piquillacta (S5) and Andahuaylillas (S5) leave from the middle of the street outside Tullumayo 207. For S80 they'll drive you into the ruins at Tipón and Piquillacta, wait and bring you back.

➡ You can also get to the these destinations, and Saylla, by catching a minibus headed for Urcos (S5) from a terminal just off Av de la Cultura opposite the regional hospital. Shared taxis to Lucre (S3, one hour) depart from Huascar, between Av Garcilaso and Manco Capac, between 7am and 7pm.

➡ Minibuses for Limatambo (S12, two hours) and Curahuasi (S15, three hours) leave Arcopata when full, a couple of blocks west of Meloc, until about 3pm.

CAR & MOTORCYCLE

Given all the headaches and potential hazards of driving yourself around, consider hiring a taxi for the day – it's cheaper than renting a car. If you must, you'll find a couple of car-rental agencies in the bottom block of Av El Sol.

Motorcycle rentals are offered by a couple of agencies in the first block of Saphi heading away from the Plaza de Armas.

TRAIN

Cuzco has two train stations. **Estación Huanchac** (☎084-58-1414; ⏲7am-5pm Mon-Fri, to midnight Sat & Sun), near the end of Av El Sol, serves Juliaca and Puno on Lake Titicaca. **Estación Poroy**, east of town, serves Ollantaytambo and Machu Picchu. The two stations are unconnected, so it's impossible to travel directly from Puno to Machu Picchu. (Downtown Estación San Pedro is used only for local trains, which foreigners cannot board.)

You can take a taxi to Poroy (S30) or the station in Ollantaytambo (S80) from Cuzco. Return trips are slightly more expensive.

You can buy tickets at Huanchac station, and there are ATMs in the station, but the easiest way is directly through the train companies.

From January through March there is no train service between Cuzco and Aguas Calientes (for Machu Picchu) because of frequent landslides on the route. Instead, there's a bus from Estación Huanchac to Ollantaytambo where you can board a train there for the remainder of the trip.

To Ollantaytambo & Machu Picchu

The only way to reach Aguas Calientes (and access Machu Picchu) is via train (three hours).

Fares vary according to departure hours: more desirable times are usually more expensive. It is common for trains to sell out, especially at peak hours, so buy your ticket as far ahead of time as possible.

The quickest 'cheaper' way to get from Cuzco to Aguas Calientes is to take a *combi* (minibus) to Ollantaytambo and catch the train from there. In low season (between December and March), service from the Cuzco terminal is discontinued and replaced with a bus from Cuzco to Ollantaytambo from where you continue by train.

Peru Rail (Map p200; www.perurail.com; Estación Huanchac; ⏲7am-5pm Mon-Fri, to noon Sat) The flagship service to Aguas Calientes, with multiple departures daily from Estación Poroy, 20 minutes outside of Cuzco. There are three service categories: Expedition (from S223 one way), Vistadome (from S261 one way) and the luxurious Hiriam Bingham (from S1153 one way). The Hiram Bingham includes brunch, afternoon tea, entrance to Machu Picchu and a guided tour. It runs daily except Sunday.

Inca Rail (Map p200; ☎084-25-2974; www.incarail.com; Portal de Panes 105, Plaza de Armas; ⏲8am-9pm Mon-Fri, 9am-7pm Sat, to 2pm Sun) Has three departures daily from Ollantaytambo and four levels of service. Children get a significant discount. Environmentally sustainable business practice.

To Puno

Peru Rail (Map p200; www.perurail.com; Estación Huanchac; tickets S838; ⏲7am-5pm Mon-Fri, 7am-noon Sat) Andean Explorer, a luxury train with a glass-walled observation car, goes to Puno. Trains depart from Estación Huanchac at 8am, arriving at Puno around 6pm, on Monday, Wednesday and Saturday from November to March, with an extra departure on Friday from April to October. Lunch is included.

Getting Around

TO/FROM THE AIRPORT

The airport is about 6km south of the city center. The *combi* lines Imperial and C4M (S0.70, 20 minutes) run from Av El Sol to just outside the airport. A taxi to or from the city center to the airport costs S20. An official radio taxi from within the airport costs S25. With advance reservations, many hotels offer free pickup.

BUS

Local rides on public transportation cost only S0.70, though it's easier to walk or just take a taxi than to figure out where any given *combi* is headed.

TAXI

There are no meters in taxis, but there are set rates. At the time of research, trips within the city center cost S5, and to destinations further afield, such as El Molino, were S8. Check with your hotel whether this is still correct, and rather than negotiate, simply hand the correct amount to your driver at the end of your ride; he is unlikely to argue if you seem to know what you're doing. Official taxis, identified by a lit company telephone number on the roof, are more expensive than taxis flagged down on the street, but they are safer.

Unofficial 'pirate' taxis, which only have a taxi sticker in the window, have been complicit in muggings, violent assaults and kidnappings of tourists. Before getting into any taxi, do as savvy locals do and take conspicuous note of the registration number.

AloCusco (☎084-22-2222) A reliable company.

TRAM

Tranvia (tickets S25; ⏲Mon-Sat) A free-rolling tourist tram that conducts a 1½-hour hop-on, hop-off city tour. It leaves at 8:30am, 10am, 11:30am, 2pm, 3:30pm, 5pm and 6:30pm from the Plaza de Armas.

AROUND CUZCO

The four ruins closest to Cuzco are Sacsaywamán, Q'enqo, Pukapukara and Tambomachay. They can all be visited in a day – far less if you're whisked through on a guided tour. If you only have time to visit one site, Sacsaywamán is the most important, and less than a 2km trek uphill from the Plaza de Armas in central Cuzco.

The cheapest way to visit the sites is to take a bus bound for Pisac and ask the driver to stop at Tambomachay, the furthest site from Cuzco (at 3700m, it's also the highest). It's an 8km walk back to Cuzco, visiting all four ruins along the way. Alternatively, a taxi will charge roughly S70 to visit all four sites.

Each site can only be entered with the *boleto turístico* (p205). They're open daily from 7am to 6pm. Local guides hang around offering their services, sometimes quite persistently. Agree on a price before beginning any tour.

Robberies at these sites are uncommon but not unheard of. Cuzco's tourist police recommend visiting between 9am and 5pm.

Sacsaywamán

This immense **ruin** (Map p200; boleto turístico adult/student under 26 with ISIC card S130/70) of both religious and military significance is 2km from Cuzco. The long Quechua name means 'Satisfied Falcon,' though tourists will inevitably remember it by the mnemonic 'sexy woman.' Sacsaywamán feels huge, but only about 20% of the original structure remains. Soon after the conquest, the Spaniards tore down many walls and used the blocks to build their own houses, leaving the largest and most impressive rocks, especially the main battlements.

In 1536 the fort was the site of one of the most bitter battles of the Spanish conquest. More than two years after Pizarro's entry into Cuzco, the rebellious Manco Inca recaptured the lightly guarded Sacsaywamán and used it as a base to lay siege to the conquistadors in Cuzco. Manco was on the brink of defeating the Spaniards when a desperate last-ditch attack by 50 Spanish cavalry led by Juan Pizarro, Francisco's brother, succeeded in retaking Sacsaywamán and putting an end to the rebellion. Manco Inca survived and retreated to the fortress of Ollantaytambo, but most of his forces were killed. Thousands of dead littered the site after the Incas' defeat, attracting swarms of carrion-eating Andean condors. The tragedy was memorialized by the inclusion of eight condors in Cuzco's coat of arms.

The site is composed of three different areas, the most striking being the magnificent three-tiered zigzag fortifications. One stone, incredibly, weighs more than 300 tons. It was the ninth *inca*, Pachacutec, who envisioned Cuzco in the shape of a puma, with Sacsaywamán as the head, and these 22 zigzagged walls as the teeth of the puma. The walls also formed an extremely effective defensive mechanism that forced attackers to expose their flanks.

Opposite is the hill called Rodadero, with retaining walls, polished rocks and a finely carved series of stone benches known as the Inca's Throne. Three towers once stood above these walls. Only the foundations remain, but the 22m diameter of the largest, Muyuc Marca, gives an indication of how big they must have been. With its perfectly fitted stone conduits, this tower was probably used as a huge water tank for the garrison. Other buildings within the ramparts provided food and shelter for an estimated 5000 warriors. Most of these structures were torn down by the Spaniards and later inhabitants of Cuzco.

Between the zigzag ramparts and the hill lies a large, flat parade ground that is used for the colorful tourist spectacle of Inti Raymi, held every June 24.

To walk up to the site from Cuzco's Plaza de Armas takes 30 to 50 minutes, so make sure you're acclimatized before attempting it. Arriving at dawn will let you have the site almost to yourself, though solo travelers shouldn't come alone at this time of day.

Another option is to take a taxi tour which also includes Q'enkqo, Pukapukara and Tambomachay (S70).

The *boleto turístico* is valid for 10 days and covers 16 other sites.

Q'enqo

The name of this small but fascinating ruin means 'zigzag.' A large limestone rock, it's riddled with niches, steps and extraordinary symbolic carvings, including the zigzagging channels that probably gave the site its name. Scramble up to the top to find a flat surface used for ceremonies: look carefully to see laboriously etched representations of a puma, a condor and a llama. Back below, you can explore a mysterious subterranean cave with altars hewn into the rock. Q'enqo is about 4km northeast of Cuzco, on the left of the road as you descend from Tambomachay.

Pukapukara

Just across the main road from Tambomachay, this commanding structure looks down on the Cuzco valley. In some lights the rock looks pink, and the name literally means 'Red Fort,' though it is more likely to have been a hunting lodge, a guard post and a stopping point for travelers. It is composed of several lower residential chambers, storerooms and an upper esplanade with panoramic views.

Tambomachay

In a sheltered spot about 300m from the main road, this site consists of a beautifully wrought **ceremonial stone bath** (⏲dawn-dusk) channeling crystalline spring water through fountains that still function today. It is thus popularly known as El Baño del Inca (Bath of the Inca), and theories connect the site to an Inca water cult. It's 8km northeast of Cuzco.

THE SACRED VALLEY

Tucked under the tawny skirts of formidable foothills, the beautiful Río Urubamba Valley, known as El Valle Sagrado (The Sacred Valley), is about 15km north of Cuzco as the condor flies, via a narrow road of hairpin turns. Long the home of attractive colonial towns and isolated weaving villages, in recent years it has become a destination in its own right. Star attractions are the markets and the lofty Inca citadels of Pisac and Ollantaytambo, but the valley is also packed with other Inca sites. Trekking routes are deservedly gaining in popularity. Adrenaline activities range from rafting to rock climbing. Most activities can be organized in Cuzco or at some hotels in Urubamba.

A multitude of travel agencies in Cuzco offer whirlwind tours of the Sacred Valley, stopping at markets and the most significant archaeological sites. If you have a day or two to spare, spend it exploring this peaceful, fetching corner of the Andes at your own leisure. The archaeological sites of Pisac, Ollantaytambo and Chinchero can be visited with a *boleto turístico* (p205), which can be bought directly on-site.

Pisac

☎084 / POP 900 / ELEV 2715M

It's not hard to succumb to the charms of sunny Pisac, a bustling and fast-growing colonial village at the base of a spectacular Inca fortress perched on a mountain spur. Its pull is universal and recent years have seen an influx of expats and new age followers in search of an Andean Shangri-la. Indeed, it's a magnet for spiritual seekers. The local tourism industry has responded by offering everything from yoga retreats and cleanses to guided hallucinogenic trips. Yet it's also worthwhile for mainstream travelers, with ruins, a fabulous market and weaving villages that should not be missed. Located just 33km northeast of Cuzco by a paved road, it's the most convenient starting point to the Sacred Valley.

Sights & Activities

Mercado de Artesania MARKET

Pisac is known far and wide for its market, by far the biggest and most touristy in the region. Official market days are Tuesday, Thursday and Sunday, when tourist buses descend on the town in droves. However, the market has taken over Pisac to such an extent that it fills the Plaza de Armas and surrounding streets every day; visit on Monday, Wednesday, Friday or Saturday if you want to avoid the worst of the crowds.

Pisac Ruins RUINS

(boleto turístico adult/student under 26 with ISIC card S130/70; dawn-dusk) A truly awesome site with relatively few tourists, this hilltop Inca citadel lies high above the village on a triangular plateau with a plunging gorge on either side. Allow several hours to explore. To walk from town, a steep but spectacular 4km trail starts above the west side of the church. It's a two-hour climb and 1½ hour return. Worthwhile but grueling, it's good training for the Inca Trail! Taking a taxi up and walking back is a good option.

The most impressive feature is the agricultural **terracing**, which sweeps around the south and east flanks of the mountain in huge and graceful curves, almost entirely unbroken by steps (which require greater maintenance and promote erosion). Instead, the terracing is joined by diagonal flights of stairs made of flagstones set into the terrace walls. Above the terraces are cliff-hugging footpaths, watched over by caracara falcons and well defended by massive stone doorways, steep stairs and a short tunnel carved out of the rock. Vendors sell drinks at the top.

This dominating site guards not only the Urubamba Valley below, but also a pass leading into the jungle to the northeast. Topping the terraces is the site's **ceremonial center**, with an *intihuatana* (literally 'hitching post of the sun'; an Inca astronomical tool), several working water channels, and some painstakingly neat masonry in the well-preserved **temples**. A path leads up the hillside to a series of ceremonial baths and around to the military area. Looking across the Kitamayo Gorge from the back of the site, you'll also see hundreds of holes honeycombing the cliff wall. These are **Inca tombs** that were plundered by *huaqueros*

The Sacred Valley

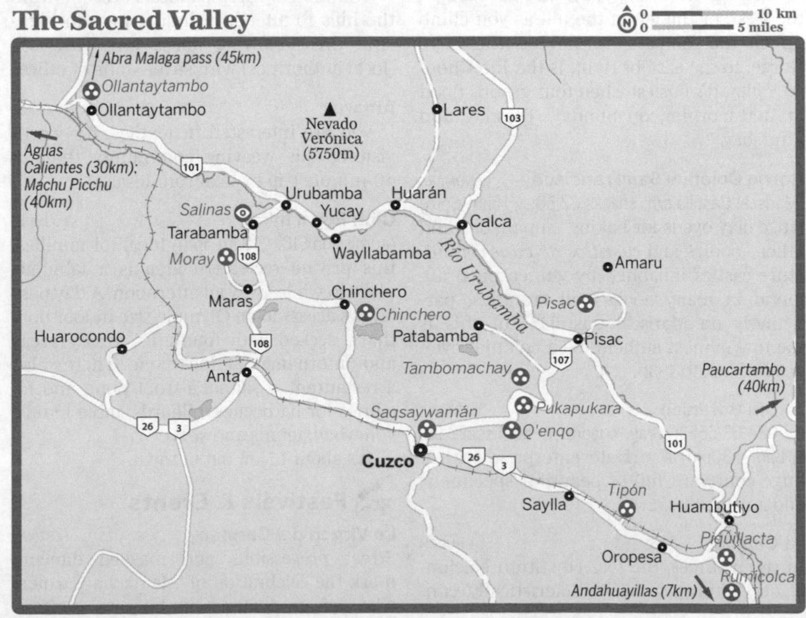

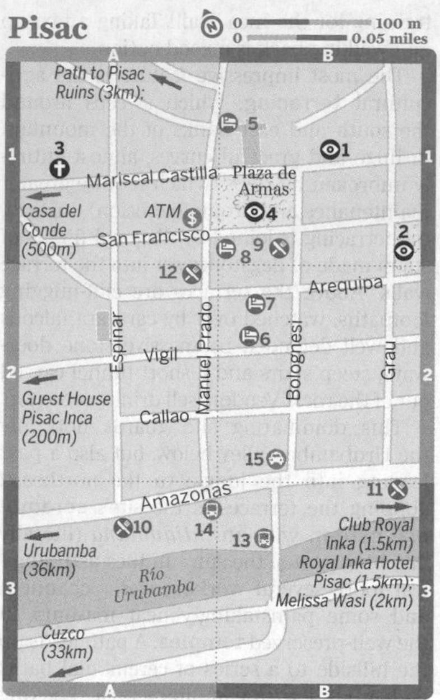

Pisac

Sights

1 Horno Colonial San Francisco....B1
2 Jardín Botanico....B1
3 La Capilla....A1
4 Mercado de Artesania....B1

Sleeping

5 Hospedaje Beho....B1
6 Hotel Pisac Quishu....B2
7 Kinsa Ccocha Inn....B2
8 Pisac Inn....B1

Eating

9 Mullu....B1
Restaurante Cuchara de Palo....(see 8)
10 Restaurante Valle Sagrado....A3
11 Restaurante Yoly....B3
12 Ulrike's Café....A2

Transport

13 Buses....B3
14 Buses to Cuzco....A3
15 Taxis to Ruins....B2

(grave robbers), and are now completely off-limits to tourists.

For those taking the footpath, there are many crisscrossing trails, but if you aim toward the terracing, you won't get lost. To the west, or the left of the hill as you climb up on the footpath, is the Río Kitamayo Gorge; to the east, or right, is the Río Chongo Valley. It's busiest when tour groups flood in mid-morning on Sunday, Tuesday and Thursday.

Horno Colonial San Francisco LANDMARK
(Mariscal Castilla s/n; snacks S2.50; 6am-6pm) Huge clay ovens for baking empanadas and other goodies and *castillos de cuyes* (miniature castles inhabited by guinea pigs) are found in many nooks and crannies, particularly on Mariscal Castilla. But this is the town's most authentic – a colonial oven dating back to 1830.

Jardín Botanico GARDENS
(084-63-5563; Grau, cuadra 4; admission S8; 8am-4:30pm) A private enterprise with a huge courtyard full of beautiful specimens and a resident cat.

La Capilla CHURCH
In recent times, the INC (Instituto Nacional de Cultura), in a characteristically controversial move, demolished the church in the main square in order to reconstruct it in colonial style. Masses, which have moved to a nearby chapel, are worth visiting. On Sunday, a Quechua-language mass is held at 11am.

Traditionally dressed locals descend from the hills to attend, including men in highland dress blowing horns and *varayocs* (local authorities) with silver staffs of office.

Amaru VILLAGE
If you are interested in textiles, it's worth visiting this weaving community that's a 40-minute trip by taxi from Pisac.

Club Royal Inka SWIMMING
(admission S10; 8am-4pm) Ideal for families, this private recreation area is a fabulous place to while away an afternoon. A day pass allows access to an Olympic-size indoor pool that's decked with fountains, grassy areas and an ornamental duck pond. There's also a restaurant, a sauna, a trout pond and facilities for barbecues, billiards, table tennis, volleyball, tennis and *sapo*.

It's about 1.5km out of town.

Festivals & Events

La Virgen del Carmen FESTIVAL
Street processions and masked dancing mark the celebration of 'Mamacha Carmen' who defeats demons climbing on rooftops

and balconies. This renowned celebration of the Virgin of Carmen takes place from around July 15 to July 18.

Sleeping

Foreign-run mystical and spiritual retreats on the outskirts of town offer packages with shamanic ceremonies; some are vastly more commercial than others.

Hotel Pisac Quishu GUESTHOUSE $
(084-43-6921; www.pisacinca.com; Vigil 242; s/d S50/100, s/d without bathroom S40/70, all incl breakfast;) A small, family-run lodging overseen by friendly host Tatiana. There's a handful of colorful rooms around a tiny courtyard and kitchen use. A larger, sister guesthouse is a 10-minute walk away.

Kinsa Ccocha Inn HOTEL $
(084-20-3101; kinsaccocha_inn@hotmail.com; Arequipa 307A; s/d S60/80, tr/q without bathroom S75/100;) With a fertile fig tree in its stony patio, this simple lodging has a nice vibe and thoughtful touches, such as plenty of power plugs, good towels and strong, hot showers. Breakfast is not offered, but there's an adjoining cafe.

Guest House Pisac Inca GUESTHOUSE $
(084-50-9106; www.pisacinca.com; Calle Huayna Picchu s/n; s/d/tr 136/179/223, s/d without bathroom 56/99) A few blocks away from the center, this ample guesthouse is freshly minted. Rooms center on a large, grassy area. Some have kitchenettes. There's also a roof deck with views. It's run by the same hospitable family that runs Hotel Pisac Quishu.

Hospedaje Beho GUESTHOUSE $
(084-20-3001, 984-848-538; hospedajebehopisac@gmail.com; Intihuatana 113; s/d S40/80, s/d without bathroom S30/70;) On the path to the ruins, this family-run lodging beyond a handicrafts shop offers no-frills accommodations with warm showers. The raggedy, rambling garden is a tranquil haven from the madness of the market streets just outside. Also offers airport transfers and car rentals.

Club Royal Inka CAMPGROUND $
(084-20-3066, 084-20-3064; camping per person S25;) Camping doesn't get any better than this. Pitch a tent in your own designated, fenced-off site with a fireplace, a light and a power plug, and enjoy all the amenities of the club, including the Olympic-size pool. There is also a playground for kids.

★ **Pisac Inn** INN $$
(084-20-3062; www.pisacinn.com; Plaza de Armas; s/d/tr incl breakfast S185/230/295;) Location, location, location! This lovely plaza hotel features an inviting courtyard and romantic rooms with down bedding, dark blue walls and Andean decor. Rooms with king-size beds are a slight upgrade. Unlike others, it's open year-round, with good off-season discounts. The location means some rooms get noisy early when merchants are setting up outside. German, English and French are spoken.

Melissa Wasi LODGE $$
(s/d S181/294, 4-person cabin S417;) Guests rave about the warm treatment at this attractive established lodge situated on a shady lane. It also serves as a spiritual retreat center. The restaurant has nightly chef-prepared dinners and English is spoken. Wi-fi is only available in common areas. Located 2km from Pisac.

La Casa del Conde GUESTHOUSE $$
(084-78-7818; www.cuzcovalle.com; s/d/ste incl breakfast S185/247/309;) La Casa del Conde is a lovely country house, nestled into the foothills with blooming flower patches. Family-run and brimming with personality, it has pleasant rooms, with down duvets, heating and cable TV. There's no car access. It's a 10-minute walk uphill from the plaza, but a *mototaxi* (three-wheeled motorcycle rickshaw taxi) can leave you at the chapel that's five minutes away.

Royal Inka Hotel Pisac HOTEL $$
(084-20-3066, 084-20-3064; www.royalinkahotel.pe; s/d incl breakfast S147/205;) Once a large hacienda, this hotel is surprisingly unpretentious. Rooms are generous, many with views of the ruins, surrounded by well-tended flower gardens and conservatories. Guests can access the facilities of Club Royal Inka across the road, plus the on-site spa and Jacuzzi. The wi-fi only works in some areas. Located about 1.5km from the plaza up the road to the ruins.

Eating

Restaurante Yoly PERUVIAN $
(084-20-3114; Amazonas s/n; menú S5; 6am-10pm) Popular with locals, this bare-bones restaurant offers home-cooked set meals with soup and drink included.

Restaurante Valle Sagrado PERUVIAN $
(084-20-3009; Amazonas s/n; menú S8-23; 8am-9pm) The *menú turistico* here is somewhat fancier; if you want to eat what the locals are eating (and pay only what they are paying), order the basic *menú*.

Ulrike's Café CAFE $$
(084-20-3195; Manuel Prado s/s; veggie/meat menú S22/25, mains S15-33; 9am-9pm;) This sunny cafe is consistently tasty, serving up a great vegetarian *menú*, plus homemade pasta, melt-in-the-mouth cheesecake and a fluffy carrot cake that is legendary. There's a book exchange, DVDs and special events. English, French and German are spoken.

Mullu FUSION $$
(084-20-3073; www.mullu.pe; San Francisco s/n, 2nd fl; mains S14-32; 9am-9pm) The balcony may be the best spot to watch market-day interactions in the plaza below. Chill and welcoming, the menu is fusion (think Thai meets Amazonian and flirts with highland Peruvian). Traditional lamb is tender to falling-off-the-bone; soups and blended juices also satisfy.

Restaurante Cuchara de Palo INTERNATIONAL $$
(084-20-3062; Plaza de Armas; mains S15-38; 7:30-9:30am & noon-8pm) Inside Pisac Inn, this fine-dining restaurant offers organic salads and original dishes like pumpkin ravioli drizzled with corn and cream. Service can be slow but it has great ambience, with candle-lit courtyard tables.

Information

There's an ATM in the Plaza de Armas. There are slow cybercafes around the plaza and a minisupermarket on Bolognesi.

Getting There & Around

Buses to Urubamba (S3, one hour) leave frequently from the downtown bridge between 6am and 8pm. Minibuses to Cuzco (S5, one hour) leave from Calle Amazonas when full. Many travel agencies in Cuzco also operate tour buses to Pisac, especially on market days.

For the Pisac ruins, minivans (S25 to S30 per van, one way) near the plaza leave regularly or hire a taxi from near the bridge into town to drive you up the 7.5km paved road.

Pisac to Urubamba

Between Pisac and Urubamba is a series of pretty villages (as well as the non-touristy but fairly uninteresting town of Calca), which can easily be explored in a day. **Yucay** and **Huarán** offer boutique accommodation and food options, and make excellent bases for leisurely exploration of the safe, scenic Sacred Valley and its many intriguing side valleys.

A visit to the community of **Patabamba** offers a fascinating participative demonstration of the weaving process, all the way from picking the plants to making dyes, to shearing sheep and setting up a loom – with explanations of the meanings of colors and patterns. There are also excellent trekking options. Campsites and homestays are available with advance notice. Prices vary wildly, depending on group size and transport needed. Both **Journey Experience** (www.thejoex.com) and **Chaski Ventura** (www.chaskiventura.com) offer visits.

In Huarán, country inn **Greenhouse** (984-770-130; www.thegreenhouseperu.com; Km 56.9, Carr Pisac-Ollantaytambo; s/d/tr S232/309/417;) offers respite replete with dogs lounging on their pillows and hammocks in the lush garden. Large rooms are well-appointed and afford complete privacy. As green as its name, it features solar panels, composting and recycling, uses recycled river water for gardening and offers guests water refills. There's a healing room with massage, acupuncture and reiki offered. Family dinners (S70) gather guests around a common table. To get here, you can grab a bus between Pisac and Urubamba or grab a taxi (S15) from Urubamba.

Also in Huarán, adventure tour operator **Munaycha** (984-770-381; www.munaycha.com; Km 60.2, Carretera Pisac–Ollantaytambo) comes highly recommended. Among other trips, it guides Lares treks, as well as more local options, and a variety of mountain-bike trips. We have heard rave reviews about trek-bike combinations to Huaipo Lake near Chinchero. Buses running between Pisac and Urubamba pass regularly.

Urubamba

084 / ELEV 2870M / POP 17,500

A busy and unadorned urban center, Urubamba is a transportation hub surrounded by bucolic foothills and snowy peaks. The advantages of its lower altitude and relative proximity to Machu Picchu make it popular with both high-end hotels and package tours. While there is little of historical interest, nice countryside and great weather make it a convenient base from which to explore the extraordinary salt flats of Salinas and the terracing of Moray.

Since Urubamba is quite spread out, the mode of transportation of choice are *mototaxis* (three-wheeled motorcycle rickshaw taxis). The Plaza de Armas is five blocks east and four blocks north of the terminal, bounded by Calle Comercio and Jirón Grau.

Activities

Many outdoor activities that are organized from Cuzco take place near here, including horseback riding, rock climbing, mountain biking, paragliding and hot-air balloon trips.

Perol Chico HORSE RIDING
(☎950-314-065; www.perolchico.com; overnight packages from US$590) This place is run by Dutch-Peruvian Eduard van Brunschot Vega, with an excellent ranch outside Urubamba with Peruvian *paso* horses. Eduard organizes horseback-riding tours that last up to two weeks. An overnight in the Sacred Valley with rides to Salinas, Maras and Moray includes all meals and luxury accommodations. Advance bookings are required.

Cusco for You HORSE RIDING
(☎084-79-5301, 987-841-000; www.cuscoforyou.com; Carretera a Salineras de Maras; day trips US$170) Highly recommended for horseback-riding and trekking trips from one to eight days long. Horseback-riding day trips go to Moray and Salinas and other regional destinations. Ask about special rates for families and groups.

Sacred Wheels BICYCLE TOUR
(☎954-700-844; www.sacredwheels.com) Even the casual rider can enjoy these mountain-bike tours that visit the valley and urban Urubamba.

Sleeping

A new hub of luxury hotels, Urubamaba has surprisingly few mid-to-low end offerings. Most hotels are lined up along the highway, west of town and the bus terminal, on the way to Ollantaytambo.

Los Jardines HOTEL $
(☎084-20-1331; www.losjardines.weebly.com; Jr Convención 459; s/d/tr S60/80/90) Noted for its accommodating service, this family hotel occupies a walled compound with a large adobe home and flowering gardens that make it feel like the city isn't even there. Rooms are basic but clean, some feature large picture windows. The buffet breakfast served in the garden is extra (S12). It's within walking distance of the plaza.

Llama Pack HOSTEL $
(www.llamapackperu.com; dm incl breakfast S35) Located outside of town on the main road, this affable hostel sits behind an all-encompassing cement wall. There are several bunk rooms and a tidy shared kitchen and living area. The owners have lots of information on trekking and bike touring, they also run llama treks to Lares and other parts. Reservations required, since no one regularly attends the door.

Hostal los Perales GUESTHOUSE $
(☎084-20-1151; www.ecolodgeurubamba.com; Pasaje Arenales 102; r per person S35) Tucked down a hidden country lane, this welcoming family-run guesthouse offers good-value, basic rooms around lovely overgrown gardens. Its elderly owners are sweet, serving banana pancakes and tomato jam from their own

COMMUNITY TOURISM IN THE SACRED VALLEY

In recent times, rural communities of the valley have become far more accessible to visitors. While usually hospitable to passersby, they feature little infrastructure for visitors, so it's best to organize a visit in advance.

➡ **La Tierra de los Yachaqs** (☎971-502-223; www.yachaqs.com) A rural tourism network. Guests visit Andean communities, trek to highland lakes and learn about natural medicine and artisan traditions.

➡ **Parque de la Papa** (☎084-24-5021; www.parquedelapapa.org; Pisac) Day treks and cooking workshops are some of the offerings of this new nonprofit which promotes potato diversity and communal farming.

➡ For a guided trip to visit traditional communities, check out these recommended operators: **Journey Experience** (www.thejoex.com), **Chaski Ventura** (www.chaskiventura.com) and **Respons** (www.respons.org).

tree for breakfast. It's easy to get lost, so take a *mototaxi* (S1) from the terminal.

★Las Chullpas CABINS $$

(☎084-20-1568; www.chullpas.pe; Pumahuanca Valley; s/d/tr/q incl breakfast S140/200/270/300; @📶) Hidden 3km above town, these rustic woodland cottages make for the perfect getaway. Rooms feature comfortable beds and fireplaces. The site, nestled among thick eucalyptus trees, is spread out with inviting pathways and lounge areas with hammocks. There is also an open kitchen serving vegetarian food, holistic treatments and a sweat lodge (available on request).

Much of the food is grown organically on site, and efforts are made towards composting and recycling. The affable Chilean owner also guides treks, especially to the Lares Valley. Highly recommended. Come with good directions; the roads are unmarked and not all taxi drivers know it.

★Sol y Luna BOUTIQUE HOTEL $$$

(☎084-20-1620; www.hotelsolyluna.com; Fundo Huincho lote A-5; d/tr from S905/1199; @📶🏊) A living fairy tale, this luxury Relais & Chateaux property runs wild with whimsy. Fans of folk art will be overwhelmed – its 43 *casitas* (cabins) feature original murals and comic, oversized sculptures by noted Peruvian artist Federico Bauer. The playful feel spills over to bold tropical hues and a decor of carved wooden beds, freestanding tubs and dainty chandeliers.

French-Swiss owned, it all conspires to charm you. Avant-garde circus productions with former Cirque de Soleil artists provide evening entertainment. For daytime fun, Peruvian *paso* horses can be ridden on the 15 hectares and beyond. With eccentric atmosphere, its acclaimed restaurant Wayra is the creation of Lima's Malabar-famed chef. There's also a more casual open-air offering featuring food tours and chef visits.

Río Sagrado Hotel LUXURY HOTEL $$$

(☎084-20-1631; www.riosagradohotel.com; d incl breakfast from S1190; @📶) A design haven of cottage-style rooms with rough-hewn beams and exquisite accents of Ayacucho embroidery, this Belmond property is the epitome of understated luxury. The steep hillside location affords privacy for rooms set on terraced pathways perfumed with jasmine blooms. There's also river views from hammocks set amid cascading waterfalls. Facilities include a spa, hot tubs, sauna and restaurant.

K'uychi Rumi BUNGALOW $$$

(☎084-20-1169; www.urubamba.com; d/q incl breakfast S432/710; @📶) 'Rainbow Stone' in Quechua, this walled compound of two-story cottages tucked into gardens offers a lost retreat. It's family-friendly, small and personable, popular among European travelers. There are various configurations, but most are two-bedroom with kitchenette, fireplace and terrace balcony, linked by a labyrinthine trail with hummingbirds zipping around and very friendly dogs that guard the property.

It's between Km 74 and Km 75 on the main highway, more than 2km west of town.

Tambo del Inka LUXURY HOTEL $$$

(☎084-58-1777; www.libertador.com.pe; d/ste from S661/1282; @📶🏊) Just like Hogwarts, Tambo del Inca features its own train station – handy for a morning jaunt to Machu Picchu. Stark and commanding, this LEED-certified hotel (with its own water treatment plant and UV air filters) occupies an immense riverside spread with giant eucalyptus trees. The eucalyptus is a staple of interior decor and even spa treatments.

The hotel's best features: the chromotherapeutic indoor–outdoor pool which changes colors at night, and a hipster lounge with round tables and leather armchairs, back-lit by an immense mural of fractured onyx. Rooms are appealing and comfortable, but it seems cheeky that standards like breakfast and wi-fi cost extra.

Casa Andina LUXURY HOTEL $$$

(☎in Lima 01-213-9739; www.casa-andina.com; 5th Paradero, Yanahuara; d/ste incl breakfast from S386/426; @📶) In a lovely countryside setting, this good-value Peruvian chain has 92 rooms in townhouse-style buildings on manicured lawns. The main lobby and restaurant occupies an inviting high-ceiling glass lodge. Classic rooms offer standard amenities and plasma TVs. Among activities are riding, biking and visits to Maras and Moray.

✕ Eating & Drinking

High-end hotels have good restaurants open to the public. There are a few touristic *quintas* (houses serving typical Andean food) along the highway east of the *grifo* (gas station).

Kaia CAFE $

(☎084-20-1192; Calle Berriozabel III; mains S12-22; ⏱noon-6pm Sun-Thu, to 9pm Fri-Sat) A great addition to Urubamba, this garden cafe offers flavorful vegetarian fare, a lunchtime set menu (S18 to S24) and even homemade baby food (S8). There's also lentil burgers, tacos, homemade hot sauce and sides of crunchy pickled vegetables. Delicious fresh juices come spiked with *maca* (a natural energy booster) or honey. With occasional live music.

★**Huacatay** PERUVIAN $$

(☎084-20-1790; Arica 620; mains S32-50; ⏱1-9:30pm Mon-Sat) In a little house tucked down a narrow side street, Huacatay makes a lovely night out. Though not every dish is a hit, the tender alpaca steak, served in a port reduction sauce with creamy quinoa risotto and topped with a spiral potato chip, is the very stuff memories are made of. Staff aim to please and there's warm ambience.

Tres Keros Restaurant Grill & Bar NOVOANDINA $$

(☎084-20-1701; cnr hwy & Señor de Torrechayoc; mains from S26; ⏱lunch & dinner) Garrulous chef Ricardo Behar dishes up tasty gourmet fare, smokes his own trout and imports steak from Argentina. Food is taken seriously here, and enjoyed accordingly. It's 500m west of town.

Shopping

Seminario Cerámicas CERAMICS

(☎084-20-1002; www.ceramicaseminario.com; Berriozabal 405; ⏱8am-7pm) The internationally known local potter Pablo Seminario creates original work with a pre-conquest influence. His workshop – actually a small factory – is open to the public and offers a well-organized tour through the entire ceramics process.

Information

Banco de la Nación (Mariscal Castilla s/n) changes US dollars. There are ATMs at the *grifo* (gas station) on the corner of the highway and the main street, Mariscal Castilla, and along the highway to its east. **Clínica Pardo** (☎984-10-8948), on the highway a couple of blocks west of the *grifo*, offers medical attention.

Getting There & Around

Urubamba serves as the valley's principal transportation hub. The bus terminal is about 1km west of town on the highway. Buses leave every 15 minutes for Cuzco (S4, two hours) via Pisac (S4, one hour) or Chinchero (S3, 50 minutes). Buses (S1.50, 30 minutes) and *colectivos* (S2.50, 25 minutes) to Ollantaytambo leave often.

Colectivos to Quillabamba (S35, five hours) leave from the *grifo*.

A standard *mototaxi* ride around town costs S1.

Salinas

Salinas (admission S10; ⏱9am-4:30pm) is among the most spectacular sights in the whole Cuzco area, with thousands of salt pans that have been used for salt extraction since Inca times. A hot spring at the top of the valley discharges a small stream of heavily salt-laden water, which is diverted into salt pans and evaporated to produce a salt used for cattle licks. It all sounds very pedestrian but the overall effect is beautiful and surreal.

To get here, cross the Río Urubamba over the bridge in Tarabamba, about 4km down the valley from Urubamba, turn right and follow a footpath along the south bank to a small cemetery, where you turn left and climb up a valley to the salt pans of Salinas. It's about a 500m uphill hike.

A rough dirt road that can be navigated by taxi enters Salinas from above, giving spectacular views. Tour groups visit via this route most days. A taxi from Urubamba to visit Salinas and the nearby Moray costs around S120. You can also walk or bike here from Maras. If it's hot, walk the downhill route from Maras and arrange ahead a taxi pickup.

Chinchero

☎084 / POP 900 / ELEV 3762M

Known to the Incas as the birthplace of the rainbow, this typical Andean village combines Inca ruins with a colonial church, some wonderful mountain views and a colorful Sunday market. On a high plain with sweeping views to snow-laden peaks, it's quite beautiful.

Since it is very high, it's unwise to spend the night until you're somewhat acclimated. Entry to the historic precinct, where the ruins, the church and the museum are all found, is by the *boleto turístico* (adult/student under 26 with ISIC card S130/70), valid for 10 days and covering 17 sites across the region, including Cuzco.

Sights & Activities

Iglesia Colonial de Chinchero CHURCH
(adult/student under 26 with ISIC card S130/70; ⏲8am-5:30pm) Among the most beautiful churches in the valley, this colonial church is built on Inca foundations. The interior, decked out in merry floral and religious designs, is well worth seeing. Admission is via the *boleto turístico* tourist card (valid for 10 days and for 16 other sites across the region).

Mercado de Chinchero MARKET
The Chinchero market, held on Tuesday, Thursday and especially Sunday, is less touristy than its counterpart in Pisac and well worth a special trip. On Sunday, traditionally dressed locals descend from the hills for the produce market, where the ancient practice of *trueco* (bartering) still takes place; this is a rare opportunity to observe genuine bartering.

Centro de Textiles Tradicionales HANDICRAFTS
(Manzanares s/n) The best artisan workshop in town.

Ruinas Inca RUINS
The most extensive ruins here consist of terracing. If you start walking away from the village through the terraces on the right-hand side of the valley, you'll also find various rocks carved into seats and staircases.

Museo del Sitio MUSEUM
(☎084-22-3245; adult/student under 26 with ISIC card S70/35; ⏲9am-5pm Tue-Sun) A small archaeological museum opposite the church houses a collection heavy on broken pots. Admission is via the partial *boleto turístico* tourist ticket (valid for two days and for nearby ruins).

Wayllabamba HIKING
On the far side of the valley, a clear trail climbs upward before heading north and down to the Río Urubamba Valley (about four hours). At the river, the trail turns left and continues to a bridge at Wayllabamba. Cross it for the Sacred Valley road to Calca (turn right, about 13km) or Urubamba (turn left, about 9km).

You can flag down any passing bus until mid-afternoon, or continue walking to Yucay, where the trail officially ends. In Yucay you'll find a colonial church, an Inca ruin, and more than one charming accommodation option.

Sleeping & Eating

Other than the restaurants attached to accommodations (open to non-guests), there are few eating options in town.

La Casa de Barro INN $$
(☎084-30-6031; www.lacasadebarro.com; cnr hwy & Miraflores; s/d/tr incl breakfast S185/247/294) A colorful architect-designed adobe with Italian influence, it's a wonderful retreat for couples or families. There's curvy, rambling stairways and nooks, an overgrown garden, and tasteful rooms with snug quilts. It's also ideal for children, with a playroom and swings. Staff can arrange excursions around the region. The restaurant's set menu is S60, with a vegetarian version available for S50.

Hospedaje Mi Piuray GUESTHOUSE $
(☎084-30-6029; www.hospedajemipiuraycusco.com; Garcilaso 187; s/d/tr/q incl breakfast S70/100/110/120) A welcoming family hostelry with large, neat rooms with pastel accents and a sunny courtyard. There's also an on-site restaurant and bar.

Getting There & Away

Combis and *colectivos* traveling between Cuzco (S5 and S6 respectively, 45 minutes) and Urubamba (S4 and S6 respectively, 30 minutes) stop on the corner of the highway and Calle Manco Capac II; just flag down whatever comes along. They will also drop you off at intermediate points such as the turnoff to Maras.

Moray & Maras

The impressively deep amphitheater-like terracing of **Moray** (admission via boleto parcial S70; ⏲dawn-dusk), reached via the small town of **Maras** (admission S10), is a fascinating spectacle. Different levels of concentric terraces are carved into a huge earthen bowl, each layer of which has its own microclimate, according to depth. Some theorize that the Incas used the terraces as a kind of laboratory to determine the optimal conditions for growing crops of each species. There are three bowls, one of which has been planted with various crops as a kind of living museum.

Though refreshingly off the beaten path, this site is not challenging to reach. Take any transportation bound between Urubamba and Cuzco via Chinchero and ask to be let off at the Maras/Moray turnoff. Taxis usually wait at this turnoff to take tourists to Moray and back for around S50, or both Moray and

Salinas and back to the turnoff for around S70. A taxi from Urubamba to visit both Salinas and Moray costs around S100.

You could also tackle the 4km walk to the village of Maras yourself. From there, follow the road another 9km to Moray.

From Maras, you can walk or bike to Salinas, about 6km away. The trail starts behind the church. The Maras taxi company rents out bikes for this purpose – this is a fun, fast, single-track ride.

Ollantaytambo

084 / POP 700 / ELEV 2800M

Dominated by two massive Inca ruins, the quaint village of Ollantaytambo (known to locals and visitors alike as Ollanta) is the best surviving example of Inca city planning, with narrow cobblestone streets that have been continuously inhabited since the 13th century. After the hordes passing through on their way to Machu Picchu die down around late morning, Ollanta is a lovely place to be. It's perfect for wandering the mazy, narrow byways, past stone buildings and babbling irrigation channels, pretending you've stepped back in time. It also offers access to excellent hiking and biking.

Currently, Ollantaytambo suffers for being a thoroughfare between Cuzco and the jungle. Since there are no alternate roads, huge semi trucks and buses barrel through the narrow main street (barely missing pedestrians). Locals question the disruption of town life, along with the effect of excessive exhaust on the ruins, but talk of an alternative road has not materialized in any immediate plans.

There are a couple of internet cafes and ATMs in and around Plaza de Armas. There are no banks, but several places change money.

EXPLORE MORE OLLANTA

Charmed by this small town? There's plenty to do if you want to extend your stay:

- Explore **Pinkulluna ruins**, with great views of town. Take the entry on Calle Lari. The trail is very steep, so hike carefully and wear boots with good traction.
- Day hike to **Intipunku** (p257), an old Inca lookout.
- Hike or mountain bike to **Pumamarka**, a nearly forgotten Inca ruin, a half-day trip. Local hotels can give you directions.

Sights & Activities

Ollantaytambo Ruins RUINS

(adult/student under 26 with ISIC card S130/70; 7am-5pm) Both fortress and temple, these spectacular Inca ruins rise above Ollantaytambo, making a splendid half-day trip. (Admission is via the *boleto turístico* tourist card, valid for 10 days and for 16 other sites across the region.)

The huge, steep terraces that guard Ollantaytambo's spectacular Inca ruins mark one of the few places where the Spanish conquistadors lost a major battle.

The rebellious Manco Inca had retreated to this fortress after his defeat at Sacsaywamán. In 1536, Hernando Pizarro, Francisco's younger half-brother, led a force of 70 cavalrymen to Ollantaytambo, supported by large numbers of indigenous and Spanish foot soldiers, in an attempt to capture Manco Inca.

The conquistadors, showered with arrows, spears and boulders from atop the steep terracing, were unable to climb to the fortress. In a brilliant move, Manco Inca flooded the plain below the fortress through previously prepared channels. With Spaniards' horses bogged down in the water, Pizarro ordered a hasty retreat, chased down by thousands of Manco Inca's victorious soldiers.

Yet the Inca victory would be short lived. Spanish forces soon returned with a quadrupled cavalry force and Manco fled to his jungle stronghold in Vilcabamba.

Though Ollantaytambo was a highly effective fortress, it also served as a temple. A finely worked **ceremonial center** is at the top of the terracing. Some extremely well-built walls were under construction at the time of the conquest and have never been completed. The stone was quarried from the mountainside 6km away, high above the opposite bank of the Río Urubamba. Transporting the huge stone blocks to the site was a stupendous feat. The Incas' crafty technique to move massive blocks across the river meant carting the blocks to the riverside then diverting the entire river channel around them.

The 6km hike to the Inca quarry on the opposite side of the river is a good walk from Ollantaytambo. The trail starts from

Ollantaytambo

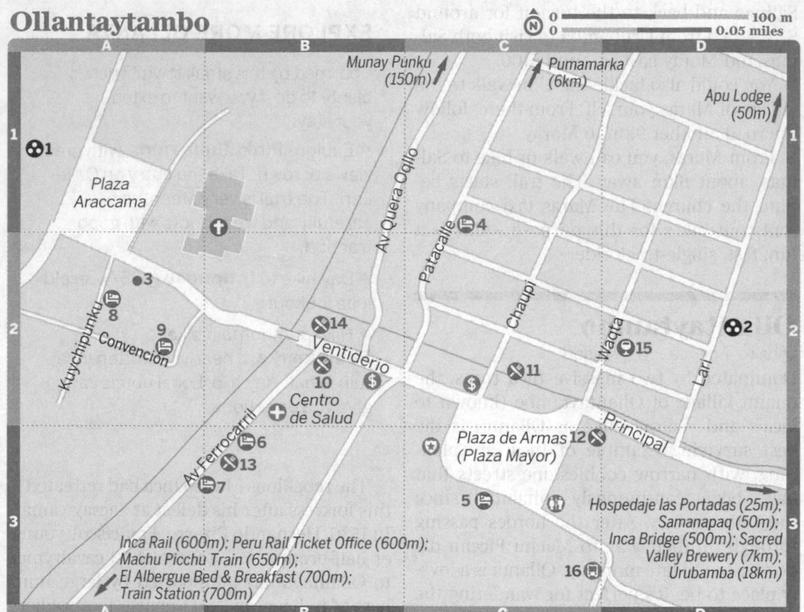

the Inca bridge by the entrance to the village. It takes a few hours to reach the site, passing several abandoned blocks known as *piedras cansadas* – tired stones. Looking back toward Ollantaytambo, you can see the enigmatic optical illusion of a pyramid in the fields and walls in front of the fortress. A few scholars believe this marks the legendary place where the original Incas first emerged from the earth.

Choco Museo COOKING COURSE
(☎084-43-6753; Ventiderio s/n; workshop per person S35-75; ⏲9am-6:30pm) The Chocolate Museum has several outlets; this one has chocolates and cacao-based goodies for sale as well as daily chocolate-making workshops.

Ortiz Adventures Tours MOUNTAIN BIKING
(☎084-46-6735, 992-532-448; josemanuel_jjm@hotmail.com) Mountain-biking tours to Moray and Maras, Pumamarka, and other destinations more apt for advanced riders.

Sota Adventure ADVENTURE SPORTS
(☎984-455-841; www.sotaadventure.com) Sota Adventure comes highly recommended by readers, particularly for horseback riding. The family-run business also offers mountain biking and multiday hikes.

Festivals & Events

Día de los Reyes Magos FESTIVAL
Epiphany is celebrated on January 5 to 8, when residents of surrounding communities arrive on foot to Ollanta to celebrate the arrival of the three kings. Following a procession, there are traditional dances and a bullfight.

Señor de Choquechilca FESTIVAL
Occurring during Pentecost in late May or early June, the town's most important annual event commemorates the local miracle of the Christ of Choquechilca, when a wooden cross appeared by the Inca bridge. It's celebrated with music, dancing and colorful processions.

Sleeping

There are lots of budget and midrange accommodations east of the Plaza de Armas.

Casa de Wow HOSTEL $
(☎084-20-4010; www.casadewow.com; Patacalle s/n; dm S62, s S124, d with/without bathroom S155/185; @ 📶) A cozy little home away from home run by Wow, a local artist. Bunks are snug and couples have a shot at the fantastic handmade Inca royalty bed (though unlike the original, these raw beams are held to-

Ollantaytambo

gether with rope, not llama innards). Sign the world's biggest guestbook before leaving.

Hospedaje las Portadas GUESTHOUSE $
(☎084-20-4008; las.portadas@yahoo.com; Principal s/n; dm S15, s/d S30/50, s/d without bathroom S20/35) Although all of the tourist and local buses pass by outside, this friendly, family-run place still manages to achieve tranquillity. It has a flowery courtyard, a grassy lawn and a rooftop terrace made for stargazing. Rooms are dated, with tired pillows, but it's still a steal.

Chaska Wasi HOSTEL $
(☎084-20-4045; www.hostalchaskawasi.com; Plaza de Armas s/n; dm/d incl breakfast S20/60; @📶) Backpackers enjoy the company of the lovely, helpful Katy and her tribe of cats. Cheerful but quite basic rooms with electric showers are good value.

★**Apu Lodge** INN $$
(☎084-79-7162; www.apulodge.com; Lari s/n; s/d/q incl breakfast S170/190/280; @📶) Backed against the ruins, this modern lodge with a sprawling lawn is a real retreat, thanks to the welcoming staff and the helpful attention of its Scottish owner. Ample, cozy rooms feature powerful hot showers that melt your muscle aches. Wi-fi is available in the common area. Breakfast includes yogurt, cereal, fresh fruit and eggs.

★**El Albergue Bed & Breakfast** B&B $$
(☎084-20-4014; www.elalbergue.com; Estación de Tren; d incl breakfast from S282; @📶) On the train platform, this romantic pit stop exudes Andean charm. Surrounded by green lawns with lush flowerbeds, tasteful tiled rooms feature dark hardwood trim, tapestries and quality linens in an early 20th-century building. There are portable heaters, games for kids and sauna access. It's 800m (all uphill) from the village center but there's an excellent on-site restaurant.

La Casa del Abuelo HOTEL $$
(☎084-43-6747; lacasadelabuelo78@gmail.com; Calle Convencion 143; s/d incl breakfast S86/170) Lauded for the attentive, often multilingual, service, this small and recently built multistory hotel sits at the end of the street. Attractive rooms still in pristine shape feature down duvets. Breakfast features real brewed coffee. A solid option.

Samanapaq INN $$
(☎084-20-4042, 999-583-243; www.samanapaq.com; cnr Principal & Alameda de las Cien Ventanas; d/tr incl breakfast S291/381; 📶) Recommended for the family welcome and mellow Great Dane Venus, this sprawling complex features lawns for the kids to run on, comfortable shared spaces and 20 motel-style rooms with massage-jet showers. With buffet breakfast. Has a pottery workshop on-site.

Munay Punku GUESTHOUSE $$
(☎084-62-4263; www.munaypunku.com; Av Quera Oqllo 704; s/d/tr S120/150/200; 📶) A spacious, homey three-story on the outskirts of town toward the ruins of Pumamarka. Ruth and her family are good hosts, rooms are spacious and beds are firm with good bedding. Offers river and countryside views.

Hotel Muñay Tika HOTEL $$
(☎084-20-4111; www.munaytika.com; Av Ferrocarril s/n; s/d/tr incl breakfast S90/110/130; @📶) Though the native corn drying in the courtyard might say otherwise, this hotel is modern and spacious. Rooms with tinted windows feature parquet floors and down duvets. The garden is a nice area to hang out in.

K'uychi Punku Hostal HOTEL $$
(☎084-20-4175; kuychipunkuhostal@yahoo.com; Kuyuchipunku s/n; s/d/tr incl breakfast S50/100/150; 📶) Run by the wonderful Bejar-Mejía family, this recommended hotel

may be open to bargaining. Lodgings are in an Inca building with 2m-thick walls and a modern section with less personality. A breakfast including eggs and fresh juice is served in Ollanta's most photographed outdoor dining room.

Hostal las Orquídeas HOTEL **$$**
(☎084-20-4032; www.hotellasorquideasllantaytambo.com; Av Ferrocarril s/n; s/d/tr incl breakfast S85/125/180;) Has a small, grassy courtyard and rooms with parquet floors, down bedding and TVs.

Eating

Uchucuta PERUVIAN **$**
(☎951-141-514; Ventidero s/n; mains S22-39; ⏲noon-10pm) Forgive the stark setting with cafeteria lighting. This unassuming restaurant serves wonderful, artfully presented Peruvian fare. Its version of chicken cordon bleu is stuffed with spinach and served with a timbale of fluffy, flavorful fried rice. There's also juicy alpaca steaks and homemade pastas. With a spotless open kitchen and friendly service.

Il Piccolo Forno ITALIAN **$**
(☎996-400-150; Calle del Medio, also known as Chaupi; mains S15-25; ⏲noon-9pm) Thin-crust pizzas and green salads with crisp chicken chunks are the standouts at this tiny eatery run by an Italian-Peruvian couple. It's a great option when you want to sate your hunger without much ado.

La Esquina CAFE **$**
(☎084-20-4078; mains S12-18; ⏲7am-9pm;) This corner cafe and bakery has an intimidating menu crafted to strain weak eyes. Highlights include the original salad bowls with fresh greens, veggies and quinoa. The breakfasts are also tasty.

Tutti Amore ICE CREAM **$**
(Av Ferrocarril s/n; ice creams S5; ⏲8:30am-7pm) Andres from Rosario, Argentina, serves up homemade gelato-style ice cream, including some exotic jungle-fruit flavors worth a try. It's halfway down the hill to the train station.

★El Albergue Restaurante INTERNATIONAL **$$**
(☎084-20-4014; Estación de Tren; mains S22-41; ⏲5:30am-10am, noon-3pm & 6-9pm) This whistle-stop cafe serves elegant dinners of well-priced, classic Peruvian fare. It's inviting, with an open kitchen bordered by heaping fruit bowls and candles adorning each linen-topped table. Start with the *causas* (potato dish) or organic greens from the garden. Lamb medallions with *chimichurri* (herb sauce) are a standout, as well as the molle-pepper steak with spice from the tree outside.

It also serves local artisan beer. Those less hungry can order homemade pasta in half-portions. For train passengers, it may be worth stopping by the patio option Café Mayu for an espresso or homemade *aguantamayo* cheesecake.

Hearts Café CAFE **$$**
(☎084-20-4078; cnr Ventiderio & Av Ferrocarril; mains S10-28; ⏲7am-9pm;) Serving healthy and hearty food, beer and wine and fabulous coffee, Hearts is a longtime local presence, with some organic produce and box lunches for excursions. Breakfasts like *huevos rancheros* (fried eggs with beans served on a tortilla) target the gringo palette perfectly, and the corner spot with outdoor tables was made for people-watching.

Drinking & Nightlife

Ganso BAR
(☎984-30-8499; Waqta s/n; ⏲2pm-late) Treehouse meets circus meets *Batman*! The hallucinatory decor in tiny, friendly Ganso is enough to drive anyone to drink. A firepole and swing seats are the icing on the cake.

Sacred Valley Brewery BREWERY
(⏲Sat & Sun) Located 7km outside of town toward Urubamba, this affable American-style brewery serves four varieties of pints, including a very smooth and quaffable amber. Check out its Facebook page for news on monthly barbecues.

Getting There & Away

BUS & TAXI

Frequent *combis* and *colectivos* shuttle between Urubamba and Ollantaytambo (S1.50 and S3 respectively, 30 minutes) from 6am to 5pm. To Cuzco, it's easiest to change in Urubamba, though occasional departures leave direct from the Ollantaytambo train station to Cuzco's Puente Grau (*combis* S15, two hours; *colectivos* S15, 1½ hours).

Even though Ollantaytambo is closer to Santa María (for those traveling on to Santa Teresa) and Quillabamba, buses pass through here already full. Backtrack to Urubamba's bus terminal to get a seat.

TRAIN

Ollantaytambo is a transportation hub between Cuzco and Machu Picchu: the cheapest and quickest way to travel between Cuzco and Machu Picchu is to catch a *combi* between Cuzco and Ollantaytambo (two hours), then the train between Ollantaytambo and Aguas Calientes (two hours). Two companies currently offer the service. Rates change according to peak times.

Inca Rail (☎084-43-6732; www.incarail.com; Av Ferrocarril s/n) Three departures daily from Ollantaytambo and four classes (one-way S191 to S423). Children get significant discounts.

Peru Rail (www.perurail.com; Av Ferrocarril s/n; ⊙5am-9pm) Service to Aguas Calientes with multiple departures daily. With three classes of service, though some trips feature extras. One-way fares: Expedition (from S197), Vistadome (from S58) and the luxurious Hiram Bingham (from S1153).

Getting Around

Ollantaytambo Travel (☎084-62-4263, 984-537-329; www.ollantaytambotravel.com) A reliable taxi service with responsible drivers available for taxi tours throughout the Sacred Valley and private airport transfers (S110 for three passengers).

MACHU PICCHU & THE INCA TRAIL

Shrouded by mist and surrounded by lush vegetation and steep escarpments, the sprawling Inca citadel of Machu Picchu is one icon that lives up to every expectation. Like the Mona Lisa, the pyramids and San Francisco's Golden Gate Bridge, this icon has been seared into our collective consciousness, though nothing can diminish the thrill of being here. If you have the time and the interest, hiking to Machu Picchu via the scenic Inca Trail, as its ancient inhabitants once did, offers a full-immersion experience. But no pilgrimage is without its challenges. All visitors must pass through the gateway to Machu Picchu, Aguas Calientes. Part tourist trap, part Wild West, this shabby town is isolated from the rest of the region and only accessible by railway.

Aguas Calientes

☎084 / POP 1000 / ELEV 2410M

Also known as Machu Picchu Pueblo, this town lies in a deep gorge below the ruins. A virtual island, it's cut off from all roads and enclosed by stone cliffs, towering cloud forest and two rushing rivers. Despite its gorgeous location, Aguas Calientes has the feel of a gold rush town, with a large itinerant population, slack services that count on one-time customers and an architectural tradition of rebar and unfinished cement. With merchants pushing the hard sell, it's hard not to feel overwhelmed. Your best bet is to go without expectations.

Yet spending the night offers one distinct advantage: early access to Machu Picchu, which turns out to be a pretty good reason to stay.

Note that the footpath from the train station to the Machu Picchu bus stop is stepped. Wheelchairs should be directed across the small bridge to Sinchi Roca and through the center of town.

Sights & Activities

A new visitor center and small museum from the Ministerio de Cultura may be added by 2017 at the Puente Ruinas.

Museo de Sitio Manuel Chávez Ballón MUSEUM

(admission S22; ⊙9am-5pm) This museum has superb information in Spanish and English on the archaeological excavations of Machu Picchu and Inca building methods. Stop here before or after the ruins to get a sense of context (and to enjoy the air-conditioning and soothing music if you're walking back from the ruins after hours in the sun).

There's a small botanical garden with orchids outside, down a cool if nerve-testing set of Inca stairs. It's by Puente Ruinas, at the base of the footpath to Machu Picchu.

Las Termas HOT SPRINGS

(admission S10; ⊙5am-8:30pm) Weary trekkers soak away their aches and pains in the town's hot springs, 10 minutes' walk up Pachacutec from the train tracks. These tiny, natural thermal springs, from which Aguas Calientes derives its name, are nice enough but far from the best in the area, and get scummy by late morning. Towels can be rented cheaply outside the entrance.

Sleeping

Lodgings here are consistently overpriced – probably costing two-thirds more than counterparts in less-exclusive locations.

Supertramp Hostel HOSTEL $

(☎084-43-5830; www.supertramp.com; Chaskatika s/n; dm S30-34, d with shared bathroom S90, all incl breakfast; wi-fi) Cloaked in psychedelic murals, this recommended but sometimes

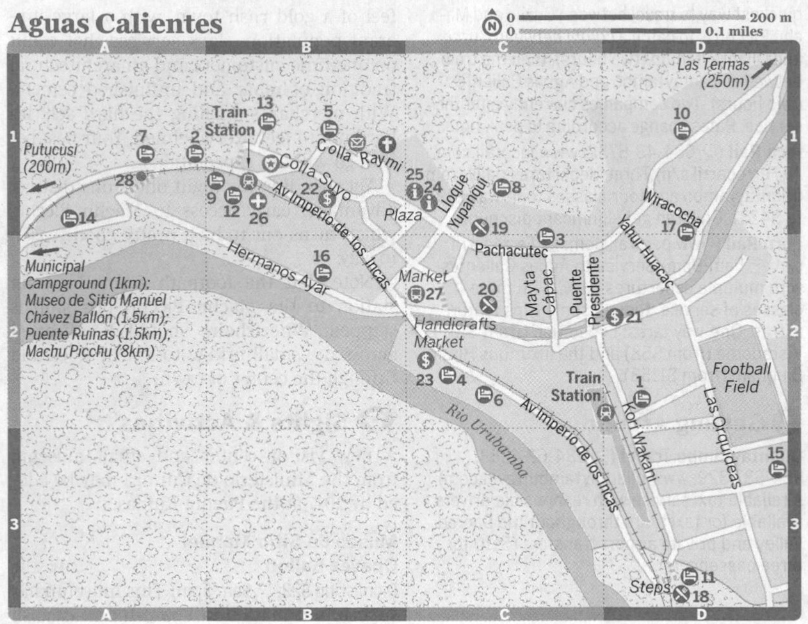

Aguas Calientes

Sleeping

1	Casa Andina	D2
2	Ecopackers	A1
3	El Mapi	C2
4	Ferre Machu Picchu	C2
5	Gringo Bill's	B1
6	Hatun Inti	C2
7	Hospedaje los Caminantes	A1
8	Hostal Muyurina	C1
9	Hotel Presidente	B1
10	La Cabaña Hotel	D1
11	Machu Picchu Pueblo Hotel	D3
12	Machupicchu Hostal	B1
13	Rupa Wasi	B1
14	Sumaq Machu Picchu Hotel	A1
15	Supertramp Hostel	D3
16	Tierra Viva	B2
17	Wiracocha Inn	D1

Eating

18	Café Inkaterra	D3
19	Indio Feliz	C1
20	La Boulangerie de Paris	C2
	Tree House	(see 13)

Information

21	ATM	D2
22	ATM	B1
23	BCP	C2
24	Centro Cultural	C1
25	iPerú	C1
26	Medical Center	B1

Transport

27	Machu Picchu Bus Tickets & Bus Stop	C2
28	Trains to Hydroelectric Station (Transport to Santa Teresa)	A1

cramped hostel has good, helpful staff and a small adjoining cafe that whips up salads and gourmet burgers. Early starters can get egg breakfasts with coffee, toast and jam at 4:30am. With train station pick-up available.

Ecopackers HOSTEL $
(084-21-1121; Av Imperio de las Incas 136; dm S44-47, d S150) While service lags compared to its Cuzco counterpart, this clean and convenient hostel is still a good find. The building and its installations are new, leading out to a moss-covered courtyard with a pool table. Dorms have two to three bunks, and there's laundry service and a bar-restaurant. Grab those free earplugs at the reception – you will need them!

Hospedaje los Caminantes GUESTHOUSE $
(084-21-1007; los-caminantes@hotmail.com; Av Imperio de los Incas 140; per person with/without bathroom S35/20;) Great value, this big,

multistory guesthouse has dated but clean rooms with laminate floors. Features include reliable hot water and a few balconies. The train whistle at 7am is an unmistakable wake-up call. Breakfast isn't included, but is available (S8 to S10) at the strangely upscale in-house cafe.

Municipal Campground CAMPGROUND **$**
(sites per tent S15) This small, charming campground has toilets, showers and kitchen facilities for rent. It's a 20-minute walk downhill from the center of town on the road to Machu Picchu, before the bridge.

Wiracocha Inn HOTEL **$$**
(☎084-21-1088; www.wiracochainn.com; Wiracocha 206; s/d incl breakfast S247/309) On a side street crowded with midrange hotels, this newer option has well-kept and polished rooms, amiable service and a sheltered patio area near the river. Rooms feature down bedding and TVs.

Hotel Presidente HOTEL **$$**
(☎084-21-1065; reservas@siahotels.com; Av Imperio de los Incas s/n; s/d/tr incl breakfast from S190/240/270; @📶) A solid and very secure option featuring small double beds and flat-screen TVs. For the same price it's worth asking for a room with river views, not just for the scenery but to get as far from the train tracks as possible.

Hostal Muyurina HOTEL **$$**
(☎084-21-1339; www.hostalmuyurina.com; Lloque Yupanqui s/n; s/d/tr incl breakfast S120/150/270; 📶) Sparkling new and keen to please, Mayurina is a friendly option. Rooms have phones and TV.

Machupicchu Hostal HOTEL **$$**
(☎084-21-1095; reservas@siahotels.com; Av Imperio de los Incas 520; s/d/tr incl breakfast S150/160/220; @📶) One of the tidy midrange inns by the train tracks, this place has buffet breakfasts and a small flower-festooned interior courtyard. Small, dark rooms echo with sounds of the guesthouse, and you will certainly hear every train.

★**Machu Picchu Pueblo Hotel** LODGE **$$$**
(☎in Lima 01-610-0400; www.inkaterra.com; d casitas from S2040, villas from S3457; ❄@📶🏊) 🌿 Luxuriant and set amid tropical gardens, these Andean-style cottages (many with their own private pool) connected by stone pathways are pure indulgence. The devil is in the details: iPod docks, subtle, classy decor, and showers with glass walls looking out onto lush vegetation. The on-site spa has a bamboo-eucalyptus sauna, but the best feature is the (included) guided excursions.

Choose from bilingual tours for bird-watching, tea plantation visits and orchid walks, or take a trip to the hotel's conservation site protecting the rare Andean spectacled bear. Rates include half-board and kids under 12 stay for free.

El Mapi DESIGN HOTEL **$$$**
(☎084-21-1011; www.elmapihotel.com; Pachacutec 109; d S699; ❄@📶) Spare and ultramodern, this design hotel occupies a central spot in the middle of town. Lofty ceilings, burnished steel and oversized nature photos create a cool, stripped down atmosphere, though the stark, all-white rooms take it a little too far. Perks include enjoying a welcome pisco sour at the stylish bar and the enormous buffet breakfast which provides ample fuel for a day in the ruins.

There's also a warm landscaped pond for dips, a full-service restaurant serving buffet lunch (S42 to S56) and an on-site boutique.

Casa Andina HOTEL **$$$**
(☎084-21-1017; www.casa-andina.com; Prolongacion Imperio de Los Incas E - 34; d/tr/ste S431/924/862; 📶) A comfortable classic, this upscale Peruvian chain features truly modern rooms with earthy terra-cotta accents, sparkling installations and glass showers. There's also stunning river views behind the double-pane glass. With flat-screen TVs, safe boxes, an on-site restaurant and all the usual amenities.

Sumaq Machu Picchu Hotel HOTEL **$$$**
(☎084-21-1059; www.sumaqhotelperu.com; Hermanos Ayar s/n; d incl breakfast from S1377; ❄@📶) This high-end hotel has a soothing interior, thanks to the double-pane windows and neutral palette with splashes of bold color. There are 60 rooms and more on the way, with views of either river and mountains, or a hillside with artificial cascades. Includes an elevator, multiple eating and drinking areas, and a full spa with sauna and Jacuzzi. Offers a free cooking class to guests.

The Machu Picchu bus stops conveniently at the door.

Rupa Wasi HOTEL **$$$**
(☎084-21-1101; www.rupawasi.net; Huanacaure s/n; d/ste incl breakfast from S232/294; 📶) Hidden away up a steep flight of stairs, Rupa Wasi clings to the hillside with wooden

stairways and moss-strewn stone pathways. It's quaint and a little wild, but the price only reflects its proximity to Machu Picchu. Cabin-style rooms feature down duvets and views; a nice American breakfast is served in the Tree House cafe. Accepts credit cards.

Tierra Viva HOTEL **$$$**
(☎084-21-1201; www.tierravivahoteles.com; Av Hermanos Ayar 401; s/d/ste incl breakfast S604/665/725; @📶) A respected Peruvian boutique chain has set up shop in this five-story hotel. While the design isn't as smooth as at its other outlets, rooms still work a modern-minimalist charm, displaying Andean weavings (for purchase to benefit a regional foundation). There's a glass-walled breakfast room, elevator access and pleasant staff.

Gringo Bill's HOTEL **$$$**
(☎084-21-1046; www.gringobills.com; Colla Raymi 104; d/tr/ste incl breakfast S279/381/417; @📶🏊) One of the original Aguas Calientes lodgings, friendly Bill's features well-heeled rooms in a multi-tiered construction. Rooms are smart, some recently added, with beds covered in thick cotton quilts and large bathrooms. Suites feature massage jet tubs and TVs. The mini pool only has space for two. Larger suites easily accommodate families.

Hatun Inti HOTEL **$$$**
(☎084-23-4312; www.grupointi.com; Av Camino de los Incas 606; s/d incl half-board S556/618) A well-heeled high-end option with subdued style, wonderful beds and ample rooms. All feature flat-screen TVs, safe boxes and Jacuzzi tubs. A buffet breakfast and dinner or lunch at the on-site restaurant is included.

Ferre Machu Picchu BOUTIQUE HOTEL **$$$**
(☎084-21-1337; www.hotelferremachupicchu.com; Av Imperio de los Incas 634; d/ste incl breakfast S417/618) A multi-story hotel with a set of attractive riverside rooms with modern decor. It's good value, but we wish they used gentler cleaning products. The elevator was still under construction when we visited. Takes Visa.

La Cabaña Hotel HOTEL **$$$**
(☎084-21-1048; www.lacabanamachupicchu.com; Pachacutec 805; s/d/tr incl breakfast S402/464/525; @📶) Further uphill than most of the hotels, this welcoming spot features woody, cozy heated rooms, in part thanks to down duvets decorated with flower petals and chocolates. Still, it hardly merits the steep price tag. There's buffet breakfast, plus complimentary tea and fruit round the clock.

Eating

Touts standing in the street will try to herd you into their restaurant, but take your time making a selection. Standards are not very high in most places – if you go to a restaurant that hasn't been recommended, snoop around to check the hygiene first. Since refrigeration can be a problem, it's best to order vegetarian if you're eating in low-end establishments.

La Boulangerie de Paris BAKERY **$**
(☎084-79-7798; Jr Sinchi Roca s/n; snacks S3-10; ⏰5am-9pm; 📶) We don't know how these Frenchmen got here, we're just thankful. This small cafe sells *pain au chocolat*, fresh croissants, espresso drinks and desserts, with a few gluten-free items. You can also order boxed lunches.

★**Indio Feliz** FRENCH **$$**
(☎084-21-1090; Lloque Yupanqui 4; mains S34-48; ⏰11am-10pm) Hospitality is the strong suit of French cook Patrik at this multi-award-winning restaurant, but the food does not disappoint. Start with *sopa a la criolla* (a potent and flavorful broth, served with hot bread, homemade butter and optional chilis). There are also nods to traditional French cooking – like Provençal tomatoes, crispy-perfect garlic potatoes and a melt-in-your-mouth apple tart.

The candlelit decor shows the imagination of a long-lost castaway with imitation Gauguin panels, a carved figurehead damsel, colonial benches and vintage objects. The *menú* (S69) is extremely good value for a decadent dinner. Indio Feliz has wheelchair access and was in the process of adding an upstairs bar and terrace when we visited, which provides another reason not to leave here.

Tree House FUSION **$$**
(☎084-21-1101; Huanacaure s/n; mains S38-52; ⏰4:30am-10pm) The rustic ambience of Tree House provides a cozy setting for its inviting fusion menu served alongside South American wines, craft beers and cocktails. Dishes like chicken soup with wontons and ginger, red quinoa risotto and crispy trout are lovingly prepared. For dessert, lip-smacking fruit crumble. With raw and vegan options. Reserve ahead. It's part of the Rupa Wasi hotel.

Café Inkaterra PERUVIAN **$$$**
(☎084-21-1122; Machu Picchu Pueblo Hotel; menú lunch/dinner S54/90; ⊙11am-9pm; ✎) Upstream from the train station, this tucked-away riverside restaurant is housed in elongated thatched rooms with views of water tumbling over the boulders. There's only a set menu (starter, main dish and dessert), with gluten-free and vegetarian options. The perfectly executed *lomo saltado* (beef strips stir-fried with tomatoes and potatoes) features a flavorful sauce and crisp red onions.

 Drinking & Nightlife

There isn't much nightlife in Aguas Calientes. Desperate restaurants offer a four-for-one happy hour (probably not the best way to prepare for running up Wayna Picchu).

ℹ Information

Currency and traveler's checks can be exchanged in various places at highly unfavorable rates, so it's best to bring plenty of Peruvian currency from Cuzco.

BCP (Av Imperio de los Incas s/n) If this runs out of money (weekends are busiest), there are four others in town, including one on Av Imperio de los Incas.

Centro Cultural (Machu Picchu Tickets; ☎084-81-1196; Av Pachacutec; ⊙5:30am-8:30pm) This new cultural center is the only spot in town selling Machu Picchu entrance tickets.

iPerú (☎084-21-1104; cuadra 1, Pachacutec; ⊙9am-1pm & 2-6pm Mon-Sat, to 1pm Sun) A helpful information center for everything Machu Picchu.

Medical Center (☎084-21-1005; Av Imperio de los Incas s/n; ⊙emergencies 24hr) Located by the train tracks.

Post Office (Colla Raymi s/n)

 Getting There & Away

There are only three options to get to Aguas Calientes, and hence to Machu Picchu: trek it, catch the train via Cuzco and the Sacred Valley, or travel by road and train via Santa Teresa.

BUS

There is no road access to Aguas Calientes. The only buses go up the hill to Machu Picchu (round-trip S72, 25 minutes) from 5:30am to 3:30pm; buses return until 5:45pm.

TRAIN

Buy a return ticket to avoid getting stranded in Aguas Calientes – outbound trains sell out much quicker than their inbound counterparts. All train companies have ticket offices in the train station, but you can check their websites for up-to-date schedules and ticket purchases.

To Cuzco (three hours), **PeruRail** (www.perurail.com) has service to Poroy and taxis connect to the city, another 20 minutes away.

To Ollantaytambo (two hours), both Peru Rail and **Inca Rail** (www.incarail.com) provide service.

To Santa Teresa (Hidroelectrica Station, 45 minutes), Peru Rail travels at 8:53am, 2:55pm and 9:50pm daily, with other departures for residents only. Tickets (US$26) can only be bought from Aguas Calientes train station on the day of departure, but trains actually leave from the west end of town, outside the police station. You can also do this route as a guided multisport tour.

Machu Picchu

For many visitors to Peru and even South America, a visit to the Inca city of Machu Picchu is the long-anticipated highpoint of their trip. In a spectacular location, it's the best-known archaeological site on the continent. This awe-inspiring ancient city was never revealed to the conquering Spaniards and was virtually forgotten until the early part of the 20th century. In the high season, from late May until early September, 2500 people arrive daily. Despite this great tourist influx, the site manages to retain an air of grandeur and mystery, and is a must for all visitors to Peru.

The site is most heavily visited between 10am and 2pm. June through August are the busiest months.

History

Machu Picchu is not mentioned in any of the chronicles of the Spanish conquistadors. Apart from a couple of German adventurers in the 1860s, who apparently looted the site with the Peruvian government's permission, nobody apart from local Quechua people knew of Machu Picchu's existence until American historian Hiram Bingham was guided to it by locals in 1911. You can read Bingham's own account of his 'discovery' in the classic book *Inca Land: Explorations in the Highlands of Peru,* first published in 1922 and now available as a free download from Project Gutenberg (www.gutenberg.org).

Bingham was searching for the lost city of Vilcabamba, the last stronghold of the Incas, and he thought he had found it at Machu Picchu. We now know that the remote ruins at Espíritu Pampa, much deeper in

Machu Picchu

This great 15th-century Inca citadel sits at 2430m on a narrow ridgetop above the Río Urubamba. Traditionally considered a political, religious and administrative center, new theories suggest that it was a royal estate designed by Pachacutec, the Inca ruler whose military conquests transformed the empire. Trails linked it to the Inca capital of Cuzco and important sites in the jungle. As invading Spaniards never discovered it, experts still dispute when the site was abandoned and why.

At its peak, Machu Picchu was thought to have some 500 inhabitants. An engineering marvel, its famous Inca walls have polished stone fitted to stone, with no mortar in between. The citadel took thousands of laborers 50 years to build – today its cost of construction would exceed a billion US dollars.

Making it habitable required leveling the site, channeling water from high mountain streams through stone canals and building vertical retaining walls that became agricultural terraces for corn, potatoes and coca. The drainage system also helped combat heavy rains (diverting them for irrigation), while east-facing rooftops and farming terraces took advantage of maximum sun exposure.

The site is a magnet to mystics, adventurers and students of history alike. While its function remains hotly debated, the essential grandeur of Machu Picchu is indisputable.

TOP TIPS

» **Visit** before mid-morning crowds

» **Allow** at least three hours to visit

» **Wear** walking shoes and a hat

» **Bring** drinking water

» **Gain** perspective walking the lead-in trails

ADAMK92/GETTY IMAGES ©

Intihuatana

'Hitching Post of the Sun', this exquisitely carved rock was likely used by Inca astronomers to predict solstices. It's a rare survivor since invading Spaniards destroyed *intihuatanas* throughout the kingdom to eradicate pagan blasphemy.

Temple of the Three Windows

Enjoy the commanding views of the plaza below through the huge trapezoidal windows framed by three-ton lintels. Rare in Inca architecture, the presence of three windows may indicate special significance.

MARKUS DANIEL/GETTY IMAGES ©

Wayna Picchu

This 2720m peak with ladders, caves and a small temple can be climbed in a 45- to 90-minute scramble. Take care, the steep steps are slippery when wet. Purchase a coveted permit ahead with admission.

POWEROFFOREVER/GETTY IMAGES ©

Central Plaza

This sprawling green area with grazing llamas separates the ceremonial sector of Machu Picchu from the more mundane residential and industrial sectors.

Entrance to Wayna Picchu trail

Principal Temple

Residential Sector

Industrial Sector

House of the High Priest

Ceremonial Baths

Fountains

To Main Entrance

To Agricultural Terraces

Temple of the Sun

This off-limits rounded tower is best viewed from above. Featuring the site's finest stonework, an altar and trapezoidal windows, it may have been used for astronomical purposes.

GLOWIMAGES/GETTY IMAGES ©

Royal Tomb

Speculated to have special ceremonial significance, a natural rock cave sits below the Temple of the Sun. Though off-limits, visitors can view its step-like altar and sacred niches from the entrance.

GEORGE HOLTOR/GETTY IMAGES ©

Temple of the Condor

Check out the condor head carving with rock outcrops that resemble outstretched wings. Behind, an off-limits cavity reaches a tiny underground cell that may only be entered by bending double.

the jungle, are actually the remains of Vilcabamba. The Machu Picchu site was initially overgrown with thick vegetation, forcing Bingham's team to be content with roughly mapping the site. Bingham returned in 1912 and 1915 to carry out the difficult task of clearing the thick forest, when he also discovered some of the ruins on the so-called Inca Trail. Peruvian archaeologist Luis E Valcárcel undertook further studies in 1934, as did a Peruvian-American expedition under Paul Fejos in 1940 and 1941.

Despite scores of more recent studies, knowledge of Machu Picchu remains sketchy. Even today archaeologists are forced to rely heavily on speculation and educated guesswork as to its function. Some believe the citadel was founded in the waning years of the last Incas as an attempt to preserve Inca culture or rekindle their predominance, while others think that it may have already become an uninhabited, forgotten city at the time of the conquest.

A more recent theory suggests that the site was a royal retreat or the country palace of Pachacutec, abandoned at the time of the Spanish invasion. The site's director believes that it was a city, a political, religious and administrative center. Its location, and the fact that at least eight access routes have been discovered, suggests that it was a trade nexus between Amazonia and the highlands.

It seems clear from the exceptionally high quality of the stonework and the abundance of ornamental work that Machu Picchu was once vitally important as a ceremonial center. Indeed, to some extent, it still is: Alejandro Toledo, the country's first indigenous Andean president, impressively staged his inauguration here in 2001.

Sights & Activities

Don't miss the Museo de Sitio Manuel Chávez Ballón (p249) by Puente Ruinas at the base of the climb to Machu Picchu. Buses headed back from the ruins to Aguas Calientes will stop upon request at the bridge. From here it's under a half-hour walk back to town.

Inside the Complex

Unless you arrive via the Inca Trail, you'll officially enter the ruins through a ticket gate on the south side of Machu Picchu. About 100m of footpath brings you to the mazelike main entrance of Machu Picchu proper, where the ruins lie stretched out before you, roughly divided into two areas separated by a series of plazas.

Note that the names of individual ruins speculate their use – in reality, much is unknown. To get a visual fix of the whole site and snap the classic postcard photograph, climb the zigzagging staircase on the left immediately after entering the complex, which leads to the Hut of the Caretaker.

Hut of the Caretaker of the Funerary Rock RUIN

An excellent viewpoint to take in the whole site. It's one of a few buildings that has been restored with a thatched roof, making it a good shelter in the case of rain. The Inca Trail enters the city just below this hut. The carved rock behind the hut may have been used to mummify the nobility, hence the hut's name.

Ceremonial Baths RUIN

If you head straight into the ruins from the main entry gate, you pass through extensive terracing to a beautiful series of 16 connected ceremonial baths that cascade across the ruins, accompanied by a flight of stairs.

Temple of the Sun RUIN

Just above and to the left of the ceremonial baths is Machu Picchu's only round building, a curved and tapering tower of exceptional stonework.

Royal Tomb RUIN

Below the Temple of the Sun, this almost hidden, natural rock cave was carefully carved by Inca stonemasons. Its use is highly debated; though known as the Royal Tomb, no mummies were actually ever found here.

Sacred Plaza PLAZA

Climbing the stairs above the ceremonial baths, there is a flat area of jumbled rocks, once used as a quarry. Turn right at the top of the stairs and walk across the quarry on a short path leading to the four-sided Sacred Plaza. The far side contains a small viewing platform with a curved wall, which offers a view of the snowy Cordillera Vilcabamba in the far distance and the Río Urubamba below.

Temple of the Three Windows RUIN

Important buildings flank the remaining three sides of the Sacred Plaza. The Temple of the Three Windows features huge trapezoidal windows that give the building its name.

Principal Temple RUIN

The 'temple' derives its name from the massive solidity and perfection of its construction. The damage to the rear right corner is the result of the ground settling below this corner rather than any inherent weakness in the masonry itself.

House of the High Priest RUIN

Little is known about these mysterious ruins, located opposite the Principal Temple.

Sacristy RUIN

Behind and connected to the Principal Temple lies this famous small building. It has many well-carved niches, perhaps used for the storage of ceremonial objects, as well as a carved stone bench. The Sacristy is especially known for the two rocks flanking its entrance; each is said to contain 32 angles, but it's easy to come up with a different number whenever you count them.

Intihuatana RUIN

This Quechua word loosely translates as the 'Hitching Post of the Sun' and refers to the carved rock pillar, often mistakenly called a sundial, at the top of the Intihuatana hill. The Inca astronomers were able to predict the solstices using the angles of this pillar. Thus, they were able to claim control over the return of the lengthening summer days. Its exact use remains unclear, but its elegant simplicity and high craftwork make it a highlight.

Central Plaza PLAZA

The plaza separates the ceremonial sector from the residential and industrial areas.

Prison Group RUIN

At the lower end of this area is the Prison Group, a labyrinthine complex of cells, niches and passageways, positioned both under and above the ground.

Temple of the Condor RUIN

This 'temple' is named for a carving of the head of a condor with rock outcrops as outstretched wings. It is considered the centerpiece of the Prison Group.

Intipunku

The Inca Trail ends after its final descent from the notch in the horizon called **Intipunku** (Sun Gate; ⏲checkpoint closes around 3pm). Looking at the hill behind you as you enter the ruins, you can see both the trail and Intipunku. This hill, called Machu Picchu (Old peak), gives the site its name.

Access here from Machu Picchu ruins may be restricted. It takes about an hour to reach Intipunku. If you can spare at least a half-day for the round-trip, it may be possible to continue as far as Wiñay Wayna. Expect to pay S15 or more as an unofficial reduced-charge admission fee to the Inca Trail, and be sure to return before 3pm, which is when the checkpoint typically closes.

READ UP ON THE RUINS

If you are wondering what it's like to hike the Inca Trail, or its lesser-known alternatives, pick up Mark Adams' *Turn Right at Machu Picchu* (2010). Not a hero's tale, the humorous travelogue is a first-person account of one adventure editor bumbling out into the wild. On the way, it provides an entertaining layperson's look at Inca history and the striving explorations of Hiram Bingham.

Inca Drawbridge

A scenic but level walk from the Hut of the Caretaker of the Funerary Rock takes you right past the top of the terraces and out along a narrow, cliff-clinging trail to the Inca drawbridge. In under a half-hour's walk, the trail gives you a good look at cloud-forest vegetation and an entirely different view of Machu Picchu. This walk is recommended, though you'll have to be content with photographing the bridge from a distance, as someone crossed the bridge some years ago and tragically fell to their death.

Cerro Machu Picchu

A 1½- to two-hour climb brings you to the top of Machu Picchu mountain, to be rewarded with the site's most extensive view – along the Inca Trail to Wiñay Wayna and Phuyupatamarka, down to the valley floor and the impressive terracing near Km 104 (where the two-day Inca Trail begins) and across the site of Machu Picchu itself.

This **walk** (S24) is more spectacular than Wayna Picchu, and less crowded, though a ticket is now required, purchased at the time of your entry. Allow yourself plenty of time to enjoy the scenery – and catch your breath!

Wayna Picchu

Wayna Picchu is the small, steep mountain at the back of the ruins. Wayna Picchu is normally translated as 'Young Peak,' but the word *picchu,* with the correct glottal pronunciation, refers to the wad in the cheek of a coca-leaf chewer. Access to Wayna Picchu is limited to 400 people per day – the first 200 in line are let in at 7am, and another 200 at 10am. A **ticket** (S24) which includes a visit to the Moon Temple may only be obtained when you purchase your entrance ticket. These spots sell out a week in advance in low season and a month in advance in high season, so plan accordingly.

At first glance, it would appear that Wayna Picchu is a difficult climb but, although the ascent is steep, it's not technically difficult. However, it is not recommended if you suffer from vertigo. Hikers must sign in and out at a registration booth located beyond the central plaza between two thatched buildings. The 45- to 90-minute scramble up a steep footpath takes you through a short section of Inca tunnel.

Take care in wet weather as the steps get dangerously slippery. The trail is easy to follow, but involves steep sections, a ladder and an overhanging cave, where you have to bend over to get by. Part way up Wayna Picchu, a marked path plunges down to your left, continuing down the rear of Wayna Picchu to the small **Temple of the Moon**. From the temple, another cleared path leads up behind the ruin and steeply onward up the back side of Wayna Picchu.

The descent takes about an hour, and the ascent back to the main Wayna Picchu trail longer. The spectacular trail drops and climbs steeply as it hugs the sides of Wayna Picchu before plunging into the cloud forest. Suddenly, you reach a cleared area where the small, very well-made ruins are found.

Cerro Machu Picchu is a very good alternative if you miss out.

Sleeping & Eating

Most people either arrive on day trips from Cuzco or stay in Aguas Calientes.

Machu Picchu Sanctuary Lodge HOTEL **$$$**
(084-21-1038; www.sanctuarylodgehotel.com; d/mountain view/ste US$625/950/1750) Run by Belmond, this exclusive hotel has one feature no other can match: location. Attention is impeccable and rooms are comfortable, with sober decor, docking stations and eat-in options. There's also a spa, manicured gardens and personalized guide service for the ruins. There's two restaurants, including a popular lunch buffet open to non-guests (S120; 11:30am to 3pm).

Though it's the only place to stay at Machu Picchu, the advantage is minor, since buses start running early to the ruins and the early closing time means even hotel guests are denied that cherished panoramic sunset photo. It's often full, so book at least three months ahead.

Information

Machu Picchu Historical Sanctuary (www.machupicchu.gob.pe; adult/student S128/65; 6am-4pm) Entrance tickets often sell out: buy them in advance in Cuzco (p232). Guests can only enter until 4pm though those inside are not expelled until 5pm. Check for changes in online purchasing: it is possible to use debit cards, but only for adult entry (to the ruins, Wayna Picchu and Cerro Machu Picchi). Student and child admission cannot be purchased online.

The site is limited to 2500 visitors daily, with 400 paid spots for hiking Wayna Picchu and Mt Machu Picchu. While the government has tried enforcing set, limited hours for each visit, at present entrance remains more loosely controlled.

Plan your visit early or late in the day to avoid the worst of the crowds. A visit early in the morning midweek during the rainy season guarantees you more room to breathe, especially during February, when the Inca Trail is closed.

Walking sticks or backpacks over 20L are not allowed into the ruins. There are **baggage check offices** (per item S5; 6am-4pm) outside the entrance gate.

Local **guides** (per person S150, in groups of 6 to 10 S30) are readily available for hire at the entrance. Their expertise varies, look for one wearing an official guide ID from DIRCETUR. Agree on a price in advance, clarify whether the fee is per person or group, and agree on the tour length and maximum group size.

For really in-depth explorations, take along a copy of *Exploring Cuzco* by Peter Frost.

DANGERS & ANNOYANCES

Inside the ruins, do not walk on any of the walls – this loosens the stonework and prompts a cacophony of whistle blowing from the guards. Overnighting here is also illegal: guards do a thorough check of the site before it closes. Disposable plastic bottles and food are not allowed in the site, though vigilance is a bit lax. It's best to eat outside the gate, use camping-type drink bottles and pack out all trash, even organic waste. Water is sold at the cafe just outside the entrance, but only in glass bottles.

Use of the only toilet facilities, just below the cafe, will set you back S1.

Tiny bugs like sand flies abound. You won't notice them biting, but you may be itching for a week. Use insect repellent.

The weather at Machu Picchu seems to have only two settings: heavy rain or bright, burning sunlight. Don't forget rain gear and sun block.

Getting There & Around

From Aguas Calientes, frequent buses for Machu Picchu (round-trip S72, 25 minutes) depart from a ticket office along the main road from 5:30am to 3:30pm. Buses return from the ruins when full, with the last departure at 5:45pm.

Otherwise, it's a steep walk (8km, 1½ hours) up a tightly winding mountain road. First there's a flat 20-minute walk from Aguas Calientes to Puente Ruinas, where the road to the ruins crosses the Río Urubamba, near the museum. A breathtakingly steep but well-marked trail climbs another 2km up to Machu Picchu, taking about an hour to hike (but less coming down!).

The Inca Trail

The most famous hike in South America, the four-day Inca Trail, is walked by thousands every year. Although the total distance is only about 38km, the ancient trail laid by the Incas from the Sacred Valley to Machu Picchu winds its way up and down and around the mountains, snaking over three high Andean passes en route, which have collectively led to the route being dubbed 'the Inca Trial.' The views of snowy mountain peaks, distant rivers and ranges, and cloud forests flush with orchids are stupendous – and walking from one cliff-hugging pre-Columbian ruin to the next is a mystical and unforgettable experience.

The Hike

Most trekking agencies run buses to the start of the trail, also known as Piscacucho or Km 82 on the railway to Aguas Calientes.

After crossing the Río Urubamba (2600m) and taking care of registration formalities, you'll climb gently alongside the river to the trail's first archaeological site, **Llactapata** (Town on Top of the Terraces), before heading south down a side valley of the Río Cusichaca. If you start from Km 88, turn west after crossing the river to see the little-visited site of **Q'ente** (Hummingbird), about 1km away, then return east to Llactapata on the main trail.

The trail leads 7km south to the hamlet of **Wayllabamba** (Grassy Plain; 3000m), near which many tour groups will camp for the first night. You can buy bottled drinks and high-calorie snacks here, and take a breather to look over your shoulder for views of the snowcapped **Nevado Verónica** (5750m).

Wayllabamba is situated near the fork of the Ríos Llullucha and Cusichaca. The trail crosses the Llullucha, then climbs steeply up along the river. This area is known as **Tres Piedras** (Three White Stones; 3300m), though these boulders are no longer visible. From here it is a long, very steep 3km climb through humid woodlands.

The trail eventually emerges on the high, bare mountainside of **Llulluchupampa** (3750m), where water is available and the flats are dotted with campsites, which get very cold at night. This is as far as you can reasonably expect to get on your first day, though many groups will actually spend their second night here.

From Llulluchupampa, a good path up the left-hand side of the valley climbs for a two- to three-hour ascent to the pass of **Warmiwañusca**, also colorfully known as 'Dead Woman's Pass.' At 4200m above sea level, this is the highest point of the trek, and leaves many a seasoned hiker gasping. From Warmiwañusca you can see the Río Pacamayo (Río Escondido) far below, as well as the ruin of Runkurakay halfway up the next hill, above the river.

The trail continues down a long and knee-jarringly steep descent to the river, where there are large campsites at **Paq'amayo**. At an altitude of about 3600m, the trail crosses the river over a small footbridge and climbs toward **Runkurakay** (Egg-Shaped Building); at 3750m this round ruin has superb views. It's about an hour's walk away.

Above Runkurakay, the trail climbs to a false summit before continuing past two small lakes to the top of the second pass at 3950m, which has views of the snow-laden Cordillera Vilcabamba. You'll notice a change in ecology as you descend from this pass – you're now on the eastern, Amazon slope of the Andes and things immediately get greener. The trail descends to the ruin of **Sayaqmarka** (Dominant Town), a tightly constructed complex perched on a small mountain spur, which offers incredible

Inca Trail

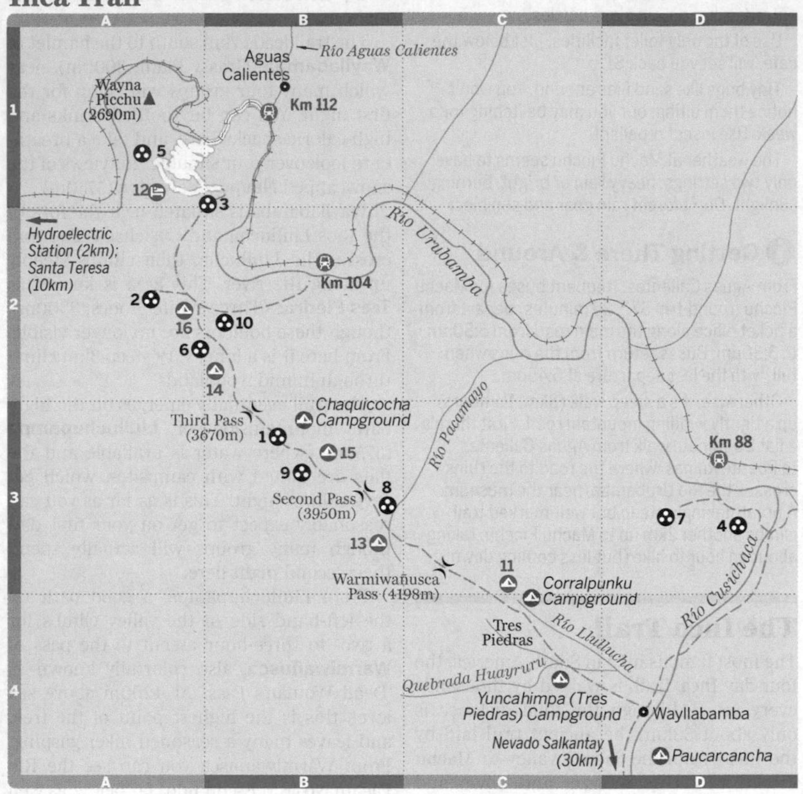

views. The trail continues downward and crosses an upper tributary of the Río Aobamba (Wavy Plain).

The trail then leads on across an Inca causeway and up a gentle climb through some beautiful cloud forest and an **Inca tunnel** carved from the rock. This is a relatively flat section and you'll soon arrive at the third pass at almost 3600m, which has grand views of the Río Urubamba Valley, and campsites where some groups spend their final night, with the advantage of watching the sun set over a truly spectacular view, but with the disadvantage of having to leave at 3am in the race to reach the Sun Gate in time for sunrise. If you are camping here, be careful in the early morning as the steep incline makes the following steps slippery.

Just below the pass is the beautiful and well-restored ruin of **Phuyupatamarka** (City Above the Clouds), about 3570m above sea level. The site contains six beautiful ceremonial baths with water running through them. From Phuyupatamarka, the trail makes a dizzying dive into the cloud forest below, following an incredibly well-engineered flight of many hundreds of Inca steps (it's nerve-racking in the early hours; use a headlamp). After two or three hours, the trail eventually zigzags its way down to a collapsed red-roofed white building that marks the final night's campsite.

A 500m trail behind the old, out of use, pub leads to the exquisite little Inca site of **Wiñay Wayna** (Huiñay Huayna), which is variously translated as 'Forever Young,' 'To Plant the Earth Young' and 'Growing Young' (as opposed to 'growing old'). Peter Frost writes that the Quechua name refers to an orchid *(Epidendrum secundum)* that blooms here year-round. The semitropical campsite at Wiñay Wayna boasts one of the most stunning views on the whole trail, especially at sunrise. For better or worse, the famous

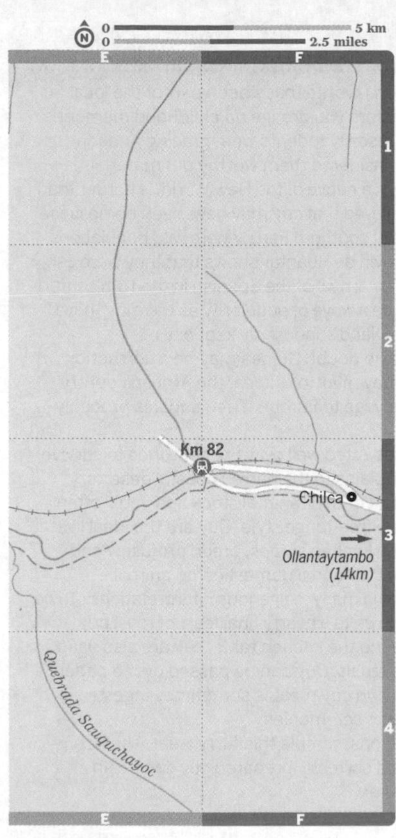

Inca Trail

Sights

1	Inca Tunnel	B3
2	Intipata	A2
3	Intipunku	B1
4	Llactapata	D3
5	Machu Picchu	A1
6	Phuyupatamarka	A2
7	Q'ente	D3
8	Runkurakay	B3
9	Sayaqmarka	B3
10	Wiñay Wayna	B2

Sleeping

11	Llulluchupampa Campground	C3
12	Machu Picchu Sanctuary Lodge	A1
13	Paq'amayo Campground	B3
14	Phuyupatamarka Campground	B2
15	Sayaqmarka Campground	B3
16	Wiñay Wayna Campground	A2

pub located here is now deteriorated and no longer functioning. A rough trail leads from this site to another spectacular terraced ruin, called **Intipata**, best visited on the day you reach Wiñay Wayna; consider coordinating it with your guide if you are interested.

From the Wiñay Wayna guard post, the trail winds without much change in elevation through the cliff-hanging cloud forest for about two hours to reach **Intipunku** (Sun Gate) – the penultimate site on the trail, where it's tradition to enjoy your first glimpse of majestic Machu Picchu while waiting for the sun to rise over the surrounding mountains.

The final triumphant descent takes almost an hour. Trekkers generally arrive long before the morning trainloads of tourists, and can enjoy the exhausted exhilaration of reaching their goal without having to push past enormous groups of tourists fresh off the first train from Cuzco.

CUZCO TO PUNO

The rickety railway and the paved road to Lake Titicaca shadow each other as they both head southeast from Cuzco. En route you can investigate ancient ruins and pastoral Andean towns that are great detours for intrepid travelers who want to leave the Gringo Trail far behind. Most of the destinations here can be reached on day trips from Cuzco. Inka Express (p233) and Turismo Mer (p233) run luxury bus tours between Cuzco and Puno that visit some but not all of these places. Local and long-distance highway buses run more frequently along this route and are less expensive.

Tipón

A demonstration of the Incas' mastery over their environment, this extensive **Inca site** (boleto turístico adult/student under 26 with ISIC card S130/70; 7am-6pm) consists of some impressive terracing at the head of a small valley with an ingenious irrigation system. It's about 30km from Cuzco, just before Oropesa.

Take any Urcos-bound bus from opposite the hospital in Av de la Cultura in Cuzco, or a *colectivo* from Av Huascar 28, and ask to be let off at the Tipón turnoff (S1, 40 minutes). A steep dirt road from the turnoff climbs the 4km to the ruins. You can also contract a taxi tour from Cuzco (S120) to drive you into the ruins, wait and bring you back.

THE GUINEA PIG'S CULINARY RISE

Love it or loathe it, *cuy* (guinea pig) is an Andean favorite that's been part of the local culinary repertoire since pre-Inca times. And before you dredge up childhood memories of cuddly mascots in protest, know that these rascally rodents were gracing Andean dinner plates long before anyone in the West considered them worthy pet material.

Pinpointing the gastronomic history of the *cuy*, a native of the New World, is harder than trying to catch one with your bare hands. It's believed that *cuy* may have been domesticated as early as 7000 years ago in the mountains of southern Peru, where wild populations of *cuy* still roam today. Direct evidence from Chavín de Huántar shows that they were certainly cultivated across the Andes by 900 BC. The arrival of the Spanish in the 18th century led to the European debut of *cuy*, where they rode a wave of popularity as the must-have exotic pet of the season (Queen Elizabeth I of England supposedly kept one).

How they earned the name guinea pig is also in doubt. Guinea may be a corruption of the South American colony of Guiana, or it may refer to Guinea, the African country that *cuy* would have passed through on their voyage to Europe. Their squeals probably account for the latter half of their name.

Cuy are practical animals to raise and have adapted well over the centuries to survive in environments ranging from the high Andean plains to the barren coastal deserts. Many Andean households today raise *cuy* as part of their animal stock and you'll often see them scampering around the kitchen in true free-range style. *Cuy* are the ideal livestock alternative: they're high in protein, feed on kitchen scraps, breed profusely and require much less room and maintenance than traditional domesticated animals.

Cuy is seen as a true delicacy, so much so that in many indigenous interpretations of *The Last Supper*, Jesus and his disciples are sitting down to a hearty final feast of roast *cuy*.

An integral part of Andean culture, even beyond the kitchen table, *cuy* are also used by *curanderos* (healers) in ceremonial healing rituals. *Cuy* can be passed over a patient's body and used to sense out a source of illness, and *cuy* meat is sometimes ingested in place of hallucinogenic plants during shamanistic ceremonies.

If you can overcome your sentimental inhibitions, sample this furry treat. The rich flavors are a cross between rabbit and quail, and correctly prepared *cuy* can be an exceptional feast with thousands of years of history.

Admission is with the *boleto turístico* tourist card only, which is valid for 10 days and covers 16 other sites in the region.

Piquillacta & Rumicolca

Urcos-bound buses from Cuzco pass both these sites, which are located 1km apart.

Piquillacta RUIN

(boleto turístico adult/student under 26 with ISIC card S130/70; ⏲7am-6pm) Meaning 'Place of the Flea,' Piquillacta is the only major pre-Inca ruin in the area. Built around AD 1100 by the Wari culture, it's a large ceremonial center of crumbling two-story buildings, all with entrances that are strategically located on the upper floor, surrounded by a defensive wall. The stonework here is much cruder than that of the Incas, and the floors and walls were paved with slabs of white gypsum, of which you can still see traces.

Admission is with the *boleto turístico* tourist card only, which is valid for 10 days and covers 16 other sites in the region.

Rumicolca GATE

FREE The huge Inca gate of Rumicolca is built on Wari foundations. The cruder Wari stonework contrasts with the Inca blocks. It's interesting to see indigenous people working with the mud that surrounds the area's swampy lakes – the manufacture of adobe (mud bricks) is one of the main industries of this area.

Andahuaylillas

☎084 / POP 840 / ELEV 3123M

Don't confuse this place with Andahuaylas, west of Cuzco. Andahuaylillas is more than 45km southeast of Cuzco, about 7km before the road splits at Urcos. This pretty Andean village is most famous for its lavishly decorated **Iglesia de San Pedro** (admission S15;

⌚7am-5:30pm), which is almost oppressive in its baroque embellishments. Admission is with the Ruta del Barrocco Valle Sur (Southern Valley Baroque Route) ticket, which also includes the Capilla de la Virgen Purificada in Canincunca and the Templo San Juan Bautista in Huaro.

The church dates from the 17th century and houses many carvings and paintings, including a canvas of the Immaculate Conception attributed to Esteban Murillo. There are reportedly many gold and silver treasures locked in the church, and the villagers are all involved in taking turns guarding it 24 hours a day. Is the rumor true or not? All we can tell you is that the guards take their job *very* seriously.

Near the church is the shop of the **Q'ewar Project**, a women's cooperative that makes distinctive dolls clad in traditional costumes, and the eclectic **Museo Ritos Andinos** (admission by donation; ⌚7am-6pm), whose somewhat random displays include a mummified child and an impressive number of deformed craniums.

To reach Andahuaylillas (up to S7, one hour), take any Urcos-bound bus from the terminal just off Av de la Cultura in Cuzco.

Raqchi

☎084 / POP 320 / ELEV 3480M

The little village of Raqchi, 125km southeast of Cuzco, is wrapped around **Templo de Viracocha** (admission S10), an Inca ruin that looks from the road like a strange alien aqueduct. These are the remains of a temple which was once one of the holiest shrines in the Inca empire. Twenty-two columns made of stone blocks helped support the largest-known Inca roof; most were destroyed by the Spanish, but their foundations are clearly seen. The remains of many houses and storage buildings are also visible, and reconstruction is an ongoing process.

The people of Raqchi are charming and environmentally conscious, working periodically to eradicate litter left by visitors. And they are famous potters – many of the ceramics on sale in the markets of Pisac and Chinchero come from here.

You can experience life in Raqchi by organizing a homestay. Families offer accommodations in basic but comfortable guest rooms, with private bathrooms and showers. Packages include all meals, a nighttime fiesta and a highly recommended day of **guided activities**. These include a visit to the ruins (admission not included), a heart-pumping hike up to the local *mirador* (lookout) and a ceramics workshop. Contact the South American Explorers (p232) in Cuzco for more information.

On the third Sunday in June, Raqchi is the site of a colorful **fiesta** with much traditional music and dancing.

Raqchi to Abra La Raya

About 25km past Raqchi is bustling **Sicuani**, a market town of 12,000 people, halfway from Cuzco to Puno. There's no real reason to stop here except to break the journey. A few economical places to stay are located near the bus terminal.

Twenty minutes past Sicuani – just before Abra La Raya, the high pass that marks the boundary between the Cuzco and Puno departments – are the **Aguas Calientes de Marangani** (admission S5; ⌚dawn-dusk). This complex of five fabulously hot thermal pools is linked by rustic bridges over unfenced, boiling tributaries. Quite a sight, it isn't odd to see locals washing themselves, their kids and their clothes in the pools. Consider it an accessible, off-the-beaten-track experience.

You can count on local transportation to hop between Cuzco, Andahuaylillas, Raqchi, Sicuani and the baths from early morning until at least 3pm.

CUZCO TO THE JUNGLE

There are three overland routes from Cuzco to the jungle. The least-developed, cheapest and quickest goes northwest from Ollantaytambo over the Abra Málaga Pass, to the secondary jungle around Quillabamba and into little-visited Ivochote and Pongo de Mainique beyond.

The other two routes are more popular but are rarely accessed by road. You can get to the area around Parque Nacional Manu through Paucartambo, Tres Cruces and Shintuya, or to Puerto Maldonado via Ocongate and Quince Mil. To get deep into these areas, most people go on organized tours which include light-plane flights in and out, or in some cases, 4WD road transportation.

Some of these roads are muddy, slow and dangerous. Think twice before deciding to travel overland, and don't even contemplate it in the wettest months (January to April).

BE SAFE IN THE JUNGLE

An increased activity of narcotraffickers and Shining Path guerillas in specific jungle areas in recent times may alter advisable routes for travel and trekking. The government has increased military presence in these areas for security and has added a military base in Kiteni. However, it is always wise to consult with knowledgeable guides and tour operators, or an unaffiliated organization like South American Explorers (p232), before heading out. Areas that may be of concern include Vilcabamba, Ivochote, Kiteni and beyond, though this is subject to change. It is important to use good, responsible local guides and never go on your own.

Independent travelers can request the *Peruvian Jungle Information Packet,* available at the South American Explorers (p232) in Cuzco.

Cuzco to Ivochote

Soon after Ollantaytambo, the road leaves the narrowing Sacred Valley and climbs steeply over the 4350m Abra Málaga. From here it's a dizzying, scenic, mostly unpaved descent straight into Amazonia. Dusty **Santa María** has bus company offices and a couple of very basic *hospedajes* (small, family-owned inns) and restaurants. It marks the junction where you turn off for Santa Teresa and the back-door route to Machu Picchu, or continue down to Quillabamba.

Santa Teresa

☎084 / POP 460 / ELEV 1900M

The makeshift feel of Santa Teresa persists thanks to its repeated flooding. A landslide in February 2015 washed out the only bridge into town. Before that, there was flood damage in 2010, 1998 and a decade before. Thus vulnerable to the elements, Santa Teresa struggles to position itself in tourism, despite being a back-door gateway to Machu Picchu. So far, the only takers are mostly backpackers seeking a cheaper access point to Machu Picchu.

In the tiny center, most buildings are prefabricated emergency-relief shells and, strangely, the most permanent construction is the puzzling Plaza de Armas statue. The real attractions are a few kilometers outside town – the Cocalmayo hot springs and the Cola de Mono zipline are both worth the time and effort required to get to them.

Activities

Cola de Mono ADVENTURE SPORTS

(☎084-78-6973, 984-992-203; www.canopyperu.com; 2hr zipline S160; rafting S150) South America's highest zipline is a must for thrill seekers. A total of 2500m of cables with six separate sections whiz high above the spectacular scenery of the Sacsara Valley.

The owners of Cola de Mono, river guides from way back, also run half-day rafting on the spectacular, and so far little-exploited, Santa Teresa river and camping on their extensive grounds.

To get there, it's a pleasant 2km (half-hour) stroll east – just follow the road out of town or take a taxi.

Llactapata HIKING

Hike to the hydroelectric station via Llactapata, a six-hour walk up and over a hill on the well-marked Inca Trail, affording views of Machu Picchu and access to a half-cleared ruin. The trail is well-marked and can be done without a guide, though they can indicate ruins, as well as the flora and fauna. Start early as it gets hot on the trail.

Hire a taxi (S40, 30 minutes) to drop you off at the start in Lucmabamba. You can take a *colectivo* back from the Hydroelectrica, or continue on to Machu Picchu.

Baños Termales Cocalmayo HOT SPRINGS

(admission S10; ⏲24hr) These stunningly landscaped, council-owned natural hot springs are truly a world-class attraction. As if huge, warm pools and a natural shower straight out of a jungle fantasy weren't enough, you can buy beer and snacks.

It's 4km from town. You can reliably catch a *colectivo* from Santa Teresa to Cocalmayo at around 3pm, when vehicles head down to collect Inca Jungle Trail walkers arriving from Santa María. Otherwise, you may have to brave the unshaded, dusty walk (with cars driving too fast) or pay a taxi around S36 round-trip. Pools washed out in the river flooding of 2010 have been rebuilt, though camping areas have not.

Tour de Cafe TOUR

(tours S195) Run by Eco Quechua, this 2½-hour tour visits a family coffee farm steeped in local tradition – see the *cuys* (guinea pigs) being raised in the kitchen! You can also pick tropical fruit and see a fish farm in action.

Not a modern operation, this is old-style cultivation in transition, in the process of introducing new techniques to improve productivity. It's an interesting visit and 50% of the visitor fee goes to help local farmers.

Sleeping & Eating

A handful of *hospedajes* in the center offer bare-bones accommodations. Hot meals are available at the market and the rotisserie chicken restaurants on the plaza – choose based on cleanliness.

Hotel El Sol HOTEL **$**
(☎084-63-7158; Av Calixto Sanchez G-6; s/d S40/70) This partially finished cement multistory is one of the best deals in town, though prices may go up as the building does! A friendly place, it features nice, clean rooms with bright sheet sets, hot-water bathrooms and cable TV.

Eco Quechua LODGE **$$**
(☎084-63-0877, 984-756-855; www.ecoquechua.com; Sauce Pampa; r S188-278, 3-day packages from US990; 📶) Staying at this thatched lodge lets you sample jungle living right outside of Santa Teresa, with optional adventure tour packages that also include Machu Picchu visits. Rooms feature mosquito nets, but still bring repellent. The open-air living room is cloaked in thick vegetation. It's rustic and pricey, but undoubtedly the most ambient spot around. A fun choice for groups.

Information

There are no banks or ATMs in Santa Teresa – you must bring all the cash you need. You may be able to change dollars at an extremely unfavorable rate. Internet access is poor, but also available in a few cafes.

Cusco Medical Assistance in Carrión provides 24-hour medical attention.

Getting There & Away

To get to Santa Teresa from Cuzco, take a bus headed for Quillabamba from the Santiago terminal, get off in Santa María, and catch a local *combi* or *colectivo* (S25, one hour) to Santa Teresa. These shared vans and wagons take on the winding, dirt road to Santa Teresa like Formula One competitors – try to chose one who seems more conservative, it's a lot to stomach.

YELLOW RIVER LODGE

A cozy place in Quellomayo, 25 minutes outside of Santa María on the alternative route to Machu Picchu, this welcoming family **homestay** (☎084-63-0209; www.quellomayo.com; r per person S69) is an organic farm harvesting coffee, chocolate and tropical fruit. Simple rooms have comfortable beds and colorful walls, but you'll spend most of your time exploring the lush surroundings. Home-cooked meals (S25) are available at the restaurant.

There's a riverside campground, including a shower, grill and adobe oven. If you want to learn more about coffee, there are roasting workshops on-site.

To get there, take a bus from Cuzco to Santa María (S30, four hours) and grab a taxi (S50) from there or trek via an old Inca trail – the website has details, including regional transportation options.

To get to Machu Picchu, train tickets on this route are sold only at the **Peru Rail** (⏰6-8am & 10am-3pm daily, 6-8pm Wed & Sun) ticket office at the bus station. Daily trains (US$26 one way) leave from the hydroelectric station, about 8km from Santa Teresa, at 7:54am, 3pm and 4:35pm. Be at the bus terminal an hour prior to your train to catch a *combi* (S7, 25 minutes). The 13km train ride to Aguas Calientes takes 45 minutes. Some choose to walk by the railway tracks instead, an outstandingly cheap way to get to Machu Picchu; it takes around four very dusty and sweaty hours.

You can also do this route as part of one of the guided multisport tours on offer.

Combis going directly to Quillabamba (two hours) depart from Santa María's Plaza de Armas every 15 minutes. *Colectivos* to Santa María leave often from the bus terminal. From Santa María you can connect to Cuzco (S40, five hours).

Quillabamba

☎084 / POP 8800 / ELEV 1050M

Welcome to the jungle! Quillabamba's tropical vibe is palpable, with heat that becomes oppressive by 9am, music that blares all night, and the land-that-time-forgot feel to most hotels and restaurants.

Quillabamba itself has few attractions and sees little tourism, but there are some outstanding, watery natural attractions nearby. The streets north and south of the

Mercado Central, rather than the eternally somnolent Plaza de Armas, are Quillabamba's commercial center.

Activities

Locals are justifiably proud of **Sanbaray** (admission S5; ⏲8am-late), a delightful complex of swimming pools, lawns, bars and a decent trout restaurant. It's a 10-minute *mototaxi* ride (S4) from the center.

La Balsa, hidden far down a dire dirt track, is a bend in the Río Urubamba that's perfect for swimming and river tubing. Enterprising locals sell beer and food here on weekends.

Mandor, **Siete Tinajas** and **Pacchac** are beautiful waterfalls where you can swim, climb and eat jungle fruit straight off the tree. Siete Tinajas and Pacchac are accessible via public transportation for a few soles each to Charate; a taxi to Mandor with waiting time will set you back S35.

Tours

Eco Trek Peru ADVENTURE TOUR
(☎in Cuzco 084-24-7286; www.ecotrekperu.com) This agency has passionate specialists in multiday trips in this part of the world.

Roger Jara GUIDED TOUR
(rogerjaraalmiron@hotmail.com) Guided trips to all the main attractions, as well as remnant virgin jungle near Quillabamba. Roger can also guide you through the area's big draws, Pongo de Mainique and Vilcabamba. He speaks some English.

Sleeping

There are many cheap, cold-water hostels around the Plaza de Armas and the Mercado.

Hostal Don Carlos HOTEL $
(☎084-28-1150; www.hostaldoncarlosquillabamba.com; Jirón Libertad 556; s/d/tr S75/110/120; @) With an on-site cafe, this colonial-style hotel features bright, ample rooms around a sunny interior courtyard. Rooms have hot showers and minibars. It's half a block from the Plaza de Armas.

Hostal Alto Urubamba HOTEL $
(☎084-28-1131, 084-28-2516; www.hostalaltourubamba.com; 2 de Mayo 333; s/d/tr S55/75/95, s/d/tr without bathroom S25/35/45) Clean, comfortable-enough rooms with fans encircle a sunny courtyard in this dementedly noisy, long-established traveler favorite.

Eating & Drinking

Locals love their *cevicherías* with fresh river fish – ask a taxi driver for their favorite. *Heladerías* (ice-cream shops) are also deservedly popular.

Pizzería Carlo PIZZA $
(☎084-28-1558; Jr Espinar 309; pizzas from S15; ⏲6pm-10:30pm Tue-Sun) This restaurant fires up wood-oven pizzas and serves lasagna in big portions. It's a local hangout after dark.

Heladería la Esquina ICE CREAM $
(cnr Espinar & Libertad; sandwiches from S5; ⏲8am-11pm Mon-Sat) This retro cafe serves up delicious juices, cakes, ice cream and fast-food snacks. Service is grouchy, but the 1950s-diner decor makes up for that.

Niko's BAR
(Pio Concha s/n) For a drink, try Niko's.

Information

BCP (Libertad 549) and Banco Continental on Bolognesi near the corner of Grau have ATMs and change US dollars. There's arm-chewingly slow internet access at a few places around the Plaza de Armas. Limited tourist information is available on the 3rd floor of the Municipalidad.

Getting There & Away

Walk south along Torre four blocks past Plaza Grau, to Plaza de Banderas, to find transportation to Huancacalle. Turn right at the end of Plaza de Banderas to find minivans (S35, five to seven hours) to Cuzco in the first block, and the *terminal terrestre* (bus station) a block later. Buses for Cuzco (S25) leave from here several times a day before 8am and between 1:30pm and 9:30pm. Minivans leave early in the morning and in the evening. All stop at Ollantaytambo and Urubamba en route, but charge full fare wherever you get off.

Minivans leave from Quillabamba's market area for Kiteni (three to six hours) and Ivochote (six to eight hours), further into the jungle.

Getting Around

The basic *mototaxi* fare around town is S3.

Huancacalle

☎084 / POP 300 / ELEV 3200M

Peaceful, pretty Huancacalle is best known as the jumping-off point for treks to Vilcabamba, but many more hikes from three to 10 days long are possible from here, including to Puncuyo, Inca Tambo, Choquequirao and Machu Picchu. The town's biggest building is **Hostal Manco Sixpac** (relative in Cuzco 971-823-855; per person without bathroom S20), run by the Cobos family of local guides. It's the only lodging with hot water. You can organize mules and guides here.

Manco Inca's huge palace fortress of **Vitcos** (also known as Rosaspata) is an hour's walk up the hill, and from there you can continue to the amazing, sacred white rock of **Yurac Rumi**. The whole easy-to-follow circuit, which starts just over the bridge at the end of the road, takes a leisurely three hours, including plenty of time for photos and admiration of both scenery and ruins.

Vilcabamba

The real 'lost city of the Incas,' Vilcabamba – also known as Espíritu Pampa – is what Hiram Bingham was looking for when he stumbled on Machu Picchu. The beleaguered Manco Inca and his followers fled to this jungle retreat after being defeated by the Spaniards at Ollantaytambo in 1536. The long, low-altitude trek, which takes four to nine days, is very rugged, with many steep ascents and descents before reaching Vilcabamba, 1000m above sea level. You can start at either Huancacalle or Kiteni.

This area may be insecure; consult with knowledgeable guides and tour operators, or an unaffiliated organization like South American Explorers (p232) in Cuzco, before heading out.

Cuzco to Manu

Paucartambo

POP 1300 / ELEV 3200M

This small village lies on the eastern slopes of the Andes, about 115km and three hours northeast of Cuzco along a cliff-hanging road, paved only until Huancarán.

Paucartambo is famous for its riotously colorful celebration in honor of the **Virgen del Carmen**, a festival held annually from July 15 to 18, with hypnotic street dancing, wonderful processions and all manner of weird costumes. The highly symbolic dances are inspired by everything from fever-ridden malaria sufferers to the homosexual practices of the Spanish conquistadors.

Accommodations for the festival need to be organized in advance; you either have to find a room in one of a few basic hotels or hope a local will give you some floor space. Many tourist agencies in Cuzco run buses specifically for the fiesta and can help arrange accommodations with local families.

Transportes Gallito de las Rocas (084-22-6895; Diagonal Angamos, 1st block off Av de la Cultura) buses depart Cuzco to Paucartambo (S12, three hours) daily and to Pilcopata (S26, 10 to 12 hours) on Monday, Wednesday and Friday. Look for 'Paucartambo' painted on a lamp post between auto shops to find the office.

Tres Cruces

About two hours beyond Paucartambo is the extraordinary jungle view at Tres Cruces, a lookout off the Paucartambo–Shintuya road. The sight of the mountains dropping away into the Amazon Basin is gorgeous in itself, but is made all the more magical by the sunrise phenomenon that occurs from May to July (other months are cloudy), especially around the time of the winter solstice on June 21. The sunrise here gets optically distorted, causing double images, halos and an incredible multicolored light show. At this time of year, many travel agencies and outdoor adventure outfitters run sunrise-watching trips from Cuzco.

During Paucartambo's Fiesta de la Virgen del Carmen, minibuses run back and forth between Paucartambo and Tres Cruces all night long. You can also take a truck en route to Pilcopata and ask to be let off at the turnoff to Tres Cruces (a further 13km walk). Alternatively, ask around in Paucartambo to hire a truck. Make sure you leave in the middle of the night to catch the dawn, and take plenty of warm clothing. Camping is possible but take all your own supplies.

Tres Cruces is within Parque Nacional Manu.

Cuzco to Puerto Maldonado

Almost 500km long, this road takes a day to travel in the dry season. Most travelers choose to fly from Cuzco to Puerto Maldonado. Now paved, this route is part of the Interoceánica, a highway that unites the east and west coasts of South America for the first time.

Various companies depart from Cuzco's *terminal terrestre* for Puerto Maldonado between 3pm and 4.30pm daily. CIVA (S60, 17 hours, departs 4pm) is probably

THE Q'OYORITI PILGRIMAGE

Rivers and mountains are *apus* (sacred deities) for the Andean people, possessed of a vital force called *kamaq*. At 6384m, Ausangate is the Cuzco department's highest mountain and the most important *apu* in the area. The subject of countless legends, it's the *pakarina* (mythical place of sacred origin) of llamas and alpacas, and controls their health and fertility. Condemned souls are also doomed to wander its freezing heights as punishment for their sins.

Ausangate is the site of the traditional festival of **Q'oyoriti** (Star of the Snow), held in late May or early June between the Christian feasts of the Ascension and Corpus Christi. Despite its overtly Catholic aspect – it's officially all about the icy image of Christ that appeared here in 1783 – the festival remains primarily and obviously a celebration and appeasement of the *apu*, consisting of four or more days of literally nonstop music and dance. Incredibly elaborate costumes and dances – featuring, at the more extreme end, llama fetuses and mutual whipping – repetitive brass-band music, fireworks and sprinklings of holy water all contribute to a dizzy, delirious spectacle. Highly unusual: no alcohol is allowed. Offenders are whipped by anonymous men dressed as *ukukus* (mountain spirits) with white masks that hide their features, who maintain law and order.

Many *cuzqueños* (inhabitants of Cuzco) believe that if you attend Q'oyoriti three times, you'll get your heart's desire. Pilgrims buy an *alacita* (miniature scale model) of houses, cars, trucks, petrol stations, university degrees, driver's licenses or money at stalls lining the pilgrimage pathway. The items are blessed at the church. Repeat three years in a row and see what happens.

Q'oyoriti is a pilgrimage – the only way in is by trekking three or more hours up a mountain, traditionally in the wee hours to arrive around dawn. The sight of a solid, endless line of people quietly wending their way up or down the track and disappearing around a bend in the mountain is unforgettable, as is Q'oyoriti's eerie, otherworldly feel. The majority of attendees are traditionally dressed *campesinos* (peasants) for whom seeing a foreigner may be a novelty (they may even point you out).

Discomfort is another aspect of the pilgrimage. Q'oyoriti takes place at an altitude of 4750m, where glaciers flow down into the Sinakara Valley. It's brutally cold, and there's no infrastructure, no town, just one big elaborate church (complete with flashing lights around the altar) built to house the image of El Señor de Q'oyoriti (Christ of Q'oyoriti). The temporary toilets are a major ordeal. The blue plastic sea of restaurants, stalls and tents is all carried in, on foot or donkey. The whole thing is monumentally striking: a temporary tent city at the foot of a glacier, created and dismantled yearly to honor two mutually contradictory yet coexisting religions in a festival with dance and costumes whose origins no one can remember.

the best option. If you want to split up the journey, the best places to stop are Ocongate and Quince Mil, which have basic accommodations.

The route heads toward Puno until soon after Urcos, where the road to Puerto Maldonado begins. About 75km and 2½ hours from Cuzco, you come to the highland town of **Ocongate**, which has a couple of basic hotels around the plaza.

From here, trucks go to the village of **Tinqui**, an hour's drive beyond Ocongate, which is the starting point for the spectacular seven-day trek encircling Ausangate (6384m), the highest mountain in southern Peru.

After Tinqui, the road drops steadily to **Quince Mil**, 240km from Cuzco, less than 1000m above sea level, and the halfway point of the journey. The area is a gold-mining center, and the hotel here is often full. After another 100km, the road into the jungle reaches the flatlands, where it levels out for the last 140km into Puerto Maldonado.

Ausangate

Snowcapped Ausangate (6384m), the highest mountain in southern Peru, can be seen from Cuzco on a clear day. Hiking a circuit around its skirts is the most challenging alpine hike in the region. It takes five to six days and crosses four high passes (two over 5000m). The route begins in the rolling brown *puna* (grasslands of the Andean plateau) and features stunningly varied scenery, including fluted icy peaks, tumbling glaciers, turquoise lakes and green marshy valleys. Along the way you'll stumble across huge herds of alpacas and tiny hamlets unchanged in centuries.

The walk starts and finishes at Tinqui, where there are warm **mineral springs** and a basic hotel, and mules and *arrieros* (mule drivers) are available for about S30 per day each. Average price is US$520 for an organized, tent-based five-day trek with operators such as **Apus Peru** (☎084-23-2691; www.apus-peru.com) or specialist guides.

For a luxurious, lodge-based experience of Ausangate, check out **Andean Lodges** (☎084-22-4613; www.andeanlodges.com; 3-day package from US$870). Ecofriendly technologies are used in bathrooms and restaurants. Treks range from three-days to a week, with lodging and all included.

CUZCO TO THE CENTRAL HIGHLANDS

Traveling by bus from Cuzco to Lima via Abancay and Nazca takes you along a remote route closed from the late 1980s until the late 1990s due to guerilla activity and banditry. It is now much safer, and paved. You should still check recent news reports before heading out this way as rainy season landslides can really slow a trip. Going west from Abancay to Andahuaylas and Ayacucho is a tough ride on a rough road rarely used except by the most hardcore travelers.

Cuzco to Abancay

There are several worthwhile stops along this four-hour, 200km ride. It's possible to make a day out of visiting one or two, bus-hopping your way to Abancay. Start by catching a *colectivo* to Limatambo (S12, two hours) from Arcopata in Cuzco.

Limatambo, 80km west of Cuzco, is named after the Inca site of Rimactambo, also popularly known as **Tarawasi** (☎Cuzco 084-58-2030; admission S10), which is situated beside the road, about 2km west of town. The site was used as a ceremonial center, as well as a resting place for the *chasquis* (Inca runners who delivered messages over long distances). The exceptional polygonal retaining wall, noteworthy for its 28 human-sized niches, is in itself worth the trip from Cuzco. On the wall below it, look for flower shapes and a nine-sided heart amid the patchwork of perfectly interlocking stones. There are basic, hard-to-find accommodations in Limatambo.

The natural thermal baths of **Cconoc** (☎Abancay 083-32-1664; admission S2.50) are a 3km walk downhill from a turnoff 10km east of minor transportation hub **Corahuasi**, 1½ hours east of Abancay. It has a restaurant, a bar, taxis and a basic hotel. For information, call Dircetur in Abancay (p270).

The Inca site of **Saihuite** (☎Abancay 083-32-1664; admission S10), 45km east of Abancay, has a sizable, intricately carved boulder called the Stone of Saihuite, which is similar to the famous sculpted rock at Q'enqo, near Cuzco, though it's smaller and more elaborate. The carvings of animals are particularly intricate. Ask to be let off at the turnoff to the ruins, from where it is a 1km walk downhill.

Cachora, 15km from the highway from the same turnoff as Saihuite, is the most common starting point for the hike to Choquequirao. There are a few guesthouses, a campground and local guides and mules for hire.

Choquequirao

Remote, spectacular, and still not entirely cleared, the ruins of Choquequirao are often described as a mini Machu Picchu. This breathtaking site at the junction of three rivers currently requires a challenging four-day hike to get there and back.

Many see it as 'the next big thing' in Inca ruins tourism. In fact, the Peruvian government has already approved controversial plans to put in a tramway, the country's first, with a capacity of 3000 visitors daily. The construction will bring this remote attraction to within 15 minutes of the nearby highway. Conservationists worry about its potential impact.

For now, you can still go without the crowds. Travelers can organize this walk on their own easily, but be aware that essential footbridges can get washed out, making the hike impossible. Inquire with operators first, even if you plan on going on your own.

A guided, four-day trek costs US$1050 per person (with two trekkers) on average. **Apus**

Peru (☎084-23-2691; www.apus-peru.com) joins this trek up with the Inca Trail, for a total of nine days of spectacular scenery and an ever-more-impressive parade of Inca ruins culminating in Machu Picchu.

Abancay

☎083 / POP 13,800 / ELEV 2378M

This sleepy rural town is the capital of the department of Apurímac, one of the least-explored regions in the Peruvian Andes. Travelers may opt to use it as a rest stop on the long, tiring bus journey between Cuzco and Ayacucho.

Jirón Arequipa, with banks, is the main commercial street; its continuation, Av las Arenas, has restaurants and entertainment.

Sights & Activities

During the dry season (late May to September), hikers and climbers head for the sometimes snowcapped peak of **Ampay** (5228m), about 10km northwest of town. Its 3635-hectare **Santuario Nacional Ampay** features good camping and birding.

Festivals & Events

Abancay has a particularly colorful **Carnaval** held in the week before Lent, which is a chance to see festival celebrations unaffected by tourism. It includes a nationally acclaimed folk-dancing competition. Book ahead or arrive before the festivities start. **Abancay Day**, the anniversary of the town's founding, is on November 3.

Sleeping & Eating

Accommodations are geared more toward business travelers than tourists. There are plenty of restaurants and cafes on Arenas, with a fair share of rotisserie joints and *chifas* (Chinese restaurants). Abancay's nightlife centers on Arenas and Pasaje Valdivia just off it.

Hotel Saywa HOTEL $
(☎084-32-4876; www.hotelsaywa.com; Arenas 302; s/d/tr incl breakfast S65/100/135; 📶) A friendly spot with good options for solo travelers. Attractive rooms have parquet floors and TV; there's also an on-site tour agency.

Hotel Turistas HISTORIC HOTEL $$
(☎084-32-1017; www.turismoapurimac.com; Díaz Bárcenas 500; s/d S100/150; @📶) A colonial mansion with a whiff of former grandeur, it's nonetheless a city landmark. Rooms are plain for what you might imagine, but comfortable, with phones and TVs. Breakfast is included but the coffee is not recommended. Be sure to ask for the 18% tax to be discounted. Solo travelers upgrade to an executive room (S50 extra).

Villa Venecia PERUVIAN $$
(☎084-23-4191; Av Bella Abanquina; mains from S18; ⏰11am-4pm) Worth the short taxi ride (it's behind the stadium), Villa Venecia is Abancay's most noteworthy restaurant. Serving up every local food imaginable, it's the living embodiment of the Peruvian mantra *'bueno, barato y bastante'* (good, cheap and plentiful). The *tallarines* (spaghetti) are an Abancay specialty and the tamales are wonderful.

Information

Dircetur (☎084-32-1664; informes@dirceturapurimac.gob.pe; Av Arenas 121, 1st fl) Provides information on area attractions, including Cconoc hot springs and Saihuite.

Getting There & Around

Colectivos to Corahuasi via Saihuite (S12, 1½ hours) leave from Jirón Huancavelica, two blocks uphill from Arenas. Vehicles to Cachora leave from one block further uphill. Buses towards Cuzco, Andahuaylas and Lima leave from the *terminal terrestre*.

Various companies go to Cuzco (S20 to S30, five hours), clustered around 6am, 11am and 11pm. Dozens depart to Lima (S60 to S180, 14 to 18 hours) daily, mostly in the afternoon and between 10:30pm and midnight. Departures to Andahuaylas (S10, five hours) cluster around 11:30am and 11:30pm. The faster, more comfortable minibuses to Andahuaylas (S25, four hours) are a little bit reckless.

Terminal departure tax is S1. Taxis go to the center (S4).

Central Highlands

Best Places to Eat

- ➡ La Choza de Omar (p274)
- ➡ Daylo Cocina Peruana-Fusion (p283)
- ➡ Leopardo (p292)
- ➡ Via Via (p305)

Best Places to Stay

- ➡ Villa Jennifer (p280)
- ➡ Hacienda La Florida (p283)
- ➡ La Casa de la Abuela (p290)
- ➡ Via Via (p303)

Why Go?

If it's breathtaking ancient ruins or immersion in uninterrupted wilderness that you crave during your Peruvian voyage, listen up. The rocky, remote central highlands can match the country's better-known destinations for these things and more: with the almost absolute absence of other travelers.

This sector of the Andes is Peru at its most Peruvian: at its zenith from Easter to July for the greatest of its myriad fiestas. Travel here is not for the faint-hearted. But adventure-spirited souls will discover better insights into local life than are possible elsewhere: bonding with locals on bumpy buses, perhaps, or hiking into high hills to little-visited Inca palaces.

Life in this starkly beautiful region is lived largely off the land: donkeys ply roads more than cars and bright indigenous dress predominates in communities secreting Peru's best handicrafts. The region's rearing, lake-studded mountains, it often seems, shield the central highlands from the 21st century.

When to Go

Ayacucho

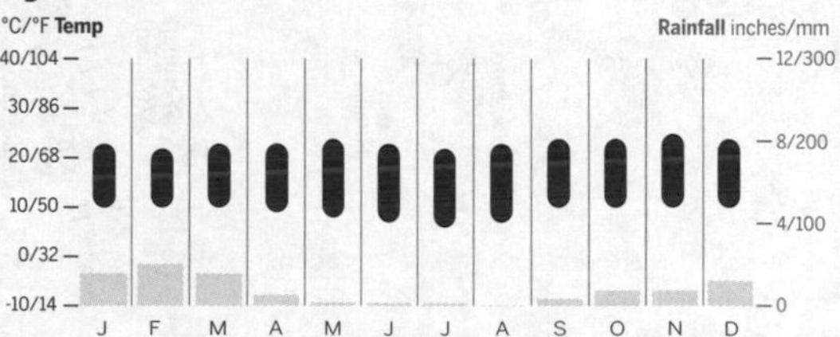

Jan Hot, rain-prone summer weather as Huancayo celebrates New Year with quirky festivities.

Mar/Apr Peru's biggest and best Easter party unfolds during Ayacucho's Semana Santa.

Jul & Aug Dry weather with chilly, starry nights conducive to toddies and thermal baths.

Central Highlands Highlights

1 Hiking out to the isolated northern Inca and pre-Inca ruins near **Canta** (p274), **La Unión** (p279) or **Tantamayo** (p279).

2 Savoring the taste of by-gone farming lifestyles with a stay at an age-old hacienda in **Tarma** (p281).

3 Poring over 25,000 colonial-era books in the convent of **Santa Rosa de Ocopa** (p287) at Concepción.

4 Taking to the tracks on the world's second-highest railway to **Huancayo** (p287).

5 Hunting for handicrafts in the villages of the **Río Mantaro Valley** (p285) around Huancayo.

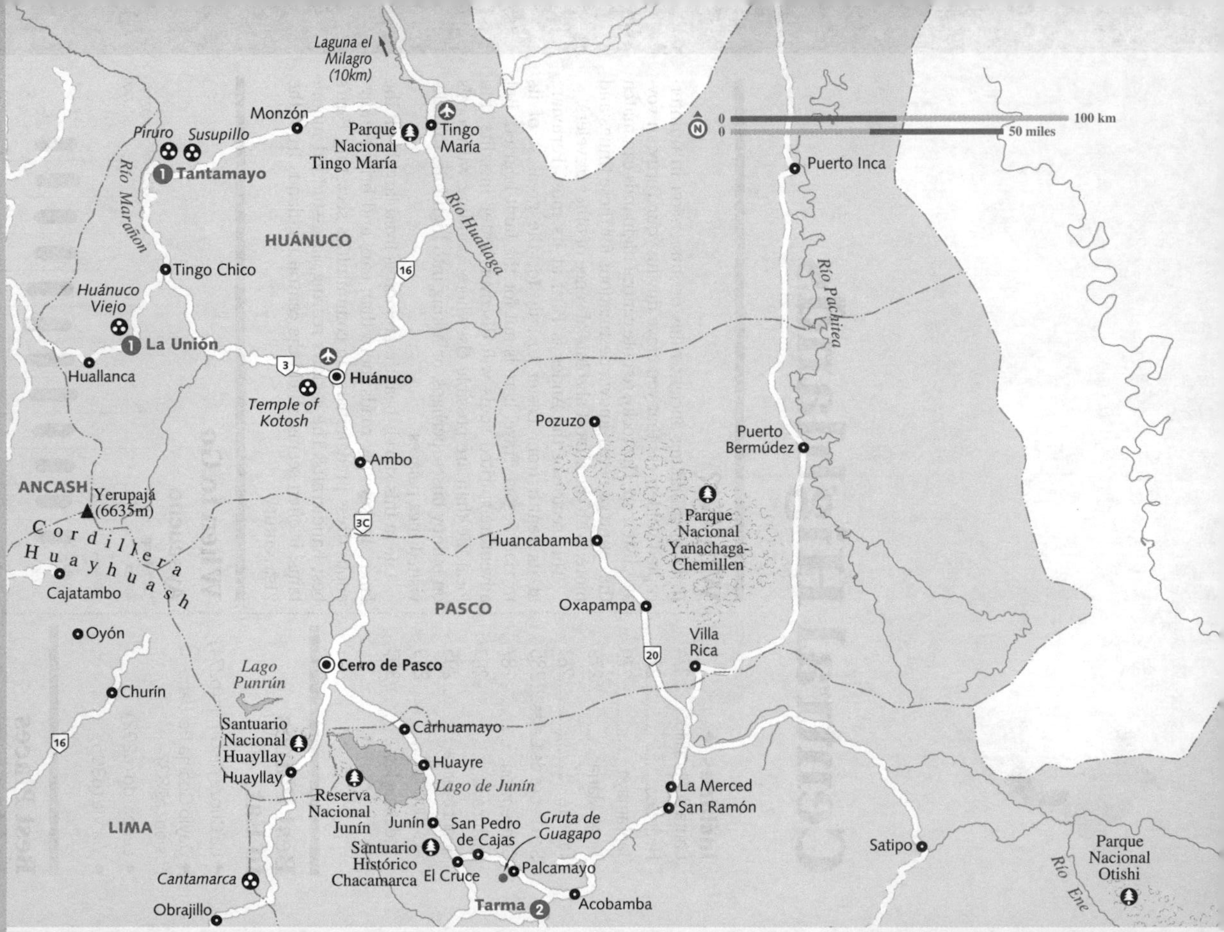

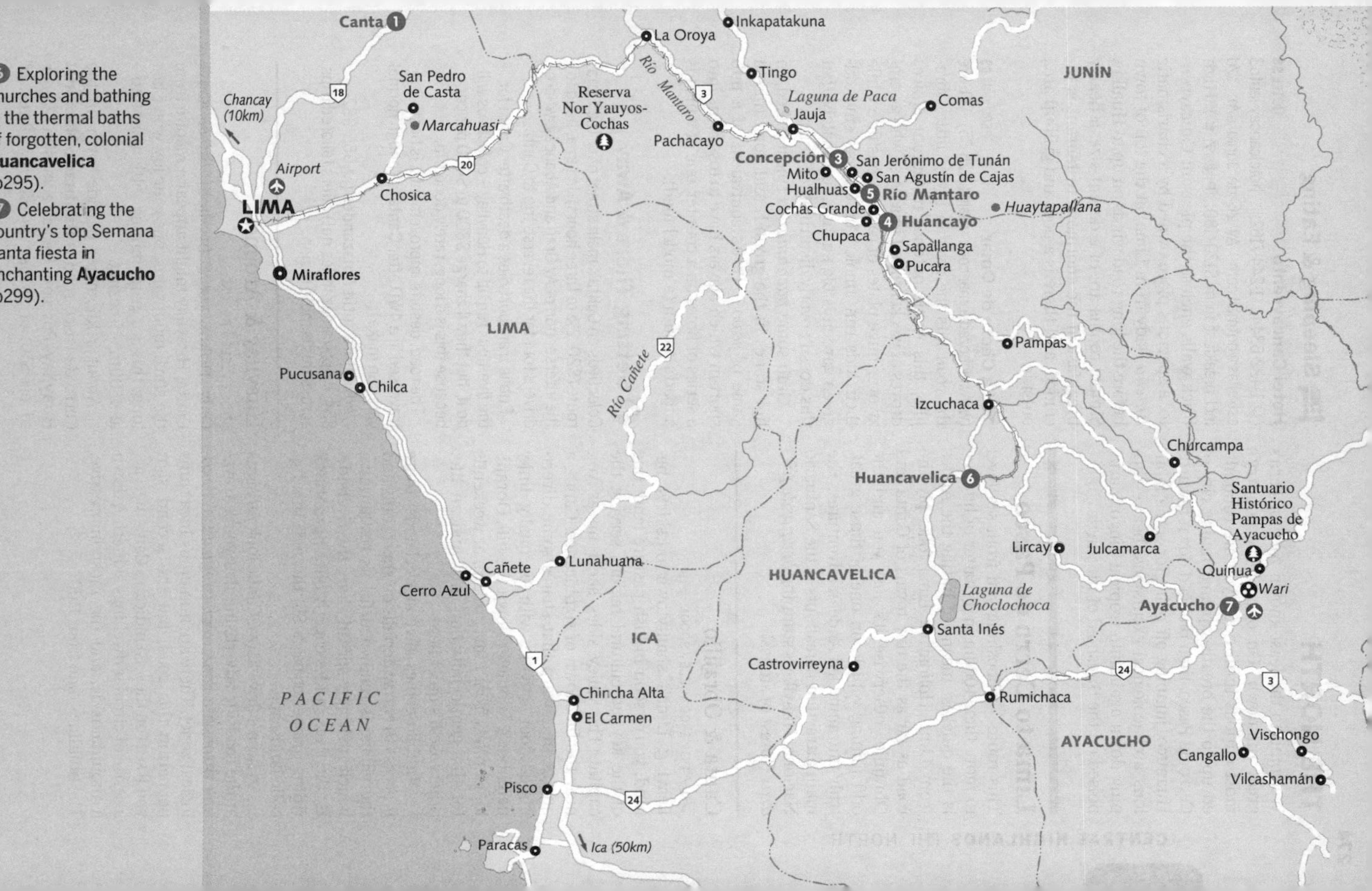

6 Exploring the churches and bathing in the thermal baths of forgotten, colonial **Huancavelica** (p295).

7 Celebrating the country's top Semana Santa fiesta in enchanting **Ayacucho** (p299).

THE NORTH

Welcome to the least-known zone of Peru's great unknown. On one of the country's most curious thrill rides, you are catapulted up to the breath-sapping mining city of Cerro de Pasco, then plunged down towards Huánuco, jumping-off point for some fabulous archaeological excursions, before dipping down again into tropical Tingo María, poised on the threshold of the jungle.

Lima to Cerro de Pasco

This route – whooshing you from sea level to more than 4000m in a matter of hours – is the quickest means of hitting the Andes from Lima. Holidaying Lima folks ply the road as far as the tiny towns of Canta and Obrajillo: otherwise it's just you and the odd mining vehicle on one of those great, truly untrammeled Andean adventures. The main attraction hereabouts is the Santuario Nacional Huayllay's stunning *bosque de piedras* (forest of stones).

Canta & Obrajillo

☎1 / POP 2800 / ELEV 3000M

Leaving Lima's shantytown outskirts behind, you're soon in lush pasture land: one of the key agricultural regions serving the capital. The valley sides sheer up as you near the first town of significance, Canta, a quaint time warp that shares some diverting outdoor activities with its equally dinky neighbor a kilometer down the hill, Obrajillo. Families from Lima rock up at weekends for this gentle initiation into Andean life; otherwise it's quiet here.

Obrajillo comes alive at weekends: there is access to two waterfalls on short trails and the village is renowned for its restaurants, which invitingly spread along the riverside. By the river, guides eagerly offer **horseback riding** (per person per hr S5) through this bucolic landscape.

An hour's drive above Canta, look for signs at the roadside advertising that you're traveling through a *zona arqueologica* (archaeological zone). There are numerous Inca ruins peppering this road, but the second sign you'll see (on the left) indicates Cantamarca – a series of circular dwellings skittering down a mountainside, and the most impressive. The buildings date from 1100.

Sleeping & Eating

Hotel Cancayvento HOTEL $$
(☎1-422-6344, 1-244-7162; hotelcancayvento3estrellas@hotmail.com; Av 26 de Junio s/n; s/d incl breakfast from S120/180; P@📶🏊) High brick walls enclose the pleasant Cancayvento, a spacious place owned by a charismatic *limeña* (lady from Lima) at the top of town before the long road winds on up to Huallay. Simple rooms are of a decent size, a hearty breakfast in the enormous restaurant is included, and there is a pool and grill-up area outside.

★**La Choza de Omar** PERUVIAN $$
(www.lachozadeomar.com; mains S25-35) Where the road hits the river in idyllic little Obrajillo, this rustic outdoor restaurant entices droves of weekending Lima types who go crazy over huge plates of carnivorous fare while their kids run amok. The Choza's emerald-green garden is big enough, fortunately, that this doesn't overly disturb other diners.

Grab some *pachamanca* (meat baked on hot stones in the ground) and don't miss a game of *sapo* – Peru's equivalent of a pub sport in which players have to toss coins into a series of holes on a counter, one of which is a toad's mouth (a model toad).

Getting There & Away

Colectivos on Canta's main street offer the Lima route (S20, 2½ to three hours). In Lima, head to the intersection of Av Grau and Abancay, where drivers tout for the reverse trip to Canta.

Public transport dies a death after Canta for the five-hour run up to Huayllay – *colectivos* will do it, but they'll charge S300 to S400 per car, because this is a long, rarely done trip.

The road, despite improvements, is best traversed in a 4WD after Canta, although normal cars can make it.

Adventure outfit **Amazandes** (☎965-982-854; http://amazandes.net) offers tailored trips across this remote region.

Huayllay & Around

☎063 / ELEV 4500M

Only 110km, yet a five-hour drive, above Canta, Huayllay might appear a respite from the stark mountains, but your joy won't last long: this is a gritty mining settlement and – at 4500m – freezing.

About a kilometer outside town on the Cerro de Pasco road is **Santuario Nacional Huayllay** (Bosque de Piedras; admission S2; guided tour S30) or *bosque de piedras* (forest of stones). It's the world's largest and highest rock forest with rock formations looming out of the desolate *pampa* (pampas grass) in such shapes as an elephant, a king's crown and an uncannily lifelike grazing alpaca. The area is highly rated for rock climbing. The sanctuary, comprising a vast area of several kilometers, also has thermal baths and (you might need a guide to find these) prehistoric cave paintings. Señor Raul Rojas of Hostal Santa Rosa in Cerro de Pasco is a recommended guide and charges S50 per person for day trips here. Guides also await at the site.

Going solo, you might miss out on some formations, but it's doable. *Colectivos* traverse the Huayllay–Cerro de Pasco road. In Cerro de Pasco, *colectivos* depart from Parque Minero, near the bus terminal (S6, 45 minutes).

Cerro de Pasco

☎063 / POP 66,000 / ELEV 4333M

With its altitude-sickness-inducing height above sea level and its punishingly bitter, rain-prone climate, this dizzyingly high altiplano mining settlement is never going to be a favorite traveler destination. First impressions, however, are still striking: houses and streets spread haphazardly around a gaping artificial hole in the bare hills several kilometers wide. The Spanish discovered silver here in the 17th century and this, along with other mineral wealth, has made Cerro a lucrative Peruvian asset. It has also worked hard at image improvement recently and boasts decent hotels to take your mind off the cold and industrial clamor. Besides being the highest place of its size in the world, Cerro attracts the odd traveler as a springboard for visiting some of Peru's most spectacular rock formations. If you are traveling by *colectivo* taxi around the altiplano, it is also handy for picking up a connecting ride.

Change your money at **BCP** (Arenales 162), which has an ATM. It's below Hotel Arenales, near the bus station. Emergency health care is available at **Clínica Gonzales** (☎063-42-1515; Carrión 99)

Uphill from the bus station on Plaza Daniel Carrión, **Hostal Santa Rosa** (☎063-42-2120; Libertad 269; s/d without bathroom S25/30) has basic, spacious rooms sharing three bathrooms and one highly prized hot shower. The owner is a guide, with information on how to visit the Santuario Nacional Huayllay rock formations. On the opposite side of the plaza is chirpy **Plaza Apart Hotel** (☎063-42-3391; Prado 118; s/d S80/120) with big, well-appointed, welcoming rooms and cable TV. Food? Miners like big portions, with taste and ambience further down the priority order, if Cerro's eateries are anything to go by.

The bus terminal, five blocks south of the Plaza de Armas, has buses to Huánuco (S10, three hours), Huancayo (S15, four hours), Lima (S30 to S40, eight hours), La Oroya (S10, 2½ hours) and Tarma. Faster *colectivos* from the bus terminal charge S20 to Huánuco. For Tarma you will likely have to change taxis at El Cruce where the Tarma road branches off (total fare to Tarma S25).

WORTH A TRIP

AN AUTHENTIC DOSE OF ALTIPLANO: LAGO DE JUNÍN

South of Cerro de Pasco, towards Tarma, on Hwy 3, the *real* altiplano opens up. Altiplano means 'high plain' and that's exactly what you get: bare, yellow, treeless grassland above 4000m altitude, battered by strong winds, that few besides intermittent herds of llamas can stomach long. But it's a trade-off: bleakness, in return for beauty.

By the village of Huayre is the main entrance to the interesting **Lago de Junín**, which, at about 30km long and 14km wide, is Peru's largest lake after Titicaca, and the highest lake of its size in the Americas: known for its spectacular birdlife. Some authorities claim one million birds live on and around the lake at any one time. These include one of the western world's rarest species, the Junín Grebe, and, among the nonwinged inhabitants, wild cuy. The lake and its immediate surroundings are part of the 53-sq-km Reserva Nacional Junín.

From Huayre, a 1.5km path leads to the lake. Otherwise it can be quite hard to actually visit or even see the lake as it is mostly surrounded by swampy marshlands.

Huánuco

☎062 / POP 175,000 / ELEV 1894M

Huánuco lay on the important Inca route from Cuzco to Cajamarca, the key settlement in the north of the empire, and developed as a major way station accordingly. The Incas chose Huánuco Viejo, 150km west, as their regional stronghold, but the exposed

Huánuco

Huánuco

Sights

1	Iglesia San Francisco	B1

Sleeping

2	Grand Hotel Huánuco	C2
3	Hostal Huánuco	B2
4	Hotel Real	B2
5	Hotel Santorini	C2
6	Hotel Trapiche Suites	B2

Eating

7	Chifa Khon Wa	C2
8	La Piazzetta	C2
9	Lookcos Burger Grill	B1

Drinking & Nightlife

10	Alambique	B2

Information

11	Banco Continental	B2
12	BCP	B2
13	Hospital Regional Hermillo Valdizán Medrano	D2

Transport

14	Bahía Continental	C2
15	Colectivos to La Unión	A3
16	Colectivos to Tingo María	C3
17	LC Peru	C1
18	Transportes Chavín	A3
19	Turismo Central	A3

location prompted the Spanish to move the city to its current scenic setting on the banks of the Río Huallaga in 1541.

Little is left of its colonial past, but the profusion of archaeological remains in the surrounding mountains is the main reason to linger in this busy little place. Locals boast Huánuco's perfect elevation gives it the best climate in Peru: indeed, after the tempestuous climes of the altiplano, the city seems positively balmy. It certainly makes for a convenient and tempting stopover on the Lima–Pucallpa jungle route.

Nearby is one of Peru's oldest Andean archaeological sites, the Temple of Kotosh (aka the Temple of the Crossed Hands), while up in the hills sit the still-more impressive ancient ruins of Huánuco Viejo and Tantamayo.

Sights

Sights in the city itself are thin on the ground: you might try seeing if **Iglesia San Francisco** (cnr Huallayco & Beraún) is open – it's Huánuco's most appealing church with lavish baroque-style altars and interesting *escuela cuzqueña* (Cuzco school) paintings – but don't hold your breath.

Temple of Kotosh RUINS
(admission incl guided tour S5; ⌚8am-5:30pm) This temple ruin is also known as the Temple of the Crossed Hands because of the life-sized mud molding of a pair of crossed hands, which is the site's highlight. The molding dates to about 2000 BC and is now at Lima's Museo Nacional de Antropología, Arqueología e Historía del Perú; a replica remains. Little is known about Kotosh, one of the most ancient Andean cultures. The site is easily visited by taxi (S12, including a 30-minute wait and return).

In the hills 2km above the site, **Quillaromi** cave has impressive prehistoric paintings. Kotosh is about 5km west of town off La Unión road.

Festivals & Events

Dance of the Blacks TRADITIONAL DANCE
Huánuco's most singular festival sees revelers remember the slaves brought to work in the area's mines by donning black masks, dressing up brightly and drinking – lots. It's held January 1, 6 and 18.

Sleeping

On the southeast side of the plaza is a glut of uninspiring options offering basic accommodations with a plaza price tag.

★**Hostal Huánuco** GUESTHOUSE $
(☎062-51-1617; www.facebook.com/Hostalhuanucos.r.l; Huánuco 777; s with/without bathroom S35/20, d S50) This traditional mansion simply exudes character, with old-fashioned tiled floors, a 2nd-floor terrace overlooking a garden and hall walls covered with art and old newspaper clippings. Delightful – if worn – rooms contain characterful old furniture and have comfortable beds. Showers are hot but can take an age to warm up: ask in advance.

Hotel Trapiche Suites BOUTIQUE HOTEL $$
(☎062-51-7091; hoteltrapichehuanuco@hotmail.com; General Prado 636; s/d S87/137;) Boutique hotels are clearly well received in Huánuco: this, the sole exponent of the genre, is booked out weeks in advance. Funky artwork features on the walls above huge, comfy, colorful beds; there are copiously stocked minibars and telephones. It's clearly aiming at well-to-do business types and offers a viable luxury alternative to the city's other more staid top hotels.

Hotel Santorini HOTEL $$
(☎062-51-5130; Beraún, btwn Valdizán & Bolivar; s/d S80/100) The sounds of your own footsteps echo in immaculate yet empty hallways. The rooms (and the cable TVs within) are big. The beer in the minibar could be cooler, but at least it's there. The showers could be hotter, but at least they're there, too. A clean, reasonable, respectable guarantee of a night's sleep.

Grand Hotel Huánuco HOTEL $$$
(☎062-51-4222; http://grandhotelhuanuco.com; Beraún 775; s/d S170/230; P) On the Plaza de Armas is this grande dame of Huánuco hotels. Its public areas are airy and pleasant, high-ceilinged rooms have solid parquet floors as well as a phone and a fuzzy, mainly Spanish-language cable-TV service. A sauna, billiard room, Jacuzzi, pretty good restaurant and bar are on the premises.

Their Inka Comfort Restaurant is open 7am to 10pm (mains from S15).

Eating

The 24-hour cafe at the **Hotel Real** (☎062-51-1777; www.realhotelhuanuco.com.pe; Jirón 2 de Mayo 1125; s/d S90/120) is an excellent choice for midnight munchies or predawn breakfasts. For more formal dining try the stately dining room at the Grand Hotel Huánuco.

★**Tradiciones Huanuqueñas** PERUVIAN $
(Huallayco 2444; S12-30; ⌚8am-5pm) This is the quintessential eating experience in Huánuco, which is why it gets our vote. Dishes remain true to the Peruvian Andes, prices remain down to earth and portions pose challenges for most appetites. Add on a green, quiet, out-of-town setting and the question is: why not? A *mototaxi* from the center costs S5.

Lookcos Burger Grill BURGERS $
(Castillo 471; meals S7.50-15; ⌚6pm-midnight) This large, two-floor squeaky-clean restaurant serves mean burgers and sandwiches, sports a balcony, and a bar blaring out a diverse selection of ear-splitting *reggaetón* come nightfall.

La Piazzetta PIZZA $
(Beraún 845-847; medium pizza S21-24; ⌚6-11pm Mon-Sat) This upscale restaurant does quality Italian food including tasty pizzas. Service is prompt and there is a good range of Chilean and Argentinean wines.

Chifa Khon Wa CHINESE $
(www.khonwa.pe; General Prado 820; mains S16-32; ⌚noon-midnight) The largest and most popular Chinese eatery in town.

Drinking & Nightlife

Alambique BAR
(Beraún 635; ⌚6pm-late) A mellow kind of place with a small dance floor downstairs and a cozy upstairs area for drinks: go on, come knock back some of their house sangria!

Information

Almost identical sets of internet joints grace most blocks. Huánuco has no tourist office but does have a handy online **information site** (www.huanuco.com).

BCP (Jirón 2 de Mayo 1005) With a Visa ATM.

Hospital Regional Hermillo Valdizán Medrano (☎062-51-8139; www.hospitalvaldizanhco.gob.pe; Hermillo Valdizán 950)

Getting There & Away

AIR

LC Peru (☎962-673-710, 062-51-8113; www.lcperu.pe; Jirón 2 de Mayo 1321) flies to and from Lima daily. The airport is 5km north of town. Take a cab (S10) to get there.

BUS & TAXI

Buses go to Lima (S25 to S50, eight hours), Pucallpa (S25 to S35, 11 hours), La Merced (S20, six hours) and Huancayo (S20, six hours), with companies all over town.

A *colectivo* taxi is best for La Unión (S25, four hours) or Tantamayo (S30, five hours), as the ascent is on a narrow corkscrew road. Head to the *cuadra* of Tarapaca between San Martín and Huallayco to find several La Unión *colectivo* companies clamoring for your business.

Take a Pucallpa-bound bus (S10, 3½ hours) or a *colectivo* taxi (S20, two hours) for Tingo María from the river end of General Prado.

For Cerro de Pasco, minibuses (S10, three hours) and *colectivo* taxis (S20, two hours) leave

MINING OR UNDERMINING? THE ISSUES WITH THE ALTIPLANO'S MINERAL WEALTH

Mining is Peru's *numero uno* source of income, and the central highlands accounts for a sizable chunk of it. But with the affluence that the extraction of zinc, lead, silver, copper and gold brings – Peru ranks within the world's top four exporters for each – questions concerning the distribution of that wealth and the detriment that extraction brings to the environment are raised. And Peru's major mining centers are some of the poorest and most polluted places in the country, if not the continent.

Mining or mineral processing is the economic lifeblood of Cerro de Pasco (one of South America's main zinc and lead mines) and La Oroya (the Highlands' main ore smelting center). Yet it could also be the ruination of these cities. Contamination rates are high: La Oroya constantly graces 'most polluted places in the world' lists and Cerro de Pasco can't be far behind. While Doe Run, the company that owns the La Oroya smelter, has now shut down production, there have since been clamors to restart operations from residents despite their awareness of the risks.

Huelgas (strikes) over working and living conditions are regularly reported, but also poignantly in evidence are the conditions people are prepared to endure to keep their jobs in this industry. Nowhere is this more evident than in Cerro de Pasco, where the pit owned by Volcan Compañia Minera is in the middle of the city (it is ironically referred to as Peru's biggest Plaza de Armas). Not only do nine out of 10 children have above-average levels of minerals in their blood (according to research by the US-based Centers for Disease Control), but also, with the majority of available water supplying the mine, running tap water is only available for limited hours. A significant percentage of the city's population lives in poverty.

However, there is a more imminent danger. Houses cluster around the rim, and subsidence from the ever-present hole outside the properties is a problem. In 2008, Volcan was allowed to buy a portion of the historic city center. With the pit poised to eat up the heart of Cerro de Pasco, Peruvian congress passed a bill proposing an audacious and costly solution to the problem: relocating the entire city some 20km away. But this, officials estimate, could take US$500 million and over a decade to execute. And time, for many residents, is running out. Watch the space. Soon, Cerro de Pasco might not be there at all: a victim, like many Peruvian mining towns, of its own success.

from Paradero de Cayhuayna, a 1km *mototaxi* ride from the center, as do *colectivos* to La Oroya and the Tarma turn off at El Cruce (S40, 3½ hours).

Bahía Continental (☎062-51-9999; Valdizán 718) One of the more luxurious options. Regular bus to Lima at 10am plus *bus-camas* at 9:30pm, 10pm and 10:15pm (the last is the most comfortable).

Transportes Chavín (San Martín btwn Mayro & Tarapaca) *Colectivos* to Tantamayo aren't as common as to La Unión – not least because the road is worse – but these guys offer daily morning services, leaving around 5am. Ideally, come here the day before to book your berth.

Turismo Central (☎062-51-1806; Tarapaca 552) To Pucallpa 8am and 8pm, Huancayo 9:30pm.

La Unión

POP 6300 / ELEV 3200M

La Unión is the first (only) significant community on the bumpy road from Huánuco to Huaraz: an exciting way to connect the central highlands and the Cordillera Blanca. From here you can hike to the extensive Inca ruins of **Huánuco Viejo** (admission S5; ⊙8am-6pm) on a swathe of barren pampa at 3700m. From behind the central market, a steep flight of steps leads up to a water tower, from where the defined path continues through beautiful altiplano landscapes (1½ to two-hour walk). Once you've climbed up to the plain, look for a road and the ruins visible on open ground to the right. Locals will point you in the right direction. Minivans leaving from the market throughout the day (S3) can take you to within a 20-minute walk of the site. There are 2 sq km of ruins and more than 1000 buildings and storehouses altogether here. Most impressive is the *usnu*, a huge 4m-high ceremonial platform with engravings of animals (monkeys with lion faces) adorning the entrance. A key figure in the Inca resistance against the Spanish, Illa Tupac defended Huánuco Viejo until 1543, significantly after many Inca settlements had fallen. Looking at the site's defensive advantages today, it's easy to see how.

La Unión has a handy **Banco de la Nación** (Jirón 2 de Mayo 798) with what is surely Peru's remotest Visa ATM. **Hostal Inka House** (Virgen del Carmen 123; r from S20) has adequate accommodation in a central location near the market.

All transport arrives/departs from the bus terminal on Commercio at the west end of town. Companies leave around 6pm to 8pm for Lima (S20 to S30, 10 hours) while a couple of buses daily (plus numerous *colectivos*) ply the route east to Huánuco (S15, five hours) and to Tantamayo (S10, three hours). La Unión Huánuco has a service to Huaraz that departs at the ungodly hour of 3am, taking five hours (S15).

Tantamayo

ELEV 3400M

Tantamayo is connected only by rough track to the outside world, ensconced in a green-brown patchwork of fields standing out from the stark, precipitous sides of the Upper Marañon Valley. From this serene, chilly village flows a river that will, hundreds of kilometers downstream, morph into the Amazon itself. Tantamayo was capital of the pre-Columbian Yarowilca culture, remains of which are scattered throughout the nearby hills. The most impressive ruins are those at **Piruro** and **Susupillo**. This culture was one of the oldest known in Peru and very architecturally advanced. Buildings were constructed with up to six floors connected via internal spiral staircases, giving them a different appearance to the constructions of the Incas, whom many believe were unable to emulate the superior Yarowilca style.

Piruro is easiest to visit: a 1½-hour walk down from Tantamayo and up the other side of the valley. The path is hard to find: be sure to ask. For Susupillo, vehicles can take you to the village of Florida, a 20-minute drive from Tantamayo, from where you can hike to the site.

There are basic lodgings in Tantamayo, although La Unión has more choice. Tantamayo boasts public phones (these can't dial internationally) but no listed ones, no cell phone reception and no banks. *Colectivos*, minibuses and buses from Huánuco make the journey in five to eight hours (bus S20, *colectivo* S30). Tantamayo is also connected to La Unión (three hours) from where you can catch onward buses to Lima.

Tingo María

☎062 / POP 55,000 / ELEV 649M

This languid, humid university and market town lies in the *ceja de la selva* (eyebrow of the jungle; on the cusp between mountains and jungle): its back rests against the mountains – as the conical, forested hills that flank it testify – but its feet are firmly fixed in the lush, sticky vegetation of the

Amazonas region. Tingo María, or Tingo for short, is a popular weekend destination for holidaying *limeños,* while travelers pause here en route to the Amazon.

The main attraction is Parque Nacional Tingo María: a lush forested wilderness with caves and great bathing spots. Sadly, this adventure comes with its dangers.

Sights

Parque Nacional Tingo María PARK
(admission S5) This 180-sq-km park lies to the south of town, around the mouth of the Río Monzón, a tributary of the Río Huallaga. The most distinguishing feature is the **Bella Durmiente** (Sleeping Beauty), a hill overlooking the town, which, from some angles, looks like a recumbent woman wearing an Inca crown. The park is not without its dangers for tourists, and it is advised to take a guide with you whichever site you choose to visit.

Also in the park is **La Cueva de las Lechuzas** (the Cave of the Owls), which, despite its name, is known for the colony of oilbirds that lives inside. In addition, there are stalactites, stalagmites and bats around the cave entrance, but the oilbirds are undeniably the main attraction.

The caves are about 6km away from Tingo; taxis can take you there. Guides will show you around during daylight hours (6am to 6pm). The best times for park visits are in the morning, when sunlight shines into the cave mouth, or dusk, when the oilbirds emerge. Don't use your flashlight to see the birds, as this disturbs their sleeping and breeding patterns.

There are myriad great **bathing spots** in and around the park. Recommended are the **San Jacintillo Medicinal Springs**, 1km before the Cave of the Owls; and **Velo de las Ninfas** and **Cueva de los Tambos**, 9km south of Tingo. There is a nominal entrance fee of S3 to S5 at each spot.

The Cave of the Owls has police protection, but the road there is still risky, as are more remote destinations.

Sleeping & Eating

★**Villa Jennifer** LODGE $$
(☎062-79-4714; www.villajennifer.net; Castillo Grande Km 3.4; dm S50, s/d from S110/130; ⏲restaurant 10:30am-6pm; 📶🏊) Located north of Tingo's airport is this peaceful tropical hacienda and lodge, run by a Danish-Peruvian couple. They have done wonders out of a lush expanse of tropical bushland bounded by rivers on two sides. Suave rustic accommodations range from simple rooms with shared bathrooms to airy minihomes that can sleep up to 10 people.

One common feature of all accommodations is the relaxation space: terraces, sunbeds, patios.

Listing the other highlights of a stay takes a while. A menagerie of animals makes an entertaining sideshow (crocodiles, tortoises, a sloth and some monkeys particularly vociferous at 7am feeding time). You could also play table tennis, darts or table soccer, or catch a movie in the DVD lounge. In the excellent restaurant, be sure to try the local fruit *anonas* (custard apples), which are delectable. There are also two swimming pools and minigolf, and not to be missed is the 30-minute hike up to a *mirador* (lookout) on a sheer conical hill above the property.

Information

There have been reports of travelers being robbed and raped at gunpoint en route to destinations within Parque Nacional Tingo María. It is strongly recommended that you do not venture into the countryside around Tingo without a guide and ensure you return well before dark. Increased police protection at key park attractions has improved security, but remember that this is a remote area.

Furthermore, the Huallaga Valley that runs north of Tingo to Tarapoto is a cocaine production area and also one of the last bastions of the Sendero Luminoso (Shining Path). Risk to tourists from drugs traffickers and the Sendero Luminoso is very low but care should still be taken.

BCP (Raimondi 249) Also changes US cash. It has a Visa ATM.

Main Post Office (Plaza Leoncio Prado)

Getting There & Away

AIR

Flights between Tingo and Lima run daily with **LC Peru** (☎062-56-1672; www.lcperu.pe; Raymondi 571).

BUS & TAXI

Transport here mostly serves Lima and destinations in between such as Huánuco, as well as local villages and Pucallpa. The road between Tingo and Pucallpa can be risky and is best done in daylight.

Buses to Lima (S40 to S60, 12 hours) are operated by, among others, **Transportes León de Huánuco** (☎062-56-2030, 962-56-2030; Pimentel 164). Buses usually leave at 7am or 7pm. Some operators go to Pucallpa (S20, nine hours). A faster service to Pucallpa is with

Turismo Ucayali (cnr Tito Jaime Fernández s/n, cuadra 2), which has *colectivos* (S45, 4 ½ hours).

From around the gas station on Av Raimondi near the León de Huánuco bus terminal, *colectivos* depart to Huánuco (S20, 2½ to three hours) and other destinations.

Selva Tours (☎062-56-1137; Raimondi 205-207) has cars north to Tocache (S40, three to four hours) and eventually Tarapoto (S95, nine hours). Tarapoto vehicles go direct if there's the demand but normally you'll have to change at Tocache or Janjui or both. Do this journey only in daylight, and only if you must.

By *mototaxi* to the Cueva de las Lechuzas it's about S25 for the round-trip, including a wait at the cave.

LIMA TO TARMA

This is the most-used artery from Lima up into the heart of the central highlands in the Río Mantaro Valley. However, most travelers whiz straight past the pretty places en route – which include rock formations, Inca ruins, caves and craft villages. Don't join them – make a stop-off here.

San Pedro de Casta & Marcahuasi

Isolated San Pedro de Casta (population 1300, elevation 3200m) is the perfect precursor to your Central Andes adventure. The road from **Chosica** (p105) twists spectacularly upward for 40km around a sheer-sided valley before arriving at this mountainside town clustered around a ridge and resounding with the bellows of *burros* (donkeys).

People come here principally to visit the little-known archaeological site of Marcahuasi, a nearby 4-sq-km plateau at 4100m. Marcahuasi is famed for its weirdly eroded rocks shaped into animals such as camels, turtles and seals, which have a mystical significance for some people (who claim they are signs of a pre-Inca culture or energy vortices).

Because of the altitude, it's not advisable to go to Marcahuasi from Lima in one day; acclimatize overnight in San Pedro. It takes two hours to hike the 2km up to the site; you can sometimes catch a bus part of the way if it's not engaged on other municipality business (departing 7:30am from the plaza most days), then hike for 45 minutes. A **Centro de Información** (☎01-571-2087; Plaza de Armas, San Pedro; ⊙9am-3pm Mon-Fri) has limited information and maps; staff can arrange guides for S10. Mules and horses can also be hired for similar prices.

You can camp at Marcahuasi but carry water: the few lakes there aren't fit to drink from. In San Pedro, there is a basic hotel just off the plaza, and local families usually have beds (ask at the information center). Simple plaza restaurants serve a *menú* (set meal) for about S5.

Getting there entails taking a bus from Lima to Chosica; minibuses to Chosica can be picked up in Central Lima from Arica at Plaza Bolognesi (S3.50, two hours). Then ask for Transportes Municipal San Pedro, which leaves from the bus yard by Parque Echenique on the main drag (Carretera Central) in Chosica at 9am and 3pm (S6, four hours). The bus back to Choisica leaves at 2pm.

Tarma

☎064 / POP 46,000 / ELEV 3050M

Travelers seldom make it to Tarma, but they should. One of the region's most welcoming cities with a balmy climate by altiplano standards, this is a great stopover – surrounded on all sides by scrubby, brown-dirt mountains secreting some intriguing day trips, but poised on the cusp of the *ceja de la selva* (eyebrow of the jungle) with a road linking the central Andes to the Amazon Basin and its associated attractions. *Limeños* (inhabitants of Lima) come here on the way to experiencing the nearest accessible tract of jungle to their desert capital and the city is now cottoning-on to tourism with facilities ever-improving. Tarma can also be used as a base for exploring *la selva central* (Central Amazon).

The area has a long history too. Hidden in the mountains around town are Inca and pre-Inca ruins that have yet to be fully excavated. Tarma was one of the first places to be founded by the Spanish after the conquest (1538 is the generally accepted date): the surviving legacy from this time are the gorgeous colonial haciendas – some of Peru's best – making atmospheric locales in which to spend the night.

⊙ Sights

Tarma itself, ushering you in under the gorgeous archway of its main thoroughfare, is quite appealing, without wowing you. Local excursions include one of Peru's key pilgrimage sites, El Señor de Muruhuay (the Christ

Tarma

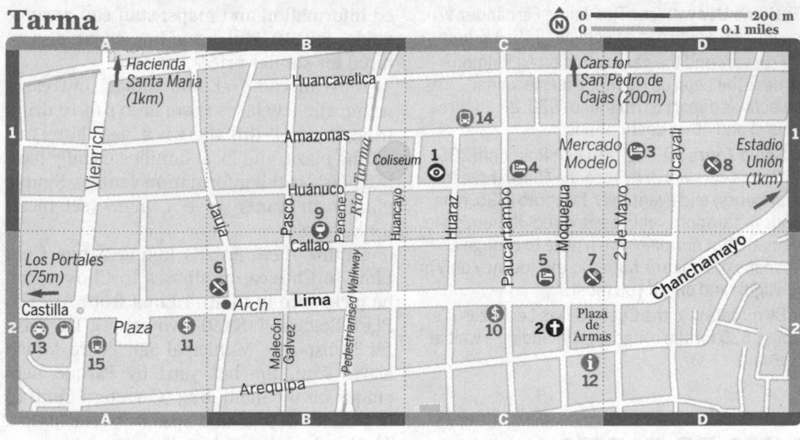

Tarma

Sights

1 Astronomical Observatory C1
2 Cathedral C2

Sleeping

3 El Vuelo del Condor D1
4 Hospedaje el Dorado C1
5 Los Balcones C2

Eating

6 Daylo Cocina Peruana-Fusion B2
7 Restaurant Chavín de Grima C2
8 Restaurant Señorial/El Braserito D1

Drinking & Nightlife

9 La Colonia 'H' B1

Information

10 BCP C2
11 Casa de Cambio A2
12 Tourist Office C2

Transport

13 Colectivos A2
Edatur .... (see 15)
14 Los Canarios C1
15 Terminal Terrestre A2
Transportes La Merced .... (see 15)

of Muruhuay) near Acobamba (9km from Tarma) and San Pedro de Cajas (41km away).

Astronomical Observatory OBSERVATORY
(☎064-32-2625; Huánuco 614; admission S5; ⊙8-10pm Fri) Tarma is high in the mountains and the clear nights of June, July and August provide ideal opportunities for stargazing, though the surrounding mountains do limit the amount of observable heavens. A small astronomical observatory is run by the owners of Hospedaje Central: admission includes a talk (in Spanish) on constellations and a peek at some stars. Closed for refurbishment at the time research, the observatory was sheduled to reopen mid-2016.

Cathedral CHURCH
(Plaza de Armas) The town's cathedral is modern (1965), and it contains the remains of Tarma's most famous son, Peruvian president Manuel Odría (1897–1974). He organized construction of the cathedral during his presidency. The old clock in the cathedral tower dates from 1862.

Tarmatambo ARCHAEOLOGICAL SITE
Of the myriad archaeological ruins near Tarma, best known is Tarmatambo, 6km south. Former capital of the Taruma culture and later a major Inca administrative center, the fairly extensive remains include storehouses, palaces and an impressive, still-used aqueduct system. Ask at the tourist office about guides to take you there and to other sites: going solo, these ruins are difficult to find. Independent travelers: take a Jauja-bound bus to Tarmatambo village, on the main road below the ruins.

From Tarmatambo, a rarely-used **Camino del Inca** forges over the hills down to Jauja: there's basic accommodations in Tarmatambo but it's then a strenuous (but beautiful) all-day hike to Jauja (40km).

Festivals & Events

The big annual attraction is undoubtedly Easter. For good information on this and other regional festivities (in Spanish) visit www.tarma.info.

Semana Santa RELIGIOUS
(Mar/Apr) Many processions are held in Tarma during Holy Week, including several by candlelight after dark. They culminate on the morning of Easter Sunday with a marvelous procession to the cathedral along an 11-block route entirely carpeted with flower petals, attracting thousands of Peruvian visitors. Hotels fill fast and increase prices by up to 50% at these times.

Tarma Tourism Week FESTIVAL
(late Jul) Features dress-up parades, music, dancing and much raucous merriment.

Sleeping

Choices in Tarma itself are limited to unspectacular budget options and one expensive resort hotel. A short ride from town, some attractive farmhouse B&Bs compensate with atmospheric hacienda-style accommodations. Most budget hotels have hot water, usually in the morning, though they may claim all day.

Hospedaje el Dorado GUESTHOUSE $
(064-32-4151; www.hospedajeeldoradotarma.com; Huánuco 488; s with/without bathroom S30/20, d S50) Sizable, clean, occasionally worn rooms face a leafy internal courtyard and come with cable TV and hot showers. Friendly staff and an in-house cafeteria help make this central Tarma's most backpacker-friendly sleeping option.

El Vuelo del Condor GUESTHOUSE $
(064-32-3602; Jirón 2 de Mayo 471; s/d/tr S50/75/90;) Amid the market bustle, this is a clean, secure, well-appointed place: nothing fancy, but reliable wi-fi and hot water; doubles and triples are the rooms with windows on the market action.

★ **Hacienda La Florida** HACIENDA $$
(064-34-1041; www.haciendalaflorida.com; s/d incl breakfast S125/215;) Located 6km from Tarma on the Acobamba road, this 300-year-old working hacienda is owned by a welcoming Peruvian-German couple, Pepe and Inge. Prettily decorated rooms boasting wooden parquet floors and private bathrooms flank a large courtyard. There's space for campers (per person S15) and the filling breakfasts have a delectable German slant. Contact them by phone; email is rarely checked.

Visitors can stroll the trails on the property, partake in farm life, or in various two-day workshops (minimum of six people) on relaxation techniques and cooking classes. El Señor de Muruhuay sanctuary is a one-hour hike away, and tours to other local sights are available.

Los Balcones HOTEL $$
(064-32-3600; www.losbalconeshoteltarma.com; Lima, btwn Paucartambo & Moquegua; s/d incl breakfast S100/195;) It does appear idyllic, a convenient half-block from the Plaza de Armas in revamped colonial style, but something is lacking. Inside, despite the rooms ticking all the boxes, a certain soullessness wafts around.

Los Portales HOTEL $$$
(064-32-1411; www.losportaleshoteles.com.pe; Castilla 512; s/d/ste incl breakfast S220/320/670;) Set in secluded gardens in the west of town, the refined mustard facade of the 'LP' secretes 44 standard hotel rooms with cable TV and wi-fi access. There's even a children's playground. Rates include continental breakfast and the restaurant provides room service. The two suites have Jacuzzis. This is the best choice for accommodations in Tarma city itself.

The town's best disco, Kimera, is also on the premises along with a popular fast-food chicken outlet.

Hacienda Santa María HACIENDA $$$
(064-32-1232; www.haciendasantamaria.com; Vista Alegre 1249; r per person incl breakfast S120;) Calle Vienrich becomes Vista Alegre to the northeast of town and after 1km arrives at this charming hacienda: a white-walled, 18th-century colonial house with wooden balconies perfect for surveying the surrounding lush, flower-abundant grounds strung with hammocks. Rustic rooms are full of old furniture. There is also a clutch of alternative local tours that the owners can arrange.

Eating & Drinking

★ **Daylo Cocina Peruana-Fusion** FUSION $
(064-32-3048; cnr Lima & Jauja; mains S12-25; noon-11pm) With one stylish opening, Daylo has whirled Tarma's eating scene from the culinary wasteland category right up into refined dining. The food in this intimately designed venue veers away from traditional Peruvian, but doesn't lose sight of these influences. A 'Chinese style' ceviche goes down

a treat with a Chilean wine, for example. And we've rarely seen carpaccio done so well in Peru. For evenings, it's best to reserve.

Restaurant Chavín de Grima PERUVIAN $
(Lima 270; meals S14-25; ⏱7am-10pm) For breakfasts and cheap set lunches on the Plaza de Armas you won't go far wrong by heading to this veritable institution. A wholesome two-course *menú del dia* (set menu of the day) is a mere S5.

Restaurant Señorial/ El Braserito PERUVIAN $
(Huánuco 138/140; mains S12-24; ⏱8am-3pm & 6-11pm) Two restaurants rolled into one (just one side is opened if it's slow), this is the local favorite. It's seen better days but there's something inexplicably appealing about the array of meaty options complemented by the nonstop *telenovelas* (Spanish-language soaps) and inane reality shows blaring from the TV. The wholesome menu features the usual Peruvian standards, including *cuy* (guinea pig) and *trucha* (trout).

La Colonia 'H' BAR
(Callao 822; ⏱until 2am) The best place for a beer or three.

Information

Casas de cambio (foreign-exchange bureaus) are at the western end of Lima. Internet cabins are on almost every block.

BCP (Lima at Paucartambo) You can change money here; it also has an ATM.

Tourist Office (☎964-638-750, 943-873-366; Arequipa, btwn Moquegua & Jirón 2 de Mayo; ⏱8am-1pm & 3-6pm Mon-Fri) On the Plaza de Armas, a newly built tourist office shows Tarma's intent to bolster tourism (although it's often closed). It proffers information about nearby attractions, such as Tarmatambo, San Pedro de Cajas, Gruta de Huagapo and some of the nearer jungle sights – and can point you in the right direction for organized tours.

Getting There & Around

Most public transport now arrives and departs from the sparkling new **Terminal Terrestre** at the end of Lima by the arched entrance to central Tarma. There are no shortage of buses to Lima here (S20 to S30, six hours). Buses to the central jungle destinations such as La Merced (bus S10, *colectivo* S15, two hours) do leave from here, although for greater flexibility you can go to the Estadio Unión and wait for the frequently passing *colectivos* and *combis*. To forge further into the jungle, La Merced has plenty more transport options.

BUS

Some bus companies have their own terminals in Tarma.

Edatur (Terminal Terrestre) Has good services down to the jungle, including a bus to Oxapampa (S18, four to five hours) at 10:30am. San Ramón, La Merced and Satipo are also served.

Los Canarios (☎064-32-3357; Amazonas 694) The best option for going to Huancayo, with small buses (S10, three hours) via Jauja (S7, two hours) leaving almost hourly from 5am to 6pm.

Transportes La Merced (Terminal Terrestre) Lima at 11:30am, 1:30pm, 10pm, 11pm and 11:45pm.

OTHER TRANSPORT

By the gas station at the intersection of Lima, Vienrich and Castilla, *colectivo* taxis take up to four passengers to Lima (S30 each) or local destinations such as Junín or La Oroya (S15), or Huancayo (S20). If you want to go to Cerro de Pasco or Huánuco, you can take *colectivos* from here, too, though you will have to change at El Cruce (the crossroads of the Tarma and La Oroya–Cerro de Pasco roads).

From Estadio Unión a *mototaxi* (motorcycle taxi) here costs S2. Amazon-bound vehicles head via Acobamba (S2, 10 minutes) down to San Ramón and La Merced. The journey to La Merced is spectacular, dropping about 2.5km vertically to the jungle in the space of just over an hour. For destinations beyond La Merced, change at La Merced's convenient bus terminal.

Cars for San Pedro de Cajas (S5) leave from the northern end of Moquegua.

Acobamba

☎064 / POP 13,500 / ELEV 2950M

Colorful Acobamba, about 9km from Tarma, has profited substantially from and is famous for the religious sanctuary of **El Señor de Muruhuay**, a white shrine visible on a hill 1.5km away.

The sanctuary, one of Peru's top pilgrimage sites, is built around a rock etching of Christ crucified. The image supposedly appeared to smallpox sufferers during a regional epidemic, healing them when authorities had left them for dead. Historians claim it was carved with a sword by a royalist officer who was one of the few survivors after losing the major independence Battle of Junín, but this story has less cachet and legends relating to the image's miraculous appearance persist. A small chapel replaced the previous roughly thatched hut at the site in 1835 and the present sanctuary, inaugurated in 1972, is a modern building with an electronically controlled bell tower and is decorated with huge weavings from San Pedro de Cajas.

The feast of El Señor de Muruhuay, held throughout May, has been celebrated annually since 1835. There are religious services, processions, dances, fireworks, ample opportunities to sample local produce and even a few gringos. Stalls sell *chicha* (fermented corn beer) and *cuy* (guinea pig), but be wary unless your stomach is travel-hardened. Visitors usually stay in nearby Tarma, although Acobamba has accommodations.

San Pedro de Cajas

☎064

Forty kilometers up in the hills from Tarma, peaceful San Pedro is the production center for the country's finest *tapices* (tapestries). Most of the village is involved in making these high-quality woven wall hangings, depicting moving scenes from rural Peruvian life. You can watch locals weaving in workshops around the Plaza de Armas: it's one of Peru's best opportunities for witnessing handicraft production – and purchasing the results.

The **Casa del Artesano** (Plaza de Armas; ⏲9am-7pm) is one of the largest workshops. On the same street, down from the plaza, basic *hospedajes* (family-run inns) offer rooms. *Colectivos* from Tarma (S5, one hour) serve San Pedro regularly.

About 28km up on the way to San Pedro (just past the village of Palcomayo) you'll pass the **Gruta de Huagapo**, a huge limestone cave that ranks among Peru's largest subterranean systems. A proper descent into the Gruta de Huagapo requires caving equipment and experience: tourist facilities consist only of a few ropes. The cave contains waterfalls, squeezes and underwater sections (scuba equipment required). It is possible to enter the cave for a short distance, but you soon need technical gear.

RÍO MANTARO VALLEY

Back in the mists of time – so local legend runs – two huge snakes had a battle, with the loser falling to earth to form the Río Mantaro. The meandering river, opening out on a wide, fertile agricultural plain southeast of Tarma, reveals a gentler side to the mostly rugged highlands: undulating pastoral panoramas, the sophisticated modern city of Huancayo and, dotted in-between, a number of villages internationally renowned for the quality of their handicrafts. For those who still crave remoter adventures, there is the wild Reserva Nor Yauyos-Cochas, a number of high-altitude hikes and even kayaking opportunities right down the valley.

Festivals are a way of life here. Residents say that there is a festival occurring each day of the year, and chancing upon some colorful celebration is highly likely.

The valley, split by the Río Mantaro throughout its length, runs northwest-southeast between Jauja and Huancayo. South of Jauja, the road branches to follow both the west and east sides of the Río Mantaro Valley to Huancayo. Local bus drivers refer to these as *derecha* (right, or west) and *izquierda* (left, or east).

From Huancayo, some classic Andean travel routes connect through the hard-going but delightfully scenic valleys south to Huancavelica, Ayacucho, Andahuaylas and eventually on to Cuzco.

Jauja

☎064 / POP 15,000 / ELEV 3250M

Coming from Lima, the first place you pass along this route is Jauja, a small, bustling colonial town of narrow traffic-swamped streets about 60km southeast of Tarma and 50km north of Huancayo. It offers some decent accommodations, which can be used as a base for sampling attractions including a lakeside resort and several interesting hikes.

Sights

Jauja was Francisco Pizarro's first capital in Peru, though this honor was short-lived. Some finely carved wooden altars in the main **church** are all that remain of the early colonial days. Before the Incas, this area was home to an important Huanca indigenous community, and **Huanca ruins** can be seen on a hill about 3km southeast of town. A brisk walk or *mototaxi* will get you there.

Some good general information can be found at the town's website (www.jaujamiperu.com; in Spanish).

A well-preserved **Camino del Inca** (Inca road) runs from Jauja to Tarma. The most spectacular section is from Tingo (30 minutes from Jauja by taxi) to Inkapatakuna (30 minutes from Tarma), a scenic but tough all-day hike.

Laguna de Paca LAKE

This small lakeside resort, 4km outside Jauja, offers restaurants, rowboats and fishing.

A boat ride around the lake will cost S5 to S10 per passenger (depending on how many passengers there are). There are ducks and gulls, and you can stop at Isla del Amor – a tiny artificial island. A *mototaxi* out to the lake costs S4.

Reserva Nor Yauyos-Cochas NATURE RESERVE
The huge Reserva Nor Yauyos-Cochas is an iconic Andean smorgasbord of glimmering blue-green mountain lakes nestled within towering peaks and home to the Pariacaca Glacier. You'll need your own 4WD vehicle (rent one in Lima or Huancayo) to get there.

The entrance, half an hour west of Jauja on the Lima road, is at Pachacayo.

Sleeping & Eating

Many visitors stay in Huancayo and travel to Jauja by minibus or *colectivo*.

Out by Laguna de Paca, a string of lakeshore restaurants attempt to entice diners with shrill, piped Andean music. Music aside, the lakeside tables are pleasant to sit at. Most offer a creditable plate of *pachamanca* (meat, potatoes and vegetables cooked in an earthen 'oven' of hot rocks). Another specialty here is clay-baked *trucha* (river trout) seasoned with chilies, garlic and lemon, wrapped in banana leaves and baked in Laguna mud: delicious. Jauja also has several simple, central restaurants.

Hostal María Nieves GUESTHOUSE $
(☎064-36-2543; Gálvez 491; s with/without bathroom S40/35, d with/without bathroom S50/40) The friendly owner at this *hostal* is accustomed to hosting the odd stray gringo and offers nine homely rooms of which three have private bathrooms. Breakfast is available on request.

El Paraíso PERUVIAN $
(Ayacucho 917; mains S15; ⏲lunch & dinner) The best eatery in town is this vast plant-filled restaurant popular with locals who are attracted by bargain specialties such as *trucha* (river trout) from Laguna de Paca and *picante de cuy* (roast guinea pig in a spicy sauce). It's just south of the main plaza.

Getting There & Around

Jauja has the regional airport with daily flights to/from Lima courtesy of **LC Peru** (☎064-21-4514; www.lcperu.pe; Ayacucho 322), which only has an office in Huancayo. The airport is south of town by the roundabout off the Huancayo road.

Buses, minibuses and taxis all congregate at the south side of town by the bus yard at the intersection of Ricardo Palma with Calle 28 de Julio about 800m from the Plaza de Armas. During the day, frequent, inexpensive minibuses (S3) and *colectivos* (S5) leave from here for Huancayo (50 minutes) via Concepción. Minibuses also leave for Tarma (S7, 1½ hours) and La Oroya (two hours). *Colectivos* will also leave to

RÍO MANTARO VALLEY VILLAGES

Two main road systems link Huancayo with the villages of the Río Mantaro Valley: *izquierda* is the east and *derecha* is the west side of the river, as you head into Huancayo from the north. It is best to confine your sightseeing on any given day to one side or the other; few bridges link the two sides.

Perhaps the most interesting excursion on the east side is a visit to the twin villages of **Cochas Grande** and **Cochas Chico**, about 11km from Huancayo. These villages are the major production centers for the incised gourds that have made the district famous. Oddly enough, the gourds are grown mainly on the coast, in the Chiclayo and Ica areas. Once transported into the highlands, they are dried and scorched, then decorated using woodworking tools. Gourd carving can be seen at various houses in the village.

On the west side, the town of **Chupaca** has an interesting livestock market. Starting early, you can visit and continue by bus to **Ahuac**, then (hiking or by minibus) a further 2km up to **Laguna Ñahuimpuquio**, which offers restaurants and boat rides. From the east shore a path climbs to a ridge for great valley views and the ruins of **Arwaturo**, constructed to maximize illumination by the sun's rays.

Other villages known for their handicrafts include: **San Agustín de Cajas** (wicker furniture); **Hualhuas** (wool products, including ponchos and weavings); and **San Jerónimo de Tunán** (filigree silverwork).

While most trading is done in Huancayo, the villages are easily visited from the city. They have few facilities but there is no substitute for the experience of seeing the crafts in the villages themselves. The key is an ability to speak some Spanish and make friends with locals.

these destinations if there is demand: they normally only leave when they have five passengers (that means two in the front seat).

Mototaxis run anywhere in town for around S1.50. Take a *mototaxi* to get to Laguna de Paca (S4).

Concepción

064 / ELEV 3283M

From Concepción, a village halfway between Jauja and Huancayo on the *izquierda* side of the valley, you can travel to charming Ocopa village, home to the famous convent of **Santa Rosa de Ocopa** (admission S5; 9am-noon & 3-6pm Wed-Mon). Admission is by 45-minute guided tour every hour or once large-enough groups have congregated (seven-person minimum). There is a 50% student discount. The building, set around beautiful gardens and courtyards, was built by the Franciscans in the early 18th century as a center for missionaries heading into the jungle. During the years of missionary work, the friars built up an impressive collection of indigenous artifacts and stuffed jungle wildlife, now displayed in the convent's museum. There is a large collection of colonial religious art, mainly in the *escuela cuzqueña* (Cuzco School) style – a combination of Spanish and Andean artistic styles. The highlight, however, is the fantastic 2nd-floor library of some 25,000 volumes, many dating back as far as the 15th century.

Frequent *colectivos* (Monday to Saturday) leave from the plaza in Concepción for Ocopa, about 5km away. *Mototaxis* charge S20 for the return trip, including an hour's wait. Concepción is easily visited by taking a Huancayo–Jauja *izquierda* bus.

Huancayo

064 / POP 365,000 / ELEV 3244M

The central altiplano's megametropolis, bustling Huancayo mixes its modern facade with a strong underlying sense of tradition. For many travelers, this self-confident, cosmopolitan city will be their first experience of the Peruvian highlands – it stands within a lush valley on an exciting overland mountain route to Cuzco – and while its charms are less obvious than those of other Andean locales, Huancayo does not disappoint.

Some of Peru's finest dining outside of Lima and Cuzco awaits within the teeming streets, yet once you've sipped your espresso and sampled the region's renowned cuisine in well-appointed restaurants, prepare yourself for Peru's most interesting handicrafts – sold in the markets here and in the valley beyond – and vibrant, varied fiestas that take place almost daily.

There are, too, opportunities to learn Spanish or Quechua, to master musical instruments or to dabble in Andean cooking. For the adventurous, the dusty nearby hills hide weird rock formations and spectacular lakes, while further afield, Andes trekking, extreme mountain biking and jungle tramping await. To top it all, Huancayo is the terminus for two of Peru's (and South America's) best railway journeys, including the world's second-highest railway over the Andes to/from Lima.

MARKET DAYS AROUND HUANCAYO

Each village and town in the Río Mantaro Valley has its own *feria* (market day).

Monday San Agustín de Cajas, Huayucachi

Tuesday Hualhuas, Pucara

Wednesday San Jerónimo de Tunán, Jauja

Thursday El Tambo, Sapallanga

Friday Cochas

Saturday Matahuasi, Chupaca, Marco

Sunday Huancayo, Jauja, Mito, Comas

Sights

Huancayo is a sizeable town; you'll end up doing a lot of walking. Most attractions lie outside the center. In the city itself, the most notable landmark is the **Iglesia de La Merced**, on the first block of Real, where the Peruvian Constitution of 1839 was approved.

Museo Salesiano MUSEUM

(Arequipa 105; adult/child S5/3; 9am-1pm & 3-6pm Mon-Fri, 9am-noon Sat) The museum can be entered from the Salesian school, and displays fauna epitomizing Peru's three contrasting geographic regions, plus pottery and archaeology exhibits. Hours vary.

Cerro de la Libertad VIEWPOINT

(cnr Giráldez & Torre Tagle; dawn-dusk) Head northeast on Giráldez for a great view of the city. About 2km from the town center is a popular recreational and dining locale

Huancayo

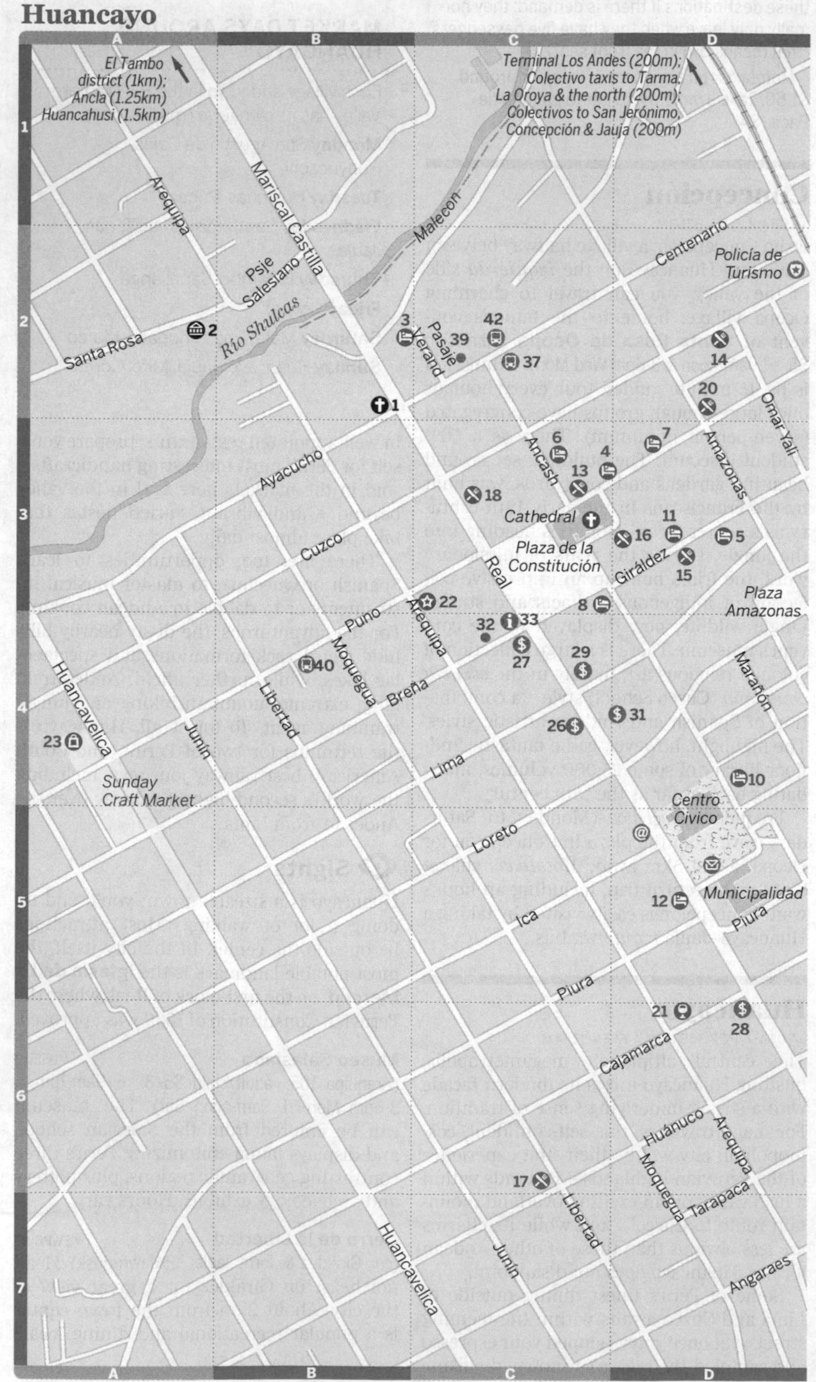
El Tambo district (1km); Ancla (1.25km) Huancahusi (1.5km)
Terminal Los Andes (200m); Colectivo taxis to Tarma, La Oroya & the north (200m); Colectivos to San Jerónimo, Concepción & Jauja (200m)
Arequipa
Mariscal Castilla
Malecon
Psje Salesiano
Río Shulcas
Santa Rosa
Pasaje Verand
Centenario
Policía de Turismo
Omar Yali
Amazonas
Ancash
Ayacucho
Cathedral
Plaza de la Constitución
Giráldez
Cuzco
Real
Plaza Amazonas
Puno
Arequipa
Moquegua
Breña
Libertad
Marañon
Huancavelica
Junín
Lima
Sunday Craft Market
Centro Civico
Loreto
Municipalidad
Ica
Piura
Piura
Cajamarca
Huánuco
Arequipa
Moquegua
Tarapaca
Libertad
Junín
Huancavelica
Angaraes

where, apart from the city view, there are artwork stalls and a playground.

Parque de la Identidad Huanca PARK

In the suburb of San Antonio, 3km northeast of the center, this is a fanciful park full of stone statues and miniature buildings representing the area's culture.

Activities

Incas del Perú ADVENTURE TOUR

(064-22-3303; www.incasdelperu.org; Giráldez 675) Ever-active Lucho Hurtado of Incas del Perú, located in the same building as the restaurant La Cabaña, organizes many activities. Lucho is a local who speaks English and knows the surrounding area well. He arranges demanding, multiday mountain-bike tours and Andean mountain-trekking expeditions to the lake and glacier in the nearby mountains; the cost for trekking for one person starts at S1170 for a three-day/two-night excursion.

There are also treks on offer down the eastern slopes of the Andes and into high jungle on foot, horseback or public transport. It isn't luxurious, but it's a good chance to experience something of the real rural Peru: you can stay on Lucho's father's ranch in the middle of nowhere in the high jungle of the central Amazon. Five-day/four-night trips are S975 per person including food. Accommodations are rustic and trips can involve camping.

Incas del Peru also arrange Spanish and Quechua lessons, including meals and accommodations with a local family (if you wish), from about S600 to S900 per week. Lessons can be modified to fit your interests. You can also learn to cook regional dishes, engage in the local handicraft of gourd carving or discover how to play Andean panpipes.

Torre Torre HIKING

The eroded geological formations of Torre Torre (*torre* means 'tower'; some outcrops here are thus shaped) lie 2km up in the hills beyond Cerro de la Libertad. Initially head east from Cerro de la Libertad on Taylor, from where a fairly obvious path ascends to the formations.

To make a longer route, continue along the ridge keeping Huancayo to your left (west). You'll eventually reach another rock formation, known as Corona del Fraile (crown of the monk), a round-topped rock surrounded by a crown of eucalyptus trees, below which are several waterfalls.

Huancayo

Sights
1 Iglesia de La Merced........B2
2 Museo Salesiano........A2

Activities, Courses & Tours
Incas del Perú........(see 30)

Sleeping
3 Blub Hotel Spa........B2
4 Hostal El Marquez........C3
5 Hostal Las Lomas........D3
6 Hotel Confort........C3
7 Hotel los Balcones........D3
8 Hotel Olímpico........C3
9 Hotel Presidente........E6
10 Hotel Turismo........D4
11 Isha Hotel........D3
12 Susan's Hotel........D5

Eating
13 Café Coqui........C3
14 Chicharronería Cuzco........D2
15 Chifa Centro........D3
16 Detrás de la Catedral........D3
La Cabaña........(see 30)
17 Leopardo........C6
18 Sofa Café Paris........C3
19 Supermercado Plaza Vea........E3
20 Zalema Social Coffee........D2

Drinking & Nightlife
21 Insomnico........D6

Entertainment
22 Antojitos........C3
La Cabaña........(see 30)

Shopping
Casa del Artesano........(see 33)
23 Feria Dominical........A4
24 Mercado Mayorista........F3
25 Real Plaza Mall........E3

Information
26 Banco Continental........C4
27 BCP........C4
28 BCP........D6
29 Casa de Cambio........C4
30 Incas del Perú........F2
31 Interbank........D4
32 Lavandería Cisne........C4
33 Tourist Office........C4

Transport
34 Buses to Cochas........F2
35 Colectivos to Huancavelica........E6
36 Combis to Chupaca........F2
37 Cruz del Sur........C2
38 Expreso Molina........E7
39 LC Peru........C2
40 Los Canarios........B4
41 Transportes Ticllas........E6
42 Turismo Central........C2

You can return to Huancayo from this end of the ridge. While safe enough during daylight hours, beware the packs of stray dogs, particularly in the houses below Torre Torre.

Festivals & Events

There are hundreds of fiestas in Huancayo and surrounding villages – supposedly almost every day somewhere in the Río Mantaro Valley. For more information, ask at the tourist office.

Año Nuevo TRADITIONAL DANCE
(Jan 1-6) New Year festivities in Huancayo are some of Perú's most unusual. Dances performed include the *huaconada*, in which revelers dress up to look like quirky old men with big noses, representing village elders who, in times past, would drop by the houses of lazy or mischief-making villagers and whip them into behaving for the coming year. Plenty of butt-whipping still takes place.

Mito, an hour north of Huancayo, and where the *huaconada* originates, also has vivid celebrations.

Semana Santa RELIGIOUS
(Mar/Apr) One of the biggest events in Huancayo, big religious processions attract people from all over Peru in the week leading up to Easter.

Fiestas Patrias FESTIVAL
(Jul 28 & 29) Peru's Independence Days are celebrated with processions by the military and schools. Hotels fill up and raise their prices during these times.

Sleeping

★ **La Casa de la Abuela** HOSTEL $
(064-23-4383; www.incasdelperu.com; Prolongacion Cusco & José Gálvez; dm/s/d without bathroom incl breakfast S30/50/70; P@) Now in a new location a 25-minute walk from central Huancayo, La Casa de la Abuela is run by Incas del Peru and makes every effort to welcome tired travelers. This brightly painted house is clean and friendly, with inviting chill-out areas, kitchen facilities, cable TV and DVD.

It's popular with backpackers, who can chose from amenable dorms or compact rooms with shared bathrooms. Rates include a great continental breakfast with bread and homemade jam and real, freshly brewed coffee. Good tourist information is available too. It's worth being further from the center to be here.

Hotel los Balcones HOTEL $
(☎064-21-1041; www.losbalconeshuancayo.com.pe; Puno 282; s/d/tr S/50/60/75; @) Sporting plenty of namesake hard-to-miss balconies, this is an attractive, modern, airy and spacious hotel. Tastefully furnished rooms come with cable TV, phone, alarm clock and reading lights: there's complimentary internet access and a busy in-house restaurant too. Look no further for reasonably priced city-center comfort.

Hotel Confort HOTEL $
(☎064-23-3601; Ancash 237; s/d S30/40) We're going to put our neck on the line here: this is among the best deals in Huancayo city center. As for the *confort* (comfort), S30 won't get you much more anywhere in Peru. Cleaned conscientiously, this is a real survivor: around for decades. In a little-anticipated move, a branch of the city's smartest cafe, Coqui, has opened underneath.

Hostal Las Lomas HOSTEL $
(☎064-23-7587; laslomashyo@yahoo.es; Giráldez 327; s/d S50/60) Spotless hot-water bathrooms and excellent mattresses make this backpacker-accustomed place a fine, central choice. Rooms vary in size; many are quite large, some get lots of street noise. In-house laundry service.

Blub Hotel Spa HOTEL $$
(☎064-22-1692; www.blubhotelspa.com; Psje Verand 187; s/d incl breakfast S160/210;) Overlooking the river (or its bone-dry bed), the tucked-away Blub has well-appointed, inviting rooms with big flat-screen cable TVs, telephones, minibars, '70s-style bathrooms and, as the name implies, a sauna. Why 'Blub'? It's a crying shame, but the staff we asked didn't have the foggiest either.

Hotel Turismo HOTEL $$
(☎064-23-1072; www.hoteles-del-centro.com; Ancash 729; s/d S195/215;) This pleasant-looking old building has wooden balconies, public areas with a certain faded grandeur and good views of the shoe-shines at work outside the Centro Civico. Rooms vary in size and quality but all have bathrooms.

Hostal El Marquez HOTEL $$
(☎064-21-9026; www.elmarquezhuancayo.com; Puno 294; s/d/ste incl breakfast S150/190/220; @) The El Marquez is an anomaly. It's comfortable, and better than most, yet is inexplicably lacking in character and in service, and, price-wise, has a delusional idea of its own worth. Recently done-up, carpeted rooms get all the expected trappings, while three suites feature Jacuzzis, king-sized bed and minibar. A small cafe offers room service.

Isha Hotel BUSINESS HOTEL $$
(☎064-23-1389; Av Giraldez 246; s/d incl breakfast S150/170; @) Av Giraldez is desperately ugly at this point, but Isha Hotel attempts to brighten it. It's the best newcomer among Huancayo's central hotels, approached, in somewhat unorthodox fashion, through a Chinese restaurant (reception is on the 2nd floor). Rooms are very smart, although a fair few don't have windows. There's a business center (computers, good wi-fi) and conference room.

Susan's Hotel HOTEL $$
(☎064-20-2251; www.susanshotel.com; Real 851; s S70, d S70-110;) A clean and cheerful-enough midrange option that hasn't quite shaken off the snarly service from its more budget-focused days, Susan's has a warren of rooms with good-sized bathrooms, cable TV, writing desks and firm mattresses. Rooms are dark; get one at the rear for peace and quiet, and head to the nice 5th-floor restaurant for light and views.

Hotel Olímpico HOTEL $$
(☎064-21-4555; Ancash 408; s/d S80/120;) If you insist on *actual* plaza views, this is the best of the somewhat ailing hotel trio on the south side of Plaza de la Constitución. Guests report service as decent overall, and it's not much of a hike to the restaurant of the same name underneath. There is cable TV in all the ample, but often gloomy, rooms.

Hotel Presidente HOTEL $$$
(☎064-23-1275; http://huancayoes.hotelpresidente.com.pe; Real 1138; s/d/ste incl breakfast S240/285/360; P@) Good modern hotel; sports large, nicely carpeted rooms and spacious bathrooms.

Eating

Good news for snack lovers: the blocks of Real south of the Plaza abound with cake shops and stalls selling strips of grilled *pollo* (chicken) and *lomo* (beef), often in kebab format.

Huancayo has some fabulous restaurants: regional specialties include *papas a la huancaína* (boiled potatoes in a creamy sauce of cheese, oil, hot pepper, lemon and egg yolk, served with boiled egg and olives). The city is also known for its trout, reared in nearby lakes.

The cool new going-out/eating-out area is Parque Túpac Amaru. The best supermarket is downstairs in the **Real Plaza Mall** (cnr Giraldez & Ferrocarril; ⏲9am-10pm).

★Leopardo PERUVIAN **$**
(cnr Libertad & Huánuco; mains S19-34; ⏲6:30am-7:30pm) This joint is *so* Huancayo, right down to the model train in the central dining area, effortlessly combining common people's cafeteria with upscale restaurant. Go for Andean with *mondongo* (broth made with maize, tripe, minced pork hoof and vegetables), or go coastal with *tacu tacu* (a concoction of beans, rice and chili fried golden-brown and served with steak).

It's so popular it opened an identical restaurant (right across the street) and won the undying affection of at least one hungry travel writer.

Sofa Café Paris CAFE **$**
(Puno 252; snacks from S3; ⏲4-11pm; 📶) With the chilled vibe you'd hope from the name, this is a lively venue with a wrap-around mezzanine level to oversee the action below. It favors Nirvana over Andean music and is frequented by trendy young *huancaínos* (Huancayo residents). It does elaborate coffees (it has what must be Huancayo's second coffee machine) and cakes, alongside other more substantial Peruvian fare.

We've spotted the retro pics of London on the walls too, though – did they run out of moody Paris images, one wonders?

Café Coqui BAKERY **$**
(Puno 298; snacks from S3; ⏲7am-10:30pm) This modern bakery/coffee shop is a contender for the best breakfast stop in the Central Andes, serving tasty sandwiches, pastries, empanadas, real espresso and other coffees. It's lively from morning until evening and now even does a line in pizzas and other more substantial fare. It's resting on its laurels just a tad, however.

La Cabaña INTERNATIONAL **$**
(Giráldez 675; mains around S20; ⏲5-11pm; 📶) This haunt is popular with locals and travelers alike for its relaxed ambience, hearty food and tasty pisco (grape brandy) sours. When you're suitably mellow, order a scrumptious pizza or graze on trout, juicy grills and al dente pastas. It's worth a visit for its wacky decor alone. The soundtrack? Rock-and-roll classics!

Detrás de la Catedral PERUVIAN **$**
(Ancash 335; mains S14-24; ⏲11am-11pm) This well-run, attractive place exudes a woody, warm feeling and has garnered plenty of regular patrons with its broad menu, which is a few steps up from the usual chicken-and-rice choices. Enjoy filling burgers (veggie or carnie), specials such as *asado catedral* (barbecued meats done in house style) and tasty desserts such as chocolate-drenched *pionono helado* (pastry with caramel filling). Surrealist paintings grace the walls.

Zalema Social Coffee CAFE **$**
(www.facebook.com/zalemacoffee; Amazonas 461; snacks from S3, lunches S10; ⏲12:30-11pm Mon-Sat) Watch this neat little Bohemian space: if it keeps on like this it's going places. Understated decoration themed around the other passion of the owners (mountain climbing), a laid-back feel, decent coffee, an open fire come evenings and humble but tasty local food, much of it tapas-style, are just some of the reasons why.

Chicharronería Cuzco LATIN AMERICAN **$**
(Cuzco 173; mains S5-10) Traditional plates of *chicharrón* (deep-fried pork) at this carnivore-centric hole-in-the-wall are about S7.

La Italia ITALIAN **$**
(Torres 441; small pizza/pasta dishes S18-24; ⏲6-11pm Mon-Sat) One of a growing group of quality eateries around Parque Túpac Amaru, this has the best Italian food for many, many miles around. It's owned by an Italian; let no more be said.

Chifa Centro CHINESE **$**
(www.chifacentro.com.pe; Giráldez 245; meals S10-20) Serves up Huancayo's tastiest Chinese food in huge portions.

Huancahuasi PERUVIAN **$$**
(☎064-24-4826; www.huancahuasi.com; Mariscal Castilla 2222; mains S16.50-36; ⏲9am-6pm) Northwest of town, Real becomes Mariscal Castilla in El Tambo district. The local eatery of choice is this classy establishment. A flower-filled courtyard and walls decorated with San Pedro de Cajas tapestries and poems set the ambience for tucking into regional goodies such as *pachamanca* (meat cooked in an earthen 'oven' of hot rocks).

Other delights include *papas a la huancaína* (potatoes with a creamy cheese sauce) and *ceviche de trucha* (river-trout ceviche). It's all well presented and the service comes with a smile. Lunchtime is best for a visit. A taxi ride from the center is S3.

Ancla CEVICHE $$
(Los Manzanos 830; ceviche plates S25-35) Do not dismiss the Andes for ceviche until you feast on the exquisite offerings here.

Drinking & Nightlife

There are no standout nightclubs – many are out of center and can be dangerous late at night. Try the more central new-kid-on-the-block **Insomnico** (cnr Cajamarca & Moquegua; ⊙8pm-4am Fri & Sat).

★**La Cabaña** TRADITIONAL MUSIC
(Giráldez 675; ⊙5-11pm) Contemplate this. A man collects wondrous and miraculous things from old fruit machines to antiquated aguardiente-making equipment throughout his life and then arranges them around a lively, cozy bar that makes delicious pisco sours (if you're feeling hot) or *calientitos* (if you're feeling cold). Heart- and belly-warming.

Peña Restaurant Turistico Wanka Wanka TRADITIONAL MUSIC
(Jirón Parra del Riego 820; ⊙from 8pm Fri & Sat) In El Tambo, this *peña* (bar or club featuring live folkloric music) attracts local bands such as Kjantu and has good *cumbia* and folk music. Take a taxi here (S3).

Antojitos LIVE MUSIC
(Puno 599; ⊙5pm-late Mon-Sat) Local bands perform at this bar-restaurant most nights from 9pm. Lennon posters, Pink Floyd on the stereo, and burgers and pizzas to chow down on.

Shopping

Huancayo is the central altiplano's best shopping destination by a distance, whether you desire traditional markets (there are two main markets here), souvenirs or American-brand jeans. If you have really come to Huancayo for designer clothes, visit **Real Plaza Mall** (cnr Giraldez & Ferrocarril; ⊙9am-11pm).

Mercado Mayorista MARKET
(⊙daily) The colorful produce market spills out from the covered Mercado Mayorista, east along the railway tracks. In the meat section you can buy Andean delicacies such as frogs, guinea pigs and chickens, while an incredible variety of unpronounceable fruits and vegetables also beckon. Don't miss trying the *tokuc* (rotten potato drink). Many stalls open by 4am and stay open until midnight.

Stallholders are friendly and let you try before you buy. Wandering through the different sections, the smells of different products rise up to hit you: it's like a sensory crash course in the ingredients of classic Peruvian dishes. It's one of Peru's most interesting city markets, without doubt. The most important day is Sunday, coinciding with Huancayo's weekly craft market.

Feria Dominical HANDICRAFTS
(Huancavelica; ⊙Sun) This craft market occupies numerous blocks along Huancavelica to the northwest of Piura, offering weavings, textiles, embroidered items, ceramics and wood carvings. *Mates burilados* (carved gourds) and many other items from various villages in the Río Mantaro valley are sold here – handy if you don't have time to trek out to the villages yourself. Keep an eye on your valuables.

Casa del Artesano SOUVENIRS
(Plaza de la Constitución; ⊙9am-6pm) Handy Casa del Artesano on the south corner of the plaza, is an indoor crafts market with a wide range of art souvenirs for sale in a secure environment.

Information

BCP, Interbank, Banco Continental and other banks and *casas de cambio* (foreign-exchange bureaus) are on Real. Most banks open on Saturday morning and have ATMs. You'll need to walk under a block along Real to find some of the city center's abundant internet cafes: S1.50 seems to be the going hourly rate and most do international phone calls.

Clínica Ortega (☎064-23-2921; Carrión 1124; ⊙24hr) English is spoken. Southwest of the center.

Incas del Perú (☎064-22-3303; www.incasdelperu.org; Giráldez 675; ⊙10am-midnight) A recommended source for information on just about anything in the area.

Lavandería Cisne (Breña 154; per kilo S5; ⊙8am-10pm) Laundry that offers both self-service and drop-off.

Main Post Office (Centro Cívico)

Policía de Turismo (☎064-21-9851; Ferrocarril 580) Can help with tourist information, as well as with emergencies.

Tourist Office (Casa del Artesano, Real 481; ⊙8am-noon & 5-9pm Mon-Sat) Located upstairs in the indoor crafts market with limited information.

Getting There & Away

BUS

Huancayo is slowly organizing its bus terminals, with **Terminal Los Andes** (cnr Av Ferrocarril & Los Andes) at the northern end of Av Ferrocarril handling most bus departures north to Tarma and the central jungle.

From Terminal Los Andes, an S4 taxi ride from central Huancayo, there are departures at least hourly for Satipo (S20 to S25, six to seven hours) via Tarma (S10, two hours), San Ramón (S15 to S17, 4¼ hours) and La Merced (S15 to S17, 4½ hours). Many services continue as far as Mazamari (S25 to S27, 7½ hours).

For Lima (west) and destinations in the southern valleys such as Huancavelica and Ayacucho, bus companies still have their own offices and departure points scattered around the city center.

As it is the most-trawled route, ticket prices to Lima vary wildly. One-way tickets range from S40 to S60. For S60 to S80 you get a bed seat on a *bus-cama;* for S40 you get an ordinary seat that usually reclines a little. Travel time is seven hours.

All companies below are worth noting for the routes they offer – due to the enormous amount of competition, it is worth taking your time deciding if you value either the money you shell out or the comfort you travel in.

Cruz del Sur (☎064-22-3367, 064-22-1767; Ayacucho 281) The most luxurious Lima-bound buses. Eight daily services – with night-time *bus-cama* services from S65 to S78. This is the booking office. Its bus station is located at Ferrocarril 151 (get a taxi there).

Expreso Molina (☎064-22-4501; Angaraes 334) The recommended service for Ayacucho (on the now fully paved road). Morning departure (S25) and night departures (S35) for the seven-hour journey. There's also a service via the longer but safer route via Rumichaca (S40, 10 hours).

Los Canarios (☎064-21-5149; Puno 739) Serves Tarma almost hourly (S10, three hours) and will stop at Jauja and Concepción.

Selva Tours (Terminal Los Andes) A surefire bet for services to Satipo and on to Mazamari in the central Amazon jungle.

Turismo Central (☎064-22-3128; Ayacucho 274) Buses north to Huánuco (S50, seven hours), Tingo María (S50, 10 hours) and Pucallpa (S70, 22 hours). It also has an office located in Terminal Los Andes.

Transportes Ticllas (☎954-175-420; Ferrocarril 1590) Frequently serves Huancavelica (S13, three to four hours).

TAXI

Colectivos for Huancavelica (S25, 2½ hours) leave when full (four-passenger minimum) from *cuadra* 16 of Av Ferrocarril near the Transportes Ticclas bus station. *Colectivos* for Andean destinations to the north including Tarma (S20) and La Oroya (S18) now leave from a convenient location outside Terminal Los Andes. *Colectivos* for Jauja (S7, 50 minutes) via San Jerónimo and Concepción (S3, 30 minutes) leave from here too.

TRAIN

Huancayo has two unconnected train stations in different parts of town.

A special tourist train, the Ferrocarril Central Andino (p102), runs fortnightly up from Lima's **Estación Desamparados** (☎01-263-1515; Ancash 203) between mid-April and October. In Huancayo, it arrives into (and departs from) the **central train station** (Av Ferrocarril, opposite Real Plaza Mall).

The 12-hour trip leaves Lima at 7am Friday and departs Huancayo for the return trip at the rather inconvenient time of 6pm Sunday. For this return night leg, bring along warm clothes and perhaps a blanket.

It's a fabulous run, reaching 4829m and passing La Galera, which clocks in as one of the world's highest passenger railway stations (the Tibetans are the record holders, followed by the Bolivians). It operates on a single-gauge track and is popular with train enthusiasts the world over. The best ways to book are either to visit the Incas del Perú website (www.incasdelperu.org), where there is an online booking form, or the train's official website. Train packages start at US$105 one-way through Incas del Peru.

The **Chilca train station** (☎064-21-6662; Prado cuadra 17 s/n) for Huancavelica is at the southern end of town. The train leaves Huancayo at 6.30am on Monday, Wednesday and Friday, returning at the same time from Huancavelica on Tuesday, Thursday and Saturday. Tickets are S9 for 1st class and S12 for buffet class. Buffet class is comfortable, with padded seats and guaranteed seating; 1st class has reserved seats with less padding. The real draw of this train is that it is one used by locals (as opposed to just tourists) and so has plenty of color: umpteen food vendors and even a blind violinist who plays for tips. Updates on the service can be obtained from Lucho Hurtado of Incas del Perú.

The ticket office is open from 6am until noon: the station is a fair hike from town so take a taxi.

Getting Around

Local buses to nearby villages leave from the central street intersections. Just show up and wait until a bus appears: most routes have buses every few minutes. Cochas buses (from Giráldez and Huancas) are cream-brown and come every 15 minutes; *combis* to Chupaca leave from the same intersection. Ask other passengers if you're unsure. The tourist office is a good source of local bus information. Taxis charge a standard S4 for rides around town.

THE SOUTHERN VALLEYS

The roads get rougher and are often blocked by impromptu fiestas, the valleys get sheerer and lonelier and, like strange treasures in a chest with the lid only just lifted, the colonial architecture gleams in the sharp mountain light. You have arrived in the most quintessentially Andean swathe of the central highlands. The two outstanding jewels are the cities of Huancavelica and Ayacucho, both developing in magnificent opulence on the back of silver mines discovered in the nearby hills in the 16th and 17th centuries. The region has a sadder chapter to its history, too, as the stronghold of the Sendero Luminoso (Shining Path) revolutionary group that terrorized Peru in the 1980s and made this entire area off-limits for travelers. Today these valleys are some of the poorest parts of Peru, but they know how to have a party like no one else: Ayacucho's Semana Santa is the country's best fiesta.

Huancavelica and Ayacucho, together with Andahuaylas further south, form part of an exciting alternative route down to Cuzco.

Huancavelica

☎067 / POP 40,000 / ELEV 3690M

It's a mystery why more travelers don't visit this pretty colonial city. It's bursting with beautiful churches, charming plazas and mineral springs and lies picturesquely nestled within craggy peaks. These days it's even easily accessible, with a good road connecting it to Huancayo 147km north. Still, few people make it here and therein lies another attraction: Huancavelica is a safe, serene spot to take a break from the Gringo Trail and soak up life as locals live it. This entails partying at one of the frequent fiestas, browsing the markets or, for the most part, just watching the colorful cross-section of society pass by.

Huancavelica was a strategic Inca center and shortly after the conquest, the Spanish discovered its mineral wealth. By 1564 the Spaniards were sending indigenous Peruvian slaves to Huancavelica to work in the mercury and silver mines. The present town was founded in 1571 under the name of Villa Rica de Oropesa (Rich Town of the Lord), somewhat ironic given that Huancavelica is today the poorest city in Peru. Bear in mind the city suffers from frequent bone-chilling winds and icy temperatures at night.

Sights

Instituto Nacional de Cultura MUSEUM

(INC; ☎067-45-3420; Raimondi 205; ⏲8:30am-1pm & 3:30-6:30pm Tue-Sun) FREE The INC, in a colonial building on Plaza San Juan de Dios, has information and displays about the area: plus a bundle of interesting information if you ask. There is a great bookshop here, while a small **museum** (closed at the time of research) features Inca artifacts, fossils, displays of local costumes and paintings by Peruvian impressionist artists.

Minas de Santa Barbara MINE, HIKE

FREE The ghostly mines of Santa Barbara, high in the hills above Huancavelica, and accessed by a tough but rewarding 1½ hour hike, are the city's most poignant site – and a warning to the mining companies now flocking to the central highlands. Closed since a collapse ended two centuries of mineral extraction in 1786, Santa Barbara was once one of the most profitable mines in the Americas. Buildings – including accommodations and a church – enjoy a lonely, lovely location well worth visiting.

The path is accessed from a long flight of steps, which heads straight up from above Hospedaje San José in Huancavelica. Above the treeline after the steps end, aim for some TV masts on a hill, just below which the path picks up a metaled track leading to the mine.

Laguna de Choclococha LAKE

One of many lakes adorning the Rumichaca road, this body of water 70km south of Huancavelica can be visited by taking the Rumichaca-bound bus at 4:30am. It's about two hours to Choclococha 'town' (then a 10-minute walk); the same bus can pick you up again on its return to Huancavelica at 2pm (check with the driver). This lake, at 4700m, is dazzling on a sunny day when the surrounding mountains are mirrored in its waters. Birdlife includes condors and there is good hiking, fishing and restaurants.

Churches

Huancavelica churches are noted for their silver-plated altars, unlike the altars in the rest of Peru's colonial churches, which are usually gold-plated. There are several churches of note here, although they are

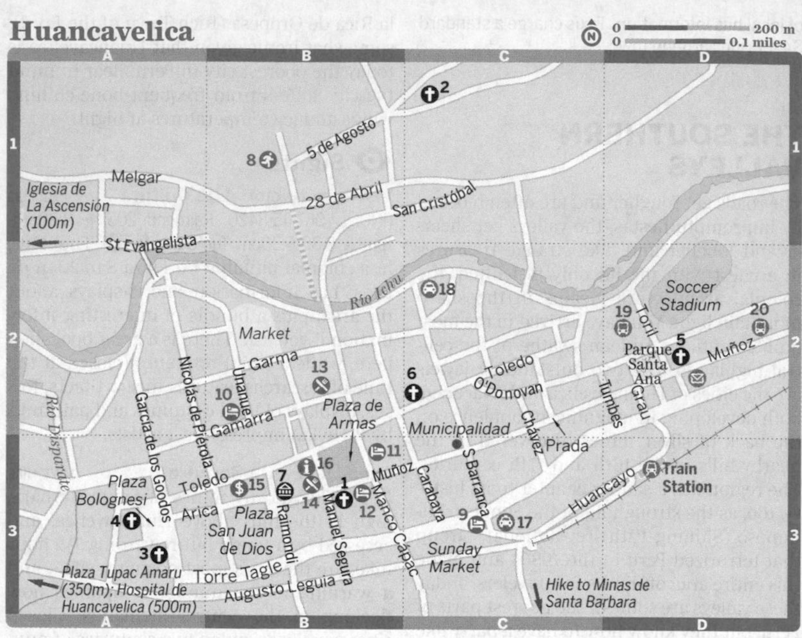

Huancavelica

Sights

1 Cathedral B3
2 Iglesia de San Cristóbal C1
3 Iglesia de San Francisco A3
4 Iglesia de San Sebastián A3
5 Iglesia de Santa Ana D2
6 Iglesia de Santo Domingo C2
7 Instituto Nacional de Cultura B3

Activities, Courses & Tours

8 San Cristóbal Mineral Springs B1

Sleeping

9 Hospedaje San José C3
10 Hostal Ccori B2
11 Hotel Ascensión B3
12 Hotel Presidente Huancavelica B3

Eating

13 Oregano Pastas y Pizzas B2
14 Pollos y Parrilladas El Centro B3

Information

15 BCP B3
16 Tourist Office B3

Transport

17 Colectivos to Lircay C3
18 Combi/Colectivo Terminal (Colectivos to Huancayo) C2
19 Expreso Lobato D2
20 Transportes Ticllas D2

generally closed to tourists. However, you can go as a member of the congregation when they are open for services, usually early in the morning on weekdays, with longer morning hours on Sunday.

The oldest church in Huancavelica is **Iglesia de Santa Ana** (Toril at Parque Santa Ana), founded in the 16th century. Dating from the 17th century are **Iglesia de San Francisco** (Garcia de las Goodos at Plaza Bolognesi), renowned for its 11 intricately worked altars; **Iglesia de Santo Domingo** (Toledo btwn Carabaya & S Barranca), with famous statues of Santo Domingo and La Virgen del Rosario, which were made in Italy; **Iglesia de San Sebastián** (Plaza Bolognesi), which has been well restored; **Iglesia de San Cristóbal** (cnr Calle 5 de Agosto & Pablo Solis); and **Iglesia de La Ascensión** (Plaza Mariano Santos Mateo).

Cathedral CATHEDRAL
(Muñoz at Plaza de Armas) Built in 1673, Huancavelica's most spectacular religious building has been restored and contains what

some say is the best colonial altar in Peru, with ornate cedar woodwork, as well as *escuela cuzqueña* (Cuzco school) paintings.

Activities

San Cristóbal Mineral Springs BATHHOUSE
(pool/private shower S1.50/3; 8am-5pm) These mineral springs are fed into two large, slightly murky swimming pools. The lukewarm water supposedly has curative properties. You can rent a towel, soap and a bathing suit if you've forgotten yours (though the selection is limited and unlovely). You can reach the springs via a steep flight of stairs – enjoy the view of the city as you climb. Baths are often closed on Thursdays for cleaning.

Saccsachaca SPRINGS
(admission S1; 8am-5pm) Some 2km east of the center are these scenic springs, accessed via the bridge at the end of Javier Heraud off Donovan. On the other side, follow the rough road that climbs above the river via the first of the two pools (Los Incas) and continue to the best, Tres Boas. Here a spread of natural pools and waterfalls tumble invitingly down the valley side above the river. Water is not hot, however, and you should bring your own swimming things.

Festivals & Events

Huancavelica's vibrant fiestas are renowned and, due to the mostly indigenous population, feel particularly authentic. Colorful traditional festivities occur on major Peruvian holidays, such as Carnaval, Semana Santa, Todos Santos and Christmas. Huancavelica's Semana Turística (Tourism Week) is held in late September and early October. Check with the INC (p295) for upcoming festivals.

Fiesta de las Cruces RELIGIOUS
(May) The festival of the crosses is held for six days in May. Revelers bear crosses, local bands play music in the plazas and proceedings culminate in bull fights.

Sleeping

Huancavelica does, in fact, boast more than a dozen places to stay, though most of them are budget options that don't offer hot water. There's always the town's natural mineral baths to soak away the aches and pains.

Hospedaje San José GUESTHOUSE $
(067-45-1014; Huancayo s/n; s with/without bathroom S35/15, d with/without bathroom S45/30) At the southern end of Baranca by the market, a cluttered entrance leads up to surprisingly large rooms with comfortable beds and hot water. Many rooms get good views over town.

Hotel Ascensión HOTEL $
(067-45-3103; Manco Cápac 481; r with/without bathroom S60/50;) Facing the more expensive Hotel Presidente across Huancavelica's delightful Plaza de Armas, this hotel is a great deal, with decent, clean rooms and hot-water showers.

Hostal Ccori GUESTHOUSE $
(067-45-1125; cnr Gamarra & Unanue; s/d S35/70) Nice rooms face into a pleasant green courtyard garden; all are generously proportioned but only the doubles have private bathrooms.

Hotel Presidente Huancavelica HISTORIC HOTEL $$
(067-45-2760; http://huancavelicaes.hotel-presidente.com.pe; Plaza de Armas; s/d/ste incl breakfast S240/285/360;) Presentable old Hotel Presidente Huancavelica is, truth be told, very pricey for what you actually get: but the location couldn't be better. Rooms are much plainer than the gorgeous facade, but do benefit from guaranteed hot showers, telephone, cable TV and a laundry service – not to forget a handy restaurant.

Eating

There are few standout restaurants, but plenty of chicken places and *chifas* (Chinese restaurants).

★ **Pollos y Parrilladas El Centro** PARRILLA $
(cnr Manuel Segura & Muñoz; mains about S15; 11am-11pm) There are two large parts to this plaza-facing restaurant – separated by the kitchen – and at lunchtime they need every inch of space, as seemingly all of Huancavelica's residents descend to eat. A good grilled steak is what to go for here – it comes served on its own cooker and it's *muy sabroso* (very tasty).

Oregano Pastas y Pizzas PIZZA $
(Gamarra, btwn Manuel Segura & Manco Capac; pizzas S20-30; 6pm-late) Cozy, sophisticated venue with Huancavelica's best Italian food.

Shopping

There are small daily markets, but Sunday is market day, and the best day to see locals in traditional dress. The main market snakes

AYACUCHO – THE TOUGH WAY!

Sometimes life is too easy, right? Well if you are moving on from Huancavelica in the direction of Ayacucho, opportunities abound to make proceedings a little more of a challenge (besides, the main buses are at night, and who wants to travel in the dark and miss all that cracking scenery?)

The 'easiest' daytime option to Ayacucho is to take a 4:30am (!) minibus to Rumichaca. In the west of Huancavelica from Plaza Tupac Amaru, **San Juan Bautista** minibuses depart daily (S10, six hours). Then wait for an Ayacucho-bound bus coming from the coast. Most days buses from Lima don't get to Rumichaca until about 2pm.

Another possibility, involving still more stunning scenery and more amounts of time on still more bone-jarring transport, is to take a *colectivo* from outside Hospedaje San José in Huancavelica to Lircay (S25, three hours). From the market In Lircay, pick up another *colectivo* bound to Julcamarca and then to Ayacucho (S30, four hours). The caveat with Ayacucho-bound *colectivos* in Lircay is that few people want to take them (it's too far!) so you might wind up having to pay for the whole car (S120). Ensure you get to Lircay early to maximize your chances of onward transportation to either Julcamarca or Ayacucho.

up Barranca then continues along Torre Tagle behind the cathedral. Handicrafts are sold almost every day on the north side of the Plaza de Armas and also by the Municipalidad. Colorful wool leggings are especially popular.

Information

More than a dozen central places provide internet access.

BCP (Toledo s/n) Has a Visa ATM and changes money.

Hospital de Huancavelica (☎067-45-3369; Av Andrés Céceres)

Main Post Office (Pasaje Ferrua 105) Near Iglesia de Santa Ana.

Tourist Office (Manuel Segura 140; ⏰9am-1:30pm & 3:30-6:30pm Mon-Fri, 9am-1:30pm Sat) Provides good directions (in Spanish) for local hikes, such as the 6km tramp to Santa Barbara mines, as well as transport information. Can arrange tours on request for groups.

Getting There & Away

Huancavelica now sports a paved road connecting it to Huancayo (the easiest means of approach). This is a beautiful route that ascends on mountain contours then loops down to a narrow river valley and Izcuchaca before opening out again into lush alpine meadowland with thatched-roof settlements (some prettily painted) and strolling herds of llamas. You can also reach Huancavelica directly from Pisco via a 4850m pass, and from Ayacucho via Rumichaca or Lircay. Buses ply all these routes but are of the ponderous local variety – filled with locals and their goods.

The most interesting way to Huancavelica, however, is by train from Huancayo (albeit slightly slower than the buses and taking a route along the valley bottom).

If you are in a hurry, from Huancayo it's a good idea to take a *colectivo*.

BUS

Major buses usually depart from the Terminal Terrestre, inconveniently located about 2km to the west of the town center. A taxi here costs S3. Buy your bus tickets in the downtown offices, and be sure to ask about where the buses depart from – which seems to change on whim. From the Terminal Terrestre, several companies offer nightly departures to Ayacucho via Rumiachaca (S30 to S40, seven to eight hours)

Companies serving Huancayo (S13, three hours) include **Transportes Ticllas** (Muñoz 154) with almost hourly daily departures. Other companies go less often or at night, or may go via Huancayo en route to Lima.

For Lima (S30 to S60, 10 to 13 hours) companies go via Huancayo or via Pisco. The higher price tag is for more luxurious *bus-camas*. Via Huancayo is usually a little faster but it depends on road conditions. The Pisco route is freezing at night; bring warm clothes. Several companies with offices clustering around Parque Santa Ana offer Lima services including **Expreso Lobato** (☎067-36-8264; O'Donovan 519) which has comfortable overnight buses via Huancayo.

TAXI

Colectivos for Huancayo (S25, 2½ hours) leave when full (four-passenger minimum). They leave from the *combi/colectivo* terminal on Garma by the river – or hang around on Muñoz for more than a few minutes and the offers for Huancayo transport will begin.

TRAIN

Trains currently leave for Huancayo at 6:30am on Tuesday, Thursday and Saturday.

Ayacucho

066 / POP 181,000 / ELEV 2750M

The name of this mesmerizing colonial city, originating from the Quechua *aya* (death, or soul) and *cuchu* (outback), offers a telling insight into its past. Ayacucho's status as isolated capital of a traditionally poor department provided the perfect breeding ground for Professor Abimael Guzmán to nurture the Sendero Luminoso (Shining Path) Maoist revolutionary movement, bent on overthrowing the government and causing thousands of deaths in the region during the 1980s and 1990s. Yet the city's historically poor links with the outside world have also helped foster a fiercely proud, independent spirit evident in everything from the unique festivals to its booming cultural self-sufficiency.

The shadow of Ayacucho's dark past has long been lifted, but travelers are only just rediscovering its treasures. Richly decorated churches dominate the vivid cityscape alongside peach- and pastel-colored colonial buildings hung with wooden balconies. Among numerous city festivities, Ayacucho boasts Peru's premier Semana Santa celebrations, while in the surrounding mountains lie some of the country's most significant archaeological attractions.

Perhaps Ayacucho's greatest allure is the authenticity with which it pulls off its charms. Its development has been tasteful, its commercialization blissfully limited and, if you take to the pedestrianized, cobbled city central streets early enough, it is easy to imagine yourself transported back several centuries to its colonial heyday. That said, these days designer-clad students and businesspeople are increasingly in evidence and behind many colonial facades are plenty of sumptuous accommodations and suave restaurants. What is clear is that Peru's most enticing Andean city after Cuzco is experiencing a resurgence – one well worth witnessing.

History

Some of Peru's first signs of human habitation were allegedly discovered in the Pikimachay caves, near Ayacucho (today there is nothing of interest to be seen there).

Five hundred years before the rise of the Incas, the Wari dominated the Peruvian highlands and established their capital 22km northeast of Ayacucho. The city's original name was San Juan de la Frontera de Huamanga (locals still call it Huamanga) and it grew rapidly after its founding in 1540 as the Spanish sought to defend it against attack from Manco Inca. Ayacucho played a major part in the battles for Peruvian independence, commemorated by an impressive nearby monument.

Ayacucho's first paved road connection with the outside world (to Lima) came only in 1999, which conveys how isolated the city previously was. But it's turned to face the 21st century, doesn't discuss the dark days of the 1980s much, and welcomes travelers with good cheer.

AYACUCHO'S CHURCHES

Ayacucho, the 'Ciudad de las Iglesias' (City of Churches), boasts more than 30 churches and temples. Here is a crash course:

Templo de San Cristóbal (Jirón 28 de Julio, cuadra 6) This is the oldest city church, dating from 1540.

Iglesia de Santa Clara (Grau at Nazareno) Attracts thousands of pilgrims annually for the image of Jesus of Nazareth supposedly inside.

Iglesia de Santo Domingo (Jirón 9 de Diciembre at Bellido) One of the most photogenic churches, dating from 1548. Allegedly built with the stone of a former Inca fortress, it contains some superb examples of *churrigueresque*-style painting.

Iglesia de La Merced (Jirón 2 de Mayo at San Martín) Dating from 1550, full of colonial art and with one of Peru's oldest convents (1540) attached.

Iglesia de Santa Teresa (Jirón 28 de Julio) Gorgeous church-cum-monastery with an altar studded in seashells.

Iglesia de San Francisco de Asis (Jirón 28 de Julio) Visually striking stone church containing *retablos* (ornamental religious dioramas) and an attractive 17th-century adjoining convent. It's opposite the market.

Ayacucho

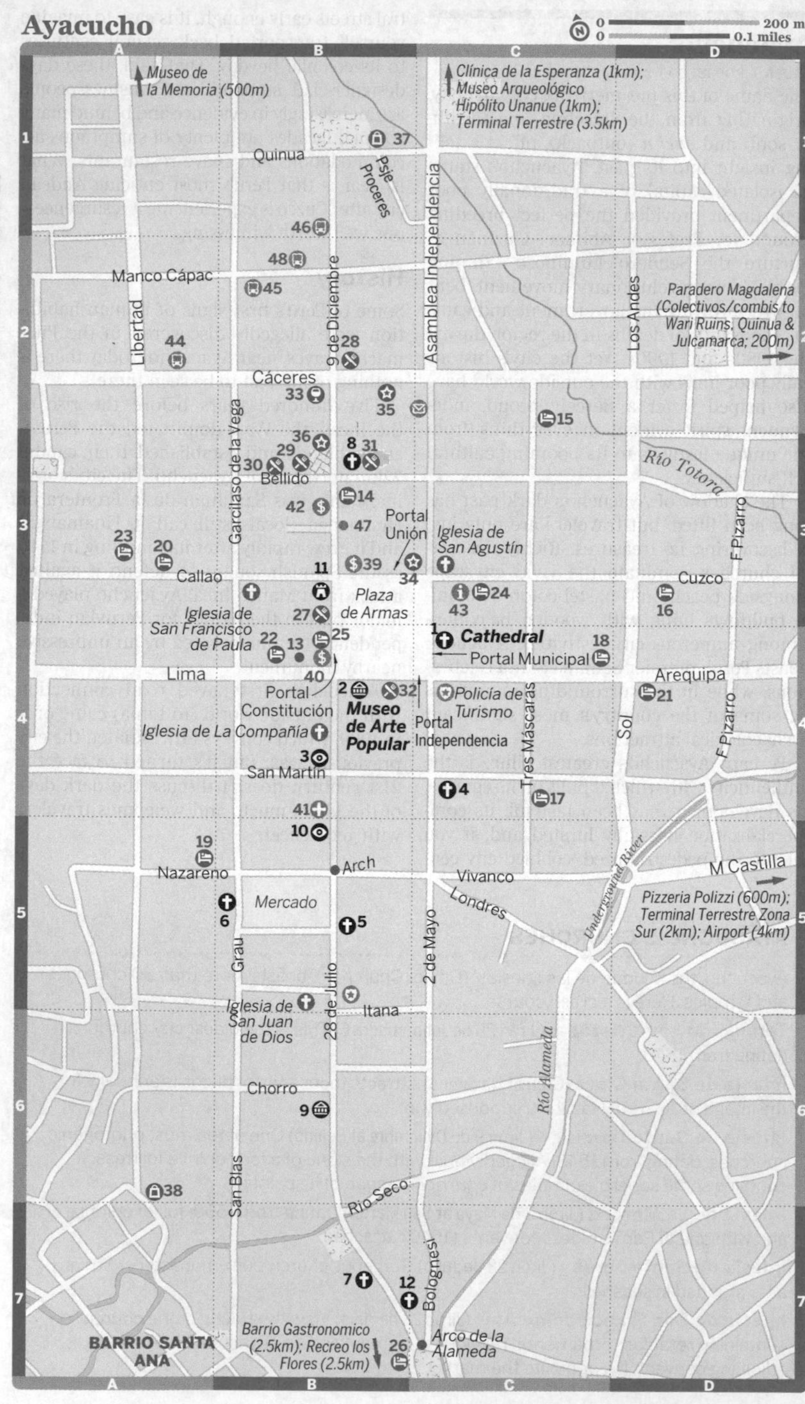

0 200 m
0 0.1 miles
Museo de la Memoria (500m)
Clínica de la Esperanza (1km); Museo Arqueológico Hipólito Unanue (1km); Terminal Terrestre (3.5km)
Quinua
Psje Proceres
Asamblea Independencia
Manco Cápac
Libertad
9 de Diciembre
Los Andes
Paradero Magdalena (Colectivos/combis to Wari Ruins, Quinua & Julcamarca; 200m)
Cáceres
Garcilaso de la Vega
Río Totora
Bellido
Portal Unión
Iglesia de San Agustín
F Pizarro
Callao
Cuzco
Plaza de Armas
Iglesia de San Francisco de Paula
Cathedral
Portal Municipal
Lima
Arequipa
Portal Constitución
Museo de Arte Popular
Portal Independencia
Policía de Turismo
Tres Máscaras
Sol
Iglesia de La Compañía
San Martín
Underground River
Nazareno
Arch
Vivanco
M Castilla
Londres
Mercado
Pizzeria Polizzi (600m); Terminal Terrestre Zona Sur (2km); Airport (4km)
Grau
2 de Mayo
28 de Julio
Iglesia de San Juan de Dios
Itana
Río Alameda
Chorro
San Blas
Rio Seco
Bolognesi
Barrio Gastronomico (2.5km); Recreo los Flores (2.5km)
BARRIO SANTA ANA
Arco de la Alameda

Ayacucho

Top Sights
1 Cathedral C4
2 Museo de Arte Popular B4

Sights
3 Centro Turístico Cultural San Cristóbal B4
4 Iglesia de La Merced C4
5 Iglesia de San Francisco de Asis B5
6 Iglesia de Santa Clara B5
7 Iglesia de Santa Teresa B7
8 Iglesia de Santo Domingo B3
9 Museo Andrés Avelino Cáceres B6
10 Plaza Moré B5
11 Prefectura B3
12 Templo de San Cristóbal B7

Activities, Courses & Tours
Via Via .... (see 25)
13 Wari Tours B4

Sleeping
14 Ayacucho Hotel Plaza B3
15 Hostal Ayacuchano C2
16 Hostal Florida D3
17 Hostal Tres Máscaras C4
18 Hotel El Mesón C4
19 Hotel La Crillonesa A5
20 Hotel San Francisco de Paula A3
21 Hotel Santa María D4
22 Hotel Santa Rosa B4
23 Hotel Sevilla A3
24 La Colmena Hotel C3
25 Via Via B4
26 Via Via B7

Eating
27 Café Miel B3
28 Creamz B2
29 El Niño B3
30 Guilles B3
31 La Casona B3
32 Las Tinajas B4
Mamma Mia .... (see 10)
Via Via .... (see 25)

Drinking & Nightlife
33 Taberna Magía Negra B2

Entertainment
34 Centro Cultural B3
35 Rock B2
36 Tupana Wasi B3

Shopping
37 Craft Market B1
38 Edwin Pizarro A6

Information
39 BBVA Banco Continental B3
40 Casa de Cambio B4
41 Inka Farma B4
42 Interbank B3
43 iPerú C3

Transport
44 Cruz del Sur A2
45 Expreso Internacional Palomino B2
46 Expreso Molina B1
47 LC Peru B3
48 Turismo Libertadores B2

Sights

Sights in Ayacucho consist primarily of churches and museums. While the listed museums have posted (yet nevertheless frequently altering) opening times, churches are a law unto themselves. Some list their visiting times on the doors; with others you will have to take potluck. During Semana Santa churches are open for most of the day; at other times ask at the tourist office, which publishes the guide *Circuito religioso* with information on opening hours. Joining the congregation for Mass (usually 6am to 8am Monday to Saturday) is an interesting way of seeing inside the churches. Entrance to the churches is free but donations are appreciated.

The **Plaza de Armas** (also known as Plaza Mayor de Huamanga) is one of Peru's most beautiful plazas and should be a starting point for city explorations. The four sides of the plaza, clockwise from the east, are Portal Municipal, Portal Independencia, Portal Constitución and Portal Unión. Around here are many gorgeous colonial mansions, including the offices of the department of Ayacucho, the **Prefectura** (Jirón 28 de Julio). Ask at the tourist office for details on how to visit these buildings, which are often open during office hours.

★Cathedral — CHURCH

(Portal Municipal) This spectacular 17th-century cathedral on the Plaza de Armas has a religious-art museum. The moody facade doesn't quite prepare you for the intricacy of the interior, with its elaborate gold-leaf altar being one of the best examples of the *churrigueresque* style (in which cornices and other intricate, Spanish-influenced workmanship is mingled with Andean influences, often evinced by the wildlife depicted).

★Museo de la Memoria — MUSEUM

(Prolongación Libertad 1229; admission S2; 9am-1pm & 3-5pm) In an unlikely location 1.5km northwest of the center is Ayacucho's most haunting museum, remembering the impact the Sendero Luminoso (Shining Path) had on Peru in the city that was most deeply affected by the conflict. Its simple displays (in Spanish) are nonetheless moving: there are eyewitness accounts of the horrors that went on and a particularly poignant montage of photos of mothers who had children killed in the fighting.

★Museo de Arte Popular MUSEUM
(Portal Independencia 72; ⏲8am-1pm & 2-4:30pm Mon-Fri) FREE The popular art here covers the *ayacucheño* (natives of Ayacucho) spectrum – silverwork, rug- and tapestry-weaving, stone and woodcarvings, ceramics (model churches are especially popular) and the famous *retablos* (ornamental religious dioramas). These are colorful wooden boxes varying in size and containing intricate papier-mâché models: Peruvian rural scenes or the nativity are favourites, but interesting ones with political or social commentary can be seen here. Photographs show how Ayacucho changed during the 20th century. Opening hours here change frequently.

Museo Andrés Avelino Cáceres MUSEUM
(Jirón 28 de Julio 508-512; admission S2; ⏲9:30am-1pm & 3-6pm Mon-Fri, 9:30am-1pm Sat) Housed in the Casona Vivanco, a gorgeous 16th-century mansion. Cáceres was a local man who commanded Peruvian troops during the War of the Pacific (1879–83) against Chile. Accordingly, the museum houses maps and military paraphernalia from that period, as well as intriguing *retablos* and colonial art: check the painting of the Last Supper – with *cuy* (guinea pig)!

Museo Arqueológico Hipólito Unanue MUSEUM
(Av Independencia s/n; admission S4; ⏲9am-1pm & 3-5pm Tue-Sun) In the Centro Cultural Simón Bolívar at the university, located more than 1km north from the city center along Independencia – you can't miss it. Wari ceramics make up most of the small exhibition, along with relics from the region's other various civilizations. While there, visit the university library for a free exhibition of mummies, skulls and other niceties. The buildings are set in a botanical garden. The best time to visit the museum is in the morning: afternoon hours sometimes aren't adhered to.

Mirador de Carmen Alto VIEWPOINT
This *mirador* (lookout) offers fabulous views of Ayacucho, as well as decent restaurants. Taxis here charge S5, otherwise catch a bus from the Mercado Central or walk (one hour).

Centro Turístico Cultural San Cristóbal SQUARE
(Jirón 28 de Julio 178) This is a remodeled colonial building with the courtyard transformed into a hip little mall. Here you'll find bars, restaurants and coffee shops, along with art galleries, craft stores and flower stands. A nice place to hang during the day.

Plaza Moré SQUARE
(Jirón 28 de Julio 262) Similar to Centro Turístico Cultural San Cristóbal, only better in quality and quantity for restaurants and shops.

Courses

Via Via COOKING COURSE
(☎066-31-2834; www.viaviacafe.com/en/ayacucho; Portal Constitución 4) Runs a cooking course where you can make a *lomo saltado* (strips of beef stir-fried with onions, tomatoes, potatoes and chili) and a pisco sour (and then consume them): S50 per person for 1½ hours.

Tours

Several agencies arrange tours; most cater to Peruvian tourists and guides mainly speak Spanish. Ask about tours in other languages.

Wari Tours ADVENTURE TOUR
(☎066-31-1415; Lima 138) Experience-rich multilingual tours to regional destinations. Half-day tours cost around S50.

Festivals & Events

The tourist office here is a good source of information about the many minor fiestas held throughout the department.

Semana Santa RELIGION
(⏲Mar/Apr) Held the week before Easter, this is Peru's finest religious festival and attracts visitors from all over the country. Rooms in most hotels fill well in advance so book well ahead. The tourist office has lists of local families who provide accommodations for the overflow.

Each year, iPerú (p306) prints a free brochure of events with street maps of the main processions. Celebrations begin on the Friday before Palm Sunday and continue for 10 days until Easter Sunday. The first day is marked by a procession in honor of La Virgen de los Dolores (Our Lady of Sorrows), during which it is customary to inflict 'sorrows' on bystanders by firing pebbles out of slingshots. Gringos have been targets, so be warned.

Each succeeding day sees solemn yet colorful processions and religious rites, which reach a fever pitch of Catholic tradition. They culminate on the Saturday before Easter Sunday with a huge all-night party including dawn fireworks to celebrate the resurrection of Christ. If you want to party too, stay on your guard, as proceedings are notoriously wild. Crime in the city escalates dramatically during festivities: robbery and rape are not unheard of.

In addition to the religious services, Ayacucho's Semana Santa celebrations include art shows, folk-dancing competitions, local music concerts, street events, sporting events (especially equestrian ones), agricultural fairs and the loving preparation of traditional meals.

Sleeping

Ayacucho isn't short on accommodations, but in addition to the myriad small hotels and *hospedajes* (small, family-owned inns) with generally limited facilities, there is an ever-growing number of plusher (yet still reasonably priced) options with creature comforts such as round-the-clock hot water. During Semana Santa prices rise markedly – by 25% to even 75%.

Hostal Tres Máscaras GUESTHOUSE $
(☎066-31-2921; hoteltresmascaras@yahoo.com; Tres Máscaras 194; s/d without bathroom S30/50, with bathroom S53/70) The pleasing walled garden and friendly staff make this an enjoyable place to stay, and garden-facing rooms are of a generous size. Hot water is on in the morning and later on request. A room with TV is S5 extra. Continental and American breakfast is available for S7 and S8 respectively.

Hotel La Crillonesa HOTEL $
(☎066-31-2350; www.hotelcrillonesa.com; Nazareno 165; s/d from S40/60) A popular and helpful hotel, it offers a rooftop terrace with photogenic views, a TV room, tour information and 24-hour hot water. Its rather small, clean rooms have comfy beds and generally functioning cable TV. The best rooms are right at the top.

Hostal Ayacuchano HOTEL $
(☎066-31-9891; Tres Máscaras 588; s/d S20/40) Amply sized, inoffensively decorated well-furnished, occasionally dim rooms get cable TV and, in some cases, even balconies. Not all singles have private bathrooms, but the bathrooms in some doubles are the sanitary surprises of Ayacucho: spacious, with actual baths and hot water to boot.

Hotel El Mesón HOTEL $
(☎066-31-2938; www.hotelelmesonayacucho.com; Arequipa 273; s/d S50/70) This is a great, central bargain, with voluminous rooms (each with a cable TV that isn't a lot smaller) set way back on the other side of a courtyard.

Hostal Florida GUESTHOUSE $
(☎066-31-2565; Cuzco 310; s/d S35/50) This traveler-friendly *hostal* has a relaxing courtyard garden and clean rooms (those on the upper level are better) with bathrooms and TV, hot water in the morning and later on request. There is a basic cafeteria too.

★**Via Via** HOTEL $$
(☎066-31-2834; www.viaviacafe.com/en/ayacucho; Portal Constitucion 4; s/d S115/150; wi-fi) One of the more imaginative sleeping options in central Ayacucho is Via Via, with an enviable plaza location and cool, vibrantly decorated rooms themed around different continents. Travelers will feel like they've landed in a veritable oasis, all centered on a plant-filled courtyard. English and Dutch are spoken, and their popular restaurant hangout is alongside.

They've now opened a second **Via Via** (☎066-31-7040; Bolognesi 720; s/d S95/125; P) hotel in the colonial property formerly known as Hotel El Marqués de Valdelirios.

Hotel Sevilla HOTEL $$
(☎066-31-4388; www.hotelsevillaperu.com; Libertad 635; s incl breakfast S75, d incl breakfast 100-120; wi-fi) The Sevilla is one of the nicest, brightest, best-value hotels in Ayacucho, and more backpacker-friendly than most. Ample, cozy rooms get desks, minibars and microwaves. Accommodations are set back across a courtyard from the street. There is a downstairs restaurant, and breakfast is enjoyed from the top-floor cafe commanding great views across the city.

Hotel Santa Rosa HOTEL $$
(☎066-31-4614; www.hotelsantarosa.com.pe; Lima 166; s/d incl breakfast S95/130; wi-fi) Less than a block from the Plaza de Armas, this capacious hotel with its twin courtyards has spacious, airy and cozily furnished rooms. Some come with a fridge (a luxury in the Central Andes) and all have TV, DVD player and phone. The bathrooms are large and the showers have oodles of hot water. There's also a decent and well-priced on-site restaurant.

Hotel Santa María HOTEL $$
(☎/fax 066-31-4988; Arequipa 320; s/d S95/125; 📶) Of the places opened during the hotel rush of the late '90s, this one seems to have got it right. It looks impressive from the outside and the rooms are very comfortable, quite spacious and tastefully decorated.

Hotel San Francisco de Paula HOTEL $$
(☎066-31-2353; www.hotelsanfranciscodepaula.com; Callao 290; s/d incl breakfast S80/130; 📶) This rather rambling, oldish hotel isn't flash, but it is presentable, with public areas decorated with bizarre indigenous art. It has a restaurant and bar and decent-sized, tiled rooms get the usual midrange facilities. Outside doubles are better as the inside singles can be very poky. Below par for the hotels of this price in the center.

La Colmena Hotel HOTEL $$
(☎066-31-1318; Cuzco 140; s S70, d S100-120) This popular hotel is often full by early afternoon, partly because it's one of the longest-standing places in town and partly because it's only steps from the plaza. It's a great building that has spruced itself up significantly of late. It also has a locally popular restaurant and an agreeable courtyard.

Ayacucho Hotel Plaza HOTEL $$$
(☎066-31-2202; fax 066-31-2314; Jirón 9 de Diciembre 184; d S283) Once considered the best in town, this is an impressive-looking colonial building and the interior does admittedly exude a certain kind of colonial charm. However, for what you pay, the rooms are oh-so-plain and in reality no more than adequate. The better rooms have balconies (request one) and some have plaza views. That said, no centrally located top-end hotels have yet given it a run for its money.

Eating

Regional specialties include *puca picante* (potato and beef stew in a spicy red peanut and pepper sauce, served over rice), *patachi* (wheat soup with various beans, dried potatoes and lamb or beef) and *mondongo* (corn soup cooked with pork or beef, red peppers and fresh mint). *Chicharrónes* (deep-fried pork scratchings) and *cuy* (guinea pig) are also popular. Vegetarians may accordingly be challenged to find meatless fare: *chifas* (Chinese restaurants) are the best bets.

Within the Centro Turístico San Cristóbal, some upbeat eats provide quality food and atmospheric, if touristy, dining, while Plaza Moré further down has gone one step further and offers eateries that are positively gourmet: an indication of the changing face of Ayacucho. After all, how many Andean towns can boast a Barrio Gastronómico (gastronomic neighborhood) – José Olaya?

Café Miel CAFE $
(Portal Constitución 4; snacks from S2; ⏲10am-10pm) Breakfast is the best time to visit this reader-recommended place with its chirpy atmosphere strangely reminiscent of an English tearoom – we're talking great fruit salads and some of Ayacucho's best (freshly brewed) coffee. It serves hearty lunches and phenomenal chocolate cake too.

Creamz ICE CREAM $
(cnr Cáceres & Jirón 9 de Diciembre; ice cream S8; ⏲10am-9pm) Flavors at this ice-cream parlor include Belgian chocolate, *chicha morada* (an iconically Peruvian, sweet, unfermented, purple corn drink) and Baileys: there's real machine-made coffee too.

Guilles SANDWICHES $
(Bellido, btwn Garcilaso de la Vega & Jirón 9 de Diciembre; sandwich & juice S10-15; ⏲8am-1pm & 4-9pm) Show up here for the best sandwiches and smoothies in Ayacucho – if not in the entire central highlands.

El Niño PARRILLA $
(Jirón 9 de Diciembre 205; mains around S15; ⏲11am-2pm & 5-11pm) In a colonial mansion with a sheltered patio and tables overlooking a garden, El Niño specializes in grills and serves a variety of Peruvian food. The individual *parrillada* (grilled-meat platter) is good, although in practice it's sufficient for two modest eaters. This is one of the city's better restaurants.

Recreo Las Flores PERUVIAN $
(José Olaya 106; meals S12-21.50; ⏲8am-6pm) *Cuy, cuy* and more *cuy* (guinea pig): let's hope you like it if you're eating here. Inside it resembles a vast Communist-style cafeteria but over by the windows that feeling is less apparent. This and several other places nearby form 'Barrio Gastronómico' in the Conchapata district south of the center.

La Casona PERUVIAN $
(Bellido 463; mains S12-35; ⏲7am-10:30pm) This popular, ambient courtyard restaurant has been recommended by several travelers for its big portions. It focuses on Peruvian food such as the excellent *lomo saltado* (strips of beef stir-fried with onions, tomatoes, potatoes and chili) and often has regional specialties.

THE SHINING PATH: AN ONGOING CONFLICT

The Sendero Luminoso's (Shining Path's) activities in the 1980s focused on deadly political, economic and social upheaval. They caused violent disruption, particularly across the central highlands and Amazon jungle, which were almost completely off-limits to travelers. Things finally changed when the Sendero Luminoso's founder, Guzmán, a former Ayacucho university professor, was captured and imprisoned for life in 1992. Guzmán was followed quickly by his top lieutenants. This led to a lull in activities, but fragmented groups of Sendero Luminoso revolutionaries carried on in remote areas of Peru. These groups split from the Maoist philosophy of Guzmán, and in recent years their most notable activity has been drug trafficking (the US State Department confirms the link).

The last major clash in this region was in April 2009, when Shining Path rebels killed 13 army officers. A high-profile incident in August 2011 saw tourists on a high-end tour to Choquequirao, a major Inca site in the Cuzco region, politely asked to hand over valuables to help the cause of the revolution. This sparked media reports of a Sendero Luminoso re-emergence, however, since then, no major incidents have been reported.

The number of remaining Sendero Luminoso members is, according to the *Wall Street Journal*, only around 500. Activity is mostly in remote Amazon valleys which, not by coincidence, contain significant cocaine production areas and are not safe for tourists to visit. Outside those areas, the threat to tourists remains minor, and most places can be visited as safely as anywhere else in Peru. The majority of Peruvians have no allegiance to any faction of the Sendero Luminoso, or to the military searching for their remainder.

★Pizzeria Polizzi PIZZA **$$**
(☎066-317255; Av del Ejercito s/n; medium pizza S21-28.) Not all the culinary stars that shine in Ayacucho shine in the center. This pizzeria twinkles in a galaxy all of its own out on Av del Ejercito (although it's planning a second central branch). The food is superb but even that pales into insignificance beside the gushing Italian-style service (although it should be emphasized this is an Italian-Peruvian enterprise). They do takeaway.

Get a taxi here, and tell the driver to aim for the gas station Grifo Santa Rosa.

★Via Via INTERNATIONAL **$$**
(☎066-31-2834; Portal Constitucion 4; mains S17-28; ⌚10am-10pm Mon-Thu, to midnight Fri & Sat;) With its upstairs plaza-facing balcony, Via Via has the best views with which to accompany your meal in Ayacucho. It's ethically sourced, organic food – but this is Peruvian-European fusion cuisine, so you'll find something to sate you – like *quinnoto* (a risotto with quinoa) or *salteado de alpaca* (strips of alpaca meat stir-fried with onions, tomatoes, potatoes and chili), and crisp South American wine to wash it down.

It's a traveler-friendly hangout, the like of which the city had never seen before, and does everything right.

Mamma Mia ITALIAN **$$**
(Jirón 28 de Julio 262; medium pizzas S25; ⌚4pm-midnight;) An exceptional pizza stop, manned by a Ukrainian. He has pooled his extensive catering experience and come up with a truly atmospheric place where you can laze away the late afternoon with real coffee and great cakes, or come later for delicious pizza and pasta. Round off your meal with a Mamma Mia cocktail: vodka, coconut rum, peach schnapps and melon. Find it in Plaza Moré.

Las Tinajas STEAK **$$**
(Portal Municipal; mains S15-31; ⌚noon-midnight) An elegant choice with plaza- or courtyard-facing dining, ultra-professional service and – well – damned good steak. Part of the mini-chain found in other Peruvian cities.

Drinking & Nightlife

This is an important university city, so you'll find a few bar-clubs to dance or hang out in, mostly favored by students.

Taberna Magía Negra BAR
(Jirón 9 de Diciembre 293; ⌚4pm-midnight Mon-Sat) It's been around longer than most and the youth of today prefer the newer venues, but this bar-gallery has local art, beer, pizza and great music.

Rock DISCO
(Cáceres 1035; ⌚10pm-2am Wed-Sat) The liveliest local disco, known locally as Maxxo, where gringos, as well as locals, go to strut their stuff. There is another disco on the same block playing mostly salsa.

RETABLOS

You will see *retablos* (vibrantly decorated boxed dioramas or 'scenes' from Peruvian life) in other parts of Peru, but Ayacucho is the proud capital of this particular handicraft. Typical *retablos* feature religious scenes, but there are also fascinating social, political and cultural ones produced, too. The common denominator is the intricacy of the figures, engaged in a variety of activities, which are protected inside a box with doors. They make for some unique souvenirs of the Peruvian highlands.

Tupana Wasi LIVE MUSIC
(Jirón 9 de Deciembre 206, 2nd fl; ⌚7pm-late Mon-Sat) Good live bands, from folkloric to rock, perform here, and there's live music nightly.

☆ Entertainment

Centro Cultural LIVE PERFORMANCE
(Portal Unión) The students and the hipsters flock here for regular open-air performances (music, comedy, the works) in the courtyard, while upstairs there is now a decent eatery, Mestizo. Events are posted on billboards at the entrance way.

Shopping

Ayacucho is a renowned handicraft center: a visit to the Museo de Arte Popular will give you an idea of local products. The tourist office can recommend local artisans who will welcome you to their workshops. The Santa Ana *barrio* (neighborhood) is well known for its crafts: there are various workshops around Plazuela Santa Ana. A **craft market** (Independencia & Quinua) is open during the day.

Edwin Pizarro HANDICRAFTS
(☎966-180-666) The *retablos* (ornamental religious dioramas) from Edwin Pizarro's workshop in Barrio Belén are highly recommended. He's renowned locally as one of the best artisans in the business, and will personalize his lovingly made creations by adding figures appropriate to the customer. The workshop is a tough 15-minute walk above central Ayacucho (opposite Templo de Belén) and can be hard to find: a taxi's not a bad idea.

ℹ Information

Internet cafes are on almost every block, particularly along the pedestrianized section of Jirón 9 de Deciembre. Almost every hotel now offers wi-fi.

BBVA Banco Continental (Portal Unión 28) Visa ATM.

Casa de Cambio (Portal Constitución) On the southwest corner of the Plaza de Armas.

Clínica de la Esperanza (☎066-31-2180; www.hospitalregionalayacucho.gob.pe; Independencia 355; ⌚8am-8pm) English is spoken.

Inka Farma (Jirón 28 de Julio 250; ⌚7am-10:30pm)

Interbank (Jirón 9 de Diciembre 183)

iPerú (☎066-31-8305; cnr Cusco & Asamblea; ⌚9am-6pm Mon-Sat, to 1pm Sun) One of Peru's best tourist offices. Helpful advice; English spoken.

Police (Jirón 28 de Julio 325; ⌚24hr)

Policía de Turismo (☎066-31-7846; Jirón 2 de Mayo 100) Handles emergencies.

Serpost (Asamblea 293) It's 150m from the Plaza de Armas.

ℹ Getting There & Around

AIR

The airport is 4km from the town center. Taxis charge about S10. Flight times and airlines can change without warning, so check airline websites for latest schedules. Daily flights to Lima are with **LC Peru** (☎066-31-2151; Jirón 9 de Diciembre 139) at 6:45am.

BUS

Most buses (to long-distance north- and south-bound destinations, including Lima) arrive and depart from the grandiosely named **Terrapuerto Libertadores de America** (Terminal Terrestre; end of Perez de Cuellar) bus terminal to the north of the city center, although you can still buy tickets at the downtown offices (it's best to ask when buying your ticket where your bus departs from). A taxi to the terminal costs S8.

Transport connections with Lima are via the relatively fast and spectacular Hwy 24 that traverses the Andes via Rumichaca to Pisco. Night departures outnumber day departures, but day trips are naturally more interesting for the wild scenery en route. Choose your bus and company carefully. Ticket prices to/from Lima are wide-ranging – from S40 for a regular seat to S90 for a reclining armchair that you can sleep in. The trip takes around nine hours. Take warm clothing if traveling by night.

Heading north to Huancayo (S30 to 40, seven hours), there is now a paved road, although there are still vertiginous drops with precious little protection. Change in Huancayo for onward services to Huánuco, Tingo María, Pucallpa and Satipo.

Heading southeast, the road to Andahuaylas (S30, six hours) and on to Cuzco (S50 to 60, 14 to 15 hours) is fully paved, but few companies thus far have the licenses to run the route, meaning limited choices. Both of these trips boast fantastic scenery, and are worth doing in daylight.

AROUND AYACUCHO

Ayacucho has several interesting excursions in the vicinity. You can reach them via day tours with agencies in Ayacucho for about S60 per person.

The extensive **Wari Ruins** (Huari; admission S3; 8am-5:30pm), 20km above Ayacucho on the road to Quinua, are some of the most significant surviving remains of the Wari culture, scattered among fields of bizarre opuntia cacti: a moody spot to contemplate this once powerful civilization. Information is in Spanish only. Don't leave the site too late to look for return transport – vehicles get hopelessly full in the afternoon.

A further 17km beyond the Wari ruins is the pretty village of **Quinua**, with a **museum** with erratic hours, besides which is the room where, after the War of Peruvian Independence, Spanish royalist troops signed their surrender, leading to the end of colonialism in Peru. The 40m-high white **obelisk** (admission S1), intermittently visible for several kilometers as you approach Quinua, lies 15 minutes' walk above town via Jirón Sucre and commemorates the Battle of Ayacucho, the decisive conflict in the war. From here, you can elect to go **horse-riding** on rather scrawny-looking steeds to waterfalls where swimming is possible. Quinua is 34km northeast of Ayacucho. The whole area is protected as the 300-hectare **Santuario Histórico Pampas de Ayacucho**.

The ruins of **Vilcashuamán** (admission S2), a former Inca stronghold (considered the geographical center of the Inca empire), lie some 115km south of Ayacucho near **Vischongo**. Little remains of the city's early magnificence, but an intact five-tier pyramid called an *usnu* survives, topped by a huge stone-carved double throne. From the Vilcashuamán turnoff it's only 2km to Vischongo, where you can base yourself overnight (basic accommodations). You can also take a 1½-hour hike to a **Puya raimondii forest**.

From **Terminal terrestre zona sur**, which handles southbound regional departures, the main destinations of note to travelers are Vischongo and the ruins of Vilcashuamán. All manner of vehicles here will offer the route, with Vilcashuamán tarriffs ranging from S20 in a *combi* to S30 in a *coletivo*. Departures are early in the morning: get here around 5am to stake your claim to a berth. A taxi to the terminal is S4.

Pickup trucks and buses go to many local villages, including Quinua (S3, one hour), and to the Wari ruins (also S3, 40 minutes), departing from the **Paradero Magdalena** at the traffic circle at the east end of Cáceres. Northwest-bound *colectivos* to Julcamarca (2½ hours) from where you can also travel via Lircay (a further two hours) to Huancavelica (another three to four hours) leave from Paradero Magdalena too (around 4:30am). With changeovers in Julcamarca and Lircay, likely travel time to Huancavelica is eight to nine hours and costs S120 in total.

Cruz del Sur (066-31-2813; www.cruzdelsur.com.pe; Cáceres, btwn Libertad & Garcilaso de la Vega) Top-notch, executive-style service, with comfortable seats, to Lima; meals thrown in. Departs from their own terminal, with a bakery across the way to stock up on snacks. Prices vary depending on when and how you purchase the ticket, but start around the S70 mark.

Expreso Internacional Palomino (066-32-7543; cnr Manco Cápac & Libertad) Near the top end of the market for Lima departures. Offers three evening *cama* services with varying levels of quality. Prices start at S80 one-way.

Expreso Molina (066-31-9989; Jirón 9 de Diciembre 473) A good company to know about, with departures from their own terminal in the center. They're not top for comfort, but they serve Lima (two daily departures and no less than seven night departures), Huancayo (one daily, five night departures) and Huancavelica (nightly departures).

Expreso Turismo Los Chankas (066-31-2391; Terrapuerto Libertadores de America) Currently the only through service to Cuzco (otherwise, you need to change in Andahuaylas) – departures are 7:30am (Monday to Saturday) and 8:30pm (daily). True, the road is now paved, but breaking this long journey in Andahuaylas is a good idea.

Transportes Sarmiento (Terrapuerto Libertadores de America) Reliably regular, albeit cramped, little minivans for skittering along the new road to Andahuayas (S30). Departures are between 7am and 9am daily.

Turismo Libertadores (066-31-9115; Manco Cápac, btwn Garcilaso de la Vega & Jirón 9 de Diciembre) One of the best of the cheap options to Lima: the one daytime and four nightly departures are S50.

Andahuaylas

083 / POP 6800 / ELEV 2980M

Andahuaylas, 135km west of Abancay on the way to Ayacucho, is the second-most important town in the department of Apurímac, and a convenient halfway stop on the rough but scenic route between Cuzco and Ayacucho.

Sights

Andahuaylas has a Sunday market that is worth perusing; otherwise the main attraction, the beautiful **Laguna de Pacucha**, is 17km from town and accessible by bus or taxi.

Sondor RUIN
(admission S10; ⏲8am-5pm) About 15km past the end of Laguna de Pachucha in the municipality of Pachuca stands the imposing hilltop site of Sondor, constructed by the Chanka culture. The Chankas were traditional enemies of the Incas, but evidently shared their appreciation of a good view. Evidence suggests the top of the central pyramid in the complex (accessed by some 500 steps!) was an important sacrifice spot.

Festivals & Events

The annual **Fiesta de Yahuar** (Blood Feast) is on July 28, when traditional dances and music are performed. In the village of Pacucha, the festival includes lashing a condor to the back of a bull and allowing the two to fight in a representation of the highland people's struggle against the Spanish conquistadors.

Sleeping & Eating

You can't always expect a hot shower in Andahuaylas hotels, but you can undoubtedly count on cable TV. Go figure.

El Encanto de Oro Hotel HOTEL $
(☎083-42-3066; www.hotelandahuaylas.com; Av Casafranca 424; s/d incl breakfast S50/60; 📶) Features spotlessly clean rooms of varying shapes and sizes, all with frilly curtains and phones. Friendly and caring, near the market.

Hotel Residencial El Eden HOTEL $
(☎083-42-1746; Ricardo Palma 450; s S40-100 d S60-150; 📶) The implication in the name is that you've found paradise; not totally true, but this is the best-located hotel – nice, clean and safe, accommodating of all budgets. Higher tariffs are for rooms with Jacuzzi.

Imperio Chanka HOTEL $$
(☎083-42-3065; Vallejo 384; s/d incl breakfast S60/90; 📶) With a modern, vaguely appealing look, this multi-story cement building features good, clean rooms that are well looked after. There's also an on-site restaurant.

El Portal CAFE $
(Plaza de Armas; snacks from S3; ⏲8am-9pm) Good coffee makes the rough journey out to Andahuaylas. Rather pleasant.

Puma de Piedra PERUVIAN $$
(www.restaurantepumadepiedra.com; Los Sauces s/n; mains S12-34; ⏲9am-11pm) Simply the best. This is where you want to be when it gets hot in Andahuaylas – a lovely landscaped garden where sensational Andean cuisine is served. The 24-hour opening claim on their Facebook page? We wish it were true.

Information

There's a Western Union office and several *casas de cambio* (foreign-exchange bureaus) on Ramón Castilla. **BCP** (Ramón Castilla s/n) has an ATM and changes US dollars.

Getting There & Away

AIR

LC Peru (☎in Lima 083-20-5128; www.lcperu.pe; Ricardo Palma 318) flies daily to Lima. A taxi to the airport costs about S25.

BUS

The Terminal Terrestre is the ramshackle main bus station, just southwest of the center alongside the river on Malecón Mil Amores. That said, some companies depart from their own bus stations here (all conveniently near Terminal Terrestre).

Heading east, **Expreso los Chankas** (☎083-42-2441; Malećon Grau s/n) and **Molina Union** (☎083-42-1248; Malecón Mil Amores), among a host of other companies with minivans, run daily buses to Cuzco (S30, 10 hours) via Abancay (S10, five hours) with departures usually in the evening between 5pm and 7pm.

Several companies with offices in Terminal Terrestre run faster, more comfortable and expensive minibuses throughout the day to Abancay (S15 to S20, four hours) where many more Cuzco-bound services await.

Heading west, Expreso Los Chankas has daily services to Ayacucho around 7am and 8pm (S35, five to six hours), although Sunday services are unreliable. **Transportes Sarmiento** (☎958-808-124; Terminal Terrestre) do the same route in similar time for S30 and run more regularly, but their minivans are more cramped.

For Lima (S70 to S130, 20 hours), the best direct services are run by **Expreso Internacional Palomino** (cnr Av del Ejercito & Ricardo Palma). Higher price tags are for fully reclining seats.

For Laguna de Pachucha and Sondor, you can catch a microbus to Sondor (S3, one hour) from the corner of Av Martinelli and Av Casafranca. Go in the morning – transport peters out by 4pm. You can also take a taxi.

North Coast

Includes ➡

Best Places to Eat

- La Sirena d'Juan (p355)
- El Celler de Cler (p321)
- Cafe 900 (p338)
- Capuccino (p347)
- Restaurant Big Ben (p331)

Best Places to Stay

- Sunset Hotel (p354)
- Loki del Mar (p353)
- Chaparrí Ecolodge (p343)
- Playa Colán Lodge (p345)
- Hospedaje El Mochilero (p319)

Why Go?

This savage shore has some of the best surfing in the world and plenty of tanned travelers to keep you company. It's also home to a jaw-dropping array of archaeological sites, colonial cities and evocative desertscapes straight out of *Mad Max*. In this land of rock and desert sand you will also find a few verdant valleys, while up north, Peru's only mangrove forests cling for their lives.

There's a lot of hyperbole to be had – one of the world's longest left breaks challenges surfers in Puerto Chicama, South America's oldest civilization vexes archaeological explorers at Caral, and the massive pre-Columbian adobe complex at Chan Chan was once the largest city in the Americas.

Whether surfing-off your jags from the backpacker hubs of Máncora and Huanchaco, or going lo-fi in resurgent fishing villages like Zorritos and Cabo Blanco, there are unique adventures to be found up-and-down this rugged North Shore.

When to Go

Trujillo

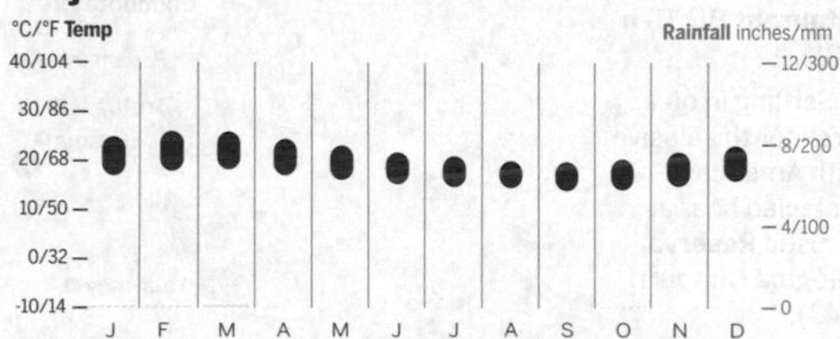

Mar Summer's sizzling sun remains, but prices smolder back down to earth.

Apr–Nov The further north you go, the shinier the sun and fewer the people.

Nov–Feb Surf's up (and so are summer prices) in Máncora, Huanchaco and Puerto Chicama.

North Coast Highlights

1 Wandering the high-walled adobe ruins of **Chan Chan** (p325), marveling at 700-year-old friezes.

2 Indulging in sun, surf and sand in **Máncora** (p352), Peru's premier beachside hot spot.

3 Ogling the vast wealth of once-buried booty at the North Coast's best museum, **Museo Tumbas Reales de Sipán** (p342) outside Chiclayo.

4 Dragging your board up the coast in search of that elusive perfect swell at **Huanchaco** (p329), **Playa Lobitos** (p349), **Puerto Chicama** (p333), **Pacasmayo** (p333) and **Máncora** (p352).

5 Hiding yourself away in the (nearly) undiscovered sands at **Pimentel** (p335), **Zorritos** (p357) and **Colán** (p345).

6 Finding ceviche salvation in the coastal desert at **Mar Picante** (p322) and **Restaurant Big Ben** (p331).

7 Settling in on a search for the elusive South American spectacled bear at the rustic **Reserva Ecológica Chaparrí** (p343).

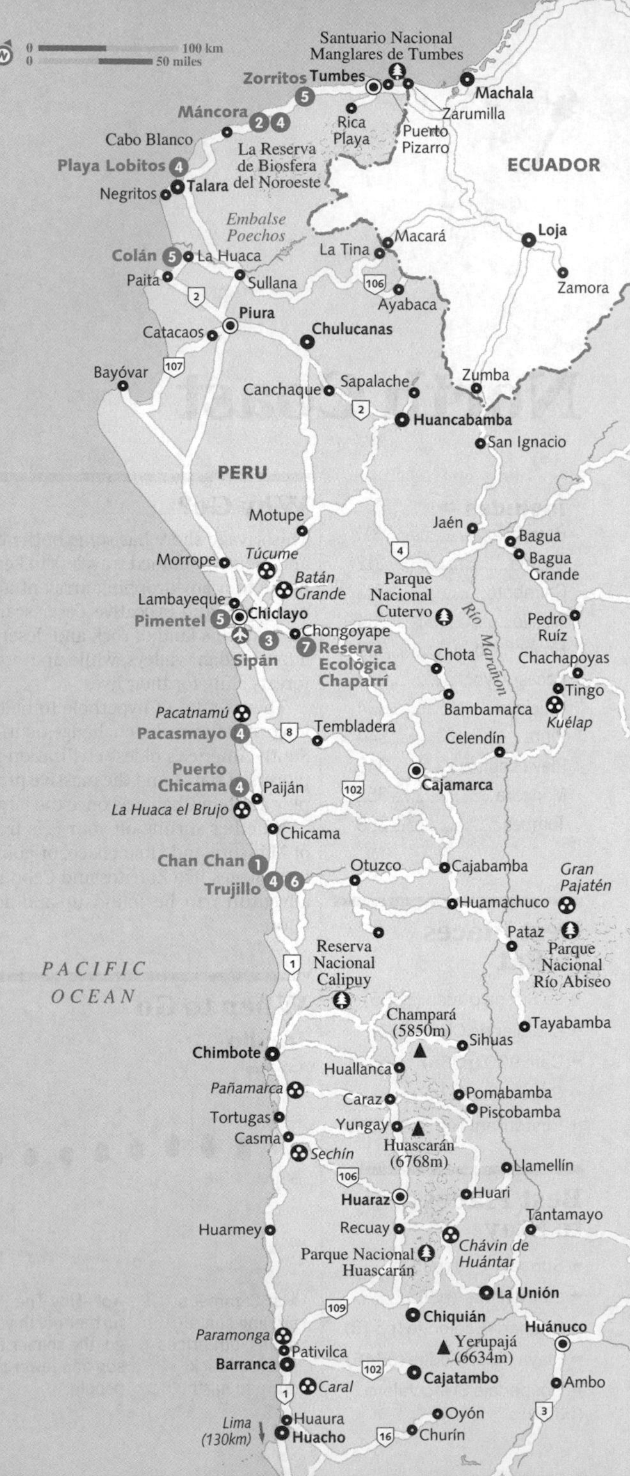

Barranca

☎01 / POP 54,000

Loud and unruly Barranca is used primarily as a transit hub to Huaraz or as a stopover for visits to the nearby Caral archaeological site. The town's action centers on the plaza, where you'll find gangs of roller-skating kids, couples taking romantic *paseos* (walks), a yellow church and a spouting fountain.

Neighboring Pativilca, located 10km further north, is where the road branches off to Huaraz and the Cordillera Blanca. This spectacular route climbs inland via cactus-laden cliffs, cathedrals of sheer rock, with desert brown slowly turning into a carpet of greenery as you climb up to Huaraz.

Sights

Caral ARCHAEOLOGICAL SITE

(www.zonacaral.gob.pe; admission S11, guide S20; 9am-4pm) Caral culture arose in the Supe Valley some 4500 to 5000 years ago, making it one of the world's earliest large cities, alongside those in Mesopotamia, Egypt, India and China. This ancient culture was a conglomeration of 18 city-states and controlled the three valleys of Supe, Pativilca and Fortaleza, with the main seat of government at Caral. The monumental ruins are located about 25km inland from Barranca.

Considering how few people visit Caral, the site is well set out for visitors. There are plaques in both Spanish and English illustrating points of interest. Weekends are a great time to visit because handicrafts and local food are for sale at the site.

These ruins confounded Peruvian archaeologists when they proved to be part of the oldest civilization in all of South America. Before Caral's discovery, the city of Chavín de Huántar near Huaraz, built around 900 BC, held that particular title. At the site, six stone-built pyramids (most of which have been excavated) were found alongside amphitheaters, ceremonial rooms, altars, adobe complexes and several sunken circular plazas. Most of the pyramids have stairways leading to their peaks, where offerings were once made; the stairs can be climbed for great views of the lush Supe River valley.

The people of Caral-Supe were experts in agriculture, construction, public administration and making calendars and musical instruments. Evidence of elaborate religious ceremonies among elites suggests a highly stratified culture in which classes were organized according to their labor in society; archaeologists at Caral believe that men and women may have enjoyed considerable equality. Among the many artifacts you'll see at the site are millennia-old bone flutes and Peru's oldest *quipus* (a system among Andean cultures of tying cords in knots to convey information). A large geoglyph – a design carved into earth – called Chupacigaro attests to the Caral people's sophisticated measurements of the movements of the stars. Unesco declared the Sacred City of Caral a World Heritage site in 2009.

Explora Tours (☎99-367-9948; Ugarte 190, Barranca; tours 4hr/7hr S35/40) offers guided tours including transportation from Barranca; inquire at Hostal Continental. Lima Tours (p101) arranges expensive private tours to Caral and Paramonga from Lima on request.

Colectivo (shared transportation) taxis depart from Calle Berenice Davila in Barranca to the nearby hamlet of Caral fairly regularly for S10 (two hours). Alternatively, elusive private taxis will cost around S80 for the return journey (including waiting time); some charge S20 per hour for the same route. The road out here is rough and may be impassable during the December to March wet season.

Paramonga RUIN

(www.muniparamonga.gob.pe; admission S10, guide S10; Tue-Sun 9am-5pm) The adobe temple of Paramonga is situated 4km beyond the turnoff for the Huaraz road and was built by the Chimú culture, which was the ruling power on the north coast before it was conquered by the Incas. The fine details of the massive temple have long been eroded, yet the multi-tiered construction is nonetheless impressive and affords fantastic panoramas of the lush valley.

Colectivos from Barranca (S2.50, 25 minutes) leave from the corner of Ugarte and Lima and will drop you off at a spot 3km from the entrance. A private return taxi here, including wait time, will cost about S40 but are hard to come by.

Sleeping & Eating

Most hotels are along the Antigua Panamericana Norte, Barranca's main street.

Hostal Continental HOTEL $

(☎01-235-2458; Ugarte 190; s/d from S40/55; wi-fi) Though still oozing dilapidation, this is the best budget choice, offering basic rooms in a solid location a block from Plaza de Armas. Ask for a room in the back to save on street noise.

Hotel Chavín HOTEL $$
(☎01-235-5025; www.hotelchavin.com.pe; Gálvez 222; s S85, d S165-185;) Barranca's big-shot hotel has comfortable rooms that are perfectly preserved in a resplendent '70s style contrasting with striking new hardwood floors and flat-screen TVs. There's a karaoke bar and pool area out back, plus a decent attached restaurant, making this a one-stop shop for Barranca waylays.

Seichi CAFE $
(A Ugarte 184; mains S7.50-13, menús S13; closed dinner Sun) This modern cafe churns out tasty, home-cooked *menús*, with a smile to boot. Hard to find fault here.

Mary's PIZZA $
(Av Arica 101, Plaza de Armas; mains s5-7.50) This little corner coffee shop and pizzeria has a large window with views onto the plaza. The fruit juices are excellent, while the sandwiches and pizzas are passable. The service is top-tier.

Cafetería El Parador CAFE $
(Hotel Chavín, Gálvez 222; breakfasts S9-15, sandwiches S6-12; 7am-11pm) This diner attached to Hotel Chavín has a few breakfast combos, watered-down coffee and sandwiches in a classic cafe setting with bar seating, pie displays and plenty of chrome.

Getting There & Away

Turismo Barranca (☎99-613-6847; Primavera 250), two blocks east of Plaza de Armas, leaves every 10 minutes for Lima (S15, four hours) from 2:30am to 10pm. Alternatively, flag down one of the many buses heading in that direction. Most buses from Lima going up the coast can also drop you in Barranca. For Huaraz, catch a *colectivo* (S2) to the Pecsa gas station in Pativilca, 3km from the Huaraz turnoff. From there, *colectivos* leave when full (S30, three hours); infrequent buses from Lima also stop to pick up passengers. For something more fixed, **Z Buss** (☎964-404-463) departs four times daily from Pativilca (S20, four hours, 11am, noon, 3pm and 5:30pm).

Casma

☎043 / POP 24,700

A small and unflustered Peruvian coastal town; there is little to do in Casma except watch the whirring of passing buses. The big draw here is the archaeological site of Sechín, about 5km away. Casma's once-important colonial port (11km from town) was sacked by various pirates during the 17th century; the town today is merely a friendly blip on the historical radar.

From here, the Pan-American Hwy branches off for Huaraz via the Callán Pass (4225m). This route is tough on your backside but offers excellent panoramic views of the Cordillera Blanca. Most points of interest in town lie along the Pan-American Hwy, between the Plaza de Armas in the west and the petrol station in the east.

Sights

Sechín ARCHAEOLOGICAL SITE
(admission S5; 8am-6pm) One of Peru's granddaddy archaeological sites, Sechín is located 5km southeast of Casma and dates from about 1600 BC. It is among the more important and well-preserved ruins along this coast, though it has suffered some damage from grave robbers and natural disasters.

The warlike people who built this temple remain shrouded in mystery. The site consists of three exterior walls of the main temple, which are completely covered in gruesome 4m-high bas-relief carvings of warriors and captives being vividly eviscerated. Ouch! Inside the main temple are earlier mud structures that are still being excavated: you can't go in, but there is a model in the small on-site museum. Stop by the museum first if you're in need of a guide, as you may be able to pick up a Spanish-speaking caretaker for S30.

To get here, a *mototaxi* (three-wheeled motorcycle rickshaw taxi) from Casma costs around S6. Other early sites in the Sechín area have not been excavated due to a lack of funds. From the museum, you can see the large, flat-topped hill of **Sechín Alto** in the distance. The nearby fortress of **Chanquillo** consists of several towers surrounded by concentric walls, but it is best appreciated from the air. Aerial photographs are on display at the museum.

The entry ticket to Sechín also allows you to visit the Mochica ruins of **Pañamarca**, 10km inland from the Pan-American Hwy on the road to Nepeña. These ruins are badly weathered, but you can see some of the covered murals if you ask the guard.

Sleeping & Eating

Hostal Gregori HOTEL $
(043-58-0573; Ormeño 579; s/d/tr S30/50/60;) Your best bet in town has a pretty interior courtyard punctuated by a handful of statues. The rooms have firmish beds and refurbished bathrooms with cement and glass sink vanities. Pop on the flat-screen for a late-night escape to TV land.

El Tío Sam PERUVIAN, CHINESE $
(043-71-1447; Huarmey 138; mains S14-20) Part *chifa* (Chinese restaurant), part regional cuisine, this is your best bet in Casma, bipolarity notwithstanding. In fact, their ceviche, which outclasses the town, was Ancash's best back in 2010. There are also lots of fried things, too, along with good-looking steaks and seafood.

La Careta STEAK $$
(Peru 885; mains S9.50-34.50; from 6pm, closed Tue) This popular, orange-tableclothed meatery serves sizzling grills nightly amid an odd decorative duo of bullfighting paintings and model cars. All plates come with fries and a salad – not bad – though the indoor potted plants are the most impressive 'greens' in the house.

Information

There's a branch of **BCP** (Bolívar 111) here. Several internet cafes line the plaza.

Getting There & Away

Colectivo taxis to Chimbote leave frequently from a fairly set spot a half block east of Plaza de Armas.

Most bus companies are on Ormeño in front of the petrol station at the eastern end of town. Many buses stop here to pick up extra passengers. **Cruz del Norte/Transportes Huandoy** (043-41-1633; www.transportescruzdelnorte.com; Ormeño 121) offer frequent services to Lima and three daily departures for Huaraz at 9am, 2pm and 9pm (the latter, along with Yungay Express, has buses that take the scenic route via the Callán Pass). Faster minivans to Huaraz also leave from in front of this office when full.

Tepsa (01-617-9000; www.tepsa.com.pe; Huamay 356) has comfortable buses to Lima departing at 1am daily. **Erick El Rojo** (044-47-4957; www.turismoerickelrojo.pe; Ormeño 145) has five daily departures to Trujillo and one 7:30pm departure to Tumbes.

For Sechín, *mototaxis* (S6) make the run. They are all around town, but there's an honest cluster operating as Motocars Virgen de Fatima on Plaza San Martín.

Ticket prices fluctuate with the quality of the bus/classes.

Casma Buses:

DESTINATION	COST (S)	DURATION (HR)
Chimbote	6	1
Huaraz	20-25	2½-3
Lima	20-65	5½
Máncora	50-60	11
Trujillo	10	3
Tumbes	50-60	12-13

Chimbote

Chimbote is Peru's largest fishing port. With fish-processing factories lining the roads in and out of town, you'll probably smell it before you see it. The odor of fermenting fish may take a while to get used to, but the quiet, open plaza in the town's heart is less overwhelming. The fishing industry has declined from its 1960s glory days due to overfishing, but you'll still see flotillas moored offshore every evening as you take a sunset walk along the *malecón*. This roguish port town is a transit hub, not a tourist destination, but you may have to stay overnight if you're catching an early morning bus to Huaraz via the hair-raising Cañón del Pato route.

Sleeping

Hospedaje Chimbote HOTEL $
(043-51-5006; Pardo 205; s/d S30/40, without bathroom S20/30) A team of siblings owns this lovely budget option, which has been in the family since opening in 1959. Cell-like rooms here have windows onto the corridor, which is a bright, freshly painted joy for these prices. Hot water comes with en-suite rooms only.

Hotel San Felipe HOTEL $$
(043-32-3401; www.hotelcasinosanfelipe.com; Pardo 514; s/d/ste incl breakfast S80/115/160; P @) Across from the Plaza de Armas, the town's best option is family run with a helpful smile. Equipped with elevators, this hotel with its gaudy facade offers clean business-style rooms with strong hot showers and cable TV. Be sure to take your continental breakfast on the 5th-floor terrace with plaza views.

A glitzy downstairs casino will help you live out your Las Vegas card-shark fantasies.

Hostal Chifa Canton HOTEL $$

(☎043-34-4388; Bolognesi 498; s/d incl breakfast S95/120; P 📶) This hotel wins points for architectural originality with an odd front turret, cantilevered top floor and amazingly mismatched materials all harkening to a Peruvian take on the Orient. It has large, carpeted rooms with modernish amenities and lumpy pillows. Some rooms look out over the sea.

Eating

The *chifa* at **Hostal Chifa Canton** (Bolognesi 498; mains S8.50-35.50) is superb. There are plenty of good spots along Bolognesi and Pardo in the vicinity of Plaza de Armas as well.

Mar & Luna SEAFOOD $

(cnr Villavicencio & Malecón; mains S13-23) This retro-pop pub cranks out hits from the '70s, '80s and '90s, and serves up plentiful seafood favorites like ceviche and *chupe de cangrejo* (seafood stew). There's a giant guitar on the ceiling that pays tribute to *Sgt. Pepper's Lonely Hearts Club Band* and rock posters throughout. It's probably the liveliest spot in town and has good views to the ocean.

Capuccino Café CAFE $$

(Villavicencio 455; mains S20-30) Try this little cafe for espresso and higher-end Peruvian fusion.

Getting There & Away

BUS

For Casma (S6, 45 minutes), *colectivos* depart from the corner of Pardo and Balta.

All long-distance buses leave from the Terminal Terrestre 'El Chimbador,' about 5km east of town across from the municipal stadium (S6 taxi ride or catch *colectivo* 25 on Pardo for S1.50). There's an internet cafe in the terminal.

America Express (☎01-424-1352; www.americaexpress.com.pe) has buses leaving for Trujillo every 15 minutes from 5:25am to 9:30pm. Dozens of companies run mostly overnight buses to Lima, leaving between 10pm and midnight, though a few depart in daylight. Reputable companies, several of which also have offices lined up along Bolognesi with the banks, include **Oltursa** (☎01-708-5000; www.oltursa.pe), **Línea** (☎043-35-4000; www.linea.pe), **Civa** (☎01-418-1111; www.excluciva.pe) and **Cruz Del Sur** (☎0-801-11111; www.cruzdelsur.com.pe). The last has the most frequent and most comfortable departures at 11am, 2:30pm, 11:15pm and 11:30pm. Cruz del Sur also has international trips to Buenos Aires (S776) and Santiago (S530).

Buses to Huaraz and the Cordillera Blanca run along one of three routes: via the dazzling yet rough road through the Cañón del Pato, via an equally rough road that climbs through the mountains from Casma, or via the longer, comfortably paved route through Pativilca. Travel times on these routes range from seven to nine hours. **Yungay Express** (☎043-35-0855) has an 8:30am bus to Caraz and Huaraz through the Cañón del Pato, and 1pm and 10pm buses via Casma. **Movil Tours** (☎01-716-8000; www.moviltours.com.pe) has 12:30pm, 11:10pm, 11:50pm and 12:30am departures to Huaraz via Casma that also stop in Caraz. It pays to book Huaraz buses a day in advance.

Sample travel times and costs from Chimbote are shown in the table (prices fluctuate with the quality of the bus/classes).

Chimbote Buses:

DESTINATION	COST (S)	DURATION (HR)
Caraz	20	6-7
Chiclayo	23-40	6
Huaraz	20-65	5-8
Lima	40-85	6-7
Máncora	90-120	11
Piura	35-80	8
Trujillo	12-15	2
Tumbes	40-120	12

Trujillo

☎044 / POP 709,500

Stand in the right spot and the glamorously colonial streets of old Trujillo look like they've barely changed in hundreds of years. Well, there are more honking taxis now – but the city still manages to put on a dashing show with its polychrome buildings and profusion of colonial-era churches. Most people come here to visit the remarkable pre-Incan archaeological sites nearby, spending just a short time wandering the compact city center.

The behemoth Chimú capital of Chan Chan is nearby. It was the largest pre-Columbian city in the Americas, making it the top attraction in the region. Other Chimú sites bake in the surrounding desert, among them the immense and suitably impressive Moche Huacas del Sol y de la Luna (Temples of the Sun and Moon), which date back 1500 years.

Beach bums may consider staying in the laid-back surfer village of Huanchaco (p329), just 20 minutes up the road.

History

The area has been inhabited for millennia, with several prominent pre-Incan civilizations popping up in the fertile oasis.

Francisco Pizarro founded Trujillo in 1534, and he thought so highly of this patch of desert he named it after his birthplace in Spain's Estremadura. Spoiled by the fruits of the fertile Moche Valley, Trujillo never had to worry about money – wealth came easily. With life's essentials taken care of, thoughts turned to politics and life's grander schemes, and so the city's reputation for being a hotbed of revolt began. The town was besieged during the Inca rebellion of 1536 and in 1820 was the first Peruvian city to declare independence from Spain.

The tradition continued into the 20th century, as bohemians flocked, poets put pen to paper (including Peru's best poet, César Vallejo), and rebels raised their fists defiantly in the air. It was here that the Alianza Popular Revolution Americana (APRA) workers' party was formed – and many of its members were later massacred.

Sights

Trujillo's colonial mansions and churches, most of which are near the Plaza de Armas, are worth seeing, though they don't keep very regular opening hours.

Hiring a good local guide is recommended if you are seriously interested in history. The churches are often open for early morning and evening masses, but visitors at those times should respect worshippers and not wander around.

The creamy pastel shades and beautiful wrought-iron grillwork fronting almost every colonial building are unique Trujillo touches.

Plaza de Armas

Trujillo's spacious and spit-shined main square, surely the cleanest in the Americas and definitely one of the prettiest, hosts a colorful assembly of preserved colonial buildings and an impressive statue dedicated to work, the arts and liberty. Elegant mansions abound, including **Hotel Libertador** (Independencia 485).

At 9am on Sundays there is a flag-raising ceremony on the Plaza de Armas, complete, on special occasions, with a parade, *caballos de paso* (pacing horses) and performances of the *marinera* (a typical coastal Peruvian dance involving much romantic waving of handkerchiefs).

Basilica Menor Catedral CHURCH
(Plaza de Armas s/n; museum S4; church 10-11am, museum 9am-1pm & 4-7pm Mon-Fri, 9am-noon Sat) Known simply as 'La Catedral,' this bright, canary-yellow church fronting the plaza was begun in 1647, destroyed in 1759, and rebuilt soon afterward. The cathedral has a famous basilica (but unless you are attending Mass, you have a one-hour window each day to pop in) and a museum of religious and colonial art that is pricier than it is worth, though there are intriguing frescoes in the downstairs basement (along with a few bats).

Casa de Urquiaga HISTORIC BUILDING
(Pizarro 446; 9:15am-3:15pm Mon-Fri, 10am-1pm Sat) FREE Owned and maintained by Banco Central de la Reserva del Perú since 1972, this beautiful colonial mansion's history dates to 1604, though the original house was completely destroyed in the earthquake of 1619. Rebuilt and dramatically preserved since, it now houses exquisite period furniture, including a striking writer's desk once used by Simón Bolívar, who organized much of his final campaign to liberate Peru from the Spanish empire from Trujillo in 1824.

There is also a small collection of Moche, Nazca, Chimu and Vicús pottery. It's a working bank, so security is high for a free attraction.

East of Plaza de Armas

Palacio Iturregui NOTABLE BUILDING
(Pizarro 688; 9am-5pm daily) This bright yellow 19th-century mansion is unmistakable and impossible to ignore unless you're color blind. Built in neoclassical style, it has beautiful window gratings, 36 slender interior columns and gold moldings on the ceilings. General Juan Manuel Iturregui lived here after he famously proclaimed independence.

Today, it's a private social club, so visits are restricted. You can pop into the interior courtyard any time of day, but visiting the ornate rooms is restricted to the listed opening hours.

Trujillo

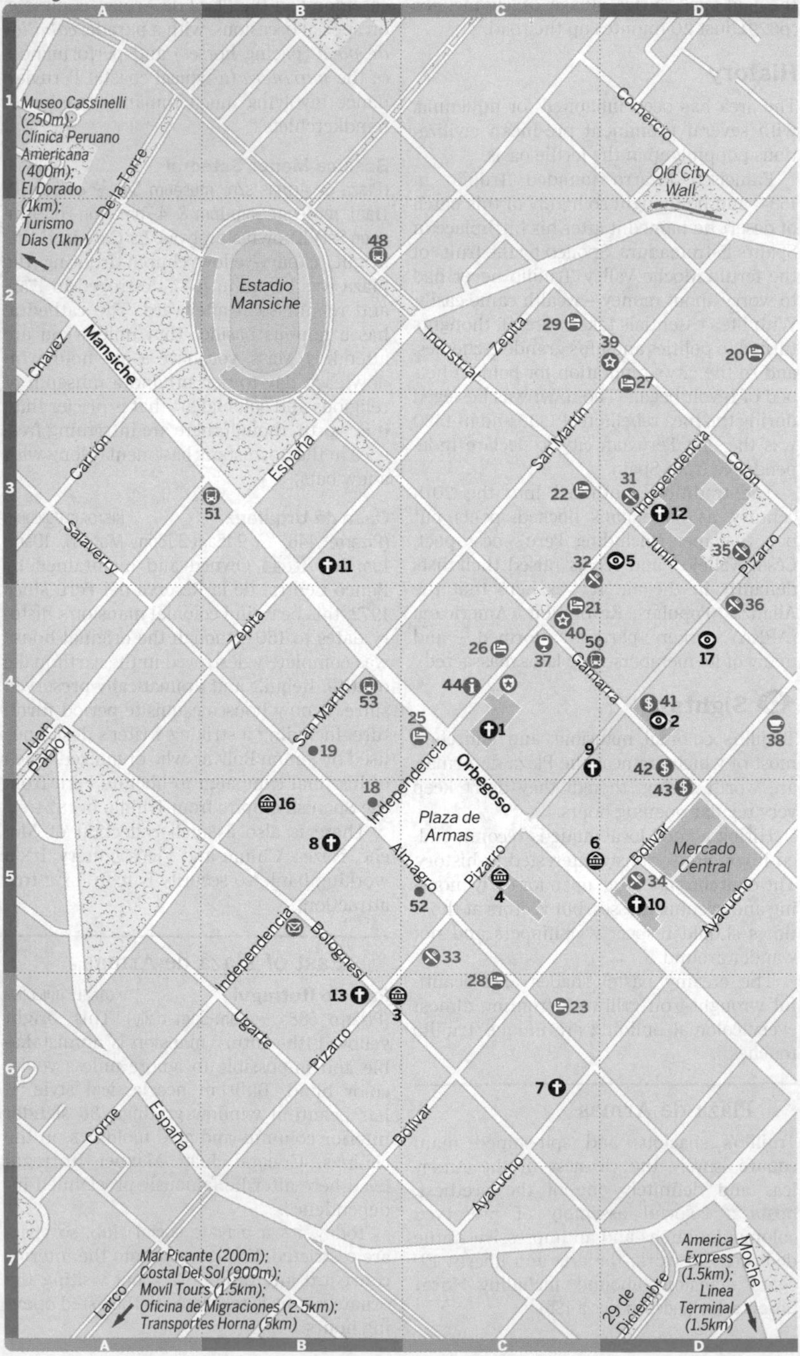

A
B
C
D
1
2
3
4
5
6
7
Museo Cassinelli (250m); Clínica Peruano Americana (400m); El Dorado (1km); Turismo Días (1km)
De la Torre
Estadio Mansiche
Chavez
Mansiche
Carrión
España
Salaverry
Zepita
San Martín
Juan Pablo II
Industrial
Zepita
Comercio
Old City Wall
San Martín
Independencia
Colón
Junín
Pizarro
Gamarra
Orbegoso
Plaza de Armas
Independencia
Almagro
Pizarro
Bolívar
Mercado Central
Ayacucho
Independencia
Bolognesi
Ugarte
Pizarro
Corne
España
Bolívar
Ayacucho
Larco
Mar Picante (200m); Costal Del Sol (900m); Movíl Tours (1.5km); Oficina de Migraciones (2.5km); Transportes Horna (5km)
29 de Diciembre
Moche
America Express (1.5km); Linea Terminal (1.5km)

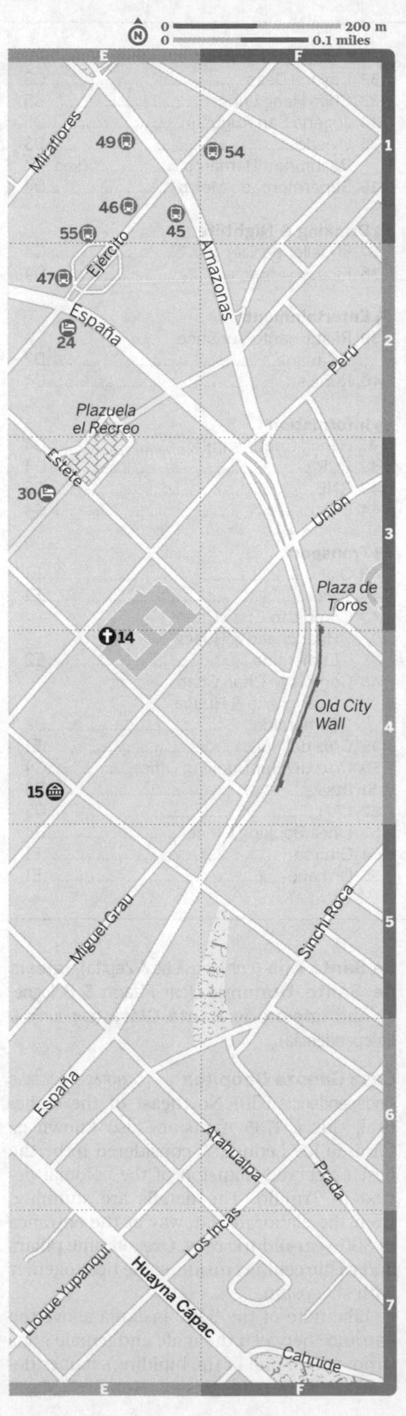

Museo de Arqueología MUSEUM

(Junín 682; admission S5; 9am-5pm Mon-Sat, to 1pm Sun) This well-curated museum features a rundown of Peruvian history from 12,000 BC to the present day, with an emphasis on Moche, Chimu and Inca civilizations as well as the lesser-known Cupisnique and Salinar cultures. But it's also worth popping in for the house itself, a restored 17th-century mansion known as La Casa Risco, which features striking cedar pillars and gorgeous painted courtyard walls.

Casa de la Emancipación NOTABLE BUILDING

(Pizarro 610) Now the Banco Continental, this building features a mishmash of colonial and Republican styles and is best known as the site where Trujillo's independence from colonial rule was formally declared on December 29, 1820. Check out the unique cubic Cajabamba marble stone flooring; there are also galleries dedicated to revolving art exhibitions, Peruvian poet César Vallejo and period furniture. It hosts live music events as well – look for posters around town on your visit.

Iglesia de la Merced CHURCH

(Pizarro) Worth a flyby is the 17th-century Iglesia de la Merced, which has a striking organ and cupola. Uniquely, an altar here is painted on the wall, an economical shortcut when funds ran out for a more traditional gold or carved-wood alternative. The church is not currently open to visitors.

Iglesia del Carmen CHURCH

(cnr Colón & Bolívar) Iglesia del Carmen is home to an impressive Carmelite museum. Unfortunately, the church was not open for visitors at time of research.

Iglesia de San Agustín CHURCH

(cnr Orbegoso & Bolívar; 9am-noon & 4-7:30pm) Iglesia de San Agustín has a finely gilded high altar and dates from 1558.

Iglesia de Belén CHURCH

(Ayacucho s/n) This noteworthy central church has twin towers and was built around the turn of the 17th century.

Casa de Mayorazgo de Facala HISTORIC BUILDING

(Pizarro 314; 9:30am-1pm & 4-7pm Mon-Fri) The 1709 Casa de Mayorazgo de Facala mansion now houses Scotiabank, and is a great example of colonial architecture.

Trujillo

Sights
1 Basilica Menor Catedral....C4
2 Casa de la Emancipación....D4
3 Casa de Mayorazgo de Facala....B6
4 Casa de Urquiaga....C5
5 Casa Ganoza Chopitea....D3
6 Casona Orbegoso....C5
7 Iglesia de Belén....C6
8 Iglesia de la Compañía....B5
9 Iglesia de la Merced....C4
10 Iglesia de San Agustín....D5
11 Iglesia de Santa Ana....B3
12 Iglesia de Santa Clara....D3
13 Iglesia de Santo Domingo....B6
14 Iglesia del Carmen....E4
15 Museo de Arqueología....E4
16 Museo de Zoología....B5
17 Palacio Iturregui....D4

Activities, Courses & Tours
18 Chan Chan Tours....B5
Colonial Tours....(see 21)
19 Trujillo Tours....B4

Sleeping
20 Hospedaje El Mochilero....D2
21 Hostal Colonial....C4
22 Hostal el Ensueño....C3
23 Hotel Chimor....C6
24 Hotel El Brujo....E2
25 Hotel Libertador....C4
26 House-Lodge el Conde de Arce....C4
27 La Hacienda....D2
28 Los Conquistadores Hotel....C6
29 Munay Wasi Hostel....C2
30 Pullman Hotel....E3

Eating
31 Café Bar Museo....D3
32 Casona Deza....C3
33 Chifa Heng Lung....C5
34 Jugería San Augustín....D5
35 Oviedo....D3
Restaurant Demarco....(see 35)
36 Supermercado Metro....D4

Drinking & Nightlife
37 El Celler de Cler....C4
38 Picasso Lounge....D4

Entertainment
39 Restaurante Turístico Canana....D2
40 Runa's....C4

Information
41 Banco Continental....D4
42 BCP....D4
43 GNB....D5
44 iPerú....C4

Transport
45 Cial....E1
46 Civa....E1
47 Combis to Chan Chan, Huanchaco & Huaca Esmeralda....E2
48 Combis to Chan Chan, Huanchaco & Huaca Esmeralda....B2
49 Cruz del Sur....E1
50 Cruz del Sur Booking Office....C4
51 Ittsa....B3
52 LAN....C5
53 Línea Booking Office....B4
54 Oltursa....F1
55 Ormeño....E1

Casona Orbegoso HISTORIC BUILDING
(Orbegoso 553) Named after a former president of Peru, this beautiful 18th-century corner manor is home to a collection of well-worn art and period furnishings, but its stuck-in-time feel is being increasingly ensured by its ongoing closure for renovations. There was no estimated reopening date when we came through.

North & West of Plaza de Armas

There are several interesting churches near the Plaza de Armas that are not open for visitation but are well worth viewing from the outside on a walking tour of the city: **Iglesia de la Compañía** (Independencia), now part of the Universidad Nacional de Trujillo, **Iglesia de Santa Ana** (cnr Mansiche & Zepita), **Iglesia de Santo Domingo** (cnr Pizarro & Bolognesi) and **Iglesia de Santa Clara** (cnr Junín & Independencia).

Casa Ganoza Chopitea NOTABLE BUILDING
(Independencia 630) Northeast of the cathedral, this c 1735 mansion, also known as Casa de los Léones, is considered to be the best preserved mansion of the colonial period in Trujillo. The details are stunning, from the elaborate gateway at the entrance to 300-year-old frescoes, Oregon pine pillars and rustic ceilings inside, some tied together with sheepskin.

Take note of the 'JHS' insignia above the entrance between the male and female lions (from which one of the building's names derives). It stands for 'Jesus,' 'Hombre' (Man),

'Salvador' (Savior) and stems from the building's time as a convent (as does the lazy Susan by the bathrooms). Best of all, perhaps, is that it now houses the wonderful Casona Deza cafe (p322).

Museo Cassinelli MUSEUM

(N de Piérola 607; admission S7; ⏲9am-1pm & 3-6pm Mon-Sat) This private archaeological collection housed in the basement of a Repsol gas station (the one on the west side of the intersection, not the east side) is fascinating, with some 2000 ceramic pieces on display (curated from a collection owned by Italian immigrants) that certainly don't belong under a gritty gas dispensary.

Have a look at the bird-shaped whistling pots, which produce clear notes when air is blown into them (ask the curator to show you). Superficially the pots are very similar, but when they are blown each produces a completely different note that corresponds to the calls of the male and female birds. The mummified eight-month-old female fetus, born premature, is estimated to date from AD 250 and will blow your mind as well.

Museo de Zoología MUSEUM

(San Martín 368; admission S2; ⏲9am-6pm) This museum is mainly a taxidermic collection of Peruvian animals (many so artificially stuffed they look like nightmarish caricatures of their former selves).

Tours

There are dozens of tour agencies in Trujillo. Some agencies supply guides who speak English but don't know much about the area; some supply guides who are well informed but don't speak English. Entrance fees are *not* included in the listed tour prices. Most full-day tours cost around S65, including transport and guide. If you prefer your own guide, it's best to go with a certified official guide who knows the area well. Ask at iPerú (p323) for a list of certified guides and contact details.

Trujillo Tours CULTURAL TOUR

(☎044-23-3091; www.trujillotours.com; Almagro 301; ⏲7:30am-1pm & 4-8pm) This friendly operation has three- to four-hour tours to Chan Chan and Huanchaco, and Moche Huacas del Sol y de la Luna, as well as city tours. Tours are available in English, French, Portuguese and German.

Chan Chan Tours CULTURAL TOUR

(☎044-24-3016; chanchantourstrujillo@hotmail.com; Independencia 431; ⏲8am-1pm & 3-8pm) Right on Plaza de Armas, this established agency organizes trips to Chan Chan and Moche Huacas Sol y de la Luna, as well as trips further afield. The guides speak some English.

Colonial Tours TOUR

(☎044-29-1034; www.colonialtoursnorteperu.com; Independencia 616) Full-day guided tours to all the major archaeological sites.

Festivals & Events

La Fiesta de la Marinera DANCE

This is the national *marinera* contest; held in the last week in January.

El Festival Internacional de la Primavera FESTIVAL

(International Spring Festival) Trujillo's major festival is celebrated with parades, national dancing competitions (including, of course, the *marinera*), *caballos de paso* displays, sports, international beauty contests and other cultural activities. It all happens in the last week in September and better hotels are booked out well in advance.

Sleeping

Some travelers prefer to stay in the nearby beach town of Huanchaco. Many budget and midrange hotels can be noisy if you get the streetside rooms. For a city of its size and history, Trujillo lags way behind when it comes to design and boutique hotels.

★**Hospedaje El Mochilero** HOSTEL $

(☎044-29-7842; www.elmochileroperu.com; Independencia 887; dm/d S20/50) It feels more like a youth hostel than anywhere else in Trujillo. They have hammocks out back, two big dorm rooms that sleep 10 to 12 (bring your ear plugs), funk-show-brother pumped-in music, plus cool common areas for chillaxing megathons. There's basic cane cabins out back if you want to sleep in the open air. All in all, good vibes.

Hostal Colonial HISTORIC HOTEL $

(☎044-25-8261; www.hostalcolonial.com.pe; Independencia 618; dm/s/d/tr S35/90/110/140; 📶) This tastefully renovated, rose-colored colonial mansion has a great location just a block from the Plaza de Armas. It's a top contender in both the midrange and budget categories. It's an HI affiliate, with two- to

OFF THE BEATEN TRACK

OTUZCO: PERU'S FAITH CAPITAL

The small provincial mountain town of Otuzco is only two hours away from Trujillo, making it the only place in Peru where you can go coast-to-Andean peaks in such a short amount of time. The cobblestone streets, cool weather and relaxed pace of life make this a great day trip or stopover on the mountain route to Cajamarca. The modern church here dramatically houses the Virgen de la Puerta (Virgin of the Door) outside its walls on the 2nd floor balcony of the town cathedral. This patron saint is the impetus behind the popular Peruvian pilgrimage on December 15 (one of South America's most important), when pilgrims of all ages leg it the 73km from Trujillo as a test to their faith. What? Not impressed? Let's not forget Trujillo is at sea level and Otuzco sits at a cool 2641m. The town's conviction has earned it the title of Peru's Capital de la Fe (Capital of Faith).

The trip itself is worthwhile (we mean the drive, of course), as you'll be greeted by excellent mountain scenery through coastal subtropical crops and into the highland agricultural regions.

There are some modest places to stay, the best being the cheap **Hostal Los Portales** (hotellosportalesdeotuzco@hotmail.com; Santa Rosa 680; s with/without bathroom S30/15, d with/without bathroom S45/30, tr with/without bathroom S60/30). A few inexpensive restaurants serve Peruvian food – **Restaurante Otuzco** (Tacna 451; menús S4-5) has a good reputation with locals.

Tours Pacifico (044-43-6138; Progreso 301) heads to Otuzco from Trujillo (S6 to S8, 1½ hours) six times daily. You can pick up a *colectivo* to Huamachuco (S10, 3½ hours) at the crossroads 3.5km south of town. They pass at 10am, 2:30pm and 8pm. A taxi to the crossroads is S1.

five-bedroom dorms, and plenty of private rooms spread out over three levels.

Chatty and helpful staff, a tour desk, popular cafe, gorgeous courtyards, open spaces and a garden synergistically come together to keep attracting travelers. Some of the cozy rooms have balconies and great views of Iglesia de San Francisco opposite.

Munay Wasi Hostel GUESTHOUSE $
(044-23-1462; munaywasi@hotmail.com; Colón 250; dm S35, s/d/tr without bathroom incl breakfast S50/70/90) A pleasant, family-run budget option that woos travelers with a nice courtyard, eight rooms with hot water (as well as a small communal lounge, a guest kitchen and a wholly different atmosphere than most spots in Trujillo). The shared bathrooms have been newly remodeled.

House-Lodge el Conde de Arce GUESTHOUSE $
(044-29-5117; nathalyarrascue@hotmail.com; Independencia 577; dm S20, s/d S45/60) With a giant, cluttered patio, this is a simple, safe budget lodging right in the center of town. It's one hot, disorganized mess, but the rooms are spacious and empty out onto a bright cement courtyard. It's all overseen by the young, friendly and English-speaking Nathaly, the daughter of the longtime owner.

Hostal el Ensueño GUESTHOUSE $
(99-441-1131; www.elensuenohostal.com; Junín 336; s S50/60) This hot-as-Hades guesthouse has its own personal Jesus poster at the entrance. The rooms are as clean as St Peter's Pearly Gates, with tiled floors and dated furniture. Make sure to get a room with a fan.

La Hacienda HISTORIC HOTEL $$
(044-23-2234; www.lahaciendatrujillo.pe; San Martín 780; s/d/tr S95/125/160) This Republican-era historic hotel has a gorgeous al fresco interior patio with it's own singing lionhead fountain. The rooms could be nicer, but you get plenty of space and flat-screen TVs – plus a hodgepodge of furniture that could have been picked up at any number of estate sales throughout the ages.

There's a dip-pool and sauna in the slightly ghetto grotto spa area.

Hotel Chimor HOTEL $$
(044-20-2252; www.hotelchimor.com; Almagro 631; s/d/tr S110/160/220) This is a very solid midrange choice for comfort and modernity. The contempo rooms can get a little hot, but they are quite sharp, with built-in desks, flat-screen TVs and leather headboards. It's friendly and central, and borders on boutique cool.

Hotel El Brujo HOTEL **$$**
(☎044-22-3322; www.elbrujohotel.com; Independencia 978; s/d incl breakfast S151/201; ❄@📶) This is a solid (though slightly boring) midrange option. It is clean and quiet, and its location close to several northern bus stations adds to the convenience factor. Despite the rad Brujo wall sculture in the lobby, it's very business-like, with modern, carpeted rooms and all the requisite amenities (minibar, cable TV and writing desk).

Pullman Hotel HOTEL **$$**
(☎022-28-7866; www.pullmanhoteltrujillo.com.pe; Pizarro 879; s/d incl breakfast S110/160; ❄@📶) The modern lobby here faces a pedestrian street near the Plazuela el Recreo and therefore doesn't suffer from much street noise. Neat and spotless, the parquet- or tile-floored rooms feature modern amenities, and some funky architectural touches like innovative ceiling fans and ceiling cut-outs. The common areas still retain an institutional air.

You might well get better bang for your buck at other midrange options.

Hotel Libertador HISTORIC HOTEL **$$$**
(☎044-23-2741; www.hotellibertador.com.pe; Independencia 485; s/d incl breakfast S387/417; P❄@📶🏊) The classy dame of the city's hotels, the 79-room Libertador is in a beautiful building that's the Audrey Hepburn of Trujillo – it wears its age with refined grace. It earns its four stars with a beautiful and lush courtyard pool, archways aplenty and modern rooms with all expected amenities.

Rooms are centered on a bright atrium that encompasses the three floors, but try to avoid the streetside rooms unless you want to watch the goings-on, as they tend to be noisy.

Costal Del Sol RESORT **$$$**
(☎044-48-4150; www.costadelsolperu.com; Los Cocoteros 505; s/d incl breakfast S510/580; P❄@📶🏊) This chain hotel has a large resort compound about a 10-minute taxi ride from the city center. The resort has a grand circular pool, spa, treatment rooms and steam baths, and expansive grounds patrolled by a troupe of alpacas (that must hate the heat). Rooms are classy and elegant.

You'll won't feel like you are in Trujillo at all, but it's probably the best high-end resort in town.

Los Conquistadores Hotel HOTEL **$$$**
(☎044-48-1650; www.losconquistadoreshotel.com; Almagro 586; s/d incl breakfast S273/343; P❄@📶) A few steps away from the Plaza de Armas, this art-deco-inspired hotel has some of the best contemporary rooms in the city center. The newly remodeled bathrooms have concrete and ceramic touches, though the air-fresheners can be a little overpowering. All in all, it's a strong top-end contender, but if you want a pool, you should look elsewhere.

Eating

The 700 *cuadra* of Pizarro is where Trujillo's power brokers hang out and families converge, and they're kept well fed by a row of trendy yet reasonably priced cafes and restaurants. Some of the best eateries in Trujillo are found a short taxi ride outside the town center.

Jugería San Augustín JUICE, SNACKS **$**
(Bolívar 526; juice S2-5, sandwiches S6-8; ⏲8:30am-1pm & 4-8pm Mon-Sat, 9am-1pm Sun) You can spot this place by the near-constant lines snaking around the corner in summer as locals queue for the drool-inducing juices. But don't leave it at that. The chicken and *lechón* (suckling pig) sandwiches, slathered with all the fixings, are what you'll be telling friends back home about on a postcard.

Chifa Heng Lung CHINESE **$**
(☎044-24-3351; Pizarro 352; mains S10.50-42.50, menús S7-9.50; ⏲to 11:30pm) Owned by a Chinese family of veteran chefs, this vaguely upscale, tasty option packs a wallop of flavorful infusion for Peruvinized palates. The menu is a predictable list of Cantonese dishes, but very long on options and flavors.

Café Bar Museo CAFE **$**
(cnr Junín & Independencia; mains S6-15, cocktails S18-22; ⏲closed Sun) This locals' favorite shouldn't be a secret. The tall, wood-paneled walls covered in artsy posters and the classic marble-top bar makes it feel like a cross between an English pub and a Left Bank cafe.

Supermercado Metro SELF-CATERING **$**
(Pizarro 700; ⏲9am-9pm daily) For self-caterers.

★**El Celler de Cler** PERUVIAN
(cnr Gamarra & Independencia; mains S24-48; ⏲6pm-1am) This atmospheric spot is the only place in Trujillo to enjoy dinner (coupled with an amazing cocktail) on a 2nd-floor

balcony; the wrap-around number dates to the early 1800s. The food is upscale, featuring pasta and grills, and delicious. Antiques fuel the decor, from a '50s-era American cash register to an extraordinary Industrial Revolution pulley lamp from the UK.

While the food and ambience are great, it's the creative cocktails that really shine, don't miss the classic *chilcano de pisco* (pisco, ginger ale and lime juice), souped up here with any number of twists (*rocoto, ají limo, maracuya* etc). Try to go after rush hour or on a weekend as, ambience notwithstanding, the streets below are noisy.

Mar Picante PERUVIAN **$$**
(www.marpicante.com; Húsares de Junín 412; mains S18-30; ⏲10am-5pm) If you come to Trujillo without sampling this bamboo-lined seafood palace's *ceviche mixto* ordered with a side of something spicy, you haven't lived life on the edge. You'll get raw fish, crab, scallops and onions, marinated as usual in lime juice, piled on top of yucca and sweet potato with a side of toasted corn *(canchas)* and corn on the cob.

This is the North Coast's best ceviche! Service is swift and friendly as well, no small feat considering it's always packed. Take a taxi (S3.50) or leg it southwest on Larco from the center. Húsares de Junín splits off to the southeast 200m south of España.

Casona Deza PERUVIAN **$$**
(Independencia 630; mains S22-35; 📶) 🍃 Expect excellent espresso, house-made desserts and tasty pizzas and sandwiches, often sourced organically, at this spacious, atmospheric cafe that occupies one of the city's most fiercely preserved colonial homes.

The Casa Ganoza Chopitea mansion (c 1735) was resurrected via auction by a local team of brothers passionate about Trujillo. Whether you're here for coffee, wine, sustenance or architectural oohing and aahing, it's an addictive spot.

Restaurant Demarco PERUVIAN **$$**
(☎044-23-4251; Pizarro 725; mains S10-45; ⏲7:30am-11pm; 📶) An elegant choice with veteran cummerbund-bound waiters who fawn over you like in the '40s, this tableclothed classic offers a long list of sophisticated meat and seafood dishes along with good-value lunch specials (S14.50) and pizzas.

They have mouthwatering *chupe de camarones*, a seafood stew of jumbo shrimp simmering in a buttery broth with hints of garlic, cumin and oregano, and the desserts are excellent, from classic tiramisu to mile-high *tres leches* (a spongy cake made with evaporated milk).

Oviedo BREAKFAST, CAFE **$$**
(Pizarro 758; mains S19-28; ⏲8am-midnight) If you're sick of the tiny plate of eggs your hotel is throwing at you in the morning, check out Oviedo's long list of breakfasts – from a simple continental to a hearty *criollo* (spicy Peruvian fare with Spanish and African influences) that comes with a pork chop.

Drinking & Nightlife

Runa's LIVE MUSIC
(Independencia 610; cover S15) This cool colonial bar has an outside patio and live music on weekends. The airy feel is a nice break from the cachophonous discos nearby. The cover charge generally includes a drink.

Picasso Lounge CAFE, BAR
(Bolívar 762) This shotgun-style cafe and bar approaches Trujillo's trendiness tipping point and is a great place to check out some contemporary local art. Exhibitions change every two months. When the bartender is on (Thursday to Saturday from 8pm), there's a well-rounded cocktail list with some creative pisco concoctions.

Entertainment

Trujillo's local newspaper **La Industria** (www.laindustria.com) is the best source for information about local entertainment, cultural exhibitions and other events.

Restaurante Turístico Canana LIVE MUSIC
(☎044-23-2503; San Martín 791; admission S20; ⏲from 11pm Thu-Sat) Although this place serves good Peruvian coastal food, late Thursday to Saturday is the time to go. Local musicians and dancers perform, starting at around 11pm, and you just might find yourself joining in. Better start drinking now.

Information

DANGERS & ANNOYANCES

Single women tend to receive a lot of attention from males in Trujillo – to exasperating, even harassing, levels. If untoward advances are made, firmly state that you aren't interested. Inventing a boyfriend or husband sometimes helps get the message across.

At night, it's advisable to take cabs. Ask your hotel or restaurant to find you a *taxi de confianza* (trustworthy cab – generally with a bubble on top). A good rule: if no women or kids are around, it's probably not safe to be walking about.

Like many other cities, the noise pollution levels in Trujillo are high. Civic groups have attempted to protest the constant bleating of taxi horns.

EMERGENCY

Policía de Turismo (044-29-1770; Independencia 572) Shockingly helpful. Tourist police wear white shirts around town and some deputies speak English, Italian and/or French.

IMMIGRATION

Oficina de Migraciónes (044-28-2217; www.migraciones.com.pe; Larco, cuadra 12; 8am-4:15pm Mon-Fri, 9am-1pm Sat) Handles visas for foreign residents and tourist visa extensions.

MEDICAL SERVICES

Clínica Peruano Americana (044-24-2400; Mansiche 802) The best general medical care in town, with English-speaking doctors. It charges according to your means, so let the clinic know if you don't have medical insurance.

MONEY

Changing money in Trujillo is a pleasure; some of the banks are housed in well-preserved colonial buildings and all have ATMs that accept Visa and MasterCard. If lines are long, visit the *casas de cambio* (foreign-exchange bureaus) near Gamarra and Bolívar, which give good rates for cash.

Banco Continental (Pizarro 620) Bank housed in the handsome Casa de la Emancipación.

BCP (Gamarra 562) Bank with ATM.

GNB (Gamarra 574) ATM and bank.

POST

Serpost (Independencia 286) Postal services.

TOURIST INFORMATION

Local tour companies can also provide you with some basic information on the area.

iPerú (044-29-4561; www.peru.travel; Independencia 467, oficina 106; 9am-6pm Mon-Sat, to 2pm Sun) Provides tourist information and a list of certified guides and travel agencies.

Getting There & Away

AIR

The airport (TRU) is 10km northwest of town. **LAN** (044-22-1469; www.lan.com; Pizarro 340) has three daily flights between Lima and Trujillo. On average, fares range from S343 to S486. **Avianca** (0-800-1-8222; www.avianca.com; Real Plaza, César Vallejo Oeste 1345) flies the same route twice per day for as low as S150.

BUS

Buses often leave Trujillo full, so booking a little earlier is advised. Several companies that go to southern destinations have terminals on the Panamericana Sur, the southern extension of Moche, and Ejército; check where your bus actually leaves from when buying a ticket.

Línea has services to most destinations of interest to travelers and is one of the more comfortable bus lines.

There's an enclave of bus companies around España and Amazonas offering Lima-bound night buses (eight hours).

If you want to travel to Huaraz by day, you'll need to go to Chimbote and catch a bus from there. For more frequent buses to Cajamarca and the northern Highlands, head to Chiclayo.

For Otuzco, *combis* depart between the 17th and 18th *cuadras* of Prolongacíon Unión northeast of town. **Tours Pacifico** (044-42-7137; Prolongacíon Unión, cuadra 22) heads up the mountain six times per day in buses.

America Express (01-424-1352; www.americaexpress.com.pe; La Marina 315) A S5 taxi ride south of town, with buses to Chimbote every 20 minutes between 4am and 10:30pm.

Cial (044-20-1760; www.expresocial.com; Ejército & Amazonas 395) A 10pm bus to Lima.

Civa (01-418-1111; www.civa.com.pe; Ejército 285) A 10pm bus to Lima.

Cruz del Sur (0-801-11111; www.cruzdelsur.com.pe; Amazonas 437) One of the biggest and priciest bus companies in Peru. It goes to Lima five times a day and Guayaquil at 11:45pm on Sunday, Wednesday and Friday. They also have a booking office (Gamarra 439; 9am-9pm Mon-Sat) in the centre.

El Dorado (044-29-1778; Nicolás de Piérola 1070) Has rudimentary buses to Piura five times daily (12:30pm, 8pm, 8:30pm, 10:20pm, 11pm) and four to Máncora and Tumbes (12:30pm, 8pm, 8:30pm, 9pm).

Ittsa (044-25-1415; www.ittsabus.com; Mansiche 143) Has buses for Piura (9am, 1:30pm, 11:15pm, 11:30pm, 11:45pm), as well as 11 Lima-bound departures from 9am to 11:15pm.

Línea (044-29-7000; www.linea.pe) The company's booking office (044-24-5181; cnr San Martín & Obregoso; 8am-9pm Mon-Sat) is conveniently located in the historical center, although all buses leave from the terminal (044-29-9666; Panamerica Sur 2855), a S5 taxi ride away.

Línea goes to Lima nine times daily between 8:30am and 10:45pm; to Piura at 1:30pm and 11pm; to Cajamarca at 10:30am, 1pm, 10pm and 10:30pm; to Chiclayo six times between 6am and 7pm, stopping at Pacasmayo and Guadalupe; to Chimbote four times a day (5:30am, 11am, 2pm and 7pm); and to Huaraz at 9pm and 9:15pm.

Móvil Tours (01-716-8000; www.moviltours.com.pe; Panamerica Sur 3955) Specializes in very comfortable long-haul tourist services. It has a 10pm service to Lima; 10am, 9:40pm and 10:20pm departures to Huaraz, the first two continuing on to Caraz; a bus at 4:45pm to Chachapoyas; and a 3pm bus to Tarapoto.

A taxi to the station is S5 or catch a red-signed A *combi* (California/Esperanza) on Av España and hop off at Ovalo Larco.

Oltursa (☎ 01-708-5000; www.oltursa.pe; Ejército 342) Offers three daily departures at noon, 10pm and 11pm. Oltursa shares an authorized booking agency with Ittsa on Plaza de Armas, but this office sometimes charges commissions.

Ormeño (☎ 044-25-9782; Ejército 233) Has two night buses to Lima leaving at 7pm and 10pm, as well as one night bus (9pm) to Máncora and Tumbes, continuing on to Guayaquil, on the Ecuadorean coast. Additionally, they have a Monday and Friday departure (10pm) to Quito, continuing on to Bogotá in Colombia.

Transportes Horna (☎ 044-25-7605; America Sur 1368) Has seven daily departures to Huamachuco and three buses to Cajamarca (1:30pm, 8pm and 11:30pm).

Turismo Días (☎ 044-20-1237; www.turdias.com; N de Piérola 1079) Opposite El Dorado, has four departures to Cajamarca (10am, 1:15pm, 10:30pm and 11pm) and two to Cajabamba (8pm and 9pm).

AROUND TRUJILLO

Green-signed B *combis* to Huaca Esmeralda (S1), Chan Chan (S1) and Huanchaco (S1.50) pass the corners of España and Ejército, and España and Industrial every few minutes. Buses for La Esperanza go northwest along the Carretera Panamericana and can drop you off at Huaca Arco Iris.

For Huacas del Sol y de la Luna, take a taxi (S4) to the Primax gas station at Ovalo Grau southeast of the centre, where *combis* (S1.50) pass every 15 minutes or so. Note that these buses are worked by professional thieves; keep valuables hidden and watch your bags carefully. A taxi to most of these sites will cost S10 to S15.

El Complejo Arqueológico la Huaca el Brujo, about 60km northwest of Trujillo, is harder to reach. The safest route is catching a bus in Trujillo, bound for Chocope (S3.50, 1½ hours) from Ovalo del Papa southwest of town. Switch for a *colectivo* to Magdalena de Cao (S2.50, 20 minutes), where you'll need to negotiate with a *mototaxi* to take you to and from the site with waiting time (S5 each way plus something for waiting is about right; few tourists visit this site so options are slim – do not bank on randomly grabbing something after your visit). There are also Chocope-bound buses from the Provincial Bus Terminal Interurbano southeast of central Trujillo, but this neighborhood is best avoided by tourists.

Trujillo Buses:

DESTINATION	COST (S)	DURATION (HR)
Bogotá	495	56
Cajabamba	25-35	12
Cajamarca	16-135	6-7
Caraz	50-65	8
Chachapoyas	65-85	15
Chiclayo	20-45	3-4
Chimbote	10-65	2
Guayaquil (Ec)	138-201	18
Huaraz	45-65	5-9
Lima	30-110	8-9
Máncora	30-70	8-9
Otuzco	6-10	2
Piura	25-45	6
Quito (Ec)	234	32
Tarapoto	95-115	18
Tumbes	39-100	9-12

Getting Around

The **airport** is 10km northwest of Trujillo and reached cheaply on the Huanchaco *combi*, though you'll have to walk the last kilometer. It takes around 30 minutes. A taxi from the city center costs S15.

A short taxi ride around town costs about S3.50. For sightseeing, taxis charge about S20 (in town) to S25 (out of town) per hour.

Around Trujillo

The Moche and Chimú cultures left the greatest marks on the Trujillo area, but they were by no means the only cultures in the region. In a March 1973 *National Geographic* article, Drs ME Moseley and CJ Mackey claimed knowledge of more than 2000 sites in the Río Moche valley and many more have been discovered since.

Five major archaeological sites can be easily reached from Trujillo by local bus or taxi. Two of these are principally Moche, dating from about 200 BC to AD 850. The other three, from the Chimú culture, date from about AD 850 to 1500. The recently excavated Moche ruin of Huaca el Brujo (p328) can also be visited, but it's not as convenient.

Joining a tour to the archaeological sites isn't a bad idea, even for budget travelers. The ruins will be more interesting and meaningful with a good guide. Alternately, you could hire an on-site guide.

Around Trujillo

The entrance ticket for Chan Chan is also valid for the Chimú sites of Huaca Esmeralda and Huaca Arco Iris, as well as the Chan Chan museum, but it must be used within two days. All sites are open from 9am to 4pm and tickets are sold at every site, except Huaca Esmeralda.

Sights

Chan Chan RUIN
(admission S10, guide per person S15, minimum 3 people; 9am-4pm, museum closed Mon) Built around AD 1300 and covering 20 sq km, Chan Chan is the largest pre-Columbian city in the Americas, and the largest adobe city in the world. Although it must have been a dazzling sight at one time, devastating El Niño floods and heavy rainfall have severely eroded much of the outer portions of the city. You can still visit the impressive restored Tschudi complex and revel in the broad plazas, royal burial chamber and intricate designs that remain.

The best option for a visit is with an organized guided tour from Trujillo or with a local site tour guide, as signage is extremely limited. Much of the site is covered with tent-like structures to protect from erosion.

At the height of the Chimú empire, Chan Chan housed an estimated 60,000 inhabitants and contained a vast wealth of gold, silver and ceramics. The wealth remained more or less undisturbed after the Incas conquered the city, but once the Spaniards hit the stage, the looting began. Within a few decades, little but gold dust remained. Remnants of what was found can be seen in museums nearby.

The Chimú capital consisted of 10 walled citadels, also called royal compounds. Each contained a royal burial mound filled with vast quantities of funerary offerings, including dozens of sacrificed young women and chambers full of ceramics, weavings and jewelry. The **Tschudi Complex**, named after a Swiss naturalist, is the only section of Chan Chan that's partially restored. It is possible that other areas will open in the future, but until they are properly policed and signed, you run the risk of being mugged if you visit them.

At the Tschudi Complex you'll find an entrance area with tickets, snacks, souvenirs, bathrooms, the small **Museo de Sitio Chan Chan** (incl with Chan Chan ticket) with information in English and Spanish, and guides. The complex is well marked by fish-shaped pointers, so you can see everything without a guide if you prefer.

Also called the **Palacio Nik-An**, the complex's centerpiece is a massive, restored Ceremonial Courtyard, whose 4m-thick interior walls are mostly decorated with recreated geometric designs. The ground-level designs closest to the door, representing three or four sea otters, are the only originals left and remarkably better preserved than many of the recreations. A ramp at the far side of the high-walled plaza enters the 2nd level (early wheelchair access?). Though all the Chan Chan walls have crumbled with time, parts of Tschudi's walls once stood more than 10m high.

Head out of the **Ceremonial Courtyard** and walk along the outside wall, one of the most highly decorated and best restored

PRE-COLUMBIAN PEOPLES OF THE NORTH COAST

Northern Peru has played host to a series of civilizations stretching as far back as 5000 years. Listed below are the major cultures that waxed and waned in Peru's coastal desert.

Huaca Prieta

One of first peoples on the desert scene, the **Huaca Prieta** (p329) lived at the site of the same name from around 3500 BC to 2300 BC. Though primarily hunters and gatherers, they also grew cotton and varieties of beans and peppers, and subsisted mainly on seafood. They were pre-ceramic people who had developed netting and weaving, but didn't use jewelry. At their most artistic, they decorated dried gourds with simple carvings. Homes were single-room shacks half buried in the ground; most of what is known about these people has been deduced from their middens (dumps that still show evidence of shells, bones, excrement and other artifacts that help archeaologists piece the puzzle together).

Chavín

Based around Huaraz in Peru's central Andes, the Chavín also had a significant cultural and artistic influence on coastal Peru, particularly between the years 800 BC and 400 BC.

Moche

Evolving from around AD 100 to AD 800, the Moche created ceramics, textiles and metalwork, developed the architectural skills to construct massive pyramids and still had enough time for art and a highly organized religion.

Among all their expert productions, it's the ceramics that earn the Moche a ranking in Peru's pre-Inca civilization hall of fame. Considered the most artistically sensitive and technically developed of any ceramics found in Peru, Moche pots are realistically decorated with figures and scenes that leave us with a very descriptive look at everyday life. Pots were modeled into lifelike representations of people, crops, domestic and wild animals, marine life and monumental architecture. Other pots were painted with scenes of ceremonial activities and everyday objects.

Some facets of Moche life illustrated on pots include punishments, surgical procedures (such as amputation and the setting of broken limbs) and copulation. One room in Lima's Museo Larco is devoted to pots depicting a cornucopia of sexual practices, some the products of very fertile imaginations. **Museo Cassinelli** (p319) in Trujillo also has a fine collection. A few kilometers south of Trujillo, there are two main Moche sites: **Huaca del Sol** and **Huaca de la Luna** (p328).

The Moche period declined around AD 700, and the next few centuries are somewhat confusing. The Wari culture, based in the Ayacucho area of the central Peruvian Andes, began to expand after this time, and its influence was reflected in both the Sicán and Chimú cultures.

of Tschudi's walls. The adobe friezes show waves of fish rippling along the entire length of the wall above a line of seabirds. Despite their time-worn appearance, the few rougher-looking originals retain a fluidity and character somehow lacking in the contemporary version.

At the end of this wall, the marked path goes through the labyrinthine **Audience Rooms**. Their function is unclear, but their importance is evident in both the quantity and quality of the decorations – the rooms have the most interesting friezes in Tschudi. Living so close to the ocean, the Chimú based much of their diet on seafood, and the importance of the sea reached venerable proportions. Fish, waves, seabirds and sea mammals are represented throughout the city, and in the Audience Rooms you'll find all of them in the one place. For the Chimú, both the moon and the sea were of religious importance (unlike the Incas, who worshipped the sun and venerated the earth).

Further on, the **Second Ceremonial Courtyard** also has a ramp to the 2nd level. West of this Plaza, you visit the **Gran Hachaque Ceremonial**, a freshwater pool surrounded by a verdant border of reeds and grasses. This was no doubt an important space for ceremonial life.

To the left is an area of several dozen small, crumbling cells that has been called the **Almacenes** (warehouses). Perhaps soldiers lived here, or the cells may have been used for storage. Next is the **Mausoleum**, where a king was buried along with human

Sicán

The Sicán were probably descendants of the Moche and flourished in the same region from about AD 750 to 1375. Avid agriculturalists, the Sicán were also infatuated with metallurgy and all that glitters. The Sicán are known to many archaeologists for their lost-wax (mold-cast) gold ornaments and the manufacture of arsenical copper, which is the closest material to bronze found in pre-Columbian New World archaeology. These great smiths produced alloys of gold, silver and arsenic copper in vast quantities, using little more than hearths fired by *algarrobo* (carob tree) wood and pipe-blown air to achieve the incredible 1000°C temperatures needed for such work.

Artifacts found at Sicán archaeological sites suggest that this culture loved to shop, or at least trade. They were actively engaged in long-distance trade with peoples along the length and breadth of the continent, acquiring shells and snails from Ecuador, emeralds and diamonds from Colombia, bluestone from Chile and gold from the Peruvian highlands.

With a structured and religiously controlled social organization, the Sicán engaged in bizarre and elaborate funerary practices, examples of which can be seen at the Museo Nacional Sicán in Ferreñafe.

Unfortunately, as was the case with many pre-Inca societies, the weather was the ultimate undoing of the Sicán. Originally building their main city at Batán Grande, northeast of Trujillo, they were forced to move to Túcume when rains devastated the area in the 13th century.

Chimú

The Chimú were contemporaries of the Sicán and were active from about AD 850 to 1470. They were responsible for the huge capital at **Chan Chan** (p325), just north of Trujillo. The artwork of the Chimú was less exciting than that of the Moche, tending more to functional mass production than artistic achievement. Gone, for the most part, was the technique of painting pots. Instead, they were fired by a simpler method than that used by the Moche, producing the typical blackware seen in many Chimú pottery collections. While the quality of the ceramics declined, skills in metallurgy developed, with gold and various alloys being worked.

The Chimú are best remembered as an urban society. Their huge capital contained about 10,000 dwellings of varying quality and importance. Buildings were decorated with friezes, the designs molded into mud walls, and important areas were layered with precious metals. There were storage bins for food and other products from across the kingdom, which stretched along the coast from Chancay to the Gulf of Guayaquil (southern Ecuador). There were huge walk-in wells, canals, workshops and temples. The royal dead were buried in mounds with a wealth of offerings. The Chimú were conquered by the Incas in 1471 and heavy rainfall has severely damaged the adobe moldings of this once vast metropolis.

sacrifices and ceremonial objects. To the left of the main tomb, a pyramid containing the bodies of dozens of young women was found.

The final area is the **Assembly Room**. This large rectangular room has 24 seats set into niches in the walls, and its amazing acoustic properties are such that speakers sitting in any one of the niches can be clearly heard all over the room.

The **site museum** contains exhibits explaining Chan Chan and the Chimú culture. It is on the main road, about 500m before the Chan Chan turnoff. The museum has a few signs in Spanish and English but a guide is still useful. A sound-and-light show plays in Spanish every 30 minutes. The aerial photos and maps showing the huge extension of Chan Chan are fascinating, as tourists can only visit a tiny portion of the site.

Combis to Chan Chan (S1.50) leave Trujillo every few minutes, passing the corners of España and Ejército, and España and Industrial. A taxi from Trujillo runs S10.

Huaca Esmeralda RUIN

(incl with Chan Chan ticket) Halfway between Trujillo and Chan Chan, this Chimú temple is to the south of the main road, four blocks behind the Mansiche Church. Thieves reportedly prey on unwary tourists wandering around, so go with a large group or a guide and keep your eyes open.

Huaca Esmeralda was buried by sand and was accidentally discovered by a local landowner in 1923. He attempted to uncover the ruins, but El Niño of 1925 began the process of erosion, which was exacerbated by the floods and rains of 1983. Although little restoration work has been done on the adobe friezes, it is still possible to make out the characteristic Chimú designs of fish, seabirds, waves and fishing nets.

Green-signed B *combis* to La Huaca Esmeralda leave Trujillo every few minutes; they pass the corners of España and Ejército, and España and Industrial.

Huaca Arco Iris RUIN

(Rainbow Temple; incl with Chan Chan ticket) Also known locally as Huaca del Dragón, Huaca Arco Iris is in the suburb of La Esperanza, about 4km northwest of Trujillo. Dating from the 12th century, it is one of the best preserved of the Chimú temples – simply because it was buried under sand until the 1960s. Its location was known to a handful of archaeologists and *huaqueros* (grave robbers), but excavation did not begin until 1963. Unfortunately, the 1983 El Niño caused damage to the friezes.

The *huaca* (tomb) used to be painted, but these days only faint traces of yellow hues remain. It consists of a defensive wall more than 2m thick enclosing an area of about 3000 sq meters, which houses the temple itself. The building covers about 800 sq meters in two levels, with a combined height of about 7.5m. The walls are slightly pyramidal and covered with repeated rainbow designs, most of which have been restored. Ramps lead the visitor to the very top of the temple, from where a series of large bins, found to contain the bones of infants – possibly human sacrifices – can be seen. This may have been a fertility temple since in many ancient cultures the rainbow represents rain, considered to be the bringer of life.

There is a tiny on-site **museum**, and local guides are available to show you around.

Buses for La Esperanza go northwest along the Carretera Panamericana and can drop you off at Huaca Arco Iris.

Huacas del Sol y de la Luna RUIN

(www.huacasdemoche.pe; site admission S10, museum $5; ⌚9am-4pm) The Temples of the Sun and the Moon are more than 700 years older than Chan Chan and are attributed to the Moche period. They are on the south bank of the Río Moche, about 10km southeast of Trujillo. The entrance price includes a guide. The Huaca del Sol is not currently open to visitation as research continues on the site.

Huaca del Sol is the largest single pre-Columbian structure in Peru, although about a third of it has been washed away. The structure was built with an estimated 140 million adobe bricks, many of them marked with symbols representing the workers who made them.

At one time the pyramid consisted of several different levels connected by steep flights of stairs, huge ramps and walls sloping at 77 degrees. The last 1500 years have wrought their inevitable damage, and today the pyramid looks like a giant pile of crude bricks partially covered with sand. The few graves within the structure suggest it may have been a huge ceremonial site. Certainly, its size alone makes the pyramid an awesome sight.

Size isn't everything, however. The smaller but more interesting **Huaca de la Luna** is about 500m away across the open desert. This structure is riddled with rooms that contain ceramics, precious metals and some of the beautiful polychrome friezes for which the Moche were famous. The *huaca* (tomb or grave) was built over six centuries to AD 600, with six succeeding generations expanding on it and completely covering the previous structure.

Archaeologists are currently onion-skinning selected parts of the *huaca* and have discovered that there are friezes of stylized figures on every level, some of which have been perfectly preserved by the later levels built around them. It's well worth a visit; you'll see newly excavated friezes every year, and the excellent **Museo Huacas de Moche** (admission S3; ⌚9am-4:30pm) is a long-time-coming permanent home for numerous objects excavated from the site. There's a research center and theater as well.

As you leave, check out the souvenir stands, some of which sell pots made using the original molds found at the site. Also look around for *biringos*, the native Peruvian hairless dogs that hang out here. Their body temperature is higher than the normal dog and they have traditionally been used as body warmers for people with arthritis.

Combis for the Huacas del Sol y de la Luna pass Ovalo Grau in Trujillo every 15 minutes or so. It's also possible to take a taxi (S15).

Complejo Arqueológico la Huaca del Brujo

This **archaeological complex** (admission S10; ⌚9am-4pm), 60km from Trujillo, consists of the Huaca Prieta site, the recently excavated Moche site of Huaca Cao Viejo with its brilliant mural reliefs, and Huaca el Brujo, which is only starting to be excavated. The complex is on the coast and is hard to find without a guide. It's technically not open to the public as there is little to see so far, but tour agencies in Trujillo can arrange a visit to the area on request.

Reaching the complex on your own is complicated. The safest route is catching a bus in Trujillo bound for Chocope (S3.50, 1½ hours) from Ovalo del Papa southwest of town. Switch for a *colectivo* to Magdalena de Cao (S2.50, 20 minutes), where you'll need to negotiate with a *mototaxi* to take you to and from the site with waiting time. There is very little public transport out this way.

Huaca Cao Viejo RUIN

FREE The main section of Huaca Cao Viejo is a 27m truncated pyramid with some of the best friezes in the area. They show magnificently multicolored reliefs – much more color than you see at the *huacas* closer to Chiclayo – with stylized life-sized warriors, prisoners, priests and human sacrifices.

There are also many burial sites from the Lambayeque culture, which followed the Moche. The people who live near this *huaca* insist that it has positive energy and ceremonies are occasionally performed here when someone needs to soak up a bit of the good vibes.

Huaca Prieta RUIN

Huaca Prieta has been one of the most intensively studied early Peruvian sites. However, for nonarchaeologists, it's generally more interesting to read about than to tour. Although it's simply a prehistoric pile of refuse, it does afford extensive vistas over the coastal area and can be visited along with the other *huacas* in the archaeological complex.

Huanchaco

044 / POP 41,800

This once-tranquil fishing hamlet, 12km outside Trujillo, woke up one morning to find itself a brightly highlighted paragraph on Peru's Gringo Trail. The village's fame came in large part from the long, narrow reed boats you'll see lining the *malecón*. A small number of local fishermen still use these age-old crafts today, and you may even sight some surfing in with the day's catch. Though you can almost picture Huanchaco on postcards of days gone by, the beach is distinctly average. Nevertheless, the slow pace of life attracts a certain type of beach bum and the town has managed to retain much of its villagey appeal. Today, Huanchaco is happy to dish up a long menu of accommodations and dining options to tourists and great waves for budding surfers. Come summertime, legions of local and foreign tourists descend on its lapping shores, and this fast-growing resort town makes a great alternative base for exploring the ruins surrounding Trujillo.

Sights

The curving, gray-sand beach here is fine for swimming during the December to April summer, but expect serious teeth chatter during the rest of the year. The good surf, perfect for beginners, draws its fair share of followers and you'll see armies of bleached-blond surfer types ambling the streets with

A DYING ART – CABALLITOS DE TOTORA

Huanchaco's defining characteristic is that a small number of local fisherfolk are still using the very same narrow reed boats depicted on 2000-year-old Moche pottery. The fishermen paddle and surf these neatly crafted boats like seafaring cowboys, with their legs dangling on either side – which explains the nickname given to these elegantly curving steeds, *caballitos de tortora* (little horses). The inhabitants of Huanchaco are among the few remaining people on the coast who remember how to construct and use the boats, each one only lasting a few months before becoming waterlogged. The fishermen paddle out as far as a mile, but can only bring in limited catches because of the size of their vessels (which now also integrate styrofoam for bouyancy).

The days of Huanchaco's reed-boat fisherfolk is likely numbered. Recent reports say that erosion and other environmental factors are affecting the beds where the fisherfolk plant and harvest the reeds, and many youngsters are opting to become surf instructors, professionals or commercial fishers rather than following in their parents' hard-paddled wake.

boards in hand. Expect decent waves year-round. The beach break starts about 800m south of the pier – with a rock and sand bottom. It rarely connects for longer rides, but you can get plenty of fun lefts and shortish rights anywhere on the beach.

There is a S0.50 charge between 10:30am and 6:30pm to enter the town pier, a picturesque sight with a gazebo at its terminus.

Santuario de la Virgen del Socorro CHURCH
(9am-12:30pm & 4-7pm) FREE This church above town is worth a visit. Built between 1535 and 1540, it is said to be the second-oldest church in Peru. There are sweeping views from the restored belfry.

Activities

You can rent surfing gear (S30 per day for a wetsuit and surfboard) from several places along the main drag. Lessons cost about S50 for an 1½- to two-hour session. Check at Otra Cosa for local volunteering opportunities.

Muchik Surf School SURFING
(044-63-3487; www.escueladetablamuchik.com; Av Victor Larco 650) Huanchaco's longest-running surf school is said to be the most reliable.

Un Lugar SURFING
(94-957-7170; www.unlugarsurfschoolperu.com; Atahualpa 225) Two blocks back from the main beach road. This rustic surf school/guesthouse is run by highly skilled Juan Carlos and provides private two-hour lessons. It also rents boards and suits, and organizes surfing safaris to Puerto Chicama and other iconic Peruvian surf spots. Bare-bones bamboo treehouse-style rooms are also available for S15 per person.

Wave SURFING
(044-58-7005; Larco 850) Surf school that rents surfing gear.

SKIP VOLUNTEERING
(www.skipperu.org) Supporting Kids in Peru (SKIP) is a nonprofit organization that works with economically disadvantaged children in El Porvenir. Accommodation is included in the volunteer fee, which runs about US$540 a month.

Otra Cosa VOLUNTEERING
(044-46-1302; www.otracosa.org; Las Camelias 431) Started by the folks at the Otra Cosa restaurant, this nonprofit is now run by a UK outfit. They do education, music and sport outreaches in the neighboring communities. Volunteering costs around US$300 per month with accommodation options.

Festivals & Events

Carnaval FESTIVAL, RELIGIOUS
(Feb/Mar) A big event in Huanchaco.

Festival del Mar CULTURAL
This festival re-enacts the legendary arrival of Takaynamo, founder of Chan Chan. Expect surfing and dance competitions, cultural conferences, food, music and much merrymaking. Held every other year (even-numbered years) during the first week in May.

Sleeping

Most guesthouses are located in the southern end of town in the small streets running perpendicular to the beach. You can get discounts of up to 50% outside festival and holiday times, so be sure to ask.

★**Naylamp** GUESTHOUSE $
(044-46-1022; www.hostalnaylamp.com; Larco 1420; camping S15-18, dm/s/d S20/40/60; @) At the northern end of Huanchaco, and top of the pops in the budget stakes, Naylamp has one building on the waterfront and a second, larger building behind the hotel. Great budget rooms share a spacious sea-view patio, and the lush camping area has perfect sunset views. Kitchen, laundry service, hammocking zone and a cafe are all thrown in. The beds have mosquito nets so you can leave your windows open at night. Ask for a room up top to catch cooling ocean breezes.

Surf Hostal Meri HOSTEL $
(044-53-8675; www.surfhostelmeri.com; La Rivera 720; dm/s/d S20/30/50; @) Full of tattered antique furniture, this rustic place across the street from the beach is vaguely hippie-esque with a good communal hostel surf-til-you-turn-gray vibe. This doubles as a surf school, and there are ample public spaces to hang out, including a couple of great hammocks and sun-drenched sea-view decks. The restaurant serves a broad mix of international favorites. Extend your stay with volunteer opportunities.

Hostal Huanchaco HOTEL $
(044-46-1272; www.huanchacohostal.com; Plaza de Armas; s/d S65/120; P) On the town's small Plaza de Armas, this cozy little place

has spartan rooms and a handsome backyard concealing a secluded pool and garden. There are plenty of arty touches to make it feel homey, and it has a decidedly family-friendly air.

Hospedaje My Friend HOSTEL $
(044-46-1080; www.myfriendsurfhostal.com; Los Pinos 158; dm/d S15/30;) This hole-in-the-wall attracts droves of backpackers and surfers with only a few *nuevo soles* left in their pockets. The little cafe downstairs serves breakfast, there's a peaced-out upstairs terrace, and you can arrange surf lessons here too. The dorms have five beds, and you get electricity-heated showers, lockers and plenty of hot-and-tanned travelers to hang out with.

Hospedaje Oceano GUESTHOUSE $
(044-46-1653; www.hospedajeoceano1.com; Los Cerezes 105; r per person S15;) Ideally located between one of the town's most lush and pleasant *plazoletas* and the ocean, this superbly welcoming family-run spot will have you feeling like kin within minutes of arrival. From the outside, it's indistinguishable from any number of dismissible Peruvian guesthouses, but the great Mediterranean-inspired rooms offer a pleasant surprise upon popping your bags down.

Best of all? The family makes addictive homemade *cremoladas* (Italian ices; S2), which are listed on the daily-changing menu complete with their requisite health benefits (cappuccino and coconut are extraordinary).

La Casa Suiza HOSTEL $
(044-63-9713; www.lacasasuiza.com; Los Pinos 308; dm/s/d S25/35/85;) The Swiss House's spacious and sparkling rooms have Peru-themed, airbrushed murals. The little cafe downstairs prepares crunchy-crust pizzas, and the patio upstairs hosts a nice view and the occasional barbecue. It's less of a surfer hangout than the other budget spots in town, but retains a cool vibe nevertheless.

McCallum Lodging House GUESTHOUSE $
(044-46-2350; mccallumlodginghouse.wordpress.com; Los Ficos 305; dm/s/d/tr S15/25/45/60;) This family-run guesthouse levels the playing field of its crude construction with friendliness and camaraderie – travelers gather around the nice communal kitchen and hammock-strewn concrete garden and discuss the day's waves. Rooms are basic but clean with 24-hour hot water.

Hotel Caballito de Totora BOUTIQUE HOTEL $$
(044-46-2636; www.hotelcaballitodetotora.com.pe; La Rivera 348; s/d/tr incl breakfast S145/205/290;) Although regular rooms can be a little stuffy, the suites here are the best single rooms in Huanchaco, decked in modern motifs that wouldn't be out of place in Miami. They offer perfect sea views, wide, circular tubs and private patios to boot. A cozy bar adds to the ambience. It's the one hotel in Huanchaco that feels truly boutique.

Hotel Bracamonte HOTEL $$
(044-46-1162; www.hotelbracamonte.com.pe; Los Olivos 160; s/d incl breakfast from S148/171;) Popular, friendly, welcoming and secure behind high walls and a locked gate, the Bracamonte is one of the oldest of Huanchaco's nicer hotels and it remains one of the top choices. Nice gardens, a games room, barbecue, restaurant, bar and toddlers' playground make it great for families; the executive rooms are probably the best maintained in Huanchaco.

Ask for a higher room to catch ocean breezes. It's located at the entrance to town by the river bed. Overall, it's the most equipped and near resort-like choice.

Eating

Not surprisingly, Huanchaco has oodles of seafood restaurants, especially near the *caballitos de tortora* stacked at the north end of the beach. Entertainment is of the reggae and beer variety. On weekends, *trujillanos* descend on the town and things are a little more lively.

Otra Cosa VEGETARIAN $
(Larco 921; dishes S6-13; from 8am;) This Dutch-Peruvian beachside pad is Huanchaco's requisite travelers' hub, serving up yummy vegetarian victuals like falafel, crepes, Spanish tortillas, Dutch apple pie and tasty curry-laced burritos (one of which is *almost* a breakfast burrito). Coffee is organic as well. The restaurant has a great record for giving back to the community.

★**Restaurant Big Ben** PERUVIAN $$
(044-46-1378; www.bigbenhuanchaco.com; Larco 836; mains S17-40; 11:30am-5:30pm;) This sophisticated seafooder at the far north end of town specializes in lunchtime ceviches (S39 to S46) and is the best in town for top-notch seafood. Though ceviche is the main draw, the menu is also heavy on fresh

fish, *sudados* (seafood stews) and prawn dishes, all of which go down even better on the 3rd-floor patio with ocean views.

Restaurante Mococho PERUVIAN, SEAFOOD **$$**
(www.facebook.com/restaurantemococho; Bolognesi 535; menú S45; ⏲1-3pm, closed Mon) This tiny place sits secluded in a walled garden where the legend of chef Don Victor is carried on by his widow and son, Wen. It's not cheap, but it's fresh and excellent, despite the Halls served as an after-meal mint.

Local fisherman knock on the door here every morning shouting, 'Hey Chinese! The catch of the day is ...' and Wen, the only Chinese-Peruvian restaurateur in town, serves up just two dishes with whatever's fresh that day: a ceviche appetizer and a steamed whole fish (filets for solo diners) in a sharply colored, wildly flavorful *criollo* sauce.

El Caribe PERUVIAN **$$**
(Athualpa 150; mains S20-25; ⏲10am-5pm) This is a local favorite for the reasonably priced seafood and *comida criolla* (local cuisine). Ceviche here is half the price of the expensive options and double the price of the cheapies, but do you really want to eat raw fish for under S10? Their grouper *(mero)* ceviche was featured in *Saveur* magazine.

 Drinking & Entertainment

Jungle Bar Bily BAR, SEAFOOD
(Larco 420; cocktails S12-18; ⏲closed Mon; 📶) Travelers gravitate to this quasi-Polynesian-themed bar due to location (across from the pier), good music (U2, R.E.M.) and a popular S15 ceviche, among other good-value seafood. Happy hour (6pm to 10pm) nets a 50% discount on selected cocktails.

ℹ Information

Most services are in Trujillo, a short ride away. There's a **Post Office** (Manco Cápac 220; ⏲9am-7pm Mon-Fri, to 1pm Sat) a block back from the pier, and next to the *municipalidad* (town hall) are three ATMs that accept MasterCard and Visa cards. Be careful walking the streets late at night, as robberies are not uncommon.

ℹ Getting There & Away

Some bus companies (Línea and TRC Express) keep a ticket office in Huanchaco, but buses depart from Trujillo. *Combis* to Huanchaco frequently leave from Trujillo (S1.50). To return, just wait on the beachfront road for the bus as it returns from the north end. A taxi to or from Trujillo should cost S12.

Puerto Chicama (Puerto Malabrigo)

☎044

The small fishing outpost of Puerto Chicama might not look like much, but it's the offshore action that draws a dedicated following. Puerto Chicama, also known as Puerto Malabrigo, lays claim to one of the longest left-hand point breaks in the world. Originally a busy port for the sugar and cotton grown on nearby haciendas, Puerto Chicama now draws adrenaline-seeking surfers who try their luck catching that rare, long ride. Peru's national surfing championships are usually held here in April.

The lengthy left break is caused by a shallow, flat beach, and on the right wave on the right day at the right time, it's possible to hitch a 3.2km ride here on a 2m wave! Good waves can be found year-round, but the marathon breaks only come about when the conditions are just so, usually between March and June. The water is very cold for much of the year, except for December through March. You can rent boards at Los Delfines for S25 per half-day.

🛏 Sleeping & Eating

All the hotels are located south of the *muelle* (pier) on the high-outcrop overlooking the beach.

Surf House Chicama BUNGALOW **$**
(☎044-57-6138; r per person S40-45; 📶) Formerly known as El Inti, this spot has a sea-view terrace restaurant and plenty of surfer brahs. There are a few garden bamboo bungalows here and an outstanding 2nd-floor suite that outclasses the town with amazing sea views from the deep Jacuzzi tub.

El Hombre HOTEL **$**
(☎044-57-6077; www.facebook.com/hotelelhombre; s/d S40/80, without bathroom S20/40) El Hombre is the original surfers' hostel and is run by the daughter of local legend 'El Hombre,' a surfer guru who's been at it for more than 40 years. Facing the ocean, the hostel has dead simple rooms, great communal bathrooms, wholesome meals (S10 to S14) and a communal TV often seen flickering with surf videos. There's a shared kitchen, and many rooms have ocean views.

Los Delfines de Chicama HOTEL $$
(☎044-34-3044; delfinesdechicama@gmail.com; d/tr/ste S180/275/370; P) This large surfer hotel has simple painted brick rooms that somehow feel more formal than their counterparts in the village. All rooms have private balconies. As the balcony doors do not lock, we recommend asking for a 2nd-floor option. There's a pool outback and a second-story restaurant with views out to sea.

Getting There & Away

Some surf shops in Huanchaco, including Un Lugar and The Wave, arrange surfing safaris to Puerto Chicama. The easiest independent route is catching an El Dorado bus to Puerto Malabrigo (S6, two hours). A faster route is a *colectivo* to the town of Paiján, 40km further north on the Carretera Panamericana (S7, 1½ hours). From here you can catch *colectivos* for the 16km to Puerto Chicama (S2, 20 minutes).

Pacasmayo

☎044 / POP 25,700

This lively, mostly forgotten beach town is crammed with colonial buildings in various states of disrepair and is blessed with a pretty stretch of beach and a throwback *malecón* (esplanade). Dedicated surfers often drop in, particularly from May to August, when there is a decent offshore break. It's also a great place to spend some time away from the more popular resort towns and get swept up in the aging nostalgia of the whole place.

Sights & Activities

Pacatnamú RUIN
A few kilometers north, just before the village of Guadalupe, a track leads toward the ocean and the little-visited ruins of Pacatnamú, a large site that was inhabited by the Gallinazo, Moche and Chimú cultures and is regarded by archaeologists as one of the coast's most impressive.

Muelle Pacasmayo PIER
(admission S1) What's said to be the longest pier in Peru has a storied history. Constructed between 1870 and 1874, it initially clocked in at a whopping 743.4m. Today, it stands at 544m after a chunk was swept out to sea in 1924. In the '40s, two overloaded train cars fell into the sea from the pier as well.

Balin Surf Shop SURFING
(Junín 84) Rents boards and does repairs.

Sleeping & Eating

There are several cheap, basic-but-clean hotels in town and some swisher converted colonial mansions and new constructions along the beach.

Hotel Pakatnamú HISTORIC HOTEL $$
(☎044-52-2368; www.actiweb.es/hotelpakatnamu; Malecón Grau 103; s/d/ste incl breakfast S100/130/250; @) This freshly painted bright yellow colonial building along the waterfront has more storied character than others, despite abrupt color changes from one hallway to the next. The plush rooms here come with TV and fridge – some even have built-in car tape decks (sorry no USB attachments). The furnishings are equally anachronistic. There's a cozy restaurant and the open-ended hallways spill out onto a wonderful sea-view terrace.

La Estación Gran Hotel HOTEL $$
(☎044-52-1515; www.hotellaestacion.com.pe; Malecón Grau 69; s/d/ste incl breakfast S110/160/200; @) The majestic, restored Republican-era facade doesn't carry over to the interiors, but there is a great rooftop terrace, small pool and ground-floor bar-restaurant (mains S20 to S30). The rooms are dated – not rundown, but dated (like John Travolta).

The restaurant is one of the best in town, try the fabulous *pescado a lo macho* (catch of the day topped with a creamy shellfish sauce with *ají* and garlic).

Hostal El Mirador HOTEL $$
(☎044-52-1883; www.pacasmayoperu.com; Aurelio Herrera 10; s/d/q from S60/120/210; P) All tiles, bricks and Brazilians, this surfers' hang-pad has good rooms varying from *económico* (basic) to *de lujo* (luxury); all have hot water, communal balconies and wall-mounted flat-screen TVs with international channels; the nicest rooms have kitchens and DVD players. It's located just one block inland below the Christ statue.

Information

There are **BCP** (Ayacucho 20), **BBVA** (Calle 2 de Mayo 9) and **Banco de la Nación** (Calle 8 de Julio & Lima) ATMs in town, though BCP is the most convenient on Plaza de Armas. Internet is ubiquitous.

Getting There & Away

Emtrafesa (www.emtrafesa.com.pe; 28 de Julio 104) has frequent buses to Trujillo (S8, 1¾ hours), Chiclayo (S9, 1¾ hours), Cajamarca (S20 to S30, 4½ hours, 2pm and 11:30pm) and points further north.

Chiclayo

074 / POP 553,200

Spanish missionaries founded a small rural community on this site in the 16th century. Either by chance or through help from above, Chiclayo has prospered ever since. In one of the first sharp moves in Peruvian real estate, the missionaries chose a spot that sits at the hub of vital trade routes connecting the coast, the highlands and the deep jungle. Chiclayo's role as the commercial heart of the district has allowed it to overtake other once-vital organs of the region, such as the nearby city of Lambayeque, and this bustling metropolis shows few signs of slowing down.

La Ciudad de la Amistad (the City of Friendship) holds a friendly, outstretched hand to the wayward venturer. While it's shaking hands hello, it will probably slip in a bold mix of unique regional dishes to tickle your taste buds. Known for its *brujos* (witch doctors), the fascinating market here is a Wal-Mart of shamanistic herbs, elixirs and other sagely curiosities. While the town itself is pretty light on tourist attractions, the dozens of tombs with Moche and Chimú archaeological booty surrounding the area should not be missed.

A strong alternative for ruins-goers is staying in the nearby beachtown of Pimentel.

Sights & Activities

In 1987 a royal Moche tomb at Sipán (p341), 30km southeast of Chiclayo, was located by researchers. This find proved to be extraordinary, as archaeologists recovered hundreds of dazzling and priceless artifacts from the site. Excavation continues. Partly because of these rare treasures, the Chiclayo area has single-handedly cornered the Peruvian market for exceptionally well-designed museums; a case in point is the excellent Bruning Museum (p342) in Lambayeque, 11km north of Chiclayo. Other sites worth visiting are the ruins at Túcume (p343), another great museum in Ferreñafe (p343), and a number of coastal villages.

The **Plaza de Armas** is a great place to amble as it fills nightly with sauntering couples, evangelical preachers and an army of underemployed shoe shiners.

Travelers with kids might want to check out the **children's playground** at the west end of Aguirre.

Mercado Modelo MARKET

(Arica btwn Balta & Cugilevan; 7am-8pm Mon-Sat, to 2pm Sun) This is one of Peru's most interesting markets, sprawling over several blocks. Most notable for tourists is the *mercado de brujos* (witch-doctors' market) in the southwest corner. This area is a one-stop shop for medicine men and has everything you might need for a potent brew: whale bones, amulets, snake skins, vials of indeterminate tonics, hallucinogenic cacti and piles of aromatic herbs.

If you'd like to make contact with a *brujo* for a healing session, this is a good place to start, but be wary of sham shamans. It's best to go with a reliable recommendation.

Cathedral CHURCH

(Plaza de Armas) This cathedral was built in the late 19th century. In contrast, the Plaza de Armas (Parque Principal) wasn't inaugurated until 1916, which gives an idea of how new the city is by Peruvian standards.

Paseo de las Musas PARK

This pleasant, narrow city park showcases classical-style statues of mythological figures.

Tours

Agencies offer frequent inexpensive tours of Sipán, Túcume, Ferreñafe, Batán Grande, Pimental/Santa Rosa, Reserva Ecológica Chaparrí, and the museums in Lambayeque. Tours to the archeaological sites cost between S45 and S60. Reserva Ecológica Chaparrí tours cost between S130 and S140. Prices do not include admission fees.

Sipán Tours CULTURAL TOURS

(074-22-9053; www.sipantours.com; Calle 7 de Enero 772; 8:30am-1:30pm & 4:30-8:30pm) This 25-year-old agency offers guided tours to all the major archaeological sites and the nearby beach towns. Ask about a new rural tourism project that takes you on a culinary tour through the countryside with homestays en route.

Moche Tours SIGHTSEEING TOURS

(074-23-2184; www.mochetourschiclayo.com.pe; Calle 7 de Enero 638; 8am-8pm Mon-Sat, to noon Sun) Highly recommended for cheap daily tours with Spanish- or English-speaking guides.

WORTH A TRIP

CHICLAYO BEACH TOWNS

Just 20 minutes from Chiclayo there's a string of three lovely beach towns – Puerto Etén, Santa Rosa and Pimentel. Both Puerto Etén and Pimentel make noteworthy alternatives to staying in noisy Chiclayo. *Combis* here from Chiclayo cost S1.50 to S2.80, departing from the corner of Vicente de la Vega and Ortiz. The towns are listed here from south to north.

Puerto Etén Sporting a brand-new *malecón*, a long honey-brown beach and slightly muddled waters, this little village is just 20 minutes from Chiclayo. There's a handful of beach-view seafood joints, pretty Republican-era architecture and a few beat-down hotels.

Santa Rosa A modern ruin – organic, pungent and powerful – this rough fishing village is really quite entrancing. The dry-docked ships make for interesting Instagram opps, and there's still some *caballitos de tortora* used here. Miracles have been reported at the cozy church.

Pimentel The poshest of the beach towns, Pimentel has a long pier, a broad *malecón* fronted by high-end, glassed-in houses, and the nicest beach for miles. Unfortunately, the waves here are rarely surfable – conversely, they are highly swimmable – and an afternoon stroll along the boardwalk and through some of the stick-frame, centuries-old houses is a fun retreat. One block inland from the pier, **Hostal Garuda** (☎074 45-2964; Quiñones 109; s/d S35/60; 📶) is a yellow-fronted, 100-year-old house with a clutch of friendly guest rooms; the rooms out back are more modern and sit around a playful garden.

Sleeping

Hostal Sicán HOTEL $

(☎074-20-8741; hsican@hotmail.com; Izaga 356; s/d/tr incl breakfast S40/55/75; 📶) This appealing pick has lots of polished wood and wrought iron creating an illusion of grandeur. The rooms are small, comfortable and cool. All feature wood paneling, as well as tasteful bits of art and a TV. A great choice, it sits on one of Chiclayo's most charming brick-lined streets.

Hostal Victoria HOTEL $

(☎074-22-5642; victoriastar2008@hotmail.com; Izaga 933; s/d/tr S30/50/60; 📶) This is a great find just east of the main plaza. It's quiet, sanitary and has colorful rooms spruced up by tiny ceramics and textiles here and there. There's a friendly family vibe to the whole place.

Ejecutivo Hotel HOTEL $

(☎074-20-6147; Calle 7 de Enero 1351; s S25, d S30-45; 📶) This price is right at this secure spot. It's got clean bright rooms with polka-dotted art-deco inspired sheets. The bathrooms are sterile, but lack toilet seats. The rooms don't have fans, and it can get hot here at night. The neighborhood here is a bit sketchy at night – take a cab.

Hospedaje San Lucas GUESTHOUSE $

(☎074-20-6888; www.chiclayohostel.com; Aguirre 412; s/d S20/35; @📶) Elementary but trim and tidy, this shoestringer steps up successfully to its 'Welcome Backpackers' motto. There's a nice city view from the top floor, electric hot showers and some locally made laurel wood furniture to give it some flare.

Pirámide Real HOTEL $

(☎074-22-4036; piramidereal@hotmail.com; Izaga 726; s/d S30/40; 📶) Blink and you'll miss the tiny entrance to this place. Things don't get any bigger inside, but if you're willing to forgo space, there's clean and tidy rooms with writing desks, hot water and cable TV – a reasonably good deal at this price range. There are only matrimonial rooms, though (no twins), so it's suitable for couples, not buds.

Hotel Mochiks BOUTIQUE HOTEL $$

(☎074-20-6620; www.hotelmochiks.com; Tacna 615; s/d incl breakfast S135/180; ❄@📶) This polished upstart made an immediate impression on the hotel scene in the city, owing much of its success to a sense of style that was previously MIA. Tall and narrow, the lobby, cafe and 2nd-floor bar are decked out in chromes and moody reds, which contrast perfectly with the smallish but soothing beige-toned rooms.

Everything is new and well-maintained; the trendiness is held in check with small indigenous Moche touches here and there. At 25 rooms, it's the perfect size.

Sun Palace HOTEL $$

(☎074-20-4729; www.hotelsunpalacechiclayo.com; Calle 7 de Enero 1368; s/d incl breakfast S90/130;

Chiclayo

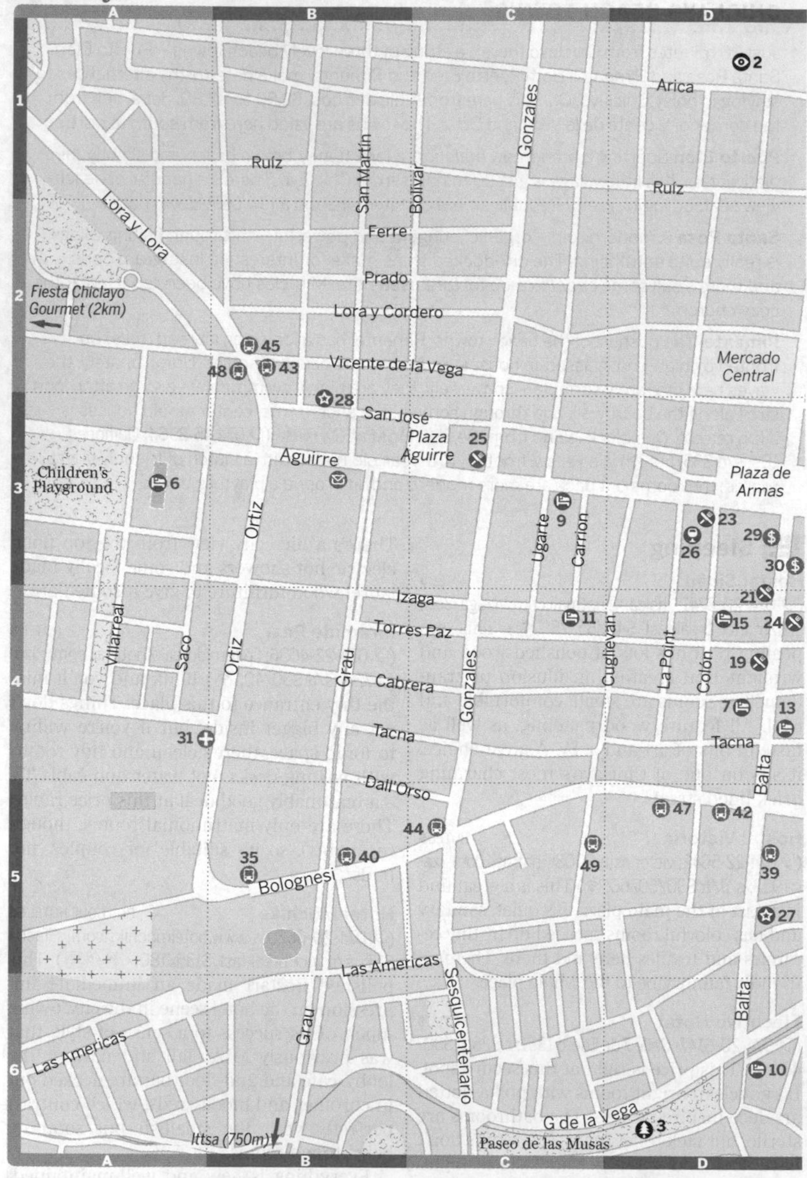

@) This fab 23-room choice makes no bones about it: lime and tangerine are its favorite colors and you will be pummeled with them at every turn – like being churned in an art-deco frosty-freeze machine.

It makes for a fun and festive choice that's top-loaded with value and personality: a minimalist cafe, trapezoidal bathroom mirrors, suites with Jacuzzi tubs, and efficient and friendly staff.

Hostal Colibrí HOTEL **$$**
(☎ 074-22-1918; www.hotelcolibriperu.com; Balta 010-A; s/d incl breakfast S60/100; 📶) Overlooking the leafy Paseo de las Musas, the newish Colibrí is a longish walk from the center but is top value. Brightly lit and brightly painted, it's a modern choice, with a friendly front desk, a burger joint in the bottom and a 2nd-floor coffee/cocktail bar with patio views of the park. Funky bathrooms, too.

Hotel Paraíso HOTEL **$$**
(☎ 074-22-8161; www.hotelesparaiso.com.pe; Ruiz 1064; s/d incl breakfast S100/110, air-con extra S30; ❄ @ 📶) Brighter and cheerier than its immediate neighbors, the value equation falls in Hotel Paraíso's favor, boasting all the mod cons of far fancier hotels for a fraction of the price. Spotless cell-like rooms boast decent furniture, hot showers and cable TV. The staff could take some lessons from Ms Manners.

Latinos Hostal HOTEL **$$**
(☎ 074-23-5437; latinohotelsac@hotmail.com; Igaza 600; s/d S90/140; ❄ @ 📶) An excellent choice, this hotel is thoroughly maintained with perfect little rooms. Some of the corner rooms have giant curving floor-to-ceiling windows for great street views and plenty of light. The staff is very helpful.

Casa Andina Select Chiclayo HOTEL **$$$**
(☎ 074-23-4911; www.casa-andina.com; Villarreal 115; r/ste incl breakfast S616/788; P ❄ @ 📶 🏊) The Peruvian boutique chain Casa Andina swooped in and gobbled up this aging relic, formerly the Gran Hotel Chiclayo. It's like a business hotel with an Andean pulse. There's a pleasant terrace and pool area, spa, fitness center and restaurant, plus modern, clean rooms that are sparkly new.

Costa Del Sol BUSINESS HOTEL **$$$**
(☎ 074-22-7272; www.costadelsolperu.com; Balta 399; s/d incl breakfast S285/350; P ❄ @ 📶 🏊) This fully loaded business hotel is one of Chiclayo's best, though reviews have been mixed. It must now answer to a higher multinational power in the form of Ramada, who took the reins in 2012. All the creature comforts are here, including pool, gym, sauna and massage rooms. We aren't chain hotel fans, mind you, but this is Chiclayo.

Eating

Chiclayo is one of the best places to eat on the North Coast. *Arroz con pato a la chiclayana* (duck and rice cooked in cilantro and beer) and *tortilla de manta raya* (Spanish omelet made from stingray) are endless sources of culinary pride. For dessert, try the local street sweet called a King Kong, a large cookie filled with a sweet caramel

Chiclayo

Sights
1 Cathedral ... E3
2 Mercado Modelo ... D1
3 Paseo de las Musas ... D6

Activities, Courses & Tours
4 Moche Tours ... E3
5 Sipán Tours ... E3

Sleeping
6 Casa Andina Select Chiclayo ... A3
7 Costa Del Sol ... D4
8 Ejecutivo Hotel ... E1
9 Hospedaje San Lucas ... C3
10 Hostal Colibrí ... D6
11 Hostal Sicán ... C4
12 Hostal Victoria ... F3
13 Hotel Mochiks ... D4
14 Hotel Paraíso ... E2
15 Latinos Hostal ... D4
16 Pirámide Real ... E4
17 Sun Palace ... E1

Eating
18 Cafe 900 ... E4
19 Chez Maggy ... D4
20 El Pescador ... F3
21 Hebron ... D4
22 Heladería Hoppy ... F5
23 Mi Tia ... D3
24 Restaurant Romana ... D4
25 Supermercado Metro ... C3

Drinking & Nightlife
26 Tribal Lounge ... D3

Entertainment
27 Premium Boulevard ... D5
28 Sabor y Son Cubano ... B3

Information
29 Banco Continental ... D3
30 BCP ... D3
31 Clínica del Pacífico ... A4
32 iPerú ... E3
33 Oficina de Migraciónes ... E6

Transport
34 Avianca ... E5
35 Cial ... B5
36 Civa ... E5
37 Colectivos to Ferreñafe ... F2
38 Cruz del Sur ... E5
39 Empresa Transcade ... D5
Emtrefesa ... (see 39)
40 Ittsa ... B5
41 LAN ... E4
42 Línea ... D5
Minibus Terminal ... (see 47)
43 Minibuses to Lambayeque & Pimentel ... B2
44 Móvil Tours ... C5
45 Oltursa ... B2
Oltursa Sales Office ... (see 24)
46 Ormeño ... F6
47 Tepsa ... D5
48 Transportes Chiclayo ... B2
49 Turismo Dias ... C5

cream made of milk and sugar; it's available everywhere.

El Pescador SEAFOOD, PERUVIAN $
(San José 1236; mains S10-20; 11am-6pm) This little local's secret packs in the droves for outstanding seafood and regional dishes at laughable prices. The ceviches here are every bit as good as places charging double or even triple the price; and weekend specials like *cabrito con frijoles* (goat with beans; Saturday) and *arroz con pato* (duck with rice; Sunday) are steals.

Owner Oscar and his brother (the chef) work their tails off to make sure you're happy.

Mi Tia BURGERS $
(Aguirre 662; burgers S1-6) Lines run very deep at this no-frills Peruvian haunt, whose burger stand draws legions of *céntimo* pushers for burgers (loaded with fries) that are practically free if you take them away (S1 to S4). Inside, they're pricier (S2 to S6), along with a long list of country staples served by smiling staff. It does a *suspiro de limeña* (milk caramel and meringue) just big enough that you don't feel guilty.

Heladería Hoppy DESSERTS $
(www.heladoshoppychiclayo.blogspot.com; CC Real Plaza; scoops S4-8) If you're jonesin' for something other than industrialized ice cream, they do a decent job here with the homemade stuff, especially considering all the Italians went to Brazil and Argentina. Good flavors include pisco sour and *lúcuma*; there are milkshakes and snacks as well.

Supermercado Metro SELF-CATERING $
(cnr Gonzáles & Aguirre; 8am-10pm) Solid supermarket.

★ **Cafe 900** PERUVIAN $$
(www.cafe900.com; Izaga 900; mains S13-28; 8am-11pm Mon-Thu, to 1pm Fri & Sat;) Live music, slowly spinning ceiling fans, exposed

wood and adobe that connect you with the elements are the hallmarks of the best bar-slash-cafe-slash-restaurant in Chiclayo. It's certainly tops on ambience, and the food is simple, direct, unpretentious and affordable.

Restaurant Romana PERUVIAN **$$**
(Balta 512; mains S13-25; 7am-1am;) This popular place serves a bunch of different dishes, all of them local favorites. If you're feeling brave, try the *chirimpico* for breakfast: it's stewed goat tripe and organs and is guaranteed to either cure a hangover or give you one.

If not, the *humitas* (steamed dough with corn and cheese wrapped in corn husks) are a tasty, can't-beat treat at S3.50. For other meals, there's pasta, steaks, seafood, chicken or pork *chicharrónes* (breaded and fried) with yucca – you name it.

Chez Maggy PIZZA **$$**
(www.pizzeriaschezmaggy.com; Balta 413; pizzas S12-31; 6-11pm) It's not how Papa Giuseppe used to make it, but the wood-fired pizzas at this Peruvian small-chain restaurant have a pretty darn good crust and fresh toppings. They have convenient personal-size pizzas for solo diners.

Hebron PERUVIAN **$$**
(074-22-2709; www.hebron.com.pe; Balta 605; mains S16-30, tourist menu S20; 24hr;) This flashy, contemporary and bright two-story restaurant is a luxury *pollería* (restaurant specializing in roast chicken). They have a fairly complete tourist menu that'll keep you well energized.

Fiesta Chiclayo Gourmet REGIONAL **$$$**
(074-20-1970; www.restaurantfiestagourmet.com; Salaverry 1820; mains S35-49) Few things are as satisfying as scraping those last bits of slightly charred rice off the bottom of an iron-clad pan and savoring all that's great about a rice dish like *arroz con pato a la chiclayana*, made here with farm-raised duck that must be a black-feathered quacker not a day over three months old.

Blindsiding your palate with a wholly unexpected delight is *ceviche a la brasa* (traditional raw fish served warm in corn husks after an 11th-hour searing). The pisco sours are constructed tableside, service is exquisite, and the best of this region's world-famous cuisine is outrageously great. Call for a reservation here or visit a sister restaurant in Lima, Trujillo or Tacna. A S5 taxi ride covers the 2km from the centre.

Drinking & Nightlife

Tribal Lounge BAR
(Lapoint 682; cocktails S12-22; closed Mon) An actual living, breathing bar in Chiclayo, this rock-themed spot is run by a local who returned from San Francisco after a decade. Good cocktails as well as live music (acoustic on Thursday, rock on Friday and Saturday from midnight). Great spot for a tipple.

Sabor y Son Cubano BAR, CLUB
(074-27-2555; saborysoncubano.blogspot.com; San José 155; cover S10; closed Sun) This spot gives the over-35 crowd somewhere to shake their rumps on the weekends, with tropical, classic salsa and merengue setting the pace.

Premium Boulevard CLUB
(www.premiumboulevard.com; Balta 100; cover S5-10; closed Sun) This massive club packs in nearly 1500 revelers at capacity, spread between a small karaoke room, a large disco and an absolutely massive concert hall that caters to national and international acts. There's a boisterous vibe fueled typically by salsa, merengue, *cumbia*, *bachata* and *reggaetón*.

Information

EMERGENCY

Policía de Turismo (074-49-0892; Saenz Peña 830) Useful for reporting problems.

IMMIGRATION

Oficina de Migraciónes (074-20-6838; www.migraciones.gob.pe; La Plata 30; 8:30am-12:30pm & 2-4pm) Near Paseo de Las Museos; handles visa issues.

MEDICAL SERVICES

Clínica del Pacífico (074-22-8585; www.clinicadelpacifico.com.pe; Ortiz 420) The best medical assistance in town.

MONEY

There are several banks on *cuadra* 6 of Balta as well as a bevy of ATMs convenient to the bus stations inside Supermarcado Metro, across from the Emtrafesa station. Money-changers outside the banks change cash quickly at good rates.

Banco Continental (Balta 643)

BCP (Balta 630) Has a 24-hour Visa and MasterCard ATM.

POST

Serpost (Aguirre 140; 9am-7pm Mon-Fri, to 1pm Sat) West of Plaza Aguirre.

TOURIST INFORMATION

iPerú (Saenz Peña 838; ⏲7am-4:30pm Mon-Fri) The best spot for tourist info in town; with other spots at the Municipalidad de Chiclayo building at Calle San José 823, and at the Museo de Tumbas Reales in Lambayeque. If they're closed, hit up the tour agencies.

ℹ Getting There & Away

AIR

The airport (CIX) is 1.5km east of town; a taxi ride there is S5. **LAN** (☎074-27-4875; www.lan.com; Izaga 770) departs from Lima to Chiclayo daily at 4am and 8:10pm, returning to Lima at 5:50am, 6:15pm and 10pm. More economical is **Avianca** (☎0-800-1-8222; www.avianca.com; Cáceres 222, CC Real Plaza), departing from Lima at 6:10am and 3:30pm and heading back from Chiclayo at 8:20am and 5:55pm. Prices for the latter can be as low as S97.

BUS

Cruz del Sur, Movil Tours, Línea, Ittsa and Oltursa usually have the most comfortable buses.

Tepsa's terminal next to its ticketing office hosts a dozen small companies that have at least six buses throughout the day to Cajamarca; two night buses to Tumbes, both departing at 8:30pm; buses at 8pm, 8:30pm (Monday to Saturday) and 7:30pm (Sunday) to Chachapoyas; at least six departures daily to Tarapoto; a 10am, 7pm and 10:30pm bus to Yurimaguas; and frequent services to Jaén. These times tend to change with the setting of each moon, so check the schedule ahead of time.

The minibus terminal at the corner of San José and Lora y Lora has regular buses to Lambayeque and Pimentel.

Buses for Ferreñafe, Sipán, Monsefú and Chongoyape leave frequently from **Terminal de Microbuses Epsel** (Nicolás de Piérola, at Oriente).

Combis to Túcume leave from Leguia 1306 north of the centre.

Cial (☎074-20-5587; www.expresocial.com; Bolognesi 15) Has a 7:30pm Lima bus.

Civa (☎01-418-1111; www.civa.com.pe; Bolognesi 714) Has the cheapest *comfortable* Lima buses at 5pm and 8:45pm; also 8pm and 8:30pm; Jaén buses at 9:30am and 9:30pm; Tarapoto buses at 5:45pm and 6:30pm; and a Chachapoyas bus at 6pm. They are now also serving Guayaquil at 6:15pm, which is more comfortable and way more convenient than Ormeño.

Cruz del Sur (☎0-801-1111; www.cruzdelsur.com.pe; Bolognesi 888) Has four departures to Lima between 7am and 8pm.

Empresa Transcade (☎074-23-2552; Balta 110) Has buses to Jaén (S14) at 8:30am and 8:30pm.

Emtrefesa (☎074-22-5538; www.emtrafesa.com; Balta 110) Has a bus to Jaén (at 10:45pm) and many departures for Trujillo and Pacasmayo.

Ittsa (☎074-23-3612; www.ittsabus.com; Grau 497) *Bus-cama* to Lima at 8pm.

Línea (☎074-23-2951; Bolognesi 638) Has a comfortable Lima service at 8pm and regular hourly services to Trujillo and Piura. Also has buses to Chimbote at 9:15am, 7:30pm and 11pm; buses to Cajamarca at 10am, 11:30am, 10pm and 10:45pm; and buses to Jaén at 2:15pm and 11pm.

Móvil Tours (☎01-716-8000; www.moviltours.com.pe; Bolognesi 199) Has two Lima buses at 7:30pm *(bus-cama)* and 8pm; a Tarapoto bus at 6:30pm; and a Chachapoyas bus at 9pm.

Oltursa (☎01-716-5000; www.oltursa.pe; Vicente de la Vega 101) You can purchase tickets at the terminal or at the downtown Sales Office (cnr Balta & Izaga). Four *bus-cama* services to Lima between 7pm and 9pm.

Ormeño (☎074-23-4206; www.grupo-ormeno.com.pe; Haya de la Torre 242) The most comfortable services to Ecuador and beyond, including a 3am departure to Tumbes and Guayaquil as well as Bogotá on Tuesdays and Fridays at 1am.

Tepsa (☎074-23-6981; www.tepsa.com.pe; Bolognesi 504) *Bus-cama* services to Lima at 8:30pm (Monday to Saturday) and 7:30pm (Sunday).

Transportes Chiclayo (☎074-50-3548; www.transporteschiclayo.com; Ortiz 10) Has buses to Piura every half-hour from 4:30am to 8:30pm; and to Máncora and Tumbes at 10am and 9:30pm. There is also one Cajamarca departure at 11pm and one bus to Tarapoto at 6pm.

Turismo Dias (☎074-23-3538; www.turdias.com; Cuglievan 190) This affordable carrier heads to Lima at 8pm, also offering departures to Cajamarca at 6:45am, 5pm, 9:45pm and 10:30pm.

Chiclayo Regional Minibuses:

DESTINATION	COST (S)	DURATION (HR)
Batán Grande	5	¾
Chongoyape	3.50	1½
Ferreñafe	2	½
Lambayeque	1.50	¼
Pimentel	1.60	½
Monsefú	2	¼
Sipán	3.50	¼
Túcume	2.50	1

Chiclayo Long-Distance Buses:

DESTINATION	COST (S)	DURATION (HR)
Bogotá	486	48
Cajamarca	16-40	6
Chachapoyas	30-50	10
Chimbote	20-25	6
Guayaquil (Ec)	81	17
Jaén	20-25	6
Lima	40-125	12-14
Máncora	30-35	6
Pacasmayo	9	2
Piura	15-21	3
Tarapoto	45-120	14
Tumbes	25-50	8
Yurimaguas	65-70	20

Around Chiclayo

Given the doubling of guide prices in the last few years, it hardly makes sense to travel independently to most of the archaeological sites around Chiclayo – you'll find the organized tours far more convenient.

Sipán

The story of **Sipán** (Huaca Rayada; ☎074-80-0048; admission S10; ⏲9am-5pm) reads like an Indiana Jones movie script: buried treasure, *huaqueros*, police, archaeologists and at least one killing. The archaeological site was discovered by *huaqueros* from the nearby hamlet of Sipán. The Moche site is located about 30km southwest of Chiclayo. The story of Sipan's discovery is almost as interesting as the remarkable collection of artifacts that were found in its tombs.

When local archaeologist Dr Walter Alva saw a huge influx of intricate objects on the black market in early 1987, he realized that an incredible burial site was being ransacked in the Chiclayo area. Careful questioning led Dr Alva to the Sipán mounds. To the untrained eye the mounds look like earthen hills, but in AD 300 these were huge truncated pyramids constructed from millions of adobe bricks.

At least one major tomb had already been pillaged by looters, but fast protective action by local archaeologists and police stopped further plundering. Luckily, several other tombs that the grave robbers had missed were unearthed, including an exceptional royal Moche burial that became known as the Lord of Sipán. One *huaquero* was shot and killed by police in the early, tense days of the struggle over the graves. The Sipán locals were not too happy at losing what they considered their treasure trove. To solve this problem, the locals were invited to train to become excavators, researchers and guards at the site, which now provides steady employment for many. The full story was detailed by Dr Alva in the October 1988 and June 1990 issues of *National Geographic*, and the May 1994 issue of *Natural History*.

The Lord of Sipán turned out to be a major leader of the Moche people, indicated by his elaborate burial in a wooden coffin surrounded by hundreds of gold, ceramic and semiprecious mineral objects, as well as an entourage consisting of his wife, two girls, a boy, a military chief, a flag-bearer, two guards, two dogs and a llama. Another important tomb held the *sacerdote* (priest), who was accompanied into the afterlife with an equally impressive quantity of treasures, as well as a few children, a guardian whose feet were cut off and a headless llama. Archaeologists don't understand why the body parts were removed, but they believe that important members of the Moche upper class took with them in death those who composed their retinues in life.

Some of the tombs have been restored with replicas to show what they looked like just before being closed up more than 1500 years ago. Opposite the entrance is the **Museo de Sitio Sipán** (admission S10 or incl with site ticket; ⏲9am-5pm Mon-Fri) opened in January 2009, which is worth a visit – but note that the most impressive artifacts, such as the Lord of Sipán and the Sacerdote, were placed in the Museo Tumbas Reales de Sipán in Lambayeque, after going on world tour. Spanish- and English-speaking guides can be hired (S30).

Daily guided tours are available from tour agencies in Chiclayo for around S45. Alternatively, buses for Sipán (S3.50, 45 minutes) leave frequently from Chiclayo's Terminal de Microbuses Epsel.

Lambayeque

☎074 / POP 47,900

About 11km north of Chiclayo, Lambayeque was once the main town in the area but now plays second fiddle to Chiclayo. The only reason to stop is for a visit to the town's world-class museums, some of the best in Peru.

Sights

The two museums in Lambayeque are both within a 15-minute walk of the plaza.

★Museo Tumbas Reales de Sipán MUSEUM

(www.museotumbasrealessipan.pe; admission S10; ⏲9am-5pm Tue-Sun) Opened in November 2002, the Museum of the Royal Tombs of Sipán is the pride of northern Peru – as well it should be. With its burgundy pyramid construction rising gently out of the earth, it's a world-class facility specifically designed to showcase the marvelous finds from Sipán. Photography is not permitted and all bags must be checked.

Visitors are guided through the museum from the top down and are shown some of the numerous discoveries from the tomb in the same order that the archaeologists found them – this small detail alone, rare in the museum world, adds a fascinating context to visits. The first hall contains detailed ceramics representing gods, people, plants, llamas and other animals.

On the 2nd floor there are delicate objects like impossibly fine turquoise-and-gold ear ornaments showing ducks, deer and the Lord of Sipán himself. The painstaking and advanced techniques necessary to create this jewelry place them among the most beautiful and important objects of pre-Columbian America.

Finally, the ground floor features exact reproductions of how the tombs were found. Numerous dazzling objects are displayed, the most remarkable of which are the gold pectoral plates representing sea creatures such as the octopus and crab. Even the sandals of the Lord of Sipán were made of precious metals, as he was carried everywhere and never had to walk. Interestingly, since nobility were seen as part animal god, they used the *nariguera* (a distinctive nose shield) to conceal their very human teeth – and the fact that they were no different from everyone else.

The exhibits on how they went about excavating this remarkable archeaological find. are as interesting as the artifacts on display.

The lighting and layout is exceptional (though it's take a minute to get used to the dark interior lighting). The signage is all in Spanish, but English- speaking guides are available for S30.

Bruning Museum MUSEUM

(www.museobruning.com; admission S8; ⏲9am-5pm) This museum, once a regional archaeological showcase, is now greatly overshadowed by the Museo Tumbas Reales de Sipán; however, it still houses a good collection of artifacts from the Chimú, Moche, Chavín and Vicus cultures.

Budding archaeologists will enjoy the displays showing the development of ceramics from different cultures and the exhibits explaining how ceramics and metalwork were made. Architecture and sculpture lovers may find some interest in the Corbusier-inspired building, bronze statues and tile murals adorning the property. Models of several important sites are genuinely valuable for putting the archaeology of the region into perspective. English-speaking guides charge S30.

La Casa de Logia HOUSE

La Casa de Logia, a block south of the main plaza, has a 67m-long, 400-year-old balcony,

HUAQUEROS – MODERN-DAY TOMB RAIDERS

Since the Spanish conquest, *huaqueros* (tomb raiders) have worked the ancient graves and archeaological ruins of Peru, unearthing antiquities and selling them to anybody prepared to pay.

To a certain extent, one can sympathize with a poor *campesino* (peasant) hoping to strike it rich, but the *huaquero* is one of the archaeologist's greatest enemies. With over 400 years of activity, their efforts have been so thorough that archaeologists rarely find an unplundered grave. In some cases, archaeologists are now hiring *huaqueros* to do field research, but the age-old practice continues to this day. *Huaqueros* are especially active around Semana Santa (Holy Week), when the treasures of the earth are said to come to the surface. Increased patrols and visibility have made it harder to move antiquities, and to a certain degree, have diminished *huaquero* activity in the north.

According to reports from Peru's leading newspaper *El Comercio*, new threats are coming from private businesses opening quarries atop burial bounds, and from squatters who are setting up shantytowns in the middle of the desert.

said to be the longest balcony in Peru. Most people visit here on an organized tour from Chiclayo.

Getting There & Away

The minibus terminal at the corner of San José and Lora y Lora in Chiclayo has regular buses to Lambayeque (S1.50, 20 minutes), which will drop you off a block from the Bruning Museum.

Ferreñafe

074 / POP 34,500

Sicán culture thrived in the Lambayeque area between AD 750 and 1375, around the same time as the Chimú. The main Sicán site at Batán Grande lies in remote country to the north and is best visited on a tour from Chiclayo or Pacora. Ferreñafe, 18km northeast of Chiclayo, is worth visiting for the excellent Museo Nacional Sicán.

Museo Nacional Sicán MUSEUM
(admission S8; 9am-5pm Tue-Sun) This splendid museum displays replicas of the 12m-deep tombs found at the Sicán site at Batán Grande, among the largest tombs found in South America.

Enigmatic burials were discovered within – the Lord of Sicán was buried upside down, in a fetal position with his head separated from his body. Beside him were the bodies of two women and two adolescents, as well a sophisticated security system to ward off grave robbers: the red *sinabrio* dust, toxic if inhaled.

Another important tomb contained a nobleman sitting in a cross-legged position and wearing a mask and headdress of gold and feathers, surrounded by smaller tombs and niches containing the bodies of one man and 22 young women. The museum is worth the ride out, and it's never crowded. Guided tours from Chiclayo to Ferreñafe and Túcume cost around S45 per person, or buses for Ferreñafe (S1.50) leave frequently from Chiclayo's Terminal de Microbuses Epsel.

Túcume

This little-known **archeaological site** (www.tucume.com; admission S8; 8am-4:30pm Tue-Sun) lies around 30km to the north of Lambayeque on the Carretera Panamericana. A vast area – with more than 200 hectares of crumbling walls, plazas and no fewer than 26 pyramids – it was the final capital of the Sicán culture, who moved their city from nearby Batán Grande around AD 1050 after that area was devastated by the effects of El Niño.

The pyramids you see today are a composite of structures made by several civilizations; the lower levels belonged to the Sicán while the next two levels, along with the distinctive surrounding walls, were added by the Chimú. While little excavation has been done and no spectacular tombs have been found, it's the sheer size of the site that makes it a memorable visit.

The site can be surveyed from a stunning *mirador* (lookout) atop Cerro Purgatorio (Purgatory Hill). The hill was originally called Cerro la Raya (Stingray Hill), but the name was changed after the Spaniards tried to convert local people to Christianity by dressing as demons atop the hill and throwing nonbelievers to their deaths. There is a small but attractive on-site **museum** (Cerro la Raya; incl with site ticket; closed Mon) with some interesting tidbits. Guides are available for S30.

From Chiclayo (S2.50), *combis* depart from Leguia 1306 north of the center. You can also catch one from Lambayeque (ask at the Bruning Museum). Guided tours cost around S50 per person.

Reserva Ecológica Chaparrí Wildlife

This 34,000-hectare private **reserve** (www.chaparri.org; admission S10, reservations required; 7am-5pm), located 75km east of Chiclayo, was established in 2000 by the community of Santa Catalina and the famous Peruvian wildlife photographer Heinz Plenge. It offers a completely unique atmosphere for this coast. This is one of the few places in the world where you can spot the rare spectacled bear in its natural habitat; 25 or so have been accounted for (there are also two in rehabilitation captivity).

This area is an ornithologist's dream, with more than 237 species of birds, including rare white-winged guans, Andean condors, king vultures and several species of eagle. A large number of threatened species are also found here, including pumas, collared anteaters and Andean weasels. Nearly a third of these vertebrates are not found anywhere else in the world. And there's a friendly fox or two.

You can spend the night in the wonderfully rustic **Chaparrí EcoLodge** (074-45-2299; www.chaparrilodge.com; r per person incl full board & 1-day guide S351-396) where well-appointed adobe and bamboo bungalows await under the looming mountain of the same name. Advanced reservations are required. There's solar-heated hot water and solar-powered electricity and each room has its own patio with hammock. It's not fancy, but it's nice enough that you'll be sweetly surprised upon arrival. The food is of the homey Peruvian comfort variety served on a communal table next to a gurgling stream. It's pretty ideal if you are a nature lover.

You can visit the reserve on your own as a day trip by catching a bus from Chiclayo's Terminal de Microbuses Epsel to Chongoyape (S3.50), from where you must contact the local guide association, **Acoturch** (☎97-889-6377) and arrange a required guide and transport for about S140 for up to three people to tour the reserve. If you can't get through to the association, pop in to the corner shop Fotografia Carrasco where the family can arrange everything as well as set up campers in a very rustic campground in a beautiful setting above Chongoyape.

Alternatively, Moche Tours and Sipán Tours in Chiclayo arranges day tours, including transportation and guide, for S130 to S140 per person (minimum four people).

Batán Grande & Chota

About halfway from Chiclayo to Chongoyape a minor road on your left leads to the Sicán ruins of **Batán Grande**. This is a major archaeological site where about 50 pyramids have been identified and several burials have been excavated. With the urging of Dr Walter Alva, among others, the site was transformed into the **Santuario Histórico Bosque de Pomac**, but there is no tourist infrastructure.

The protected reserve lies within one of the largest dry tropical forests in the world and hosts more than 50 species of birds; healthy stands of *algarrobo* (carob tree) offer beautiful shade along the way. *Combis* to Batán Grande leave from Chiclayo's Terminal de Epsel (S5), but it is best to go on an organized tour.

One of the best ways to visit this area is on horseback from **Rancho Santana** (☎97-971-2145; www.cabalgatasperu.com; camping with/without tent rental S10/5, r per person incl breakfast S35) in Pacora, about 45km northeast of Chiclayo. Readers rave about their experiences riding typical Peruvian Paso horses at this rustic, animal-packed Swiss-owned ranch, which also has a simple but spacious bungalow with hammocks and super-sized bathroom; fresh milk and simple meals are whipped up if needed or guests may use the kitchen facilities. The owners are highly knowledgeable of Lambayeque cultures and will pick you up in Chiclayo for half-day to three-day *cabalgatas* (horse rides) through the Pomac Forest, Batán Grande and the pyramids at Túcume. The owners care for their horses exceptionally well and can make even the most inexperienced rider feel comfortable. The tours are a great value at S45 for a half-day to S360 for three days.

A rough but scenic road climbs east from Chongoyape into the Andes until it reaches Chota (at an altitude of around 2400m), a 170km journey that takes about eight hours. Two or three buses a day from Chiclayo travel there, from where a daily bus makes the rough journey via Bambamarca and Hualgayoc to Cajamarca (five hours).

Piura

☎073 / POP 387,200

After several hours of crossing the vast emptiness of the Sechura Desert, Piura materializes like a mirage on the horizon, enveloped in quivering waves of heat. It's hard to ignore the sense of physical isolation forced on you by this unforgiving environment; the self-sufficiency imposed upon early settlers may explain why they identify as Piuran rather than Peruvian.

Being so far inland, the scorching summer months will have you honing your radar for air-conditioning, as you seek out chilled venues in which to soothe your sweltering skin. But the lovely narrow cobbled streets and charismatic colonial houses of central Piura make up for the fact that there's little else for tourists to do here. Its role as a hub for the spokes of the northern towns means that you'll probably end up spending some time here, sighing in relief at the occasional afternoon breeze.

Literature fans will find wandering Piura's streets, listening to its sounds and watching its people an interesting excercise. This desert oasis was home to Peru's emminent novelist, Mario Vargas Llosa, during his formative years, and much of the Nobel-prize-winning author's work grabs from life in Piura. Literary explorers should definitely check out his seminal second novel *La casa verde* (*The Green House*, 1966), as well as his latest endeavour, *El héroe discreto* (*The Discreet Hero*, 2013), both of which are partially set in Piura.

OFF THE BEATEN TRACK

BEACHSIDE COLÁN IS PURE PIURADISE

If you want to lose a few days in an authentic Peruvian beach town that foreigners haven't yet embraced, look no further than **Colán**, 15km north of Paita, Piura's main port some 50km west of the city.

Paita itself is a dusty, crumbling colonial port town that looks like it sprouted organically from the desert and has a roguish, Wild West feel to it, but as soon as Colán comes into view after you've turned off the main highway, you feel that sense of discovery so often lost in a world of Google Earth and iReports. Not only is Colán home to the oldest colonial church in Peru (it looks like something out of a Cormac McCarthy novel), this white-sand beach is a trendy summer destination for the Peruvian jet set – and is practically deserted the rest of the year. The curving bay has a shallow beach that's excellent for swimming. Loads of restaurants line the main drag, and there are a few great places to plop yourself down for a few days.

There are buses every 15 minutes to Paita from the Terminal Interprovincial Gechisa in Piura (S4, one hour). *Colectivos* leave from the main terminal in Paita, near the market, to Colán (S4, 20 minutes) and Sullana (S6, 1¼ hours).

Playa Colán Lodge (073-32-6778; www.playacolanlodge.com.pe; 1.5km south of town on beach; 2-/4-/5-person bungalows S199/252/331;) This is the best place to stay in Colán. Built from a combination of natural materials, it has an upmarket Robinson Crusoe feel and hosts cute, pastel-colored bungalows along the beach. There are lots of hammocks, shady palm trees, a tennis court, a curvy and delicious pool, plus an excellent on-site restaurant.

Luna Nueva (073-66-1761; www.lunanuevadecolan.com; 10m right of T-Junction; s incl breakfast S809-90, d incl breakfast S160-180;) Luna Nueva gives you a beat-box taste of Máncora with modern-tones, a blue-lit restaurant, and smallish, slightly cramped rooms. The loud music out front ends when you head to the block of rooms by the beach, where you'll find a central pool and a bunch of kayaks that are free for guests.

Hospedaje Frente del Mar (96-966-914; just north of T-Junction; s S35, d S70-100) The best budget spot in town. The rooms are hot and the beds are spongy. But it's friendly and clean, and there's a laid-back porch looking onto the beach. The new top-floor rooms are the best.

Sights

Jirón Lima, a block east of the Plaza de Armas, has preserved its colonial character more than most areas in Piura.

Museo Municipal Vicus MUSEUM
(mvicus.blogspot.com; Huánuco 893; 9am-5pm Tue-Sat, 9am-1pm Sun) FREE This four-story monolith offers a sparse but decent look into Vicus culture, highlighted by the underground **Sala de Oro** (admission S4; 9am-5pm Tue-Fri) where some excellent pieces are displayed, including a gold belt decorated with a life-sized gold cat head that puts today's belt buckles to shame.

Casa Grau MUSEUM
(073-32-6541; Tacna 66; 8am-1pm & 3-6pm Mon-Fri, to noon Sat) FREE This restored colonial home is the birthplace of Admiral Miguel Grau, born on July 27, 1834. The house was restored by the Peruvian navy and is now a naval museum. Admiral Grau was a hero of the War of the Pacific against Chile (1879–83), and the captain of the British-built warship *Huáscar*.

Cathedral CHURCH
(Plaza de Armas) The cathedral was originally constructed in 1588, when Piura was finally built in its current location. The impressive early-17th-century gold-covered side altar of the Virgin of Fatima was once the main altar in the church. Famed local artist Ignacio Merino painted the canvas of San Martín de Porres in the mid-19th century.

Sleeping

Hospedaje San Carlos GUESTHOUSE $
(073-30-6447; Ayacucho 627; s/d S45/75;) Winning the budget stakes by a nose, this little *hospedaje* has immaculate and trim rooms, each with TV. The back rooms are best for light sleepers.

Piura

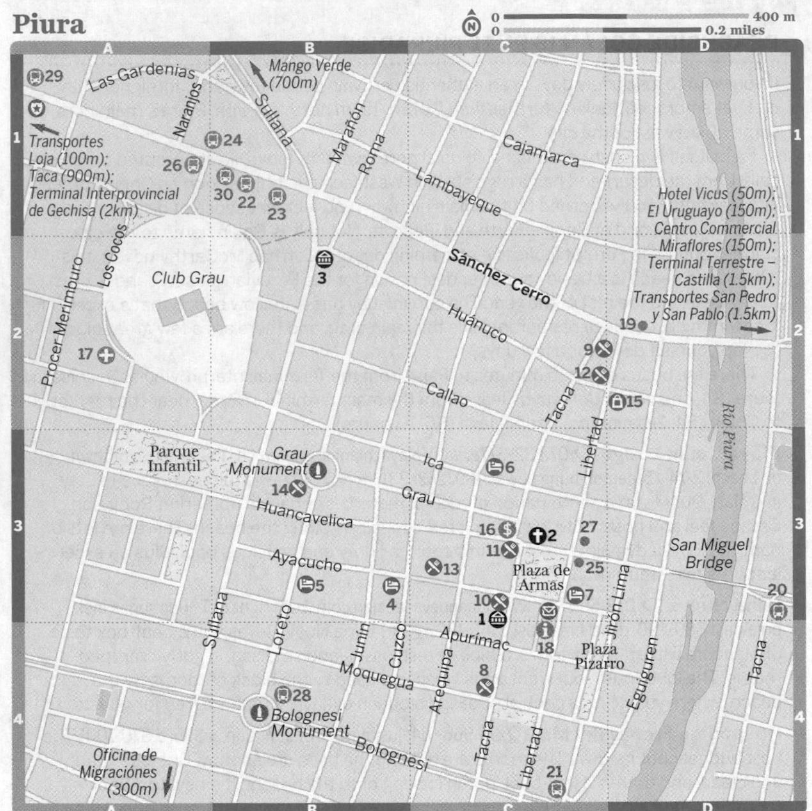

Hotel Vicus HOTEL **$**
(☎073-34-3201; Guardia Civil B-3; s/d/tr S60/80/105; ❄@📶🏊) Though upkeep isn't what it should be and the Canadiana illustration reprints from Peter John Strokes' *Old Niagara on the Lake* are out of place, we dig this perfectly reasonable spot. Rooms are spaced out around a drive-in, motel-style layout with a lush communal patio and have everything you might crave, including three matrimonial rooms with air-con.

It's a nice location just across the bridge from the centre, comparatively quiet, and the best nightlife is a block away. Enough said.

Mango Verde B&B **$$**
(☎073-32-1768; www.mangoverde.com.pe; Country 248; s/d incl breakfast S160/S180, without air-con S140/S150; ❄📶) About 2km north of Plaza de Armas in a leafy residential area, this smart, 19-room B&B ups the charm ante and manages to be both industrial and cozy at the same time (wonderfully inviting common terraces with plush patio furniture next to steel staircases and exposed concrete).

Pottery from Catacaos and well-curated art add a bit of color to things and rooms are simple-ish with all the mod cons. It's not mind-blowing, but it tries harder than the rest.

Hotel Las Arenas HOTEL **$$**
(☎073-30-7583; hotellasarenaspiura@hotmail.com; Loreto 945; s/d incl breakfast S110/S140, without air-con S90/S120; ❄@📶🏊) It was a low bar, but this remodeled *casona* now offers a smidgeon more character than the other spots in town. It earns its top Piura honors for the small but enchanting pool with inviting wicker loveseats and copious potted plants, mismatched (depending on the era) but endearing flooring and well-maintained-if-ever-so-dated rooms.

There's a small cafe and they'll knock S10 off the price for foreigners.

Piura

Sights

1 Casa Grau ... C3
2 Cathedral ... C3
3 Museo Municipal Vicus ... B2

Sleeping

4 Hospedaje San Carlos ... B3
5 Hotel Las Arenas ... B3
6 Intiotel ... C3
7 Los Portales ... C3

Eating

8 Capuccino ... C4
9 Chifa Canton ... C2
10 Don Parce ... C3
11 Heladería el Chalán ... C3
12 Matheo's ... C2
13 Snack Bar Romano ... C3
14 Supermercado Multiplaza ... B3

Shopping

15 Centro Artesanal Norte ... D2

Information

16 BCP ... C3
17 Clínica San Miguel ... A2
18 iPerú ... C4

Transport

19 Avianca ... D2
Buses to Catacaos ... (see 20)
20 Civa ... D3
21 Cruz del Sur ... C4
22 El Dorado ... B1
23 Eppo ... B1
24 Ittsa ... B1
25 LAN ... C3
26 Linea ... A1
27 Peruvian Airlines ... C3
28 Tepsa ... B4
29 Terminal Terrestre – Castilla ... A1
30 Transportes Chiclayo ... B1

Los Portales HISTORIC HOTEL $$$
(073-32-8887; www.losportales.com.pe; Libertad 875; r incl breakfast S440-660;) Live out dreams of conquistador grandeur in this beautiful and fully refurbished colonial building on the Plaza de Armas. Handsome public areas with iron grillwork and black-and-white checkered floors lead to a poolside restaurant and rooms with large cable TV, minibar and great beds.

The new rooms out back are quieter, but lack the artisanry of the historic chambers.

Intiotel BUSINESS HOTEL $$$
(073-28-7600; www.intiotel.com; Arequipa 691; s/d/ste incl breakfast S210/273/420;) This modern newcomer is the trendy choice, with industrially sterile hallways that lead to spotless-but-dark rooms with tasteful art and retro silver minibars, flat-screen TVs and nice bathrooms. There's a business center and round-the-clock room service.

Eating

To tuck into some regional delicacies, a lunchtime trip to the nearby town of Catacaos is a must. Vegetarians will be pleased by Piura's wealth of meatless options.

Snack Bar Romano PERUVIAN $
(Ayacucho 580; mains S7.50-15, menús S6-22; closed Sun) With an excellent list of several daily *menús,* this local favorite has been around as long as its middle-aged waiters. It gets the double thumbs-up for ceviches, *sudados* (seafood stews) and local specialties.

Matheo's VEGETARIAN $
(073-30-8096; Libertad 487; meals S9-14;) With two central locations, Matheo's serves as an antidote to the hills of *parrillada* found all over Peru. The all-veggie menu has lots of I-can't-believe-it's-not-meat versions of local dishes. The second branch is at Tacna 532.

Heladería el Chalán DESSERTS $
(Tacna 520; snacks S6.50-19) This fast-food joint has numerous outlets whipping up burgers and sandwiches, but our money's on the excellent selection of juices and the dozens of flavors of cool, cool ice cream. Try *manjar blanco* (milk caramel) or *límon* (lime) – it's all so good, you'll wish the owners canvassed Piura less and spread the love to Chiclayo and Trujillo. Additional branches at Grau 173 and 453.

Supermercado Multiplaza SELF-CATERING $
(Ovalo Grau) For self-caterers.

★ **Capuccino** CAFE $$
(www.facebook.com/capuccinogourmet; Tacna 786; mains S22-45; closed Sun;) The real deal. This modern cafe offers gourmet sandwiches and salads that are great for lunch (though it's shockingly empty). There's more sophisticated fare for a fine night out with a bottle of wine at dinner.

Creativity shines here – *lomo saltado* lasagna, *mero* (grouper) in soy and *maracuyá* sauce – and the desserts that you might be missing from home (Toblerone cheesecake, pecan pie) are astonishing. For caffeine freaks, it's tops in the centre for espressos

(S4.50), and these are the best fries you'll have had in weeks.

Chifa Canton CHINESE **$$**
(cnr Sánchez Cerro & Tacna; mains S22-32) Peruvian Chinese restaurants almost always guarantee a good meal and this nearly fancy *chifa* is no exception. It's a bummer about the street noise, but the food is fresh and flavorful and the perfect antidote when you tire of ceviche. Meals might just be big enough for two.

Don Parce PERUVIAN **$$**
(☎073-30-0842; www.donparce.com; Tacna 642; mains S16-33, menú S39; 📶) Immensely pleasant spot serving a long list of Peruvian standards as well as daily specials in a convenient, colonial atmosphere off the Plaza de Armas. The best deal is a three-course lunch *menú*, always with a hearty, meaty main dish.

El Uruguayo STEAK **$$$**
(cnr Guardia Civil & Cayeta, Centro Commercial Miraflores; steaks S25-70; ⏲from 6:30pm) Beef lovers unite at this Uruguayan steakhouse that has fallen out of favor in Trujillo but remains fresh meat, so to speak, in Piura. Cuts range from 200g to 500g and are categorized by region (Uruguay, Argentina, América) and they do a bang up job with the condiments (*chimichurri*, vinaigrette, *ají*).

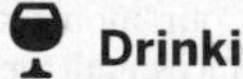

Drinking

All of Piura's worthwhile nightlife takes place in Centro Commercial Miraflores, a small shopping center east of the centre on the corner of Guardia Civil and Cayeta.

For a great bar, check out **Atiko** (cocktails S12-22).

If you really need to shake your rump, head upstairs to **Queens** (cover S25-30), which gets rowdy on weekends when it fills with gringos and well-heeled Peruvians shakin' their money-makers to an eclectic international music mix.

Don't worry – if any of these close, something else will open here.

Shopping

Centro Artesanal Norte HANDICRAFTS
(cnr Huánuco & Libertad; ⏲9:30am-1:30pm & 4-8pm Mon-Fri, to 1:30pm Sun) This artisan center is actually a tiny mall of about a dozen different craft shops featuring regional specialties from baskets to weavings to Chulucanas pottery. With fair and negotiable prices, it's a great stop if you don't have time to go to the outlying craft towns.

Information

Internet is ubiquitous and most lodgings offer laundry facilities.

MEDICAL SERVICES

Clínica San Miguel (www.clinicasanmiguelpiura.com; Los Cocos 111-153; ⏲24hr) Excellent medical care.

MONEY

Casas de cambio are at the Ica and Arequipa intersection. **BCP** (Grau 133) bank has an ATM.

POLICE

Police Station (Sánchez Cerro s/n) For reporting robberies.

POST

Serpost (cnr Ayacucho & Libertad; ⏲9am-7pm Mon-Fri, to 1pm Sat) On the plaza.

BORDER CROSSING: ECUADOR VIA LA TINA

The border post of La Tina lacks hotels, but the Ecuadorean town of Macará (3km from the border) has adequate facilities. La Tina is reached by *colectivos* (S12, 2½ hours) leaving from Sullana, 40km north of Piura, throughout the day. A better option is **Transportes Loja** which has three daily buses from Piura (9:30am, 1pm and 9pm) that conveniently go straight through here and on to Loja (S28, eight hours).

The border is the international bridge over the Río Calvas and is open 24 hours. Formalities are relaxed as long as your documents are all in order. There are no banks, though you'll find money changers at the border or in Macará. A new bridge and completely revamped immigration facilities, with both Peruvian and Ecuadorean immigration offices sharing the same building on the bridge, make the crossing easy-peasy.

Travelers entering Ecuador will find taxis (US$1) and *colectivos* (US$0.50) to take them to Macará. Most nationalities are simply given a T3 tourist card, which must be surrendered when leaving, and granted 90 days' stay in Ecuador. There is a Peruvian **consulate** (☎07-269-4030; www.consuladoperumacara.com; Bolivar 134) in Macará. See Lonely Planet's *Ecuador & the Galápagos Islands* for further information on Ecuador.

TOURIST INFORMATION

iPerú (☎073-32-0249; Ayacucho 377; ⏰9am-6pm Mon-Sat, to 1pm Sun) Has tourist information; the airport also has an iPerú counter.

Oficina de Migraciónes (☎073-33-5536; www.migraciones.gob.pe; cnr Sullana & Integración) Handles visa issues.

Getting There & Away

AIR

The airport (PIU) is on the southeastern bank of the Río Piura, 2km from the city center. Schedules change often.

LAN (office at the airport) flies from Lima to Piura at 6:10am, 4:45pm and 7:40pm, returning to Lima at 8:20am, 11:30am, 6:30pm and 9:50pm. Considerably cheaper is **Avianca** (☎0-800-1-8222; www.avianca.com; Sánchez Cerro 234, CC Real Plaza) leaving Lima at 5:50am and 5pm and returning at 8:15am and 8:50pm, and upstart **Peruvian Airlines** (☎011-716-6000; www.peruvian.pe; Libertad 777), which departs Lima at 6pm and returns from Piura at 8pm.

BUS

International

The standard route to Ecuador goes along the Carretera Panamericana via Tumbes to Machala. Civa is the most comfortable option, departing at 9:45pm daily. Alternatively, **Transportes Loja** (☎073-30-5446; Sánchez Cerro Km 1) goes via La Tina to Macará (S12, four hours) and Loja (S28, eight hours) at 9:30am, 1pm and 9pm. These buses stop for border formalities, then continue.

Domestic

Several companies have offices on *cuadra* 1100 of Sánchez Cerro, though for Cajamarca and across the northern Andes, it's best to go to Chiclayo and get a connection there.

East of the San Miguel pedestrian bridge, buses and *combis* leave for Catacaos (S1.50 to S2, 15 minutes). Buses to Sullana (S2, 45 minutes) and Paita (S4, one hour) leave from **Terminal Interprovincial de Gechisa** (Prolongación Sánchez Cerro) a S5 taxi ride west of town. Chulucanas and Huancabamba buses leave from **Terminal Terrestre – Castilla** (Carretera Panamericana s/n) aka 'El Bosque,' a S3.50 *mototaxi* ride east of town.

Civa (☎01-418-1111; www.civa.com.pe; cnr Tacna & Castilla, east of the San Miguel Bridge) Has 5pm, 6pm and 6:30pm buses to Lima, frequent buses to Chulucanas and two buses to Huancabamba at 9:30am and 6:30pm, the latter two leaving from Terminal Terrestre – Castilla).

Cruz del Sur (☎0-801-11111; www.cruzdelsur.com.pe; cnr Bolognesi & Lima) Has comfortable Lima buses at 3pm, 5:30pm, 6:30pm and 7:30pm as well as a lone shot to Trujillo at 3pm.

El Dorado (☎073-32-5875; www.transporteseldorado.com.pe; Cerro 1119) Has 14 buses for Tumbes between 6:30am and 12:30am that stop in Máncora.

Eppo (☎073-30-4543; www.eppo.com.pe; Carreterra Panamericana 243) Offers fast services to Máncora every half-hour from its new station behind CC Real Plaza.

Ittsa (☎044-33-3982; www.ittsabus.com; Cerro 1142) Has buses to Trujillo (9am, 1:30pm, 11:15pm), Chimbote (11pm), and a *bus-cama* to Lima at 6pm.

Línea (☎073-30-3894; www.linea.pe; Cerro 1215) Hourly buses to Chiclayo between 5am and 8pm, and 1:30pm and 11pm buses to Trujillo.

Tepsa (☎01-617-9000; www.tepsa.com.pe; Loreto 1198) Lima buses at 3pm, 5pm, 6:30pm and 9pm.

Transportes Chiclayo (☎074-50-3548; www.transporteschiclayo.com; Cerro 1121) Hourly buses to Chiclayo.

Transportes San Pedro y San Pablo (☎073-34-9271; Terminal Terrestre – Castilla) Has a *semi-cama* for Huancabamba at 6pm.

Piura Buses:

DESTINATION	COST (S)	DURATION (HR)
Chiclayo	12-20	3
Chimbote	35	8
Guayaquil (Ec)	50-60	10-12
Huancabamba	25-20	8
Lima	59-135	12-16
Loja (Ec)	28	8
Mancará (Ec)	12	4
Máncora	16-25	3
Trujillo	25-45	6
Tumbes	16-25	5

TAXI

If you are heading to Máncora, Punta Sal or Tumbes, you can catch much faster *combis* with **Sertur** (☎01-658-0071; www.serturperu.com) which depart hourly between 6:30am and 8:30pm from Terminal Interprovincial de Gechisa (S25, 3½ hours).

Playa Lobitos

☎073

This relative newcomer on Peru's surf scene has a ton of great breaks, a chilled-out beach scene and just a smidge of nightlife. The village got its start as an oil town in the 1920s,

SHOPPING FOR SHAMANS

For the daring adventurer, **Huancabamba**, deep in the eastern mountains, is well worth the rough 10-hour journey from Piura. This region is famed in Peru for the powerful *brujos* (witch doctors) and *curanderos* (healers) who live and work at the nearby lakes of Huaringas. Peruvians from all over the country flock to partake in these ancient healing techniques. Many locals (but few gringos) visit the area, so finding information and guides is not difficult.

The mystical town of Huancabamba is surrounded by mountains shrouded in mist, and lies at the head of the long, narrow Río Huancabamba. The banks of the Huancabamba are unstable and constantly eroding and the town is subject to frequent subsidence and slippage. It has earned itself the nickname La Ciudad que Camina (Town that Walks). Spooky.

When people from the West think of witchcraft, visions of pointed hats, broomsticks and bubbling brews are rarely far away. In Peru, consulting *brujos* and *curanderos* is widely accepted and has a long tradition predating Spanish colonization.

Peruvians from all walks of life visit *brujos* and *curanderos* and often pay sizable amounts of money for their services. These shamans are used to cure an endless list of ailments, from headaches to cancer to chronic bad luck, and are particularly popular in matters of love – whether it's love lost, love found, love desired or love scorned.

The **Huaringas** lake area near Huancabamba, almost 4000m above sea level, is said to have potent curative powers and attracts a steady stream of visitors from all corners of the continent. The most famous lake in the area is **Laguna Shimbe**, though the nearby **Laguna Negra** is the one most frequently used by the *curanderos*.

Ceremonies can last all night and entail hallucinogenic plants (such as the San Pedro cactus), singing, chanting, dancing and a dip in the lakes' painfully freezing waters. Some ceremonies involve more powerful substances like *ayahuasca* (Quechua for 'vine of the soul'), a potent and vile mix of jungle vines used to induce strong hallucinations. Vomiting is a common side effect. The *curanderos* will also use *icaros*, which are mystical songs and

and you'll still see some remnant Oregon Pine buildings here and there. It then turned into a military outpost. Today, it's shores are shared by surfers and oil workers.

Activities

The surf is best here in October, and April through June, but expect some waves year-round. When it's cooking, you can get 2m waves that peel for several hundred meters. Expect mostly big barreling point breaks. Beginners should check out the shorebreaks near the pier.

Sleeping & Eating

Los Muelles Surf Camp HOSTEL **$**
(☎97-869-3003; www.facebook.com/losmuelles-surfcamp; near the pier; per person camping S13-15, dm S10-15, per person r S25) While there's a slight Jonestown vibe, this place is pretty cool. Housed in the skeleton of a rundown 1920s-era bodega, the open-air surfer hangout has a 2nd-floor tent area, simple rooms with mattresses and little else, and a surfer-roots feel that harkens back to the sport's anti-establishment heyday.

From the 2nd-floor platform, you can see a handful of breaks, sip a *mate* (tea) and share tales with surfers and hangers-on from across the globe. Use of the shared kitchen costs S3.

Lobitos Lodge LODGE **$$**
(☎073-67-8723; www.lobitoslodge.com.pe; 100m south of pier on beach; s S120-180, d S180-270; P 🛜) Hands-down the nicest hotel in town, Lobitos Lodge has just eight rooms on a big swatch of beachfront property. The rooms have brand new beds, flat-screen TVs, balaconies with hammocks and a few photographs of the surfer-owner-business-magnate and his kin ripping it up. If you ask in advance, they can prepare a home-made meal.

It's worth it springing for the ocean-front rooms as the back rooms get hot.

Getting There & Away

To get here from Piura, take an Eppo (p349) bus to Talara (S9.50, two hours), then grab a *combi* (S3, 30 minutes) north to Playa Lobitos.

chants used to direct and influence the spiritual experience. Serious *curanderos* will spend many years studying the art, striving for the hard-earned title of *maestro curandero*. Many reports of dangerous *ayahuasca* practices (especially around Iquitos in the Amazon) are surfacing, and it pays to think once, twice and three times before ingesting the substance. We don't advise it. Bringing a friend is recommended, especially for single female travelers.

If you are interested in visiting a *curandero* while in Huancabamba, be warned that this tradition is taken very seriously and gawkers or skeptics will get a hostile reception. *Curanderos* with the best reputation are found closer to the lake district. The small **tourist information office** (☎073-47-3321; ⏱8am-6pm) at the bus station has an elementary map of the area and a list of accredited *brujos* and *curanderos*. In Salala, closer to the lakes, you will be approached by *curanderos* or their 'agents,' but be wary of scam artists – try to get a reference before you arrive. Know also that there are some *brujos* who are said to work *en el lado oscuro* (on the dark side). Expect to pay around S200 for a visit. If you go, hotels are rudimentary and most share cold-water bathrooms. **Hostal-El Dorado** (☎074-47-3016; Medina 116; s/d without bathroom S15/28) is on the Plaza de Armas and has a helpful owner.

At the Huancabamba bus terminal, **Civa** (☎01-418-1111; www.civa.com.pe), **Turismo Express** (☎074-34-4330) and **Transportes San Pedro y San Pablo** (☎074-47-3617) each have a morning service between 7:30am and 8am to Piura (S20, eight hours). Three afternoon buses also depart for Piura between 5pm and 7pm. To visit the lakes, catch the 5am *combi* from this terminal to the town of Salala (S5 to S7, two hours), from where you can arrange treks to the lakes on horseback (S20 to S25).

These days, busy Peruvian professionals can get online and consult savvy, business-minded shamans via instant messenger. Not quite the same thing as midnight chants and icy dunks in the remote lakes of the Andes.

Cabo Blanco

☎073

The Pan-American Hwy runs parallel to the ocean north of Talara, with frequent glimpses of the coast. This area is one of Peru's main oil fields, and pumps are often seen scarring both the land and the sea with offshore oil rigs.

About 40km north of Talara is the sleepy town of Cabo Blanco, one of the world's most famous fishing spots. Set on a gently curving bay strewn with rocks, the town has a flotilla of fishing vessels floating offshore where the confluence of warm Humboldt currents and El Niño waters creates a unique microcosm filled with marine life.

Ernest Hemingway was supposedly inspired to write his famous tale *The Old Man and the Sea* after fishing here in the early 1950s. The largest fish ever landed on a rod here was a 710kg black marlin, caught in 1953 by Alfred Glassell Jr. The angling is still good, though 20kg tuna are a more likely catch than black marlin, which have declined and are now rarely over 100kg. Fishing competitions are held here and 300kg specimens are still occasionally caught.

From November to January, magnificent 3m-high fast-charging left tubes attract hard-core surfers.

Deep-sea fishing boats with high-quality tackle can be rented through Hotel El Merlin and other hotels in the area for S1350 per six-hour day, including drinks and lunch. January, February and September are considered the best fishing months.

Sleeping

Hotel El Merlin HOTEL $
(☎073-25-6188; www.elmerlin.webs.com; s/d incl breakfast from S60/100; P 📶) The rooms all catch ocean breezes and have sweet beach-setting wallpapers, handsome stone-flagged floors, private cold showers and balconies with ocean views. With limited visitors to Cabo Blanco, this cavernous hotel can seem quite empty.

Hospedaje Cabo Blanco GUESTHOUSE $
(☎073-25-6202; Malecón s/n; s/d S40/80; 📶) This simple guesthouse at the entrance to town has two basic rooms, a shared kitchen and a little living-room area. It's a good spot for bigger groups wanting to rent out the whole house.

Getting There & Away

Cabo Blanco is several kilometers down a winding road from the Pan-American Hwy town of El Alto. From Máncora, you can take a *combi* to El Alto (S2, 30 minutes), then grab a truck or *combi* down to Cabo Blanco (S2, 15 minutes).

Máncora

073 / POP 9700

Máncora is *the* place to see and be seen along the Peruvian coast – in the summer months foreigners flock here to rub sunburned shoulders with the frothy cream of the Peruvian jet set. It's not hard to see why – Peru's best sandy beach stretches for several kilometers in the sunniest region of the country, while dozens of plush resorts and their budget-conscious brethren offer up rooms just steps from the rolling waves. On shore, most of the action is focused on the noisy main street, with plenty of good seafood restaurants and international flavors to choose from.

The consistently good surf and bathtub-warm waters draw a sun-bleached, board-toting bunch, and raucous nightlife keeps visitors busy after the sun dips into the sea in a ball of fiery flames.

Year-round sun means that this is one of the few resort towns on the coast that doesn't turn into a ghost town at less popular times.

Located about halfway between Talara and Tumbes, Máncora has the Pan-American Hwy passing right through its middle, within 100m of the surf, where it becomes Av Piura, which changes to Av Grau halfway through town. At the southern entrance to town, there's a turnoff from the Pan-American Hwy that takes you south along the coast on the Antigua Panamericana. This quiet stretch has the best high-end and midrange resorts, and direct access to Las Pocitas and Vichayito Beaches, probably the best stretch of sand around.

Activities

There are remote, deserted beaches around Máncora; ask your hotel to arrange a taxi or give you directions by bus and foot, but be prepared to walk several kilometers.

Surfing & Kitesurfing

Surf here is best from November to February, although good waves are found year-round and always draw dedicated surfers. The best expert break in town is Punta Ballenas (a steep point break with a rocky bottom that's located about five minutes' walk south of the main beach). Máncora beach itself has great beach breaks that are suitable for all abilities (but can get pretty crowded). Definitely consider taking long day or overnight trips to nearby breaks like Los Organos, Lobitos, Talara and Cabo Blanco.

You can rent surfboards from several places at the southern end of the beach in Máncora (per hour S10, per day S20) – in front of Del Wawa is the most convenient.

Laguna Surf Camp SURFING
(99-401-5628; www.vivamancora.com/lagunacamp; Veraniego s/n) The friendly Pilar at Laguna Camp does surf lessons for S60 for 90 minutes of instruction (including board rental).

Máncora Surf Shop SURFING
(www.mancorasurfshop.com; Piura 352) Máncora Surf Shop sells boards, surf clothing and organizes lessons for about S50 per hour.

Wild K KITESURFING
(www.wild-kitesurf-peru.com; Piura 261) May through September offers the best kitesurfing in Máncora (with some leftovers in January and February). Wild K does a three-day course for US$360. You can also do an hour-long intro for US$65. They rent paddle boards for half (S60) and full days (S90), and do hour-long paddleboard classes (S90).

Biking

Amancay BICYCLE RENTAL
(94-794-6470; www.amancaybikes.com; Piura Interior s/n) Rents bikes for one hour (S15), four hours (S40) and eight hours (S70), and does three-hour guided bike tours to EcoFundo (S80). The best biking spot is to Eco-Fundo or along the Antigua Panamericana.

Mud Baths

About 11km east of town, up the wooded Fernández Valley, a natural **hot spring** (admission S3) has bubbling water and powder-fine mud – perfect for a face pack. The slightly sulfurous water and mud is said to have curative properties. The hot spring can be reached by *mototaxi* (S50 including waiting time).

Diving & Snorkeling

The snorkeling and diving aren't great here, but an afternoon excursion can be fun. Snorkeling tours (S80) take you out to swim with sea turtles along the pier of a small fishing village called El Ñuro, located 23km south of Máncora at the end of Los Órganos beach. Most of the diving is done from nearby petroleum platforms, with 70m descents. Expect limited visibility, schools of fish and octopus.

Spondylus Dive Center DIVING
(☎99-989-1268; www.buceaenperu.com; Piura 216) Máncora's only dive shop is the first PADI-certified operation in Peru. They offer three-day open-water courses for S990, half-day dives for S300 (no diving credentials required), and two fun dives for S300 for certified divers.

Trekking
To see some of the interior of this desert coast, hire a pickup (around S75, including waiting time) to take you up the Fernández Valley, past the mud baths and on until the road ends (about 1½ hours). Continue for two hours on foot through mixed woodlands with unique birdlife to reach Los Pilares, which has pools ideal for swimming. You can also visit these areas as part of a tour.

Tours

Several operators in town offer a mix of tours, including snorkeling (S80 to S100), a nine-hour trip north to the Manglares (S60 to 100), Chiclayo and Sipán (S99), and Piura and around (S89). Your tourist bucks do more for small local economies if you stay the night in these far-off places.

Iguana Tours ADVENTURE TOUR
(☎073-63-2762; www.iguanastrips.com; Piura 245) Iguana's organizes full-day trips to the Los Pilares dry forest, which include wading through sparkling waterfalls, swimming, horseback riding, a soak in the mud baths and lunch for S180 per person, along with other standard tours.

Discovery Tours ADVENTURE TOUR
(☎073-51-1593; www.discoveryperu_chiclayo.com; Piura 300) This mainstream operator offers all the major tours.

Eco Fundo La Caprichosa ZIPLINING
(☎073-25-8572; www.ecofundolacaprichosa.com) This 'eco fun park' does a S100 canopy tour – the two-hour trip takes you over 1600m on four lines – and horseback rides for S20. It's located 10 minutes inland by *mototaxi* (S15).

Sleeping

Rates for accommodations in Máncora are seasonal, with the January to mid-March high season commanding prices up to 50% higher than the rest of the year, especially at weekends. During the three major holiday periods (Christmas to New Year, Semana Santa and Fiestas Patrias) accommodations can cost triple the low-season rate, require multinight stays and be very crowded; this time is generally best avoided. High-season rates are given here.

South of town, along Antigua Panamericana, you'll find great midrange and high-end accommodation. A *mototaxi* between here and town costs between S5 and S10.

★**Loki del Mar** HOSTEL $
(☎073-25-8484; www.lokihostel.com; Av Piura 262; dm S28-39, r S96, all incl breakfast;

THE NORTH COAST'S TOP SURF BREAKS

Dedicated surfers will find plenty of action on Peru's North Coast, from the longest break in the world at Puerto Chicama to consistently good surf at Máncora. Most spots have reliable swell year-round, and there are plenty of beginner spots in between.

Los Organos Located about 14km south of Máncora. Has a rocky break with well-formed tubular waves reaching up to 2m; it's for experienced surfers only.

Cabo Blanco (p351) A perfect pipeline ranging between 1m and 3m in height and breaking on rocks; again, experienced surfers only.

Puerto Chicama (p332) On a good day, this is the longest break in the world (up to 3km!); it has good year-round surfing for all skill levels.

Máncora Popular and easily accessible, with consistently decent surf up to 2m high; it's appropriate for all skill levels.

Huanchaco (p329) Long, well-formed waves with a pipeline; it's suitable for all skill levels.

Playa Lobitos (p349) Eight-plus named breaks in a back-to-basics surf setting.

) Social butterflies flock to this mother of all beach hostels, which is really a self-contained resort masquerading as a backpackers' hangout. Tucked away in the whitewashed building are spacious dorm rooms with extra wide beds and a few private rooms for those seeking a hostel vibe without the communal snoring.

The party revolves around the massive pool, bar and lounge area, where beer pong rules are clearly laid out and a running board of (mostly) free activities keeps everyone entertained. As far as hostels go, it's punching above its weight class.

Kokopelli HOSTEL **$**
(073-25-8091; www.hostelkokopelli.com; Piura 209; dm S32-40, r S100, all incl breakfast;) Part of a successful chain of Peruvian hostels, this is the most intimate hostel in town. It doesn't have beach access, but there's a small pool, cool bar area, colorful dorm rooms boasting loads of exposed brick and three private rooms with in-room safes, a rarity in Peruvian hostels. It's a great alternative if your first choice is booked.

Laguna Surf Camp BUNGALOW **$**
(99-401-5628; www.vivamancora.com/lagunacamp; Veraniego s/n; dm/s/d S30/90/120, bungalows S80-120;) This laid-back pad is a hidden gem, one block back from the beach in its own little rustic oasis. Older Indonesian-style bamboo bungalows sit around a pleasant sandy garden right near the water and lots of swinging, shady hammocks will provide days of entertainment. New five-bed dorms are a boon for budgeteers.

The cheery owner, Pilar, who is also a surf instructor, is a joy and nailed the essence of Máncora years ago.

Del Wawa HOTEL **$$**
(073-25-8427; www.delwawa.com; 8 de Octubre s/n; s/d S50/100;) This surfer's mecca is set up right on the beach, and perhaps rides that wave a little too casually at times – lots of chipped paint and dangerously rusty hot water heaters in some rooms kill the mood and an aloof front desk doesn't reverse that trend.

But brightly colored adobe rooms facing the ocean are hard to beat for location, as are the newer, warm-colored 2nd-floor rooms in a back annex. It has the most idyllic common area on the town beach with great views of the best breaks from a gaggle of comfy, umbrella-shaded beach lounges and there's surfboard rental, and kitesurfing instruction.

Hostal Las Olas HOTEL **$$**
(073-25-8099; www.lasolasmancora.com; s/d/tr incl breakfast from S140/160/240;) This great couples' spot dons a Mediterranean-esque olive tone on the outside and minimalist white rooms with wood accents on the inside. The small, cozy restaurant looks onto the beach's best breaks and is a surf-spotter's dream.

Newer 2nd- and 3rd-floor rooms are larger with expansive terraces and ocean views, but the cheapest rooms sit under a staircase that sounds like an earthquake when people who've sprung for the best rooms bound up to revel in their better abodes.

Marcilia Beach Bungalows BUNGALOW **$$**
(073-69-2902; www.marciliadevichayito.com; Antigua Panamericana Km 1212; r per person incl breakfast with/without sea view S100/80;) A friendly trilingual Peruvian couple started these rustic bungalows on Vichayito Beach after years working the cruise-ship circuit. Each rustic bungalow has electric hot water and very nice bathrooms, but the real coup here is the one that sits seaside: book it and you'll feel like the entire stretch of beach is your own private paradise.

★ **Sunset Hotel** BOUTIQUE HOTEL **$$$**
(073-25-8111; www.sunsetmancora.com; Antigua Panamericana 196; s/d incl breakfast S360/450;) The intimate, boutique-styled Sunset wouldn't be out of place on the cover of a glossy travel mag. It has beautifully furnished interiors and great aqua-themed rock sculptures, the good-sized rooms supply solid mattresses, hot showers, balconies and views of the seascape.

The pool is tiny and ocean access is rocky, though a short walk brings you to a sandy beach – if you can tear yourself away from the hotel's Italian restaurant, one of the area's best.

Casa de Playa RESORT **$$$**
(073-25-8005; www.casadeplayamancora.net; Antigua Panamericana Km 1217; s/d incl breakfast S200/280;) This wonderfully friendly place offers up modern, slick dwellings colored in warm orange and yellow tones and constructed with lots of gently curving lines. Half the room interiors are dressed in smoothed exposed concrete, which contrasts well with the plethora of colorful common areas – all are reached via lush corridors strewn with all manner of vibrant plants.

All the large rooms have hot water, arty bits and a balcony with a hammock and fine sea views. An inviting two-story lounge hangs out over the sea.

Hotelier HOTEL $$$
(073-25-8702; www.hotelier.pe; Antigua Panamericana Km 1217; s/d incl breakfast from S200/270;) If you travel for food, this artsy choice is your resting place. The owner, Javier Ruzo, is the son of one of Peru's most famous chefs, Teresa Ocampo, who spent 30 years at the helm of a Peruvian cooking show on TV (think the Peruvian Julia Childs).

Javier, a published chef himself and all-around character, carries on the family tradition at the fabulous restaurant here, but beyond that, he's also an artist and photographer whose work (poems, paintings, photos) gives unique personality to each of the rooms.

DCO Suites BOUTIQUE HOTEL $$$
(073-25-8171; www.hoteldco.com; ste incl breakfast from S710;) This relative newcomer upped the ante into the stratosphere for trendsetters and it remains the discerning choice of jetsetters, rock stars, honeymooners and other deep-pocketed nomads.

Though the color scheme – a jarring turquoise and white – is seriously polarizing, the spacious rooms come with his-and-hers kimono-style robes, rain-style showers and lovely curved sandstone walls that fit together like an architectural jigsaw puzzle.

Service, privacy and luxury are the trump cards here, whether on the curtained beach *cabañas*, at the remarkable outdoor spa or in the small infinity pool.

Eating

Seafood rules the culinary roost in Máncora. Other ingredients tend to be pricier due to transportation costs. There are several mini-markets along the strip for self-caterers.

Green Eggs & Ham BREAKFAST $
(Grau 503; meals S15-18; 7:30am-4:30pm) There's nothing silly about this Dr Seuss-inspired breakfast spot, which counts a battalion of gringo fans for its homesick-remedy breakfasts (pancakes, French toast, hash browns). Yes, you'll like them Sam I Am, but the real coup is the 2nd-floor patio – a straight shot through a thatch of tall palms to the crashing waves.

Angela's Place BREAKFAST $
(Piura 396; breakfasts S6.50-14, mains S5-12; from 8am;) Angela the Austrian bread wizard started selling her delicious sweet potato, yucca and wheat breads from her bicycle years ago. Now you can get them at her cheery cafe on the main drag, along with creative and substantial vegetarian (and vegan) dishes, energizing breakfast combos and sweet pastries.

Beef Grill BURGERS, STEAKHOUSE $
(Piura 253; burgers S18-23; from 5pm) The North Coast's best burgers are an ideal antidote to the seafood blues, but there are more serious slabs of meat coming out of the kitchen too.

Jugería Mi Janett JUICES
(Piura 677; juices S3-6) For juices so big and so tasty they can easily replace your breakfast. Head over to the best juice joint in town, where massive jugs of your favorite tropical fruits are freshly squeezed daily.

★La Sirena d'Juan PERUVIAN $$
(073-25-8173; Piura 316; mains S30-35; closed Tue;) Local boy done good, Juan has turned his intimate little main drag seafooder into northern Peru's best restaurant. Yellowfin tuna fresh from Máncora's waters is the showstopper here, whether it's prepared as a *tiradito* (a sort of Peruvian sashimi) in yellow curry or grilled with a mango-*rocoto*-red-pepper chutney.

Also on the menu are creative raviolis and Peruvian classics given a foodie upgrade (baby goat in black beer, for example). Service in the small, French farmhouse-style space is personalized and on point. It's expensive for Máncora, but you'd probably pay triple this at home.

Reservations are not a bad idea in high season.

Tao SOUTHEAST ASIAN $$
(Piura 240; mains S12-35; closed Mon) The aromas of Southeast Asia waft out onto Piura from the interior of this Thai-Chinese hot spot. Travelers flock here for the taste-bud flip – red, yellow, green and panang curries, fusion stir-fries and noodles.

All make good use of local tuna, but pork, beef, chicken and veggies are on the menu as well. It's upscale, but is always packed with backpackers looking for a culinary upgrade for the evening.

Ají MEXICAN $$
(Piura Interna s/n; mains S20-30;) Away from the honks and exaust of the main drag, this friendly retreat serves up ample Mexican dishes and a smattering of standard pub fare like hot wings and barbecue chicken. The open-air restaurant has a small bar, and the owner, Eric, is a cool surfer dude with plenty of tips.

Donde Teresa PERUVIAN $$$
(073-25-8702; Antigue Panamericana Km 1217, Hotelier; mains S32-70;) Before Gastón Acurio, there was Teresa Ocampo, Peru's most recognizable celebrity chef (famous before Peruvian food was even famous). She lives in Texas now, but her son, Javier, keeps the dream alive a short S5 *mototaxi* ride away on Los Pocitas Beach.

Recommended dishes include a smoked *ají de gallina*, stir-fried rice with seafood, anything with yellowfin tuna, and a memorable pisco-dunked bread pudding.

Javier has lived in France, China and God knows where else, so his skills are honed and he even spears his own catches of the day on occasion! If this restaurant weren't fabulous, Peruvians would riot. Call ahead in January, February and July.

Drinking & Nightlife

Most restaurants offer two-for-one happy-hour specials, with the party starting along Piura, then moving to the dancehall bars along the beach. Loki (p353) has a DJ party Friday and Saturday nights (you may need to present a passport).

Information

All in all, it's pretty safe, but there have been some reports of late-night robberies. Be wary of your bags in *mototaxis*, as there are limited reports of taxi drivers running off with people's bags. Don't walk the beach alone at night.

Many travelers extend their stays by volunteering in the hostels or finding employment in a restaurant or bar – fun for the traveler, not great for locals who also compete for these jobs.

There is no information office, but the website www.vivamancora.com has tons of useful information. There are BCP, BBVA, Globalnet and Banco de la Nación ATMs along the strip, but only the last is a bank. You'll find scattered internet access on the strip as well.

Banco de la Nación (Piura 625) Change US dollars here.

Medical Center (073-20-8743; www.medicalcentermancora.com; Antigue Panamericana s/n; 24hr) If you get stung by a ray or break a bone, head to this full-service clinic at the far northern entrance to town.

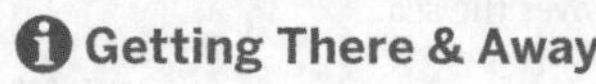

Getting There & Away

AIR

The best way to get here by plane is to fly to Piura with **LAN** (073-30-2145; www.lan.com; Grau 140), Avianca (p349) or Peruvian Airlines (p349), or to Tumbes with **LAN** (072-52-4481; www.lan.com; Bolognesi 250), catching ground transportation from there.

BUS

Many bus offices are in the center, though most southbound trips originate in Tumbes. *Combis* leave for Tumbes (S10, two hours) regularly; they drive along the main drag until full. *Buscamas* from Máncora go direct to Lima (14 hours); other services can drop you in intermediate cities on the way to Lima (18 hours). Regular minibuses run between Máncora and Punta Sal (S3, 30 minutes).

Cial (96-540-2235; Piura 520) Has a Lima-bound bus at 5:30pm.

Cifa (94-181-6863; www.cifainternacional.com; Grau 2121) Cheap daily buses to Guayaquil (S60) and Cuenca (S60) in Ecuador.

Civa (01-418-1111; www.excluciva.pe; Piura 704) Has an economical 3:30pm service to Lima, as well as nicer buses at 5:30pm and 6:30pm; and a midnight bus to Guayaquil.

Cruz del Sur (0-801-1111; www.cruzdelsur.com.pe; Grau 208) Has a *bus-cama* service to Lima at 5:30pm; buses to Trujillo and Chimbote on Tuesday Wednesday, Friday and Saturday at 10:30pm; and you can catch its Guayaquil-bound bus from Lima at 9am on Monday, Tuesday, Thursday and Saturday.

El Dorado (073-25-8161; www.transporteseldorado.com.pe; Grau 213) Six buses a day to Piura between 9:30am and 9:30pm; buses for Chiclayo (9:30am, 9:30pm, 11:30pm, midnight) and Trujillo (9:30am, 9:30pm, 11pm). A Tumbes-bound bus also grabs passengers seven times a day.

Emtrafesa (072-52-5850; www.emtrafesa.com; Grau 193) Heads to Chiclayo at 9:30pm and 10pm; Trujillo at 8:30pm, 9:30pm and 10pm.

Eppo (073-25-6262; Piura 679) Fast and regular hourly buses to Sullana and Piura between 4:15am and 7pm. Will drop you at Organos for S2.

Oltursa (01-708-5000; www.oltursa.pe; Piura 509;) Lima *bus-cama* (with wi-fi) at 5:30pm and 6pm Monday to Saturday; 4pm and 4:30pm Sunday.

Sertur (01-658-0071; www.serturperu.com; Piura 624) Faster *colectivo* vans to Piura (departing hourly from 7am to 9pm) and Tumbes (departing hourly from 8am to 6pm).

Tepsa (☎01-617-9000; www.tepsa.com.pe; Grau 113) Lima bus at 6pm.

Máncora Buses:

DESTINATION	COST (S)	DURATION (HR)
Chiclayo	39-100	6
Chimbote	80	14
Guayaquil (Ec)	60-108	9
Lima	60-145	14-18
Piura	20-95	3½
Sullana	12.50	2½
Trujillo	30-87	9-10
Tumbes	10-60	2

Punta Sal

☎072 / POP 3300

The long, curvy bay at Punta Sal, 25km north of Máncora, has fine sand and is dotted with rocky bits – but it's still great for a dip in the ocean. The sea here is calm and the lack of surfer types means that this tranquil oasis of resorts is particularly popular with families.

Sleeping & Eating

Las Terrazas de Punta Sal HOTEL $

(☎072-50-7701; www.lasterrazasdepuntasal.com.pe; s/d without bathroom S25/50, r with bathroom from S80; @) One of the few budget options on this beach, Las Terrazas has solid rooms inside the main house, as well as some poky small bamboo rooms at the back – choose wisely! The terrace restaurant here has awesome sunset views.

Hotel Caballito de Mar BOUTIQUE HOTEL $$

(☎072-54-0058; www.hotelcaballitodemar.com; r per person incl full board S105-150; @) The 23 ocean-view rooms at Hotel Caballito de Mar literally climb up the sea cliff and have pretty bamboo accents and private patios. Hit the restaurant, bar, Jacuzzi, TV room, games room and the gorgeous pool that practically dips its toe into the sea. Activities such as fishing, boating, horseback riding, waterskiing and surfing can be arranged. It's located in the main town section of Punta Sal.

Punta Sal Suites & Bungalows RESORT $$$

(☎072-59-6700; www.puntasal.com.pe; s incl full board from S333-440, d per person incl full board S280-390; P@) Off the Pan-American Hwy at Km 1192 – about 10 minutes north of Punta Sal proper – this seaside oasis has all the good stuff you'd expect from a resort retreat. The way to go is the bungalows that can sleep up to five and are fully decked with tropical furnishings and have excellent beach vibes.

The individual rooms lack beach views. Perfect for families, it has mini-golf, laundry facilities, banana-boat rides, waterskiing, tennis, volleyball, table tennis, billiards and a wooden-decked pool – and what resort would be complete without a near-life-size replica of a conquistador galleon?

Getting There & Away

Regular minibuses run between Máncora and Punta Sal (S3, 30 minutes).

Zorritos

☎072 / POP 9400

About 35km south of Tumbes, Zorritos is the biggest fishing village along this section of coast. While the thin beach here isn't as nice as beaches further south, it is home to interesting coastal birdlife. Look for frigate birds, pelicans, egrets and other migratory birds. A new *malecón* with a gleaming building that remains uninhabitated promises bigger things for little Zorritos.

Sleeping & Eating

Dining options are limited, but there are a few eateries (mostly seafood joints) fronting the *malecón*.

Grillo Tres Puntas Ecohostel LODGE $

(☎072-79-4830; www.casagrillo.net; Panamericana Norte Km 1235; campsites S15, r with/without bathroom per person S55/30, all incl breakfast; @) Grillo Tres Puntas Ecohostel was constructed (mainly by volunteers) from natural materials such as bamboo and cane. Everything here, including water, is recycled. Breezy, rustic cabins with balconies and hammocks sit on the beach and campsites have electricity and a shade roof.

There is an artistic elevated patio fashioned from driftwood – great for sunset beers. All rooms share interesting outdoor communal bathrooms covered in mosaic tiles and seashells. Hiking to nearby mud baths can be arranged and they also run popular five-day hostal-and-camping tours that take in beaches, trekking, lagoons and mud baths and cost only S600 per person – including everything! It's supremely rustic but pretty idyllic at the same time.

HANDICRAFT HAVENS: CATACAOS & CHULUCANAS

A bustling small town 12km southwest of Piura, **Catacaos** is the self-proclaimed capital of *artesanía* (handicrafts) in the region. And justifiably so: its **arts market** (⊙10am-4pm) is the best in northern Peru. Sprawling for several blocks near the Plaza de Armas, here you will find excellent weavings, gold and silver filigree jewelry, wood carvings, ceramics (including lots of pieces from Chulucanas), leather goods and more. The weekends are the best and busiest times to visit. *Combis* and *colectivos* leave frequently for Catacaos from Av Tacna in Piura (S1.50 to S2, 15 minutes).

Located about 55km east of Piura, just before the Sechura Desert starts rising into the Andean slopes, **Chulucanas** is known Peru-wide for its distinctive ceramics – rounded, glazed, earth-colored pots that depict humans. Chulucanas' ceramics have officially been declared a part of Peru's cultural heritage and are becoming famous outside Peru.

The best place to buy ceramics around here is in La Encantada, a quiet rural outpost just outside of Chulucanas, whose inhabitants work almost exclusively in *artesanía*. La Encantada was home to the late Max Inga, a local legend who studied ceramic artifacts from the ancient Tallan and Vicus cultures and sparked a resurgence in the art form. The friendly artisans are often happy to demonstrate the production process, from the 'harvesting' of the clay to the application of mango-leaf smoke to get that distinctive black-and-white design. The village is reached from Chulucanas by a 30-minute *mototaxi* ride (S10) down a 7km dirt road. A good place to start your hunting is **Ceramica Inge** (Los Ceremistas 591), but a visit to Chulucanas is probably for die-hards only, as lugging this excellent but fragile pottery around Peru with you would be less than ideal. Civa has frequent buses to Chulucanas from Piura's Terminal Terrestre – Castilla (S4, one hour).

Puerta del Sol HOTEL $

(☎98-593-2412; puertadelsol@rosillotours.com; Piaggio 109; r per person incl breakfast S50-60; 📶) Right in Zorritos, Puerta del Sol is a skinny little *hospedaje* that is just too lovely for words. It has a miniature garden dissected by a winding, yellow-brick path and patches of vibrant lawn. The only accessory missing is a garden gnome. The rooms are simple and neat, and beach access is available, but there are no views.

Costa Azul RESORT $$

(☎01-446-1644; www.costaazulperu.com; Piaggio s/n; s/d/tr incl breakfast from S180/200/250; 📶🏊) While it gets a two-outta-ten on the friendliness scale, you can't beat the option of having three hotels combined into the one – choose from rustic to upmarket. Costa Azul offers rustic accommodations, next door Brisas brings nicer touches, while the Noelani is the cushiest of all, with its own infinity pool.

ℹ Getting There & Away

Combis to Zorritos leave regularly from Tumbes (S2.50, about one hour). Coming from the south, just catch any bus heading toward Tumbes.

Tumbes

☎072 / POP 99,700

Only 30km from the Ecuadorean border, Tumbes sits in a uniquely green part of coastal Peru, where dry deserts magically turn into mangroves and an expanse of ecological reserves stretches in all directions. As Peruvian dumps go, it comes in the top 10 – it's dirty, crumbling and occasional floods bring flies everywhere – but you'll probably need to go here if you are headed to Ecuador, and the nearby eco-reserves are worth a visit (though many are choosing to visit these on a day-tour from Máncora).

There are some very interesting kitsch mosiac structures, a riverwalk and a sweet Jesus statue that may just spark your imagination with their garishness.

A flashpoint for conflict during the border war between Ecuador and Peru (1940–41), Tumbes remains a garrison town with a strong military presence.

Sights

There are several **old houses** dating from the early 19th century on Grau, east of the Plaza de Armas. These rickety abodes are made of split-bamboo and wood and it seems like they are defying gravity through sheer will. The plaza has several outdoor restaurants and is a nice place to relax. The **pedestrian streets** north of the plaza (especially Bolívar) have several large, modern monuments and are favorite hangouts for young and old alike.

Museo de Cabeza de Baca MUSEUM
(admission S5; 8:30am-4pm Mon-Sat) About 5km south of Tumbes, off the Pan-American Hwy, is an overgrown archaeological site that was the home of the Tumpis people and, later, the site of the Inca fort visited by Pizarro. The story is told in this tiny site museum, which also displays some 1500-year-old ceramic vessels, including Chimú and Inca. One display case is dedicated to artifacts seized by customs before they were illegally trafficked out of the country.

Tours

Preference Tours GUIDED TOURS
(072-52-5518; turismomundial@hotmail.com; Grau 427; 9am-7:30pm Mon-Sat, to 11am Sun) This friendly shop runs some of the most economical tours in town. Puerto Pizarro tours cost S60 per person, Santuario Nacional Los Manglares de Tumbes tours are S95 per person, Cerros de Amotape costs S97.50 a head. All rates are for two people minimum.

Sleeping

Be sure your room has a working fan if you're here in the sweltering summer (December to March). During the wet season and the twice-yearly rice harvests, mosquitoes can be a big problem, and there are frequent water and electricity outages. In the lower end of the budget range, watch your valuables carefully.

Hotel Roma HOTEL $
(072-52-4137; hotelromatumbes@hotmail.com; Bolognesi 425; s/d S45/70;) Boasting top Plaza de Armas real estate, the Roma is an upper-level budget option and provides guests with clean, comfortable rooms with hot shower, high-octane fans, phone and cable TV. Accustomed to dealing with foreigners, it extends a warm welcome, but can be noisy – there's even an in-house intercom system that's switched on at all hours.

Hospedaje Lourdes GUESTHOUSE $
(072-52-2966; Mayor Bodero 118; s/d S40/60;) Clean, safe and friendly, the Lourdes offers austere (for Tumbes) rooms with fans, phones, TV and hot showers.

★ **Casa César** BOUTIQUE HOTEL $$
(072-52-2883; www.casacesartumbes.com; Huáscar 311; s/d incl breakfast from S110/160;) These former budget digs got the kind of makeover normally reserved for reality TV. It's now a full-on midrange boutique hotel that is professional, friendly and easy on the eyes. Sleek, high-design furniture colors up the minimalist white aesthetic at play here.

The 20 rooms are named after local fauna and are split between less sleek standards and colorful and bright executives. For Tumbes, it's a step up and the price is right.

Hotel Rizzo Plaza HOTEL $$
(072-52-3991; www.rizzoplazahotel.com; Bolognesi 216; s/d incl breakfast S116/138; @) Just steps from the Plaza de Armas, the ritzy Rizzo gets solid reviews from travelers. With a business center, it leans vaguely to a suit-and-tie set, with a professional staff, smallish bathrooms and way too many faux plants.

Hotel Costa del Sol BUSINESS HOTEL $$$
(072-52-3991; www.costadelsolperu.com; San Martín 275; s/d incl breakfast S300/400; @) This is the most upscale hotel in town, providing a decent restaurant, a pleasant bar and garden, and a Jacuzzi, swimming pool with a children's section, small casino and gym. The comfortable rooms could be way better – and don't compare to the other offerings by the chain – but it's about as good as you get. Offers free airport transfers.

Eating

There are several bars and restaurants on the Plaza de Armas, many with shaded tables and chairs outside – a real boon in hot weather. It's a pleasant place to sit and watch the world go by as you drink a cold beer and wait for your bus.

Moka CAFE $
(Bolognesi 252; snacks S5-10; 8am-1pm & 4:30-11pm) This modern cafe is so wildly out of place in Tumbes that it turns heads. You'll find loads of scrumptious cakes, flavored frappés, juices, milkshakes and not-quite-right espresso (but from a proper machine nonetheless). The good menu of 'croissant-wiches' makes for a lovely quick bite or breakfast (try chicken salad with avocado).

BORDER CROSSING: ECUADOR VIA TUMBES

Shady practices at the border crossing between Ecuador and Peru at Aguas Verdes earned it the dubious title of 'the worst border crossing in South America.' A new integrated one-stop office and increased police presence have made it safer in recent years, but keep on your toes.

A new **CEBAF** (Centro Binacional de Atención de Frontera; ⌚24hr) office in Huaquillas means you now get off your bus at the immigration control, present your Peruvian tourist card to immigration authorities, then step a few feet over to have your passport stamped for Ecuador.

Very few nationalities need a visa for Ecuador, but everyone needs a Tarjeta Andina embarkation card, available for free at the immigration office. You must surrender your Tarjeta Andina when you leave Ecuador. If you lose it, there is no monetary penalty but you will not be allowed to re-enter Ecuador for 90 days. Exit tickets out of Ecuador and sufficient funds (US$20 per day) are legally required, but rarely asked for. Tourists are allowed only 90 days per year in Ecuador without officially extending their stay at a consulate – if you have stayed more, you may be fined between US$200 and US$2000 when you leave.

You are strongly advised to take a direct bus across the border with a major bus company like Cruz del Sur, Civa, Ormeño or Cifa. The cheaper option is to take a local bus to the border and switch busses after passing immigration; it'll save you a few bucks, but can cost you dearly (see scams, below).

Aguas Verdes is basically a long, dusty street full of vendors that continues into the near-identical Ecuadorean border town of Huaquillas via the international bridge across the Río Zarumilla. If you are forced to stay the night at the border, there are a few basic hotels in Aguas Verdes, but they're all noisy and pretty sketchy. There are some nicer options in Huaquillas, but really you're better off hanging back in Tumbes for the night or making the two-hour bus trip to the city of Machala, where there are much better facilities.

Scams

By taking a direct bus, and simply getting off and on the bus at one stop, you avoid many scams. One common one run in the past happens if you take local transit to the border, where you may be hoodwinked into switching buses, where they eventually convince you that you'll need to contribute to bribe the border police. You're also likely to encounter plenty of touts and money changers passing false bills. Don't change your money here.

The Ecuadorian border town of Huaquillas is best avoided. It's far better to take the bus straight through to Machala or Guayaquil further on in Ecuador.

See Lonely Planet's *Ecuador & the Galápagos Islands* for more information.

Classic Restaurant PERUVIAN **$**
(☎072-52-4301; Tumbes 185; mains S20-27, menú S7; ⌚8am-5pm) Small, quiet as a funeral home and dignified, Classic Restaurant is a wonderful place to escape torrid Tumbes and relax with a long lunch, as many of the town's better-connected locals do. The food is good and mainly coastal, but secretly we love this place for its air-con. The daily *menú* is a steal.

Sí Señor PERUVIAN **$$**
(Bolívar 115; mains S15-35) On a quiet corner of the plaza with pleasant streetside tables outside and quixotic, slow-turning fans inside, Sí Señor is the long-standing staple doing all manner of everything, with a heavy emphasis on fish and seafood. The dizzying menu of Peruvian faves and seafood dishes will leave you giddy.

Las Terrazas PERUVIAN **$$**
(☎072-52-1575; Araujo 549; mains S15-30) A little bit out of the town center, this popular place is well worth the S1.50 *mototaxi* ride. Packed with hungry diners daily, it serves up heaping plates of seafood, and will ceviche or cook anything from fish to lobster and octopus. It's all prepared in the northern coastal style and they have music Friday through Monday from 3pm.

Information

Apart from offering tours to local sights, Tumbes tour companies can also provide some tourist information.

DANGERS & ANNOYANCES

The border crossing has a bad reputation, but new infrastructure and immigration offices may be helping.

EMERGENCY

Policía de Turismo (Poltur; ☎97-288-0013; San Pedro 600, 2nd fl) Tourist police.

IMMIGRATION

Ecuadorian Consulate (☎072-52-5949; Bolívar 129, 3rd fl) On the Plaza de Armas.

Oficina de Migraciónes (☎072-52-3422; www.migraciones.gob.pe; Carretera Panamericana Km 1275.5) Along the Pan-American Hwy, 2km north of town. Handles visa issues.

MEDICAL SERVICES

Clinica Feijoo (☎072-52-5341; www.clinica-feijoo.blogspot.com; Castilla 305) One of the better medical clinics in Tumbes.

MONEY

Banco Continental (Bolívar 129) Bank and ATM.

BCP (Bolívar 261) Changes traveler's checks and has an ATM.

POST

Serpost (San Martín 208; ⏲9am-7pm Mon-Fri, to 1pm Sat) Postal service on the block south of Plaza Bolognesi.

TOURIST INFORMATION

iPerú (☎072-50-6721; Malecón III Milenio, 3rd fl) Provides useful tourist information. Walk south on Bolognesi to the waterfront to find it.

Getting There & Away

AIR

The airport (TBP) is 8km north of town. LAN (p356) has a daily flight from Lima to Tumbes leaving at 5:30pm and returning to Lima at 7:55pm. Fares rise from S379 for foreigners.

BUS

You can usually find a bus to Lima within 24 hours of your arrival in Tumbes, but they're sometimes (especially during major holidays) sold out a few days in advance. You can take a bus south to another major city and try again from there.

Some companies offer a limited-stop special service, with air-con, bathrooms and very loud video; some have deluxe, nonstop *bus-cama* services.

Slower services stop at Piura, Chiclayo and Trujillo. If you are heading to Máncora or Piura, much faster *colectivo* minivans are the best way to go.

If you're going to Ecuador, it's easiest to go with Cifa, an Ecuadorean company, or Ormeño. Civa leaves in the middle of the night and Cruz del Sur only departs three days per week. All stop at the border for you to complete passport formalities.

From around the market area, *colectivos* for Puerto Pizarro leave from the corner of Castilla and Feijoo; for Zorritos, *combis* depart from Castilla near Ugarte; for Rica Playa, *combis* depart from Ugarte 404 near Castilla. Ask locals as the stops aren't marked.

For Máncora, faster, air-conditioned minivans congregate around the corner of Tumbes and Piura. On the southwest corner of the same intersection, slower, cheaper *combis* also depart regularly. Buses to Casitas leave at 1pm (S10, five hours).

Cial (☎072-52-6350; www.expresocial.com; Tumbes 958) *Bus-cama* to Lima at 3:30pm.

Cifa (☎072-52-5120; www.cifainternacional.com; Tumbes 958) Heads to Machala (you must switch in Huaquillas) and Guayaquil six times daily, both in Ecuador, about every two hours from 6am to 5pm.

Civa (☎01-418-1111; www.civa.com.pe; Tumbes 587) Cheaper *semi-cama* Lima services at 1:30pm and 4:30pm and a *bus-cama* at 3:30pm. A Guayaquil bus departs at 2am.

Cruz del Sur (☎0-801-11111; www.cruzdelsur.com.pe; Tumbes 319) *Bus-cama* to Lima at 3:30pm and Guayaquil on Monday, Thursday and Saturday at 11am.

El Sol (☎072-50-9252; Piura 403) Economy buses to Chiclayo (S26) at 8:15am and 9:30am. Also a service to Lima (S55) via Chiclayo (S20) and Trujillo (S28) at 8:20pm.

Oltursa (☎01-708-5000; www.oltursa.pe; Tumbes 948) *Bus-cama* service to Lima at 3:30pm and 4pm (Monday to Saturday), 2pm and 2:30pm Sunday. Also heads to Trujillo and Chiclayo daily at 8pm.

Ormeño (☎072-52-2894; www.grupo-ormeno.com.pe; Tumbes 1187) Lima departure at 7:30pm via Chiclayo and Trujillo. Also has a direct bus to Guayaquil at 9:30am.

Sertur (☎01-658-0071; www.serturperu.com; Tumbes 502) Faster minivans to Máncora and Piura every 30 minutes from 5:30am to 8:30pm.

Tepsa (☎01-617-9000; www.tepsa.com.pe; Tumbes 199) To Lima at 4pm.

Transportes Chiclayo (☎074-50-3548; www.transporteschiclayo.com; Tumbes 570) Daily buses to Chiclayo via Máncora at 12:30pm and 9pm.

Transportes El Dorado (☎072-52-3480; www.transporteseldorado.com.pe; Tacna 251) Thirteen daily buses to Piura and departures to Chiclayo and Trujillo at 7:30pm, 9pm and 10:30pm.

Tumbes Buses:

DESTINATION	COST (S)	DURATION (HR)
Chiclayo	30-100	8
Guayaquil (Ec)	80-100	6
Lima	60-175	16-18
Machala (Ec)	12	3
Máncora	35-60	1½-2
Piura	35-95	4-5
Puerto Pizarro	1.50	¼
Rica Playa	4	1½
Trujillo	39-100	11
Zorritos	2.50	¾

Getting Around

A taxi to the airport is about S20. There are no *combis* to the airport.

Puerto Pizarro

072

About 14km north of Tumbes, the character of the oceanfront changes from the coastal desert, which stretches more than 3000km north from central Chile to northern Peru, to the mangrove swamps that dominate much of the Ecuadorean and Colombian coastlines. There's an explosion of **birdlife** here, with up to 200 different migrating species visiting these areas. Boats can be hired to tour the mangroves; one tour goes to a **crocodile sanctuary** where you can see Peru's only crocodiles being nursed back from near extinction. The nearby **Isla de Aves** can be visited (but not landed on) to see the many nesting seabirds, especially between 5pm to 6pm, when huge flocks of birds return to roost for the night. Boats line the waterfront of Puerto Pizarro and cost S30 per hour per boat; you can do a tour of the mangroves and the above-mentioned sites for S40 per boat for up to six people. You pay an entrance fee to Puerto Pizarro of S3.50.

Two good options are **Turmi** (97-298-6199; Grau s/n), the boatmen's association, which is your best bet for small groups and independent travelers; and **Manglaris Tours** (972-634-241; Grau s/n), which has bigger boats and prices as cheap as S7 per person for the standard tour. Both hang out along the walkway to the pier. Tour companies in Tumbes also provide guided tours to the area.

A quick and easy independent day trip from Tumbes is a visit to **Isla Hueso de Ballena**, which has a few lunch restaurants. They are all pretty ramshackle, but **Restaurante Hueso de Ballena** (mains S25-28; 9am-6pm) is pretty ideal, right on the sand with a few hammocks as well. It promises an 'orgy of shellfish' and is a good place to try the local specialty, *conchas negras* (black shells), as well as ceviche, seafood rices, *chicharrónes* and soups, with ingredients all plucked fresh from the water. Boats will take you out to the restaurants and back for S25, including wait time.

There are regular *combis* between Puerto Pizarro and Tumbes (S1.50, 15 minutes).

Reserva de Biosfera del Noroeste

The Northwestern Biosphere Reserve consists of four protected areas that cover 2344 sq km in the department of Tumbes and northern Piura. A lack of government funding means that there is little infrastructure or tourist facilities – much of what exists was funded by organizations such as the Fundación Peruana para la Conservación de la Naturaleza (FPCN; also called ProNaturaleza), with assistance from international bodies such as the WWF.

Information about the area is available from the Tumbes office of **Sernanp** (072-52-6489; www.sernanp.gob.pe; Panamericana Norte 1739, Tumbes; 8:30am-12:30pm & 3:30-5:30pm Mon-Fri), the government department in charge of administering this region. You will need to get permission papers to visit any of the protected areas on your own; these are free and take minutes to organize. You should check with your consulate, as well as with local operators in Tumbes or Máncora, about security in the park.

Tour companies in Tumbes can arrange tours to the two most visited areas, Parque Nacional Cerros de Amotape and Santuario Nacional los Manglares de Tumbes, as can Grillo Tres Puntas Ecohostel (p357) in Zorritos. There are few roads into these areas and visiting during the wet months of December to April can prove very difficult.

Parque Nacional Cerros de Amotape

The tropical dry forest ecosystem of Cerros de Amotape is protected by this 1515-sq-km national park, which makes up the lion's share of the Biosfera and is home to flora and fauna including jaguars, condors and anteaters, though parrots, deer and peccaries are more commonly sighted. Large-scale logging, illegal hunting and overgrazing are some of the threats facing this habitat, of which there is very little left anywhere in Peru. The best place to spot a wide range of wild animals is the Zona Reservada de Tumbes, now encompassed within Amotape itself. The forest is similar to the tropical dry forest of other parts of Amotape, but because it lies more on the easterly side of the hills, it is wetter and has slightly different flora and fauna, including crocodiles, howler monkeys and nutria. You can also see various orchids and a wide variety of birds.

Guides are essential for spotting wildlife and can be arranged in the town of **Rica Playa**, a small, friendly village located just within the park. Although there are no hotels here, you can camp and local families will sell you meals.

Agencies in Tumbes also organize tours for S97.50 per person (minimum two), only visiting the park May through November.

Santuario Nacional los Manglares de Tumbes

This national sanctuary was established in 1988 and lies on the coast, separate from the other three dry-forest areas. Only about 30 sq km in size, it plays an essential role in conserving Peru's only region of mangroves. Entrance to the sanctuary is S10.

You can travel here by going to Puerto Pizarro and taking a dirt road northeast to the tiny community of **El Bendito**. From here, ask around for someone to guide you by canoe. Guided tours are available from Puerto Pizarro as well, though the mangroves here are not technically within the protection of the sanctuary. A visit here is tide-dependent. Agencies in Tumbes also arrange tours for S95 per person (minimum two).

Huaraz & the Cordilleras

Includes ➡

Best Places to Eat

- Café Andino (p373)
- Chili Heaven (p374)
- Mi Comedia (p374)
- Buongiorno (p399)
- Taita (p373)

Best Places to Stay

- Albergue Churup (p372)
- Lazy Dog Inn (p373)
- Llanganuco Mountain Lodge (p391)
- Cuesta Serena (p373)
- Andes Lodge Peru (p402)

Why Go?

Ground zero for outdoor-adventure worship in Peru, the Cordilleras are one of the preeminent hiking, trekking and backpacking spots in South America. Every which way you throw your gaze, perennially glaciered white peaks razor their way through expansive mantles of lime-green valleys. In the recesses of these prodigious giants huddle scores of pristine jade lakes, ice caves and torrid springs. The Cordillera Blanca is one of the highest mountain ranges in the world outside the Himalaya, and its 18 ostentatious summits of more than 6000m will not let you forget it for a second.

Huaraz is the fast-beating heart linking the trekking trails and roads that serve as the mountains' arteries. Plans of daring ice climbs, mountain-biking exploits and rock-climbing expeditions are hatched over ice-cold beers in fireplace-warmed hostels and bars, often only interrupted by a brief sojourn into the eastern valley to the enigmatic 3000-year-old ruins of Chavín de Huántar.

When to Go

Huaraz

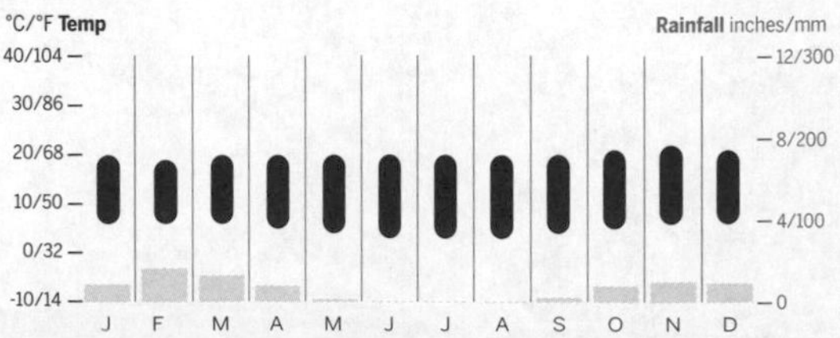

May–Sep The Cordilleras' dry season offers the best trekking conditions.

Oct–Dec A relaxed post-season atmosphere in Huaraz; more quality guides available.

Dec–Apr Wet and rainy, but appropriately geared trekkers enjoy the silence.

HUARAZ

☎043 / POP 64,100 / ELEV 3091M

Huaraz is the restless capital of this Andean adventure kingdom and its rooftops command exhaustive panoramas of the city's dominion: one of the most impressive mountain ranges in the world. Nearly wiped out by the earthquake of 1970, Huaraz isn't going to win any Andean-village beauty contests anytime soon, but it does have personality – and personality goes a long way.

This is first and foremost a trekking metropolis. During high season the streets buzz with hundreds of backpackers and adventurers freshly returned from arduous

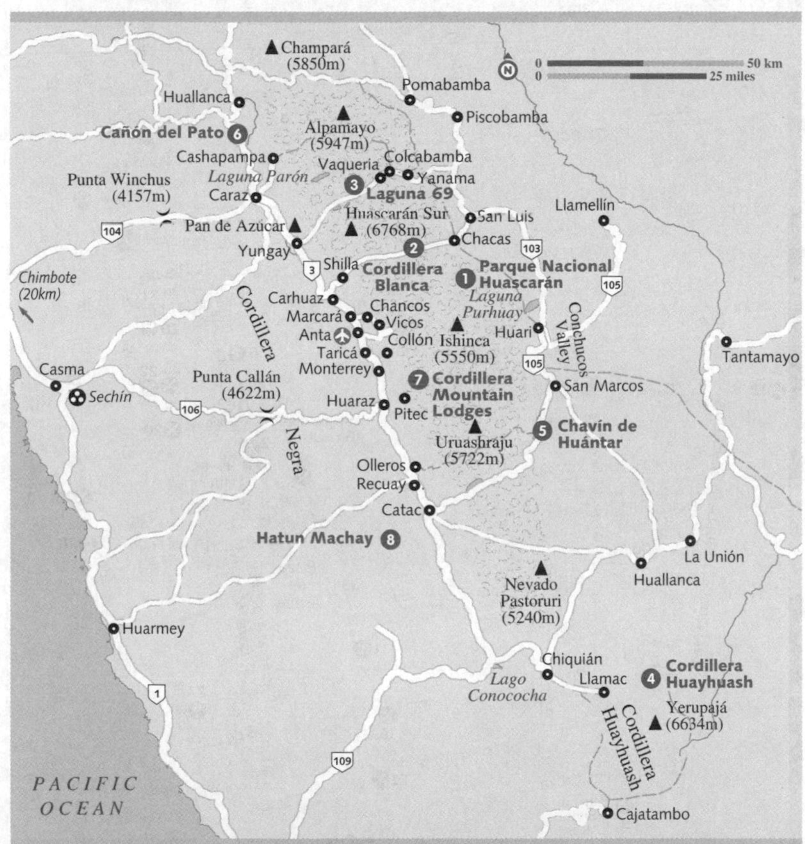

Huaraz & the Cordilleras Highlights

1 Traipsing for weeks around the magnificent peaks of **Parque Nacional Huascarán** (p379).

2 Riding the astonishing new highway between Huaraz and Chacas, where panoramas of the **Cordillera Blanca** (p378) lie before you like a painting.

3 Marveling at the blue waters of **Laguna 69** (p383).

4 Heading into the wilderness on the epic **Cordillera Huayhuash** (p384) circuit.

5 Journeying through mysterious passageways amid the ruins of **Chavín de Huántar** (p397).

6 Taking a white-knuckle ride through the sheer walls of the **Cañón del Pato** (p392).

7 Resting in an idyllic Cordillera mountain lodge like the **Lazy Dog Inn** (p373) or **Llanganuco Mountain Lodge** (p391).

8 Scrambling up boulders or climbing sheer rock faces at **Hatun Machay** (p395).

Huaraz

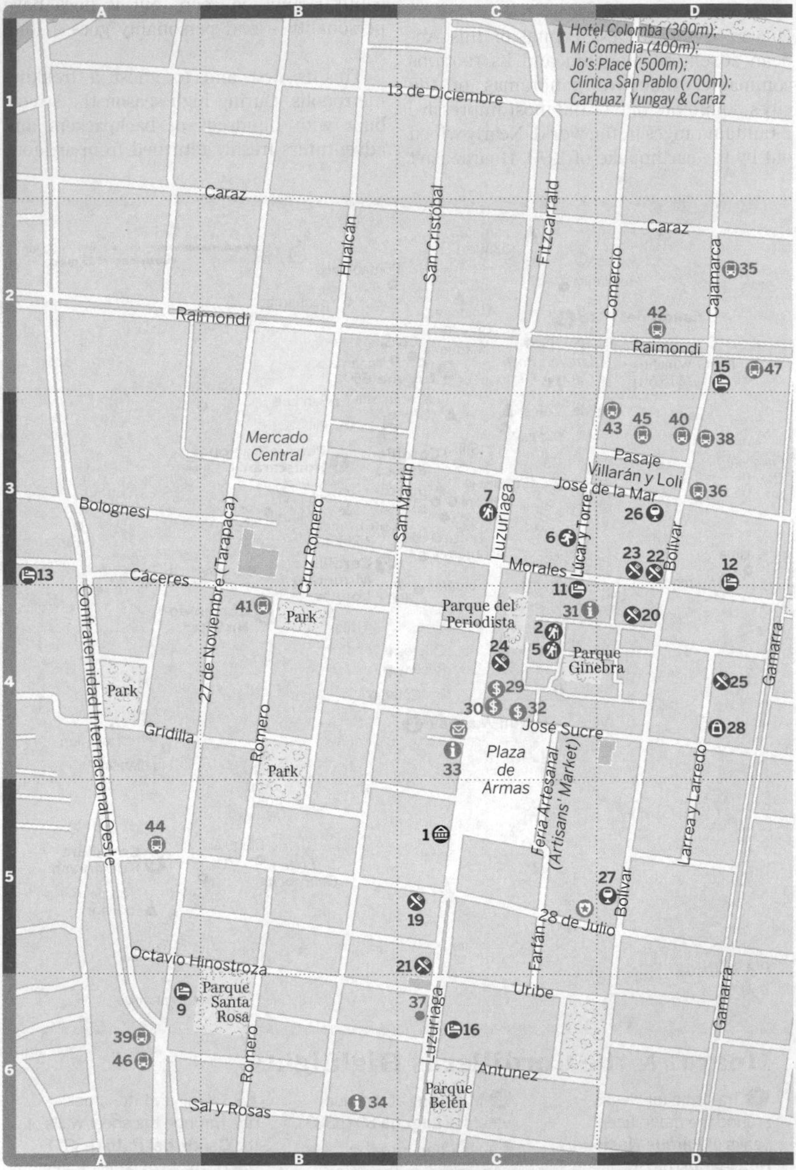

A B C D

Hotel Colomba (300m); Mi Comedia (400m); Jo's Place (500m); Clínica San Pablo (700m); Carhuaz, Yungay & Caraz

13 de Diciembre
Caraz
Hualcán
San Cristóbal
Fitzcarrald
Comercio
Cajamarca
Raimondi
Mercado Central
Pasaje Villarán y Loli
José de la Mar
Bolognesi
27 de Noviembre (Tarapaca)
Cruz Romero
San Martín
Luzuriaga
Lúcar y Torre
Bolívar
Morales
Cáceres
Park
Parque del Periodista
Parque Ginebra
Gamarra
Confraternidad Internacional Oeste
Gridilla
José Sucre
Romero
Plaza de Armas
Feria Artesanal (Artisans' Market)
Larrea y Larredo
28 de Julio
Farfán
Octavio Hinostroza
Uribe
Parque Santa Rosa
Antunez
Parque Belén
Sal y Rosas

hikes or planning their next expedition as they huddle in one of the town's many fine watering holes. Dozens of outfits help plan trips, rent equipment and organize a list of adventure sports as long as your arm. An endless lineup of quality restaurants and hopping bars keep the belly full and the place lively till long after the tents have been put away to dry. Mountain adventures in the off-season can be equally rewarding, but the vibe is more subdued and some places go into hibernation once the rains set in.

Sights

Monumento Nacional Wilkahuaín RUIN
(adult/student S5/2; ⌚9am-5pm Tue-Sun) This small Wari ruin about 8km north of Huaraz is remarkably well preserved, dating from about AD 600 to 900. It's an imitation of the temple at Chavín done in the Tiwanaku style. Wilkahuaín means 'grandson's house' in Quechua. The three-story temple has seven rooms on each floor, each originally filled with bundles of mummies. The bodies were kept dry using a sophisticated system of ventilation ducts. Another smaller set of ruins, **Wilkahuaín Pequeno**, can be seen nearby.

The two-hour walk up to Wilkahuaín is a fairly easy first hike and can be a rewarding glimpse into Andean country life, passing farms and simple *pueblos* (villages). To get here take a taxi to 'El Pinar' (S7) from where there are two paths leading to the ruins – a direct route via the main road or a longer but more scenic route via Marian. Alternatively, a taxi direct to the ruins will set you back around S25. Avoid taking the path from the ruins down to the baths at Monterrey as robberies are common on this stretch.

Museo Regional de Ancash MUSEUM
(Plaza de Armas; adult/child S5/1; ⌚8:30am-5:15pm Tue-Sat, 9am-2pm Sun) The Museo Regional de Ancash houses one of the most significant collections of ancient stone sculptures in South America. Small but interesting, it has a few mummies, some trepanned skulls and a garden of stone monoliths from the Recuay culture (400 BC–AD 600) and the Wari culture (AD 600–1100).

Jirón José Olaya ARCHITECTURE, MARKET
On the east side of town, Jirón José Olaya is the only street that remained intact through the earthquakes and provides a glimpse of what old Huaraz looked like; go on Sunday when a street market sells regional foods.

Mirador de Retaqeñua LOOKOUT
Mirador de Retaqeñua is about a 45-minute walk southeast of the center and has great views of the city and its mountainous backdrop. It's best to take a S15 taxi here as robberies have been reported on the trail.

Activities

Trekking & Mountaineering

Whether you're arranging a mountain expedition or going for a day hike, Huaraz is the place to start – it is the epicenter for planning and organizing local Andean adventures. Numerous outfits can prearrange entire trips so that all you need to do is show up at the right place at the right time. Many visitors go camping, hiking and climbing in the mountains without any local help and

Huaraz

Sights
1 Museo Regional de Ancash C5

Activities, Courses & Tours
2 Andean Kingdom C4
3 Eco Ice Peru F5
4 Huascarán F5
5 Montañero C4
6 Mountain Bike Adventures C3
7 Quechuandes C3
8 Respons Sustainable Tourism Center F6

Sleeping
9 Albergue Benkawasi A6
10 Albergue Churup F5
11 Aldo's Guest House C4
12 Cayesh Guesthouse D3
13 Edward's Inn A3
14 El Jacal E5
Familia Meza Lodging .... (see 6)
15 Hostal Schatzi D2
16 La Aurora C6
17 La Casa de Zarela F5
18 Olaza's Bed & Breakfast F5

Eating
Café Andino .... (see 6)
19 California Café C5
20 Chili Heaven D4
21 El Fogón C5
La Brasa Roja .... (see 16)
22 Novaplaza D3
23 Rinconcito Mineiro D3
24 Rossonero C4
25 Taita D4

Drinking & Nightlife
26 El Tambo D3
Los 13 Buhos .... (see 20)
27 Tio Enrique D5

Shopping
28 Tejidos Turmanyé D4

Information
29 Banco de la Nacion C4
30 BCP C4
31 Casa de Guías C4
32 Interbank C4
33 iPerú C4
34 Parque Nacional Huascarán Office B6
Policía de Turismo .... (see 33)

Transport
35 Combis to Carhuaz, Yungay & Caraz D2
36 Cruz del Sur D3
37 LC Perú C6
38 Línea D3
39 Minibuses to Recuay & Catac A6
40 Móvil Tours D3
41 Olguita Tours B4
42 Oltursa D2
43 Transportes Alas Peruanas D3
44 Transportes El Rápido A5
45 Transportes El Veloz D3
Transportes Renzo .... (see 42)
46 Turismo Nazario A6
47 Yungay Express D2

you can too if you have the experience. Just remember, though, that carrying a backpack full of gear over a 4800m pass requires much more effort than hiking at low altitudes.

Rock Climbing

Rock climbing is one of the Cordillera Blanca's biggest pastimes. There are good climbs for beginners at Chancos, while the area around Los Olivos offers something for all skill levels. Avid climbers will find some gnarly bolted sport climbs at Recuay and Hatun Machay. For some big-wall action that will keep you chalked up for days, head to the famous Torre de Parón, known locally as the Sphinx. Most trekking tour agencies offer climbing trips, both for beginners and advanced, as part of their repertoire. Many also rent gear and with a bit of legwork and some information gathering you could easily arrange your own do-it-yourself climbing expedition.

Ice Climbing

With enough glaciers to sink your ice axe into for the rest of your life, the Cordillera Blanca is a frozen heaven for folks who want to learn ice climbing or attack new peaks and heights. Since many summits require a degree of technical know-how, ice climbing is a big activity in the Cordillera, and many tour and trekking operators can arrange excursions, equipment rental and lessons. The best trekking agencies have years of experience with ice climbing and safe equipment. In Parque Nacional Huascarán a certified guide is required.

Mountain Biking

Mountain Bike Adventures MOUNTAIN BIKING
(☎043-2-4259; www.chakinaniperu.com; Lúcar y Torre 530, 2nd fl; ⏲9am-1pm & 3-8pm) Mountain Bike Adventures has been in business for more than a decade and receives repeat visits from mountain bikers for its decent

selection of bikes, knowledgeable and friendly service, and good safety record. It offers guided tours, ranging from an easy five-hour cruise to 12-day circuits around the Cordillera Blanca. Rates start at around S160 for a day circuit.

The owner is a lifelong resident of Huaraz who speaks English and has spent time mountain biking in the USA – he knows the region's single-track possibilities better than anyone.

Volunteering

Agencies specializing in community and sustainable tourism may also be able to help you arrange different kinds of volunteer activities in the region. It's best to organize volunteering activities in advance although agencies sometimes take short-term applicants. For the latest on volunteering, check out the community notice boards at popular gringo cafes and hangouts around Huaraz.

Seeds of Hope VOLUNTEERING
(☎94-352-3353; www.peruseeds.org) This aid organization works with Huaraz' poorest children and provides accommodations to volunteers for a small fee.

Teach Huaraz Peru VOLUNTEERING
(☎043-42-5303; www.teachhuarazperu.org) Arranges English-teaching and other kinds of experiences for volunteers; homestays with local families are available.

Community Tourism

Respons Sustainable Tourism Center CULTURAL TOUR
(☎043-42-7949; www.responsibletravelperu.com; Eulogio del Río 1364, La Soledad; 9am-1pm & 3-7pm) Respons works as a clearinghouse for information about local community tourism and arranges homestays in Humachucco, which is a good base for exploring Lagunas Llanganuco and 69, and Vicos, a very traditional mountain community. You will stay in bungalows next to family homes and eat meals with your hosts. It also arranges trips to Huaripampa, where visitors learn about traditional weaving.

Activities in the villages range from preparing traditional food to participating in farming and craft production. There is also a small shop in the office selling fair-trade products from local artisans. Almost anything you do with the agency will benefit local families and contribute to the growing community-tourism movement in the region.

Other Activities

Skiers will not find ski lifts in the Cordillera Blanca, but there is limited mountain **skiing** for die-hards who want to climb with skis. Ask locally for current conditions. **River running** (white-water rafting) is sometimes offered on the Río Santa, but it's a very polluted river (mine-tailings upstream and raw sewage certainly don't help things) and people have fallen ill doing it. It's not recommended.

Horseback riding is a possibility; although there is no dedicated outfit in Huaraz, horses can be arranged by many travel agencies. The Lazy Dog Inn (p373) outside Huaraz has its own horses and does treks to the surrounding mountains. Respons Sustainable Tourism Center offers a couple of one-day rides around the village of Yungar in the Cordillera Negra.

Parapenting (parasailing) is increasing in popularity, though you will need to bring your own equipment. Jangas, 20 minutes north of Huaraz; Wilcacocha, 40 minutes southeast; and Huata near Caraz are popular Cordillera Negra launching spots.

Tours

Day Tours

Dozens of agencies along Luzuriaga can organize outings to local sites, including several day excursions. Most of the trips are run by the transportation companies so regardless of who you book through, you'll probably end up on the same bus.

One popular tour visits the ruins at Chavín de Huántar; another passes through Yungay to the beautiful Lagunas Llanganuco, where there are superb vistas of Huascarán and other mountains; a third takes you through Caraz to Laguna Parón, which is surrounded by ravishing glaciated peaks; and a fourth travels to the glacier at Nevado Pastoruri, the most accessible in the Cordillera.

All of these trips run between S35 and S60 each; prices may vary depending on the number of people going, but typically include transportation (usually in minibuses) and a guide (who often doesn't speak English). Admission fees and lunch are extra. Trips take a full day; bring a packed lunch, warm clothes, drinking water and sunblock. Tours depart daily during the high season, but at other times departures depend on demand. Do not take a day trip to Chavín de Huántar on a Monday – the ruins and museum are closed.

TREMORS & LANDSLIDES

Records of *aluviones*, a deadly mix of avalanche, waterfall and landslide, date back almost 300 years, but three recent ones have caused particular devastation. The first occurred in 1941, when an avalanche in the Cojup Valley, west of Huaraz, caused the Laguna Palcacocha to break its banks and flow down onto Huaraz, killing about 5000 inhabitants and flattening the city. Then, in 1962, a huge avalanche from Huascarán roared down its western slopes and destroyed the town of Ranrahirca, killing about 4000 people.

The worst disaster occurred on May 31, 1970, when a massive earthquake, measuring nearly 8.0 on the Richter scale, devastated much of central Peru, killing an estimated 70,000 people. About half of the 30,000 inhabitants of Huaraz died, and only 10% of the city was left standing. The town of Yungay was buried by the *aluvión* caused by the quake and almost its entire population of 25,000 was buried with the city (see boxed text, p390).

Since these disasters, a government agency (Hidrandina) has been formed to control the lake levels by building dams and tunnels, thus minimizing the chance of similar catastrophes. Today, warning systems are in place, although false alarms do occur.

Trekking & Mountaineering

All activity within Parque Nacional Huascarán – whether mountaineering or hiking – technically requires that you are accompanied by a certified guide although in practice this is not enforced at all park entrances. Even so, it is well worth taking a guide even for nontechnical activities as conditions change rapidly in the mountains and altitude sickness can seriously debilitate even experienced hikers. Furthermore a good guide will ensure you see things you otherwise may have missed.

All guides must be licensed by the Peruvian authorities and registered with the national-parks office. Mountaineers and trekkers should check out Casa de Guías (p375), the headquarters of the **Mountain Guide Association of Peru**. It maintains a list of its internationally certified guides, all of whom are graduates of a rigorous training program. Bear in mind that international certification is not necessary to work in the park and there are also some excellent independent guides from other associations certified to work in the region.

Many agencies arrange full trekking and climbing expeditions that include guides, equipment, food, cooks, porters and transportation. Depending on the number of people, the length of your trip and what's included, expect to pay from under S100 for an easy day out to up to S750 for more technical mountains per person per day. Try not to base your selection solely on price, as you often get what you pay for. Do your research: things change, good places go bad and bad places get good.

One of the best resources for guides in Huaraz is other travelers who have just come back from a trek and can recommend (or not recommend) their guides based on recent experience. The **South American Explorers Club** (p100) in Lima is also an excellent source of information and maps.

Quechuandes TREKKING, ROCK CLIMBING
(☎943-562-339; www.quechandes.com; Luzuriaga 522) A very well organized agency that gets rave reviews for its quality guides and ethical approach to treks. Management will assess your level before sending you out into the mountains or renting gear to ensure you are up to the task. In addition to offering treks and summit expeditions, its staff are experts in rock climbing and bouldering.

It also offers mountaineering courses and has an indoor climbing wall in the office. The detailed website offers a great overview of treks and climbs in the region.

Skyline Adventures TREKKING, MOUNTAINEERING
(☎043-42-7097; www.skyline-adventures.com; Pasaje Industrial 137) Based just outside Huaraz, this high-end operator comes highly recommended and provides guides for treks and mountain climbs. Leads six- and 12-day mountaineering courses.

Montañero TREKKING, MOUNTAINEERING
(☎043-42-6386; www.trekkingperu.com; Parque Ginebra; ⏲9am-12pm & 4-8pm) This high-end agency arranges both treks and climbs. It also sells quality gear.

Eco Ice Peru TREKKING
(www.ecoice-peru.com; Figueroa 1185; ⏲8am-6pm) Run by a gregarious and passionate

young guide, this new agency gets top reviews from travelers for its customer service. Treks often end with a dinner at the owner's pad in Huaraz.

Andean Kingdom TREKKING
(☎944-913-011; www.andeankingdom.com; Parque Ginebra) A laid-back but enthusiastic agency offering the usual excursions as well as off-the-beaten path treks and a variety of climbing trips.

Huascarán TREKKING
(☎043-42-2523; www.huascaran-peru.com; Campos 711) A well-established operator offering the full gamut of excursions.

Festivals & Events

Carnaval RELIGIOUS
(Feb/Mar) Carnaval in Huaraz is very busy, with Peruvian tourists flooding into town, many of whom will get soaked in water fights on the city's take on **Mardi Gras (Fat Tuesday)**. On **Ash Wednesday** colorful funeral processions for *ño carnavalón* (king of carnival) converge on the Plaza de Armas. Here, his 'will' is read, giving the opportunity for many jabs at local politicians, police and other dignitaries, before the procession continues to the river where the coffin is thrown in. Participants dress in colorful costumes with papier-mâché heads, some of which are recognizable celebrities.

El Señor de la Soledad CULTURAL
(May) Huaraz pays homage to its patron (the Christ of Solitude) beginning May 3. This weeklong festival involves fireworks, music, dancing, elaborately costumed processions and lots of drinking.

Festival de Andinismo MOUNTAINEERING
(Jun) Held annually, it attracts mountaineers from several countries, and competitions and exhibitions are held.

Sleeping

Hotel prices can double during holiday periods and rooms become very scarce. Perhaps because Huaraz is seen as a trekking, climbing and backpacking center, budget hotels predominate. Hostels employ individuals to meet buses, but beware of overpricing – don't pay anybody until you've seen the room.

Jo's Place GUESTHOUSE $
(☎043-42-5505; josplacehuaraz@hotmail.com; Villazón 278; campsites per person S10, dm S15, r with/without bathroom S50/40; @ 📶) Bright splashes of color and a rambling grassy area mark this cheap and chilled guesthouse with a variety of simple but functional rooms spread over four floors, connected by spiral staircases. Full English breakfasts are prepared on request. If you don't need luxury, it's hard to beat the value here.

MARTES GUERRA

You might want to invest in a waterproof suit or brave the high-altitude chill in your bathing suit if you are in Huaraz on Carnaval's Fat Tuesday, a day of intense water fights throughout the city. Known as Martes Guerra (War Tuesday), thousands of kids run around the city with buckets searching for public sources of water and have huge water fights. Women, senior citizens and tourists are prime targets. Police are everywhere, even the military, but none of them can control these wild water bandits. Stay inside your hotel if you don't want to get drenched!

Albergue Benkawasi GUESTHOUSE $
(☎043-43-3150; www.huarazbenkawasi.com; Parque Santa Rosa 928; dm/s/d S25/50/70; @ 📶) With coke-bottle glass windows, plaid bedspreads and brick walls, the Benkawasi has a kind of '70s mountain chalet feel to it. The owner and his English-speaking Peruvian-Lebanese wife are young and fun, and the accommodations are excellent value.

Familia Meza Lodging GUESTHOUSE $
(☎94-369-5908; Lúcar y Torre 538; r per person S25; 📶) In the same building as Café Andino (p373), this charming family guesthouse has cheery rooms and is decorated throughout with homey touches. What's more, the owners are friendly and helpful enough to cure the worst bout of homesickness. Bathrooms and hot showers are shared and there's a top-floor communal area with a small kitchen.

Hostal Schatzi GUESTHOUSE $
(☎043-42-3074; www.hostalschatzi.com; Bolívar 419; s/d/t S50/80/90; 📶) Plenty of leafage in the pleasant courtyard here manages to keep the concrete at bay. Charismatic little rooms surround this garden and inside have exposed wood-beam ceilings and great top-floor views (ask for No 6). It's a reliable bet.

Aldo's Guest House GUESTHOUSE $
(☎043-42-5355; Morales 650; dm/s/d/tr 25/35/50/75; @ 📶) Budget travelers love

little Aldo's, a cheery, homey place decorated with bright colors and located right in the center of town. Rooms have cable TV and private bathrooms with hot showers, and you can use the kitchen. There is another slightly cheaper branch near Parque Belén.

Cayesh Guesthouse GUESTHOUSE **$**
(043-42-8821; Morales 867; dm S20, s/d S35/50, without bathroom S30/40;) A solid budget choice offering simple rooms with comfortable beds and kitchen access; fluent English is spoken.

Edward's Inn GUESTHOUSE **$**
(043-42-2692; Bolognesi 121; dm/s/d S25/35/70; @) Rooms in this popular place all have hot water, but are otherwise elementary. There is a nice grassy bit and the owner is very knowledgeable about the region.

★ **Albergue Churup** BOUTIQUE HOSTEL **$$**
(043-42-4200; www.churup.com; Figueroa 1257; dm S30, s/d incl breakfast S85/120; @) This immensely popular family-run hostel continues to win the top budget-choice accolade. Immaculate and comfortable rooms share comfortable, colorful lounging areas on every floor. The building is topped by a massive, fireplace-warmed lounge space with magnificent 180-degree views of the Cordillera.

If that isn't enough, the affable Quirós family, especially the heir to this tourism throne, Juan, are consummate hosts and offer a communal kitchen and a travel office that rents out trekking gear. It's so popular, a new, equally homey annex, Churup II, has opened a block over on Arguedas. Reservations are essential.

La Aurora HOTEL **$$**
(043-42-6824; www.laaurorahotel.com; Luzuriaga 915; s/d/t incl breakfast from S120/220/270) Don't be put off by the entrance shared with a *pollería* (restaurant specializing in roast chicken); go up the elevator to find some of the most comfortable accommodations in town. The bright new rooms feature wooden floors, luxurious bathrooms with marble sinks, and flourishes of local flavor such as straw lampshades and woven bedspreads.

Breakfast is served on the fantastic terrace with views of Huascarán and Churup. Outstanding value.

Hotel San Sebastián HOTEL **$$**
(043-42-6960; www.sansebastianhuaraz.com; Italia 1124; s/d incl breakfast S180/218; @) A fetching white-walled and red-roofed urban sanctuary, this four-story hotel is a neocolonial architectural find. Balconies and arches overlook a grassy garden and inner courtyard with a soothing fountain, and all rooms have a writing desk, good beds, hot shower and cable TV. Most have balconies as well, but if you don't get one, there are plenty of communal terraces.

El Jacal HOTEL **$$**
(043-42-4612; www.jacalhuaras.com; Sucre 1044; s/d incl breakfast S80/105;) This popular family-run hotel combines a homely vibe, attentive service and comfortable modern facilities. The rooms are not huge, but are clean and inviting, while the enclosed rooftop terrace affords fine views of the surrounding mountains.

Olaza's Bed & Breakfast GUESTHOUSE **$$**
(043-42-2529; www.olazas.com; Arguedas 1242; s/d/tr incl breakfast S80/100/150; @) This smart little hotel has spacious bathrooms and comfortable beds, but the best part is the big lounge area upstairs and massive panoramic terrace. The owner is an established figure in the Huaraz trekking and tourism scene; he can provide advice no matter where you want to go (as long as he's around). Bus-station pickup is included.

Casa Hotel HOTEL **$$**
(043-22-1028; www.casahotelhouse.com.pe; Maguiña 1467; s/d/t S90/120/170) In a quiet street up the hill from all the action, this remodeled hotel features well-finished rooms with all the mod cons including quality mattresses, good shower heads and wall-mounted flat-screen TVs. The rooftop terrace comes complete with a foosball table and is a great place to hang out.

La Casa de Zarela GUESTHOUSE **$$**
(043-42-1694; Arguedas 1263; dm/s/d/t S40/80/120/150;) Zarela's helpfulness is legendary and the 18 rooms here are neat and comfortable, but the best thing about this quality guesthouse is the abundance of patios, terraces and common areas that mean even when full it never feels crowded. There is a bright kitchen on the top floor for guests.

Hotel Colomba HOTEL **$$**
(043-42-1501; www.huarazhotel.com; Francisco de Zela 210; s/d incl breakfast from S170/240; @) The rooms at this wonderfully surprising oasis are speckled around a dense and compulsively trimmed hedge forest, some

spilling out onto a long, relaxing veranda. The sprawling gardens conceal a kids' playground, making it a great choice for families looking for secure and enclosed grounds for their kids to safely run amok.

Cuesta Serena BOUTIQUE HOTEL **$$$**
(981-400-038; www.cuestaserena.pe; via Carhuaz, Anta; r incl 2 meals S630-930) Out near the airport, this high-end hotel is a great place to stay to avoid the noise of Huaraz while remaining accessible to transportation and local attractions. The elegant rooms are set in lovely manicured gardens, which offer fantastic views of the Cordillera Blanca. They manage to be both luxurious and homely, making the place feel like a private country retreat.

Food here gets great reviews. Reservations are essential.

Andino Club Hotel HOTEL **$$$**
(043-42-1662; www.hotelandino.com; Pedro Cochachín 357; s/d from S343/424, d with balcony S473;) Because the structure itself feels a little bit too much like a chain hotel, you sacrifice on cozy charm at this 54-room, Swiss-run hotel, but the immaculate rooms all have great views and are packed with the requisite mod cons. Balcony rooms are worth the splurge for the postcard views to Huascarán peak, wood-burning fireplaces and plant-lined terraces.

The excellent on-site restaurant, **Chalet Suisse**, serves international and Peruvian food in addition to Swiss specialties.

Lazy Dog Inn LODGE **$$$**
(94-378-9330; www.thelazydoginn.com; r S420;) Run by rugged and proud Canadians Diana and Wayne, this deluxe ecolodge steeped in sustainable and community tourism is at the mouth of the Quebrada Llaca, 8km east of Huaraz. It's made entirely of adobe and built by hand. You can either stay in comfortable double rooms in the main lodge or in fancier private cabins, with fireplaces and bathtubs.

Lots of trekking opportunities are available, including numerous day hikes right from the lodge, as well as day trips on horseback. Long- and short-term volunteer opportunities are also available.

Eating

Restaurant hours are flexible in Huaraz, with shorter opening times during low-season slow spells and longer hours at busy times.

Taita PERUVIAN **$**
(Larrea y Laredo 633, 2nd fl; mains S5.50-18; 11am-3pm) This atmospheric local's haunt is an excellent spot to try *chocho,* the alpine answer to ceviche, with the fish replaced with *lupine* (an Andean legume). It also does ceviche, *leche de tigre* (ceviche juice) and *chicharrones* (deep-fried pork rinds). It's a top spot.

The walls here are covered head-to-toe in historical photos of beauty queens, sports teams, school classes and other Huaracino Kodak moments.

Café Andino CAFE **$**
(www.cafeandino.com; Lúcar y Torre 530, 3rd fl; breakfast S8-24, mains S18-25;) This modern top-floor cafe has space and light in spades, comfy lounges, art, photos, crackling fireplace, books and groovy tunes – it's the ultimate South American traveler hangout and meeting spot. You can get breakfast anytime (Belgian waffles, *huevos rancheros*), snacks you miss (nachos). It's the best place in town for information about trekking in the area.

American owner Chris is the go-to java junkie in the Cordilleras and roasts his own organic beans here. He was responsible for first bringing excellent brew to town in 1997 – he showed up a year earlier and had to resort to using a rock to smash organic beans he'd brought from Alaska, straining it through a bandanna for his morning jolt. Seriously.

Rustika PERUVIAN **$**
(Ricardo Palma 200; mains S12-25; 9:30am-11:30pm) For a full-on local experience, trek up the hill to this atmospheric restaurant constructed from logs and colored glass. It serves tasty typical dishes including ceviche and barbecue *cuy* (guinea pig). Tables are tucked into various nooks and crannies, but the best place to eat is out on the terrace – it offers great mountain views with a Peruvian pop-music soundtrack.

California Café BREAKFAST, CAFE **$**
(www.huaylas.com; Jiron 28 de Julio 562; breakfast S13-25; 7:30am-6:30pm, to 2pm Sun;) Managed by an American from California, this hip traveler magnet does breakfasts at any time, plus light lunches and salads – it's a funky, chilled space to while away many hours. You can spend the day listening to the sublime world-music collection or reading one of the hundreds of books available for exchange.

Rinconcito Mineiro PERUVIAN $
(Morales 757; menús S8-16, mains S12-35; 7am-11pm;) This popular place is *the* spot to tuck into homey and cheap Peruvian daily *menús* (set meals). The daily blackboard of 10 or so options includes an excellent *lomo saltado* (strips of beef stir-fried with onions, tomatoes, potatoes and chili), plus grilled trout, *tacu-tacu* (a Peruvian fusion dish of rice, beans and a protein) and the like. It's all served in a welcoming and clean space, tastefully decorated with regional crafts.

La Brasa Roja PERUVIAN $
(Luzuriaga 915; mains S11.50-27; noon-11pm) This upscale *pollería* (restaurant specializing in roast chicken) is the ultimate budget refueling stop. Not only is the chicken perfect, but you get five sauces – count 'em, five! – instead of the usual three (black olive and mustard make a surprise appearance). The other mains are hit and miss but if you're lucky you'll get a live violinist. No lie.

Rossonero DESSERTS $
(Luzuriaga 645, 2nd fl; desserts S5.50-8.50; 8am-11pm;) This modern den of decadence, billed as a 'sofa-cafe,' is really more of an upscale dessert diner. We're talking numerous variations of *tres leches* (a very sweet dairy pudding) and cheesecakes, pecan pie and chocolate cake – you name it – and artisanal house-made ice creams such as *manjar blanco* (milk caramel) with cinnamon and port.

Novaplaza SELF-CATERING $
(cnr Bolivar & Morales; 7am-11:30pm) A good supermarket to pick up supplies for trekking or self-catering.

★ **Mi Comedia** ITALIAN $$
(Centenario 351; mains S25-32; 5-11pm Mon-Sat) Pizzerias are ubiquitous in Huaraz but once you've eaten in this friendly place you won't go anywhere else. The pizzas are prepared right in the dining room and all feature a delicious crust and farm-fresh tomato sauce. There is also a small selection of excellent pasta dishes. Reservations are advisable.

Chili Heaven INDIAN, THAI $$
(Parque Ginebra; mains S17-35; noon-11pm) Whether you send your appetite to India or Thailand, the fiery curries at this hot spot will seize your taste buds upon arrival, mercilessly shake them up and then spit them back out the other side as if you've died and gone to chili heaven (hence the name). They also bottle their own hot sauces. A critical Peruvian food antidote.

El Fogón STEAK $$
(Luzuriaga 928, 2nd fl; mains S11-39; noon-3pm & 6-11pm) A bright, modern and slightly upscale twist on the traditional Peruvian grill house, this place will grill anything that moves – including the usual chicken, trout and rabbit, plus great *anticuchos* (beef skewers). It also does a fine lunch *menú* for S9. Vegetarians will go hungry though.

Drinking & Nightlife

Huaraz is the best place in this part of the Andes to take a load off.

★ **Los 13 Buhos** BAR
(Parque Ginebra; 11am-late) A supremely cool cafe-bar in newly upgraded Parque Ginebra digs. The owner, Lucho, was the first craft-beer brewer in Huaraz and offers five tasty choices, including red and black ales. It also prepares top Thai curries and fantastic *menús*. It's the best bar in town for kicking back over cold home brews and liquid-courage inspired conversation.

Tio Enrique BAR
(Bolivar 572; 5-11pm) If you like beer, you'll like this cozy Swiss-themed drinking hole with a long bar and communal pine tables. Popular with hard-core climbers it serves around three dozen varieties of imported beers from the UK, Belgium and Germany as well as tasty sausages grilled at the door by the charismatic apron-toting owner.

El Tambo BAR, CLUB
(José de la Mar 776; 9pm-4am) If you're hankering to shake your groove-thang, this is the most popular disco in town, complete with dance-floor trees and loads of nooks and crannies so you can hide yourself away. Fashionable with both *extranjeros* (foreigners) and Peruvians, the music swings from techno-*cumbia* to Top 20, salsa and reggae, and most things in between.

Shopping

Inexpensive thick woolen sweaters, scarves, hats, socks, gloves, ponchos and blankets are available if you need to rug up for the mountains; many of these are sold at stalls on the pedestrian alleys off Luzuriaga or at the *feria artesanal* (artisans' market) off the Plaza de Armas. A few shops on Parque Ginebra, plus several agencies that rent equipment, also sell quality climbing gear and clothes.

Tejidos Turmanyé CLOTHING
(www.arcoiristurmanye.com; Larrea y Loredo, cuadra 6; ⏲11am-1pm & 4-8pm Mon-Sat) Sells handsome locally made weavings and knit garments to support a foundation that provides occupational training to young mothers.

Information

DANGERS & ANNOYANCES

Time to acclimatize is important. The altitude here will make you feel breathless and may give you a headache during your first few days, so don't overexert yourself. The surrounding mountains will cause altitude sickness if you venture into them without spending a few days acclimatizing in Huaraz first.

Huaraz is a safe city that experiences little crime; unfortunately, robberies of trekkers and tourists do happen, especially in the area of the Mirador de Retaqeñua and the Wilkahuaín ruins, and early in the morning when groggy backpackers arrive on overnight buses. In these cases, stay alert and walk with a group or hire a taxi to avoid problems.

EMERGENCY

Casa de Guías (☎043-42-1811; www.casadeguias.com.pe; Parque Ginebra 28G; ⏲9am-1pm & 4-8pm Mon-Fri, 8am-noon Sat) Runs mountain safety and rescue courses and maintains a list of internationally certified guides. Also mounts rescue operations to assist climbers in emergencies. If you are heading out on a risky ascent, it's worth consulting this place first.

Policía de Turismo (☎043-42-1341; Luzuriaga 724; ⏲24hr) On the west side of Plaza de Armas.

MEDICAL SERVICES

Clínica San Pablo (☎043-42-8811; www.sanpablo.com.pe; Huaylas 172; ⏲24hr) North of town, this is the best medical care in Huaraz. Some doctors speak English.

MONEY

These banks have ATMs and will exchange US dollars and euros.

Banco de la Nacion (Luzuriaga 680)

BCP (Luzuriaga 691)

Interbank (José Sucre 687)

POST

Serpost (Luzuriaga 702; ⏲8:30am-8pm Mon-Fri, to 5:30pm Sat) Postal services.

TOURIST INFORMATION

English newspaper *The Huaraz Telegraph* (www.huaraztelegraph.com) is a good source of information about the region.

iPerú (☎043-42-8812; iperuhuaraz@promperu.gob.pe; Pasaje Atusparia, Oficina 1, Plaza de Armas; ⏲9am-6pm Mon-Sat, to 1pm Sun) Has general tourist information but little in the way of trekking info.

Parque Nacional Huascarán Office (☎043-42-2086; www.sernanp.gob.pe; Sal y Rosas 555; ⏲8:30am-1pm & 2:30-6pm Mon-Fri, to noon Sat) Staff have limited information about visiting the park.

Getting There & Away

AIR

LC Perú (☎043-42-4734; www.lcperu.pe; Luzuriaga 904) operates flights from Lima to Huaraz every day at 5:30am; the return journey leaves at 7:05am. The Huaraz airport is actually at Anta, 23km north of town. A taxi will cost about S40.

BUS

Combis (minibuses) for Caraz, Carhuaz and Yungay leave every few minutes during the day from a lot on Cajamarca near Raimondi. These will drop you in any of the towns along the way. Minibuses south along the Callejón de Huaylas to Recuay, Catac and other villages leave from the corner terminal at Calle 27 de Noviembre and Confraternidad Internacional Oeste.

A plethora of companies have departures for Lima, so shop around for the price/class/time you prefer. Most depart midmorning or late evening. Some buses begin in Caraz and stop in Huaraz to pick up passengers. During high season it is recommended that you book your seats at least a day in advance.

Buses to Chimbote cross the 4225m-high Punta Callán which provides spectacular views of the Cordillera Blanca before plummeting down to Casma and pushing north.

Many small companies with brave, beat-up buses cross the Cordillera Blanca to the towns east of Huaraz. Of the long-haul companies, Oltursa and Línea are recommended.

Cruz del Sur (☎043-42-8726; Bolívar 491) Has 11am and 10pm luxury nonstop services to Lima.

Línea (☎043-42-6666; Bolívar 450) Has excellent buses at 9:15pm and 9:30pm to Chimbote and Trujillo.

Móvil Tours (www.moviltours.com.pe) ticket office (Bolívar 452); tTerminal (☎043-42-2555; Confraternidad Internacional Oeste 451) Buses to Lima at 9:30am, 1pm and 2:30pm and four night buses between 10pm and 11pm. Has 9:40pm, 10:20pm and 11:10pm buses to Chimbote via Casma, the first two of which continue on to Trujillo.

Olguita Tours (☎043-39-6309, 943-644-051; Mariscal Caceres 338) Departures to Chavín and Huari at 4am, 7:30am, 11am, 12:20pm and 8:30pm.

Oltursa (☎043-42-3717; www.oltursa.pe; Raimondi 825) These are the most comfortable Lima buses; departures at 12:15pm and 10:30pm.

Transportes Alas Peruanas (☎943-990-020; Lucar y Torre 444) Buses to Chimbote via Casma at 4am, 8:15am, 10:45am, 1:15pm, 3:30pm and 8:45pm. Convenient for onward connections to Trujillo.

Transportes El Rápido (☎043-42-2887; Calle 28 de Julio, cuadra 1) Buses leave at 5am and 2pm to Chiquián via Recuay; 6am, 1pm and 3pm to Huallanca and La Unión.

Transportes El Veloz (☎043-22-1225; Pasaja Villarán y Loli 143) Buses to Pomabamba at 7:15am and 6:30pm, as well as Chacas and San Luis at 5pm.

Transportes Renzo (☎043-42-5371; Raymundi 821) Has a rambling 6:45am and 7pm service to Pomabamba, stopping at Chacas and Piscobamba. Another service leaves at 7am for San Luis via Chacas.

Turismo Nazario (☎043-77-0311; Tarapaca 1436) Has a 5am bus to Chiquián with continuing service to Llamac.

Yungay Express (☎043-42-4377; Raimondi 930) Has departures to Chimbote via Casma at 7:45am, 9am, 12:45pm, 2pm, 4pm and 10pm.

Getting Around

A taxi ride around central Huaraz costs about S3, rising a couple of soles to reach the outer neighborhoods.

THE CORDILLERAS

Huaraz lies sandwiched in a valley carved out by the Río Santa, flanked to the west by the brown Cordillera Negra and to the east by the frosted Cordillera Blanca. A paved road runs along the valley, more commonly known as the Callejón de Huaylas, and links a string of settlements while furnishing visitors with perfect views of lofty elevations.

The Cordillera Negra, though an attractive range in its own right, is snowless and often eclipsed by the stunning, snow-covered crown of the Cordillera Blanca.

The Cordillera Blanca, about 20km wide and 180km long, is an elaborate collection of toothed summits, razor-sharp ridges, turquoise-colored lakes and green valleys draped with crawling glaciers. More than 50 peaks of 5700m or higher grace this fairly small area. North America, in contrast, has only three mountains in excess of 5700m and Europe has none. Huascarán, at 6768m, is Peru's highest mountain and the highest pinnacle in the tropics anywhere in the world.

South of the Cordillera Blanca is the smaller, more remote, but no less spectacular Cordillera Huayhuash. It contains Peru's second-highest mountain, the 6634m Yerupajá, and is a more rugged and less frequently visited range.

Where once pre-Columbian and Inca cultures used the high valleys as passageways to eastern settlements, backpackers and mountaineers now explore and marvel at the spectacle of Mother Nature blowing her own trumpet.

The main trekking areas of the Cordilleras include sections of the Cordillera Blanca, which is mostly encompassed by Parque Nacional Huascarán, and the Cordillera Huayhuash, to the south of Huaraz. There's something here for scramblers of all skills and fitness levels: from short, easy hikes of a day or two, to multiweek adventures requiring technical mountain-climbing skills. Foreigners flock here yearly and favorite hikes such as the Santa Cruz trek can see a lot of hiking-boot traffic in the high season. While the more remote 10-day Cordillera Huayhuash Circuit doesn't see half as many visitors as the Santa Cruz trek, savvy travelers are rapidly discovering its rugged beauty and appreciating the friendly highland culture. Dozens of shorter routes crisscross the Cordillera Blanca and can provide an appetizing taste of the province's vistas, or can be combined with longer treks to keep you walking in the hills for months on end.

Trekking & Mountaineering

When to Go

People hike year-round, but the dry season of mid-May to mid-September is the most popular time to visit, with good weather and the clearest views. It's still advisable to check the latest weather forecasts, however, as random heavy snowfalls, winds and electrical storms are not uncommon during this period. December to April is the wettest time, when it is often overcast and wet in the afternoons and trails become boggy. With the appropriate gear and some preparation, hiking is still possible and some trekkers find this season more rewarding, as many of the most popular trails are empty. For serious mountaineering, climbers pretty much stick to the dry season.

The management body for Parque Nacional Huascarán, Sernamp (Servicio Nacional de Áreas Naturales Protegidas por el Estado; the government agency administering national parks, reserves, historical sanctuaries and other protected areas under the Ministry of Environment), technically requires the use of local licensed guides for all activity in Parque Nacional Huascarán, including day hikes, trekking and climbing.

Trail Guidebooks & Maps

The most comprehensive guide to trekking in the region is *Peru's Cordilleras Blancas & Huayhuash* by Neil and Harriet Pike. It contains detailed route maps and altitude charts, and ranks treks by difficulty. Another great resource for the Huayhuash region is the detailed *Climbs and Treks of the Cordillera Huayhuash of Peru* (2005) by Jeremy Frimer, though it's sold out and only available for consultation in Huaraz.

The best overview of climbing glaciers in the Cordillera Blanca is Brad Johnson's *Classic Climbs of the Cordillera Blanca Peru* (2003), which was reprinted in 2009. For rock climbing and bouldering, check out *Huaraz: The Climbing Guide* by David Lazo and Marie Timmermans.

Felipe Díaz' 1:300,000 *Cordilleras Blanca & Huayhuash* is a popular map for an overview of the land, with towns, major trails and town plans, though it's not detailed enough for remote treks.

The Alpenvereinskarte (Austrian Alpine Club) produces the most detailed and accurate maps of the region; look for the regularly updated 1:100,000 *Cordillera Blanca Nord, Cordillera Blanca Sur* and *Cordillera Huayhuash*. These maps are available in Caraz, Huaraz and at South American Explorers' clubhouses for around S80 each. Cheaper but with a similar scale

CHOOSING A TREK OPERATOR

Before you lay out your cold, hard cash for a guided trek make sure you know what you're getting. Ask the company or guide to list the services, products and price they're offering on your contract. In the event that they don't live up to their promises you may or may not be able to do anything about it, but a list ensures that the company understands exactly what you expect.

On your end, it is critical that you are crystal clear with your guides about your experience and fitness level. Also important is that you are properly acclimatized before setting out on a trek. All too often, parties set out for big treks and climbs just after arriving in Huaraz, with the predictable result of altitude sickness and having to turn back. Take the time to adjust in Huaraz, do a couple of acclimatization hikes, and *then* enjoy a trouble-free, multiday trek.

It is standard to provide food and shelter for the guides, cooks and *arrieros* (mule drivers), which should be discussed beforehand. Remember that prepackaged dehydrated meals are not staples in the Cordillera Blanca. You will almost certainly be eating whole, local foods that weigh more and require more effort to carry.

Below are some suggested questions to ask before choosing your guide; keep in mind that the answers will make a difference in the price.

➡ Can I meet our guide ahead of time? This is an opportunity to meet the person you'll spend a lot of time with for multiple days and nights, and if necessary, to confirm ahead of time that he/she speaks English.

➡ Will we use public or private transportation?

➡ Will there be a cook and an *arriero*?

➡ Will there be a separate cooking tent and a separate bathroom tent?

➡ How many meals and snacks will we get every day? Many trekkers complain about inadequate breakfasts and too few energizing noshes.

➡ How many people will be on our trek? Larger numbers mean lower prices, but make sure you're comfortable trekking with a dozen strangers.

➡ Can I check the equipment before we set off? If you don't have your own sleeping bag, make sure that the one provided is long enough and warm enough (good to -15°C), and inspect the tents for holes and rain resistance.

ARTESONRAJU'S 15 MINUTES OF FAME

If you think the dramatic peak of Artesonraju (5999m) looks familiar, that's because the mountaintop spent a chunk of the '80s and '90s as the peak featured in Paramount Pictures' live-action logo. The famous view is of its northeast face as seen from Quebrada Arhuaycocha (also known as Mirador Alpamayo).

are the *Cordillera Blanca* and *Cordillera Huayhuash* topo maps distributed by Skyline Adventures, available at Café Andino and agencies around Huaraz.

Tours & Guides

Even experienced mountaineers would do well to add a local guide, who knows exactly what has been happening in the mountains, to their group. The Casa de Guías (p375) and trekking agencies in Huaraz (p370) and Caraz (p392) are good places to start your search for qualified mountain guides, *arrieros* (mule drivers) and cooks. Qualified guides and *arrieros* are issued with photo identification by the tourism authority – ask for credentials. Not all registered guides are of the same level, but for a small commission, many agencies will put you in touch with one of their recommended guides, although in high season they will usually be tied up with organized trips.

If your Spanish is up to it and you're not in a great hurry, you can hire *arrieros* and mules in trailhead villages, particularly Cashapampa, Colcabamba and Vaqueria, among others. Horses, donkeys and mules are used as pack animals, and while llamas are occasionally provided, they are expensive and cannot carry as much weight. Try to get a reference for a good *arriero* and establish your trekking goals (ie pace, routes) before you depart. Check the state of the pack animals before you hire them – some *arrieros* overwork their beasts of burden or use sick or injured animals.

The Dirección de Turismo and the guides' union generally set prices. Expect to pay around S30 per day for a horse, S20 for a donkey or mule and S50 per day for an *arriero*. Official rates for guides are S210 per day for a trekking guide, S360 for a climbing guide and S660 to S750 for a technical climbing guide. It's often possible to negotiate lower rates even with experienced registered guides.

Prices do not include food and it is customary that you provide meals and shelter for any hired staff – confirm what's included before you set off. In the case of *arrieros* you may have to pay for their return journey if your trek does not begin and end at the same point.

Equipment & Rentals

If you lack the experience or equipment required to mountain it, fear not, as dozens of businesses offer guides and gear rental, and organize entire adventures for you, right down to the *burros* (donkeys). If you go on a tour, trekking agencies will supply everything from tents to ice axes. Most of them also rent out gear independently.

Reliable rental agencies for decent climbing gear are Quechuandes (p370), Andean Kingdom (p371) and Huascarán (p371).

It often freezes at night, so make sure you have an adequately warm sleeping bag, wet-weather gear (needed year-round), and a brimmed hat and sunglasses. Strong sunblock and good insect repellent are also a must and can be found easily in Huaraz if you've left them at home.

Information

To get the lowdown on trekking and the latest conditions, your first port of call should be Casa de Guías (p375), which has information on weather, trail conditions, guides and mule hire. Some topographic maps are sold here.

Trekking and equipment-rental agencies are also good sources of local knowledge and can advise on a variety of hikes. For more impartial advice, be sure to visit popular Huaraz haunts such as Café Andino (p373) and California Café (p373), whose foreign owners keep abreast of local developments, sell hiking maps and guides, and freely dole out advice alongside tasty treats.

Cordillera Blanca

One of the most breathtaking parts of the continent, the Cordillera Blanca is the world's highest tropical mountain range and encompasses some of South America's highest mountains. Andean leviathans include the majestic Nevado Alpamayo (5947m), once termed 'the most beautiful mountain in the world' by the Austrian Alpine Club. Others include Nevado Huascarán (at

6768m, Peru's highest), Pucajirca (6046m), Nevado Quitaraju (6036m) and Nevado Santa Cruz (Nevado Pucaraju; 6259m).

Situated in the tropical zone, the Cordillera Blanca stands to be affected greatly as global warming increases; there exists significant evidence that the glaciers of the Cordillera Blanca show a measurable decrease in their volume and that the snow line has receded in recent decades. Other threats to the park include litter and high-altitude grazing on endangered *qeñua* (*Polylepis*) trees.

Parque Nacional Huascarán

Peruvian mountaineer César Morales Arnao first suggested protecting the flora, fauna and archaeological sites of the Cordillera Blanca in the early 1960s, but it didn't become a reality until 1975, when the national park was established. This 3400-sq-km park encompasses practically the entire area of the Cordillera Blanca above 4000m, including more than 600 glaciers and nearly 300 lakes, and protects such extraordinary and endangered species as the giant *Puya raimondii* plant, the spectacled bear and the Andean condor.

Visitors to the park can register (bring your passport) and pay the park fee at the park office in Huaraz although most of the main entrances to the park also sell tickets. This is S10 per person for a day visit or S65 for a 10-day pass. Park officials may not sell park permits to trekkers or climbers who are not using the services of a local registered agency or a local licensed guide.

Money from fees is used to help maintain trails, pay park rangers and offset the effects of the legions of visitors to the area. It makes sense that as foreign visitors are among those frequenting the area and causing the greatest change, they should contribute to the financing of the national park with their user fees.

Santa Cruz Trek

The classic Cordillera Blanca trek takes visitors along the Quebrada Huarípampa, across the Punta Union Pass (4760m) and down through the spectacular Quebrada Santa Cruz Valley. The completion of a major local transit route to the Lagunas Llanganuco and beyond means that the trek is now shorter and can be completed in three days by acclimatized parties; however, four days allows more scope for viewing alpine flora and a side trip to the base of Alpamayo which affords spectacular panoramas.

It can be hiked in either direction – and agencies in town offer both – but here we describe the trek beginning in Vaqueria, as for those without private transportation it is easier to finish in Cashapampa. Beginning in Vaqueria also avoids a grueling, hot and dusty ascent at the very beginning of the hike and ensures the best scenery comes later in the trek.

Head-turning sights along the way include emerald lakes, sensational views of

PICK YOUR PEAK

With 18 glaciated summits over 6000m and more than 50 over 5700m, the Cordillera Blanca is one of the most important ranges in the world for high-altitude climbers. Add to that the sheer multitude of options, generally short approaches and almost no red tape or summit fees (although you have to pay your park fee) and the appeal is obvious. While Huascarán Sur is the undisputed granddaddy and Alpamayo voted 'most beautiful' by climbers and photographers the world over, Pisco is certainly the most popular climb for its straightforward accessibility and moderate technical requirements.

But that may change. Global warming in the Cordillera Blanca has caused glaciers to retreat and undergo significant transformations, and well-plied routes have altered dramatically in recent years.

Here are 10 popular climbs (and major summits) of the Cordillera Blanca, offering everything from relatively easy routes to hard-core ice climbing:

Huascarán Sur (6768m)	Alpamayo (5947m)
Chopicalqui (6345m)	Pisco (5752m)
Copa Sur (6188m)	Ishinca (5550m)
Quitaraju (6036m)	Urus (5497m)
Tocllaraju (6034m)	Maparaju (5326m)

many of the Cordillera's peaks, beds of brightly colored alpine wildflowers and stands of red *qeñua* trees. Another less thrilling sight here, as in many trekking areas, is the constant sight of cow patties dimpling the valleys and meadows. Watch your step!

The Santa Cruz is one of the most popular routes in Peru for international trekkers and is clearly signposted for much of its 50km length. Each day requires between five and eight hours of hiking, with ascents ranging from 150m to 900m; the final day requires a knee-busting 800m descent.

Heading out from Vaqueria, the first day involves a short and relatively easy ascent through the hamlet of **Huaripampa** and its traditional thatched-roof Quechua houses. Guinea pigs (destined for the dinner table) can often be seen running around in shallow wooden platforms underneath the roofs. After passing the village, the trail follows the Quebrada Huaripampa to a camp at Paria (3850m).

The second day is the toughest, but trekkers gain major bragging rights as they push up past Laguna Morococha and through a spiralling rocky buttress over the Punta Union Pass, which appears from below as

Santa Cruz Trek

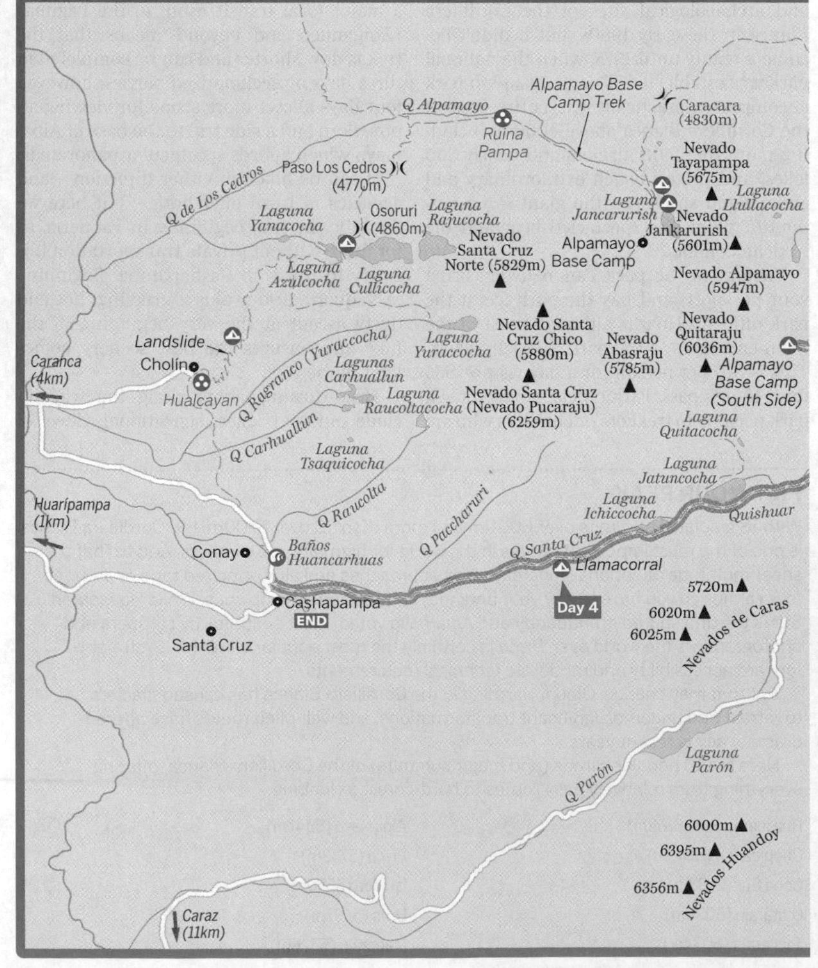

an angular notch in a seemingly unbroken rocky wall above. The panoramas from both sides of the pass are captivating. To the west lies the Quebrada Santa Cruz and its lakes while to the southeast, the Quebrada Huaripampa plunges steeply downwards. After crossing the pass, it's usual to pitch tents at Taullipampa (4250m), which sits in a gorgeous meadow at the foot of the majestic Nevado Taulliraju (5830m). The glacial icefall on the flanks of Taulliraju is very active and large chunks regularly break off, especially in the afternoon sun. To the south, Nevado Artesonraju (6025m) and Nevado Paria (5600m) dominate the skyline.

The reward on day three for the hard legwork so far is a long but easy hike through some spectacular mountain scenery past small waterfalls, lakes and interconnected marshy areas. From Taullipampa, the trail heads toward the large Laguna Jatuncocha. It was in this area that a 2012 avalanche on the northeast flank of Nevado Artisonraju blew out the ice-and-mud dam holding the small Laguna Arteson Bajo and the lake contents emptied into the valley and washed away a significant portion of the trail. The path has now been repaired although the small Laguna Icchicocha which once formed

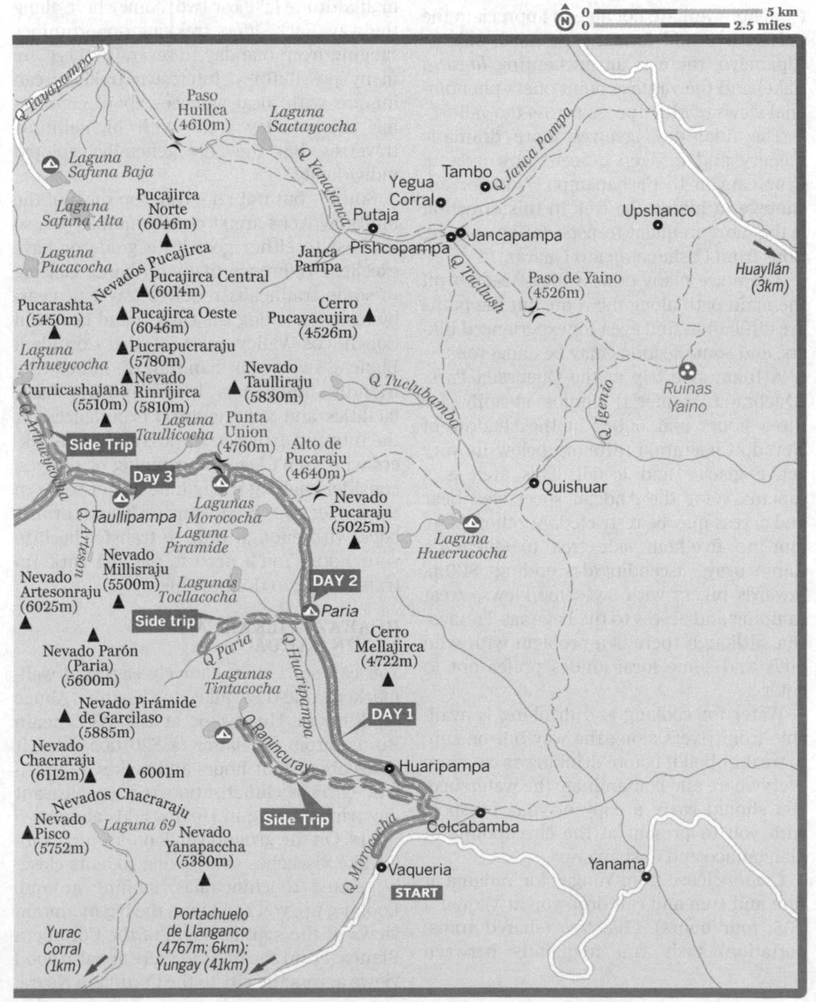

> **FAST FACTS: SANTA CRUZ**
>
> **Duration:** Four days
>
> **Distance:** 50km
>
> **Difficulty:** Moderate
>
> **Start:** Vaqueria (3700m)
>
> **Finish:** Cashapampa (2900m)

a double act with Jatuncocha is now more of a marshy area than an alpine lagoon.

Before you reach Jatuncocha, it is possible to take a side trip to Alpamayo Base Camp (South Side) underneath the magnificent Nevado Alpamayo (5947m). Although from here you are not able to appreciate the perfect pyramid form of the north side of Alpamayo, there is an enchanting *laguna* (lake) and the vantage point offers phenomenal views of other peaks across the valley.

The final day involves more dramatic scenery and a steep descent down Santa Cruz canyon to Cashapampa. A major advantage in hiking the trek in this direction is the more frequent transportation connections from Cashapampa to Huaraz.

There are many other valleys leading off the main path along the route but the paths are difficult to find even for experienced hikers, and some sections may be dangerous.

A 10km side trip at the Quebrada Paria (Quebrada Vaqueria) climbs steadily for three hours and 600m in the shadow of Nevado Chacraraju (6108m), below its very active glacier and icefall. This area is a sanctuary for the Andean spectacled bear and access may be restricted. Another 11km, four- to five-hour side trek to Quebrada Ranincuray, ascending/descending 800m, rewards hikers with awesome views, great camping and access to the Lagunas Tintacocha, although there is a problem with wild bulls and some local guides prefer not to enter.

Water for cooking and drinking is available from rivers along the way but be sure to treat or boil it before drinking as cows are everywhere and contaminate the watershed. You should carry a copy of your passport with you to present at the checkpoints at Llanganuco and Cashapampa.

Combis leave from Yungay for Yanama at 7am and 1pm and can drop you at Vaqueria (S15, four hours). *Colectivo* (shared transportation) taxis run frequently between Caraz and the trailhead at Cashapampa (S8, 1½ hours).

Other Cordillera Blanca Treks & Hikes

While the Santa Cruz trek attracts the lion's share of visitors, dozens of other trekking possibilities in the Cordillera Blanca supply scenery and vistas just as jaw-dropping (minus the crowds). A series of *quebradas* (valleys) – Ishinca, Cojup, Quilcayhuanca, Shallap and Rajucolta (listed north to south) – run parallel to each other from the area around Huaraz up into the heart of the Cordillera Blanca, and most of them have a high-altitude lake (or two) somewhere along the way. Each offers trekking opportunities ranging from one day to several – there are many possibilities. Interested trekkers can inquire with local agencies about connecting these valley treks with high-altitude traverses, but they are generally explored individually.

Some – but not all – trails on most of the multiday treks aren't clearly marked yet, so it's best to either go with a guide or have excellent reference maps on hand. Getting to some trailheads requires travel to nearby towns or along the rugged and beautiful Conchucos Valley (east of the Cordillera Blanca), where a handful of ludicrously friendly indigenous towns provide basic facilities and vivid cultural experiences for the intrepid explorer. For less ambitious hikers who aren't keen on camping or refuges, consider making a day hike out of some of the longer trips by starting early and turning back with enough time to transfer back to your hotel. You'll need to pay the park entrance (S10) to do these hikes.

HUARAZ–WILKAHUAÍN–LAGUNA AHUAC

You can start this relatively easy and well-marked one-day hike to Laguna Ahuac (4560m) in Huaraz or at the Wilkahuaín Ruins. From the latter (a S20 taxi ride), it takes about four hours and makes an excellent early acclimatization trip or pleasant day trip; starting in Huaraz adds about two hours. On the ground you'll notice furry rabbit-like viscachas (burrowing rodents closely related to chinchillas) sniffing around. Looking up, you can't miss the big mountain views of the southern end of the Cordillera Blanca. From the *laguna* there are also good views across the city to the Cordillera Negra.

LAGUNA CHURUP

The hamlet of **Pitec** (3850m), just above Huaraz, is the best place to start this six-hour hike to the beautiful Laguna Churup (4450m) at the base of Nevado Churup. You can select from approaching along either the left-hand or right-hand side of the valley; most folks opt for the left approach where there are new cables to assist your progress. The steep rock wall here may test those who have issues with heights.

This day hike is often chosen as an acclimatization hike, but note the altitudes and the 600m ascent – make sure you're ready before charging into this one.

A taxi from Huaraz to Pitec will cost about S60; *combis* for Llupa (S3, 30 minutes) leave Huaraz from the corner of Gamarra and Las Americas about every 30 minutes (ask to be dropped off at the path to Pitec); from there it's a one-hour walk to Pitec. You'll need to be back at Llupa by 5pm to catch the last *colectivo* back.

LAGUNA 69

This vivid blue lake surrounded by snow-covered peaks is the jewel of the Cordilleras and a challenging second acclimatization hike. While it's possible to take it slow and spend the night close to the lake in a tent, it's most commonly visited as a day trip from Huaraz.

It's a fairly long and tough six-hour round-trip hike from the trailhead to the lake, which sits right at the base of of Chacraraju (6112m). However, you will be rewarded with great views of Chopicalqui (6345m), Huascarán Sur (6768m) and Norte (6655m) along the way.

The trails to Laguna 69 start near the Yurac Corral (3800m), on the northern tip of a big bend in the Llanganuco road.

Some agencies in Huaraz offer a tour to the lake including transportation, breakfast and a guide for S45. If you want to hike on your own, some agencies also offer a transportation-only option for S30 with a bus that will drop you at the trailhead and wait for you to return. Alternatively, a taxi from Huaraz will charge around S180 round-trip. All of these will stop on request at the Lagunas Llanganuco, which are right next to the road on the way up.

QUILCAYHUANCA & COJUP VALLEYS

This three- to four-day hike leaving from Pitec is one of the most beautiful in the Cordillera, but it's a difficult trek. You'll need to be well acclimatized to tackle it, as pack animals don't make it up over the 5000m Paso Choco. It's one thing to hike at altitude, and another altogether with a 15kg pack on your back.

The path winds up the Quebrada Quilcayhuanca through *qeñua* trees and grassy meadows until reaching the Laguna Cuchillacocha and Tullpacocha. Along the way, you pass breathtaking views of Nevado Cayesh (5721m), Maparaju (5326m), Tumarinaraju (5668m) and a half-dozen other peaks over 5700m. It then climbs to the soaring Paso Choco and descends through the Quebrada Cojup past another pair of *lagunas*. Because this trek is not well marked, it's best to go with a guide (or have advanced navigation skills and a good topo map).

An easier version is a hike up and out through the Quilcayhuanca valley back to Pitec on a two-day trek with a night in tents at 4000m. You'll still need to carry your gear but your backpack will be much lighter. This good alternative is less strenuous than the Santa Cruz trek, but also takes in spectacular mountain vistas.

INCA TRAIL

This three- to six-day hike along a stretch of Inca trail linking Huari and the city of Huánuco, doesn't get much attention possibly because the scenery is not as spectacular as in other parts of the Cordillera. It's a fairly gentle trek crossing well-preserved parts of the old Inca trail and ending up in Huánuco Viejo, which was one of the most important military sites of the Incas in northern Peru.

Very few visitors walk this stretch and details on the ground are hard to come by, but it is possible to find local guides to show you the way – ask around in Huaraz or in Huari.

CALLEJÓN DE CONCHUCOS TREKS

If you're short on time but still want to cross the Cordillera, the relatively easy two- to three-day **Olleros to Chavín de Huántar trek** is a good choice, although you'll be further from the big peaks here and the mountain views aren't as impressive as in other parts of the park.

You can start the 40km trek in either town, though most people start at the trailhead in Canray Chico, just outside Olleros in the Callejón de Huáylas, on the western side of the Cordillera Blanca. You can arrange llamas here as pack animals. Pretty villages and pre-Inca roads with great views of the Uruashraju (5722m), Rurec (5700m) and Cashan (5716m) mountains dot the landscape heading up to the 4700m Punta Yanashallash Pass. Your finishing point on the Callejón de Conchucos side is absolutely gorgeous. Best of all, in Chavín you can soak your weary bones in hot springs and get up early the next day to visit the ruins, without the usual throng of tourists. Dedicated riders have mountain-biked this route. Taxis from Huaraz to Canray cost around S50.

If this trek whets your appetite for ambling, you can continue to Huari by bus and start the similar level **Huari to Chacas trek**, making your way along the eastern flanks of the Cordillera Blanca. Be sure to camp near the Laguna Purhuay – this picturesque spot deserves an overnight visit. The easy two- to three-day route passes several other lakes, reaches its zenith at a 4550m pass and finishes in the misty high-altitude tropical forests of the Parhua Valley (3500m).

After a rest in the fetching town of Chacas, you can continue on to do the one- to two-day **Chacas to Yanama trek**. This is the shortest of the three hikes and has the lowest pass of the lot, at a 'mere' 4050m. From Chacas you hike through the municipalities of Sapcha and Potaca and can either finish the trek at Yanama or continue to the Keshu Valley, which has several good places to camp. Colcabamba, a few hours further on from Yanama, is near one end of the Santa Cruz trek – endurance hikers can tag this trek onto the end of their Herculean circuit before returning to Huaraz.

QUEBRADA AKILLPO-ISHINCA

Beautiful Quebrada Akillpo is somewhat off the tour radar, making this tough three-day trek a great choice for experienced trekkers who want to get away from the high-season crowds. The trail begins at Joncopampa and ascends through a spectacular forest of *qeñua* trees before emerging near Laguna Akillpo at the base of the Akillpo glacier. From here there is a tricky 4900m pass beneath Nevado Tocllaraju with difficult descents bordered by precipices. After this, the trail continues down past the Refugio Ishinca (4390m) into the Ishinca Valley. Donkeys are not able to cross the pass. The path is not well marked and the difficult terrain means a knowledgeable guide is essential.

If you don't have the experience to complete the full circuit, a one- or two-day trek up into the Quebrada Akillpo and back allows you to see the remarkable forest, and also serves as a good acclimatization hike. The shorter trip will take you to the end of the forest before turning back, while the longer trek reaches the *laguna* but not the pass.

For even easier access to the valley you can rent horses in Joncopampa to explore part of the trail. Taxis from Huaraz to Joncopampa cost around S180 round-trip.

Los Cedros-Alpamayo

This is one of the more dazzling and demanding treks of the Cordillera and an alternative to the epic Huayhuash circuit. The 90km route involves very long ascents to high passes, incredible alpine scenery (including the regal north side of Nevado Alpamayo) and traditional Quechua communities with no road access. Starting in Cashapampa (one end point of the Santa Cruz trek) or Hualcayan and ending in Pomabamba, it is only recommended for experienced and acclimatized hikers who are familiar with navigation. The route is relatively straightforward, but not signposted. There are no real alternative routes, so once you're in you either have to follow it to the end or head back out from where you began. You can treat yourself to well-earned dips in hot mineral spring baths at both ends of this trek.

Cordillera Huayhuash

Often playing second fiddle to Cordillera Blanca, its limelight-stealing cousin, the Huayhuash hosts an equally impressive medley of glaciers, summits and lakes – all packed into a hardy area only 30km across. Increasing numbers of travelers are discovering this rugged and remote territory, where trails skirt around the outer edges of this stirring, peaked range. Several strenuous high-altitude passes of over 4500m throw down a gauntlet to the hardiest of trekkers. The feeling of utter wilderness, particularly along the unspoiled eastern edge, is the big draw and you are more likely to have majestic Andean condors for company than other trekking groups.

In the waning moments of 2001, Peru's Ministry of Agriculture declared the Cordillera Huayhuash a 'reserved zone,' giving a transitory measure of protection to nearly 700 sq km of almost-pristine land. Since then, the ministry has backed away from official support as a unique, private- and community-managed conservation effort has taken root. Several communities whose traditional territory lies at the heart of the Huayhuash range are formally recognized as 'Private Conservation Areas.' Nine districts along the circuit, **Llamac**, **Pocpa**, **Jirishanca**, **Quishuarcancha**, **Tupac Amaru**, **Guñog**, **Uramasa**, **Huayllapa** and **Pacllón**, now charge user fees of S15 to S40, with costs for the basic circuit S195 at time of writing and continuing to rise on a yearly basis. Part of the fees goes toward improved security for hikers and part goes to continued conservation work and improved facilities, although the standard of toilets in some parts of the circuit remain far from acceptable. Support this grassroots preservation attempt by paying your fees, carrying enough small change and by always asking for an official receipt.

Note that open fires are prohibited throughout the Huayhuash region as wood is scarce. If you're hiking on your own, make sure you bring a gas cooker.

Cordillera Huayhuash Circuit

Circling a tight cluster of high peaks, including Yerupajá (6634m), the world's second-highest tropical mountain, this stunning trek crosses multiple high-altitude passes with spine-tingling views. The dramatic lakes along the eastern flanks provide great campsites (and are good for trout fishing) and give hikers a wide choice of routes to make this trek as difficult as they want.

Daily ascents range from 500m to 1200m, but a couple of days in the middle and at the end of the trek involve major descents, which can be just as tough as going uphill. The average day involves about 12km on the trail, or anywhere from four to eight hours of hiking, although you may experience at least one 10- to 12-hour day.

Most trekkers take extra rest days along the way, partly because the length and altitude make the entire circuit very demanding, and partly to allow for the sensational sights to sink in. Others prefer a shorter version and can hike for as few as five days along the remote eastern side of the Huayhuash.

Described here is the classic Huayhuash Circuit trek, but many side trips and alternate routes along the way can add a day or two to your trekking time.

FAST FACTS: CORDILLERA HUAYHUASH

Duration: Nine days

Distance: 115km

Difficulty: Demanding

Start: Pocpa/Matacancha

Finish: Llamac

Nearest towns: Chiquián, Llamac and Cajatambo

If you are trekking with an agency you may begin your trek at Matacancha, but if you don't have private transportation you will need to begin from Pocpa near **Llamac**, the last town for several days as the trail leaves 'civilization.' In Pocpa it's possible to arrange *arrieros* and pack animals, and there are several local families offering accommodations and basic meals.

On the first stretch of the trek, you'll follow the Río Llamac through the village of Palca to Matacancha, where you'll spend the night. The second day takes you over a 4700m pass and down to Laguna Mitacocha (4230m). On day three, you'll see more excellent mountain panoramas and eventually reach a cliff that overlooks Laguna Carhuacocha (4138m) and the glaciated mountains behind Siula Grande (6344m) and Yerupajá looming in the distance.

Continuing on the main trail, parties hit a short section of paved Inca trail, about 1.5m wide and 50m long, the remnants of an Inca road heading south from the archaeological site of Huánuco Viejo near La Unión. Over the next couple of days work your way toward Laguna Carnicero (4430m), Laguna Mitucocha, the top of Portachuelo de Huayhuash (4750m), and Laguna Viconga (4407m). After several glaciated mountain crowns come into view, including the double-peaked Cuyoc (5550m), you can either camp and continue the main circuit, or you can head southwest along the Río Pumarinri Valley toward Cajatambo, leaving the circuit early.

If you keep going, get ready for the challenging 5000m-plus Punta Cuyoc Pass. On day six, the trail crests a small ridge on Pumarinri (5465m), giving trekkers face-on views of Cuyoc. Look out for the hardy *Stangea henricii*, a grayish-green, flat, rosette-

Cordillera Huayhuash Circuit

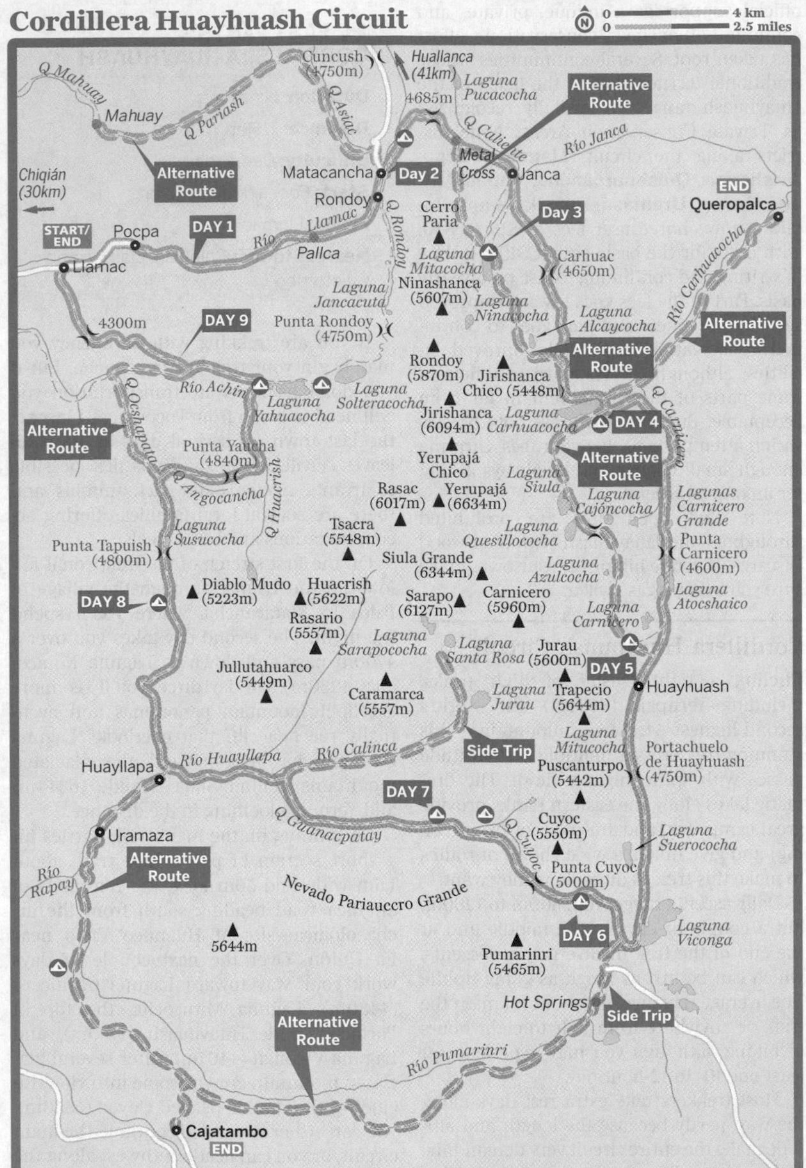

shaped plant of overlapping tongue-like leaves that only grows above 4700m.

On the seventh day you can continue the direct circuit by hiking past the village of Huayllapa; exit the circuit through Huayllapa and the town of Uramaza to Cajatambo, or make a side trip up the Río Calinca Valley to Lagunas Jurau, Santa Rosa and Sarapococha, where there are some of the best mountain panoramas of the entire trek. The traditional circuit will take you past the glacier-clad pyramid of Jullutahuarco (5449m) and a stupendous 100m-high waterfall. Push on to a small

HUAYHUASH HOGWASH

Some travelers have complained that the community gatekeepers on the Cordillera Huayhuash Circuit sometimes try to resell used receipts or purposely write down the wrong date on your receipt in order to fine you later in a random check at the campsite, so keep a keen eye on your transactions and don't head out until all is squared away.

lake near Punta Tapuish (4800m) for good high-altitude camping.

The following day the trail drops gently to Laguna Susucocha (4750m) shortly before a junction (4400m) with Quebrada Angocancha. The trail skirts boggy meadows and climbs into rock and scree before reaching Punta Yaucha (4840m), offering wonderful views of the range's major peaks, including Yerupajá to the east and many of the minor glaciated high points to the southeast. Go fossil-hunting in this area for imprints of ammonites and other creatures that once dwelled under the sea – and imagine the Andes relegated to the ocean's bottom. Finally, the path descends to the wonderfully scenic Laguna Yahuacocha.

The last day is short, with an early arrival in Llamac, from where public transportation to Chiquián and on to Huaraz leaves at 11:15am. Trekkers should be prepared for aggressively territorial dogs along the way; bending down to pick up a rock usually keeps them off – though refrain from throwing it unless you absolutely must.

Cordillera Negra

The poor little Cordillera Negra lives literally in the shadows of its big-brother range, the Cordillera Blanca, whose towering glaciated peaks to the east block the morning sun and loom dramatically over everything around them. The 'Black Range,' which gets its name from its obvious contrast to the more beautiful 'White Range,' will probably always look a bit dressed down – with its arid, mud-brown, merely hilly silhouette – against the Cordillera Blanca's stunning icy and craggy profile. Still, the Negra has an important role to play in the area's ecology as it blocks warm Pacific winds from hitting the Blanca's glaciers and contributing to their thaw. It's also an important agricultural and mining area for the local population.

While not offering the big-mountain recreational offerings available on the other side of the Callejón de Huaylas, the Cordillera Negra has some great attractions, especially for rock climbers, who will find excellent bolted climbs in Recuay and Hatun Machay. Mountain-bikers have access to seemingly unlimited kilometers of roads and trails over the rugged landscape; bike-guiding companies in Huaraz know these old byways well.

Day hikers can also explore these routes. Hire a taxi to take you to Punta Callan (4225m) above Huaraz or to Curcuy (4520m) above Recuay and walk down to town. Another suggested hike is a three-hour ascent to the Mirador Quitabamba near Jangas. Take a *colectivo* toward Carhuaz, getting off at La Cruz de la Mina and hike up the hill.

The villages here don't see a lot of tourists, and you'll be interacting with indigenous people who in many cases live an untouched, traditional lifestyle.

Laguna Wilkacocha

In the Cordillera Negra, just 10km from Huaraz, the tranquil Laguna Wilkacocha (3700m) is a popular first acclimitization hike. The lake is well worth a visit in its own right, but is often frequented by visitors who plan bigger outings in the Cordillera Blanca.

The views from here across to the Cordillera Blanca are absolutely spectacular and take in many snow-covered peaks including Huantsan, Shaqsha, Vallunaraju and Ranrapalca.

The trail begins at the Puente Santa Cruz on the highway south of Huaraz and passes several small traditional villages on the way up. A guide is recommended as the path is not clear, and some visitors have enraged locals by trampling all over their crops. It takes around two hours going up and an hour on the return.

Colectivos heading from Huaraz to Recuay will drop you at Puente Santa Cruz (S2, 20 minutes). Alternatively, a taxi from Huaraz can take you all the way to the lake for S40 and then wander down at your own pace to take a *colectivo* back to town.

NORTH OF HUARAZ

As the Río Santa slices its way north through the Callejón de Huaylas, a road shadows its every curve past several subdued towns to Caraz and on to the menacingly impressive Cañón del Pato. The Andean panorama of the Cordillera Blanca looms over the length of the valley like a wall of white-topped sentries, with the granddaddy of them all, Huascarán, barely 14km away from the road as the condor flies. Many hiking trailheads are accessible from towns along this route and two roads valiantly cross the Cordillera, a freshly paved one linking Carhuaz to Chacas and an unsealed one from Yungay to Yanama.

Monterrey

043 / POP 1100 / ELEV 2800M

Huddled around a scattered spine of tourist facilities, this tiny *pueblo,* 9km north of Huaraz, earns a spot on the map for its natural **hot springs** (admission S4; 7am-4:30pm). Buses terminate right in front.

The hot springs are divided into public pools, which are sometimes far from warm, and private rooms which offer the sort of scalding action you're looking for. Facilities here are very basic and the private facilities have a distinct public hospital feel – don't expect a romantic soak.

> **WORTH A TRIP**
>
> **CHANCOS**
>
> Set among some lovely rural scenery above the town of Marcará, community-run thermal bath complex **Baños Termales de Chancos** (Vicos; pool/baths/sauna S1/2/5; 6am-6pm) has a couple of a piping-hot pools and baths, but the real reason to come here is for the natural sauna caves carved into the mountainside. Temperatures are posted on the doors to each cave – our favorites are caves 5, 6 and 7. There is also massage service and special thermal baths infused with wild herbs.
>
> *Colectivos* to the baths (S1.50, 15 minutes) leave when full from the bridge in Marcará. If in a hurry, just pay for all the seats. Any *combi* running from Huaraz to Cuarhuaz can drop you in Marcará (S3, 30 minutes).

However there is no need to wrinkle your nose at the brown color of the water, it's due to high iron content rather than questionable hygiene practices. It's best to visit early in the morning before the crowds.

Sleeping & Eating

Though there is a great hotel and some fine restaurants in Monterrey, it works best as a day trip from Huaraz. On Sundays, many restaurants serve a traditional Peruvian feast called *pachamanca* (*pacha* means 'earth' and *manca* means 'oven' in Quechua), a magnificent bounty of chicken, pork, lamb, guinea pig, corn, potatoes and other vegetables cooked for several hours over hot stones.

★ El Patio de Monterrey HOTEL $$$

(043-42-4965; www.elpatio.com.pe; s/d incl breakfast S203/357;) The fanciest venture around, this hotel has colonial-style architecture around a toothsome hacienda, complemented by colonial-style furniture. Most of the ship-shape rooms are spacious and have bathtubs and TV, while some sleep up to four and have a fireplace. The rooms are surrounded by a bountiful garden strewn with wagon wheels and fountains. Dinner is available in the fireplace-heated restaurant-bar.

El Cortijo PERUVIAN $$

(Carretera Huaraz; mains S25-40; 8am-7pm) This excellent restaurant grills ostrich (when they can get it in Peru) alongside *cuy* (guinea pig) and other meats. Outdoor tables are arranged around a fountain (complete with a little boy peeing) in a grassy flower-filled garden, with swings for children.

Getting There & Away

Local *combis* from Huaraz go north along Luzuriaga, west on Calle 28 de Julio, north on Calle 27 de Noviembre, east on Raymondi and north on Fitzcarrald. Try to catch a bus early in the route, as they fill up quickly. The fare for the 20-minute ride is S1. A taxi ride between Huaraz and Monterrey costs about S7.

Carhuaz

043 / POP 15,400 / ELEV 2638M

Carhuaz, 35km north of Huaraz, lays claim to one of the prettiest plazas in the valley, with a combination of rose gardens and towering palms that make lingering here a pleasure. The Sunday **market** is a kaleidoscopic treat

REMOTE RIFUGI

Established by the pioneering Father Ugo de Censi, a priest of the Salesian order, the Italian nonprofit organization Don Bosco, based in Marcará, runs three remote **refuges** (97-111-0088; www.rifugi-omg.org; per bed S90; May-Sep) deep within the belly of the Cordillera. Each refuge is heated and has a radio, hot water, basic medical supplies and charges S90 per night for bed, breakfast and dinner.

Profits go to local aid projects. Refuges include Refugio Perú (4765m), a two-hour walk from Llanganuco and a base for climbing Pisco; Refugio Ishinca (4350m), a three-hour walk from Collón village in the Ishinca Valley; and Refugio Huascarán (4670m), a four-hour walk from Musho. A fourth refuge at Contrahierba (4100m) only opens on demand.

Trekkers, mountaineers and sightseers are all welcome. Outside peak season you will need to make reservations at least one week in advance and have a group of at least four people who will commit to two nights of accommodation.

as *campesinos* (peasants) descend from surrounding villages to sell a medley of fresh fruits, herbs and handicrafts. A paved road passes over the Cordillera Blanca from Carhuaz, via the beautiful Quebrada Ulta and the new Punta Olímpica tunnel, to Chacas and San Luis.

Carhuaz' annual **La Virgen de La Merced fiesta** is celebrated from September 14 to 24 with processions, fireworks, dancing, bullfights and plenty of drinking – so much that the town is often referred to as *Carhuaz borachera* (drunk Carhuaz)!

You'll find a Banco de la Nación with a Visa/Plus ATM on the Plaza de Armas.

Sleeping & Eating

Don't miss the town's ubiquitous treat, *raspadilla*, a slurpee of ice slathered in fruity syrup.

Hotel La Merced HOTEL $
(043-39-4280; Ucayali 724; s/d S25/45) One of the town's oldest running ventures, boasting lots of windows for Cordillera adulation and plenty of religious posters with the odd ABBA piece thrown in. Rooms are clean and have hot showers.

Alojamiento Cordillera Blanca GUESTHOUSE $
(94-389-7678; Aurora 247; s/d S24/45) Forget hospitality, but if you want to arrive Saturday night and wake up in the thick of the market, here are cramped but clean rooms.

★**Hotel El Abuelo** INN $$
(043-39-4456; www.elabuelohotel.com; Calle 9 de Diciembre 257; s/d incl breakfast S144/195; @) The haughtiest place to stay in town is this excellent boutique inn. It has immaculate and charming rooms spread between the main house and a new annex that affords fine views of the Cordillera Negra. All the rooms receive plenty of natural light and the modern, fully equipped bathrooms boast hot-water sinks. Prices include a buffet breakfast with fruit and juices sourced from the hotel orchard.

Montaña Jazz HOTEL $$$
(043-63-0023; www.montanajazzperu.com; via Chucchun s/n; bungalows S330-450) Within walking distance from Carhuaz but with a distinctly rural vibe, these comfortable and well-equipped bungalows make a great base for exploring the Callejón de Huaylas. Set in an ample garden with mountain vistas flooded with birdsong, rooms are elegant and spacious and most feature fireplaces, modern bathrooms and functional private kitchens.

If you don't feel like cooking, the friendly owners serve Italian-style meals on the porch. They can also arrange activities throughout the region.

Restaurante Gusto y Sabores PERUVIAN $
(Merced 459; menús S6; noon-9pm) This popular local spot does a flavorful set meal served with a hearty soup.

Gerardos Chickens PERUVIAN $
(cnr 2 de Mayo & La Merced; mains S9; 5-10pm) Does a good roasted chicken. It's across from the Huaraz terminal.

Getting There & Away

Passing minibuses to Yungay (S3, 30 minutes) and Caraz (S3.50, 45 minutes) pick up on the highway near the corner of La Merced. *Combis* to Huaraz (S3, 50 minutes) leave from a small terminal on the first block of La Merced. Buses and *colectivos* from Huaraz to Chacas and San Luis stop on the corner of La Merced and Amazonas, one block from the plaza.

Yungay

043 / POP 21,900 / ELEV 2458M

Light on overnight visitors, serene little Yungay has relatively few tourist services but is a well organized and neat little town. It is the access point for the popular Lagunas Llanganuco and Laguna 69, via a dirt road that continues over the Cordillera to Yanama and beyond. Surrounded on all sides by lush hills wafting brisk mountain air, it's difficult to believe the heart-wrenching history of this little junction in the road.

The original village of Yungay is now a rubble-strewn zone about 2km south of the new town and marks the site of the single worst natural disaster in the Andes. The earthquake of May 31, 1970, loosened 15 million cubic meters of granite and ice from the west wall of Huascarán Norte. The resulting *aluvión* (debris landslide) dropped over three vertical kilometers on its way to Yungay, 15km away. The town and almost all its 25,000 inhabitants were buried.

Sleeping & Eating

Hostal Gledel GUESTHOUSE $

(043-39-3048; Aries Graziani; s/d without bathroom S15/25) The gregarious and generous Señora Gamboa rents out 13 spartan rooms with decent mattresses brightened by colorful bedspreads, plus there's hot water. Expect at least one hug and a sample of her cooking during your stay. This is both the cheapest and best place to stay in town – it's deservedly popular.

Hotel Rima Rima HOTEL $

(043-39-3257; rodriortiz@movistar.es; Grau 275; s/d/tw S45/75/80;) The most comfortable hotel in town, Rima Rima has modern spacious rooms with cable TV. The rooms at the back have great views of the Cordillera Negra, but if you don't snare one, there's a rooftop terrace with even better vistas.

Restaurant Turístico Alpamayo PERUVIAN $

(043-39-3090; mains S14-24, menús S7; 7:30am-6pm) Surrounded by gardens just off the main highway at the north end of town,

DON'T MISS

CAMPO SANTO

On May 31, 1970, when the most of the world was watching the Mexico–Soviet Union FIFA World Cup opening match, a nearly 8.0 magnitude earthquake jolted the Peruvian departments of Ancash and La Libertad. The 45-second shake turned an 83-sq-km area into a disaster zone, but it was the loosening of an estimated 50 million cubic meters of rock, ice and snow that broke away from the north face of Mt Huascarán that caused the most cataclysmic disaster in Andean history. The resulting *aluvión* (debris avalanche) barreled 15km down the mountainside at average speeds between 280km/h and 335km/h, burying the entire town of Yungay and nearly all of its inhabitants by the time it came to rest. An entire town, gone in three minutes.

The site of old Yungay (Yungay Viejo), **Campo Santo** (admission S2; 8am-6pm) is overseen by a towering white statue of Christ standing on a knoll above the town's original, Swiss-designed cemetery, from where he overlooks the path of the *aluvión*. Ironically, it was this very cemetery that helped save the lives of 92 of the town's residents, who had just enough time to charge up its steps and elevate themselves out of the path of the *aluvión*. Those, along with some 300 residents attending a circus at the town stadium, were the only survivors out of an estimated 25,000 residents.

Flower-filled gardens follow the solemn pathway of the *aluvión*, with occasional gravestones and monuments commemorating the thousands of people who lie buried beneath. At the old Plaza de Armas, you can just see the remains of the cathedral tower, what's left of a crushed Expreso Ancash bus and four palm-trees that survived the onslaught (one of them remarkably still alive). A replica of the cathedral's facade has been built in honor of the dead. Nearly every *Yungayano* born before 1955 is buried here in a grave dug by Mother Nature.

Vendors at the entrance draw your attention to a slew of before and after photos, which are well worth a look to gain some context of the absolute destruction of this disaster. The entire site has been declared a national cemetery and excavations of any kind are prohibited.

Alpamayo is a pleasant spot, with a garden gazebo, to dig into some trout, *cuy* (guinea pig) or *chicharrones* (fried pork skins).

Pilar's PERUVIAN $
(Plaza de Armas; mains S8-28; ⏲7:30am-10pm, closed Wed) Right on the plaza, friendly Pilar's knocks up good-quality typical Peruvian dishes.

Outside Town

Humacchuco Community Tourism Project GUESTHOUSE $$
(☎043-42-7949; www.responsibletravelperu.com; r per person incl meals & activities S393) Members of the Humacchuco community maintain comfortable bungalows as part of an established sustainable-tourism program. Here visitors can learn about the local culture and natural-resource management, savor a *pachamanca* and go on guided hikes, including a day trip to Laguna 69. You can tailor your own program through Respons (p369) in Huaraz.

★**Llanganuco Mountain Lodge** LODGE $$$
(☎94-366-9580; www.llanganucolodge.com; r incl full-board S450-750) About 45 minutes by taxi from Yungay toward the Lagunas Llanganuco, this recommended lodge run by Brit Charlie Good is in a prime position for serious acclimatization, exploring the lakes area or charging the Santa Cruz trek. It is perched at 3500m next to newly excavated Keushu ruins on the shore of a translucent lagoon.

Lodge rooms are big on space and comfort with down-feather beds and balconies affording great views of the three highest peaks in the range. Tito, an aspiring chef, handles the excellent food, and Shackleton, Dino and Zulu, the Rhodesian ridgebacks, handle mascot duties along with a pair of alpacas. From Yungay, taxis departing in front of the town hospital charge S50 for the ride here. Advanced reservations are essential.

Getting There & Away

Minibuses run from a small terminal along the highway to Caraz (S2, 15 minutes), Carhuaz (S3.50, 30 minutes) and Huaraz (S5, 1¼ hours). Buses from Caraz to Lima pick up passengers at the Plaza de Armas. A couple of *combis* leave from the terminal heading for Yanama (S15, 7am, three hours) via the dirt road over the Cordillera Blanca, with another service leaving from near the police station around 1pm. They pass through Vaqueria, the launching point for the Santa Cruz trek.

Lagunas Llanganuco

A dirt road ascends 1350m from Yungay winding over 28km to the Llanganuco Valley and its two stunning lakes, which are also known as Laguna Chinancocha and Laguna Orconcocha. Nestled in a glacial valley just 1000m below the snow line, these pristine lagoons practically glow under the sun in their bright turquoise and emerald hues. There's a half-hour trail hugging Chinancocha past a jetty and picnic area to where sheer cliffs plunge into the lake. You can take a boat out on the lake for S3.50. Llanganuco is a popular day trip from Huaraz although it is a six-hour drive round-trip. Continuing on the road past the lake you'll see a *mirador* with killer views of the mountain giants of Huascarán (6768m), Chopicalqui (6345m), Chacraraju (6108m), Huandoy (6395m) and others. The road continues over the pass of Portachuelo (4760m) to Yanama on the other side of the Cordillera Blanca.

To reach the Lagunas Llanganuco, you can take a tour from Huaraz or use *colectivos* or taxis from Yungay. Round-trip *colectivos* leave from Yungay's small terminal on the main highway (S30), allowing about two hours in the lake area. A national-park admission fee of S10 is charged. Alternatively you can take a *combi* heading to Yanama, but it costs the same and you may have difficulty getting back to town. A private round-trip taxi from Yungay will cost around S100 to S120. Go in the early morning for the clearest views, especially in the low season.

Caraz

☎043 / POP 26,200 / ELEV 2270M

With an extra helping of superb panoramas of the surrounding mountains and a more kick-back attitude than its rambunctious brother Huaraz, Caraz makes a tranquil alternate base of operations. Trekking and hiking trails meander in all directions – some are day trips, others are much longer sojourns.

One of the few places in the valley spared total destruction by earthquakes or *aluvión,* the town still has a gentle whiff of colonial air. Its lazy Plaza de Armas wouldn't be out of place in a much smaller *pueblo.*

Caraz is the departure point for rugged treks into the remote northern parts of the Cordillera Blanca, which are some of the best in the region. The north side of Alpa-

DEAD NUN'S CANYON

The Spanish version of the History Channel profiled the Cañón del Pato in its 2012 *Rutas Mortales: Los Andes* TV show, where the perceived-to-be weakly named Cañón del Pato (Duck Canyon) was changed to the far more frightening El Cañón de la Monja Muerta (Dead Nun's Canyon). Scary!

mayo (5947m), considered by some to be the most beautiful mountain in the world for its knife-edged, perfectly pyramidal northern silhouette, is accessible from here.

Sights

Laguna Parón LAKE

This postcard pastel-blue lake (4200m), 25km east of Caraz, is surrounded by spectacular snow-covered peaks, of which Pirámide de Garcilaso (5885m), at the end of the lake, looks particularly brilliant. The challenging rock-climbing wall of Torre de Parón, known as the **Sphinx**, is also found here. The road to the lake goes through a canyon with 1000m-high granite walls – this drive is as spectacular as the better-known Llanganuco trip.

Fit and acclimatized hikers can trek to the lake in one long day, but it's easier to catch local transportation to Pueblo Parón and hike the remaining four hours up to the lake. If you go on your own, be aware that you cannot circumnavigate the lake. The north shore is fine, but there is a very dangerous section on the south shore that is impassable due to potential falls up to 100m where the trail briefly disappears in favor of an unmarked section where slippery vegetation grows flush against the mountain surface. Two foreigners have attempted – and two have died.

A private taxi from Caraz right to the lakeshore runs from S120 return with two hours wait time – each additional hour will cost around S10.

Cañón del Pato CANYON

If you continue north from Caraz along the Callejón de Huaylas, you will wind your way through the outstanding Cañón del Pato. It's here that the Cordillera Blanca and the Cordillera Negra come to within kissing distance for a battle of bedrock wills, separated in parts by only 15m and plummeting to vertigo-inducing depths of up to 1000m. The harrowing road snakes along a path hewn out of sheer rock, over a precipitous gorge and passing through 54 tunnels.

Gargantuan, crude walls tower above the road on all sides, and as the valley's hydroelectric plant comes into sight you realize that it's dramatic enough to house the secret lair of a James Bond arch-villain. The most dramatic stretch of the road is between Caraz and Huallanca, especially between tunnels 10 and 18, where the canyon is at its narrowest point. Sit so that you're looking out of the right-hand side of the bus (as you face the driver) for the best views along the way.

Punta Winchus NATURE RESERVE

A remote 4157m pass in the Cordillera Negra is the center of a huge stand of 5000 rare *Puya raimondii* plants. This is the biggest-known stand of these 10m-tall members of the pineapple family, which take 100 years to mature and in full bloom flaunt up to 20,000 flowers each! On a clear day you have an astounding 145km panorama from the Cordillera Blanca all the way to the Pacific Ocean. It's 45km west of Caraz and reached by tour vehicles.

Activities

For detailed hiking information you can visit one of the two main trekking outfits in Caraz.

Pony Expeditions OUTDOORS

(☎043-39-1642; www.ponyexpeditions.com; José Sucre 1266) English- and French-speaking regional expert Alberto Cafferata provides equipment rental (including bicycles), transportation, guides and *arrieros*, and organises various excursions including mountaineering expeditions, mountain treks, and vehicle and cycling trips through the Cañón del Pato. Books, maps, fuel and other items are for sale at the shop.

Apu Aventura TREKKING, CLIMBING

(☎043-39-1130; www.apuaventura.pe; Parque San Martín 103) English-speaking Luis is an experienced guide who can help arrange treks, horse riding, climbing and equipment rental. He also offers quad-bike tours in the Cordillera Negra. The office is inside Los Pinos Lodge.

Sleeping

Caraz has yet to see the tourist development of Huaraz and offers straightforward

Caraz

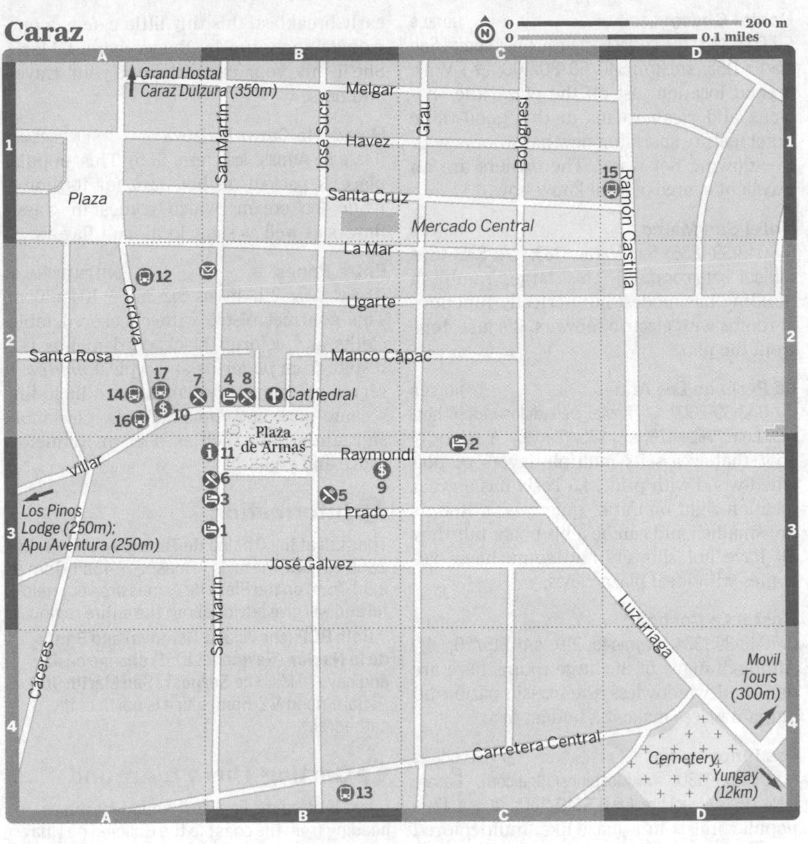

Caraz

Activities, Courses & Tours
Pony Expeditions ....(see 5)

Sleeping
1 Hostal Chavín B3
2 Hostal La Casona C3
3 Hotel San Marco B3
4 La Perla de Los Andes B2

Eating
5 Café de Rat B3
6 Cafetería El Turista B3
7 Entre Panes A2
8 Heladería Caraz Dulzura B2

Information
9 Banco de la Nación B3
10 BCP A2
11 Oficina de Turismo B3

Transport
12 Colectivos to Huallanca A2
13 Colectivos to Yungay & Huaraz B4
14 Cooperativa Ancash A2
15 Terminal Santa Cruz D1
16 Transportes Julio Cesar A2
17 Yungay Express A2

facilities and budget sleeping options. Prices remain quite stable throughout the year.

Grand Hostal Caraz Dulzura HOTEL $
(☎043-39-1523; www.hostalcarazdulzura.com; Sáenz Peña 212; s/d/tr incl breakfast S45/70/120; 📶) About 10 blocks north of the plaza along Cordova, this quiet lodge provides good bang for your buck. Rooms are bright and have electric hot showers and comfortable beds. A new wing in an adjoining garden was on the drawing board when we visited.

Hostal Chavín HOTEL $

(☎043-39-1171; chavinhostel@hotmail.com; San Martín 1135; s/d/tr/q S40/60/80/100; 📶) With a good location just off the plaza, the spacious and clean rooms in this good-value hotel feature sparkling new bathrooms with free-flowing hot water. The owners are an excellent source of local know-how.

Hotel San Marco HOTEL $

(☎043-39-1836; San Martín 1133; s/d S35/45, s without bathroom S15) This large, rambling building has modest but perfectly functional rooms with electric showers. It's just steps from the plaza.

La Perla de Los Andes HOTEL $

(☎043-39-2007; hostal_perladelosandes@hotmail.com; Villar 179; s/d S35/55; 📶) A friendly spot that wears its multiple layers of polished wood with pride, La Perla has a great location right on Caraz' quiet plaza. Rooms are smallish and can be a bit noisy, but they all have hot showers and some have balconies with ideal plaza views.

Hostal La Casona HOTEL $

(☎043-39-1334; Raymondi 319; s/d S15/20; @) Although many of the large rooms here are dark and windowless, the classic patio and bargain prices make it a budget fave.

Los Pinos Lodge LODGE $$

(☎043-39-1130; www.lospinoslodge.com; Pasaje 9 No 116; s/d incl breakfast S140/160; @📶) This popular inn is in a maze-like, multicolored mansion that is thoughtfully decorated inside and out. It offers outstanding rooms, although some seem a bit on the pricey side for Caraz, so take a look around. There are several great garden courtyards and the owner, Luis, organizes trekking and tours of the area.

Eating

Café de Rat CAFE $

(pizzas S17-32; ⏲8-11am & 6-10pm) Don't mind the name, the menu has been cleared of rodents. This atmospheric wood-beamed restaurant and cafe serves sandwiches, pizza and pasta. It also has a book exchange, darts, a bar and music. This is a top spot to hang out, especially on the upstairs balcony with fireplace and plaza views. Find it above Pony Expeditions (p392).

Cafetería El Turista BREAKFAST, PERUVIAN $

(San Martín 1127; breakfast S5-12; ⏲6:30am-noon & 5-8pm) A great place to grab an early breakfast, this tiny little cafe is a one-woman show run by the exuberant Maria. She'll talk your ear off about your travels and hers.

Heladería Caraz Dulzura ICE CREAM $

(Plaza de Armas; ice cream S1-5) This popular place is packed on hot days for its homemade ice cream, which comes in classic flavors as well as some local-fruit flavors.

Entre Panes INTERNATIONAL $$

(Daniel Villar 211; mains S12-38; ⏲10am-10pm) This gourmet bistro with checkered tablecloths and colorful blackboard menus is a respite from *pollerías* and typical *menús*. It serves up interesting sandwiches including sesame pork and *lomo saltado*, plus more substantial fare such as beef in Roquefort sauce and goulash.

Information

The staff at the **Oficina de Turismo** (☎043-48-3860 ext 143; Plaza de Armas; ⏲7:45am-1pm & 2:30-7pm) on the Plaza de Armas are very helpful and will give advice about the entire region.

Both **BCP** (cnr Villar & Cordova) and **Banco de la Nación** (Raymondi 1051) change cash and have ATMs. The **Serpost** (San Martín 909; ⏲8am-noon & 2-6pm) office is north of the cathedral.

Getting There & Around

Caraz is often the final destination for buses heading from the coast to the Callejón de Huaylas. Most coastal buses go via Huaraz.

BUS

Long Distance

Transportes Julio Cesar (☎94-492-8824; cnr Cordova y Villar) has a comfortable Lima bus at 8:30pm and a Trujillo service at 7:45pm. **Cooperativa Ancash** (☎043-39-1126; Cordova 915) has good-value Lima buses at 11am, 7pm and 8pm.

Móvil Tours (☎043-39-1184; Pasaje Santa Teresita 334) has the most comfortable Lima *bus-cama* (bed bus) at 9pm as well as good economic services at 7:30am, 9am, 1pm and 8:30pm. It also has service to Chimbote via Casma at 8:10pm and 9:30pm.

Yungay Express (☎043-39-1492; Cordova 830) has one bus a day to Chimbote via the Cañón del Pato leaving at 9am and three via Casma at 7am, noon and 8pm.

Caraz Area

Colectivos to Yungay, Carhuaz and Huaraz leave from the bus station on Carretera Central.

TAXI

Colectivo taxis for Cashapampa (S8, 1½ hours) for the northern end of the Santa Cruz trek leave when full from the **Terminal Santa Cruz** (Jiron Ramón Castilla) near the market. *Colectivos* to Pueblo Parón (S8, one hour), which is about 9km from the famous Laguna Parón, leave from the same terminal. It's best to get there early in the morning when departures are more frequent.

Colectivos to Huallanca (S7, one hour), for the Cañón del Pato, leave from the small **terminal** (Cordova 818) on Jirón Cordova when full.

Mototaxis (S1.50) trundle around town, but Caraz is easily managed on foot.

SOUTH OF HUARAZ

Covering the southern extent of the Cordillera Blanca and the majestic Cordillera Huayhuash, this part of the Andes refuses to be outdone in the 'breathtaking mountain scenery' stakes. Several peaks here pass the 6000m mark, huddling to form a near-continuous, saw-toothed ridge of precipitous summits. **Yerupajá** (6617m), Peru's second-highest mountain, is the icing on the Cordillera cake and is followed in height by its second lieutenant **Siulá Grande** (6344m), where climber Joe Simpson fell down into a crevice and lived to tell the tale in the book and movie *Touching the Void*. The rugged and rewarding 10-day Cordillera Huayhuash Circuit (p385), accessed through the town of Llamac, is the glittering star attraction.

The Puente Bedoya bridge, about 18km south of Huaraz, marks the beginning of a 2km dirt road to the community of **Olleros**, the starting point for the three-day trek across the Cordillera Blanca to Chavín de Huántar. Respons Sustainable Tourism Center (p369) in Huaraz arranges a colorful day trip (S90 for two people, less per person for larger groups) to the village of **Huaripampa**, just a few minutes south of Huaraz, to see two local women dye and weave wool with plants from their own gardens and on their own hand looms.

Recuay (population 2900), a town 25km from Huaraz, is one of the few municipalities to have survived the 1970 earthquake largely unscathed. **Catac** (population 2300), 10km south of Recuay, is an even smaller hamlet and the starting point for trips to see the remarkable *Puya raimondii* plant.

Further south, about 70km from Huaraz on the road to Lima and in the vicinity of the village of Pampas Chico, **Hatun Machay** (admission S5) is a rock-climber's paradise. There are dozens of climbing routes throughout this 'rock forest' nestled high in the Cordillera Negra. There is a large rustic refuge (dorm beds S30) with kitchen facilities that is popular with those learning to climb and experienced climbers planning hard-core ascents. If that weren't enough, two treks around the area take you past archaeological remains of rock carvings and a view of the Pacific Ocean (on a clear day), and make for great half-day acclimatization hikes. A taxi here from Catac will cost around S50.

Chiquián

☎043 / POP 3600 / ELEV 3400M

A subdued hill town, Chiquián was traditionally the base of operations for folk trekking the Cordillera Huayhuash Circuit. Now, however, it can be bypassed using the new (unpaved) road that extends to the trailheads at Pocpa and Llamac, though if you plan on spending the night in the area, you will be infinitesimally more comfortable here. Great views of the Huayhuash come into view as you drive into town.

The annual festival in late August is held in honor of **Santa Rosa de Lima** and celebrated with dances, parades, music and bullfights.

Sleeping & Eating

★Hotel Los Nogales GUESTHOUSE $
(☎043-44-7121; www.hotelnogaleschiquian.com; Comercio 1301; s/d from S35/60; wi-fi) Colorful, clean and attractive, this is a great place a couple of blocks from the central plaza. A variety of comfortable rooms surround an impossibly charming colonial-style courtyard garden. Meals are available on request. The owners and employees are very friendly and the hot water, cable TV, wi-fi and room-service coffee seals the deal.

Gran Hotel Huayhuash HOTEL $
(☎043-44-7049; cnr 28 de Julio & Amadeo; s/d S30/60, s without bathroom S25, all incl breakfast; @ wi-fi) What it lacks in atmosphere, this contemporary choice in a multistory building makes up for with comfort. The spacious rooms have hot water and flat-screen TVs as standard, although there is no cable. Some rooms also afford fine mountain vistas.

Miky PERUVIAN $
(2 de Mayo s/n, 2nd fl; menús S5-12, mains S15; 7am-9pm, closed Sun) If you wonder why

most restaurants in Chiquián are empty, it's because pretty much the entire town dines at this festive, well-run restaurant that serves a top-quality *menú*. Fantastic soups are served as a first course, after which you can take your pick from a list of tasty mains.

Getting There & Away

If you're interested in heading straight to Chiquián and the Cordillera Huayhuash, you'll find direct buses from Lima. However, as you'll probably need a few days to acclimatize, note that Huaraz offers a wider selection of distractions. **Turismo Cavassa** (☎043-44-7036; Bolognesi 421) has buses direct to Lima (S30, eight hours) at 8am and 8pm as well as services to La Uníon, from where there are connections to Huánuco.

If you're starting the Huayhuash Circuit, catch the 8am **Turismo Nazario** (☎043-77-0311; Comercio 1050) bus to Pocpa via Llamac (S15, 2½ hours). The same company runs a bus to Huaraz at 2pm (S8, two hours) that connects with the bus arriving from Pocpa and Llamac. **Transportes El Rapido** (☎043-44-7096; Figueredo 209) goes to Huaraz at 5am and 2pm (S10).

The ride between Huaraz and Chiquián, whether the fogged-in morning run from Huaraz (sit on the left) or the afternoon ride back from Chiquián (sit on the right), affords some of the most beautiful scenery you will see in Peru.

Llamac

☎043 / ELEV 3300M

The ramshackle brick-and-mud village of Llamac was once the launching point for the Huayhuash Circuit but now that the public bus continues on to the trailhead at Pocpa, closer to the Matacancha rest site, many hikers only visit Llamac to pick up transportation back to Chiquián upon exiting the circuit.

There are few services here, though there's a small Plaza de Armas with a diminutive church draped in bougainvillea. The trail leading to Laguna Yahuacocha sits behind the municipal building on the same plaza.

There is a S20 entry fee for foreigners to enter Huayhuash, the first in the fee circuit. You will be expected to pay even if just passing through on the bus – hold on to your receipt to avoid paying again when you finish your trek.

Sleeping & Eating

If you miss the bus or are too tired to continue on to Chiquián or Huaraz after your trek there are a couple of basic accommodations options in town.

Hotel Nazario GUESTHOUSE $
(☎990-300-731; Grau s/n; r per person with/without bathroom S20/15) In an unmissable large concrete building, Hotel Nazario has neat rooms with good natural light and mountain views. There is a communal TV room and it also serves meals (S5 to S10). The helpful owners can organize *arrieros* and pack animals for treks.

Casa Fidel Hospedaje GUESTHOUSE $
(☎043-77-0714, 968-282-571; San Pedro s/n; s/d without bathroom S15/30, r S35) Casa Fidel Hospedaje has very basic rooms with low ceilings, some with private bathrooms and cable TV. Travelers congregate in the small dining room over meals (S7 to S20) and pretend to be entertained by the large flat-screen TV, which has recently been hooked up to cable, relegating the expansive DVD collection to gather dust on the shelf.

Getting There & Away

Turismo Nazario (☎990-300-731; Grau s/n) departs Chiquián for Llamac and Pocpa (S15, 2½ hours) at 8am daily. Upon arrival in Pocpa, the bus turns right around and passes back through Llamac at 11:15am, before continuing on to Chiquián.

CALLEJÓN DE CONCHUCOS

The Conchucos Valley (locally called the Callejón de Conchucos) runs parallel to the Callejón de Huaylas on the eastern side of the Cordillera. Sprinkled liberally with remote and rarely visited gems, this captivating dale is steeped in history and blessed with isolated, postcard-perfect Andean villages so tranquil that they'd fall into comas if they were any sleepier. Interlaced with excellent yet rarely visited hiking trails, this untapped region begs for exploration. Tourist infrastructure is still in its infancy, with a handful of welcoming but modest hotels and erratic transportation along rough, unpaved roads that can be impassable in the wet season, and are plagued by breakdowns and accidents. If you do make the effort to get here, the highland hospitality of Quechua-speaking *campesinos* and awe-inspiring scenery will more than make up for the butt-smacking, time-consuming bumps in the road.

Chavín de Huántar, at the south end of the valley, is the most accessible area of the lot and lays claim to some of the most important and mysterious pre-Inca ruins on the continent. Access to the northern part of the valley is via the new Tunel Olímpica, said to be the highest road tunnel on the continent and gateway to the striking mountain town of Chacas and the remote outpost of Pomabamba. Direct transportation between the two regions is almost nonexistent; if you don't want to double back through Huaraz you'll either need a lot of patience or serious stamina and solid hiking boots.

Chavín de Huántar

043 / POP 9200 / ELEV 3250M

The unhurried town of Chavín abuts the northern end of the ruins and is too often whizzed through by visitors on popular day trips from Huaraz. A shame really, as this attractive Andean township has excellent tourist infrastructure, a slew of nature-centered activities and some of the best-value accommodations in the Cordilleras. If you decide to overnight here, you can visit the impressive archaeological site in the early morning and have it all to yourself.

The main drag of Chavín town is Calle 17 de Enero Sur, which leaves the peaceful Plaza de Armas southbound, passing rows of restaurants, internet cafes and the entrance to the archaeological site. The **Banco de la Nación** (Plaza de Armas; 7am-5:30pm Mon-Fri, 9am-1pm Sat) has a Visa/Plus ATM. A small but helpful **tourist information office** (043-45-4235 ext 106; Bolivar s/n; 8am-12:30pm & 2:30-5:30pm Mon-Fri) operates out of the Municipalidad building just off the plaza.

Sights

Chavín de Huántar ARCHAEOLOGICAL SITE

(admission S10; 9am-4pm Tue-Sun) The quintessential site of the Mid-Late Formative Period (c 1200–500 BC), Chavín de Huántar is the most intriguing of the many relatively independent, competitive ceremonial centers constructed throughout the central Andes. It is a phenomenal achievement of ancient construction, with large temple-like structures aboveground and labyrinthine (now electronically lit) underground passageways. Although looters and a major landslide have affected the site, it is still intact enough to provide a full-bodied glimpse into one of Peru's oldest complex societies.

Chavín is a series of older and newer temple arrangements built between 1200 BC and 500 BC, but most structures visible today came from a big building effort between 900 and 700 BC. In the middle is a massive central square, slightly sunken below ground level, which like the overall site has an intricate, extensive and well-engineered system of channels for drainage. From the square, a broad staircase leads up to the portal in front of the largest and most important building, called the Castillo, which has withstood some mighty earthquakes over the years. Built on three different levels of stone-and-mortar masonry (sometimes incorporating cut stone blocks), the walls here were at one time embellished with tenon heads (blocks carved to resemble human heads with animal or perhaps hallucinogen-induced characteristics backed by stone spikes for insertion into a wall). Only one of these remains in its original place, although the others may be seen in the local museum related to the site.

A series of tunnels underneath the Castillo are an exceptional feat of engineering, comprising a maze of complex corridors, ducts and chambers. In the heart of this complex is an exquisitely carved, 4.5m-tall monolith of white granite known as the Lanzón de Chavín. In typical terrifying Chavín fashion, the low-relief carvings on the Lanzón represent a person with snakes radiating from his head and a ferocious set of fangs, most likely feline. The Lanzón, almost certainly an object of worship given its prominent, central placement in this ceremonial center, is sometimes referred to as the Smiling God – but its aura feels anything but friendly.

Several beguiling construction quirks, such as the strange positioning of water channels and the use of highly polished mineral mirrors to reflect light, led Stanford archaeologists to believe that the complex was used as an instrument of shock and awe. To instill fear in nonbelievers, priests manipulated sights and sounds. They blew on echoing Strombus trumpets, amplified the sounds of water running through specially designed channels and reflected sunlight through ventilation shafts. The disoriented cult novitiates were probably given hallucinogens such as San Pedro cactus shortly before entering the darkened maze. These tactics endowed the priests with awe-inspiring power.

To get the most from your visit, it's worth hiring a local guide to show you around (S40) or go on a guided day trip (including transportation) from Huaraz; this latter option is by far the most budget-friendly way to see these ruins, although it means you'll be wandering with the crowds.

Museo Nacional de Chavín MUSEUM
(☎043-45-4011; 17 de Enero s/n; ⏰9am-5pm Tue-Sun) FREE This outstanding museum funded jointly by the Peruvian and Japanese governments, houses most of the intricate and horrifyingly carved tenon heads from Chavín de Huántar, as well as the magnificent Tello Obelisk, another stone object of worship with low relief carvings of a caiman and other fierce animals. The obelisk had been housed in a Lima museum since the 1945 earthquake that destroyed much of the original museum, and was only returned to Chavín in 2009.

The museum is located around 2km from the ruins on the other side of town.

Activities

Horseback riding on Peruvian pacing horses can be arranged through the Cafetería Renato for S40 per hour (including a guide).

From Chavín you can **hike** for a few hours into a lofty valley, in the direction of Olleros, to a high pass with stirring views of Huantsán (6395m) – the highest mountain in the southern Cordillera Blanca.

Don Donato HIKING
(☎043-45-4136; Tello Sur 275) Don Donato of the Asociación de Servicios de Alta Montaña offers a four-day trek that circles the back side of the Cordillera Blanca, passes by several alpine lakes and exits through the Carhuascancha valley. You'll need to bring your own food, tent and sleeping bags.

Quercos Thermal Baths BATHHOUSE
(admission S4) The sulfur Quercos thermal baths, a 30-minute walk south of town, house numerous windowless bath cubicles which fail to take advantage of their riverside setting. Still, the waters work wonders on post-hike muscles. Keep your eyes peeled for a small, signed path that leads down to the river. A taxi from town costs S10.

Sleeping & Eating

Chavín has a surprisingly good selection of accommodations. Most of the town's eateries can be found along Calle 17 de Enero Sur and around the plaza. Restaurants have a reputation for closing soon after sunset, so dig in early.

Hostal Inca GUESTHOUSE $
(☎043-45-4021; Plaza de Armas; s/d S35/70, bungalow S120) The reputation of this secure, popular place is as solid as its colonial foundations and boasts very respectable rooms (though some of the showers are a little tight) with views over the tiled roofs of town. There's a small garden tended by the somewhat cranky couple that runs it.

Finca Renato CAMPGROUND $
(☎943-974-062; per tent S10) Perched on a hillside overlooking town, this 6-hectare farm has icy showers but offers fantastic views over rooftops to the ruins. You can rent a tent for an additional S5. Bungalows were on the drawing board at the time of research. Ask for details at Cafetería Renato.

Hostal Chavín Turístico GUESTHOUSE $$
(☎043-45-4051; chavinturistico1@gmail.com; Maytacapac 120; r S90) This new, family-run option is the best place to stay, offering well-appointed rooms with cute bedspreads, large bathrooms and – perhaps most refreshingly – no chipped paint or rusty pipes. It's quiet, well-maintained and clean as a whistle. If it's not busy you may be able to negotiate a cheap single room.

La Casona GUESTHOUSE $$
(☎043-45-4116; www.lacasonachavin.com.pe; Plaza de Armas 130; s/d S70/140) Nestled in an imposing house with a beautiful courtyard right on the plaza, this hotel could be great but many of the rooms are dark with low ceilings and flickering fluorescent lights. The rooms at the front with plaza views are better.

Cafetería Renato BREAKFAST, PERUVIAN $
(☎943-974-062; Plaza de Armas; breakfast S6-14; ⏰from 7am) On the casual Plaza de Armas, this cozy place serves yummy local and international breakfasts alongside homemade yogurt, cheese and *manjar blanco* (homemade caramel spread). There's a lovely garden you can laze in while waiting for your bus and the owners organize horse-riding trips from here.

Chavín Turístico PERUVIAN $
(☎043-45-4051; Calle 17 de Enero Sur 439; mains S14-25; ⏰7am-8pm) A solid option, especially for *trucha al ajo* (garlic trout) and trout *sudado* (in sauce), this place has rickety tables

around a tiny courtyard and a chalkboard of traditional dishes. The food is tasty and local archaeologists say it's the most reliable choice in town.

★ **Buongiorno** PERUVIAN $$
(Calle 17 de Enero Sur s/n; mains S18-30; ⏲7am-7pm Tue-Sun) Churning out sophisticated dishes that outpunch its location's weight class, Buongiorno is a pleasant surprise in a cordial garden setting. The *lomo a la pimienta,* a Peruvian fave of grilled steak in wine, cream and cracked-pepper sauce (S27), is three-star Lima quality and the trout ceviche is also a popular choice.

The cooks here often dart out to the extensive gardens and grab some fresh organic herbs – a nice touch. It's 50m across the bridge from the entrance to the ruins. Atmosphere takes a dive at dinner – go for lunch.

ℹ Getting There & Away

The paved road across the Cordillera Blanca to Chavín passes the Laguna Querococha at 3980m from where there are views of the peaks of Pucaraju (5322m) and Yanamarey (5237m). The road continues through the Kahuish Tunnel (4516m above sea level), which cuts through the Kahuish Pass. As you exit the tunnel and descend toward Chavín, look out for the massive statue of Christ blessing your journey. It was built by Italian missionaries.

In Chavín, all transportation is supposed to leave from the shiny new bus station south of the plaza but in reality only Lima-bound services tend to call in here. All local buses pick-up and drop off where the highway bends at the plaza. **Olguita Tours** (☎941-870-525; Gran Terminal Terrestre) has regular departures to Huaraz (S12, three hours) as well as Huari (S6, two hours) to the north. *Combis/colectivos* head to Huaraz (S20/S25, 2½ hours) from the oddly

CHAVÍN PERIOD

Named after the site at Chavín de Huántar (p397), this is considered one of the oldest major cultural periods in Peru, strutting its stuff on the pre-Inca stage from 1200 BC to 500 BC. The Chavín and its contemporaries wielded their influence with great success, particularly between the formative years of 800 BC to 500 BC when they excelled in the agricultural production of potatoes and other highland crops, animal husbandry, ceramic and metal production, and engineering of buildings and canals. Chavín archaeologists have formerly referred to this time of political ascendance as the Chavín Horizon, though Early Horizon or Late Formative is also used.

The principal Chavín deity was feline (jaguar or puma), although lesser condor, eagle and snake deities were also worshipped. Representations of these deities are highly stylized and cover many Chavín-period sites and many extraordinary objects, such the Tello Obelisk in the Museo Nacional de Chavín; the Lanzón, often referred to as the Smiling God, which stands in mystical glory in the tunnels underneath the Chavín site; and the Raimondi Stela at the Museo Nacional de Antropología, Arqueología e Historia del Perú in Lima. The Raimondi Stela (which is currently considered too fragile to move to Chavín) has carvings of a human figure, sometimes called the Staff God, with a jaguar face and large staffs in each hand – an image that has shown up at archaeological sites along the northern and southern coasts of Peru and which suggests the long reach of Chavín interactions. The images on all of these massive stone pillars are believed to indicate a belief in a tripartite universe consisting of the heavens, earth and a netherworld, or as an alternative theory goes, a cosmos consisting of air, earth and water, though these remain elaborate guesses – archaeologists at the site have seen no good evidence to support any of these theories.

As a major ceremonial center, the most powerful players in Chavín were its priests who impressed the upper ranks of society with complex rituals that were occasionally terrifying. One theory says priests relied on sophisticated observation and understanding of seasonal changes, rain and drought cycles, and the movement of the sun, moon and stars to create calendars that helped the Chavín reign as agriculturalists, though there is as yet no evidence that calendars were created. Others believe that Chavín leaders were getting to the point of being free of system-serving, and heading for authority based on belief rather than for serving an agricultural purpose. Some archaeologists have argued that women also served as priests and played a powerful role during the Chavín period. Chavín, it seems, remains a rather polarizing mystery.

named Plaza Chupa, a block north of the quaint Plaza de Armas.

Both **Flor Movil** (☎958-809-378; Gran Terminal Terrestre) and **Turismo Rosario** (☎944-988-425; Gran Terminal Terrestre) have 7:30pm departures to Lima (S40, 10 hours) while **Turismo Andino** (☎ in Lima 01-427-3111; Gran Terminal Terrestre) has a less convenient service leaving at 3am.

To continue north along the east side of the Cordillera Blanca, most of the buses originating in Huaraz continue to Huari (S6, two hours). *Colectivos* leave frequently from near the Plaza de Armas to San Marcos (S2, 20 minutes) from where you can catch *colectivos* to Huari (S6, 45 minutes). If you plan on continuing further north, **Transportes Solitario** (☎ in Lima 01 426-6934; Gran Terminal Terrestre) runs a somewhat unreliable service to Pomabamba via Huari four times a week, passing Chavín on Wednesday, Thursday, Friday and Sunday at around 3pm, although their safety record is less than stellar. Call to check schedules before making plans. Other than these buses, there is no other public transportation beyond Huari.

Hikers can walk to Chavín from Olleros in about three days; it's an uncrowded trek.

North of Chavín

The road north of Chavín goes through the villages of San Marcos (after 8km), Huari (40km, two hours), San Luis (100km, five hours), Pomabamba and eventually Sihuas. The further north you go, the more inconsistent transportation becomes, and it may stop altogether during the wet season. Note that buses on this route are usually not in the best condition and breakdowns are common. This road also has more than its share of accidents.

From Sihuas, it is theoretically possible to continue to Huallanca (at the end of Cañón del Pato) via Tres Cruces and thus return to the Callejón de Huaylas, although transportation is infrequent at best. This round-trip is scenic, remote and rarely made by travelers.

There are two roads that offer picturesque crossings back to El Callejón de Huaylas. The road from Chacas to Carhuaz, via the new Tunel Olímpica, is spectacular. A road from Yanama to Yungay takes passengers over yet another breathtaking pass (4767m) and into the valley made famous by the Lagunas Llanganuco, with top views of the towering Huascarán, Chopicalqui and Huandoy peaks.

Huari

☎043 / POP 10,300 / ELEV 3150M

A small Quechua-speaking town barely clinging to the mountainside, Huari has nearly 360-degree mountain panoramas from its steep streets. Market day here is Sunday, when *campesinos* from surrounding towns descend on Huari to hawk fruits and vegetables. The annual town **fiesta**, Señora del Rosario, is held in early October and has a strange tradition of cat consumption (residents from Huari are jokingly referred to in Quechua as *Mishikanka,* which literally means 'Deep-Fried Cats' but more figuratively 'Cat Eaters'). The town has a small and modern Plaza de Armas and a larger Plaza Vigil (known as El Parque) one block away, where you'll find the bus-company offices (buses leave from a terminal a few blocks away). There is a **Banco de la Nación** near the market with a Visa/Plus ATM.

For sweeping panoramas of the valley, keep walking uphill on Jiron Simón Bolivar until you come to a *mirador* (lookout). A good day hike is to **Laguna Purhuay**, a beautiful mountain lake about 5km away. It's also possible to hire a taxi to take you here for S60 round-trip.

LAND OF THE LOST

When the Antamina Mining Company needed a paved road to move mining equipment from Yanacancha to the Conococha crossroads (some 200km east of Huaraz), they simply built it themselves. During the excavation in 2009, they made a startling discovery: more than 100 footprints and fossilized remains of at least 12 species of prehistoric animals that paleontologists have dated to the Early Cretaceous Period (about 120 million years ago). Complete skeletons of large marine reptiles known as sauropterygians were found in addition to skeletal remains of other extinct species of crocodiles, flying reptiles called pterosaurs, fish-like reptiles called ichthyosaurs and…dinosaur footprints!

The site, known as **Huellas de los Dinosaurios**, is between Kms 77 and 83 on the highway between San Marcos and Huallanca. In order to visit you'll need to hire a private car in Huallanca.

An excellent two- or three-day trek continues past the lake to emerge at the village of Chacas. Another three- to four-day hike follows the old Inca highway to Huánuco.

Sleeping & Eating

There are several cheap places to stay in town, but the pick of the bunch is **Hostal Huagancu** (943-523-186; Sucre 335; s/d S30/40) which offers bright, comfortable rooms with shiny tiled floors, wooden furniture and cable TV. Nearby, **Hostal Paraíso** (975-440-261; Simón Bolívar 263; s/d S20/30, without bathroom S10/20) has decent rooms with fresh paint jobs and a courtyard with some greenery. No hotels in town have internet connections, but there are several internet cafes around town.

Getting There & Away

For fast connections to Chavín and Huaraz, get a *colectivo* to San Marcos from behind the market (S6, 45 minutes). **Olguita Tours** (954-470-914; Plaza Vigil) has regular buses to Huaraz (S15, 4½ hours). There are a number of companies offering direct service to Lima (S40, 10 hours) from offices around Plaza Vigil.

For Pomabamba (S25, 6½ hours), **El Solitario** (in Lima 01 426-6934; Av Magisterial 285) passes by on the main road around 5pm on Wednesday, Thursday, Friday and Sunday. Schedules are irregular so call in advance to be sure. You'll have more options if you go to Huaraz first, but this is well out of the way and in the wrong direction.

If you want to forge ahead on your own timeframe to San Luis, where you can catch onward travel to Chacas and Pomabamba, a taxi is anywhere between S250 and S300 depending on your negotiation skills. The road is rough and beautiful.

Chacas

This ornate mountain town sits atop a hillcrest at 3360m, surrounded by fertile hills and with guest appearances by the occasional snowcapped Cordillera peak. The charismatic main plaza is dominated by a brilliant church built by a religious nonprofit Italian aid organization, Don Bosco, based in Marcará and established by the pioneering Father Ugo de Censi, a priest of the Salesian order.

White-walled houses around the plaza look idyllic against the mountain backdrop and many have intricate wooden balconies and brightly colored doors and window shutters, just screaming to have their picture taken. Look out for the impossibly petite, smiling Andean ladies who sit meditatively spinning wool on every second corner. This is an excellent place to while away a few days. The town has few fixed-line phones, but there's an internet cafe on Jirón Lima half a block downhill from the plaza. There is a small branch of **Banco de la Nación**, but the closest ATM is in San Luis.

You can do great two- to three-day treks from here to Huari or Yanama, from where energetic hikers can continue on to do the Santa Cruz trek (p379).

Sleeping & Eating

Idyllic as it is, the problem with lingering here is food: although if you are fortunate enough to swing by on Sunday Italian staff at the religious mission knock out mean pizzas in a small restaurant by the church. Otherwise check out **Chacas Gourmet** (Cochachi s/n; 11am-9pm) a couple of blocks downhill from the plaza, which offers a good variety of very reasonably priced local dishes. Pretty much your only choice for breakfast is **Zazón Andino** (Lima s/n; menús S5; 7am-9pm) on the plaza, which also manages to churn out a few decent *menú* choices.

Hostal Asunción GUESTHOUSE $
(956-490-064; Bolognesi 370; s/d S30/60, without bathroom S15/30) This place on the Plaza de Armas has neat and appealing rooms, especially the pair at the front which boast windows onto the plaza with church views.

Hospedaje Alameda GUESTHOUSE $
(975-686-420; Lima 305; s/d S30/40, without bathroom S15/20) Hospedaje Alameda offers a friendly welcome and modest rooms with warm beds and hot water, although those with shared bathrooms are barely big enough to put down your luggage.

Hostal Pilar HOTEL $$
(in Monterrey 043-42-3813; Ancash 110; s/d S50/100, without bathroom S30/60) The most atmospheric place to stay in town is rambling Hostal Pilar, which feels like a well-loved country estate complete with branding irons and other cowboy garb hanging from the walls. Rooms surround a large courtyard and vibrant garden, and have high ceilings, wooden floors and individual tanks for piping-hot water.

WORTH A TRIP

YANAMA

Yanama is a tiny, mountain-enveloped *pueblo* (village), where the most exciting thing to happen in the past decade is a connection to the electricity grid in 2005. The town is about a 1½-hour walk (or a 20-minute drive) from the end of the popular Santa Cruz trek and makes a good stopover point for trekkers and mountain-bikers to refuel and recharge. The town **Festival of Santa Rosa** is held here in August.

Combis link Yungay with Yanama, passing the famed Lagunas Llanganuco and the village of Vaqueria, the starting point for the Santa Cruz trekking circuit. Facilities are rudimentary in Yanama and showers can be as frosty as the mountain air.

Andes Lodge Peru (043-76-5579; www.andeslodgeperu.com; Jirón Gran Chavín s/n; s/d S70/150, s/tw without bathroom S60/100, all incl breakfast; @) is just a couple of blocks from the Plaza de Armas and is one of the best mountain lodges in the Callejón de Huaylas. Coming back to the home-cooked meals, blazing hot showers, snug beds with down comforters, and ever-helpful Peruvian owners after a day in the mountains is a revelation. All the area excursions can be arranged, including to Laguna 69 and visits to local farmers and weavers. All rooms come with breakfast – add S30 per person per day for full board.

A couple of *hospedajes* (small, family-owned inns) supply austere rooms for around S15 per person, but the best cheapie in town is **Hostal El Pino** (971-500-759; s/d without bathroom S15/25), behind the church. Exceptionally friendly, it's basic but has comfortable beds and electric showers, plus misty views of the mountains. The same owners run the best restaurant in town, **Restaurant El Pino II** (Plaza de Armas; menús S12), on the plaza, where you'll need to stop in if you want to sleep at the guesthouse.

Colectivos from Yungay to Yanama leave from one block east of the police station at 7am and 1pm, although the latter service is less punctual. Return services leave Yanama from the plaza around 3am and between noon and 1pm (S15, 4½ hours). The ride – obviously – is stunning.

Getting There & Away

Transportes Renzo (95-957-1581; Lima 37) and **Transportes El Veloz** (043-78-2836; Buenos Aires s/n) both go to Huaraz (S15 to S20, 3½ hours), the former at 1pm, the latter at 5am and 2pm, via the Tunel Punta Olímpica and Carhuaz.

Both companies also have services to Pomabamba (S20, four hours), which originate in Huaraz and pass through around 10am. There is a further Pomabamba service at around 10pm, but it's not recommended to travel on this road at night due to robberies and accidents.

Combis for San Luis (S5, one hour) depart from Bolognesi at Buenos Aires, one block east of the plaza. There is no transportation from this side of the valley to Yanama although any Pomabamba-bound bus can drop you at the turnoff, from where it's a 22km trek up to the town. A taxi from San Luis will set you back at least S200.

Turismo Andino (043-78-2994; Buenos Aires s/n), **Transporte Rosario** (Buenos Aires s/n) and **Chavín Express** (Buenos Aires s/n) all have Lima-bound buses passing through around 5pm (S45, 14 hours), although these services also travel through Huaraz so you're better off picking up a more comfortable bus there.

Pomabamba

043 / POP 16,300 / ELEV 2950M

Known as the City of Cedars (check out the specimen on the plaza), Pomabamba is a great place to spend some time between trekking trips. Soak in a lung-full of the crisp mountain troposphere and the small-town ambience. Several cross-Cordillera treks begin and end at this township and you'd be forgiven for failing to notice that this is supposed to be the 'largest' settlement north of Huari.

There are several sets of **hot springs** (admission S1) lying in wait for weary hikers on the outskirts of town, although like many thermal baths in the region, atmosphere is distinctly lacking. Many locals come here with soap and shampoo to bathe, as hot showers aren't ubiquitous in town.

Sleeping & Eating

Pomabamba has a better range of accommodations compared to other Cordillera Blanca mountain towns. There are a number of *pollerías* (roast-chicken restaurants) and *chífas* (Chinese restaurants) in town but we can't really recommend any of them and you'll probably end up snacking on bread rolls with avocado from street vendors like we did.

Hotel Mirador HOTEL **$**
(043-45-1067; cnr Moquequa & Centenario; s/d S40/60, s without bathroom S30) Easily the most comfortable choice in town, the excellent-value Hotel Mirador is located up the steep set of steps from the plaza. It offers bright and spacious rooms with fantastic views and pine furniture. Try to snag one with a private balcony.

Hospedaje Los Begonias GUESTHOUSE **$**
(043-45-1057; lasbegonias_20@yahoo.es; Huamachuco 274; s/d/tw S30/50/60) This good budget spot is in a charming colonial house with a lush entryway and a large hardwood balcony. Rooms follow suit with great hardwood floors and private bathrooms with hot showers. A less atmospheric annex has opened a few doors down but the rooms there are noisy.

Alojamiento Estrada GUESTHOUSE **$**
(043-50-4615; Huaraz 209; r S20) The cheapest place to crash in Pomabamba is the genial Alojamiento Estrada, behind the Plaza de Armas church. It has a small courtyard and a hands-on owner who'll dote on you with grandmotherly curiosity, a welcome turn of events from some of the gruff receptions travelers receive outside Huaraz. Hot water is available with an hour's notice.

Hostal Leo HOTEL **$**
(043-45-1307; Peru s/n; s/d S35/40, without bathroom S20/30) A step up the budget scale but down the hospitality hierarchy is Hostal Leo, on the plaza itself, with good-value modern rooms spread over three floors.

Davis David PERUVIAN **$**
(Huaraz 269; menús S5; 6am-9pm) Davis David feels like a typical spit-on-the-floor saloon bar except for Peppa Pig blasting out of the flat-screen at earsplitting volume. It serves a respectable daytime *menú* and has many local followers.

Information

There is a Visa/Plus ATM at **Banco de la Nación** (Huamachuco, cuadra 5) and internet is available around town. It's sometimes possible to arrange trekking guides from here – ask at your hotel.

Getting There & Away

Combis go to Sihuas and Piscobamba daily from the town center. Buses to Huaraz and Lima leave from the Plaza de Armas or just off it on Jirón Huaraz. Several companies leave for Lima (S50, 18 hours) at 11am and can drop you in Huaraz (S30, eight hours).

Transportes Renzo (043-45-1088; Huaraz 430) heads to Huaraz (S30, eight hours) via Chacas (S20, four hours) at 8:30am and 7pm daily. Likewise, **Transportes El Veloz** (94-303-6951; Peru s/n) does the same route at 8:30am and 6:45pm.

El Solitario (945-951-763; Huaraz s/n) has a direct service to Chavín de Huantar (S30, 10 hours) via Huari on Monday, Friday and Sunday at 10am. While it's a long and testing ride, it's faster than passing through Huaraz.

Northern Highlands

Includes ➡

Best Places to Eat

- La Patarashca (p436)
- La Olla de Barro (p431)
- La Casa de Seizo (p430)
- El Tejado (p419)
- El Batan del Tayta (p420)

Best Places to Stay

- Posada del Purhuay (p410)
- Gocta Andes Lodge (p424)
- Kentitambo (p428)
- Chirapa Manta (p434)
- Pumarinri Amazon Lodge (p435)

Why Go?

Vast tracts of unexplored jungle and mist-shrouded mountain ranges guard the secrets of the northern highlands like a suspicious custodian. Here, Andean peaks and a blanket of luxuriant forests stretch from the coast all the way to the deepest Amazonian jungles. Interspersed with the relics of Inca kings and the jungle-encrusted ruins of cloud-forest-dwelling warriors, connections to these outposts are just emerging from their infancy.

Cajamarca's cobbled streets testify to the beginning of the end of the once-powerful Inca empire, and remnants of the work of these famed Andean masons still remain. The hazy forests of Chachapoyas have only recently revealed their archaeological bounty: the staggering stone fortress of Kuélap, which clings for dear life to a craggy limestone peak. At the jungle gateway of Tarapoto, the Amazon waits patiently on the periphery, as it has for centuries, endowed with a cornucopia of wildlife and exquisite good looks.

When to Go

Cajamarca

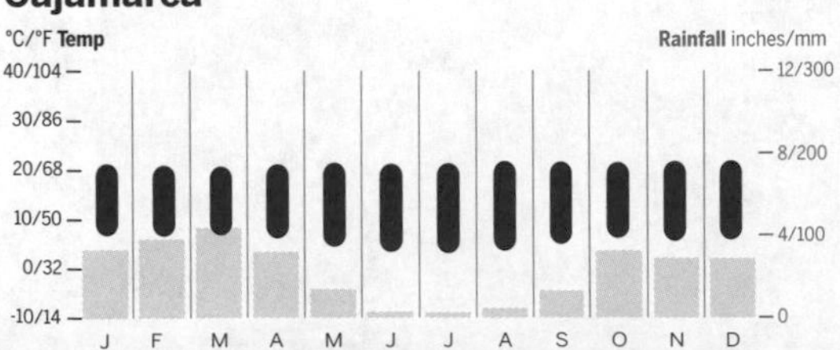

Jan–Apr Rain-soaked but vibrantly lush and full of life, with waterfalls in full, gushing glory.

Feb & Mar Let the rowdy mayhem commence: Carnaval is on in Cajamarca.

Jun–Oct The rains – and the landslides – are a thing of the past. Enjoy the sunshine.

Cajamarca

📞076 / POP 246,500 / ELEV 2750M

The most important town in the northern highlands, Cajamarca is a dainty but strong-willed colonial metropolis, cradled in a languid valley and stonewalled by brawny mountains in every direction. Descending into the vale by road, Cajamarca's mushroom field of red-tile-roofed abodes surely confesses a secret desire to cling to its village roots. Fertile farmland carpets the entire valley and Cajamarca's streets belong as much to the wide-brimmed-hat-wielding *campesinos* (peasants) bundled in brightly colored scarves, as the young city slickers who frequent the boutique restaurants and bars.

In the colonial center, majestic churches border the capacious Plaza de Armas. From here, once-decadent baroque mansions spread out along the narrow streets, many enclosing elegant hotels and fine restaurants.

Things move slowly here. The controversial Yanacocha gold mine brought new money, highly paid engineers and a heaping dose of unruly discontent to the town. But with the mine scaling back production and its successor in limbo, Cajamarca is shifting down a gear and once again turning to the traditional pursuits of making cheese and yogurt, while also investing in the nascent tourism industry.

History

In about 1460, the Incas conquered the local Cajamarca populace and Cajamarca evolved

Northern Highlands Highlights

1. Scrambling through **Kuélap** (p424), an immense stone citadel high in the cloud forest.
2. Getting within a hairbreadth of the jungle at **Tarapoto** (p431) without leaving the comfort of the paved highway.
3. Taking a high-adrenaline dip under 771m of falling water at the beautiful **Catarata de Gocta** (p424)
4. Getting close-up looks at recently discovered mummies and the marvelous spatuletail hummingbird near **Leimebamba** (p426).
5. Wallowing a few days away in the underrated colonial ambience of **Cajamarca** (p405).
6. Wandering through magnificent ruins atop a windswept plateau at **Marcahuamachuco** (p415).
7. Taking the bus ride of a lifetime on the cliff-teetering road from **Cajamarca to Chachapoyas** (p413).
8. Having a raucous night out sampling root-soaked jungle elixirs in **Chachapoyas** (p420) or **Tarapoto** (p436).

Cajamarca

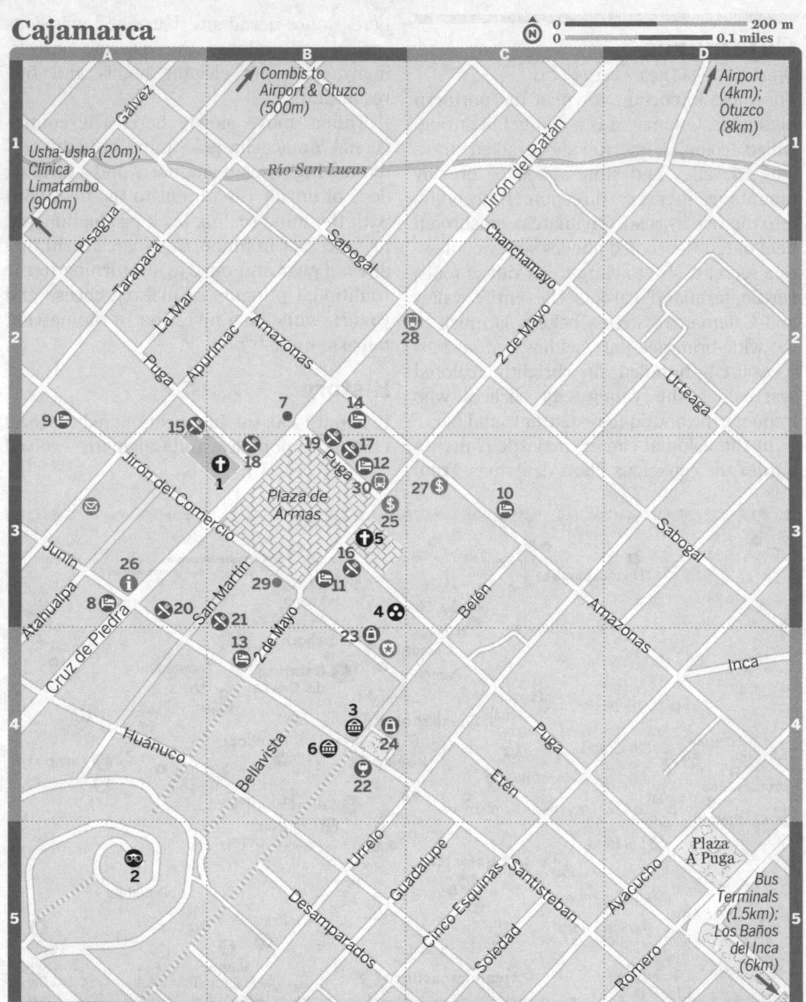

into a major city on the Inca Andean highway linking Cuzco and Quito.

After the death of the Inca (king) Huayna Capac in 1525, the remaining Inca empire, which then stretched from southern Colombia to central Chile, was pragmatically divided between his sons, with Atahualpa ruling the north and Huascar the south. Obviously not everyone was in concord, as civil war soon broke out and in 1532 Atahualpa and his victorious troops marched southward toward Cuzco to take complete control of the empire. Parked at Cajamarca to rest for a few days, Atahualpa, the new Inca emperor, was camped at the natural thermal springs, known today as Los Baños del Inca, when he heard the news that the Spanish were nearby.

Francisco Pizarro and his force of 168 Spaniards arrived in Cajamarca on November 15, 1532, to a deserted city; most of its 2000 inhabitants were with Atahualpa at his hot-springs encampment. The Spaniards spent an anxious night, fully aware that they were severely outnumbered by the nearby Inca troops, who were estimated to be between 40,000 and 80,000. The Spaniards plotted to entice Atahualpa into the

Cajamarca

Sights

1 Catedral de Cajamarca ... B3
2 Cerro Santa Apolonia ... A5
3 El Complejo de Belén ... B4
4 El Cuarto del Rescate ... B3
5 Iglesia de San Francisco ... B3
6 Museo de Arqueológico & Etnografía ... B4

Activities, Courses & Tours

7 Clarín Tours ... B2
Mega Tours ... (see 12)

Sleeping

8 El Cabildo ... A3
9 El Portal del Marques ... A2
10 Hospedaje Los Jazmines ... C3
11 Hostal Casona del Inca ... B3
12 Hostal Plaza ... B3
13 Hotel Cajamarca ... B4
14 Las Americas Hotel ... B2

Eating

15 Cascanuez Café Bar ... A2
16 Don Paco ... B3
17 Heladería Holanda ... B3
18 Querubino ... B3
19 Salas ... B3
20 Sanguchon.com ... A3
21 Vaca Loca ... B3

Drinking & Nightlife

22 Taita ... B4

Shopping

23 Artesanias El Rescate ... B4
24 Colors & Creations ... B4

Information

25 Interbank ... B3
26 iPeru ... A3
27 Scotiabank ... C3

Transport

28 Combis to Los Baños del Inca ... C2
29 LC Perú ... B3
30 Línea Ticket Office ... B3

plaza and, at a prearranged signal, capture the Inca should the opportunity present itself.

Upon Atahualpa's arrival, he ordered most of his troops to stay outside while he entered the plaza with a retinue of nobles and about 6000 men armed with slings and hand axes. He was met by the Spanish friar Vicente de Valverde, who attempted to explain his position as a man of God and presented the Inca with a Bible. Reputedly, Atahualpa angrily threw the book to the ground and Valverde needed little more justification to sound the attack.

Cannons were fired and the Spanish cavalry attacked Atahualpa and his troops. The indigenous people were terrified and bewildered by the fearsome onslaught of never-before-seen cannons and horses. Their small hand axes and slings were no match for the well-armored Spaniards, who swung razor-sharp swords from the advantageous height of horseback to slaughter 7000 indigenous people and capture Atahualpa. The small band of Spaniards was now literally conquistadors (conquerors).

Atahualpa soon became aware of the Spaniards' lust for gold and offered to fill a large room in the town once with gold and twice with silver in return for his freedom. The Spanish agreed and slowly the gold and silver began pouring into Cajamarca. Nearly a year later the ransom was complete – about 6000kg of gold and 12,000kg of silver had been melted down into gold and silver bullion. At today's prices, this ransom would be worth almost S180 million, but the artistic value of the ornaments and implements that were melted down to create the bullion is impossible to estimate.

Atahualpa, suspecting he was not going to be released, sent desperate messages to his followers in Quito to come to Cajamarca and rescue him. The Spaniards, panic-stricken by these messages, sentenced Atahualpa to death. On July 26, 1533, Atahualpa was led out to the center of the Cajamarca plaza to be burned at the stake. At the last hour, Atahualpa 'accepted' baptism and, as a reward, his sentence was changed to a quicker death by strangulation.

Most of the great stone Inca buildings in Cajamarca were torn down and the stones used in the construction of Spanish homes and churches. The great plaza where Atahualpa was captured and later killed was in roughly the same location as today's Plaza de Armas. The Ransom Chamber, or El Cuarto del Rescate, where Atahualpa was imprisoned, is the only Inca building still standing.

Sights

Cajamarca's genial Plaza de Armas has a well-kept garden and a fine central **fountain** which dates from 1692 and commemorates the bicentenary of Columbus' landing in the Americas. Come evening, the town's inhabitants congregate in the plaza to stroll and mull over the important events of the day – a popular pastime in this area of northern Peru.

Two churches face the plaza: the cathedral and the Iglesia de San Francisco. Both are often imaginatively illuminated in the evenings, especially on weekends.

El Complejo de Belén HISTORIC BUILDING
(cnr Belén & Comercio; adult/student S5/2; ⏲9am-1pm & 3-8pm Tue-Wed, 9am-8pm Thu-Sat, 9am-1pm Sun) Construction of this sprawling colonial complex, church and hospital, made entirely from volcanic rock, occurred between 1627 and 1774. The hospital was run by nuns, and 31 tiny, cell-like bedrooms line the walls of the T-shaped building. The baroque church next door is one of Cajamarca's finest and has a prominent cupola and a well-carved pulpit.

Among several interesting wood carvings is one is of an extremely tired-looking Christ sitting cross-legged on a throne, propping up his chin with a double-jointed wrist and looking as though he could do with a pisco sour after a hard day's miracle working. Look out for the oversized cherubs supporting the elaborate centerpiece, which represents the weight of heaven. The outside walls of the church are lavishly decorated.

Iglesia de San Francisco CHURCH, MUSEUM
(2 de Mayo; admission S5; ⏲10am-noon & 4-6pm Mon-Fri, 10am-noon Sat) Inside Iglesia de San Francisco you'll find elaborate stone carvings and decadent altars. Visit the church's **Museo de Arte Religioso** (Religious Art Museum) to see 17th-century religious paintings by indigenous artists. It also has the creepy **catacombs**: in one room you'll see the orderly tombs of monks, and in another are the skeletons recovered from indigenous graves found at the site, laying bare and without ceremony.

The intricately sculpted Capilla de la Dolorosa to the right of the nave is considered one of the finest chapels in the city.

El Cuarto del Rescate RUIN
(The Ransom Chamber; Puga; adult/student S5/2; ⏲9am-1pm & 3-8pm Tue-Wed, 9am-8pm Thu-Sat, 9am-1pm Sun) The Ransom Chamber, the only Inca building still standing in Cajamarca, is where Inca ruler Atahualpa was imprisoned. The small room has three trapezoidal doorways and a few similarly shaped niches in the inner walls – signature Inca construction. Visitors are not permitted to enter the room, but from outside it's possible to observe the red line marking the original ceiling of the structure – the point to which it was to be filled with treasure to secure Atahualpa's release.

In the entrance to the site are a couple of modern paintings depicting Atahualpa's capture and imprisonment. The stone of the building is weathered as it has only recently been covered by a large protective dome. The ticket to El Cuarto del Rescate includes El Complejo de Belén and Museo Arqueológico & Etnografíco if they are all visited on the same day.

Catedral de Cajamarca CATHEDRAL
(Batán; ⏲8-11am & 4-6pm) The Catedral de Cajamarca is a squat building that was begun in the late 17th century and only recently finished. Like most of Cajamarca's churches, this cathedral has no belfry. This is because the Spanish Crown levied a tax on finished churches and so the belfries were not built, leaving the church unfinished and thereby avoiding the tax.

Museo de Arqueológico & Etnografía MUSEUM
(cnr Belén y Commercio; admission S5; ⏲9am-1pm & 3-6pm Tue-Sat, 9am-1pm Sun) This small but interesting museum housed inside the Antigua Hospital de Mujeres, just a few meters from El Complejo de Belén, has exhibits of pre-Columbian pottery and stone statues, as well as displays on local costumes and clothing, domestic and agricultural implements, musical instruments, and crafts made from wood, bone, leather and stone.

The facade has a fascinating statue of a woman with four breasts – it was carved by local artisans and supposedly represents an affliction (supernumerary nipples, that is) commonly found in one of the nearby towns.

Cerro Santa Apolonia LOOKOUT
(admission S1; ⏲7am-7pm) This garden-covered viewpoint, overlooking the city from the southwest, is a prominent Cajamarca landmark. It is easily reached by climbing the stairs at the end of Calle 2 de Mayo and

THERE'S GOLD IN THEM THERE HILLS

The hills outside Cajamarca are laced with gold. Tonnes of it – but don't reach for your shovel and pan just yet, as this gold is not found in the kind of golden nuggets that set prospectors' eyes ablaze. It's 'invisible gold,' vast quantities of minuscule specks that require advanced and noxious mining techniques to be pried out of their earthly ore.

The Yanacocha mine, with a majority stake owned by Denver-based Newmont Mining Corporation, has quarried open pits in the countryside surrounding Cajamarca, becoming one of the most productive gold mines in the world. More than US$7 billion worth of the shiny stuff has been extracted so far. That, combined with plenty of new jobs and an influx of international engineers into Cajamarca, has meant a surge in wealth for the region – but for many locals, all that glitters is not gold.

In 2000, a large spill of toxic mercury raised doubts about Yanacocha's priorities: gold over safety seemed to be the marching cry. The mine makes its profits by washing vast quantities of mountainside with cyanide solution, a hazardous technique that uses masses of water that local farmers also depend on. An internal environmental audit carried out by the company in 2004 verified villagers' observations that water supplies were being contaminated and fish stocks were disappearing.

In the autumn of 2004, disillusioned *campesinos* (peasants) rallied against the opening of a new mine in the area of Quilish, and clashed violently with the police employed to protect the mine's interests. After weeks of conflict, the company eventually gave in and has since reevaluated its priorities, and improved its safety and environmental record.

In an attempt to quell future mining protests, President Ollanta Humala's administration passed the Prior Consultation Law in 2012, which requires mining companies to negotiate with local communities before initiating any new extraction projects. Nevertheless, trouble brewed that same year when Newmont's proposed US$4.8 billion Conga gold and copper mine project set Cajamarca off again. Despite claims from Newmont that the project will create up to 7000 jobs in the region, inject US$50 billion into the local economy and not harm the region's watersheds, locals weren't buying it. Under the slogan 'Conga No Va' (roughly translated as 'No to Conga!'), a far more serious general regional strike that lasted months brought days of daily marches and protests throughout Cajamarca, Celendín and the surrounding region, resulting in at least eight dead.

At the time of writing, and with production at Yanacocha nearing its end, the future of Conga remained in limbo, with some residents supporting the project and many others, particularly in rural areas, passionately against it. It remains a thorny subject here and you'll see protests against the mine burned into the foliage on hillsides surrounding the town. With nearly 50% of Cajamarca's territory concessioned to mining companies, the majority of which encompass many river sources, this is a prominent issue that won't disappear anytime soon.

following the path that spirals around the hilltop. The pre-Hispanic carved rocks at the summit are mainly from the Inca period, but some are thought to originally date back to the Chavín period (p493).

One of the rocks, which is known as the Seat of the Inca, has a shape that suggests a throne, and the Inca (king) is said to have reviewed his troops from this point.

Tours

There are a few tour companies that can provide information and inexpensive guided tours of the city and its surroundings. Many companies claim to have English-speaking guides, but only a few really pass muster. Tours to Cumbemayo and Outzco are convenient and worth the S25 price tag. Tack on an extra S10 per trip for an English guide. The companies will often pool tours.

It's also possible to organize your own group and make trips further afield to Kuntur Wasi, Ventanillas de Combayo and other attractions.

Clarín Tours SIGHTSEEING TOUR
(☎076-36-6829; www.clarintours.com; Del Batán 161) Friendly tour company with low prices and good customer service.

Mega Tours SIGHTSEEING TOUR
(☎076-34-1876; www.megatours.org; Puga 691) A popular option for cheap sightseeing tours.

Festivals & Events

Carnaval FESTIVAL

The Carnaval festivities here are reputed to be one of the most popular and rowdy events in the country. They're held in the last few days before Lent.

Sleeping

Hotel rates (and other prices) rise during festivals and special events, and are also usually slightly higher in the dry season (May to September).

★ Hospedaje Los Jazmines HOTEL $

(076-36-1812; www.hospedajelosjazmines.com.pe; Amazonas 775; s/d/tr S50/80/110, without bathroom S40/60/80; @) In a land of ubiquitous colonial courtyards, this friendly inn is a value standout for its lush version and even more extensive back gardens. With comfy rooms, piping hot water and a great central location it is a top choice, even more so considering the profits help sustain an orphanage for special-needs children in Baños de Inca.

In keeping with the social vibe, there is an on-site Espresso Bar independently run by the folks at Heladería Holanda (p412), which does some of the best coffee/espresso in town, and has become a small traveler hangout and work space.

Hostal Plaza HOTEL $

(076-36-2058; Puga 669; s/d/tr S30/50/70;) Right on the plaza, this budget traveler's favorite is set in a rambling old colonial mansion with two interior courtyards. The 10 good-value private rooms are fairly basic, although they are colorfully decorated with kitschy objects. Rooms have cable TV and 24-hour hot water.

Casa Mirita HOMESTAY $

(076-36-9361; www.casa-mirita.blogspot.com; Cáceres 1337; s without bathroom S20, r S30; @) This simple homestay is a *mototaxi* (three-wheeled motorcycle rickshaw taxi) ride (S3) to a residential neighborhood southeast of the center. It's an interesting choice for long-term stayers or those looking to be off the gringo grid. Two sisters, Mirita, the cook, and Vicki, a tourism official, run the show. Rooms are rustic and there's a kitchen, or meals cost S10.

There is an experience to be had here, but it's a hike into an area where few (if any) gringos go.

★ Posada del Purhuay HISTORIC HOTEL $$

(076-36-7028; www.posadapurhuay.com.pe; Km 4.5 Carretera Porcón; s/d/tr incl breakfast S210/260/315; @) This luxuriously restored 1822 hacienda, sitting on 23 hectares off the road to Granja Porcón, is a true find. The relaxing grounds are meticulously groomed, leading to a lovely colonial hotel offering discerning service and a step-back-in-time appeal. Spacious rooms, chock-full of antiquated charm and period furnishings, surround an impeccable courtyard and fountain. Family getaway? Check. Tuck-yourself-away romantic retreat? Check.

A taxi here will cost around S15.

El Portal del Marques HISTORIC HOTEL $$

(076-36-8464; www.portaldelmarques.com; Del Comercio 644; s/d/tr incl breakfast S197/241/296; @) Set around a neat garden, this restored colonial mansion has modern, well-presented rooms with flat-screen TVs,

CARNAVAL CAJAMARCA

The Peru-wide pageantry of Carnaval is celebrated at the beginning of Lent, usually in February. Not all Carnavals are created equal, however. Ask any Peruvian where the wildest celebrations are, and Cajamarca will invariably come out trumps.

Preparations begin months in advance; sometimes, no sooner have Carnaval celebrations wound down than planning for the following year begins. Cajamarcans take their celebrations seriously. The festival is nine days of dancing, eating, singing, partying, costumes, parades and general rowdy mayhem. It's also a particularly wet affair and water fights here are worse (or better, depending on your point of view) than you'd encounter elsewhere. Local teenagers don't necessarily limit themselves to soaking one another with water – paint, oil and other unsightly liquids have all been reported.

Hotels fill up weeks beforehand, prices skyrocket and hundreds of people end up sleeping in the plaza. Considering it's one of the most rambunctious festivals in Peru, it certainly seems worth it.

good mattresses, minifridges and in-room safes. The service is friendly and professional and there is a popular bar-restaurant in the front courtyard.

Qhapac Ñan Hotel HOTEL $$

(956-037-357; www.qhapacnanhotel.com; Nogales, Villa Universitaria; s/d S120/170) Convenient to the bus offices, this new hotel in a residential neighborhood offers very comfortable modern rooms with firm beds, well-equipped bathrooms and fast internet. Service is very efficient and there is an on-site restaurant.

Hostal Casona del Inca HISTORIC HOTEL $$

(076-36-7524; www.casonadelincaperu.com; 2 de Mayo 458; s/d/tr incl breakfast S140/190/230;) You might begin questioning your sobriety when you notice that all the brightly painted walls of this plaza-side colonial building seem to be on a slight angle. Don't worry – they are, but the aged carnival fun-house appearance just adds to the charm. The clean and cozy rooms boast exposed wooden beams and some have ample plaza views.

Some rooms have tiny bathrooms so ask to compare options.

Las Americas Hotel BUSINESS HOTEL $$

(076-36-3951; www.lasamericashotel.com.pe; Amazonas 622; s/d incl breakfast S160/230, ste S320;) Breaking away from the 'cozy colonial hotel' pack, this contemporary property is all business. The 38 rooms face onto a central atrium lined with plants. All rooms have minifridges, cable TV and excellent mattresses; three have Jacuzzi tubs and six have balconies. A restaurant provides room service and there's a criminally underused rooftop terrace with plaza and church views.

Hotel Cajamarca HISTORIC HOTEL $$

(076-36-2532; www.hotelcajamarca.com.pe; 2 de Mayo 311; s/d/tr incl breakfast S165/230/260;) This spacious, presentable hotel in a colonial mansion is spread over two levels surrounding a wonderful covered courtyard with a fountain. All rooms include modern bathrooms and elegant wooden furniture.

El Cabildo HISTORIC HOTEL $$

(076-36-7025; elcabildoh@gmail.com; Junín 1062; s/d/tr incl breakfast S100/130/180;) One of the town's best-value sleeping options, this huge historic mansion conceals an eclectic collection of graceful older rooms with slightly worn carpet, but a homely vibe. Some rooms have split levels and all have gleaming wooden furniture and tasteful decorations. At the mansion's heart, a gorgeous courtyard area is filled with greenery, a fountain and a cacophony of sculptures and statues.

Hostal Laguna Seca RESORT $$$

(076-58-4300; www.lagunaseca.com.pe; s/d incl breakfast & airport transfer S376/464;) Situated 6km from Cajamarca just outside Los Baños del Inca, this Swiss-Peruvian-owned resort has fairly generic rooms with all the mod cons. Its big selling point is its deep tubs for private soaking in thermal waters. The much nicer executive rooms (S524) offer king-sized beds.

Horseback riding (per half hour S21) is available and massages and spa health treatments pamper the hedonists among us. It all falls just on the happy side of the cheesy resort see-saw.

Eating

Don Paco PERUVIAN $

(076-36-2655; Puga 726; set menu S8, mains S12-22; 11am-10pm) Tucked away near the plaza, Don Paco has a big following among residents and expats. There's something for everyone, including typical breakfasts and great renditions of Peruvian favorites, plus more sophisticated *novocajamarquino* (new Cajamarcan) fare such as chicken cordon bleu with Andean ham and local cheese in a pomegranate sauce, and the recommended duck breast with *sauco* (elderberry) sauce.

Salas PERUVIAN $

(Puga 637; mains S12-32; 8am-10pm) Down a narrow entrance off the Plaza de Armas, this old-school diner is a big hit among the senior crowd who come for the carefully prepared typical *Cajamarquino* dishes. Everything the bow-tied waiters bring out is delicious. Order from the changing specials menu to try interesting local plates. There is another branch on Cruz de Piedra.

Castope PERUVIAN $

(Luis Rebaza Negra 557; mains S15-18; 9am-6pm) This unpretentious restaurant near the bus terminals looks decidedly like a warehouse, but it needs to be big to cater to the hordes of locals who come to dine here. The menu has a wide range of local favorites, including fried *cuy* (guinea pig), *cecina con mote* (shredded dried pork with corn) and *frito cajamarquino* (fried pork with potatoes).

There are other branches near El Quinde and in Baños de Inca.

Sanguchon.com FAST FOOD $
(www.sanguchon.com.pe; Junín 1137; sandwiches from S8.50-12; 6pm-midnight;) This wildly popular, hipster hamburger and sandwich joint features an extensive menu of hand-held drunken eats. It has 16 varieties of burgers and another half dozen sauces – the combinations are staggering. The tasty food is very convenient, as it's a rowdy bar as well.

Vaca Loca PIZZERIA $
(San Martín 330; pizzas S13-39; 6-11pm) Set in an inviting colonial house with a warm paint job, the Mad Cow pays homage to the local dairy culture with bovine-print furniture and cow art. But the reason to come here is for the quality pies. They're covered with delicious local cheese and a wide selection of toppings, including gourmet offerings such as artichoke and wild mushroom.

Heladería Holanda DESSERTS $
(www.heladosholanda.com.pe; Puga 657; ice cream sS2-4; 9am-7pm) Don't miss the tiny entrance on the Plaza de Armas; it opens into a large, Dutch orange cafe selling possibly the best ice cream in northern Peru. The staff will shower you with samples of the 20 or so changing flavors, the best of which are local and regional fruits. The Dutch owner buys them direct from family farms following a fair-trade philosophy.

In addition to the sweets, staff members are single mothers and the deaf, an ongoing social project started by the owner. It has locations at El Quinde Shopping Center and Los Baños del Inca as well.

Cascanuez Café Bar CAFE $
(076-36-6089; Puga 554; mains S16-27; 7:30am-10pm;) A nice cafe for breakfast and light meals but most folks flock here for a decadent means to their sweet-tooth ends – nine varieties of *tres leches* cake alone (try chocolate).

El Quinde Shopping Center SELF-CATERING $
(www.elquinde.com; Av Hoyos Rubio, cuadra 7; 10am-10pm) This shopping center has the closest supermarket to town (Metro), about 2.5km north of the Plaza de Armas.

Querubino PERUVIAN $$
(076-34-0900; Puga 589; mains S17-36; 12:30-4pm & 7-11pm, closed Tue) Classy Querubino has real chefs doing upscale versions of Peruvian classics, plus the occasional creative curveball and seasonally changing specials. The menu is dominated by meat and seafood, but try the *gnocchi a la huancaina,* a wondrous invention of fresh pasta doused in *huancaina* sauce (fresh white cheese, yellow chili) with *lomo fino* (tenderloin) – it's creamy, rich and delicious.

Drinking & Nightlife

★Usha-Usha BAR
(Puga 142; admission S5; 9pm-late) For an intimate local experience, head to this hole-in-the-wall dive bar run by eccentric local musician Jaime Valera, who has managed to cultivate a heap of charisma in such a small space. He sings his heart out with his musician friends and you walk out with an unforgettable travel memory.

Taita BAR
(cnr Santisteban & Belén; 8pm-late Fri & Sat) Find a spot to down your pisco sours in one of the rooms full of vintage furniture upstairs, then head down to the courtyard to hit the dance floor in this atmospheric bar right by Belén.

Shopping

Small shops selling local and Peruvian crafts line the stairwells along Calle 2 de Mayo south of Junín.

Artesanias El Rescate HANDICRAFTS
(Del Commercio 1029; 9am-8pm) This open-air arcade has around a dozen small shops selling handicrafts from around the region, including woven bags and ponchos.

Colors & Creations HANDICRAFTS
(076-34-3875; Belén 628; 9am-1pm & 3-7pm Mon-Sat, 10am-1pm & 3-6pm Sun) An artisan-owned-and-run cooperative selling excellent-quality crafts.

Information

There's internet access practically on every block.

EMERGENCY

Policía de Turismo (Tourist Police; 076-36-4515; Del Comercio 1013) Special force dealing with crimes against tourists.

MEDICAL SERVICES

Clínica Limatambo (☎0800-20-900; www.limatambo.com.pe; Puno 265) Has the best medical service; west of town.

MONEY

Interbank (☎076-36-2460; Calle 2 de Mayo 546)

Scotiabank (Amazonas 750)

POST

Serpost (Apurimac 624; ⏰8am-7pm Mon-Sat) Postal service.

TOURIST INFORMATION

iPeru (☎076-36-5166; iperucajamarca@promperu.gob.pe; Cruz de Piedra 601; ⏰9am-6pm Mon-Sat, to 1pm Sun) Incredibly helpful tourist office that has detailed maps outlining how to visit attractions around town and beyond.

Getting There & Away

AIR

The airport is 4km outside town off the road to Otuzco. Taxis charge S10 into downtown. The combination of difficult terrain and frequent heavy rains mean cancellations and delays are fairly common here. Reconfirm your flight before heading out to the airport. It would be unwise to book tight connections when leaving from Cajamarca.

LC Perú (☎076-36-3115; www.lcperu.pe; Jirón del Comercio 1024) flies this route most economically, with two daily flights leaving Lima for Cajamarca at 5:10am and 3:10pm, returning at 7:15am and 5:15am.

LAN (www.lan.com; Centro Commercial El Quinde) has three flights between Lima and Cajamarca, leaving the capital at 5:40am, 10:30am and 3:30pm, returning from Cajamarca at 7:35am, 12:40pm and 4:50pm.

BUS

Cajamarca continues its ancient role as a crossroads, with buses heading to all four points of the compass. Most bus terminals are close to *cuadra* 3 of Atahualpa, about 1.5km southeast of the center (not to be confused with the Atahualpa in the town center), on the road to Los Baños del Inca.

The major route is westbound to the Carretera Panamericana near Pacasmayo on the coast, then north to Chiclayo (six hours) or south to Trujillo (six hours) and Lima (15 hours).

The old southbound road has recently been paved and travel on this route is no longer a bone-rattling nightmare. Frequent services head to Cajabamba (three hours) from where onward buses travel to Huamachuco and Trujillo.

The trip to Trujillo takes almost twice as long on this narrow road than it does along the newer paved road via Pacasmayo, although the route is only 60km longer. The scenery is prettier and the towns are nicer on the longer route, but buses are generally less comfortable and are less frequent. It's not recommended to travel this route beyond Cajabamba at night as robberies have been reported.

The rough northbound road to Chota (five hours) passes through wild and attractive countryside via Bambamarca, which has a busy market on Sunday morning. Buses connect Chota to Chiclayo along a rough road.

The staggeringly scenic eastbound road winds to Celendín, then bumps its way across the Andes, past Chachapoyas and down into the Amazon lowlands.

Combis (minibuses) for Ventanillas de Otuzco (S1, 20 minutes) leave from the corner of Tayabambo and Los Gladiolos, near the market district. These pass the airport, although jamming yourself into a crowded van with your backpack will require some finesse and diplomacy. *Combis* for Baños del Inca (S1, 25 minutes) leave frequently from the corner of Del Batán and Chanchamayo.

Bus operators include the following:

Civa (☎076-36-1460; www.civa.com.pe; San Martín 957) Good bus to Lima at 5pm.

Cruz del Sur (☎076-36-2024; Atahualpa 884) Nice *bus-cama* (bed bus) with seat-back screens to Lima at 6:30pm.

Línea (☎076-34-0753; Atahualpa 316) Has the most comfortable Lima-bound *bus-camas* with departures at 6pm and 6:30pm. There are Chiclayo departures at 10:45am, 1:30pm, 10:50pm and 11pm, and Trujillo at 10:30am, 1pm, 10pm, 10:15pm, 10:30pm and 10:40pm. It also has a ticket office on the Plaza de Armas.

Tepsa (☎076-36-3306; Sucre 422) Comfortable *bus-cama* Lima service at 6:30pm.

Transportes Chiclayo (☎076-36-4628; www.transporteschiclayo.com; Atahualpa 283) Has a Chiclayo-bound bus at 11pm which is good for transferring north to Mancorá or Tumbes.

Transportes Rojas (☎076-34-0548; Atahualpa 309) Service to Celendín at 3pm.

Transportes Union (☎971-178-423; Atahualpa 293) Runs regular services to Cajambamba in minivans and buses.

Turismo Dias (☎076-34-4322; Atahualpa 307) Regular buses to Trujillo and Chiclayo; and a direct bus to Piura at 10:30pm, the best option for getting to Mancorá. Buses depart from its terminal at Vía de Evitamiento 1370.

Virgen del Carmen (☎98-391-5869; Atahualpa 333-A) Departs at 4:30am and 3pm daily for Chachapoyas via Celendín and Leimebamba.

Cajamarca Buses:

DESTINATION	COST (S)	DURATION (HR)
Bambamarca	15	3½
Cajabamba	10-20	3
Celendín	10	3½
Chachapoyas	50	12
Chiclayo	20-45	6
Leimebamba	35	10
Lima	80-136	15
Piura	45	9
Trujillo	20-40	6

Around Cajamarca

Los Baños del Inca

Atahualpa was camped by these natural **hot springs** (admission S2, private baths per hour S4-6, sauna or massage S10-20; ⏲5am-8pm), known as 'The Baths of the Inca', when Pizarro arrived. Now you can take a dip in the same waters that an Inca king used to bathe his war wounds – though the pools have probably been cleaned since then. Set around flourishing grounds, this attractive compound has hot water channeled into private cubicles (S6 to S25 per 30 minutes), some large enough for up to six people at a time. Unfortunately all the private baths are indoors, which makes it impossible to admire the mountain scenery while soaking. If you want to be outdoors, dip into the public pool (S3), although it too is mostly enclosed and the generic concrete design is not particularly appealing. There are also steam rooms and massages available for S10 and S20 each. This place gets hundreds of visitors daily, so it's best to come in the morning to avoid the rush.

There's a **Complejo Recreativo** (admission S2.50; ⏲5am-7pm) opposite the main bath complex that has swimming pools and a waterslide. It's a big hit with local kids.

The *baños* (baths) are 6km from Cajamarca and have a few hotel possibilities. *Combis* for Los Baños del Inca (S1, 25 minutes) leave from Chanchamayo and Plaza a Puga in Cajamarca; or take an organized tour from Cajamarca (S15). Bring your own towel as none are provided, though you may purchase one from a few entrepreneurial vendors. Afterward, pop across the street for a sweet cool down at Heladería Holanda (p412).

Cumbemayo

About 20km southwest of Cajamarca, Cumbemayo (derived from the Quechua *kumpi mayo,* meaning 'well-made water channel') is an astounding feat of pre-Inca engineering. These perfectly smooth aqueducts were carved around 2000 years ago and zigzag at right angles for 9km, all for a purpose that is as yet unclear, since Cajamarca has an abundant water supply. Other rock formations are carved to look like altars and thrones. Nearby caves contain **petroglyphs**, including some that resemble woolly mammoths. The countryside is high, windswept and slightly eerie. Superstitious stories are told about the area's eroded rock formations, which look like groups of shrouded mountain climbers.

Public transport to Cumbemayo is sporadic and getting there on your own takes some planning. *Combis* serving the village of Chetilla pass by the entrance to the site and leave Av Perú between Jirón Ica and Jirón Loreta at 4:30am, 6am, noon and 1:30pm. The last *combi* back to Cajamarca passes Cumbemayo around 1:40pm.

The site can be reached on foot via a signed road from behind Cerro Santa Apolonia in Cajamarca. The hike follows sections of the *Qhapac Ñan* (Inca paths) and takes about four hours if you take the obvious shortcuts and ask every passerby for directions.

Ventanillas de Otuzco & Combayo

These pre-Inca necropolises have scores of funerary niches built into the hillside, hence the name *ventanillas* (windows). **Ventanillas de Otuzco** (admission adult/child S5/1; ⏲9am-6pm) is in alluring countryside, 8km northeast of Cajamarca, and is easily walkable from either Cajamarca or Los Baños del Inca (ask for directions). Alternatively, *combis* to Ventanillas de Otuzco (S1, 20 minutes) leave frequently from the corner of Jirón Los Gladiolos and Jirón Tayabamba, north of the Plaza de Armas in Cajamarca.

The larger and better-preserved **Ventanillas de Combayo** FREE are 30km away and are most easily visited on a tour from Cajamarca (between S20 and S25). If you want to go on your own, irregular *colectivos* (S5, 1½ hours) depart when full from the second block of Avenida Hoyos Rubios 2 from 5am to 4pm. Leave early to ensure return transport.

Kuntur Wasi

Perched on a mountaintop overlooking the small town of San Pablo, the seldom visited pre-Inca **Kuntur Wasi ruins** (admission adult/child S5/1; ⌚9am-5:30pm Tue-Sun) are well worth the trip from Cajamarca.

The site is considered one of the cradles of Andean culture; four distinct cultures used the area for their ceremonies, with the first constructions taking place around 1100 BC. The main structure is a large u-shaped temple consisting of three elevated platforms around which are located numerous tombs. Archaeologists have unearthed fascinating relics here including magnificent gold work.

While the ruins are not the most spectacular in the region (apart from the walls and central plaza, most of the excavated structures have been filled in), the views from the site are spectacular.

The real drawcard here is the **museum** (☎976-679-484; museo.kunturwasi@gmail.com; adult/child S4/1; ⌚9am-5pm Tue-Sun), located at the foot of the ruins in the hamlet of Kuntur Wasi. It displays many objects found at the site, including amazing gold crowns and

RUINS OF HUAMACHUCO

Despite being in the envious position of having two first-class pre-Hispanic ruins on its doorstep, the pleasant mountain town of Huamachuco receives very few visitors.

Without doubt the major star is the massive pre-Inca mountain fort of **Marcahuamachuco** FREE, a spectacular collection of rugged ruins that sprawls over a windswept plateau at a dizzying 3600m.

The 3km-long site dates from around 400 BC and has immense defensive perimeter walls and towering ceremonial buildings. Research suggests that the complex formed a center of religious worship – different communities from all corners of Huamachuco lands would visit to worship the gods that were believed to reside on the mountain peaks surrounding the site on all sides. The largest archaeological site in the northern mountains, it is divided into four main sections, two of which, Cerro del Castillo and Cerro de Las Monjas, are open to visitors on a well-marked circuit.

Marcahuamachuco is located at the end of a sketchy dirt road, 10km from town. A private vehicle to the entrance can be arranged on the Via de Evitamiento near the Casa de Arcos and will cost from S60 to S80, depending on how long you want to stay at the site.

Although dwarfed by its famous neighbor, the easily accessed ruins of **Wiracochapampa** are also well worth a visit. Despite the close proximity of the sites, the structures here are not directly connected to those at Marcahuamachuco. Research suggests the buildings here were completed around 700 AD and served as a ceremonial center of the Wari culture.

Unlike many other large pre-Hispanic settlements in the region which cling to soaring peaks, these structures were built low in a valley. The ruins are centered around a large central plaza, surrounded on three sides by a compact maze of rooms, and divided by high rock walls, which contain numerous tombs. From the center of Huamachuco it's a 45-minute hike to Wiracochapampa. Otherwise a *mototaxi* should cost around S8.

The **tourism office** (☎076-44-0048; www.munihuamachuco.gob.pe; Sucre 165) can organize guides to both archaeological sites, as well as other attractions in the area. A block from the plaza in Huamachuco, the small **Museo Municipal Wamachuko** (cnr Sucre & San Martin; ⌚9am-noon & 2-5pm Mon-Fri) FREE houses ceramics from the Huamachuco period.

For accommodations, try **Hostal Plaza** (cnr José Balta & San Martín; r S40-50) which offers good-value rooms right on the main square – get one with a plaza view, the internal rooms are noisy. For eats, head to **Antojitos** (Ramón Castilla 534; mains S14; ⌚7-11am & 6-11pm), which does a tasty mixed grill, as well as filling traditional breakfasts.

Colectivos (shared transportation) leave for Cajabamba (S10, 1½ hours) when full from the small terminal on the east side of town. **Tunesa Express** (☎076-44-1157; cnr José Balta & Suarez) has regular express services linking Huamachuco with Trujillo (S35, six hours).

jewelry. Be aware that pieces in the museum are sometimes loaned out to other institutions and unlabeled replicas are put in their place. Ask the staff to identify the original pieces.

Kuntur Wasi is just outside the sleepy town of San Pablo. A *mototaxi* from town to the museum costs S3. The archaeological site is a steep 800m hike up the trail behind the museum.

Combis to San Pablo (S10, 1½ hours) depart regularly from the small terminal on Jirón Angamos, in front of Grifo Continental in Cajamarca. The last van back leaves San Pablo at 5:30pm; you may want to reserve your place in advance.

Cajabamba

☎076 / POP 30,600 / ELEV 2655M

First stop on the old highway from Cajamarca to Trujillo is the friendly town of Cajabamba, which sits on a natural ledge overlooking farms and plantations. The red-tiled roofs, and a neat Plaza de Armas surrounded by buildings with identical beige and brown paint jobs, lend the place a colonial aesthetic.

Several sights are within an hour's walk of Cajabamba, including the fetching mountain lagoons of **Ponte** and **Quengococha**. Slightly further afield, but worth a visit, is the **Cascada Cochecorral**, an elegant layered waterfall that appears as though the river is flowing down a massive flight of concrete stairs. There is very little tourism infrastructure in town, but the Alcaldia (Mayor's office) on the main plaza may be able to assist with organizing transport and a guide. The feast of **La Virgen del Rosario** is celebrated around the first Sunday in October with processions, dances and general bucolic carousing.

The most comfortable place to stay is **Hostal La Casona** (☎076-35-8285; Bolognesi 720; s/d S30/50; 📶), which has cute rooms with hot showers and cable TV at a good price. Follow the locals and head to **Pio's Chicken** (Jiron Grau s/n; mains S8; ⏱noon-10pm) for possibly the best barbecued chicken in northern Peru, as well as *arroz chaufa* (mixed fried rice) and other typical plates.

There's a Banco de la Nación in town with a Visa/Plus ATM. **Transportes Union** (☎976-990-890; Grau 145) has regular departures to Cajamarca (S10, three hours) from 5am to 7pm. *Combis* and *colectivos* to Huamachuco (S10, 1½ hours) leave when full from the small terminal beside the police station. There are a bunch of bus companies on Avenida Martinez near the market offering express services to Trujillo (S25, seven hours).

Celendín

☎076 / POP 28,000 / ELEV 2625M

Easily reached by a partly unpaved road from Cajamarca, Celendín is a delightfully sleepy little town that receives few travelers except for those taking the wild and scenic route to Chachapoyas. Celendín is particularly known for high-quality straw hats, which can be bought at its interesting Sunday market. It's an ideal place to observe traditional highland life and interact with local indigenous people, who will certainly take an interest in your unexpected visit.

Hot springs (admission S3) and mud baths to soothe aching muscles can be found at Llanguat, a 30-minute drive with private transport. You can also take a 7am *combi* from the Plaza de Armas (S6, 45 minutes). It returns around noon.

Dutch-run organization **Proyecto Yannick** (☎076-77-0590; www.proyectoyannick.org) offers volunteer opportunities working in community projects and with children with Down syndrome.

Tour operators **Orange Tours** (www.celendinperu.com) offers a variety of trips around Celendín including visits to the hot springs, although it has no office so you'll have to email before arrival.

The annual fiesta of **La Virgen del Carmen** goes from July 1 to August 6, but the best days for tourists, with fireworks, a procession, and bullfighting with matadors from Mexico and Spain in a traditional wooden construction, are from July 28 to August 3.

Sleeping & Eating

Hotel Villa Madrid HOTEL $

(☎076-55-5123; villamadridcelendin@hotmail.com; cnr Pardo & Dos de Mayo; s/d S40/50; P 📶) Just off the Plaza de Armas, Hotel Villa Madrid is the best choice in town with spacious modern rooms set around an internal courtyard.

Hostal Turistas HOTEL $

(☎076-55-5047; Gálvez 507; s/d S45/60; 📶) Close to the plaza, family-run Hostal Turistas is a fine choice with nine comfortable rooms and friendly service.

La Reserve PERUVIAN $

(José Gálvez 420; meals S4-32; ⏲7am-10pm) A popular eating choice, with multilevel seating and a warm ambience. The menu is ample but stick to the Peruvian dishes and you'll eat well.

Information

Banco de la Nación (Calle 2 de Mayo 530) Bank that can change US dollars and has a Visa/Plus ATM.

Getting There & Away

Virgen del Carmen (☎076-55-5187; www.turismovirgendelcarmen.com.pe; Cáceres 112), located behind the market, goes to Chachapoyas (S35, eight hours) via Leimebamba (S25, six hours) at 8am and 6pm. It also runs services to Cajamarca (S10, 3½ hours) at 5am and 3pm.

Chachapoyas

☎041 / POP 28,700 / ELEV 2335M

Also known as Chachas, Chachapoyas is a laid-back town awash in white and surrounded by swaths of high-altitude cloud forests. The town was founded early on in the Spanish conquest and was the base from which the exploitation of the Amazon region was launched. It remained an important junction on jungle-coast trade routes until a paved road was built in the 1940s through nearby Pedro Ruíz, bypassing Chachapoyas altogether. The unlikely capital of the department of Amazonas, this pleasant colonial settlement is now a busy market town and makes an excellent base for exploring the awesome ancient ruins left behind by the fierce civilization of the Chachapoya (People of the Clouds).

Vast zones of little-explored cloud forest surround the city of Chachapoyas, concealing some of Peru's most fascinating and least known archaeological treasures. Although the ravages of weather and time, as well as more recent attentions of grave robbers and treasure seekers, have caused damage to many of the ruins, some have survived remarkably well. Kuélap is by far the most famous of these archaeological sites, though dozens of other ruins lie besieged by jungle and make for tempestuous exploration.

History

The Chachapoya culture was conquered – but never fully subdued – by the Incas a few decades before the Spaniards arrived. When the Europeans showed up, local chief Curaca Huamán supposedly aided them in their conquest to defeat the Inca. Because of the relative lack of Inca influence, the people didn't learn to speak Quechua and today Spanish is spoken almost exclusively. Local historians claim that San Juan de la Frontera de las Chachapoyas was the third town founded by the Spaniards in Peru (after Piura and Lima).

Sights

Instituto Nacional de Cultura Museo MUSEUM

(INC; Ayacucho 904; ⏲8am-1pm & 3-5pm Mon-Fri) FREE This small museum on the plaza houses mummies found throughout the region, plus ceramics from several pre-Columbian periods and one of the original sarcophagi from Karajía.

Mirador Luya Urco VIEWPOINT

A 10-minute stroll northwest along Salamanca brings you to this lookout with a city panorama.

Mirador Huancas VIEWPOINT

(admission S1; ⏲7:30am-5:30pm) A S30 round-trip taxi ride will take you to Mirador Huancas, which has soaring views of the Utcubamba valley. It's also possible to take a *colectivo* (S3, 25 minutes) from the bus terminal. It's an easy 1½-hour hike back along the road.

Activities

Trekking

Trekking to the numerous impressive sights and ruins around Chachapoyas is becoming increasingly popular and is easy to arrange in town. The most popular trek is the four- or five-day **Gran Vilaya trek**, from Choctámal to the Marañón canyon, through pristine cloud forest and past several ruins and the heavenly **Valle de Belén**.

Another popular adventure heads out to the Laguna de los Cóndores, a three-day trip on foot and horseback from Leimebamba. Treks to any of the other ruins in the district can be arranged and tailored to suit your needs.

Chachapoyas

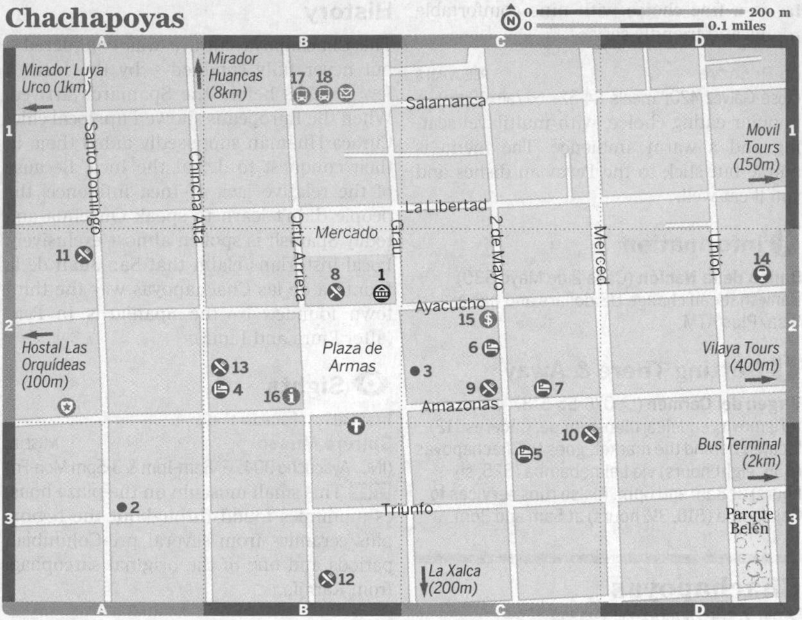

Chachapoyas

Sights

1 Instituto Nacional de Cultura Museo B2

Activities, Courses & Tours

2 International Language Center A3
3 Turismo Explorer C2

Sleeping

4 Casa Vieja Hostal B2
5 Chachapoyas Backpackers C3
6 Hotel Karajía C2
7 La Casona Monsante C2

Eating

8 Café Fusiones B2
9 Dulcería Santa Elena C2
10 El Batan de Tayta C3
11 El Tejado A2
12 La Tushpa B3
13 Terra Mia Café B2

Drinking & Nightlife

14 La Reina D2

Information

15 Banco de la Nación C2
16 iPerú B2

Transport

17 Civa B1
18 Virgen del Carmen B1

Courses

International Language Center LANGUAGE COURSE
(041-47-8807; www.ilc-peru.com.pe; Triunfo 1060; 8am-10pm) In addition to Spanish lessons for S50 per hour (discounts available for longer courses), the friendly owner freely doles out tourist information and often has paid positions for English teachers. It has luggage storage if you need to stow your bags for a day or two.

Tours

All the budget tour agencies are found near the Plaza de Armas. Ask around for other travelers' experiences before you choose an agency. Expect to pay S100 to S150 per person for multiday treks (a little more for groups of less than four) and between S35 and S90 for day tours.

Turismo Explorer GUIDED TOUR
(041-47-8162; www.turismoexplorerperu.com; Grau 549) This company has a great reputa-

tion among travelers and offers short trips and multiday treks. It has professional guides who speak excellent English.

Vilaya Tours TOUR
(☎041-47-7506; www.vilayatours.com; Amazonas 261) A recommended high-end operator run by experienced British guide Rob Dover. It offers tailor-made tours and treks focusing on archaeological sites and nature destinations.

Sleeping

Most places in Chachapoyas fall squarely in the budget category.

★Chachapoyas Backpackers HOSTEL $
(☎041-47-8879; www.chachapoyasbackpackers.com; 2 de Mayo 639; d/tr S60/90, dm/s/d without bathroom S18/30/42; @🛜) Offering cheap, clean rooms with kitchen access in a central location, this new hostel run by an amiable local couple is already a favorite with budget travelers. Owner and former guide José is extremely helpful and knowledgeable about the region. He can organize tours through his agency or provide detailed explanations if you want to go it alone.

Hotel Karajía HOTEL $
(☎041-31-2606; Calle 2 de Mayo 546; s/d S35/60, without bathroom S20/30; 🛜) A simple cheapie with a bright paint job and the occasional frilly touch such as toilet-seat covers and kaleidoscopic bedspreads. Rooms are basic and some are a little dark but they are adequate to crash for the night after a hard trek.

★La Xalca HOTEL $$
(☎041-47-9106; www.laxalcahotel.com; Grau 940; s/d/tr incl breakfast S120/170/250; P🛜) This elegant and spacious new hotel has been carefully constructed in traditional colonial style. Walk through the spacious lobby to find a lovely central courtyard overlooked by a wide wooden balcony on all sides and surrounded by ample communal spaces decked out with comfy leather sofas. The comfortable rooms feature top-of-the-line mattresses and get plenty of natural light.

Casa Vieja Hostal BOUTIQUE GUESTHOUSE $$
(☎041-47-7353; www.casaviejaperu.com; Chincha Alta 569; s/d incl breakfast S115/175; @🛜) Comfortable quarters in a classy converted mansion make this a popular choice, although some rooms could do with a bit of a makeover, so have a look around. The better rooms have handcrafted wood accents, decorative or working fireplaces, and big windows facing onto the verdant garden.

Hostal La Villa de Paris HOTEL $$
(☎041-63-1310; www.hotelvilladeparis.com; Prolongación 2 de Mayo, cuadra 5; s/d incl breakfast S95/140; @🛜🏊) Only 1.5km south from the main square, this lovely colonial-style hotel, furnished with lots of wood and antiques, has the feel of a much more expensive place. Large windows and balconies bring in the light.

La Casona Monsante HOTEL $$
(☎041-47-7702; www.lacasonamonsante.com; Amazonas 746; r/tr S120/170) This large colonial mansion is an atmospheric yet unpretentious place to lay your head, with spacious rooms set around a large, plant-filled stone courtyard. When demand is low, good-value single rooms go for S60.

Hostal Las Orquídeas GUESTHOUSE $$
(☎041-47-8271; www.hostallasorquideas.com; Ayacucho 1231; s/d/tr incl breakfast S80/110/120; @🛜) This upscale guesthouse offers tile-floor rooms that are bright and open, and the public area is decorated with cheerful colors and some wood and artsy accents. Some rooms are more appealing than others; the renovated rooms at the front of the building offer carpeted walls and granite-slab bathrooms although the TVs are still old-school.

Eating

Moving east across the Andes, Chachapoyas is the first place where you begin finding Amazonian-style dishes, though with local variations. *Juanes* (steamed rice with fish or chicken, wrapped in a banana leaf) are made with yucca instead of rice. *Cecina,* a dish made from dehydrated pork in the lowlands, is often made with beef.

El Tejado PERUVIAN $
(Santo Domingo 426; mains S15-25; ⏲noon-4pm) This charming little spot doesn't look much from the outside, but a lovely interior courtyard and dining room awaits. It's a great lunch spot, with *menús* (set meals) for S8 Monday to Friday. The specialty is *tacu-tacu* (a Peruvian fusion dish of rice, beans and a protein), seen here in nine varieties.

Its version of *lomo saltado* (strips of beef stir-fried with onions, tomatoes, potatoes and chili) is conversation-stopping good.

La Tushpa STEAKHOUSE, PERUVIAN $
(Ortiz Arrieta 753; mains S15-30; ⌚1-11pm) Service is infamously slow but always worth the wait at this classic steakhouse. The meat-heavy menu is highlighted by the *cuadril* (tri-tip), a succulent beef cut, and interesting creations such as *lomo fino* (sirloin) with a spicy pisco sauce. There's a good deal of pork and chicken to choose from as well, all with delicious house sauces.

Café Fusiones CAFE, BREAKFAST $
(www.cafefusiones.com; Ayacucho, Plaza de Armas; breakfast S8-11, light meals S4-15; ⌚7am-1pm & 2-9:30pm; 📶) The traveler congregation gathers at this artsy cafe on the plaza that serves organic coffee and espresso, good breakfasts (including regional choices such as *juanes*), lentil burgers and other light meals. There is also a book exchange, travel agency and fair-trade shop selling regional products.

Terra Mia Café BREAKFAST, PERUVIAN $
(Chincha Alta 557; breakfast S12.50-13.50; ⌚7am-10:30pm; 📶) A chic spot with the fanciest espresso machine in town. Its wonderful menu has regional and international breakfasts (ahem...waffles!), plus sandwiches and salads all served up in a cozy and clean atmosphere with colonial archways and indigenous-motif seat cushions. Service could be a lot better though.

Dulcería Santa Elena DESSERTS $
(Amazonas 800-804; cakes S2-5; ⌚8am-9pm) The crotchety old man here serves the town's best pastries and cakes; if he likes you, though, he might throw something in for free.

★ **El Batan de Tayta** PERUVIAN $$
(☎959-865-539; La Merced 604; mains S15-46; ⌚11am-11pm Sun-Thu, to midnight Fri & Sat) This hip bar-restaurant serves creative versions of traditional dishes and great fusion cuisine, plated with style on pieces of granite and inverted terra-cotta roof tiles. Try the *arroz shutito con bife y chica de jora* (creamy rice with tenderloin and a touch of maize liquor) or house specialty *cuy borracho* (literally 'drunk guinea pig'; *cuy* with Andean potatoes and herb sauce).

To accompany your meal there is a full menu of exotic sours, *chilcanos* (a broth of fish chunks flavored with the native cilantro herb) and cocktails made from local gourmet ingredients. If you're feeling brave, order the *caspioleta de hormigas* (S25) – an outlandish cocktail featuring edible ants, vanilla, cognac and cinnamon.

Drinking & Nightlife

Chachapoyas is famous for its artisan liqueurs, which come in all sorts of herbal and fruit flavors – working your way through them all makes for a definite good time.

★ **La Reina** BAR
(Ayacucho 520; ⌚9am-1pm & 3pm-1am Mon-Sat, 7pm-midnight Sun) An artsy spot to lubricate your mind very cheaply on exotic fruit and Amazonian liqueurs by the shot (S1.50) or the jar (from S18). There are 11 to choose from, including *mora* (blackberry), the most popular; *maracuyá* (passion fruit), the best; and seven *raíces* and *chuchuhuasi,* two notorious Amazonian aphrodisiacs.

The same owners run the best disco in town, a few blocks down at Ayacucho 345.

ℹ Information

Banco de la Nación (cnr Ayacucho & 2 de Mayo) Has a Visa/MasterCard ATM.

BCP (Plaza Burgos) Changes US dollars and has an ATM.

iPerú (☎041-47-7292; iperuchachapoyas@promperu.gob.pe; Ortiz Arrieta 582; ⌚9am-6pm Mon-Sat, to 1pm Sun) Excellent maps, transportation information and recommendations.

Policía Nacional (☎041-47-7017; Amazonas 1220)

Serpost (Salamanca 940; ⌚8am-1pm & 2-7pm Mon-Fri, 8am-1pm Sat) Postal services; in the market district.

ℹ Getting There & Away

AIR

Although Chachapoyas has an airport, at the time of writing no carriers flew in or out of it.

BUS & TAXI

Apart from luxury long-distance buses, all transport leaves from the new **terminal** (Triunfo cuadra 2) on the eastern edge of town.

The frequently traveled route to Chiclayo and on to Lima starts along the vista-lined route to Pedro Ruíz along the Río Utcubamba. The very comfortable **Movil Tours** (☎041-47-8545; Libertad 464) has an express bus to Lima at 11am, as well as a bus to Trujillo at 7:30pm and Chiclayo at 8pm. **Civa** (☎041-47-8048; cnr Ortiz

ROADS TO CHACHAPOYAS: A TEST OF NERVES OR STAMINA

Having sufficiently soaked up both the coastal sun and highland colonial atmosphere in the mountains, travelers often find themselves itching for a little cloud forest and jungle action. Off to Tarapoto and Chachapoyas you go, right? Not so fast. First, you must decide: do you have the heart, patience and nerves of steel to brave the astonishingly scenic but hopelessly nerve-wracking mountain route via Celendín and Leimebamba? Or would you be more comfortable taking the long way round on the highway from Chiclayo? Decisions. Decisions.

Via Celendín

This rough but beautiful road climbs over a 3085m pass before plummeting steeply to the Río Marañón at the shabby and infernally hot village of **Balsas** (975m), 55km from Celendín. The road climbs again, through gorgeous cloud forests and countryside swathed in a lush quilt a million shades of green. It emerges 57km later at **Abra de Barro Negro** (Black Mud Pass; 3678m), which offers the highest viewing point of the drive, over the Río Marañón, more than three vertical kilometers below. Ghostly low-level clouds and mists hug the dispersed communities in this part of the trip and creep eerily among the hills. The road then drops for 32km to Leimebamba at the head of the Río Utcubamba valley and follows the river as it descends past Tingo and on to Chachapoyas.

Although the road has recently been paved, it remains a narrow, high-altitude twist fest. With no guardrails in sight, your life teeters precariously on the edge around every corner. Your only hope is that the driver knows the nuances of the road intimately. Travelers should carry water and food (and maybe a valium), as the few restaurants en route are poor.

Despite the thrills, accidents involving buses on this route are very rare, with most drivers taking a very slow and steady approach. Heading north, the left side of the bus affords the most scenic viewing time, but the right side is less nauseating for those who fear heights.

Via Chiclayo

Considerably longer and immeasurably less thrilling is the usual route for travelers to Chachapoyas. From the old Panamericana 100km north of Chiclayo, a paved road heads east over the Andes via the 2145m Porculla Pass, the lowest Peruvian pass going over the Andean continental divide. The route then tumbles to the Río Marañón valley. About 190km from the Panamericana turnoff, you reach the turnoff to the town of Jaén, the beginning of a newly opened route to Ecuador. Continuing east, a short side road reaches the town of Bagua Chica in a low, enclosed valley (elevation about 500m), which Peruvians claim is the hottest town in the country. The bus usually goes through Bagua Grande (population 28,830) on the main road, and follows the Río Utcubamba valley to the crossroads town of Pedro Ruíz, about 1½ hours from Bagua Grande. From here, a paved southbound road branches to Chachapoyas, 54km and about one hour away.

Arrieta y Salamanca) has a daily bus to Chiclayo (6:30pm) and Lima (1pm).

Virgen del Carmen (☎041-79-7707; Terminal Terrestre) runs comfortable buses on the scenic mountain route to Cajamarca via Celendín and Leimebamba daily at 5am and 8pm, though staff may be a little stingy about selling a seat only to Leimebamba. A number of companies operate direct *combi* service to Leimebamba.

To continue further into the Amazon Basin, **Turismo Selva** (☎961-659-443; Terminal de Transporte) runs direct minivans to Tarapoto via Moyobamba at 6:30am, 8:30am, 10:30am and 12:30pm. There is also a 2:30pm service just to Moyobamba.

Alternatively, take one of the frequent *combis* to Pedro Ruíz where you can pick up an eastbound bus to continue on to Tarapoto (S35, seven hours), which pass most frequently between 4pm and 11pm.

For Jaén and the border route to Ecuador, you'll need to catch a *combi* to Bagua Grande, which leave frequently from 4am to 6pm and switch for a *combi* to Jaén (S5, one hour).

A taxi for a full-day trip to sites around Chachapoyas and Leimebamba costs S250 to S300.

Chachapoyas Buses:

Destination	Cost (S)	Duration (hr)
Bagua Grande	10	2¼
Cajamarca	50	12
Celendín	30	8
Chiclayo	30-75	9
Kuélap	15	2½
Leimebamba	10	2½
Lima	90-150	22
Moyobamba	24	5
Pedro Ruíz	5	1
Tarapoto	35	7
Tingo Viejo	6	1

Around Chachapoyas

Relics of Chachapoya and Inca civilizations, and daring, rugged scenery speckle the mountains surrounding Chachapoyas. Scores of archaeological sites dot this area, most of them unexcavated and many reclaimed by vivacious jungle.

Gran Vilaya

The name Gran Vilaya refers to the bountiful valleys that spread out west of Chachapoyas, reaching toward the rushing Río Marañón. Abutting the humid Amazon, this region sits in a unique microcosm of perennially moist high-altitude tropics and cloud forests – an ecological anomaly that gave rise to the Chachapoya culture's moniker: 'People of the Clouds'.

The fertility of this lush area was never a big secret – the valley successfully supported the huge populations of the Chachapoya and Inca cultures, and to date more than 30 archaeological sites have been found dotting the mountains. Important sites such as **Paxamarca**, **Pueblo Alto**, **Pueblo Nuevo** and **Pirquilla** lie connected by winding goat-tracks as they did hundreds of years ago, completely unexcavated, and can be visited on multiday hikes. Immaculately constructed Inca roads weave up and around the hills, past many ruined cities camouflaged by centuries of jungle.

The breathtaking, impossibly green and silt-filled **Valle de Belén** lies at the entrance of Gran Vilaya. The flat valley floor here is dissected by the mouth of the widely meandering Río Huaylla, coiled like a languid serpent. Filled with grazing cattle, horses and surrounded on all sides by mist-covered hills, the vistas here are mesmerizing.

Most travel agencies in Chachapoyas offer multiday trekking tours of this region with the classic four-day circuit beginning at Cohechán and ending at Kueláp via Choctámal. Hikers should be in good physical condition as the trek requires some serious ascents at altitude.

Karajía

This extraordinary funerary site hosts **six sarcophagi** perched high up a sheer cliff face. Each long-faced tomb is constructed from wood, clay and straw and is uniquely shaped like a stylized forlorn individual. The characters stare intently over the valley below, where a Chachapoya village once stood; you can see stone ruins scattered among the fields today.

Originally there were eight coupled sarcophagi, but two have collapsed, opening up the adjoining coffins – which were found to contain mummies, plus various crafts and artifacts relating to the deceased. Look out for scattered bones below the coffins. Only important individuals were buried with such reverence: shamans, warriors and chieftains. The skulls above the tombs are thought to have been trophies of enemies or possibly human sacrifices. Locals charge a S5 admission fee.

Karajía is a 40-minute walk from the tiny outpost of Cruz Pata, which is two hours from Chachapoyas. Minibuses from Chachapoyas travel to Luya (S7, 50 minutes), from where minibuses go to Cruz Pata (S5, 50 minutes). All said and done, a day tour from Chachapoyas (S50) is the way to go; the hiking and drive time is a big investment to stare with binoculars for a few minutes at a set of cliffs 100m away.

Revash

Near the town of Santo Tomás, Revash is an excellent site of several brightly colored funerary buildings tucked into limestone cliff

BORDER CROSSING: ECUADOR VIA JAÉN

If your next port of call is Ecuador, remember that you don't have to spend days on winding roads to get back to the Peruvian coast. From Jaén, a good northbound road heads 107km to San Ignacio (population 10,720) near the Ecuadorian border, on the other side of which you'll find the town of Zumba.

Begin at the fast-growing agricultural center of Jaén (population 70,690), which has all the services of a midsized town...along with a reputation for street crime and, judging by the signs, a serious dengue problem (bring repellent). The best hotel in town is **Casa del Sol** (076-43-4478; Mariscal Castilla 140; s/d/tr S70/120/170;), just off the plaza, which has spotless modern rooms, some with Jacuzzi. A block away, **Hotel Cancún** (076-43-3511; Palomino 1413; s/d S35/45;) is a solid budget choice, with hot-water showers and cable TV. For a bite, **Restaurante El Sabor** (Plaza de Armas; meals S10-12; 8am-10pm) on the plaza does a whole lot of everything for all budgets.

From Jaén, *autos* (shared taxis; S20, 2½ hours) and *combis* (S15, 2½ hours) leave for **San Ignacio** from **Empresa Transporte Jaén-San Ignacio** (Pakumuros 2093, Pueblo Libre; 4am-8pm). In San Ignacio there's a simple hotel and places to eat. Change in San Ignacio for a *colectivo* (shared transportation) for the rough road to **La Balsa** (S15, two hours) on the Río Blanco, dividing Peru from Ecuador. There used to be a *balsa* (ferry) here (hence the name), but there's now a new international bridge linking the countries.

Once in Ecuador, curious yet typical *rancheras* (trucks with rows of wooden seats) await to take you on the uncomfortable and unpredictable (because of the weather) 10km drive to **Zumba** (US$2.75, 1½ to 2½ hours). From here, buses go to **Loja** (US$7.50, six hours), where you can continue on to the famed 'valley of longevity' of **Vilcabamba**. If you leave Jaén at dawn, you should be able to make it to Vilcabamba in one day.

ledges. Looking a bit like attractive, yet inaccessible, cottages, these *chullpas* (ancient Andean funerary towers) are made of small, mud-set stones that were plastered over and embellished with red and cream paints. This bright taste in decor is still clearly visible today.

While much of the site was looted long ago, the skeletons of 11 adults and one child, along with a wealth of artifacts such as musical instruments and tools made from bones, were found inside by archaeologists. A number of pictographs decorate the walls of the cliff behind the tombs, and a now-empty funerary cave, originally containing more than 200 funerary bundles, lies 1km from the main set of tombs.

The shortest route to the site is to take a Leimebamba-bound *combi* and get off in Yerbabuena, from where it's a 1½-hour hike or a S20 ride in a *mototaxi* to the entrance at Cruz de San Bartolo. From the entrance it's a further 4.5km hike to the archaeological site. If you're up for the hunt, ask around in San Bartolo for a man who can set you up with horses. A day tour from Chachapoyas is about S80 and also visits the museum in Leimebamba.

La Jalca (Jalca Grande)

Lovely little mountain town La Jalca, also known as Jalca Grande, is a small, cobblestoned municipality that has managed to retain much of its historical roots, though modernization is slowly creeping its way in. Quechua is still spoken by older residents here and Chachapoya-influenced architecture can be seen around the town. Look for **Choza Redonda**, a traditional Chachapoya house that was supposedly continually inhabited until 1964. It was used as a model for the re-creation of Chachapoya houses in Kuélap and Levanto. The roof has collapsed but it remains one of the best-preserved indigenous houses in the region.

At the ruins of **Ollape**, a 30-minute walk west of La Jalca, you can see several house platforms and circular balconies decorated with complex designs.

There is one direct *combi* from Chachapoyas to La Jalca (S10, two hours) leaving at 3pm from the bus terminal and returning to Chachapoyas at 5am. Otherwise, take a Chachapoyas–Leimebamba bus and ask to be let off at the La Jalca turnoff, from where it's a three-hour hike up the hill.

DON'T MISS

CATARATA DE GOCTA

This 771m waterfall, **Catarata de Gocta** (admission S10; ⏲6am-4pm), somehow escaped the notice of the Peruvian government, international explorers and prying satellite images until 2005, when German Stefan Ziemendorff and a group of locals put together an expedition to map the falls and record their height. Various claims ranging from the third-loftiest waterfall on earth to the 15th resulted in an international firestorm in the always-exciting contest to rank the world's highest cascades.

Whether you're hung up on numbers or not, there is no doubt that Gocta is impressive and fairly accessible. It's easiest to go with a tour company from Chachapoyas for about S30 – it will provide transportation and a local guide for the two-hour hike to the falls – as transport to the site is irregular. If you are determined to go it alone, catch a *combi* (minibus) from Chachapoyas to Pedro Ruíz (S5, 45 minutes) and ask to be let off at the Puente de Cocahuayaco. If you are lucky, you'll find a *mototaxi* or passing *combi* to take you to the falls entrance at Cocachimba, otherwise it's a 1½-hour hike. From the entrance, it's another two-hour hike to the base of the falls. The communal tourism association arranges guides for S30.

If you're feeling particularly physical, it's possible to visit both the upper and lower cascades on an eight-hour circuit. Take any Pedro Ruíz–bound *combi* to the turnoff to San Pablo. From here it's a two-hour hike to San Pablo village, from where a trail leads to the base of the upper cascade. Doubling back on the same path, another trail on the left-hand side leads down the mountain to a fantastic lookout with a clear view of both cascades, and then across a suspension bridge to the base of the lower section. From here you exit along the main trail to Cocachimba. You will need to leave Chachapoyas at 6am in order to complete the loop.

The classy **Gocta Andes Lodge** (☎041-63-0552; www.goctalodge.com; s/d S209/249; 🏊), in Cocachimba, is one of the special spots in the northern highlands, sitting on a severely idyllic setting with unimpeded views to the falls, both from the rooms and the small infinity pool. Spacious but simple rooms feature lovely kaleidoscopic textiles, cozy down comforters, vaulted ceilings and balconies, which frame the falls like a painting.

If you can't swing the cash, the village supports a small cottage tourism industry with several cheaper options, a few restaurants and shops.

Yalape

On the road between Chachapoyas and Levanto, these ruins of limestone residential buildings make an easy day trip from Chachas. With good views of Levanto below and Kuélap in the distance, Yalape has some decent defense walls with some frieze patterns, all impressed with lots of forest growth.

Across the road from the ruins is a reconstructed Chachapoya house built on the original stone base.

Combis to Levanto (S5, one hour) leave at 5am and 11am from the terminal and can drop you at the entrance. The *combis* turn around in Levanto and head straight back down. It's a 12km hike back down the hill to Chachapoyas along stretches of Inca trail. It is paved with stone in some parts and muddy in others – bring boots.

Kuélap

ELEV 3100M

Matched in grandeur only by the ruins of Machu Picchu, this fabulous, ruined citadel city in the mountains southwest of Chachapoyas is the best preserved and most dramatic of the district's extraordinary archaeological sites. This monumental stone-fortified citadel crowns a craggy limestone mountain and affords exceptional panoramas of a land once inhabited by the Chachapoya. The site receives remarkably few visitors, although that might change with the construction of a proposed cable car. Those who make it here get to witness one of the most significant and impressive pre-Columbian ruins in all of South America.

Sights & Activities

Constructed between AD 500 and 1493, and rediscovered in 1843, **Kuélap** (adult/child

S15/2; ⌚8am-5pm) is made up of millions of cubic feet of remarkably preserved stone. Juan Crisóstomo Nieto, a judge working in the Chachapoyas area who discovered the ruins, originally said more stone was used in its construction than for the Great Pyramid of Egypt, a comparison that mathematically makes no sense, but nonetheless conveys his intended message: there's a lot of stone here! Though the stonework is not as elaborate as that of the Incas, the 700m-long oval fortress is surrounded by an imposing, near-impenetrable wall that towers on average around 20m high. Entrance into this stronghold is via three deep, lean gates which some believe to be an ingenious security system that forced attacking parties into easily defeated single files.

Insidc are three levels scattered with the remnants of more than 400 circular dwellings. Some are decorated with zigzag and rhomboid friezes, and all were once topped by soaring thatched roofs. One dwelling has been reconstructed, although shoddy work means it's in danger of collapse. In its heyday, Kuélap housed up to 3500 people and, surrounded by wispy cloud, must have been a breathtaking sight.

The most impressive and enigmatic structure, named **El Tintero** (Inkpot), is in the shape of a large inverted cone. Inside, an underground chamber houses thc remains of animal sacrifices, leading archaeologists to believe that it was a religious building of some kind. Kuélap resident archaeologist Alfredo Narvez has now excavated graves and llama skeletons around El Tintero to further support this theory. A 1996 hypothesis by a team from the University of San Diego suggests it may have also been a solar calendar. Another building is a lookout tower with excellent 360-degree vistas. The mountain summit on which the whole city sits is surrounded by abundant greenery, towering bromeliad-covered trees and exotic orchids. Keep an eye out for the citadel's only modern residents – a herd of llamas, but don't get too close as they sometimes spit and kick.

Tour groups usually arrive at the ruins around 11:30am and leave by 3pm, so consider spending the night nearby if you are after a more individual experience.

From the car park and ticket office it is a 25-minute hike uphill to the citadel.

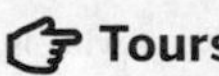

Tours

The guardians at Kuélap are very friendly and helpful; one is almost always on hand to show visitors around and answer questions. Don José Gabriel Portocarrero Chávez runs the ticket booth and has been there for years; he no longer guides but can set you up with a Spanish-speaking guide from the association (S30).

Sleeping & Eating

Kuélap itself has limited sleeping options, although there are a couple of basic *hospedajes* in family homes down an often-muddy trail from the ruins. Ask for Doña Teodula or Doña Juana; both offer basic rooms with cold showers and budget meals can be arranged. Bringing your own sleeping bag is recommended.

The next closest sleeping choices and a step up in quality are in the hamlet of María, a two-hour walk from Kuélap and connected to Chachapoyas by daily minibuses. Here you will find a cottage industry of half a dozen charming and near-identical *hospedajes* (rooms per person S15) – they all go to the same sign-maker for their signs. All offer clean, modest rooms with electric hot water and some will cook hearty meals for guests for about S10.

Hospedaje el Torreón HOTEL $
(☎94-170-8040; Av Kuélep s/n; s/d S20/30) This basic hotel is your best bet in María, with perfectly decent rooms accented with colorful bedspreads, plus hot water. The friendly owner doesn't cook, though, so you'll need to hit a restaurant or buy some of her cakes that she sells to townsfolk.

Hospedaje León GUESTHOUSE $
(☎94-171-5685; s/d S15/30) In Tingo Viejo, 3km below Tingo Nuevo at the far base of Kuélap, is this basic place with tiny, bucolic rooms and electric hot water. It's run by a friendly older couple who capitalized on a tourism vision years ago. This is about as good as it gets around Tingo Viejo.

Estancia Chillo LODGE $$
(☎979-340-444, 041-63-0510; www.estanciaelchillo.com; r per person incl breakfast & dinner S140) Five kilometres south of Tingo Viejo, this is one of the coolest and quirkiest places to stay in the area. The beautiful hacienda-style compound has rustic and well-designed rooms with the requisite gaudy bedspreads,

rounded out by ranch props, wagon wheels, brightly colored pet parrots wandering the grounds and dangling bougainvillea. All fixtures were handmade by the owner Oscar Arce Cáceres.

You can organize guides from here (per day S150) as well as horses or donkeys to explore nearby ruins.

Getting There & Around

By far the easiest way to visit Kuélap is on a guided tour from Chachapoyas (S35), even if you just use the transport and then split off from the group. Getting to Kuélap on your own is a bit of a mission. A 9.8km trail climbs from the south end of Tingo Viejo to the ruins, situated about 1200m above the town. It is relatively easy to follow, but it's an exhausting, often hot, climb; allow at least six hours. Remember to bring water as none is available along the trail. During rainy season (October to April), especially the latter half, the trail can become very muddy and travel can be difficult. You can also hike to Kuélap from María in under two hours.

Transportes Roller (Terminal Terrestre) has one bus to Kuélap (S15, 2½ hours), via Tingo Viejo, Choctámal and María, leaving Chachapoyas at 4am and returning from Kuélap at 6am, although it only runs when there is sufficient demand. A more regular but less convenient service run by **Evangelio Poder de Dios** (Terminal Terrestre) leaves the terminal in Chachapoyas at 2pm, returning from the ruins at 5am the next day. Once at Kuélap you can ask about getting a ride back to Chachapoyas with returning tour-group *combis*. Frequent *combis* (S8, 50 minutes) run between Tingo Viejo and Chachapoyas.

A round-trip taxi from Chachapoyas to Kuélap will set you back S200 to S250, depending on how long you want to spend at the site. A proposed new cable car from Tingo Nuevo would make visiting the site easier, although it may also bring a detrimental increase in visitors to the poorly protected structures.

Leimebamba

041 / POP 4200 / ELEV 2050M

This convivial cobblestoned town – often spelled 'Leymebamba' – lies at the head of the Río Utcubamba. It has an endearingly laid-back allure that is maintained by its relative isolation: it is flanked by towering mountains and the nearest big city is a couple of hours away via a narrow road. Horses are still a popular form of transport around town and the friendliness of the townsfolk is legendary in the region. Surrounded by a multitude of archaeological sites from the Chachapoya era, this is a great place to base yourself while exploring the province.

Sights & Activities

★Museo Leimebamba MUSEUM
(www.museoleymebamba.org; adult/student S15/8; 10am-4:30pm) The mummies found at Laguna de los Cóndores are housed in the Museo Leimebamba, 3km south of town. The museum is owned by the local community and is housed in a wonderfully constructed complex with multitiered roofs that pays tribute to indigenous architecture. The mummies are stored behind glass in a climate-controlled room. Most are wrapped in bundles, although some have been unwrapped for your gruesome viewing pleasure.

Other well-presented artifacts on display include ceramics, textiles, wood figures and photos of Laguna de los Cóndores. A taxi/*mototaxi* from town costs S7/5 respectively.

La Congona RUIN
The most captivating of the many ancient ruins strewn around Leimebamba, La Congona is definitely worth the three-hour hike needed to get here. The flora-covered site contains several well-preserved circular houses, one of which, oddly for Chachapoya culture, sits on a square base. Inside, the houses are adorned with intricate niches; outside, wide circular terraces surround each house.

This archaeological site is renowned for the intricate decoration on the buildings and particularly for the numerous sophisticated masonry friezes. A tall tower can be climbed by a remarkable set of curving steps for wide-angle panoramas of the surrounding valley.

The site is reached from Leimebamba along a path beginning at the lower end of Calle 16 de Julio. A guide is recommended; expect to pay around S150 for the complete eight-hour circuit. It's also possible to rent horses in town to make the journey.

Laguna de los Cóndores ARCHAEOLOGICAL SITE
This part of Peru hit the spotlight in 1996 when a group of farmers found six *chullpas* on a ledge 100m above a cloud-forest lake. This burial site was a windfall for archaeologists, and its 219 mummies and more than 2000 artifacts have given researchers a glimpse past the heavy curtain of history

THE CHACHAPOYA

The Chachapoya (People of the Clouds), controlled the vast swath of land around present-day Chachapoyas from AD 500 to around 1493, when the Incas conquered the area and ended the Chacha isolation. Very little is known about this civilization, whose inhabitants were thought to be great warriors, powerful shamans and prolific builders who were responsible for one of the most advanced civilizations of Peru's tropical jungles. Today, among the many dozens of cliff tombs and hamlets of circular structures left behind, archaeologists match wits with grave robbers in a race for a deeper understanding of the Chachapoya.

The Chachapoya were heavily engaged in trade with other parts of Peru. However, isolated in their cloud-forest realm, they developed independently of these surrounding civilizations. The Chachapoya speculatively cultivated a fierce warrior cult; depicted trophy heads as well as left human skulls show evidence of trepanation and intentional scalping. The eventual expansion of the Inca empire in the 15th century was met with fierce resistance, and sporadic fighting continued well after the initial conquest.

Environmentalists long before Greenpeace, the Chachapoya built structures that were in perfect harmony with their surroundings and that took advantage of nature's aesthetic and practical contributions. The Chachapoya religion is believed to have venerated some of the salient natural features of these territories; the serpent, the condor and the puma were worshipped as powerful representatives of the natural world as were caves, lakes and mountains.

The unique use of circular construction was complemented by intricate masonry friezes, which used zigzags and rhomboids. The buildings were covered by thatch roofs, which were tall and steep to facilitate the runoff of the area's frequent rains. Hundreds of ruins illustrate Chachapoya architecture, but none stand out as much as the impressive fortified citadel of Kuélap (p424), surrounded by a colossal 20m-high wall and encompassing hundreds of dwellings and temples.

that conceals the details of the Chachapoya civilization.

So spectacular was the find that a Discovery Channel film was made about it and a museum was built in Leimebamba to house the mummies and cultural treasures. Some of the tombs, plastered and painted in white or red-and-yellow ochre, are decorated with signature Chachapoya zigzag friezes. All lie huddled against the cliff on a natural ledge overlooking the stunning Laguna de los Cóndores.

The only way to get to the laguna is by a strenuous 10- to 12-hour journey on foot and horseback from Leimebamba. The standard tour is three days: one day to hike in, a day of sightseeing and an eight- to nine-hour return journey. Horses and guides can be arranged either in Leimebamba or at travel agencies in Chachapoyas.

Tours

Local guides can arrange trips to the tombs and various other sites; some are easily visited on a day trip, while others require several days.

The best place to find professional guides is at the **Asociación Comunal de Turismo** (95-107-2028; jabierfarje@hotmail.com), a community-run cooperative on the main plaza. It offers a package to Laguna de los Cóndores for S540 that includes guide, admission, horses, accommodations, food, ponchos and rubber boots. All you need to bring is a spare set of clothes, a flashlight and some bug spray. It also offers an extended version of the trek that takes in Laguna Quinticocha, which offers panoramic views of the area.

Another recommended hike is La Petaca, an area south of town that was a center of Chachapoya agriculture. Along the trail there are numerous ruins of ceremonial and residential structures.

For longer trips, it's best to reserve before you arrive in Leimebamba.

Sleeping & Eating

La Casona GUESTHOUSE **$$**
(041-83-0106; www.casonadeleymebamba.com; Amazonas 221; s/d incl breakfast S120/205;) This friendly, rambling guesthouse run

by a brother-sister team is chock-full of antiquated character and homespun charm. Old rooms feature polished hardwood floors while all feature new bathrooms with hot water. Some also have little balconies looking onto the quiet street below, while others have views over the town's tiled roofs and surrounding mountains.

Nelly, the matriarch here, runs a mean kitchen for guests. Breakfast is a real treat, with an espresso machine along with home-made cheese, butter and milk from their own cows.

★Kentitambo GUESTHOUSE $$$

(☎97-111-8273; www.kentitambo.com; s/d incl breakfast S348/498; 📶) This wonderfully romantic guesthouse in front of the museum is an exclusive getaway for discerning nature lovers. King-sized beds and filtered rain-water showers are highlights of the colorful, rustic bungalows built in earthquake-proof *quincho* style. But the real coup is the spacious front porch with hammocks that reach into the surrounding nature – perfect for ogling the exotic birdlife congregating on the property.

Reservations are essential. It's located next to KentiKafé.

★Sabor del Mishqui PERUVIAN $

(☎95-269-3474; Amazonas 338; menús S7-15; ⏰7am-9pm) Relocated from near the museum to the center of town, Leimebamba's best chef whips up fantastic home-style set meals that include soup, salad, a wide choice of mains and pudding. They are tasty, filling and outrageously good value.

KentiKafé CAFE $

(snacks S3.50-10; ⏰8:30am-5:30pm; 📶) Just a short stroll across the street from Museo Leimebamba and perched on a hill with views of the valley below, KentiKafé serves gourmet coffee, homemade cakes and wonderful sandwiches. The surrounding garden is visited by 17 hummingbird species – including the marvelous spatuletail.

It maintains about a dozen feeders through which the birds drink some 5kg of sugar per day. You can lie in wait for glimpses of the spatuletail while sipping your espresso; or pay S10 to visit the feeders further afield in a quieter area away from espresso-cup clanking.

Shopping

AMAL HANDICRAFTS

(San Augín 429; ⏰9am-6pm) Located on the plaza, AMAL is a women's artisan co-operative selling top-grade handicrafts and local weavings. Better than the shop, however, is heading up to the small workshop about a five-minute walk along the road to the museum. Here, you can see them in action and choose your own material to custom-design anything from purses to backpacks.

Information

There is a no-name internet spot two blocks downhill from Virgen del Carmen. Leimebamba doesn't have an ATM; bring cash.

Getting There & Away

Raymi Express (☎942-152-181; Amazonas 420) has minivans that depart for Chachapoyas (S8, 2½ hours) at 5am, 6am, 6:30am and noon daily. **Hidalgo Tours** (Bolívar 608) goes at 6am for the same price.

Virgen del Carmen (☎96-483-3033; Plaza de Armas) has a bus to Chachapoyas (S10, 2½ hours) from Celendín that passes through at about 2pm. In the reverse direction, heading toward Celendín (S20, six hours) and Cajamarca (S30, eight hours), they pass at about 8am and 10pm.

Amazonas Express runs the Chachapoyas–Celendín route with minivans, with departures at 7:30am and 9:30pm to Celendín (S25, six hours), and at 1pm and 11pm to Chachapoyas (S10, two hours).

Pedro Ruíz

This dusty transit town sits at the junction of the Chiclayo–Tarapoto road and the turnoff to Chachapoyas. When traveling from Chachapoyas, you can board east- or westbound buses here. The highway on both sides of the town is particularly susceptible to landslides. If it's wet, check on conditions before making plans.

The journey east from Pedro Ruíz is spectacular, climbing over two high passes, traveling by a beautiful lake and dropping into fantastic high-jungle vegetation in between.

Pedro has a Visa/MasterCard ATM on Av Marginal across from the PetroPeru gas station.

DARLING, YOU LOOK MARVELOUS!

You don't have to be a big-time bird-watcher to get turned on by the marvelous spatuletail *(Loddigesia mirabilis)*, a rare and exquisitely beautiful hummingbird that lives in limited habitats of scrubby forest between 2000m and 2900m in northern Peru's Utcubamba Valley. As with most bird species, the males get the prize in the looks category, and the marvelous male is no exception, with his shimmering blue crown and green throat, and a sexy set of curved and freakishly long quills that splay out from his backside and end in wide, feather 'rackets' or 'spatules.' He can independently maneuver these long plumes into extravagant mating displays, crossing the two spatuletail feathers over each other or swinging them in front of his head as he hovers in front of a female.

According to some Peruvians in the Utcubamba Valley, the spatuletail's most spectacular anatomical feature is its heart, which is considered an aphrodisiac when eaten. The hunting of the birds for this purpose has probably contributed to keeping its numbers low – perhaps less than 1000 pairs remain – although conservation efforts in the region have led to increased awareness about the precarious status of the bird, whose habitat is quickly diminishing due to deforestation and agricultural development, and the need to protect it. Leading this effort are local conservation centers such as KentiKafé (p428) in Leimebamba or the **Marvelous Spatuletail Interpretation Center** (www.ecoan-peru.com; admission S30, s/d incl breakfast S198/363; ⏲6am-6pm), known colloquially as Heumbo, 15 minutes west of Pomacochas on the road to Pedro Ruíz. The Interpretation Center maintains feeders on a 12-hectare private reserve that attracts this and many other hummingbirds; you'll have a great chance of seeing the marvelous spatuletail in all its glory. The views over the valley and the plunging road from the center are also spectacular – you can spend the night here as well.

Sleeping & Eating

The main avenues, Cahuide and Marginal, are lined with local restaurants. **Virgen de Chuquichaca** (Av Marginal; menú S6-9, mains S10-15; ⏲7am-9pm) is purportedly the cleanest and the *lomo saltado* worked out for us.

Casablanca Hotel HOTEL **$**
(☎941-902-878; Marginal 122; s/d/tr S30/70/90) The pick of the none-too-inspiring hotels in Pedro Ruíz is by the road junction, but try to get a room away from the noisy highway. Rooms are basic but perfectly decent with cable TV and hot water.

Getting There & Away

Buses from the coast pick up passengers heading to Rioja or Moyobamba (S25 to S30, five hours) and Tarapoto (S30 to S35, seven hours), and in the opposite direction to Chiclayo (S30, seven hours) and Lima (S70 to S135, 18 to 22 hours). The most comfortable choice is **Movil Tours** (☎83-0085; Cahuide 653), which departs east at 6am and 11am and west for Lima at 2pm, 2:30pm and 7:30pm. **Civa** (☎94-172-7323; Marginal s/n) heads east at 2pm and west to Chiclayo and Lima at 1pm.

Among the more economical choices is **TSP** (☎99-845-5075; Cahuide 890), heading to Tarapoto at 4pm, 8pm and 10pm, and Lima at 5pm and 8pm. There are several other options as well.

If coming from Tarapoto, Los Diplomados, next to the PetroPeru gas station, runs *combis* to Chachapoyas (S5) from 4am to 6pm every 30 minutes or so.

Moyobamba

☎042 / POP 83,500 / ELEV 860M

Moyobamba, the capital of the department of San Martín, was founded in 1542, but earthquakes (most recently in 1990 and 1991) have contributed to the demise of any historic buildings. Nevertheless, Moyobamba is a pleasant enough town to spend a few days in and local tourist authorities working together with local communities have developed a number of ecological activities in the area. The region is famed for its orchids; there's an **orchid festival** in October and a giant orchid statue guards the town's entrance.

Sights & Activities

Reserva Tingana NATURE RESERVE
(☎042-78-2803, 942-958-538; www.tingana.org; tour S70-100) This community-run nature reserve protects a swath of forest on the upper Río Mayo that is home to monkeys and a

DON'T MISS

STRICTLY FOR THE BIRDS...& THE MONKEYS

The 2960-hectare **Abra Patricia-Alto Nieva Private Conservation Area** (☎041-816-814; www.ecoanperu.org; admission S75, s/d incl meals & admission S444/726, without bathroom S396/660), about 40 minutes east of Pedro Ruíz on the road to Moyobamba (reachable by S35 *colectivo* from Nuevo Cajamarca), is a birdwatcher's paradise managed by the Association of Andean Ecosystems (ECOAN). More than 300 species call this area home, 23 of which are considered globally threatened.

ECOAN's **Owlet Lodge** offers large and exceptionally clean, quiet rooms for nature lovers and anyone who just wants to get away from the noise of civilization. The gourmet meals are served in a dining room with views of mountainous forest that has never seen the swipe of a chainsaw. Although an obvious favorite of bird-watching tour groups (who come to see such endemic species as yellow-scarved tanager, Lulu's tody-tyrant and the extremely rare long-whiskered owlet), it's also the best place to see the critically endangered yellow-tailed woolly monkey.

wide variety of birds, frogs and butterflies. The tourism cooperative offers day tours that include breakfast, lunch and a boat trip. To get here, take a *colectivo* from in front of the Universidad Cesar Vallejo to Puerto La Boca. The guides will pick you up from here in a boat. Reservations are essential.

Mirador Tahuishco VIEWPOINT

(Malecon San Juan) Head to this viewpoint seven blocks northeast of the plaza for supreme panoramas of the river valley below. There are a number of noisy bars in the street behind, disturbing what would be an otherwise peaceful spot. Stairs head down the mountainside to the river port below. Another more tranquil lookout is located a few blocks downstream at **Mirador San Juan**.

Waqanki Orchid Center GARDENS

(www.waqanki.com; Carretera a Baños de San Mateo; admission S10; ⏲7:30am-5pm) About 3km outside town you'll find some 380 species of orchids growing in a beautiful forest. There is also a hummingbird garden and restaurant. Book in advance for birdwatching trips in the forest with a professional guide (US$80).

Baños Termales de San Mateo HOT SPRINGS

(admission S2; ⏲5am-8pm) These well-maintained hot springs, 5km south of town, have six *pozos* (large baths) of varying temperatures in a pleasant garden setting. *Mototaxis* cost S6. On weekends the baths get crowded with locals.

Upper Río Mayo BOAT TOUR

(Puerto de Tahuishco) Short sightseeing trips in narrow boats on the Río Mayo are run out of the impressive new Embarcadero Turístico north of the plaza. It's best to go in the early morning or evening when you'll see more birdlife. Expect to pay S50 to S120 per boat depending on how far you want to travel.

A *mototaxi* to the port costs around S7 or walk down the stairs from Mirador Tahuishco.

Sleeping & Eating

La Casa de Seizo BUNGALOW $

(☎042-78-4766; rumipata@hotmail.com; Contiguo a Los Baños de San Mateo; s/d/tw S60/80/90; 📶) A short walk from the San Mateo hot springs, La Casa de Seizo (formerly Hospedaje Rumipata) is in a verdant and idyllic setting outside Moyobamba. Well appointed exposed-brick rooms are where you'll sleep off the food. Meals are S10 to S20 but the experience is priceless.

The Japanese-Peruvian/Venezuelan couple running the show couldn't be sweeter or better cooks: whether Seizo plucks a tilapia from the pond and turns it into sashimi before your eyes, whips up his garlic-ginger fish or feeds you his cafe-smoked chicken, you are in a for a real treat.

There are two *hospedajes* operating on the property – follow the track right to the end.

El Portón GUESTHOUSE $

(☎042-56-2900; casahospedajeelporton@hotmail.com; San Martín 449; s/d S50/70; 📶) This tranquil downtown choice offers rooms surrounding a well-manicured garden. Rooms are smallish but everything is tidy, and little touches of knickknack charm here and there and a welcoming vibe give it a leg up on the competition.

Hospedaje Santa Rosa GUESTHOUSE **$**
(☎042-50-9890; Canga 478; s/d from S17/35; 📶) A solid shoestring pick, it has a few rudimentary rooms with private bathrooms set around a brick patio. The occasional potted plant helps liven up the concrete-jungle feel.

★**La Casa de Mi Sueño** HOTEL **$$**
(☎042-56-2286; www.lacasademisueno.com; Edmundo del Aguila cuadra 1, Puerto Tahuishco; s/d S90/150; P📶) Set among gorgeous gardens with two lakes surrounded by bamboo and orchids, this peaceful small hotel near the river feels a world away from the horn-honking of downtown. The comfortable modern rooms have excellent bathrooms and balconies hung with hammocks, from where you can spot birds in the green areas below.

★**La Olla de Barro** AMAZONIAN, REGIONAL **$**
(☎042-56-3450; www.laolladebarro.com; cnr Canga & Filomeno; mains S6-18) Don't miss this local institution, set up tiki-lounge-style, where you can double-dare your friends to try fried ants or alligator, all while you savor the phenomenal *inchicapi* (chicken soup with peanuts, cilantro and yucca). This is the best place in town to sample local jungle dishes and river fish, plus exotic regional fruit sours such as *camu-camu* and *cocona*.

Avoid endangered wild *paiche* (local river fish) from October to February, when its fishing is prohibited due to near extinction.

El Matador STEAKHOUSE **$**
(Puno 501; mains S12-23; ⏲6-11:45pm Mon-Sat) Great little upscale (for Moyobamba) steakhouse serving chicken and just five slabs of *carne* (meat) on the *parilla* (grill): sirloin, tri-tip, beefsteak, pork chop and barbecue ribs. There are a few more reds on the wine list than average.

ℹ Information

BCP (Calle de Alvarado 903)

Dircetur (☎956-919-486; www.turismosanmartin.gob.pe; San Martín 301; ⏲7:30am-1pm & 2:30-5:30pm Mon-Fri) Useful departmental tourism office on the corner of the plaza, offering advice for trips throughout the region.

Oficina de Información Tursitica (Plaza de Armas; ⏲8am-1pm & 2:30-5:15pm Mon-Fri) Municipal tourism office dedicated to all things Moyobamba.

ℹ Getting There & Away

Combis to Rioja (S2, 30 minutes), Chachapoyas (S24, seven hours) and Tarapoto (S10, two hours) leave frequently from **Turismo Selva** (Callao 394). *Colectivos* to Tarapoto (S20, two hours) leave from around the corner on Jirón Benavides. For long-distance departures, the bus terminal is on Grau, about 1km from the center. Most buses running between Tarapoto and Chiclayo call in here.

Tarapoto

☎042 / POP 73,000 / ELEV 356M

Tarapoto, the busiest town in the department of San Martín, straddles the base of the Andean foothills and the edge of the vast jungles of eastern Peru. A sweltering rainforest metropolis, it dips its toe into the Amazon Basin while managing to cling to the rest of Peru by the umbilical cord of a long paved road back to civilization. From here you can take the plunge deeper into the Amazon, or just enjoy the easily accessible jungle lite, with plenty of places to stay and eat, and reliable connections to the coast. There's a bunch of natural sights to explore nearby, from waterfalls to lagoons, and river-running opportunities will entertain the adventure-seeking contingent.

👁 Sights

There is little to do in Tarapoto itself, apart from just hanging out in the town's Plaza Mayor, but you can make several excursions to nearby towns, waterfalls and lakes. There is a small regional **museum** (Maynas 174; ⏲8am-noon & 12:30-8pm Mon-Fri) run by the university on Maynas but it was closed for refurbishment at the time of writing.

Laguna Azul LAKE
Also called Laguna de Sauce, this popular local spot is reached by crossing the Río Huallaga, 45km away, on a vehicle raft ferry and continuing by car for another 45 minutes. Day tours (S85 per person, minimum two people) and overnight excursions are available. You'll find good swimming, boating and fishing here, and accommodations, ranging from camping to upscale bungalows, are available. There are also a couple of waterfalls nearby and some fairly undeveloped thermal springs, just after the river crossing.

Several *combis* (S15, two hours) go each day to nearby Sauce from a bus stop on Marginal Sur cuadra 7 in the Banda de Shilcayo district, east of the town. Taxi drivers know it.

Tarapoto

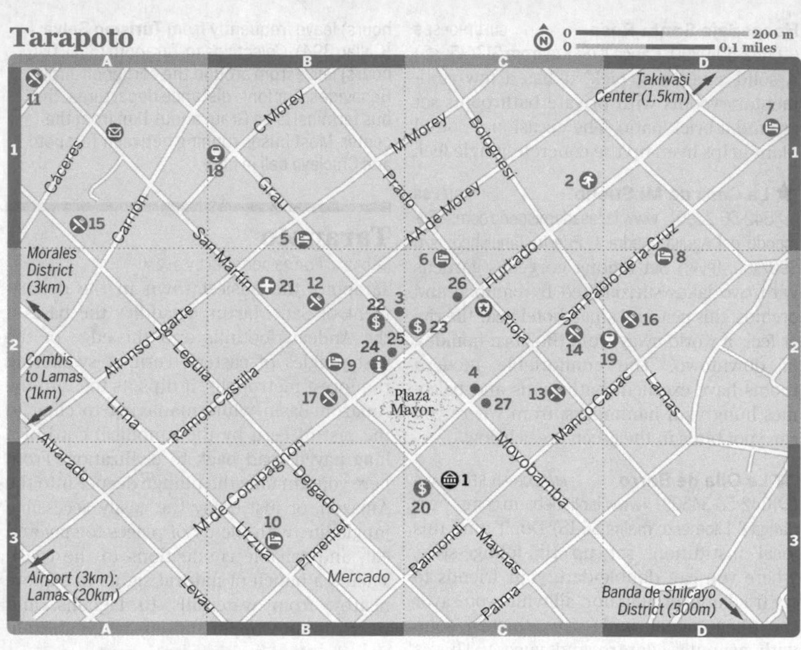

Tarapoto

Sights
- 1 Museo Regional ... C3

Activities, Courses & Tours
- 2 Ecorutas ... C1
- 3 Martín Zamora Tours ... B2
- 4 Shilcayo Travel Tours ... C2

Sleeping
- 5 Alojamiento Grau ... B1
- 6 Casa de Palos ... C2
- 7 El Mirador ... D1
- 8 La Patarashca ... D2
- 9 La Posada Inn ... B2
- 10 Sol de Selva ... B3

Eating
- 11 Brava Grilled ... A1
- 12 Café d' Mundo ... B2
- 13 Chifa Tai Pai ... C2
- 14 El Brassero ... C2
- 15 El Rincón Sureño ... A1
- 16 La Patarashca ... D2
- 17 Supermercado la Inmaculada ... B2

Drinking & Nightlife
- Café Plaza ... (see 17)
- 18 La Alternativa ... B1
- 19 Stonewasi Taberna ... D2

Information
- 20 BCP ... C3
- 21 Clínica San Martín ... B2
- 22 Interbank ... B2
- 23 Scotiabank ... C2
- 24 Tourist Information Office ... B2

Transport
- 25 LAN ... B2
- 26 Peruvian ... C2
- 27 Star Perú ... C2

Alto Shilcayo NATURE RESERVE

(fin Prolongación Alerta; admission S10; ⏲7am-6pm) Just 3km from downtown Tarapoto lies this section of the Aréa de Conservación Regional Cordillera Escalera, which protects dense jungle around the upper Río Shilcayo. The zone is populated by monkeys and many bird species, and there are five rarely visited waterfalls plus a fantastic natural lookout. Some trails become unpassable when very wet.

The local community has formed a tourism cooperative and offers guides for a number of treks, ranging from short trips to the waterfalls to two-night treks finishing on the other side of the reserve at the Yurimaguas highway. They also run a simple jungle *hostal* (guesthouse; per visitor S20) in the middle of the reserve.

Cataratas de Ahuashiyacu WATERFALL
(Carretera Yurimaguas, Km 13) This 40m waterfall is about 45 minutes from Tarapoto toward Yurimaguas. There's a small restaurant nearby and a locally favored swimming spot. Four-hour tours cost around S35 per person. It's possible to reach the entrance, a short walk from the falls, on public *combis* heading toward Yurimaguas. Heading back to town can be a problem though, as most vans return full and you may have to wait for a ride.

Also popular are the **Cataratas de Huacamaillo**, which involve two hours of hiking and wading across the river several times – as a result, they're far less crowded. Tours cost around S85 per person.

To reach the falls on your own, take a *colectivo* from Jirón Comandante Chirinos to the Puente de San Antonio de Cumbaza, from where the trail begins. Taking a guide is recommended.

Chazuta VILLAGE
This small village is famed throughout the region for its elegant pottery. It has artisanal workshops, a small museum showcasing pre-Inca funerary urns, and a port on the Río Huallaga with great fishing. Nearby is the impressive 40m, three-level Tununtunumba waterfalls and the Chazutayacu thermal baths.

Combis (S10, two hours) leave from Jirón Olaya cuadra 13. The recently paved road is subject to landslides so check conditions before making plans.

Lamas VILLAGE
This town, a short drive from Tarapoto, is remarkable in the way that it is split into two distinct halves with *mestizo* (person of mixed indigenous and Spanish descent) residents positioned on the upper plateau while the indigenous community resides on the lower. A large faux-European castle has been constructed on the edge of the upper town, a bizarre sight that serves to reinforce the weird colonial vibe.

The large indigenous population has an annual **Feast of Santa Rosa de Lima** in the last week of August. It's very easy to visit the town on your own; minibuses and *colectivos* (S5, 30 minutes) leave for Lamas regularly from the 10th cuadra of Jirón Urgarte. Alternatively, guided tours from Tarapoto cost around S35.

Activities

Rafting

The local river-running specialists run whitewater rafting trips on the Río Mayo, 30km from Tarapoto, and for those with experience, on the wilder Río Huallaga.

The Río Mayo (half-day trips, from S80 per person) is mostly class II and III whitewater, and is more of a sightseeing trip than a full-on adventure. Kayaks are available for rent with mandatory guide (half-day S100).

Try safety-first **Ecorutas** (☎042-52-3082; www.ecorutas.pe; Hurtado 435) whose owner, Julio, speaks a bit of English; or **Kuriyacu** (☎042-52-1511, 94-279-3388; www.kuriyacu.com), who can arrange guides in English and French.

Rehabilitation

Takiwasi Center HEALTH & FITNESS
(☎042-52-2818; www.takiwasi.com; Prologación Alerta 466) *Brujos* (witch doctors) play a pivotal role in the *pueblos* (villages) of the jungle. A few kilometers north of Tarapoto, in a small jungle village, is the Takiwasi Center, a rehabilitation and detox center started in the early 1990s by French physician Jacques Mabit. The center combines traditional Amazonian medicines and plants, as used by *brujos* or *curanderos* (healers), with psychotherapy.

This treatment is not for the fainthearted and we don't recommend it. Intense 'vomit therapy' and *ayahuasca* (hallucinogenic brew made from jungle vines) are used as part of the healing process. Rehabilitation programs for all kinds of ailments are organized with variable costs, though no one is turned away for lack of funds. Information and introductory sessions can be organized.

Tours

Martín Zamora Tours GUIDED TOURS
(☎042-52-5148; www.martinzamoratarapoto.com; Grau 233; ⏲8am-1pm & 4-7:30pm) Tarapoto's go-to operator for day tours, cultural trips, and longer excursions to local lakes and waterfalls.

Shilcayo Travel Tours TOUR
(☎042-78-2832; www.shilcayotraveltours.com; cnr Moyobamba & De la Cruz) An experienced and reliable local operator offering the full set of

tours in the area. The tour desk is located inside the handicrafts market on the plaza.

Sleeping

You don't need to go far from town to find lush jungle surrounds. There are a string of nature lodges on the banks of the Rio Shilcayo just north of the center.

El Mirador GUESTHOUSE **$**
(042-52-2177; www.elmiradortarapoto.com; San Pablo de la Cruz 517; s/d incl breakfast S60/80, with air-con S100/150;) Travelers swoon over this budget spot, probably because of the welcoming family vibe; or perhaps it's the excellent breakfast served on the terrace with hammocks and jungle views? Rooms in the main house are nothing beyond basic, with fans, hot showers and cable TV; whereas those in the new annex are more spacious with air-con and bright-yellow bathrooms.

As it's a few blocks from the center, you won't suffer as much *mototaxi* noise.

La Posada Inn GUESTHOUSE **$**
(042-52-2234; laposada_inn@latinmail.com; San Martín 146; s/d incl breakfast S60/80, with air-con S75/100;) This quaint hotel has beamed ceilings and an inviting wooden staircase. The rooms are a mixed bag: some have balconies, some have air-con. Even though it's right in the town center, La Posada manages to remain quiet.

Alojamiento Grau GUESTHOUSE **$**
(042-52-3777; Grau 243; s/d/tr S35/45;) On a busy street, this place has clean, elementary rooms with exposed-brick walls and windows to the inside. A solid budget option.

★ **Chirapa Manta** LODGE **$$**
(997-435-611; www.chirapamanta.com; San Roque de Cumbaza; s/d/tr S80/120/150) This tranquil ecological retreat, surrounded by birdlife and butterflies, is a top choice. It's set among lush vegetation on the banks of the upper Río Cumbaza, a 40-minute drive from Tarapoto. The comfortable rooms have electric hot water and well-functioning dry toilets, plus they feature clay walls embedded with colored glass.

The lodge feels totally isolated yet is just a short walk to the charming village of San Roque. Guests have access to the kitchen and meals are also available. The friendly management organizes hikes and ecological excursions in the area, including to local waterfalls with deep swimming holes.

La Patarashca GUESTHOUSE **$$**
(042-52-7554; www.lapatarashca.com; De la Cruz 362; s/d incl breakfast S90/140, with air-con S100/190;) This popular guesthouse is tucked away on sprawling grounds flush with jungle-like fauna. It has a good-sized swimming pool, spacious common areas, and two floors of comfortable rooms adorned with nice furniture and crafty lamps that feel homey and welcoming. A few ornery macaws drive home a sense of place, as does the best regional restaurant in town, attached by a walkway.

Cordillera Escalera Lodge LODGE **$$**
(042-78-1672; www.cordilleraescalera.com; Prolog Alerta 1521; s/d/tr S145/180/220) Set in a beautiful garden surrounded by jungle around 1.5km out of town, this well-run lodge has cute little bungalows with sweeping views of forested mountains. The rooms are simple yet functional with good mattresses, fans and hot water, and they reverberate with the sounds of the jungle.

It's a bit of a hike up the hill to the bungalows, but worth it for the sweeping views from the hammock on your balcony. Apart from breakfast there are no meals served, but guests are free to use the well-equipped kitchen.

A *mototaxi* here costs S8.

Casa de Palos GUESTHOUSE **$$**
(94-031-7681; www.casadepalos.pe; Prado 155; s/d incl breakfast S110/175;) This small, nine-room guesthouse boasts 'boutique' rooms with unfinished concrete flooring and rustic woven headboards, giving it a smidgen more character for this price range. Rooms surround a jungle-like makeshift courtyard full of chirping canaries and tiny gawking monkeys. The attached cafe on the expansive open-air terrace offers free tasting of regional coffees to guests.

Shimiyacu Lodge LODGE **$$**
(966-609-151; www.shimiyaculodgetarapoto.com; s/d/tr incl breakfast S150/170/210) This small lodge next to Reserva Cordillera Escalera offers an authentic Amazon experience just 3km from town. Perched on a hillside are a handful of well-designed, thatched A-frame bungalows that look out over the lush jungle canopy. Each has an open dining area separated from the jungle

by screens on three sides and an enclosed main bedroom with polished wooden floors.

Bungalows also have hot-water bathrooms and a small room upstairs. Apart from breakfast – which features home-baked wholewheat bread – no meals are offered, but there is a small kitchen hut for guests and delivery from town can be arranged. Many *mototaxis* don't like to make the bumpy 15-minute trip out here so phone the lodge to organize a ride with one of its regular drivers.

Mitu Wasi HOTEL $$

(042-52-1866; www.mituwasiecohospedaje.com; Jorge Chavez 1153, Barrio Huayco; s/d/tr S120/145/190;) Behind a nondescript urban facade lies this peaceful family-run hotel boasting a collection of neat and comfortable bungalows in a seemingly endless long garden.

Just a *mototaxi* ride from the center, it's a pleasant escape from the bustle of the city while still convenient to transport. The friendly management goes out of their way to make guests feel at home.

Sol de Selva HOTEL $$

(042-52-4817; www.soldeselvaperu.com; Pedro de Urzúa 161; s/d/tr S80/120/150;) If green areas are not a priority, this new hotel two blocks from the plaza offers some of the best value in town. The rooms are spotless and decked out with modern facilities, while the friendly staff are efficient in organizing activities throughout the region.

Tucan Suites HOTEL $$$

(042-52-8383; www.tucansuites.com; 1st de Abril 315; r S289-449, apt from S389;) This chic apartment-hotel in the *barrio* (neighborhood) of Banda de Shilcayo is Tarapoto's first four-star hotel. Spacious one- and two-bedroom suites feature chrome-tiled kitchenettes and soundproof glass, another city first (and wholly welcomed). Eight of the duplex rooms have open-air kitchenettes and the restaurant drops out onto a trilevel pool terrace. You'll sleep no sounder in town than here.

The attached restaurant is run by a skilled *nikkei* (Peruvian of Japanese descent) chef who serves up wonderfully executed creative cuisine. Worth a visit even if you're not staying here.

★ **Pumarinri Amazon Lodge** LODGE $$$

(042-52-6694; www.pumarinri.com; Carretera Chazuta Km 16; s/d/ste incl breakfast S199/239/339;) Located 30km east of Tarapoto on the banks of the Río Huallaga and surrounded by transitional mountain rainforest, this thatched-roof retreat is a perfect escape from the *mototaxi* blues. Most rooms are upscale-basic but very comfortable with expansive river-view terraces.

Excursions from the tranquil setting include nearby waterfalls, treks to spot the poison dart frog, boat tours, and bird-spotting some 260 recorded species within a 16km radius. Upon return, the kitchen staff fish your *gamitana* straight from their own breeding pond. Three-day, two-night packages (S599) including all meals, excursions and transfers are perfect value.

Eating

Don't leave Tarapoto without trying *inchicapi* or *juanes*.

Restaurante La Alameda PERUVIAN $

(frente Hospital Minsa; mains S6-15; 5-11pm) For an authentic Tarapoto dining experience, head to this popular open-air street-side grill. Pull up a chair at a communal table and order from the extensive menu of seriously cheap regional cuisine. Take your pick from enormous whole barbecued fish, *juanes* with shrimp or grilled kebabs. Wash it down local-style with a glass of *chicha morada* (purple-corn drink).

There is a relaxed social vibe here so you'll probably get a chance to practice your Spanish over dinner.

El Brassero STEAKHOUSE $

(San Pablo de la Cruz 254; mains S15-28; noon-2pm & 7-11pm) Pork ribs are the specialty at this great grill, served up simple, *a la pimienta* (in pepper sauce), with oregano or sweet and sour. Staff rake everything over the coals, including burgers, chicken and chorizo, and it's all supremely tasty. Stop by at lunchtime for good-value S8 *menús*.

Brava Grilled BURGERS $

(San Martín 615; burgers S9-13; 9am-noon & 5pm-midnight) Big, tasty beef patties and a variety of quality fresh ingredients heaped on real buns make for the best burgers in town, even if the fries are disappointing. Wash them down with a real milkshake.

Supermercado la Inmaculada SELF-CATERING $
(Calle de Compagnon 126; ⌚8:30am-10pm) This supermarket has everything you might need for self-catering.

★**La Patarashca** PERUVIAN $$
(www.lapatarashca.com; Lamas 261; mains S19-38; ⌚noon-11pm; 📶) Outstanding regional Amazon cuisine is on tap at this casual 2nd-floor place. Don't miss the salad of *chonta,* thin strips of local hearts of palm, with avocados doused in vinaigrette; or the namesake *patarashcas,* heaping platters of giant shrimp served in a warm bath of tomatoes, sweet peppers, onions, garlic and *sacha culantro* (cilantro) wrapped in a *bijao* leaf.

Café d' Mundo ITALIAN $$
(Calle de Morey 157; pizzas S16-18, mains S24-35; ⌚6pm-midnight) This dark and sexy restaurant-bar is illuminated nightly by moody candlelight. It has outdoor seating and snug indoor lounges. Good pizzas are the mainstay (try the caprese with avocado), but interesting regional lasagnas and pastas adorn the small menu. The full bar will help you pass the rest of the evening. Service plays second fiddle to food and atmosphere.

Chifa Tai Pai CHINESE $$
(Rioja 252; mains S17-45; ⌚11:30am-2pm & 5-11pm) If you haven't taken to jungle cuisine, this is the yin to its yang, an excellent *chifa* (Chinese restaurant) dishing out huge vibrant portions of Chinese-Peruvian fusion. The namesake plate, *Tai Pai a la plancha,* is a heaping kitchen-sink dish of chicken, pork, duck and shrimp served on a sizzling hot plate. Portions can easily serve two.

El Rincón Sureño STEAKHOUSE $$$
(☎042-52-2785; Leguia 458; steaks S20-85) The nicest restaurant in town is a swish-looking establishment with farmstead paraphernalia and cummerbund-bound waiters. Locals swear the meat is top-notch, but we have found it to be inconsistent. For Tarapoto, the wine list is impressive.

Drinking

★**La Alternativa** BAR
(Grau 401; ⌚9am-1am) Like drinking in a medieval pharmacy or maybe a Tarantino film, a night out here hearkens to a time when alcohol was literally medicine (like, for ailments, not for your emotional problems), and your local apothecary was the place to get sauced on God-knows-what elixir that happened to be inside the bottle.

Shelves here are stacked pharmaceutical-style with dusty bottles of natural concoctions combining roots and vines, and cane liquor including 15 different aphrodisiac varieties. It's a recipe for total mayhem.

Stonewasi Taberna BAR
(Lamas 218; ⌚noon-3am) Pretenders come and go, but this local institution is still the place to see and be seen in Tarapoto. Recycled sewing tables streetside are chock-full of punters, *mototaxi* drivers and the town's bold and beautiful thronging to a theme of international rock and house music.

Café Plaza CAFE
(San Martín 109; ⌚7:30am-11pm; 📶) This modern corner cafe is the spot to double-down on serious espresso and people-watching. Its plaza location makes it a fine place to sit and sip a drink, but give the meals a very wide berth.

Information

BCP (Maynas 130) Has several ATMs.
Clínica San Martín (San Martín 274; ⌚24hr) The best medical care in town.
Interbank (Grau 119) ATM.
Policía Nacional (☎042-52-2141; cnr Rioja & Hurtado)
Scotiabank (Hurtado 215) Cashes traveler's checks and has an ATM.
Serpost (San Martín 482; ⌚8am-6pm Mon-Sat) Postal services.
Tourist Information Office (☎042-52-6188; Hurtado s/n; ⌚7:30am-11pm) The municipal tourist office on Plaza Mayor. Local police keep it open when tourism officials go home.

Getting There & Away

AIR

The **airport** (TPP; ☎042-53-1165) is 3km southwest of the center, a S4 *mototaxi* ride.

LAN (☎042-52-9318; www.lan.com; Hurtado 183) has two scheduled flights per day leaving Lima at 9:20am and 8:20pm, returning to Lima at 11am and 10pm. A third flight in between departs at various hours, depending on the day of the week.

Star Perú (☎042-52-8765; San Pablo de la Cruz 100; ⌚9am-7pm Mon-Fri, to 5pm Sat, to noon Sun) has a flight from Lima to Tarapoto at 12:30pm, returning at 5:45pm, with another variable departure time. It also travels direct to Pucallpa four times a week.

Peruvian (www.peruvian.pe; Ramirez 277; ⏲9am-7pm) flies from Lima to Tarapoto at 8:45am and 6pm, returning at 10:30am and 7:45pm.

BUS & TAXI

Several companies head west on the paved road to Lima via Moyobamba, Chiclayo and Trujillo, generally leaving between 8am and 4pm. All these companies can be found along the same *cuadra* of Salaverry and its cross streets in the Morales district, an S2 *mototaxi* ride from the town center.

Civa (☎042-52-2269; www.civa.com.pe; Salaverry 840) Has a comfortable 3:10pm bus to Lima, stopping at Chiclayo and Trujillo.

Ejetur (☎042-52-6827; Salaverry 810) Has cheap services to Chiclayo and Trujillo at 8:30am and 1pm.

Movil Tours (☎042-52-9193; www.moviltours.com.pe; Salaverry 880) Top-end express buses to Lima leave at 8am and 1pm, with a 3pm departure to Trujillo and a 4pm bus to Chiclayo.

Transmar Express (☎042-53-2392; Amoraca 117) Departs at 10am on Monday, Wednesday and Friday for the ride to Pucallpa via Juanjuí, Tocache Nuevo and Tingo María. Also has cheap buses to Lima.

Turismo Selva (☎042-52-5682; Alfonso Ugarte 1130) Runs minivans to Yurimaguas, Moyobamba and Chachapoyas.

Tarapoto Buses:

DESTINATION	COST (S)	DURATION (HR)
Chazuta	10	2
Chiclayo	50-80	14
Jaén	40	9-12
Juanjuí	15	3
Lamas	5	¾
Lima	90-165	26-30
Moyobamba	15-20	2
Pedro Ruíz	40-45	7
Piura	60	16-17
Pucallpa	100	16-18
Sauce	15	4
Tingo María	80	13
Tocache Nuevo	50	8
Trujillo	65-150	15-18
Yurimaguas	15-20	2½

ℹ Getting Around

Mototaxis cruise the streets like circling sharks. A short ride in town is around S2, to the bus stations S3 to S4.

Amazon Basin

ELEV 0-1800M

Includes ➡

Best Places to Eat

- Burgos's Restaurante (p444)
- Al Frio y al Fuego (p480)
- Amazon Bistro (p481)
- Belén Mercado (p480)

Best Places to Stay

- Hacienda Concepción (p454)
- Manu Paradise Lodge (p459)
- Carolina Egg Gasthaus (p466)
- La Casa Fitzcarraldo (p479)
- Samiria Ecolodge (p487)

Why Go?

The best-protected tract of the world's most biodiverse forest, the strange, sweltering, seductive country-within-a-country that is Peru's Amazon Basin, is changing. Its sheer vastness and impenetrability has long protected its indigenous communities and wildlife from external eyes. Tribes exist here that have never had contact with outside civilization. More plant types flourish in one rainforest hectare than in any European country, and fauna is so fantastic it defies the most imaginative sci-fi comic.

But as the 21st century encroaches on this expanse of wilderness, exploitation of the forest's abundant natural resources threatens to irreversibly damage it. Sure, the Peruvian Amazon offers phenomenal wildlife-spotting, forays into untamed forest from the jungle's best lodges and raucous city life, but it also begs for protection. Remember that as, forging through it by rough road and raging river, you'll feel like the explorers who first brought attention to this region.

When to Go

Iquitos

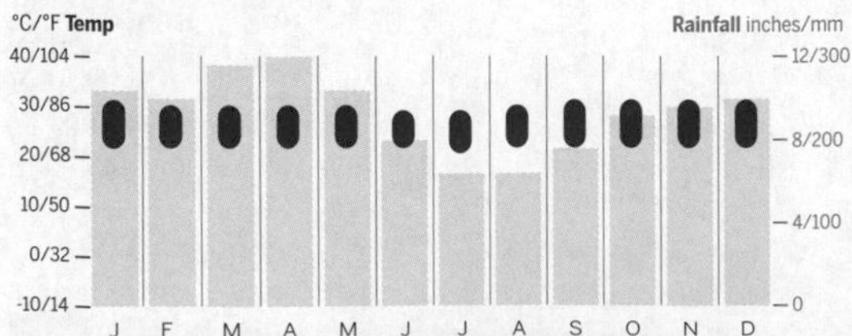

Jan Rising temperatures and water levels; a perfect time to visit the waterfalls near La Merced.

Apr & May Rains subside, heralding courtship season for many birds.

Jun The rainy season ends: cue the jungle's best parties, like debauched San Juan in Iquitos.

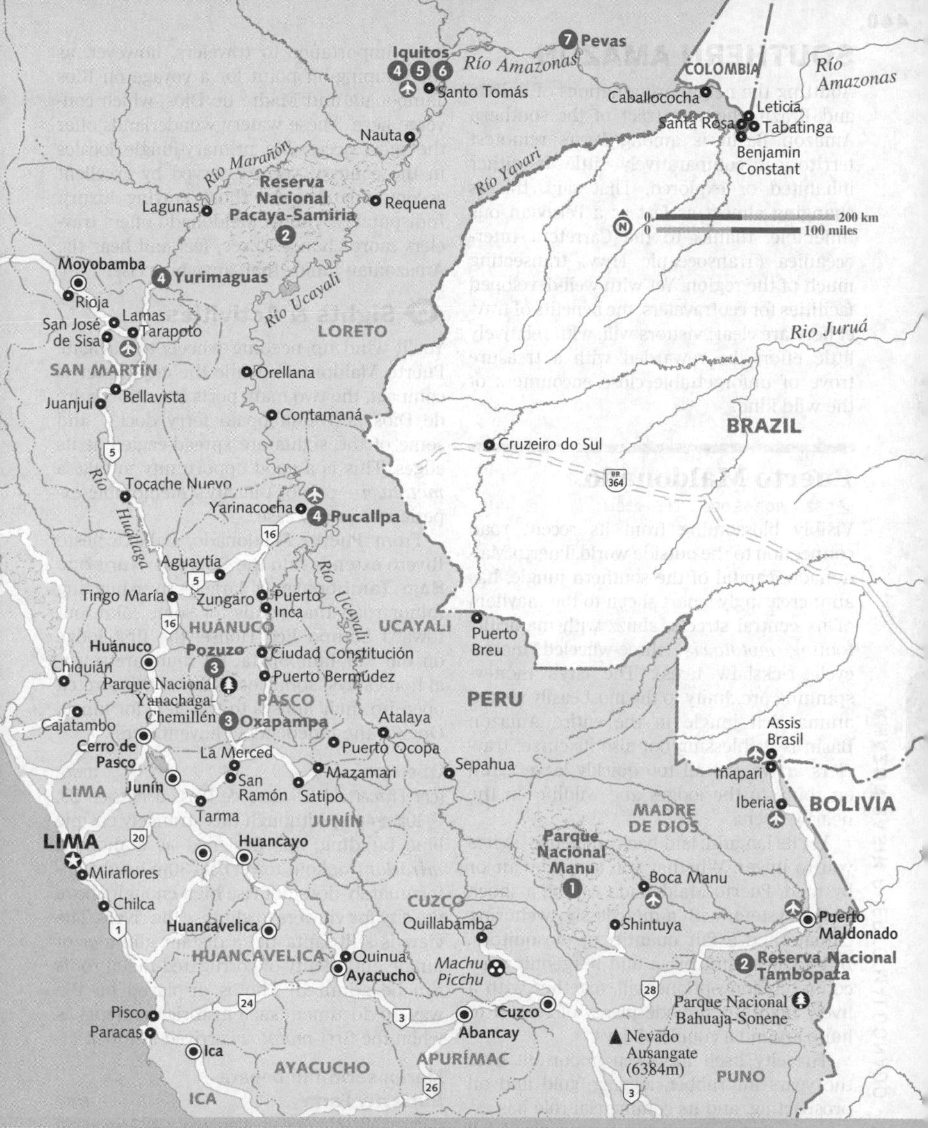

Amazon Basin Highlights

1. Traveling overland through a smorgasbord of Peruvian scenery via mountains, cloud forest and jungle to **Parque Nacional Manu** (p460).
2. Spotting animals and birds at the upper echelons of the **Río Tambopata** (p447) and the **Reserva Nacional Pacaya-Samiria** (p473).
3. Discovering the central Amazon's thriving German heritage in **Oxapampa** (p465) and nearby **Pozuzo** (p465).
4. Swinging in a hammock on a riverboat trip from **Pucallpa** (p466) or **Yurimaguas** (p471) to **Iquitos** (p473).
5. Rising early for a trip to Peru's premier jungle market in the floating district of **Belén** (p476) in Iquitos.
6. Tucking into the wondrous and often downright weird eating scene of **Iquitos** (p480).
7. Admiring world-class art in the remote rainforest at the gallery of Francisco Grippa in **Pevas** (p486).

SOUTHERN AMAZON

Abutting the neighboring nations of Bolivia and Brazil, the vast tract of the southern Amazon Basin is among Peru's remotest territories: comparatively little is either inhabited or explored. That said, this is changing almost as fast as a Peruvian bus timetable, thanks to the Carretera Interoceánica (Transoceanic Hwy) transecting much of the region. Yet with well-developed facilities for ecotravelers, the benefits of travel here are clear: visitors will, with relatively little effort, be rewarded with a treasure trove of unforgettable close encounters of the wild kind.

Puerto Maldonado

082 / POP 56,000 / ELEV 250M

Visibly blossoming from its recent road connection to the outside world, Puerto Maldonado, capital of the southern jungle, has an increasingly smart sheen to the mayhem of its central streets, abuzz with manically tooting *mototaxis* (three-wheeled motorcycle rickshaw taxis). The city's money-spinning proximity to the most easily visited animal-rich jungle in the entire Amazon Basin is its blessing but also its curse: travelers arrive, yet all too quickly leave again en route to the lodges and wildlife on the nearby rivers.

Yet its languid, laid-back ambience invites you to linger. Whether you arrive by air or by road, Puerto Maldonado will be a shock to the system, with a mercilessly sweltering climate and a fair quantity of mosquitoes. But its beautiful plaza and burgeoning accommodation options will, together with a lively nightlife, provide plenty of reason to hang around a couple of days.

The city itself has been important over the years for rubber, logging, gold and oil prospecting, and its commercial role has assumed greater dimensions as a port of call on the Carretera Interoceánica. It's of foremost importance to travelers, however, as the jumping-off point for a voyage on Ríos Tambopata and Madre de Dios, which converge here. These watery wonderlands offer the most accessible primary-jungle locales in the country, yet are served by excellent accommodations for those craving luxury. Indisputably, Puerto Maldonado offers travelers more chance to see, feel and hear the Amazonian jungle than anywhere else.

AMAZON FAST FACTS

Percentage of country covered: 60%

Main city: Iquitos

Major industries: Tourism, coffee, agriculture, fishing, cocaine processing, petroleum

Average yearly rainfall: 3000mm

Sights & Activities

You'll wind up needing wheels to navigate Puerto Maldonado: while the city center is compact, the two main ports (the Río Madre de Dios and Tambopata ferry docks) and some of the sights are spread-eagled at its edges. This is a good opportunity to take a *mototaxi* – one of the city's memorable experiences in any case.

From Puerto Maldonado, Calle Ernesto Rivero extends into the **Corredor Turístico Bajo Tambopata**, a largely river-hugging minor road that winds for some 15km out toward Sotupo Eco House, the first lodge on the Río Tambopata. En route are several homestays; some locals along this stretch open up their houses to travelers for lunch. One for the independent adventurers.

Obelisco TOWER

(cnr Fitzcarrald & Madre de Dios; admission S3; 10am-4pm) Although this strangely cosmic blue building was designed as a modern *mirador* (lookout tower), its 30m height unfortunately does not rise high enough above the city for viewers to glimpse the rivers. The view is still fantastic: a distant glimmer of jungle and plenty of corrugated-metal roofs can be admired! Photos displayed on the way up document such historic moments as when the first *mototaxi* arrived in town.

Mariposario Tambopata Butterfly Farm FARM

(Map p448; http://perubutterfly.com; Av Aeropuerto Km 6; admission US$5) Peru boasts the greatest number of butterfly species in the world (some 3700) and you can see many of them here at this well-run butterfly-conservation project, initiated in 1996. There are also displays on rainforest conservation. Butterflies are nice, but at this price remember you'll see lots of species for free in the jungle proper.

Río Madre de Dios Ferry Dock PORT

(Puerto Capitanía; Map p441) This dock close to the Plaza de Armas is a cheap way of see-

Puerto Maldonado

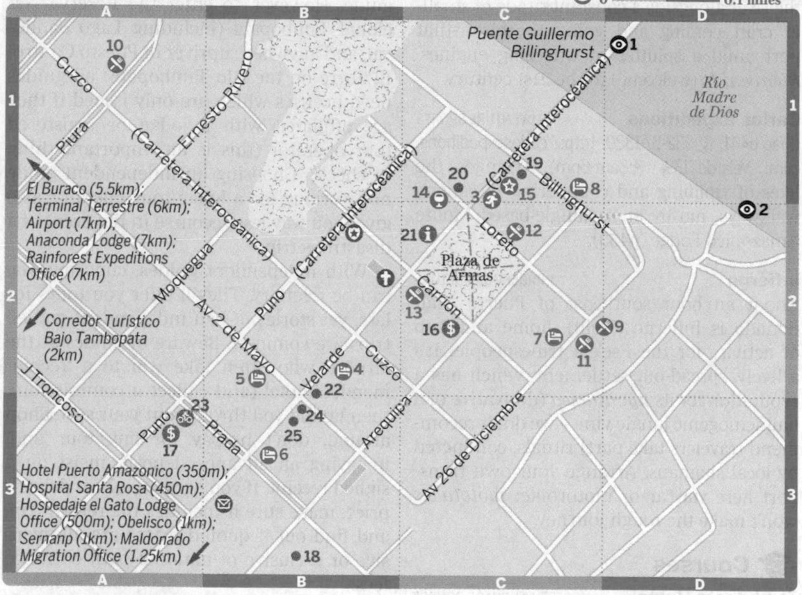

El Buraco (5.5km); Terminal Terrestre (6km); Airport (7km); Anaconda Lodge (7km); Rainforest Expeditions Office (7km)

Corredor Turístico Bajo Tambopata (2km)

Hotel Puerto Amazonico (350m); Hospital Santa Rosa (450m); Hospedaje el Gato Lodge Office (500m); Obelisco (1km); Sernanp (1km); Maldonado Migration Office (1.25km)

Puerto Maldonado

Sights

- 1 Puente Guillermo Billinghurst (Puente Intercontinental) ... D1
- 2 Río Madre de Dios Ferry Dock ... D2

Activities, Courses & Tours

- 3 Carlos Expeditions ... C1
- Tambopata Hostel ... (see 7)

Sleeping

- 4 Hospedaje Rey Port ... B2
- 5 Hospedaje Royal Inn ... B2
- 6 Paititi Hostal ... B3
- 7 Tambopata Hostel ... C2
- 8 Wasai Lodge ... C1

Eating

- 9 Burgos's Restaurante ... D2
- 10 El Califa ... A1
- 11 El Catamaran ... C2
- 12 Los Gustitos del Cura ... C2
- 13 Pizzería El Hornito/Chez Maggy ... C2

Drinking & Nightlife

- 14 Tsaica ... C1

Entertainment

- 15 Discoteca Witite ... C1

Information

- 16 BCP ... C2
- 17 Casa de Cambio ... A3
- 18 Cayman Lodge Amazonie ... B3
- Collpas Tambopata Inn ... (see 7)
- 19 Corto Maltes ... C1
- 20 Estancia Bello Horizonte ... C1
- Monte Amazonico Lodge ... (see 3)
- 21 Municipalidad ... C2
- Wasai Tambopata Lodge ... (see 8)
- 22 Willy Mejía Cepa Lodge ... B2

Transport

- 23 El Gato ... A3
- 24 LAN ... B3
- 25 Star Perú ... B3

ing a little of the action on a major Peruvian jungle river (the Río Madre de Dios), which is about 500m wide at this point. River traffic is colorful – multiple *peki-pekis* (canoes powered by two-stroke motorcycle engines with outlandishly long propeller shafts) set off from here.

However, the number of boats is vastly reduced since the opening of **Puente Guillermo Billinghurst (Puente Intercontinental)**, the bridge now carrying the Carretera Interocéania across the river a few hundred meters to the northwest. Gone are the days when a furor of decrepit catamarans ferried

Brazil-bound drivers and the vehicles across the river alongside a constant tirade of smaller craft coming and going to this-or-that port amid a splutter of wheezing engines. *Bienvenido* (welcome) to the 21st century.

Carlos Expeditions ADVENTURE SPORTS
(Map p441; ☎082-57-1320; http://carlosexpeditions.com; Velarde 139; ⊙8am-6pm) Arranges the likes of ziplining and clambering in canopy walkways, mostly at its jungle-based Monte Amazonico Lodge (p453).

Infierno INDIGENOUS CULTURE
About an hour southeast of Puerto Maldonado is Infierno (Hell!), home and hub of activity for the Ese'eja tribespeople. It's a lively, spread-out settlement, which has a reputation for its *ayahuasca* (derivative of a hallucinogenic jungle vine – we don't recommend travelers take part) rituals, conducted by local shamans. Arrange your own transport here via car or motorbike: *mototaxis* won't make the rough journey.

Courses

Tambopata Hostel LANGUAGE COURSE
(Map p441; ☎082-57-4201; www.tambopatahostel.com; Av 26 de Diciembre 234) Tambopata Hostel can arrange fun salsa classes, basic Spanish lessons and Peruvian cookery classes for very reasonable prices.

Tours

Most visitors arrive with prearranged tours and stay at a jungle lodge – convenient, but by no means the only possibility. You can also arrange a tour upon arrival by going to the lodge offices in town, where you'll likely get a significant discount on a tour that would cost more in Lima or Cuzco.

TASTING THE CARRETERA INTEROCEANÍCA?

Cuzco-based adventure-biking outfit, **Tasting the Road** (☎973-219-765; www.tastingtheroad.com) specializes in two things: running exciting Peruvian pedal-athons, and combining these with flavorsome forays to discover the local cuisine. It offers an eight-day bike tour along the Carretera Interoceanica between Cuzco and Puerto Maldonado, capped off by a stay in a jungle lodge. It's an adrenaline-pumping cycle between the Andes and the Amazon – almost 500km of it!

You can, too, look for an independent guide. However, to enter the Reserva Nacional Tambopata (including Lago Sandoval, and anywhere upriver of Puesto Control El Torre on the Río Tambopata) all guides need licenses which are only issued if they are affiliated with a lodge or registered tour operator (this is an important thing to check). Choosing an independent guide not working for a lodge/tour operator also gives you way less recourse in the event of a disastrous trip.

With independent guides, choosing one can be a lottery. They'll offer you tours for less, yet stories of bad independent guided trips are common. Beware of guides at the airport, who often take you to a 'recommended' hotel (and collect a commission), then hound you throughout your stay. Shop around, don't prepay for any tour and, if paying an advance deposit, insist on a signed receipt. If you agree to a boat driver's price, make sure it includes the return trip, and find out if quoted prices are all-inclusive or exclusive of national park entrance fees.

Almost all of the best guides with official licenses granted by the Ministerio de Industria y Turismo work full time for one of the area's jungle lodges. Guides charge from S100 to S180 per person per day, depending on the destination and number of people. Going with more people reduces the cost; in fact, some guides will only take tours with a three-person minimum.

Most tours, either with a lodge or with an independent guide, leave from the Río Madre de Dios ferry dock, heading downriver on the Río Madre de Dios or upriver on the Río Tambopata (meaning a large expense on a jungle trip is the gas the boat will expend). Some lodges/independent guides now cut hours off a Río Tambopata trip by heading to the community of Alto Tambopata Filadelfia (45 minutes on the Carretera Interoceaníca toward Cuzco, then an hour down a rough track).

Gerson Medina Valera GUIDED TOUR
(☎082-57-4201; www.tambopatahostel.com) Gerson has tons of experience in bird-watching tours and speaks fluent English. His one- to three-day Lago Sandoval tours (around S130 per person per day) are inclusive of all costs. He'll even let you know the chances of seeing every type of Tambopata animal and bird so you'll know what to expect on your

tour. He also arranges tailored fishing trips for around S150 per person daily.

Nilthon Tapia Miyashiro GUIDED TOUR
(982-788-174; nisa_30@hotmail.com) A well-known, experienced guide, also reachable through Tambopata Hostel.

Jony Valles Rengifo GUIDED TOUR
(982-704-736; jhony.com@hotmail.es) Speaks English and French.

Roldan Maron Salcedo GUIDED TOUR
(982-754-904; leo88_rms@hotmail.com) Experienced tour guide.

Sleeping

Besides the plethora of basic budget places, you can now choose from pleasant backpacker accommodations or comfortable hotels/lodges in the city itself. Note that not all lodges have reservations offices in Puerto Maldonado; some only have offices in Cuzco, Lima or the USA.

Outside Puerto Maldonado are around 20 jungle lodges.

★ Tambopata Hostel HOSTEL $
(Map p441; 082-57-4201; www.tambopatahostel.com; 26 de Diciembre 234; dm S30, s with/without bathroom S50/40 d with/without bathroom S80/70; P) Puerto Maldonado finally has the backpacker accommodations it desperately needed. This clean, relaxing hostel has a mix of dorm and private rooms abutting a garden courtyard with hammocks, and a nice breakfast is included in the price. You can even brush up on your Peruvian street talk courtesy of the board in the common room.

Also runs cookery and Spanish courses. There are secure lockers and a kitchen to use, and the owner is one of the town's best jungle guides.

Hospedaje Rey Port GUESTHOUSE $
(Map p441; 082-57-1938; Velarde 457; s S10-30, d S50;) This one's for bargain hunters, generations of whom have been sniffing out the Rey Port's 'charms.' Rooms are a tad grubby, with fans/cable TV. Ground-floor courtyard rooms with shared bathrooms may be cheapest, but the top floor has large rooms with private bathrooms starting at S20: lots of light, which shows up the views...and the dirt.

Hospedaje Royal Inn GUESTHOUSE $
(Map p441; 082-57-3464; 2 de Mayo 333; s/d with fan S35/50, d with air-con S80;) A good choice for travelers, sporting lots of large, clean rooms with fans. The courtyard has seen better days, but still, get a room here as street-facing digs are noisy. Cable TV comes with each room.

★ Anaconda Lodge LODGE $$
(Map p448; 082-79-2726; www.anacondajunglelodge.com; Av Aeropuerto Km 6; s with/without bathroom S100/S50, d with/without bathroom S160/S80, tr S220; P) The most original airport hotel in South America? Cocooned in its own tropical garden on the edge of town, this lodge has a more remote feel than its location would suggest. There are eight double-room bungalows with shared bathroom and four luxury bungalows with private facilities; all are mosquito netted.

There's also camping space (per person S20), a small pool and a spacious two-floor restaurant-bar serving great Thai food and pancake breakfasts. But we *luuurve* the honeymoon suite – erotic furniture with an oriental theme! These guys also organize kayak trips.

Wasai Lodge LODGE $$
(Map p441; 082-57-2290; www.wasai.com; Billinghurst at Arequipa; s/d S190/220;) This lodge is a striking complex of comfortable wooden bungalows overlooking the Río Madre de Dios. A few rooms offer air-con for an extra S30. Minibars, hot showers, cable TV and river views, however, are standard. Room lighting is pretty abysmal, so bring a flashlight for good measure. There is a good restaurant (mains S15 to S25), room service,

BEST JUNGLE LODGE FOR...

Remoteness Tahuayo Lodge (p486)

Luxury Ceiba Tops (p487)

Bird-watching Tambopata Research Center (p453), Cock-of-the-Rock Lodge (p460)

Animal-spotting Manu Wildlife Center (p461)

Learning about the rainforest Otorongo Lodge (p486)

Adventure activities Monte Amazonico Lodge (p453)

Classy cooking Hacienda Concepción (p454)

Indigenous encounters Casa Matsiguenka Lodge (p461)

WARNING: AYAHUASCA

Throughout your travel in the Peruvian Amazon, you will come across numerous places offering the chance to partake of *ayahuasca*. This is the derivative of a hallucinogenic jungle vine, used to attain a purgative trancelike state by shamans (witch doctors) for centuries and now very popular with Westerners. *Ayahuasca* is invariably taken as part of a ceremony that can last anything from hours to days, depending upon who is conducting the rituals.

Be wary of taking *ayahuasca:* it can have serious side effects, including severe dehydration, convulsions, dramatic rises in blood pressure and – if taken regularly – blindness. If mixed with the wrong substances, it has even been known to be fatal. Also, for the purists, know that some places mix LSD in with the *ayahuasca* to intensify the 'trip'.

Be sure, too, to do research into the type of ceremony you're signing up for. Among some shamans offering a genuine ritualistic experience (although the aforementioned health risks still apply), there are charlatans out there who have also been known to rob and on occasion rape unsuspecting gringos under the influence. And such cases *are* reported on a yearly basis.

Lonely Planet does not recommend taking *ayahuasca* and those who wish to do so do it at their own risk.

If you are convinced an *ayahuasca* ceremony is for you, remember that doing it properly involves a necessary dietary adjustment beforehand.

a bar and a pool. The lodge arranges various trips on the region's rivers, usually involving a stay at the well-regarded jungle lodge.

Paititi Hostal HOTEL **$$**

(Map p441; ☎082-57-4667; Prada 290; s/d incl breakfast S100/120;) A relatively flash, central place, the Paititi has a series of spacious, airy rooms, many full of attractive old wooden furniture, along with telephones and cable TV. A continental breakfast is included, and there's even hot water at night – very un-Amazon.

Hotel Puerto Amazonico HOTEL **$$$**

(☎082-57-2170, 082-50-2354; www.hotelpuertoamazonico.com; León Velarde 1080; s/d incl buffet breakfast S196/238;) Puerto Maldonado needed this: it might be a little overpriced, but you can't argue that the rooms are probably the city's best. The more you pay, the more the size of your flat-screen TV increases.

Eating

Regional specialties include *juanes* (rice steamed with fish or chicken in a banana leaf), *chilcano* (a broth of fish chunks flavored with the native cilantro herb) and *parrillada de la selva* (a barbecue of marinated meat, often game, in a Brazil-nut sauce). A *plátano* (plantain) is served boiled or fried as an accompaniment to many meals.

Also consider the riverfront restaurant at Wasai Lodge, or delicious Thai food at Anaconda Lodge.

El Califa PERUVIAN **$**

(Map p441; Piura 266; mains S9-21; 9am-5pm Mon-Fri) *The* local restaurant in town, in the game for decades. An ocean of tables is attended with no-nonsense service. Portions are large, cheap and tasty, and you can try a variety of jungle classics, from *chancho* (rainforest pig) to *parrillada de la selva*.

Los Gustitos del Cura DESSERTS **$**

(Map p441; Loreto 258; snacks S3-8; 8am-10pm) For a sweet treat or the best ice cream in town, drop in to this French-owned patisserie with a pleasant courtyard at the rear. Sandwiches, cakes and drinks are dished up, and local objets d'art are on sale.

★ Burgos's Restaurante PERUVIAN **$$**

(Map p441; cnr 26 de Diciembre & Loreto; mains S15-25; 11am-4pm & 5pm-midnight) This has quickly developed into Puerto Maldonado's standout restaurant. It calls itself an exponent of Novo Amazonica cuisine – for you foodies, that's like Novo Andino, only making those bold culinary adaptations to jungle dishes – but this is still more about dependable Peruvian Amazon staples, cooked to perfection rather than with particular innovation.

It's a huge, airy, courteously staffed restaurant, with a couple of terraces sporting lush river views, and serves plenty of vegetarian options alongside its fish-focused specialties.

El Catamaran CEVICHE $$
(Map p441; Jirón 26 de Deciembre 241; mains S20-30; ⏲7:30am-3pm) Gravitate to this quiet place to feast on great freshwater ceviche (raw seafood marinated in lime juice), along with the contingent of local dignitaries: there's a nice decked seating area out back with river views.

Pizzería El Hornito/ Chez Maggy PIZZERIA $$
(Map p441; ☎082-57-2082; Carrión 271; large pizzas S28-31; ⏲6pm-late) This popular upstairs hangout on the Plaza de Armas serves pasta and amply sized, wood-fired pizzas – the best in town – complete with lashings of *telenovelas* (Peruvian soap operas) on large TVs. Yeah, it does takeout.

Drinking & Nightlife

The city's nightlife, while nothing beside Lima or Cuzco, is some of the Amazon's liveliest. Discos mostly just have recorded music, but bars and clubs pound away until the early hours of a weekend.

Tsaica BAR
(Map p441; Loreto 329) Lively, and with funky indigenous art on the walls.

El Buraco BAR
(cnr Avs Universitaria, La Joya & Aeropuerto; ⏲9pm-late Fri-Sun) This has morphed into the most popular open-air bar – start with a beer and you'll be finishing with a dance. Good live music Friday and Saturday.

Discoteca Witite CLUB
(Map p441; Velarde 151; ⏲9pm-late Fri & Sat) Well, we preferred Witite with the gaudy clapboard but the smartened-up version is still the classic place to party – a party which goes on all night. It's on the new pedestrianized street near the plaza.

Shopping

Proximity to local tribes means many lodges around town, such as Posadas Amazonas on the Río Tambopata, are better for purchasing local handicrafts than the town itself.

Information

IMMIGRATION

The border town of Iñapari has regular border-crossing facilities to enter Brazil.

Maldonado Immigration Office (☎082-57-1069; Av 15 de Agosto 658; ⏲8am-1pm & 2:30-4pm Mon-Fri) To leave Peru via Puerto Heath (river) or Iberia (road) for Bolivia, get your passport stamped here (morning's best). Travelers can also extend their visas or tourist cards here.

INTERNET ACCESS

Internet is slower here than in other Peruvian cities and costs about S2 per hour. There are multiple cybercafe choices along Velarde, heading southwest from the plaza.

LAUNDRY

Lavandería (Velarde 926; ⏲7am-7pm daily) Wash your repulsive jungle rags here.

MEDICAL SERVICES

Hospital Santa Rosa (☎082-57-1019, 082-57-1046; www.hospitalsantarosa.gob.pe; Cajamarca 171) Provides basic services.

MONEY

Perhaps unsurprisingly, Brazilian reais and Bolivian bolivianos have become much easier to exchange here since the opening of the Carretera Interocéanica: ask where is currently giving the best exchange rate.

BCP (Map p441; Plaza de Armas) On Plaza de Armas; changes US cash or traveler's checks and has a Visa ATM.

Casa de Cambio (Map p441; Puno at Prada) Standard rates for US dollars.

POLICE

Police station (Map p441; ☎082-80-3504; cnr Carrión & Puno)

POST

Post office (Map p441; Velarde) Southwest of the Plaza de Armas.

TOURIST INFORMATION

Tourist booth (airport) Run by the Ministerio de Industria y Turismo; provides limited information on tours and jungle lodges.

Getting There & Away

Most travelers fly here from Lima or Cuzco, but bus is now a viable option too. The long river trips from Manu or Bolivia are (when possible) only for hardened, adventurous travelers.

AIR

The airport is 7km outside town. Scheduled flights leave every day to/from Lima via Cuzco

BORDER CROSSING: BRAZIL VIA PUERTO MALDONADO

A good paved road, part of the Carretera Interocéanica (Transoceanic Hwy), goes from Puerto Maldonado to Iberia and on to Iñapari, 233km from Puerto Maldonado, on the Brazilian border. Along the road are small settlements of people involved in the Brazil-nut-farming, cattle-ranching and logging industries. After about 170km you reach **Iberia**, which has very basic hotels. The village of **Iñapari** is another 70km beyond Iberia.

Peruvian border formalities can be carried out in Iñapari. Stores around the main plaza accept and change both Peruvian and Brazilian currency; if leaving Peru, it's best to get rid of any nuevos soles here. Small denominations of US cash are negotiable, and hotels and buses often quote rates in US dollars. From Iñapari, you can cross over the new bridge to **Assis Brasil**, which has better hotels (starting from around US$10 per person).

US citizens need to get a Brazilian visa beforehand, either in the USA or Lima. It's 325km (six to seven hours) by paved road from here to the important Brazilian city of Rio Branco, via Brasiléia (100km, two hours).

For more detailed coverage of Brazil, pick up Lonely Planet's *Brazil* from the Lonely Planet online shop (http://shop.lonelyplanet.com).

with **LAN** (Map p441; ☎082-57-3677; Velarde 503; ⏰8am-6:30pm Mon-Sat) and **Star Perú** (Map p441; ☎082-57-3564; cnr Velarde & 2 de Mayo; ⏰8am-1pm & 4-8pm Mon-Fri, 8am-6:30pm Sat, noon-6:30pm Sun). Schedules and airlines change from one year to the next, but numerous travel agents in the town center have the latest details.

BOAT

Hire boats at the Río Madre de Dios ferry dock for local excursions or to take you downriver to destinations like Lago Sandoval, Río Heath and the Bolivian border (see the advice under **Tours**, p442). It's difficult to find boats going up the Madre de Dios (against the current) to Manu; Cuzco is currently a better departure point for Manu. Occasionally, people reach Puerto Maldonado by boat from Manu (with the current) or from the Bolivian border (against the current). However, transportation is infrequent: be prepared for waits of several days.

Heading upriver on Río Tambopata, all passengers must stop at Puesto de Control La Torre (checkpoint), where passports and Sernanp permits (S30 or S65 depending on the duration of your stay) are needed. Get these from the **Sernanp office** (☎082-57-1247; www.sernanp.gob.pe/sernanp; Cajamarca btwn Ancash & 28 de Julio) in town.

Boats to jungle lodges leave from both the Río Madre de Dio and Río Tambopata docks, depending on the lodge location. When transporting visitors upriver, some Río Tambopata lodges avoid several hours of river travel by taking road and then rough track to Philadelphia (about 1¾ hours), and continuing by boat from there. This needs to be arranged in advance, however.

The Tambopata ferry dock is 2km south of the center and reachable by *mototaxi*. Here, a public boat leaves on Mondays at 8am, chugging upriver to Baltimore. It returns from Baltimore on Friday morning. Passage costs S20 or thereabouts, depending on how far you go.

BUS & TAXI

Trucks, minibuses and *colectivos* (shared taxis) leave Puerto Maldonado for Laberinto (1½ hours), passing the turnoff to Baltimore at Km 37 on the Cuzco road (from here you can walk three hours to the Río Tambopata where, if you're staying at a Baltimore homestay, boats will pick you up if it's been arranged in advance). Laberinto-bound transport leaves frequently from the corner of Av 28 de Julio and Tacna.

For Iñapari (S30, three hours), near the borders with Brazil and Bolivia, leave with **Empresa de Transportes Turismo** (cnr 28 de Julio & Fitzcarrald) via *colectivo* (departing when they have four passengers) or minivan. Other companies on the same block also advertise this trip. A minivan is a few soles cheaper, but the journey is a significantly more uncomfortable, protracted experience.

Terminal Terrestre (Av Circunvalación Norte s/n) is 6km northwest of the center; from there, buses ply the Carretera Interocéanica southwest to Cuzco and northeast to Rio Branco, Brazil. Numerous companies leave either during the morning or at night (around 8pm) to Cuzco (S35 to S70, 10 hours). Top tariffs are for fully reclining seats. Options to Río Branco are more scant but include **Movil Tours** (☎989-176-306) departing Tuesday and Friday at midday (S100, nine to 10 hours). It's advisable to buy your ticket as far in advance of travel as possible.

Getting Around

Mototaxis take two or three passengers (and light luggage) to the airport for S7. Short rides around town cost S2 or less (S1 if you bag one of the *mototaxi* Honda 90s).

You can rent motorcycles if you want to see some of the surrounding countryside; go in pairs in case of breakdowns or accident. There are several motorcycle-rental places, mainly on Prada between Velarde and Puno. They charge about S5 to S10 per hour and have mainly small, 100cc bikes. Driving one is fun, but crazed local drivers and awful road conditions can make this option intimidating. Bargain for all-day discounts.

Try **El Gato** (Map p441; cnr Puno & Gonzales Prada; per hour/day S5/40).

Around Puerto Maldonado

Four key watery areas are of interest to tourists, and two converge right in Puerto Maldonado.

With its headwaters actually in Bolivia, the Río Tambopata churns through a large portion of southern Peru. Upriver (southwest) of Puerto Maldonado, it winds through much of Reserva Nacional Tambopata, and on balance contains the region's best selection of jungle lodges.

The Río Tambopata is a major tributary of the Río Madre de Dios (p453), which it meets in Puerto Maldonado. Having come from Parque Nacional Manu, this vast torrent of water zigzags east, skirting the border of Reserva Nacional Tambopata, toward the Peru–Bolivia border at Puerto Heath. The parts of interest to Puerto Maldonado travelers are all downriver, and accordingly reaching the several lodges on this river is much easier than getting to Río Tambopata's lodges.

Lago Sandoval (p454) is an idyllic lake east of Puerto Maldonado, accessed from the Río Madre de Dios. It's a wildlife-watching haven, particularly known for its giant river otters, plus a couple of good lodges. To see Lago Sandoval, you'll need to pay the Reserva Nacional Tambopata entrance fee.

Perhaps 60km from Puerto Maldonado down the Río Madre de Dios, you hit Puerto Heath, the Peru–Bolivia border, and with it the Río Heath (p455). Running approximately north–south, this river forms the border for much of its length and offers one basic lodge. It flows through the very remote Parque Nacional Bahuaja-Sonene.

One or more of these areas are where almost all visitors will base themselves for their southern jungle experience. Ríos Tambopata, Madre de Dios and Heath are, of course, vast, and offer many contrasts along their wildlife-rich banks. Lago Sandoval is the only area you can hope to do justice to on a single visit.

All lodges quote prices in US dollars, and usually include transportation. Luggage per person is limited, but can be stored in lodge offices in Puerto Maldonado.

Activities include nature and fishing trips, visiting indigenous communities and even ziplining. Lodges provide rubber boots for traversing muddy jungle paths.

Río Tambopata

Boats go up the river, past several good lodges, and into the **Reserva Nacional Tambopata** (Map p448; admission S30 per day, S65 2-3 days), an important protected area divided into the reserve itself and the **zona de amortiguamiento** (buffer zone). The park entrance fee needs to be paid at the **Sernanp office** (☎082-57-1247; www.sernanp.gob.pe/sernanp) in Puerto Maldonado. However, if, as is very likely, you are on a guided tour, you'll pay the fee at the relevant lodge office. An additional fee is required if you are heading into the reserve proper (such as to the Tambopata Research Center) rather than just the buffer zone.

Travelers heading up the Río Tambopata must register their passport numbers at **Puesto Control El Torre** (Guard Post; Map p448) next to Explorer's Inn and show their national park entrance permits. Visiting the reserve is only really possible if you book a guided stay at one of the lodges within it. One of the reserve's highlights is the **Collpa de Guacamayos** (Macaw Clay Lick), one of the country's largest natural clay licks. It attracts hundreds of birds and is a spectacular sight.

The community of **Baltimore**, just after Refugio Amazonas lodge, is the only real settlement on the river, and has a few simple *hospedajes* (homestays). Baltimore is accessible by taking a Laberinto-bound bus from Puerto Maldonado and getting off at Km 37. From there, a footpath goes to Baltimore (about three hours). No public transport exists to points further upriver.

NEED TO KNOW

Allow plenty of time for your Amazon adventure: erratic weather causes delays, in forms such as landslides, broken boats and cancelled flights. Even on a good day, road and river transport is prone to overcrowding and severe hold-ups.

Around Puerto Maldonado

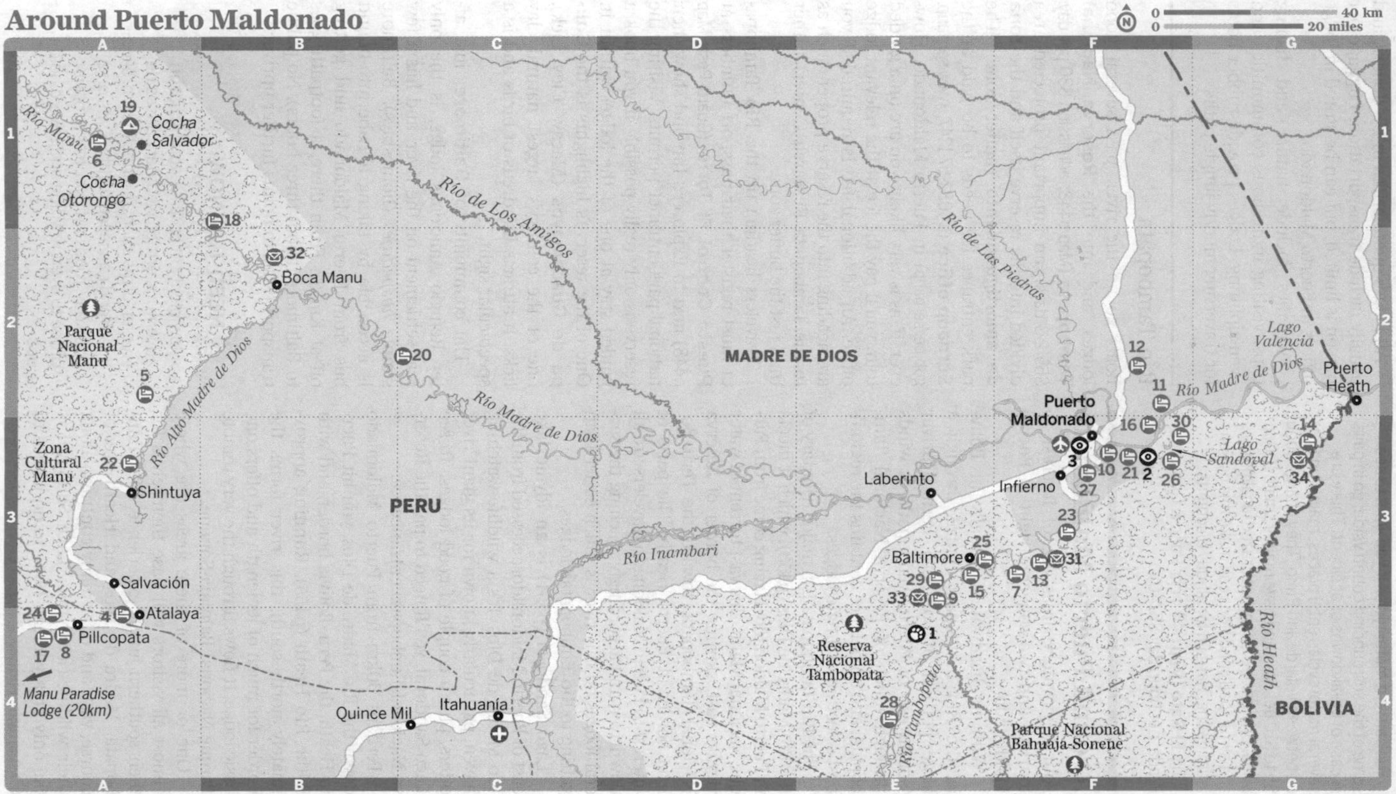

0 40 km
0 20 miles

Río Manu
19
Cocha Salvador
6
Cocha Otorongo
18
32
Boca Manu
Parque Nacional Manu
5
Río Alto Madre de Dios
Zona Cultural Manu
22
Shintuya
Salvación
24
4
Atalaya
Pillcopata
17
8
Manu Paradise Lodge (20km)
Río de Los Amigos
20
Río Madre de Dios
PERU
Quince Mil
Itahuanía
Río Inambari
MADRE DE DIOS
Río de Las Piedras
Laberinto
Baltimore
25
29
33
9
15
7
13
31
23
1
Reserva Nacional Tambopata
28
Río Tambopata
Parque Nacional Bahuaja-Sonene
Puerto Maldonado
3
Infierno
27
10
21
2
26
16
12
11
30
Río Madre de Dios
Lago Valencia
Lago Sandoval
Puerto Heath
14
34
Río Heath
BOLIVIA

Around Puerto Maldonado

Sights
1 Collpa Chuncho......E4
2 Hacienda Concepción Research Center......F3
3 Mariposario Tambopata Butterfly Farm......F3

Activities, Courses & Tours
Rainforest Expeditions......(see 3)

Sleeping
4 Amazonia Lodge......A4
Anaconda Lodge......(see 3)
5 Bonanza Ecological Reserve......A2
6 Casa Matsiguenka Lodge......A1
7 Cayman Lodge Amazonie......F3
8 Cock-of-the-Rock Lodge......A4
9 Collpas Tambopata Inn......E3
10 Corto Maltes......F3
11 Eco Amazonia Lodge......F2
12 Estancia Bello Horizonte......F2
13 Explorer's Inn Tambopata Ecolodge......F3
Hacienda Concepción......(see 2)
14 Heath River Wildlife Center......G3
15 Hospedaje el Gato......E3
16 Inkaterra Reserva Amazonica......F3
17 Manu Cloud Forest Lodge......A4
18 Manu Lodge......B1
19 Manu Tented Camp......A1
20 Manu Wildlife Center......C2
21 Monte Amazonico Lodge......F3
22 Pantiacolla Lodge......A3
23 Posada Amazonas......F3
24 Rainforest Lodge......A4
25 Refugio Amazonas......E3
26 Sandoval Lake Lodge......F3
27 Sotupa Eco House......F3
28 Tambopata Research Center......E4
29 Wasai Tambopata Lodge......E3
30 Willy Mejía Cepa Lodge......F3

Information
31 Puesto Control El Torre......F3
32 Puesto Control Limonal......B2
33 Puesto Control Malinowsky......E3
34 Puesto Control San Antonio......G3
Refugio Amazonas......(see 3)

After Collpas Tambopata Inn is a second control point, **Puesto Control Malinowski**, with displays on wildlife and accommodations for scientists/researchers only. Just beyond the control point is one of the best clay licks in the Reserva, **Collpa Chuncho** (Map p448; admission S30), where you can see one of the colorful cacophony of feeding macaws for which Tambopata region is renowned.

Sleeping

Lodges are listed in the order you approach them from Puerto Maldonado. Where Reserva Nacional Tambopata entrance fees are payable, they're mentioned below.

★Sotupa Eco House — LODGE $$

(Map p448; ☎950-416-257; www.sotupa.pe; s/d US$150/180, per couple 3 days & 2 nights US$675) The first lodge on the Río Tambopata, accessible also by road, is close enough to Puerto Maldonado for a one-night break. Perched on a pea-green grassy expanse atop a cliff, it still feels isolated. The cabins are idyllic, 9.5km of trails beckon, and as you swing from your garden hammock, know no other lodges boast a chill-out area with these river views.

A bungalow on stilts (US$325 per night), separate from the rest of the complex, is great for families. It sits at the end of the Corredor Turístico Bajo Tambopata. No Reserva Nacional Tambopata entrance fees necessary.

Posada Amazonas — LODGE $$$

(Map p448; www.perunature.com; s/d 3 days & 2 nights US$570/864) About two hours from Puerto Maldonado along Río Tambopata, followed by a 10-minute uphill walk, this posada is on the land of the Ese'eja tribe, and tribal members are among the guides. Book online or at **Rainforest Expeditions** (Map p448; ☎082-57-2575; www.perunature.com; Av Aeropuerto, Km 6, CPM La Joya) in Puerto Maldonado.

There are excellent chances of seeing macaws and parrots on a small salt lick nearby, and giant river otters are often found swimming in lakes close to the lodge. Guides at the lodge are mainly English-speaking Peruvian naturalists with varying interests. Your assigned guide stays with you throughout the duration of your stay.

Visits are also made to the Centro Ñape ethnobotanical center, where medicine is produced for the Ese'eja community. There is a medicinal-plant trail and a 30m-high observation platform giving superb views of the rainforest canopy. The lodge has 30 large double rooms with private showers and open (unglazed) windows overlooking the rainforest. Mosquito nets are provided. Electricity is available in the evenings; otherwise everything is candle- or lamp-lit.

No Reserva Nacional Tambopata entrance fees necessary.

THE CARRETERA INTEROCÉANICA: ROAD TO RICHES & RUIN

Few events in history have had such an immediate effect on the Amazon rainforest as the construction of the Carretera Interocéanica (Transoceanic Hwy) has: following its completion in July 2011, it now links the Pacific coast of Peru with the Atlantic coast of Brazil via paved road. At a cost of more than US$2800 million, the road is now a massive export opportunity for both countries (former Peruvian president Alejandro Toledo estimated the road would signify a 1.5% annual increase in Peru's GDP). The more than 2500km of newly constructed road breaches the dual hazards of the Andes and the rainforest to link the Peruvian coast at San Juan de Marcona near Nazca via Cuzco to the southern Amazon, through Puerto Maldonado, to the Brazilian border at Iñapari. From there the road runs to Rio Branco in Brazil and feeds into the Brazilian road system.

The effects of the road, good and bad, are already being felt. Thousands of new jobs have been created and Puerto Maldonado, the main city on the route not previously connected by asphalted highway, is thriving from increased tourism (Cuzco is now only 10 hours away by road) and commerce.

But for the estimated 15 uncontacted tribes that inhabit the once-isolated southeastern corner of Peru, the road now slicing through their territory heralds the risk of disease and the loss of hunting grounds. According to one NGO, Survival International, the possibility of migration a road creates without the facilities to back up such a migration would, along with the destruction of natural habitat, have a disastrous effect on such peoples. And if there are 15 human groups at risk, there are infinitely more species of plants and animals. The total area of destroyed rainforest as a result of the Transoceanic's construction equates to a third of the size of the UK and, according to various studies on roads in the Brazilian Amazon, is likely to have a significant effect on rainforest deforestation for 40km to 60km on either side.

Yet the devastation the building of the road has caused is less significant than the devastation that people who now have improved access to the remote rainforest could bring. Newspapers from the *Peruvian Times* to the *Guardian* have reported on the *prosibars* (bars with often-underage prostitutes) springing up along routes which can now be traversed with greater ease by the loggers and miners that already posed an ecological threat to this part of the Amazon. Illegal mining has since become a serious enough issue to call in the army to quell it. Ecosystems here are renowned for being among the world's most diverse and undisturbed. They still are. But, one wonders, for how much longer.

The same outfit has two other lodges on the Tambopata: Refugio Amazonas and the Tambopata Research Center.

Explorer's Inn Tambopata Ecolodge LODGE **$$$**

(Map p448; www.explorersinn.com; s/d 4 days & 3 nights US$769/1138) About 58km from Puerto Maldonado (three to four hours by river) and featuring 15 rustic double and 15 triple rooms, all with bathrooms and screened windows. Around since the 1970s, this is a more open lodge than those closer to Puerto Maldonado, in a pleasant grassy clearing. Book online or at the **Puerto Maldonado office** (☎082-57-3029; Terminal Terreste piso 2, Avenida Circunvalación s/n).

The central lodge room sports a restaurant, a bar and a small museum; outside is a soccer pitch and a medicinal garden.

The place is located in the former 55-sq-km Zona Preservada Tambopata (itself now surrounded by the much larger Reserva Nacional Tambopata). More than 600 species of bird have been recorded in this preserved zone, which is a world record for bird species sighted in one area. Despite such (scientifically documented) records, the average tourist won't see much more here than at any of the other Río Tambopata lodges during the standard two-night visit, which misses out on the macaw clay lick at Collpa Chuncho.

The 38km of trails around the lodge can be explored independently or with naturalist guides. German, English and French are spoken.

Collpas Tambopata Inn LODGE **$$**

(Map p448; www.tambopatahostel.com; per person 2 days & 1 night US$150) This lodge seems too good to be true: a real budget option for travelers, yet situated further upriver than every other lodge save the Tambopata Re-

BORDER CROSSING: BOLIVIA VIA PUERTO MALDONADO

There are three ways of reaching Bolivia from the Puerto Maldonado area.

First and easiest is to go to Brasiléia in Brazil and cross the Río Acre by ferry or bridge to **Cobija** in Bolivia, where there are hotels, banks, an airstrip with erratically scheduled flights further into Bolivia, and a rough gravel road with several river crossings to the city of **Riberalta** (seven to 12 hours depending on season).

From **Iberia** in Peru on the Carretera Interocéanica (Transoceanic Hwy) to Iñapari, a road also runs to Cobija, but public transportation mostly uses the Iñapari/Assis Brasil route.

Alternatively, hire a boat at Puerto Maldonado's Madre de Dios dock to take you to the Peru–Bolivia border at **Puerto Pardo**. A few minutes from Puerto Pardo by boat is **Puerto Heath**, a military camp on the Bolivian side. The trip takes half a day and can cost up to US$100 (but is negotiable) – the boat will carry several people. With time and luck, you may also be able to find a cargo boat that's going there anyway and will take passengers much more cheaply.

It's possible to continue down the river on the Bolivian side, but this can take days (even weeks) to arrange and isn't cheap. Travel in a group to share costs, and avoid the dry months of July to September, when the river is too low. From Puerto Heath, continue down the Río Madre de Dios as far as Riberalta (at the confluence of the Madre de Dios and Beni, far into northern Bolivia), where road and air connections can be made: a classic (if tough) Amazon adventure the like of which no road trip can compete with. Basic food and shelter (bring a hammock) can be found en route. When river levels allow, a cargo and passenger boat runs from Puerto Maldonado to Riberalta and back about twice a month, but this trip is rarely done by foreigners.

If you've had your fill of river transport by Puerto Heath, you can switch to a dirt road which runs to **Chivé** (1½ hours by bus), where there are very basic accommodations and from where minivans depart each morning around 8am to Cobija (six hours).

Always get your Peruvian exit stamp in Puerto Maldonado. Bolivian entry stamps can be obtained in Puerto Heath or Cobija. Visas are not available, however, so get one ahead of time in Lima or your home country if you need it. US citizens need to pay US$135 in cash for a visa to enter Bolivia (US$160 if purchased in the US).

Formalities are generally slow and relaxed.

For more detailed coverage of Bolivia, pick up Lonely Planet's *Bolivia* from the Lonely Planet online shop (http://shop.lonelyplanet.com).

search Center. Completed in summer 2015, it's also the newest lodge on Río Tambopata; the owner brings many years' experience in the Puerto Maldonado tourist business to the venture.

Book online or at the **Puerto Maldonado office** (Map p441; ☎082-57-4201; Av 26 de Diciembre 234).

On a sloping stretch of land near Puesto Control Malinowski, 28-person capacity Collpas Tambopata allows its guests to go foraging for their dinner (with a touch of guidance of course) and has a football pitch for those with energy still to burn after a day's jungle exploration.

Try to bag a tour with the owner, one of the region's best jungle guides. Volunteers at this lodge are welcomed (then you stay for free).

Guests arrive by road/rough track to Filadelfia and continue by boat from there to cut down transportation time and costs (meaning one-night stays are possible). This is also the nearest lodge to Collpa Chuncho.

No Reserva Nacional Tambopata entrance fees necessary.

Cayman Lodge Amazonie LODGE **$$$**
(Map p448; www.cayman-lodge-amazonie.com; s/d 4 days & 3 nights US$510/750) Some 70km from Puerto Maldonado, this lodge is run by the effervescent French Anny and her English-speaking Peruvian partner, Daniel. It's an open, relaxing environment with lush tropical garden. Rooms are on the small side, but are more than comfortable, with window meshes to thwart the mosquitoes. Book online or at the **Puerto Maldonado office** (Map p441; ☎082-57-1970; Arequipa 655).

Activities include visits to the oxbow Lagunas Sachavacayoc and Condenado.

There is also a five- to seven-day shamanism program, where you can learn about

PUNK CHICKENS

Listen carefully as your boat passes the banks of the Río Tambopata. If you hear lots of hissing, grunting and sounds of breaking vegetation, it is likely that you have stumbled upon the elaborate mating ritual of one of the Amazon's weirdest birds, the hoatzin. This is an oversized wild chicken with a blue face and a large crest on its head (hence the nickname 'punk chicken'). Scientists have been unable to classify this bird as a member of any other avian family, mainly due to the two claws the young have on each wing. To evade predators, hoatzin chicks will fall out of the nest to the river and use their claws to help them scramble back up the muddy banks. The clawed wing is a feature of no other airborne creature since the pterodactyl. The hoatzin's appearance is outdone by its terrible smell (caused by an exclusively leaf-based diet, which necessitates their having multiple micro-organisms in their stomachs to aid digestion), which may well be the first indication they are nearby. Good news for the hoatzin: their odd odor makes their flesh taste bad, so they are rarely hunted. In this age of rainforest depletion, they are one of the few native birds with a flourishing population.

tropical medicine and even be treated for ailments. One of the more arresting features here is the hammock house, from where you can watch the sun set over the Río Tambopata. A large bar and restaurant area add to the conviviality. Reserve entrance fees are not included.

Refugio Amazonas LODGE **$$$**
(Map p448; www.perunature.com; 4 days & 3 nights s/d US$854/1232) This lodge is a fairly lengthy (80km) boat ride up the river. It's built on a 20-sq-km private reserve in the buffer zone of the Reserva Nacional Tambopata. While it feels isolated, rooms are very comfortable and the lodge is not lacking in creature comforts. Book online or at the **Puerto Maldonado office** (Map p448; ☎082-57-2575; Av Aeropuerto Km 6, CPM La Joya).

A large reception, dining and drinking area, with neatly varnished walkways leading off to the rooms, helps create one of the southern jungle's sleekest lodges (there is even an art gallery and massage available).

Activities include a Brazil-nut trail and camp and, for children, a dedicated rainforest trail. The increased remoteness usually means better opportunities for spotting wildlife. Book with Rainforest Expeditions (p449).

★ **Hospedaje el Gato** LODGE **$$$**
(Map p448; ☎941-223-676; www.baltimoreperu.org.pe; per person 2 days & 1 night from US$150) One of those rare jungle lodges catering to *mochileros* (backpackers), this rustic refuge in Baltimore is 90km from Puerto Maldonado up on a cliff by a bubbling tributary of the Río Tambopata, complete with waterfalls and bathing spots. In terms of the 'rainforest experience' it gives the pricier lodges hereabouts a run for their money. Book online or at the **Puerto Maldonado office** (☎082-63-2961; Junín, Mza Lote 2).

To get there, you could take the passenger boat departing Puerto Maldonado's Tambopata ferry dock at 8am on Mondays, returning from Baltimore around the same time on Fridays. Or you could take a Laberinto-bound *colectivo*/minivan to Km 37 on the Carretera Interoceaníca, then hike (three hours) down to the riverbank opposite the *hospedaje,* where a boat can collect you. With either of these options, the cost is vastly lower (just S80 per person per night with activities and food thrown in) than the standard rates quoted above (which are for a standard package with airport pickup).

Wasai Tambopata Lodge LODGE **$$$**
(Map p448; www.wasai.com; per person 2 days & 1 night US$279) Just after Baltimore, this lodge is one of the furthest from Puerto Maldonado along the Río Tambopata. Unlike most others hereabouts, it doesn't feature programmed eco-activities. Just relax, read a book, enjoy a beer or amble around the 20km of well-signed trails. Fishing and canoe paddling are other optional pursuits. Book online or at the **Puerto Maldonado office** (Map p441; ☎082-57-2290; Billinghurst at Arequipa).

The lodge consists of four large bungalows and two smaller ones, and can accommodate a maximum of 40 guests. There is a tall observation tower from where you get good views of the surrounding jungle, and a chill-out room which boasts a library and wi-fi! Guests can now arrive by road/rough track to Filadelfia and continue by boat from there to cut down transportation time and costs (meaning one-night stays are possible). Four-day, three-night tours (per person US$588) take in Tambopata and Lago Sandoval, but not the Tambopata reserved zone.

No Reserva Nacional Tambopata entrance fees necessary.

Tambopata Research Center LODGE $$$

(Map p448; www.perunature.com; 5 days & 4 nights s/d US$1249/1944) About seven hours' river travel from Puerto Maldonado, this important research facility and lodge is known for a famous salt lick nearby that attracts four to 10 species of parrot and macaw on most mornings. The lodge itself is fairly simple, with 18 double rooms sharing four showers and four toilets. Book online or at the Rainforest Expeditions (p449) in Puerto Maldonado.

As for the research, this focuses on why macaws eat clay, their migration patterns, their diet, nesting macaws and techniques for building artificial nests. If you're interested in seeing more macaws than you ever thought possible, this lodge is worth the expense, although the owners point out that occasionally, due to poor weather or other factors, macaws aren't found at the lick.

A stopover is usually made at Refugio Amazonas on the first and last nights of a trip here. The last section of the ride is through remote country, with excellent chances of seeing capybaras and maybe more unusual animals. Have your passport ready at the **Puesto Control Malinowsky** (Map p448).

Río Madre de Dios

This important river surges eastward past Puerto Maldonado, heading into Bolivia, Brazil and the Amazon proper. In wet season it is brown-colored, flows swiftly and looks very impressive, sweeping huge logs and other jungle flotsam and jetsam downstream. Besides its selection of easily visited lodges, which include the southern jungle's most luxurious, this is also the access route both to Lago Sandoval and – further down its course – Lago Valencia and Río Heath.

Sights & Activities

Lago Sandoval is easily accessible from many lodges here. A couple of canopy walkways (Inkaterra Reserva Amazonica and Monte Amazonico Lodge) provide a distraction from normal jungle activities. Monte Amazónico Lodge even has a zipline.

Hacienda Concepción Research Center VISITOR CENTER

(Map p448; www.wcupa.edu/aceer) Formerly the ITA Aceer Tambopata Research Center, Inkaterra's reconstructed lodge, 8km downriver from Puerto Maldonado, is an important research center of interest to ecotourists, with an exhibition on conservation, occasional lectures and a laboratory for scientists. It's built on the site of the house of one of the first doctors to practice in the Amazon.

Next door, the Hacienda Concepción lodge has a good restaurant and accommodations. Inkaterra's Reserva Amazonica lodge is only 7km away.

Sleeping

Lodges are mentioned in the order by which you approach them from Puerto Maldonado.

Corto Maltes LODGE $$$

(Map p448; www.cortomaltes-amazonia.com; per person 3 days & 2 nights US$287) The closest lodge to Puerto Maldonado on the Río Madre de Dios is traveler friendly and upbeat. Only 5km from town, this lodge offers 27 comfortable, fully screened, high-ceilinged bungalows with solid mattresses – two bungalows even have king-size beds! Book online or at the **Puerto Maldonado office** (Map p441; ☎082-57-3831; Billinghurst 229).

Eye-catching Shipibo indigenous wall art and hammock-laced patios light up all the bungalows, as do cheerful decorative touches in the public areas. Electricity is available from dusk until 10:30pm, and showers have hot water. The French owners pride themselves on the excellent European–Peruvian fusion cuisine. Prices are based on two-person minimum group size.

Monte Amazonico Lodge LODGE $$$

(Map p448; http://carlosexpeditions.com; per person 3 days & 2 nights US$175; 🏊) Adrenaline-pumping adventures take priority over wildlife-watching here. This popular lodge near Lago Sandoval, with its two spick-and-span blocks of wooden, tin-roofed rooms, has canopy walkways and a zipline. A decent pool, a resident tapir and a nicely done common area with table football completes the agreeable overall effect. Book online or at the **Puerto Maldonado office** (Map p441; ☎082-57-1320; Velarde 139).

Kayaking and fishing are also possibilities. You can head here just for the day for US$80 per person. Book through Carlos Expeditions (p442).

★**Hacienda Concepción** LODGE **$$$**
(Map p448; ☎in UK 0800-458-7506, in US 800-442-5042; www.inkaterra.com; s/d 3 days & 2 nights US$429/740, cabins s/d US$521/844) This bright, enticing lodge is one of the southern Amazon's best. Facilities might be classic top-end Inkaterra but the big draw is that its prices are not. Its spacious rooms, fashioned out of reclaimed timber have an early-20th-century glamor, and there's a securely mosquito-netted bar, chill-out area and restaurant (serving incredible food). Book online or at **Inkaterra** (☎01-610-0400; central@inkaterra.com; Andalucía 174, Miraflores) in Lima.

The serene location could hardly be better, with an on-site rainforest learning center and laboratory, its own private *cocha* (an indigenous word for 'lagoon') nearby and Lago Sandoval a stone's throw away. Electricity is from 5:30am to 9:30am and 6pm to 11pm: it's one of the few jungle lodges with cell-phone reception and wi-fi. Rooms are spread around the 2nd floor, surveying the forest clearing with a broad wraparound terrace, while cabins have secluded *cocha* views – good enough, according to staff, for celebrities such as Mick Jagger to favor.

Inkaterra Reserva Amazonica LODGE **$$$**
(Map p448; ☎in UK 0800-458-7506, in US 800-442-5042; www.inkaterra.com; 3 days & 2 nights cabin s/d occupancy US$673/1082) Down the Madre de Dios, almost 16km from Puerto Maldonado, this luxurious lodge offers a good look at the jungle. Tours here include 10km of private hiking trails, and a series of swaying, narrow, jungle-canopy walkways up to 35m above the jungle floor for flora and fauna observation. Book online or at Inkaterra in Lima.

A huge, traditionally thatched, cone-shaped, two-story reception, restaurant, bar (built spectacularly around a fig tree), library and relaxation area greet the traveler. Some of the southern Amazon's best meals are served here; travelers with special dietary needs can be accommodated. There are occasional alfresco barbecues, sitting areas upstairs for imbibing views or spotting birdlife, and a separate building housing a good interpretation center. Guides speak English, French or Italian. About 40 rustic individual cabins have bathrooms and porches with two hammocks. Six suites boast huge bathrooms, writing desks and two queen-size beds each.

Eco Amazonia Lodge LODGE **$$$**
(Map p448; www.ecoamazonia.com; per person 3 days & 2 nights US$295-310;) Roughly 30km from Puerto Maldonado, this lodge boasts a huge, thatch-roofed restaurant and bar, with fine river views from the 2nd floor. Guides speak English, French and Italian; the knowledgeable manager also speaks Japanese. Fifty rustic, tin-roofed completely screened bungalows each have a bathroom and a small sitting room. Book online or at the **Cuzco office** (Map p200; ☎084-23-6159; reservas@ecoamazonia.com; Garcilaso 210, Office 206).

There is also a games room and a pool here. Several trails lead from this lodge, including a tough 14km hike to a lake, and several shorter walks. Boat tours to local lakes and along the rivers are also offered.

Estancia Bello Horizonte LODGE **$$$**
(Map p448; www.estanciabellohorizonte.com; per person 3 days & 2 nights US$180-230;) A superb getaway 20km from Puerto Maldonado on the east side of the Río Madre de Dios. Accommodations, which comprise of bungalows with smallish, comfortable rooms with bathrooms, are built in local wood and are poised on a ridge overlooking the rainforest; each has a hammock for lounging in. Book online or at the **Puerto Maldonado office** (Map p441; Loreto 252, Puerto Maldonado).

The main building contains a relaxing dining, reading, drinking and chill-out space, and child-friendly grounds include a soccer pitch, a volleyball court, a swimming pool and signposted jungle walks.

The final approach to the lodge is along a 6km private road through dense jungle.

Lago Sandoval

An attractive jungle lake, Lago Sandoval is surrounded by different types of rainforest and is about two hours from Puerto Maldonado by boat down the Madre de Dios, followed by a 3km hike. Permits to visit the lake (included on licensed guide tours and lodge stays) are S30 for the day, or S65 for two- to three-day visits. The best way to see wildlife is to stay overnight in one of the two lodges and take a boat ride on the lake, though day trips to the lake are offered. For about S100 (several people can travel for this price), a boat from Puerto Maldonado will drop you at the beginning of the hiking trail and pick you up later. From the dock the trail is obviously marked, although in poor condition. With luck, you might see caiman, turtles, exotic birds, monkeys and maybe the endangered giant river otters that live in the lake.

At the lake, you can continue 2km on a narrower, less-maintained trail to the inexpensive Willy Mejía Cepa Lodge, or take a boat ride across the lake to Sandoval Lake Lodge, the best lodge hereabouts.

Willy Mejía Cepa Lodge LODGE **$**
(Map p448; turismomejia@hotmail.com; r per person around US$50) The Mejías have been offering basic accommodations to budget travelers for two decades. The lodge can sleep 20 people in bungalow-style rooms with shared bathrooms. Bottled drinks are sold. Prices include simple family meals, accommodations and excursions (in Spanish). Book online or at the **Puerto Maldonado office** (Map p441; ☎982-684-700, 997-906-139; Velarde 487 interior). Room prices vary: ask about discounts, which are frequently given according to group size and season.

Sandoval Lake Lodge LODGE **$$$**
(Map p448; ☎in US 888-870-7378; www.inkanatura.com; per 3 days & 2 nights s/d US$535/840) These spacious premises crest a hilltop about 30m above Lago Sandoval and surrounded by primary forest. The big draw is the lake itself, which provides excellent wildlife-watching opportunities. Rooms, with heated showers and ceiling fans, are the best in the area. The restaurant-bar area is huge, airy and conducive to relaxing and chatting. Book online or at Inkaterra in Lima.

Another big attraction is the getting there. After hiking the 3km to the lake, you board canoes to negotiate narrow canals through a flooded palm-tree forest inhabited by red-bellied macaws, then silently paddle across the beautiful lake to the lodge.

With luck, you may spot the endangered giant river otter, several pairs of which live in the lake (early morning is best). Various monkey species and a host of birds and reptiles can also be seen. Hikes into the forest are offered, and the knowledgeable guides are multilingual.

The lodge was built from salvaged driftwood; the owners pride themselves on the fact that no primary forest was cut during construction (this is also true of some other lodges, though not always mentioned). Book with InkaNatura (p458).

Lago Valencia

Just off the Río Madre de Dios and near the Bolivian border, Lago Valencia is about 60km from Puerto Maldonado. At least two days are needed for a visit here, though three or four days are recommended. This lake reportedly offers the region's best **fishing**, as well as good **bird-watching** and **wildlife-watching** (bring your binoculars). There are trails into the jungle around the lake. Lodges nearer Puerto Maldonado can arrange tours, as can independent guides.

Río Heath

About two hours south of the Río Madre de Dios and along the Río Heath (the latter forming the Peru–Bolivia frontier), the **Parque Nacional Bahuaja-Sonene** (Map p448; admission S30), which Reserva Nacional Tambopata borders, has some of the best wildlife in Peru's Amazon region, including such rarities as the maned wolf and spider monkey, although these are not easily seen. Infrastructure in the park, one of the nation's largest, is limited, and wildlife-watching trips are in their infancy here. Bahuaja-Sonene comprises part of the vast Tambopata-Madidi wilderness reserve that spans a nigh-on 14,000 sq km tract across Peru and Bolivia. Park entrance fees should be paid at Sernanp (p446) in Puerto Maldonado, as checkpoints along the way don't sell tickets.

The simple, 10-room **Heath River Wildlife Center** (Map p448; www.inkanatura.com; s/d 4 days & 3 nights US$913/1512) is owned by the Ese'eja indigenous people of Sonene, who provide guiding and cultural services. Trails into Parque Nacional Bahuaja-Sonene are available, and field biologists have assessed this area as one of the most biodiverse in southeastern Peru – it's too early to tell if the Carretera Interoceánica's construction could change this. Capybaras are frequently seen, and guided tours to a nearby *colpa* (clay lick), a popular attraction for macaws and parrots, are arranged. Hot water is provided and park entrance fees are included. The first and last nights of tours are spent at Sandoval Lake Lodge; book through InkaNatura (p458).

MANU AREA

The Manu area encompasses Parque Nacional Manu and much of the surrounding jungle and cloud forest. Covering almost 20,000 sq km (about the size of Wales), the park is one of the best places in South America to scout out a whole shebang of tropical wildlife.

The park is divided into three zones. The largest sector is the *zona natural,* comprising 80% of the total park area and closed to unauthorized visitors. Entry to this sector is restricted to a few indigenous groups, mainly the Matsiguenka (also spelled Machiguenga), some of whom continue to live here as they have for generations; some groups have had almost no contact with outsiders and do not seem to want any. Fortunately, this wish is largely respected – although tensions and clashes between tribes and settled villages have been reported more of late. A handful of researchers with permits are also allowed in to study the wildlife.

The second sector, still within the park proper, is the *zona reservada* (reserved zone, recently rebranded as the Manu river sector), where controlled research and tourism are permitted. There are a couple of official accommodation options here. This is the northeastern sector, comprising about 10% of the park area.

The third sector, covering the southeastern area, is the *zona cultural* (cultural zone, recently rebranded as the cultural history zone), where most other visitor activity is concentrated.

To travel between the *zona cultural* and the *zona reservada,* you'll need to take the Río Madre de Dios to the park's main transit village, Boca Manu. Finally, outside the national park boundaries southeast of Boca Manu are, ironically, some of the very best wildlife-watching opportunities, especially at the macaw and tapir licks around the Manu Wildlife Center.

The Parque Nacional Manu website (www.visitmanu.com) has more information.

AMAZON INFORMATION

One of the best independent resources is **South American Explorer** (www.saexplorers.org), with offices in Lima and Cuzco; otherwise, see lodge websites such as www.manuexpeditions.com (Manu) and www.inkaterra.com (southern Amazon).

Tours

It's important to check exactly where the tours are going: Manu is a catchall word that includes the national park and much of the surrounding area. Some tours, such as to the Manu Wildlife Center, don't actually enter Parque Nacional Manu at all (although the wildlife center is recommended for wildlife-watching nonetheless). Some companies aren't allowed to enter the park, but offer what they call 'Manu tours' outside the park or act as agents for other operators. Other companies work together and share resources such as lodges, guides and transportation services. This can mean the agency in whose office you sign up for the tour isn't the agency you end up going with. Most will combine a Manu experience with a full Peru tour on request. Confusing? You bet!

The companies we recommend are all authorized to operate within Manu by the national park service and maintain some level of conservation and low-impact practices. The number of permits to operate tours into Parque Nacional Manu is limited; only a few thousand visitors are allowed in annually. Intending visitors must book well in advance. Be flexible with onward travel plans as delays are common. Entering by bus and boat (on the Río Alto Madre de Dios) and returning by boat (the Río Madre de Dios) and flight from Puerto Maldonado is the best means of seeing Manu.

Tour costs depend on whether you camp or stay in a lodge, whether you arrive and depart overland or by air and whether you enter the *zona reservada.* A tour inside the zone won't necessarily get you better wildlife-viewing – although, since it's virgin jungle here, the chances of seeing larger animals are greater. If your budget allows, the more expensive companies really are worth considering. They offer more reliable and trained multilingual guides, better equipment, a wider variety of food, suitable insurance and emergency procedures. Perhaps most importantly, there are more guarantees that your money is going partly toward preserving Manu, as many of these companies fund conservation costs.

All companies provide transportation, food, purified drinking water, guides, permits and camping equipment or screens in lodge rooms. It's the traveler's responsibility to bring personal items such as a sleeping bag (unless staying in a lodge), insect repellent, sunblock, flashlight with

JUNGLE CHECKLIST

First jungle voyage? You'll find things far more relaxing than the movies make out. The jungle, you'll see, has largely been packaged to protect delicate tourists. With lodge facilities and the below kit list, you should be ready for most eventualities.

- ☐ Two pairs of shoes, one for jungle traipsing, one for camp.
- ☐ Spare clothes – in this humidity clothes get wet quickly; take a spare towel too.
- ☐ Binoculars and a zoom lens camera, for wildlife in close-up.
- ☐ Flashlight for night walks.
- ☐ Mosquito repellent with DEET – bugs are everywhere.
- ☐ Sunblock and sunglasses – despite that foliage, you'll often be in direct sun.
- ☐ First-aid kit for basics such as bites, stings or diarrhea.
- ☐ Plastic bags to waterproof gear and pack nonbiodegradable litter to take back with you.
- ☐ Lightweight rainproof jacket.
- ☐ Sleeping bag, mat or hammock if sleeping outside.
- ☐ Books – cell phones rarely work and neither do TVs; electricity is often limited to several hours daily.

spare batteries, suitable clothing and bottled drinks. Binoculars and a camera with a zoom lens are highly recommended.

All lodges and tour operators in the big-money business of Manu excursions quote prices in US dollars.

Crees ADVENTURE TOUR
(www.crees-manu.org; 1-week trip s/d per person from US$1695/2650) Crees runs 'voluntourism' one-week trips into the *zona reservada*. These depart every fortnight April to December: participants can help with projects such as reforestation and jaguar monitoring, while at the same time getting to see parts of the jungle the tourist otherwise couldn't reach. Book online or at the **Cuzco office** (☎084-26-2433; www.crees-manu.org; Urb Mariscal Garmarra B-5, Zona 1).

If one week isn't enough for you, it also runs long-term volunteer projects (up to 16 weeks), based at its Manu Learning Centre, where you'll be directly helping communities in and around Manu.

Bonanza Tours ADVENTURE TOUR
(Map p200; ☎084-50-7871; www.bonanzatoursperu.com; Suecia 343, Cuzco) Run by Ryse Choquepuma and his brothers, who grew up in Manu and know it better than most. Tours are to the family home, which has been converted into the well-appointed Bonanza Ecological Reserve. The land here virtually backs onto the park proper and there are trails as well as a clay lick that attracts plenty of wildlife.

Swims in hot springs and coconut-cutting lessons are included, as is a special late-night creepy-crawly-hunting sojourn.

The four-day and three-night option with two nights at the family lodge and one at their lodge near Pilcopata is US$490. Bonanza also runs longer tours into the *zona reservada*.

Pantiacolla Tours ADVENTURE TOUR
(Map p200; ☎084-23-8323; www.pantiacolla.com; Garcilaso 265 interior, 2nd fl, Cuzco) Pantiacolla is frequently recommended by a variety of travelers for its knowledgeable and responsibly executed tours, helped by the fact that its staff members were raised in the area. It also helps fund conservation of Manu, so ecologically, there's no better bet. Runs shorter trips, but it's the seven-day tours to Manu that are the real crowd-puller (per person US$1580).

This trip is all overland, including two nights in the reserved zone, and a mixture of camping and lodge accommodations, then carrying on downriver and returning via the Carretera Interoceaníca. The agency offers a variety of other tours, including the opportunity to study Spanish at its jungle lodge.

Manu Expeditions ADVENTURE TOUR
(☎084-22-5990; www.manuexpeditions.com; Los Geranios 2-G, Urb Mariscal Gamarra) Manu Expeditions, co-owners of Manu Wildlife Center, have more than two decades of Manu experience. Its guides are excellent,

but if you are lucky enough to go with the owner, British ornithologist and long-time Cuzco resident Barry Walker, you will really be in excellent hands, particularly if birding is your interest.

A popular trip leaves Cuzco every Monday (except January to March, when it's the first Monday of the month only) and lasts nine days, including overland transportation to Manu with two nights of camping at the company's Cocha Salvador Tented Camp, three nights at Manu Wildlife Center, three nights at other lodges and a flight back to Cuzco.

This costs US$2998 per person, based on two people sharing a room. The overland section can include a mountain-biking descent if arranged in advance. Shorter, longer and customized trips are offered.

Manu Nature Tours ADVENTURE TOUR
(Map p208; ☎084-25-2721; www.manuperu.com; Pardo 1046, Cuzco) This outfit operates the respected Manu Lodge, the only fully appointed lodge within the reserve. There's a 20km network of trails, and guided visits to lakes and observation towers are also provided. A four-day tour, in and out by bus and boat (single US$1330, double US$2060), uses the outfit's Manu Lodge for two nights (fixed departures each Friday May to October).

Manu trips have a bilingual naturalist guide and all meals are provided. For an extra fee, mountain biking or river running (white-water rafting) can be incorporated into the road descent. Longer tours (up to eight days) are also available.

Amazon Trails Peru ADVENTURE TOUR
(Map p200; ☎084-43-7374; www.amazontrails-peru.com; Tandapata 660) This outfit has a growing reputation for providing the best service among the cheaper tour operators. Tours provide a great deal of quirky insider information en route. High-power binoculars are also provided, increasing chances of decent wildlife sightings. Six-day tours to the *zona reservada* start from US$1515 (four-person minimum).

If you're heading on to Puerto Maldonado, onward boat/bus transport can be arranged to save backtracking to Cuzco.

At its cloud-forest-based Bambu Lodge you can also try your hand at rafting.

InkaNatura Travel TOUR
(www.inkanatura.com) InkaNatura, which has offices in **Cuzco** (☎984-691-838, 084-23-1138, 084-25-5255; www.inkanatura.com; Ricardo Palma J1 Urb Santa Mónica & Plateros 361) and Lima (p78), is a highly respected international agency and co-owner of the Manu Wildlife Center. The operators can combine a visit here with trips to other parts of the southern Peruvian rainforest, including Pampas del Heath near Puerto Maldonado, where it also has a lodge (the Heath Wildlife Center).

Cuzco to Manu

This spectacular journey provides opportunities for some excellent bird-watching at the lodges en route, as well as some of Peru's most dramatic scenery changes. The route runs from bare Andean mountains into cloud forest before dropping into a steamy tangle of lowland jungle.

You can get as far as Boca Manu, an hour before the entrance point for the *zona reservada,* independently. This is challenging but possible: most lodges en route will let you stay, but giving them advance notice is advised. However, to either enter the *zona reservada* or maximize your chances of seeing wildlife, you will need a guide and therefore a tour.

If traveling overland, the first stage of the journey involves taking a bus or truck (or minivan if you are on a tour) from Cuzco via Paucartambo (S12, three hours) to Pilcopata and Shintuya. Buses run by **Gallito de las Rocas** (☎084-22-6895; Av Diagonal Angamos 1952, Cuzco) leave at 5am on Monday, Wednesday and Friday for Pilcopata (S26, 10 to 12 hours in good weather), returning from Pilcopata on the same days at 6pm. Get a taxi to the departure point – it's difficult to find independently – and look for 'Paucartambo' painted on a lamppost between auto shops to find the office.

Cheaper trucks also leave sporadically from the Coliseo Cerrado in Cuzco for Shintuya (about 24 hours in the dry season). Breakdowns, extreme overcrowding and delays are common, and during the rainy season (even during the dry) vehicles slide off the road. It's safer, more comfortable and more reliable to take the costlier tourist buses offered by Cuzco tour operators. Many tour companies in Cuzco offer trips to Manu.

Sights & Activities

After the pretty town of Paucartambo, the road continues for 1½ hours to the entrance to Parque Nacional Manu (*zona cultural;* admission S10 for independent travelers at the turnoff to Tres Cruces, a further 13km). The next six hours to Pilcopata are through spectacular **cloud forest**, occupying a humid elevation of some 1600m and home to thousands of bird species, many of which are yet to be officially identified. There are several lodges at which you can enjoy phenomenal **bird-watching** (including, if you are lucky, the rarely glimpsed cock-of-the-rocks, with striking scarlet plumage and elaborate mating dances).

The next village, **Pilcopata**, is the end of the public bus route and indeed contact with the outside world of all kinds: the last public phone (and cell-phone reception) before Manu is here, along with Manu's main police station. There are basic hotels (beds around S15) and stores too. Pickup trucks leave early every morning for Atalaya (45 minutes) and Shintuya (three hours).

The road beyond Pilcopata can be nigh-on impassable in wet season, which is why most vehicles give up the ghost at **Atalaya**, and switch to boat (all Manu tour agencies continue by boat from here). To continue by rough road beyond here to **Salvación** (where there is a national park office) and **Shintuya** (with limited basic accommodations) is possible, but slightly pointless, as there are more boats available for continuing downriver in Atalaya. Just past Shintuya, **Itahuanía** has Manu's emergency hospital.

The long boat journey down the Río Alto Madre de Dios from Atalaya to **Boca Manu**, at the junction with the Río Manu, can take almost a day. Boca Manu village has basic facilities and is known for building the region's best riverboats: it is interesting to see these vessels in various stages of construction. Independent travelers: again, bear in mind that if you are not on a tour with a licensed Manu tour agency you will not be permitted entry into the *zona reservada,* although continuing on down the Río Manu to the Manu Wildlife Center (p461) and Puerto Maldonado *may* be possible.

Because of the long process of reaching Boca Manu from Cuzco, some companies prefer using the other route to Manu (a flight into Puerto Maldonado followed by a road trip on the Carretera Interoceaníca and a trip *up* the Madre de Dios).

Sleeping

There are several good lodges on this route. While none are in the *zona reservada* or the *zona natural* of Parque Nacional Manu, they nevertheless can provide great wildlife-watching opportunities. Don't assume entering the *zona reservada* is an automatic guarantee of seeing better wildlife. Lodges are congregated either in the cloud forest or on the Río Alto Madre de Dios after Atalaya; most let independent tourists stay, but tour groups on lodge-affiliated tours get priority. If you are set on staying at a recommended lodge, it's advisable to reserve at least a night in advance.

Cloud Forest

Rainforest Lodge LODGE **$$**

(Map p448; per person incl meals US$40) A cheap option, and a good journey-breaker, is this rustic lodge around 10 hours from Cuzco near Pilcopata (you could hit the village nightlife from here). There are eight cabins here sleeping up to 20 people, with shared bathrooms. It's at the base of the cloud forest (one hour's drive from the best cloud forest bird-watching). Book through Bonanza Tours (p457).

Manu Paradise Lodge LODGE **$$$**

(www.manuparadiselodge.com; 4 days & 3 nights s/d US$1819/2122) Around six hours from Cuzco and overlooking the scenic Río Kosñipata valley, this lodge sleeps 16 people in spacious rooms with private hot-water bathrooms. It looks quite modern, unlike the more rustic lodges further into the park. Among its assets are an attractive dining room–bar with a fireplace and telescopes for wildlife-viewing. Book online.

It advertises its wide variety of tours (three to six nights) on its website. Rafting and mountain-biking tours can be arranged, but the primary attraction is bird-watching (its classic bird-watching tour is what is priced above).

Manu Cloud Forest Lodge LODGE **$$$**

(Map p448; ☎084-25-2721; per person per day d US$130) Six to seven hours drive from Cuzco, Manu Cloud Forest Lodge is a basic 16- to 20-bed lodge providing six rooms with hot showers, a restaurant and bird-watching opportunities in the high cloud forest. Transportation and use of the sauna cost extra. Book through Manu Nature Tours (p458).

Rates include room and full board only: adding all activities/services on to a stay brings the cost to around US$300 per person daily.

Cock-of-the-Rock Lodge LODGE **$$$**

(Map p448; www.inkanatura.com; s/d incl meals 3 days & 2 nights US$994/1642) A few minutes' walk from a *lek* (mating ground) for cocks-of-the-rocks, this lodge offers exceptional cloud-forest bird-watching at 1600m elevation. The owners claim you can get photos of male cocks-of-the-rock displaying about 7m from your camera. The InkaNatura-owned lodge has a restaurant and 12 rustic double cabins with private bathrooms and hot water. Book online or through InkaNatura, which has offices in Cuzco (p458) and Lima (p78).

Rates include round-trip transportation from Cuzco, which takes on average eight hours one way (with points-of-interest stops).

Río Alto Madre de Dios

This is the upper echelons of the Río Madre de Dios; upriver of Boca Manu. It is harder to stay at some of these lodges independently, as you need a boat to reach them, and there are few available boats not affiliated with a particular tour agency.

Amazonia Lodge LODGE **$$**

(Map p448; www.amazonialodge.com; r per person incl meals US$85) In an old colonial hacienda in the Andean foothills, Amazonia provides travelers with slightly different environs to bed down (although a refurbishment is long overdue and the river has swamped some of the grounds). Expect clean, comfortable beds and communal hot showers. Book online or through any of the tour agencies in Cuzco.

The lodge has forest trails, excellent bird-watching (guided tours are offered) and no electricity. As it's just across the river from Atalaya (itself about eleven hours from Cuzco), you can usually charter a local boat to ferry you across.

Pantiacolla Lodge LODGE **$$**

(Map p448; s with/without bathroom US$175/155, d with/without bathroom US$230/200) There are 11 double rooms here, eight with shared bathrooms and three with private ones. Rates include meals but not transportation or tours, though right near the lodge are forest trails (some reascending into cloud forest at 900m), a parrot lick and hot springs. Various transportation and guided-tour options are available. Book with Pantiacolla Tours (p457).

It is necessary to give advance notice for the boat to the lodge (about 1½ hours from Atalaya by boat, or 12½ hours' journey from Cuzco), which is on the fringe of the national park, just before Itahuanía village.

Bonanza Ecological Reserve LODGE **$$**

(Map p448; per person incl meals US$85) Past Itahuanía toward the community of Bonanza, this family-run, 32-person-capacity lodge has cabins abutting a large clearing that also has a large restaurant area and a two-floor hammock-strung chill-out zone; bathrooms are shared and there's solar-paneled electricity throughout. From here trails lead off into dense jungle which backs onto Manu's *zona natural*. Book through Bonanza Tours (p457).

The highlight here is the treehouse peeping out on a clay lick which tapirs visit, and two 15m observation towers for improved animal-viewing. A canopy walkway is planned. There are also canoes available for nearby river trips. The lodge is around three hours from Atalaya by boat, or 14 hours' journey from Cuzco.

Parque Nacional Manu

This national park starts in the eastern slopes of the Andes and plunges down into the lowlands, hosting great diversity over a wide range of cloud forest and rainforest habitats. The most progressive aspect of the park is the fact that so much of it is very carefully protected – a rarity anywhere in the world.

After Peru introduced protection laws in 1973, Unesco declared Manu a Biosphere Reserve in 1977 and a World Natural Heritage site in 1987. One reason the park is so successful in preserving such a large tract of virgin jungle and its wildlife is that it is remote and relatively inaccessible to people, and therefore has not been exploited by rubber tappers, hunters and the like (although there is an ongoing dispute between local Amazonians and Hunt Oil, to which the government gave a concession to for hydrocarbon extraction in Manu's *zona cultura*).

It is illegal to enter the park without a guide. Going with an organized group can be arranged in Cuzco or with international tour operators. It's an expensive trip; budget travelers should arrange their trip in Cuzco and be flexible with travel plans. Travelers often report returning from Manu several days late. Don't plan an international airline connection the day after a Manu trip!

Permits, which are necessary to enter the park, are arranged by tour agencies. Transportation, accommodations, food and guides are also part of tour packages. Most visits are for a week, although three-night stays at a lodge can be arranged.

The best time to go is during the dry season (June to November); Manu may be inaccessible or closed during the rainy months (January to April), except to visitors staying at the two lodges within the park boundaries.

Virgin jungle lies up the Río Manu northwest of Boca Manu. At the Puesto Control Limonal (Guard Post), about an hour from Boca Manu, a park entrance fee of S150 per person is payable (usually included in your tour). Continuing beyond is only possible with a guide and a permit. Near the control point are a few trails.

Two hours upstream is the oxbow lake of **Cocha Juárez** where giant river otters are often encountered. About four hours further, **Cocha Salvador**, one of the park's largest, most beautiful lakes, has guided camping and hiking possibilities. Half an hour's boat ride away is **Cocha Otorongo**, another oxbow lake with a wildlife-viewing observation tower. These are not wide-open habitats like the African plains. Thick vegetation will obscure many animals, and a skilled guide is very useful in helping you to see them.

During a one-week trip, you can reasonably expect to see scores of different bird species, several monkey species and possibly a few other mammals. Jaguars (sightings are on the increase in the *zona reservada*), tapirs, giant anteaters, tamanduas, capybaras, peccaries and giant river otters are among the common large Manu mammals. But they are elusive, and you can consider a trip very successful if you see two or three large mammals during a week's visit. Smaller mammals you might see include kinkajous, pacas, agoutis, squirrels, brocket deer, ocelots and armadillos. Other animals include river turtles and caiman (which are frequently seen), snakes (which are less often spotted) and a variety of other reptiles and amphibians. Colorful butterflies and less pleasing insects also abound.

There are two lodges within the park, plus a tented camp: you can't stay at any of these accommodations independently, but all are included on tours, by the owners and by other agencies.

At **Manu Lodge** (Map p448), two simple, slightly decrepit blocks containing 12 double rooms are screened and have comfortable beds; a separate building has cold showers and toilets. The lodge is on Cocha Juárez, about 1km from the Río Manu. For an extra fee, you can climb up to a canopy platform; river running can also be arranged. A 20km network of trails from the lodge around the lake and beyond provides ample opportunities for spotting wildlife, including giant otters. Contact Manu Nature Tours (p458).

Manu Tented Camp (Map p448) lies beyond Manu Lodge, by Cocha Salvador. This modern camp has raised platforms supporting large walk-in screened tents. Decent showers, toilets and meals are available. Contact InkaNatura (p458). Manu Expeditions occasionally uses the more rustic **Casa Matsiguenka Lodge** (Map p448; ☎084-22-5990; www.manuexpeditions.com; Los Geranios, 2-G, Urb Mariscal Gamarra), built in traditional style by the Matsiguenka tribespeople.

More primitive camping, usually on the sandy beaches of the Río Manu or on the foreshore of a few of the lakes, is another possibility. Tour operators can provide all necessary equipment. During the rainy season (January to April) these beaches are flooded and the park is closed to camping. Campers should come prepared with plenty of insect repellent.

Manu Wildlife Center & Around

A two-hour boat ride southeast of Boca Manu on the Río Madre de Dios takes you to **Manu Wildlife Center** (Map p448; s/d 5 days & 4 nights US$2282/3872). The center is a jungle lodge owned by InkaNatura Travel (p458) and Manu Expeditions (p457), both of which take reservations. Although the lodge is not in the Manu Biosphere Reserve, it is recommended for its exceptional wildlife-watching and birding opportunities. There are 22 screened double cabins with hot showers, a dining room and a bar-hammock room. The lodge is set in tropical gardens. Note that some tours start with a flight into Puerto Maldonado and travel up the Río Madre de Dios to reach Manu Wildlife Center from there. This is a great opportunity to explore a little-plied section of this majestic river. Other options can also include one to two nights camping within the park itself.

There are 48km of trails around the wildlife center, where 12 species of monkey, as well as other wildlife, can be seen. Two canopy platforms are a short walk away, and one is always available for guests wishing to view the top of the rainforest and look for birds that frequent the canopy.

A 3km walk through the forest brings you to a natural salt lick, where there is a raised platform with mosquito nets for viewing the nightly activities of the tapirs. This hike is for visitors who can negotiate forest trails by flashlight. Chances to see animals are excellent if you have the patience, although visitors may wait for hours. Note that there isn't much happening at the lick during the day.

A short boat ride along the Madre de Dios brings visitors to another well-known salt lick that attracts various species of parrot and macaw. Most mornings you can see flocks in the hundreds. The largest flocks are seen from late July to September. As the rainy season kicks in, the numbers diminish and in June birds don't visit the salt lick at all. May and early July aren't reliable either, though ornithologists report the presence of the birds in other nearby areas during these months, which birders can usually spot.

The macaw lick is visited on a floating catamaran blind, with the blind providing a concealed enclosure from which 20 people can view the wildlife. The catamaran is stable enough to allow the use of a tripod and scope or a telephoto lens, and gets about halfway across the river. Boat drivers won't bring the blind too close to avoid disturbing the birds.

In addition to the trails and salt licks, there are a couple of nearby lakes accessible by catamaran where giant otters may be seen (as well as other wildlife). If you wish to see the macaw and tapir lick, the lakes and the canopy, and hike the trails in search of wildlife, you should plan on a three-night stay at the Manu Wildlife Center. Shorter and longer stays are workable.

Near the Manu Wildlife Center, rustic **Tambo Blanquillo Lodge** (☎Cuzco 084-23-4517, Lima 01-249-9342; Av Nicolás de Piérola 265, Barranco, Lima) has rooms with shared and private bathrooms. Some companies in Cuzco combine this cheaper option with a tour including other lodges in the Manu area, but prices vary. Staying just at Blanquillo isn't possible. Tour operators include Pantiacolla Tours (p457).

If you continue down the Madre de Dios past gold-panning areas to Puerto Maldonado, you won't see much wildlife. Amazon Trails Peru (p458) can also organize onward boat/bus transportation, but transportation to Puerto Maldonado is infrequent; almost all visitors return to Cuzco.

CENTRAL AMAZON

For a quick Amazon fix on long weekends and holidays, *limeños* (inhabitants of Lima) usually head for this relatively accessible area of the Amazon, reachable in eight hours by bus. The tropical Chanchamayo province, which accounts for most of this region, is as different to the coastal desert or the Andean mountains as can be. The last hour of the journey here is particularly remarkable for the rapid change in vegetation and climate as you slip down the Andes into the vibrant green of La Selva Central, as it is known in Spanish. Comprising the two main towns of La Merced and San Ramón, plus a scattering of remoter communities, the area is noted for coffee and fruit production. Despite popularity with Peruvian holidaymakers, the region offers the traveler a good insight into Amazon life in all its sweaty clamor. An adventurous back route also awaits for the intrepid: forging via Satipo through Peru's central belt of Amazon to the port of Pucallpa, jumping-off point for river trips deeper into the jungle.

La Merced & San Ramón

☎064 / POP 52,000 / ELEV 800M

San Ramón is 295km east of Lima and La Merced is 11km further along. Chanchamayo's two key settlements are quite likable in a languid sort of way. Resistance to colonists by the local Asháninka people meant that these towns were not founded until the 19th century. Today they are popular Peruvian holiday destinations, and great bases for exploring the luxuriant countryside nearby, characterized by photogenic forested hills and waterfalls that tumble into the Río Chanchamayo valley. Accommodation bookings are recommended at busy periods, when room rates almost double.

Sights & Activities

A few markets hereabouts add some colour to proceedings: a daily **market** in La Merced, and an interesting weekend **market**, visited by local *indígenas* (people of indigenous descent), at San Luis de Shuaro, 22km beyond La Merced. Asháninka tribespeople occasionally come into La Merced to sell handicrafts.

Viewpoints VIEWPOINT
(Av 2 de Mayo, La Merced) The stairs at the northwest end of Av 2 de Mayo afford a good view of the town, and from the balcony at the southwest end there's a photogenic river viewpoint.

Catarata El Tirol WATERFALL
There are many impressive waterfalls around San Ramón, but this 35m cascade is the most visited. El Tirol crashes down 5km east of San Ramón off the La Merced road. You can take a taxi the first 2km; the last 3km is along shady forest paths and streams.

Off the Pichanaqui road, beyond La Merced at Puente Yurinaki, are the higher waterfalls of **Catarata Velo de la Novia** and **Catarata Bayoz**. Agencies in La Merced or Tarma arrange tours to all three falls.

Isla Las Turunas ADVENTURE SPORTS
(☎942-600-089; La Merced) At the southern end of Calle las Guanábanas, south of the San Ramón–La Merced road, this leafy, lagoon-dotted enclave has been made into a fun, well-run adventure park, with kayaking and a zipline, plus an inviting pool for cool-off time. The restaurant rustles up mean *tacacho con cecina* (roasted banana and meat balls with smoked pork).

Sleeping

La Merced harbors most decent digs; some luxury lodges beckon just outside San Ramón.

La Merced

You don't have to look far in the central blocks to find a cheap *hospedaje* for S20 per person or less.

Hotel Rey HOTEL $
(☎064-53-1185, 064-53-2375; www.hotelrey.net; Junín 103; s/d S60/80) A popular place, and the owners know it. Bright, inviting hallways (public phones on each) lead to rooms with fans, cable TV and hot showers. A top-floor restaurant serves decent food and views out over the sea of tin roofs.

Hotel Elio's HOTEL $
(☎064-53-1229; Palca 281; s/d S40/50) Just off the plaza, with spacious rooms that make the beds look almost lost; there are writing desks, fans, cable TV and spotless bathrooms. Street-facing rooms are very noisy.

Tropical Hotel Suite HOTEL $$
(☎064-53-2069; info@tropicalhotelsuite.pe; Arica 282; s/d S80/120) Bandying about a lime-green colour scheme to support the 'tropical' part of its title, this is the only hotel in town with sufficient height to write its name lengthways down the building (seven floors, lofty by La Merced standards). Rooms are sizable and very clean – and green, of course. A sparkling midrange choice.

Hotel Heliconia HOTEL $$
(☎064-53-1394; www.heliconiahotel.com; Junín 992; s/d/tr incl breakfast S100/150/200; ❄📶) The best of La Merced's hotels, the air-conditioned rooms here are ginormous and all come with fridges and sparkling bathrooms. Breakfast is enjoyed in a cheerful setting and views are mostly onto Parque Integración.

San Ramón

The town itself is unexceptional. However, the best places to stay in this region lie outside, on the La Merced road.

★**Gad Gha Kum Lodge** LODGE $$$
(☎064-77-5964, 064-33-1935; www.elmensajerolodge.com; Carretera Central Km 98; cabins s/d S180/250) This is the nicest of several good lodges nearby: vast peaceful grounds, their own private waterfall trail, large, well-appointed cabins with terraces, a pretty pool and a central thatched restaurant.

THE AMAZON: MAIN POINTS OF ENTRY

Puerto Maldonado (southern Amazon) Connected by road, river and air.

La Merced/San Ramon (central Amazon) Connected by road.

Pucallpa (central Amazon) Connected by road, river and air.

Yurimaguas (northern Amazon) Connected by road and river.

Iquitos (northern Amazon) Connected by river and air.

There is also camping space, and the lodge is well-known for its massage treatments. Another world altogether from the frenetic La Selva Central towns nearby. La Merced–San Ramón minibuses run past the entrance.

Eating

Options are pretty basic.

Chifa Felipe Siu CHINESE $
(Progreso 434, San Ramón; meals around S15; 11am-2pm & 6:30-11pm) The best place to eat Chinese food in the Amazon.

Restaurant Shambari Campa PERUVIAN $$
(Tarma 389, La Merced; mains S18-27; 6:30am-12:30am) On the plaza, this famous hole-in-the-wall restaurant provides a menu so extensive you can be lost for choice, but includes sensational *chancho* (rainforest wild pig).

Shopping

Chanchamayo Highland Coffee COFFEE
(064-53-1198; http://highlandproducts.com.pe) Here you can sample and buy the coffee for which Chanchamayo is famous. (Peru is one of the world's largest coffee producers but nearly all gets exported.) It's gimmicky but enjoyable, and besides the shop, you can browse displays on coffee production and check out old coffee-producing machinery. It's 1km northeast of the main bus terminal on the Satipo road. These days it does a tempting range of local jams and ice creams too.

Information

Both towns have a BCP with an ATM, and plenty of public telephones. La Merced has better facilities: here, it's a challenge to find a block *without* an internet cafe.

Hospital Selva Central (064-53-1408; cnr Los Robles & Los Cauchos, La Merced)

Police station (Julio Piérola at Passuni, La Merced)

Post office (Av 2 de Mayo, La Merced)

Getting There & Away

AIR

The Chanchamayo airstrip is a 30-minute walk from San Ramón. *Mototaxis* will take you there (around S3). Small planes can theoretically be chartered to almost anywhere in the region but the strip is virtually deserted most days.

BUS

The main bus terminal is a 1km downhill walk east of the center of La Merced; most buses arrive and leave from here. This is well organized, but as much transportation relies on *colectivos* (that leave when full). Schedules are haphazard – go down there as early as possible and ask around.

Direct buses go from Lima to Chanchamayo, though many travelers break the journey at Tarma. Try to travel the 70km stretch from Tarma to San Ramón in daylight for the views during the spectacular 2200m descent.

Many companies run to Lima (S35 to S50, eight hours) from La Merced, including **Expreso Molina Unión** (988-893-599; Av José De Aguirrezabal s/n), with its own separate terminal 1km from the main bus terminal along the San Ramón road. Other outfits like Transportes Salazaar also go to Lima, with several daily and/or nightly departures. Their offices are all located at the main bus terminal or across the road on Prolongación Tarma.

Frequent buses from various companies go to Tarma (around S10, 2½ hours) and on to Huancayo (S15 to S20, 4½ hours) via Jauja.

Transportation into the jungle is by large minibus or pickup truck. *Colectivos* ply some routes for a slightly higher price. Minibuses leave for Pichanaqui (S5, 1½ hours) and Satipo (S10, 2½ hours) about every half hour, also departing frequently to Oxapampa (S10, three hours), where you can change for services to Pozuzo (four hours further on).

TAXI

Colectivos seating four passengers go to Tarma (S20, 1¾ hours), Oxapampa (S15, two hours), Pichanaqui (S10, one hour) and Satipo (S21, two hours) from marked stands within the bus-terminal complex.

Getting Around

Minibuses linking La Merced with San Ramón and the hotels in between leave frequently (S1.50, 15 minutes) from outside the bus terminal. Drivers try charging more if they think you're staying at one of the flash hotels outside San Ramón. *Mototaxis* charge S1 to drive you from the terminal up into La Merced center.

Satipo

064 / POP 42,000 / ELEV 630M

This amiable jungle town is the center of a coffee- and fruit-producing region 130km by road southeast of La Merced. This road was paved in 2000 to provide an outlet for produce, and Satipo grew rapidly in response. It's of interest to travelers as the start of a way-off-the-beaten-path track and river journey to Pucallpa (although few foreigners attempt the odyssey).

The attractive main plaza has a BCP (ATM) and lots of ice-cream and cake shops. Tour agencies in town offer trips to local waterfalls (there are some real stunners nearby) and petroglyphs.

The pick of Satipo's mushrooming accommodations scene is **Hostal San Luis** (☎064-54-5319; cnr Grau 173 & Leguía; s/d S60/90; ❄🏊), where decent-sized rooms are served by a cafeteria downstairs. There's a pool too.

Minibuses and *colectivos* leave regularly for Pichanaqui, where you can change for La Merced, or head direct to La Merced (S21, two hours) less frequently. Larger buses leave from the main bus station, **Terminal Terrestre**, on the southwestern edge of town. The main destination is again La Merced (S10), where you can change for a better range of services to Lima and Huancayo.

Bunched around the corner of Francisco Irazola and Bolognesi, *colectivos* leave for Mazamari (S5, 30 minutes), Puerto Ocapa (S25, two hours) and eventually, via a deteriorating road, to Atalaya, at the intersection of Ríos Urubamba, Tambo and Ucayali. From here, it's possible to find boats heading to Pucallpa, 450km downstream (a trip taking up to three days). If undertaking this trip, be aware that this is remote jungle and not without dangers, one of which is armed plantation saboteurs.

Oxapampa

☎063 / POP 14,000 / ELEV 1800M

Two key periods in history have shaped this pretty ranching and coffee center, 75km north of La Merced. The first was during the mid-19th century when it attracted some 200 settlers from Germany, the descendants of which (many still blonde-haired and blue-eyed) inhabit Oxapampa and its surrounds. The second? The last few years! Local land has been sold off at basement prices, enticing a new wave of settlers, this time largely from Lima. New businesses have opened, many of which are attractive guesthouses and restaurants, which keeps the town's tourist appeal buoyant. Add a cracking nearby national park and Peru's best music fest and you have one of the most intriguing locales in the Amazon. Buildings have a Tyrolean look, Austrian-German food is prepared, an old-fashioned form of German is still spoken by some families, and numerous Germanic customs are preserved. There is a BCP with ATMs on the main plaza.

Sights

Parque Nacional Yanachaga-Chemillén NATIONAL PARK

(admission S10) North of Oxapampa rear the cloud-capped hills of this little-visited park, preserving spectacular cloud forest and diverse flora and fauna, including the rare spectacled bear. The most accessible entrance is from a turning near Carolina Egg Guesthaus on the eastern edge of town. A 7km track, of which 5km is doable by car, corkscrews up to the entrance. A glorious two-hour hike then leads to the top of the forest at Abra Esperanza (2420m and chilly).

A second park entrance lies at Yuritunqui (take a Pozuzo-bound minibus for 60km and ask the driver where to get off). Basic *refugios* can be found at each entrance, and just below Abra Esperanza. Further information can be obtained at Oxapampa's **INRENA** (Instituto Nacional de Recursos Naturales; ☎063-46-2544; Jr Pozuzo, cuadra 3 s/n) office.

Pozuzo VILLAGE

The inexorably Germanic Pozuzo, four hours north of Oxapampa by daily minibus, is picture-book Tyrolean from the architecture to the residents, straight out of a Brothers Grimm fairy tale (well, almost).

Festivals & Events

Selvámanos MUSIC

(www.selvamanos.org) Held in Parque Nacional Yanachaga-Chemillén every June since 2010, this is one of Peru's most talked-about festivals. It's a great showcase of Peruvian contemporary music: innovative new rock, electronica, reggae and wacky takes on *cumbia* (Colombian salsa-like dance and musical style). It's also a force behind simultaneously run Semana Kultura, where various musical and cultural events occur in towns around here.

Sleeping & Eating

★**Carolina Egg Gasthaus** GUESTHOUSE $$

(☎063-46-2331; http://carolinaegg.com; Av San Martin 1085; s/d incl breakfast S70/120; P❄📶🏊) Across from Oxapampa's bus station, this is an oasis of pretty wooden cabins and rooms run by descendants of one of the town's original German settlers. It's set way back from the road in a gorgeous garden, with a couple of shady terraces, a pool and a restaurant. Perhaps the only breakfast in Peru where you're served strudel!

Ulcumano Ecolodge LODGE $$$
(☎972-679-060; http://ulcumanoecolodge.com; nr Chonabamba; s/d S229/458) A bird-watcher's paradise in Chontabamba district, 10km outside Oxapampa, this lodge is perched in the forest and is named for the endangered Ulcumano tree. The species was sought after to build many houses hereabouts, but survives in the grounds here. Six cabins sleep 18 people, the property's bird list surpasses 150 and there's a restaurant strung with hammocks.

Specialized hiking tours are offered into Parque Nacional Yanachaga-Chemillén, and there are mountain-biking excursions too.

Das Tee Haus CAFE $
(dasteehausoxa@gmail.com; Mullembruck 548; snacks & light meals S3-12; ⌚6am-noon & 3:30-8:30pm) This is about the only place to sample a really good coffee (ironically) in Peru's entire coffee-producing region. But that's not all: this wonderful German-owned teahouse has great home-baked cakes, tasty lasagnas, teas (of course) and an affiliated butchers next door vending further delicacies, including Floralp cheese.

La Nonna PIZZERIA $$
(cnr Grau & Mariscal Castilla; pizzas S20-40; ⌚6pm-midnight) On the corner of the plaza. Delicious thin-crust pizzas served.

Vatter Otto BAR
(cnr Grau & Mariscal Castilla; ⌚6pm-late) Stays open, reputedly, until the last punter fancies leaving.

Shopping

Floralp FOOD
(www.floralp-sa.com; Carretera a Chontabamba Km 2; ⌚9am-9pm) Peru won't wow you with its cheese – unless you find your whey to Oxapampa. Come to the factory shop here and, besides purchasing a few flavorsome cheeses, you might get lucky with a factory tour.

Getting There & Away

Pozuzo buses (S20) run the four-hour route from the plaza in Oxapampa at 6am, 10am and 2pm along a rough road. Oxapampa's pleasant bus station is eight blocks from the center on the paved La Merced road. La Merced transportation (buses S10, *colectivos* S15) leaves from here, and there are also direct Lima buses in the evenings.

Pucallpa

☎061 / POP 205,000 / ELEV 154M

The busy port of Pucallpa has a distinctly less jungle-like appearance than other Amazonian towns. Although this is an important distribution center for goods along the broad, brown Río Ucayali, which sweeps past the city en route to join the Río Amazonas, the rainforest feels far away.

After all those miles of tropical travel to get here, Pucallpa seems underwhelming and bland, and hasty modern development in the center barely disguises the shantytown simplicity a few blocks further out. Still, it's started tarting itself up with an attractive pedestrianized boulevard, and is a starting point for a spectacular river adventure north to Iquitos – and, if time and inclination allow, on to Brazil and the Atlantic.

Beyond the city sprawl, there is reason for the traveler to linger: lovely Lago Yarinacocha, with river lodges to relax at and interesting indigenous communities to visit.

Sights

Many travelers visit nearby Yarinacocha, which is more interesting than Pucallpa and has some good accommodations.

Parque Natural ZOO
(adult/child S3/1; ⌚9am-5pm) About 4km from the center of Pucallpa, off the airport road, enter through the mouth of a tiger into this Amazon zoo ensconced in lush grounds. Many animals from the *selva* (jungle) can be found here, although the majority could be spotted in the wild on any decent rainforest excursion. Buses heading to the airport can drop you outside, or take a *mototaxi* for about S4.

Sleeping

Most places here have rooms with bathrooms, fans and cable TV.

Hostal Arequipa GUESTHOUSE $$
(☎061-57-1348; www.hostal-arequipa.com; Progreso 573; s S60-100, d S70-120; ❄📶) This is a popular, professional and often-full midrange choice, and has hot water, minibars, a restaurant, and aesthetic public areas decorated with Shipibo art. The pricier rooms with air-con also include a continental breakfast.

Hospedaje Komby GUESTHOUSE $$
(☎061-59-2074, 061-57-1562; www.elkombypucallpa.com; Ucayali 360; s S65-80, d S85-130; ❄📶🏊) In a quandary about whether to aim for budget or luxury? Komby has rooms that veer between the two brackets. Accommodations overall are clean but basic, brightened by the small pool. Higher tariffs are for rooms with air-con.

Grand Hotel Mercedes HOTEL $$
(☎061-57-5120; www.grandhotelmercedes.com; Raimondi 610; s S115-158, d S155-255; ❄🏊) Pucallpa's first good hotel has recently had a sprucing up. All rooms now have air-con and minibars, although be aware the difference in quality between old and new rooms is greater than the price difference. Yet there is a dated elegance to this clean, comfortable place, with its gorgeous garden courtyard and swimming pool.

★**Manish Hotel Ecológico** CABAÑAS $$$
(☎061-57-7167; www.manishhotel.com.pe; Av Lloque Yupanqui s/n; s/d incl breakfast S180/230, 4-person bungalow incl breakfast S420; P❄📶🏊) Escape Pucallpa's dusty thoroughfares in this serene expanse of leafy grounds, dotted with terra-cotta-roofed cabins. For families, taking one of the bungalows can mean downtime on the terrace for the grown-ups while the kids can safely run wild betwixt the palms and the pool.

Hotel Sol del Oriente HOTEL $$$
(☎061-57-5510; www.hotelessoldeloriente.com; San Martín 552; s/d/ste S230/285/460; P❄📶🏊) This is about the best you'll get in Pucallpa proper. It's not that flash, but it's comfortable. Set around a swimming pool, the somewhat old-fashioned rooms are of a decent size and have cable TV, minibars and good, always-hot showers. You get a welcome cocktail on arrival. A gym is on-site.

Eating & Drinking

Pucallpa does cafes and ice-cream parlors well, but noteworthy restaurants less so. The heat in the middle of the day means that restaurants tend to open by 7am for breakfast.

Delicious cakes and ice cream can be found at cafes such as **Fuente Soda Tropitop** (Sucre 401; snacks from S3-12; ⏰7am-midnight). If you are planning a longer trip, stock up at **Supermercado Los Andes** (Portillo 545).

WARNING: PUERTO BERMÚDEZ

Although it is possible to travel via Puerto Bermúdez to Pucallpa from La Merced, we do not currently recommend it.

Chez Maggy PIZZERIA $$
(www.chezmaggylosmaderos.com; Inmaculada 643; medium pizzas S24-27; ⏰5pm-midnight) Maggy whips up pizzas nothing short of superb, and from a wood-burning oven. The interior is modern and not plasticized like some neighboring restaurants. The unusual, tropical-tasting sangria goes down well with all dishes.

Chifa Mey Lin CHINESE $$
(Inmaculada 698; mains S19-29; ⏰6-11pm) This place gets the gong for being the best of Pucallpa's *chifas* (Chinese restaurants). Choosing where to sit in the roomy interior can be a challenge. Plates are BIG and to top it off there is also karaoke next door.

El Rincón Ingles PUB
(www.facebook.com/ElRinconInglesPucallpa; cnr Alamedas & Jr Masisea; ⏰6pm-midnight Tue-Thu, to 3am Fri & Sat) No typo: an English pub in Pucallpa. English-owned, with UK and Belgian draft beers, plus pub grub. Your only difficulty will be finding the place – a 15- to 20-minute *mototaxi* ride outside of the center. Specify to the driver *'al costado de Polleria Junior.'*

Shopping

The local Shipibo tribespeople wander the streets of town selling souvenirs. More of their work is seen near Yarinacocha.

Information

Internet cafes abound on every block, including several on *cuadra* (block) 3 of Tacna. Several banks have ATMs and change money and traveler's checks. Foreign-exchange bureaus are

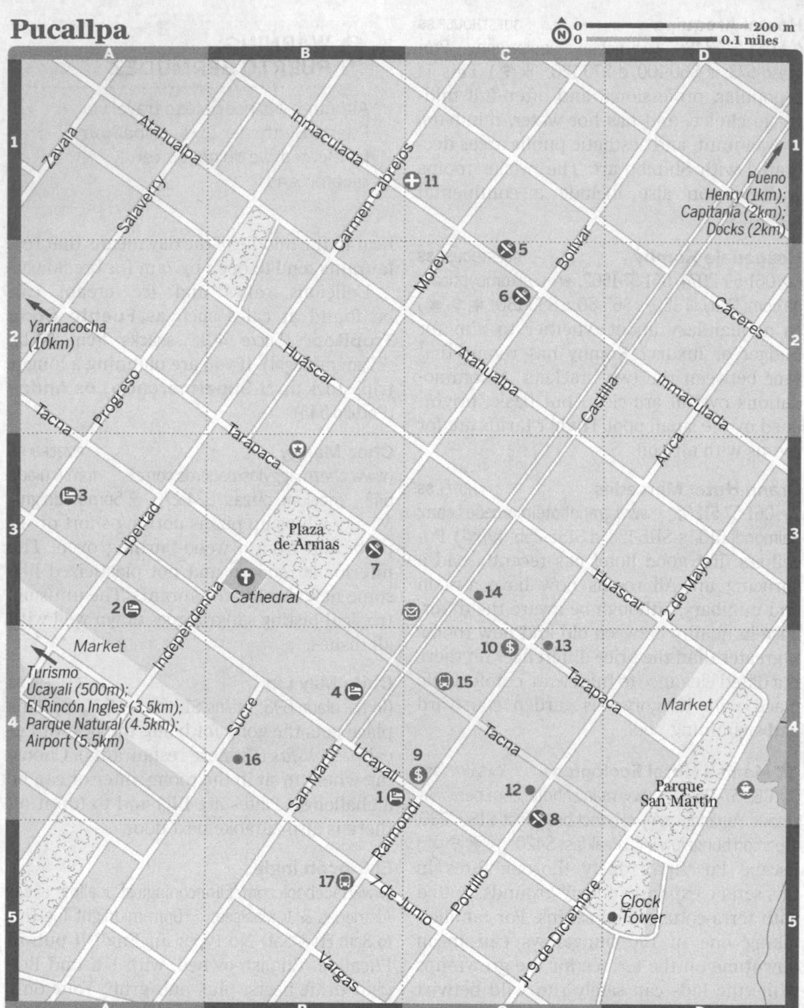

found along the fourth, fifth and sixth *cuadras* of Raimondi. For jungle guides, go to Yarinacocha.

Clínica Monte Horeb (☎061-57-1689; Inmaculada 529; ⏱24hr) Good medical services.

Lavandería Gasparinet (Portillo 526; ⏱9am-1pm & 4-8pm Mon-Sat) Self-service or drop-off laundry.

Viajes Laser (☎061-57-1120, 961-900-513; www.laserviajes.pe; Raimondi 399) Western Union is here, at one of Pucallpa's better travel agencies.

Getting There & Away

AIR

Pucallpa's decent-sized airport is 5km northwest of town. The best connections are with **Star Perú** (☎061-59-0585; 7 de Junio 865), with direct flights leaving from Lima at 8:30am and 4:30pm – the morning flight continues to Iquitos. For Pucallpa–Lima, the times are 1pm and 6:10pm. Another option is **LAN** (Tarapacá 805) with three daily (but much pricier) flights to Lima.

Other towns and settlements – including Atalaya (on the Río Ucayali), Contamaná, Tara-

Pucallpa

Sleeping

1 Grand Hotel Mercedes.......................B4
2 Hospedaje Komby A3
3 Hostal Arequipa A3
4 Hotel Sol del Oriente B4

Eating

5 Chez Maggy C2
6 Chifa Mey Lin..C2
7 Fuente Soda Tropitop B3
8 Supermercado Los Andes..................C4

Information

9 Banco Continental..............................C4
10 BCP...C4
11 Clínica Monte Horeb..........................C1
12 Lavandería Gasparinet.......................C4
13 Viajes Laser C4
Western Union...............................(see 13)

Transport

14 LAN...C3
15 León de Huánuco................................C4
16 Star Perú..B4
17 Transportation to Amazon Towns B5

poto and Yurimaguas – are served by small local airlines using light aircraft; ask at the airport.

BOAT

Pucallpa's port moves depending on water levels. During high water (January to April) boats moor at the dock abutting Parque San Martín in central Pucallpa itself.

As water levels drop, the port falls back to several spots along the banks, including **Puerto Henry** (Manco Capác s/n) and eventually to about 3km northeast of the town center, reached by *mototaxi* (S3). The town port stretches some way: different boats for different destinations depart from different areas, usually referred to by the name of the nearest intersecting road.

Wherever the port is, riverboats sail the Río Ucayali from Pucallpa to Iquitos (S80 to S100, slinging your own hammock and with basic meals, three to five days). Cabins with two or four bunks and private bathrooms come with better food service and cost anything from about S150 to S400, depending on the quality and indeed your powers of negotiation.

Boats announce their departure dates and destinations on chalkboards on the boats themselves, but these can be unreliable. Talk to the captain or the cargo loadmaster for greater dependability. They must present boat documents on the morning of their departure day at the **Capitanía** (☎ 061-59-0193; M Castilla 754); come here to check for the latest reliable sailing information. Many people work here, but only the official in charge of documents knows the real scoop and can give you accurate sailing information. Passages are daily when the river is high, but in the dry season low water levels result in slower, less frequent passages.

The quality of the boats varies greatly both in size and comfort. Choose a boat that looks good. The *Henry V* is one of the better-equipped outfits, with a 250-passenger capacity.

This is not a trip for everyone. Come prepared – the market in Pucallpa sells hammocks, but mosquito repellent may be of poor quality. Bottled drinks are sold on board, but it's worth bringing some large bottles of water or juice.

When negotiating prices for a riverboat passage, ask at any likely boat, but don't pay until you and your luggage are aboard your boat of choice, then pay the captain and no one else. Always get to the port well in advance of when you want to leave: it can take hours hunting for a suitable vessel. Most boats leave either at first light, or in the late afternoon or evening.

The river journey to Iquitos can be broken at various communities, including Contamaná (about S30, 15 to 20 hours) and Requena, and continued on the next vessel coming through (although there's precious little to do in these villages). Alternatively, ask around for speedboats to Contamaná (about S100, five hours), which depart at 6am most days. The return trip (six to seven hours) goes against the current.

Smaller boats occasionally head upriver toward Atalaya; ask at the Capitanía or the town port.

Jungle 'guides' approaching you on the Pucallpa waterfront are not recommended. For jungle excursions, look for a reliable service in Yarinacocha.

BUS

The sprucing up of Pucallpa's center hasn't been quite so sexy for bus companies, all of which now depart from disparate terminals straggled along the airport road around 4km from the center, after Parque Natural. One or two companies still have central booking offices. For departures, get a taxi (about S5) out to the relevant bus terminal.

A direct bus to Lima (S70 to S90) takes 18 to 20 hours in the dry season; the journey can be broken in Tingo María (S20, nine hours) or Huánuco (S25, 12 hours). The road is paved but vulnerable to flooding and erosion. This journey has become safer since the posting of armed police units along parts of the route; still, it's better to do the Pucallpa–Tingo María section in daylight.

León de Huánuco (☎ 061-57-5049; Tacna 765), with a central booking office, serves Lima at 8pm, stopping at Tingo María and Huánuco. There is also a 10pm *bus-cama* (bed bus) service. Another good company is **Turismo Central** (061-60-0122). However, it's often best to get a taxi out to Km 4 of the airport road and do the rounds of the offices for the service best suiting your schedule.

Turismo Ucayali (061-57-2735; Centenario 150) has cars to Tingo María (S45, 4½ hours) leaving hourly throughout the day.

A few companies on *cuadra* 7 of Raimondi have trucks and buses to more remote Amazon towns like Puerto Inca. Departures are nevertheless from points along the airport road 4km from the center.

Getting Around

Mototaxis to the airport or Yarinacocha are about S7; taxis are S10.

Yarinacocha

About 10km northwest of central Pucallpa, Yarinacocha is a lovely oxbow lake where you can go canoeing, observe wildlife, and visit indigenous communities and purchase their handicrafts. The lake, once part of the Río Ucayali, is now landlocked, though a small canal links the two bodies of water during the rainy season. Boat services are provided here in a casual atmosphere. It's well worth spending a couple of days here.

The lakeside village of **Puerto Callao** is a welcome relief from the chaos of downtown Pucallpa's streets. It's still a ramshackle kind of place with only a dirt road skirting the busy waterfront. Buzzards amble among pedestrians, and *peki-peki* boats come and go to their various destinations all day.

Here you'll find limited accommodations, as well as some decent food. You can also hire **boats** here – in fact, you'll be nabbed as soon as you turn up by boat touts seeking to lure you to their vessel. Choose your boat carefully: make sure it has new-looking life jackets and enough petrol for the voyage, and pay at the end of the tour. Wildlife to watch out for includes freshwater pink dolphins, sloths and meter-long green iguanas, as well as exotic birds such as the curiously long-toed wattled jacana (which walks on lily pads) and the metallic-green Amazon kingfisher. If you like **fishing**, the dry season is apparently the best time.

Tours

Lots of *peki-peki* boat owners offer tours. Take your time choosing; the first offer is unlikely to be the best. Guides are also available for walking trips into the surrounding forest, including some overnight hikes.

A highly recommended guide is **Gilber Reategui Sangama** (messages 061-57-9018; http://sacredheritage.com/normita), who owns the boat *La Normita* in Yarinacocha. He has expedition supplies (sleeping pads, mosquito nets, drinking water) and is both knowledgeable and environmentally aware. He speaks some English, is safe and reliable, and will cook meals for you. He charges about S210 per person per day, with a minimum of two people, for an average of three to five days. Gilber lives at the lakeside village of Nueva Luz de Fátima, and offers tours to stay with his family; his father is a shaman with 50 years' experience. Contact him in advance to arrange a tour. Some other guides will claim Gilber is unavailable or no longer works. Don't believe all you hear.

A good boat driver will float slowly along, so that you can look for birdlife at the water's edge, or *perezosos* (sloths) in the trees. Sunset is a good time to be on the lake.

Boat trips to the Shipibo villages of either **San Francisco** (also reached by road) or, better, **Santa Clara** (reached only by boat), are also popular. For short trips, boat drivers charge around S25 an hour for the boat; these can carry several people. Bargaining over the price is acceptable.

Sleeping & Eating

Several inexpensive restaurants and lively bars line the Puerto Callao waterfront.

La Maloka Ecolodge LODGE **$$**
(061-59-6900; lamaloka@gmail.com; Puerto Callao; s/d S120/180;) This is the only decent place to stay in Puerto Callao. It is worth forking out for the comfort. La Maloka Ecolodge is located at the right-hand end of the waterfront. It is built right out on the water, with the amply sized but unadorned rooms sitting on stilts over the lake. There is a relaxing outdoor restaurant-and-bar area overlooking the lake; pink dolphins regularly flash their flippers for guests.

La Jungla BUNGALOWS
(961-971-865, 061-57-1460; bungalows per person S80) This enthusiastically run place on Yarinacocha's far shore northeast of the Puerto Callao dock has several rustic bungalows open to guests, each sleeping up to four people. There is a zoo, a resident tapir and a spacious bar-restaurant. The owner's father can guide you in the surrounding jungle.

NORTHERN AMAZON

Raw, vast and encapsulating the real spirit of the Amazon, the northern Amazon Basin is home to the eponymous river that wells up from the depths of the Peruvian jungle before making its long, languorous passage through Brazil to the distant Atlantic Ocean. Settlements are scarce in this remote region: Yurimaguas in the west and Iquitos in the northeast are the only two of any size.

Yurimaguas

065 / POP 72,000 / ELEV 181M

This sleepy, unspectacular port is one of the Peruvian Amazon's best-connected towns and the gateway to the northern tract of the Amazonas. It's visited by travelers looking for boats down the Río Huallaga to Iquitos and the Amazon proper or by those wanting to experience one of Peru's most animal-rich paradises, the Pacaya-Samiria reserve, accessible from here. There is little to detain visitors from continuing their Amazon adventure. Go to Lagunas for a jungle guide, although touts will approach you in Yurimaguas. A paved road connects Yurimaguas with Tarapoto to the south.

Sleeping & Eating

You might have better luck encountering El Dorado than a hotel with hot water. Budget hotels flank the *cuadras* of Jáuregui west of the plaza. For eating, there is a paucity of choice, particularly if fried chicken isn't your thing; try the hotel restaurants.

Alojamiento Yacuruna GUESTHOUSE $
(965-735-767; Malecón Shanusi 200; r per person from S25) This is a great rustic retreat right by the river. Simple, nicely decorated rooms have shared bathrooms. Tours are offered both to local sites and the Pacaya-Samiria reserve. Access it via steps down from the plaza.

Río Huallaga Hotel & Business Center BUSINESS HOTEL $$
(065-35-3951; www.riohuallagahotel.com; Arica 111; s/d S180/220;) Courteous service; spacious, clean, well-designed rooms; a swimming pool and bar; a three-floor restaurant (perhaps the best in town) with cracking Río Huallaga views from the top deck; and even its own tour agency. For all this, the town's best hotel has a high asking price.

The whole place is built on multiple levels, and tucked away at the bottom are cheapie rooms (still not bad) for a mere S40 per person.

Posada Cumpanama GUESTHOUSE $$
(065-35-2957; http://posadacumpanamaperu.com; Progreso 403; s/d S75/85) If you're looking for decent digs without an inflated price tag, Posada Cumpanama comes in handy. Large rooms and a cute little bar, arranged around a pool in a walled enclave quiet enough to allow beauty sleep.

Cebicheria El Dorado PERUVIAN $
(Aguirre 113; mains S18-25; 8am-4:30pm) Getting a taxi to this spot, slightly out of the center, is the best idea for breakfast or lunch. Nothing fancy, mind, but agreeable enough – and the portions are exceedingly generous.

Shopping

Stores selling hammocks for river journeys are on the north side of the market, which is located on Jáuregui two blocks west of the central plaza..

Information

It is better to arrange Pacaya-Samiria tours in nearby Lagunas. Banco Continental (with a Visa ATM) and BCP will change US cash and traveler's checks. Internet and phone booths come and go frequently but there are a few around the plaza.

Cabinas de Internet (Jauregui on Plaza; per hour S2; 7:30am-11pm) Lots of terminals: wi-fi in Yurimaguas isn't reliable.

Getting There & Around

AIR

No airline company currently serves Yurimaguas. The nearest main-line airport is at Tarapoto, with connections to Lima and Iquitos.

BOAT

The main port 'La Boca' is 13 blocks north of the center. Cargo boats from Yurimaguas follow the Río Huallaga onto the Río Marañón and Iquitos, taking between two and four days with numerous stops for loading and unloading cargo. There are usually departures daily, except Sunday. Passages cost about S100 on deck to Nauta for Iquitos (sling your own hammock and receive basic food) or around S130 for a bunk in double or quadruple cabins on the top deck, where the food is better and your gear safer; at Nauta, switch to road for the remainder of the journey to Iquitos (one hour). Bottled water, soft drinks and snacks are sold on board; bring insect repellent and a hat. Taking your own food and water supplies is also advisable. The Eduardo boats (of which there are five) are considered the best (although readers have reported graphic animal cruelty on these). The journey can be broken at Lagunas (S30, 10 to 12 hours), just before the Río Huallaga meets the Marañón.

Transporte Rapido (☎962-562-270, 980-382-870; La Boca) has fast boats to Lagunas, which continue on to Iquitos – leaving from the La Boca port. Leaving Yurimaguas at the ungodly hour of 2:30am daily, they hit Lagunas around 7:30am or 8am, getting to Iquitos about 6pm.

Smaller slow boats and fast boats to Lagunas (S100, 4½ to 5½ hours) leave from the more convenient town port 200m northwest of the Plaza de Armas.

BUS

The paved road now makes Yurimaguas easily accessible by Amazon standards.

Buses and taxis arrive and depart from offices 2km southwest of the center. For Tarapoto (S15, three hours), several companies leave from numberless offices on the Tarapoto road, or nearby on Calle Pastaza.

Likewise, there are multiple companies with *colectivos* to Tarapoto (S20, two hours) from *cuadra* 5 and *cuadra* 6 of Sifuentes. These include **Empresa San Martín** (☎065-35-1438; Victor Siffuentes S/N), but there is nothing really to choose between them: it's a matter of which one leaves first, which will happen only when they've touted four passengers.

TAXI

Mototaxis charge S1.50 to take you anywhere around town.

Lagunas

☎065 / POP 14,300 / ELEV 148M

Travelers come to muddy, mosquito-rich Lagunas because it is the best embarkation point for a trip to the Reserva Nacional Pacaya-Samiria. It's a spread-out, remote place; there are stores, but stock (slightly pricier than elsewhere in Peru) is limited, so it's wise to bring your own supplies as back-up. There are no money-changing facilities and hardly any public phones.

Tours

Spanish-speaking guides are locally available to visit Pacaya-Samiria. It is illegal to hunt within the reserve (though fishing for the pot is OK). The going rate is a rather steep S120 to S150 per person per day for a guide, a boat and accommodations in huts, tents and ranger stations. Food and park fees are extra, although the guides can cook for you.

Several years ago, there was such a plethora of guides in Lagunas that to avoid harassment and price-cutting, an official guides association was formed. This then split into two separate organizations with the highly regarded **Estypel** (☎065-40-1080; www.estypel.com.pe; Jr Padre Lucero 1345), headed by the reputable guide Juan Manuel Rojas Arévalo, the only survivor of these two.

There's also **Huayruro Tours** (☎965-662-555, 065-40-1186; www.peruselva.com; Alfonso Aiscorbe 2), an increasingly prominent association that is great for helping plan tours (agency staff speak English; their guides are Spanish-speaking but know the reserve extremely well). It offers tours of up to 22 days and is involved in programs like turtle reintroduction within the reserve.

Sleeping & Eating

Accommodations are improving, but still very basic. Hostels provide cheap meals; if you like chicken and fried banana, try the basic restaurant on the plaza.

Hostal Samiria GUESTHOUSE $

(☎065-40-1061; Fitzcarrald; s/tr S25/50) This is probably Lagunas' best option. Rooms are smallish but clean enough, with Spanish-language TV and OK bathrooms. The best feature is the secluded central courtyard that the rooms face onto, which includes a hammock area. It's situated near the market. A restaurant is on the cards.

Hostal Paraiso Verde GUESTHOUSE $

(☎959-941-566; contacto@hostalaparaisoverde.com; Daniel A Carrión 320; r per person from S25) Clean tiled rooms typify the upper end of the upward curve in Lagunas' accommodations standards. There are fans and TVs – but of course both stop with the almost-nightly electricity cut-offs, like elsewhere in town.

Getting There & Away

Regular boats downriver from Yurimaguas to Lagunas take about 10 to 12 hours and leave Yurimaguas' La Boca port between 7am and 8am most days. Times are posted on boards at the port in both Yurimaguas and Lagunas for a day in advance. Fast boats from Yurimaguas head off either at 2:30am (from La Boca) or between 7am and 8am from the port near the Plaza: they take 4½ to 5½ hours.

Action time is, indeed, between 7am and 8am in Lagunas' ramshackle port. This is when many fast boats rock up for the journey upriver to Yurimaguas (S40, 5½ to 6½ hours) and downriver to Iquitos (S100, 10 hours).

Reserva Nacional Pacaya-Samiria

At 20,800 sq km, **Reserva Nacional Pacaya-Samiria** (3-day pass S60) is the largest of Peru's parks and reserves. Pacaya-Samiria provides local people with food and a home, and protects ecologically important habitats. An estimated 42,000 people live on and around the reserve; juggling the needs of human inhabitants while protecting wildlife is the responsibility of some 30 rangers. Staff also teach inhabitants how to best harvest the natural renewable resources to benefit the local people and to maintain thriving populations of plants and animals.

The reserve is the home of aquatic animals such as Amazon manatees, pink and grey river dolphins, two species of caiman, giant South American river turtles and many other bird and animal species.

The area close to Lagunas has suffered from depletion: allow several days to get deep into the least disturbed areas. With 15 days, you can reach Lago Cocha Pasto, where there are reasonable chances of seeing jaguars and larger mammals. Other noteworthy points in the reserve include Quebrada Yanayacu, where the river water is black from dissolved plants; Lago Pantean, where you can check out caimans and go medicinal-plant collecting; and Tipischa de Huana, where you can see the giant *Victoria regia* waterlilies, big enough for a small child to sleep upon without sinking.

Official information is available at the reserve office in Iquitos (p482), with more limited information available in Yurimaguas and Lagunas.

The best way to visit the reserve is to go by dugout canoe with a guide from Lagunas and spend several days camping and exploring. Alternatively, comfortable ships visit from Iquitos.

If coming from Lagunas, Santa Rosa is the main entry point, where you pay the park entrance fee (often included in tour prices).

The best time to go is during the dry season, when you are more likely to see animals along the riverbanks. Rains ease off in late May; it then takes a month for water levels to drop, making July and August the best months to visit (with excellent fishing). September to November isn't too bad, and the heaviest rains begin in January. The months of February to May are the worst times to go. February to June tend to be the hottest months, with animal-viewing best in early morning and late afternoon.

Travelers should bring plenty of insect repellent and plastic bags (to cover luggage), and be prepared to camp out.

Iquitos

☎065 / POP 472,000 / ELEV 130M

Linked to the outside world by air and by river, Iquitos is the world's largest city that cannot be reached by road. It's a prosperous, vibrant jungle metropolis teeming with the usual, inexplicably addictive Amazonian anomalies. Unadulterated jungle encroaches beyond town in full view of the air-conditioned, elegant bars and restaurants that flank the riverside; motorized tricycles whiz manically through the streets yet locals mill around the central plazas eating ice cream like there is all the time in the world. Mud huts mingle with magnificent tiled mansions; tiny dugout canoes ply the water alongside colossal cruise ships. You may well arrive in Iquitos for the greater adventure of a boat trip down the Amazon, but whether it's sampling rainforest cuisine, checking out the buzzing nightlife or exploring one of Peru's most fascinating markets in the floating shantytown of Belén, this thriving city will entice you to stay awhile.

Because everything must be 'imported,' costs are higher than in other cities.

History

Iquitos was founded in the 1750s as a Jesuit mission, fending off attacks from indigenous tribes that didn't want to be converted. In the 1870s the great rubber boom boosted the population 16-fold, and for the next 30 years Iquitos was at once the scene of ostentatious wealth and abject poverty. Rubber barons became fabulously rich, while rubber tappers (mainly local tribespeople and poor *mestizos* – people of mixed indigenous and Spanish descent) suffered virtual enslavement and sometimes death from disease or harsh treatment.

By WWI, the bottom fell out of the rubber boom as suddenly as it had begun. A British entrepreneur smuggled some rubber-tree seeds out of Brazil, and plantations were seeded in the Malay Peninsula. It was much

Iquitos

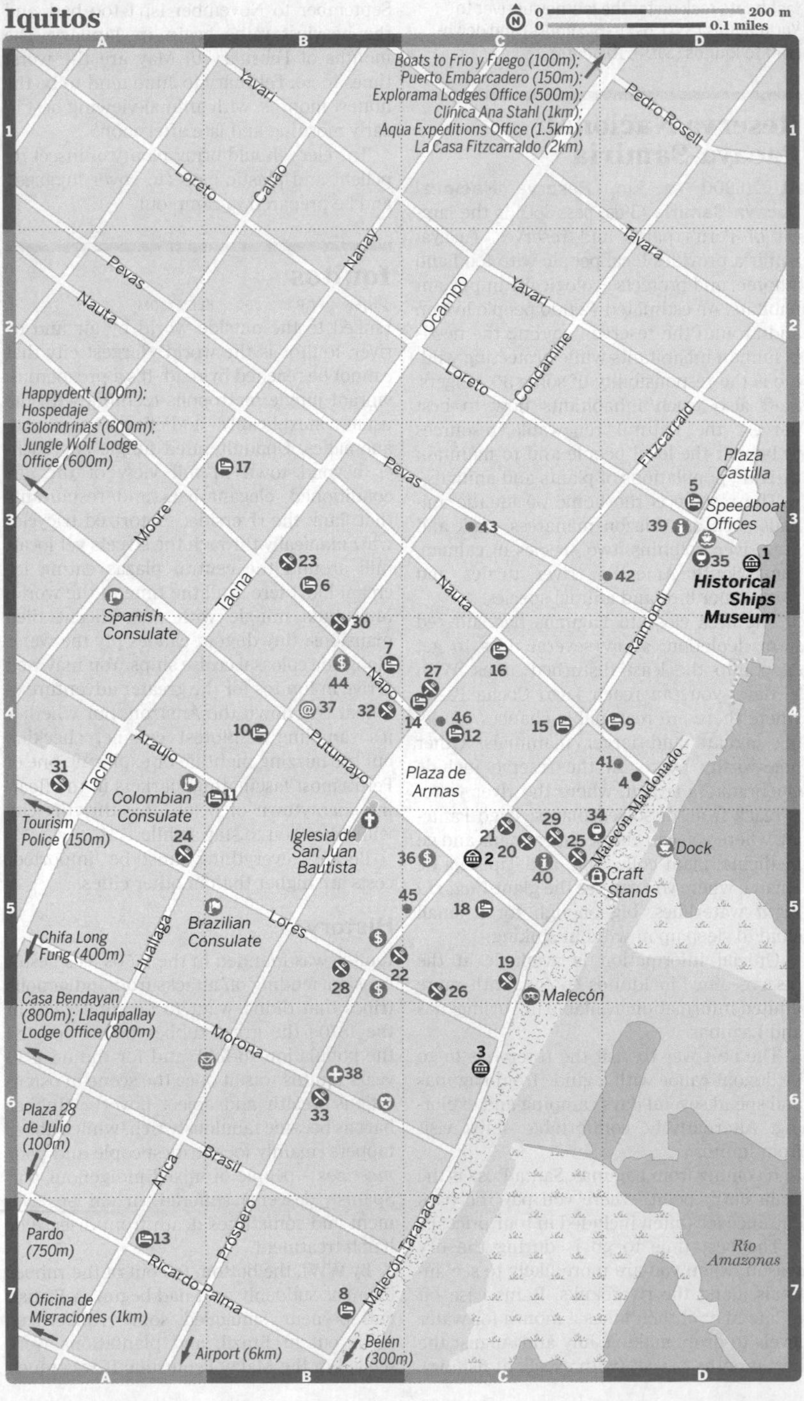

0 200 m
0 0.1 miles

Boats to Frio y Fuego (100m); Puerto Embarcadero (150m); Explorama Lodges Office (500m); Clínica Ana Stahl (1km); Aqua Expeditions Office (1.5km); La Casa Fitzcarraldo (2km)

Yavari
Pedro Rosell
Loreto
Callao
Nanay
Tavara
Pevas
Nauta
Ocampo
Yavari
Condamine
Loreto
Fitzcarrald
Happydent (100m); Hospedaje Golondrinas (600m); Jungle Wolf Lodge Office (600m)
17
Pevas
Plaza Castilla
5
Speedboat Offices
39
43
Moore
23
6
35
1
Historical Ships Museum
42
Nauta
Tacna
Spanish Consulate
30
Raimondi
7
16
44
Napo
27
37
32
14
46
12
15
9
10
Araujo
Putumayo
41
4
31
Tacna
Colombian Consulate
11
Plaza de Armas
Malecón Maldonado
Tourism Police (150m)
34
24
29
21
25
Iglesia de San Juan Bautista
20
Dock
36
2
40
Craft Stands
45
18
Chifa Long Fung (400m)
Huallaga
Brazilian Consulate
Lores
22
19
28
26
Malecón
Casa Bendayan (800m); Llaquipallay Lodge Office (800m)
Morona
3
38
33
Plaza 28 de Julio (100m)
Arica
Brasil
Próspero
Pardo (750m)
13
Ricardo Palma
Malecón Tarapaca
Río Amazonas
Oficina de Migraciones (1km)
8
Airport (6km)
Belén (300m)

Iquitos

Top Sights
1 Historical Ships Museum D3

Sights
2 Casa de Fierro C5
3 Museum of Indigenous Amazon Cultures C6

Activities, Courses & Tours
4 Dawn on the Amazon Tours & Cruises D4

Sleeping
5 Casa Morey D3
6 El Dorado Express B3
7 El Dorado Isabel B4
8 Flying Dog Hostel B7
9 Hostal El Colibrí D4
10 Hostal Florentina B4
11 Hotel Acosta B4
12 Hotel El Dorado Plaza C4
13 Hotel Victoria Regia A7
14 La Casa Chacruna C4
15 La Casa Del Francés C4
16 Marañón Hotel C4
17 Nativa Apartments B3
18 Otorongo Lodge C5

Eating
19 Amazon Bistro C5
20 Antica C5
21 Ari's Burger C5
22 Cafe Express B5
23 Comma y Punto B3
Dawn on the Amazon Café (see 4)
24 El Sitio A5
25 Fitzcarraldo Restaurant-Bar C5
26 Gran Maloca C5
27 Huasai C4
28 Ivalú B5
29 Karma Cafe C5
30 Kikiriki B4
31 Mercado Central A4
32 Mitos y Cubiertos B4
33 Supermercado Los Portales B6

Drinking & Nightlife
34 Arandú Bar C5
35 Musmuqui D3

Information
36 BCP C5
37 Cyber B4
38 InkaFarma B6
39 iPerú D3
40 iPerú C5
41 Lavandería Imperial D4
42 Paseos Amazonicos D3
43 Reserva Nacional Pacaya-Samiria Office C3
44 Western Union B4

Transport
45 LAN C5
46 Star Perú C4

cheaper and easier to collect the rubber from orderly rubber tree plantations than from wild trees scattered in the Amazon Basin.

Iquitos suffered subsequent economic decline, supporting itself with a combination of logging, agriculture (Brazil nuts, tobacco, bananas and *barbasco* – a poisonous vine used by indigenous peoples to hunt fish and now exported for use in insecticides) and the export of wild animals to zoos. Then, in the 1960s, a second boom revitalized the area. This time the resource was oil, and its discovery made Iquitos a prosperous modern town. In recent years tourism has also played an important part in the area's economy.

Sights

Iquitos' cultural attractions, while limited, dwarf those of other Amazon cities, especially boosted by the arrival of two new museums. The cheery Malecón (riverside walk) runs between Nauta and Ricardo Palma; despite the following diversions, it is perhaps the main sight!

Remnants of the rubber-boom glory days include *azulejos*, handmade tiles imported from Portugal to decorate the mansions of the rubber barons. Many buildings along Raimondi and Malecón Tarapaca are lavishly decorated with these tiles. Some of the best are various government buildings along or near the Malecón.

★Historical Ships Museum MUSEUM
(Plaza Castilla; S10; ⏲8am-8pm) Moored below Plaza Castilla is the diverting new Historical Ships Museum, on a 1906 Amazon riverboat, the gorgeously restored three-deck *Ayapua*. The exhibitions reflect the Amazon River's hodgepodge past: explorers, tribes, rubber barons and the filming of the 1982 Herzog movie *Fitzcarraldo*. Included in the entrance price is a half-hour historic boat ride on the river (Río Itaya out to the Río Amazonas proper).

Museum of Indigenous Amazon Cultures MUSEUM

(Malecón Tarapaca 332; S15; ⏲8am-7:30pm) This new and intuitively presented museum takes you on a romp through the traits, traditions and beliefs of the tribes of the Amazon Basin, with a focus on the Peruvian Amazon. Some 40 Amazonian cultures are represented.

Casa de Fierro HISTORIC BUILDING

(Iron House; cnr Putumayo & Raymondi) Every guidebook mentions the 'majestic' Casa de Fierro (Iron House), designed by Gustave Eiffel (of Eiffel Tower fame). It was made in Paris in 1860 and imported piece by piece into Iquitos around 1890, during the opulent rubber-boom days, to beautify the city. It's the only survivor of three different iron houses originally imported here. It resembles a bunch of scrap-metal sheets bolted together, was once the location of the Iquitos Club and is now, in humbler times, a general store.

Belén

★Belén NEIGHBOURHOOD

At the southeast end of town is the floating shantytown of Belén, consisting of scores of huts, built on rafts, which rise and fall with the river. During the low-water months, these rafts sit on the river mud and are dirty and unhealthy, but for most of the year they float on the river – a colorful and exotic sight. Seven thousand people live here, and canoes float from hut to hut selling and trading jungle produce.

The best time to visit the shantytown is at 7am, when people from the jungle villages arrive to sell their produce. To get here, take a cab to 'Los Chinos,' walk to the port and rent a canoe to take you around.

The market here, located within the city blocks in front of Belén, is the raucous, crowded affair common to most Peruvian towns. All kinds of strange and exotic products are sold among the more mundane bags of rice, sugar, flour and cheap household goods. Look for the bark of the *chuchuhuasi* tree, which is soaked in rum for weeks and used as a tonic (it's served in many of the local bars). *Chuchuhuasi* and other Amazon plants are common ingredients in herbal pain-reducing and arthritis formulas manufactured in Europe and the USA. The market makes for exciting shopping and sightseeing, but do remember to watch your wallet.

UPROOTING BELÉN

The order has come from on high: Belén – perhaps the character-defining district of Iquitos – needs to be moved. The main reason cited is sanitation. When water levels are high, this shantytown-cum-market on the river floats, but it sits on the stinking mud when the water drops. But how do you relocate an entire district, and to where? It's proving a headache. At the time of writing, a few families of the hundreds living here have signed up for the scheme. The rest have strongly opposed it. Without residents' consent, and with a relocation threatening the only livelihood most of them know (fishing and river trade), any uprooting of Belén will be a struggle taking many months if not years.

Activities

Golf

Amazon Golf Club GOLF

(☎065-22-3730; www.amazongolfcourse.com; Quistacocha; per day incl golf-club rental S75; ⏲6am-6pm) Amazing as it may seem, you can play a round or two on the nine holes of the only course in the entire Amazon. Founded in 2004 by a bunch of nostalgic expats, the 2140m course was built on bush land around 15km outside Iquitos and boasts, apart from its nine greens, a wooden clubhouse with a bar. Hole 4 is a beauty: you tee onto an island surrounded by piranha-infested waters. Don't go fishing for lost balls!

River Cruises

Cruising the Amazon is an expensive business: the shortest trips can cost over US$1000. It's a popular pastime, too, and advance reservations are often necessary (and often mean discounts). Cruises naturally focus on the Río Amazonas, both downriver (northeast) toward the Brazil–Colombia border and upriver to Nauta, where the Ríos Marañón and Ucayali converge. Beyond Nauta, trips continue up these two rivers to the Pacaya-Samiria reserve. Trips can also be arranged on the three rivers surrounding Iquitos: the Itaya, the Amazonas and the Nanay. Operators quote prices in US dollars. A useful booking website for most of the following is www.amazoncruise.net.

★ **Dawn on the Amazon Tours & Cruises** CRUISE
(065-22-3730; www.dawnontheamazon.com; Malecón Maldonado 185; per person day trips incl lunch US$79, multiday cruises per day from US$150) This small outfit offers the best deal for independent travelers. The *Amazon I* is a beautiful 11m wooden craft with modern furnishings, available for either day trips or longer river cruises up to two weeks. Included are a bilingual guide, all meals and transfers. You can travel with host Bill Grimes and his experienced crew along the Amazon, or along its quieter tributaries (larger cruise ships will necessarily stick to the main waterways).

While many cruise operators have fixed departures and itineraries, Bill's can be adapted to accommodate individual needs. The tri-river cruise is a favorite local trip: while on board, fishing and bird-watching are the most popular activities.

Aqua Expeditions CRUISE
(965-83-2517, 065-60-1053, in US 866-603-3687; www.aquaexpeditions.com; Av La Marina s/n; 3-night Marañón & Ucayali cruise per person in suite from US$3135) Aqua operates two luxury riverboats, which depart twice weekly for the Pacaya-Samiria reserve. The 40m *MV Aqua* has 12 vast, luxury suite cabins (each over 22 sq meters) while the *MV Aria* has equally splendid accommodations, but in 16 similarly sized suites and with an on-board Jacuzzi. Both boats have beautiful observation lounges. Cruises last three, five or seven days.

The office is 1km along Av La Marina from the center.

Cruise boats come with a full crew and bilingual guides. Meals are included and small launches are carried for side trips. Activities can involve visiting indigenous communities (for dancing and craft sales), hikes, and bird- and pink-dolphin-watching (on big ships, don't expect to see too much rare wildlife).

Festivals & Events

San Juan CULTURAL
(Jun 22-27) This is the big annual debauch, a festival that has grown around the saint's day of San Juan Bautista (St John the Baptist) on June 24 (the main party day). It's celebrated in most Amazon towns but Iquitos honors the saint most fervently with dancing, cockfights, and above all feasting and frivolity.

Juanes (turmeric-smeared rice blended with chicken, olives or sliced egg and wrapped in a jungle leaf) is the typical food consumed. On the night of 23 June locals partake in the river dunk, as this is the day of the year when the waters of the Itaya are said to have healing properties.

Great Amazon River Raft Race SPECTATOR SPORT
(www.amazonriverinternationalraftrace.com/en; Sep/Oct) Held in September or October, this is an annual race down the river between Nauta and Iquitos in hand-built craft.

Sleeping

The range of accommodations in Iquitos is as broad as a cruise ship seems when bearing down on a canoe: basic budget to five-star luxury are catered for, with a plethora of enterprises attempting top-end and failing.

Mosquitoes are rarely a serious problem in town, so mosquito netting is not always provided.

The best hotels tend to be booked up on Friday and Saturday, and during major festivals such as San Juan. The busiest season is from May to September, when prices may rise slightly. Due to the competition, even budget hotels have decent standards, many offering bathrooms and fans. Every place that's midrange or higher has air-con and a private bathroom, normally with hot water. Prices tend to rise around holidays.

Hospedaje Golondrinas GUESTHOUSE $
(065-23-6428; www.hospedajegolondrinas.com; Putumayo 1024; dm/s/d S20/35/46;) Quickly growing in clout as a backpacker hangout because of a combination of reasonable prices and well-maintained rooms, Hospedaje Golondrinas manages to throw in a pool and offers great budget jungle tours out to its lodge, Jungle Wolf.

La Casa Chacruna GUESTHOUSE $
(065-53-3189; www.facebook.com/lacasachacruna; Napo 312; d S60) Hard to believe, but across the way from Iquitos' most expensive hotel, you could save a sweet S500 and stay in a place with the same plaza views. La Casa Chacruna wins the prize for the city's most innovative interior decor, too, and a constant supply of good coffee is available in the common room.

Downsides? It's a little cramped and the plaza location can get noisy. But this place fills a niche between the hostels and the hotels, and fills it attractively.

HERZOG'S AMAZON

Eccentric German director Werner Herzog, often seen as obsessive and bent on filming 'reality itself,' shot two movies in Peru's jungle: *Aguirre, the Wrath of God* (1972) and *Fitzcarraldo* (1982). Herzog's accomplishments in getting these movies made at all – during havoc-fraught filming conditions – are in some ways more remarkable than the finished products.

Klaus Kinski, the lead actor in *Aguirre,* was a volatile man prone to extreme fits of rage. Herzog's documentary *My Best Fiend* details such incidents as Kinski beating a conquistador extra so severely that his helmet, donned for the part, was all that saved him from being killed. Then there was the time near the end of shooting when, after altercations with a cameraman on the Río Nanay, Kinski prepared to desert the film crew on a speedboat. Herzog had to threaten to shoot him with a rifle to make him stay. (To tell both sides of the story, however, *My Best Fiend* also reveals that Herzog admitted to once trying to firebomb Kinski in his house, and according to other members of the film crew Herzog often overexaggerated.) Kinski's biography, *Kinski Uncut* (albeit partly ghostwritten by Herzog), paints a picture of the director as a buffoon who had no idea how to make movies.

Filming *Fitzcarraldo,* the first choice for the lead fell ill and the second, Mick Jagger, abandoned the set to do a Rolling Stones tour. With a year's filming already wasted, Herzog called upon Kinski once more. Kinski soon antagonized the Matsiguenka tribespeople being used as extras – one even offered to murder him for Herzog. While filming near the Peru–Ecuador frontier, a war between the two nations erupted and soldiers destroyed the film set. Then there was the weather: droughts so dire that the rivers dried and stranded the film's steamship for weeks, followed by flash floods that wrecked the boat entirely. (Some of these are chronicled in *Conquest of the Useless: Reflections from the Making of Fitzcarraldo,* Herzog's film diaries, translated into English in 2009.) To hear another side to events during filming, chat to the folks at La Casa Fitzcarraldo, owned by the daughter of the executive producer of *Fitzcarraldo* the movie.

Herzog could certainly be a hard man to work with, filming many on-set catastrophes and using them as footage in the final cut. The director once said he saw filming in the Amazon as 'challenging nature itself.' The fact that he completed two films in the Peruvian jungle against such odds is evidence that in some ways, Herzog did challenge nature – and triumphed.

Flying Dog Hostel HOSTEL $
(☎in Lima 01-445-6745; www.flyingdogperu.com; Malecón Tarapaca, btwn Brasil & Ricardo Palma; dm/s/d/tr incl breakfast S26/75/90/99; @📶) The Flying Dog, part of the same hostel chain you'll find in Lima and Cuzco, is leader of the pack for traditional backpacker digs: clean, bright rooms, hot water and kitchen facilities. The doubles are a tad pricey for what you get but some have private bathrooms.

Hostal El Colibrí GUESTHOUSE $
(☎065-24-1737; Nauta 172; s S60, d S70-90; ❄) A very good budget choice close to the river and the main square, with pleasant, airy singles and doubles sporting fans and TVs. It's now risen up by three floors of rooms, and with its small cafeteria has the air of a hotel. Higher tariffs are for air-con.

La Casa Del Francés GUESTHOUSE $
(☎065-23-1447; http://en.lacasadelfrances.com; Raimondi 183; dm/s/d S20/45/60) A secure, hammock-strung courtyard leads back to this decent budget choice. The colonial rooms show the wear and tear of generations of budget-minded backpackers, but they're alright.

Hostal Florentina GUESTHOUSE $
(☎065-23-3591; Huallaga 212; r S60-90; ❄) Rooms in this old colonial house are smallish but very quiet. They come with cable TV, mosquito nets and sparkling bathrooms, and are tucked well back from the road with a hammock-hung courtyard at the rear. Lower rates are for rooms with fans, higher for rooms with air-con.

Casa Bendayan BOUTIQUE HOTEL $$
(☎965-982-854, 065-50-0489; www.casabendayan.com; Brasil 1209; r incl breakfast S135-195; ❄📶🏊) Head and shoulders above the many other new entrants in the midrange (and indeed top-end) hotel markets in Iquitos is this five-room place. The rooms are enormous, and are enhanced by bright, bold color schemes, a pool, rooftop racquetball and a barbecue area. It's refreshingly absent of the snobbishness of other luxury accommodations, and it has well-regarded jungle tours, using its Llaquipallay Lodge.

Nativa Apartments APARTMENT $$
(☎065-60-0270; www.nativaapartments.com; Nanay 144; apt S177-330; ❄📶) If what you want in Iquitos is a clean, safe, quiet, friendly home-from-home where you can do your own cooking in a generously sized apartment, there is no need to keep searching.

Marañón Hotel HOTEL $$
(☎065-24-2673; www.hotelmaranon.com; Nauta 289; s/d incl continental breakfast S99/150; ❄📶🏊) This place, looking a little like a stranded ferry, has light tiles everywhere and a restaurant with room service. The rooms have good-sized bathrooms, minibars and indeed all the usual amenities. Good value.

★**La Casa Fitzcarraldo** GUESTHOUSE $$$
(☎065-60-1138, 065-60-1139; http://lacasafitzcarraldo.com; Av La Marina 2153; r incl breakfast S180-420; P❄📶🏊) Sequestered within a serene walled garden 3km north of the city, this is most interesting accommodation. The house takes its title from Werner Herzog's film – Herzog and co stayed here during the filming of *Fitzcarraldo*. Stay in the mahogany-floored Mick Jagger room, the luxuriantly green Klaus Kinski suite (with its beautiful butterfly picture) or five other individually designed rooms.

There is a tree house (with wi-fi!), a lovely swimming pool (nonresidents S10) and a huge breakfast included in the price, as well as a bar-restaurant, minicinema and several four-legged residents to check out. Unique stills from the filming of *Fitzcarraldo* line the walls of the public areas. The place is a S2.50 *mototaxi* ride from the center; airport pickup is included in room prices however.

Casa Morey BOUTIQUE HOTEL $$$
(☎065-23-1913; www.casamorey.com; Loreto 200; s/d incl breakfast S210/285; ❄📶🏊) This former mansion of the rubber baron Luis F Morey dates from 1910 and has been renovated to its former elegance, with 14 extravagantly large suites, plenty of original *azulejos*, voluminous bathrooms with baths, river views, a courtyard with a small pool and a library with a stupendous collection of Amazon-related literature.

The grandiose dining area makes for charming breakfast environs (though the tiling here isn't original).

Hotel El Dorado Plaza BUSINESS HOTEL $$$
(☎065-22-2555; www.grupo-dorado.com; Napo 258; s/d incl breakfast from S784/896; ❄📶🏊) With a prime plaza location, this modern hotel is the town's priciest (undoubtedly) and best (possibly), with 64 well-equipped, spacious rooms (some with plaza views, others overlooking the pool). Jacuzzi, sauna, gym, restaurant, several suites, 24-hour room service, two bars and attentive staff make this a five-star hotel. Rates for rooms are often discounted when the hotel is not busy.

The same group runs the slightly cheaper **El Dorado Isabel** (☎065-23-2574; Napo 362; s/d incl buffet breakfast from S264/297; ❄📶🏊), where you can still use the plaza hotel facilities, and cheaper-again **El Dorado Express** (☎065-23-5718; www.doradoexpress.com; Napo 480; s/d from S180/210), where the same offer applies.

Hotel Victoria Regia HOTEL $$$
(☎065-23-1983; www.victoriaregiahotel.com; Ricardo Palma 252; s/d incl breakfast S330/372; ❄@🏊) A blast of icy, air-conditioned air welcomes guests to this comfortable hotel. It has excellent beds and sizable rooms that include fancy reading lights and minibars, plus hairdryers and baths in the bathrooms. One of the suites has a Jacuzzi. The indoor pool and fine restaurant-bar attract upscale guests and business people.

The reality, though, is that this is not significantly better than several city hotels that charge about S100 less. Various promotions can reduce the quoted rates.

Hotel Acosta HOTEL $$$
(☎065-23-1761; www.hotelacosta.com; cnr Araujo & Huallaga; s/d S198/231; ❄📶) Owned by the same people as the Victoria Regia; you can be sure you're in good hands at this smart hotel. Ample rooms are finished in delicate earthy tones; they all come with minibars, air-con, safes and writing desks. There is a ground-floor restaurant.

Eating

The city has excellent restaurants, but be aware that many regional specialties feature endangered animals, such as *chicharrón de lagarto* (fried alligator) and *sopa de tortuga* (turtle soup). *Paiche,* a local river fish, is making a comeback thanks to breeding programs. More environmentally friendly esoteric dishes include ceviche made with river fish, *chupín de pollo* (a tasty soup of chicken, egg and rice) and *juanes*.

For self-catering supplies, visit **Supermercado Los Portales** (Próspero at Morona).

★ Belén Mercado MARKET $
(cnr Prospero & Jirón 9 de Diciembre; menús from S5) There are great eats at Iquitos' markets, particularly the Belén *mercado* where a *menú*, including *jugo especial* (jungle juice) costs S5. Look out for specialties including meaty Amazon worms, *ishpa* (simmered sabalo fish intestines and fat) and *sikisapa* (fried leaf-cutter ants; abdomens are supposedly tastiest), and watch your valuables. Another good market for cheap eats is **Mercado Central** (Lores cuadra 5).

Cafe Express CAFE $
(Prospero 285; snacks/breakfasts S3-10; ⏲7am-4pm) Wondering what to do for breakfast? Don't wonder. This is the spot. Grab a newspaper from the old dude outside and pull up a pew with the locals for a dose of the infamously curt service (part of the fun) and then the tasty grub. If it ain't broke, don't fix it.

Antica ITALIAN $
(☎065-24-1672; Napo 159; mains S22-24; ⏲7am-midnight) The Antica is the best Italian restaurant in town. It's primarily a pizza place – there's an impressive wood-fired pizza oven – but pasta also takes a predominant spot on the menu with the lasagna being an excellent choice. Chow down at solid wooden tables and choose from the range of fine imported Italian wines.

Ari's Burger AMERICAN $
(☎065-23-1470; Próspero 127; meals S9-23; ⏲7am-3am) On the corner of the Plaza de Armas, this clean, chirpy and brightly lit joint is known locally as *gringolandia* (gringo land). Two walls are open to the street, allowing great plaza- and people-watching. It's almost always open and serves American-style fast food (with cute Amazonian caveats like the burger with *paiche*, a local fish). Popular with tourists and locals alike.

Mitos y Cubiertos PERUVIAN $
(Napo 337; menús S12, mains around S15; ⏲11am-11:30pm) Resembling the inside of an *ayahuasca* vision, Mitos y Cubiertos is probably *the* place to be cool in an understated way in Iquitos right now. The menu loosely hinges around the national classics, but there are veggie options, bruschetta and imaginative pasta to add a tad of pizzazz.

El Sitio PARRILLA $
(cnr Lores & Huallaga; parrillas around S10; ⏲6-11pm) Wide varieties of delicious grilled meats, which are grilled on the street outside. It stays open until it's all gone.

Comma y Punto CEVICHE $
(Napo 488; mains S16-25; ⏲9am-5pm) The 'Comma and the Full Stop' has raced into the lead in the contest (keenly fought) for the city's best ceviche.

Huasai PERUVIAN $
(www.huasairestaurant.com; Fitzcarrald 131; menús S14; ⏲7:30am-4pm) Efficient service, a variety of dependable tasty meat and fish lunch specials and great juices are the cornerstones of this good-value, centrally located restaurant.

Ivalú PERUVIAN $
(Lores 215; snacks from S3; ⏲8am-early afternoon) One of the most popular local spots for juice and cake and tamales (corn cakes filled with chicken or fish and wrapped in jungle leaves). As for the opening: go earlier, before they sell out!

Chifa Long Fung CHINESE $
(San Martín 454; mains S10-20; ⏲noon-2.30pm & 7pm-midnight) Of the several inexpensive *chifas* (Chinese restaurants) near the Plaza 28 de Julio, the Long Fung is a little more expensive but worth it.

Kikiriki FAST FOOD $
(☎065-23-2020; Napo 159; quarter chicken from S10) How does a Peruvian cock crow? '*Kikiriki.*' This is a great place for grilled chicken. Have it served on a bed of fried banana, the jungle way, with a dash of the legendary hot green sauce. Delivery is possible. Several other branches around town too.

★ Al Frio y al Fuego FUSION $$
(☎965-607-474; www.alfrioyalfuego.com; Embarcadero Av La Marina 138; mains S20-40; ⏲noon-4pm & 7-11pm Tue-Sat, noon-5pm Sun) Take a

boat out to this floating foodie paradise in the middle of the mouth of the Río Itaya to sample some of the city's best food. The emphasis is on river fish (such as the delectable *doncella*), but the *parrillas* (grills) are inviting too. The address given is the boat embarkation point.

Come here at night for the best overall view of Iquitos, beautifully lit up beyond the restaurant's swimming pool.

★ Amazon Bistro INTERNATIONAL **$$**
(Malecón Tarapaca 268; breakfasts S12, mains S20-40; 6am-midnight;) This is laid out with TLC by the Belgian owner, with a New York-style breakfast bar (OK, Amazon version thereof) and upper-level mezzanine seating looking down on the main eating area. The cuisine refuses to be pigeonholed: there are Argentine steaks, not to mention the Belgian influence, which creeps across in the crepes, and with the L'escargot and the range of Belgian beers.

Then there is the city's best coffee, which goes down rather nicely in conjunction with a fresh croissant. The bistro is best for breakfast but not bad for an evening drink either.

Dawn on the Amazon Café INTERNATIONAL **$$**
(Malecón Maldonado 185; mains S18-32; 7:30am-10pm;) This traveler magnet on the Malecón, with its tempting row of street-front tables, sports a menu divided up into North American, Peruvian, Spanish and (logically) Chinese. Travel wherever your taste buds desire but bear in mind that the steamed fresh fish is very good. Ingredients are all non-MSG and those on gluten-free diets are catered for.

Fitzcarraldo Restaurant-Bar INTERNATIONAL **$$**
(065-50-7545; www.restaurantefitzcarraldo.com; Napo 100; mains S15-40; noon-late;) The Fitzcarraldo is an upscale option on the riverside strip, with very good food and service. It does good pizzas (delivery available) and various local and international dishes. Try the S80 Amazon tasting platter – all the jungle specialties on one massive plate. And beware of that icy air-con!

Gran Maloca PERUVIAN **$$**
(Lores 170; menús S15, mains S25-42; noon-11pm;) Enter the bygone world of the rubber-boom glory days at this atmospheric Amazonian restaurant. Expect silk tablecloths, wall-length mirrors and imaginative

MUST-TRY FOODS

Juane Steamed rice with pork or chicken, wrapped in a jungle leaf.

Ceviche The Amazon version of the citrus-marinated seafood, with freshwater fish.

Parrilladas de la selva Jungle barbecue, with meat marinaded in Brazil-nut sauce.

regional delicacies such as *chupín de pollo*, Amazon venison with toasted coconut and the scrumptious Loretan omelet with jungle leaves.

The air-con will leave you wondering why you didn't just plan a vacation to Antarctica

Karma Cafe CAFE **$$**
(Napo 138; mains S7-30; 9am-midnight;) This chilled atmospheric place does a little bit of everything and does it well: Thai, Indian, vegetarian, Peruvian, cocktails. Offers a 'make your own' breakfast, a popular happy hour and great live music several nights per week. An interior garden and pool should be open by the time you read this.

Drinking & Nightlife

Iquitos is a party city. The Malecón is the cornerstone of the lively nightlife scene.

Arandú Bar BAR
(Malecón Maldonado 113; till late) The liveliest of several thumping Malecón bars, great for people-watching and always churning out loud rock-and-roll classics.

Musmuqui BAR
(Raimondi 382; to midnight Sun-Thu, to 3am Fri & Sat) Locally popular lively bar with two floors and an extensive range of aphrodisiac cocktails concocted from wondrous Amazon plants.

El Pardo CLUB
(cnr Caceres & Alzamora; until 5am most nights) Our favorite of the batch of party places, this complex is in a sort of stadium, with a vast open-air dance space. It is its own restaurant too.

Shopping

There are a few stands along the Malecón selling jungle crafts, some of high quality, some (not always the same ones) pricey.

A good place for crafts is **Mercado de Artesanía San Juan**, on the airport road – bus and taxi drivers know it. Don't buy items made from animal bones and skins, as they are made from jungle wildlife. It's illegal to import many such items into the US and Europe.

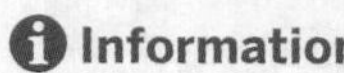

Information

DANGERS & ANNOYANCES

Street touts and self-styled jungle guides tend to be aggressive, and many are both irritatingly insistent and dishonest. They are working for commissions, and usually for bog-standard establishments. It is best to make your own decisions by contacting hotels, lodges and tour companies directly. Exercise particular caution around Belén, which is very poor and where petty thieving is quite common. That said, violent crime is almost unknown in Iquitos.

EMERGENCY

National police (065-23-1123; Morona 126) Most central police station.

Policía de Turismo (965-935-932, 065-24-2081; Lores 834)

IMMIGRATION

If arriving from or departing for Brazil or Colombia, get your entry/exit stamp at the border.

Brazilian Consulate (065-23-5151; Lores 363)

Colombian Consulate (065-23-1461; Calvo de Araujo 431)

Oficina de Migraciónes (065-23-5371; Mariscal Cáceres, cuadra 18)

INTERNET ACCESS

Places charge about S3 per hour; the wi-fi in hotels usually offers a better connection.

Cyber (Putumayo 374) Lots of machines; serves beer; almost always open – why not?

LAUNDRY

Lavandería Imperial (Nauta cuadra 1; per load S12; 8am-8pm Mon-Sat)

MEDIA

Amazon River Monthly (www.iquitostimes.com) A free about-monthly newspaper in English, aimed at tourists, delivered to all hotels and restaurants.

MEDICAL SERVICES

Clínica Ana Stahl (065-25-2535; www.facebook.com/caas.iquitos; La Marina 285; 24hr) Private clinic 2km north of the center.

Happydent (Putumayo 786) Dentist.

InkaFarma (Prospero 397; 7am-midnight) Reliable.

MONEY

Several banks change traveler's checks, give advances on credit cards or provide an ATM, including **BCP** (Próspero & Putamayo), which has secure ATMs. For changing US cash quickly, street money changers are located on Próspero between Lores and Brasil. Most are OK, but a few run scams where they replace a S100 note with a S20 note. Exercise caution when changing money on the street; it's best to do this in a bank. For the Peru/Brazil/Colombia tri-border, the border towns have money changers anyway. Transfer money at **Western Union** (065-23-5182; Napo 359).

POST

Serpost (Arica 402; 8am-6pm Mon-Fri, to 5pm Sat)

TOURIST INFORMATION

Various jungle guides and jungle lodges also give tourist information, obviously promoting their services, which is fine if you are looking for them but otherwise rarely helpful.

iPerú (065-23-6144; Napo 161; 9am-6pm Mon-Sat, to 1pm Sun) There's also a branch at the airport (065-26-0251; Main Hall, Francisco Secada Vignetta Airport; whenever flights are arriving/departing).

Reserva Nacional Pacaya-Samiria Office (065-60-7299; Pevas 339; 7am-3pm Mon-Fri)

Getting There & Away

AIR

Iquitos' small but busy airport, 7km from the center, currently receives flights from Lima, Pucallpa, Tarapoto and Panama City.

Charter companies at the airport have five-passenger planes to almost anywhere in the Amazon, if you have a few hundred US bucks going spare.

Copa Airlines (in Panama 1-800-359-2672; www.copaair.com) Twice-weekly flights to Panama City (Wednesday and Saturday).

LAN (065-23-2421; Próspero 232) LAN Peru has five to seven daily runs to Lima – several via Tarapoto and Pucallpa.

Star Perú (065-23-6208; Napo 260) Star Perú operates two daily flights to and from Lima: the morning flight stops at Pucallpa and the afternoon flight at Tarapoto. Fares are about US$100 to Lima and US$75 to Pucallpa or Tarapoto.

BOAT

Iquitos is Peru's largest, best-organized river port. You can theoretically travel all the way from Iquitos to the Atlantic Ocean, but most boats out of Iquitos today ply only Peruvian waters, and voyagers necessarily change boats at the Colombia–Brazil border. If you choose to arrive by river, you'll end up at one of three ports, which are between 2km and 3km north of the city center.

Puerto Masusa

Puerto Masusa (Los Rosales), about 3km north of the town center, is where cargo boats depart for Yurimaguas (upriver; three to six days) and Pucallpa (upriver; four to seven days); but these trips are better undertaken in the other direction, with the current. Fares cost S80 to S100 for hammock space and S130 to S180 for a tiny (often cell-like) cabin. Boats leave most days for both places; there are more frequent departures for the closer intermediate ports en route. For Yurimaguas, the Eduardo boats have the best reputation.

Downriver boats to the Peruvian border with Brazil and Colombia leave from Puerto Masusa too. There are about two or three departures weekly for the two-day journey (per person S80). Boats will stop at Pevas (hammock space S40, about 15 hours) and other ports en route. Boats may dock closer to the center if the water is very high (from May to July).

Henry Boats Port

Closer to the center, the more organized **Henry Boats port** (☎965-678-622; Av La Marina s/n; ⏰7am-7pm) runs services along the Iquitos–Pucallpa route.

At both ports chalkboards tell you which boats are leaving when, for where, and whether they accept passengers. Although there are agencies in town, it's usually best to go to the dock and look around; don't trust anyone except the captain for an estimate of departure time. Be wary: the chalkboards have a habit of changing dates overnight! Boats often leave hours or even days late.

You can often sleep aboard the boat while waiting for departure, and this enables you to get the best hammock space. Never leave gear unattended – ask to have your bags locked up when you sleep.

Puerto Embarcadero

Tiny Puerto Embarcadero, closest to the center, near the join of Av La Marina/Calle Ocampo is for speedboats to the tri-border (with Colombia and Brazil). These depart between 5am and 6am daily except Monday. You'll need to purchase your ticket in advance. Speedboat offices are bunched together on Raimondi near the Plaza Castilla. Standard fares are S170 to Pevas or S200 for the 10- to 12-hour trip to Santa Rosa, on the Peruvian side, including meals.

You *may* be able to book a berth on a Leticia-bound cruise ship if space is available, although this is more likely coming from Leticia to Iquitos (the captain is more likely to take pity on you if you're stranded in Leticia).

Getting Around

Squadrons of *mototaxis* are the bona fide transport round town. They are fun to ride, though they don't provide much protection in an accident. Always enter *mototaxis* from the sidewalk side – passing traffic pays scant heed to embarking passengers – and keep your limbs inside at all times. Scrapes and fender bending are common. Most rides around Iquitos cost a standard S1.50 to S3; to the airport it's about S8 for a *mototaxi* and S15 for the harder-to-spot cabs. Your accommodations will always order you a taxi on request.

Buses and trucks for several nearby destinations, including the airport, leave from near Plaza 28 de Julio. Airport buses are marked Nanay-Belén-Aeropuerto: they'll head south down Arica to the airport.

A paved road extends 102km through the jungle as far as Nauta on the Río Marañón, near its confluence with the Río Ucayali. Riverboat passengers from Yurimaguas usually now alight at Nauta and pick up a local bus to Iquitos, thus making the journey shorter by some six hours; Pacaya-Samiria–bound cruises and several jungle lodges now depart from Nauta too.

Minivans to Nauta take 1½ hours and depart from the corner of Próspero and José Gálvez. There are swimming opportunities at the creeks and beaches en route.

Around Iquitos

About 16km from town, past the airport, **Santo Tomás** is famous for its pottery and mask making. A few bars here overlook Mapacocha, a lake formed by an arm of the Río Nanay. You can rent boats by asking around (motorboat with driver about S30). **Santa Clara** is about 15km away, on the banks of the Río Nanay. There are white-sand beaches during low water (July to October), and boats for rent. Both villages can be reached by *mototaxi* (about S15) or a S2 minivan ride from the Nauta van stop.

Corrientillo is a lake near the Río Nanay. There are a few bars around the lake, which is locally popular for swimming on weekends and has good sunsets. It's about 15km from town; a *mototaxi* will charge about S15.

Sights

Pilpintuwasi Butterfly Farm WILDLIFE RESERVE

(☎065-23-2665; www.amazonanimalorphanage.org; Padre Cocha; adult/student S15/9; ⏰9am-4pm Tue-Sun) A visit to the fascinating Pilpintuwasi Butterfly Farm is highly

BORDER CROSSING: THE PERU–COLOMBIA–BRAZIL BORDER ZONE

Even in the middle of the Amazon, border officials adhere to formalities and will refuse passage if documents are not in order. With a valid passport and visa or tourist card, border crossing is not a problem.

When leaving Peru for Colombia or Brazil, you'll get an exit stamp at a Peruvian guard post just before the border (boats stop there long enough for this; ask the captain).

The ports at the three-way border are several kilometers apart, connected by public ferries. They are reached by air or boat, but not by road. The biggest, nicest border town, **Leticia**, in Colombia, boasts by far the best hotels and restaurants, and a hospital. You can fly from Leticia to Bogotá on almost-daily commercial flights. Otherwise, infrequent boats go to **Puerto Asis** on the Río Putumayo; the trip takes up to 12 days. From Puerto Asis, buses go further into Colombia.

The two small ports in Brazil are **Tabatinga** and **Benjamin Constant**; both have basic hotels. Tabatinga has an airport with flights to Manaus. Get your official Brazilian entry stamp from the Tabatinga police station if flying on to Manaus. Tabatinga is a continuation of Leticia, and you can walk or take a taxi between the two with no immigration hassles, unless you are planning on traveling further into Brazil or Colombia. Boats leave from Tabatinga downriver, usually stopping in Benjamin Constant for a night, then continuing on to Manaus, a week away. It takes about an hour to reach Benjamin Constant by public ferry. US citizens need a visa to enter Brazil. Make sure you apply in good time – either in the USA or in Lima.

Peru is on the south side of the river, where currents create a constantly shifting bank. Most boats from Iquitos will drop you at the small village of Santa Rosa, which has Peruvian immigration facilities. Motor canoes reach Leticia in about 15 minutes. For travelers to Colombia or Brazil, Lonely Planet has guidebooks for both countries.

If you are arriving from Colombia or Brazil, you'll find boats in Leticia and Tabatinga for Iquitos. You should pay US$10 to US$15 for the nigh-on two-day trip on a cargo riverboat, or US$65 for a *mas rápido* (fast boat; 12 to 14 hours), which leave daily. Prices and departures are the same for the opposite journey too, although downriver from Iquitos to the tri-border is quicker. Up or down river, you may be able to get passage on a cruise ship, but note that this will make stops en route.

Remember that however disorganized things may appear, you can always get meals, money changed, beds and boats simply by asking around.

recommended. Ostensibly this is a conservation and breeding center for Amazonian butterflies. Butterflies aplenty there certainly are, including the striking blue morpho *(Morpho menelaus)* and the fearsome-looking owl butterfly *(Caligo eurilochus)*. But it's the farm's exotic animals that steal the show. Raised as orphans and protected within the property are several mischievous monkeys, a tapir, an anteater and Pedro Bello, a majestic jaguar.

To get there, take a boat from Bellavista-Nanay, a small port 2km north of Iquitos, to the village of Padre Cocha. Boats run all day. The farm is signposted: a 15-minute walk through the village from the Padre Cocha boat dock.

Laguna Quistacocha LAKE

(admission S3) This lake, 15km south of Iquitos, is served by minibus (S2) several times an hour from near Plaza 28 de Julio (corner of Bermúdez and Moore), as well as *mototaxis* (S15). There's a small **zoo** of local fauna (much improved of recent years) and an adjoining **fish hatchery**, which has 2m-long *paiche*, endangered until recently, due to habitat loss and its popularity as food; attempts to rectify the situation are being made with the breeding program here.

A pedestrian walk circles the lake, swimming is possible and paddleboats are available for hire (S5 to S10). There are several restaurants and a hiking trail to the Río Itaya. It's fairly crowded with locals on the weekend but not midweek.

Tours

Jungle 'guides' will approach you everywhere in Iquitos. Some will be independent operators, and many will be working on behalf of a lodge. Travelers have mixed experiences with private guides. All guides should have a permit or license – if they don't, check with the tourist office. Get references for any guide, and proceed with caution. The better lodges often snap up the best guides quickly.

Walter Soplin ADVENTURE TOUR
(☎965-303-113; per person per night from US$50) Walter's hard-core adventure trips go deep into the incredibly flora-and-fauna-rich Tamshiyacu-Tahuayo Reserve around seven to eight hours' boat ride from Iquitos. This is back-to-basics stuff: you're sleeping in small-scale cabins, situated near one of the Amazon's remotest communities, Nuevo Jerusalem, and scattered around a blackwater lake. Because of the distances involved, you really need to sign up for the seven-day and six-night tour.

Sleeping

In this northern tract of the Peruvian jungle, there are many good lodges accessible from Iquitos that provide a rewarding rainforest experience.

Numerous lodges exist both up- and down-river from Iquitos. Take your time choosing: a bewildering variety of programs and activities are available and quality varies considerably. There is the usual mix of luxury options, where relaxation plays a key part, and more rustic lodges offering camping, hiking, fishing (July to September are the best months) and adventurous side trips. Most lodges have offices in Iquitos.

Many of these lodges can be reserved from abroad or in Lima, but if you show up in Iquitos without a reservation you can certainly book a lodge or tour and it'll cost you less. If planning on booking after you arrive, avoid major Peruvian holidays, when places swarm with local holidaymakers. June to September (the dry months and summer vacation for North American/European visitors) is also busy.

Lodges are some distance from Iquitos, so river transport is included in the price. Most of the area within 50km of the city is not virgin jungle: chances of seeing big mammals here are remote and interaction with local tribespeople is geared toward tourists. Nevertheless, much can be seen of the jungle way of life, and birds, insects and small mammals can be observed. More-remote lodges have more wildlife.

A typical two-day trip involves a river journey of two or three hours to a jungle lodge with reasonable comforts and meals, a jungle lunch, a visit to an indigenous village to buy crafts and to see dances (where tourists often outnumber tribespeople), an evening meal at the lodge, maybe an after-dark canoe trip to look for caiman by searchlight, and jungle walks to scout out other wildlife. A trip like this will set you back about US$300, depending on the operator, the distance traveled and the comfort of the lodge. On longer trips you'll get further away from Iquitos and see more of the jungle, and the cost per night drops.

All prices quoted here are approximate; bargaining is often acceptable, and meals, tours and transportation from Iquitos are included in prices. Lodges will provide containers of purified water for you to drink when there, but bring extra water for the journey.

The big new concentration of lodges is on the Ríos Yarapa and Cumaceba, still with pristine wildlife but far more accessible (in wet season 1½ to two hours from Nauta) due to a change in the river course.

Jungle Wolf Lodge LODGE $$
(☎065-23-6428; www.junglewolfexpeditions.com; Putumayo 1024; per person per day from US$70) One for the budget hunters! This lodge is really very nice for the price, and it's right up the Río Cumaceba, a tributary of the Yarapa, and gets no passing river traffic, which in turn can mean more serenity and more wildlife sightings. Travel is by bus to Nauta, then boat.

Amazonas Sinchicuy Lodge LODGE $$$
(3 days & 2 nights per person s/d US$313/534) On a small tributary of the Amazon 30km northeast of Iquitos. The 32 rooms, which can sleep up to four, have private cold showers and are lantern-lit. Some rooms are wheelchair accessible. This lodge can be visited on a day trip from Iquitos. Lodge office is located in **Iquitos** (☎065-23-1618; www.paseosamazonicos.com; Pevas 246).

The palm-thatched Tambo Yanayacu Lodge, 60km northeast of Iquitos, has 10 rustic rooms with private bathrooms.

Stays at these two lodges can be combined into one trip, including visits to local Yagua communities.

Cumaceba Lodge LODGE $$$
(☎065-23-2229; www.cumaceba.com; Putumayo 184-188; 3 days & 2 nights per person US$240-335) Rustic Cumaceba Lodge, in operation since 1995, is about 35km downriver from Iquitos.

WORTH A TRIP

PEVAS

Pevas, about 145km downriver from Iquitos, is Peru's oldest town on the Amazon. Founded by missionaries in 1735, Pevas boasts about 5000 inhabitants but no cars, post office or banks (or attorneys!); the first telephone was installed in 1998. Most residents are *mestizos* (people of mixed indigenous and Spanish descent) or indigenous people from one of four tribes. Pevas is the most interesting town between Iquitos and the border.

The main attraction in Pevas is the studio-gallery of one of Peru's best-known living artists, **Francisco Grippa**. Grippa handmakes his canvases from local bark, similar to that formerly used by local tribespeople for cloth. The paintings on view are the outcome of Grippa's two decades' observation of Amazonian people, places and customs. You can't miss the huge house with its red-roofed lookout tower on the hill above the port. The artist also has rooms on his property sometimes offered to visitors; otherwise, basic accommodations exists within the town center. Come dusk, fried-chicken vendors fire up grills around town.

Leticia-bound cargo boats make request stops at Pevas, as do daily (except Monday) fast boats to the tri-border (the same applies if you are coming from Leticia). These slow cargo boats (S40, around 15 hours) or fast boats (S170, downriver/upriver 3½/five hours) also connect Pevas with Iquitos. Tour operators also sometimes incorporate a Pevas trip into packages. Arriving independently, there's an element of risk – you might get stuck here for a while – but a boat *will* eventually turn up.

It has 15 screened rooms with private showers, and focuses on local adventure trips – although not in primary jungle. Guides speak English, French and even Japanese.

The same company also run Amazonas Botanical Lodge, which places an emphasis on studying rainforest plants in addition to wildlife-watching.

Otorongo Lodge LODGE **$$$**
(www.otorongoexpeditions.com; 5 days & 4 nights per person d US$500) Travelers give great feedback about this rustic-style lodge, 100km from Iquitos. Set down a peaceful tributary off the Amazon and surrounded by walkways to maximize appreciation of the surrounding wildlife, it has 12 rooms with private bathrooms and a relaxing common area. It's run by a falconer who imitates an incredible number of bird sounds. Lodge office is in **Iquitos** (☎965-75-6131, 065-22-4192; Departamento 203, Putumayo 163).

Staying here gets you up close and personal to a huge variety of wildlife, and so this lodge comes recommended for a magical, personal experience of the Amazonian wilderness.

The five-day option can include lots of off-the-beaten-path visits to nearby communities, and camping trips deeper in the jungle. Otorongo offers passersby (!) en route to the Colombian border a daily rate of US$50. Ask about its 'extreme fishing' and jungle-survival programs: the owner is an expert on these.

Tahuayo Lodge LODGE **$$$**
(☎in US 800-262-9669, 813-907-8475; www.perujungle.com; 8 days & 7 nights per person US$1295) You'll hear the phrase 'Pacaya-Samiria' bandied around a lot in these parts but this is only one of several reserves in the northern jungle. This lodge, 140km from Iquitos, is the only one with access to the 2500-sq-km Tamshiyacu-Tahuayo reserve, an area of pristine jungle where a record 93 species of mammal have been recorded.

The 15 lodge cabins are located 65km up an Amazon tributary, built on high stilts and connected by walkways; half have private bathrooms. There is a laboratory with a library here too. Wildlife-viewing opportunities are among the best of any lodge: they usually include a peek at the pygmy marmosets that nest near the lodge. Visitors can also stay at the nearby Tahuayo River Research Center, which boasts an extensive trail network.

Explorama LODGE **$$$**
(3 days & 2 nights per person s/d US$549/998) About 80km from Iquitos on the Amazon, near its junction with the Río Napo, this was one of the first lodges constructed in the Iquitos area (1964) and remains attractively rustic. The lodge has several large, palm-thatched buildings; the 55 rooms have private cold-water bathrooms. Covered walkways join the buildings and lighting is by kerosene lantern. Lodge offices are in

Iquitos (☎065-25-2530; www.explorama.com; Av La Marina 340).

Guides accompany visitors on several trails that go deeper into the forest. You could arrange a trip to visit this along with one or more of Explorama's other lodges (each of which is very different) combined with a visit to the Canopy walkway located near the company's ExplorNapo Lodge. Sample rates are given; contact Explorama for other options and combinations – and discounts.

Ceiba Tops LODGE **$$$**
(3 days & 2 nights per person s/d US$580/1040; ❄@🏊) About 40km northeast of Iquitos downriver on the Amazon, this is the area's most well-appointed lodge and resort. There are 75 luxurious rooms and suites, all featuring comfortable beds and furniture, fans, screened windows, porches and spacious bathrooms with hot showers. Landscaped grounds surround a pool complex, complete with hydromassage, waterslide and hammock house. Run by Explorama.

The restaurant adjoins a bar with live Amazon music daily. Short guided walks and boat rides are available for a taste of the jungle; there is primary forest nearby containing *Victoria regias* (giant Amazon waterlilies). This lodge is a recommended option for people who really don't want to rough it. It even hosts business incentive meetings.

ExplorNapo LODGE **$$$**
(5 days & 4 nights per person s/d US$1280/2360) On the Río Napo, 157km from Iquitos, this simple lodge, run by Explorama, has 30 rooms with shared cold-shower facilities. The highlights are guided trail hikes in remote primary forest, bird-watching, an ethnobotanical garden of useful plants (curated by a local shaman) and a visit to the nearby Canopy Walkway (half-hour walk).

A major highlight of any trip to the Peruvian Amazon, the canopy walkway is suspended 35m above the forest floor to give visitors a bird's-eye view of the rainforest canopy and its wildlife. Bear in mind that because of the distance involved, you spend the first and last night of a five-day/four-night package at the Explorama lodge.

ExplorTambos Camp is located 160 km from Iquitos, a two hour walk from ExplorNapo, and is a self-declared 'primitive' camp sleeping a maximum of 16. It has better wildlife-watching than at any of Explorama's other lodges because of the isolated location.

ACTS Field Station LODGE **$$$**
(srmadigosky@widener.edu) Around 150km from Iquitos, near the Canopy Walkway, with 20 rustic rooms. Book ahead, because accommodations are often used by researchers and workshop groups. Scientists and researchers wishing to use the accommodations here should contact head of scientific research Dr S Madigosky at the email address above. The station is visited by tourists as part of a program including nights at other lodges.

★**Llaquipallay** LODGE **$$$**
(☎959-338-607, 065-500-489; www.llaquipallay-expeditions.com; Brasil 1209; per person 2 days & 1 night US$180) Just before the mouth of the Río Yarapa, a gentle narrow tributary of the Ucayali on the edge of Reserva Nacional Pacaya-Samiria, this lodge remains surrounded by water for most of the year and thus feels a more intimate, isolated experience than those many other lodges offer. Rooms are simple but securely netted against mosquitoes, and the bathrooms probably have the best views in the jungle!

The place is run by a local family, who cook superbly, and the fun-loving owner makes the guest experience unique. The excellent guides, and the proximity of a small nearby community to which cultural trips are organized, enhances the attraction of a stay here. Travel is by bus to Nauta, then boat.

Treehouse LODGE **$$$**
(☎in US 435-879-5839; http://treehouselodge.com; 3 days & 2 nights s/d US$895/1390) The Treehouse looks very cool – the eight luxurious apartments perched high up in the branches here above the Río Yarapa are some of the Amazon's most impressive accommodations. But, as is often the case with owners who live far away, standards of service are poor, with staff unhelpful and unwelcoming. For comfort, this gets the nod; for the jungle experience it offers, a big fat zero. Travel is by bus to Nauta, then boat.

★**Samiria Ecolodge** LODGE **$$$**
(www.samiriaecolodge.com; Napo 475; 3 days & 2 nights per person US$400) It's not significantly more 'eco' than other lodges around, but this brand-new beauty on the Río Marañon is significantly flashier. Shiny, dark-wood 56-sq-meter cabins, with cotton-sheeted

king beds and futons, form part of an exquisite thatched complex, which also has a restaurant, bar and coffee bar. Tour activities, including a crash course in local botany, get good reports.

★ **Muyuna Amazon Lodge** LODGE $$$
(☎065-24-2858; www.muyuna.com; office, Ground Fl, Putumayo 163, Iquitos; 3 days & 2 nights s/d US$440/735) About 140km upriver from Iquitos on the Río Yanayacu, this intimate lodge is surrounded by 10 well-conserved lakes in a remote area less colonized than jungle downriver, which makes for a great rainforest experience – and a luxurious one. Fifteen trim, stilted, thatched bungalows here each sleep between two and six people and have lovely bathrooms and a balcony with a hammock.

The helpful Peruvian owners have a very hands-on approach to maintaining their lodge, ensuring that recycling occurs, staff set an ecofriendly example to visitors, and guests are happy. During high water, the river rises up to the bungalows, which are connected to the lodge's dining building with sweeping covered, raised walkways.

Lighting is by kerosene lanterns. The bilingual guides are excellent and they guarantee observation of monkeys, sloths and dolphins, as well as rich avian fauna typical of the nearby Amazonian *varzea* (flooded forest), including the piuri – the wattled curassow *(Crax globulosa),* a critically endangered bird restricted to western Amazonia, which can only be seen in Peru at Muyuna. One of the most unforgettable activities, however, is setting out from here by canoe at night and paddling through the maze of blackwater tributaries, where the foliage – and often the wildlife – gets within touching distance.

Understand Peru

Peru Today

From the happening capital of Lima to cobblestoned Andean villages, Peru leaves an indelible impression as a place of incredible diversity, bustling commerce and innovation. In 2011 it became one of the world's fastest-growing economies. Though the pace of progress has slowed, there are still many positives. That doesn't mean there are no tangles to be worked out. Environmental woes, a growing drug trade and political uncertainty are all concerns without an easy out. But by and large, Peru is finding its way.

Best in Print

The Last Days of the Inca (Kim MacQuarrie; 2007) The history-making clash between civilizations.

Aunt Julia & the Scriptwriter (Mario Vargas Llosa; 1977) A classic unconventional love story.

Cradle of Gold (Christopher Heaney; 2010) Readable biography of Hiram Bingham, the 'real' Indiana Jones.

At Play in the Fields of the Lord (Peter Matthiessen; 1965) Inspired by Amazon conflicts.

Best Music

Uchpa Quechua band lacing Peruvian punk rock with blues.

NovoLima Internationally popular Afro-Peruvian and electronic music.

Bareto Alt rock and Peruvian rhythms.

Arturo 'Zambo' Cavero Legendary crooner.

Pauchi Sasaki Modern violinist incorporating diverse influences.

Etiquette

Manners Transactions begin with a formal *buenos días* or *buenas tardes*.

Photos Ask before photographing people in indigenous communities – payment may be requested.

Antiquities It is illegal to buy pre-Columbian antiquities and take them out of Peru.

Unparalleled Boom

Between the violence of the Conquest, the chaos of the early republic and the succession of dictatorships that swallowed up much of the 20th century, stability has been a rare commodity in Peru. But the new millennium has treated the country with uncharacteristic grace. Peru's economy has grown every year since 2003. Foreign investment is up and the country's exports – in the areas of agriculture, mining and manufacturing – have been strong. Tourism is also big: the number of foreign travelers going to Peru almost tripled between 2003 and 2014 from 1.3 to 3.2 million, according to World Bank data.

In addition, since 2000, a succession of peaceful elections has provided political stability. In 2011 former army officer Ollanta Humala was elected to the presidency. The son of a Quechua labor lawyer from Ayacucho, he has made social inclusion a theme of his presidency. One of his early acts was to make it a legal requirement for native peoples to be consulted on mining or other extractive activities in their territories.

As Humala's term comes to a close, political bickering, a stalled economy and the absence of a clear successor all put Peru into a moment of uncertainty during this relatively stable period of growth.

Cultural Renaissance

The good times have resulted in a surge of cultural productivity – much of it revolving around food. Once considered a place to avoid, Lima is now a foodie bastion, where gastronomic festivals attract visitors from all over the world. La Mistura, an annual culinary gathering organized by celebrity chef Gastón Acurio, drew half a million people in 2013.

The relentless focus on food has had a ripple effect on other aspects of the culture. Young fashion designers produce avant-garde clothing lines with alpaca knits. Innovative musical groups fuse folk and electronica. And the contemporary-arts scene has been refreshed with the opening of the Museo Mario Testino, a top-to-bottom renovation of Museo de Arte de Lima (MALI), and galleries blossoming in the capital's bohemian quarters.

A Ways to Go

None of this means there aren't serious challenges. Though the country's poverty rate has been roughly cut in half since 2002, the economic boom has not trickled down to everyone: rural poverty, for one, is nearly double the national average.

In addition, Sendero Luminoso (Shining Path), the Maoist guerrilla group that took the country to the brink of civil war in the 1980s, has seen a comeback with a small political following and offshoots reportedly in the drug trade. Peru now rivals Colombia in terms of cocaine production, which represented 17% of the GDP in 2009. Coca and cocaine production also affects Peru's environment through deforestation in remote growing areas and chemical contamination that's a byproduct of production.

Above all, there are environmental pressures. Antimining strikes in Cajamarca and Arequipa continue the regional civil unrest, enmeshed with regional corruption and environmental concerns. The Amazon is now bisected by the Carretera Interocéanica (Transoceanic Hwy), an important overland trade route connecting Peru and Brazil both physically and economically. The engineering marvel has generated deep apprehension among scientists about its future impact on one of the world's last great wilderness areas.

AREA: **1,279,996 SQ KM**

POPULATION: **30.4 MILLION**

GDP: **$371.3 BILLION**

GDP GROWTH: **2.4%**

INFLATION: **3.2%**

UNEMPLOYMENT: **6%**

if Peru were 100 people

45 would be indigenous
37 would be mestizo (mixed indigenous & white)
15 would be white
3 would be black or Asian

belief systems

(% of population)

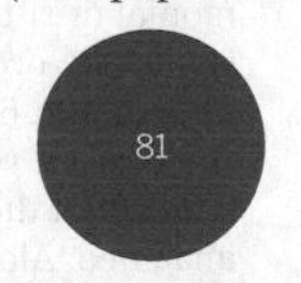

Roman Catholic

Evangelical

Other

population per sq km

PERU

US

UK

≈ 25 people

History

In 1532, when Francisco Pizarro landed to conquer Peru in the name of God and the Spanish Crown, the region had already seen the epic rise and fall of civilizations. Yet the conquest changed everything: the economics, political systems, religion and language. Modern history has been a series of aftershocks from that seismic clash between Inca and Spaniard. The conflict remains embedded in the Peruvian psyche. With it came new cultures, new races, new voices, new cuisines – ultimately, a new civilization.

Earliest Settlers

The Tiwanaku were a pre-Inca culture that settled the area around Lake Titicaca and are, in many ways, closely linked with the Wari. Margaret Young-Sanchez' *Tiwanaku: Ancestors of the Inca* provides a lushly illustrated compendium of their art and history.

There is some debate about how long, exactly, there has been a human presence in Peru. Some scholars have suggested that humans occupied the Andes as far back as 14,000 BC (with at least one academic reporting that it could precede even that early date). The most definitive archaeological evidence, however, puts humans in the region at around 8000 BC. Caves in Lauricocha (near Huánuco) and Toquepala (outside Tacna) bear paintings that record hunting scenes from that era. The latter shows a group of hunters cornering and killing what appears to be a group of camelid animals.

In 4000 BC taming of llamas and guinea pigs began in the highlands, followed by the domestication of potatoes, gourds, cotton, *lúcuma* (an earthy Andean fruit), quinoa, corn and beans. By 2500 BC, once-nomadic hunters and gatherers clustered into settlements along the Pacific, surviving on fishing and agriculture. These early Peruvians lived in simple one-room dwellings, but also built many structures for ceremonial or ritual purposes. Some of the oldest – raised temple platforms facing the ocean and containing human burials – date from the third millennium BC.

In recent years studies at some of these archaeological sites have revealed that these early societies were far more developed than previously imagined. Along with Egypt, India and China, Peru is considered one of the six cradles of civilization (a site where urbanization accompanied agricultural innovation) – the only one located in the southern hemisphere. Ongoing excavations at Caral, on the coast about 200km north

TIMELINE

8000 BC

Hunting scenes are painted in caves by hunter-gatherers near Huánuco in the central highlands and in Toquepala in the south – early evidence of humans in Peru.

c 3000 BC

Settlement of Peru's coastal oases begins; some of the first structures are built at the ceremonial center of Caral, north of present-day Lima.

3000 BC

Potatoes, squash, cotton, corn, *lúcuma* fruit and quinoa begin to be domesticated; at this point, llamas, alpacas and guinea pigs had likely been tamed for 1000 years.

of Lima, continue to uncover evidence of what is the oldest civilization in the Americas.

Roughly contemporary to these developments on the coast, a group in the highlands built the enigmatic Temple of Kotosh near Huánuco, whose structures are an estimated 4000 years old. The site features two temple mounds with wall niches and decorative friezes. It represents some of the most sophisticated architecture produced in the highlands during the period.

Clay & Cloth

In the centuries from 1800 BC to about 900 BC, ceramics and a more sophisticated textile production came into being. Some of the earliest pottery from this time comes from coastal archaeological sites at Las Haldas in the Casma Valley, south of Chimbote, and the Huaca La Florida, an unmapped temple structure in the heart of Lima. During this time, ceramics developed from basic undecorated bowls to sculpted, incised vessels of high quality. In the highlands, the people of Kotosh produced skilled pieces fashioned from black, red or brown clay.

The epoch also saw the introduction of looms, which were used to produce plain cotton cloths, as well as improvements in agriculture, including early experimentation with the terrace system.

The portrayal of indigenous people in pop culture tends to be that of benign stewards of vast wilderness. But Charles C Mann's *1491: New Revelations of the Americas Before Columbus* reveals that the continent was a place of great urbanization and high technological skill. The Incas are prominently featured.

Chavín Horizon

Lasting roughly from 1000 BC to 300 BC, and named after the site of Chavín de Huántar, the Chavín Horizon was a rich period of development for Andean culture, when artistic and religious phenomena appeared, perhaps independently, over a broad swath of the central and northern highlands, as well as the coast. The salient feature of this era is the repeated representation of a stylized feline deity, perhaps symbolizing spiritual transformations experienced under the influence of hallucinogenic plants. One of the most famous depictions of this many-headed figure can be found on the Raimondi Stela, a bas-relief carving which resides at the Museo Nacional de Antropología, Arqueología e Historia del Perú in Lima.

Chavín's feline also figures prominently in ceramics of the era, particularly the stark, black-clay specimens referred to as Cupisnique, a style that flourished on the northern coast.

Methods of working with gold, silver and copper were also developed during this time, and there were important advances in weaving and architecture. In short, this was a period when culture truly began to blossom in the Andes.

1000 BC

The Chavín Horizon begins, a period in which various highland and coastal communities share uniform religious deities.

200 BC

The Nazca culture on the coast starts construction of a series of giant glyphs that adorn the desert to this day.

AD 1

The southern coast sees the rise of the Paracas Necropolis culture, known for its intricate textiles that depict stylized images of warriors, animals and gods.

200

The Tiwanaku begin their 400-year domination of the area around Lake Titicaca, into what is today Bolivia and northern Chile.

INTRIGUE IN PACHACAMAC

The widespread looting of Peru's archaeological treasures has left many ruins with more puzzling questions than answers. So the discovery in May 2012 of an untouched 80-person burial chamber in Pachacamac (p103) is considered nothing less than a coup. Archaeologists from the Free University of Brussels discovered an 18m (60ft) oval chamber in front of the Temple of Pachacamac, hidden under newer burials. The perimeter was laced with infants and newborns encircling over 70 skeletons in the center of the tomb. The mummies were wrapped in textiles and buried with valuables, offerings, and even dogs and guinea pigs. According to *National Geographic,* investigators think the tomb may contain pilgrims who were drawn to the site to seek cures for serious illnesses.

Birth of Local Cultures

After 300 BC, numerous local settlements achieved importance at a regional level. South of Lima, in the area surrounding the Península de Paracas, lived a coastal community whose most significant phase is referred to as Paracas Necropolis (AD 1–400), after a large burial site. It is here that some of the finest pre-Columbian textiles in the Americas have been unearthed: colorful, intricate fabrics that depict oceanic creatures, feline warriors and stylized anthropomorphic figures.

To the south, the people of the Nazca culture (200 BC–AD 600) carved giant, enigmatic designs into the desert landscape that can only be seen from the air. Known as the Nazca Lines, these were mapped early in the 20th century – though their exact purpose remains up for debate. The culture is also known for its fine textile and pottery works, the latter of which used – for the first time in Peruvian history – a polychrome (multicolored) paint technique.

During this time, the Moche culture settled the area around Trujillo between AD 100 and 800. This was an especially artistic group (they produced some of the most remarkable portrait art in history), leaving behind important temple mounds, such as the Huacas del Sol y de la Luna (Temples of the Sun and Moon), near Trujillo, and the burial site of Sipán, outside Chiclayo. The latter contains a series of tombs that have been under excavation since 1987 – one of the most important archaeological discoveries in South America since Machu Picchu.

A catastrophic drought in the latter half of the 6th century may have contributed to the demise of the Moche as a culture.

Wari Expansion

As the influence of regional states waned, the Wari, an ethnic group from the Ayacucho Basin, emerged as a force to be reckoned with for 500 years

500

In the north, the Moche culture begins construction on the Huaca del Sol y de la Luna, adobe temples situated outside present-day Trujillo.

600

The Wari emerge from the Ayacucho area and consolidate an empire that covers a territory from Cuzco to Chiclayo; they are closely linked, stylistically, to the Tiwanaku culture of Bolivia.

c 800

The fiercely independent Chachapoyas build Kuélap, a citadel in the northern highlands composed of upwards of 400 constructions – including their trademark circular dwellings.

c 850

The Chimú begin development of Chan Chan (outside present-day Trujillo), a sprawling adobe urban center.

beginning in AD 600. They were vigorous military conquerors who built and maintained important outposts throughout a vast territory that covered an area from Chiclayo to Cuzco. Though their ancient capital lay outside present-day Ayacucho (the ruins of which can still be visited), they also operated the major lowland ceremonial center of Pachacamac, just outside Lima, where people from all over the region came to pay tribute.

As with many conquering cultures, the Wari attempted to subdue other groups by emphasizing their own traditions over local belief. Thus from about AD 700 to 1100, Wari influence is noted in the art, technology and architecture of most areas in Peru. These include elaborate, tie-dyed tunics, and finely woven textiles featuring stylized human figures and geometric patterns, some of which contained a record-breaking 398 threads per linear inch. They are most significant, however, for developing an extensive network of roadways and for greatly expanding the terrace agriculture system – an infrastructure that would serve the Incas well when they came into power just a few centuries later.

Guns, Germs & Steel, the Pulitzer Prize–winning book by Jared Diamond, is a thoughtful examination of why some societies triumphed over so many others. The battle for Cajamarca and Atahualpa's capture by the Spanish is discussed at length.

Regional Kingdoms

The Wari were eventually replaced by a gaggle of small nation-states that thrived from about 1000 until the Inca conquest of the early 15th century. One of the biggest and best studied of these are the Chimú of the Trujillo area, whose capital was the famed Chan Chan, the largest adobe city in the world. Their economy was based on agriculture and they had a heavily stratified society with a healthy craftsman class, which produced painted textiles and beautifully fashioned pottery that is distinctive for its black stain.

Closely connected to the Chimú are the Sicán from the Lambayeque area, renowned metallurgists who produced the *tumi*, a ceremonial knife with a rounded blade used in sacrifices. (The knife has since become a national symbol in Peru and replicas can be found in crafts markets everywhere.)

To the south, in the environs of Lima, the Chancay people (1000–1500) produced fine, geometrically patterned lace and crudely humorous pottery, in which just about every figure seems to be drinking.

In the highlands, several other cultures were significant during this time. In a relatively isolated and inaccessible patch of the Utcubamba Valley in the northern Andes, the cloud-forest-dwelling Chachapoyas people erected the expansive mountain settlement of Kuélap, one of the most intriguing and significant highland ruins in the country. To the south, several small altiplano (Andean plateau) kingdoms near Lake Titicaca left impressive *chullpas* (funerary towers). The best remaining examples are at Sillustani and Cutimbo.

The formation of chiefdoms in the Amazon began in this period too.

1100–1200

The Incas emerge as a presence in Cuzco; according to legend, they were led to the area by a divine figure known as Manco Cápac and his sister Mama Ocllo.

1438–71

The reign of Inca Yupanqui – also known as Pachacutec – represents a period of aggressive empire-building for the Incas; during this time, Machu Picchu and Saqsaywamán are built.

1492

Funded by the Spanish Crown, Genoa-born explorer Christopher Columbus arrives in the Americas.

1493

Inca Huayna Cápac begins his reign, pushing the empire north to Colombia; his untimely death in 1525 – probably from smallpox – would leave the kingdom fatally divided.

Important Inca Emperors

Manco Cápac (c 1100s), Cuzco's founder

Mayta Cápac (1200s), began expansion

Inca Yupanqui (1400s), 'Pachacutec'

Huayna Cápac (1400s–1500s), expanded north

Atahualpa (1497–1533), last sovereign

Enter the Incas

According to Inca lore, their civilization was born when Manco Cápac and his sister Mama Ocllo, children of the sun, emerged from Lake Titicaca to establish a civilization in the Cuzco valley. Whether Manco Cápac was a historical figure is up for debate, but what is certain is that the Inca civilization was established in the area of Cuzco at some point in the 12th century. The reign of the first several *incas* (kings) is largely unremarkable, and for a couple of centuries they remained a small, regional state.

Expansion took off in the early 15th century, when the ninth king, Inca Yupanqui, defended Cuzco – against incredible odds – from the invading Chanka people to the north. After the victory, he took on the boastful new name of Pachacutec (Transformer of the Earth) and spent the next 25 years bagging much of the Andes. Under his reign, the Incas grew from a regional fiefdom in the Cuzco valley into a broad empire of about 10 million people known as Tawantinsuyo (Land of Four Quarters). The kingdom covered most of modern Peru, in addition to pieces of Ecuador, Bolivia and Chile. This was made more remarkable by the fact that the Incas, as an ethnicity, never numbered more than about 100,000.

Pachacutec allegedly gave Cuzco its layout in the form of a puma and built fabulous stone monuments in honor of Inca victories, including Sacsaywamán, the temple-fortress at Ollantaytambo and possibly Machu Picchu. He also improved the network of roads that connected the empire, further developed terrace agricultural systems and made Quechua the lingua franca.

Atahualpa's Brief Reign

Inca kings continued the expansions of the empire first started by Pachacutec. Pachacutec's grandson, Huayna Cápac, who began his rule in 1493, took over much of modern-day Ecuador all the way into Colombia. Consequently, he spent much of his life living, governing and commanding his armies from the north, rather than Cuzco.

By this time, the Spanish presence was already being felt in the Andes. Smallpox and other epidemics transmitted by European soldiers were sweeping through the entire American continent. These were so swift, in fact, that they arrived in Peru before the Spanish themselves, claiming thousands of indigenous lives – including, in all likelihood, that of Huayna Cápac, who succumbed to some sort of plague in 1525.

Without a clear plan of succession, the emperor's untimely death left a power vacuum. The contest turned into a face-off between two of his many children: the Quito-born Atahualpa, who commanded his father's army in the north, and Huáscar, who was based in Cuzco. The ensuing

A classic of the genre, John Hemming's *The Conquest of the Incas*, first published in 1970, is a must-read for anyone wanting to understand the rise and fall of the short-lived Inca empire.

1532

Atahualpa wins a protracted struggle for control over Inca territories; at virtually the same time, the Spanish land in Peru – in less than a year, Atahualpa is dead.

1572

Túpac Amaru, the monarch who had established an Inca state independent of the Spanish at Vilcabamba, is captured and beheaded by colonial authorities.

1609

Mestizo writer and thinker El Inca Garcilaso de la Vega publishes *Los Comentarios Reales* (The Royal Commentaries), a celebrated narrative of Inca life before and after the conquest.

1611

Diego Quispe Tito, one of the most renowned painters of the so-called 'Cuzco School' movement of religious painting, is born in the southern highlands.

struggle plunged the empire into a bloody civil war, reducing entire cities to rubble. Atahualpa emerged as the victor in April 1532. But the vicious nature of the conflict left the Incas with a lot of enemies throughout the Andes – which is why some tribes were so willing to cooperate with the Spanish when they arrived just five months later.

The Spanish Invade

In 1528 explorer Francisco Pizarro and his right-hand-man Diego de Almagro landed in Tumbes, a far-flung outpost on the north coast of Peru. There, a crew of welcoming native people offered them meat, fruit, fish and corn beer. To the Spaniards' delight, a cursory examination of the city revealed an abundance of silver and gold. The explorers quickly returned to Spain to court royal support for a bigger expedition.

They returned to Tumbes in September 1532, with a shipload of arms, horses and slaves, as well as a battalion of 168 men. Tumbes, the rich town they had visited just four years earlier, had been devastated by epidemics, as well as the recent Inca civil war. Atahualpa, in the meantime, was in the process of making his way down from Quito to Cuzco to claim his hard-won throne. When the Spanish arrived, he was in the highland settlement of Cajamarca, enjoying the area's mineral baths.

Pizarro quickly deduced that the empire was in a fractious state. He and his men charted a course to Cajamarca and approached Atahualpa with royal greetings and promises of brotherhood. But the well-mannered overtures quickly devolved into a surprise attack that left thousands of Incas dead and Atahualpa a prisoner of war. (Between their horses, their armor and the steel of their blades, the Spanish were practically invincible against fighters armed only with clubs, slings and wicker helmets.)

In an attempt to regain his freedom, Atahualpa offered the Spanish a bounty of gold and silver. Thus began one of the most famous ransoms in history – with the Incas attempting to fill an entire room with the precious stuff in order to placate the unrelenting appetites of the Spanish. But it was never enough. The Spanish held Atahualpa for eight months before executing him with a garrote at the age of 31.

The Inca empire never recovered from this fateful encounter. The arrival of the Spanish brought on a cataclysmic collapse of indigenous society. One scholar estimates that the native population – around 10 million when Pizarro arrived – was reduced to 600,000 within a century.

Tumultuous Colony

Following Atahualpa's death, the Spanish got to work consolidating their power. On January 6, 1535, Pizarro sketched out his new administrative

Historic Churches

Iglesia de Santo Domingo, Lima

Catedral de Ayacucho

Iglesia de La Compañía de Jesus, Cuzco

Iglesia de San Pedro, Andahuaylillas

Monasterio de Santa Catalina, Arequipa

1613
Guamán Poma de Ayala pens a 1200-page missive to the Spanish king detailing poor treatment of natives; it lies forgotten until 1908, when it's discovered in a Danish archive.

1671
Santa Rosa de Lima, the patron saint of Peru and the Americas, is canonized by Pope Clement X.

1717
The Spanish Crown establishes the Viceroyalty of New Granada, covering modern-day Ecuador, Colombia and Panama – reducing the Peruvian viceroyalty's power and reach.

1781
Inca noble Túpac Amaru II (born José Gabriel Condorcanqui) is brutally executed by the Spanish in Cuzco after leading an unsuccessful indigenous rebellion.

Browse original research materials dating back to the colony on the website of the Biblioteca Nacional (National Library; www.bnp.gob.pe and click Biblioteca Virtual).

center in the sands that bordered the Río Rímac on the central coast. This would be Lima, the so-called 'City of Kings' (named in honor of Three Kings' Day), the new capital of the viceroyalty of Peru, an empire that for more than 200 years would cover much of South America.

It was a period of great turmoil. As elsewhere in the Americas, the Spanish ruled by terror. Rebellions erupted regularly. Atahualpa's half-brother Manco Inca (who had originally sided with the Spanish and served as a puppet emperor under Pizarro) tried to regain control of the highlands in 1536 – laying siege to the city of Cuzco for almost a year – but was ultimately forced to retreat. He was stabbed to death by a contingent of Spanish soldiers in 1544.

Throughout this, the Spanish were doing plenty of fighting among themselves, splitting into a complicated series of rival factions, each wanting control of the new empire. In 1538 De Almagro was sentenced to death by strangulation for attempting to take over Cuzco. Three years later, Pizarro was assassinated in Lima by a band of disgruntled De Almagro supporters. Other conquistadors met equally violent fates. Things grew relatively more stable after the arrival of Francisco de Toledo as viceroy, an efficient administrator who brought some order to the emergent colony.

THE MAKING OF PERU'S SAINTS

The first century of the Peruvian colony produced an unusual number of Catholic saints – five in all. There was the highly venerated Santa Rosa of Lima (1556–1617), a devout *criolla* (Spaniard born in Peru) who took a vow of chastity and practiced physical mortification. (She wore a cilice and slept on a bed of broken glass and pottery.) In addition, there was San Juan Macías (1585–1645), who counseled the needy, and San Martín de Porres (1579–1639), the New World's first black saint.

Why so many? A lot of it had to do with the Spanish program to systematically replace the old indigenous order with its own traditions. Catholic authorities, through a process known as the Extirpation, aimed to eradicate indigenous religious belief by prohibiting ancestor worship and holding ceremonies in which pre-Columbian religious idols were burned. The whole process gave rise to a crop of holy figures that Catholic officials could hold up as examples of piousness. Priests preached the wonders of everyday people who rejected worldly possessions and displayed extreme humility – qualities that the Church was eager to cultivate in its newfound flock. Countless figures were canonized during this time, and those who attained sainthood remain an integral part of Peruvian spiritual culture to this day.

You can see relics from these saints at the Iglesia de Santo Domingo in Lima.

1810

Painter Pancho Fierro, a watercolorist known for recording daily life, is born in Lima; his paintings helped define a uniquely Peruvian identity.

1821

José de San Martín declares Peru independent.

1824

True sovereignty finally comes to Peru after Simón Bolívar's forces vanquish the Spanish in battles at Junín and Ayacucho.

1826

The last of the Spanish military forces depart from Callao, after which the country descends into a period of anarchy.

Until independence, Peru was ruled by a series of these Spanish-born viceroys, all of whom were appointed by the Crown. Immigrants from Spain held the most prestigious positions, while *criollos* (Spaniards born in the colony) were confined to middle management. *Mestizos* – people of mixed blood – were placed even further down the social scale. Full-blooded *indígenas* resided at the bottom, exploited as *peones* (expendable laborers) in *encomiendas*, a feudal system that granted Spanish colonists land titles that included the property of all the indigenous people living in that area.

Tensions between *indígenas* and Spaniards reached a boiling point in the late 18th century, when the Spanish Crown levied a series of new taxes that hit indigenous people the hardest. In 1780 José Gabriel Condorcanqui – a descendant of the Inca monarch Túpac Amaru – arrested and executed a Spanish administrator on charges of cruelty. His act unleashed an indigenous rebellion that spread into Bolivia and Argentina. Condorcanqui adopted the name Túpac Amaru II and traveled the region fomenting revolution.

The Spanish reprisal was swift – and brutal. In 1781 the captured indigenous leader was dragged to the main plaza in Cuzco, where he would watch his followers, his wife and his sons killed in a daylong orgy of violence, before being drawn and quartered himself. Pieces of his remains were displayed in towns around the Andes as a way of discouraging further insurrection.

A full scan of Guamán Poma de Ayala's 17th-century manuscript (complete with illustrations), in which he documents colonial atrocities against indigenous people, can be found on the Danish National Library's website at www.kb.dk/permalink/2006/poma/info/en/frontpage.htm.

Independence

By the early 19th century, *criollos* in many Spanish colonies had grown increasingly dissatisfied with their lack of administrative power and the Crown's heavy taxes – leading to revolutions all over the continent. In Peru, the winds of change arrived from two directions. Argentine revolutionary José de San Martín led independence campaigns in Argentina and Chile, before entering Peru by sea at the port of Pisco in 1820. With San Martín's arrival, royalist forces retreated into the highlands, allowing him to ride into Lima unobstructed. On July 28, 1821, independence was declared. But real independence wouldn't materialize for another three years. With Spanish forces still at large in the interior, San Martín would need more men to fully defeat the Spanish.

Enter Simón Bolívar, the Venezuelan revolutionary who had been leading independence fights in Venezuela, Colombia and Ecuador. In 1823 the Peruvians gave Bolívar dictatorial powers (an honor that had been bestowed on him in other countries). By the latter half of 1824, he and his lieutenant, Antonio José de Sucre, had routed the Spanish in decisive battles at Junín and Ayacucho. The revolutionaries had faced

1845

Ramón Castilla begins the first of four nonconsecutive presidential terms, bringing some degree of stability to Peru.

1872

Scholar Ricardo Palma publishes the first of a series of books – known as the *Tradiciones Peruanas* – that chronicle a distinctly *criollo* (creole) folklore.

1879–83

Chile wages war against Peru and Bolivia over nitrate-rich lands in the Atacama Desert; Peru loses the conflict – in addition to its southernmost region of Tarapacá.

1892

Poet César Vallejo is born in the highlands; he lives for only 46 years, but his spare phrasing and socially conscious themes make him one of the continent's transformative literary figures.

staggering odds, but nonetheless managed to capture the viceroy and negotiate a surrender. As part of the deal, the Spanish would retire all of their forces from Peru and Bolivia.

From the 16th to 19th centuries, many women in Lima donned head scarves that obscured everything but one eye, leading locals to dub them *las tapadas* (the covered ones).

New Republic

The lofty idealism of the revolution was soon followed by the harsh reality of having to govern. 'Peru the young nation', proved to be just as anarchic as 'Peru the viceroyalty'. Between 1825 and 1841, there was a revolving door of regime changes (two dozen) as regional *caudillos* (chieftains) scrambled for power. The situation improved in the 1840s with the mining off the Peruvian coast of vast deposits of guano the nitrate-rich bird droppings that reaped unheard-of profits as fertilizer on the international market (nineteenth-century Peruvian history is – literally – rife with poop jokes).

The country would find some measure of stability under the governance of Ramón Castilla (a *mestizo*), who would be elected to his first term in 1845. The income from the guano boom – which he had been key in exploiting – helped Castilla make needed economic improvements. He abolished slavery, paid off some of Peru's debt and established a public school system. Castilla served as president three more times over the course of two decades – at times, by force; at others, in an interim capacity; at one point, for less than a week. Following his final term, he was exiled by competitors who wanted to neutralize him politically.

He died in 1867, in northern Chile, attempting to make his way back to Peru. (Visitors can see his impressive crypt at the Panteón de los Proceres in central Lima.)

Peru's exports of guano in the mid-19th century totaled more than US$20 million a year – more than US$517 million a year by today's standards. In 1869, the country was exporting more than half a million tons of the nitrate-rich fertilizer per year.

War of the Pacific

With Castilla's passing, the country once again descended into chaos. A succession of *caudillos* squandered the enormous profits of the guano boom and, in general, managed the economy in a deplorable fashion. Moreover, military skirmishes would ensue with Ecuador (over border issues) and Spain (which was trying to dominate its former South American colonies). The conflicts left the nation's coffers empty. By 1874, Peru was bankrupt.

This left the country in a weak position to deal with the expanding clash between Chile and Bolivia over nitrate-rich lands in the Atacama Desert. Borders in this area had never been clearly defined and escalating tensions eventually led to military engagement. To make matters worse for the Peruvians, President Mariano Prado abandoned the country for Europe on the eve of the conflict. The war was a disaster for Peru at every level (not to mention Bolivia, which lost its entire coastline).

1895

Nicolás de Piérola is elected president, beginning a period of relative stability buoyed by a booming world economy.

1911

US historian Hiram Bingham arrives at the ruins of Machu Picchu; his 'discovery' of the ancient city is chronicled in *National Geographic*.

1924

Northern political leader Víctor Raúl Haya de la Torre founds APRA, a populist, anti-imperialist political party that is immediately declared illegal.

1928

Journalist and thinker José Carlos Mariátegui publishes the *Seven Interpretive Essays on Peruvian Reality*, which heavily critiques the feudal nature of his country's society.

Despite the very brave actions of military figures such as Navy Admiral Miguel Grau, the Chileans were simply better organized and had more resources, including the support of the British. In 1881 they led a land campaign deep into Peru, occupying the capital of Lima, during which time they ransacked the city, making off with the priceless contents of the National Library. By the time the conflict came to a close in 1883, Peru had permanently lost its southernmost region of Tarapacá, and it wouldn't regain the area around Tacna until 1929.

A New Intellectual Era

As the 20th century loomed, things were looking up for Peru. A buoyant world economy helped fuel an economic recovery through the export of sugar, cotton, rubber, wool and silver. And, in 1895, Nicolás de Piérola was elected president, beginning an era known as the 'Aristocratic Republic.' Hospitals and schools were constructed and de Piérola undertook a campaign to build highways and railroads.

This period would witness a sea change in Peruvian intellectual thought. The late 19th century had been an era in which many thinkers (primarily in Lima) had tried to carve out the notion of an inherently Peruvian identity – one largely based on *criollo* experience. Key among them was Ricardo Palma, a scholar and writer renowned for rebuilding Lima's ransacked National Library. Beginning in 1872, he published a series of books on *criollo* folklore known as the *Tradiciones Peruanas* (Peruvian Traditions) – now required reading for every Peruvian schoolchild.

But as one century gave way to the next, intellectual circles saw the rise of *indigenismo*, a continent-wide movement that advocated for a dominant social and political role for indigenous people. In Peru, this translated into a wide-ranging (if fragmented) cultural movement.

Most Influential Writers

- *El Inca Garcilaso de la Vega, chronicler*
- *Ricardo Palma, folklorist*
- *Abraham Valdelomar, essayist*
- *César Vallejo, poet*
- *José Carlos Mariategui, political theorist*
- *Mario Vargas Llosa, novelist*

A NOBEL FOR PERU

In 2010 Mario Vargas Llosa (b 1936), Peru's most famous living writer, was awarded the Nobel Prize in literature for work that explored the vagaries of love, power and corruption. The honorific caps an extraordinary life: as a young man, Vargas Llosa had an affair with an uncle's sister-in-law, whom he later married (an incident he fictionalized in *Aunt Julia and the Scriptwriter*). In the '70s, he came to blows with Colombian Nobel laureate Gabriel García Márquez for reasons that have never been revealed. The following decade he ran for the presidency – and lost. Over his life he has produced novels, short stories, plays and political essays. Upon winning the Nobel, he told a reporter: 'Death will find me with my pen in hand.'

1932

More than a thousand APRA party followers are executed by the military at the ancient ruins of Chan Chan, following an uprising in Trujillo.

1948

General Manuel Odría assumes power for eight years, encouraging foreign investment and cracking down on the APRA movement.

1962

Mario Vargas Llosa publishes *La ciudad y los perros* (*The Time of the Hero*), an experimental novel set at a military academy in Lima.

1968

General Juan Velasco Alvarado takes power in a coup d'état; in his seven years in office, he promulgates a populist agenda that involves 'Peruvianization' of all industry.

Historian Luis Valcárcel attacked his society's degradation of the indigenous class. Poet César Vallejo wrote critically acclaimed works that took on indigenous oppression as themes. And José Sabogal led a generation of visual artists who explored indigenous themes in their paintings. In 1928, journalist and thinker José Carlos Mariátegui penned a seminal Marxist work – *Seven Interpretive Essays on Peruvian Reality* – in which he criticized the feudal nature of Peruvian society and celebrated the communal aspects of the Inca social order. (It remains vital reading for the Latin American left to this day.)

In this climate, in 1924, Trujillo-born political leader Victor Raúl Haya de la Torre founded the Alianza Popular Revolucionaria Americana (American Popular Revolutionary Alliance), otherwise known as APRA. The party espoused populist values, celebrated 'Indo-America' and rallied against US imperialism. It was quickly declared illegal by the autocratic regime of Augusto Leguía – and remained illegal for long stretches of the 20th century. Haya de la Torre, at various points in his life, lived in hiding and in exile and, at one point, endured a 15-month stint as a political prisoner.

Photographer Martín Chambi (1891–1973) was known for his beguiling black and white photographs of Cuzco in the early 20th century. These provide a revealing portrait of the city before the age of mass tourism. To see images, go to www.martinchambi.org.

Dictatorships & Revolutionaries

After the start of the Great Depression in 1929, the country's history becomes a blur of dictatorships punctuated by periods of democracy. Leguía, a sugar baron from the north coast, ruled on a couple of occasions: for his first period in office (1908–12) he was elected; for the second (1919–30), he made it in via coup d'état. He spent his first term dealing with a morass of border conflicts and the second, stifling press freedom and political dissidents.

Legúia was followed by Colonel Luis Sánchez Cerro, who served a couple of short terms in the 1930s. (Though his time in office was turbulent, Sánchez would be celebrated in some sectors for abolishing a conscription law that required able-bodied men to labor on road-building projects. The law affected poor indigenous men disproportionately, since they couldn't afford to pay the exemption fee.) By 1948 another dictator had taken power: former army colonel Manuel Odría, who spent his time in office cracking down on APRA and encouraging US foreign investment.

The most fascinating of Peru's 20th-century dictators, however, is Juan Velasco Alvarado, the former commander in chief of the army who took control in 1968. Though he was expected to lead a conservative regime, Velasco turned out to be an inveterate populist – so much so that some APRA members complained that he had stolen their party platform away from them. He established a nationalist agenda that included 'Peruvian-

1970

A 7.7-magnitude earthquake in northern Peru kills almost 80,000 people, leaves 140,000 injured and another 500,000 homeless.

1980

Guerrilla group Sendero Luminoso (Shining Path) takes its first violent action – burning ballot boxes – in the Ayacucho region; the incident draws little notice from the press.

1980

Fernando Belaúnde Terry becomes the first democratically elected president after a 12-year military dictatorship, but his term is plagued by economic instability and violence in the Andes.

1983

In one of the more high-profile massacres of the internal conflict, eight journalists are murdered in the Andean town of Uchuraccay.

izing' (securing Peruvian majority ownership) various industries. In his rhetoric he celebrated the indigenous peasantry, championed a radical program of agrarian reform and made Quechua an official language. He also severely restricted press freedom, which drew the wrath of the power structure in Lima. Ultimately, his economic policies were failures, and in 1975, in declining health, he was replaced by another, more conservative military regime.

Internal Conflict

Peru returned to civilian rule in 1980, when President Fernando Belaúnde Terry was elected to office. It was the first election in which leftist parties were allowed to participate, including APRA, which was now legal. Belaúnde's term was anything but smooth. Agrarian and other social reforms took a back seat as the president tried desperately to jump-start the moribund economy.

Shining Path founder Abimael Guzmán took the name Sendero Luminoso (Shining Path) from a maxim by writer and Communist Party founder José Carlos Mariátegui: 'Marxism-Leninism will open the shining path to revolution.'

It was at this time that a radical Maoist group from the poor region of Ayacucho began its unprecedented rise. Founded by philosophy professor Abimael Guzmán, Sendero Luminoso (Shining Path) wanted nothing less than an overthrow of the social order via violent armed struggle. Over the next two decades, the situation escalated into a phantasmagoria of violence, with the group assassinating political leaders and community activists, carrying out attacks on police stations and universities and, at one point, stringing up dead dogs all over downtown Lima. (Its actions earned the group a place on the US State Department's list of foreign terrorist organizations.) At the same time, another leftist guerrilla group sprang into action: the Movimiento Revolucionario Túpac Amaru (MRTA), which focused its attacks on the police and the armed forces.

To quell the violence, the government sent in the military, a heavy-handed outfit that knew little about handling a guerrilla insurgency. There was torture and rape, plus disappearances and massacres, none of which did anything to put a stop to Sendero Luminoso. Caught in the middle were tens of thousands of poor *campesinos,* who bore the brunt of the casualties.

In the midst of this, Alan García was elected to the presidency in 1985. Initially, his ascent generated a great deal of hope. He was young, he was a gifted public speaker, he was popular – and he was the first member of the storied APRA party to win a presidential election. But his economic program was catastrophic (his decision to nationalize the banks and suspend foreign-debt payments led to economic ruin), and, by the late 1980s, Peru faced a staggering hyperinflation rate of 7500%. Thousands of people were plunged into poverty. There were food shortages

1985
Alan García becomes president, but his term is marked by hyperinflation and increased attacks by terrorist groups; he flees the country in 1992, clouded by allegations of embezzlement.

1987
Archaeologists working near Lambayeque uncover a rare, undisturbed tomb of a Moche warrior-priest known as El Señor de Sipán.

1990
Alberto Fujimori is elected president; his authoritarian rule leads to improvements in the economy, but charges of corruption plague his administration.

1992
Sendero Luminoso detonates truck bombs in Miraflores, Lima, killing 25 and wounding scores more; following this act, public opinion turns decisively against the guerrillas.

IN THE WAKE OF THE INTERNAL CONFLICT

One of the most remarkable things to come out of Alejandro Toledo's presidency (2001–06) was the establishment of the country's Comisión de la Verdad y Reconciliación (Truth and Reconciliation Commission), which examined the innumerable acts of mass violence from the internal conflict (1980–2000). Though the panel wasn't endowed with prosecutorial powers, its public hearings nonetheless proved to be an emotional and cathartic act. Men and women of all ages and races came forward to testify to the massacres, rapes and disappearances that had occurred at the hands of the military and various guerrilla groups during this terrible period.

In August 2003, the commission issued its final report, revealing that the death toll from that era was more than twice the original estimate: almost 70,000 people had been killed or disappeared. Along with the final report, the commission also staged an exhibit of photography called Yuyanapaq ('to remember' in Quechua) that is now housed at Lima's Museo de la Nación. Even as the years pass, this poignant installation remains a profoundly moving experience.

and riots. Throughout this, Sendero Luminoso and MRTA stepped up attacks. The government was forced to declare a state of emergency.

Two years after completing his term, García fled the country after being accused of embezzling millions of dollars. He would return to Peru in 2001, when the statute of limitations on his case finally ran out.

Fujishock

With the country in a state of chaos, the 1990 presidential elections took on more importance than ever. The contest was between famed novelist Mario Vargas Llosa and Alberto Fujimori, a little-known agronomist of Japanese descent. During the campaign, Vargas Llosa promoted an economic 'shock treatment' program that many feared would send more Peruvians into poverty, while Fujimori positioned himself as an alternative to the status quo. Fujimori won handily. But as soon as he got into office, he implemented an even more austere economic plan that, among other things, drove up the price of gasoline by 3000%. The measures, known as 'Fujishock,' ultimately succeeded in reducing inflation and stabilizing the economy – but not without costing the average Peruvian dearly.

Fujimori followed this, in April 1992, with an *autogolpe* (coup from within). He dissolved the legislature and generated an entirely new congress, one stocked with his allies. Peruvians, not unused to *caudillos*, tolerated the power grab, hoping that Fujimori might help stabilize the economic and political situation – which he did. The economy grew. And by the end of the year, leaders of both Sendero Luminoso and MRTA had

1992

Abimael Guzmán, the founder of Sendero Luminoso, is captured in Lima after he is found hiding out above a dance studio in the well-to-do neighborhood of Surco.

1994

Chef Gastón Acurio opens Astrid y Gastón in the Lima neighborhood of Miraflores; the restaurant helps catapult Peruvian cuisine to international levels.

1996

Guerrillas from the Movimiento Revolucionario Túpac Amaru (MRTA) storm the Japanese ambassador's residence in Lima and hold 72 hostages for four months.

2000

Fujimori flees to Japan after videos surface showing his intelligence chief bribing officials and the media; the Peruvian legislature votes him out of office.

been apprehended (though not before Sendero Luminoso had brutally assassinated community activist María Elena Moyano and detonated lethal truck bombs in Lima's tony Miraflores district).

The internal conflict, however, wasn't over. In December 1996, 14 members of MRTA stormed the Japanese ambassador's residence and hundreds of prominent people were taken hostage; the captors demanded that the government release imprisoned MRTA members, among other things. Most of the hostages were released early on, though 72 men were held until the following April – at which point, Peruvian commandos stormed the embassy, killing every last captor and releasing the surviving hostages.

By the end of his second term, Fujimori's administration was plagued by allegations of corruption. He ran for a third term in 2000 (which was technically unconstitutional) and remained in power despite the fact that he didn't have the simple majority necessary to claim the election. Within the year, however, he was forced to flee the country after it was revealed that his security chief Vladimiro Montesinos had been embezzling government funds and bribing elected officials and the media. (Many of these acts were caught on film: the 'Vladivideos' – all 2700 of them – riveted the nation when they first aired in 2001.) Fujimori formally resigned the presidency from abroad, but the legislature rejected the gesture, voting him out of office and declaring him 'morally unfit' to govern.

Peru, however, hadn't heard the last of Fujimori. In 2005 he returned to South America, only to be arrested in Chile on long-standing charges of corruption, kidnapping and human-rights violations. He was extradited to Peru in 2007 and, that same year, was convicted of ordering an illegal search. Two years later, he was convicted of ordering extrajudicial killings, and three months after that, was convicted of channeling millions of dollars in state funds to Montesinos. In 2009 he also pleaded guilty to wiretapping and bribery. He is currently serving 25 years in prison. Montesinos, in the meantime, is doing 20 – for bribery and selling arms to Colombian rebels.

Forgotten Continent: The Battle for Latin America's Soul is an acclaimed (if dense) political tome by *Economist* contributor Michael Reid. Published in 2009, it examines the continent's strained relations with the US and Europe, as well as its economic and political development in the last three decades.

The 21st Century

The new millennium has, thus far, been pretty good to Peru. In 2001 shoeshine-boy-turned-Stanford-economist Alejandro Toledo became the first person of Quechua ethnicity ever to be elected to the presidency. (Until then, Peru had had *mestizo* presidents, but never a full-blooded *indígena*.) Unfortunately, Toledo inherited a political and economic mess. This was amplified by the fact that he lacked a majority in congress, hampering his effectiveness in the midst of an economic recession.

2001

Alejandro Toledo becomes the first indigenous person to govern an Andean country.

2003

The country's Truth and Reconciliation Commission releases its final report on Peru's internal conflict: estimates of the dead reach 70,000.

2005

Construction of the Transoceanic Hwy, which opens an overland trade route between Peru and Brazil, begins in the southern Amazon Basin.

2006

Alan García is elected to a second, nonconsecutive term as president after a run-off contest.

Toledo was followed in office by – of all people – APRA's Alan García, who was reelected in 2006. His second term was infinitely more stable than the first. The economy performed well and the government invested money in upgrading infrastructure such as ports, highways and the electricity grid. But it wasn't without problems. For one, there was the issue of corruption (García's entire cabinet was forced to resign in 2008 after widespread allegations of bribery) and there has been the touchy issue of how to manage the country's mineral wealth. In 2008 García signed a law that allowed foreign companies to exploit natural resources in the Amazon. The legislation generated a backlash among various Amazon tribes and led to a fatal standoff in the northern city of Bagua in 2009.

For dedicated students of Peruvian history, *The Peru Reader* by Orin Starn, Carlos Iván Degregori and Robin Kirk provides an indispensable collection of articles covering every historical era, from excerpts of Spanish chronicles to essays on the cocaine economy.

The Peruvian congress quickly revoked the law, but this issue remains a challenge for president Ollanta Humala, elected in 2011. Having campaigned on a broader inclusion of all social classes, he passed the Prior Consultation Law, a historic new law to guarantee indigenous rights to consent to projects affecting them and their lands. The former army officer was initially thought to be a populist in the Hugo Chávez vein (the Lima stock exchange dropped precipitously when he was first elected). But his administration has been quite friendly to business. Though the economy has functioned well under his governance, civil unrest over a proposed gold mine in the north, as well as a botched raid on a Sendero Luminoso encampment in the highlands, sent his approval rating into a tailspin by the middle of 2012.

While the explosive growth spurt of the early part of the millennium has slowed down, the country remains far more stable than in previous decades. There is no clear forerunner for 2016 elections, though the first lady is expected to run (Humala himself is ineligible for another consecutive term), as well as Keiko Fujimori and former president Alan García.

2009

Fujimori is convicted of embezzling; this is in addition to prior convictions for authorizing an illegal search and ordering military death squads to carry out extrajudicial killings.

2011

Populist former army officer Ollanta Humala assumes the presidency after winning a tight run-off election against Fujimori's daughter Keiko.

2011

A state of emergency is declared in four provinces following massive resident protests against mining projects with environmental concerns.

2014

A Greenpeace protest that puts a message in the Nazca lines irreparably damages the World Heritage Site and causes international outrage.

Life in Peru

With a geography that encompasses desert, highland and jungle, Peru is relentlessly touted as a land of contrasts. This also applies to the lives of its people: the country is a mix of rich and poor, modern and ancient, agricultural and urban, indigenous and white. Day-to-day existence can be difficult – but it can also be profoundly rich. For centuries, this has been the story of life in Peru.

Population

Peru is essentially a bicultural society: there is the indigenous part and the European-influenced part. The largest cohort consists of Peruvians who speak Spanish and adhere to *criollo* tradition, the cultural legacy of the Peru-born Spaniards who administered the colony. This group is a racial mix of those who are white (15% of the population) and those who are *mestizo,* people of mixed indigenous and European heritage (another 37%). The country's positions of leadership and affluence are generally occupied by individuals from this group, especially those who are white and fair-skinned.

About 45% of Peru's population is pure *indígena* (people of indigenous descent), making it one of three countries in Latin America to have such high indigenous representation. A disproportionate share of *indígenas* inhabit rural areas in the Andes and work in agriculture.

Afro-Peruvians, Asians and other immigrant groups are also represented, but cumulatively make up only 3% of the population.

A whopping 78% of Peruvians live in cities. This represents a significant shift from the 1960s, when more than half the population inhabited the countryside. Urban migration has put a strain on municipal infrastructure, particularly in the capital, and issues of effective sanitation and electrification remain challenges, especially for the informal squatter settlements known as *pueblos jovenes* (young towns).

It was a Peruvian priest, Gustavo Gutiérrez, who first articulated the principles of liberation theology – the theory that links Christian thought to social justice – in 1971. He now teaches in the United States.

Lifestyle

Though the recent economic boom has been good to the country, there is still a yawning disparity between rich and poor. The minimum monthly wage stands at US$238. According to the World Bank, around 24% of the population lives below the poverty line. Though the official national unemployment rate is only 7.6%, underemployment is rampant, especially in Lima and other cities.

In rural areas, the poor survive largely from subsistence agriculture, living in traditional adobe or tin houses that often lack electricity and indoor plumbing. In cities, the extreme poor live in shantytowns, while the lower and middle classes live in concrete, apartment-style housing or small stand-alone homes. More affluent urban homes consist of large stand-alone houses, often bordered by high walls. Across the board, homes are generally shared by more than one generation.

VIVA EL PERÚ...¡CARAJO!

With vastly different peoples inhabiting such an extreme landscape, national identity has always been a slippery concept in Peru. Yet if there's something that binds its people together, it's a sturdy sense of defiance.

In the 1950s Peruvian journalist Jorge Donayre Belaúnde penned a poem to his homeland called 'Viva el Perú...¡Carajo!' (Long Live Peru...Damn It!). The verse is an epic, warts-and-all tribute to Peru, depicting life in Andean villages as well as sprawling urban shantytowns. Peruvians, wrote Donayre, aren't scared off by difficult circumstances – not by cataclysmic earthquakes, difficult geography or the corrupt habits of their politicians. In the face of adversity, there is an intractable sense of assurance.

In the half century since Donayre first wrote those words, that hasn't changed one bit. *Viva el Perú... ¡Carajo!*

Social Graces

Peruvians are polite, indeed formal, in their interactions. Handshakes are appropriate in business settings, but among good friends an *abrazo* (back-slapping hug) is in order. Women will often greet each other with a kiss, as will men and women. Indigenous people don't kiss and their handshakes, when offered, tend to have a light touch.

Locals are used to less personal space than some Western travelers may be accustomed to: expect close seating on buses.

Religion

Though there is freedom of religion, Peru remains largely Roman Catholic. More than 81% of the population identifies as such (though only 15% of them attend services on a weekly basis). The Church enjoys support from the state: it has a largely tax-exempt status and Catholicism is the official religion of the military. Moreover, all of the Church's bishops, and up to an eighth of its overall clergy, receive monthly government stipends. This has generated outcries from some evangelical groups that do not receive the same generous treatment. Even so, evangelicals and other Protestants are a growing force, representing up to 13% of the nation's population.

Everything you ever needed to know about every regional Peruvian soccer team – large and small – is available at www.peru.com/futbol (in Spanish).

Women in Peru

Women can vote and own property, but the situation remains challenging in a country that is informally ruled by machismo. Particularly in rural areas, female literacy is far behind that of male counterparts (27% illiteracy among women versus 7% among men). Women's wages average just over half of earnings by men. That said, the overall situation has improved. A number of laws barring domestic violence and sexual assault have been passed, and women now make up 28% of the country's professional class (senior officials, managers and legislators) and almost a third of the congress.

Spectator Sports

Fútbol (soccer) is the most sanctified spectator sport. The season runs from late March to November. Though there are many teams, their abilities aren't always exceptional: Peru hasn't qualified for the World Cup since 1982 – though it did take home the Copa América trophy in 2004. The best teams are from Lima, and the traditional *clásico* is the match between Alianza Lima and the Universitario de Deportes (La U).

Bullfighting is also well attended, particularly in Lima, where it is most popular. The traditional season runs from October to early December, when Lima's Plaza de Acho attracts international matadors.

Peru's Cuisine

In Peru, fusion was always a natural part of everyday cooking. Over the last 400 years, Andean stews mingled with Asian stir-fries, and Spanish rice dishes absorbed Amazonian flavors, producing the country's famed *criollo* (creole) cooking. More recently, a generation of experimental young innovators has pushed local fare to gastronomic heights. The short of it is that you'll never go hungry in Peru: from humble spots in Moyobamba to trendy boîtes in Miraflores, this is a country devoted to keeping the human palate entertained.

Embracing Local Cuisine

Peru, once a country where important guests were treated to French meals and Scotch whiskey, is now a place where high-end restaurants spotlight deft interpretations of Andean favorites, including quinoa and *cuy* (guinea pig). The dining scene has blossomed. And tourism outfits have swept in to incorporate a culinary something as part of every tour. In 2000 the country became the site of the first Cordon Bleu academy in Latin America, and in 2009 *Bon Appétit* magazine named Lima the 'next great food city.' In Lima, La Casa de La Gastronomia Peruana is a new museum fully dedicated to celebrating the country's complex culinary heritage. In 2015 Peru won 'best culinary destination' from the World Travel Awards for the third time. Of Peru's 3.1 million annual visitors, 40% do gastronomic tourism. And maybe you should too.

First published in 2001, *The Exotic Kitchens of Peru* by Copeland Marks is not only a comprehensive guide to traditional cooking, but a good source of insight into the history of many dishes.

Foodie fever has infected Peruvians at every level, with even the most humble *chicharrón* (fried pork) vendor hyperattentive to the vagaries of preparation and presentation. No small part of this is due to mediagenic celebrity chef Gastón Acurio, whose culinary skill and business acumen (he owns dozens of restaurants around the globe) have given him rock-star status.

Staples & Specialties

Given the country's craggy topography, there are an infinite number of regional cuisines. But at a national level much of the country's cooking begins and ends with the humble potato, which originally hails from the Andes. (All potatoes can be traced back to a single progenitor from Peru.)

Standout dishes include *ocopa* (potatoes with a spicy peanut sauce), *papa a la huancaína* (potato topped with a creamy cheese sauce) and *causa* (mashed potato terrines stuffed with seafood, vegetables or chicken). Also popular is *papa rellena,* a mashed potato filled with ground beef and then deep-fried. Potatoes are also found in the chowder-like soups known as *chupe* and in *lomo saltado,* the simple beef stir-fries that headline every Peruvian menu.

Other popular items include tamales (corn cakes), which are made in various regional variations, such as *humitas* (created with fresh corn) and *juanes* (made from cassava).

Coast

The culinary website Yanuq (www.yanuq.com) has an extensive online database of Peruvian recipes in English and Spanish.

The coast is all about seafood – and ceviche, naturally, plays a starring role. A chilled concoction of fish, shrimp or other seafood marinated in lime juice, onions, cilantro and chili peppers, it is typically served with a wedge of boiled corn and sweet potato. The fish is cooked in the citrus juices through a process of oxidation. (Some chefs, however, have begun to cut back on their marinating time, which means that some ceviches are served with a sushi-like consistency.) Another popular seafood cocktail is *tiradito,* a Japanese-inflected ceviche consisting of thin slices of fish served without onions, sometimes bathed in a creamy hot-pepper sauce.

Cooked fish can be prepared dozens of ways: *al ajo* (in garlic), *frito* (fried) or *a la chorrillana* (cooked in white wine, tomatoes and onions), the latter of which hails from the city of Chorrillos, south of Lima. Soups and stews are also a popular staple, including *aguadito* (a soupy risotto), *picante* (a spicy stew) and *chupe* (bisque), all of which can feature fish, seafood and other ingredients.

Other items that make a regular appearance on seafood menus are *conchitas a la parmesana* (scallops baked with cheese), *pulpo al olivo* (octopus in a smashed-olive sauce) and *choros a la chalaca* (chilled mussels with fresh corn salsa). On the north coast, around Chiclayo, omelets made with manta ray *(tortilla de manta raya)* are a typical dish.

None of this means that pork, chicken or beef aren't popular. *Ají de gallina* (shredded chicken-walnut stew) is a Peruvian classic. In the north, a couple of local dishes bear repeat sampling: *arroz con pato a la chiclayana* (duck and rice simmered in cilantro, typical of Chiclayo) and *seco de cabrito* (goat stewed in cilantro, chilis and beer).

Along the coast, where the Asian presence is most significant, you will also find the Peruvian-Chinese restaurants known as *chifas*. The cuisine is largely Cantonese-influenced: simple dishes low on heavy sauces.

TOP EATS

Collectively, Lonely Planet's writers spent months on the road and ate hundreds of meals. Herewith, a list of the places so good they brought tears to our eyes and unbridled joy to our palates:

Arequipa At Zig Zag, the succulent combination meat plate of alpaca, beef and lamb – cooked over hot volcanic rocks – is a carnivore's delight.

Cajamarca Antifusion restaurant Salas meticulously prepares the full gamut of typical *cajamarquiño* dishes according to classic recipes.

Cuzco Elegant Uchu serves stone-grilled alpaca with piquant sauces. You can also order off the menu of Marcelo Batata upstairs – twice-baked Andean potatoes are a must!

Huancayo Dip into the creamiest *papas a la huancaína* (steamed potatoes served with a cheese sauce) in a flower-filled courtyard at Huancahuasi.

Iquitos Set at the mouth of the Río Itaya, Al Frío y al Fuego has excellent nighttime views of Iquitos and scrumptious dishes crafted from Amazon river fish.

Lima The aphrodisiacal ceviche found in El Mercado, La Mar and Al Toke Pez.

Máncora Hyperfresh yellowfin tuna drawn straight from the Pacific is worth the price at La Sirena d'Juan.

Tarapoto At La Patarashca don't miss the namesake dish: traditional platters of fresh-grilled Amazon fish or shrimp doused in tomatoes, garlic and cilantro.

Trujillo The bamboo-lined Mar Picante is known for serving up behemoth orders of divine *ceviche mixto,* piled high with shrimp, fish, crab and scallops.

Highlands

In the chilly highlands, it's all about soups, which tend to be a generous, gut-warming experience, filled with vegetables, squash, potatoes, locally grown herbs and a variety of meats. *Sopa a la criolla* (a mild, creamy noodle soup with beef and vegetables) is a regular item on menus, as is *caldo de gallina* (a nourishing chicken soup with potatoes and herbs). In the area around Arequipa, *chupe de camarones* (chowder made from river shrimp) is also a mainstay.

The highlands are also known as the source of all things *cuy*. It is often served roasted or *chactado* (pressed under hot rocks). It tastes very similar to rabbit and is often served whole. River trout – prepared myriad ways – is also popular.

Arequipa has a particularly dynamic regional cuisine. The area is renowned for its *picantes* (spicy stews served with chunks of white cheese), *rocoto relleno* (red chilis stuffed with meat) and *solterito* (bean salad).

For special occasions and weddings, families will gather to make *pachamanca:* a mix of marinated meats, vegetables, cheese, chilis and fragrant herbs baked on hot rocks in the ground.

Cuy – otherwise known as guinea pig – was an important source of protein for pre-Columbian people all over the Andes. In recent years Peru has begun testing the export market: the guinea pig is high in protein, but low in fat and cholesterol.

Amazon

Though not as popular throughout the entire country, Amazon ingredients have begun to make headway in recent years. Several high-end restaurants in Lima have started giving gourmet treatment to jungle mainstays, with wide acclaim. This includes the increased use of river snails and fish (including *paiche* and *doncella*), as well as produce such as *aguaje* (the fruit of the moriche palm), yucca (cassava) and *chonta* (hearts of palm). *Juanes* (a bijao leaf stuffed with rice, yucca, chicken and/or pork) is a savory area staple.

Desserts

Desserts tend to be hypersweet concoctions. *Suspiro limeña* is the most famous, consisting of *manjar blanco* (caramel) topped with sweet meringue. Also popular are *alfajores* (cookie sandwiches with caramel) and *crema volteada* (flan). Lighter and fruitier is *mazamorra morada,*

A PISCO PRIMER

It is the national beverage: pisco, the omnipresent grape brandy served at events from the insignificant to the momentous. Production dates back to the early days of the Spanish colony in Ica, where it was distilled on private haciendas and then sold to sailors making their way through the port of Pisco. In its early years, pisco was the local firewater: a great way to get ripped – and wake up the following morning feeling as if you had been hammered over the head.

By the early 20th century, the pisco sour (pisco with lime juice and sugar) arrived on the scene, quickly becoming the national drink. In recent decades, as production has become more sophisticated, piscos have become more nuanced and flavorful (without the morning-after effects).

The three principal types of Peruvian pisco are Quebranta, Italia and acholado. Quebranta (a pure-smelling pisco) and Italia (slightly aromatic) are each named for the varieties of grape from which they are crafted, while acholado is a blend of varietals that has more of an alcohol top-note (best for mixed drinks). There are many small-batch specialty piscos made from grape must (pressed juice with skins), known as *mosto verde*. These have a fragrant smell and are best sipped straight.

The most common brands include Tres Generaciones, Ocucaje, Ferreyros and La Botija, while Viñas de Oro, Viejo Tonel, Estirpe Peruano, LaBlanco and Gran Cruz are among the finest. Any pisco purchased in a bottle that resembles the head of an Inca will make for an unusual piece of home decor – and not much else.

a purple-corn pudding of Afro-Peruvian origin that comes with chunks of fruit.

During October, bakeries sell *turrón de Doña Pepa*, a sticky, molasses-drenched cake eaten in honor of the Lord of Miracles.

The dessert *turrón de Doña Pepa* was first made by a slave woman, in 1800, to honor the Christ of Miracles after she regained the use of her paralyzed arms.

Drinks

The main soft-drink brands are available, but locals have a passion for Inca Kola – which tastes like bubblegum and comes in a spectacular shade of nuclear yellow. Fresh fruit juices are also popular, as are traditional drinks such as *chicha morada*, a refreshing, nonalcoholic beverage made from purple corn and spices.

Though the country exports coffee to the world, many Peruvians drink it instant: some restaurants dish up packets of Nescafé or an inky coffee reduction that is blended with hot water. In cosmopolitan and touristy areas, cafes serving espresso and cappuccino have proliferated. Tea and *mates* (herbal teas) such as *manzanilla* (chamomile), *menta* (mint) and *mate de coca* (coca-leaf tea) are also available. Coca-leaf tea will not get you high, but it can soothe stomach ailments and it's believed to help in adjusting to high altitude.

Beer & Wine

The craft-beer trend has come to Peru, with interesting innovations such as quinoa beer. Small-batch brewers have popped up in Huaraz, Cuzco and Lima. The best-known mainstream brands of beer are Pilsen Callao, Brahma, Cristal and Cusqueña, all of which are light lagers. Arequipeña and Trujillana are regional brews served in and around those cities. In the Andes, homemade *chicha* (fermented corn beer) is very popular. It tastes lightly sweet and is low in alcoholic content. In rural Andes villages, a red flag posted near a door indicates that *chicha* is available.

NOVOANDINA & THE PERUVIAN NEW WAVE

The current Peruvian gastronomic renaissance has its roots in the 1980s. The country was in turmoil. The economy was in a free fall. And newspaper publisher Bernardo Roca Rey was experimenting with Andean ingredients in his kitchen: roasting *cuy* (guinea pig), using rare strains of potatoes and producing risottos made with quinoa (a dish now known as *quinotto*). At the same time, Cucho La Rosa, the chef at El Comensal (since closed), was upgrading Peruvian recipes by improving cooking techniques: gentle steaming instead of boiling; searing instead of frying. These early figures detailed their discoveries in newspaper articles and recipe booklets. The cuisine was dubbed *novoandina* (Peruvian nouvelle cuisine) – but given the challenges of that period, it never quite ignited as a full-blown movement.

By 1994, however, circumstances had changed. The economy was in recovery and the political situation was beginning to improve. When Gastón Acurio (who studied cooking at Le Cordon Bleu in Paris) opened Astrid y Gastón in Lima, he applied many of the same principles as the *novoandina* pioneers before him: interpreting Peruvian cooking through the lens of haute cuisine. The restaurant quickly became a place of pilgrimage. Other innovative new-wave chefs have since followed, including Rafael Piqueras and Pedro Miguel Schiaffino. Collectively, they have expanded the definition of *novoandina*, adding European, Chinese and Japanese ingredients and influences – in the process, transforming Peruvian food into a global cultural phenomenon.

Today's *novoandina* is pushing even further, experimenting with molecular gastronomy, and ancient foods and growing techniques. Chef Virgilio Martínez of Central is developing terraced crops to experiment with growing practices similar to those used by the Incas. Meanwhile, even among everyday diners, the local palate becomes ever bolder.

Local wines have improved greatly over the years. The best local labels are Tabernero, Tacama, Ocucaje and Vista Alegre. Pisco is also very popular.

Sumptuous photographs and recipes are available in Tony Custer and Miguel Etchepare's hardback two-volume tome *The Art of Peruvian Cuisine*. Visit www.artperucuisine.com for mouthwatering previews.

Where to Eat & Drink

For the most part, restaurants in Peru are a community affair, and local places will cater to a combination of families, tourists, teenagers and packs of chatty businesspeople. At lunch time, many eateries offer a *menú* (a set meal consisting of two or three courses). This is generally good value. Note: if you request the *menú*, you'll get the special. If you want the menu, ask for *la carta*.

Cevicherías – places where ceviche is sold – are popular along the coast, and most commonly open for lunchtime service, as most places proudly serve fish that is at its freshest. In the countryside, informal local restaurants known as *picanterías* are a staple. In some cases these operate right out of someone's home.

Quick Eats

Peru has a vibrant street-food culture. The most popular items are *anticuchos* (beef-heart skewers), ceviche, tamales, boiled quail eggs and *choclo con queso* (boiled corn with cheese). Also popular, and quite delicious, are *picarones* (sweet doughnut fritters), usually served with sweet syrup.

For a cheap and tasty meal, check out the many *pollerías* (spit-roasted chicken joints) found just about everywhere.

Vegetarians & Vegans

In a country where many folks survive on nothing but potatoes, there can be a general befuddlement over why anyone would choose to be vegetarian. This attitude has started to change, however, and some of the bigger cities have restaurants catering exclusively to vegetarians. In recent years Lima and Cuzco have become progressive centers for vegetarian and sustainable dining, with raw food, organic and vegan options that finally befit their ambitious fine-dining scenes.

In addition, one can always find vegetarian dishes at a regular Peruvian restaurant. Many of the potato salads, such as *papas a la huancaína, ocopa* and *causa* are made without meat, as is *palta a la jardinera*, an avocado stuffed with vegetables. *Sopa de verduras* (vegetable soup), *tortilla* (Spanish omelet) and *tacu-tacu* (beans and rice pan-fried together) are other options. *Chifas* can also be a good source of vegetarian meals. Before ordering, however, ask if these are *platos vegetarianos* (vegetarian dishes). The term *sin carne* (without meat) refers only to red meat or pork, so you could end up with chicken or seafood instead.

Vegans will have a harder time in conventional restaurants. Peruvian cuisine is based on eggs and dairy and infinite combinations thereof. There are grocery stores and a handful of eateries with gluten-free options, mostly in tourist centers.

Most Influential Chefs

Gastón Acurio at Astrid y Gastón and others

Virgilio Martínez at Central

Pedro Miguel Schiaffino at Malabar and ámaZ

Rafael Osterling at Rafael and El Mercado

Ancient Peru

A *pachacuti*, according to the Incas, was a cataclysmic event dividing the different ages of history. For the indigenous cultures of 16th-century Peru, the arrival of the Spanish was the most earth-shattering *pachacuti* imaginable. The conquerors obliterated native history: melting gold objects, immolating religious icons and banning long-held traditions. Not a single Andean culture left behind a written language. Historians are still piecing together Peru's pre-Columbian history. Thankfully, the physical legacy – from sumptuous textiles and striking ceramics to monumental structures – is bountiful.

For an excellent primer to Peru's pre-Hispanic art, pick up Ferdinand Anton's *The Art of Ancient Peru*. The descriptions are concise and accessible and the book comes laden with almost 300 large-scale photographic images.

Caral

Just a couple of hundred kilometers north of Lima is one of the most exciting archaeological sites in Peru. It may not look like much – half a dozen dusty temple mounds, a few sunken amphitheaters and remnants of structures crafted from adobe and stone – but it is. This is the oldest-known city in the Americas: Caral.

Situated in the Supe Valley, this early society developed almost simultaneously with the cultures of Mesopotamia and Egypt about 5000 years ago, and it predates the earliest civilizations in Mexico by about 1500 years. Little is known about the people that built this impressive 626-hectare urban center. But archaeologists, led by Ruth Shady Solís, the former director of Lima's Museo Nacional de Antropología, Arqueología e Historia del Perú, have managed to unearth a few precious details.

Caral was a religious center that venerated its holy men and paid tribute to unknown agricultural deities. Inhabitants cultivated crops such as cotton, squash, beans and chilies, collected fruits and were knowledgeable fishers. Archaeological finds include pieces of textile, necklaces, ceremonial burials and crude, unbaked clay figurines depicting female forms. The first serious digs began in the area in 1996 and much of the complex has yet to be excavated – expect further discoveries.

Chavín

If Caral is evidence of early urbanization, then Chavín de Huántar, near Huaraz, represents the spread of a unified religious and artistic iconography. In a broad swath of the northern Andes, from roughly 1000 BC to 300 BC, a stylized feline deity began to appear on carvings, friezes, pottery and textiles. As with Caral, there is only patchy information available about the era's societies, but its importance is without question: in Peru, this moment heralds the true birth of art.

The website www.arqueologia.com.ar/peru gathers useful links (in Spanish) related to archaeology news in Peru. The site contains timelines and some basic photo galleries devoted to different cultural groups.

It is still debated whether the temple at Chavín de Huántar represented a capital or merely an important ceremonial site, but what is without doubt is that the setting is extraordinary. With the stunning Cordillera Blanca as a backdrop, the remnants of this elaborate ceremonial complex – built over hundreds of years – include a number of temple structures, as well as a sunken court with stone friezes of jaguars. Here, archaeologists have found pottery from all over the region filled with *ofrendas* (offerings), including shells from as far away as the Ecuadorean coast, and carved bones (some human) featuring supernatural motifs. The site's most remarkable feature is a maze of disorienting galleries beneath the temple complex, one of which boasts a nearly 5m-tall rock carving of a fanged anthropomorphic deity known as the Lanzón – just the sort of fierce-looking creature that is bound to turn anyone into a believer.

Paracas & Nazca

The Chavín Horizon, when Chavín civilization emerged, was followed by the development of a number of smaller, regional ethnicities. Along the country's south coast, from about 700 BC to AD 400, the Paracas culture – situated around modern-day Ica – produced some of the most renowned textiles ever created. The most impressive of these were woven during the period known as the Paracas Necropolis (AD 1 to 400), so named for a massive grave site on the Península de Paracas uncovered by famed Peruvian archaeologist Julio Tello in the 1920s.

Published by Harvard University's Peabody Museum, *The Moche of Ancient Peru: Media and Messages*, by Jeffrey Quilter, is an outstanding introduction to the history, art and architecture of the Moche culture of the north coast.

The historical data on the culture is thin, but the magnificent textiles recovered from the graves – layers of finely woven fabrics wrapped around mummy bundles – provide important clues about day-to-day life and beliefs. Cloths feature flowers, fish, birds, knives and cats, with some animals represented as two-headed creatures. Also significant are the human figures: warriors carry shrunken trophy heads, and supernatural anthropomorphic creatures are equipped with wings, snake tongues and lots of claws. (There are some fantastic examples at the Museo Larco in Lima.) Many of the mummies found at this site had cranial deformations, most of which showed that the head had been intentionally flattened using two boards.

During roughly the same period, the Nazca culture (200 BC to AD 600), to the south, was producing an array of painted pottery, as well as incredible weavings that showcased everyday objects (beans, birds and fish), in addition to supernatural cat- and falcon-men in an array of explosive colors. The Nazca were skilled embroiderers: some weavings feature tiny dangling figurines that must have induced blindness in their creators. (Well-preserved examples can be seen at the Museo Andrés del Castillo in Lima.)

The culture is best known, however, for the Nazca Lines, a series of mysterious geoglyphs carved into a 500-sq-km area in the southern Peruvian desert. Recently, new Japanese research has suggested that two different groups made the glyphs. The lines became the center of a worldwide scandal in 2014. Greenpeace activists entered the site on foot, without authorization, to leave an environmental message (saying 'Time for change, the future is renewable'), which inadvertently damaged the site. See (p<OT>) for more details.

Moche

When it comes to ceramics, there is no Andean civilization that compares to the Moche, a culture that inhabited the Peruvian north coast from about AD 100 to AD 800. Though not inherently urban, they built

DRONES & RUINS

When the Nazca lines were damaged in a Greenpeace climate-change protest, the Peruvian government dispatched drones to survey the damage. They're also being used to protect ancient sites in other ways, such as to document the encroachment of developers and squatters into protected areas. Drones have proved handy in conservation, tracing the effects of El Niño storms on Chan Chan. State-of-the-art technology called octocopters are outfitted with a high-definition swivel camera for precision monitoring – that's a lot of high tech in service to the ancients.

sophisticated ceremonial centers, such as the frieze-laden Huacas del Sol y de la Luna, outside modern-day Trujillo, and the elaborate burial site of Sipán, near Chiclayo. They had a well-maintained network of roads and a system of relay runners who carried messages, probably in the form of symbols carved onto beans.

Top Ruins Sites

- *Machu Picchu, Sacred Valley*
- *Chan Chan, Trujillo*
- *Sillustani, Puno*
- *Chavín de Huántar, Huaraz*
- *Huacas del Sol y de la Luna, Trujillo*
- *Kuélap, Chachapoyas*

But it's their portrait pottery that makes the Moche a standout: lifelike depictions of individuals (scars and all) are so skillfully rendered they seem as if they are about to speak. Artisans often created multiple portraits of a single person over the course of a lifetime. One scholar, in fact, recorded 45 different pieces depicting the same model. Other ceramics showcase macho activities such as hunting, combat and ritual sacrifice. This doesn't mean, however, that the Moche didn't know a thing or two about love – they are famous for their downright acrobatic depictions of human sex (on view at Lima's Museo Larco).

Wari

From about AD 600 to 1100, the Andes saw the rise of the first truly expansive kingdom. The Wari were avid empire builders, expanding from their base around Ayacucho to a territory that occupied most of the highlands, in addition to a piece of the northern coast. Expert agriculturalists, they improved production by developing the terrace system and creating complex networks of canals for irrigation.

Like many conquering cultures in the region, the Wari built on what was already there, usurping and adding to extant infrastructure created by smaller regional states. The coastal ceremonial center of Pachacamac, for instance, was originated by the Lima culture, but expanded by the Wari.

This doesn't mean that there aren't definitive Wari sites to be seen. The remains of what was once a 1500-hectare city is located outside Ayacucho, and there is a Wari ceremonial center in Piquillacta, near Cuzco. Unfortunately, the Wari's architecture was cruder than that of the Incas and so the buildings have not aged gracefully.

The Wari culture was highly skilled in weaving, producing elegant fabrics with elaborate, stylized designs. The Wari were masters of color, using as many as 150 distinct shades which they incorporated into woven and tie-dyed patterns. Many textiles feature abstract, geometric designs, as well as supernatural figures – most common is a winged deity holding a staff.

In 2013, the first intact, unlooted Wari imperial tomb was discovered north of Lima at El Castillo de Huarmey. Inside the 1200-year-old royal tomb, which has been described as the 'Temple of the Dead,' three Wari queens were accompanied by numbers of seated mummies, alabaster drinking cups, decorated ceramic vessels and gold weaving tools. Thirty tons of loose stone fill had been protecting the site from grave robbers. In 2015 another ceremonial site known as Tenahaha in the Cotahuasi Valley was unearthed, revealing hundreds of mummies and artifacts which will eventually illuminate more of the Wari culture.

Tejidos Milenarios del Perú: Ancient Peruvian Textiles is a sumptuously illustrated encyclopedia of Peruvian textiles, from Chavín and the Incas. It's a legacy so rich that the tome spans more than 800 pages and weighs more than 10kg.

Chimú & Chachapoyas

Following the demise of the Wari, a number of small nation-states emerged in different corners of the country. They are too numerous to detail here, but there are two that merit discussion because of the art and architecture they left behind.

The first of these is the Chimú culture, once based around present-day Trujillo. Between about AD 1000 and AD 1400, this sophisticated society built the largest known pre-Columbian city in the Americas. Chan Chan is a sprawling, 36-sq-km complex, which once housed an estimated 60,000 people. Though over the centuries this adobe city has been worn down by the elements, parts of the complex's geometric friezes have been restored, giving a small inkling of what this metropolis must have been

FATHER OF PERUVIAN ARCHAEOLOGY

Much of what we know about some of Peru's most important pre-Columbian cultures we owe to a single man: Julio C Tello (1880–1947), the acclaimed 'Father of Peruvian Archaeology.' A self-described 'mountain Indian,' Tello was born in the highland village of Huarochirí, in the mountains east of Lima. He earned a medical degree at the Universidad Nacional Mayor de San Marco Lima and later studied archaeology at Harvard University – no small achievement for a poor, indigenous man in turn-of-the-20th-century Peru.

In the 1920s he undertook a series of groundbreaking archaeological studies of the Wari centers around Ayacucho and the temple complex at Chavín de Huántar, where an ornate stela – the Tello Obelisk – is named in his honor (it's on view at the Museo Nacional de Chavín). He also discovered hundreds of mummy bundles on the Península de Paracas in 1927 – one of the most important sources of information about this pre-Inca culture. Most significantly, Tello brought scientific rigor to Peru's burgeoning archaeological efforts. In the 19th century digs often resulted in more destruction than conservation, and looting was widely accepted. Tello helped get laws passed that offered legal protection to important archaeological sites.

For more on this charismatic figure, pick up a copy of *The Life and Writings of Julio C Tello: America's First Indigenous Archaeologist*, published by University of Iowa Press. The publication is the first to gather his key writings.

like in its heyday. The Chimú were accomplished artisans and metallurgists – producing, among other things, some absolutely outrageous-looking textiles covered top-to-bottom in tassels.

In the interior of the northern highlands is the cloud-forest citadel of Kuélap, built by the Chachapoyas culture in the remote Utcubamba Valley, beginning around AD 800. It is an incredible structure – or, more accurately, series of structures. The site is composed of more than 400 circular dwellings in addition to unusual, gravity-defying pieces of architecture, such as an inverted cone known as El Tintero (The Inkpot). The compound caps a narrow ridge and is surrounded, on all sides, by a 6m- to 12m-high wall, making the city practically impenetrable. This has led at least one historian to theorize that if the Incas had made their last stand against the Spanish here, rather than outside Cuzco, history might have been quite different.

Incas

Peru's greatest engineers were also its greatest empire builders. Because the Incas made direct contact with the Spanish, they also happen to be the pre-Columbian Andean culture that is best documented – not only through Spanish chronicles, but also through narratives produced by descendants of the Incas themselves. (The most famous of these scribes is El Inca Garcilaso de la Vega, who lived in the 16th century.)

At its acme, the Inca empire was larger than imperial Rome and boasted 40,000km of roadways. A network of *chasquis* (relay runners) kept the kingdom connected, relaying fresh-caught fish from the coast to Cuzco in 24 hours.

The Incas were a Quechua civilization descended from alpaca farmers in the southern Andes. Over several generations, from AD 1100 until the arrival of the Spanish in 1532, they steadfastly grew into a highly organized empire that extended over more than 37° latitude from Colombia to Chile. This was an absolutist state with a strong army, where ultimate power resided with the *inca* (emperor). The political history is fascinating.

The society was bound by a rigid caste system: there were nobles, an artisan and merchant class, and peasants. The latter supplied the workers for the Incas' many public-works projects. Citizens were expected to pay tribute to the crown in the form of labor (typically three months of the year), enabling the development and maintenance of monuments, canals and roadways. The Incas also kept a highly efficient communications

BEST ARCHAEOLOGICAL MUSEUMS

- Museo Nacional de Antropología, Arqueología e Historia del Perú (p76), Lima
- Museo Larco (p76), Lima
- Museo Inka (p205), Cuzco
- Museo Nacional de Chavín (p398), Chavín de Huántar
- Museo Santuarios Andinos (p146), Arequipa
- Museo Tumbas Reales de Sipán (p342), Lambayeque
- Museo Nacional Sicán (p343), Ferreñafe

system consisting of a body of *chasquis* (relay runners), who could make the 1600km trip between Quito and Cuzco in just seven days. (By comparison, it takes the average traveler three to four days to hike the Inca Trail from Ollantaytambo to Machu Picchu – a mere 43km!) As brutal as the regime was (bloody wars, human sacrifice), the Incas also had a notable social-welfare system, warehousing surplus food for distribution to areas and people in need.

On the cultural front, the Incas had a strong tradition of music, oral literature and textiles. Their fabrics were generally composed of bold, solid colors in an array of abstract, geometric prints. But they are best known for their monumental architecture. The capital of Cuzco, along with a series of constructions at Sacsaywamán, Pisac, Ollantaytambo and the fabled Machu Picchu, are all incredible examples of the imperial style of building. Carved pieces of rock, without mortar, are fitted together so tightly that it is impossible to fit a knife between the stones. Most interestingly, walls are built at an angle and windows in a trapezoidal form, so as to resist seismic activity. The Incas kept the exteriors of their buildings austere, opting to put the decoration on the inside, in the form of rich wall hangings made of precious metal.

Nestled into spectacular natural locales, these structures, even in their ruined state, are an unforgettable sight. Their great majesty was something the Spanish acknowledged, even as they pried them apart to build their own monuments. 'Now that the Inca rulers have lost their power,' wrote Spanish chronicler Pedro Cieza de León in the 16th century, 'all these palaces and gardens, together with their other great works, have fallen, so that only the remains survive. Since they were built of good stone and the masonry is excellent, they will stand as memorials for centuries to come.' León was right. The Inca civilization did not survive the Spanish *pachacuti*, but its architecture did – a reminder of the many grand societies we are just beginning to understand.

Indigenous Peru

While Peru's social order has been indelibly stamped by Spanish custom, its soul remains squarely indigenous. According to the country's census bureau, this crinkled piece of the South American Andes harbors 52 different ethnicities, 13 distinct linguistic families and 1786 native communities. In fact, almost half of Peru's population of more than 30 million identifies as Amerindian. Together, these groups account for an infinite number of rituals, artistic traditions and ways of life – a cultural legacy that is as rich as it is long-running.

Postconquest Life

In the wake of the Spanish conquest, colonial authorities transformed the ways in which people lived in the Andes. Indigenous people who had only ever known an agricultural life were forced to live in *reducciones* (mission towns) by colonial authorities. These urbanized 'reductions' provided the Church with a centralized place for evangelism and allowed the Spanish to control the native people politically and culturally. In these *reducciones,* indigenous people were often prohibited from speaking their native language or wearing traditional dress.

By the 17th century, after the Spanish had consolidated their power, many indigenous people were dispersed back to the countryside. But rather than work in the self-sustaining *ayllus* (collectives) that had existed in pre-Columbian times, *indígenas* were forced into a system of debt peonage. For example: a native family was granted a subsistence plot on a Spanish landowner's holdings. In exchange, the *campesino* (peasant) provided labor for the *patrón* (boss). In many cases, *campesinos* were not allowed to leave the land on which they lived.

This system remained firmly in place into the 20th century.

In Spanish, *indígena* (indigenous) is the appropriate term. The word *indio* – 'Indian' in English – can be insulting, especially when used by outsiders. The slang *cholo* (translating roughly to 'Indian peasant') has long been considered derogatory, though some Peruvians use it as a term of empowerment.

A 20th-Century Shift

The last 100 years have marked a number of significant steps forward. Since the indigenist social movements of the 1920s, various constitutions and laws have granted legal protection to communal lands (at least on paper, if not always in practice).

In 1979 the Peruvian constitution officially recognized the right of people to adhere to their own 'cultural identities,' and the right to bilingual education was officially established. (Until then, the public school system had made a systematic effort to eliminate the use of native languages and pressured indigenous people to acculturate to Spanish *criollo* society.) And, the following year, literacy voting restrictions were finally lifted, allowing indigenous people to fully participate in the political process.

In 2011 President Humala passed a law that required native peoples to be consulted on all mining and extraction activities on their territories. Yet, conflict still runs deep. In September 2014 four indigenous activists were murdered en route to a meeting to discuss illegal logging.

Pressures of Poverty & Environment

Even as *indígenas* continue to make strides, there are obstacles. Indigenous people make up almost twice as many of the country's extreme poverty cases as Peruvians of European descent. In addition, access to basic services is problematic. Nearly 60% of indigenous communities do not have access to a health facility, and the country has a high maternal mortality ratio (higher than Iraq or the Gaza Strip). This affects indigenous women disproportionately.

Racism remains a potent societal force in Peru. Yet a DNA study recently published by *National Geographic* shows that the inhabitants of Lima have 68% indigenous blood.

Perhaps the biggest issue facing some ethnicities is the loss of land. Drug trafficking and the exploitation of natural resources in ever more remote areas are putting increased pressure on indigenous communities whose territories are often ill-defined and whose needs are poorly represented by the federal government in Lima. According to Aidesep, a Peruvian indigenous organization representing various rainforest ethnic groups, oil prospecting and extraction is occurring in more than 80% of indigenous territories in the Amazon. In late 2014 the remote Mashco-Piro, a tribe that had never been contacted until recently, raided a *mestizo* (mixed descent) village for supplies after being displaced from their own lands by logging and drug trafficking.

Multitude of Cultures

Indigenous cultures are identified by their region or name, such as the Arequipa or Chachapoyas. But with more than a thousand highly localized regional cultures in the Peruvian Andes alone, it is easiest to identify groups by the language they speak. Quechua – the lingua franca of the Incas – is predominant. It is the most commonly spoken native language in the Americas and is heard all over the Andes. In Peru, more than 13% of the national population claims it as a birth language.

Aymara is the second-most spoken indigenous language – with nearly 2% of Peruvians speaking it from birth, primarily in the area around Lake Titicaca. Nearly 1% of Peruvians speak one of another 50 or so smaller, regional dialects. These include the numerous Amazon cultures that inhabit the rainforest.

Quechua

The descendants of the Incas (along with the myriad peoples the Incas conquered) inhabit much of Peru's Andean spine, representing the biggest indigenous cohort in the country. The department of Cuzco, however, remains the symbolic center of Quechua life. Traditional Quechua refer to themselves as *runakuna* and refer to mixed-raced *mestizos* or indigenous people who adopt Spanish-Peruvian culture as *mistikuna*. The ritual chewing of coca is regarded as a major point of self-identification among *runakuna*. However, such distinguishing characteristics are becoming increasingly blurred as more indigenous people adopt at least some *criollo* customs in order to participate in the greater economy.

English Words Derived from Quechua

- Coca
- Condor
- Guano
- Llama
- Pampa
- Puma
- Quinoa

Regardless, many people continue to speak the language, chew coca and wear traditional dress. For men, this generally consists of brightly woven ponchos and the ear-flap hats known as *chullos*. Women's outfits are more elaborate and flamboyant: a bowler or flat-topped hat accompanies some sort of woven wrap or sweater, and multiple layers of handwoven or shiny skirts. (The layered-skirt look is considered very feminine.) Elements of traditional and Western dress are often combined.

Aymara

Though subjugated by the Quechua-speaking Incas in the 15th century, the Aymara have maintained a distinct language group and identity.

OLLANTAY: QUECHUA'S GREAT LITERARY EPIC

Ollantay tells the story of a pair of star-crossed lovers: Ollanta, a celebrated warrior of humble birth, and Cusi Cuyllur, a captivating Inca princess. Because Ollanta is not a noble, societal mores dictate that he cannot marry his beloved. But he nonetheless draws up the courage to ask Emperor Pachacutec for his daughter's hand in marriage. The emperor becomes enraged at the audacity of the young lovers, and expels Ollanta from Cuzco and throws his daughter in jail. Battles ensue, a child is born and after much palace intrigue, the lovers are reunited.

Ollantay is a work of classic Quechua – the version of Quechua spoken at the time of the conquest. But because the Incas didn't leave behind a written language, its origins are quite murky: no one knows who composed it, or when. Its first recorded appearance is in the manuscripts of an 18th-century priest named Antonio Valdés, who worked in the department of Cuzco. Some scholars have surmised that Valdés may have written *Ollantay*. Others say that it was one of the many epic poems transmitted orally among the Incas, and that Valdés simply recorded it. Others figure Valdés may have tailored an indigenous work to suit Spanish tastes. Regardless, it is a popular theater drama in Peru – and remains one of the great works of art in Quechua.

Traditionally an agricultural society, they were reduced to near-slave status through debt peonage and, later, in the silver mines of Bolivia. Within Peru, they are clustered in the area around Puno and Lake Titicaca.

While identification with indigenous custom is strong, Spanish elements are present in spiritual life. *Indígenas* have largely adapted Catholic deities to their own beliefs. Like the Quechua, many Aymara practice syncretic religious beliefs that closely link indigenous custom to Catholic thought. In Puno, there is a large festival in honor of La Virgen de la Candelaria every February 2 (Candlemas). The Virgin, however, is closely identified with Pachamama (Peruvian earth goddess), as well as natural elements such as lightning and fertility.

Cultures of the Amazon

The vast Peruvian Amazon is home to more than 330,000 indigenous people, representing more than five dozen different ethnicities; some are closely related while others couldn't be more different in terms of tradition and language.

Within this group, the biggest demographic is made up of the Asháninka people (also known as Campa). Comprising roughly a quarter of the indigenous population in the Peruvian Amazon, they inhabit numerous river valleys east of the central highlands. (Because of this location, the Asháninka suffered mightily during the internal conflict of 1980–2000, when the Sendero Luminoso – Shining Path – made incursions to the east.)

The second-largest Amazon group is the Aguaruna, who occupy the Marañón, Nieva and Santiago river valleys to the north. The group not only resisted Inca attempts at conquest, they also fended off the Spanish. In fact, they still occupy their preconquest lands, and survive by practicing horticulture, hunting and fishing.

There are countless other smaller ethnic groups, including the Shipibo, Matsiguenka and the small, so-called 'uncontacted tribes' that have made headlines in recent years. These groups are extremely vulnerable to land loss and pollution caused by oil and mineral extraction. For the most remote groups, the biggest problem can boil down to simple immunity: in the 1980s more than half of the Nahua people in the southern Amazon died after contracting diseases from loggers and oil-company agents.

For a well-written examination of Quechua life in Peru, read Catherine Allen's *The Hold Life Has: Coca and Cultural Identity in an Andean Community*. This intriguing ethnography, last updated in 2002, covers everything from belief systems to the rituals of daily life in the southern highlands.

Music & the Arts

The country that has been home to both indigenous and European empires has a wealth of cultural and artistic tradition. Perhaps the most outstanding achievements are in the areas of music (both indigenous and otherwise), painting and literature – the latter of which received plenty of attention in 2010, when Peruvian novelist Mario Vargas Llosa won the Nobel Prize.

Music

Of the infinite varieties of music that exist all over Peru, the Afro-Peruvian tunes from the coast are perhaps the grooviest. For an excellent primer, listen to the David Byrne–produced compilation *Afro-Peruvian Classics: The Soul of Black Peru.*

Like its people, Peru's music is an intercontinental fusion of elements. Pre-Columbian cultures contributed bamboo flutes, the Spaniards brought stringed instruments and the Africans gave it a backbone of fluid, percussive rhythm. By and large, music tends to be a regional affair: African-influenced *landó* with its thumbing bass beats is predominant on the coast, high-pitched indigenous *huayno,* heavy on bamboo wind instruments, is heard in the Andes and *criollo* waltzes are a must at any dance party on the coast.

Over the last several decades, the *huayno* has blended with surf guitars and Colombian *cumbia* (a type of Afro-Caribbean dance music) to produce *chicha,* a danceable sound closely identified with the Amazon region, growing in popularity even with cool urban youth. (Well-known *chicha* bands include Los Shapis and Los Mirlos.) *Cumbia* is also popular. Grupo 5, which hails from Chiclayo, is currently a favorite in the genre.

On the coast, guitar-inflected *música criolla* (*criollo* music) has its roots in both Spain and Africa. The most famous *criollo* style is the *vals peruano* (Peruvian waltz), a three-quarter-time waltz that is fast moving and full of complex guitar melodies. The most legendary singers in this genre include singer and composer Chabuca Granda (1920–83), Lucha Reyes (1936–73) and Arturo 'Zambo' Cavero (1940–2009). Cavero, in particular, was revered for his gravelly vocals and soulful interpretations. *Landó* is closely connected to this style of music, but features the added elements of call-and-response. Standout performers in this vein include singers Susana Baca (b 1944) and Eva Ayllón (b 1956).

Peru is making significant contributions to today's alt-rock scene, with fusion bands such as Uchpa, NovaLima, Bareto, La Sarita and the award-winning Lucho Quequezana integrating Quechua, Afro-Peruvian and other influences. Band La Mente sets a party tone and Bareto remakes Peruvian *cumbia* classics with great appeal.

Must-Read Fiction

The War of the End of the World (Mario Vargas Llosa; 1981)

War by Candlelight (Daniel Alarcón; 2006)

Chronicle of San Gabriel (Julio Ramón Ribeyro; 2004)

Visual Art

The country's most famous art movement dates to the 17th and 18th centuries, when the artists of the Cuzco School produced thousands of religious paintings, the vast majority of which remain unattributed. Created by native and *mestizo* (person of mixed indigenous and Spanish descent) artists, the pieces frequently feature holy figures laced in gold paint and rendered in a style inspired by mannerist and late Gothic art, but bearing traces of an indigenous color palette and iconography. Today, these hang in museums and churches throughout Peru and reproductions are sold in many crafts markets.

TRADITIONAL CRAFTS

Peru has a tradition of producing extraordinary crafts and folk art. Here's what to look for:

➡ **Textiles** You'll see intricate weavings with elaborate anthropomorphic and geometric designs all over Peru. Some of the finest can be found around Cuzco.

➡ **Pottery** The most stunning pieces of pottery are those made in the tradition of the pre-Columbian Moche people of the north coast. But also worthwhile is Chancay-style pottery: rotund figures made from sand-colored clay. Find these at markets in Lima.

➡ **Religious crafts** These abound in all regions, but the *retablos* (three-dimensional ornamental dioramas) from Ayacucho are the most spectacular.

One of the most well-known artistic figures of the 19th century is Pancho Fierro (1807–79; the illegitimate son of a priest and a slave), who painted highly evocative watercolors of the everyday figures that occupied Lima's streets: fishmongers, teachers and Catholic religious figures clothed in lush robes.

In the early 20th century, an indigenist movement led by painter José Sabogal (1888–1956) achieved national prominence. Sabogal often painted indigenous figures and incorporated pre-Columbian design in his work. As director of the National School of Arts in Lima, he influenced a whole generation of painters who looked to Andean tradition for inspiration, including Julia Codesido (1892–1979), Mario Urteaga (1875–1957) and Enrique Camino Brent (1909–60).

Literature

Mario Vargas Llosa (b 1936) is Peru's most famous writer, hailed alongside 20th-century Latin American luminaries such as Gabriel García Márquez, Julio Cortázar and Carlos Fuentes. His novels evoke James Joyce in their complexity, meandering through time and shifting perspectives. Vargas Llosa is also a keen social observer, casting a spotlight on the naked corruption of the ruling class and the peculiarities of Peruvian society. His more than two dozen novels are available in translation. The best place to start is *La ciudad y los perros* (The Time of the Hero; 1962), based on his experience at a Peruvian military academy. (The soldiers at his old academy responded to the novel by burning it.)

César Vallejo is one of the world's most renowned poets, influencing writers all over the West. Now his complete works – in English and Spanish – are available in a single volume, *The Complete Poetry of César Vallejo: A Bilingual Edition*, 2009.

Another keen observer includes Alfredo Bryce Echenique (b 1939), who chronicles the ways of the upper class in novels such as *El huerto de mi amada* (My Beloved's Garden; 2004), which recounts an affair between a 33-year-old woman and a teenage boy in 1950s Lima. Demonstrating a distinctly Peruvian penchant for dark humor is Julio Ramón Ribeyro (1929–94). Though never a bestselling author, he is critically acclaimed for his insightful works, which focus on the vagaries of lower-middle-class life. His work is available in English in *Marginal Voices: Selected Stories* (1993). If you are just learning to read Spanish, his clearly and concisely written pieces are an ideal place to start exploring Peruvian literature.

Also significant is Daniel Alarcón (b 1977), a rising Peruvian-American writer whose award-winning short stories have appeared in the *New Yorker* magazine. His debut novel, *Lost City Radio* (2007), about a country recovering from civil war, won a PEN award in 2008.

If Vargas Llosa is the country's greatest novelist, then César Vallejo (1892–1938) is its greatest poet. In his lifetime, he published only three slim books – *Los heraldos negros* (The Black Heralds; 1919), *Trilce* (1922) and *Poemas humanos* (Human Poems; 1939) – but he has long been regarded as one of the most innovative Latin American poets of the 20th century. Vallejo frequently touched on existential themes and was known for pushing the language to its limits, inventing words when real ones no longer suited him.

The Natural World

Few countries have topographies as rugged, forbidding and wildly diverse as Peru. It lies in the tropics, south of the equator, straddling three strikingly different geographic zones: the arid Pacific coast, the craggy Andes and a good portion of the Amazon Basin. Regardless of which part you visit, you'll never travel a straight line. Between snaking rivers, plunging canyons and zigzagging mountain roads, navigating Peru's landscape is about circumventing natural obstacles, a path of excitement and jaw-dropping beauty.

The Land

The origin of the word 'Andes' is uncertain. Some historians believe it comes from the Quechua *anti*, meaning 'east,' or *anta*, an Aymara-derived term that signifies 'copper-colored.' Interestingly, the mountains don't stop at the Pacific coast; 100km offshore is a trench that is as deep as the Andes are high.

At 1,285,220 sq km Peru is the third-largest country in South America. It is five times larger than the UK, almost twice the size of Texas and one-sixth the size of Australia. On the coast, a narrow strip of land, which lies below 1000m in elevation, hugs the country's 3000km-long shoreline. Consisting primarily of scrubland and desert, it eventually merges, in the south, with Chile's Atacama Desert, one of the driest places on earth. The coast includes Lima, the capital, and several major agricultural centers – oases watered by dozens of rivers that cascade down from the Andes. These settlements make for a strange sight: barren desert can give way to bursts of green fields within the course of a few meters. The coast contains some of Peru's flattest terrain, so it's no surprise that the country's best road, the Carretera Panamericana (Pan-American Hwy), borders much of the Pacific from Ecuador to Chile.

The Andes, the world's second-greatest mountain chain, form the spine of the country. Rising steeply from the coast, and growing sharply in height and gradient from north to south, they reach spectacular heights of more than 6000m just 100km inland. Peru's highest peak, Huascarán (6768m), located northeast of Huaraz, is the world's highest tropical summit and the sixth-tallest mountain in the Americas. Though the Peruvian Andes resides in the tropics, the mountains are laced with a web of glaciers above elevations of 5000m. Between 3000m and 4000m lie the agricultural highlands, which support more than a third of Peru's population.

The eastern Andean slopes receive much more rainfall than the dry western slopes and are draped in lush cloud forests as they descend into the lowland rainforest of the Amazon. Here, the undulating landscape rarely rises more than 500m above sea level as various tributary systems feed into the mighty Río Amazonas (Amazon River), the largest river in the world. Weather conditions are hot and humid year-round, with most precipitation falling between December and May.

Travellers' Wildlife Guides: Peru (2014), by David Pearson and Les Beletsky, helpfully lists the country's most important and frequently seen birds, mammals, amphibians, reptiles and ecosystem habitats.

Wildlife

With its folds, bends and plunging river valleys, Peru is home to countless ecosystems, each with its own unique climate, elevation, vegetation and soil type. As a result, it boasts a spectacular variety of plant and animal life. Colonies of sea lions occupy rocky outcroppings on the coast, while raucous flocks of brightly colored macaws descend on clay licks in the Amazon. In the Andes, rare vicuñas (endangered relatives of the alpaca) trot about in packs as condors take to the wind currents. Peru is one of only a dozen or so countries in the world considered to be 'megadiverse.'

Wildlife enthusiasts come to Peru to see a rainbow of birds, as well as camelids, freshwater dolphins, butterflies, jaguars, anacondas, macaws and spectacled bears – to name but a few.

Birds

Peru has more than 1800 bird species – that's more than the number of species found in North America and Europe together. From the tiniest hummingbirds to the majestic Andean condor, the variety is colorful and seemingly endless; new species are discovered regularly.

A comprehensive overview of Peru's avian life is contained in the 656-page Princeton Field Guide *Birds of Peru* (2010) by Thomas Schulenberg.

Along the Pacific, marine birds of all kinds are most visible, especially in the south, where they can be found clustered along the shore. Here you'll see exuberant Chilean flamingos, oversized Peruvian pelicans, plump Inca terns sporting white-feather mustaches and bright-orange beaks, colonies of brown boobies engaged in elaborate mating dances, cormorants, and endangered Humboldt penguins, which can be spotted waddling around the Islas Ballestas.

In the highlands, the most famous bird of all is the Andean condor. Weighing up to 10kg, with a 3m-plus wingspan, this monarch of the air (a member of the vulture family) once ranged over the entire Andean mountain chain from Venezuela to Tierra del Fuego. Considered the largest flying bird in the world, the condor was put on the endangered species list in the 1970s, due mostly to loss of habitat and pollution. But it was also hunted to the brink of extinction because its body parts were believed to increase male virility and ward off nightmares. Condors usually nest in impossibly high mountain cliffs that prevent predators from snatching their young. Their main food source is carrion and they're most easily spotted riding thermal air currents in the canyons around Arequipa.

Other prominent high-altitude birds include the Andean gull (don't call it a seagull!), which is commonly sighted along lakes and rivers as high as 4500m. The mountains are also home to several species of ibis, such as the puna ibis, which inhabits lakeside marshes, as well as roughly a dozen types of cinclodes, a type of ovenbird (their clay nests resemble ovens) endemic to the Andes. Other species include torrent ducks, which nest in small waterside caves, Andean geese, spotted Andean

WATCHING WILDLIFE IN PERU

A lot of travelers come to Peru specifically to observe the extraordinary animal life: sea lions, vicuñas, scarlet macaws and monkeys. A few tips on making the most of your wildlife-watching:

- Be willing to travel – the coast has limited fauna and some highland areas have been hunted out; remote is the way to go.
- Hire a knowledgeable local guide – they know what to look for, when and where.
- Get up *really* early – animals tend to be most active at dawn and dusk.
- Bring a pair of lightweight binoculars – they will improve wildlife observation tremendously.
- Be quiet: animals tend to avoid loud packs of chatty humans, so keep chitchat to a whisper; in the Amazon, opt for canoes instead of motorboats – you'll see much more.
- Have realistic expectations: vegetation can be thick and animals shy – you're not going to see everything in a single hike.

FREQUENT FLYERS

For many bird enthusiasts in Peru, the diminutive hummingbirds are among the most delightful to observe. More than 100 species have been recorded in the country, and their exquisite beauty is matched by their extravagant names. There's the 'green-tailed goldenthroat,' the 'spangled coquette,' the 'fawn-breasted brilliant' and 'amethyst-throated sunangel.' Species such as the redheaded Andean hillstar, living in the *puna* (high Andean grasslands), have evolved an amazing strategy to survive a cold night. They go into a state of torpor, which is like a nightly hibernation, by lowering their body temperature by up to 30°C, thus drastically slowing their metabolism.

One of the most unusual species of hummingbird is the marvelous spatuletail, found in the Utcubamba Valley in northern Peru. Full-grown adult males are adorned with two extravagant feathery spatules on the tail, which are used during mating displays to attract females.

flickers, black-and-yellow Andean siskins and, of course, a panoply of hummingbirds.

Swoop down toward the Amazon and you'll catch sight of the world's most iconic tropical birds, including boisterous flocks of parrots and macaws festooned in brightly plumed regalia. You'll also see clusters of aracaris, toucans, parakeets, toucanets, ibises, regal gray-winged trumpeters, umbrella birds with gravity-defying feathered hairdos, crimson colored cocks-of-the-rock, soaring hawks and harpy eagles. The list goes on.

Mammals

The Amazon is home to a bounty of mammals. More than two-dozen species of monkeys are found here, including howlers, acrobatic spider monkeys and wide-eyed marmosets. With the help of a guide, you may also see sloths, bats, pig-like peccaries, anteaters, armadillos and coatis (ring-tailed members of the raccoon family). And if you're really lucky, you'll find giant river otters, capybaras (a rodent of unusual size), river dolphins, tapirs and maybe one of half a dozen elusive felines, including the fabled jaguar.

A Neotropical Companion, by John Kricher, provides an introduction to the wildlife and ecosystems of the New World tropics, including coastal and highland regions.

Toward the west, the cloud forests straddling the Amazon and the eastern slopes of the Andean highlands are home to the endangered spectacled bear. South America's only bear is a black, shaggy mammal that grows up to 1.8m in length, and is known for its white, mask-like face markings.

The highlands are home to roving packs of camelids: llamas and alpacas are the most easily spotted since they are domesticated, and used as pack animals or for their wool; vicuñas and guanacos live exclusively in the wild. On highland talus slopes, watch out for the viscacha, which looks like the world's most cuddly rabbit. Foxes, deer and domesticated *cuy* (guinea pigs) are also highland dwellers, as is the puma (cougar or mountain lion).

On the coast, huge numbers of sea lions and seals are easily seen on the Islas Ballestas. While whales are very rarely seen offshore, dolphins are commonly seen. In the coastal desert strip, there are few unique species of land animals. One is the near-threatened Sechuran fox, the smallest of the South American foxes (found in northern Peru), which has a black-tipped tail, pale, sand-colored fur and an omnivorous appetite for small rodents and seed pods.

FOR THE DOGS: PERUVIAN HAIRLESS

Visit many of the ancient sites around coastal Peru and you'll be greeted by a strangely awesome canine sight: hairless dogs – some with small mohawks on the crown of their heads – bounding about the ruins. A pre-Inca breed whose roots in the Andes date back almost 3000 years, the *perro biringo* or *perro calato* (naked dog), as it is known, has been depicted in Moche, Chimú and Chancay pottery.

Over the centuries, as cutesy breeds from abroad have been introduced to Peru, the population of Peruvian hairless has declined. But, in recent years, they've started to make a comeback, with dedicated Lima breeders working to keep the species alive, and the government employing them as staple attractions at pre-Columbian sites. In 2009 they were even awarded with their own commemorative stamp. The dogs may not be pretty, but they are generally friendly. And they do have one thing going for them: no fur means no fleas.

Reptiles, Amphibians, Insects & Marine Life

The greatest variety of reptiles, amphibians, insects and marine life can be found in the Amazon Basin. Here, you'll find hundreds of species, including toads, tree frogs and thumbnail-sized poison dart frogs (indigenous peoples once used the frogs' deadly poison on the points of their blow-pipe darts). Rivers teem with schools of piranhas, *paiche* and *doncella* (both are types of freshwater fish), while the air buzzes with the activity of thousands of insects: armies of ants, squadrons of beetles, as well as katydids, stick insects, caterpillars, spiders, praying mantises, transparent moths, and butterflies of all shapes and sizes. A blue morpho butterfly in flight is a remarkable sight: with wingspans of up to 10cm, their iridescent-blue coloring can seem downright hallucinogenic.

Naturally, there are all kinds of reptiles, too, including tortoises, river turtles, lizards, caimans and, of course, that jungle-movie favorite: the anaconda. An aquatic boa snake that can measure more than 10m in length, it will often ambush its prey by the water's edge, constrict its body around it and then drown it in the river. Caimans, tapirs, deer, turtles and peccaries are all tasty meals for this killer snake; human victims are almost unheard of (unless you're Jennifer Lopez and Ice Cube in a low-rent Hollywood production). Far more worrisome to the average human is the bushmaster, a deadly, reddish-brown viper that likes to hang out inside rotting logs and among the buttress roots of trees. Thankfully, it's a retiring creature, and is rarely found on popular trails.

Andean Botanical Information System (www.sacha.org) is a veritable online encyclopedia of flowering plants in Peru's coastal areas and the Andes.

Plants

At high elevations in the Andes, especially in the Cordilleras Blanca and Huayhuash, outside Huaraz, there is a cornucopia of distinctive alpine flora and fauna. Plants encountered in this region include native lupins, spiky tussocks of *ichu* grass, striking *queñua* (Polylepis) trees with their distinctive curly, red paperlike bark, in addition to unusual bromeliads. Many alpine wildflowers bloom during the trekking season, between May and September.

In the south, you'll find the distinctive *puna* ecosystem. These areas have a fairly limited flora of hard grasses, cushion plants, small herbaceous plants, shrubs and dwarf trees. Many plants in this environment have developed small, thick leaves that are less susceptible to frost and radiation. In the north, you can find some *páramo* (high-altitude Andean grasslands), which have a harsher climate, are less grassy and have an odd mixture of landscapes, including peat bogs, glacier-formed valleys, alpine lakes, wet grasslands and patches of scrubland and forest.

GIANT FLOWERS OF THE MOUNTAINS

Reaching the staggering height of more than 10m, with an explosive, flower-encrusted cigar shape that looks to be straight out of a Dr Seuss book, the *Puya raimondii* certainly takes the award for most unusual flora. The world's tallest flowering plant is a member of the pineapple family and can take up to a century or more to mature. In full bloom, each plant flaunts up to 8000 white flowers, each resembling a lily. It blooms only once in its lifetime, after which the plant dies. Some of the most famous stands of *Puya raimondii* can be found in the Peruvian Andes, in the rocky mountains outside Huaraz, near Catac and Punta Winchus.

Vegetation of the Cloud Forest & Rainforest

As the eastern Andean slopes descend into the western Amazon uplands, the scenery once again changes. Here, tropical cloud forests – so named because they trap (and help create) clouds that drench the forest in a fine mist – allow delicate forms of plant life to survive. Cloud-forest trees are adapted to steep slopes, rocky soils and a rugged climate. They are characterized by low, gnarled growth, dense small-leafed canopies, and moss-covered branches supporting a host of plants such as orchids, ferns and bromeliads. The mist and the dense vegetation give the cloud forest a mysterious, fairy-tale appearance.

In the Amazon rainforest, the density is astonishing: tens of thousands of species of plant can be found living on top of and around each other. There are strangler figs (known as *matapalos*), palms, ferns, epiphytes, bromeliads, flowering orchids, fungi, mosses and lianas, to name a few. Some rainforest trees – such as the 'walking palm' – are supported by strange roots that look like stilts. These are most frequently found where periodic floods occur; the stilt roots are thought to play a role in keeping the tree upright during the inundation.

Top Protected Areas

- *Cañón del Colca, Arequipa*
- *Cordillera Blanca, Ancash*
- *Lake Titicaca, Puno*
- *Parque Nacional Manu, Amazon*
- *Islas Ballestas, Pisco*

One thing that often astounds visitors is the sheer immensity of many trees. A good example is the *ceiba* (also called the 'kapok' or cotton silk tree), which has huge flattened trunk supports, known as buttresses, around its base. The trunk of a ceiba can easily measure 3m across and will grow straight up for 50m before the first branches are reached. These spread out into a huge crown with a slightly flattened appearance. The staggering height of many Amazon trees, some reaching a height of 80m-plus, creates a whole ecosystem of life at the canopy level, inhabited by creatures that never descend to the forest floor.

Desert Coast

In stark contrast to the Amazon, the coastal desert is generally barren of vegetation, apart from around water sources, which may spring into palm-fringed lagoons. Otherwise, the limited plant life you'll glimpse will consist of cacti and other succulents, as well as *lomas* (a blend of grasses and herbaceous species in mist-prone areas). On the far north coast, in the ecological reserves around Tumbes, is a small cluster of mangrove forests, as well as a tropical dry-forest ecosystem, of which there is little in Peru.

National Parks

Peru's vast wealth of wildlife is protected by a system of national parks and reserves with 60 areas covering almost 15% of the country. The newest is the Sierra del Divisor Reserve Zone, created in 2006 to protect 1.5 million hectares of rainforest on the Brazilian border. All of these protected areas are administered by the Instituto Nacional de Recursos

Nacionales (Inrena; www.inrena.gob.pe), a division of the Ministry of Agriculture.

Unfortunately, resources are lacking to conserve protected areas, which are subject to illegal hunting, fishing, logging and mining. The government simply doesn't have the funds to hire enough rangers and provide them with the equipment necessary to patrol the parks. That said, a number of international agencies and not-for-profit organizations contribute money, staff and resources to help with conservation and education projects.

One of the most engaging books on rainforest life is Adrian Forsyth and Ken Miyata's *Tropical Nature: Life and Death in the Rain Forests of Central and South America*. Partially researched in the Amazon Basin, it is an essential, highly enjoyable primer on life in the lowland tropics.

Environmental Issues

Peru faces major challenges in the stewardship of its natural resources, with problems compounded by a lack of law enforcement and its impenetrable geography. Deforestation and erosion are major issues, as is industrial pollution, urban sprawl and the continuing attempted eradication of coca plantations on some Andean slopes. In addition, the Carretera Interoceánica through the heart of the Amazon may imperil thousands of square kilometers of rainforest.

Reduced growth in mining earnings in recent years has led the government to install protectionist measures, much to the detriment of the environment. A new law enacted in July 2014 weakened environmental protections by removing Peru's environmental ministry's jurisdiction over air-, soil-, and water-quality standards.

Deforestation, Air & Water Problems

At the ground level, clear-cutting of the highlands for firewood, of the rainforests for valuable hardwoods, and of both to clear land for agriculture, oil drilling and mining, has led to severe erosion. In the highlands, where deforestation and overgrazing of Andean woodlands and *puna* grass is severe, soil quality is rapidly deteriorating. In the Amazon rainforest, deforestation has led to erosion and a decline in bellwether species such as frogs. Erosion has also led to decreased water quality in this area, where silt-laden water is unable to support microorganisms at the base of the food chain.

COCA CULTIVATION PAST & PRESENT

Cultivation of the coca plant dates back at least 5000 years and its traditional uses have always included the practical and the divine. In pre-Hispanic times, chewing coca was a traditional treatment for everything from a simple toothache to exhaustion. It has also long been used in religious rituals as a sacred offering. When the Spaniards arrived in the 15th century, they attempted to outlaw the 'heathen' practice of cultivating this 'diabolical' plant. However, with coca-chewing an essential part of life for the colony's indigenous labor pool (it is a mild appetite suppressant and stimulant – on par with coffee), the Spanish ultimately reversed their policies.

Today, there continues to be a struggle surrounding coca, but it has to do with its derivative product, cocaine (in which a paste derived from coca leaves is treated with kerosene and refined into a powder). In an attempt to stem the flow of this narcotic, the US led eradication programs of coca plants in Peru in the early 2000s. These programs have done little to curb coca's cultivation (or the cocaine trade), but the herbicides employed have damaged some agricultural lands in indigenous communities. Critics of the US-sponsored programs – including Peruvian *cocaleros* (coca-growers' associations) and President Evo Morales of Bolivia – have called for regulation of eradication.

In 2014, President Ollanta Humala announced that Peru would stop its coca-eradication campaign, which had ardent support from the US, while stepping up promoting other crops in coca-heavy regions, such as coffee and cocoa.

Potable water is an issue for a large number of Peruvians: in urban areas 87% of the population has access to clean water, in rural areas, the percentage drops to 62% of residents. There is also the problem of water pollution caused by mining in the highlands. Sewage contamination along the coast has led to many beaches around some coastal cities being declared unfit for swimming. In the south, pollution and overfishing have led to the continued decline of the Humboldt penguin (its numbers have declined by more than a third since the 1980s).

Air pollution is another grave issue in Peru, especially in Lima where industrial pollutants and vehicle emissions were gauged at four times over the legal limit in 2009.

Protective Steps

In the early 1990s, Peru took steps to formulate a national environmental and natural resource code, but the government (occupied with a bloody guerrilla war in the highlands) lacked the funding and political will to enforce it. In 1995 Peru's congress created a National Environmental Council (Conam) to manage the country's national environmental policy. Though there have been some success stories (eg flagrant polluters being fined for poor practices), enforcement remains weak.

Monga Bay (www.mongabay.com) is an online resource for news and information related to the Amazon and rainforests around the world.

Some positive measures are being taken to help protect the country's environment. Peruvian government and private interests within the tourism industry have come together to develop sustainable-travel projects in the Amazon. In 2012 the Peruvian government created three new protected areas in the northern Amazon territory of Loreto, spanning nearly 600,000 hectares. The areas represent a world hot spot of biological and cultural diversity known as the Putumayo Trinational Conservation Corridor, a joint effort at regional-style management by the governments of Peru, Ecuador, and Colombia.

Peru's first environment minister, Antonio Brack – who passed away in 2014 – took an aggressive stance on deforestation, copying other Amazonian nations in a plea for Western help in conservation, and pledging to curb forest fires and reduce logging rates. Unfortunately, official policy tends to have little relevancy in remote, unmonitored areas.

Illegal mining is a major environmental hazard. In 2014 an economic emergency was declared by the government in 17 indigenous communities along the Río Marañón in the Amazon Basin because oil contamination posed a significant threat to the population. Liquid mercury, used to extract gold, contaminates water sources and kills fish.

Lima has started using a local technology known as Super Tree to combat air pollution. The device (not an actual tree) uses thermodynamic pressure to purify the air; it's the equivalent of having 1200 trees, not a small number in this deforested country. By-products are mud and nonpotable water.

Survival Guide

Directory A–Z

Accommodations

- Peru has accommodations to suit every budget, especially in tourist hubs and cities.
- Many lodgings offer laundry service and free short-term luggage storage (ask for a receipt).
- *Habitación simple* refers to a single room. A *habitación doble* features twin beds while a *habitación matrimonial* has a double or queen-sized bed.
- Street noise can be an issue in any lodging, so select your room accordingly. It's always OK to ask to see a room before committing.
- Homestays are sometimes offered by Spanish schools. Campgrounds are few.

Rates

Note that prices may fluctuate with exchange rates.

Extra charges Foreigners do not have to pay the 18% hotel tax (sometimes included in rates quoted in soles), but may have to present their passport and tourist card to photocopy. A credit-card transaction surcharge of 7% or more does not include the home bank's foreign-currency exchange fee. US dollars may be accepted, but the exchange rate may be poor.

Packages In the remote jungle lodges of the Amazon and in popular beach destinations such as Máncora, all-inclusive resort-style pricing is more the norm.

High season In Cuzco, demand is very high during the high season (June to August). Other busy times include Inti Raymi, Semana Santa (Easter Week) and Fiestas Patrias, when advance reservations are a must. In Lima, prices remain steady throughout the year; look for last-minute specials online. Paying cash always helps; ask for discounts for long-term stays.

Reservations

Airport arrival Since many flights into Lima arrive late at night, it's inadvisable to begin searching for a place to sleep upon arrival. Reserve your first night ahead; most hotels can also arrange airport pickup.

When to book Around the country, reservations are a necessity for stays during a major festival (such as Inti Raymi in Cuzco) or a holiday such as Semana Santa, when all of Peru is on vacation. In the Amazon, reservations are needed at remote lodges. In smaller villages and areas off the beaten path, service tends to be on a first-come, first-served basis.

Late arrival Cheap budget places may not honor a reservation if you arrive late. Even if you've made a reservation, it is best to confirm your arrival time. Late check-in is not a problem at many midrange and top-end hotels, in which case a deposit may be required.

Advance payment Some lodges, especially in the Amazon, may require all or part of the payment up front. Make sure your travel plans are firm if you are paying in advance, as securing refunds can be a challenge.

Discounts Reserving online is convenient, but off-season walk-in rates may be lower. At top-end hotels, however, last-minute online deals are the norm, so always check a hotel's website for discounts and special promotional packages.

Apartments

Short-term rentals, primarily in Lima, increasingly attend mid- to high-end needs.

Check www.vrbo.com and www.airbnb.com for listings.

Hostels

Hostels are diverse and plentiful in Peru, from run-down to boutique, from party hostel to mellow haven with the gamut of amenities. There

BOOK YOUR STAY ONLINE

For more accommodations reviews by Lonely Planet authors, check out http://lonelyplanet.com/peru/hotels. You'll find independent reviews, as well as recommendations on the best places to stay. Best of all, you can book online.

are also **Hostelling International** (www.hihostels.com) affiliates.

Hotels

BUDGET

Hostales (guesthouses), *hospedajes* (small inns) and *albergues* (family-run inns)are Peru's cheapest accommodations. In this price range, expect to find small rooms, with a shared or private bathroom. In the major cities, these options will generally include hot showers; in more rural and remote areas, they likely will not. Some budget inns will include a very simple breakfast in the rate, such as instant coffee with toast.

Avoid rooms that appear insecure; test the locks on doors and windows. Shopping around makes a difference.

MIDRANGE

Rooms generally have private bathrooms with hot-water showers and small portable heaters or fans. Some are also equipped with air-conditioning. Amenities may include cable TV, in-room telephones and safes. Continental or American-style breakfasts are usually included.

TOP END

Peru's top hotels are generally equipped with en suite bathrooms with bathtubs, international direct-dial phones, handy dual-voltage outlets, central heating or air-conditioning, hairdryers, in-room safes, cable TV and internet access (either through high-speed cable or wi-fi); some may come with minifridges, microwaves or coffeemakers.

A large high-end spot may also feature a bar, cafe or restaurant (or several), as well as room service, concierge services and an obliging, multilingual staff.

Expect the biggest places (particularly in Lima) to come with business centers, spas and beauty salons. In the Amazon, where conditions tend to be isolated, high-end lodgings have fewer amenities and are more rustic.

Customs Regulations

- Peru allows duty-free importation of 3L of alcohol and 20 packs of cigarettes, 50 cigars or 250g of tobacco. You can import US$300 of gifts. Legally, you are allowed to bring in such items as a laptop, camera, portable music player, kayak, climbing gear, mountain bike or similar items for personal use.
- It is illegal to take pre-Columbian or colonial artifacts out of Peru, and it is illegal to bring them into most countries. If purchasing reproductions, buy only from a reputable dealer and ask for a detailed receipt. Purchasing animal products made from endangered species or even just transporting them around Peru is also illegal.
- Coca leaves are legal in Peru, but not in most other countries, even in the form of tea bags. People subject to random drug testing should be aware that coca, even in the form of tea, may leave trace amounts in urine.
- Check with your own home government about customs restrictions and duties on any expensive or rare items you intend to bring back. Most countries allow their citizens to import a limited number of items duty-free, though these regulations are subject to change.

SLEEPING PRICE RANGES

Lodgings in Peru are considerably more expensive in tourist areas, such as Lima and Cuzco & the Sacred Valley. All prices listed are high-season rates for double rooms that include private bathroom, unless otherwise specified.

Lima and Cuzco & the Sacred Valley

$ less than S125

$$ S125–S380

$$$ more than S380

Provinces

$ less than S85

$$ S85–S250

$$$ more than S250

Discount Cards

An official International Student Identity Card (ISIC), with a photograph, can get you a 50% discount at some museums and attractions and for organized tours. Senior discount cards are not recognized.

HOT SHOWERS

Peru's budget accommodations don't always have hot water, and some only have it for certain hours of the day. Early birds often use up all the hot water, so plan accordingly.

Electric showerheads require care. Switch them on for a hot shower and wait a few minutes. Water is hotter if the pressure is low. Don't fiddle with the heating unit while the water is on or you may get a shock.

Electricity

Electrical current is 220V, 60Hz AC. Standard outlets accept round prongs, some have dual-voltage outlets which take flat prongs. Even so, your adapter may need a built-in surge protector.

Embassies & Consulates

Most foreign embassies are in Lima, with some consular services in major tourist centers such as Cuzco.

It is important to realize what your embassy can and can't do if you get into trouble. Your embassy will not be sympathetic if you end up in jail after committing a crime, even if such actions are legal in your own country. If all your money and documents are stolen, the embassy can help you get a new passport.

Call in advance to double-check operating hours or schedule an appointment. While many consulates and embassies are staffed during regular business hours, attention to the public is often more limited. For after-hours and emergency contact numbers, check individual websites.

Oficinas de migraciónes (immigration offices) are where you'll need to go to receive an exit stamp or secure a new entry card.

Australian Embassy (Map p70; ☎01-630-0500; www.peru.embassy.gov.au; Av La Paz 1049, piso 10, Miraflores, Lima; ⏲9am-5pm Mon-Fri)

Belgian Embassy (Map p70; ☎01-241-7566; www.diplomatie.be/lima; Av Angamos Oeste 380, Miraflores, Lima; ⏲8:30am-4pm Mon-Fri)

Bolivian Consulate (Map p176; ☎051-35-1251; fax 051-35-1251; Arequipa 136, 3rd fl, Puno; ⏲8am-4pm Mon-Fri).

Bolivian Embassy (Map p68; ☎01-440-2095; www.boliviaenperu.com; Los Castaños 235, San Isidro, Lima)

Brazilian Embassy (Map p70; ☎01-512-0830; www.embajadabrasil.org.pe; Av José Pardo 850, Miraflores, Lima 18)

Canadian Embassy (Map p70; ☎01-319-3200; www.canadainternational.gc.ca/peru-perou; Bolognesi 228, Miraflores, Lima; ⏲8am-12:30pm & 1:15-5pm Mon-Thu, 8am-12:30pm Fri) With a helpful website.

Chilean Embassy (Map p68; ☎01-710-2211; chileabroad.gov.cl/peru; Javier Prado Oeste 790, San Isidro, Lima 27)

Colombian Consulate (☎065-23-1461; Calvo de Araujo 431, Iquitos)

Colombian Embassy (☎01-462-0294; peru.embajada.gov.co; Calle Clemente X, 335, San Isidro, Lima)

Ecuadorian Consulate (☎072-52-5949; Bolívar 129, 3rd fl, Plaza de Armas, Tumbes)

Ecuadorian Embassy (Map p68; ☎01-212-4027; peru.embajada.gob.ec; Las Palmeras 356, San Isidro, Lima 27)

French Embassy (Map p68; ☎01-215-8400; www.ambafrance-pe.org; Av Arequipa 3415, San Isidro)

German Embassy (☎01-203-5940; www.lima.diplo.de; Av Dionisio Derteano 144, 7th & 8th fl, San Isidro, Lima)

Irish Consulate (Map p70; ☎01-242-9516; consul@irishperu.com; Av Paseo de la Republica 5757-B, Miraflores, Lima) Lima has only an honorary consul with limited services.

Israeli Embassy (Map p68; ☎01-418-0500; lima.mfa.gov.il; Centro Empresarial Platinum Plaza II, Av Andres Reyes 437, piso 13, San Isidro, Lima; ⏲9am-12:30pm Mon-Fri)

Italian Embassy (☎01-463-2727; www.amblima.esteri.it; Av Guiseppe Garibaldi 298, Jesús María, Lima; ⏲8:30-11am Mon-Fri)

Netherlands Embassy (Map p70; ☎01-213-9800; peru.nlembajada.org; Av José Larco 1301, Torre Parque Mar, 13th fl, Miraflores, Lima; ⏲8:30am-12:45pm & 1:30-5pm Mon-Thu, 8:30am-1pm Fri)

Spanish Consulate (Map p68; ☎01-513-7930; www.consuladolima.com.pe; Calle Los Pinos, San Isidro, Lima; ⏲8:30am-1pm Mon-Fri)

Swiss Embassy (☎01-264-0305; www.eda.admin.ch/lima; Av Salaverry 3240, San Isidro,

Lima; ⌚8am-1pm & 2-4:30pm Mon-Thu, 8am-2pm Fri)

UK Embassy (Map p70; ☎01-617-3000; www.ukinperu.fco.gov.uk; Av José Larco 1301, Edificio Parquemar, 22nd fl, Miraflores, Lima 18)

US Embassy (☎01-618-2000; lima.usembassy.gov; Av Encalada, cuadra 17, Surco, Lima) This place is a fortress – call before showing up in person.

PERUVIAN ADDRESSES

A post-office box is known as an *apartado postal* (abbreviated 'Apartado,' 'Apto' or 'AP') or a *casilla postal* ('Casilla' or 'CP'). Some addresses have *s/n* (short for *sin numero*, or 'without a number') or *cuadra* ('block,' eg Block 4) after the street name.

Only addresses in Lima and neighboring Callao require postal codes. Those used most often by travelers are Lima 1 (Central Lima), Lima 4 (Barranco), Lima 18 (Miraflores) and Lima 27 (San Isidro). Note that the word 'Lima' is essential to these postal codes.

Gay & Lesbian Travelers

Peru is a strongly conservative, Catholic country. In 2015 the Peruvian Congress rejected a bill for gay and lesbian civil unions, despite the adoption of similar measures in neighboring countries in the Southern Cone. While many Peruvians will tolerate homosexuality on a 'don't ask; don't tell' level when dealing with foreign travelers, gay rights remain a struggle. As a result, many gays and lesbians in Peru don't publicly identify as homosexual.

Public displays of affection among homosexual couples is rarely seen. Outside gay clubs, it is advisable to keep a low profile. Lima is the most accepting of gay people, but this is on a relative scale. Beyond that, the tourist towns of Cuzco, Arequipa and Trujillo tend to be more tolerant than the norm. Social media platforms Tinder and Grindr are good places to find out more about the gay scene.

FYI: the rainbow flag seen around Cuzco and in the Andes is *not* a gay pride flag – it's the flag of the Inca empire.

Information

Gay Lima (lima.gaycities.com) A handy guide to the latest gay and gay-friendly spots in the capital, along with plenty of links.

Global Gayz (www.globalgayz.com) Excellent, country-specific information about Peru's gay scene and politics, with links to international resources.

Purpleroofs.com (www.purpleroofs.com) Massive LGBTIQ portal with links to a few tour operators and gay-friendly accommodations in Peru.

Tours

Lima Tours (Map p60; ☎01-619-6900; www.limatours.com.pe; Nicolás de Piérola 589, 18th fl, Central Lima) A travel agency that is not exclusively gay, but that organizes gay-friendly group trips around the country.

Rainbow Peruvian Tours (Map p68; ☎01-215-6000; www.perurainbow.com; Río de Janeiro 216, Miraflores, Lima) Gay-owned tour agency based in Lima, with a multilingual website.

Insurance

Having a travel-insurance policy to cover theft, loss, accidents and illness is highly recommended. Always carry your insurance card with you. Not all policies compensate travelers for misrouted or lost luggage. Check the fine print to see if it excludes 'dangerous activities,' which can include scuba diving, motorcycling and even trekking. Also check if the policy coverage includes worst-case scenarios, such as evacuations and flights home.

Worldwide travel insurance is available at www.lonelyplanet.com/travel-insurance. You can buy, extend and claim online anytime – even if you're already on the road.

You must usually report any loss or theft to local police (or airport authorities) within 24 hours. Make sure you keep all documentation to make any claim. For health insurance, see p550.

Internet Access

- Most regions have excellent internet and reasonable prices; hotels and hostels typically have wi-fi or computer terminals.
- Family guesthouses, particularly outside urban areas, lag behind in this area.
- Internet cafes are widespread.
- Rates start at S1 per hour; higher in remote areas.

Language Courses

Peru has schools in Lima, Cuzco, Arequipa, Huaraz, Puerto Maldonado and Huancayo. You can also study Quechua with private teachers or at one of the various language institutes in Lima, Cuzco and Huancayo.

Legal Matters

Legal assistance Your own embassy is of limited help if you get into trouble with the law in Peru, where you are presumed guilty until proven innocent. If you are the victim, the *policía de turismo* (tourist police; Poltur) can help, with limited English. Poltur stations are found in major cities.

Bribery Though some police officers (even tourist police) have a reputation for corruption, bribery is illegal. Beyond traffic police, the most likely place officials might request a little extra is at land borders. Since this too is illegal, those with time and fortitude can and should stick to their guns.

Drugs Avoid having any conversation with someone who offers you drugs. Peru has draconian penalties for possessing even a small amount of drugs; minimum sentences are several years in jail.

Police Should you be stopped by a plainclothes officer, don't hand over any documents or money. Never get into a vehicle with someone claiming to be a police officer, but insist on going to a real police station on foot.

Protests It's not recommended to attend political protests or to get too close to blockades – these are places to avoid.

Detention If you are imprisoned for any reason, make sure that someone else knows about it as soon as possible. Extended pretrial detentions are not uncommon. Peruvians bring food and clothing to family members who are in prison, where conditions are extremely harsh.

Complaints For issues with a hotel or tour operator, register your complaint with the **National Institute for the Defense of Competition and the Protection of Intellectual Property** (Indecopi; ☎01-224-7800; www.indecopi.gob.pe) in Lima.

> **EATING PRICE RANGES**
>
> Mid- to high-end restaurants charge a 10% service fee and a 19% tax. The following price ranges refer to a main dish.
>
> **$** less than S20
>
> **$$** S20–S60
>
> **$$$** more than S60

Maps

The best road map of Peru is the 1:2,000,000 *Mapa Vial* published by Lima 2000 and available in better bookstores. The 1:1,500,000 *Peru South and Lima* country map, published by International Travel Maps, covers the country in good detail south of a line drawn east to west through Tingo María, and has a good street map of Lima, San Isidro, Miraflores and Barranco on the reverse side.

For topographical maps, go to the **Instituto Geográfico Nacional** (IGN; ☎01-475-3030, ext 119; www.ign.gob.pe; Aramburu 1190-98, Surquillo, Lima; ⏲8am-6pm Mon-Fri, to 1pm Sat), with reference maps and others for sale. In January the IGN closes early, so call ahead. High-scale topographic maps for trekking are available, though sheets of border areas might be hard to get. Geological and demographic maps and CD-ROMs are also sold.

Topographic, city and road maps are also at the South American Explorers' clubhouses in Lima (p100) and Cuzco (p232).

Up-to-date topo maps are often available from outdoor outfitters in major trekking centers such as Cuzco, Huaraz and Arequipa. If you are bringing along a GPS unit, ensure that your power source adheres to Peru's 220V, 60Hz AC standard and always carry a compass.

Money

- Peru uses the nuevo sol (S).
- Carrying cash, an ATM card, as well as a credit card that can be used for cash advances in case of emergency, is advisable.
- Credit-card fraud is rampant. Tell your bank you will be in Peru and use your card with care.
- Ask for *billetes pequeños* (small bills), as S100 bills are hard to change in small towns or for small purchases.
- *Casas de cambio* (foreign-exchange bureaus) are fast, have longer hours and often give slightly better rates than banks.
- Many places accept US dollars.
- Do not accept torn money as it will likely not be accepted by Peruvians.
- Avoid changing money on the street as counterfeits are a problem.

ATMs

- *Cajeros automáticos* (ATMs) proliferate in nearly every city and town in Peru, as well as at major airports, bus terminals and shopping areas.
- ATMs are linked to the international Plus (Visa) and Cirrus (Maestro/MasterCard) systems, as well as American Express and other networks.
- Users should have a four-digit PIN. To avoid problems, notify your bank that you'll be using your ATM card abroad.
- If your card works with Banco de la Nacion it may be the best option as it doesn't charge fees (at least at the time of writing).
- Both US dollars and nuevos soles are readily available from Peruvian ATMs.
- Your home bank may charge an additional fee for each foreign ATM transaction.
- ATMs are normally open 24 hours.
- For safety reasons, use ATMs inside banks with security guards, preferably during daylight hours. Cover the keyboard for pin entry.

Cash

The nuevo sol (new sun) comes in bills of S10, S20, S50, S100 and (rarely) S200. It is divided into 100 céntimos, with copper-colored coins of S0.05, S0.10 and S0.20, and silver-colored S0.50 and S1 coins. In addition, there are bimetallic S2 and S5 coins with a copper-colored center inside a silver-colored ring.

US dollars are accepted by many tourist-oriented businesses, though you'll need nuevo soles to pay for local transportation, meals and other incidentals.

Counterfeit bills (in both US dollars and nuevo soles) often circulate in Peru. Merchants question both beat-up and large-denomination bills. Consumers should refuse them too.

To detect fakes, check for a sheer watermark and examine a metal strip crossing the note that repeats Peru in neat, not misshapen, letters. Colored thread, holographs and writing along the top of the bill should be embossed, not glued on.

Credit Cards

Midrange and top-end hotels and shops accept *tarjetas de crédito* (credit cards) with a 7% (or greater) fee. Your bank may also tack on a surcharge and additional fees for each foreign-currency transaction. The most widely accepted cards in Peru are Visa and MasterCard.

Money Changers

The best currency for exchange is the US dollar, although the euro is accepted in major tourist centers. Other hard currencies can be exchanged, but usually with difficulty and only in major cities. All foreign currencies must be in flawless condition.

Cambistas (moneychangers) hang out on street corners near banks and *casas de cambio* and give competitive rates (there's only a little flexibility for bargaining), but are not always honest. Officially, they should wear a vest and badge identifying themselves as legal. They're useful after regular business hours or at borders where there aren't any other options.

> **A NOTE ABOUT PRICES**
>
> Prices are generally listed in Peruvian nuevo soles. However, many package lodgings and higher-end hotels will only quote prices in US dollar, as will many travel agencies and tour operators. In these cases, we list prices in US dollars. Both currencies have experienced fluctuations in recent years, so expect many figures to be different from what you have read.

Taxes, Tipping & Refunds

- Expensive hotels add a 19% sales tax and 10% service charge; the latter is generally not included in quoted rates. Non-Peruvians may be eligible for a refund of the sales tax only.
- A few restaurants charge combined taxes of more than 19%, plus a service charge (*servicio* or *propina*) of 10%.
- Otherwise, tip waitstaff 10% for good service. Taxi drivers do not generally expect tips (unless they've assisted with heavy luggage), but porters and tour guides do.
- There is no system of sales-tax refunds for shoppers.

Opening Hours

Hours are variable and liable to change, especially in small towns, where hours are irregular. Posted hours are a guideline. Lima has the most continuity of services. In other major cities, taxi drivers often know where the late-night stores and pharmacies are.

Banks 9am to 6pm Monday to Friday, 9am to 1pm Saturday

Government offices and businesses 9am to 5pm Monday to Friday

Museums Often close on Monday

Restaurants 10am to 10pm, many close between 3pm and 6pm

Shops 9am to 6pm Monday to Friday, some 9am to 6pm Saturday

Post

The privatized postal system is run by **Serpost** (www.serpost.com.pe). Its service is fairly efficient and reliable, but surprisingly expensive. Most international mail will take about two weeks to arrive from Lima; longer from the provinces.

Public Holidays

Major holidays may be celebrated for days around the official date.

Fiestas Patrias (National Independence Days) is the biggest national holiday, when the entire nation seems to be on the move.

New Year's Day January 1

Good Friday March/April

Labor Day May 1

Inti Raymi June 24

Feast of Sts Peter & Paul June 29

National Independence Days July 28–29

Feast of Santa Rosa de Lima August 30

Battle of Angamos Day October 8

All Saints Day November 1

Feast of the Immaculate Conception December 8

Christmas December 25

PRACTICALITIES

➡ **Newspapers** Peru's government-leaning *El Comercio* (www.elcomercioperu.com.pe) is the leading daily. There's also the slightly left-of-center *La República* (www.elcomercioperu.com.pe) and the *Peruvian Times* (www.peruviantimes.com) and *Peru this Week* (www.peruthisweek.com) in English.

➡ **Internet resources** Helpful resources in English are www.expatperu.com and www.theperuguide.com.

➡ **Magazines** The most well-known political and cultural weekly is *Caretas* (www.caretas.com.pe), while *Etiqueta Negra* (etiquetanegra.com.pe) focuses on culture. A good bilingual travel publication is the monthly *Rumbos* (www.rumbosdelperu.com).

➡ **TV** Cable and satellite TV are widely available for a fix of CNN or even Japanese news.

➡ **Weights and measures** Peru uses the metric system but gas (petrol) is measured in US gallons.

Safe Travel

Travelers may experience periodic protests, thefts and bus drivers who act as if every bend in the road should be assaulted at Autobahn speeds. Certainly, the country is not for the faint of heart. As with every other place on earth, a little common sense goes a very long way.

Thefts, Muggings & Other Crime

The situation has improved significantly in recent years, especially in Lima. Yet street crimes such as pickpocketing, bag-snatching and muggings are still common. Sneak theft is by far the most widespread type of crime, while muggings happen with less regularity. Even so, they do happen.

Use basic precautions and a reasonable amount of awareness, however, and you probably won't be robbed. Some tips:

➡ Crowded places such as bus terminals, train stations, markets and fiestas are the haunts of pickpockets; wear your day pack in front of you or carry a bag that fits snugly under your arm.

➡ Thieves look for easy targets, such as a bulging wallet in a back pocket or a camera held out in the open; keep spending money in your front pocket and your camera stowed when it's not in use.

➡ Passports and larger sums of cash are best carried in a money belt or an inside pocket that can be zipped or closed – or better yet, stowed in a safe at your hotel.

➡ Snatch theft can occur if you place a bag on the ground (even for a few seconds), or while you're asleep on an overnight bus; never leave a bag with your wallet and passport in the overhead rack of a bus.

➡ Don't keep valuables in bags that will be unattended.

➡ Blending in helps: walking around town in brand-new hiking gear or a shiny leather jacket will draw attention; stick to simple clothing.

➡ Leave jewelry and fancy watches at home.

➡ Hotels – especially cheap ones – aren't always trustworthy; lock valuables inside your luggage, or use safety deposit services.

➡ Walk purposefully wherever you are going, even if you are lost; if you need to examine your map, duck into a shop or restaurant.

➡ Always take an official taxi at night and from the airport or bus terminals. If threatened, it's better just to give up your goods than face harm.

CRIMINAL TACTICS

Distraction Some thieves work in pairs or groups. One person creates a distraction as another robs. This can take the form of a bunch of kids fighting in front of you, an elderly person 'accidentally' bumping into you or perhaps someone spilling something on your clothes. Some may slit open your bag, whether it's on your back or on the luggage rack of a bus.

Armed muggings In some cases, there have been robberies and armed muggings of trekkers on popular hiking trails around Huaraz, and jungle treks in the south. Going as part of a group with a local guide may help prevent this. In addition, the area around Tingo María, on the eastern edge of the central highlands, is a renowned bandit area, with armed robberies and other crimes regular occurrences. Keep any activities in the area, including bus rides, to daylight hours.

Express kidnapping In recent years, 'express' kidnappings have been recorded, particularly in some of the unsavory neighborhoods that surround the airport in Lima, and even just outside the airport. An armed attacker (or attackers) grabs someone out of a taxi or abducts them off the street, then forces them to go to the nearest bank to withdraw cash using their ATM cards. Victims who do not resist their attackers generally don't suffer serious physical harm.

REPORTING CRIME

The *policía de turismo* can be found in major cities and tourist areas and can be helpful with criminal matters. If you are unsure how to locate them, contact the main office in Lima (p99). If you are the victim of a crime, file a report with the tourist police immediately. At some point, inform your country's embassy about what has happened. They won't be able to do much, but embassies do keep track of crime geared at foreigners as a way of alerting other travelers to potential dangers.

If you have taken out travel insurance and need to make a claim, Poltur will provide you with a police report. Stolen passports can be reissued at your embassy, though you may be asked for an alternative form of identification first. After receiving your new passport, go to the nearest Peruvian immigration office to get a new tourist card.

Corruption & Scams

Police The military and police (even sometimes the tourist police) have a reputation for corruption. While a foreigner may experience petty harassment (usually to procure payment of a bribe), most police officers are courteous to tourists or just leave them alone.

Touts Perhaps the most pernicious things travelers face are the persistent touts that gather at bus stations, train stations, airports and other tourist spots to offer everything from discounted hotel rooms to local tours. Many touts – among them, many taxi drivers – will say just about anything to steer you to places they represent. They will tell you the establishment you've chosen is a notorious drug den, it's closed down or is overbooked. Do not believe everything you hear. If you have doubts about a place you've decided to stay at, ask to see a room before paying up.

Travel agents It is not advisable to book hotels, travel arrangements or transportation through independent touts. Often, they will demand cash up front for services that never materialize. Stick to reputable, well-recommended agencies and you'll be assured a good time.

IMPORTANT DOCUMENTS

All important documents (passport, credit cards, travel-insurance policy, driver's license etc) should be photocopied or photographed before you leave home. Leave one copy at home or on a cloud drive and keep another with you, separate from the originals.

Transport Issues

When taking buses, choose operators carefully. The cheapest companies will be the most likely to employ reckless drivers and have roadside breakdowns. Overnight travel by bus can get brutally cold in the highlands (take a blanket or a sleeping bag). In some parts, nighttime trips are also subject to the vagaries of roadside bandits, who create impromptu road blocks then relieve passengers of their valuables. Armed robberies have been reported on the night buses between Trujillo and Cajabamba.

Environmental Hazards

Some of Peru's natural hazards include earthquakes and avalanches. Rescues in remote regions are often done on foot because of the inability of helicopters to reach some of the country's more challenging topography. Perhaps the most common hazard is travelers' diarrhea, which comes from consuming contaminated food or water. Other problems include altitude sickness, animal and insect bites, sunburn, heat exhaustion and even hypothermia. You can take precautions for most of these.

Protests & Other Conflict

Protests During the internal conflict, through the 1980s and into the 1990s, terrorism, civil strife and kidnappings meant that entire regions were off limits to both foreign and domestic travelers. Now travelers visit much of the country without problems. Even so, public protests remain a familiar sight. Generally speaking, these have little effect on tourists. It is worth staying aware of current events while in the country; and if a road is blocked or an area cut off, respect the situation. Being a foreigner will not grant you immunity from violence.

Shining Path In the news, a Sendero Luminoso (Shining Path) resurgence has brought isolated incidents of violence in the main coca-growing areas in the provinces of Ayacucho, Cuzco (the trekking route to Espiritu

GOVERNMENT TRAVEL ADVICE

The following government websites offer travel advisories and information on current hot spots.

Australian Department of Foreign Affairs (☎1300-139-281; www.smarttraveller.gov.au)

British Foreign Office (☎0845-850-2829; www.fco.gov.uk/en/travelling-and-living-overseas)

Canadian Department of Foreign Affairs (☎800-267-6788; www.dfait-maeci.gc.ca)

US State Department (☎888-407-4747; travel.state.gov)

Pampa), Huancavelica, Huánuco, Junín and San Martín. These are generally directed at the Peruvian military or the police. Even so, it is worth exercising caution: avoid transit through isolated areas in these regions at night and always check with reputable tour operators before heading out on a remote trekking route.

Drug trafficking Drug-trafficking areas can be dangerous, especially at night. Travelers should avoid the upper Río Huallaga valley between Tingo María and Juanjui, Puerto Bermudez, and the Río Apurímac valley near Ayacucho, where the majority of Peru's illegal drug-growing takes place. Exercise similar caution near the Colombian border, where trafficking also goes on.

Landmines

A half century of armed conflict over the Cordillera del Condor region on Peru's northeastern border with Ecuador was finally resolved in 1998. However, unexploded ordinance (UXO) in the area has not been completely cleaned up. Only use official border crossings and don't stray from the path when traveling in this region.

Telephone

A few public pay phones operated by Movistar and Claro are still around, especially in small towns. They work with coins or phone cards which can be purchased at supermarkets and groceries. Often internet cafes have 'net-to-phone' and 'net-to-net' capabilities (such as Skype), to talk for pennies or even for free.

Cell Phones

In Lima and other larger cities, you can buy cell phones in stands at the supermarket that use SIM cards for about S40, then pop in a SIM card that costs from S15. Credit can be purchased in pharmacies and supermarkets. Claro is a popular pay-as-you-go plan. Cell-phone rentals may be available in major cities and tourist centers. Cell-phone reception may be poor in the mountains or jungle.

Phone Codes

When calling Peru from abroad, dial the international access code for the country you're in, then Peru's country code (51), then the area code without the 0 and finally, the local number. When making international calls from Peru, dial the international access code (00), then the country code of where you're calling to, then the area code and finally, the local phone number.

In Peru, any telephone number beginning with a 9 is a cell-phone number. Numbers beginning with 0800 are often toll free only when dialed from private phones. To make a credit-card or collect call using AT&T, dial 0800-50288. For an online telephone directory, see www.paginasamarillas.com.pe.

Phone Cards

Called *tarjetas telefónicas*, these cards are widely available and are made by many companies in many price ranges, with some designed for international calls.

Time

- Peru is five hours behind Greenwich Mean Time (GMT). It's the same as Eastern Standard Time (EST) in North America. At noon in Lima, it's 9am in Los Angeles, 11am in Mexico City, noon in New York, 5pm in London and 4am (following day) in Sydney.
- Daylight saving time (DST) isn't used in Peru, so add an hour to all of these times between the first Sunday in April and the last Sunday in October.
- Punctuality is not one of the things that Latin America is famous for, so be prepared to wait around. Buses rarely depart or arrive on time. Savvy travelers should allow some flexibility in their itineraries.
- Bring your own travel alarm clock – tours and long-distance buses often depart before 6am.

Toilets

Peruvian plumbing leaves something to be desired. There's always a chance that flushing a toilet will cause it to overflow, so you should avoid putting anything other than human waste into the toilet. Even a small amount of toilet paper can muck up the entire system – that's why a small, plastic bin is routinely provided for disposing of the paper. This may not seem sanitary, but it is definitely better than the alternative of clogged toilets and flooded floors. A well-run hotel or restaurant, even a cheap one, will empty the bin and clean the toilet daily. In rural areas, there may be just a rickety wooden outhouse built around a hole in the ground.

Public toilets are rare outside of transportation terminals, restaurants and museums, but restaurants will generally let travelers use a restroom (sometimes for a charge). Those in terminals usually have an attendant who will charge you about S0.50 to enter and then give you a few sheets of toilet paper. Public restrooms frequently run out of toilet paper, so always carry extra.

Travelers with Disabilities

Peru offers few conveniences for travelers with disabilities. Features such as signs in Braille or phones for the hearing-impaired are virtually nonexistent, while wheelchair ramps and lifts are few and far between, and the pavement is often badly potholed and cracked. Most hotels do not have wheelchair-accessible rooms, at least not rooms specially designated as such. Bathrooms are often barely large enough for an able-bodied person to walk into, so few are accessible to wheelchairs.

Nevertheless, there are Peruvians with disabilities who get around, mainly through the help of others.

Access-Able Travel Source (www.access-able.com) Partial listings of accessible transportation and tours, accommodations, attractions and restaurants.

Apumayo Expediciones (☎/fax 084-24-6018; apumayo.com; Jr Ricardo Palma Ñ-11, Urb Santa Monica Wanchaq, Cuzco) An adventure-tour company that takes disabled travelers to Machu Picchu and other historic sites in the Sacred Valley.

Conadis (Map p64; ☎01-332-0808; www.conadisperu.gob.pe; Av Arequipa 375, Santa Beatriz, Lima) Governmental agency for Spanish-language information and advocacy for people with disabilities.

Emerging Horizons (www.emerginghorizons.com) Travel magazine for the mobility-impaired, with handy advice columns and news articles.

Mobility International (☎541-343 1284; www.miusa.org; 132 E Broadway, Suite 343, Eugene, USA) Advises disabled travelers on mobility issues and runs an educational exchange program.

Visas

- With a few exceptions, visas are not required for travelers entering Peru. Tourists are permitted a 183-day, nonextendable stay, stamped into passports and onto a tourist card called a Tarjeta Andina de Migración (Andean Immigration Card). Keep it – it must be returned upon exiting the country. If you need the full amount of time, ask the immigration officer at the point of entry, since they have a tendency to issue 30- or 90-day stays.
- If you lose your tourist card, visit an *oficina de migraciónes* (immigration office; www.migraciones.gob.pe) for a replacement. Information in English can be found online. Extensions are no longer officially available.
- Anyone who plans to work, attend school or reside in Peru for any length of time must obtain a visa in advance. Do this through the Peruvian embassy or consulate in your home country.
- Carry your passport and tourist card on your person at all times, especially in remote areas (it's required by law on the Inca Trail). For security, make a photocopy of both documents and keep them in a separate place from the originals.

Volunteering

General advice for finding volunteer work is to ask at language schools; they usually know of several programs suitable for their students. South American Explorers (SAE) has an online volunteer database and also folders with reports left by foreign volunteers at the SAE clubhouses in Lima (p100) and Cuzco (p232).

Both nonprofit and for-profit organizations can arrange volunteer opportunities, if you contact them in advance.

Action Without Borders (www.idealist.org) Online database of social-work-oriented jobs, internships and volunteer opportunities.

Cross-Cultural Solutions (☎in UK 0845-458-2781, in USA 800-380-4777; www.crossculturalsolutions.org) Educational and social-service projects in Lima and Ayacucho; program fees include professional in-country support.

Earthwatch Institute (☎in USA 800-776-0188; www.earthwatch.org) Pay to help scientists on archaeological, ecological and other real-life expeditions in the Amazon Basin and the Andes.

Global Crossroad (☎in UK 0800-310-1821, in USA 866-387-7816; www.globalcrossroad.com) Volunteer, internship and job programs in the Andes. Summer cultural-immersion programs for 18- to 29-year-olds include language instruction, homestays, volunteer work and sightseeing.

Global Volunteers (☎in USA 800-487-1074; www.globalvolunteers.org; 375 E Little Canada Rd, St Paul, USA) Offers short-term volunteer opportunities helping orphans in Lima.

HoPe Foundation (☎084-24-9885, in the Netherlands 0413-47-3666; www.stichting-hope.org; Casilla 59, Correo Central, Cuzco) Provides educational and health care support in the Andes.

Kiya Survivors/Peru Positive Action (☎in UK 1273-721902; www.kiyasurvivors.org; 1 Sussex Rd, Hove, UK) Organizes two- to six-month volunteer placements for assistant teachers and therapists to work with special-needs children in Cuzco, Urubamba in the Sacred Valley and Máncora on the north coast.

ProWorld Service Corps (ProPeru; ☎in UK 0-18-6559-6289, in USA 877-429-6753; www.proworldsc.org) This highly recommended organization offers two- to 26-week cultural, service and academic experiences, including in the Sacred Valley and the Amazon. It has links with affiliated NGOs throughout Peru and can organize placements for individuals or groups.

Volunteers for Peace (VFP; ☎802-259-2759; www.vfp.org; 7 Kilburn Street, Ste 316, Burlington, Vermont, USA) Places volunteers in short-term work-camp programs, usually in Lima or Ayacucho. Program fees are more than reasonable and may be partially paid directly to local communities.

Women Travelers

Machismo is alive and well in Latin America. Most female travelers to Peru will experience little more than shouts of *mi amor* (my love) or an appreciative hiss. If you are fair-skinned with blond hair, be prepared to be the center of attention. Peruvian men consider foreign women to have looser morals than Peruvian women and will often make flirtatious comments to single women.

Unwanted attention Staring, whistling, hissing and catcalls in the streets are run-of-the-mill. Many men make a pastime of dropping *piropos* (cheeky, flirtatious or even vulgar 'compliments'). However, these are generally not meant to be insulting. Most men rarely follow up on the idle chatter (unless they feel you've insulted their manhood). Ignoring provocation and staring ahead is generally the best response. If someone is persistent, try an ardor-smothering phrase such as *soy casada* (I'm married). If you appeal directly to locals, you'll find most Peruvians to be protective of lone women, expressing surprise and concern if you tell them you're traveling without your family or husband.

Bricheros It's not uncommon for fast-talking charmers, especially in tourist towns such as Cuzco, to attach themselves to gringas. Known in Peru as *bricheros*, many of these young Casanovas are looking for a meal ticket, so approach any professions of love with extreme skepticism. This happens to men too.

First impressions Outside of a few big cities, it is rare for a woman to belly up to a bar for a beer, and the ones that do tend to be prostitutes. If you feel the need for an evening cocktail, opt for a restaurant. Likewise, heavy drinking might be misinterpreted by some men as a sign of promiscuity. When meeting someone, make it very clear if only friendship is intended. This goes double for tour and activity guides. When meeting someone for the first time, it is also wise not to divulge where you are staying until you feel sure that you can trust them.

Sexual Assault

As in any part of the world, the possibilities of rape and assault do exist. Use your big-city smarts (even in small towns). Travelers who are sexually assaulted can report it to the nearest police station or to the tourist police. However, Peruvian attitudes toward sexual assaults favor the attackers, not the survivors. Rape is often seen as a disgrace, and it is difficult to prosecute. Because the police tend to be unhelpful, we recommend calling your embassy or consulate to ask for advice, including on where to seek medical treatment, which should be an immediate priority. A few tips:

- Do not hitchhike or take unlicensed taxis (licensed taxis have a number on the door and an authorization sticker on the windshield).
- Avoid walking alone in unfamiliar places at night.
- If a stranger approaches you on the street and asks a question, answer it if you feel comfortable – but don't stop walking as it could allow potential attackers to surround you.
- Avoid overnight buses through bandit-ridden areas.
- Be aware of your surroundings; attacks have occurred in broad daylight around well-touristed sites and popular trekking trails.
- When hiring a private tour or activity guide, seek a recommended or reliable agency.

Practicalities

- In highland towns, dress is generally fairly conservative and women rarely wear shorts, opting instead for long skirts. Shorts, miniskirts and revealing blouses may draw unwanted attention.
- Tampons are difficult to find in smaller towns, so stock up in major cities.
- Birth-control pills and contraceptives (even condoms) are scarce outside metropolitan areas and not always reliable, so bring your own from home. Rates of HIV infection are on the rise.
- Abortions are illegal, except to save the life of the mother.

Useful Organizations

Centro de La Mujer Peruana Flora Tristán (Map p64; ☎01-433-1457; www.flora.org.pe; Parque Hernán Velarde 14, Lima; ⏲1-5pm Mon-Fri) Feminist social and political advocacy group for women's and human rights in Peru, with a Spanish-language website and a library in Lima.

Instituto Peruano de Paternidad Responsable (Inppares; ☎01-583-9012; www.inppares.org.pe) Planned Parenthood–affiliated organization that runs a dozen sexual and reproductive health clinics for both women and men around the country, including in Lima.

Work

It's increasingly difficult to obtain residence and work permits for Peru, and likewise to get jobs without a proper work visa. Some jobs teaching English in language schools may not require one, but this is illegal. Occasionally, schools advertise for teachers, but more often, jobs are found by word of mouth. Schools expect you to be a native English speaker, and the pay is low. If you have teaching credentials, so much the better.

American and British schools in Lima sometimes hire teachers of math, biology and other subjects, but usually only if you apply in advance. They pay much better than the language schools, and might possibly be able to help you get a work visa if you want to stay. In Lima, the South American Explorers (p100) clubhouse and international cultural centers may have contacts with schools that are looking for teachers.

Most other jobs are obtained by word of mouth, but the possibilities are limited.

Transportation

GETTING THERE & AWAY

Flights, cars and tours can be booked online at lonelyplanet.com/bookings.

Entering the Country

Travelers should have their passport valid for at least six months beyond their departure date. When arriving by air, US citizens must show a return ticket or open-jaw onward ticket.

Upon arrival, immigration officials may only stamp 30 days into a passport though the limit is 180 days. If this happens, explain how many more days you need, supported by an exit ticket for onward or return travel.

Bribery (known colloquially as *coima*) is illegal, but some officials may try to procure extra 'fees' at land borders. See p535 for more.

Air

Peru (mainly Lima) has direct flights to and from cities all over the Americas, as well as continental Europe. Other locations require a connection. The international departure tax is included in ticket costs.

Airports & Airlines

Located in the port city of Callao, Lima's **Aeropuerto Internacional Jorge Chávez** (☎01-517-3500, schedules 01-511-6055; www.lap.com.pe) has terminals sparkling with shopping and services. A major hub, it's serviced by flights from North, Central and South America, and two regular direct flights from Europe (Madrid and Amsterdam). Check the airport website or call for updated departure and arrival schedules for domestic and international flights. Cuzco has the only other airport with international services.

Tickets

Peak season From most places in the world, South America can be a relatively costly destination. The high season for air travel to and within Peru is late May to early September, as well as around major holidays. Look for lower fares outside peak periods.

Discounts Shopping around online can turn up cheaper tickets. Students with international student identity cards (ISIC is one widely recognized card) and anyone under 26 can often get discounts with budget or specialty travel agencies. A good option to check out is **STA Travel** (www.statravel.com), with offices around the globe.

Tax Tickets bought in Peru are subject to a 19% tax (included in the ticket price).

Reconfirming flights It is essential to reconfirm all flights 72 hours in advance, either by phone or online, or you may get bumped off the flight. If you are traveling in remote areas, have a reputable travel agent do this for you.

CLIMATE CHANGE & TRAVEL

Every form of transport that relies on carbon-based fuel generates CO_2, the main cause of human-induced climate change. Modern travel is dependent on airplanes, which might use less fuel per mile per person than most cars but travel much greater distances. The altitude at which aircraft emit gases (including CO_2) and particles also contributes to their climate change impact. Many websites offer 'carbon calculators' that allow people to estimate the carbon emissions generated by their journey and, for those who wish to do so, to offset the impact of the greenhouse gases emitted with contributions to portfolios of climate-friendly initiatives throughout the world. Lonely Planet offsets the carbon footprint of all staff and author travel.

Peru Air Routes

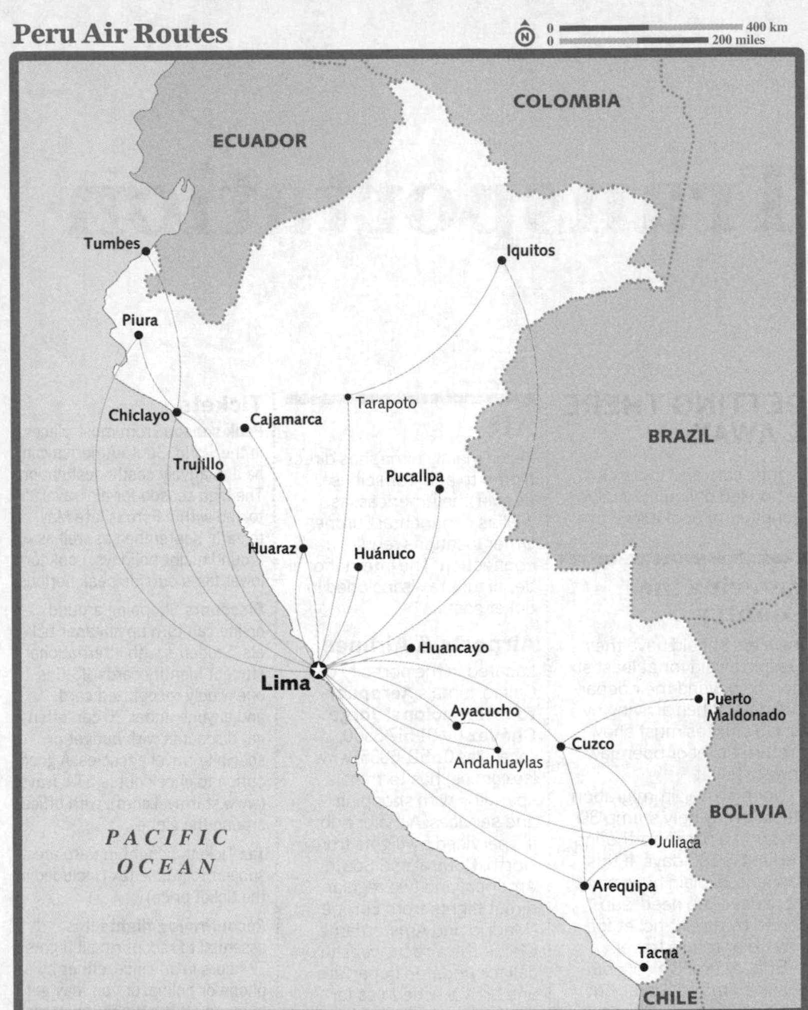

Australia & New Zealand

Santiago, Chile tends to be the most common gateway city from Australia and New Zealand, though some carriers connect through the US as well.

South American Travel Centre (☎03-9642-5353; www.satc.com.au) In Australia, this agency specializes in travel to Latin America.

Canada

There are direct flights to Lima from Toronto, but most trips require a connection in the US or Mexico City.

Continental Europe

There are direct flights from Amsterdam and Madrid, but connections through the USA, Central America or Colombia are often cheaper.

Latin America

There are direct flights from a large number of Latin American cities to Peru, including Bogotá, Leticia, Buenos Aires, Caracas, Guayaquil, La Paz, Mexico City, Panama City, Quito, Rio de Janeiro, San José (Costa Rica), Santiago (Chile) and São Paulo. LAN, Copa and TACA are the principal Latin American airlines that fly to Lima.

Al Mundo Viajes (almundo.com.ar) Travel agency in Mexico, Argentina and Uruguay.

Student Travel Bureau (STB; ☎11-3038-1551; www.stb.com.br) Travel agency in Brazil.

UK & Ireland

Flights from the UK or Ireland connect through gateway cities in continental Europe, North America and Brazil.

In the UK, a number of agencies specialize in travel to Latin America.

Journey Latin America (JLA; ☎020-3582-8751; www.journeylatinamerica.co.uk)

North-South Travel (☎01245 608 291; www.northsouthtravel.co.uk) North-South Travel donates part of its profit to projects in the developing world.

USA

There are direct (nonstop) flights to Lima from Atlanta, Dallas-Fort Worth, Houston, Los Angeles, Miami and New York. In other cases, flights will connect either in the US or in Latin American gateway cities such as Mexico City and Bogotá.

Exito Travel (☎800-655-4053; www.exitotravel.com)

Latin America for Less (☎1-817-230-4971; www.latinamericaforless.com)

Land & River

Because no roads bridge the Darien Gap, it is not possible to travel to South America by land from the north (unless you spend a week making your way through swampy, drug-dealer-infested jungle). Driving overland from neighboring Bolivia, Brazil, Chile, Colombia and Ecuador requires careful logistical planning.

Ormeño (☎01-472-1710; www.grupo-ormeno.com.pe) is the main international bus company that goes to Chile, Ecuador, Colombia, Bolivia and Argentina. Smaller regional companies do cross-border travel, but on a more-limited basis. The only rail service that crosses the Peru border is the train between Arica, Chile, and Tacna on Peru's south coast.

Getting to Peru by boat is possible from points on the Amazon River in Brazil and from Leticia, Colombia. There are also port cities on Peru's Pacific coast.

With any form of transport, it may be a bit cheaper to buy tickets to the border, cross over and then buy onward tickets on the other side, but it's usually much easier, faster and safer to buy a cross-border through ticket. When traveling by bus, check carefully with the company about what is included in the price of the ticket, and whether the service is direct or involves a transfer, and possibly a long wait, at the border.

Bolivia

Peru is normally reached overland from Bolivia via Lake Titicaca; the border crossing at Yunguyo is much safer and a lot less chaotic than its counterpart at Desaguadero. There are many transportation options for both of these routes, most of which involve changing buses at the Peru–Bolivia border before reaching Puno. It's possible, but a logistical feat, to cross into Bolivia from Puerto Maldonado.

Brazil

You can travel overland between Peru and Brazil via Iñapari. Traveling from Iquitos, it's more straightforward to go along the Amazon to Tabatinga in Brazil via Leticia, Colombia.

Chile

Traveling on the Pan-American Hwy, the major crossing point is between Arica, Chile, and Tacna on Peru's south coast.

Long-distance buses to Tacna depart from Lima, Arequipa and Puno. *Colectivo* (shared) taxis are the fastest and most reliable way to travel between Tacna and Arica. It's also possible to make the crossing, albeit much more slowly, by train; border formalities are done at the respective stations. Flights to Tacna from Arequipa are cheap but book up quickly. Alternatively, Ormeño runs through buses from Lima all the way to Santiago, Chile. From Arequipa, Ormeño goes to Santiago, Chile, and Buenos Aires.

Colombia

It is easiest to travel between Peru and Colombia via Ecuador. Ormeño has through buses between Lima and Bogotá via Ecuador. This long-haul trip is better done in stages, though.

If you are in the rainforest, it is more straightforward to voyage along the Amazon by boat between Iquitos and Leticia, Colombia, from where there are flights to Bogotá.

Ecuador

The most common way to get to or from Ecuador is along the Pan-American Hwy via Tumbes, where there is a new border building. Another route is via La Tina to Loja in Ecuador. A third way is via Jaén.

Cifa (☎072-52-5120; www.cifainternacional.com; Tumbes 958) runs buses between Tumbes in Peru and Machala or Guayaquil in Ecuador.

Transportes Loja (☎073-30-5446) runs buses between Piura in Peru and Machala or Loja in Ecuador. Ormeño has weekly through buses between Lima and Quito.

Tours

Travelers who prefer not to travel on their own, or have a limited amount of time have ample tours to choose from. Travel with knowledgeable guides comes at a premium. It's worth it for highly specialized outdoor activities like river running, mountaineering, bird-watching or mountain biking.

If you want to book a tour locally, Lima, Cuzco, Arequipa, Puno, Trujillo, Huaraz, Puerto Maldonado and

Iquitos have the most travel agencies offering organized tours. For more specialized, individual or small-group tours, you can hire a bilingual guide starting at US$20 an hour or US$80 a day plus expenses (exchange rates may affect this); tours in other languages may be more expensive. Students or unregistered guides are cheaper – some are good, others aren't.

For more guide listings, check out www.leaplocal.org, a resource promoting socially responsible tourism.

From Australia & New Zealand

Aspiring Adventures (☎in USA & Canada 1-877-438-1354, in Australia 03 489 7474; www.aspiringadventures.com) A small, enthusiastic outfit that's Kiwi-Australian run with extensive experience in Cuzco and the Sacred Valley. Does biking, classic trips and food-focused tours.

Majestic Peru (☎944-214-899; majesticperu.com) A responsible independent operator with a sustainable ethos, good guides and a selection of interesting activities beyond your typical package tour.

Peregrine Adventures (☎855-832-4859; www.peregrineadventures.com) Hotel-based and trekking trips.

Tucan Travel (☎in Australia 1300 769 249, in Cuzco 084-241-123; www.tucantravel.com; 217 Alison Rd, Randwick, Sydney) Long-running tour operator specializing in Latin America provides a wide variety of options in Peru; also has an office in Cuzco.

From Canada & the USA

With easy flight connections, the USA has more companies offering tours of Peru than the rest of the world.

Adventure Life (☎406-541-2677, 800-344-6118; www.adventure-life.com; 712 W Spruce St, Ste 1, Missoula, MT 5980) Andean trekking, Amazon exploring and multisport itineraries; reputable agency that uses bilingual guides, family-run hotels and local transportation.

Explorations (☎800-446-9660, 239-992-9660; www.explorationsinc.com; 27655 Kent Rd, Bonita Springs, FL 34135) Amazon trips include biologist-escorted cruises, lodge-based expeditions and fishing trips in the Reserva Nacional Pacaya-Samiria.

G Adventures (☎1-416-260-0999; www.gadventures.com; 19 Charlotte St, Toronto, ON M5V 2H5) The premier Canadian agency with offices in Vancouver, Boston, USA, and London, UK. Budget-priced tours include hotel-based, trekking, Amazon and cultural trips.

International Expeditions (☎205-428-1700, 800-230-7665; www.ietravel.com; One Environs Park, Helena, AL 35080) Offers Amazon tours, staying in jungle lodges or on river boats, with an emphasis on natural history and bird-watching.

Mountain Travel Sobek (☎510-594-6000, 888-831-7526; www.mtsobek.com; 1266 66th St, Emeryville, CA 94608) Luxury trekking tours along the Inca Trail or in the Cordillera Blanca, and occasional rafting trips on the Río Tambopata.

Sacred Rides (☎647-999-7955, 888-423-7849; sacredrides.com; 261 Markham St, Toronto, ON M6J 2G7) A mountain-biking specialist that organizes various multiday bike tours throughout the Peruvian Andes.

Southwind Adventures (☎303-972-0701, 800-377-9463; www.southwindadventures.com; PO Box 621057, Littleton, CO 80162) Peruvian-American tour operator with trekking, cycling, rafting and boat-cruise itineraries in the Andes, the Amazon and the Galapagos Islands.

Wilderness Travel (☎510-558-2488, 800-368-2794; www.wildernesstravel.com; 1102 Ninth St, Berkeley, CA 94710) Offers luxury treks, from four nights to two weeks, throughout the highlands and the Amazon.

Wildland Adventures (☎206-365-0686, 800-345-4453; www.wildland.com; 3516 NE 155th St, Seattle, WA 98155) Environmentally sound, culturally sensitive treks around the Sacred Valley and the Cordillera Blanca, as well as Amazon tours.

From the UK & Continental Europe

Andean Trails (☎in UK 44-131-467-7086; www.andeantrails.co.uk; 33 Sandport St, Lieth, Edinburgh, Scotland EH6 5QG) Mountain-biking, climbing, trekking and rafting tours in some unusual spots.

Exodus (☎in UK 44-208-675-5550; www.exodus.co.uk; Grange Mills, Weir Rd, London SW12 ONE, England) Award-winning, responsible-travel operator offering long-distance overland trips and shorter cultural and trekking adventures.

Hauser Exkursionen (☎in Germany 89-235-0060; www.hauser-exkursionen.de; Spiegelstrasse 9, D-81241 Munich, Germany) A German sustainable-tour operator.

Huwans Clubaventure (☎in France 04 96 1510 20; www.clubaventure.fr; 18 rue Séguier, 75006 Paris, France) A reputable French company organizing treks and tours.

Journey Latin America (☎in UK 020-3432-9702; www.journeylatinamerica.co.uk; 12 & 13 Heathfield Tce, Chiswick, London W4 4JE, UK) Cultural trips and treks in the Cordilleras Blanca and Huayhuash and to Machu Picchu.

GETTING AROUND

Peru has a constant procession of flights and buses connecting the country. In particular, driving routes to the jungle have improved drastically. Keep in mind, poor weather conditions can cancel flights and buses. Strikes can be another obstacle in regional travel – consult travel experts on the routes you will be taking.

Air

Domestic-flight schedules and prices change frequently. New airlines open every year, as those with poor safety records close. Most big cities are served by modern jets, while smaller towns are served by propeller aircraft.

Airlines in Peru

Most domestic airlines have offices in Lima. Smaller carriers and charters are also an option. The most remote towns may require connecting flights, and smaller towns are not served every day. Many airports for these places are no more than a dirt strip.

Be at the airport two hours before your flight departs. Flights may be overbooked, baggage handling and check-in procedures tend to be chaotic, and flights may even leave *before* their official departure time because of predicted bad weather.

Most airlines fly from Lima to regional capitals, but service between provincial cities is limited.

LAN (LPE; ☎01-213-8200; www.lan.com) Peru's major domestic carrier flies to Arequipa, Chiclayo, Cuzco, Iquitos, Juliaca, Piura, Puerto Maldonado, Tacna, Tarapoto, Trujillo and Tumbes. Additionally it offers link services between Arequipa and Cuzco, Arequipa and Juliaca, Arequipa and Tacna, Cuzco and Juliaca, and Cuzco and Puerto Maldonado.

LC Peru (☎01-204-1313; www.lcperu.pe; Av Pablo Carriquirry 857, San Isidro) Flies from Lima to Andahuaylas, Ayacucho, Cajamarca, Huánuco, Huaraz, Iquitos and Huancayo (Jauja) on smaller turbo-prop aircraft.

Peruvian Airlines (www.peruvianairlines.pe) Flies to Lima, Arequipa, Cuzco, Piura, Iquitos and Tacna.

Star Perú (SRU; ☎01-705-9000; www.starperu.com) Domestic carrier, flying to Ayacucho, Cajamarca, Cuzco, Huancayo (Jauja), Iquitos, Pucallpa, Puerto Maldonado, Talara and Tarapoto; with link service between Tarapoto and Iquitos.

Tickets

Most travelers travel in one direction overland and save time returning by air. You can sometimes buy tickets at the airport on a space-available basis, but don't count on it.

Peak season The peak season for air travel within Peru is late May to early September, as well as around major holidays. Buy tickets for less popular destinations as far in advance as possible, as these infrequent flights book up quickly. It's almost impossible to buy tickets just before major holidays, notably Semana Santa (the week leading up to Easter) and Fiestas Patrias (the last week in July). Overbooking is the norm.

Discounts Domestic flights are usually cheaper when advertised on the Peruvian website (vs its international version), so if you can wait until you arrive in Peru to buy regional tickets, you may save money.

Reconfirming flights In remote areas, buying tickets and reconfirming flights is best done at airline offices; otherwise, you can do so online or via a recommended travel agent. Ensure all flight reservations are *confirmed and reconfirmed* 72 and 24 hours in advance; airlines are notorious for overbooking and flights are changed or canceled with surprising frequency, so it's even worth calling the airport or the airline just before leaving for the airport. Confirmation is especially essential during the peak travel season.

Bicycle

Safety The major drawback to cycling in Peru is the country's bounty of kamikaze motorists. On narrow, two-lane highways, drivers can be a serious hazard to cyclists. Cycling is more enjoyable and safer, though very challenging, off paved roads. Mountain bikes are recommended, as road bikes won't stand up to the rough conditions.

Rentals Reasonably priced rentals (mostly mountain bikes) are available in popular tourist destinations, including Cuzco, Arequipa, Huaraz and Huancayo. These bikes are rented to travelers for local excursions, not to make trips all over the country. For long-distance touring, bring your own bike from home.

Transporting bicycles Airline policies on carrying bicycles vary, so shop around.

Boat

There are no passenger services along the Peruvian coast. In the Andean highlands, there are boat services on Lake Titicaca. Small motorized vessels take passengers from the port in Puno to visit various islands on the lake, while catamarans zip over to Bolivia.

In Peru's Amazon Basin, boat travel is of major importance. Larger vessels ply the wider rivers. Dugout canoes powered by outboard engines act as water taxis on smaller rivers. Those called *peki-pekis* are slow and rather noisy. In some places, modern aluminum launches are used.

Cargo Boat

Some travelers dream of plying the Amazon while swinging in a hammock aboard a banana boat with cargo on the lower deck. It's possible to travel from Pucallpa or Yurimaguas to Iquitos and on into Brazil this way.

Departures At ports, chalkboards with ships' names, destinations and departure times are displayed; these are usually optimistic. The captain has to clear documents with the *capitanía* (harbor master's office) on the day of departure, so directly ask the captain for updates. Nobody else really knows. Departure time often depends on a full cargo. Usually, you can sleep on the boat while waiting if you want to save on hotel bills. Never leave your luggage unattended.

Sleeping Bring your own hammock, or rent a cabin for the journey. If using a hammock, hang it away from the noisy engine room and not directly under a light, as these are often lit late at night, precluding sleep and attracting insects. Cabins are often hot, airless boxes, but are lockable. Sanitary facilities are basic and there's usually a pump shower on board.

Eating Basic food is usually included in the price of the passage, and may be marginally better on the bigger ships, or if you are in cabin class. Finicky eaters or people with dietary restrictions should bring their own food. Bottled soft drinks are usually available.

Bus

Buses are the usual form of transportation for most Peruvians and many travelers. Fares are cheap and services are frequent on the major long-distance routes, but buses are of varying quality. Remote rural routes are often served by older, worn-out vehicles. Seats at the back of the bus yield a bumpier ride.

Many cities do not have a main bus terminal. Buses rarely arrive or depart on time, so consider most average trip times as best-case scenarios. Buses can be significantly delayed during the rainy season, particularly in the highlands and the jungle. From January to April, journey times may double or face indefinite delays from landslides and bad road conditions.

Fatal accidents are not unusual in Peru. Avoid overnight buses, on which muggings and assaults are more likely to occur.

Classes

Luxury buses Invariably called Imperial, Royal, Business or Executive, these higher-priced express services feature toilets, videos and air-conditioning. Luxury buses serve paltry snacks and don't stop.

Bus-camas Feature seats which recline halfway or almost fully. Better long-distance buses stop for bathroom breaks and meals in special rest areas with inexpensive but sometimes unappetizing fare. Almost every bus terminal has a few kiosks with basic provisions.

Económico For trips under six hours, you may have no choice but to take an *económico* bus, and these are usually pretty beaten up. While *económico* services don't stop for meals, vendors will board and sell snacks.

Costs & Reservations

Schedules and fares change frequently and vary from company to company; therefore, quoted prices are only approximations.

Fares fluctuate during peak and off-peak travel times. For long-distance or overnight journeys, or travel to remote areas with only limited services, buy your ticket at least the day before. Most travel agencies offer reservations but shockingly overcharge for the ticket. Except in Lima, it's cheaper to take a taxi to the bus terminal and buy the tickets yourself.

You can check schedules online (but not make reservations, at least not yet) for the major players, including the following:

Cruz del Sur (www.cruzdelsur.com.pe)

Oltursa (www.oltursa.com.pe)

Ormeño (☎022-779-3443; www.grupo-ormeno.com.pe)

Transportes Línea (www.transporteslinea.com.pe)

Luggage

Watch your luggage in bus terminals very carefully. Some terminals have left-luggage facilities.

Bags put into the luggage compartment are generally safe. Hand luggage is a different matter. Items may be taken while you sleep. For this reason, never use the overhead compartments and bring only items which can fit below your legs or on your lap.

Car & Motorcycle

➡ Distances in Peru are long so it's best to bus or fly to a region and rent a car from there. Hiring a taxi is often cheaper and easier.

➡ At roadside checkpoints police or military conduct meticulous document checks. Drivers who offer an officer some money to smooth things along consider it a 'gift' or 'on-the-spot fine' to get on their way. Readers should know that these transactions are an unsavory reality in Peru and Lonely Planet does not condone them.

➡ When filling up with gas, make sure the meter starts at zero.

Driver's License

A driver's license from your own home country is sufficient for renting a car. An International Driving Permit (IDP) is only required if you'll be driving in Peru for more than 30 days.

Rental

Major rental companies have offices in Lima and a few other large cities. Renting a motorcycle is an option mainly in jungle towns, where you can go for short runs around town on dirt bikes, but not much further.

Economy car rental starts at US$25 a day without the 19% sales tax, 'super' collision-damage waiver, personal accident insurance and so on, which together can climb to more than US$100 per day, not including excess mileage. Vehicles with 4WD are more expensive.

Make sure you completely understand the rental agreement before you sign. A credit card is required, and renters normally need to be over 25 years of age.

Road Rules & Hazards

Bear in mind that the condition of rental cars is often poor, roads are potholed (even the paved Pan-American Hwy), gas is expensive, and drivers are aggressive, regarding speed limits, road signs and traffic signals as mere guides, not the law. Moreover, road signs are often small and unclear.

- Driving is on the right-hand side of the road.
- Driving at night is not recommended because of poor conditions, speeding buses and slow-moving, poorly lit trucks.
- Theft is all too common, so you should not leave your vehicle parked on the street. When stopping overnight, park the car in a guarded lot (common in better hotels).
- Gasoline or petrol stations (called *grifos*) are few and far between.

Hitchhiking

Hitchhiking is never entirely safe in any country in the world and is not recommended. Travelers who decide to hitchhike should understand that they are taking a serious risk. Hitchhikers will be safer if they travel in pairs and let someone know where they are planning to go. In Peru hitchhiking is not very practical, as there are few private cars, buses are so cheap and trucks are often used as paid public transportation in remote areas.

Local Transportation

In most towns and cities, it's easy to walk everywhere or take a taxi. Using local buses, *micros* and *combis* can be tricky, but very inexpensive.

Bus

Local buses are slow and crowded but cheap. Ask locals for help, as there aren't any obvious bus lines in most towns.

A faster, more hair-raising alternative is to take *micros* or *combis,* sometimes called *colectivos* (though the term usually refers to taxis). Typically, *micros* and *combis* are minibuses or minivans stuffed full of passengers. They can be identified by stickers along the outside panels and destination placards in the front windows. You can flag one down or get off anywhere on the route. A conductor usually leans out of the vehicle, shouting out destinations. Once inside, you must quickly squeeze into any available seat, or be prepared to stand. The conductor comes around to collect the fare, or you can pay when getting off. Safety is not a high priority for *combi* drivers. The only place for a passenger to safely buckle up is the front seat, but in the event of a head-on collision (not an unusual occurrence), that's the last place you'd want to be.

Taxi

Taxis seem to be everywhere. Private cars that have a small taxi sticker in the windshield aren't necessarily regulated. Safer, regulated taxis usually have a lit company number on the roof and are reached by phone. These are more expensive than taxis flagged down on the street, but are more reliable.

Fares Always ask the fare in advance, as there are no meters. It's acceptable to haggle; try to find out what the going rate is before taking a cab, especially for long trips. The standard fare for short runs in most cities is around S5.

Tipping Tipping is not the norm, unless you have hired a driver for a long period or he has helped you with luggage or other lifting.

Long-distance trips Hiring a private taxi for long-distance trips costs less than renting a car and takes care of many of the problems with car rental. Not all taxi drivers will agree to drive long distances, but if one does, you should carefully check the driver's credentials and vehicle before hiring.

Train

The privatized rail system, **PeruRail** (*www.perurail.com*), has daily services between Cuzco and Aguas Calientes, aka Machu Picchu Pueblo, and services between Cuzco and Puno on the shores of Lake Titicaca three times a week. Passenger services between Puno and Arequipa have been suspended indefinitely, but will run as a charter for groups. **Inca Rail** (Map p200; ☎084-25-2974; www.incarail.com; Portal de Panes 105, Plaza de Armas; ⏱8am-9pm Mon-Fri, 9am-7pm Sat, to 2pm Sun) also offers service between Ollantaytambo and Aguas Calientes.

Train buffs won't want to miss the lovely **Ferrocarril Central Andino** (☎01-226-6363; www.ferrocarrilcentral.com.pe), which reaches a head-spinning altitude of 4829m. It usually runs between Lima and Huancayo weekly from mid-April through October. In Huancayo, cheaper trains to Huancavelica leave daily from a different station. Another charmingly historic railway makes inexpensive daily runs between Tacna on Peru's south coast and Arica, Chile.

Health

It's not unusual to suffer from altitude sickness in the Andes or tummy problems, despite Peru's wonderful culinary reputation. Peru's many climates mean that travellers will face different risks in different areas. While food-borne as well as mosquito-borne infections happen, many of these illnesses are not life-threatening. However, they can certainly ruin your trip. Besides getting the proper vaccinations, it's important that you take insect repellent and exercise care in what you eat and drink.

BEFORE YOU GO

Since most vaccines don't produce immunity until at least two weeks after they're given, visit a physician four to eight weeks before departure.

Ask your doctor for an International Certificate of Vaccination (otherwise known as the 'yellow booklet'), which will list all the vaccinations you've received. This is mandatory for countries that require proof of yellow-fever vaccination upon entry, but it's a good idea to carry it wherever you travel.

Bring medications in their original containers, clearly labeled. A signed, dated letter from your physician describing all medical conditions and medications, including generic names, is also a good idea. If carrying syringes or needles, be sure to have a physician's letter documenting their medical necessity.

Most doctors and hospitals expect payment in cash, regardless of whether you have travel health insurance.

Insurance

All travelers should have health insurance. If yours does not cover medical expenses abroad, consider supplemental insurance. Find out in advance if your insurance plan will make payments directly to providers or reimburse you later for overseas health expenditures.

Recommended Vaccinations

The only required vaccine for Peru is yellow fever, and that's only if you're arriving from a yellow-fever-infected country in Africa or the Americas. It is strongly advised, though, for those visiting the jungle, as are malaria pills.

Diseases found in Peru include mosquito-borne infections such as malaria, yellow fever and dengue fever, although these are rare in temperate regions.

Medical Checklist

- ☐ antibiotics
- ☐ antidiarrheal drugs (eg loperamide)
- ☐ acetaminophen (Tylenol) or aspirin
- ☐ anti-inflammatory drugs (eg ibuprofen)
- ☐ antihistamines (for hay fever and allergic reactions)
- ☐ antibacterial ointment (eg Bactroban; for cuts and abrasions)
- ☐ steroid cream or cortisone (for poison ivy and other allergic rashes)
- ☐ bandages, gauze, gauze rolls
- ☐ adhesive or paper tape
- ☐ scissors, safety pins, tweezers
- ☐ thermometer
- ☐ pocket knife
- ☐ insect repellent containing DEET (for the skin)
- ☐ insect spray containing permethrin (for clothing, tents and bed nets)
- ☐ sunblock
- ☐ oral rehydration salts
- ☐ iodine tablets (for water purification)
- ☐ acetazolamide (Diamox; for altitude sickness)

Websites

World Health Organization (www.who.int/ith) Free download of *International Travel and Health*.

MD Travel Health (www.mdtravelhealth.com) Travel-health recommendations.

IN PERU

Availability of Health Care

Lima has high-quality 24-hour medical clinics, and English-speaking doctors and dentists. See the guide at the website for the **US embassy** (lima.usembassy.gov/emergency_services.html). Rural areas may have the most basic medical services. You may have to pay in cash, regardless of whether you have travel insurance.

Life-threatening medical problems may require evacuation. For a list of medical evacuation and insurance companies, see the website of the **US State Department** (travel.state.gov/content/passports/en/go/health/insurance-providers.html).

Pharmacies are known as *farmacias* or *boticas*, identified by a green or red cross. They offer most of the medications available in other countries.

Infectious Diseases

Many of the following diseases are spread by mosquitoes. Take precautions to minimize the chance of being bitten. This will also protect against other insect-borne diseases like Baronellois (Oroya fever), leishmaniasis and Chagas' disease.

Cholera

An intestinal infection, cholera is acquired through contaminated food or water, resulting in profuse diarrhea, which may cause life-threatening dehydration. Treatment includes oral rehydration and possibly antibiotics.

Dengue Fever

A viral infection, dengue is transmitted by mosquitoes, which breed primarily in puddles and water containers. It is especially common in densely populated, urban environments, including Lima and Cuzco.

Flu-like symptoms include fever, muscle aches, joint pains, headache, nausea and vomiting, often followed by a rash. The body aches may be uncomfortable, but most cases resolve in a few days.

Take analgesics such as acetaminophen/paracetamol (Tylenol) and drink plenty of fluids. Severe cases may require hospitalization.

Malaria

Malaria is transmitted by mosquito bites, usually between dusk and dawn. High spiking fevers may be accompanied by chills, sweats, headache, body aches, weakness, vomiting or diarrhea. Severe cases may lead to seizures, confusion, coma and death.

Taking malaria pills is strongly recommended for all areas in Peru except Lima and its vicinity, the coastal areas south of Lima, and the highland areas (including around Cuzco, Machu Picchu, Lake Titicaca and Arequipa). Most cases in Peru occur in Loreto in the country's northeast, where

REQUIRED & RECOMMENDED VACCINATIONS

VACCINE	RECOMMENDED FOR	DOSAGE	POSSIBLE SIDE EFFECTS
chickenpox	travelers who've never had chickenpox	2 doses one month apart	fever; mild case of chickenpox
hepatitis A	all travelers	1 dose before trip; booster 6-12 months later	soreness at injection site; headaches; body aches
hepatitis B	long-term travelers in close contact with the local population	3 doses over 6-month period	soreness at injection site; low-grade fever
measles	travelers born after 1956 who have had only one measles vaccination	1 dose	fever; rash; joint pains; allergic reactions
rabies	travelers who may have contact with animals and may not have access to medical care	3 doses over 3-4 week period	soreness at injection site; headaches; body aches
tetanus-diphtheria	all travelers who haven't had a booster within 10 years	1 dose lasts 10 years	soreness at injection site
typhoid	all travelers	4 capsules by mouth, 1 taken every other day	abdominal pain; nausea; rash
yellow fever	all travelers	1 dose lasts 10 years	headaches; body aches; severe reactions are rare

transmission has reached epidemic levels.

Typhoid Fever

Caused by ingestion of food or water contaminated by *Salmonella typhi*, fever occurs in virtually all cases. Other symptoms may include headache, malaise, muscle aches, dizziness, loss of appetite, nausea and abdominal pain. Either diarrhea or constipation may occur. Possible complications include intestinal perforation or bleeding, confusion, delirium or, rarely, coma.

The vaccine is usually given orally, but is also available as an injection. The treatment drug is usually a quinolone antibiotic such as ciprofloxacin (Cipro) or levofloxacin (Levaquin).

Yellow Fever

A life-threatening viral infection, yellow fever is transmitted by mosquitoes in forested areas. Flu-like symptoms may include fever, chills, headache, muscle aches, backache, loss of appetite, nausea and vomiting. They usually subside in a few days, but one person in six enters a second, toxic phase characterized by recurrent fever, vomiting, listlessness, jaundice, kidney failure and hemorrhage which can lead to death. There is no treatment except for supportive care.

Yellow-fever vaccination is strongly recommended for all those who visit any jungle area of Peru at altitudes less than 2300m (7546ft). Most cases occur in the departments in the central jungle. Get vaccinated at least 10 days before any potential exposure; it remains effective for about 10 years.

Environmental Hazards

Altitude Sickness

Altitude sickness may result from rapid ascents to altitudes greater than 2500m (8100ft). In Peru, this includes Cuzco, Machu Picchu and Lake Titicaca. Being physically fit offers no protection. Symptoms may include headaches, nausea, vomiting, dizziness, malaise, insomnia and loss of appetite. Severe cases may be complicated by fluid in the lungs (high-altitude pulmonary edema) or swelling of the brain (high-altitude cerebral edema). If symptoms persist for more than 24 hours, descend immediately by at least 500m and see a doctor.

The best prevention is to spend two nights or more at each rise of 1000m. Diamox may be taken starting 24 hours before ascent. A natural alternative is ginkgo.

It's also important to avoid overexertion, eat light meals and abstain from alcohol. Altitude sickness should be taken seriously; it can be life threatening when severe.

Hypothermia

To prevent hypothermia, dress in layers: silk, wool and synthetic thermals are all good insulators. Essentials include a hat and a waterproof outer layer. Carry food and lots of fluid. An emergency space blanket can be highly useful.

Symptoms are exhaustion, numbness (particularly toes and fingers), shivering, slurred speech, irrational or violent behavior, lethargy, stumbling, dizzy spells, muscle cramps and violent bursts of energy.

To treat, go indoors and replace wet clothing with dry. Take hot liquids – no alcohol – and some high-calorie, easily digestible food. Do not rub victims, as rough handling may cause cardiac arrest.

Mosquito Bites

The best prevention is wearing long sleeves, long pants, hats and shoes (rather than sandals). Use insect repellent with 25% to 35% DEET. Protection usually lasts about six hours. Children age two to 12 should use formulas with 10% DEET or less, which lasts about three hours.

Insect repellents containing certain botanical products, including eucalyptus oil and soybean oil, are effective but last only 1½ to two hours.

If sleeping outdoors or in accommodations where mosquitoes can enter, use a mosquito net with 1.5mm mesh, preferably treated with permethrin, tucking edges under the mattress.

Sunburn & Heat Exhaustion

Stay out of the midday sun, wear sunglasses and a wide-brimmed sun hat, and use sunblock with high SPF, UVA and UVB protection. Be aware that the sun is more intense at higher altitudes.

Dehydration or salt deficiency can cause heat exhaustion. Drink plenty of fluids and avoid excessive alcohol or strenuous activity when you first arrive in a hot climate. Long, continuous periods of exposure can leave you vulnerable to heatstroke.

Water

Tap water in Peru is not safe to drink. Boiling water vigorously for one minute is the most effective means of water purification. At altitudes over 2000m (6500ft), boil for three minutes.

You can also disinfect water with iodine or water-purification pills or use a water filter or Steripen. Consult with outdoor retailers on the best option for your travel situation.

Women's Health

Travel to Lima is reasonably safe if you're pregnant, but finding quality obstetric care outside the capital may be difficult. It isn't advisable for pregnant women to spend time at high altitudes. The yellow-fever vaccine should not be given during pregnancy.

Language

Latin American Spanish pronunciation is easy, as most sounds have equivalents in English. Read our colored pronunciation guides as if they were English, and you'll be understood. Note that kh is a throaty sound (like the 'ch' in the Scottish loch), v and b are like a soft English 'v' (between a 'v' and a 'b'), and r is strongly rolled. There are also some variations in spoken Spanish across Latin America, the most notable being the pronunciation of the letters ll and y. In our pronunciation guides these are represented with y because they are pronounced like the 'y' in 'yes' in much of Latin America. Note, however, that in some parts of Peru (and the rest of the continent) they sound like the 'lli' in 'million'. The stressed syllables are indicated with italics in our pronunciation guides.

The polite form is used in this chapter; where both polite and informal options are given, they are indicated by the abbreviations 'pol' and 'inf'. Where necessary, both masculine and feminine forms of words are included, separated by a slash and with the masculine form first, eg *perdido/a* (m/f).

BASICS

Hello.	*Hola.*	o·la
Goodbye.	*Adiós.*	a·*dyos*
How are you?	*¿Qué tal?*	ke tal
Fine, thanks.	*Bien, gracias.*	byen *gra*·syas
Excuse me.	*Perdón.*	per·*don*
Sorry.	*Lo siento.*	lo *syen*·to
Please.	*Por favor.*	por fa·*vor*
Thank you.	*Gracias.*	*gra*·syas
You're welcome.	*De nada.*	de *na*·da
Yes./No.	*Sí./No.*	see/no

My name is ...
Me llamo ... me *ya*·mo ...

What's your name?
¿Cómo se llama Usted? *ko*·mo se *ya*·ma oo·*ste* (pol)
¿Cómo te llamas? *ko*·mo te *ya*·mas (inf)

Do you speak English?
¿Habla inglés? *a*·bla een·*gles* (pol)
¿Hablas inglés? *a*·blas een·*gles* (inf)

I don't understand.
Yo no entiendo. yo no en·*tyen*·do

ACCOMMODATION

I'd like a single/double room.
Quisiera una habitación individual/doble. kee·*sye*·ra *oo*·na a·bee·ta·*syon* een·dee·vee·*dwal*/*do*·ble

How much is it per night/person?
¿Cuánto cuesta por noche/persona? *kwan*·to *kwes*·ta por *no*·che/per·*so*·na

Does it include breakfast?
¿Incluye el desayuno? een·*kloo*·ye el de·sa·*yoo*·no

campsite	*terreno de cámping*	te·*re*·no de *kam*·peeng
guesthouse	*pensión*	pen·*syon*
hotel	*hotel*	o·*tel*
youth hostel	*albergue juvenil*	al·*ber*·ge khoo·ve·*neel*
air-con	*aire acondicionado*	*ai*·re a·kon·dee·syo·*na*·do

WANT MORE?

For in-depth language information and handy phrases, check out Lonely Planet's *Latin American Spanish Phrasebook*. You'll find it at **shop.lonelyplanet.com**, or you can buy Lonely Planet's iPhone phrasebooks at the Apple App Store.

KEY PATTERNS

To get by in Spanish, mix and match these simple patterns with words of your choice:

When's (the next flight)?
¿Cuándo sale (el próximo vuelo)? — kwan·do *sa*·le (el *prok*·see·mo *vwe*·lo)

Where's (the station)?
¿Dónde está (la estación)? — don·de es·*ta* (la es·ta·*syon*)

Where can I (buy a ticket)?
¿Dónde puedo (comprar un billete)? — don·de *pwe*·do (kom·*prar* oon bee·*ye*·te)

Do you have (a map)?
¿Tiene (un mapa)? — tye·ne (oon *ma*·pa)

Is there (a toilet)?
¿Hay (servicios)? — ai (ser·*vee*·syos)

I'd like (a coffee).
Quisiera (un café). — kee·*sye*·ra (oon ka·*fe*)

I'd like (to hire a car).
Quisiera (alquilar un coche). — kee·*sye*·ra (al·kee·*lar* oon *ko*·che)

Can I (enter)?
¿Se puede (entrar)? — se *pwe*·de (en·*trar*)

Could you please (help me)?
¿Puede (ayudarme), por favor? — *pwe*·de (a·yoo·*dar*·me) por fa·*vor*

Do I have to (get a visa)?
¿Necesito (obtener un visado)? — ne·se·*see*·to (ob·te·*ner* oon vee·*sa*·do)

bathroom	*baño*	*ba*·nyo
bed	*cama*	*ka*·ma
window	*ventana*	ven·*ta*·na

DIRECTIONS

Where's ...?
¿Dónde está ...? — *don*·de es·*ta* ...

What's the address?
¿Cuál es la dirección? — kwal es la dee·rek·*syon*

Could you please write it down?
¿Puede escribirlo, por favor? — *pwe*·de es·kree·*beer*·lo por fa·*vor*

Can you show me (on the map)?
¿Me lo puede indicar (en el mapa)? — me lo *pwe*·de een·dee·*kar* (en el *ma*·pa)

at the corner	*en la esquina*	en la es·*kee*·na
at the traffic lights	*en el semáforo*	en el se·*ma*·fo·ro
behind ...	*detrás de ...*	de·*tras* de ...
in front of ...	*enfrente de ...*	en·*fren*·te de ...
left	*izquierda*	ees·*kyer*·da
next to ...	*al lado de ...*	al *la*·do de ...
opposite ...	*frente a ...*	*fren*·te a ...
right	*derecha*	de·*re*·cha
straight ahead	*todo recto*	*to*·do *rek*·to

EATING & DRINKING

Can I see the menu, please?
¿Puedo ver el menú, por favor? — *pwe*·do ver el me·*noo* por fa·*vor*

What would you recommend?
¿Qué recomienda? — ke re·ko·*myen*·da

Do you have vegetarian food?
¿Tienen comida vegetariana? — tye·nen ko·*mee*·da ve·khe·ta·*rya*·na

I don't eat (red meat).
No como (carne roja). — no *ko*·mo (*kar*·ne *ro*·kha)

That was delicious!
¡Estaba buenísimo! — es·*ta*·ba bwe·*nee*·see·mo

Cheers!
¡Salud! — sa·*loo*

The bill, please.
La cuenta, por favor. — la *kwen*·ta por fa·*vor*

I'd like a table for ...	*Quisiera una mesa para ...*	kee·*sye*·ra oo·na *me*·sa *pa*·ra ...
(eight) o'clock	*las (ocho)*	las (*o*·cho)
(two) people	*(dos) personas*	(dos) per·*so*·nas

Key Words

appetisers	*aperitivos*	a·pe·ree·*tee*·vos
bottle	*botella*	bo·*te*·ya
bowl	*bol*	bol
breakfast	*desayuno*	de·sa·*yoo*·no
children's menu	*menú infantil*	me·*noo* een·fan·*teel*
(too) cold	*(muy) frío*	(mooy) *free*·o
dinner	*cena*	*se*·na
food	*comida*	ko·*mee*·da
fork	*tenedor*	te·ne·*dor*
glass	*vaso*	*va*·so
hot (warm)	*caliente*	kal·*yen*·te
knife	*cuchillo*	koo·*chee*·yo
lunch	*comida*	ko·*mee*·da
main course	*segundo plato*	se·*goon*·do *pla*·to
plate	*plato*	*pla*·to
restaurant	*restaurante*	res·tow·*ran*·te

spoon	*cuchara*	koo·*cha*·ra
with	*con*	kon
without	*sin*	seen

Meat & Fish

beef	*carne de vaca*	*kar*·ne de *va*·ka
chicken	*pollo*	*po*·yo
duck	*pato*	*pa*·to
fish	*pescado*	pes·*ka*·do
lamb	*cordero*	kor·*de*·ro
pork	*cerdo*	*ser*·do
turkey	*pavo*	*pa*·vo
veal	*ternera*	ter·*ne*·ra

Fruit & Vegetables

apple	*manzana*	man·*sa*·na
apricot	*albaricoque*	al·ba·ree·*ko*·ke
artichoke	*alcachofa*	al·ka·*cho*·fa
asparagus	*espárragos*	es·*pa*·ra·gos
banana	*plátano*	*pla*·ta·no
beans	*judías*	khoo·*dee*·as
beetroot	*remolacha*	re·mo·*la*·cha
cabbage	*col*	kol
carrot	*zanahoria*	sa·na·*o*·rya
celery	*apio*	*a*·pyo
cherry	*cereza*	se·*re*·sa
corn	*maíz*	ma·*ees*
cucumber	*pepino*	pe·*pee*·no
fruit	*fruta*	*froo*·ta
grape	*uvas*	*oo*·vas
lemon	*limón*	lee·*mon*
lentils	*lentejas*	len·*te*·khas
lettuce	*lechuga*	le·*choo*·ga
mushroom	*champiñón*	cham·pee·*nyon*
nuts	*nueces*	*nwe*·ses
onion	*cebolla*	se·*bo*·ya
orange	*naranja*	na·*ran*·kha
peach	*melocotón*	me·lo·ko·*ton*
peas	*guisantes*	gee·*san*·tes
(red/green) pepper	*pimiento (rojo/verde)*	pee·*myen*·to (*ro*·kho/*ver*·de)
pineapple	*piña*	*pee*·nya
plum	*ciruela*	seer·*we*·la
potato	*patata*	pa·*ta*·ta
pumpkin	*calabaza*	ka·la·*ba*·sa
spinach	*espinacas*	es·pee·*na*·kas
strawberry	*fresa*	*fre*·sa
tomato	*tomate*	to·*ma*·te
vegetable	*verdura*	ver·*doo*·ra
watermelon	*sandía*	san·*dee*·a

QUESTION WORDS

What?	*¿Qué?*	ke
When?	*¿Cuándo?*	*kwan*·do
Where?	*¿Dónde?*	*don*·de
Who?	*¿Quién?*	kyen
Why?	*¿Por qué?*	por ke

Other

bread	*pan*	pan
butter	*mantequilla*	man·te·*kee*·ya
cheese	*queso*	*ke*·so
egg	*huevo*	*we*·vo
honey	*miel*	myel
jam	*mermelada*	mer·me·*la*·da
oil	*aceite*	a·*sey*·te
pasta	*pasta*	*pas*·ta
pepper	*pimienta*	pee·*myen*·ta
rice	*arroz*	a·*ros*
salt	*sal*	sal
sugar	*azúcar*	a·*soo*·kar
vinegar	*vinagre*	vee·*na*·gre

Drinks

beer	*cerveza*	ser·*ve*·sa
coffee	*café*	ka·*fe*

SIGNS

Abierto	Open
Cerrado	Closed
Entrada	Entrance
Hombres/Varones	Men
Mujeres/Damas	Women
Prohibido	Prohibited
Salida	Exit
Servicios/Baños	Toilets

(orange) juice	*zumo (de naranja)*	*soo·mo* (de na·*ran*·kha)
milk	*leche*	*le*·che
red wine	*vino tinto*	*vee*·no *teen*·to
tea	*té*	te
(mineral) water	*agua (mineral)*	*a*·gwa (mee·ne·*ral*)
white wine	*vino blanco*	*vee*·no *blan*·ko

EMERGENCIES

Help!	*¡Socorro!*	so·*ko*·ro
Go away!	*¡Vete!*	*ve*·te

Call ...!	*¡Llame a ...!*	*ya*·me a ...
a doctor	*un médico*	oon *me*·dee·ko
the police	*la policía*	la po·lee·*see*·a

I'm lost.
Estoy perdido/a. es·*toy* per·*dee*·do/a (m/f)

I'm ill.
Estoy enfermo/a. es·*toy* en·*fer*·mo/a (m/f)

I'm allergic to (antibiotics).
Soy alérgico/a a (los antibióticos). soy a·*ler*·khee·ko/a a (los an·tee·*byo*·tee·kos) (m/f)

Where are the toilets?
¿Dónde están los baños? *don*·de es·*tan* los *ba*·nyos

SHOPPING & SERVICES

I'd like to buy ...
Quisiera comprar ... kee·*sye*·ra kom·*prar* ...

I'm just looking.
Sólo estoy mirando. so·lo es·*toy* mee·*ran*·do

Can I look at it?
¿Puedo verlo? *pwe*·do *ver*·lo

I don't like it.
No me gusta. no me *goos*·ta

How much is it?
¿Cuánto cuesta? *kwan*·to *kwes*·ta

AYMARA & QUECHUA

The few Aymara and Quechua words and phrases included here will be useful for those traveling in the Andes. Aymara is spoken by the Aymara people, who inhabit the area around Lake Titicaca. While the Quechua included here is from the Cuzco dialect, it should prove helpful wherever you travel in the highlands too.

In the following lists, Aymara is the second column, Quechua the third. The principles of pronunciation for both languages are similar to those found in Spanish. An apostrophe (') represents a glottal stop, which is the 'nonsound' that occurs in the middle of 'uh-oh.'

Hello.	*Kamisaraki.*	*Napaykullayki.*
Please.	*Mirá.*	*Allichu.*
Thank you.	*Yuspagara.*	*Yusulipayki.*
Yes.	*Jisa.*	*Ari.*
No.	*Janiwa.*	*Mana.*

How do you say ...?	*Cun saña-sauca'ha ...?*	*Imainata nincha chaita ...?*
It's called ...	*Ucan sutipa'h ...*	*Chaipa'g sutin'ha ...*
Please repeat.	*Uastata sita.*	*Ua'manta niway.*
How much?	*K'gauka?*	*Maik'ata'g?*

father	*auqui*	*tayta*
mother	*taica*	*mama*
food	*manka*	*mikíuy*
river	*jawira*	*mayu*
snowy peak	*kollu*	*riti-orko*
water	*uma*	*yacu*

1	*maya*	*u'*
2	*paya*	*iskai*
3	*quimsa*	*quinsa*
4	*pusi*	*tahua*
5	*pesca*	*phiska*
6	*zo'hta*	*so'gta*
7	*pakalko*	*khanchis*
8	*quimsakalko*	*pusa'g*
9	*yatunca*	*iskon*
10	*tunca*	*chunca*

That's too expensive.
Es muy caro. es mooy *ka*·ro

Can you lower the price?
¿Podría bajar un poco el precio? po·*dree*·a ba·*khar* oon *po*·ko el *pre*·syo

There's a mistake in the bill.
Hay un error en la cuenta. ai oon e·*ror* en la *kwen*·ta

ATM	*cajero automático*	ka·*khe*·ro ow·to·*ma*·tee·ko
internet cafe	*cibercafé*	see·ber·ka·*fe*
market	*mercado*	mer·*ka*·do
post office	*correos*	ko·*re*·os
tourist office	*oficina de turismo*	o·fee·*see*·na de too·*rees*·mo

TIME & DATES

What time is it?	*¿Qué hora es?*	ke o·ra es
It's (10) o'clock.	*Son (las diez).*	son (las dyes)
It's half past (one).	*Es (la una) y media.*	es (la *oo*·na) ee *me*·dya
morning	*mañana*	ma·*nya*·na
afternoon	*tarde*	*tar*·de
evening	*noche*	*no*·che
yesterday	*ayer*	a·*yer*
today	*hoy*	oy
tomorrow	*mañana*	ma·*nya*·na
Monday	*lunes*	*loo*·nes
Tuesday	*martes*	*mar*·tes
Wednesday	*miércoles*	*myer*·ko·les
Thursday	*jueves*	*khwe*·ves
Friday	*viernes*	*vyer*·nes
Saturday	*sábado*	*sa*·ba·do
Sunday	*domingo*	do·*meen*·go

TRANSPORT

boat	*barco*	*bar*·ko
bus	*autobús*	ow·to·*boos*
plane	*avión*	a·*vyon*
train	*tren*	tren
first	*primero*	pree·*me*·ro
last	*último*	*ool*·tee·mo
ticket office	*taquilla*	ta·*kee*·ya
timetable	*horario*	o·*ra*·ryo

NUMBERS

1	*uno*	*oo*·no
2	*dos*	dos
3	*tres*	tres
4	*cuatro*	*kwa*·tro
5	*cinco*	*seen*·ko
6	*seis*	seys
7	*siete*	*sye*·te
8	*ocho*	*o*·cho
9	*nueve*	*nwe*·ve
10	*diez*	dyes
20	*veinte*	*veyn*·te
30	*treinta*	*treyn*·ta
40	*cuarenta*	kwa·*ren*·ta
50	*cincuenta*	seen·*kwen*·ta
60	*sesenta*	se·*sen*·ta
70	*setenta*	se·*ten*·ta
80	*ochenta*	o·*chen*·ta
90	*noventa*	no·*ven*·ta
100	*cien*	syen
1000	*mil*	meel

bus stop	*parada de autobuses*	pa·*ra*·da de ow·to·*boo*·ses
train station	*estación de trenes*	es·ta·*syon* de *tre*·nes
A ... ticket, please.	*Un billete de ..., por favor.*	oon bee·*ye*·te de ... por fa·*vor*
1st-class	*primera clase*	pree·*me*·ra *kla*·se
2nd-class	*segunda clase*	se·*goon*·da *kla*·se
one-way	*ida*	*ee*·da
return	*ida y vuelta*	*ee*·da ee *vwel*·ta

Does it stop at ...?
¿Para en ...? *pa*·ra en ...

What stop is this?
¿Cuál es esta parada? kwal es *es*·ta pa·*ra*·da

What time does it arrive/leave?
¿A qué hora llega/sale? a ke o·ra *ye*·ga/*sa*·le

Please tell me when we get to ...
¿Puede avisarme cuando lleguemos a ...? *pwe*·de a·vee·*sar*·me *kwan*·do ye·*ge*·mos a ...

I want to get off here.
Quiero bajarme aquí. *kye*·ro ba·*khar*·me a·*kee*

I'd like to hire a ...	*Quisiera alquilar ...*	kee·*sye*·ra al·kee·*lar* ...
4WD	*un todo-terreno*	oon to·do·te·*re*·no
bicycle	*una bicicleta*	*oo*·na bee·see·*kle*·ta
car	*un coche*	oon *ko*·che
motorcycle	*una moto*	*oo*·na *mo*·to
helmet	*casco*	*kas*·ko
hitchhike	*hacer botella*	a·*ser* bo·*te*·ya
mechanic	*mecánico*	me·*ka*·nee·ko
petrol/gas	*gasolina*	ga·so·*lee*·na
service station	*gasolinera*	ga·so·lee·*ne*·ra
truck	*camion*	ka·*myon*

Is this the road to ...?
¿Se va a ... por esta carretera? — se va a ... por es·ta ka·re·*te*·ra

Can I park here?
¿Puedo aparcar aquí? — *pwe*·do a·par·*kar* a·*kee*

The car has broken down.
El coche se ha averiado. — el *ko*·che se a a·ve·*rya*·do

I have a flat tyre.
Tengo un pinchazo. — *ten*·go oon peen·*cha*·so

GLOSSARY

albergue – family-owned inn
altiplano – literally, a high plateau or plain; specifically, it refers to the vast, desolate Andean flatlands of southern Peru, Bolivia, northern Chile and northern Argentina
aluvión – fast-moving flood of ice, water, rocks, mud and debris caused by an earthquake or a bursting dam in the mountains
arequipeño – inhabitant of Arequipa
arriero – animal driver, usually of *burros* or *mulas* (mules)
avenida – avenue (Av)
ayahuasca – potent hallucinogenic brew made from jungle vines and used by shamans and traditional healers

barrio – neighborhood
bodega – winery, wine shop, wine cellar or tasting bar
boleto turístico – tourism ticket
bruja/brujo – shaman, witch doctor, or medicine person
burro – donkey
bus-cama – long-distance, double-decker buses with seats reclining almost into beds; toilets, videos and snacks are provided on board

caballito – high-ended, cigar-shaped boat; found near Huanchaco
calle – street
campesino – peasant, farmer or rural inhabitant
cañón – canyon
carretera – highway
casa – home, house
casa de cambio – foreign-exchange bureau
cerro – hill, mountain
chullpa – ancient Andean burial tower, found around Lake Titicaca
cocha – lake, from the indigenous Quechua language; often appended to many lake names
colectivo – shared transportation; usually taxis, but also minibuses, minivans or boats
combi – minivan or minibus (usually with tiny seats, and as many passengers as possible)
cordillera – mountain chain
criolla/criollo – Creole or native of Peru; also applies to coastal Peruvians, music and dance; *criollo* food refers to spicy Peruvian fare with Spanish, Asian and African influences
cuadra – city block
curandera/curandero – traditional healer
cuzqueño – inhabitant of Cuzco (also Cusco or Qosq'o)

escuela cuzqueña – Cuzco school; colonial art movement that combined Spanish and Andean artistic styles

feria – street market with vendor booths

garúa – coastal fog or mist
grifo – gas (petrol) station
gringa/gringo – all foreigners who are not from South or Central America and Mexico
guanaco – large, wild camelid that ranges throughout South America, now an endangered species in Peru

hospedaje – small, family-owned inn
hostal – guesthouse, smaller than a hotel and with fewer amenities
huaca – sacred pyramid, temple or burial site
huaquero – grave robber
huayno – traditional Andean music using instrumentation with roots in pre-Columbian times

iglesia – church
inca – king
indígena – indigenous person (male or female)
Inrena – Insituto Nacional de Recursos Naturales (National Institute for Natural Resources);

government agency that administers national parks, reserves, historical sanctuaries and other protected areas

Inti – ancient Peruvian sun god; husband of the earth goddess Pachamama

isla – island, isle

jirón – road (abbreviated Jr)

lavandería – laundry

limeño – inhabitant of Lima

marinera – a typical coastal Peruvian dance involving the flirtatious waving of handkerchiefs

mestizo – person of mixed indigenous and Spanish descent

micro – a small bus used as public transport

mirador – watchtower, observatory, viewpoint

mototaxi – three-wheeled motorcycle rickshaw taxi; also called *motocarro* or *taximoto*

museo – museum

nevado – glaciated or snow-covered mountain peak

nuevo sol – the national currency of Peru

oficina de migraciónes – immigration office

Pachamama – ancient Peruvian earth goddess; wife of the sun god Inti

pampa – large, flat area, usually of grasslands

Panamericana – Pan-American Highway (aka Interamericana); main route joining Latin American countries

parque – park

peña – bar or club featuring live folkloric music

playa – beach

pongo – narrow, steep-walled, rocky, jungle river canyon that can be a dangerous maelstrom during high water

pueblo – town, village

puna – high Andean grasslands of the *altiplano*

puya – spiky-leafed plant of the bromeliad family

quebrada – literally, a break; often refers to a steep ravine or gulch

quero – ceremonial Inca wooden drinking vessel

río – river

selva – jungle, tropical rainforest

sillar – off-white volcanic rock, often used for buildings around Arequipa

soroche – altitude sickness

taximoto – see *mototaxi*

terminal terrestre – bus station

totora – reed of the papyrus family; used to build the 'floating islands' and traditional boats of Lake Titicaca

turismo vivencial – homestay tourism

vals peruano – Peruvian waltz, an upbeat, guitar-driven waltz played and danced to in coastal areas

vicuña – threatened wild relative of the alpaca; smallest living member of the camelid family

Behind the Scenes

SEND US YOUR FEEDBACK

We love to hear from travelers – your comments keep us on our toes and help make our books better. Our well-traveled team reads every word on what you loved or loathed about this book. Although we cannot reply individually to your submissions, we always guarantee that your feedback goes straight to the appropriate authors, in time for the next edition. Each person who sends us information is thanked in the next edition – the most useful submissions are rewarded with a selection of digital PDF chapters.

Visit **lonelyplanet.com/contact** to submit your updates and suggestions or to ask for help. Our award-winning website also features inspirational travel stories, news and discussions.

Note: We may edit, reproduce and incorporate your comments in Lonely Planet products such as guidebooks, websites and digital products, so let us know if you don't want your comments reproduced or your name acknowledged. For a copy of our privacy policy visit lonelyplanet.com/privacy.

OUR READERS

Many thanks to the travelers who used the last edition and wrote to us with helpful hints, useful advice and interesting anecdotes:

Abby Furnish, Adriana Kaufmann, Ailniery Wu, Alberto Garro, Aleix Megias, Aleksei Trofimov, Alfonso Mendocilla, Amy Wattridge, Andrea Meichtry, Andrea Polvicino, Andreas Dehlholm-Lambertsen, Andreas Pecnik, Andrew Agnew, Andy Aegerter, Anne de la Vega, Ansie Serbon, Badong Abesamis, Benjamin Kutz, Bertolt Eicke, Blanquart Noemie, Brooke Aldrich, Candida Silva, Carlos Manay, Carol Janney, Celine Heinbecker, Charles Motley, Christa Jenni, Christian Jay, Christoph Frigge, Danielle Breitenbuecher, Dave Dalpiaz, David Johnson, Davide Camisa, Deborah Galef, Desiree Weins, Diego Corimanya, Edwin Junco, Elizabeth MacLean, Erica Lazarow, Francesco Davi, Guy Duke, Hanna Hommes, Havala Hanson, Helen O'Leary, Jackie Chase, Jandra Fischer, Jean-Philippe Hardy, Jenna Lindsay, Jenny Blaker, Jesus Villacorta, Jim Doherty, JoAnn Spangler, Johan Desser, Johan Reinhard, Jorge Riveros-Cayo, Kate Convissor, Kathy Kieffer, Kelsi Luhnow, Kiara Gallop, Kristina Solheim, Laura King, Laura Sanfilippo, Laurent Tschumi, Lisa Bucolo, Lynn Haanen, Marco Rodriguez, Marie Rognes, Mary de Sousa, Massimiliano Malloni, Michele Oechsle, Mitch Gruber, Nicole McGrath, Patricia Kohlmann, Paul Dumont, Pedro Obando, Philip Jensen, Rick Vecchio, Roberto Filho, Rudy Bovee, Ryan Bates, Sabine Gerull, Sandeep Gaonkar, Sandy Lee, Sebastian Engel, Sheena Gilby, Sonia Matlochova, Sophie Young, Stefan Hey, Stefan Pielmeier, Stefanie Hess, Susan Waldock, Sveta Karelsky, Tawny Welch, Tessa Hermanussen, Tiffany Doan, Veronika Arnyas-Turcsanyi, Vetillart Tania, Walter Soplin, Wendelin Zahoransky, Wendy Grayburn, Wesley Reisser, Willeke Norder and Yvonne Streit.

AUTHOR THANKS

Carolyn McCarthy

Many thanks go out to the Peruvian chefs and street vendors who played a key role in my contentment. I am also grateful for the friendship, advice and assistance of Jorge Riveros Cayo, Arturo Rojas, Mandy Kalitsis, Louise Norton, Elizabeth Shumaker, John Leivers, Paolo Greer and Illa Liendo. To my hard working co-authors, a chilled pisco sour and cheers.

Greg Benchwick

Muchísimas gracias to my coordinating author Carolyn McCarthy and the trailblazers who worked on previous editions. These books are a team effort and my dynamic destination editor MaSovaida Morgan and the rest of the LP Crew are amazing! While I came close to throwing him from the car, my co-pilot for adventures in the north, Santiago, did reveal many unique insights into the Peruvian (and human) condition. Thanks for going the extra mile to Maria Isabel at Sipán Tours, Peter at Aproturpisco, and beautiful Sandra at Desert Travel in Ica. Last, but never least, this book is for Violeta.

Alex Egerton

Thanks to all those who helped out on the road in Peru – too many to mention – but big shouts to Adriana Von Hagen, Rob and Jose in Chachas, Susan in Celendin, and Lluis and the drunk Chileno guinea pigs in Amazonas. In Huaraz and surrounds, special thanks to Juan, Pablo, Marie and David, Alberto, Rex, Julio, Chris, and the Respons team. At LP, thanks to Carolyn for being supportive as usual and MaSovaida for bringing it all together.

Phillip Tang

In Arequipa, thanks to Paul and José-Luis for hospitality. Thanks Luis for the night walk and mirador. To Ingrid for condor adventures; LA Raúl and Nuvia for laughs. Justo Béjar and José Lopera in Lima; and Gabriel, Yoko and Kristian in La Paz. Mostly, thanks to the Aussies and Mexicans who made returning a joy: Lisa N'paisan, Shane, Lee, Vek Lewis, Wendy Risteska, Ben and Waimei Garcia-Lee, Craig Burgess, Jocsan L Alfaro, Manuel Aveleyra García, Alberto R Romero and Ernesto A Alanis Cataño.

Luke Waterson

Wow – another list here as long as an epic Andean bus journey! Firstly, Marcel: thank you for an unforgettable trans-Andean jeep ride. Lucho (in Huancayo), Pauline (in Ayacucho), Gerson and Donald (in Puerto Maldonado), Ryse and Katie (in Cuzco), James (in Yurimaguas) and Bill and Analia (in Iquitos) also deserve a special mention, as do the myriad taxi, bus, boat and plane drivers/pilots who DIDN'T crash and wove together the fabric of yet another unforgettable trip to this unforgettable land.

ACKNOWLEDGMENTS

Climate map data adapted from Peel MC, Finlayson BL & McMahon TA (2007) 'Updated World Map of the Köppen-Geiger Climate Classification', *Hydrology and Earth System Sciences*, 11, 163344.

Cover image: Young girl in traditional dress, Michael Melford/Alamy

THIS BOOK

This 9th edition of Lonely Planet's *Peru* guidebook was researched and written by Carolyn McCarthy, Greg Benchwick, Alex Egerton, Phillip Tang and Luke Waterson. The previous edition was also written by Carolyn, with Carolina A Miranda, Kevin Raub, Brendan Sainsbury and Luke Waterson. This guidebook was produced by the following:

Destination Editor
MaSovaida Morgan

Product Editors
Catherine Naghten, Martine Power

Senior Cartographer
Mark Griffiths

Book Designer
Virginia Moreno

Assisting Editors Susie Ashworth, Judith Bamber, Helen Koehne, Kellie Langdon, Charlotte Orr, Monique Perrin, Gabrielle Stefanos

Assisting Cartographer
David Kemp

Cover Researcher
Naomi Parker

Thanks to Bruce Evans, Ryan Evans, Larissa Frost, Andi Jones, Kate Mathews, Wayne Murphy, Karyn Noble, Kirsten Rawlings, Julie Sheridan, Ellie Simpson, Ross Taylor, Angela Tinson, Tony Wheeler, Tracy Whitmey

Index

Map Pages **000**
Photo Pages **000**

Map Pages **000**
Photo Pages **000**

D

E

Map Pages **000**
Photo Pages **000**

Map Pages **000**
Photo Pages **000**

Map Legend

Sights

- Beach
- Bird Sanctuary
- Buddhist
- Castle/Palace
- Christian
- Confucian
- Hindu
- Islamic
- Jain
- Jewish
- Monument
- Museum/Gallery/Historic Building
- Ruin
- Shinto
- Sikh
- Taoist
- Winery/Vineyard
- Zoo/Wildlife Sanctuary
- Other Sight

Activities, Courses & Tours

- Bodysurfing
- Diving
- Canoeing/Kayaking
- Course/Tour
- Sento Hot Baths/Onsen
- Skiing
- Snorkeling
- Surfing
- Swimming/Pool
- Walking
- Windsurfing
- Other Activity

Sleeping

- Sleeping
- Camping

Eating

- Eating

Drinking & Nightlife

- Drinking & Nightlife
- Cafe

Entertainment

- Entertainment

Shopping

- Shopping

Information

- Bank
- Embassy/Consulate
- Hospital/Medical
- Internet
- Police
- Post Office
- Telephone
- Toilet
- Tourist Information
- Other Information

Geographic

- Beach
- Gate
- Hut/Shelter
- Lighthouse
- Lookout
- Mountain/Volcano
- Oasis
- Park
- Pass
- Picnic Area
- Waterfall

Population

- Capital (National)
- Capital (State/Province)
- City/Large Town
- Town/Village

Transport

- Airport
- Border crossing
- Bus
- Cable car/Funicular
- Cycling
- Ferry
- Metro station
- Monorail
- Parking
- Petrol station
- Subway/Subte station
- Taxi
- Train station/Railway
- Tram
- Underground station
- Other Transport

Note: Not all symbols displayed above appear on the maps in this book

Routes

- Tollway
- Freeway
- Primary
- Secondary
- Tertiary
- Lane
- Unsealed road
- Road under construction
- Plaza/Mall
- Steps
- Tunnel
- Pedestrian overpass
- Walking Tour
- Walking Tour detour
- Path/Walking Trail

Boundaries

- International
- State/Province
- Disputed
- Regional/Suburb
- Marine Park
- Cliff
- Wall

Hydrography

- River, Creek
- Intermittent River
- Canal
- Water
- Dry/Salt/Intermittent Lake
- Reef

Areas

- Airport/Runway
- Beach/Desert
- Cemetery (Christian)
- Cemetery (Other)
- Glacier
- Mudflat
- Park/Forest
- Sight (Building)
- Sportsground
- Swamp/Mangrove

OUR STORY

A beat-up old car, a few dollars in the pocket and a sense of adventure. In 1972 that's all Tony and Maureen Wheeler needed for the trip of a lifetime – across Europe and Asia overland to Australia. It took several months, and at the end – broke but inspired – they sat at their kitchen table writing and stapling together their first travel guide, *Across Asia on the Cheap*. Within a week they'd sold 1500 copies. Lonely Planet was born.

Today, Lonely Planet has offices in Franklin, London, Melbourne, Oakland, Beijing and Delhi, with more than 600 staff and writers. We share Tony's belief that 'a great guidebook should do three things: inform, educate and amuse'.

OUR WRITERS

Carolyn McCarthy

Coordinating Author, Lima, Cuzco & the Sacred Valley Author Carolyn McCarthy first discovered *cumbia* camping on the Inca Trail many years ago. On this trip she embarked on a quest for the perfect ceviche (with success). She has contributed to more than 30 titles for Lonely Planet, including *Panama*, *Trekking in the Patagonian Andes*, *Argentina*, *Chile*, *Colorado*, *The Southwest* and national parks guides. She has also written for *Outside*, *BBC Magazine*, *National Geographic* and other publications. For more information, see www.carolynmccarthy.pressfolios.com or follow her on Instagram @masmerquen and Twitter @RoamingMcC.

Greg Benchwick

North Coast, South Coast Greg Benchwick has been trucking around South America for the past 15 years. For this trip, the Lonely Planet veteran covered over 5000km of coastline, going that extra mile to explore offbeat surf destinations along the way. Greg has written speeches for the United Nations, interviewed Grammy-award winners and created dozens of videos and web features for LonelyPlanet.com, *National Geographic Traveler* and other international publications. He is an expert on sustainable travel, international development, food, wine and having a good time.

Read more about Greg at:
https://auth.lonelyplanet.com/profiles/gregbenchwick

Alex Egerton

Huaraz & the Cordilleras, Northern Highlands A journalist by trade, Alex writes about travel and culture in destinations all over Latin America but has a particular passion for the Andes and the seldom visited jungle-covered parts of the map. Based in southern Colombia, he makes regular trips down to Peru in search of the best spicy eats and most spectacular/sketchy mountain bus rides. When not on the road for work, you'll find him hiking in the mountain plains or watching way too much football.

Published by Lonely Planet Publications Pty Ltd
ABN 36 005 607 983
9th edition – April 2016
ISBN 978 1 74321 557 9

10 9 8 7 6 5 4
Printed in Singapore

Phillip Tang

Arequipa & Canyon Country, Lake Titicaca A degree in Latin America studies brought Phillip Tang to these shores, and over a decade later he still finds himself feeling breathless (only slightly literally) pondering a canyon in Colca or the ocean in Miraflores. He writes about travel on his two loves, Asia and Latin America, and has contributed to Lonely Planet's guides to China, Japan and Mexico, and has written about Peru for other publishers. Find his Peru Insta-photos from this visit through philliptang.co.uk.

Luke Waterson

Central Highlands, Amazon Basin Back for his 3rd edition of Lonely Planet's *Peru*, Luke has a love for getting off the beaten track, which is evident in him writing the Central Highlands and Amazon Basin chapters of this guide. He specialises in writing about Andean and Amazonian South America as a travel writer and as a novelist: his debut novel, *Roebuck: Adventures of an Admirable Adventurer* is set in the 16th-century South American jungle. He writes on Latin America for the *Independent*, the *Telegraph* and the BBC, and runs a travel-and-culture blog about his current home, Slovakia: Englishmaninslovakia.com. Luke also wrote the 'Peru's Cuisine' chapter.